Vide
iterum
alicuiz
extentis
modum
falcem
magnā
rosam
quā ft.
tertium &'
duplicat'
primū ele
mentum
divisa sunt. Item 2 iūcta falafer. iiij. nūsiū
te scribo in principatus ante omīs quem cō
sumpsisti gladio templa ydolorum post
paululum resuscitato tres autem annos
in mūdo vivens senex uade in infernum
duabus tribulationibus in medio.

Thomas E. Marston (1904–84)

Catalogue

of Medieval and Renaissance Manuscripts

in the Beinecke Rare Book

and Manuscript Library

Yale University

VOLUME III: MARSTON MANUSCRIPTS

medieval & renaissance
texts & studies

Volume 100

Catalogue

of Medieval and Renaissance Manuscripts in the Beinecke Rare Book and Manuscript Library Yale University

VOLUME III: MARSTON MANUSCRIPTS

BY

Barbara A. Shailor

Medieval & Renaissance Texts & Studies
Binghamton, New York
1992

Library of Congress Cataloging-in-Publication Data

Beinecke Rare Book and Manuscript Library.
Catalogue of Medieval and Renaissance manuscripts in the Beinecke Rare Book and Manuscript Library, Yale University.

(Medieval & Renaissance texts & studies ; v. 34, 48, 100)
Includes bibliographical references and indexes.
Contents: v. 1. MSS 1–250—v. 2. MSS 251–500—v. 3. Marston manuscripts.
1. Beinecke Rare Book and Manuscript Library—Catalogs.
2. Manuscripts—Connecticut—New Haven—Catalogs.
3. Manuscripts, Latin (Medieval and modern)—Catalogs.
4. Manuscripts, Greek (Medieval and modern)—Catalogs.
5. Manuscripts, Medieval—Connecticut—New Haven—Catalogs.
6. Manuscripts, Renaissance—Connecticut—New Haven—Catalogs.
I. Shailor, Barbara A., 1948– . II. Title. III. Title: Catalog of Medieval and Renaissance manuscripts in the Beinecke Rare Book and Manuscript Library, Yale University. IV. Series. V. Series: Medieval & Renaissance texts & studies ; v. 34, etc.
Z6621.B4213 1984 011'.31 84-667
ISBN 0-86698-065-2 (v. 1)
ISBN 0-86698-030-X (v. 2)
ISBN 0-86698-115-2 (v. 3)

This book is made to last.
It is set in Baskerville, smythe-sewn
and printed on acid-free paper
to library specifications

Printed in the United States of America

Contents

Abbreviations

Abbey Cat.	J. J. G. Alexander and A. C. de la Mare, *The Italian Manuscripts in the Library of Major J. R. Abbey* (New York and London, 1969).
Achten-Knaus	G. Achten and H. Knaus, *Deutsche und niederländische Gebetbuchhandschriften der Hessischen Landes- und Hochschulbibliothek Darmstadt* (Darmstadt, 1959).
Anthologia latina	A. Riese, ed., *Anthologia latina sive poesis latinae supplementum, I, Carmina in codicibus scripta* (Leipzig, 1894–1906).
Aristoteles Latinus	G. Lacombe, *Aristoteles Latinus.* Pars prior (Rome, 1939); Pars posterior (Cambridge, 1955).
Avril and Gousset	F. Avril and M.-T. Gousset, *Manuscrits enluminés d'origine italienne*, v. 2 = XIIIe siècle (Paris, 1984).
Avril and Zaluska	F. Avril and Y. Zaluska, *Manuscrits enluminés d'origine italienne*, v. 1 = VIe–XIIe siècles (Paris, 1980).
Bertalot	L. Bertalot, *Initia humanistica latina: Initienverzeichnis lateinischer Prosa und Poesie aus der Zeit des 14. bis 16. Jahrhunderts* (Tübingen, 1985–).
BHG^{3}	*Bibliotheca hagiographica graeca*, ediderunt Socii Bollandiani, 3rd ed. (Brussels, 1957).
BHL	*Bibliotheca hagiographica latina*, ediderunt Socii Bollandiani.
B. L.	British Library.
Bloomfield, *Virtues and Vices*	M. W. Bloomfield, et al., *Incipits of Latin Works on the Virtues and Vices, 1100–1500 A. D.* (Cambridge, Mass., 1979).

B. N. — Bibliothèque Nationale.

Branner — R. J. Branner, *Manuscript Painting in Paris during the Reign of Saint Louis: A Study of Styles* (Berkeley, 1977).

Briquet — C. M. Briquet, *Les filigranes: Dictionnaire historique des marques du papier...1282 jusqu'en 1600*, facs. of the 1907 edition with supplementary material, ed. A. Stevenson (Amsterdam, 1968).

Bursill-Hall, *Census* — G. L. Bursill-Hall, *A Census of Medieval Latin Grammatical Manuscripts*, Grammatica Speculativa, 4 (Stuttgart-Bad Cannstatt, 1981).

CAG — *Commentaria in Aristotelem graeca*, 23 vols. + 3 supp. vols. (Berlin, 1882–1909).

Canart — P. Canart, "Scribes grecs de la Renaissance," *Scriptorium* 17 (1963) pp. 56–82.

CC — Corpus christianorum.

CC Cont. Med. — Corpus christianorum: Continuatio mediaevalis.

CLA — E. A. Lowe, *Codices latini antiquiores* (Oxford, 1934–71).

Colophons — *Colophons de manuscrits occidentaux des origines au XVIe siècle*, 6 vols. (Fribourg, 1965–82).

Copinger — W. A. Copinger, *Supplement to Hain's Repertorium bibliographicum* (Berlin, 1926).

Cosenza — M. E. Cosenza, *Biographical and Bibliographical Dictionary of the Italian Humanists and of the World of Classical Scholarship in Italy, 1300–1800* (Boston, 1962–67).

CPL — *Clavis patrum latinorum*, ed. E. Dekkers, *Sacris erudiri* 3 (2nd ed., 1961).

CSEL — Corpus scriptorum ecclesiasticorum latinorum.

CTC — V. Brown, F. E. Cranz, P. O. Kristeller, eds., *Catalogus translationum et commentariorum: Mediaeval and Renaissance Latin Translations and Commentaries* (Washington, D.C., 1960–).

De la Mare, *New Research* — A. C. de la Mare, "New Research on Humanistic Scribes in Florence," in A. Garzelli, ed., *Miniatura*

	fiorentina de Rinascimento 1440–1525, 2 vols. (Florence, 1985).
De Marinis, *La legatura*	T. De Marinis, *La legatura artistica in Italia nei secoli XV e XVI*, 3 vols. (Florence, 1960).
De Meyier	K. A. de Meyier, "Scribes grecs de la Renaissance. Additions et corrections aux répertoires de Vogel-Gardthausen, de Patrinélis et de Canart," *Scriptorium* 18 (1964) pp. 258–66.
De Ricci	S. de Ricci, *Census of Medieval and Renaissance Manuscripts in the United States and Canada* (New York, 1935–40).
Delaissé, Marrow and de Wit, *Waddesdon Manor*	L. M. J. Delaissé, J. Marrow and J. de Wit, *Illuminated Manuscripts.* The James A. de Rothschild Collection at Waddesdon Manor, v. 8 (Fribourg, 1977, for the National Trust by the Office du Livre).
Derolez	A. Derolez, *Codicologie des manuscrits en écriture humanistique sur parchemin*, Bibliologia 5–6 (Turnhout, 1984).
DNB	*Dictionary of National Biography.*
Dutschke	D. Dutschke, *Census of Petrarch Manuscripts in the United States*, Censimento dei codici petrarcheschi, 9 (Padua, 1986).
EETS	Early English Text Society.
Emden, BRUC	A. B. Emden, *A Biographical Register of the University of Cambridge to A. D. 1500* (Cambridge, 1963).
Emden, BRUO	A. B. Emden, *A Biographical Register of the University of Oxford to A. D. 1500* (Oxford, 1957–59).
Eubel	C. Eubel, et al., *Hierarchia catholica medii aevi...*, 8 vols. (Münster in Westphalia, 1913– ; reprinted Padua, 1960).
Exhibition Catalogue	W. Cahn and J. Marrow, eds., "Medieval and Renaissance Manuscripts at Yale: A Selection," Yale University Library *Gazette* 52 (1978) pp. 173–284.
Faye and Bond	C. U. Faye, *Supplement to the Census of Medieval and Renaissance Manuscripts in the United States and Canada.*

	Continued and edited by W. H. Bond (New York, 1962).
Garzelli, *Miniatura fiorentina*	A. Garzelli, ed., *Miniatura fiorentina de Rinascimento 1440–1525*, 2 vols. (Florence, 1985).
Gazette	Yale University Library *Gazette*.
GKW	*Gesamtkatalog der Wiegendrucke* (1925–).
Glorieux	P. Glorieux, *Répertoire des maîtres en théologie de Paris au XIIIe siècle*, Études de philosophie médiévale 17–18 (Paris, 1933–34).
Graux and Martin	C. Graux and A. Martin, *Rapport sur une mission en Espagne et en Portugal. Notices sommaires...*, in *Nouvelles archives des missions scientifiques et littéraires* 2 (1892) pp. 1–322.
Hain	L. F. T. Hain, *Repertorium bibliographicum, in quo libri omnes ab arte typographica inventa usque ad annum MD* (Stuttgart, 1826–38).
Harlfinger	D. and J. Harlfinger, *Wasserzeichen aus griechischen Handschriften* (Berlin, v. 1: 1974; 2: 1980).
Hauréau	B. Hauréau, *Initia operum scriptorum latinorum medii potissimum aevi ex codicibus manuscriptis...*, 8 vols. (Turnhout, 1973–74).
HBS	Henry Bradshaw Society.
HE	C. Wordsworth, ed. *Horae Eboracenses*, Surtees Society 132 (1920).
Heawood	E. Heawood, *Watermarks, Mainly of the 17th and 18th Centuries* (Monumenta Chartae Papyraceae I) (Hilversum, 1950).
Iter italicum	P. O. Kristeller, *Iter italicum accedunt alia itinera*, 5 vols. (London and Leiden, 1963–90).
Kaeppeli, SOPMA	T. Kaeppeli, *Scriptores ordinis praedicatorum medii aevi*, 3 vols. (Rome, 1970–80).
IMEV	C. Brown and R. H. Robbins, *The Index of Middle English Verse* (New York, 1943). *Supplement* by R. H. Robbins and J. L. Cutler (Lexington, 1965).

IUPI — M. Santagata, *Incipitario unificato della poesia italiana*, 2 vols. (Modena, 1988).

Karpozilos — A. Karpozilos, "The Yale University Manuscripts of Andreas Darmarius," *Hellenika* 26 (1973) pp. 67-71.

Ker, MLGB — N. R. Ker, *Medieval Libraries of Great Britain*, 2nd ed. (London, 1964).

Ker, MMBL — N. R. Ker, *Medieval Manuscripts in British Libraries* (Oxford, 1969-).

Lambert, BHM — B. Lambert, *Bibliotheca Hieronymiana Manuscripta*, Instrumenta Patristica, IV, 4 vols. in 6 pts. (Steenbrugge, 1969-72).

Leclercq, 1951 — J. Leclercq, "Manuscrits cisterciens dans les bibliothèques d'Italie," *Analecta Sacri Ordinis Cisterciensis* 7 (1951) pp. 71-77.

Leclercq, 1961 — J. Leclercq, "Textes et manuscrits cisterciens dans les bibliothèques des États-Unis," *Traditio* 17 (1961) pp. 163-83.

Leroquais, LH — V. Leroquais, *Les livres d'heures, manuscrits de la Bibliothèque Nationale* (Paris, 1927-43).

Lieftinck, *Maatschappij* — *Codices 168-360 Societatis cui nomen Maatschappij der Nederlandsche Letterkunde* descripsit G. I. Lieftinck. Biblioteca Universitatis Leidensis. Codices Manuscripti, v. 1 (Leiden, 1948).

Lyell Cat. — A. C. de la Mare, *Catalogue of the Collection of Medieval Manuscripts Bequeathed to the Bodleian Library Oxford by James P. R. Lyell* (Oxford, 1971).

Meertens — M. Meertens, *De Godsvrucht in de Nederlanden; naar Handschriften van Gebedenboeken der XVe Eeuw*. Leuvense Studiën en Tekstuitgaven 1-3, 6 (1930-34).

MGH — *Monumenta Germaniae historica.*

Missale Romanum — R. Lippe, ed., *Missale Romanum Mediolani 1474* in Henry Bradshaw Society 17, 33 (1899, 1907).

MSS datés — *Catalogue des manuscrits en écriture latine portant des indications de date, de lieu ou de copiste* (Paris, 1959-).

Nichipor — W. N. Nichipor, "Marginalia," Yale University Library *Gazette* 58 (1984) pp. 186-87.

OCT	Oxford Classical Texts.
Olivier	J.-M. Olivier, "Les manuscrits grecs de l'Archivo-Biblioteca del Calbildo metropolitano (La Seo) de Saragosse," *Scriptorium* 30 (1976) pp. 52–57.
Omont	H. Omont, *Facsimilés des manuscrits grecs des XVe et XVIe siècles* (Paris, 1887).
Pächt and Alexander	O. Pächt and J. J. G. Alexander, *Illuminated Manuscripts in the Bodleian Library*, 3 vols. (Oxford, 1966–73).
Parkes, *Cursive Book Hands*	M. B. Parkes, *English Cursive Book Hands 1250–1500* (Oxford, 1969).
Parkes, *Keble College*	M. B. Parkes, *The Medieval Manuscripts of Keble College Oxford* (London, 1979).
Patrinelis	C. G. Patrinelis, "Ἕλληνες κωδικογράφοι," Ἐπετῆρις τοῦ Μεσαιωνικοῦ Ἀρχείου, vols. 8–9 (1958–59) (Athens, 1961) pp. 62–125.
Perdrizet	P. Perdrizet, *Le calendrier parisien à la fin du moyen âge. Publications de la Faculté des Lettres de l'Université de Strasbourg* 63 (Paris, 1933).
PG	*Patrologiae cursus completus, series graeca*, accurante J.-P. Migne.
Phillipps Studies	A. N. L. Munby, *Phillipps Studies* (Cambridge, 1951–60).
Piccard	G. Piccard, *Die Wasserzeichenkartei Piccard im Hauptstaatsarchiv Stuttgart* (Stuttgart, 1961–).
PL	*Patrologiae cursus completus, series latina*, accurante J.-P. Migne.
Plummer, *Last Flowering*	J. Plummer, *The Last Flowering: French Painting in Manuscripts 1420–1530*, exhib. cat. (New York and London, 1982).
PMLA	*Publications of the Modern Language Association of America.*
PO	*Patrologia orientalis* (Paris, 1907–).
Reynolds, *Texts and Transmission*	L. D. Reynolds, et al., *Texts and Transmission: A Survey of the Latin Classics* (Oxford, 1983).

RH	U. Chevalier, *Repertorium hymnologicum*, v. 1–4 (Louvain, 1892–1921); v. 5–6 (Brussels, 1920–21).
Richard	M. Richard, *Répertoire des bibliothèques et des catalogues de manuscrits grecs.*, 2nd ed. (Paris, 1958); *Supplément* (1964).
Robinson, *Cambridge*	P. R. Robinson, *Catalogue of Dated and Datable Manuscripts c. 737–1600 in Cambridge Libraries* (Cambridge, 1988).
Sarum Missal	J. W. Legg, *The Sarum Missal, edited from three early manuscripts* (Oxford, 1916).
Schneyer	J. B. Schneyer, *Repertorium der lateinischen Sermones des Mittelalters für die Zeit von 1150–1350.* Beiträge zur Geschichte der Philosophie und Theologie des Mittelalters 43 (Münster, 1969–).
Sinclair	K. V. Sinclair, *Descriptive Catalogue of Medieval and Renaissance Western Manuscripts in Australia* (Sydney, 1969).
Sonet	J. Sonet, *Répertoire d'incipit de prières en ancien français. Société de Publications Romanes et Françaises* 54 (Geneva, 1956).
SR	*Statutes of the Realm*; with references to 1810–28 ed., v. 1.
Stegmüller	F. Stegmüller, *Repertorium biblicum medii aevi* (Madrid, 1950–).
Stegmüller, *Sent.*	F. Stegmüller, *Repertorium commentariorum in Sententias Petri Lombardi* (Würzburg, 1947).
Tenneroni	A. Tenneroni, *Inizii di antiche poesie italiane religiose e morali* (Florence, 1909).
Teubner	Bibliotheca scriptorum graecorum et romanorum teubneriana.
The Medieval Book	B. A. Shailor, *The Medieval Book*, exhib. cat. (New Haven, 1988; reprinted Toronto, 1991).
Thomson, *Latin Bookhands*	S. H. Thomson, *Latin Bookhands of the Later Middle Ages 1100–1500* (Cambridge, 1969).
Thorndike and Kibre	L. Thorndike and P. Kibre, *A Catalogue of Incipits of Mediaeval Scientific Writings in Latin*, 2nd ed. (Cambridge, Mass., 1963).

Ullman — B. L. Ullman, *Petrarch Manuscripts in the United States*, Censimento dei codici petrarcheschi, 1 (Padua, 1964); also in *Italia medioevale e umanistica* 5 (1962) pp. 443–75.

Vogel and Gardthausen — M. Vogel and V. Gardthausen, *Die griechischen Schreiber des Mittelalters und der Renaissance. Beihefte zum Zentralblatt für Bibliothekswesen* 33 (Leipzig, 1909).

Walters Art Gallery, *Bookbinding* — *The History of Bookbinding, 525–1950 A. D.*, exhib. cat., The Walters Art Gallery (Baltimore, 1957).

Walther, *Initia* — H. Walther, *Initia carminum ac versuum medii aevi posterioris latinorum*, Carmina medii aevi posterioris latina, i, 2nd ed. (Göttingen, 1969).

Walther, *Sprichwörter* — H. Walther, *Lateinische Sprichwörter und Sentenzen des Mittelalters*, Carmina medii aevi posterioris latina, ii (Göttingen, 1963–86).

Watson, *B. L.* — A. G. Watson, *Catalogue of Dated and Datable Manuscripts c. 700–1600 in the Department of Manuscripts, The British Library* (London, 1979).

Watson, *Oxford* — A. G. Watson, *Catalogue of Dated and Datable Manuscripts c. 435–1600 in Oxford Libraries* (Oxford, 1984).

Weale, *South Kensington* — W. H. J. Weale, *Bookbindings and Rubbings of Bindings in the National Art Library, South Kensington Museum* (London, 1894, 1898).

Wilmart — A. Wilmart, *Auteurs spirituels et textes dévots du moyen âge latin* (Paris, 1932).

Ziskind Catalogue — B. M. W. Knox, "The Ziskind Collection of Greek Manuscripts," Yale University Library *Gazette* 32 (1957) pp. 38–56.

Introduction

THE THIRD VOLUME OF THE *Catalogue of Medieval and Renaissance Manuscripts in the Beinecke Rare Book and Manuscript Library of Yale University* is devoted to the Marston Collection – a group of some 230 manuscripts collected by Thomas E. Marston preserved in the Beinecke Library as a distinct *fond*, separate from the General Collection of early manuscripts. MSS 1–500 of the General Collection are described in the first two volumes of this series (Vol. I: 1984; Vol. II: 1987).

Acquired by the late Thomas Marston primarily during the 1940s and 1950s, the collection is extremely rich in classical authors and major Renaissance texts; the Marston manuscripts, which constitute one of the major private North American collections of the 20th century, compare favorably with the manuscripts acquired by Philip Hofer, C. L. Ricketts, Henry Huntington, and Phyllis G. and John D. Gordan.

It is the purpose of this introduction to survey briefly the life and collection of Thomas E. Marston (1904–84), and to outline the format and layout of the individual entries and index.

THOMAS EWART MARSTON, BORN IN CHICAGO IN 1904, had throughout his life a close affiliation with Yale University. A graduate of Yale College in 1927 with the A. B. degree, he entered the Yale Graduate School in 1929 in the areas of Egyptology and ancient history. Marston then entered the Harvard Graduate School, where he received both the M. A. (1936) and Ph. D. (1939) degrees in European history. His doctoral dissertation, on *Britain's Imperial Role in the Red Sea Area, 1800–70*, was published in 1961. During World War II and the Korean War he served in several military capacities, both as an evaluation analyst in the Army Air Force and later as colonel in the United States Army Intelligence. After military service he returned to Yale where he became Curator of Classics, and then of Medieval and Renaissance Literature until his retirement in 1973. Marston was an active and generous Trustee of the Yale University Library Associates for the fifty-one years between 1933 and his death in 1984; he made frequent pledges to the Yale library for the acquisition of rare books and manuscripts.

It was during Thomas Marston's early years at Yale that he began collecting medieval and Renaissance manuscripts. The late Cora E. Lutz remembered vividly a course in Latin satire taught by G. Lincoln Hendrickson, Professor of Classics, in which both she and Thomas Marston were students. While other members of the class were studying the works of Juvenal and Persius from modern printed books, Marston was eagerly buying and using both early manuscripts and incunables for his texts. Many of these Juvenal volumes, which formed the nucleus of his early collection and which were presented by him to Yale in 1936 in memory of his father, are now catalogued as part of the general collections within the Beinecke Library.

Over the years Marston developed wide-ranging collecting interests. His service in the Middle East inspired him to acquire a small number of early Turkish, Arabic, Greek, Persian, Ethiopic and Slavonic manuscripts. He was an avid collector of 15th- and 16th-century printed books, with a special interest in Roman poets such as Catullus, Horace, Tibullus, and Martial. In 1939 he gave to the Yale Library a collection of first editions of W. Somerset Maugham, in addition to 35 autograph letters, four publisher's contracts, and four sets of corrected proofs of stories by Maugham. In 1960 he presented 87 maps to the library.

Throughout his career as collector, however, Marston was most enthusiastic about Western manuscripts produced in the Middle Ages and Renaissance. Although Marston began his collecting with the Latin classics, he soon broadened his scope to include texts written in later periods and he developed in time more far-reaching principles for adding volumes for his personal library. In a letter dated 1 May 1961 Marston wrote to the University Librarian, James T. Babb:

> The collection is designed around these aspects:
> 1. to show a typical monastic library of the Twelfth Century,
> 2. to show a typical humanistic library of the Fifteenth Century, and
> 3. to provide representative texts illustrating Thirteenth and Fourteenth Century intellectual activity.

Hence, in addition to the works of Ovid, Juvenal, Persius, Seneca, and Cicero, he actively sought out the texts, translations, and commentaries by Leonardo Bruni, Ambrogio Traversari, Guarino of Verona, Lorenzo Valla, and other members of their literary circles. Manuscripts from 15th-century Italy, both in Latin and Italian, constitute a major portion of the Marston collection, and for some authors the collection approached comprehensiveness. Hence, the Marston collection contains a significant proportion of items that can be attributed to 15th-century Italy, written both in Latin and Italian. As a result of Marston's enthusiasm for the Renaissance, for example, the Beinecke Library now houses the largest collection of manuscripts of Leonardo Bruni's works outside of Italy (see J. Hankins, "Bruni Manuscripts in North America: a Handlist," *Nuovi studi storici* 10 [1991] pp. 55–90).

The Marston collection is also interesting from a codicological perspective.

Many of the items are in an excellent state of preservation, with early boards and flyleaves intact, and with only minor restoration and repairs. Because Marston appreciated the artistic beauty of early bookbindings, he seldom had a volume rebound. Marston was less inspired by the elaborate decoration of a volume than by the text(s) it contained; although he acquired a few manuscripts illuminated by well-known artists of considerable accomplishment, the collection is far richer in manuscripts of textual, paleographical, and codicological interest. An example of Marston's perspicacity in seeking out text manuscripts is the remarkable group of 12th- and 13th-century manuscripts whose provenance can be traced back to the Cistercian abbey of Hautecombe in Savoy.

Unfortunately, Thomas Marston's zeal in collecting manuscripts far exceeded his interest in keeping records about the items he purchased. The files in the Beinecke Library contain very little information beyond that recorded in the Faye and Bond *Supplement.* For those manuscripts not listed in Faye and Bond, there is even less information. Marston often jotted down notes, in pencil, in a somewhat cramped but regular script on the front pastedown or flyleaf of a volume. He did not usually indicate the source of his information, much of which we have not been able to verify. In those cases where the information was erroneous, we have not included reference to his notes. In other instances, we have cited his opinion, although its accuracy may be open to question.

Marston's devotion to book collecting, which began in the 1920s, extended into the 1960s. When Faye and Bond issued in 1962 their *Supplement to the Census of Medieval and Renaissance Manuscripts in the United States and Canada*, there was a total of 276 items listed under his name. For a number of reasons this list does not accurately reflect the collection as it exists today and as it is catalogued in this volume. First, since Marston continued to acquire manuscripts after 1962, the last numbered item today bears the shelf-mark "Marston MS 287." Second, before Yale purchased the bulk of the Marston manuscript collection in 1962, Marston had sold or put up for auction more than thirty manuscripts. He sold nineteen manuscripts (Marston MSS 5, 58, 65, 66, 71, 84, 108, 110, 126, 177, 183, 191, 193, 206, 207, 221, 224, 237, and item no. 1 below) in December 1961 through Sotheby's. He sold an additional thirteen manuscripts in January 1962 to Laurence Witten, who auctioned the majority of them through Sotheby's in 1962 (Marston MSS 3, 21, 68, 115, 165), in 1966 (Marston MS 173), and in 1974 (Marston MSS 44, 75, 133, 178). Third, Marston donated some volumes from his collection to the Beinecke Library and these now form part of the general collection; the descriptions of these manuscripts appear in Volumes I and II of the catalogue. Fourth, in December 1961 Marston gave five manuscripts to the Yale School of Music Library (Marston MSS 19, 20, 103, 121, and no. 1 below).

The following concordance is intended to augment and to update the list in the Faye and Bond *Supplement.* For those items currently part of the Marston Collection and described in this catalogue we provide the shelf-mark which the manuscripts had while Marston owned them (the earlier Marston shelf-marks have been replaced by the numbers assigned in the Faye and Bond, *Supplement*). For each item recorded in Faye and Bond, but *not* described in Volume III, we attempt to give either its present location (at Yale or elsewhere), or to indicate when and where it was sold. The previous shelf-mark is given when known.

Marston MS	*Old Number*	*Comment*
1	39	–
2	6	–
3	179	sold to Witten in 1962; sold at Sotheby's, 10 December 1962, lot 119, to Dawson
4	59	–
5	182	sold at Sotheby's, 11 December 1961, lot 185, to A. G. Thomas; his cat. 12 (1963), no. 5, and re-offered in his cats. 14 (1964), no. 13, and 16 (1965), no. 4; resold at Sotheby's, 10 July 1967, lot 61, to Miss H. Blane
6	184	–
7	185	–
8	29	–
9	219	–
10	69	–
11	132	–
12	–	Ferrini, cat. 1 (1987), no. 66
13	–	No information available
14	–	No information available
15	51	–
16	260	–
17	215	–
18	216	–
19	–	Yale School of Music Library MS 61 (uncatalogued)
20	–	Yale School of Music Library MS 60 (uncatalogued)
21	13	sold to Witten in 1962; sold at Sotheby's, 10 December 1962, lot 115, to Maggs
22	32	–
23	117	–
24	125	–
25	129	–
26	145	–
27	190	–
28	149	–
29	206	–
30	90	–

31	256	–
32	213	–
33	–	Beinecke MS 450 (vol. II, pp. 400–402)
34	20	–
35	170	–
36	240	–
37	253	–
38	188	–
39	62	–
40	242	–
41	–	Beinecke MS 319 (Vol. II, pp. 125–26)
42	222	–
43	228	–
44	157	sold to Witten in 1962; sold at Sotheby's, 9 December 1974, lot 43, to Dr. Knight; British Rail Pension Fund; J. Paul Getty, Jr.; H. Tenschert, cat. 25 (1990), no. 17
45	141	–
46	189	–
47	144	–
48	200	–
49	74	–
50	138	–
51	187	–
52	224	–
53	218	–
54	217?	sold to Witten in 1962; recent provenance and present location unknown
55	210	–
56	252	–
57	–	Beinecke MS 328 (vol. II, pp. 146–47)
58	177	sold at Sotheby's, 11 December 1961, lot 186, to Quaritch; private collector, Cambridge, Mass.; re-sold at Sotheby's, 13 December 1976, lot 60, to Quaritch; now Aberystwyth, National Library of Wales MS 21587 D
59	181	–
60	172	–
61	172[*sic*]	–
62	171	–
63	168	–
64	148	–
65	161	sold at Sotheby's, 11 December 1961, lot 182, to Heilbrun

66	225	sold at Sotheby's, 11 December 1961, lot 187, to Quaritch
67	139	–
68	211	sold to Witten in 1962; now Florence, Biblioteca Nazionale Nuov. Acq. 1129
69	133	–
70	153	–
71	–	sold at Sotheby's, 11 December 1961, lot 191, to A. G. Thomas; his cat. 12 (1963), no. 2
72	183	–
73	70	–
74	83	–
75	64	sold to Witten in 1962; sold at Sotheby's, 9 December 1974, lot 45, to Gleeson
76	89	–
77	96	–
78	100	–
79	101	–
80	107	–
81	114	–
82	115	–
83	166	–
84	151	sold at Sotheby's, 11 December 1961, lot 183, to Dawson; re-sold at Sotheby's, 11 December 1972, lot 39, to Traylen
85	176	–
86	36	–
87	40	–
88	11	–
89 & 89A	4	–
90	52	–
91	54	–
92	30	–
93	78	–
94	80	–
95	262	–
96	94	–
97	95	–
98	102	–
99	34	–
100	97	–
101	–	Beinecke MS 358 (vol. II, pp. 201–2)

102	116	–
103	–	Yale School of Music Library MS 59 (uncatalogued)
104	26	–
105	48	–
106	65	–
107	68	–
108	106	sold at Sotheby's, 11 December 1961, lot 184, to Davis and Orioli; re-sold at Sotheby's, 5 July 1965, lot 205, to Maggs; sold in 1966 to Canterbury University Library, Christchurch, New Zealand
109	93	sold to Witten in 1962; his sale, cat. 8 (1978), no. 98; Sotheby's, 23 June 1987, lot 92
110	86	sold at Sotheby's, 11 December 1961, lot 192, to Quaritch
111	44	–
112	7	–
113	113	–
114	71	–
115	61	sold to Witten in 1962; sold at Sotheby's, 10 December 1962, lot 120, to Maggs; B. S. Cron (*Handlist*, 1965, no. 21)
116	58	–
117	14	–
118	27	–
119	142	–
120	–	no information available
121	–	Yale School of Music Library MS 63 (uncatalogued)
122	239	–
123	202	–
124	42	–
125	135	–
126	75	sold at Sotheby's, 11 December 1961, lot 188, to A. G. Thomas; his cat. 12 (1963), no. 4; B. S. Cron (*Handlist*, 1965, no. 22)
127	22	–
128	23	–
129	92	–
130	111	–
131	72	–
132	98	–
133	169	sold to Witten in 1962; sold at Sotheby's, 9 December 1974, lot 44, to Van der Merckt

134	67	–
135	8	–
136	28	sold to Witten in 1962; his sale, cat. 6 (1975), no. 8
137	–	Beinecke MS 308 (vol. II, pp. 97–99)
138	122	–
139	10	–
140	82	–
141	91	–
142	109	–
143	–	no information available
144	150	–
145	223	–
146	—	Beinecke MS 327 (vol. II, pp. 143–46)
147	193	–
148	–	Beinecke MS 415 (vol. II, pp. 327–29)
149	174	–
150	226	–
151	123	–
152	131	–
153	128	–
154	154	–
155	251	–
156	248	–
157	130	–
158	126	–
159	136	–
160	85	–
161	41	–
162	254	–
163	163	–
164	164	–
165	45	sold to Witten in 1962; sold at Sotheby's, 9 December 1974, lot 47, to Van der Merckt; L. Moorthamers, sale, Brussels, 12 February 1977, lot 169; now Brussels, Bibliothèque Royale, IV.1101
166	2	–
167	165	–
168	195	–
169	47	–
170	–	Beinecke MS 339 (vol. II, pp. 166–69)
171	99	–
172	124	–

173	127	sold to Witten in 1962; sold at Sotheby's, 11 July 1966, lot 249, to Measures
174	50	–
175	15	–
176	249	–
177	16	sold at Sotheby's, 11 December 1961, lot 181, to Witten
178	53	sold to Witten in 1962; sold at Sotheby's, 9 December 1974, to Quaritch; now Chicago, Newberry Library MS 97.3
179	178	–
180	119	–
181	56	–
182	60	–
183	63	sold at Sotheby's, 11 December 1961, lot 190, to A. G. Thomas; his cat. 13 (1963), no. 1 and cat. 15 (1964), no. 2
184	184	–
185	105	–
186	152	–
187	197	–
188	73	–
189	192	–
190	76	–
191	265	sold at Sotheby's, 11 December 1961, lot 194, to Traylen; his cat. 58 (1963), no. 43
192	134	–
193	237	sold at Sotheby's, 11 December 1961, lot 178, to H. P. Kraus; his cat. 100 (1962), no. 3
194	250	–
195	–	Beinecke MS 338 (vol. II, pp. 165–66)
196	198	–
197	238	–
198	155	–
199	258	–
200	18	–
201	201	–
202	204	–
203	203	–
204	84	–
205	66	–
206	244	sold at Sotheby's, 11 December 1961, lot 180, to Vennor

207	259	sold at Sotheby's, 11 December 1961, lot 196, to H. P. Kraus; collection of Peter and Irene Ludwig; now Malibu, California, J. Paul Getty Museum, MS Ludwig XI.1
208	137	–
209	87	–
210	207	–
211	88	–
212	208	–
213	243	–
214	209	–
215	156	–
216	143	–
217	261	–
218	212	–
219	19	–
220	245	–
221	255	sold at Sotheby's, 11 December 1961, lot 193, to Heilbrun
222	246	–
223	108	–
224	263	sold at Sotheby's, 11 December 1961, lot 195, to Witten; to H. P. Kraus; "a private Swiss collection"; re-sold at Sotheby's, 18 June 1991, lot 90
225	25	–
226	220	–
227	110	–
228	146	–
229	112	–
230	264	–
231	35	–
232	247	–
233	5	–
234	160	–
235	162	–
236	24	–
237	12	sold at Sotheby's, 11 December 1961, lot 179, to Maggs for Major J. R. Abbey (JA.7122); Abbey sale, Sotheby's 19 June 1989, lot 3012, to H. Tenschert; his cat. 25 (1990), no. 6
238	–	Beinecke MS 506 (uncatalogued)
239	33	–

240	38	–
241	121	–
242	118	–
243	104	–
244	–	Beinecke MS 380 (vol. II, pp. 239–41)
245	49	–
246	–	Beinecke MS 326 (vol. II, pp. 141–43)
247	191	–
248	241	–
249	113	–
250	46	–
251	81	–
252	9	–
253	37	–
254	120	–
255	227	–
256	103	–
257	175	–
258	57	–
259	55	–
260	158	–
261	214	–
262	43	–
263	199	–
264	196	–
265	159	–
266	140	–
267	147	–
268	3	–
269	17	–
270	21	–
271	1	–
272	–	no information available
273	194	–
274	173	–
275	221	–
276	31	–
277	77	–
278	63	–
279	205	–
280	229	–
281	230	–

282	231	–
283	232	–
284	233	–
285	234	–
286	235	–
287	236	–

In addition to those manuscripts listed in Faye and Bond we can add a number of items formerly belonging to Thomas E. Marston, the present location of which is unknown: 1. Augustine, *Confessiones*, etc., Florence, s. XV^{2}; sold at Sotheby's, 11 December 1961, lot 189, to A. G. Thomas; his cat. 12 (1963), no. 3, re-offered in his cats. 14 (1964), no. 11, and 16 (1965), no. 1; re-sold at Sotheby's, 10 July 1967, lot 59, to Milne. 2. New Testament, Latin, with glosses, s. XII^{2}; sold at Sotheby's, 10 December 1962, lot 114, to A. G. Thomas; his cat. 12 (1963), no. 10. 3. Bible, Spain, s. XIII^{ex}; sold at Sotheby's, 10 December 1962, lot 116, to Maggs. 4. Gregory IX, pope, *Decretales, Liber Sextus*, Bologna, s. XIII/XIV; sold at Sotheby's, 10 December 1962, lot 117, to A. G. Thomas; his cat. 12 (1963), no. 7.

Two manuscripts were donated by Marston to other libraries at Yale University:

1. Yale School of Music Library MS 62 (uncatalogued; not recorded in Faye and Bond): *Opera varia*, in Greek, with musical notation throughout, Byzantium, s. XVI.
2. Yale Medical Historical Library MS 51 (Faye and Bond, p. 63).

The description of each manuscript currently in the Marston collection follows, for the most part, the methodological considerations and explanations of format as presented in Vol. I of this series (pp. xix-xxi of the Introduction). Those comments are repeated here, with some further clarification, for the reader's convenience.

I. *Heading*

The heading of each entry consists of the call number, in bold type, in the first line to the left. The number is preceded in every case by "Marston" to distinguish items in this collection from those in the general collection; the designation "Marston" should always be included in references to these manuscripts. The known or probable place of origin and date, known or approximate, appear in the first line to the right. The suprascript notations *in*, 1, *med*, 2, *ex* refer to the beginning, first half, middle, second half, end of the century; 2/4 denotes the second quarter of a century whereas, s. XIV/XV denotes the period around the turn of a century. Multiple places and/or dates appear for composite codices or for items that may have been copied in one location and period and decorated at another place or time. The second line provides an author and short title, to the left, and reference(s) to plates at the end of the volume, on the right.

II. *Contents*

As a rule we record texts in the sequence in which they occur in the manuscript and give a leaf citation for the beginning and conclusion of each article. Arabic numerals designate the particular texts (articles). Roman numerals appear if the manuscript is composed of physically discrete sections, as when booklets were bound together into a single codex. Text identifications and bibliographical citations, when available, follow immediately the incipits and explicits for an article. In the case of some texts (e. g., liturgical texts, Bible prefaces) when incipits and explicits are often not useful, a brief identification (and bibliographical citation, if appropriate) is noted instead.

Rubrics and headings written in display script are here printed in italics. Transcriptions of incipits and explicits attempt to retain the original orthography of the text; abbreviations and ligatures are expanded silently. Parallel oblique lines (//) indicate that the text begins or ends imperfectly, or that a passage has been omitted from the text. Square brackets ([]) denote editorial intervention or problems of interpretation (e.g., [?]). The use of [*sic*] is restricted to readings that may appear peculiar to the reader but which do, in fact, appear in the text. Asterisks occur when letters, words or phrases are illegible due to erasure or damage by water, rodents, etc.

III. *Physical Description*

The physical specifications of the codex (with multiple descriptions for composite items) are divided into several paragraphs arranged in the following order (it has sometimes been necessary to adopt slightly altered formats, as in the case of rolls and fragments):

a. Material on which a manuscript is written. Adjectives that describe the quality of the parchment or references to watermarks listed in standard works such as Briquet, Piccard, and Harlfinger may follow in parentheses. Number of leaves and foliation are given, with flyleaves designated by small Roman numerals before and after the numbers of leaves of the text. It is presumed that flyleaves are contemporary with a binding unless otherwise stated. Dimensions of the folio, with dimensions of the written space in parentheses, record the height and width respectively, in millimeters. After the number of columns and lines is the description of the physical arrangement of the page: bounding lines (rulings that delineate the written space), the instruments or materials used for ruling (hard point, crayon, lead, ink), and prickings. For those manuscripts produced in Italy in the fifteenth century, we refer to the helpful series of numbered diagrams included in A. Derolez, *Codicologie des manuscrits en écriture humanistique sur parchemin*, Bibliologia

5–6 (Turnhout, 1984). Because it has become apparent while cataloguing the manuscripts in the Marston collection that much of what Derolez has outlined for humanistic manuscripts written on parchment is also applicable for items originating in Italy in the fifteenth century that were written on paper and in non-humanistic scripts, we also frequently provide references to his work for manuscripts with these characteristics.

b. Collation; catchwords, leaf and/or quire signatures. If there are several designs or arrangements of catchwords and signatures, we attempt to list them and to record where they occur.

c. Scribes, scripts. Information on the identity of scribe(s), if available, occurs here or under the section devoted to Provenance.

d. Decoration. The main kinds of decoration are described hierarchically, beginning with the most elaborate and proceeding to the simplest. If this portion of the description is exceedingly long, as is true in the case of lavishly illuminated manuscripts, we divide the discussion into several distinct paragraphs. Attributions by art historians and bibliographical citations concerning the illuminator or school of illumination are noted wherever possible.

e. Imperfections. We record significant damage or repair to the item that is not mentioned elsewhere in the entry. When the manuscript is in good physical condition, the paragraph is omitted.

f. Binding. Extensive comments on the structure of the binding have been compiled by J. Greenfield. Plate 1 illustrates different designs of endbands. Those portions of the binding composed of manuscript fragments are also discussed here; often, however, their poor state of preservation or the lack of continuous text hinders us from describing them in great detail or from identifying precisely the text(s). For many of the early bindings, the description is often divided into two paragraphs, with the first discussing the internal structure and the second devoted to the boards, outer covering, hardware, and other external features.

IV. *Provenance*

This portion of the entry addresses the questions: Where and when was the manuscript produced? Who were its former owners, both individuals and institutions? When and from whom did Thomas Marston acquire the item? Since all manuscripts in the collection were purchased by the Yale University Library Associates in 1962 for Yale, this information is not repeated in each entry. Evidence of prior ownership is presented even if its importance is unclear. Opening words of the *secundo folio* are appended below the paragraph for most Western manuscripts before 1500. We provide the *secundo folio* for booklets in a composite manuscript, but not for fragments or for codices where the beginning of the volume is imperfect.

V. *Bibliography*

Bibliographical citations occur in the following order: 1. De Ricci and/or Faye and Bond; 2. *Exhibition Catalogue* prepared in 1978 by Walter Cahn and James Marrow; 3. *The Medieval Book*, catalogue of an exhibition written by Barbara A. Shailor in 1988 (reprinted by the University of Toronto Press, 1991). Other references not cited in the text of the entry are listed in chronological order of publication.

VI. *Indices*

Multiple indices (1–7) provide access to information in the descriptions:

1. MSS arranged by country (or region) of origin and by century.

2. Dated MSS.

3. General Index: persons, places, authors, etc. There are rather lengthy entries for Saints, Illuminations (listed by subjects illustrated), Bindings, the *Secundo folio* references, and Watermarks.

4. Illuminators and Scribes.

5. Provenance: individuals and institutions associated with manuscripts.

6. Other MSS cited.

7. Incipits for both identified and unidentified texts.

VII. *Plates*

Financial considerations preclude the inclusion of photographic reproductions of each item or of each part of a composite codex; we do not illustrate items that are poorly preserved. We exclude account books, diplomas, documents, and the like. The plates are arranged in approximate chronological order according to place of origin. Photographs of bindings are grouped together at the end; the drawing of endbands by Jane Greenfield occurs at the beginning.

I AM GRATEFUL TO MANY COLLEAGUES for their continuing help and support during this entire project. The Board of Advisors for this volume has offered invaluable assistance in the following ways: A. C. de la Mare examined the Italian humanistic manuscripts and offered opinions on their dates and places of origin; Consuelo W. Dutschke read all of the catalogue descriptions in draft format and provided special assistance with both the liturgical and Italian vernacular manuscripts; Jane Greenfield compiled the detailed analysis of structures for the medieval and early Renaissance bindings, as well as information on the origin and date of each binding; Richard H. Rouse, who read the descriptions in draft format and advised on the dating and place of most non-humanistic manuscripts, was especially helpful in dating and localizing items from the twelfth through fourteenth centuries.

Over the past five years many scholars have shared their expertise with me either when they were visiting in New Haven or through personal correspondence. Among those to whom I am indebted for their assistance with this volume are: J. J. G. Alexander, Thomas Amos, Lilian Armstrong, François Avril, Bernhard Bischoff, Virginia Brown, Walter Cahn, Albert Derolez, Dennis Dutschke, A. S. G. Edwards, Hugh Feiss, Mirella Ferrari, David Ganz, Michael Gullick, Jeffrey Hamburger, James Hankins, Dieter Harlfinger, Michel Huglo, Ranee Katzenstein, Laura Light, James Marrow, Paul Meyvaert, John Monfasani, Francis Newton, Timothy Noone, W. Keith Percival, Julian Plante, Emil Polak, Jean Preston, Michael D. Reeve, Kathleen L. Scott, Patricia Stirnemann, Andrew Watson, Roger Wieck. My colleague, James M. Heath, meticuously proofread the volume in preparation for publication.

The following individuals have been instrumental in helping to trace the provenance of many of the Marston manuscripts: Christopher de Hamel of Sotheby's, Joshua Lipton of H. P. Kraus, and the bookdealers Bernard Rosenthal and Laurence Witten. In addition, we are thankful to the staff of the Hill Monastic Manuscript Library and of the Institut de Recherche et d'Histoire des Textes in Paris for their assistance with identifying incipits and manuscripts.

Throughout the preparation of this volume I have had the good fortune to work with a number of the very talented graduate students at Yale; I owe special thanks to Richard Armstrong, Susan Boynton, Annette Burton, James T. Powell, and Edward Brian Roots.

This project would not have been possible without the encouragement of the administration and staff of the Beinecke Rare Book and Manuscript Library. Robert Babcock, Curator of Early Books and Manuscripts, has offered valuable advice and clarification on many catalogue entries; George Miles worked miracles with a new indexing program that much simplified the compilation of multiple indices; Stephen Parks and Vincent Giroud answered numerous questions related to English and French provenance; Ralph Franklin, Director of the Beinecke Library, has given continuous, enthusiastic support for this and other projects.

Finally, I am indebted to the National Endowment for the Humanities, which has generously funded the three volumes of this catalogue.

Marston Manuscripts

Marston MS 1 Northeastern Italy, s. XV^{med}

Aeneas Gazaeus, Theophrastus, Lat. tr. Ambrogio Traversari, etc.

1. ff. 2r–9v blank (first gathering; foliation begins on preceding flyleaf); ff. 10r–52v *Aenee Sophiste. V. CL. Dialogus qui Theophrastus inscribitur Incipit. Collocutores Egyptus Alexandrinus. Euxitheus Syrus. Theophrastus Atheniensis.* [in margin: *Egyptus*] Quo tu Euxithee uel unde. *Euxith.* E Syria Athenas ferebar o egypte ... *Taeoph.* Satis oratum est sed proficiscamur. .ΤΕΛΟΣ.

   Aeneas Gazaeus, *Theophrastus*, translated into Latin by Ambrogio Traversari; the names of the interlocutors occur in red throughout the text. *Aeneas Gazaeus et Zacharias Mitylenaeus de immortalitate animae ... Accedit Aeneae interpretatio ab Ambrosio camaldi facta* (Paris, 1836) pp. 469–510, reprinted from the Paganini edition (Venice) of 1513.

2. f. 53r–v *Diui integerrimique Viri Beati Helennij vita incipit foeliciter.* Fuit alius vir sanctus Helennius nomine a puericia hic in seruitio dei omni cum continentia et castissimis institutionibus enutritus ... nihil ei deerat eorumque poscebat a domino. Finis. ff. 54r–59v blank

   Life of St. Helenus, monk in Egypt. Text is an extract (incomplete) taken from the Latin translation by Rufinus of the *Historia monachorum*, ch. 11; PL 21.429–30.

Paper (watermarks: Briquet Fleur 6306, and unidentified shrub, ff. i–viii, in gutter; Briquet Tête humaine 15617), ff. i (contemporary parchment) + viii (contemporary paper) + 50 (two series of modern foliation) + i (contemporary parchment, stub only), 202 x 143 (133 x 79) mm. 22 long lines. Single vertical and horizontal bounding lines, full length and full width, ruled in lead. Guide lines for text in pale brown ink (Derolez 13.13). Remains of prickings in upper, lower, and outer margins.

I^8 (ff. i–viii, all blank), II^{10} (ff. 1 and 10 parchment), $III–IV^{10}$, (last six leaves blank). Catchwords perpendicular to text on inner vertical bounding line in lower margin, verso (Derolez 12.6).

Written in humanistic script by a single scribe, above top line.

One large illuminated initial, 5-line, of modest quality, in gold with black accents on a multicolored ground of red, blue and green with white vine-stem ornament and white dots. One smaller initial (unfinished), parchment color on blue ground with white vine-stem ornament. On f. 1r, in lower border an unidentified coat of arms: vert a chief sable [?], overall a lion [?] rampant gules (or purpre?) on the main field and/or in chief and with bend (tincture undetermined) overall; the whole shield overpainted in black. Headings in red.

Binding: Italy, s. xv. Vellum stays are adhered in- and outside the paper gatherings. Original sewing on three tawed skin, kermes pink, slit straps which go through tunnels in the edges of wooden boards to channels on the outside where they are pegged. The primary endband, sewn on a tawed skin core, is gilt with traces of a red secondary endband. A design is scratched on the gilt edges.

Covered in brown sheepskin with corner tongues and blind-tooled with progressively taller concentric frames alternately decorated with five small tools. Five flower-shaped bosses on each board, some wanting, and four fastenings, leaf-shaped catches on the lower board, the upper board cut in for the clasp straps which are attached with star-headed nails. Rebacked.

Written in Northeastern Italy in the middle of the 15th century; owned by an unidentified person whose mutilated arms appear on f. 1r. Inscription, s. xvi, on f. 59v: "frater bonaventura minorum [?]." Inscription, s. xviii, on front pastedown: "Ex libris B. Brunati." Inscription, s. xviii, erased but visible under ultra-violet light on front pastedown: "Iohannis Jacobi Dugatiis di Thomarijs liber." Signature, s. xviii^2, on front pastedown: "Alberti Bonetti." Unidentified circular white paper tag on spine with handwritten shelf-mark in ink: "Aeneas/4o. 72806 [portion of tag missing]/ L III O." In pencil on front pastedown: "279" and on recto of front flyleaf: "30." Acquired from C. A. Stonehill in 1949 by Thomas E. Marston (bookplate).

secundo folio: humanitatis

Bibliography: Faye and Bond, p. 64, no. 1.

Marston MS 2 Tuscany, s. $XII^{4/4}$

Canticum canticorum, with glossa ordinaria

1. ff. 1r–63r *Obsculetur* me osculo oris sui. Quia meliora sunt ubera uino. flagrantia unguentis optimis ... Fuge dilecte mi et asimilare capree. ynuloque ceruorum super montes aromatum.

Canticum canticorum.

2. ff. 1r–63r [In upper margin, f. 1r:] Sinagoga id est congregatio. quod et lapidum. Ecclesia conuocatio quod rationalium. Vtraque autem hec portio iustorum ... [in inner margin, f. 1r:] Uox ecclesie optantis christi aduentum ... [in outer margin, f. 1r:] Sinagoga dominum in carne uenire desiderat. ac uenienti deuota caritate occurrat. Tangat me dulcedine presentie sue ... [interlinear gloss:] delectet me et certificet./ Incarnatione filii. que est quasi pre/ libatio coniunctionis ... [f. 63r:] Cum in montibus figas pedes. dignare dilabi ad ualles. f. 63v blank

Glossa ordinaria; Stegmüller, v. 9, no. 11804; PL 113.1128–68.

Parchment (scraps, endpieces), ff. iii (paper; ii = modern title page, majuscule inscription within frame: "Canticum canticorum salomonis cum notis interlinearibus et marginalibus/ MS.") + 63 + iii (paper), 178 x 127 (102 x 86) mm. Written in 3 columns, with 8 lines of text and interlinear glosses in the center and up to 26 lines of gloss in the outer two columns. Double vertical bounding lines ruled in hard point on hair side. Text lines ruled faintly in lead. Remains of prickings in upper, lower, and outer (for 8 lines of text only) margins.

$I–VII^{8}$, VIII^{8} (–8). Quire signatures (e.g., a, b, c, etc.) in lower right corner, verso, or lower left corner, recto.

Text written in large round late caroline minuscule; commentary in a similar, but smaller script with many abbreviations.

One unpretentious illuminated initial, f. 1r, 3-line, yellow edged in red, against blue and red ground with yellow filigree, filled with stylized vine-stem ornament, white with green and yellow shading. For similar initials see Paris, B. N. lat. 588 (cf. Avril and Zaluska, vol. 1, pp. 53–54, no. 90, pl. XXXIX, attributed to Pistoia). First word of text in alternating letters, red and brown with yellow touches. Small initials in blue or red. Guide letters for rubricator throughout.

Binding: Italy, s. xix. Quarter bound in vellum, spine worm eaten and peeling; blue-grey paper sides. Title in rectangular frame, in ink, on spine: "Cant. Salo. MS."

Written in Tuscany, probably in Pistoia to judge from the style of decoration, in the fourth quarter of the 12th century; early provenance unknown. Belonged to Marchese Francesco Riccardi del Vernaccia (1648–1719; bookplate) and to Gustavo Cammillo Galletti of Florence (1805–68; bookstamp [effaced] on f. 1r). Collection of Baron Horace de Landau (1824–1903; bookplate stamped with numbers "2242" and "2243" on front pastedown; see his *Catalogue des livres manuscrits et imprimés composant la bibliothèque de M. Horace de Landau* [Florence, 1890] v. 2, 46); the collection was maintained by his niece Madame Finaly, of Florence (d. 1938). Unidentified rectangular paper label, white with blue frame, with "113" in ink, on front cover. Purchased from C. A. Stonehill in 1948 by Thomas E. Marston (bookplate).

secundo folio: [text:] [curre]mus in
[commentary:] [uene]ris. illa

Bibliography: Faye and Bond, p. 64, no. 2.

Marston MS 4 — Oxford, s. $XV^{3/4}$
Cicero, De officiis, De oratore, etc.

Arts. 1–4 are excerpts from an 11th- or early 12th-century supplement to Curtius Rufus, *Historia Alexandri Magni*; see E. R. Smits, "A Medieval Supplement to the Beginning of Curtius Rufus's Historia Alexandri: An Edition with Introduction," *Viator* 18 (1987) pp. 100–112.

1. f. 1r–v blank; f. 2r [Heading:] Oratio heschinis. [text:] [R]eminiscor Athenienses Alexandrum hac nostra in vrbe liberalibus artibus eruditum. Et Aristotelis ... si nos obsequentes sibi supplices que [*sic*] inuenerit.

   Oratio Aeschinis; R. Sabbadini, "Antonio da Romagno e Pietro Marcello," *Nuovo Archivio Veneto* n.s. 30 (1915) p. 241.

2. f. 2r [Heading:] Oracio demadis. [text:] [A]dmirans vehementer admiror viri Athenienses quonammodo timiditatem incutiens Eschines in deditionem et potestatem ... suis custodibus consiliis et viribus vacuam facilius diripiat.

   Oratio Demadis; Sabbadini, *op. cit.*, pp. 241–42.

3. f. 2r–v [Heading:] Oratio demostenis. [text:] [A]pud vos in questione verti videor. vtrum sumenda sint nobis arma aduersus Alexandrum ... nec dicamus nolle parere alexandro qui seruiuimus philippo.

Oratio Demosthenis contra Demadem; Sabbadini, *op. cit.*, p. 242.

4. ff. 2v–4r [Heading:] Oracio demostenis ad Alexandrum. [text:] [N]ichil habet Rex alexander vel fortuna tua maius quam vt possis . . . nullam de tuis laudibus fore quam eam quam [*hodie* crossed out] hodierno die consequuturus es.

Oratio Demosthenis ad Alexandrum; Sabbadini, *op. cit.*, pp. 243–44; Baron, p. 179. A short quotation from this oration has also been added on f. 123v.

5. f. 4r [Heading:] Responsio alexandri. [text:] [F]acundissime ac disertissime Demosthenes audiui et intellexi . . . me omnia que petunt effectutrum. ffinit. f. 4v ruled, but blank

Ps.-Alexander the Great, *Oratio*.

6. ff. 5r–82r [Heading, added in upper margin:] Marcij tullij Ciceronis Philosophi Amplissimi. liber primus Officiorum ad marcum filium suum incipit. [text:] [Q]uamquam te marce fili. annum iam audientem Cratippum. idque athenis . . . sed multo fore cariorem, si talibus monumentis preceptisque latebre. [added in the same hand as heading on f. 5r:] Excellunt cunctos hij libri philosophorum/ Libri quos scripsit tres tullius officiorum/ . . . lux orbis patrieque Salus meus tota Senatus/ hic plus sole micat cruciatus propter honestum. ff. 82v–84v blank

Cicero, *De officiis*; C. Atzert, ed., Teubner fasc. 28 (1963) pp. 1–123. Text is annotated by contemporary hands in both Latin and Middle English.

7. ff. 85r–119v [C]ogitanti michi sepe numero et memoria vetera repetenti perbeati fuisse quinte frater illi videri solent qui . . . et sic prope dicam decantatas habere debent nisi forte estimatis a. M curio causam.// ff. 120r–123v mostly blank, but with list, pen trials, etc. (see also provenance)

Cicero, *De oratore*; K. Kumaniecki, ed., Teubner fasc. 3 (1969) pp. 1–160. The text, which seems to follow MS A, is defective: breaks abruptly on f. 100v, line 5, at I.128 and resumes in I.157 [" . . . vox tragedorum gestum pene summorum // citacione non sane michi displicit adhibere si cum [space] fueris adeptus eciam ista locorum. . ."]; breaks abruptly on f. 105r, line 23, at I.193 and resumes at II.60 [" . . . hoste habet fontes omnium disputacionum suarum qui iure ciuili // scripserunt voluerunt [?] vulgo intelligi in philosophos nostros. si quando incidero quam est ornatus indicibus librorum qui sunt fere inscripti de rebus notis et. . ."]; breaks abruptly on f. 106v, line 11, at II.69 and resumes at II.19 ["... que in illa arte effici possunt a doctore tradantur // Tum catulus ne gret [*sic*] quidem inquit crasse qui in ciuitatibus suis magni et clari fuerint..."]; breaks abruptly on f. 108r, line 3, at II.30 and resumes in II.39 ["... hii postea arriserint res michi videtur esse inquit facultate preclara arte // eloquentem vel optime facere oportet vt eloquenciam laudet Debet enim ad eam laudandam ipsam illam adhibere quam laudat..."]; breaks abruptly on f. 109r, line 17, at II.50 and resumes in II.30 ["... diserte quam que in lite dicuntur obiurgacio cohortacio // mediocris ars enim earum rerum est que sciuntur oratoris..."]; breaks abruptly on f. 110v, line 3, in II.39 and resumes in an unidentified passage ["... subtiliter visus es tum laudare copiosissime Quod quidem // ei dicendum esse de rebus maximis et grauiter et ornate quia..."]; breaks abruptly and resumes on f. 110v, line 12, at II.69 ["... summa cum laude ac dignitate ipsius omne versari officium statuo // sed velut qui primarum ac ceterarum rerum genera ipsa didicerunt..."]; breaks abruptly on f. 113v, line 18, in II.90 and resumes in II. 92 ["... quem dilegeret imitando effigat etque [*sic*] exprimat // Quid enim cause cencetis [*sic*] esse cur etates extulerunt singule singula..."]; the manuscript breaks off imperfectly in II.140.

Parchment, ff. i (paper) + 123 + i (paper), 221 x 168 (ff. 2–4: 158 x 98 mm., 30 long lines; ff. 3–83: 152 x 98 mm., 28 long lines; ff. 85–119: 160 x 95 mm., 28 long lines). ff. 2–64: single vertical and single horizontal (upper and/or lower) bounding lines; remainder of text: single vertical bounding lines. Ruled in pen or crayon; remains of prickings in upper, lower, and outer margins.

I–X^8, XI^4, XII–XV^8, XVI^8 (–8).

Scribe 1: ff. 2r–4r, sloping humanistic cursive script with gothic features; above top line. Scribe 2: ff. 5r–61v, well spaced and well formed gothic script with large uncrossed tironian *et*, prominent descenders on long *s* and *f*; below top line; horizontal catchwords in lower margin to right of center with bracket on left extending below words. Scribe 3: ff. 61v–82r, upright English gothic bookhand; below top line; no remains of catchwords. Scribe 4: ff. 85r–119v, upright English gothic bookhand; below top line; catchwords enclosed in crudely executed scrolls, lower margin to right of center. Interlinear and marginal glosses in art. 6 in at least two contemporary or slightly later annotating hands.

Spaces for decorative initials and most headings remain unfilled; remains of guide letters for arts. 1–5.

Binding: England, s. xix–xx. Half bound in dark brown goatskin, goldtooled, with dark pink cloth sides. Edges spattered red. Title on spine: "Cicero/ De Officiis/ MS./ Saec. XV."

Written in the third quarter of the 15th century probably at Oxford according to A. C. de la Mare, who has also suggested that the gothic bookhands in the manuscript are very close to that in Paris, B. N. lat. 6729, a Renaissance miscellany with ex libris dated 1473 of John Gunthorpe (dean of Wells, d. 1498). The letters "N. K." (s. xvii) appear several times in the manuscript (e.g., f. 1v, 2r, etc.); early notation on f. 1r crossed out. List, s. xvii, crudely written on f. 120r: "Iacobus Rex/ Iames Kinge/ I-a-go [*sic*] Brenhin/ Avna Regina/ Anva Quene/ Agnes Brenhines/ Henricus Princeps Cambrie/ Dux Cornubie/ Comes Cestrie." The "Brenhines" (owners of the manuscript?) remain unidentified. Off-set impression of rectangular bookplate on front pastedown. Purchased from C. A. Stonehill (note on back pastedown) in 1948 by Thomas E. Marston (bookplate).

secundo folio: [f. 3:] nec

Bibliography: Faye and Bond, p. 64, no. 4.

Marston MS 6 Northern Italy, 1420s and XV$^{med-3/4}$
Cicero, Orationes, De oratore, Orator, Brutus, etc. Pl. 13

I. 1. ff. 1r–11v *Marci Tulij Ciceronis oratio pro S. Pompeio.* Quanquam michi semper frequens conspectus uester multo iocundissimus. hic autem locus ad agendum amplissimus ... reipublicae dignitatem et salutem prouinciarum atque sociorum meis omnibus commodis et rationibus preferre oportere.

Cicero, *De imperio Cn. Pompeii*; P. Reis, ed., Teubner v. 6,1 (1931) pp. 3–34.

2. ff. 11v–27v *M. T. Ciceronis oratio pro Milone.* Etsi uereor. iudices ne turpe sit pro fortissimo uiro dicere incipientem timere minimeque deceat cum. T. Annius ipse magis de rei publicae salute quam de sua perturbetur ... michi credite is maxime probabit qui in iudicibus legendis optimum et sapientissimum et fortissimum quemque delegit.

Cicero, *Pro T. Annio Milone*; A. Klotz, ed., Teubner v. 8 (1918) pp. 13–66.

3. f. 11v [In margin:] Titus Anius Milo ciuis romanus sibi infestissimum et inimicissimum romanum ciuem Publium Clodium habuit multeque inter hos duos altercationes in re publica sepe fuerunt

specialiter uero cum Milo consulatum anni peteret... Cicero ergo Milonis amicissimus [some text lost] et summo artificio contextam.

Antonio Loschi, *Argumentum orationis Milonianae.* The introductions to ten of the speeches in this codex (arts. 3, 5, 9, 11, 17, 19, 20, 23, 26, 30) were composed by Antonio Loschi between 1391 and 1405 (see R. Sabbadini, *Le scoperte dei codici latini e greci ne' secoli xiv e xv* [Florence, 1905–14; reprinted 1967] pp. 122–23); Marston MS 6 does not, however, follow the usual order of speeches noted by M. D. Reeve in *Texts and Transmission*, p. 87. In Marston MS 6 the *argumentum* of Loschi's text was either written by the scribe in the text immediately before the speech (arts. 20, 30) or was added in a smaller script in the margins next to the speech (arts. 3, 5, 9, 11, 17, 19, 23, 26).

A comparison of Loschi's introductions in Marston MS 6 with those in the text edited by Girolamo Squarciafico and printed in Venice after 2 June 1477 by Johann von Köln and Johann Manthen reveals substantial differences, particularly in the introductions to *Pro rege Deiotaro* (art. 11) and to *Pro Plancio* (art. 17).

4. ff. 27v–32r *M. T. Ciceronis oratio pro Archia poeta.* Si quid est in me ingenij Iudices quod sentio quam [*sit* added later] exiguum aut si qua exercitacio dicendi in qua me non inficior mediocriter esse uersatum ... esse in bonam partem accepta ab eo qui Iudicium exercet certe scio.

   Cicero, *Pro Archia poeta*; P. Reis, ed., Teubner fasc. 19 (1949) pp. 43–57.

5. f. 27v [In margin:] Aulus Licinius Archias poeta Anthichie natus rome uixit in amicicia et gratia multorum clarissimorum ciuium romanorum et a nonnullis grecis populis honoratus et eorum ciuitatibus donatus fuit ... ac nichil puto uirtuti poete qui hoc solo nomine omnia merito debuit consequi et eloquentie Ciceronis non impetratum fuisse.

   Antonio Loschi, *Argumentum orationis pro Aulo Licinio Archia poeta*; see art. 3 above.

6. ff. 32v–39r *M. T. Ciceronis oratio habita in senatu de reditu in patriam.* Si patres conscripti pro uestris immortalibus in me fratremque meum liberosque nostros meritis parum uobis cumulate gracias egero ... presertim cum illa amissa recuperauerim uirtutem et fidem nunquam amiserim.

Cicero, *Oratio cum senatui gratias egit*; T. Maslowski, ed., Teubner fasc. 21 (1981) pp. 3–19.

7. f. 32v [In margin:] Cum illud in ceteris orationibus satis explicatum sit quomodo Cicero propter inimicorum furorem e patria recedere. uoluit malens consulere patrie iacturam suam potius quam discrimen facere uoluit. Euersa fuit domus funditus. direpta predia et bona omnia. migrauit in Ciciliam ... haberemus [?] ista clarissima.

   Unidentified *argumentum* to Cicero, *Oratio cum senatui gratias egit*; much of text illegible.

8. ff. 39r–44r *M. T. Ciceronis oratio pro Q. Ligario.* Nouum crimen. C. Cesar et ante hunc diem inauditum propinquus meus ad te. Q. Tutero [*sic*] detulit. Q. Legarium in africa fuisse ... admonebo si illi absenti salutem dederis presentibus his omnibus te daturum. finit pro Q. ligario.

   Cicero, *Pro Q. Ligario*; A. Klotz, ed., Teubner v. 8 (1918) pp. 84–100.

9. f. 39r [In margin:] Q. Ligarius ciuis romanus cum S. Considio consule prefectus est legatus in Africam ante ciuilis belli principium deinde prouincia decedente Considio. Q. Ligarius prefectus prouincie mansit ... Cicero ipsum Ligarium hac insigni oratione defendit pro qua gratiam Cesaris nititur impetrare.

   Antonio Loschi, *Argumentum orationis pro Q. Ligario*; see art. 3 above.

10. ff. 44r–50v Incipit pro rege deiotaro. *M. T. Ciceronis oratio pro* [*Q. Ligario* crossed out] *rege Deiotaro.* Cum in omnibus causis grauioribus. C. Cesar initio dicendi commoueri soleam uehementius quam uidetur uel usus uel etas mea postulare ... Quorum alterum optare illorum crudelitatis est, Alterum conseruare clemencie tue.

    Cicero, *Pro rege Deiotaro*; A. Klotz, ed., Teubner v. 8 (1918) pp. 101–19.

11. f. 44v [In margin:] Deiotarus rex gallogrecie populo romano amicissimus cum pompeio fuit. qui post farsalicam pugnam domi se contulit. Ac donque [?] g. Cesari bella gerenti subsidia administrauit ... est subornatus a Castore nepote ex filia deiotari. quas accusationes ... coram Cesare totius fere orbis domitore.

    Antonio Loschi, *Argumentum orationis pro rege Deiotaro*; see art. 3 above.

12. ff. 50v–54v *M. T. Ciceronis oratio* [*pro rege Deitareo* crossed out] *habita ad populum pridie quam iret in exilium.* Si quandoque inimicorum impetum propulsare et propellere me cupistis defendite nunc universi unum qui ne omnes periretis ardore flamme occidentis mei capitis periculo prouidere non dubitaui . . . ut quem sepe numero uestra laude cohonestastis eundem in dubijs uite periculis uestra uirtute conseruetis.

Ps.-Cicero, *Oratio antequam in exilium iret*; M. Gianascian, *M. Tullius Cicero* in Scriptorum romanorum quae extant omnia v. 102–03 (Venice, 1968) pp. 160–72.

13. f. 50v [In margin:] Omisso titulo huius orationis quod non satis habeo compertum quis eam composuerit materiam eius brevissime attingam. Eo namque tempore quo Cicero consul erat et forte nonnulli eum scelerato illo consilio L. Cateline [*sic*] conspirarent . . . flores ex dictis Ciceronis et non habet stillum suum prout patet.

Unidentified *argumentum* to Ps.-Cicero, *Oratio antequam in exilium iret*; according to M. D. Reeve this introduction also appears in Paris, Bibliothèque de l'Arsenal 1042.

14. ff. 54v–58v *M. T. Ciceronis oratio de congratulacione sui reditus ad patriam apud quirites incipit foeliciter.* Quod precatus a Iove optimo maximo ceterisque dijs immortalibus sum quirites eo tempore cum me fortunasque meas pro uestra incolumitate . . . non posse tenere se nisi me recuperasset cunctis suffragijs iudicauit.

Cicero, *Oratio cum populo gratias egit*; T. Maslowski, ed., Teubner fasc. 19 (1981) pp. 22–32.

15. f. 54v [In margin:] Cum Cicero superiori oratione patribus conscriptis gratias egerit de restitucione sua in patriam illud animo previdit non praetermictendum esse: gracias agere populo romano qui maxime in eo restituendo senserat. Voluit itaque infinitas . . . [conclusion stained and illegible].

Unidentified *argumentum* to Cicero, *Oratio cum populo gratias egit.*

16. ff. 58v–76v *M. T. Ciceronis oratio de congratulacione sui reditus ad patriam apud quirites* [*incipit* crossed out and *finit* written above] *feliciter M. T. Ciceronis oratio pro Cn. Plancio.* Cum propter egregiam et singularem. Cn. Plancij iudices in mea salute custodenda [*sic*] fidem tam multos et bonos uiros eius honori uiderem esse fautores . . . quoniam istis uestris lacrimis recordor de illis quas pro me sepe et multum profudistis.

Cicero, *Pro Cn. Plancio*; E. Olechowska, ed., Teubner fasc. 25 (1981) pp. 1-51.

17. f. 58v [In margin; much of the text is stained and illegible, with only portions visible under ultra-violet light:] Gneus plancius ciuis romanus ex equestre ordine et latercusta [?] ... sue defensionis assignans eo quod maximis Plancij meritis sit obstrictus.

Antonio Loschi, *Argumentum orationis pro Cn. Plancio*; see art. 3 above.

18. ff. 76v–81r *M. T. Ciceronis oratio incipit pro Marcello.* Diuturni silencij patres conscripti quo eram his temporibus usus non timore aliquo sed partim dolore partim uerecundia finem hodiernus attulit dies ... quod fieri iam posse non arbitrabar magnus hic tuo facto cumulus accesserit.

Cicero, *Pro M. Marcello*; A. Klotz, ed., Teubner v. 8 (1918) pp. 69–81.

19. f. 76v [In margin; most of the text is stained and illegible, with only portions visible under ultra-violet light:] M. Marcellus ciuis romanus amplissimus atque clarissimus in dissensione ciuili fuit cum pompeio quemadmodum fuit et Cicero cum multis aliis senatoribus ... qua non possit dignitas rei publicae neque restitui neque seruari.

Antonio Loschi, *Argumentum orationis de laudibus Cesaris occasione M. Marcelli per Cesarem restituti*; see art. 3 above.

20. f. 81v [Introduction:] *Pro Silla* [sic]. Silla et Antronius [*sic*] romani ciues petentes ambo consulatum. per ambitionem obtinuerunt contra L. Torquatum patrem huius torquati ... quam ipse consul aperuit et indicauit Sillam in hac oratione defendit.

Antonio Loschi, *Argumentum orationis pro Sulla*; see art. 3 above.

21. ff. 81v–96v *M. T. Ciceronis oratio incipit pro P. Silla* [sic]. Maxime uellem iudices ut. P. Silla et antea dignitatis sue splendorem obtineret et post calamitatem acceptam. modestie fructum aliquem percipere potuisset ... mansuetudine et misericordia uestra falsam a nobis crudelitatis famam repellamus.

Cicero, *Pro P. Sulla*; H. Kasten, ed., Teubner fasc. 19 (1949) pp. 2–40.

22. ff. 96v–111v *M. T. Ciceronis oratio pro L. Flacco Valerio.* Cum in maximis periculis huius urbis atque imperij grauissimo atque acer-

bissimo rei publicae casu socio atque adiutore ... nomen clarissimum et fortissimum uel generis uel uetustatis uel hominis causa rei publicae reseruate.

Cicero, *Pro L. Flacco*; L. Fruechtel, ed., Teubner v. 6,2 (1933) pp. 182–243.

23. f. 96v [In margin:] L. Flaccus ciuis romanus unus de adiutoribus Ciceronis et defensoribus patrie in coniuratione Catiline fuit pretor in Asia et cum expleta ... [conclusion is mostly stained and illegible:] lesus est a Cicerone [one word illegible] nobili [?] est defenditur.

Antonio Loschi, *Argumentum orationis pro L. Flacco*; see art. 3 above.

24. ff. 111v–124v *M. T. Ciceronis oratio pro M. Celio incipit foeliciter.* Si quis iudices forte nunc adsit ignarus legum iudiciorum consuetudinis nostre miretur profecto que sit tanta auctoritas ... uos potissimum iudices fructus uberes diuturnosque capietis.

Cicero, *Pro M. Caelio*; A. Klotz, ed., Teubner v. 7 (1919) pp. 277–332.

25. ff. 125r–138r *M. T. C. oratio pro. P. Quintio incipit.* Que res in ciuitate due plurimum possunt he contra nos ambe faciunt in hoc tempore summa gracia et eloquencia ... quae existimacio. P. Quintium usque ad senectutem perduxit eadem usque ad rogum prosequatur.

Cicero, *Pro P. Quinctio*; A. Klotz, ed., Teubner v. 4 (1923) pp. 4–44.

26. f. 125r [In margin; one line at beginning of text lost due to trimming of upper margin:] //Quintii stante illa societate defuncti hereditas pervenit ad P. Quintium fratrem suum quem P. Q. cum uellet ... pro Quintio perorauit hac elegantissima oratione.

Antonio Loschi, *Argumentum orationis pro P. Quincino* [sic]; see art. 3 above.

27. ff. 138r–148v *M. T. Ciceronis oratio pro. L. Cornelio Balbo incipit.* Si auctoritates patronorum in iudicijs ualerent ab amplissimis uiris. L. Cornelij causa defensa est si usus a peritissimis ... uos in hac causa non de maleficio L. Cornelij sed de beneficio. Cn. Pompeij iudicaturos.

Cicero, *Pro L. Cornelio Balbo*; A. Klotz, ed., Teubner v. 7 (1919) pp. 361–400.

28. ff. 148v–169r *M. T. Ciceronis oratio pro Sex. Roscio incipit feliciter.* Credo ego uos iudices mirari quid sit quod cum tot summi oratores hominesque nobilissimi sedeant ego potissimum surrexerim ... qui natura mitissimi sumus assiduitate molestiarum sensum omnem humanitatis ex animis amittimus.

Cicero, *Pro Sex. Roscio Amerino*; H. Kasten, ed., Teubner fasc. 8 (1968) pp. 1–60.

29. ff. 169r–181r *M. T. Ciceronis pro Lucio Murena oratio incipit.* Que deprecatus ab dijs immortalibus sum iudices more institutoque maiorum illo die quo auspicato comitijs centuriatis ... hos ad magistros si qua te fortuna Cato cum ista natura detulisset non tu quidem uir melior esses nec fortior nec temperatior nec iustior// ff. 181v–184r ruled, but blank

Cicero, *Pro Murena*, with text ending imperfectly at 31.64; H. Kasten, ed., Teubner fasc. 18 (1961) pp. 1–32.

30. ff. 184v–185r [Introduction:] Aulus Cluentius abitus et Statius Albius oppianicius [*sic*] romani ciues ambo ex municipio Larinate fuerunt ab initio inimici ... quodque iddem [*sic*] facere uoluisset in filio oppianico adolescente Cicero ipsum egregie hac mirabili oratione proxsequenti [?] defendit. [followed by:] Constitucio cause in qua hec habetur oratio. Ut plane intelligamus in qua institucione hec oratio cause habeatur ... et sentencie constitucionis incidunt ut suis dicetur in locis. [followed by a final passage, 4-lines:] M. T. Ciceronis oratio sequitur que in genere iudiciali.... Et primo facit auditores dociles.

Antonio Loschi, *Argumentum orationis pro Aulo Cluentio Habito, Constitutio cause in qua hec habet oratio*; final four lines are unidentified. See also art. 3 above.

31. ff. 185v–212v *M. T. Ciceronis oratio pro Cluentio incipit.* Animaduerti iudices omnem accusatoris orationem in duas diuisam esse partes quarum altera ... Postea autem cum appropinquare huius iudicium ei [*est* crossed out] nuntiatum est confestim huc aduolauit ne aut accusatoribus diligentia aut pecunia testibus deesset aut ne forte// ff. 213r–216v ruled, but blank

Cicero, *Pro A. Cluentio*, with text ending imperfectly at 67.192; L. Fruechtel, ed., Teubner v. 6,1 (1931) pp. 37–135. According to S. Rizzo, *Catalogo dei codici della Pro Cluentio Ciceroniana* (Genoa, 1983) p. 87, the text of this oration belongs to "fam. α."

32. ff. 217r–230v *M. T. Ciceronis pro P. Sextio oratio incipit.* Si quis antea iudices mirabatur quid esset quod pro tantis opibus rei publicae tantaque dignitate imperij nequaquam satis multi ciues forti et magno animo inuenirentur ... ut si me saluum esse uoluistis eos conseruetis per quos me recuperauistis. Deo Gracias Amen. ff. 231r–233v ruled, but blank

Cicero, *Pro P. Sestio*; A. Klotz, ed., Teubner v. 7 (1919) pp. 161–250.

II. 33. ff. 234r–324r [Heading:] M. T. C. de oratore Liber primus Incipit. [text:] Cogitanti michi sepe numero et memoria vetera repetenti perbeati fuisse Quinte frater illi uideri solent qui in optima re publica ... Sed iam surgamus inquit nosque curemus et aliquando ab hac contencione disputacionis animos nostros curamque laxemus.

Cicero, *De oratore*; K. Kumaniecki, ed., Teubner fasc. 3 (1969) pp. 1–362.

34. ff. 324v–353v [Added in pencil:] de perfecto oratore ad Marium [*sic*] Brutum. [text:] Utrum difficilius aut maius esset negare tibi sepius idem roganti an efficere id quod rogares diu multumque brute dubitaui ... dum tibi roganti uoluerim obsequi uerecundia negandi scribendi me impudentiam suscepisse. Deo gratias. [added in pencil:] Explicit de oratore ad M. Brutum.

Cicero, *Orator*; P. Reis, ed., Teubner fasc. 5 (1932) pp. 1–92.

35. ff. 354r–393r [Added in pencil:] de claris oratoribus. [text:] Cum e Cilicia decedens rhodum venissem et eo michi de. Q. hortensii morte esset allatum opinione omnium maiorem animo cepi dolorem ... dico si michi accidisset ut mirarer in multis si operosa est a concursatio magis opportunorum. Marci tullii Ciceronis dialogi qui de oratore Ad brutum de claris ac illustribus oratoribus inscribuntur expliciunt. ff. 393v–398v ruled, but blank

Cicero, *Brutus*; E. Malcovati, ed., Teubner fasc. 4 (1965) pp. 1–105.

Composed of two distinct parts, ff. 398 + v (paper), 270 x 202 mm.

Part I: ff. 1–232, paper (ff. 1 and 10 only are parchment; watermarks: unidentified letter B), written space 185 x 125 mm. Some leaves with commentary in margin (e.g., f. 11) are slightly larger and now folded vertically in outer margin. 35 long lines. Single vertical bounding lines, ruled in lead. Guide lines for text in pale brown ink. Prickings in upper margin; often there are single prickings in outer margin, 3 mm. above top line and 3 mm. below bottom line. I–XVIII^{10}, XIX^{6}, XX–XXIII^{10}, XXIV^{6}. Catchwords, with dots and flourishes to left and right, center of lower margin, verso. Written by a single scribe in a fere-humanistic script characterized by the broadness of majuscule letter forms; written below top line. Elegantly decorated title-page (f. 1r), that may (as has been suggested by A. C. de la Mare and L. Armstrong) have been executed in two stages. In the first, a full border: in inner and upper margins, thin gold bar with flowers in mauve, blue and gold and stylized foliage in green with pale yellow highlights; in outer and lower margins, floral border of black inkspray with flowers in mauve and blue and with some gold accents and stylized foliage in green. In center of lower margin, a shield with unidentified coat of arms, much rubbed (gules, two augers [?] in saltire, or, banded sable) supported by two standing nude female figures with flowing blond hair (bath-maidens?). In the second stage, an historiated initial, 12-line, mauve, green and pink against gold ground, with extremely fine portrait in profile of a man wearing a two-tiered red cap and academic gown against a blue background with a geometric pattern in black and greyish blue. It has been noted that the face closely resembles portraits of Guarino da Verona found in manuscripts of his translations of Strabo's *Geography* (*olim* Phillipps 6645 and Albi, Bibliothèque municipale MS 4), as well as on a medal of Matteo de' Pasti (cf. *Exhibition Catalogue*, pp. 224–25, no. 48). 6-line initials, blue with red penwork designs alternate red with purple for the beginning of each text. Headings in red.

Part II: ff. 233–398, paper (watermarks: Briquet Tête de boeuf 15068, and Piccard Ochsenkopf VII.40), written space 192 x 130 mm. 2 columns, 40 lines. Single vertical and horizontal bounding lines ruled in hard point; text rulings in crayon. Single pricking in outer margin even with top line. Accurate collation difficult due to tight binding and absence of signatures or catchwords. Written in a small gothic script with cursive features, below top line. Red and black divided initial, 6-line, with plain designs on f. 234r; plain red initials some with simple designs, 5- to 2-line, elsewhere. Paragraph marks and initial strokes in red. The dark acidic ink has bled through many leaves; no loss of text.

Binding: France, s. xviii. Gold-tooled brown, mottled calf spine. Edges gilt. Boards, composed of paper pasteboard, are detached.

The precise origin and date of the manuscript are problematic. The text of Part I appears to have been written in the 1420s according to A. C. de la Mare, but the decoration of both the border and miniature appear to have been added in the mid-15th century. On general stylistic grounds, the illumination resembles manuscripts produced in Ferrara; J. J. G. Alexander has pointed to the similarity of the border decoration in

Marston MS 6 with that in Glasgow, University Library MS Hunter 425, which may have been produced in Bologna (Exhib. cat., *The Glory of the Page* [London, 1987] p. 138, no. 7). The portrait of Guarino certainly suggests an association with his circle of humanists. Part II appears to have been written in Northern Italy, but somewhat later, probably in the middle or third quarter of the 15th century. The pattern of stains indicates that Parts I and II were once separate; it is unclear when they were bound together. Unidentified inscription along the upper edge of f. 1r. Purchased from C. A. Stonehill in 1949 by Thomas E. Marston (bookplate).

secundo folio: [f. 2] agitur
[f. 235] poetarum

Bibliography: Faye and Bond, pp. 64–65, no. 6.
Exhibition Catalogue, pp. 224–25, no. 48.

Marston MS 7

Florence, s. XV^{in}

Cicero, Orationes, etc.

1. ff. 1r–8v M. Tullii Ciceronis Philippicarum in M. Antonium liber .I. incipit. Ante quam de re publica patres conscripti dicam ea que dicenda hoc tempore arbitror exponam uobis breuiter ... huc siquid accesserit non tam michi quam uobis rei publiceque accesserit. Philippicarum in .M. Antonium liber .II incipit.

   Cicero, *In M. Antonium oratio Philippica I*; F. Schoell, ed., Teubner fasc. 8 (1918) pp. 128–45.

2. ff. 9r–32r Quoniam meo fato patres conscripti fieri dicam ut nemo his annis uiginti rei publice fuerit hostis qui non bellum eodem tempore michi quoque indixerit ... a diis immortalibus clari nichil potest alterum ut ita cuique eueniat [corrected from *eueniet*] ut eueniet ut de re publica quis mereatur.

   Cicero, *In M. Antonium oratio Philippica II*; Schoell, *op. cit.*, pp. 147–202.

3. ff. 32r–40r Serius omnino patres conscripti quam tempus rei publice postulauit aliquando tamen conuocati sumus ... de his rebus ad hunc ordinem referant ita uti de re publica fideque sua consuerint.

   Cicero, *In M. Antonium oratio Philippica III*; Schoell, *op. cit.*, pp. 204–22.

4. ff. 40r–43v Frequentia uestrum incredibilis contioque tanta quantam meminisse non uideor ... interuallo [corrected from *intelruallo*] me auctore et principe ad spem libertatis exarsimus.

Cicero, *In M. Antonium oratio Philippica IV*; Schoell, *op. cit.*, pp. 222–29.

5. ff. 43v–50r Nichil unquam longius kalendis ianuariis mihi uisum est patres conscripti quod idem intelligebam ... Alie nationes seruitutem pati possunt populi romani res est propria libertas.

Cicero, *In M. Antonium oratio Philippica V*; *In M. Antonium oratio Philippica VI*; written as one speech, but is in fact the beginning of the Fifth Philippic and the end of the Sixth Philippic combined into a single oration; Schoell, *op. cit.*, pp. 231–45 and 262–63. The break occurs on f. 50r, line 12: "... Quam ob rem patres conscripti legatorum mentionem [*Phil. V*, ch. 12, sect. 31, Teubner p. 245] // numquam uidi tantam quanta nunc uestra est. Vnum sentitis omnes ... [*Phil. VI*, ch. 7, sect. 18, Teubner p. 262]."

6. ff. 50v–55r Paruis de rebus sed fortasse necessariis consulimur patres conscripti ... hoc ardore populi romani potes in perpetuum metu et periculo rem publicam libertare [*sic*].

Cicero, *In M. Antonium oratio Philippica VII*; Schoell, *op. cit*, pp. 263–73.

7. ff. 55r–61v Confusius hesterno die est acta res .c. pansa quam postulabat ... Profectus praeter .L. uarium senatum existimaturum eum contra rem publicam fecisse.

Cicero, *In M. Antonium oratio Philippica VIII*; Schoell, *op. cit.*, pp. 275–89.

8. ff. 61v–65r Vellem dii imortales [*sic*] fecissent patres conscripti ut uiuo potius quam mortuo honores queremus ... uti quod optimo iure sepulcrum ipsius publice datum est.

Cicero, *In M. Antonium oratio Philippica IX*; Schoell, *op. cit.*, pp. 290–98.

9. ff. 65v–70v Maximas tibi pansa gratias omnes et habere et agere debemus ... legatis suis prouintiam macedoniam obtinere quo ad ex senatus consulto successum sit.

Cicero, *In M. Antonium oratio Philippica X*; Schoell, *op. cit.*, pp. 299–312.

10. ff. 70v–79v Magno in dolore sum patres conscripti uel merore potius quem [*sic*] ex crudeli et miserabili morte ... quae cum ita sint eam quam dixi sententiam uobis patres conscripti censeo comprobandam.

Cicero, *In M. Antonium oratio Philippica XI*; Schoell, *op. cit.*, pp. 313–32.

11. ff. 79v–87v Etsi minime decere uidetur patres conscripti falli decipi errare eum cui uos maximis sepe de rebus ... idque potissimum faciendum quod maxime interesse rei publicae iudicauero.

Cicero, *In M. Antonium oratio Philippica XII*; Schoell, *op. cit.*, pp. 333–46.

12. ff. 87v–97v Belli patres conscripti quod cum impiis ciuibus sceleratisque suscepimus . . . ut proprio senatus consulto pompeius collaudatus esse uideatur.

Cicero, *In M. Antonium oratio Philippica XIII*; Schoell, *op. cit.*, pp. 347–72.

13. ff. 98r–105v M. T. Ciceronis Philippicarum Liber .XIII. et Ultimus. Sicut ex litteris que recitate sunt patres conscripti sceleratissimorum hostium exercitum cesum [corrected from *cessum*] fusumque . . . que militibus ipsis tribui oporteret si illi uixissent qui morte uixerunt. Explicit.

Cicero, *In M. Antonium oratio Philippica XIV*; Schoell, *op. cit.*, pp. 374–89.

14. ff. 105v–111v Quousque tandem abutere .o. Catilina patientia nostra . . . inter se ac nefaria sotietate conuictos [?] eternis supplicijs uiuos defunctosque mactabis.

Cicero, *Oratio in Catilinam prima*; P. Reis, ed., Teubner fasc. 6,2 (1933) pp. 5–22.

15. ff. 111v–117v Tandem aliquando quirites .L catilinam furentem audacia scelus hanelantem [*sic*] pestem . . . hanc omnibus hostium copiis terra marique superatis. a proditissimorum ciuium nefario scelere defendant.

Cicero, *Oratio in Catilinam secunda*; Reis, *op. cit.*, pp. 22–37.

16. ff. 117v–124r Incipit Liber Tertius. Rem publicam quirites uitamque omnium uestrum .bona .fortunas coniuges liberosque uestros atque hoc domicilium . . . atque ut in perpetua pace esse possitis prouidebo quirites.

Cicero, *Oratio in Catilinam tertia*; Reis, *op. cit.*, pp. 38–53.

17. ff. 124r–129v Incipit Liber Quartus. Uideo patres conscripti in me omnium ora atque oculos esse conuersos uideo uos non solum de uestro periculo . . . et ea que statueritis defendere quo ad uiuet et per se ipsum prestare possit. Inuectiuarum quatuor M. Tullij Ciceronis .in .L. Catilinam feliciter expliciunt.

Cicero, *Oratio in Catilinam quarta*; Reis, *op. cit.*, pp. 55–68.

18. ff. 130r–131r Grauiter et iniquo animo maledicta tua paterer .M.

Tullij si te scirem iudicio animi magis quam morbo petulantia ista uti ... trasfuga [*sic*]. neque in hac neque in illa parte fidem habens.

Ps.-Sallust, *Invectiva in M. Tullium Ciceronem*; M. Gianascian, ed., *C. Sallustius Crispus*, in Scriptorum romanorum quae extant omnia, v. 49 (Venice, 1965) v. 1, pp. 83–86.

19. ff. 131v–135r Ea demum tibi magna uoluptas est .C. Salusti equalem ac parem uerbis uitam agere ... Salustius debeat audire merito. sed ut ea dicam siqua ego honeste effari possim. M. Tullij Ciceronis Oratio in .C. Salustium Feliciter explicit. ff. 135v–137v ruled, but blank

Ps.-Cicero, *Invectiva in Crispum Sallustium*; Gianascian, *op. cit.*, v. 1, pp. 87–95.

Parchment, ff. iii (modern parchment) + ii (contemporary parchment; i = original pastedown with passage, now erased but partially visible under ultraviolet light, from Cicero's *Pro Q. Ligario*: "//hijs omnibus quam caret ... et in nostrum fletum in//"; in humanistic script) + 137 (early foliation runs 1–106, arts. 1–13; 1–24, arts. 14–17; 1–2, art. 18; 1–4, art. 19; skips from 82 to 84) + i (contemporary parchment, original pastedown or flyleaf?) + iii (modern parchment). 270 x 183 mm.

The manuscript was copied by two scribes who exhibit distinct formats and scripts reflecting the transition from gothic to humanistic types of book production.

Scribe I: ff. 1–107r, line 14. Written space 185–90 x 109 mm. Ca. 27–28 long lines. Ruled in hard point on hair side in several formats: single upper and/or lower vertical and double horizontal bounding lines (Derolez 13.32 and 13.33); single horizontal and vertical bounding lines in first quire (Derolez 13.12 and 13.13). Remains of prickings in upper and lower margins. Written in a very fine early humanistic bookhand, above top line; catchwords slightly toward right of center, lower margin (Derolez 12.2); remains of quire and leaf signatures (e.g., 2a, 3a, 4a, etc.).

Scribe II: ff. 107r, line 15–135r. Written space 185 x 111 mm. Ca. 27 long lines. Ruled in ink or lead. Single vertical and horizontal bounding lines (Derolez 13.12 and 13.13). Remains of prickings in upper, lower, and outer margins. Written in a semi-gothic script, below top line, in a style of writing similar to that used by Coluccio Salutati; strong gothic influence in forms of majuscules. According to A. C. de la Mare the hand resembles most closely that on f. 61r–v of Florence, Bib. Laur. 78,11, which contains corrections by Salutati himself in the main portion of the manuscript. Catchwords, surrounded by flourishes, center of lower margin (Derolez 12.1); same kind of leaf signatures as above.

I-VIII^{10}, IX^{8}, X-XIII^{10}, XIV^{10} (-10).

Twenty-three illuminated initials of fine quality, 6- to 2-line, yellow on rectangular bright blue grounds with narrow black frames. Grounds filled with restrained and stylized thin white vine-stem ornament and intricate white filigree. Most spaces for rubrics left unfilled (see also provenance below).

Binding: England, s. xix. Bound by Zaehnsdorf (London, 1842–1930) in brown goatskin, blind-tooled, with gold-tooled spine "Cicero" and "MS." Yellow edges. Discoloration on early parchment endleaves reveals traces of corner tongues.

Written in Florence probably at the beginning of the 15th century according to A. C. de la Mare, to judge from the style of scripts and early design of the vine-stem initials. Owned by the humanist Guglielmino Tanaglia (1391–1460; see A. C. de la Mare, "Humanistic Script: The First Ten Years," *Das Verhältnis der Humanisten zum Buch*, eds. F. Krafft and D. Wuttke, *Kommission für Humanismusforschung Mitteilung* 4 [Boppard, 1977] pp. 105–06, figs. 8–9). Tanaglia annotated the text in a small neat bookhand, added some headings, the foliation and running titles; he also wrote the table of contents and a quote from Juvenal (*Sat.* 10.122–25) on f. iv verso. On f. v recto is the erased bilingual ex libris (visible under ultraviolet light) of Lorenzo di Giovanni Tornabuoni (d. 1497), who was a student of Politian: "ὃ βιβλιος [?] ἐστί Λαυρεντίου τοῦ τορνυβόνου καὶ τῶν φιλῶν/ hic liber est Laurentij de Tornybonis et amicorum." Tornabuoni annotated the text in a sprawling humanistic cursive script (e.g., lower margin of f. 2r) and wrote an unidentified quotation ("Hec promissa seruanda sunt ea que quibus promisoris sunt/ Inutilia et forte plus noceant quam prosint"; perhaps a paraphrase of Cicero, *De Officiis* III.94.1?) on f. v recto and one from Demosthenes' *First Olynthiac*, sect. 20, on the recto of the final original flyleaf ("δεῖ δὲ χρημάτων καὶ ἄνευ ... τῶν δεόντων"). Unidentified shelf-marks include: "N. III. 20." in ink, s. xv–xvi, f. iv verso; "N xvj" in ink, s. xvi, on final flyleaf; "B: 4–48" in ink, f. 1r. From the collection of William Charles de Meuron, 7th Earl Fitzwilliam (1872–1943; bookplate); sold by his heir (Sotheby's, 26 April 1948, no. 474). Purchased from C. A. Stonehill (inv. no. 1213) in 1948 by Thomas E. Marston (bookplate).

secundo folio: liberatores

Bibliography: Faye and Bond, p. 65, no. 7.
The Medieval Book, p. 107, no. 103.

Marston MS 8 Italy, s. XV^{med}
Ps.-Cicero, Rhetorica ad Herennium

ff. 1–2 flyleaves; ff. 3r–78v Et sinegocijs familiaribus impediti. Vix satis otium studio suppeditare possumus ... Ergo amplius in arte rethorica nihil est. hec omnia adipiscemur si rationes preceptionis diligentia consequemur exercitationis. [added by another hand:] deo gratias. amen.

Ps.-Cicero, *De ratione dicendi ad C. Herennium*; F. Marx, ed., Teubner, fasc. 1 (1923) pp. 1–192; reissued with addenda by W. Trillitsch (Leipzig, 1964). Divisions for Books 2, 3, 4 on ff. 13r, 31r, and 46r; running headlines, probably giving number of book, now trimmed. Text has a large quantity of interlinear material (in at least three hands) that is intended to help the reader through the Latin text by providing synonyms, referents for pronouns, etc.; annotations are less frequent after f. 52v. Some marginal glosses, often partially trimmed.

Parchment (palimpsest throughout, from many different manuscripts, s. xv, primarily documents that were previously folded and a large service book with musical notation), ff. i (paper) + i (modern parchment, f. 1) + i (contemporary parchment, f. 2) + 76 (ff. 3–78) + i (modern parchment, f. 79) + i (paper), 195 x 135 (140 x 80) mm. 24 long lines. Single vertical and double horizontal bounding lines, mostly full length and full width; ruled in crayon or lead.

I-IX^8, X^4. Remains of horizontal catchwords along lower edge near gutter, verso.

Written by a single scribe in fere-humanistic script with numerous abbreviations.

Red initial, 5-line, with purple penwork flourishing that extends down inner margin, marks beginning of text, f. 3r. Plain red initial, 3-line, f. 3v. Spaces with guide letters are unfilled for remainder of codex. Initial letter for each sentence stroked with red, ff. 3r–4r only.

Binding: England, s. xix. Bound by Charles Lewis (London, 1807–36) in brown diced calf with a gold-tooled title: "Ciceronis Rhetorica MS in Membr:". Edges gilt.

Written in Italy in the middle of the 15th century. Inscription, s. xv^2, on f. 2r: "hic codex est Monasterij Sancti Iohannis baptiste in Rebdorff ordinis Canonicorum regularium diui Augustini episcopi. eystetensis dyocesis. Et continet In se Rethoricam tullij"; it presumably remained at Rebdorff until the 19th century. Probably identifiable with the following entry in the Rebdorff catalogue: P. Ruf, ed., *Mittelalterliche Bibliothekskataloge Deutsch-*

lands und der Schweiz, Bd. III, 1 (Munich, 1932) p. 306 ("Tullius, philosophus et oratorum princeps, Rhetorica, K.28"). Belonged to the Rev. Henry Drury (1778–1841; inscription on f. i recto); his sale (Evans, 3 March 1827; information not verified). Small round label with "58" handwritten, on spine; "254" in pencil on front pastedown. Bookplate of Jacques Rosenthal inside front cover. Purchased from C. A. Stonehill in 1949 by Thomas E. Marston (bookplate).

secundo folio: similes

Bibliography: Faye and Bond, p. 65, no. 8.

Marston MS 9 Florence, ca. 1460–65

Curtius Rufus, Historia Alexandri Magni, It. tr. Pier Candido Decembrio, etc.

1. ff. 1r–208v *Incomincia la hystoria d'Alexandro Magno figluolo di Philippo Re di Macedonia scripta da Quinto Curtio Ruffo hystorico....* Alexandro in questo mezo mandato Leandro con molta pecunia per condurre gente darme del peloponese ... et alla memoria del quale ogni debito honore e Referito. *Finisce el duodecimo et ultimo libro della hystoria d'Alexandro magno figliuolo di Philippo Re di macedonia ... Nellano .Mccccxxxviij. a di .xxj. d'aprile in Milano. Laus Deo Finis.*

   Curtius Rufus, *Historia Alexandri Magni*, translated into Italian and supplemented with material from Plutarch by Pier Candido Decembrio; text printed "Apud Sanctum Jacobum de Ripoli" in Florence, 1478 (GKW, v. 7, no. 7877). Missing portions of the text are clearly indicated in the manuscript by explanatory rubrics, e.g., on ff. 88v, 89r, 90v, 197r–v, 198r.

2. ff. 208v–216v *Al serenissimo prencipe et excellentissimo signore Philippo Maria duca di Milano di Pauia et Angera conte et di genoua Signore. Incomincia la comparatione di Caio Iiulio* [sic] *Cesare imperadore maximo et d'Alexandro magno Re di macedonia da P. Candido ordinata....* Io credo serenissimo prencipe che fia molte singulari et gioconde quistioni le quali non solamente da licterati et docti huomini ... uno specchio della loro gloria parue che fussino innamorati. *Finisce la comparatione di Caio Iulio Cesare ... felicemente.*

   Pier Candido Decembrio, *Comparazione di Cesare e d'Alessandro Magno*, published with art. 1 in GKW, v. 7, no. 7877.

Parchment, ff. ii (modern paper) + 216 + ii (contemporary parchment bifolium; ii = back pastedown), 292 x 215 (176 x 114) mm. 30 long lines. Double vertical bounding lines (Derolez 13.31); ruled in pale brown ink. Three single prickings in margins: 5 mm. below lowest horizontal ruling in outer margin; in inner margin 23 mm. above top line and 61 mm. below lowest horizontal ruling.

I-IX^{10}, X^{8}, XI-XXI^{10}, XXII^{10} (-9, 10). Vertical catchwords between inner bounding lines in lower margin (Derolez 12.5). Remains of two sets of quire and leaf signatures (e.g., t 4, t 5, +, etc.) in lower right corner, recto, with one set correcting the misalphabetization of the other.

Written by a single scribe in a slightly rounded humanistic bookhand with many cursive elements, below top line.

One illuminated initial, 6-line, gold against blue, green and pink ground with white vine-stem ornament, extending into inner margin to form a partial border; terminating at top and bottom in pen inkspray with buds in green and pink and gold balls with hair-line extensions. Plain initials, 3- to 2-line, in blue, mark text divisions; headings in pale red.

Binding: Italy, s. xv–xvi. Sewn on four tawed skin, slit straps laid in channels on the outside of wooden boards and pegged. Gilt edges.

Covered in brown goatskin with corner tongues, and blind-tooled with a ropework star inside painted (red) and blind-tooled circles inside a floral border, all with metallic annular dots. There are traces of four leaf-shaped fastenings, the catches on the lower board, the upper one cut in for fabric straps attached with star-headed nails. Rebacked twice.

Written in Florence ca. 1460–65 by an anonymous scribe who copied a number of vernacular texts including Beinecke MS 151 (vol. I, pp. 202–03) and Marston MS 247; he has been named by A. C. de la Mare the "Scribe of Florence, Biblioteca Laurenziana, San Marco 384" (see *New Research*, Appendix I, p. 548, no. 90, for other manuscripts by this scribe). Inscription in upper left corner on front pastedown: "1608 Di Trani nori [?] comparò lire quattro"; pasted over this was a small rectangular piece of paper, now removed, with "242h" handwritten, the number in black ink and the letter in red ink. The bookplate, s. xviii, of Graf von Chotek (partially effaced) on front pastedown (F. Warnecke, *Die deutschen Bücherzeichen* ... [Berlin, 1890] p. 47, no. 327). From an unidentified French collection, s. xviii (full-page inscription on f. i recto); although a later hand has added a note at the bottom of the leaf that the manuscript belonged to Comte Firmian (Carlo Giuseppe di Firmian, 1716–82), we have been unable to locate the book in the multi-volume catalogue of his collection. Belonged to Acton Griscom (De Ricci, v. 2, p. 1168, no. 32). Purchased from Lathrop C. Harper in 1949 by Thomas E. Marston (bookplate).

secundo folio: questa passaua

Bibliography: De Ricci, v. 2, p. 1168, no. 32; Faye and Bond, p. 65, no. 9. *The Medieval Book*, p. 107, no. 103.

Marston MS 10 — Florence, ca. 1415–20

Demosthenes, et al., Lat. tr. Leonardo Bruni — Pl. 14

1. ff. 1r–7r *Demosthenis oratio traducta a Leonardo Arretino.* Nequaquam eadem mihi uideor intelligere o uiri athenienses cum res ipsas ... uos autem sequamini quod et rei p. et uobis omnibus profuturum sit. ff. 7v–8v ruled, but blank

   Demosthenes, *Olynthica tertia*, translated into Latin by Leonardo Bruni; Baron, p. 178.

2. ff. 9r–11r *Aeschinis epistola. Leonardus transtulit. Aeschines atromiti senatui* populoque atheniensi salutem. Ego me ad remp. [*sic*] contuli trigesimo tertio etatis anno. non me hercle ex scena ut aiebat demostenes ... cui necessarium est magisquam malanopo contra nos roganti annuere. Explicit.

   Aeschines, *Epistola senatui populoque Atheniensi*, translated into Latin by Leonardo Bruni; Baron, p. 178.

3. ff. 11r–14v *Epistola philippi regis. Leonardi Ar.* Rex macedonum philippus ateniensium senatui plebique salutem. Quoniam persepe iam legatos misi qui uobiscum agerent. ut pacta conuenctionesque seruaremus ... et diis testibus inuocatis pro rebus meis pugnabo. Explicit.

   (Anaximenes of Lampsacus), *Epistola Philippi ad Athenienses*, translated into Latin by Leonardo Bruni; Baron, p. 171.

4. ff. 15r–53r *Eschinis oratio contra ctesiphontem traducta per leonardum arretinum.* Quanti conatus parentur uiri athenienses ad hoc iudicium oppugnandum. quantisque precibus nitantur ... Vos autem ex dictis et omissis iuste pro re publica decernatis.

   Aeschines, *Oratio contra Ctesiphontem*, translated into Latin by Leonardo Bruni; Baron, p. 163.

5. ff. 53r–96r *Leonardi Arretini. Demosthenis oratio. pro Ctesiphonte.* Primum quidem viri athenienses deos atque deas omnes precor ... metus et salutem indubiam prestate [added by another hand:] et finis. Deo gracias Amen. ff. 96r–97v blank

Demosthenes, *Oratio pro Ctesiphonte (De corona)*; Baron, p. 162.

Parchment (speckled on hair side), ff. ii (paper) + 97 (remains of contemporary foliation, Roman numerals) + ii (paper), 234 x 158 (165 x 83) mm. Written in 22 long lines; double vertical and single horizontal bounding lines, full length and full width (Derolez 13.33). Ruled in hard point on hair side. Prickings along outer edge (Derolez 18.1).

I^8, $II–IX^{10}$, X^9 [structure uncertain]. Catchwords in lower right corner near gutter, verso (Derolez 12.4).

Written in an expert humanistic bookhand characterized by prominent approach and finishing strokes. The headings in red are by a different scribe.

One very fine illuminated initial, 12-line, in gold on vibrant blue ground with white vine-stem ornament. The stems of the initial are divided into compartments and filled with penwork decoration in red, blue and green on parchment ground. Four small initials, 6- to 5-line, gold on vibrant blue ground with white vine-stem ornament. Headings in red.

Binding: France or Italy, s. xix. Brown calf blind- and gold-tooled, with shells and caducei in the blind-tooled borders. Edges red.

Written in Florence ca. 1415–20 according to A. C. de la Mare; possibly by the same scribe who wrote Vatican Lat. 1613; London, British Library, Harley MS 2771; Florence, Biblioteca Laurenziana 54, 29; Oxford, Bodleian Library, MS E. D. Clarke 25 (we thank A. C. de la Mare for this information); early modern provenance unknown. Belonged to Sir Thomas Phillipps (stamp and note on first flyleaf recto and verso, with nos. 922 and 2681). According to *Phillipps Studies*, v. 3, p. 147, no. 922 was acquired from Abate Luigi Celotti (ca. 1768–ca.1846; no. 111 in his second sale catalogue: Sotheby's, 14 March 1825, listed as "Demosthenis et Aeschines Orationes, in Lat. traductae a Leonardo Aretino") whereas no. 2681 was bought from Thorpe; there is, however, no internal evidence to suggest that the volume was previously composed of two separate manuscripts. Belonged to Charles Butler of Warren Wood, Hatfield (bookplate inside front cover); his sale at Sotheby's, 5 April 1911, no. 361. Purchased from Lathrop C. Harper in 1948 by Thomas E. Marston (bookplate).

secundo folio: [com]memorare

Bibliography: Faye and Bond, p. 65, no. 10.

Marston MS 11 Germany, s. XIII^{med}

Eusebius Pamphili, Historia ecclesiastica, Lat. tr. Rufinus

1. ff. 1r–2r //Dicunt esse medicorum ubi imminere urbibus uel regionibus generales uiderint morbos prouidere aliquod medicamenti uel poculi ... ita et christiani fide atque operibus id agant ut paterne superstitionis errore [added in another hand:] relicto ad uere fidei lumen conuertantur.

   Prologue of Rufinus with list of capitula for ch. 1 of Eusebius, *Historia ecclesiastica*; large space unfilled at top of f. 1r, presumably for a decorative heading and initial. The scribe copied this portion of the text twice (see art. 3 below), though the text deviates from art. 3 after chapter viii (De nece infantium apud), and continues without interruption: "conscribuntur etiam si homine rebus tamen et religione christianos fuisse ..."; recognizing the error, the scribe recopied the text afresh on f. 3r.

2. f. 2v Genealogy of the Virgin Mary in chart format, with explanation below: "Notandum quod duo ioseph in hac genealogia positi sunt. Primus frater Cleophe cui idem desponsauit ... autem genuit sanctum servatium."

3. ff. 3r–139v [Rubric damaged:] *Eusebius cesariensis episcopus et hystoriographus librum istum ex hebr**cam transtulit linguam. Rufinus uero in latinam. Prologus eiusdem ** Cromatium episcopum.* Peritorum dicunt esse medicorum ubi imminere urbibus uel regionibus ... [table of contents for Bk. 1; f. 3v:] *Incipiunt capitula. I.* Prefatio de deitate christi. *ij.* Quod deus et creator omnium ... de Syrorum lingua translata sunt. *Expliciunt capitula in nomine domini.* [text:] *Incipit liber primus.* Successiones sanctorum apostolorum et tempora que a saluatore nostro ad nos usque decursa sunt ... cum piissimis principibus precepturus premia meritorum. Explicit liber undecimus.

   Eusebius, *Historia ecclesiastica,* Lat. tr. Rufinus, preceded by the prologue of Rufinus. T. Mommsen, ed. (Leipzig, 1903–09) Bd. 2, parts 1, 2, 3 in *Die griechischen christlichen Schriftsteller der ersten drei Jahrhunderte*; Marston MS 11 not listed.

Each book is preceded by a chapter list signalled by Roman numerals. There are no titles for the chapters in the text, but only Roman numerals that do not always correspond to those in the chapter list. Book I = 16 chs., II = 28 chs., III = 39 chs., IV = 29 chs., V = 27 chs., VI = 37 chs. (numbering in text skips iv and therefore runs i–xxxviii), VII = 28 chs. labelled in chapter list and 29 in text, VIII = 19 chs. labelled in chapter list and 18 in text, IX = 10 chs., X = 40 chs. in chapter list and 36 in text, XI = 34 chs. in chapter list and 31 in text.

Parchment (thick; holes and end pieces), ff. i (paper) + 139 + i (paper), 302 x 215 (230 x 158) mm. 35–36 long lines. Single vertical and double horizontal bounding lines, full length and usually full width. Ruled in ink; remains of prickings in lower and outer margins, often with double prickings for the first of the lower horizontal bounding lines.

$I–III^8$, IV^6, $V–XII^8$, XIII^{10}, $XIV–XVII^8$, XVIII^6 (-2, 5, 6, all blank). Remains of catchwords, most enclosed by rectangles, center of lower edge, verso.

Written in gothic bookhand below top line by several scribes whose hands are uneven; text is written for the most part between the rulings.

Decorative initials, 8- to 6-line, in red, some with modest penwork designs in red and black, or with foliage type appendages, in red, mark the beginning of each book; plain red 3-line initials, with knobs, for beginnings of chapters. Rubrics, chapter numbers, and initial strokes, in red. Guide letters and instructions for rubricator.

Outer edge of f. 1v damaged and repaired resulting in some loss of text.

Binding: Germany, s. xix. Bound in a grey-beige paper case with the title, in ink, on a label on the spine: "Eusebii Caesariensis Hystoria Ecclesiastica."

Written in Germany in the middle of the 13th century, presumably at the Premonstratensian abbey of St. Peter at Weissenau (founded 1145 and suppressed 1803); contemporary inscription in upper margin of f. 1r: "Liber sancti petri in augia minori" and later inscription in lower margin of f. 1v (partially effaced): "Bibliotheca Weissenav***." Bookplate (with initials BAZW) of Abbot Benedict Rheindl of Weissenau on front pastedown (see F. Warnecke, *Die deutschen Bücherzeichen* ... [Berlin, 1890] no. 2409). Listed by P. Lehmann, *Mittelalterliche Bibliothekskataloge Deutschlands und der Schweiz* (Munich, 1918) Bd. 1, p. 409, as München, Antiquariat Jacques Rosenthal, no. 21933; Rosenthal's white oval paper tag with scalloped edges (superimposed on a rectangular label) with handwritten ink notations "21933/ III.M" and note in pencil inside front cover: "(Fol. 21933.) Coll [?] T[sch?] k 139 Blt." Unidentified shelf-marks include "Eusebius" in blue crayon on front pastedown and round circular paper tag on spine with number "456." From the collection of Sir Thomas Phillipps (no. 19049; tag on spine and number written on Rheindl bookplate with "a 32.522" added beneath). Purchased from C. A. Stonehill in 1949 by Thomas E. Marston (bookplate).

secundo folio: [reli]gio est ut

Bibliography: Faye and Bond, p. 65, no. 11.

Marston MS 15 Florence, ca. 1456-65
Leonardo Bruni, De bello italico adversus gothos, It. tr.

ff. 1r–82v *Libro primo della gherra* [sic] *italiana contro agothi composta per messere lionardo d'areço al R. P. D. Giuliano cardinale di sancto agnolo.* [letter:] Ben che a me molto piu giocondo sarebbe stato riferre la felicita che i danni d'italia niente ... [final paragraph, f. 2v:] Nel tempo di çeneno imperadore ... italia. [rubric wanting, text, f. 3r:] Dopo la morte di ualentiniano minore el quale come per certo si sa fu da suoi ucciso in roma l'omperio occidentale comincio a mancare di fermeça ... mancando loro gia ogni cosa necessaria et non auendo sperança alcuna// catchwords: dauito a totila.

Leonardo Bruni, *De bello italico adversus gothos*, in the Italian version by Ludovico Petroni made in 1456, but the text here differs significantly from that printed in Florence in 1526; ends imperfectly in the first part of Book IV. Preceded by the letter of Leonardo Bruni to Giuliano Cardinal Cesarini (1398–1444).

Parchment, ff. i (paper) + 82 + i (paper), 257 x 160 (143 x 96) mm. Written in 26 long lines. Double vertical bounding lines that do not always extend the full length of the page (Derolez 13.31); ruled in pale brown ink. Two single prickings at the top and bottom of inner margin, another single pricking in outer margin, 5 mm. below final horizontal ruling.

I^{2}, $II–VIII^{10}$. Horizontal catchwords with dots and flourishes on either side in lower margin written across inner vertical bounding line, verso (Derolez 12.3).

Written by a single scribe in fere-gothic script, above top line.

Partial border in inner margin of white vine-stem ornament, f. 1r, on blue, green and pink ground with white and blue dots. In lower border terminals extending in ink hair spray with green, pink and blue flowers and gold balls frame central medallion with a crude outline drawing of a head in profile (later addition?). Two decorated initials, 4- to 3-line, gold on blue, pink and green grounds with white vine-stem ornament. On f. 1r initial joined to partial border. Heading on f. 1r in red.

Binding: Italy, s. xviii–xix. "Alla rustica" with grey-green paper added over the spine and part of the boards. Edges yellow.

Written in Florence ca. 1456–65; early modern provenance unknown. Signature of "S. [or L.?] Haas 1894 [?]" on front pastedown. Modern notations, in pencil, on front pastedown: "50" in a circle and "281." White oval label with scalloped edge and "224" in ink on upper cover;

plain white round paper label ("S. III N/ Leon. Aretino/ XV. Jh/ 4o 73245b") on spine. Acquired from C. A. Stonehill in 1949 by Thomas E. Marston (bookplate).

secundo folio: furono

Bibliography: Faye and Bond, p. 66, no. 15.

Marston MS 16 — Germany, 1459
Ovid, Metamorphoses

1. f. 1r [Title:] Ouidius methamorphoseos. ff. 1v–2r blank; f. 2v Short table of proper names in alphabetical order, with book numbers and folio references to individual books, both of which refer to the same sequence written in upper right corner of each text leaf.

2. ff. 3r–201v In noua fert animus mutatas dicere formas/ Corpora dij ceptis. Nam uos mutastis et illas/ . . . Ore legar populi perque omnia secula fama/ Siquid habent veri vatum presagia viuam. [colophon:] Explicit Anno 1459. ff. 202r–207v blank

   W. S. Anderson, ed., Teubner (1977); a new critical edition by R. J. Tarrant is in progress (for additional information on the manuscript tradition, see *Texts and Transmission*, pp. 276–82). The text of Marston MS 16 contains interlinear and marginal notes throughout. Lactantian *tituli* and *narrationes* in margins; see D. A. Slater, ed., *Towards a Text of the Metamorphosis of Ovid* [Oxford, 1927]).

Paper (watermarks: unidentified bull's head and mountain), ff. ii (paper, ff. 1–2) + 204 (modern foliation, 3–207, omits no. 168), 344 x 235 (212 x 108) mm. Ca. 30–37 lines of verse. Leaves folded lengthwise for vertical bounding lines.

I^2, $II\text{–}XVIII^{12}$. Gatherings of twelve signed with Arabic numerals along lower edge near gutter, verso.

Written in a small neat gothic text hand with hybrida features.

Plain red 5-line initial, in outline only, f. 3r; two smaller initials of similar style, ff. 3v–4r. First letter of each verse stroked with red, ff. 3r–4r. Spaces left for decorative initials remain unfilled elsewhere in codex.

Binding: Germany, s. xv. Adhered vellum stays on the inside of the quires. Original wound sewing on three wide, tawed skin, slit straps laced through tunnels in the edges of beech boards to channels on the outside and pegged. Natural color endbands, caught up on the spine, are sewn to tawed cores laced into grooves on the outside of the boards. Front pastedown: reused paper manuscript with text side pasted face down.

Quarter bound in blue, tawed skin with a strip, now wanting, nailed along the edge. Two leaf-shaped catches with three five-petalled flowers on them on the lower board and the upper one cut in for kermes pink straps attached with metal plates; damage from a chain fastening at the head of this board, and the board broken; outer edge wanting. Title, in same [?] hand as on f. 1r, on upper and lower boards: "Ouidius methamorphoseos."

Written in Germany in 1459 (see colophon in art. 2). Acquired by Brother Henricus Karrer [?] in 1469 for the Franciscan convent of Villingen in Strasbourg, inscription on front pastedown: "Hoc opus procurauit frater henricus Karr [followed by abbreviation stroke] minister [or magister?] prouinciae argentinensis pro conuentu Viligensi fratrum minorum ac studiosis filijs eiusdem Conuentus. 1469." Monogram in the same [?] hand directly above the inscription, partially effaced: "b. w. h. k." Belonged to Pietro Girometti (MS. 1), whose manuscripts were bought by Prince Baldassarre Boncompagni in 1856 (E. Narducci, *Catalogo di manoscritti ora posseduti da D. B. Boncompagni* [Rome, 1892]; nos. 221 (296) in the Boncompagni collection (both numbers on spine, the first on a small paper label, the second in bright red ink). Unidentified inscriptions include note on f. 1r, crossed out and illegible; below in ink: "C. 1–207./ 1–202, 203, 203–206/ C. (204)-(207)"; round white paper label with saw-toothed edge on spine: "S II F/ Ouidius Ms. 1459/ fol. 21930"; on front pastedown, in pencil: "302" and "200." Remains of large square paper label wrapped around spine. Unidentified Latin note, s. xix–xx, pasted inside front cover. Purchased from C. A. Stonehill in 1949 by Thomas E. Marston (bookplate).

secundo folio: Proxima

Bibliography: Faye and Bond, p. 66, no. 16.

F. Munari, *Catalogue of the Manuscripts of Ovid's Metamorphoses*, University of London, Institute of Classical Studies, Bulletin Supplement no. 4 (London, 1957) p. 40, no. 183 (cited without shelf number).

Marston MS 17 — Roccacontrada, 1434

Petrarch, Itinerarium; Boccaccio, De montibus, silvis, fontibus, etc. — Pl. 36

1. ff. 1r–7r [Heading written three times by later hands; epistle:] Raro admodum spei nostre exitus respondent. Sepe premeditata destituunt:

insperata contingunt ... suspiramus abeuntem jam reducem exoptamus. [text, f. 1v:] Poscis Ergo vir optime quoniam me [?] non [one word omitted and added in margin, now lost] comites ... superest pagendum christi ope feliciter his spectaculis et hoc duce doctior nobis ac sanctior remeabis. *Explicit itinerarium francisci petrarce.* f. 7v blank

Petrarch, *Itinerarium breve de Ianua usque ad Ierusalem et Terram sanctam*; text is defective: lower portion of f. 1 missing. G. L. Lumbroso, ed., *L'Itinerarium del Petrarca* in *Atti della R. Accad. dei Lincei, Rendiconti*, s. IV, 4 (1888) pp. 390–403; reissued, *La guida compilata dal Petrarca ad uso d'un pellegrino* in *Memorie italiane del buon tempo antico* (Turin, 1889) pp. 16–49. A new edition, translation, and commentary is being prepared by J. Shey. Names of geographical locations written in margin by scribe of text.

2. ff. 8r–70r *Uiri clarissimi ac poete illustris Iohannis Boccatij de Certaldo ciuis florentinj de montibus et fluminibus fontibus siluis lacubus et maribus liber incipit. Prohemium.* [S]urrexeram equidem fessus a labore quodam egregio et aliquali otio ... altitudines metitur et conspicit. [text:] Aalac mons est cuius nomen alij diuidentem montem interpetrantur [*sic*] alij uero lenem id est lepidum ... Si quid uero congruum suis conformet [*sic*] scriptis comperiatur diuine bonitati et doctrine ascribatur sue. [colophon:] Sit nomen domini benedictum ex hoc/ Nunc et usque In seculum Amen/ Non nobis domine non nobis, sed nomine/ tuo da gloriam. [cf. *Colophons*, v. 6, no. 23555]/ *hic est finis. Laus altissimo. amen/ In rocha contrata sub anno domini Millesimo/ cccc° xxxiiij° die xxviij° Iulij.* f. 70v blank

Boccaccio, *De montibus, silvis, fontibus* ... ; printed in Venice (Wendelin von Speyer), 13 January 1473 (GKW 4482), and thereafter. The text has the following running headings, in red: *Montes, Silue, Fontes, Lacus, Flumina, Stagna, Maria.*

Paper, with parchment for inner and outer bifolia (watermarks: similar to Briquet Monts 11854), ff. ii (paper) + 70 + ii (paper), 289 x 220 (225 x 150) mm. 2 columns, 38–41 lines. Paper leaves: frame-ruled in lead. Parchment leaves: single vertical bounding lines in lead or ink, text rulings in pale brown ink. Remains of prickings in upper, lower, and outer margins.

I^{12} (–1), II^{12}, III^{10}, $IV–V^{12}$, VI^{14} (–14). Horizontal catchwords centered beneath written space, verso (Derolez 12.1).

Written in fere-humanistic script by a single scribe, above top line.

Plain red initial, 5-line, f. 1r; space unfilled for 10-line initial, f. 8r.

Plain red initials, 3- to 1-line, throughout. Paragraph marks in red, in art. 1. Rubrics throughout, except f. 1r.

First folio torn with loss of lower third of leaf; beginning and end of manuscript stained; some stains and wormholes affect text.

Binding: France [?], s. xviii. Brown, mottled sheepskin. Two blackish green labels (probably later additions) on gold-tooled spine: "Petrarchae Itinerarium" and "Boccatius De Montibus et Fluuiis." Contemporary green gold-tooled label on upper cover: "Fr. Petrachi. Itinerarium J. Bouatii. De. Flauiis. M. S. 1434."

Written in 1434 at Roccacontrada (since 1816 called Arcevia, in the province of Ancona; see colophon, art. 2). M. Morici ("Le opere geografiche del Petrarca e del Boccaccio copiate da un amanuense di Roccacontrada nel 1434," *La Bibliofilia* 6 [1905] pp. 321–26, with photograph of colophon) identified the scribe as don Marco di Antonio di Sante Massi of Roccacontrada who also copied another Boccaccio manuscript (see colophon cited in *Archivio storico messinese*, 2, fasc. 3–4, 150). Belonged to the Jesuit College of Agen; inscription on f. 1r: "Collegii Agen Societ. Iesu Catal. Ins." For additional information on manuscripts from Agen see N. Mann, "Petrarch Manuscripts in the British Isles," *Italia medioevale e umanistica* 18 (1975) p. 273, note 1. From the collection of Sir Thomas Phillipps (stamp with no. 1025 [1024 above cancelled] on f. ii recto; inscription with 1025 on f. 1r; tag on spine), who acquired it from Abate Luigi Celotti (ca. 1768–ca. 1846; see *Phillipps Studies*, v. 3, pp. 50–51). Rosenthal, Munich (round paper label, damaged, with "28278" on spine); unidentified label partly visible beneath Rosenthal label. Note on final rear flyleaf, recto, in pencil: "Imp. Temp. N°. 21 del 3-3-933"; "305" and "100" within a circle, both in pencil, on f. i verso. On f. ii recto traces of an unidentified bookdealer's description, in English, transcribed by Morici (*op. cit.*, p. 324). Purchased from C. A. Stonehill in 1949 by Thomas E. Marston (bookplate).

secundo folio: ciuitatem

Bibliography: Faye and Bond, p. 66, no. 17.
Ullman, p. 456, no. 46.
Dutschke, pp. 174–76, no. 69.

Marston MS 18 — Milan, ca. 1467
Francesco Filelfo, Oratio

ff. 1r–82r *Francisci Philelfi Oratio Parentalis De Divi Francisci Sphortiae Mediolanensium Ducis Felicitate.* [S]i fieri posse censerem: ut lamentationibus ac lachrymis saeuo et peracerbo naturae uulneri mederemur: quod ex incommodo fortasse magis quam ex immaturo Francisci Sphortiae ... ut non mortuum minus quam uiuum ab uno Francisco Philelfo et amatum illum, et obseruatum, et celebratum, praesentes omnes uenturique cognoscant. [colophon:] *Que quidem oratio habita est ab eodem Francisco Philelfo equite aurato laureatoque poeta in ecclesia cathedrali Mediolani die lunae vii idus martias anno a natali christiano Millesimo quadringentesimo sexagesimo septimo.* f. 82v ruled, but blank

Francesco Filelfo, *Oratio parentalis de divi Francisci Sphortiae Mediolanensium ducis felicitate*; printed in Milan and Venice in 1481 and thereafter (Hain nos. 12918–25). Brief notes by scribe, in red, in column ruled in outer margin. For other manuscripts containing this work see A. Calderini, "I codici milanesi delle opere di Francesco Filelfo," *Archivio Storico Lombardo* ser. 5, 42 (1915) nos. 33, 34, 35, and p. 394, no. 45.

Paper (watermarks, much worn, buried in gutter: similar in general design to Piccard, Ochsenkopf VII.955), ff. i + 82 (modern foliation begins on front flyleaf) + i (paper), 234 x 162 (131 x 72) mm. 16 long lines. Double vertical bounding lines and two additional vertical rulings to delineate column in margin for notes. Rulings impressed on a ruling board from the center of the gathering out; vertical rulings do not always extend to the lower edge of leaves; single pricking along lower edge.

I–X^{8} (+ 1 leaf at end). Vertical catchwords, surrounded by dots, between vertical bounding lines (Derolez 12.5).

Written by a single scribe in a neat sloping humanistic bookhand, above top line.

Space left for initial on f. 1r is unfilled; heading in majuscules, colophon, and marginalia, in pale red.

Binding: Italy, s. xix^{in}. Quarter bound in brown mottled calf; mottled yellow and green paper sides; pale brown edges. Gold-tooled spine including title, which is mostly wanting. Spine worm-eaten.

Written in Milan ca. 1467 when the oration was delivered; according to A. C. de la Mare the manuscript was very probably copied by one of Filelfo's scribes, Fabricius Elphiseus, who was secretary to Galeazzo Maria Sforza, Duke of Milan 1466–76; Elphiseus signed Paris, B. N. lat 8125 and El Escorial g. II. 9, both containing works of Filelfo and both written in a more formal style of writing than Marston MS 18. Unidentified notes and shelf-marks, s. xviii–xix, include: remains of square white label at head of spine with only "21" in ink now visible; round white paper label at tail of spine: "7797/ III M" in ink; on front pastedown, all in pencil: "Num. 36" (partially erased), "82" written twice, "50" enclosed by a circle, "307" and "81 B1" [remainder unclear]; on front flyleaf, partially erased "No 22." Purchased from C. A. Stonehill in 1949.

secundo folio: nostros cogitatus

Bibliography: Faye and Bond, p. 66, no. 18.

Marston MS 22 Oxford [?], s. XIII^{med}
Book of Hours, Sarum use Pl. 51

1. f. 1r [Added:] Christe qui lux es et dies noctis tenebras detegis. lucisque lumen crederis. lumen beatum predicans ... Memento nostri domine in graui isto corpore qui es defensor anime adesto nobis domine.

   RH 2934.

2. f. 1v [Added:] Cultor dei memento te fontis et lauacri rorem subbisse scantum [?] te crismate innouatum ... Groria [*sic*] et honor deo. summo vero regi spiritu paraclito et nunc et in perpetuum Amen.

   RH 4053.

3. ff. 2r–91r Hours of the Holy Spirit beginning defectively and Hours of the Virgin, Sarum use (worked in after the office of the Holy Spirit, except that matins and lauds of each appear to be copied straight on); after lauds of the office of the Virgin, suffrages of the Holy Spirit, John the Baptist (beginning defectively), Peter and Paul, John the Evangelist, Andrew, Many Apostles, Stephen, Laurence, Edmund king and martyr, Thomas of Canterbury (cancelled), Many Martyrs, Nicolas, Edmund confessor, Benedict, an unidentified confessor (Benedict again? breaks defectively), and unidentified virgin (? begins defectively), Susanna, Many Martyrs, relics, All Saints, for peace, the Virgin; loss of leaves throughout, as follows: ff. 2r–5v HS matins, defect. beg. (and possibly a leaf missing after f. 3 as well?); ff. 6r–17v BVM matins, defect. beg.; ff. 17v–43v BVM lauds, defect. between ff. 31v–32r, 38v–39r; ff. 43v–46r HS prime; ff. 46r–54r BVM prime; ff. 54r–57r HS terce; ff. 57r–61v BVM terce, defect. end; ff. 62r–63v HS sext, defect. beg.; ff. 63v–67v BVM sext, defect. end; f. 68r-v HS nones, defect. beg., end; ff. 69r–72v BVM nones, defect. beg., end; f. 73r-v HS vespers, defect. beg., end; ff. 74r–81v BVM vespers, defect. beg.; ff. 81v–84r HS compline; ff. 84r–91r BVM compline.

4. ff. 91v–92v [Added:] Omnipotens sempiterne deus qui es sine fine et principio qui creasti omnia ex nichilo ad cuius imperium ... vt huic famule tue [an initial?] grauide pregnanti interueniat pietatis tue auxilium vt prolem tibi gratam sine mortis periculo valead [*sic*] producere....

   Prayer for safe delivery in childbirth.

5. ff. 93r–107v Penitential Psalms, beginning defectively, and litany including Alphege (14), Thomas (15; not cancelled), Alban (16), Edmund (17), and Oswald (18) among 18 martyrs; Paulinus (8), Cuthbert (9), Dunstan (10), Swithun (11), Benedict (14), and Botulph (17) among 17 confessors; Mary Magdalen (1), Radegundis (2), Osyth (3), Scholastica (11), Juliana (12), and Ethelreda (14) among 14 virgins; ends defectively.

6. ff. 108r–112r Gradual Psalms [?], beginning defectively and ending imperfectly (Pss. 119–126 no longer present; cues only, as normal, for Pss. 127–130; Pss. 131, 132, as normal, written out in full; Ps. 133 not copied), followed straight on by Ps. 150, Kyrie, Pater noster, Requiem and several prayers for the dead: Inclina domine aurem tuam ad preces nostras quibus misericordiam tuam suplices [*sic*] deprecamur ... [HE, p. 101]; Deus qui nos patrem et matrem honorare precepisti ... [HE, p. 111]; Miserere quesumus domine animabus omnium benefactorum ... [HE, p. 101]; Fidelium deus omnium conditor et redemptor ... [HE, p. 101].

7. ff. 112r–113r Dampne deu sire pere ihesu crist isi uerraiement cume nus creumus et ueirs est. que cu seint sacrefise est icel uerrai cors ... de moi cheitive pecheresse....

   K. V. Sinclair, *French Devotional Texts of the Middle Ages: a bibliographic manuscript guide* (Westport, Conn., 1979) 2687 (p. 40).

8. ff. 113r–114r Beu sire deu si uerraiement cume uus preistes iceste chariti sacre de la uirgine marie et en cu char nasquistes....

   Sinclair, *op. cit.*, 2555 (p. 24; see also his 952, 1903, 1957, 2049–50, 2528).

9. ff. 114r–115r Beu [*a* added in margin] sire ihesu crist que le uestre beneit seintime cors. et uestre precius saunc dunastes en la seinte uerraie croiz pur tut le mund sauuer....

   Sinclair, *op.cit.*, 2565 (p. 25).

10. f. 115r-v Pericope from John (1.1–10), ending defectively: "... uenientem in hunc mundum. In mundo//"

Parchment (thick, fuzzy on hair side), ff. i (modern parchment) + 115 (modern pagination, upper right; modern foliation, lower right), 148 x 111 (112 x 60) mm. Ca. 13 long lines. Double vertical and single or double horizontal bounding lines; ruled in hard point or crayon (lead for ff. 93r–115v). Row of prickings along outer vertical bounding line, f. 91 only.

Precise collation impossible due to tight binding, repairs, and number of missing leaves.

Written in two styles of script: large gothic bookhands, often with only 3-4 words per line, by three scribes for ff. 1r, 2r–91r, 93r–115v, respectively; Anglicana scripts for ff. 1v, 91v–92v (added prayers).

The codex, now in fragmentary condition with no miniatures extant, contains the following sequence of historiated initials, some badly rubbed (*L* = large historiated initial; *S* = small historiated initial): f. 5r Head of Janus (S); f. 7r King David, head in profile (S); f. 17v Annunciation (L); f. 18r Crouching naked man (S); f. 21r Head of woman in profile (S); f. 26r Rooster (S); f. 28r Blessed Virgin Mary, portrait (S); f. 32r Peter with keys, half-length (S); f. 37r Nicolas, head of (S); f. 43v Scourging at the pillar (L); f. 45v God the Father (S); f. 46r Visitation (L); f. 46v Holy Ghost descending (S); f. 54v Carrying of the cross (L); f. 57r Annunciation to the shepherds (L); f. 57r Holy Ghost descending (S); f. 63v Nativity (L); f. 81v Three Marys at the tomb (L); f. 84r Flight into Egypt (L); f. 94r Woman praying (S); f. 101r Man praying (S); f. 112r Woman praying (S). Large historiated initials, 3-line, pink or blue with white designs on blue square ground framed with gold; both initial and frame edged in black; figures on gold ground, often rubbed and flaked; elongated dragons extend into margins for ascenders, as in initial *D*. Small historiated initials, 2-line, of similar designs and colors, but on cusped gold grounds. Other text divisions marked by 2-line initials, pink, orange, blue with simple foliage motifs in the same colors and yellow, all with designs in white and on square or cusped gold grounds that often extend far into margins. Initials on ff. 93–115 are somewhat more delicate in appearance and presumably by a different hand than those on ff. 2-91. 1-line initials in red with blue penwork designs alternate with opposing color scheme. Elaborate line-fillers, including fish and heads of long-beaked beasts, for litany (art. 5). Headings in red, ff. 2-91 only.

Manuscript has been heavily trimmed with loss of marginal decoration; staining, rubbing throughout affects illumination.

Binding: England, s. xix–xx. Rigid vellum case with note on spine "MS. Circa 1400." Red edges. Bound by Birdsell and Son (Northampton, 1792 and later).

Produced in England, probably in Oxford, in the middle of the 13th century, to judge from the style of decoration (for similar manuscripts see N. J. Morgan, *Early Gothic Manuscripts 1250–1285* [London, 1988] v. 1: pp. 119–21, no. 73; v. 1: pp. 123–24, no. 75; v. 2: pp. 66–67, no. 104; v. 2: pp. 150–52, no. 158; this manuscript not recorded in J. Backhouse, *The Madresfield Hours* [Oxford, 1975]). Commissioned by an unidentified woman given the feminine forms in arts. 3, 4 and 7. The manuscript appears to have been made by two workteams, in view of the slight differences in script and decoration exhibited by ff. 1–91 and 93–115, and the insertion of art. 4 on ff. 91v–92v. Notes in pencil, on rear flyleaf: "Bought of Ridler, about 1887." Purchased from C. A. Stonehill in 1935 by Thomas E. Marston (bookplate).

Bibliography: Faye and Bond, p. 67, no. 22.

Marston MS 23 Central Italy, s. XIV/XV
Collectanea drawn from Vincent of Beauvais

1. ff. 1r–3r De abstinentia c. 4./ De Accidia c. 5/ De Acceptione uel contentu munerum c. [5]/ De Amministratione rerum domesticarum ... DE. V. De ypocrisi et simulatione suy. 58/ DE. Z. De zelo et suy correptione. Rubrica. 59.

   Table of chapters.

2. f. 3v Nullus redarguendum me putet. si mihi copianti Prohemium huiusmodi libri fore describendum persuasi ... quo pretermisso nullum rite fundatur exordium.

   Prologue to art. 3.

3. ff. 3v–59v *Incipiunt Autoritates philosophorum et Poetarum secundum Ordinem Alphabeti de diuersis materijs Compilate et aduersis libris extracte per me fratrem Vincencium lectorem in prouincie francie ordinis fratrum predicatorum.* [f. 4r:] *Incipit tractatus Secundum Ordinem Alphabeti ut infra patebit et primo de astinentia. Videlicet Actor ait.* [A]bstinentia est virtus qua gule uoluntates in nobis restrignimus [*sic*] ... Seneca. Si uis omnia tibi subicere te ipsum primo subicias rationi. Deo gratias. [colophon:] Explicit Opus Autoritatum Philosophorum et Poetarum secundum Ordinem Alphabeti de uarijs materijs. Compilatum et a diuersis libris extractum per Venerabilem Virum fratrem Vincentium lectorem in prouincia francie Ordinis fratrum predicatorum deo gratias.

   An alphabetically arranged collection of extracts on the virtues and vices and on moral subjects drawn from Vincent of Beauvais. The text also appears in Basel, Universitätsbibliothek MS B XI 3, ff. 238–308, and Ratisbonne, Bibl. prov. 176, ff. 90–124; see P. Delahaye, "Un dictionnaire d'éthique attribué à Vincent de Beauvais," *Mélanges de science religieuse* 1 (1951) pp. 65–85.

Parchment, ff. i (paper) + 59 + i (paper), 148 x 109 (124 x 71) mm., greatly trimmed. 31 long lines. Single vertical bounding lines. Ruled in pale brown ink.

I–V^{10}, VI^{10} (–10).

Written in a small neat gothic script.

Twenty-one illuminated initials, 12- to 3-line, green, blue, pink, grey or red with white filigree against gold ground edged in black. Initials filled with curling acanthus, red, green, grey and unburnished gold against blue ground with white filigree, and ending in foliage serifs, as above. In the margins gold balls with a single hair-line spike. The style of the initials may be compared to Paris, BN lat. 6815 (cf. Avril and Gousset, v. 2, p. 179, no. 221, pl. CXXVI). Numerous flourished initials with interior harping alternate blue and red with red and pale yellow penwork. Headings in red. Paragraph marks alternate red and blue. Several marginal drawings, among them grotesques (ff. 53v, 54r) and human heads, a woman holding a flower (f. 39v), a snake impaled on a spear (f. 58v), in a nearly contemporary hand. Guide letters for the decorator in red. Space left unfilled for initial on f. 4r.

Binding: Italy, s. xix. Half bound in brown mottled calf with a gold-tooled spine and cream, blue-green, and red paste-paper sides. Red and olive green paste-paper pastedowns in a chevron pattern. Red edges.

Written in Central Italy (perhaps Bologna?) at the end of the 14th or beginning of the 15th century. Contemporary ownership inscription on scroll on f. 59v indicates the volume belonged to one Paulus: "*Si.* PA. *Ponatur.* u. *coniugatur* lu. *condectatur* [?]. s *.sotiatur. Cuius est liber sic nominatur.*" Colophon rewritten by later hand on front flyleaf; ownership note on front pastedown effaced. Unidentified shelf-marks and notes include: "N. 4" in ink on upper cover; "282" and "100" in a circle, both in pencil, on front flyleaf; "S. [?] 59" and undeciphered series of numbers [?] on back flyleaf. Purchased from C. A. Stonehill in 1949 (note on back flyleaf) by Thomas E. Marston (bookplate).

secundo folio: De doctoribus

Bibliography: Faye and Bond, p. 67, no. 23.

Marston MS 24 Italy, s. XII^in

Joannes Cassianus; Ambrosius Autpertus Pl. 56

1. ff. 1r–36r *Incipit liber primus de habitu monachorum Iohannis Cassiani. De institutis* ac regulis monasteriorum dicturi. unde conpetentius donante deo quam ex ipso habitu ... prosperis fuerimus elati. utraque uelut caduca. et mox transeuntia contemplantes. *Explicit liber de spiritu tristicie*. f. 36v blank, with only upper portion of leaf extant

   Joannes Cassianus, extracts from *De institutis coenobiorum et de octo principalium vitiorum remediis libri XII*; M. Petschenig, ed., CSEL, v. 17 (1888) pp. 8–171; the manuscript includes only I.1–2, 10–11; II.1–3, 5-6, 15–18; IV.1–43; V.3 - IX.13. There are no chapter lists in arts. 1 or 2.

2. ff. 37r–65r *Incipit collatio abbatis Moysi Prima*. Cum in heremo sithii ubi monachorum probatissimi patres et omnis commemoratur perfectio ... cum censum habeat pauperis. non abiecit diuitis uoluntatem. *Explicit collatio abbatis danielis*.

   Joannes Cassianus, *Conlationes XXIV*; M. Petschenig, ed., CSEL, v. 13 (1886) pp. 7–118 (Conlationes I-IV). See also art. 5.

3. f. 65v Miscellaneous notes, in Lat.

4. ff. 66r–68v *Oratio Sancti Ambrosii ad Beatam Trinitatem. Pro vitandis septem Principalibus viciis. Et sanctis virtutibus adquirendis*. Summa et incomprehensibilis natura. uirtus uitaque beata. lux inaccessibilis uera ... pro me exorent ipse inspiraueris. qui eternitate perhenni uiuis et regnas cuncta per secula. et in omnibus seculis. *Amen. Explicit oratio Sancti Ambrosii de viii*^o [sic] *vitiis Principalibus*.

   Ambrosius Autpertus, *Oratio contra septem vitia*; R. Weber, ed., CC cont. med. 27B (1979) pp. 935–44; Recension A.

5. ff. 68v–90v *Incipit Collatio Abbatis Piamonis De. IIII*^or *Generibus monachorum. Postquam* conspectum atque. colloquium trium illorum senum quorum collationes sancto fratre nostro eucherio compellente ... curarum flagris semper//

   Joannes Cassianus, extracts from *Conlationes XXIV*; page references here in parentheses referring to Petschenig, *op. cit.* (see also art. 2). Books XVIII-XIX (chapter list for XIX, f. 74r; pp. 506–52); XX.8–12 (pp. 561–70); XXII.1-2 (abridged), 3-6.7 (pp. 616–24); XII.1 (abridged), 2-4, 6.1–4, 7.1, 7.3, 7.4-5, 11.1, 12.1, 12.3, 13.2, 15.2 (pp. 334-35, 335-39, 341–43, 345, 346, 351, 353, 354, 356–57, 358), text ending imperfectly on f. 87v ("... trium siue ut alii//"); XXIV.9–13.4 (pp. 683–89), text ending imperfectly on f. 89v ("... indisrupta iugitate//"); XXIV.19.4–24.2 (pp. 696–700), text ending imperfectly.

Parchment (endpieces, holes, speckled on hair side), ff. 91 (modern foliation, lower right corner, skips leaf between ff. 42 and 43), ca. 315 x 185 (260 x 125) mm. Written in 41 to 50 long lines. First two gatherings: ruled in crayon, double vertical bounding lines; prominent prickings (slashes) in upper, lower and outer margins. Remaining quires: ruled in hard point, double vertical and single or double horizontal bounding lines, prominent prickings (punctures) in upper, lower and outer margins.

I–II^{8}, III^{14} (–3, 5, 9, 13; no loss of text), IV^{10}, V–VI^{8}, VII^{8} (+ 1 bifolium, half-sheet, inserted in center of quire, ff. 55A and 55B), VIII^{6}, IX–X^{8}, XI^{6}, XII (original structure uncertain, –1, a bifolium, + 1 leaf conjugate to first missing leaf). First quire signed with Roman numeral, center of lower margin, verso. Remains of catchwords, right of center in lower margin, verso.

Written by multiple scribes of varying degrees of accomplishment in late caroline minuscule and early gothic bookhand.

One decorated 5-line initial (rubbed) on f. 1r, constructed of interlacing bands in parchment, outlined in brown ink against an irregular red ground. Plain red initials, some of which are drawn vertically rather than upright, and often with small red pearl designs, appear to be executed by many different hands. Instructions to rubricator in upper margin of f. 1r. Guide letters for decorator.

Binding: Italy. s. xii. Original sewing on two tawed pigskin slit straps. The sewing supports and endband cores are laced through a tawed skin spine lining (from a palimpsest?) which extends about 50 mm. on either side and is turned in at head and tail. There is a fragment of finely woven cloth caught up by the lower sewing support and kettle stitch. Chevron endbands on tawed skin straps, one of which extends across the lower side under the lower turn-in. The lower side is reinforced with two irregular pieces of vellum. The structure of this binding is discussed in detail by M. Gullick, "From Scribe to Binder: Quire Tackets in Twelfth-Century Manuscripts," *The Compleat Binder: Studies in Bookmaking and Conservation in Honour of Roger Powell*, ed. G. Petherbridge (The Codicology Press, 1991).

A flush, tawed skin cover with overlapping corners and irregular turn-ins, wide at the fore edge. Stubs of fastenings which are extensions of the supports. Contemporary title in ink on upper cover: "liber intitulatur de habitu monachorum." Decorative panel containing a drawing of an unidentified animal smeared blue and/or green within a border of brown circles, on lower side.

Written in Italy toward the beginning of the 12th century. Early note on f. 36v mentions the name "andreas avelloni"; another inscription inside back cover: "Reddatur priori sancti andree de t[*o* or *e*; remainder illegible due to ink blotch]." Belonged to Federico Patetta (1867–1945), Professor of the History of Law at the University of Turin at the beginning of the 20th century (his note, f. 1r: "MS no. 81"). Sold by Hoepli (Milan, 3 May 1928, no. 50); bought by E. P. Goldschmidt (cat. 15, no. 7); purchased by Acton Griscom (De Ricci, v. 2, p. 1160, no. 1). Purchased from Lathrop C. Harper in 1955 by L. C. Witten (inv. no. 835), who sold it in 1956 to Thomas E. Marston (bookplate).

secundo folio: dei sentenciam

Bibliography: De Ricci, *Census*, v. 2, p. 1160, no. 1 (while in the Griscom collection); Faye and Bond, p. 67, no. 24.

The Medieval Book, no. 55, with plate of binding.

Marston MS 25 Southwestern France, s. XII[1] and XIV–XVI

Calendar; Martyrology; Benedictine Rule

1. ff. i–ii verso [a single leaf folded in half, to be read beginning with the inner, facing leaves, f. i verso, f. ii, f. i, f. ii verso]: Portion of an unidentified office, possibly that of the common of a martyr; office, for monastic use, of matins for the common of a confessor bishop.

I. 2. ff. 1–44v Calendar with obituary, giving names and offices (abbatissa, priorissa, sacristana, helemosinaria, infirmaria, reclusa, decana, conversa, puella, laica, ancilla) of the nuns of the Benedictine abbey of Notre-Dame de Saintes in Charente Inférieure in Southwestern France, and giving the names and bequests of benefactors of the monastery, and the names of contemporary rulers (Eleanor of Aquitaine, William of Poitiers, Richard the Lion-Hearted, Henry II of England, Geoffrey of Anjou, Agnes of Burgundy). The main body of this section dates from the fourteenth century (having been recopied from a twelfth century original, of which only f. 2 remains), with continual supplemental notices through the sixteenth century; the latest datable obituary is apparently that of Anna of Rohan, abbess of Notre-Dame, 1484–1523 (f. 7r, a later replacement leaf). Text is missing one leaf at the end. ff. 45–46 skipped in foliation.

II. 3. ff. 47r–128v *In christi nomine incipit epistola cromatij et eliodori episcoporum. ad iheronimum prebiterum* [sic]. Domino sancto fratri iheronimo presbitero cromatius et heliodorus episcopi in domino salutem. Cum religiosissimus augustus theodosius mediolanensium urbem fuisset ingressus ... dei martiribus exhiberi. *Rescripcio iheronimj presbiterj.* Cromatio et helidoro episcopis iheronimus presbiter. Constat deum nostrum omni die martyrum sanctorum triumphis exhibere ... [f. 48v:] in celesti gloria fecit esse sublimes. *Breuiarium ex nominibus apostolorum uel loquorum ubi predicauerunt ubi orti uel ubi occisi seu ubi sepulti sunt. de sancto petro.* Symon qui interpretatur hobediens. petrus agnoscens filius iohannis frater andree ... [f. 50v:] cui datur euangelij predicatio in iudea. *Expliciunt feste apostolorum. Liber Kalendarius per annj circulum. Mensis ianuarius habet dies xxxi. luna xxx.* Iani prima dies et septima fine minatur. Kalendas ianuarij. Circumcisio domini nostri ihesu christi. Rome. nathale almachij martyris ... gladio cesa est. Reciare. sancti hermetis exorciste. *Explicit calendarius liber.*

A version of Usuard's *Martyrology*; PL 123.601–992; 124.9–858; the body of the text written in the 12th century with some later marginal additions. The martyrology proper preceded by the Epistle of Chromatius and Heliodorus to Jerome, his reply, and a section devoted to the Twelve Apostles; each month introduced by the verse for the *dies mali*.

4. ff. 128v–168v *Incipit prologus regule sancti benedicti abbatis. Ausculta o filia* precepta magistri. et inclina aurem cordis tui. et ammonicionem pii patris libenter excipe ... que supra commemorauimus doctrine uirtutumque culmina. deo protegente peruenies. Amen.

Rule of St. Benedict, feminine version with contemporary interlinear glosses and corrections; the text of this manuscript discussed by H. Feiss, OSB, "Care for the Text: A Twelfth-Century Glossed Rule of Benedict for Notre-Dame de Saintes," *American Benedictine Review* (forthcoming).

Consists of two distinct parts, both on thick parchment 250 x 198 mm., with front flyleaves taken from a liturgical manuscript with musical notation arranged along a single red line.

Part I: ff. 1–46 (incorrect foliation in first quire: 1–8, stub only foliated 46), format irregular due to numerous additions to text. I^7 [?], $II–V^8$, VI^6 (–6, f. 46, with text). Quire and leaf signatures (e.g., bj, bij, etc.) lower right corner, recto. Some signatures, left of center in lower margin, verso. Written in a variety of scripts ranging from gothic bookhand to bâtarde. Initials, dates and headings in red. This part of the manuscript has been extensively patched and repaired.

Part II: ff. 47–168, written space: 180 x 140 mm., 23–24 long lines. Single or double horizontal (sometimes triple lower) and vertical bounding lines; ruled in hard point on flesh side. Remains of prickings in upper, lower and outer margins. I–X^8, XI^2 (ff. 127–128), XII–XVI^8. Same types of signatures and catchwords as in Part I. Written in elegant late caroline/ early gothic bookhand. Two decorated initials, ff. 47r and 129r, 6-line, in red, green and blue. Decorative headings in brown ink touched with red and green, or red touched with blue. Small initials, 4- to 1-line in red, some with foliage scrolls in red or contrasting color. Headings in red.

Binding: France, s. xv [?]. An early resewing on three double, twisted, tawed skin supports laced into wide grooves in oak boards and pegged with rectangular or square pegs.

Covered in brown sheepskin with corner tongues, blind-tooled with diagonals in an outer frame. Spine leather wanting. Leather on boards much worn.

Written for the Benedictine abbey of nuns at Notre-Dame de Saintes in Southwestern France. Part II, copied in the first half of the 12th century, exhibits Spanish influence with respect to both its script and decoration; Part I consists of one leaf (f. 2) contemporary with Part II, but the remainder was primarily written (recopied from earlier manuscript?) in the first half of the 14th century, with extensive additions dating up to and including the 15th–16th centuries. Parts I and II were probably bound together in the 15th century. For information and bibliography on the abbey, see *Gallia christiana*, rev. ed. (Paris, 1883) v. 2, 1127–31; Cottineau, v. 2, 2927–28; T. Grasilier, ed., *Cartulaires inédits de la Saintonge*, v. 2 = Cartulaire de l'abbaye royale de Notre-Dame de Saintes de l'ordre de Saint-Benoit (Paris, 1871). Belonged to Acton Griscom (De Ricci, v. 2, p. 1160, no. 2). Purchased from Lathrop C. Harper in 1956 by Thomas E. Marston (bookplate).

secundo folio: [Part I:] Obiit aquilina
[Part II:] palmam

Bibliography: De Ricci, v. 2, p. 1160, no. 2 (while in the Griscom collection); Faye and Bond, p. 67, no. 25.

Exhib. Cat., pp. 185–86, no. 12.

P. Johnson, *Equal in Monastic Profession: Religious Women in Medieval France* (Chicago, forthcoming 1991).

Marston MS 26 France, s. $XIII^{2/4}$
Petrus Pictaviensis, Compendium historiae in genealogia Christi Pl. 44

ff. 1r–5r [C]onsiderans hystorie sacre prolixitatem necnon et difficultatem scolarium circa studium sacre lectionis maxime illius que quoque in hystorie fundamento uersatur ... ordinem perduxi. [explanation for genealogical diagram:] [C]hain agricola dolens sua munera et non fratris fuisse reprobata licet a domino ... [concludes with list of apostles arranged in tiers of circles, ending with Barnabas:] inter dies ascensionis et pentecosten. f. 5v blank

Glorieux, no. 100f; Stegmüller, 6778, where it is attributed, as in other manuscripts, to Petrus Pictaviensis. One leaf (with text?) missing between ff. 1–2.

Parchment, ff. 5, 350 x 235 (264 x 200) mm. 71 ruled lines, but not all lines are used on every page. Columns vary in number, but each has vertical bounding lines in red, full length of page. Horizontal text rulings in lead. Prickings in upper, lower, and inner margins.

A single gathering of six leaves, the second wanting.

Written by a single scribe in fine gothic bookhand, above top line.

Genealogical tables accompany text throughout: drawn in red with roundels connected by pairs of parallel lines and aligned between red vertical rulings. Roundels for Adam and Eve, f. 1r, in yellow and blue, respectively; the roundels for their descendants on green ground. The plan of the temple at Jerusalem, f. 4r, in red, yellow, green and blue. The roundels for Christ, f. 5r, in blue, yellow, and red. Headings in red; spaces left for decorative initials remain unfilled.

Lower portion of f. 1 torn, with loss of text.

Binding: Germany, s. xix. Grubby blue paper wrapper. Title, in ink, on upper cover: "*Manuscript des XIIIten Jahrhunderts*. Historia mundi sec. ord. chronol. usque ad mortem Jesu Christi."

Written in France in the second quarter of the 13th century; early provenance unknown. Inscriptions, s. xix–xx, on front cover, in ink: "E. Schr. 3782," and in pencil, f. 1r: "E. Schr. fol. 3782 Pergamenthandschrift." Unidentified entry from sale cat. (no. 323), in English, pasted inside front cover. Purchased from Ludwig Rosenthal of the Netherlands in 1956 by L. C. Witten (inv. no. 989), who sold it the same year to Thomas E. Marston (bookplate).

Bibliography: Faye and Bond, p. 67, no. 26.

Marston MS 27 Spain, s. XVI$^{1/4}$

Diego Enríquez del Castillo, Crónica del Rey don Enrique IV

1. f. 1r [Later title:] Cronica del Rey Don Enrique IIII por diego enriquez. f. 1v blank; ff. 2r–7v [table:] Tabla: capitulo primero de la vida y filosomia [*sic*] del Rey. ffo. iij . . . capitulo clxix de como tornado el Rey a madrid le creçio la dolençia y murio. ffo. cc.

2. ff. 8r–9r Don juan pacheco marques de villena maestre de Santiago . . . y murio en grand prosperidad dhedad de cinqa. y cina [?]. años. ff. 9v–10v blank

   Life of Don Juan Pacheco, Marques de Villena.

3. f. 11r [Contemporary title page:] Coronica del quarto Rey don enrique de glorosa [*sic*] memoria hecha por el liçençiado diego enrriquez de Castillo su coronista Capellan y del su consejo. ff. 11v–12v blank [Contemporary foliation begins:] ff. 1r–201r Tanto [corrected from "Quanto"] los prinçipes señalados y antiguos varones de las hedades pasadas quedaron famosos . . . que nj porlo muy prospero se muestre mas alegria nj porlas aduersidades Señaladas de alta tristeza. fin. f. 201v blank

   Diego Enríquez del Castillo (1433–1504?), Chronicle of King Enrique IV of Castile (1425–74); J. de Flores, ed., *Cronica del Rey D. Enrique el quarto de este nombre, por su capellan y cronista Diego Enriquez del Castillo* (Madrid, 1787).

4. f. 202r Decretal texts concerning behavior of clerics, in Sp. ff. 202v–231v blank

5. f. 232r-v Brief law text, in Lat.

Paper (watermarks: unidentified hand), ff. i (paper) + 245 (ff. 1–12, with an unnumbered leaf between 4 and 5; followed by contemporary foliation 1–201; remainder of leaves, modern foliation 202–232) + i (paper), 293 x 206 (232 x 155) mm. Ca. 28 long lines. Single vertical bounding lines ruled in hard point.

I^{11} [?], II^{2} (ff. 11–12), III-VIII^{8}, IX^{4}, X-XXIII^{8}; collation of remaining leaves impossible due to tight binding. Remains of quire and leaf signatures (e.g., b i, bij, etc.) for quires III–XXIII only.

Written by several scribes in late Spanish bookhands with cursive and humanistic features. Some headings in large gothic display script.

Binding: Spain, s. xvi. Sewn on three tawed skin, slit straps, now broken, laced into channels in wooden boards. One plain wound endband is sewn on a tawed skin core, the other endband was added later.

Covered in brown calf blind-tooled with concentric frames, the central panel and alternate frames filled with rope interlace. The layout of the design is the same on both boards but different small tools are used in the central panels. Spine: four fillets outlining the supports and in the center of the panels a small rope tool in the center of the compartments so formed. Two fastenings, the catches on the lower board, the clasp straps later additions. The spine is mended at head and tail; some corners repaired.

Written in Spain in the first quarter of the 16th century; early provenance unknown. Traces of shelf-mark, in ink, on spine "L. 6. 25 [?]." Belonged to James P. R. Lyell (bookplate); for further information on his manuscripts see *Lyell Cat.*, pp. xv–xxix. Bought from the Lyell estate by Bernard Quaritch in 1951 and sold in 1952 (Cat. 699, no. 71; Cat. 716, no. 310). Purchased from C. A. Stonehill (inv. nos. 3135 and 11204) in 1955 by Thomas E. Marston (bookplate).

secundo folio: [table, f. 3:] c° xxviij° como llega
[text, f. 2:] por que

Bibliography: Faye and Bond, p. 66, no. 27.

Marston MS 28 — Italy, s. XIII/XIV
Epitome of Aristotle, in It.

ff. 1r–18r [O]ngne arte eivgne [*sic*] dottrina e' d'ongne operatione et d'ongne [*sic*] eleççione si pare a domandar alcun bene ... E percio che a benerdinare [*sic*] le leggi sie mestieri ragione et experiença deo gratis Amen. Explicit Ethica Aristotilis tranlata [*sic*] a magistro Tadeo in uolgare. f. 18v blank

Epitome of Aristotle's *Ethics* translated into Italian by Taddeo d'Alderotto (ca. 1235–1295). There is some confusion as to the relationship between the Italian translation by Taddeo d'Alderotto and that used/made by Bono Giamboni in his translation of Latini's *Tresor*, Book VI (L. Gaiter, ed., *Il Tesoro di Brunetto Latini volgarizzato da Bono Giamboni* [Bologna, 1880]), vol. III); see L. Frati, "L'Etica di Aristotile volgarizzata da Taddeo di Alderotto," in *Giornale storico della letteratura italiana* 68 (1916) pp. 192–95.

Parchment (palimpsest: written over an unidentified canon law text, s. $XIII^{3/4}$), ff. iii (paper) + 18 + iii (paper), 338 x 223 (252 x 170) mm. 2

columns, 35 lines. Faintly ruled in lead; prickings at four corners of each text column and in outer margin.

I^8, II^{10}. Horizontal catchwords center of lower margin, verso.

Written in a calligraphic notarial hand with tall ascenders and strongly looped forms of letters *d* and *b*, above top line.

Spaces left for decorative initials remain unfilled.

Binding: England or U.S.A. [?], s. xix/xx. Quarter bound in orange goatskin with a gold-tooled label on spine ("Aristotle. Ethica, in Italian. XIVth Century") and marbled paper sides. Edges gilt.

Written in Italy at the end of the 13th or beginning of the 14th century; remains of inscription, s. xv?, on f. 18v: "Questo libro ***." Purchased from L. C. Witten in 1956 by Thomas E. Marston (bookplate).

secundo folio: che 'll'uno

Bibliography: Faye and Bond, p. 67, no. 28.

Marston MS 29 Northern Italy, 1402
Lucan, Pharsalia Pl. 8

1. f. 1r Corduba me genuit. rapuit nero. prelia dixi ... plus michi coma placet.

   Epitaph of Lucan; *Anthologia latina* 668; B. Munk Olsen, *L'Étude des auteurs classiques latins aux XIe et XIIe siècles* v. 2 (Paris, 1985) no. 45b.

2. ff. 1r–132r Bella per Emathios plus quam ciuilia campos./ Iusque datum sceleri canimus. populumque potentem/ ... Ad campos epidaure tuos. ubi solus apertis/ Obsedit muris calcantem menia magnum. [colophon:] .deo gratias. amen: finitur lucani liber ultimus .die. 22°. Septembris anno domini. 1402. scriptus per me Nicolaum de florinis. amen.

   Lucan, *Pharsalia*; G. Luck, ed. and tr., *Lukan: Der Bürgerkrieg* (Berlin, 1985) pp. 72–504. Accompanied by extensive interlinear and marginal annotations; see art. 3.

3. ff. 1r–132r [In upper margin:] Titulus. Marcij lucij anei lucani liber primus incipit. Materia huius fuit ciuile bellum. artifex fuit lucanus. intentio. remouere homines a bello. cui parti phylosophie, supponitur morali ... [In outer margin, at first line of poetry:] Nota quod quatruplex est bellum scilicet remotum videlicet quod fit [?] inter gentes ... ;

[in outer margin, line 8:] Hic autem. tria facit primo proponit. secundo inuocat. tertio narrat ... [outer margin, f. 132r, at Bk. 10, line 543:] Respexit. quo dicit quod cesar ita circumdatus in loco illo arto in mente sua imaginatus est uidere seuam pugnantem solum ... quod cesar fuit ymaginatus. nec prosequitur ulterius. deo gratias Amen.

Commentary on art. 2.

4. ff. 132v–134r *Summa super toto opere lucani.* Disparat elatos regni comunio. regna/ Indiuisa solent dispariare gradus./ Tres dictatores statuit sibi roma rebelles./ ... Mors semiplenum stare coegit opus.

Unidentified verse summary of art. 2.

5. ff. 134r–135v *Summa super primo libro lucani.* Proponit primus liber. inuehit. inuocat atque/ Causas exponit cursus proparantis ad urbem/ ... *Summa super decimo libro.* Ut primum. primo notat ut perexit in urbem/ Egipti cesar. et ut est cleopatra locuta./ Et dapibus sumptis, ... Praua [*corrected from*: Prima] duci cesos aduersa nefandaque passo. deo gratias. amen. [colophon:] Annos mille, quater centumque rotante duosque/ Cursu, uigenam lucem ducente secundam/ Septembris, scripsit nicolaus sic opus istud./ Spirituique patri filio sit gloria semper./ Qui tres sunt unus. regit unus cunctaque trinus. f. 136r-v ruled, but blank

Verse *argumenta* of each book of the *Pharsalia*; *Anthologia latina* 806.

Paper (watermarks: unidentified bull's head concealed by script), ff. i (early parchment flyleaf) + 136 + i (early parchment flyleaf), 310 x 209 (225 x 98) mm. 31 lines of verse. Double vertical bounding lines. Ruled in lead. Prickings in upper, lower and outer margins.

I–XVIII^{8}. Catchwords, accompanied by a single dot at beginning and end, in lower margin to the right of center, verso. Remains of quire and leaf signatures (e.g., b 1, b 2, etc.), lower right corner, recto.

Written by a single scribe in well spaced gothic bookhand, above top line. Marginalia in several contemporary hands.

Crudely executed penwork initials in red, f. 1r only; spaces for decorative initials at beginning of each book have sketches in brown ink (contemporary?) or are left unfilled. Headings in red. Some guide letters for decorator.

Binding: Italy, s. xv. Vellum stays in and outside the quires. Original sewing on three tawed skin, slit straps which are laced through tunnels in the edges of wooden boards to channels on the outside and pegged. Plain, wound endbands are sewn on tawed skin cores laced or laid in grooves on the outside of the boards.

Quarter bound with brown leather, probably a later addition, as perhaps are the clasp straps. Two leaf-shaped catches and inscription in ink on the lower board: "Lucanus [?]." Front pastedown and flyleaf from a lectionary (Italy, s. XI^2) containing: on the pastedown, the end of a prophecy reading and the beginning of the epistle reading for the Saturday of the Advent Rogation Days (Is. 45.1–8; Paul, 2 Thess. 2.1–6); on the flyleaf, the end of the gospel reading for the common of many virgins (Mt. 13.45–53), both readings for the dedication of a church (Apo. 21.2–5; Lk. 19.1–10), the beginning of the epistle reading for a mass for the dead (Paul, 1 Thess. 5.1–10). Back flyleaf and pastedown from a homiliary (Northern Italy, s. X^2) containing: on the flyleaf, a homily on the Eucharist and on Christ's acceptance of his passion, according to his Father's will ("//bueret remissionem cotidie in ara mactandum . . . ut sine interitu iudeorum credat gentium multitudo passionem recuso. Sin autem//"); note that the text, which is marked in certain sections for recitation, is complete vertically, but has some cropping in the outer margin); on the pastedown, a homily on submission to the will of God, probably a continuation of the same text as on the flyleaf ("// [?] mea pater uoluntas sed tua fiat. Nobis ergo exemplum posuit ut cum hoc imminet quod fieri uolumus . . . corporisque concretam [?] per [?]//").

Written in Northern Italy in 1402 by the scribe Nicolaus de Florinis (colophons in arts. 2, 5). Belonged to a member of the Capilupi family of Mantua whose inscription, s. xv, is written on f. 135v ("Lucanus Iste Iohannis Francisci de Codelupis Optimi ingenii Iuuenis"), perhaps to be identified with the father of Benedetto Capilupi (1461–1518; *Dizionario biografico degli italiani*, v. 18, pp. 528–31). Unidentified contemporary pen trials on front and back flyleaves. Notes, s. xv–xvi, on verso of rear flyleaf: "Lucanus mei Francisci de buzono [or *buxono*?]" and on f. 136v: "Nul bien." Belonged to Giuseppe (Joseph) Martini of Lugano (his signature on front flyleaf, verso). Purchased from H. P. Kraus in 1956 by Thomas E. Marston (bookplate).

secundo folio: Etheris

Bibliography: Faye and Bond, p. 67, no. 29.

Marston MS 30 — Italy, s. XV^1

Ps.-Cicero, Rhetorica ad Herennium, It. epitome, etc. — Pl. 11

1. ff. 1r–33r [Q]uella magna dignita dilectissimo fradello de la qual la humana natura e stata doctata dal summo Creatore como lo Intellecto

ragioneuele non se puo explicare . . . Qui finise la sopra dicta Rethorica ne la qual sta tuta l'arte de lo dire la quale se puo ligieramente aver praticandolla e prendere la doctrina de Alguno excellente parlatore praticandola como se regiede.

Unidentified Italian epitome of the Ps.-Ciceronian *Rhetorica ad Herennium*. Folios 1r–28v constitute the standard introduction, parts and divisions of rhetoric, followed by a discussion of figures and tropes (each indicated by a term written in the margin): f. 24r repetitio; f. 24v conversio, conquestio, exclamatio; f. 25r interrogatio, ratiocinatio; f. 25v menbrum [*sic*]; f. 26r articulus, subietio, tradutio [*sic*]; f. 26v diffinitio, transactio; f. 27r correctio, occupatio, disiuntio; f. 27v interpretatio, commutatio; f. 28r permissio, pressio, circuitio; f. 28v superlatio, allussio, distributio de sententie, liçentia; f. 29r diminutio; f. 29v distinctio, diuisio, frequentatio; f. 30r expolitio, similitudo; f. 30v confirmatio, significatio. Two sections follow on *memoria* (ff. 31r–32v) and *pronuntiatione* (ff. 32v–33r).

2. ff. 33r–44r [Heading:] Una altra arte de memoria. [text:] [L]'arte della artificiosa memoria reverendo padre e come lo homo possa pervegnire per la memoria artificial a recordarse de piu cosse . . . E dapuo de sotto de li pesci I quali significano questo essere la quinta mercadantia e simele a questi amen.

Unidentified and anonymous treatise on memory divided into the following sections: f. 33r-v (Introduction); f. 34r-v In qual muodo se impara questa arte; ff. 34v–35r de la forma de li luoghi; ff. 35r–36v delle Imagine; f. 36v de arecordarse le ambasade; ff. 36v–37r de lo reçitare de li argomenti; ff. 37r–38r de arecordarse uno sermone; f. 38r-v de arecordarse li testamenti o testo; f. 38v de li luogi da esser ordinadi; f. 38v del moltiplicar e mutare de logi; f. 38v de le Imagine; f. 38v de lo moltiplicare de la memoria; f. 39r delle Imagine; ff. 39r-v delli nomy cognosciuti; f. 39v de cognoscere le letere (with diagram); ff. 39v–40r de li nomy cognosciuti con anima e sença; f. 40r-v del cognoscimento delli mexi delli di e delle figure de l'abicho; ff. 40v–41r delli nomy da douere metere çioe da essere messi per sillaba houer per similetudine; ff. 41r–44r delle merchandarie (ff. 41r–42v include a numbered list of 100 things found in 100 respective places in 20 rooms; f.43r includes a list of 7 items and their weights).
The text appears to be similar to a Latin memory treatise appended to the *Rhetorica ad Herennium* in London, B. L. Harley MS 3949 (ff. 45v–47v) with the incipit "Reverende Pater et domine, qualiter homo ad recordandum de pluribus rebus per memoriam artificialem. . ." (reported in Kristeller, *Iter Italicum*, v. 3, p. 177b).

3. f. 44r-v [Heading:] Una altra arte de memoria molto brieve. [text:] [S]e tu vuol tegnire ne la memoria alguna cossa houere pluxore cosse sença alguna scriptura guarda e pensa qualche luogo a ti delecteuolle ... E per questo modo seguita che sempre honor e fama tuy hauera al mondo.

4. ff. 44v–45r Rx, Ad hauere perfecta e grande memoria segondo li antiqui philosophi ... e temperado in tute le cosse e haueray la gratia del nostro Creatore.

   Recipe for an ointment to improve memory.

5. f. 45r Ad iddem. Rx noxe muscate garrof[olum] galanga gardamonj grana paradisi ... Item questa aqua da gran virtu alli spiriti et ha molte altre virtude e proprietade et cet.

   Another recipe to improve memory.

6. ff. 45v–46r Chart depicting chambers of a memory palace described in art. 2 mapped onto the fingers of both hands.

   f. 45v (Labeled at bottom of page) Man Sinestra

   (thumb, top) la tua camera alogerai cose le quale te serano necessarie;

   (thumb, bottom) El tuo studio intro el qual tu allogeray tuti i tuo sacreti e tute altre simile cosse;

   (index, top) El tuo lecto qua tu i puo metere molti e de varij tuoi pensiery de vendere o conprare;

   (index, bottom) un altra camera la tua dona e qua alogeray femene de che condicion tu vuol e schave e serue stagando quelle a servirla;

   (middle, top) In la salla dono spariuiere e qua tu meteray tuti oxelli volatiui e caze e altre cosse de dilecto e di piaxere;

   (middle, bottom) la septima camera ymagine cognosude se tu te vuole aricordare de lo p ouere z meti lo p overe lo z tuo amigo che faza qualche cosa difforme zioe rompere la bancha ha diga qualche cosa da ridere;

   (ring, top) 8ª camera di nomi longi o curti se 'l nome e longho meti la ymagine longa e del nome curto meti la ymagine curta e sença cavo;

   (ring, bottom) 9ª camera di nomy corti;

   (little finger) 10 camera de le ciptade qua tui metera lo tuo amigo che 'l suo se confaza con quel de la cipta appicha per lo pe o inçenochioni con la scripta in mano la qual lui te la punta con el nome de la cipta;

f. 46r (labeled at bottom of page) Man dextra.

(little finger, top) la tua tauola qua tuy metera tute conse necesarie al viuere per la tua caxa over per la ciptade o per altre simel conse;

(little finger, bottom) i tuoy balcony qua tui metera tuti i pexi e marcadantie tuy I uol mandar fuora de la tua ciptade over de altro luogo;

(ring, top) la tua camera le tue veste e qua metera tute cose che aspeta ad tute merchantie e altre simel conse;

(ring, bottom) la quarta camera lo papaga e qua tuy metera gli exordij di sermoni e argumenti e tute simel conse;

(middle, top) a l'intrata de sala la camera lo papa vestido pontificalmente e qua metera tute cosse che aspetara a perlati [*sic*] e a chiesia e a sacre cosse;

(middle, bottom) la segonda camera lo spechio al qual tu meteray testamenti scripture e l'e tute cosse da morti;

(index, top) a meza scalla la camera e lo doctor al qual tu meterai tute consse che aspecta alla scientia e medesine;

(index, bottom) al capo dela schala la camera e lo inperadore vistido inperalmente e qua meteray tute anbasiade e cose de zudesi çioe le substantie appicada ad vno trauo e se l'e tropo longa diuidela in piu parte;

(thumb, upper) porta lo o armado con la spada in mano per defensione e qua metera tuti i fati d'arme e simel cose e ogni altra tua defensione;

(thumb, lower) pe dela scalla la stalla con lo gran cauallo B[ianco – cf. f.36r] e qua tu metera tuti gli animali da quatro piedi. ff. 46v–50v ruled, but blank

Paper (coarse, remains of deckle edges; watermarks, along upper edge: unidentified mountain and hunting horn), ff. i (paper) + 50 (contemporary foliation 1–48 in Arabic numerals, in ink; modern, in pencil on leaves where original numbers trimmed) + i (paper), 204 x 145 (122 x 75) mm. 26 long lines. Single vertical and horizontal bounding lines in lead. Text lines ruled in ink for ff. 41v–45r and 49r–50v only. Prickings for bounding lines.

I–V^{10}. Catchwords in lower margin to left of center, verso.

Written in gothic bookhand by a single scribe, above top line.

Spaces left for initials remain unfilled, except on f. 25r where there are three poorly executed initials in red; guide letters for decorator. Paragraph marks and initial strokes, in red, ff. 1r–2r, 30r-v, 35v, 37v, 38v, 40r, 41r–42v, 43v, 44v.

Binding: Italy [?], s. xix. Half bound in vellum with a gold-tooled spine and Spanish marbled sides. Ribbon bookmark.

Written in Italy in the first half of the 15th century; early provenance unknown. Belonged to the bookdealer Giuseppe (Joseph) Martini of Lugano ["Mart 82" in pencil on back pastedown]. "188" in pencil on spine; "WW2/3/32" in pencil on front pastedown. Purchased from H. P. Kraus (*List 189*, no. 152) in 1958 by Thomas E. Marston (bookplate).

secundo folio: La gratia

Bibliography: Faye and Bond, p. 67, no. 30.

Marston MS 31 Venice, 1470s
Bartolomeo da Ferrara (attr. author), Polistorio Pl. 35

1. front pastedown: Sempre si dize che'vno fa male A ccento/ ... Che fazia in piede tenere la si[?] parole.

   Sonnet by the Franciscan Alessandro de Ritiis, or by his compatriot from L'Aquila, Buccio di Ranallo, lamenting the loss of a loaned book; printed (with variations) by C. De Lollis, "Sonetti inediti di Buccio di Ranallo," *Giornale storico della letteratura italiana* 8 (1886) pp. 242–47 at 246.

2. ff. 1r–5v blank; ff. 6r–174r *Qui Comença La quarta partte ouer el quartto libro de polistoro chome octauiano intro in Roma triomphando fo chiamato imperadore de tutto el senato ed a tuto el populo di Roma e di molte incidentie de cita e de philosophi. Rubrica Capitulo j°.* Con ço sia cosa che oramai da qui inanzi comenza nouo rezimento in roma e nouo imperio in tuto el mondo ... Et si Io non l'o scripto cusi tosto come doueua. ancor vi prego che vuj me perdonatj perche tosto e bene non se conuenne. ffinitta est vltima pars polistorij. Deo gratias amen. ff. 174v–177v ruled, but blank

   Attributed to the Dominican Bartolomeo da Ferrara (1368–1444) by L. Muratori (*Rerum Italicarum Scriptores* 24 [Milan, 1738] pp. 697–848) who published only the last portion of the text (ff. 131r–174r in Marston MS 31) which covers the years 1287–1367 (1286–1366 in the Beinecke MS).

The attribution to Bartolomeo is, however, doubted by modern scholars (see entry by A. Alecci in the *Dizionario biografico degli Italiani* [Rome, 1964] v. 6, p. 719). Kaeppeli, SOPMA 395 (with attribution to Nicolaus de Ferraria, O. S. B.). The Beinecke text is divided into 218 chapters, most introduced by rubrics and chapter numbers in Arabic numerals. At least one later hand, s. xvii–xviii, has marked certain passages and has added dates in the margin.

Paper (watermarks: Briquet Arbalète 746), ff. i (contemporary paper; watermarks: Briquet Chapeau 3387) + 174 (remains of original foliation, mostly trimmed; foliated 1–177, also in a contemporary hand, beginning with i = 1 and omitting 120 and 123) + ii (same contemporary paper as used for front flyleaf), 400 x 285 (295 x 192) mm. 2 columns, 48 lines. Single vertical bounding lines, full length, ruled in lead and crayon; rulings for text in brown ink (Derolez 13.41). Prickings in upper and lower margins.

I^4 (ruled, but blank), $II-XVIII^{10}$. Catchwords in majuscules, center of lower margin, verso (Derolez 12.1). Remains of leaf signatures in lower right corner, recto.

Written in fere-humanistic script by a single scribe, above top line.

Fully illuminated title page, f. 6r. Floral border in inner and upper margin, black inkspray with blossoms, green, blue and purple with white highlights and gold balls. Bar border between text columns, gold and red, extends from buds (mauve, green and blue with white highlights) with stylized foliage, purple, blue and green and gold with white highlights; surmounted in upper margin by half-length figure of Virgin with Child. In outer margin, elaborate partial border of stylized foliage and flowers, green, blue and purple with white and yellow highlights and gold balls, framing central wreathed medallion with triton blowing a curved horn, on gold ground with penwork filigree. In center of lower border, arms of the Marcello family of Venice (azure, a bend wavy or) on deep red ground within wreathed medallion, both with yellow highlights. Arms symmetrically flanked by 2 putti plucking fruit from wreathed medallion and holding rods, green, blue, and purple with scrolls bearing the mottoes "sola virtus" and "dulcia poma" in red, and two triton-putti, one playing a flute, the other a stringed musical instrument. One historiated initial, 6-line, of stylized foliage in green, purple, and blue with white filigree on gold ground, with a half-length figure of a crowned and bearded man, perhaps the Emperor Augustus. The design of the upper and inner border and of the historiated initial is conservative in style and close to the work of Leonardo Bellini (see *Exhibition Catalogue*, pp. 233–34, no. 58). According to L. Armstrong (*Renaissance Miniature Painters and Classical Imagery. The*

Master of the Putti and his Venetian Workshop [London, 1981] p. 117, no. 27, fig. 58) the decorative device in the outer border and the bas-de-page decoration originated in the workshop of the "Master of the Putti" whose motto appears on the scrolls. The composition in Marston MS 31 is, however, somewhat more awkward and poorly executed than the work of the Master himself.

Binding: Italy, s. xv. Parchment stays are adhered inside the quires. Rear pastedown (now lifted): parchment leaf from a lectionary, Italy (North?), s. XI^2; a parchment leaf, perhaps from the same manuscript, is concealed under front paper pastedown. Each leaf, with a stub, is folded around the front and back flyleaves, sewn, and glued down under the pastedowns. Original sewing on five tawed skin, slit straps laid in channels on the outside of beech boards and nailed. Yellow edges. Plain wound, natural color endbands are sewn on leather cores.

Covered in brown calf with narrow corner tongues. There is a large, eight-petalled fitting in the central blind-tooled panel and four corner fittings have flower and *agnus dei* designs on them. The concentric outer frames are filled with rope interlace or small roses. The Marcello arms (see above and provenance) were stamped on each board on an inlaid leather shield which is wanting on the upper board. Spine: bands outlined with triple fillets, an *X* of three fillets in the panels. Four fastenings, the catches on the lower board, the upper one cut in for red fabric straps, attached with star-headed nails.

Written in Venice in the 1470s in the workshop of the "Master of the Putti"; notes of the workshop appear in the lower margin on f. 174r ("236 letere/ 178 karte") and on the front pastedown ("Questo sie libro quarto di polistorio di karte 174/ non schrite karte 3 a drietro e karte 5 auanti"). A contemporary comment on the text has been added above the workshop note on the front pastedown: "A karta 120 che he vna charta complida sie la istoria di l'inperadore f. barbaroxa con veniziane pro defenxione di la giexa romana." Produced for a member of the Marcello family of Venice whose arms appear on f. 6r and binding. T. E. Marston believed that the manuscript may have been a presentation copy from the Florentine Arte della Lana to Niccolò Marcello upon his election as Doge of Venice in 1473; there is no evidence except for the "agnus dei" design on the binding to support this hypothesis. Contemporary note on f. 1v: "sancta doratea sancta doratea." Unidentified shelf-marks include: on upper cover a white rectangular label with "d 143" in ink (same shelf-mark on f. 2r); remains of paper label with title on spine; "349" in ink on f. 1r; "Cas: N. 73" in ink on f. 2r; "Historia di Nicolò Polistoro" on f. 5r. Acquired from Payne by Sir Thomas Phillipps (no. 3008; tag on spine;

stamp on f. 2r); Phillipps sale (Sotheby's, 1 Dec. 1947, no. 108, pl. of f. 6r). Purchased from H. P. Kraus in 1956 by Thomas E. Marston (bookplate).

secundo folio: E tra

Bibliography: Faye and Bond, pp. 67–68, no. 31.

Marston MS 32 France, s. XV^2

Paulus Venetus, Summulae naturalium

ff. 1r–171r [Title:] Summule naturalium magistri Pauli veneti ordinis heremitarum sancti Augustini physicorum liber incipit. [text:] Plurimorum astrictus precibus quorum pridem. Mee introductionis eloquium in facultate logice mentem demulserat. Vt suo in naturalibus modo propositionis physicisque doctrinis formare compendium ... hic per gratiam et in futuro per gloriam quam mihi in premium [?] tantorum laborum donare dignetur per infinita seculorum secula. Amen. Laus deo. [colophon:] Explicit ultima pars summule naturalium Acta per Reuerendum magistrum Paulum de Venetiis ordinis heremitarum Sancti Augustini. Frater petrus de sancto Amore eiusdem ordinis Scripsit Anno Domini MCCCLXXIII [*sic*]. f. 171v blank

Numerous manuscripts and early printed editions of this text composed in 1408 by Paulus Nicolettus Venetus O.E.S.A. (1369/72–1429); see C. H. Lohr, "Medieval Latin Aristotle Commentaries, Authors: Narcissus-Richardus," *Traditio* 28 (1972) pp. 317–18, no. 5 (Marston MS 32 not listed). Two additional colophons with the date 1373 (for 1473?) also occur at the conclusion of Parts 3 and 5, ff. 72r, 129v. Some contemporary marginal annotations. Folio 171, written in a different hand and on different paper, may have been copied later as a replacement leaf.

Paper (watermarks, obscured by text: similar to Harlfinger Chapeau 17 and unidentified ladder), ff. ii (paper) + 171 (contemporary foliation, Arabic numerals, 1–60 only) + ii (paper), 331 x 225 (229 x 145) mm. 2 columns, 50 lines. Single vertical bounding lines and sometimes a single upper horizontal bounding line. Ruled in light brown ink and lead. No visible remains of prickings.

$I\text{-}VI^{10}$, $VII\text{-}IX^{12}$, X^8, $XI\text{-}XVI^{10}$, XVII^8 (–8). Catchwords, with pen flourishes on all sides, center or right of center in lower margin, verso.

Written by several scribes in humanistic cursive script with gothic features, below top line; initial words of each section in gothic bookhand.

Decorated title page, f. 1r, with border, in black and red ink composed of various decorative devices: in the upper margin a bar border with a central semicircle flanked by stylized scrolls in black and red. In the outer margin, a roundel, black with red and black frame, filled with a flower of 6 petals in red; the roundel flanked by stylized scrolls. In center of lower margin a medallion framed in narrow black and red bands containing a flaming heart pierced by an arrow and an open book, also flanked by stylized scrolls. Numerous decorated initials, 30- to 4-line, black and red with interior designs of lozenges, small flowers, and wavy lines of paper ground. Plain initials and paragraph marks in red. Guide letters for rubricator throughout.

Worm-eaten; some minor loss of text.

Binding: England, s. xix. Blind-tooled brown goatskin with the same gold-tooled title on the spine and both covers: "Summule Naturalium/ Paulus de Venetiis/ M. S. 1373." Bound by Rivière (London) before 1881. Red edges.

Written probably in France in the second half of the 15th century to judge from the script, decoration, and watermarks. The colophons (see art. 1), however, give the date 1373 (perhaps an error for 1473?). The scribe remains unidentified except for this manuscript (*Colophons*, v. 5, p. 133, no. 15893). Sold by Maggs Brothers (London, Cat. 542, June 1930, no. 93, with plate of f. 1r). Belonged to E. Crawshaw (bookplate). Modern note (*bis*), in pencil, on front flyleaves: "28" within circle. Purchased from C. A. Stonehill (inv. no. 3036) in 1953 by Thomas E. Marston (bookplate).

secundo folio: Licet sit

Bibliography: Faye and Bond, p. 68, no. 32.

Marston MS 34 — Germany, s. XII$^{4/4}$, XII/XIII
Petrus Riga, Aurora

ff. 1r–136v [Prose preface:] *Incipit uetus testamentum*. Frequens sodalium meorum peticio cum quibus conuersando florem infancie exegi ... et ueritatis fulgor patenter illuxit. *Explicit prologus. Incipit* [remainder of rubric illegible; text begins:] Primo facta die. duo celum terra leguntur/ Fit firmamenti spera sequente die/ ... apud te pascha paretur//

P. E. Beichner, ed., *Aurora Petri Rigae Biblia Versificata*, Publications in Mediaeval Studies 19 in 2 vols. (Notre Dame, Ind., 1965); we provide page references to this edition in square brackets below. Stegmüller 6823–25.

The text, composed of three different parts (see also physical description and provenance below), appears in the following order. Part I: Genesis, with Petrus Riga's prose preface, f. 1r [pp. 7–8, 21–90]; Exodus, f. 23r [pp. 91–144]; Leviticus, f. 43r [with prologue and with the verses *De avibus*, Beichner, p. 171, on a half-sheet of parchment added between ff. 50–52; the scribe has noted that the verses should be inserted on f. 52v after *De piscibus*; pp. 145–78]; Numbers, f. 55r [pp. 179–203]; Deuteronomy, f. 64r [with prologue; pp. 207–17]; Joshua, f. 68v, with text ending imperfectly on f. 72r, line 243 [pp. 219–29]. f. 72v blank except for erased pen trials. Part II: Job, f. 73r [with prologue consisting of lines 9–10 and 17–18 only; heading erased], text ends complete on f. 112v, but is much rubbed and followed by numerous pen trials [pp. 669–702]. Part III: Evangelium, ff. 113r–136v beginning and ending imperfectly [lines 567–2268: pp. 447–512].

Composed of three parts, with I and III in the same format and possibly from the same manuscript, ff. i (modern parchment) + 136 + i (modern parchment).

Parts I and III: parchment, ff. 1–72 and 113–136, 162 x 115 (137 x 70) mm. 35 lines of verse. Double upper and sometimes lower horizontal bounding lines. Double or triple inner and single outer vertical bounding lines. Ruled in lead. Few remains of prickings suggest the sections were greatly trimmed. Collation for Part I: I–VI^8, VII^8 (with half-leaf, f. 51, added in), VIII^8, IX^8 (–1?). Quires signed with Roman numerals I–VIII (IX unsigned); Part III: X^8 (unsigned), XI–XII^8 (signed with Roman numerals XI and XII on first recto of each gathering). Copied by multiple scribes in small gothic bookhand, with first letter of each verse usually aligned on the second vertical bounding line. Red initials, plain or with modest designs throughout. Headings in red often added to right of text. First letter of each verse stroked in red or ochre, often by drawing a single line the length of the written space.

Part II: parchment (thick and fuzzy), ff. 73–112, 167 x 115 (122 x 84) mm. 28 lines of verse. Triple vertical bounding lines; ruled very faintly in hard point or lead. Prickings prominent in upper, lower and outer margins. I–V^8. The second gathering signed in red with the Roman numeral II. Written by multiple scribes in a larger module and a neater gothic script than that in Parts I and III; each verse is justified by the placement of the final letter along outer vertical ruling. Script has often been retraced. Plain initials and headings in red throughout.

Binding: Belgium, s. xix. Tan calf over wooden boards, blind-tooled with the Arenberg arms on the sides. Title on spine: "Sacrae Scripturae excerptae/ Circa 1225–50." Remains of old fore-edge tabs.

All three parts were written in Germany, Part II in the fourth quarter of the 12th century and Parts I and III at the end of the 12th or beginning of the 13th century. Parts I and III, given the similar format and the sequence of quire signatures, perhaps comprised at one time a single unit. It is not clear when the three parts were joined together, but probably before the early ex libris and book curse (s. xiii?) of the abbey of St. Eucharius and St. Matthias the Apostle in Trier were added in lower margin, f. 1r, and along inner margin, f. 136v: "Codex sancti Evcharii sanctique. Mathie apostoli. Quem si quis abstulerit anathema sit. Amen." For more information and bibliography on the library of this abbey see P. Becker, "Notizen zur Bibliotheksgeschichte der Abtei St. Eucharius-St. Matthias," *Armaria Trevirensia. Beiträge zur Trierer Bibliotheksgeschichte*. 2., stark erweiterte Auflage, ed. G. Franz (Wiesbaden, 1985) pp. 44–63. Early press-mark [?] in upper right corner on f. 1r: "X.[?]13." Inscription of one Gerardus on ff. 110v and 112v. From the library of the Dukes of Arenberg (binding); for a discussion of this collection see C. Lemaire, "La bibliothèque des ducs d'Arenberg, une première approche," *Liber amicorum Herman Liebaers 1984* (Brussels, 1984) pp. 81–106 (Marston MS 34 cited on p. 104). Unidentified labels on spine. "20" on square cream-colored label, "No 16/2 me Sénè [?]" in red ink on white rectangular label with serrated edge and blue border. "No 26" and "B,7" on front pastedown. Presented by Otto Rauschberg in 1956 (inscription on front pastedown) to Thomas E. Marston (bookplate).

secundo folio: Firmamenta

Bibliography: Faye and Bond, p. 68, no. 34.

Marston MS 35 — Ferrara, ca. 1460–75
Biondo Flavio, Italia Illustrata — Pl. 34

ff. 1r–149r [Dedication:] *Sanctissimo .Domino. Nostro. Domino Nicolao. Q. Summo Pontifici Blondus Flavius Forliviensis*. Cum multi historiam beatissime pater uariis extollant celebrentque sententiis . . . [text, f. 2r:] *Blondi Flavii Forliviensis Italie Illustrate liber incipit felicissime*. Italiam describere exorsi prouinciarum orbis primariam a laudibus suis incipere debuimus . . . Superius Fortorii amnis fonti Monsfalco castellum est proximum. f. 149v blank

Biondo Flavio, *Italia Illustrata* with the dedicatory preface to Pope Nicholas V (d. 1455); edited by Biondo's son Gaspare for the *editio princeps* (Rome, Johannes Philippus de Lignamine, 1474; GKW, v. 4, no. 4421). Marston MS 35 is a copy of the early B-version of the text; it contains the dedication, a number of additions later expunged, and some additions contained in the revised E-version of the text. See J. A. White, "Towards a Critical Edition of Biondo Flavio's 'Italia Illustrata': A Survey and an Evaluation of the MSS," *Umanesimo a Roma nel Quattrocento*, ed. P. Brezzi and M. De Panizza Lorch (Città di Castello, 1984) pp. 267–93 (Marston MS 35: pp. 283–84).

Parchment, ff. ii (paper) + 149 + ii (paper), 310 x 225 (180 x 130) mm. Single vertical bounding lines, full length. Additional rulings in upper margin for running titles and in outer margin for rubrics. Ruled in pale brown ink. Prickings in upper and lower margins.

I–XIV^{10}, XV^{10} (–10). Horizontal catchwords in lower margin between inner bounding lines and gutter, verso (Derolez 12.4). Vertical catchwords on inner vertical bounding line (f. 110v and thereafter).

Written in fine humanistic bookhand, below top line, by a single scribe who also wrote the running titles (epigraphic majuscules) and marginalia, in red.

Elaborately illuminated title page with historiated initial, 10–line, mauve with silver filigree against gold ground, edged in black, with a portrait of the author, seated and holding a book, against a hilly landscape and blue sky. Partial border of white vine-stem ornament against a predominantly gold ground with blue, green, and red patches with white and pale yellow dots in inner and upper margins, terminating in dense penwork scrolls with gold dots. In outer and lower margin, border of stylized flowers and foliage in red, purple, green, and blue, surrounded by dense penwork scrolls punctuated by gold dots (cf. Oxford, Bod. Lib. MS Canon. Pal. Lat. 164; Pächt and Alexander, v. 2, no. 431, pl. XLII). The style of the penwork decoration is similar to that of Evangelista da Reggio, active in Ferrara from 1477–94 (see *Abbey Manuscripts*, pp. 137–39, pls. LXI, b; LXII; LXIII). In center of lower margin, wreathed medallion with unidentified arms (or a two-headed eagle displayed, crowned [?], armed and membered gules; overall an inescutcheon gules, a fess argent), supported by two purple winged putti outlined in blue and wearing red necklaces. 14 illuminated initials, 9– to 6–line, gold, on blue, green, and red ground with white vine-stem ornament, sometimes extending into the margins. Headings, running titles, and marginalia in red.

Binding: England, s. xviii. Red goatskin gold-tooled, with the crest of Charles Chauncy on the sides (see provenance below). Gilt edges. Rebacked. The fine quality of the endleaves and leather, and the tool used on the edges of the boards and the turn-ins are similar to those in Marston MS 102 and Beinecke MS 497, both probably bound by Richard Wier, active in London and France in the 1770s (d. 1792).

Written in Ferrara ca. 1460–75 by the "Scribe of the Maffei Vergil" (Chicago, Newberry Library, 95.5); according to A. C. de la Mare the scribe was also responsible for Vienna, Österreichische Nationalbibliothek Cod. 35, signed Ferrara 1468; Cambridge, Mass., Harvard University, Houghton Library Typ 425, signed Ferrara 1463; Vatican City, Biblioteca Apostolica Vaticana, Ross. 439, signed Ferrara 1462; Brussels, Bibl. Roy. IV. 185, dated 1471. Probably produced at the court of the d'Este. Belonged to Dr. Charles Chauncy (1709–77; bookplate; crest on binding) who bequeathed his collection to his brother Nathaniel (d. 1790); sale (Leigh and Sotheby, 15 April 1790, no. 3150). Acquired by Michael Wodhull, Esq., of Thenford, Northamptonshire (1740–1816); his inscriptions on f. ii recto and rear flyleaf with dates "May 1st 1790" and "Aug. 14th 1793." After Wodhull's death the manuscript remained in his family until it was sold by J. E. Severne (Sotheby's, 12 Jan. 1886, no. 420, to Quaritch). Bought by Thomas Brooke, F. S. A., of Armitage Bridge, Huddersfield (1830–1908; bookplate); sale of Sir John Arthur Brooke of Fenay Hall, Huddersfield (Sotheby's, 25 May 1921, no. 124). Inside front cover: white square label, with grey decorative circle, within which is written "A./ II. /31." in ink. Purchased from L. C. Witten in 1956 by Thomas E. Marston (bookplate).

secundo folio: hominibus

Bibliography: Faye and Bond, p. 68, no. 35.
Exhibition Catalogue, pp. 230–31, no. 55.

Marston MS 36 — Southern France, s. $XIV^{1/4}$

Gottofredo da Trani, Summa super titulis Decretalium, etc.

1. ff. 1r–148v *Incipit summa super titulis decretalium compilata a magistro gaufrido de trano domini pape subdyacono, et capellano. Rubrica.* [prologue:] Glosarum diuersitas intelligenciam textus non numquam obtenebrat. et dum pereas . . . [text:] *De summa trinitate et fide catholica.* Post prohemium breuiter edocemur, quare hec noua compilatio facta sit . . . malui repeti quam deesse. [colophon:] Explicit liber quintus qui scripsit sit benedictus.

   Edition: Goffredus Tranensis, *Summa super titulis decretalium* (Lugduni, 1519; repr. Aalen, 1968). One leaf with text missing between ff. 60 and 61. Text is accompanied by some contemporary notes and pointing hands in margins. Finding aids consisting of chapter titles in lower right corner, recto (ff. 2–46).

2. f. 148v Two recipes for treatment of sore eyes, in Lat.

3. f. 149r List of Roman emperors from Julius Caesar to Constantine.

4. f. 149v Beginning of a word list, for the letter *A* only.

5. f. 150r (back flyleaf) blank; f. 150v Miscellaneous notes, in Lat.

Parchment, ff. ii (parchment, early flyleaves?) + 149 + ii (parchment, early flyleaves?), 410 x 225 (295 x 160) mm. 2 columns, 64 lines. Single vertical bounding lines, full length. Ruled in lead. Prickings in upper and lower margins.

I-VI^{10}, VII^{10} (-1), VIII-XV^{10}. Catchwords in lower margin under inner column, verso. First leaves of each quire signed with letters of alphabet, in red, lower right corner, recto (*a* through *v* on ff. 1–74).

Written in a rounded gothic bookhand, below top line; marginal annotations and finding aids by a contemporary hand in less formal script.

5 fine illuminated initials, 30- to 7-line, in blue or pink with white filigree on blue and red grounds framed in blue or red accentuated at the corners by gold dots. Infilled with intertwining or angular vines, some with biting head terminals, mauve or blue with white highlights and gold dots. Ascenders and descenders, red, mauve and blue terminating in spiralling serifs with biting animal heads or grotesques against cusped grounds (cf. R. Branner, *Manuscript Painting during the Reign of St. Louis* [Berkeley, 1977] fig. 282). Two initials with vines issuing from upper and lower corners, blue with white highlights ending in grotesques. 3- and 2-line calligraphic initials, red and blue with blue and red penwork. Plain initials alternating in red and blue. Headings in red; running titles (chapter numbers) alternating red and blue. Instructions to rubricator in lower margins.

Binding: France, s. xix. Early sewing on five supports with 19th-century boards covered in parchment. Title on spine: "Gofredo de Trano/ Manuscrit."

Written in Southern France in the first quarter of the 14th century; notes on final flyleaves and pastedown (s. xiv–xv), severely affected by reagents and rubbing, include: unidentified monogram; two 2-line Latin poems written in French bâtarde (s. XV^2); a note dated "1384"; the name "hugo carinfias [or tarinfias?]." Bookstamp and inscription ("Ex Biblioth. D. presidis de Montesquieu Catal. inscrip.") of the Bibliotheca Bredensis (Charles Louis de Secondant, Baron de, Marquis de Montesquieu; 1689–1755) f. 1r, lower margin. Booklabel of comte Chandon de Briailles (b. 1852; *Dictionnaire de Biographie de France*, v. 8, cols. 370–71) on first front flyleaf. "703 *bis*" in red on f. i recto; "70657659 [or 4?]" on back cover; "PP [?]/ XI–1954" in pencil on back pastedown. Purchased from Georges Heilbrun of Paris in 1955 by L. C. Witten (inv. no. 663), who sold it the same year to Thomas E. Marston (bookplate).

secundo folio: Nam

Bibliography: Faye and Bond, p. 68, no. 36.

Marston MS 37 Bologna [?], s. XIV²
Valerius Maximus, with commentary of Dionysius de Burgo Sancti Sepulchri, etc. Pl. 7

1. ff. 1r–3v Maximi ualerij uerborum suauitas me inducit et quorundam dilectorum fratrum caritas me compellit. ut operi prefati autoris iungam ego frater Giunta de sancto gemiano [?] ordinis herimitarum sancti augustini Inuentarium siue tabulam ... Abstinencia li°. iiij°. c. iij°. per totum/ Absolucio ... Vxor li. vi. c. vii. per totum.

   Alphabetical index to Valerius Maximus by Junta de Sancto Geminiano; D. Schullian, CTC 5 (1984) p. 301 (lists seven manuscripts, including Marston MS 37, which contain the index; gives bibliography and suggestions regarding the possible identity of the indexer).

2. ff. 3v–4r *Valerii Maximi factorum et dictorum memorabilium romanorum liber. primus Incipit Tabula.* De religione obseruata. 2./ De neglecta religione. 4./ ... De hijs qui infimo loco nati mendacio se clarissimis familijs inserere conati sunt. 138. f. 4v blank

   Table of contents for all nine books; folio references in Arabic numerals added by a later hand which has also foliated the main text of the manuscript and added book numbers in center of upper margin.

3. f. 5r Reuerendo in christo patri et suo domino spirituali domino Iohanni de columpna diuina prouidencia ... et consumacionis finem accepi possitis glorie sociari.

   Dedication to Giovanni Colonna of the commentary of Dionysius de Burgo Sancti Sepulchri; ed. D. Schullian, *op. cit.*, pp. 325–26.

4. ff. 5r–141r Urbis rome et cetera. Valerius huic operi suo. primo prohemium ponit in quo suum propositum ostendens ... Et ipse deus iusto seruicio colitur. In cuius cultu sincero eterna uita promictitur. In secula seculorum. Amen.

   Commentary on Valerius Maximus by Dionysius de Burgo Sancti

Sepulchri; D. Schullian, *op. cit.*, pp. 326–29 (Marston MS 37 listed on p. 327); beginning on f. 5v the commentary surrounds the text of Valerius Maximus in all four margins.

5. ff. 5v–141r *Valerij maximj factorum et dictorum memorabilium. liber primus Incipit de religione.* Urbis rome exterrarumque gencium facta simul ac dicta memoratu digna . . . credula suffragacione fultum caput imperio dementer imminens iusto inpendere supplicio coegit.

Valerius Maximus, *Factorum et dictorum memorabilium libri novem*; C. Kempf, ed., Teubner, 2nd ed. 1888, reprinted 1966, pp. 1–472. Irregularities in Marston MS 37 include: vi.2.2–3 misplaced from f. 88r to 88v; ix.5.2–3 omitted between ff. 132–133; eleven lines, ix.9.2, erased on f. 135r; text on ff. 140v–141r (after ix.15.2: "Hannibal autem canensis pugne . . . publice terrenius adfixus est") marked "uacat" in margin is unidentified.

6. f. 141v Decimus huius operis liber. qui est ultimus uel neglegencia. uel maliuolentia librariorum deperiit. Abbreviator ue titulos eius habebat integre fortasis . . . [text begins:] Varro simplicia in ytalia fuisse nomina. ait existimacionisque sue argumentum refert . . . Dictum postumum communium. auricum et postumum ebu// f. 142r-v blank

Julius Paris, *Epitome* of Valerius Maximus, ending imperfectly; Kempf, *op. cit.*, pp. 587–88.

Parchment, ff. i (contemporary parchment) + 141 (early foliation 1–141, in ink, begins on current f. 5, skips 119, and includes back flyleaf and pastedown; modern foliation, in pencil) + i (contemporary parchment). Format for ff. 1–4 varies; remainder of codex: 354 x 243 (292 x 200) mm. Text in 2 columns of 15–43 lines, surrounded by up to 78 lines of commentary. Single vertical bounding lines, full length. Ruled in crayon. Remains of prickings in upper and lower margins.

I^6 (1, 2 = front pastedown and flyleaf), II^6, $III–IV^8$, V^6, $VI–X^8$, XI^6, XII^8, XIII^6, $XIV–XVIII^8$, $XIX–XX^4$, XXI^4 (-2; 3, 4 = back flyleaf and pastedown). Catchwords with dots on either side, in left lower margin, verso. Remains of quire and leaf signatures (e.g., f i, f ii, f iii, etc.) in black or red, in lower right corner, recto. Unidentified signatures, Roman numerals, in lower left corner, verso.

Large historiated initial, f. 5r, 17-line, mauve with white filigree and stylized foliage in red and green against gold ground, thickly edged in black. Initial filled with a half-length portrait in profile of a man in black robes and a black cap, probably Dionysius de Burgo Sancti Sepulchri. Foliage serifs, blue, red, mauve, and green with gold balls thickly edged in black extending into the upper and inner margins to form a partial border, which extends as stylized foliage scrolls, blue and purple into the lower margin. Gold balls partially or completely flaked. Numerous illuminated initials, 9- to 4-line, mauve with white highlights, filled with stylized foliage, green, red and blue on blue grounds with white filigree. Initials for the text against gold grounds, thickly edged in black; initials for commentary against blue ground with white filigree. Some initials with foliage serifs, pink, red and/or blue and gold balls thickly edged in black extending into margins. Pen and ink initials, 3-line, alternate blue and red with red and purple penwork. Headings in red. Plain initials touched with yellow.

Binding: Spain, s. xv. Own parchment endleaves, one cut out in back. Original sewing on five tawed skin slit straps laid in channels on the outside of wooden boards and fastened. Yellow edges. The natural color, plain wound endbands are sewn through the spine lining on tawed skin cores which are laid in grooves on the outside of the boards. The spine is lined with vellum extending inside the boards between supports.

Covered in red-brown goatskin blind-tooled with an *X* in an outer frame and crosses made of decorated circles in the divisions. Four fastenings, truncated diamonds at head and tail and shields at the fore edge, on the lower board. The clasp straps are attached with star-headed nails. Traces of five small round bosses on each board. Traces of incised inscription near the head of the lower board. Spine leather missing. Described in Walters Art Gallery, *Bookbinding*, p. 57, no. 133.

Written in Central Italy, probably Bologna to judge from the style of decoration, in the second half of the 14th century; bound in Spain at the beginning of the 15th century; early provenance otherwise unknown. Belonged to the Spanish writer D. Martin Panzano y Abos (d. 1775; bookplate; *Enciclopedia Universal Ilustrada*, v. 41, p. 906) and to François Robert Secousse (bookplate with "No 184/31" added in ink). Unidentified bookplate on front pastedown. Purchased from C. A. Stonehill in 1955 by Thomas E. Marston (bookplate).

secundo folio: [index, f. 3r:] Pietas
[text of commentary, f. 6r:] fuit octauianus

Bibliography: Faye and Bond, p. 68, no. 37.

Marston MS 38 Florence, ca. 1450-60
Diogenes Laertius, Lat. tr. Ambrogio Traversari Pl. 19

1. front flyleaf, recto Alphabetical index of names: Anacarsis scytha, Anaximander milesius ... Zeno cittieus, Zeno eleates. Vite omnes suprascripte numero Lxxxii insupra [?]. A second hand has added folio references to each entry. Verso of flyleaf is blank.

2. ff. 1r–179r [Letter, no heading:] *Voluenti mihi quedam greca uolumina uenit ad manus la*ertii diogenis de philosophis prolixum opus. Id etsi auctori plus in legendo studii quam inscribendo.... [text, f. 2r:] *Laertii Diogenis uitae atque sententie eorum qui in philosophia claruerunt liber primus incipit. Philosophiam a barbaris initia* sumpsisse plerique autumant. Namque apud persas clauisse magos ... non sunt defuncti celeriorem obitum. *Laertii Diogenis uite atque sententie eorum qui in philosophia claruerunt. Liber decimus et ultimus explicit.* f. 179v ruled, but blank

   Diogenes Laertius, *Vitae et sententiae philosophorum*, translated into Latin by Ambrogio Traversari and preceded by his dedicatory letter to Cosimo de' Medici. Notes, corrections, and variant readings added by the scribe and at least one contemporary hand.

Parchment, ff. ii (contemporary parchment bifolium; i = front pastedown) + 180 (contemporary foliation, Roman numerals 1–179, with 120 *bis*) + ii (contemporary parchment bifolium; i excised, ii = back pastedown), 335 x 230 (205 x 125) mm. 32 long lines. Double vertical and horizontal bounding lines, full length and full width (Derolez 13.36). Ruled in hard point on hair side. Prickings in upper, lower, and outer margins (Derolez 18.1).

I–XVI^{10}, XVII–XVIII^{8}, XIX^{4}. Horizontal catchwords in lower inner margin near gutter, verso (Derolez 12.4).

Main text written in round humanistic bookhand by a single scribe; art. 1 added in humanistic cursive by a contemporary hand.

Decorated by the unidentified "Master of the Riccardiana Lactantius" (Florence, Biblioteca Riccardiana MS 544), who may have been the master for the Florentine illuminator Mariano del Buono and whose work is characterized by well drawn but badly colored animals. For other manuscripts by the same artist see Garzelli, *Miniatura fiorentina*, pp. 200–01. The decoration consists of a 3/4 border, f. 1r, of intricate white vine-stem ornament curling around thin gold bars (doubled in inner and lower margins) on a blue, green and pale pink ground dotted with white, yellow and blue, and gold balls. Incorporated into the lower border are a medal-tion (blank) framed by a laurel wreath and two narrow gold bands, a stag, and a putto with multi-colored wings in blue, green and dark red. In the inner margin are two birds in brown, orange and white. Ten illuminated initials, 9- to 4-line, gold on blue, green and pale pink background with white vine-stem ornament. Numerous smaller initials, 3- to 2-line, gold on blue and pink or green and pink grounds with white and gold filigree. Headings in black majuscules. Running headlines, in red, on ff. 1–4 only.

Some worming at beginning of text.

Binding: Italy, s. xv. A hybrid Italo-Greek binding. Sewn or resewn (the sewing is too tight to determine with certainty) on five tawed skin, slit straps. Wooden boards which are not flush at head and tail are grooved on the edges. Beaded Western endbands added.

Covered in dark brown calf, blind-tooled with a triple cross made up of gilt annular dots and rope interlace in a central panel within concentric frames alternately made up of a beaded zigzag ribbon and feathered rinceau. Similar tools are used on Marston MSS 39 and 68. Spine: bands outlined and panels diapered with triple fillets. Traces of four braid-and-pin fastenings, the pins in the edges of the lower board instead of the upper board as is usual in Greek bindings. "Diogenes ***" is added on the fore edge; "diogenes laergi" is written in bâtarde (see also provenance) on a label under horn at the head of the upper board, possibly added in northern Europe. See Walters Art Gallery, *Bookbinding*, pp. 87–88, no. 197; *The Medieval Book*, pp. 66–67, no. 60, with plate of upper board.

Written in Florence ca. 1450–60; a contemporary note on the front pastedown indicates that Brother Bogart bought the manuscript in 1465 from Ludovicus de Bancis (perhaps to be identified with Ludovico Banchi, Cosenza, v. 1, p. 380): "Ludouico de bancis. Emi ego frater Bogart hunc librum a Ludouico de Bancis pro x duc. large 1465 de mense Ianuarij." The style of bâtarde script on the horn label on the upper cover suggests either that the manuscript travelled north to Belgium after it was bound, or that it was acquired by a Belgian owner (Brother Bogart?) who added the label. On back pastedown is contemporary inscription "Angelot." Unidentified inscriptions, s. xix, on front pastedown: "Bibl. Brunnd [?] Sept. 1849" and "AGl[***]ly." Entry from sale catalogue, in Italian, pasted inside front cover. "98" in ink on entry and in pencil on front pastedown; "468" in pencil on rear pastedown. Purchased from Alexander Simkhovitch in 1955 by Thomas E. Marston (bookplate).

secundo folio: Tibi itaque Cosme

Bibliography: Faye and Bond, p. 68, no. 38.

Marston MS 39 Florence, 1453
Cicero, De oratore, Pro Milone, Pro Ligario Pl. 20

1. ff. 1r–121v *M. T. Ciceronis de. oratore ad .Q. fratrem liber primus foeliciter incipit.* Cogitanti mihi sepenumero et memoria vetera repetenti perbeati fuisse Quinte frater illi uideri solent qui in optima re publica ... et aliquando ab hac contentione disputationis animos nostros curamque laxemus: M. T. Ciceronis de oratore liber tertius et ultimus foeliciter explicit. Τελος. Φ [surrounded by dots and flourishes here and at conclusion of arts. 2 and 3]. Phylippus Corbizus manu propria scripsit MCCCC° LIII. ff. 122r–124v ruled, but blank

   Cicero, *De oratore I–III*; K. F. Kumaniecki, ed., Teubner fasc. 3 (1969) pp. 1–362. The scribe has entered into the margins both corrections to the text and variant readings that are usually marked by the abbreviations *ul* or *al*; annotations are decorated with dots and flourishes in the same manner as the catchwords.

2. ff. 125r–144v *M. T. Ciceronis oratio ad iudices pro .T. Amnio Milone foeliciter incipit.* Et si vereor iudices ne turpe sit pro fortissimo uiro dicere incipientem timere minimeque deceat ... in iudicibus legendis optimum et sapientissimum quemque legit. Φ.

   Cicero, *Pro T. Annio Milone*; A. Klotz, ed., Teubner v. 8 (1918) pp. 13–66. In art. 2 and to a lesser extent in art. 3 key rhetorical words have been entered in the margins (e. g., on f. 125r: Captat beniuolentiam a persona Milonis, Expolitio, Ratio propositionis, Distributio, Correctio). No rhetorical words appear on ff. 133v–144v.

3. ff. 145r–151v [In upper margin:] YHS. [heading:] *M. T. Ciceronis oratio ad Cesarem pro .Q. Ligario foeliciter incipit.* Nouum crimen .c. cesar et ante hunc diem inauditum propinquus meus. [to be inserted from margin: ad te .Q.] tubero detulit .Q. ligarium in africam fuisse ... Tantum te ipsum admonebo si illi absenti salutem dederis presentibus his omnibus te daturum. Τελός. Explicit. Φ. f. 152r-v ruled, but blank

   Cicero, *Pro Q. Ligario*; A. Klotz, ed., Teubner v. 8 (1918) pp. 84–100.

Paper (coarse; remains of deckle edges; watermarks: Briquet Échelle 5904, Briquet Fleur 6306, and similar to Briquet Ciseaux 3668), ff. i (paper, later addition) + 152 + i (paper, later addition), 220 x 147 (140 x 95) mm. 25 long lines. Double vertical bounding lines, full length (Derolez 13.31); ruled in hard point.

I–XII^{10}, XIII^{4}, XIV–XV^{10}, XVI^{10} (-2). Catchwords with symmetrically arranged dots and flourishes perpendicular to text between inner bounding lines, verso (Derolez 12.5). Leaf signatures (e.g., 1, 2, 3, etc.) in lower right corner, recto.

Written in a neat upright humanistic cursive by a single scribe.

Partial border, f. 1r, white vine-stem ornament on blue, green and pink ground with white and pale yellow dots. At the terminals, gold balls with hair-line extensions. Illuminated initial, 4-line, gold on blue, green and red ground as above joined to the border. In lower margin, wreathed medallion for arms (drawn with a compass), blank. Five smaller initials, 4- and 3-line, gold on blue, green and red rectangular grounds with white or pale yellow filigree and white dots. Headings and colophons in red.

Binding: Italy, s. xv. Stays cut from parchment manuscripts (text washed) inside the quires and also outside the first two. Original sewing on three tawed skin, slit straps attached to wooden boards. Beaded, chevron, natural, pink, and green endbands are sewn on tawed skin cores.

Covered in dark brown calf with narrow corner tongues and blind-tooled with two circles and corners of rope interlace in a central panel with concentric frames, one with beaded zigzag ribbon tools similar to those on Marston MSS 38 and 68, and gilt annular dots. Spine: double fillets at head and tail and outlining the bands; panels diapered with double fillets. Two fastenings, the catches on the lower board; the straps and clasps probably later additions. See Walters Art Gallery, *Bookbinding*, p. 88, no. 198.

Written in Florence in 1453 by the scribe Phylippus Corbizus who also wrote Munich, Bayerische Staatsbibliothek Clm 10719 (*Colophons*, v. 5, no. 16,069). The scribe's name and the date appear in the colophon (f. 121v) and the Greek letter Φ occurs at the conclusion of all three works. Belonged to Auguste Chardin of Paris (sale cat., Paris, 1813, no. 1212) from which it was acquired by Sir Thomas Phillipps (no. 2814, inscription on front pastedown). The manuscript passed from the collection of Giuseppe (Joseph) Martini (his inscription in pencil on front pastedown) to H. P. Kraus, who sold it to Thomas E. Marston (bookplate) in 1955.

secundo folio: singuli

Bibliography: Faye and Bond, p. 68, no. 39.

The Medieval Book, p. 35, no. 36, with pl. of f. 121v.

Marston MS 40 — Italy, s. XIII^{med}
Uguccione Pisano, Derivationes

I. 1. ff. 1r–9r [Introduction:] Ut partes quasdam que in summa Vgucionis sub figura dissimili ab alia que incipiunt continentur possit quis reperire facilius breuem hanc tabulam deo prestante compegimus que de multis absque graui labore ... [table:] Abreuio. as. c. bracos/ Abdo is. e. co [?]/ Abdomen g. hostio/ ... Xirofagus. fagin [*sic*]/ Xiromirrum. f. amarus.

Alphabetical table of words discussed in art. 5 within the entries for other words; arranged in three columns, each of which is divided into three more columns: the word to be located, followed by a letter of the alphabet (a-g) to indicate where within the entry the reader should look, followed by the main entry. For example, to find *abreuio*, the reader must locate the entry for *bracos*. The letters *a* through *g* are not, however, listed in the text proper; the reader must calculate the approximate location of the desired word.

2. f. 9r Vgutio dicor sine quo non rite docetur/ Si careat doctor, me quisque cimera nocetur [?]/ ... Que fuerint primo capitula sintque secundo/ Non est cautela duplex contraria mundo.

Unidentified poem, 10 lines.

3. ff. 9r–28v [Heading, in later hand:] Tabula ordinaria Vgutionis. [list:] Augeo Auctor Autor Anieo [?] Autor Autoritas Autenticus Autoricabilis ... Corobabel. Zoistero. Zoroastrum. Explitiunt Vgucionis tabule.

Alphabetical table of words included in art. 5; arranged in 7–8 columns per page.

4. f. 28v Hec sunt dictiones que non inueniuntur in Vgucione. Tranquillus. a. um. Presertim. Vniuersus. a. um ... scarifico. as. id est scarfare. cum uentosia. vnde hec scarificatio. [added in another hand:] Muscatum [followed by an erasure of ca. 5 lines].

Short list of words (arranged in 2 columns) not found in the *Derivationes*; many crossed out with the comment "cancellatum quia reperitur" or "reperitur."

II. 5. ff. 29r–169r [Prologue:] Cum nostri protoplausti suggestiua preuaricatione humanum genus a sue dignitatis culmine quam longe deciderit. ac triplicis incommodi ... A uerbo augmenti nostre assertionis auspitium sortiamur. [text:] Augeo. ges. get. auxi. auctum. amplificare augmentum dare. Inde hic auctor id est augmentator et debet scribi cum u. et c ... [text concludes:] Zorobabel apud hebreos ... iudee gentis extitit. Zoroastrum minimum sydus. f. 169v blank, but with off-set impression of back flyleaf or pastedown now removed

Uguccione Pisano (d. 1210), *Derivationes*; Marston MS 40 not listed in either Bursill-Hall, *Census*, or A. Marigo, *I codici manoscritti delle "Derivationes" di Uguccione Pisano* (Rome, 1936). Prologue (including additional passage found in this manuscript), incipit and explicit published by Marigo, *op. cit.*, pp. xiii–xvi.

Parchment, ff. i (modern paper) + 169 + i (modern paper), 380 x 240 mm.

Part I: written space 294 x 179 mm., ruled in crayon or lead in tabular format in three columns; prickings in lower margins. I–II^{12}, III^{4} (structure uncertain: two single [?] leaves stitched in followed by bifolium). Catchword (f. 12v) in decorative frame right of center, lower margin. Written by a single scribe in round gothic bookhand, below top line. Divided initial, blue, 8-line, with intricate red pen flourishes extending down inner margin, f. 1r. Plain red initials, 2-line, to mark new letter of the alphabet; first letter of each word in table stroked with red; more important words preceded by paragraph mark.

Part II: written space 274 x 162 mm. 2 columns, 70 lines. Single vertical bounding lines with additional ruling between columns, single lower horizontal ruling extends to outer edge. Prickings in upper, lower, and outer margins; additional prickings in outer margin for lower horizontal bounding line. I–XIV^{10} (+ 1 leaf added at end). Remains of catchwords along lower edge, right of center, verso. Written in small gothic bookhand, above top line. Many sections traced over in darker ink. Blue or red initials (some divided), 20- to 7-line, with pen flourishes in red and/or blue, for prologue (art. 5) and each letter of the alphabet. On ff. 29r, 43v, 60r: a single dragon-like grotesque, in red and blue, extends up or down the margin (for similar but more elaborate grotesques see Avril and Gousset, pl. XLII, no. 88, f. 117). Initials, 2-line, alternate red and blue with plain pen flourishing in opposite color. Text has faded and flaked throughout.

Binding: Italy, s. xiv? Original sewing on four tawed skin, slit straps laid in channels on outside of beech boards and nailed. A beaded, natural color endband.

Covered in kermes pink tawed skin with an *X* within a rectangular frame drawn on it. Traces of five round bosses on each side and four truncated diamond-shaped catches on the lower board; the upper board cut in for the straps. Rebacked.

Part II written in Italy in the middle of the 13th century; Part I added in the 14th century when the two parts may have been bound together; early provenance unknown. Unidentified shelf-mark in ink on spine ("44/16"), repeated in pencil inside front cover. Note, s. xviii, about the author and the text, pasted to f. 1v. "11303," in pencil, on f. 1v. Purchased in 1954 from C. A. Stonehill (inv. no. 3193) by Thomas E. Marston (bookplate).

secundo folio: [tabula, f. 2r:] Austroaphricus [?]
[text, f. 30r:] [fa]milia enim

Bibliography: Faye and Bond, p. 68, no. 40.

Marston MS 42 — Italy, 1406
Statius, Thebais — Pl. 9

1. ff. 1r–117r *Sursuli papiriani Statij Tolosani thebaidos Incipit liber primus.* Fraternas acies, alternaque regna prophanis/ decertata odijs, sontesque euoluere thebas/ ... Mox tibi si quis adhuc pretendit nubila liuor./ Occidet. et mariti post me referentur honores. [colophon:] Papirij surculi Statij tholosani thebaidos liber xij^{us} et ultimus explicit. die 8 Martij 1406.

   Statius, *Thebais*; A. Klotz, ed., Teubner (1908), rev. ed. Th. C. Klinnert (1973) pp. 1–475. Text here is accompanied by marginal glosses added by scribe on ff. 1r–17v (e.g., f. 1r on line 15: "*Atque adeo.* Autor deliberat se tractaturum de bello duorum fratrum. scilicet. etheoclis et polinicis"); a later hand has entered a few variant readings and marginal notes (e.g., f. 1r on line 2: "*uel sontis*").

2. ff. 117r–118r [Summary of the 12 books, in 12 lines:] Soluitur in primo fratrum concordia libro/ Denegat et fedus. repetitaque regna secundus/ ... Vltimus ogigias dat theseum uincere thebas. [*argumenta* for Bks. 2–5, 7–12:] At maia genitus superas remeabat ad auras./ Excitusque herebo iam seuus laius ibat./ ... Mox ille infrendens optat. uocatque creonta./ Quem sternit bello. graiorumque immolat umbris. f. 118v blank

   Klotz and Klinnert, *op. cit.*, for *argumenta*, pp. 476–82.

Paper (watermarks, obscured by text: similar in type to Piccard Horn

VI.110–29), ff. ii (paper) + 118 + ii (paper), 298 x 217 (200 x 85) mm. Ca. 41 lines of verse for art. 1; 2 columns of verse for art. 2. Single horizontal bounding lines ruled in pencil. Prickings in upper, lower, and outer margins.

I–VII^{16}, VIII^{6}. Catchwords centered along lower edge, verso.

Written by several scribes in scripts ranging from calligraphic *mercantesca* to a more formal gothic bookhand.

One garishly painted initial, 16-line, red and blue divided with penwork designs in both colors. Spaces left for decorative initials at beginning of remaining books are unfilled. For ff. 1r–13r only: headings, paragraph marks, underlining of passages glossed in marginalia and running headlines, all in red; for ff. 1r–16v: first letter of each verse touched with yellow.

Binding: England, s. xx. Quarter bound in alum tawed pigskin, blind-tooled, over oak boards. Title, in ink, on head edge: "Statij. thebaidos." Title on spine: "Statii Thebais/ MS. 1406."

Written in Italy in 1406 (colophon, art. 1); some annotations by an Italian hand, s. XV^{ex}. Belonged to Ercole Silva, conte di Biandrate (in the province of Novara; 1756–1840; bookplate). From the collection of Ambroise de Firmin-Didot (1790–1876; booklabel dated 1850); his sale 1883, no. 11 (unverified). Bookplate of C. S. Ascherson (d. 1945); note in pencil on his bookplate that the manuscript was in the Allen sale (Sotheby's, 30 January 1920, no. 101). Modern notes in pencil, on f. i recto "744" and "149"; on second rear flyleaf, recto: "rs/-/-" and "19302." Purchased from C. A. Stonehill in 1952 by Thomas E. Marston.

secundo folio: Indue

Bibliography: Faye and Bond, p. 69, no. 42.

Marston MS 43 — Northeastern Italy, s. XV^{2}
Treatise on Cardinal Virtues, in It. — Pl. 33

ff. 1r–30v *Qui in questo libro se intende di tractare de le quactro virtu cardinale stracte da massimo valerio et da molti altri filosafi.* [text:] *Similemente* como la misericordia et La Unita Guardano lo Rei Et la clementia Exalta la sua sedia cosi le quactro uirtu Cardinale Sono quagi A modo quactro Colonde [*sic*] le quale sostengono la sedia sua ... et per tanto lo dolce parlare di costui et la scusa del superchio bevere Et la sin// [catchword: plice]

Unidentified treatise, incomplete, on the Cardinal Virtues; material taken mostly from Valerius Maximus, with additional material from Augustine (*De civitate Dei, De beata vita, Epistolae*), Bible (Proverbs), Cicero (*De officiis*, etc.), Seneca (*Epistolae morales, De ira, De constantia*), Macrobius, Aristotle, Vegetius, the "Storie Romane" of "Arineo" (f. 6r), and "Salino" (f. 23v). The presence of the "versificatore" (f. 11r), cited in Latin (Walther, *Sprichwörter* 33507), and a similar constellation of sources suggests that Vincent of Beauvais' *Speculum Doctrinale* was a major (though not exclusive) source for this author.

The headings are as follows: f. 1v Comença A tractare de la Giustitia; f. 2r-v Como Se deueno Ordinare le Giuste legge Capitulo; ff. 2v–3r De l'oseruatione de le Legge; ff. 3v–5v De la Giustitia In conseruare la Reipubilica [*sic*]; f. 5v Poem, 6-line, beginning O quanto serria macto chil facesse . . . ; ff. 5v–6v Di conseruare la giustitia verso li nimici; ff. 6v–8r Qui se Intende di Tractare de la Giustitia In espetie [Note that between ff. 6–7 two leaves are missing which in the old foliation had been numbered ff. 42–43]; ff. 8r–9r *Qui se intende de tractare de la virtu de la prudentia overo discretione*; f. 9r-v De la Prudentia de li philosafy; ff. 9v–10r De le Parte de la Prudentia; ff. 10v–11v De Inteligentia; ff. 11v–13r De le Parte di Prouidentia; ff. 13r–14r De le parte de la Giustitia Secondo Marcobrio [*sic*]; f. 14r *Sequita di vedere de la virtu de la temperantia la quale e molta* [sic] *utile a li principi*; ff. 14v–15r De continentia Capitulo; ff. 15r–17r De L'astinentia Contra Lo Vitio de l'arabiata Luxuria; ff. 17r–18r De la castita de l'antique donne; ff. 18r–19r Del onore che faceuano Li omini Antiqui Ale Vergine; ff. 19r–20v De la Continentia Contra La Varitia; ff. 20v–21r De la Umilita de lantiqui; ff. 21r–22v De la Continentia de li philosofy; ff. 22v–24r De la Clementia; f. 24r-v De la modestia de Li antiqui Filosaphy Capitulo; ff. 25r–27r *In questa ultima parte resta da vedere de la virtu de la forteza la quale virtu e molto da comendare*; f. 27r-v De la Fidutia delli omini Antiqui; ff. 28r–29r De la Patientia che foro ne li saui filosafi; f. 29r-v De la Patientia In sostinere le pene del Corpo; f. 30r-v De la patientia Che forono ne li antiqui In perdonare de le Ingiurie.

Paper (watermarks: similar to Briquet Coutelas 5157, 5159), ff. i (paper) + 30 (early foliation 36–67; leaves with 42–43 missing) + i (paper), 285 x 195 (210 x 115) mm. 39 long lines. Double vertical and horizontal bounding lines (Derolez 13.36). Additional rulings on f. 8r to delineate space for decorative initial. Prickings in upper and lower margins.

I^{10} (–1, 2, 9, 10, with loss of text), II–III^{12}. Horizontal catchwords, surrounded by elaborate penwork designs, touched with yellow, center of lower margin, verso.

Written by a single scribe in humanistic cursive script with notarial features, above top line.

28 pen and watercolor initials, heavily influenced by Greek models, 24- to 10-line (with larger initials at the main divisions for Justice on f. 1r, Prudence on f. 8r, Temperance on f. 14r, and Strength on f. 25r), in green, red or pale purple on paper ground, with intricate designs of scrolling and intertwining vines, pale yellow with touches of unburnished gold, terminating in spiky leaves. Berries, pale purple, red or green with geometric pen designs attached to the vines. Folio 1r, ends of initial *S* terminating in dragon heads; ff. 14r and 25r, unidentified arms (or, 2 or 3 bars nebuly purpure), incorporated into the initial. Sketches, in lead, visible beneath most initials. Headings in red. Majuscules touched with yellow.

Binding: Italy, s. xix–xx. Paste-paper case binding in yellow, green and red.

Written in Northeastern Italy in the second half of the 15th century according to A. C. de la Mare; was part (ff. 36–67) of a larger codex. Unidentified arms incorporated into decorative initials on ff. 14r and 25r; early provenance unknown. Belonged to Federico Patetta (1867–1945), Professor of the History of Law at the University of Turin at the beginning of this century (his notes: f. 1r, "MS no. 131"; back pastedown, "Aij [?]. I, 458." Unidentified notes: "4552," in pencil, on front pastedown and on f. 30v. Purchased from the Turin dealer Bourlot by H. P. Kraus, who sold it in 1958 to Thomas E. Marston (bookplate).

Bibliography: Faye and Bond, p. 69, no. 43.

Marston MS 45 — France, s. XII$^{3/4}$

Seneca; Claudian, etc.

1. f. 1r *In hoc uolumine continentur epistole senece transmisse ad sanctum paulum uel pauli ad senecam. Item epistole senece ad lucilium suum numero. octoginta nouem. Item libri septem eiusdem de beneficijs uel liberalitate. Libri duo eiusdem de clementia. Liber unus supradicti de .iiij^{or}. uirtutibus Liber unus eiusdem de remedijs fortuitorum.*

   Table of contents, in red throughout, occupies only the second column.

2. f. 1v *Incipit prologus beati ieronimi presbiteri.* Lucius ennius [*written above*: uel anneus] seneca cordubensis. fotini [*sic*; *written above*: uel stratini] stoici discipulus. et patruus lucani poete. continentissime uite fuit. quem non ponerem in cathalogo sanctorum. nisi me ille epistole prouocarent . . . a nerone interfectus est.

Jerome, *Prologus beati Ieronimi presbyteri*; F. Haase, ed., Teubner (1872) v. 3, p. 476.

3. ff. 1v–2v *Incipiunt epistole ad sanctum paulum transmisse a seneca. Seneca paulo salutem*. Credo tibi paule nunciatum . . . Data kal.aug. locone [*sic*] et sauino [*sic*] consulibus.

Ps.-Seneca, *Epistolae Senecae, Neronis imperatoris magistri, ad Paulum apostolum et Pauli apostoli ad Senecam*; F. Haase, *op.cit.*, pp. 476–81. Contains all 14 letters of the correspondence, reversing the order of letters 11 and 12 as printed in Haase's text but otherwise corresponding closely to the text of his edition.

4. ff. 2v–3r *Epitaphium senecae*. Cura labor meritum . . . reddimus; ossa tibi.

Complete 6-line text of *Anthologia latina* 667, ed. Riese (Leipzig, 1894).

5. ff. 3r–79r *Incipiunt epistole Senece ad lucilium. numero. lxxx.ix*. [added in later (?) hand] *prima*; [text:] Ita fac mi lucili. uendica [*sic*] te tibi . . . ad hunc peruenire mansueta sunt. Vale.

Seneca, *Ad Lucilium epistulae morales*; L. D. Reynolds, ed., OCT (1965). Purporting to contain 89 letters, the text begins with the first and ends with the complete text of the 85th letter, the 48th letter being divided into two letters at 48.6 on f. 30r [" . . . tam seria. senes ludimus. Vale. // Mus sillaba est. . ."] and letters 86, 87 and 88 being placed between letters 84 and 85. As noted by Reynolds, this division of letter 48 is shared by all the older manuscripts. The placement of the final four letters seems to be unique to Marston MS 45. Our text therefore corresponds to the contents of v. 1 of Reynold's OCT, and to Books 1–13 of the medieval tradition, which were transmitted separately from Books 14–20. (See *Texts and Transmission*, p. 359.)

6. ff. 79r–99v *Incipiunt exceptiones librorum Annei senece de beneficijs uel liberalitate ad eburtium liberalem. amicum suum. Liber primus incipit*. Inter multos ac uarios errores temere inconsulteque uiuentium . . . iste omnibus [*sic*]. Non est. magni animi. beneficium dare. et perdere; hoc est magni animi. perdere. et dare.

Seneca, *De beneficiis libri vii*; K. Hosius, ed., Teubner (1914). The text is heavily excerpted, containing in proper order selections from all seven books.

7. ff. 100r–103v *Annei. lucij. Senece. de clementia ad neronem. liber primus incipit*. Scribere De clementia Nero cesar institui; ut quodam modo

speculi uice fungerer ... Videbit sapiens quod ingenium. qua ratione tractandum sit; quomodo in rectum praua flectantur. *Explicit liber de clementia.*

Seneca, *De clementia libri ii*; K. Hosius, ed., Teubner (1914). The text is heavily excerpted in the manner of art. 6, containing in proper order selections from both books.

8. ff. 103v–105v *Annei Senece. de iiii^{or} uirtutibus liber incipit.* Quatuor uirtutum species. multorum sapientium sententiis diffinite [*sic*] sunt. quibus animus humanus comptus ad honestatem possit accedere ... *De prudentia* Quisquis ergo prudentiam sequi desideras; tunc per rationem recte uiues ... aut ruentem compos ipse deuitet insaniam; aut deficientem puniat ignauiam.

Martin of Braga, *Formula vitae honestae*; C. W. Barlow, ed., *Martini episcopi Bracarensis opera omnia* (New Haven, 1950) pp. 236–50. Barlow does not seem to mention any manuscripts which, like Marston MS 45, omit the preface and dedication and then attribute the work to Seneca. Aside from the omission of preface and dedication, the text is complete.

9. ff. 105v–107v *Incipit liber annei. Senece de remedijs fortuitorum.* Licet cunctorum poetarum carmina gremium uestrum semper illustrent. aliquando deliberans ... Felix est. non qui aliis uidetur; sed qui sibi. Vides autem qua in domo sit ista felicitas.

Ps.-Seneca, *De remediis fortuitorum liber*; F. Haase, ed., Teubner (1872) v. 3, pp. 446–57. The text corresponds to a very early stage in the tradition, omitting the *additiones* in Haase's text.

10. f. 107v Ab alio expectes; alteri quod feceris/ ... Oratorem te puta; si tibi ipsi quod oportet persuaseris.

19 sententiae attributed to Publilius Syrus and Seneca by a modern hand in pencil at the top right hand of f. 107v. 17 occur in the text of Publilius, E. Woelfflin, ed., *Publilii Syri sententiae* (Leipzig, 1869), while the other two are found neither there nor in the works of Seneca. The order of the *sententiae*, all but four of which are arranged in alphabetical order, is as follows [line numbers refer to Woelfflin's text]: (1) P.S. 2; (2) P.S. 95; (3) P.S. 47; (4) P.S. 128; (5) P.S. 161; (6) P.S. 199; (7) P.S. 208; (8) P.S. 255; (9) Caritas in quo regnat; non aliquando unici potest; (10) P.S. 292; (11) P.S. 315; (12) P.S. Prov. 9; (13) P.S. Prov. 57; (14) P.S. Prov. 91; (15) P.S. Prov. 103; (16) P.S. Prov. 123; (17) P.S. Prov. 133; (18) Locutum me aliquando penituit; tacuisse numquam [Walther, *Sprichwörter* 37932c]; (19) P.S. Prov. 28.

11. 107v–109r *Claudianus uir illustris*. Abstulit hunc tandem rufini pena tumultum. Absoluitque deos ... Leujus communia tangunt.

Claudian, *Excerpta*; J. B. Hall, ed., Teubner (1985). The excerpts correspond exactly to the text in a manuscript described by T. Birt, *Claudii Claudiani Carmina* MGH X (1892) p. clxxv, who is referring incorrectly to what is now Beinecke Marston MS 45 as the *codex Cheltenhamensis* 4534, which, like Beinecke Marston MS 45, "Continet Senecae epist. ad paulum et alia eiusdem scriptoris." The *Cheltenhamensis* likewise prefaced its excerpts of Claudian with the rubric "Claudianus uir illustris," the only manuscript of those mentioned by Birt to do so, and followed the excerpts from Claudian with the "Willelmus signiacensis de tribus dicendi generibus (versus 23 a m. poster.)." In his article "Verses attributed to William of Saint-Thierry," *Scriptorium* 8 (1954) pp. 117–19, C. H. Talbot mentions what is now Beinecke Marston MS 45 as the only source for this work, though in his remarks on its provenance he says nothing of its having once been *Cheltenhamensis* 4534. Birt describes the *Cheltenhamensis* 4534 as "membre. saec. XII de quo rettulit Vogel," which is consistent with the date of Beinecke Marston MS 45. It is almost certain that the codex Birt is referring to is actually *Cheltenhamensis* 4572, now Beinecke Marston MS 45 (see also provenance below).

12. f. 109r *Willelmus signiacensis de tribus dicendi generibus*. Si doceas; ujtes id quo [*sic*] non rite docetur;/ Soluens atque docens ... sit clausula queque:/ Ut non ex animo fugiant dicenda; cauendum. ff. 109v–110v blank except for miscellaneous notes

William of Saint-Thierry, *De tribus dicendi generibus*; C. H. Talbot, ed., "Verses attributed to William of Saint-Thierry," *Scriptorium* 8 (1954) pp. 117–19. We offer the following corrections to Talbot's text: line 1, "quo" [not "quod"], line 10, "asciscit" [not "accescit"], line 11, "grande" [not "grandi"]; in addition, Talbot's punctuation does not reflect that of the manuscript.

Parchment (good quality), ff. ii (paper) + 110 + ii (paper), 294 x 204 (218 x 150) mm. 2 columns, 34 lines. Single vertical bounding lines. Double upper (and sometimes lower) horizontal bounding lines, often widely spaced. Ruled in crayon or lead. Remains of prickings in all margins, including inner.

I–XIII^{8}, XIV^{4}, XV^{2}. Quires signed with Roman numerals (I–II accompanied by small head of a grotesque) center of lower margin, verso.

Written in fine early gothic bookhand; arts. 11–12 in less expert hands.

Carefully drawn monochrome initials with modest penwork designs, 12- to 2-line, in red, green and blue. Headings in red.

Binding: France, s. xviii. Bound in light brown, mottled calf with a gold-tooled spine and red label: "Opera Senecae MS." Red edges. Mended at tail. Discoloration from bosses [?] of earlier binding on first and last leaves.

Written in the third quarter of the 12th century in the Cistercian abbey at Igny near Rheims (Cottineau v. 1, col. 1443; ex libris in hand of original scribe written in lower margin, ff. 49v–50r: "Liber Sancte Marie Igniacj"). The manuscript contains evidence of early use, including interlinear and marginal variant readings. Marston MS 45 served as the exemplar for Charleville-Mézières 206-II from the Cistercian abbey of Notre-Dame de Signy (we thank J. Fohlen for this information); see C. Jeudy and Y.-F. Riou, *Les manuscrits classiques latins des bibliothèques publiques de France* v. 1: Agen-Évreux (Paris, 1989) pp. 423–24. Contemporary inscription on f. 109r obliterated by reagent. Signature, f. 1r, of Claude Robert Jardel (ca. 1722–1788), antiquary and bibliophile of Braine, near Soissons; see S. Prioux, "Notice bibliographique et biographique sur Jardel de Braisne, antiquaire [1722–1788]," *Bulletin de la Société Académique de Laon* 8 (1859) p. 18. This manuscript among those acquired from Jardel by Sir Thomas Phillipps (no. 4572; see also art. 11 above). Bookstamp, f. 1r, of Friedrich von Schennis, Swiss-born artist (1852–1918). Belonged to C. S. Ascherson (bookplate; d. 1945) who acquired it, according to note on bookplate, at the J. T. Adams sale (Sotheby's, 8 Dec. 1931, no. 218). From the collection of Dr. Eric G. Millar (1877–1966; booklabel); see D. H. Turner, "List of the Medieval and Renaissance Manuscripts owned by Eric Millar," *British Museum Quarterly* 33 (1968–69) pp. 9–16, Marston MS 45 = no.64 on p. 16. Miscellaneous modern notes, in pencil, on front and rear flyleaves. Purchased from C. A. Stonehill (inv. no. 10991) in 1954 by Thomas E. Marston (bookplate).

secundo folio: [fac]tum non

Bibliography: Faye and Bond, p. 69, no. 45.

Marston MS 46 — Northern Italy, 1426
Eberhardus Bethuniensis, Graecismus — Pl. 10

ff. 1r–121v [Preface:] Quoniam ingnorantie [*sic*] nubilo turpiter excecati quidam imperiti fatuitatem exprimentes asininam chimerinas ymaginantes statuas ... de nominibus exortis a grecis secundum alphabetum. [text, f. 1v:] Est proprie meta trans grece formatio plasma/ Indeque transformatio dicatur metaplasmus/ ... Verbaque cum motu sibi iungunt diptota tum tu/ Explicit ebrardi grecismus nomine christi/ Qui dedit alpha et o sit laus gloria christo/ Defficiunt partes nature significati/ Defficiunt etiam duo dum documenta repugnant/ Desunt per sillabe desunt dum deficit usus./ *Deo Gratias Amen.* [colophon:] Grecismi dei explicit nomine liber/ Grates reddo nobis pie christe glorioseque magister/ Nox antonium scriptus fuit liber iste/ Ocurente domini milessimo quadrigentessimoque/ Anno hijs addas vigesimo sexto. Folio 37v blank, no loss of text; ff. 122r–123r ruled, but blank; f. 123v see provenance below

J. Wrobel, ed., *Eberhardi Bethuniensis Graecismus* (Breslau, 1887) pp. 1–249; text missing (xxv.56–91) between ff. 105–106: "... sine dat tibi ualde // Plus prior et peior...". Some glosses that reflect philosophical grammar (e.g., f. 1r, note on *capam cathegoriam*: "Adiectiuum secunde impositionis non debet addi subiecto prime impositionis"); marginal and interlinear notes sporadically throughout; text written on every other line to facilitate glossing.

Paper (watermarks: similar to Briquet Lettre G 8199, Briquet Lettre B 7980, Briquet Fleur 6393, Briquet Joug 7872, 7876), ff. iii (paper) + 123 + iii (paper), 290 x 207 (219 x 142) mm. 39 long lines or lines of verse; single vertical bounding lines, full length, in lead; text ruled in brown ink. Some portions of text ruled in two columns, though written in either long lines or verse. Remains of prickings in upper and lower margins.

$I–III^{10}$, IV^{8}, $V–VII^{10}$, VIII^{12}, $IX–X^{10}$, XI^{8} (-6, loss of text), $XII–XIII^{8}$. Horizontal catchwords, often elaborately decorated, in center of lower margin, verso.

Written in gothic bookhand by a single scribe, below top line.

Plain initials, paragraph marks, initial strokes, punctuation, in red. Guide letters for rubricator.

Ink has corroded some leaves; many leaves repaired in margins.

Binding: Italy, s. xix. Half bound in vellum with paper spattered with black on the sides. Gold-tooled spine with black label: "Trattato de' Grecismi in Versi Latini," and "1471" stamped along lower edge.

Written in Northern Italy to judge from the script and watermarks; signed and dated 1426 by the scribe Antonius (colophon above). Three contemporary inscriptions on f. 123v indicate the manuscript was owned by Jacobus de Vocatris (or Advocatris) who studied at the school of Magister Jacobus de Griffis: "Iste grecismus est mei Iacobi de advocatris qui suus vnus capister et nescio quid faciam"; "Iste grecismus est mei iacobi de uocatris qui sum vnus capister et nescio quid faciam et ego pergo ad scolas magistri domini iacobi de griffis et cet. ego nonquam dici plus verborum"; "Meum nomen non pono quia me laudare non volo/ Si vultis sire [*sic*] iacobus de uocatris fuit ille/ [followed by two crudely sketched animals on next line] Quod tibi [*n* followed by erasure] faceres alijs fecise cauebis/ Vulnera ne fatias que potes ipse pati." Unidentified round white paper label on spine with "6063" written in ink and "III L" added in another hand. In pencil on back pastedown: "Imp. Zemp [?] No 21 del 3-3-9330." Purchased in 1956 from Bernard M. Rosenthal (Cat. 1, no. 34) by Thomas E. Marston (bookplate).

secundo folio: Ast apposioposis

Bibliography: Faye and Bond, p. 69, no. 46.

Marston MS 47 — France or Italy [?], s. XII/XIII
Ovid, Metamorphoses — Pl. 42

1. f. 1r [Title in upper margin:] *Publij Ouidij nasonis Metamorphoseos liber incipit. qui dicitur Ouidius maior. et habet libros xv.* [text:] Orba parente suo quicumque uolumina cernis/ his saltem uestra detur in urbe locus/ ... Emendaturus si licuisset eram.

   Ovid, *Tristia* 1.7.35–40; S. G. Owen, ed., OCT (1915 and thereafter).

2. ff. 1r–120v *Incipit liber metamorfoseos.* In noua fert animus mutatas dicere formas/ corpora dij ceptis nam uos mutastis et illas/ ... Parte tamen meliore mei. super atra perhennis// [final 4 lines of text added, s. XV^{ex}, concluding:] Siquid habent veri Vatum presagia viuam. Τελος.

   W. S. Anderson, ed., Teubner (1977); a new critical edition by R. J. Tarrant is in progress (for additional information on the manuscript tradition, see *Texts and Transmission*, pp. 276–82). The text of Marston MS 47 contains interlinear and marginal notes, including words and phrases in Greek, throughout; some marginalia are contemporary; most are s. xiv–xv. Lactantian *tituli*, often in red ink, added in margins (D. A. Slater, ed., *Towards a Text of the Metamorphosis of Ovid* [Oxford, 1927]). Portions of text have been retraced by a later hand.

Parchment (much worn, pieced), ff. i (paper) + i (early parchment flyleaf) + 120 + i (paper), 295 x 160 (225 x ca. 65) mm. 50 lines of verse. Triple vertical bounding lines, full length; three or four upper and lower horizontal bounding lines and usually three or four through middle of leaf, full across. Additional pair of vertical rulings in outer margin. Ruled in lead. Remains of prickings in upper and lower margins.

I–XV^8. Contemporary quire signatures (Roman numerals), some erased, in lower margin, verso, for first 8 gatherings. Catchwords, either horizontal or vertical, appear to be later additions, s. xv.

Written by at least three scribes in scripts ranging from late caroline minuscule to early gothic bookhand, all above top line (see also provenance below). Interlinear and marginal annotations and running headlines by several hands, s. xiii–xv.

Two illuminated initials, f. 1r, severely damaged: 21-line initial *I* for first verse of art. 2 incorporates an elongated grotesque, originally purple, red, blue, and green on gold ground; 4-line initial at beginning of art. 1, gold on red ground with center totally effaced. 8-line initial for Bk. 2, f. 8v, gold on blue [?] ground, now rubbed: inhabited by winged grotesque biting its back with intertwining foliage in blue, green, orange and mauve on gold and red ground. Books 3–15 have attractive penwork initials divided red and medium blue with designs in both colors, ascenders and descenders often sweeping far into margins. Headings and paragraph marks in red. First letter of each verse (either set apart from text block between the first and second or placed directly on the second vertical bounding line) stroked with yellow.

Binding: Place uncertain, s. xix. Sewing, possibly original, on four kermes pink slit straps. Plain, wound endbands on tawed skin cores.

Tan blind-tooled goatskin over wooden boards, also possibly original as they are cut in for the straps. Title gold-tooled on spine: "Ovidii Metam./ Saec. XV. M. S. in memb."

Written at the end of the 12th or beginning of the 13th century either in France or Italy: although the physical format and the penwork initials are consistent throughout the codex and are characteristic of French manuscripts of this period, the script of ff. 66r–120v is similar to that occurring in manuscripts from Northern Italy. Marginal annotations of the 14th–15th centuries appear to be written by Italian hands. Belonged in the second half of the 15th century to Antonius Farfuzola who annotated the text, added the final four lines of Book 15, and wrote the following inscription on the early front flyleaf, verso: "Die viiij° maricij [?] 1481 tertio die quatrigessime scilicet primo ueneri inceptum fuit opus ouidij scilicet metamorfosios per dominum magistrum antonium farfuzolam." This inscription is written on the dorse of a fragment of a 15th-century legal document, in Latin, recording events in the diocese of Verona. Belonged to Sir Thomas Phillipps (no. 9033, note of T. E. Marston on first flyleaf); sold by W. H. Robinson (London, Cat. 83, 1953, p. 131 with reproduction of ff. 64v–65r) to H. P. Kraus, from whom it was purchased in 1955 by Thomas E. Marston (bookplate).

secundo folio: Ere ligabantur

Bibliography: Faye and Bond, p. 69, no. 47.

F. Munari, *Catalogue of the Manuscripts of Ovid's Metamorphoses*, University of London, Institute of Classical Studies, Bulletin Supplement no. 4 (London, 1957) p. 57, no. 287.

B. Munk Olsen, *L'Étude des auteurs classiques latins aux XIe et XIIe siècles* v. 2 (Paris, 1985) pp. 152–53, no. C99.

Marston MS 48 — Italy, after 1457
Humanistic Commonplace Book

1. ff. 1r–16r [In upper margin:] 1464. [heading:] Excerpta quedam e L. Iunio moderato Columella. Atqui ego satis mirari non possum quid ita dicendi cupidi ... Quicunque sunt habiti mortalium sapientissimi multa scisse dicuntur non omnia.

   Columella, *De agricultura*, extracts arranged according to the order of the text for books 1–12, here numbered to 13 ["5" omitted in error].

2. ff. 16v–52v [Heading:] Li. primo. In prefatione. Excerpta quedam e Plinio secundo Naturalis hystorie. [text:] Lucilius enim primus Stili uasum condidit ... hispanie Lino excussiora.

   Pliny the Elder, *Historia Naturalis*, extracts arranged according to the order of the text for Books 1–18 (ending with 18.107–08).

3. f. 53r Four lines of Latin text in the original hand "Metricis nos uirtutibus tuis et per uos magnus extollit/ et mihi caput demulces./ Magno quisque animo diuitias despicit/ Valentissima quisque corporis longe abest a sapientia," followed by a table of expenses added by a later hand, s. XVIII. f. 53v blank.

4. ff. 54r–59v [Heading:] Βαλεριους μαξιμους. [text:] Lento enim gradu ad uindictam sui diuina procedit ira: tarditatemque supplicij grauitate compensat ... infirmo uinculo coherens societas dirimatur. Τελος.

   Valerius Maximus, *Facta et dicta memorabilia*, extracts.

5. ff. 59v–74v [Heading:] λαερτειους διογενες. [text:] Museo Eumolpi filio Athene: et Lino: Mercurio: et musa urania genito Thebe inclyte

sunt . . . Nihil enim similis est mortali animanti animal homo in mortalibus bonis inuersatus. Τελος.

Diogenes Laertius, *De vita et moribus philosophorum*, Lat. tr. Ambrogio Traversari; extracts from Books 1–10 (ending with 10.122–35, the complete letter of Epicurus to Menoeceus).

6. ff. 75r–78v [Heading:] Ιωσεφους. Βελλει Ιουδαικι. Mentiri apud scientes inhonestum esse uidetur . . . eamque fugere ne fortunatissimi quid possunt. Τελος.

Josephus, *De bello Judaico*, Lat. tr. Rufinus; brief extracts.

7. ff. 78v–80r [Lower margin, f. 78v:] .C. cesaris. uita. incipit. [Heading: f. 79r] Σουετωνιους Τρανκιλλους. [text:] Consutia repudiata a.c. Cornelia cinne con. filia duxit uxorem . . . quibus de coniuratione comperta, non crederetur: nisi occisis. Τελος.

Suetonius, *De vita Caesarum*, extracts from the lives of Caesar and Augustus, with brief notes on Tiberius, Caligula, Galba, Titus and Domitian.

8. ff. 80v–83v [Heading:] Σολίνος. [text:] Sternutatio post coitum cauenda est. ne prius semen excutiat impulsus repentinus . . . captiuusque romam ueniret ne uenali poculo animam expulit.

Solinus, *Collectanea rerum memorabilium*; brief quotation and notes.

9. f. 83v [Heading:] Απουλέγιος. [text:] Ego uero inquam nihil impossibile . . . Nam quod nemo nouit: pene non sit. nouerca ad priuignum.

Apuleius, *Metamorphoses*; brief extracts from Bks. 1, 5, 9–10.

10. ff. 84r–85r [Heading:] Ιουστίνος. [text:] Ninus: rex assiriorum primus omnium bella intulit finitimis. Zoroaster rex . . . ab eo uarijs generibus mortis exponitus fuit: pudore flagitij.

Justinus, *Epitoma historiarum Pompeii Trogi*; paraphrases of the text.

11. ff. 85r–87v [Heading:] .K. Κουρτιος. [text:] Quippe semper circumiecta nemora petreque quantancumque accepere uocem . . . Male humanis ingenijs natura consuluit: quia plerumque non futura: sed transacta perpendimus. Τελος.

Curtius Rufus, *Historia Alexandri Magni*; quotes and paraphrases from Books 3–10.

12. ff. 88r–94r [Heading:] Λακταντιους. [text:] Nullus enim suauior animo cybus est, quam cognitio ueritatis . . . Loquendi ergo causa

patefactus hic meatus. [symbol of a flower followed by :] Vide ubi est hec signum: et sequitur materia [referring to a similar symbol on f. 91v, with text:] hec duo latera post debent poni.

Lactantius, extracts from *Divinae institutiones*, *De ira Dei*, *De opificio Dei*.

13. ff. 94v–100r [Heading:] Βυτροῦβιους δε αρκιτεκτουρα. [text:] Opera architecti nascitur et fabrica et ratiocinatione. Fabrica est continuata ... qua ad murum plano pede transitus esse posset. [followed by table of contents for the ten books of the *De architectura* on f. 100v]

Vitruvius, *De architectura*, extracts and paraphrases of Books 1–2, 5–8, 10; cf. art. 16.

14. ff. 101r–111v [Heading:] Ιερονιμους. ad damasum. [text:] Lectio sine stilo, somnus est. Scio hec molesta esse lectori: Sed de hebreis disputantem, non decet Aristotelis argumenta ... Ex abundantia enim cordis, os loquitur. Τελος.

Jerome, extracts from his *Epistolae* and other works; in addition, at least one extract from a work addressed to him.

15. ff. 111v–120r A. Γελλιους νοκτιουμ ακτικαρουμ. .Liber primus. Stadium pedum numero esse sexcentum. Theophrastus de amicitia librum edidit ... facultatem scribendi commentandique idoneus. Τελος αμην. *1457*.

Aulus Gellius, *Noctes Atticae*, extracts from Books 1–7 (f. 115r: "Liber octavus deest."), 9–20.

16. ff. 120v–123r Miscellaneous notes, including extracts from Vitruvius (cf. art. 13). f. 122v blank

17. ff. 123v–127r [Heading:] Plautus in amphitrione. [text:] Nam iniusta ab iustis impetrari non decet/ ... Immundas fortunas et quum est squalorem sequi. ff. 127v–130v blank

Plautus, extracts from *Amphitruo*, *Asinaria*, *Captivi*, *Aulularia*, *Curculio (Gurgulio)*, *Cistellaria*, arranged for the most part according to play.

18. ff. 131r–135r Κυκερω Δε λεγυβος. Nec dubito quin idem et cum Egeria collocutum ... Quecumque imitatio morum in principibus extuerit [?] eandem in populo secuturam. Sciscere, decernere: ferre. Quitur.

Cicero, *De legibus*; extracts primarily from Book 1.

19. ff. 135r–140r .Q. ασκονιος πεδιανος. Effigies hominum ex feno fieri solebant quibus obiectos ad spectaculum prebendum tauri irritarentur

... Orbita res duas significat: nam et Rota ipsa intelligitur: et uestigium rote in molli solo.

Asconius Pedianus, *Commentarii in Ciceronis orationes*; extracts.

20. ff. 140v–142r Βεγεφιος [*sic*]. Nemo metuit facere, quod bene se didicisse confidit ... siue Circius. a Sinistra Boreas id est aquilo.

Vegetius, *De re militari*, brief extracts.

21. ff. 142r–145v λοθυος [*sic*] σενεκα. Iram dixerunt breuem insaniam, eque enim impotens sui est decoris oblita, necessitudinum immemor ... Et magno animo breuiora feramus incomoda.

Seneca, *De ira*, brief extracts in the order of the text, followed by extracts on anger not located in Seneca.

22. ff. 145v–148r Βιθα πομπεί περ ύακοβομ ανγελί εδιθα εξ πλοθαρκο. Strabo pater pompei magni. uir bellicosissimus fuit ... duo in iunioribus obuersari feminis solent.

Plutarch, *Vita* of Pompey, Lat. tr. of Giacomo d'Angelo da Scarperia; extracts.

23. ff. 148v–149r Βιθα μαρκι βροΘί εξ πλοθαρκο. Portia filia Catonis erat. habuerat hanc ab auunculo Catone Brutus in coniugem non ex pueritia ... deinde os claudentem [*sic*] sic uitam extinxisse.

Plutarch, *Vita* of Brutus, Lat. tr., probably also by Giacomo d'Angelo da Scarperia, (see art. 22); extracts.

24. ff. 149r–153r κικερο αδ βροθομ δε φινιβος βονορομ εΘ μαλορομ. Non est omnino hic dicendi locus: sed ita sentio et sepe disseruj: Latinam linguam ... Marcum Crassum aiunt semel in uita risisse.

Cicero, *De finibus bonorum et malorum*; extracts and paraphrases mostly appearing in the order of the text, Books 1–5.

25. ff. 153r–158v Δε βιτα ετ μοριβος φιλοσοφορομ. Tales milesius philosophus, coniuge caruit: qui quum interogatus esset, cur non duceret: ait ob filiorum amorem ... Quid est quod hominem lassum fieri non sinit: Lucrum.

Walter Burley, *De vita et moribus philosophorum*; brief extracts.

26. ff. 158v–159v Κικρο δε οραθορε. In dicendo autem uitiu [*sic*] uel maximum est a uulgari genere orationis ... in oratore probari non possunt. ff. 160r–168v blank

Cicero, *De oratore*; brief extracts, all from Book 1.

27. ff. 169r–171r *C.* Πλινιη βερονενσις επιστολε. Frequenter hortaris ut epistolas quas paulo accuratius scripsissem colligerem ... Historia quoquo modo scripta delectat. Sunt enim homines natura curiosi. Vale. ff. 171v–177v blank

Pliny the Younger, *Epistolae*; extracts from Books 1–5.

28. f. 178r-v Miscellaneous notes (extracts), mostly discussions of individual Latin words.

29. ff. 179r–180v Book list, containing 90 titles mainly humanistic, most of which are followed by an evaluation in florins. See also art. 44.

30. f. 180v Word lists.

31. ff. 181r–184v [Quire(s) missing at beginning of text?] .IX Νοταβυλια α σερβιο γραμματικο. εξκερτα. Eris quasi eris dicta est. Numquam enim ad conciliationem mittitur, sicut Mercurius: sed ad disturbationem. et est ministra ... quo tusci piraticam exercuerunt nam illic metropolis fuit. f. 185r blank

Servius, *Commentaria in Vergilium*; extracts from Bks. 9–10 only (concluding in 10.184).

32. f. 185v Medical recipe to cure obstruction of the urinary tract, in Italian. ff. 186r–190v blank

33. ff. 191r–200r Φαβίους Κίντιλιανους. *Li. 1.* Illud tamen in primis testandum est, nihil precepta, atque artes ualere, nisi adiuuante ... aut certe multos infra nos uidebimus. Τελος.

Quintilian, *Institutiones oratoriae*; extracts from Books 1–12.

34. ff. 200v–204v Γεοργιους Τραπεζουντιους. Αλφονσω. *Li. primus.* Rhetorica est ciuilis scientia: qua cum assensione auditorum quoad eius fieri potest ... Tantus est enim splendor in uera laude tanta in magnitudine animi et consilij dignitas: ut. Τελος.

George of Trebizond, *Rhetorica*; extracts from Books 1–5 of a manuscript belonging to the "A" group, with additional extracts from Bk. 4 added at end. See J. Monfasani, *Collectanea Trapezuntia* ... in Medieval and Renaissance Texts and Studies 25 (Binghamton, N. Y., 1984) pp. 459–62.

35. f. 205r Unidentified passage on Plato and Aristotle (added in a later hand). f. 205v blank

36. f. 206r Unidentified words and phrases under the heading: "Plautus in amfitrione"; added by the same later hand as art. 35. ff. 206v–230r blank

37. f. 230v [Added by a later hand, s. XVIII[1]; heading:] dopo fatta la crida ed il tronbeta il Prologo dice. [text:] Ola ò signori avette pur sentito le mani al armi in via ognun figli . . . con una testa piu dura che di bronzo aconpagnata dalla perfidia dalla calumnia dalla falsita dalla bugia. f. 231r blank

Unidentified exhortation to battle.

38. f. 231v .A. Alma di questa vitta/.B. Biancha come neve/.C. Candida come gilio. . . . T. Tortora per la mia rette/.V. Voce che mi chiama à morte. ff. 232r–236r blank

Amorous phrases beginning with each letter of the alphabet, *A-V*.

39. f. 236v li [capelli], la [fronte], li [occhi] . . . il [piede], et qui finisce l' [uomo]. f. 237r blank.

Male bust with rebus of body parts.

40. f. 237v Full page sketch of male figure with mask and holding the small whip that is also associated with flagellants.

41. f. 238r Table of expenses.

42. f. 238v Sketches of rabbits, deer, and male figure. f. 239r blank

43. f. 239v Sketches of male figures and letter trials. f. 240r blank

44. ff. 240v–241r [Text contemporary or slightly later than Latin extracts, added in pale brown ink; heading:] Inventorio de tutti mei libri in questo studio.

Book inventory of 70 entries, mainly of classical authors but also including Boccaccio's *Genealogia deorum*, Dante, "sonniti et triumphi petrarce," and the *Elegantiae* of Lorenzo Valla; perhaps most are manuscript books, since only one (a copy of Solinus) is signalled "impressus." Many are described as to their bindings and are said to be accompanied by a commentary.

45. f. 241v [Added by the same later hand as art. 47; heading:] il primo maggio 1715 [text:] Sonò l'ave maria per il tempo cativo–i, adi 5 del [mese] sonò . . . i, adi 24 del [mese] sonò–ii. ff. 242r–244r blank

Record of number of times the Ave Maria was rung for bad weather for the month of May, 1715.

46. ff. 244v–245v [Text contemporary with or slightly later than Latin extracts:] [1] Io uedo i cieli riuersi nei mei danni/ e la crudel fortuna a me nimica/ e vedo hauerme perso i felici anni/ ... Ma fanne uendecta dio che non prego altro/ Se non in questo mondo al men ne l'alto; [2] Non posso piu tener la trista uoce/ che cantando non pianga el mio dolore/ e che non mostri come el cor si coce ... / e chi cridando non dimostri fuora/ A qual stracio ua chi se n'amora [9 lines, line 5 repeated]; [3] Se mai per tua cason el corpo mio/ Donna crudel fia giunto in scura fossa/ Da poi el spirto solo sia gito a dio/ ... e de qui pigli exempio chi donna ama/ che al fim [*sic*] la uita perde cum la fama; [4] Non hauera forza mai tua crudeltade/ Donna che sempre non te sia suggetto/ Ne mai non mancara mia fideltade/ ... e del mio bom seruir inuam perduto/ e del passato fior senza alcum fruto; [5] Sera tu piena si de crudeltade/ ch'io perda tempo e 'l mio lial seruire/ Non te debe mai mouere a pietade/ ... In nobile sangue regna gentileza/ Um cor villam conuien usar dureza; [6] Io so che butto le parole al uento/ e la fatica mia e la mia fede/ Io so che non ho ad uscir mai piu de stento/ ... Per fim che uenga morte a trarme fuora/ che cusi ua chi nasce in la malhora; [7] Fusti creata in mezo el paradiso/ Cum le sue mano dio te hebbe a formare/ Inprimamente si te fece el viso/ ... e poi te mando ad habitar in terra/ Sol per tenermi giorno et nocte in guerra; [8] Ochi sereni o delicato viso/ O bocha tucta piena de dolzeza/ O labre de coraglio o dolce riso/ ... Dal ciel uenesti o alma peregrina/ Non restaro laudarte o mia regina; [9] Chi uol uedere in una donna sola/ Quante [?] belleze sono in terra sparte/ venga a mirar costei e la sua gola/ ... Felice e chi presente ognhor ti uede/ Ma piu felice assai chi te possede; [10] Mai la natura non congiunse in terra/ si cosa singular come tu sei/ Ne si bel fior produsse primauera/ ... Ma poi che i cielj t'ham data tanta belleza/ humanita dei usar e non dureza; [11] O bella e bianca mam che amando moro/ Non dei mai dar soccorso a la mia uita/ O uui ochi ligiadri o crine d'oro/ ... e terovi sempre fim che sero soterra/ Ma bem ui prego pace a tanta guerra; [12] Che gloria fia la tua quando sepulto/ sera sto corpo per servirte in terra/ e che in sul duro saxo sera sculpto ... Se si fidel te fu fim che fo uiuo/ e tu a torto l'hai del mondo priuo.

Twelve Italian strambotti, in hendecasyllables with scheme abababcc, each 8 lines in length unless otherwise noted. Most are unidentified. No. 3 appears anonymously in Pesaro, Biblioteca Oliveriana, MS 54, dating from the early 1500s but containing mainly poems of the late 1400s; text published by A. Saviotti, "Rime inedite del secolo XV (dal codice oliveriano 54)," *Il Propugnatore* n.s. v. 5, pt. 2 (1892) p. 337, no.

12. Nos. 6, 11 and 12 appear in Biblioteca Apostolica Vaticana, Vat. lat. 5159, respectively, on the following folios: ff. 165v, 65r, 155r; see F. Carboni, *Incipitario della lirica italiana dei secoli XV–XX. Biblioteca Apostolica Vaticana. Fondo Vaticano Latino* Studi e Testi 297–299 and 299 bis (Vatican City, 1982), where all are attributed to Serafino Aquilano. No. 7 appears in Bologna, Biblioteca Universitaria, 46 (Busta II, n. 1), a zibaldone, s. xv–xvi, in the hand of Cesare Nappi, and may be the work of Giovan Battista Refrigerio. See also art. 48 below.

47. f. 246r [Added in the same later hand as art. 45; heading:] adi 11 maggio [text:] prestai a silvestro.

List of expenses or items on loan for month of May?

48. ff. 246v–249v [Text contemporary with Latin extracts:] [1] Chi uol uedere belleze singulare/ chi uol uedere quantuncha puo natura/ Venga a mirare costei che non ha pare/ ... Costei donne uirtu e gloriosa/ Magnanima gentile e graciosa; [2] Chi uol uedere quantuncha puo natura/ Miri e contempli el uiso de costei/ Et uedera belleze oltra mesura/ ... In lei non trouara se non um defecto/ Che ella non e pietosa al suo sugetto; [3] Se tu sapessi l'amore che io te porto/ Non me faresti donna quello che faj/ Ma de una cosa solo me conforto/ ... Et poi che m'hara morto e posto al fondo/ Io sero el seruo tuo ne l'altro mondo; [4] El non fu mai guerra si mortale/ Che qualche pace o tregua non seguesse/ Ma tu che uiui lieta del mio male/ ... Rendime el core che me'l furasti prima/ che dare el uolglio a chi ne fa piu stima; [5] Chi usa in questo mondo la pietade/ Ne l'altro se retroua fra beati/ Chi usa in questo mondo crudeltade/ ... pero risguarda donna el tuo fidele/ Melglio e de essere pietosa che crudele; [6] La morte sola et altro non potria/ Leuarmeti del core che io non te amasse/ Io te uo bene piu che a l'alma mia/ ... Et mille uolte tu me dessi bando/ Sempre ritornaria al tuo commando; [7] Io te uoria amare e tu non uoi/ Non so per qual casom tu m'habi a sdegno/ forse che pensi agli altri amanti toi/ ... Ma se me pilgli per tuo seruitore/ Sempre serai contenta del mio amore; [8] Io som disposto de uolerti amare/ et in omne cosa sempre a te seruire/ Io som disposto de non te lassare/ ... et poi ch'io sero morto li spiriti mei/ Se sforzaram uenire doue tu sei; [9] Se de' sempre gettare mei preghi al uento/ Et in danno afaticarsi la mia fede/ Et uiuer sempre cum pena e tormento/ ... o despiatato amore o crudel sorte/ prima seria contento de la morte ["prima seria" replaced by "sum piu tosto" after the word "contento" above line in same hand]; [10] Aime che non me ual merce chiamare/ Ne pianti ne suspiri ne passione/ Io uolglio li elementi radunare/ ... Et in terra

uederam li membri mei/ Morti dicendo miserere mei; [11] Quando tu uederai el mio corpo morto/ che te solea cum tanta fe seruire/ Tu sentirai li frati el disconforto/ ... Et se non sei di saxo piangerai/ Et de mia morte gran pietate haraj; [12] Quando io sero posto in sepultura/ Io uo per mia memoria um saxo forte/ El quale demonstri cum ferma scriptura/ ... Qui giace um fidel seruo inamorato/ Casom fu de sua morte um cor spietato; [13] Prima che lassi mai de esserti seruo/ In poluere n'andara sta carne e l'ossa/ Mangiare mi lassaro omne mio neruo/ ... che seruo te sero in lieto et in stento/ fim che la poluere mia se importi el uento; [14] Qual seria quello iudeo che non te amasse/ Se tu non fussi si superba in uista/ Ognom chi t'ama di uento si passe/ ... Non se conuiene a tanta tua beltade/ Ad non hauer de me qualche pietade; [15] El fu non mai che inuidia non regnasse/ Doue e el summo bene el summo amore/ El non fu mai che non se trouasse/ ... El non fu mai che fra l' inamorati/ Non glie ne fusseno de li apassionati; [16] Aime che spartira tal bem uolere/ Aime che spartira tal amistade/ Aime che me usara tal despiacere/ ... Aime che ce spartira gli sia spartita/ L'alma dal corpo e tu togli la uita; [17] Se io potesse fare quello che uorrei/ Non me faresti donna quello che fai/ Ne giorno in giorno piu crudel me sei/ ... Rendime se esser puo rendime el core/ poi che pieta non hai del mio dolore; [18] Aime dolente et crudel mia partita/ che me diuidi dal mio car Signore/ Questo e la fim de la dolente uita/ ... Lassar pur te conuengo o car mio bene/ Quello che fortuna uole esser conuene; [19] Guarda signora mia de chi te fidi/ che ogni herba uerde non e magiorana/ Et guarda cum chi parli et cum chi ridi/ ... Se questo Signora mia non farai/ Ancor u' ira tempo che te ne pentirai; [20] Potesse io cum la uoce et col cridare/ Sfogare la mia pena e 'l mio dolore/ potesse io col morire et col stentare/ ... Cussi cantando io chiamo et prego morte/ che trarre mi uenga de questa crudel sorte; [21] Io uedo bem che al mondo non e fede/ Io uedo bem che fede non se troua/ Ma elgli'e pazo che non se n'auede/ ... pero che in donna pone sua speranza/ El tempo perde et altro non auanza; [22] El non fu mai alchum leal seruir[e]/ Che non sperasse hauer qualche merc[ede]/ El non fu mai alchun lungo desire/ ... El non fu mai che in omne gentil core/ Sempre non regnasse el perfecto amore; [23] Tu non hai facto si cum altra gente/ chi gli hai seruiti et facto omne a piacere/ Et io che t'ho amato fidelmente/ ... che mille uolte anchor ne serai/ pentita amor se me abandonarai; [24] Io rompo col cridar l'aero e 'l cielo/ Si che piatoso fo ciaschum che sente/ Et io che per amarti bruso et gielo/ ... E fa' l contra iustitia et contra amore/ Ma dio te punira de [t]anto erro[re]; [25] Da poi [che] uego pur uenir la morte/ A trar de questo corpo la mia uita/ Lasso per testamento unico et forte/ ... Eh sia chi in aspra uoce dica/ Costui e morto per te crudel nimica; [26] [Qu]ando scripto uederai sul duro saxo/ costui che per sua fede iusta e morto/ E lo mio corpo li sotto sia al basso/ ... Ma 'l tuo pensier fia tardo al uiuer mio/ che' l corpo stara in terra el spirto a dio; [27] In vm sepolchro de duro marmo forte/ Voglio che incluso sia sto corpo mio/ Oue se legera la crudel morte/ ... Ma uoglio se stia sempre nel inferno/ A dolersi de ti madonna sempiterno.

Twenty-seven strambotti [or sonnets?], in Italian, most of which are unidentified. No. 3 occurs anonymously in Udine, Biblioteca Comunale MS 10 (olim 42). Nos. 4 and 5 appear in Biblioteca Vaticana Apostolica, Vat. lat. 5159, on ff. 90r and 153v; see Carboni (cited in art. 46), where the poems are attributed to Serafino Aquilano. No. 13 appears in Bologna, Biblioteca Universitaria, 46 (52, Busta II, n. 1), and may be the work of Giovan Battista Refrigerio; see art. 46 above. No. 24 appears anonymously in Biblioteca Vaticana Apostolica, Urb. lat. 729, as reported by G. Zannoni, "Strambotti inediti del secolo XV," *Rendiconti della R. Accademia dei Lincei, Classe di scienze morale, storiche e filologiche*, ser. 5, v. 1 (1892) pp. 371–87, with this incipit on p. 386. No. 27 appears anonymously in Pesaro, Biblioteca Oliveriana, MS 54, dating from the early 1500s but containing mainly poems of the late 1400s; text published by A. Saviotti, *op. cit.*, pp. 339–40, no. 21 (see art. 46 above).

49. f. 249v A note of transaction dated 16 October, 1500.

Paper (watermarks, in gutter: unidentified hunting horn, crossbow, animal [?]; in outer margin, trimmed: unidentified mountain in a circle surmounted by cross), ff. i (paper) + 249 + i (paper), 290 x 107 (ca. 240 x 85) mm. Ca. 37 lines. Most leaves have no rulings for text; occasionally, a single vertical bounding line along which initial letters are aligned; other leaves folded lengthwise, as in first gathering.

I^{52}, II^{70}, III^{58} [one quire missing?; see art. 31], IV^{70} (–70, blank?).

Written by a single scribe in a neat humanistic script with many cursive elements; later additions by several hands.

Headings and initials often highlighted in red or ochre; some paragraph marks in same colors.

Binding: Italy, s. xix. Rigid vellum case; paper label with title on spine: "Excerpta De Vetustioribus script. Latinis et Grecis, Saecul. XV."

Written in Italy ca. 1457–64 (see arts. 1 and 15), presumably for the personal use of the unidentified humanist whose book list comprises art.

29. Given the large size of the quire gatherings, the arrangement of the excerpts, and the nature of the text, it is likely that the manuscript originally existed in booklet format. Some entries, including the second book list in art. 44 and the Italian poetry in arts. 46, 48–49, were written by a second individual toward the end of the 15th or beginning of the 16th century. Another group of entries, including art. 45 (dated 1715), were carelessly added by a third person. Modern notation: "322" twice, in pencil, on back flyleaf and pastedown. Purchased from H. P. Kraus (notes on back pastedown) in 1956 by Thomas E. Marston (bookplate).

secundo folio: Nundinarum

Bibliography: Faye and Bond, p. 69, no. 48.

Marston MS 49 — Italy, 1476
Unidentified grammatical treatise; Vita vergiliana, etc.

I. 1. ff. 1r–29r //uos ipsi ut nunquam secus dictum sit. *Tu mihi familiaris es.* ego te utor familiariter. Tu mihi amicus es: ego te amico utor: Tu mihi magister es: ornatius dicitur ego te magistro utor: ego te . . . admirationis ratione mutata atque id omne exemplo cuius curiculum uno ac trigesimo die conficitur. Primus itaque dies kalende erunt Martij ij sexto nonas// ff. 29v–30v ruled, but blank

Unidentified grammatical text, imperfect at beginning and end, which draws heavily on the *Elegantiolae* of Agostino Dati and also perhaps on Lorenzo Valla, *Elegantiae* and Niccolò Perotti, *Rudimenta* and *Cornucopiae* (we thank W. K. Percival for his help with the texts in this manuscript). The work consists of miscellaneous comments on word usage presented as a series of *documenta*; primarily distinctions between synonyms (e.g., "familiaris/amicus," "munus/officium," "intelligo/animadverto") and notes on the stylistic superiority of certain Latin constructions over others (e.g., when giving a person's place of origin, one should use "Atheniensis" rather than "de Athenis"). The text quotes examples from Cicero, Aulus Gellius, Juvenal, Livy, Terence, Priscian, Servius, Donatus, Nonius Marcellus (rubrics with the names of these authors in outer margins).

II. 2. ff. 31r–52v *.P. Virgilij Maronis poete Maximi Vita foeliciter incipit.* *.P.* Virgilius Maro parentibus modicis fuit, et precipue patre: quem quidam opificem figulum . . . que in georgicis intentio quisque finis fuerit: nec minus etiam in Eneide: *Hic est finis de ipso carmine.*

Vita virgiliana: "Donatus auctus"; for this text and a full account of its transmission see K. Bayer, in *Vergil Landleben ... Vergil-Viten*, ed. J. and M. Götte (Munich, 1970) pp. 214–40, 350–70, 659–89 (with notes), 746–51.

3. ff. 53r–54v In Exponendis Auctoribus hec consideranda sunt: Vita poete. Titulus operis. Qualitas carmis [*sic*]: Intentio scribentis. Numerus librorum: Ordo librorum: Explanatio: Virgilij uita hec est: Patre Marone ... ut cuncta Virgilij maronis secreta nouisse diuino quodam modo credatur: *Explicit de ipso carmine.*

   Preface to Servius' *In Vergilii Aeneidos libros Commentarius*, with substantial abridgements: the first portion of the text is drawn directly from the *Vita Seruii* at the beginning of the Servius commentary; the remainder consists of selections taken from Servius' preface. *Seruianorum in Vergilii Carmina Commentariorum Editionis Harvardianae*, vol. 2 (1946) pp. 1 (lines 1–10), 4–5 (parts of lines 75–97). The final seven lines of text in the manuscript are unidentified.

4. ff. 54v–74r Pes in metro dicitur quod pedis fungitur officio Metra enim per pedes quodamodo [*sic*] incedunt: Pedes alij dicuntur. alij vero nothi ... [f. 62r:] apud poetas per lectionem facile deprendimus: et hec de primis syllabis dicta sufficiant. *De medijs Syllabis sequitur.* Que uero syllaba in medio constiterit isdem ferme deprenditur modis ... [f. 67v:] Quare de ultimis iam dicere pergamus: *De ultimis. syllabis. sequitur.* A. finita casualia per rectos casus corripiuntur ut syllaba. musa. illa ... Octauus modus est: quom breuem uocalem sequitur. Z. Est .H. longa in hoc Mezenti ducis exuuias: Breuis in hoc nemorosa. [*iaz* crossed out] iazintus [*sic*]. [colophon:] τελόσ. Αμην. die. 9. Iulij 1476. Finis.

   Leonicenus Omnibonus (ca. 1412–ca.1480), *De arte metrica.* Cf. Bursill-Hall, *Census*, citing only two manuscript copies: 166.27.5; 166.61.8; the treatise also occurs in Beinecke MS 66, art. 1; Rome, Biblioteca Angelica, 1371; Venice, Biblioteca Marciana, Cod. Lat. XIII, 23 (= 4414); Verona, Biblioteca Comunale 2813. Portions of the text are derived from Servius' *Commentarius in artem Donati*: ff. 57r (line 7)–58r (line 15) = H. Keil, ed., *Grammatici latini* (Leipzig, 1855–1923) v. 4, p. 423 (lines 11–34); ff. 72v (line 17)–74r = Keil, *op. cit.*, p. 424 (lines 10–36) and p. 425 (1–4).

5. ff. 74v–75v Senatui populoque romano: Lentulus sal: D. Aparuit temporibus istis: et adhuc est homo magne uirtutis nominatus christus iesus: qui dicitur a gentibus propheta veritatis ... In collo-

quio grauis: rarus: et modestus: speciosus forma inter filios hominum. Hic est finis epistole. quam misit lentulus .S.P.Q.R. de conditione domini nostri iesu christi. ff. 76r–80v ruled, but blank; quotation in contemporary humanistic hand on f. 79v: "Homo sum et humani nihil a me alienum esse puto." [Walther, *Sprichwörter*, v. 2, 11108].

Ps.-Lentulus, *Epistola de conditione Domini nostri Iesu Christi*; E. von Dobschütz, "Christusbilder," in *Texte und Untersuchungen zur Geschichte der altchristlichen Literatur*, 18 (1899), text on p. 319**. For additional bibliography and an English translation see C. E. Lutz, "The Letter of Lentulus describing Christ," *Gazette* 50 (1976) pp. 91–97.

Composed of two parts of similar format that were bound together soon after being produced.

Part I: ff. 1–30, paper (watermarks, buried in gutter: similar to Briquet Oiseau 12128 and 12130), 204 x 125 (132 x 76) mm. 20 long lines. Double vertical bounding lines, ruled in lead or, later in manuscript, hard point; rulings for text in ink. Prickings in upper and inner margins; single pricking in outer margin, 7 mm. above upper ruling. $I–III^{10}$ (at least one quire missing at beginning). Vertical catchwords on inner ruling (Derolez 12.5 and 12.6) often on verso of first leaf of each bifolium; horizontal catchwords on red scrolls in center of lower margin, final verso (Derolez 12.1). Written by a single scribe in humanistic cursive, below top line. Plain initials (1-line), headings, initial strokes, and marginalia in red.

Part II: ff. 31–80, paper (watermarks, buried in gutter: similar in general design to Harlfinger Balance 31; final quire has same watermarks as in Part I), 205 x 129 (129 x 72) mm. 20 long lines. Double vertical bounding lines in lead; rulings for text in ink. Prickings in upper and lower margins; single pricking in outer margin, 7 mm. above upper ruling. $I–V^{10}$. Vertical catchwords as in Part I and to mark end of gatherings; quire and leaf signatures (later addition). Arts. 2–4 in humanistic cursive, below top line; art. 5 in a more formal humanistic bookhand. Arts. 2–4: plain initials, headings, and initial strokes in red.

Binding: Italy, s. xv. Two pairs of tunnels in the edges of the boards, and the supports laced into one or the other of them to channels in the outside and nailed. Partly resewn.

Boards sharply bevelled, with the fore-edge bevel broken off the upper board. Quarter vellum binding, a later addition. Title in ink on lower board, partially visible under ultra-violet light: "Vita Vergilii [another word illegible]/ Documenta." Later title in ink on spine: "Varia man. scr./

vetera" and what appears to be a monogram or shelf-mark with letters *I, F, O, T, H* in ink on vellum addition.

Written in Italy; Part II is dated 1476 (art. 4) and Part I, which has the same watermarks as the final quire of Part II, is contemporary to it. Early provenance unknown. Miscellaneous notes, sketches of scrolls, and pen trials by at least two hands, s. xv–xvi, on f. 80v. The same later hand may have written both "Palladiorun [?]" in the lower margin of f. 1r and the title on the vellum addition. Purchased from C. A. Stonehill (inv. no. 13709) in 1958 by Thomas E. Marston (bookplate).

Bibliography: Faye and Bond, pp. 69–70, no. 49.

Marston MS 50 — Hautecombe [?], s. XII^{med}
Origen, Commentarius in ad Romanos, Lat. tr. Rufinus

ff. 1r–154v [Rufinus' preface and Origen's prologue, written continuously:] Uolentem me paruo subuectum nauigio ora tranquilli litoris stringere et minutos de grecorum stagnis pisciculos legere . . . poterimus compendiis exsequemur. *Explicit prologus. Incipit liber primus.* [text, f. 2v:] Paulus seruus ihesu christi. De paulo iam diximus. requiramus nunc cur seruus dicatur . . . Nobis enim. propositum est non plausum legentium. sed fructum proficientium querere. *Explicit liber decimus.*

Ends incomplete in Rufinus' epilogue; PG 14.831–1294. Three short lacunae where the scribe has left lines blank for the missing text: f. 132r: " . . . Non alta sapientes; sed humilibus consentientes. // Consentire enim humilibus et amare humiles . . . "; f. 132v: " . . . ex utraque constare; ne nos alterius // Quomodo potest fieri ut pacem cum omnibus hominibus . . . "; f. 153v: " . . . eius ex illa sine dubio sciat sibi // Videtur ergo indicare de eo quid uir fuerit. . . ." The manuscript has been carefully corrected, with tie marks used to key missing text added in margins; elaborate contemporary "Nota" signs.

Parchment, ff. ii (paper) + 154 + ii (paper), 302 x 208 (217 x 154) mm. 2 columns, 33 lines. Format of leaves varies considerably; some bifolia of different formats found within a single quire. In general, the rulings are as follow. Quires I–II: single vertical, one to three upper (and sometimes single lower) horizontal bounding lines, additional vertical ruling between columns. Quires III–VII, IX–XII: single vertical, two sets of widely spaced double bounding lines at top and bottom of written space, additional vertical ruling between columns. Quire VIII: single vertical bounding lines with additional vertical ruling between columns. Quires XIII–XIV: single vertical, double upper and lower horizontal bounding lines, additional vertical ruling between columns. Quires XV–XIX same as XIII–XIV, but without additional ruling between columns. All guide lines ruled in lead or crayon; prickings (punctures) sometimes visible in all four margins. Corrections and additions to text on rulings drawn in margin.

I–XVIII^{8}, XIX^{12} (–4, 10; no loss of text). Quires signed (i–viii) with roman numerals surrounded by dots, center of lower margin, verso; remains of other signatures. Catchwords accompany quire marks (trimmed), f. 136v.

Written by multiple scribes in well formed early gothic bookhand.

Fine painted initials, ff. 1r and 29v, red with simple green penwork designs and pale yellow wash, 8-line; smaller red, green, or dark yellow-brown monochrome initials, 7- to 1-line. On f. 141r red initial, 7-line, with pale yellow wash. Headings in red.

Binding: Italy, s. xix in. Half bound in brown sheepskin, gold-tooled, with two green, gold-tooled labels: "Hieronimi/ In Epistol/ ad Romanos/ Manuscrip" and "Saecul XII." Bright pink paper sides and edges spattered blue-green. Bound in the same distinctive style as Marston MSS 125, 128, 135, 151, 153, 158, 159, and 197, also from the Cistercian abbey of Hautecombe (see provenance). The spine of the manuscript is back bevelled at head and tail. Rust stains from the nails of four corner bosses of early binding on first two leaves.

Written in the middle of the 12th century, probably at the Cistercian abbey of Hautecombe to which it belonged; contemporary ex libris in red and black follows text on f. 154v: ".liber sancte marie altecumbe;". Located in the ancient diocese of Geneva, the abbey was founded toward the beginning of the 12th century by monks from the abbey of Aulps (see R. Clair, "Les origines de l'abbaye d'Hautecombe," *Mélanges à la mémoire du Père Anselme Dimier* [Arbois, 1982–87] tome II, v. 4, pp. 615–27). The script, format, and general style of decoration resemble those in Marston MS 197, which also belonged to this abbey. Marston MS 50 has the characteristic bright pink binding of the books of Monseigneur Hyacinthe della Torre who acquired and rebound a group of twelve manuscripts from Hautecombe at the beginning of the 19th century (see Leclercq, 1951, p. 75). Belonged to the Biblioteca del Seminario Metropolitano in Turin (Leclercq, *op. cit.*, p. 76, no. 17: number in red crayon on front pastedown). Acquired from C. A. Stonehill in 1956 by Thomas E. Marston (bookplate).

secundo folio: in his omnibus

Bibliography: Faye and Bond, p. 70, no. 50.

Marston MS 51 Southern Italy, s. XV^{med}
Giacomo Curlo, Epitoma Donati in Terentium, etc. Pl. 61

1. ff. 1r–8r *Ad illustrissimum dominum fferdinandum Sicilie ac Iherusalem regem. Iacobi curuli Ianuensis qui vocabula dudum per eum ex comentario elij donati gramatici super Therencium comicum passim excerpta in hoc volumine compilauit acque ad debitum alfabeti ordinem reduxit prohemjum incipit.* Superioribus mensibus Rex inclyte acque preclarissime diuus alfonsus pater tuus regum celeberrimus pridie quam morbo ... et in amplissimjs et ornatissimjs bibliotecis reponerent vnde nacti sunt gloriam Immortalem. Vale.

   Giacomo Curlo, preface to art. 2, addressed to Ferdinand I of Naples; printed by De Marinis, *Supplemento* (1969) pp. 34–37, from Liverpool, University Library F. 3. 2. For other manuscripts containing arts. 1–2 see P. O. Kristeller, "A New Work on the Origin and Development of Humanistic Script," *Manuscripta* 5 (1961) pp. 37–38 (Marston MS 51 not listed), and G. Germano, ed., *Jacobi Curuli Epitoma Donati in Terentium* (Naples, 1987), where this manuscript is listed as *Z* (text of this art. on pp. 3–12 and art. 2 on pp. 13–203).

2. ff. 8r–89r *Elij donati gramatici antiquissimj vocabula per eum super Therensium comicum eleganter exposita.* Abducere est per fraudem auferre Cicero per vim ac dolum abducte ab rhodio tibicine. Terencius in eunucho ... cuius rei Ennius testis est Exin Tarqujnjum bona femjna laujt et vnxit. Finjs deo gracias.

   Giacomo Curlo, *Epitoma Donati in Terentium*; alphabetical list: Abducere-Vxor. See bibliography for art. 1.

3. ff. 89v–90v *Antonij cassarinj ad Iacobum curlum virum clarissimum in traduccione apophetegmatum [*sic*] plutarchi prefacio incipit.* Nuper amoenissime Iacobe aliquantulum ocij nactus cum essem. quod michi quam perraro contingat nosti ... et studijs communibus Impesum non cupiam.

   Antonio Cassarino, preface for art. 4, addressed to Giacomo Curlo; G. Resta, "Antonio Cassarino e le sue traduzioni da Plutarco e Platone," *Italia medioevale e umanistica* 2 (1959) pp. 244–45.

4. ff. 90v–137r *Plutarchi in apotehmatibus ad traianum Cesarem prohemjum.* Artaxerses Rex persarum maxime Imperator traiane Cesar. existimans

non mjnus regium acque humanum esse parua grato ac libenti animo recipere ... [f. 91v:] *Apotehmata*. Apud persas gryppi idest qui aquilino sunt naso plurimum diliguntur ... qui eo modo edifices perinde roma Immortalis sit futura. Finjs deo gracias. ff. 137v–144v blank

Plutarch, *Apophthegmata*, Latin translation by Antonio Cassarino; Resta, *op. cit.*, pp. 245–46 for incipit and explicit only.

5. ff. 145r–199r *ffrancisci aretinj in phalaridis tyrannj agrigentinj epistolas ad illustrem principem malatestam nouellum de malatestis prohemjium.* [text:] Uellem malatesta nouelle princeps illustris tantam michi dicendi facultatem dari vt uel prestancie tue ... [Ep. 1, f. 148r:] *Phalaris Alciboo.* Policletus messenius quem prodicionis apud ciues tuos insimulas morbo me incurabili liberauit ... qui miserit laudem consecuturam.

Phalaris, *Epistolae*, translated by Francesco Griffolini of Arezzo and dedicated to Malatesta Novella of Cesena. See art. 6 for bibliography.

6. ff. 199r–201r *Ad illustrissimum Alfonsum aragonum regem ffranciscus aretinus harum quatuor phalaridis epistolarum e greco ad latinum sermonem interpres fidelissimus acque doctissimus.* Quatuor phalaridis epistolas quas nuper in alio libello Inuentas in latinum traduxi ... [f. 199v:] *Aphilanti et Thrasibulo.* Quas mutuo vobis pecunias dedimus Teucro reddidisse dicitis ... sed summe bonitatis premjum accepissent. Vale. Finis deo gracias. ff. 201v–208v blank

Phalaris, four additional *Epistolae*, translated into Latin by Francesco Griffolini of Arezzo and dedicated to King Alfonso I of Naples. The letters in arts. 5 and 6 are those in the editio princeps (Treviso, Gerardus de Lisa, 1471); however, the dedicatory letter to Francesco Pellato is not present in this manuscript.

7. ff. 209r–261v *Plinij secundi antiquissimj atque elegantissimj viri nonnulle epistole quas lege feliciter.* Caius plinius secundus Septicio salutem. Frequenter hortaris vt epistolas quas paulo accuracius scripsissem ... de vnjuersitate pronuncio de partibus experiar legendo. Vale. [added by a later hand, s. xvi, who also added the headings for Books II and III:] Desunt hoc loco sex epistolae usque ad finem tertij libri. ff. 262r–265v blank

Pliny, *Epistolae I.1–III.15*; R. A. B. Mynors, ed., OCT (1963) pp. 5–89. There are a few annotations (e.g., ff. 212v, 219r, etc.); spaces left blank for the Greek, but Latin translations regularly appear in the margins (in some instances, for example on f. 212v in *Epistola I.6.1*, the Greek is written in with the Latin translation in the margin).

Paper (slightly polished; watermarks: ff. 1–112, similar to Briquet Lettre R 8941; ff. 113–160 and 209–256, similar to Briquet Échelle 5904, 5908; ff. 161–208, 257–265, similar to Piccard Kreuz II.616, 619, 622), ff. ii (contemporary paper, i = front pastedown) + 265 (contemporary foliation, i-cclxj, in upper right corner; f. cxxxx, a blank, removed; modern foliation skips f. 140), 293 x 212 (176 x 100) mm. 24 long lines. Double horizontal and vertical bounding lines, with the vertical usually ending just below the written space and the horizontal not extending into inner margins. Ruled in hard point on versos. Only two single prickings in outer margins, near upper and lower horizontal bounding lines.

I–XVI^{16} (–f. cxxxx), XVII^{10} (10 = back pastedown?). Horizontal catchwords under written space to right, verso (Derolez 12.2).

Written in an unusual style of loose and sloping humanistic script with cursive features; angular, little shading of letters, well spaced.

Plain lumpy initials, 3- to 2-line, alternate blue and red. Headings and paragraph marks in red.

Binding: Spain [?], s. xv. Original wound sewing on four tawed skin, slit straps laced through tunnels in the edges of wooden boards to channels on the outside and pegged. Yellow edges. The beaded chevron endbands are sewn with red and yellow thread on tawed skin cores laid in grooves in the boards.

Covered in brown sheepskin with the surface mostly worn off; decorated with concentric frames, the central panel and one frame filled in with square goat [?] and flower tools standing on a point. Title in ink on a paper label, now mostly wanting. Four truncated diamond-shaped catches on the lower board have a raised design of the Virgin and child and a flower.

Written in Southern Italy in the middle of the 15th century. Before 1954 it was MS XI.50 in the Library of the Santa Iglesia del Pilar in Saragossa (Germano, *op. cit.*, p. xxii); the style of the binding suggests that the codex may have been in Spain as early as the 15th century. Acquired from C. A. Stonehill in 1954 by Thomas E. Marston (bookplate).

secundo folio: [decli]nata tempestate

Bibliography: Faye and Bond, p. 70, no. 51.

Marston MS 52 Bologna, s. XV^{med}
Suetonius, De vita Caesarum Pl. 23

ff. 1r–179r *C. Suetonii Tranquilli de XII cesaribus ac primum de C. Iul. Cesaris vita incipit feliciter.* Annum agens cesar sextum decimum patrem amisit Sequentibusque consulibus flamen dialis destinatus ... portendi statum rei publice sicut sane breui euenit. abstinentia et moderatione insequentium principum. ff. 179v–180v blank

M. Ihm, ed., Teubner (Leipzig, 1903) v. 1. Greek words and phrases have been written in the text, with Latin translations added in the margin; Greek omitted on ff. 117v and 176r.

Parchment (hair side mottled), ff. ii (contemporary parchment bifolium; i = front pastedown) + 180, 275 x 195 (180 x 108) mm. 25 long lines. Single vertical and narrowly spaced double horizontal bounding lines in which the upper ruling delineates height of minims; a similar pattern of double horizontal rulings is used for each line of text. Ruled in hard point.

$I-XXII^8$, $XXIII-XXIV^2$. Horizontal catchwords, with single dots on most sides, in lower margin written across vertical bounding line (Derolez 12.3). Remains of quire and leaf signatures (e.g., b 1, b 2, etc.) in lower margin, recto.

Written by a single scribe in a round humanistic script that inclines slightly toward the left.

Illuminated title page with partial border in upper and inner margin, white vine-stem ornament against vibrant blue, green and red ground with white dots and gold balls, terminating in pen inkspray with gold balls and large blossoms, yellow and red with gold highlights in upper margin, blue with white highlights in inner margin. Inner margin interrupted by a scrolling banderole (no inscription) in blue and red with white highlights. Floral border in lower margin, pen inkspray with flowers in blue, red, green and pink, and gold balls, surrounding a wreathed medallion with unidentified arms (azure 3 bendlets argent, a chief or with 3 birds sable beaked and membered gules) and the initials VI and M (arms and initials are later additions), on a parchment ground. 12 illuminated initials, 8- to 6-line, gold. Some against green and red grounds with yellow and white highlights, filled with yellow shaded white vine-stem ornament against blue, green and red grounds with white and yellow dots. Other initials on blue, green and red grounds with yellow shaded white vine-stem ornament, yellow and white dots. Initials on ff. 1r, 26v, 83v, 119r, 140r, 170r are enclosed within faceted rectangular frames. Headings and marginal notes by original scribe in red.

Binding: Italy, s. xv. Resewn on four supports and rebacked. Edges yellow.

Covered in brown leather over wooden boards, blind-tooled with concentric frames alternately filled with rope interlace. A triple cross in the central panel. Badly cut tools and impressions burned into the leather. Four fastenings, the catches on the lower board.

Written in Bologna in the middle of the 15th century by Simon Carpaneti who copied and signed London, B. L. Add. 11981; the arms and initials (written over an erasure) on f. 1r appear to be slightly later additions. Ownership inscriptions, s. xv–xvi, on the front pastedown: 1. "Hunc de stampis Innocentius possideo"; 2. the date 1511 written twice, the first time partially effaced; 3. ꝑ$_{B}$ n° xxv followed by a word crossed out; 4. "Manilii [or Marsilii] stampide [the name has been scratched out and written over at least once] C Suetonius Tranquillus Liber est suus."; 5. "hic liber [two words effaced, perhaps Vincentij Nerae?, with the name Innocentii stampis written above the original name]"; 6. a Greek quotation from Euripides, *Orestes* (708), with the Latin translation added above, and a heraldic or printer's device drawn below containing the name Euripides (in Greek), three blackbirds, the initials G. M. S. F. E., and the [Greek?] letters IHIO. Purchased by Thomas E. Marston (bookplate) from Lathrop C. Harper, Inc., in 1952.

secundo folio: Nam comites

Bibliography: Faye and Bond, p. 70, no. 52.
The Medieval Book, p. 35, no. 34, pl. of f. 83v.

Marston MS 53 — Germany [?], s. XV^{med}

Poggio Bracciolini, Dialogus in avariciam

ff. 1r–15v *Dialogus in auariciam Pogij florentini ad franciscum Barbarum.* Antonio ricio viro prestantissimo Stephanus Nouarie S. P. D. dyalogum hunc in auariciam poggio florentino nuper editum per me autem Rome scriptum tibi dono do atque largior ut si quando mentem tuam inuaserit ardor auaricie qui est communis omnium prelatorum morbus uideas ... [preface:] [Q]uoniam plures mortalium mi francisce non viuunt set agunt vitam ... [text, f. 1v:] Cum diebus estiuis Antonius luscus cracius [elsewhere corrected by a later hand to cincius] romanus alijque nonnulli ex pontificis secretarijs cenarent cum Bartholomeo politiano ... Sed cum satis iam collocuti sumus et nox supervenerit abeundum censeo. Ita omnes consurrexerunt. finis. [colophon:] Explicit feliciter dialogus [crossed out: nouissimus] in auariciam pogij florentini quem nemo usquam hominum Immo nec franciscus ipse Barbarus uidit. Si quid autem erroris in eo compertum fuerit non autori sed scriptori ascribat. ff. 16r–20v blank

The text is the revised version made by Poggio following the suggestions of Niccolò Niccoli. The original version was printed in Strasbourg (1513) and Basel (1538), whereas the revised edition was never printed, although it exists in many manuscripts. See H. Harth, "Niccolò Niccoli als literarischer Zensor: Untersuchungen zur Textgeschichte von Poggios 'De avaritia'," *Rinascimento*, n. s. 7 (1967) pp. 29–53 (Marston MS 53 cited as unseen on p. 40), with some readings from the two versions compared on pp. 47–49. The text has been glossed by a contemporary hand, in both Latin and German.

Paper (watermarks: similar in design and proportions, but with prominent sewing dots, to Piccard Anker II.182, 200), ff. iii (paper) + 20 + iii (paper), 285 x 210 (228 x 140) mm. 44 long lines. Frame-ruled in hard point.

I–II^{10}. Catchword, with flourishes on both sides, along lower edge in center, f. 10v.

Written in elegant bâtarde by a single scribe.

Heading, f. 1r, in red. Outline of initial, incomplete, occurs at beginning of text, f. 1v.

Binding: place uncertain, s. xx. Limp vellum case.

Although the introduction states that Stephanus Nouarie copied the manuscript in Rome for Antonius Ricius, the hand does not correspond to that in London, B. L. Harl. 2993, a manuscript written in Venice in 1437 by Stephanus Novarie (cf. *Colophons*, v. 5, no. 17485). The physical format, watermarks, script and contemporary annotations in German suggest, moreover, that Marston MS 53 was copied further North, perhaps in Germany, in the middle of the 15th century. It is possible that the introductory comments of the scribe were copied from the exemplar which was originally written in Rome. Unidentified sale notice [?], in French, in library files. Purchased from Lathrop C. Harper, Inc., in 1954 by Thomas E. Marston (bookplate).

secundo folio: racio haberi

Bibliography: Faye and Bond, p. 70, no. 53.

Marston MS 55 Florence, ca. 1445–50
Nonius Marcellus, De compendiosa doctrina Pl. 18

ff. 1r–130r *Senium est tedium et odium dictum a sene*ctute quod senes omnibus odio sunt et tedio . . . persecutus aristoteles animancium omnium ortus uictus figuras. *Finis. Amen.* f. 130v ruled, but blank

The books are in the following order: I–II, IV–XV, XVII–XX, III; W. M. Lindsay, ed., Teubner (1903), 3 vols; Aldo Lunelli, "L'editio princeps del capitolo III di Nonio," *Res Publica Litterarum* 9 (1986) pp. 193–202 (cited p. 198). The text is very corrupt: beginning in the latter portion of Book IV and Books V–XI the text of entries is often omitted and sections are frequently abridged; Books XII–XX and III are essentially complete. Passages containing Greek are handled in three ways: first, by omitting the Greek and leaving no space for its later insertion; second, by transliterating the Greek into Roman letters; third, by leaving a large blank space where the Greek was presumably to be inserted. Decorative initials appear at the beginning of each book (except for VIII which begins without a break at the conclusion of VII) and, for those books whose contents are arranged alphabetically (II–IV), at the first entry for each letter.

Parchment, ff. iii (modern parchment) + 130 + iii (modern parchment), 283 x 195 (179 x 115) mm. 39 long lines. Double vertical bounding lines, often not quite full length (Derolez 13.31); ruled in pale brown ink. Single pricking in inner margin, 68 mm. below bottom line, and in outer margin, 3 mm. below bottom line.

I–XIII^{10}. Vertical catchwords perpendicular to text in gutter (Derolez 12.7). Quire and leaf signatures (e.g., a1, a2, a3, etc.) in lower right corner, recto.

Written in a small upright humanistic cursive script by a single scribe who began copying the text with a single line of majuscules; written below top line.

According to A. C. de la Mare the decoration is possibly by the Florentine artist Giovanni Varnucci (d. 1457) in his early style. Folio 1r with partial border in upper and inner margins; white vine-stem ornament on blue, green and pink ground with grey and pale yellow dots, terminating in penwork with gold balls. At the left upper corner vine-stem ornament is inhabited by a red-winged putto being attacked by a bird. Historiated initial, 9-line, gold, against a blue, green and pink ground with white vine-stem ornament, and a medallion with the profile of a man, dressed in a red and green cap and red robes against blue ground (for a detail of this medallion see Garzelli, *Miniatura fiorentina*, p. 54, no. 58: middle photo on the left, incorrectly identified as MS 438). Numerous small initials, 4-line, gold on blue, pink and green or blue and pink rectangular grounds with white and pale yellow filigree.

Binding: England, s. xx, after 1926. Dark green pigskin, gold-tooled with the arms of C. H. St. John Hornby on the upper side; title on spine. Edges gilt.

Written in Florence ca. 1445–50; early modern provenance unknown, although stamps (now mostly erased) of the Minutoli Tegrimi family of Lucca on ff. 1r, 130r and v ("Di casa Minutoli Tegrimi") suggest it may have belonged to this family as early as the 15th century; for other manuscripts with this stamp see *Abbey Cat.*, p. 55, n. 2 and p. 53, fig. 18 for detail of stamp. Illustrated in De Marinis sale cat. VIII (1908) no. 47; bought from De Marinis in 1926 (Hoepli, Milan, cat. 44) by C. H. St. John Hornby (M. 65; booklabel inside front cover; notes on f. i recto; armorial binding). Acquired from Hornby by J. R. Abbey (bookplate), in 1946 when he acquired other manuscripts from the Hornby collection; Abbey's note in ink on final flyleaf: "J. A. 3207/ 15: 9: 1946." Belonged to H. Harvey Frost, whose collection was dispersed in the 1950s. Purchased from Davis and Orioli in 1955 by L. C. Witten (inv. no. 533), who sold it the same year to Thomas E. Marston (bookplate).

secundo folio: Numquam dum ego

Bibliography: Faye and Bond, p. 70, no. 55.

Marston MS 56 — Italy, 1465

Saints' Lives, etc., in It.

1. f. ii recto: Idus mar. Prima hetas fuit ad [*sic*] adam vsque noe et fuit annis . . . ; Seconda [*sic*] hetas fuit ad noe vsque ad abram et fuit annis . . . ; Tersia [*sic*] hetas fuit ad abram vsque ad Davit et fuit annis . . . ; Quarta hetas fuit ad Davit vsque ad tranxmigrationis populi Iudaici et fuit annis . . . ; Quinta hetas fuit ad tranxmigrasione [*sic*] vsque ad nativitate domini nostri ihesu christi et fuit annis . . . ; Sexta hetas est ad nativitate domini nostri ihesu christi vsque ad cumsumationem seculi. ff. ii verso-iii recto blank, except for notes on provenance

   List of the 6 ages of the world.

2. f. iii verso [List of contents with each entry followed by the folio number:] De lo comensamento de lo mondo; De la promera hetae; De la

terssa hetae; De la seconda hetae; Como ioxepo fo uenduo; Como moizes nasse; Como dee manda la mana in lo dezerto; Como lo nostro segnor dee de li x comandamenti a moizes; Como lo pouo d'issrael auem ree; Como davit fo cinto per ree et amassa lo zigante; Como davit fo eleto ree e incomenssa la quarta hetae; Como saramon regna in gerussallem; Como nabucdanazor preizu gerussallem e incomessa [*sic*] la quinta hetae; Como lo nostro segno nasse e incomenssa la sexta hetae; Como lo nostro segno ze in egito; Como lo nostro segno torna in terra di gudea; De lo comensamento de la passom; De como la anima de christo ze a lo linbo; De la resuressiom de messe ihesu christe; De la uendeta de messe ihesu christe faita per tito e uespexiano; De la natiuite de la nostra dona; De la nonsaciom de la nostra dona; De la senciom de la nostra dona; De monti miracoli de la nostra dona; De la passiom de l'imagem de christe; De la invenciom de la santa croxe de me[sse] ihesu christe; De la exartaciom de la santa croxe; De la invenciom de messe san miche; De lo sermon de li angeri; De antechriste e de lo di de lo zuixo; De lo sermon de li apostori e de messe san zoane apostoro; De lo sermon de messe san pe e poro apostori; De la lezenda de messe san pe apostoro; De la lezenda de messe san poro apostoro; De lo sermo[n] e de la lezenda de messe santo andrea apostoro; De la lezenda de messe san thomao apostoro; De la lezenda de messe san berthome apostoro; De lo sermon de messe san mathe apostoro e euangelista; De la soa lezenda; De lo sermon de messe san gacomo apostoro e de la soa lezenda; De lo sermon de messe san feripo apostoro e de la soa lezenda; De la lezenda de messe san Iacomo Mao; De la lezenda de messe san simon e tade apostori; De la lezenda de messe san matia apostoro; De la lezenda de messe san Marcho apostoro e eliangelista; De la lezenda de Ioxepe abarimatia; De lo sermon de li martori; De la lezenda de messe san steuam primo Martiro; De la inuenciom de lo so santissimo corpo; De la lezenda de messe san lorensso martiro; De la lezenda de messe san cremento papa e martiro; De la lezenda de messe san trope martiro e pizano; De la lezenda de messe santo vstachio martiro; De la lezenda de messe santo christoffaro martiro; De la lezenda de messe santo sebastiano Martiro; De la lezenda de messe santo biaxio Martiro; De la nassiom de messe sa zoane Batesto; De quando e lincomenssa a bateza; De la morte de messe san zoane Batesto; De lo sermon de li santi conffesoi de messe ihesu christe; De la lezenda de messe san martin uescho e conffesao; De la lezenda de messe san baxirio uescho e conffesao; De la lezenda de messe santo grigo papa e conffesao; De la lezenda de messe santo agustino uescho e conffesao; De la lezenda de messe san beneito abao e eremita; De messe san bernardo abao e conffesao; De la lezenda de messe san domenego conffesao; De la lezenda de messe san fransescho conffesao; De li soi fioreti; De li soe stimate; De la lezenda de messe santo zerbonio uescho e conffesao; De la lezenda de Barlam e de Ioxaffa; De li trenta grai de messe san geronimo; De la soa lezenda; De monte vixiomi e miracori che fe christe per li soi mereti; [added:] De rei monaci chi zenno a la paxiom de christo.

3. ff. 1r–187v De lo comensamento de lo mondo o dixe in lo libero de genexis che in lo comensamento de lo mondo dee crea lo cel e la terra e la terra era vachua e tuto lo mondo era tenebrozo e lo spirito de dee si andaua surua le aigoe e tuto lo mondo era como vna balla roanda chi fosse faita de Morte cosse cossi como terra pree fogo chi fossem misse inter vna concha d'aigoa . . . Amen.

Lives of the Saints, in It., preceded by accounts of events in the Bible from both the Old and New Testaments. Folios 51 and 61 interchanged in rebinding.

Paper (thick, coarse; watermarks: similar in design to Briquet Ciseaux 3708 dated Genoa, 1465), ff. i (paper) + ii (bifolium, original front flyleaves) + 187 (contemporary foliation in Roman numerals, trimmed, is keyed to list of contents in art. 2; modern foliation lower right corner), 332 x 236 (242 x 162) mm. Ca. 42–57 long lines. Frame-ruled in hard point; remains of prickings for bounding lines in all margins.

I–XVIII^{10}, XIX^{7} [structure uncertain due to repairs]. Horizontal catchwords surrounded by flourishes in center of lower margin, verso.

Written by several scribes in unruly *mercantesca* script, above top line. Script becomes smaller and tighter toward end of codex.

Crudely executed title page, f. 1r, consisting of floral and foliage motifs in upper margin, scroll around column in inner margin, and, in outer margin, scroll around column terminating in elongated arm with the following text on the scroll (much rubbed and stained): "christus viuit/ christus regnat/ christus inperat/ et ab omni/ malo/ nos/ deffendat/ christus/ autem/ transiens/ per medium/ illorum/ ibat." In lower margin a coat of arms (damaged; probably: or, two columns gules); the letters *B* and *C* on either side in the bases of columns in inner and outer margins. The decoration of title page in bright red and green. Plain initials (some with simple foliage designs), headings, paragraph marks, pointing hands, and hands holding crosses or symbols of passions of martyrs (e.g., gridiron for Laurence), all in bright red, green, and/or black.

Folio 1 damaged; no loss of text.

Binding: Italy, s. xix. Rigid vellum case with two red labels on spine: "Trattati di storia sacra" and "Manuscritto 1360."

Written in Italy in the second half of the 15th century, probably in 1465, since the date (damaged) "M° cccc lxv die prima Octobris," written in the upper margin of f. 1r, is in the same hand as the beginning of the text. Contemporary signature on f. iii recto ("Iste liber est batiste de clauaro .d. luce"), the initials "B" and "C" on title page, the watermarks, and the arms (cf. entry for Chiavari di *Genova* in G. B. di Crollalanza, *Dizionario Storio-Blasonico* ... [Pisa, 1886] v. 1, p. 287) suggest that the codex was produced for Battista Chiavari in either Lucca or Genoa. Signature, s. xvi, in lower margin, f. 1r: "Di Ieronimo Lomellino de'l [one word illegible] luca." Purchased from Libreria Mediolanum of Milan (Dr. E. Pozzi) in 1956 by L. C. Witten (inv. no. 1348), who sold it in 1959 to Thomas E. Marston (bookplate).

secundo folio: Morto

Bibliography: Faye and Bond, p. 70, no. 56.

Marston MS 59 Northwestern Italy, ca. 1400; Netherlands, s. XV^1
Cicero, Epistolae ad familiares Pl. 12

1. ff. 1r–185r *M. T. Ciceronis Epistolarum liber primus incipit. Marcus Cicero salutem dicit publio lentulo proconsuli.* Ego omni officio ac potius pietate erga te. ceteris satisfacio omnibus. mihi ipse nunquam satisfacio ... tuosque occulos [*sic*] etiam si te ueniens in medio foro uidero. dissaniabor. me ama. Vale. *Epistolarum. M. T. C. liber xvj et vltimus ad Tironem explicit feliciter. Amen.*

As compared with D. R. Shackleton Bailey, ed., *Cicero: Epistulae ad familiares*, 2 vols. (Cambridge, 1977), Marston MS 59 is a complete copy of all 16 books in the traditional order, with the following differences: [1] Absent are leaves 116, 165, 166, the first and last of which would have contained illumination for the beginnings of Bks. 11 and 15. Missing text for f. 116 includes end of 10.34, all of 10.35, and beginning of 11.1 ("... ita ut sint amplius equitum// moliamur. quia ubi consistamus non habemus...."); missing text for ff. 165–166 includes 14.11–24 and beginning of 15.1 ("... cura diligenter. vale. vij. idus quintiles.// populi romani existimatur...").
[2] Misplaced is a large block of text which runs from within 8.2 to within 8.9, which is inserted as a whole into letter 9.15: on f. 77v (8.2.1) Vide modo, inquis. Non// (8.9.3) mihi litteris ostenderis; on f. 88v (9.15.5) nihil est in parietibus// (8.2.1) non me hercules nihil unquam enim; on f. 94r (8.9.3) Puto etiam, si nullam spem// (9.15.5) aut in tecto vitij.

[3] Peculiarities of the division and order of letters include: 1.2 and 1.3 are written as a single letter; the first sentence of 1.5b ("Hic quae ... scribi oportere") is written as part of 1.5a; 1.9 is written as three letters; 3.3 and 3.4 are written as a single letter; 8.8 is written as two letters; 11.28 is written before 11.27; 12.22 and 12.23 are written together, but with a note by the scribe and a red paragraph mark in text indicating that there should be a division; 12.25, 12.25a and 12.26 are written as a single letter; 15.9 is written before 15.7; 16.12 is missing.

[4] Several letters appear twice in the manuscript: on f. 78r, 2.12 follows 8.9; on ff. 90v–91r, 2.9 follows 8.5; on f. 93v, 2.11 follows 8.8; on f. 154v, 2.14 follows 13.49; on f. 160v, 12.29 follows 13.77.

[5] At the beginning of the codex Greek words are written neatly; at f. 83 a different hand appears to begin; at f. 85v and apparently thereafter, the blank spaces remain unfilled.

[6] The scribe has often entered variant readings both in margins and between lines.

2. f. 185r Epistola. C. fabricij et Emilij cons. Romanorum super proditione scripta ad regem pirrhum ... Consules Romani salutem dicunt Pirrho regi. [text:] Nos pro tuis iniurijs continuo animo commoti ... tu nisi caues iacebis. Pirrhus rex consulibus et populo romano ... restituit reddiditque. f. 185v blank

Extract from Aulus Gellius, *Noctes Atticae* III.8.8: *Epistula Fabricii et Aemilii consulum ad Pyrrhum regem*; P. K. Marshall, ed., OCT (1968) v. 1, pp. 143–44.

Parchment (hairside yellow and speckled), ff. i (paper) + i (modern parchment) + 182 (early foliation in Arabic numerals 1–185; ff. 116, 165, 166 missing) + i (modern parchment) + i (paper), 263 x 180 (180 x 117) mm. 32 long lines. Single vertical bounding lines, full length; ruled in pale brown ink or lead (Derolez 13.11). Prickings in upper and lower margins. One pricking in outer margin, 55 mm. below top line (Derolez 18.3).

I-XI^{10}, XII^{10} (-6, f. 116), XIII-XVI^{10}, XVII^{10} (-5, 6, ff. 165–166), XVIII^{10}, XIX^{6} (-6). Catchwords with dots and flourishes on either side and below, in center of lower margin, verso (Derolez 12.1).

Written in a neat fere-humanistic hand by a single scribe, below top line.

14 elegant illuminated initials and partial borders at the beginning of each of the 16 books (the opening pages of Books XII and XV have been excised). Initials, 5- to 3-line, blue with white filigree or red with gold filigree on cusped grounds of gold. Most of the illuminated initials filled with bust-length portraits, presumably of Cicero's correspondents, on red,

blue, or diapered ground. Some initials filled with vine scrolls with trilobe leaves in red with white highlights against gold ground. Partial borders, scrolling vine with trilobe leaves or acanthus in blue, pink, red, and gold with white highlights and green, red, and blue with gold highlights. Small figures of angels, dressed in green with gold wings in borders or margins, some playing musical instruments, one holding an open book, one holding the cloth of Veronica. Other marginal figures include the "Agnus Dei" and a pelican piercing its breast. The figures are all characterized by white faces, small angled black eyes, and a preference for green and gold, the green with contour lines in gold. Plain initials alternate red and blue. Rubrics throughout.

Binding: France [?], s. xix. Red velvet case with a dark green gold-tooled label: "M. T. Ciceronis Epistolae Ad Familiares MS. in Membranis." Gilt edges.

The text was copied in Northwestern Italy ca. 1400 and apparently brought to Northern Europe where according to J. Marrow (letter on file) the border decoration was added between ca. 1415 and 1431 by the Dutch illuminator called the "Master of the Brno Speculum" (see Exhib. Cat., *The Golden Age of Dutch Manuscript Painting* [New York, 1990] pp. 58 and 72–74 for the Brno Speculum and another manuscript containing a miniature by the same artist); it is possible that the "Master of the Brno Speculum" is identifiable with the "Master of Mary of Guelders" (Berlin, Preussische Staatsbibliothek, MS germ. qu. 42; *Golden Age, op.cit.*, no. 17) or that he was either an associate or a follower of the "Master of Mary of Guelders." Early provenance unknown. Unidentified bookstamp consisting of the initials "A. N." enclosed in a double circle, outer thick and inner thin, f. 1r. Belonged to Edward Craven Hawtrey (1789–1862; booklabel) who was Headmaster and Provost of Eton College; his sale (Sotheby and Wilkinson, 1 July 1853, no. 536, to Boone). From the collection of Sir Thomas Phillipps (no. 24346, written in pencil inside front cover); sold by W. H. Robinson Ltd. London. Modern note, in pencil, on front pastedown "A/V/22." Acquired from Dudley M. Colman, through C. A. Stonehill, in 1954 by Thomas E. Marston (bookplate).

secundo folio: eius orationi

Bibliography: Faye and Bond, p. 71, no. 59.

Marston MS 60 Naples [?], 1450-60
Leonardo Bruni, Epistolae familiares, etc.

We thank J. Hankins for his assistance with the text of this manuscript.

1. ff. 1r–89v *Epistolae familiares* of Leonardo Bruni, in nine books. F. Luiso, *Studi su L'Epistolario di Leonardo Bruni,* (= *Istituto Storico Italiano per il Medio Evo, Studi storici* fasc. 122–124 [Rome, 1980]), for first reference cited below; L. Mehus, ed., *Leonardi Bruni Arretini Epistolarum Libri VIII* (Florence, 1741), for references in parentheses. Headings in the manuscript were added by a later hand, s. xvi^{in}.

Book 1: I.3 (I.1); I.4 (I.2), with heading: "Adversario praeponitur, Pontificisque Secretarius eligitur"; letter of Coluccio Salutati to Innocent VIII, with heading: "Colucij Gratulatio ad Pontificem. [text:] [I]nnocentio pape Linus Coluccius Salutatus post humilem recommendationem et pedum obscula beatorum. Nescio cui magis. . ." (F. Novati, ed., *Epistolario di Coluccio Salutati* [Rome, 1904] vol. 4, pp. 105–09, ep. XIV.xv); I.6 (I.3); I.5 (I.4); I.7 (I.5); I.8 (I.6); I.9 (I.7); I.1 (I.8); I.13 (I.9); I.14 (I.10); I.15 (I.11); I.16 (I.12), dated "iiij Maii, ex Mutiliana, Mccccvj"; I.17 (I.13); I.18 (I.14); I.19 (I.15). Book 2: II.23 (II.1); II.1 (II.2); II.2 (II.3); II.3 (II.4); II.4 (II.5); II.7 (II.6); II.8 (II.7); II.9 (II.8); II.10 (II.[9]); II.12 (II.10); II.13 (II.11); II.14 (II.12); II.11 (II.13); II.20 (II.14); II.21 (II.15); II.22 (II.16); II.24 (II.17); II.25 (II.18); II.26 (II.19); II.27 (II.20); II.28 (II.21); II.29 (II.22). Book 3: III.1–3 (III.1–3); III.5 (III.4); III.7 (III.5); III.8 (III.6); III.10 (III.7); III.11 (III.8); III.12 (III.9); III.14 (III.10); III.15 (III.11); III.18 (III.12); III.19 (III.13); III.21 (III.14); III.22 (III.15); III.25 (III.16); III.27 (III.17), dated "Florentie xv Kal. Aprilis"; III.26 (III.18), dated "viij Kal. Januarii Rome"; III.28 (III.19); III.29 (III.20). Book 4: IV.1 (IV.1), dated "ex Urbe vij Kal. Januarii Mccccxij"; IV.2–4 (IV.2–4); IV.5 (IV.5), dated "Florentiae, Idibus Sept. Mccccxvj"; IV.12 (IV.14); IV.6 (IV.6), dated "Florentiae, iiij Kal. Decembris Mccccxvj"; IV.7–9 (IV.7–9); IV.18 (IV.10); III.13 (IV.11); IV.10 (IV.12); IV.11 (IV.13); IV.14 (IV.15), dated "Aretii, Idibus Juniis"; IV.16 (IV.16); IV.20 (IV.17); IV.24 (IV.18), dated "Florentie, ij Kal. Februarii Mccccxxj"; IV.25 (IV.19); IV.26 (IV.20); IV.27 (IV.21); IV.29 (IV.22); IV.30 (IV.23). Book 5: V.1–2 (V.1–2); III.23 (V.3); IV.22 (V.4); IV.31 (V.5); V.5 (V.8). Book 6: VI.1 (VI.1), dated "nonas octobris Florentiae Mccccxxviiij"; VI.2–3 (VI.2–3); VI.5 (VI.4); VI.6 (VI.5); VI.9 (VI.6); VI.10 (VI.7); VI.12 (VI.8); VI.13 (VI.9); VI.15 (VI.10); VI.16 (VI.11). Book 7: VII.1–6 (VII.1–6); VII.14 (VII.7), addressed "Leonardus Bartolomeo Senensi s.p.d."; VII.15 (VII.8); VII.16 (VII.9); VII.7 (VII.10). Book 8: VIII.4 (VIII.1); VIII.9 (VIII.2); VIII.10 (VIII.3); VIII.11 (VIII.4);

VIII.12 (VIII.5); VIII.13 (VIII.6), with eight lines at the conclusion omitted, expl.: "O pecudem! neque enim appellari hominem decet, cui tam insensatum iudicium sit. Vale."; VIII.14 (VIII.7); VIII.15 (VIII.8). Book 9: IX.2 (IX.1); IX.3 (IX.2); IX.4 (IX.3); IX.5 (IX.4); IX.7 (IX.6); IX.8 (IX.7); IX.9 (IX.8); IX.10 (IX.9); IX.11 (IX.10); IX.12 (IX.11); IX.13 (IX.12); IX.14 (IX.13).

2. ff. 90r–94r [Heading in upper margin:] Leonardi Aretinj prohemium in orationibus homeri. [text:] [A]dmirari non numquam soleo: cum alia permulta diuinitus apud homerum scripta ... repellas. non tamen par gratia atque honor tibi erit. finis orationis: phoenicis: amen. f. 94v ruled, but blank

   Selected speeches from Homer, *Iliad* IX (Oratio Ulixis, Responsio Achillis, Oratio Phoenicis), translated into Latin prose by Leonardo Bruni, with his preface. D. Mansi, ed., *Stephani Baluzii tutelensis Miscellanea novo ordine* ... (Lucca, 1762) v. 3, pp. 151–54; preface only in Baron, pp. 132–34.

   Arts. 3–135, the public letters of Leonardo Bruni, are numbered 1–132 by an 18th-century hand, but actually contain 131 letters and fragments of 20 others, with salutations and texts as follow. This portion of the manuscript is a direct copy of Vatican City, Biblioteca Apostolica Vaticana, Chigi J IV 119, ff. 156r–289v (written in Arezzo, 1449), but omits a number of texts included in the Chigi manuscript. None of these texts has been located in published sources. There are no headings or decorative initials for any of the letters in Marston MS 60; in addition, it is not always clear where the salutation ends and the text begins.

3. f. 95r [M]agnifici domini amici carissimi. [text:] Displicent nobis iniurie....

4. f. 95r [M]agnifici domini amici carissimi. [text:] Nobilis ac dilectissimus ciuis noster Orlandus de Medicis....

5. f. 95r [No salutation.] [P]resentibus litteris nostris eandem Dominam Magdalenam....

6. f. 95r-v [No salutation.] [S]pectabilis miles ciuis noster carissime....

7. f. 95v [D]omini Amici Reuerendi. [text:] Accedit ad presentiam uestram Ciuis noster dilectissimus.... [arts. 7 and 8 written as a single letter].

8. f. 95v Vir amice Reuerende. [text:] Ratio exigit ut pro iustitia....

9. ff. 95v–96r [D]omine amice Reuerendissime. [text:] Quia officium est magistratus. . . .

10. f. 96r [S]erenissime ac gloriosissime princeps. [text:] Necesse est tam in paruis rebus. . . .

11. f. 96r-v [V]ir amice carissime. [text:] Quia pene omnes gubernatores.

12. f. 96v [I]llustris ac excelse domine frater et amice carissime. [text:] Si eadem conditione forent ciues uestri. . . .

13. ff. 96v–97r [S]erenissime ac gloriosissime princeps ac benefactor noster singularis. [text:] Accedit ad pedes V. M. ciuis noster dilectus Jacobus Johannis de bischaris. . . .

14. f. 97r [I]llustris et excelse domine frater et amice carissime. [text:] Reuertitur uenetias vir bonus et spiritu feruens. . . .

15. f. 97r-v [I]llustris ac excelse domine frater et amice Reuerende. [text:] Inter occupationes maximas. . . .

16. f. 97v [I]llustris ac excelse domine frater et amice Reuerende. [text:] Prudentes uiri ac uobis plurimum dilecti. . . .

17. ff. 97v–98v [I]n Cristo pater et dominus post recomendationem. [text:] Audivimus literas quasdam diffamatorias civitatis nostre. . . .

18. ff. 98v–99r [S]anctissime ac Beatissime pater post humilem recommendationem. [text:] Non dubitamus, Beatissime Pater, quin multum displiciant. . . .

19. f. 99r [R]euerendo in christo patri et domino Domino Fratri Archiepiscopo Florentino. [text:] Que cum ita sit [*sic*] atque ut audiunt ciues nostri. . . .

20. ff. 99r–101r [No salutation.] [L]icet grauissimum sit mentibus nostris aduersus Cesaream Maiestatem. . . .

21. f. 101r-v [No salutation.] [F]raternus amore et beniuolentia singularis.

22. f. 101v [S]pectabilis domina amica nostra Reuerenda. [text:] Cum sicut accepimus. Dilectus ciuis noster Simon Antonij. . . .

23. ff. 101v–102r [S]anctissime ac Beatissime pater post humilem recomendationem. [text:] Quod [sc. Quam] fauorabiliter Sanctitas Vester se habuerit. . . .

This is the same letter as art. 78 below.

24. f. 102r-v [S]erenissime atque gloriosissime princeps et domine. [text:] Etsi per alias literas ciues omnes nostros. . . .

25. f. 102v [I]llustrissime ac excelse domine frater et amice Reuerende. [text:] Alias scripsimus M. V. recomictentes negotium dilectorum ciuium nostrorum N. et C. et heredum p. de pantaleonibus. . . .

26. f. 102v [S]pectabilis uir amice Reuerende. [text:] Singularis dilectio nostra quam erga uos. . . .

27. f. 102v [D]omine amice Reuerende. [text:] Quia audiuimus M. V. per hoc ipsum tempus. . . .

28. f. 103r [M]agnifici domini amici Reuerendi. [text:] Conquestus est grauiter apud nos. . . .

29. f. 103r [S]pectabilis domine amice Reuerende. [text:] Accepimus litteras uestro nomine scriptas. . . .

30. f. 103v [M]agnifici domini fratres Reuerendi. [text:] Gratias agimus Magnifice fraternitati uestre pro hijs. . . .

31. f. 103v [S]erenissime princeps pater et benefactor noster singularissime. [text:] Cum ad uestre ciuitatis obsequia nouiter condusserimus. . . .

32. f. 103v [I]llustris ac Magnifice domine. [text:] Magnifice Vir, rogamus ut nostro intuitu Recomendatos habere uelit. fratres germanos eiusdem. . . .

33. ff. 103v–104r [U]niuersis et singulis ad quos presentes aduenerint salutem et prosperos ad uota successus. [text:] Cum egregium et circumspectum virum Marioctium. . . .

34. f. 104r [I]llustres ac Magnifici fratres et amici Reuerendi. [text:] Super materia illa differenciarum. . . .

35. f. 104r-v [M]agnifici ac prudentes viri amici Reuerendi. [text:] Si iustitiam colit ciuitas uestra. . . .

36. f. 104v [P]riores Artium ac vexilefer [*sic*] iustitie populi et comunis florentie uniuersis et singulis dominis et officialibus et ceteris omnibus quibus hee nostre littere presentabuntur. [text:] Fidem certissimam et indubitatam uobis facimus per presentes litteras nostras. . . .

37. f. 105r [D]omini fratres Reuerendi. [text:] Cum olim sequuta fuisset pax ex nouissimo bello. . . .

38. f. 105r [D]omini Fratres Reuerendi. [text:] Super querela nobis facta per Oratorem. . . .

39. f. 105r-v [S]erenissima Regina mater nostra singularis. [text:] Iam pridem et meminisse debet. . . .

40. ff. 105v–106r [M]agnifici domini Amici Reuerendi. [text:] Si prouisio facta per populum uestrum. . . .

41. f. 106r [S]erenissime princeps pater et benefactor noster singularissime. [text:] Capta fuit dudum ut S. V. meminisse confidimus. . . .

42. f. 106r-v [S]pectabilis et honorabilis amice Reuerende. [text:] Solent qui conuiuia instituunt. . . .

43. f. 106v [I]llustris ac Magnifice domine frater et amice carissime. [text:] Quia semper fuit consuetum. . . .

44. ff. 106v–107r [I]llustris ac excelse domine frater et amice carissime. [text:] Ut possit Illustris D. V. intueri. . . .

45. ff. 107r–108r [I]llustris atque excelse domine frater et amice carissime. [text:] Dum sapientiam V. D. eximiam in maximis minibusque rebus. . . .

46. f. 108r [I]llustris ac excelse domine frater et amice Reuerende. [text:] Quoniam per effectum operis manifeste deprehendimus. . . .

47. f. 108r-v [I]llustris et excelse domine frater et amice carissime. [text:] Recensentes nobiscum ipsi sanctum illud. . . .

48. ff. 108v–109r [D]omini fratres carissimi. [text:] Sepius iam querelas nobis fecerunt comunitas et homines de Montepulciano. . . .

49. f. 109r-v [M]agnifici domini fratres carissimi. [text:] Veniens ad nos. Spectabilis vir Johannes eneri [*sic*]. . . .

50. ff. 109v–110r [No salutation.] [V]ellemus nos quidem serenissima regina ut qui ferebat. . . .

51. f. 110r [M]agnifice et amice noster carissime. [text:] Audiuimus non sine displicentia. . . .

52. f. 110r [M]agnifici domini amici Reuerendi. [text:] Audito casu prouidi uiri B. sandri talani ciuis nostri dilecti. . . .

53. f. 110r-v [M]agnifici uiri. [text:] Pro liberatione eiusdem ciuis nostri rerumque suarum restitutione ad ipsum. . . .

54. f. 110v [I]llustris et excelse domine frater et amice carissime. [text:] Non est dubium mentibus nostris. . . .

55. f. 110v [R]euerende in christo pater et domine. [text:] Licet nostris mentibus desiderium insideat. . . .

56. ff. 110v–111r [No salutation.] Receptis litteris claritatis uestre in quibus ad nos scribitis. . . .

57. f. 111r-v [M]agnifice domine amice carissime. [text:] Non alienum ab offitio hominis uidetur esse. . . .

58. f. 111v [R]euerende in christo pater et domine. [text:] Exposuerunt nobis quidem negotia florentini cleri. . . .

59. f. 111v [M]agnifici uiri et amici Reuerendi. [text:] Quia nonulli deuotionis populi forte ignari. . . .

60. f. 112r [M]agnifice domine et amice carissime. [text:] Quia experientia teste didicimus. . . .

61. f. 112r [U]niuersis et singulis ad quos presentes littere nostre peruenerit [*sic*] salutem [*salutem* expunged] et prosperos ad uota successus. [text:] Fidem uobis facimus per presentes quod facto solempni discursu. . . .

62. f. 112v [M]agnifice domine et amice carissime. [text:] Notum est non solum nobis uerumetiam uniuersis. . . .

63. f. 112v [M]agnifice vir amice carissime. [text:] Scribimus Magnifico domino Johanni de Uarrano. . . .

64. ff. 112v–113r [D]omine amice carissime. [text:] Recepimus uestras litteras super negotio hominum de pontito. . . .

65. f. 113r [R]euerende in christo pater et domine. [text:] Per litteras uenerabilium religiosarum monialium sancti silvestri. . . .

66. f. 113r [S]anctissime ac Beatissime pater post humilem recomendationem et pedum oscula beatorum. [text:] Cum spectabilis miles dominus Paulus de quiperno qui potestarie offitium in hac nostra civitate exercuit. Nunc finito offitio suo domum reuertatur atque ut ab eo percepimus. . . .

67. f. 113r-v [E]gregii uiri et amici Reuerendi. [text:] Cum spectabilis miles dominus petrus de piperno qui potestarie offitium in hac nostra ciuitate exercuit nunc finito offitio suo domum reuertatur. Noluimus pretermictere. . . .

68. ff. 113v–114r [M]agnifice domine et amice carissime. [text:] Si casus maleficij umquam accidit in quo boni domini. . . .

69. f. 114r [I]llustris ac Magnifice domine. [text:] Etsi non dubitamus celsitudinem vestram in multiplicibus uarijsque casibus. . . .

70. f. 114r-v [R]euerende vir pater quam amantissime. [text:] Quanta deuotione et quanta eximia caritate florentinus populus. . . .

71. f. 114v [M]agnifici domini fratres Reuerendi. [text:] Quia per capitaneos partis guelfi ciuitatis nostre ordinatum est certum equestrem. . . .

72. f. 114v [M]agnifici domini fratres Reuerendi. [text:] Audiuimus quemdam. Stefanum donati de Rassina....

73. f. 115r [M]agnifice domine amice carissime. [text:] Quia iustitie fauor semper est comendabilis libenter....

74. f. 115r-v [No salutation.] [C]ognoscimus Serenissime princeps et clementissime domine rengnum [*sic*] Vmgarie [*sic*]....

75. f. 115v [I]llustris ac excelse domine frater et amice carissime. [text:] Fuerunt dudum res quedam et merces....

76. f. 115v [M]agnifici uiri amici carissimi. [text:] Que per uestras litteras ad gaudium et letitiam....

77. ff. 115v–116r [S]pectabiles uiri amici Reuerendi. [text:] Aduentus Nobilis uiri I. borromei a nobis missi gratissimus proculdubio....

78. f. 116r-v [S]anctissime ac Beatissime pater post humilem recomendationem. [text:] Quam fauorabil[iter sanctitas uester] se habuerit et habeat erga Reuerendum in christo patrem Amerigum florenti[e archie]piscopum....

The same letter as art. 23 above.

79. f. 116v [I]llustris et excelse domine frater et amice carissime. [text:] Coniunctio nostra et hec scribendi assiduitas....

80. ff. 116v–117r [M]agnifice domine frater et amice. [text:] Fuit dudum in principio huius belli....

81. f. 117r [S]anctissime et Beatissime pater post humilem recommendationem. [text:] Exposuit nobis Reuerendus in christo pater et dominus pilius Archiepiscopus Ianuensis....

82. f. 117r [M]agnifici domini fratres nostri Reuerendi. [text:] Relatum nobis a commissario uestro scribitis multa et facta....

83. f. 117v [S]anctissime ac beatissime pater post humilem recomendationem. [text:] Scripsit nuper sanctitas vester nobis super negotio....

84. ff. 117v–118r [S]erenissime princeps et clementissime domine. [text:] Singularis deuotio, quam ciuitas nostra erga uos....

85. f. 118v [M]agnifici domini fratres carissimi. [text:] Fraternitas uestra sic litteras nostras interpretatur....

86. f. 118v [M]agnifici domini fratres amici Reuerendi. [text:] Audiuimus captum esse in ciuitate vestra....

87. ff. 118v–119r [R]euerende vir amice carissime. [text:] Scribimus spectabilibus viris *** et brargo [*sic*]. . . .

88. f. 119r [I]llustris et excelse domine frater et amice carissime. [text:] Alias scripsimus celsitudini uestre recommendantes. . . .

89. f. 119r-v [V]enerabiles et magnifici domini amici Reuerendi. [text:] Excitat nos dilectio singularis qua venerabilem uirum. . . .

90. f. 119v [M]agnifici domini fratres Reuerendi. [text:] Examinatis litteris vestris postremis. . . .

91. f. 119v [S]erenissime princeps et clementissime domine. [text:] In hijs litteris per quas iustitiam postulatur. . . .

92. f. 120r [R]euerende in christo pater et domine. [text:] Susceptis litteris uestris in quibus securitatem. . . .

93. f. 120r-v [R]euerende in christo pater. [text:] Quam inuiti ac prope horentes scribamus. . . .

94. f. 120v [R]euerendissime in christo pater et domine. [text:] Audiuimus ex ciuibus nostris dilectis Iohannem de cordutijs. . . .

95. ff. 120v–121r [S]erenissime princeps et clementissime domine. [text:] Est clementis mansuetudinisque vestre. . . .

96. f. 121r [M]agnifici domini fratres carissimi. [text:] Ciues quidam nostri ut uobis suggeritur. . . .

97. f. 121r [N]obilis uir amice carissime. [text:] Cognouimus relatione nobis facta pro parte consulum. . . .

98. f. 121v [M]agnifici domini fratres carissimi. [text:] Si alias scripserimus, M. V., pro liberatione B. de tizano quem ratione cuiusdam blasfemie condempnatum. . . .

99. f. 121v [M]agnifice domine ami[ce carissime]. [text:] Fuit dudum captus per hostes nostros I. Io. de orlandinis. . . .

100. ff. 121v–122r [M]agnifici Reuerendi carissimi [*sic*]. [text:] Si sepius scribimus M. V. F. in fauorem ciuium nostrorum. . . .

101. f. 122r [No salutation.] [Q]uare cum iustitia sit in facto et fauor in personis. . . .

102. f. 122r [R]euerendissime pater et prestantissime domine. [text:] Honestum simul et debitum uidetur esse. . . .

103. f. 122r [M]agnifici domini et amici Reuerendi. [text:] Litteras qui-

dem uestras plenas beniuolentie et singularis caritatis accepimus. . . .

104. f. 122r-v [S]anctissime ac beatissime pater post humilem recomendationem et pedum oscula beatorum. [text:] Et per litteras oratoris nostri penes s. v. . . .

105. f. 122v [S]anctissime ac beatissime pater post humilem recomendationem et pedum obscula [*sic*] beatorum. [text:] Per gratiam summi et inefabilis creatoris nostri a quo omnia bona descendunt. . . .

106. ff. 122v–123r [M]agnifici domini. [text:] Quia certissime scimus cuncta que ad prosperitatem. . . .

107. f. 123r [M]agnifice domine amice carissime. [text:] Etsi non dubitamus quin omnes florentini ciues. . . .

108. f. 123r [R]everendissime pater et domine. [text:] Quia preces eorum qui iustitiam. . . .

109. f. 123r [M]agnifici domini fratres Reuerendi. [text:] Duas per hos dies querelas habuimus. . . .

110. f. 123r-v Sanctissime ac Beatissime pater post humilem recomendationem. [text:] Ut primum per oratores ferarie consistentes. . . .

111. ff. 123v–124r [R]euerendissime pater et domine. [text:] Etsi opera R. P. V. in hoc sanctissimo ac acceptissimo pacis negotio. . . .

112. f. 124r [No salutation:] [C]um aliquid accidit deuotis fidelibus et subiectis uestris. . . .

113. f. 124r [I]llustris atque excelse domine. [text:] Sepius iam scripsimus celsitudini uestre. . . .

114. f. 124r [I]llustris atque excelse domine. [text:] Ut de bello dudum exorto maximam non [imme]rito. . . .

115. f. 124r-v [R]euerendissime in christo pater et domine. [text:] Quoniam per dei gratiam pax. . . .

116. f. 124v [I]llustris et excelse domine amice carissime. [text:] Suscepimus litteras I. M. V. et cum illis documentum publicum ratificationis facte. . . .

117. f. 124v [R]euerendissime in christo pater et domine. [text:] Singularis fidutia quam prestitit nobis benignitas S. D. . . .

118. ff. 124v–125r [M]agnifice domine amice carissime. [text:] Scripsimus nuper ad M. V. desiderium nostrum. . . .

119. f. 125r [R]everendissime in christo pater. [text:] Quoniam in hijs que nobis scribitis. . . .

120. f. 125r-v [M]agnifice domine amice carissime. [text:] Debitum est ut talibus viribus qualem [per] presentem. . . .

121. f. 125v [M]agnifice domine amice carissime. [text:] Nos quidem libenter fauemur honori fidelium nostrorum. . . .

122. ff. 125v–126r [I]llustris et excelse domine amice carissime post salutem. [text:] Et animos ad uobis grata largitor paratos nostri semper fuit. . . .

123. f. 126r [M]agnifice domine amice carissime. [text:] Audiuimus non sine molestia animorum nostrorum. . . .

124. f. 126r [I]llustris atque excelse domine frater et amice carissime. [text:] Gerentes singularem deuotionis effectum. . . .

125. f. 126r [M]agnifici uiri amici Reuerendi. [text:] Dignum simul gratumque existimamus. . . .

126. f. 126r-v [E]gregie doctor. [text:] Non nichil admirationis actulit nobis tanta properatio recessus uestri. . . .

127. f. 126v [R]euerendissime in christo pater et domine. [text:] Etsi uestra intercessio pro Nobili illo de uiuario. . . .

128. f. 126v [R]euerendissime in christo pater et domine. [text:] Recolenda memoria clarissimi uiri colucij salutati. . . .

129. ff. 126v–127v In this art. are the exordia of 14 different letters with the following salutations and incipits:

a. [No salutation.] [Q]uia illa que sunt comunis utilitatis debent ab omnibus prompto fauore . . . ; b. [No salutation.] [Q]uia ut alias scripsimus per ipsa belli tempora . . . ; c. [No salutation.] [S]i sepius scripsimus M. fraternitati V. pro liberatione . . . ; d. [No salutation.] [A]ccidit nuper casus cuidam dilecto ciui nostro . . . ; e. [No salutation.] [F]aciunt liberalissime oblationes uestre nobis per uestras litteras . . . ; f. [No salutation.] [P]recipua singularisque fidutia Quam in uestra paternitate . . . ; g. [S]erenissime princeps et clementissime domine. Plerumque fiunt querele apud principes et dominos . . . ; h. [No salutation.] [I]n multis occupationibus et rebus agendis . . . ; i. [No salutation.] [C]ommendamus diligentiam uestram et circa opera istic facta . . . ; j. [No salutation.] [Q]uanta cum fidutia recurramus ad sublimissimam S. V. in cunctis casibus . . . ; k. [No salutation.] [F]aciunt liberalissime oblationes uestre et cum effectu operam ... ; l. [No salutation.] [E]xigunt et familie prestantia merita ... ; m. [No salutation.] [N]ollemus ut territoria et loca nostra ... ; n. [M]agnifici domini fratres carissimi. [text:] [Q]uia laudabile semper fuit et honestati consonum....

130. f. 127v [M]agnifici domini fratres Reuerendi. [text:] Comendationum genera multiplicia sunt....

131. f. 127v [M]agnifici domini fratres Reuerendi. [text:] Scripsimus litteras commendatiuas pro duobus....

132. ff. 127v–128r In this art. are one complete letter and the exordia of five additional letters: a. [M]agnifice uir amice carissime. [text:] Compellunt nos multiplicitia et maxime [*sic*] atque pene incomportabilia ... compellamur. Datum.; b. [I]llustris atque excelse domine frater et amice Reuerende. [text:] [A]licit nos dulcedo ... ; c. [No salutation.] [S]e [*sic*] ipse paruerit mandatis nostris ... ; d. [No salutation.] [Q]uotidie admiratio nobis crescit ... ; e. [No salutation.] [N]on obmictimus nos quidem quotiens ... ; f. [No salutation.] [F]iduciam capimus M. D. de M. V....

133. f. 128r-v [I]llustris et excelse domine frater et amice Reuerende. [text:] [O]ptaremus no[s quidem in hac] liberalissima....

134. f. 128v In this art. are two letters, the first giving a complete text, the second fragmentary at the end. a. [P]riores artium et uexillifer iustitie populi et comunis florentie vniuersis et singulis uicarijs capitaneis potestatibus ac ceteris officialibus et sudditis uestris ad quos presentes aduenerint. [text:] Cum Illustris princeps et generosus dominus dominus petrus ... ; b. [Priores ar]tium et uexillifer iustitie populi et comunis florentie. Specta[bilibus uiris] consulibus ciuitatis cacrouie [*sic*] uel alijs uniuersis et singulis [officialibus con]stitutis ad quos presentes litteras peruenerint. Salutem et [prosperos ad uo]ta successus. [text:] Fidem uobis et uestris singulis facimus per presentes....

135. f. 129r-v [Heading, in upper margin:] Ad regem Vngarie. [salutation:] [S]erenissime rex et gloriossime princeps post humilimam recomendationem. [text:] Gloria et magnitudo et omnis prosperitas sit in perpetuum tibi gloriosissime rex ... negotijs reportent. Datum.

136. ff. 129v–130r Ad Imperatorem oratio pro parte Comunis Florentie. [text:] [V]idimus stellam eius in oriente Et uenimus adorare eam [*sic*]. Verba sunt Macthei Euangeliste in capitulo [lacuna in ms]. Serenissime atque gloriosissime princeps. non sine probabili ratione similitudo facta est ab antiquis ... cum dabitur locus et tempus tui Maiestati seriosius exprimemus. For f. 130v see provenance below.

Leonardo Bruni, unpublished diplomatic oration, probably written for Florentine orators attending the coronation of Frederick II as King of the Romans in 1440.

Parchment, ff. i (paper) + 130 + v (paper, watermarks similar to Briquet Oiseau 12250), 255 x 185 (187 x 128) mm. 32 long lines. Frame-ruled in pale brown ink.

I^{12}, $II\text{–}VII^{10}$, VIII^{12}, $IX\text{–}XII^{10}$, XIII^{6}. Vertical catchwords perpendicular to text along inner bounding line, verso.

Written in a semi-gothic bookhand with notarial features; marginal notes, in red, by a later hand in humanistic cursive script.

Illuminated title page, f. 1r, with three-quarter border, fleshy curling acanthus, red and green with some touches in blue and gold on parchment ground, in inner, upper and outer margins (partly rubbed). Illuminated initial, composed of foliage, green, red, mauve, yellow, and gold, against blue ground, edged in yellow. In center of lower margin, unidentified arms (partially effaced) clearly painted over earlier arms. Many flourished initials alternate in blue and red with red or ochre pen designs, with flourishes often extending the whole length of page. After 23r, spaces for initials remain unfilled; remains of guide letters for decorator.

Rodent damage at end of manuscript often affects text.

Binding: Italy, s. xix. Quarter bound in vellum with semi-limp paper sides. Traces of title, in ink, on spine. Off-set impression of earlier turn-ins on f. 130v.

Written probably in Southern Italy, perhaps in Naples, in the middle of the 15th century according to A. C. de la Mare. Owned and annotated by an unidentified Italian humanist (Rome, s. XVI^{in}) who added brief marginal notations in red at the beginning of many letters, as well as the inscription on f. 130v: "M D viij Die. xj. Aprilis: hora v. noctis: obijt Guido Vbaldus Dux Vrbinj." Early monogram [?] on f. 130v at top of leaf. Notes, s. xix, in ink in margins of manuscript and on flyleaves; these notes by the same 19th century collector as those in Marston MS 61. The collector designated Marston MS 60 as "Vol. I" and Marston MS 61 as "Vol. II" since each contained letters not found in the other. There is, however, no certain evidence to indicate that the two volumes were originally intended to complement one another; except for the same style of 19th-century binding, the physical format of the two codices is completely different. Purchased from Libreria Mediolanum of Milan (Dr. E. Pozzi) in 1955 by L. C. Witten (inv. no. 775), who sold it the same year to Thomas E. Marston (bookplate).

secundo folio: sanctitati

Bibliography: Faye and Bond, p. 71, no. 60.

Marston MS 61 Northeastern Italy, s. XV$^{3/4}$
Leonardo Bruni, Epistolae familiares, etc.

We thank J. Hankins for his assistance with the text of this manuscript.

1. ff. 1r–59r *Epistolae familiares* of Leonardo Bruni, including the first two books, part of the third, and selected letters from the remaining. F. Luiso, *Studi su L'Epistolario di Leonardo Bruni* (= *Istituto Storico Italiano per il Medio Evo, Studi storici* fasc. 122–124 [Rome, 1980]), for first reference cited below; L. Mehus, ed., *Leonardi Bruni Arretini Epistolarum Libri VIII* (Florence, 1741), for references in parentheses.

   Book 1: I. 3 (I.1); I.4 (I.2); letter of Coluccio Salutati to Innocent VIII, beginning: Nescio cui magis ... (F. Novati, ed., *Epistolario di Coluccio Salutati* [Rome, 1904] vol. 4, pp. 105–09, ep. XIV.xv); I.6 (I.3); I.5 (I.4); I.7 (I.5); I.8 (I.6); I.9 (I.7); I.1 (I.8); I.13 (I.9); I.14 (I.10); I.15 (I.11); I.16 (I.12); I.17 (I.13); I.18 (I.14); I.19 (I.15). Book 2: II.23 (II.1); II.1 (II.2); II.2 (II.3); II.3 (II.4); II.4 (II.5); II.7 (II.6); [II.8 omitted]; II.9 (II.8); II.10 (II.[9]); II.12 (II.10); II.13 (II.11); II.14 (II.12); [II.11 omitted]; II.20 (II.14); II.21 (II.15); II.22 (II.16); II.24 (II.17); II.25 (II.18); II.26 (II.19); II.27 (II.20); II.28 (II.21); II.29 (II.22). Book 3: III.1 (III.1); III.2 (III.2); III.3 (III.3); III.5 (III.4); after this letter (f. 40v), catchwords "Quod ad me" as though beginning letter III.7 (III.5); f. 41r-v blank; f. 42r III.2 (III.2), repeated from 39v; f. 42r III.5 (III.4), repeated from f. 40v; f. 42r-v III.11 (III.8); ff. 42v–43r VI.16 (VI.11); f. 43r IV.27 (IV.21); f. 43r-v III.22 (III.15); ff. 43v–44r III.25 (III.16); ff. 44r–45r IV.8 (IV.8); f. 45r III.13 (IV.11), with the explicit written as perpendicular catchwords at the bottom right-hand corner of page; ff. 45v–46r IV.14 (IV.15); f. 46r-v VIII.3 (X.10); ff. 46v–48v Leonardo Bruni, Preface to his version of Aristotle's *Politics*, [heading:] Leonardo Aretini prefatio ad dominum Eugenium papam quartum. [text:] Libros Politicorum multis a me vigiliis ... tue beatitudinis prolixitate nimia detineam. [= *Epistola super translatione Politicorum Aristotelis*, in Baron, pp. 70–73]; f. 48v VIII.5 (X.11); ff. 48v–49r IX.16 (X.16); f. 49r (X.17); f. 49v VI.11 (X.18); ff. 49v–50v IX.17 (X.20); ff. 50v–51r VII.9 (X.21); f. 51r–v IX.19 (X.22); ff. 51v–52r VII.11 (X.23); f. 52r–v I.21 (X.6); ff. 52v–53r III.17 (X.2); f. 53r II.15 (X.1); ff. 53v–55r I.20 (X.19); f. 55r–v VII.14 (VII.7); f. 55v–56r VII.5 (VII.5), fragmentary at the end "... ut Mediolanum urbs tam populosissima iam dudum fuerit atque sit, et cetera" [= Mehus, *op.cit.*, II, pp. 90–91, line 5]; f. 56r-v VII.10 (X.9); ff. 56v–59r VIII.4 (VIII.1), with the postscript of the Ravenna manuscript, ed. Luiso, *op.cit.*, p. 139, note 12; f. 59r V.3 (V.6).

2. ff. 59v–60v Cicero, *Epistolae*; extracts.

3. ff. 61r–62r [Heading:] De ortu Regis francorum sic legitur in panteon particula uigesima tertia capitulo primo. [text:] Tempore igitur quo eneas post [*s* deleted] troiae destructionem in italiam uenit priamus iunior nepos magni priami . . . dicti qui ultra danubium fertur in Europam. f. 62v blank

4. 63r–78r [Heading:] Sexti Ruffi viri consularis ad Valentianum [*sic*] rerum gestarum populi romani. [text:] Breuem fieri clemetia [*sic*] tua precepit: parebo libens preceptis . . . tibi palma pacis accedat Gloriosissime principe Valentine Auguste. Τελος. f. 78v ruled, but blank

   J. W. Eadie, ed., *The Breviarium of Festus: A Critical Edition with Historical Commentary*, University of London Classical Studies V (1967) text: pp. 1–69.

Paper (several unidentified watermarks in gutter), ff. i (paper) + 78 + i (paper), 217 x 148 (ff. 1–40: 152 x 92; ff. 42–60: 150 x 96; ff. 61–78: 131 x 80) mm. Page format varies: usually single vertical bounding lines; single upper and/or lower horizontal bounding lines. Ruled in lead. Prickings in all margins except inner.

I–III^{10}, IV^{12}, V^{8}, VI^{12}, VII^{8} (–7, 8). Vertical catchwords along inner bounding line, verso.

Written by two scribes in humanistic cursive script, above top line: Scribe 1: ff. 1–60; Scribe 2: ff. 61–78.

Spaces left for headings and decorative initials remain unfilled.

Binding: Italy, s. xix. Quarter bound in vellum with semi-limp paper sides. Traces of title and designs [from palimpsest?], in ink, on spine.

Written in Northeastern Italy in the third quarter of the 15th century; some contemporary and slightly later annotations by scribe and other hands. Early provenance otherwise unknown. Notes, s. xix, in ink in margins of manuscript and on front flyleaf; these notes by the same 19th century collector as those in Marston MS 60. The collector designated Marston MS 60 as "Vol.I" and Marston MS 61 as "Vol. II" since each contained letters not found in the other. There is, however, no certain evidence to indicate that the two volumes were originally intended to complement one another; except for the same style of 19th-century binding, the physical formats of the two codices are completely different. Purchased from Libreria Mediolanum of Milan (Dr. E. Pozzi) in 1955 by L. C. Witten (inv. no. 776), who sold it the same year to Thomas E. Marston (bookplate).

secundo folio: ipsa Loci

Bibliography: Faye and Bond, p. 71, no. 61.

Marston MS 62 — Northern Italy, s. $XV^{2/4}$
Boccaccio, De mulieribus claris

1. f. 1r-v blank, except for title "De mulieribus claris" on f. 1r; f. 2r-v *De Eua prima parente. Capitulum Primum/ De Semiramide Assiriorum Regina. Capitulum Secundum/ . . . De Tertia Emilia Primi Africani coniuge. Capitulum Lxxij^m^./ De Dripetrua Laodecie Regina. Capitulum Lxxiij^m^.//*

   Table of contents, in red throughout, incomplete at end.

2. ff. 3r–80r Iohannis Boccacij de Certaldo de Mulieribus claris ad Andream de Acciaiolis de Florentia Alte Ville comitissam. Liber incipit feliciter. [dedication:] Scripsere iam dudum nonnulli ueterum sub conpendio de uiris illustribus libros. et nostro euo latiori tamen uolumine et accuratiori stilo . . . [text, f. 3v:] *De Eua Prima Parente Capitulum Primum.* Scripturus igitur quibus fulgoribus mulieres claruerunt insignes a matre omnium [?] sumpsisse exordium non apparebit indignum . . . quam in nullius comodum laceratum dentibus Inuidorum depereat. Amen. ff. 80v–82v ruled, but blank

   Boccaccio, *De mulieribus claris*, with dedication to Andrea Acciaiuoli; V. Branca, general ed., *Tutte le opere di G. Boccaccio* (Verona, 1967), v. 10 edited by V. Zaccaria, pp. 1–579.

Paper (watermarks: Briquet Tête de boeuf 14717 and similar to Piccard Ochsenkopf XII.123), ff. ii (paper) + 82, 286 x 210 (194 x 114) mm. 39 long lines. Single vertical bounding lines, ruled in lead; rulings for text in pale brown ink. Remains of prickings.

I^3 (1 = front pastedown), II^9 (structure of I–II uncertain; loss of text in art. 1), $III–VIII^{10}$, IX^{12} (12 = back pastedown). Horizontal catchwords, center of lower margin, verso.

Text written in a well spaced gothic bookhand with humanistic features by a single scribe, below top line. Art. 1 and rubrics added in similar script by another hand.

Folio 3r, partial border, of poor quality: in lower margin, a patch of green grass with two women seated, one dressed in red, the other in green and white, supporting a shield with unidentified arms (gules, 3 helmets sable [in outline only]), a later addition. From the patch of grass oak branches with leaves and acorns extend into inner and upper margins. In inner margin, a fox chasing a hare. Folio 80r, a medallion framed in red and pink and four small gold flowers, with an unidentified monogram [letters u, p, h, a, c, l, o?] in gold against blue ground. One pen-and-ink initial, 8-line, blue with pale red penwork. Plain initials alternate in red and blue. Headings in red (ff. 1r–7r only). Many initials touched with red. Guide letters for decorator throughout.

Binding: Italy, s. xv. Parchment stays from contemporary document (see provenance below) adhered to inner and outer conjugate leaves of quires. Original wound sewing on three tawed skin, slit straps fastened in channels in flush wooden boards. A primary endband, caught up on the spine, is sewn on tawed skin cores. Remains of red secondary embroidery. The spine is square and lined with tawed skin between central supports.

Covered in kermes pink, tawed skin with corner tongues, the sides divided into triangles with right angled and diagonal fillets. Three fastenings, the catches on the lower board and stubs of green fabric straps on the upper board which is cut in to accommodate them. Eight star-shaped bosses on the upper board (one wanting) and five on the lower, each board with four bosses on its spine edges. Inscription on upper cover: "de mulieribus claris." Written in ink on fore edge: "LXXXVIII" with a helmet on each side. Label on lower board wanting.

Written in Northern Italy in the second quarter of the 15th century; the design of the watermarks (Briquet 14717: Brescia 1433–42) and the geographical names (Erbusco, Montirone) mentioned on the strips of a parchment document used as binding stays suggest a place of origin near Brescia. Unidentified arms, with "Cretulia" and "Thurj" added on either side, and inscription in the lower margin of f. 2v: "Quid spectas Thurum [with 3 helmets] sunt hec insignia. Thuris/ Donarunt Sacre Iuno Minerua Venus/ Cretulia" [written below], and marginalia in arts. 1 and 2, appear to be nearly contemporary additions by a single person. Inscription, s. xvi, on f. 82v: "liber plebanj Brotij et amicorum." Stamp on f. 4r: three helmets with ribbons scrolling around shield. Purchased in 1954 from C. A. Stonehill (inv. no. 3030) by Thomas E. Marston (bookplate).

secundo folio: [text, f. 4:] aut incude

Bibliography: Faye and Bond, p. 71, no. 62.

Marston MS 63 Siena, 1465
Guarino da Verona; Francesco Barbaro, et al.

I. 1. f. 1r *Apretiatum ducatos duos/ Tabula operum que in hoc volumine sunt. Existimatus per me Ranerium constat codex in totum libras quatuor bononinorum de argento monete Rauenatis.* [table of contents:] *Guarini veronensis Ipotesia ad Ieronimum suum de vite Institutione et moribus. a foglie 2 ... De laudibus phylosophie In ethicis In Initio studij senis oratio habita per bartholomeum senensem phisichum et philosophum Insignem. a foglie 61.*

Appraisal of the codex; table of contents, in red throughout.

2. ff. 1v–3v *Ipotesia/ Guarini ueronensis oratoris et gramatici nobilissimi ad Ieronimum suum Ipotesia. De Vite Institutione et obseruantia bonorum morum.* Tandem tuas accepi litteras dilecte ... Mathe [*sic*] noua uirtute puer sic itur ad astra. *Finis. Ipothesie guarini.*

Guarino da Verona, *Ipotesia ad Hieronymum (filium) suum*, written in 1443; R. Sabbadini, ed., *Epistolario di Guarino Veronese* (Miscellanea di Storia Veneta per cura della R. Diputazione veneta di storia patria, ser. III) v. 9 (Venice, 1916) pp. 436–43, no. 785.

II. 3. ff. 4r–40r *ffrancisci barbari ueneti de re uxoria libellus incipit.* [letter:] Maiores nostri. Laurenti carissime beniuolentia uel necessitudine sibi coniunctos in nuptijs donare consueuerunt ... [text, f. 5r; no heading:] Antequam de delectu uxoris et offitio dicere Incipio de ipso coniugio prius pauca michi dicenda sunt ... uel quod ab optima fide ac animo certe tibi deditissimo proficiscitur. finis. *finis.*

Francesco Barbaro, *De re uxoria*, with the prefatory letter to Lorenzo di Giovanni de' Medici (1395–1440); A. Gnesotto, ed., *Atti e memorie della R. Accademia di scienze, lettere ed arti in Padova*, n. s. 32 (1915–16) pp. 23–100.

4. f. 40r [Heading, in margin:] *Que in bona requirantur uxore/ Rubrica.* In bona sponsa ista requiruntur ut sit frequens et deuota quo ad deum. subdita quo ad mariti obsequium. affabilis et benigna quo ad miseros ... et plus curat habere liberos dei gracia quam nature. finis. *finis.*

Anonymous text, 12 lines, listing the qualities of a good wife.

5. ff. 40r–42r *Beatus bernardus ad Raimundum militem de cura et modo rei familiaris utilius gubernarde* [sic]. *Incipit.* Gratioso et felici militi Raimundo de Castro ambrosij Bernardus In senium deductus salu-

tem et pacem. Doceri petis a nobis de cura et modo rei familiaris ... quibus ademptis bibat cum eo doloris calicem quem optauit ad quem eam deducant merita sue dapnabilis [*sic*] senectutis. *finis*.

Ps.-Bernard of Clairvaux, *Epistola de gubernatione rei familiaris*; PL 182.647–51 (Epistola 456); R. Avesani, *Quattro miscellanee medioevali e umanistiche* (Rome, 1967) pp. 42–43.

6. ff. 42r–44v *Antonii aurispe. inter Scipionem. Romanum Alexandrum. macedonicum et Anibalem cartaginensem apud Minos controuersia. quis eorum preferendus sit et laude dignior Incipit*. Cum in rebus bellicis semper. Ceteris uero animi uirtutibus aliqua etate cuntis gentibus romanos prestitisse non modo apud latinos set apud grecos ... [dialogue begins, f. 42v:] *Alexander*. Me o libice preponi decet melior equidem sum. *Anibal*. Immo uere. me ... et tertius si uidetur anibal. neque Is quidem spernendus est. *finis*. Laude pacem superis scipio. rex alter. tertius est libicus. *finis*.

   Lucian, *Contentio de presidentia P. Scipionis*, Lat. tr. Giovanni Aurispa; Hain *10275; G. Martellotti, "La 'Collatio inter Scipionem. . .'," *Classical, Medieval and Renaissance Studies in Honor of B. L. Ullman*, ed. G. Henderson, Jr. (Rome, 1964) v. 2, p. 146.

7. ff. 44v–56r *Declamande controuersie de nobilitate inter* [*Fulgentium* crossed out] *Gaium Flaminium et publium cornelium apud Senatum habite de habenda lucretia. directe Illustrissimo principi guidantonio Vrbini Comiti Initium Sequitur*. Apud maiores nostros sepe de nobilitate dubitatum est. Multi quidem in felicitate generis non nulli in affluentia ... nunc tandem. expergiscimini et contentionis summam animadvertite. Contendimus de nobilitate. Satis utriusque uita// *finis*.

   Buonaccorso da Montemagno, *Controversia de nobilitate*, text incomplete; G. B. Casotti, ed., *Prose e rime de' due Buonaccorsi da Montemagno* (Florence, 1718) pp. 2–94.

8. ff. 56v–60v *De artis oratorie laudibus. beatus senensis In Initio legendi*. Studui quantum licuit uenerandi patres maioresque carissimi. onus hoc si fieri potuisset effugere non ea de causa ut deessem laborem ... Ille se profecisse sciat. Cui Cicero ualde placebit [Quintilian, *Inst. or.*, X.1.112]. *finis Senis habita 1465*.

   Unidentified oration delivered before the faculty at the university of Siena in 1465 (see also arts. 9–10).

9. ff. 60v–63v *Illustrissimus doctor franciscus pontanus Senis nomine Vniuersitatis in Initio studij ad dominos Senenses de laudibus legum et*

litterarum sequitur. Video pro uestrorum omnium humanitate potentissimi domini atque amplissimi uiri senenses . . . si quoque longius oratio traducta est quam utere forsam [*sic*] expectationes paterentur. uenia donari exposcho. *finis.*

Francesco Pontano, unidentified oration delivered before the faculty at the university of Siena (see also arts. 8, 10).

10. ff. 63v–67r *Magistri Bartholomei senensis de Laudibus phylosophie in ethicis In Initio studij. sequitur.* Multas et uarias et eximias phylosophie laudes Insignes patres doctoresque clarissimi Instituissem dicere . . . quid de hijs rectius sentire compellar. doctrina. et auctoritate uestra. *finis.* f. 67v blank

Bartholomaeus Senensis, unidentified oration delivered before the faculty at the university of Siena (see also arts. 8–9).

Composed of two closely related parts, with one modern paper flyleaf added at beginning.

Part I: ff. 1–3, paper (watermarks: unidentified two-wheeled wagon), 282 x 202 (175 x 100) mm. Ca. 37 long lines; frame-ruled in lead. I^4 (–1, blank?). Art. 2 written in a small neat humanistic cursive by a single scribe, above top line; art. 1 and all the rubrics, foliation, and marginalia added by scribe who copied and annotated Part II. Headings, running titles, punctuation, paragraph marks, marginalia, in red.

Part II: ff. 4–67 (incorrectly foliated 4–64 by scribe who only numbered those leaves where a new text begins; a later hand added correct foliation), paper (watermarks, in gutter: similar to Briquet Chapeau 3387), written space 163 x 100 mm. 30 long lines; single or double vertical bounding lines on left of written space, single on right, all in lead; text rulings in ink. Remains of prickings in upper and lower margins; single prickings in outer margin, 5 mm. above top line. $I–VI^{10}$, VII^4. Horizontal catchwords, preceded by red paragraph mark, near gutter, verso (Derolez 12.4). Written in a slanting humanistic bookhand with gothic features by a single scribe, above top line. Illuminated initial, f. 4r, 4-line, gold on blue, green, and red ground with yellow and white filigree. In lower border wreathed medallion with ribbons on either side, bearing the arms of Rainerius de Maschis of Rimini (or, 3 bendlets sable [?], a chief gules with cross argent [?]); the initials *R* and *A*, in gold, on either side of shield. Headings, paragraph marks, punctuation and marginalia, in red.

Binding: Italy, s. xv. Sewn on three tawed skin, slit straps laced through tunnels in the edges of beech boards to channels on the outside and nailed. Natural color endbands, beaded on the spine, were sewn on tawed skin cores laid in grooves in the boards and nailed. There is tawed skin under the endband tie downs.

Covered in green [?] tawed skin with a strip of red leather, s. xix–xx, added on the spine. Two truncated diamond catches with the *IHS* monogram within a sunburst (as used by St. Bernardinus of Siena) on the lower board. The upper board is cut in for clasp straps which are a later addition. Both clasps and catches have the word *AVE*. The title *De re uxoria* written in ink on both head and tail edges. The boards are badly worm-eaten. See T. De Marinis, *La legatura artistica*, v. 1, p. 16, no. 82 and pl. IV, for similar catches.

Part II was written in Siena in 1465 by the jurist and diplomat Rainerius de Maschis of Rimini whose coat of arms appears at the foot of f. 1r with the inscription: "Ranerij de maschis militis Atque doctoris ariminensis Senarum Capitanei mccccIxv libellus sua manu et arma sunt." A similar inscription and the same arms occur in Oxford, Bod. Lib. Digby 144, a manuscript of Livy that was copied for Rainerius in Siena in 1466, which also has foliation, headings, and rubrics in his hand (*Colophons*, v. 5, no. 16449; Pächt and Alexander, v. 2, no. 281, pl. XXV; Watson, *Oxford*, v. 1, pp. 68–69, v. 2, pl. 649). A manuscript of Justinus' *Historiae* (Leyden, Bibl. Univ. Perizonianus Fo. 13), copied for Rainerius in Genoa in 1457, contains rubrics by him (see Lieftinck, v. 1, no. 208 and pls. 409–410); according to A. C. de la Mare, Rainerius apparently copied the second part (ff. 88–95) of Rimini, Bibl. Gambalunghiana 43 (D.IV.112), a manuscript of Tacitus' *Germania* written in Rome in 1476 (*Catalogo di manoscritti filosofici nelle biblioteche italiane* [Unione accademica nazionale, 1980] v. 1, pp. 129–31). Art. 2 of Part I, copied by another scribe, was apparently added later to the beginning of the manuscript, as was the table of contents written on f. 1r by Rainerius. Rainerius joined Parts I and II and had them bound together. Belonged to Federico Patetta (1867–1945), Professor of the History of Law at the University of Turin at the beginning of this century (his note, f. 1r: "MS no. 70"). Purchased from H. P. Kraus in 1955 by Thomas E. Marston (bookplate).

secundo folio: obseruare

Bibliography: Faye and Bond, p. 71, no. 63.

Marston MS 64 Northern Italy, s. $XV^{1/4}$
Alexander of Villa Dei, Doctrinale

ff. 1r–54v [Preface:] Scribere clericulis paro doctrinale nouellis/ Pluraque doctorum sociabo scripta meorum./ ... Iste fere totus liber est extractus ab illo./ ... [text, f. 1v:] *Capitulum primum de declinationibus.* Rectis as es a dat declinatio prima./ ... Nate dei deus atque tibi deus alitus alme/ Quas tres personas in idem credo deitatis./ Deo. gratias. Amen.

D. Reichling, ed., Das Doctrinale des Alexander des Villa-Dei, *Monumenta Germaniae paedagogica*, v. 12 (Berlin, 1893) pp. 7–178. Some minor interlinear and marginal glosses on ff. 1v–19v (through ch. 5).

Parchment, ff. i (paper) + i (modern parchment) + 54 + i (modern parchment) + i (paper), 264 x 184 (162 x 95) mm. 24 long lines. Single vertical bounding lines, full length, with an additional ruling within text space to delineate narrow column for the first letter of each verse. Ruled in lead or pale brown ink. Prickings in upper and lower margins. Single pricking in outer margin, 8 mm. above top line.

$I-VI^8$, VII^6. Horizontal catchwords in lower margin near gutter, verso (Derolez 12.4). Remains of quire and leaf signatures (e. g., a i, a ii, a iii, etc.) in lower right corner, recto.

Written in round gothic bookhand by a single scribe, below top line.

One historiated initial, f. 1r, 6-line, pink, red, and green with white filigree on gold ground thinly edged in black, with a half-length portrait of a teacher in red robes and a red cap holding a book, against a blue ground with white filigree. In the lower margin, arms of the Pesaro family of Venice (per pale indented or and azure; Rietstap, v. 2, p. 418), framed by scrolling acanthus, green, red, blue, and pink. Plain initials and paragraph marks both alternate blue and red. Headings in red.

Binding: England, s. xix. Light brown leather, gold-tooled. Gilt edges. Rebacked. Title on spine: "Alexander de Villa Dei Doctrinale. MS: In Memb:." Bound for Henry Drury by C. Lewis in 1820 (note on f. i recto).

Written in Northern Italy in the first quarter of the 15th century for an unidentified member of the Pesaro family of Venice whose arms occur in the lower margin of f. 1r. Belonged to the Rev. Henry Drury (1778–1841; inscription on f. i recto; see binding); his sale (Evans, 3 March 1827, no. 188; information not verified). Armorial bookplate with motto "Invictus maneo" of John Trotter Brockett (1788–1842; DNB, v. 2, pp. 1280–81); his [?] note, f. i recto, that the manuscript was acquired from Thorpe in

1832. Round leather booklabel of Edward Hailstone (1818–90; DNB, v. 8, p. 886); his sale (Sotheby's, 23 April 1891, no. 327). Belonged to William Morris, Kelmscott House, Hammersmith (1834–96; booklabel). Morris' manuscripts sold at his death to Richard Bennett; this manuscript among those re-sold by Bennett (Sotheby's, 10 Dec. 1898, no. 1190). Unidentified Sotheby sale description (no. 105) glued inside front cover. Purchased from Maggs Bros., London, in 1956 by L. C. Witten (inv. no. 1245), who sold it the same year to Thomas E. Marston (bookplate).

secundo folio: Ir uel ur

Bibliography: Faye and Bond, pp. 71–72, no. 64.

Marston MS 67 Eastern France, s. $XII^{4/4}$
Priscian, Grammatica minor Pl. 41

ff. 1r–66r Quoniam in ante expositis [*gloss above*: compositis] libris de partibus orationis in plerisque [*gloss above*: multis] apollonij sumus auctoritatem secuti. Aliorum quoque siue nostrorum [*gloss*: scilicet latinorum] siue grecorum ... Sed postquam intus sum omnium rerum satior. f. 66r-v miscellaneous pen trials, notes, doodles, including the statement: "malum est perdere propter perdidisse dixit socrates," a chart on the "Septem artes," and a note on childbirth ("Vt mulier cito pariat...").

H. Keil, ed., *Grammatici latini* (Leipzig, 1855–70) v. 3, pp. 107–377. This manuscript cited by M. Gibson, "Priscian, *Institutiones grammaticae*: A Handlist of Manuscripts," *Scriptorium* 26 (1972) p. 116, and M. Passalacqua, *I codici di Prisciano* (Rome, 1978) p. 193, no. 430. The text here is accompanied by extensive interlinear and marginal glosses in ink and lead, with the most densely written marginalia dating from the second half of the 13th century. A contemporary hand, probably the original scribe, signalled the examples cited from classical authors by placing letters (many lost due to trimming) in the outer margins of leaves: *v* for Vergil, *t* for Terence, *ho* for Horace, *l* for Lucan, etc.

Parchment (end pieces, worn, repaired), ff. 66, 241 x 172 (168 x 95) mm. 31 long lines. Single vertical bounding lines and an additional vertical ruling in outer margin; double upper horizontal bounding lines. Ruled in lead or crayon. Remains of prickings in upper and lower margins.

I–VIII^8, IX^2 (leaves not conjugate). Quires signed with Roman numerals on ff. 1v (i) and 2r (ii).

Written by a single scribe in early gothic bookhand, above top line.

8-line initial [later addition?], f. 1r, red with crude penwork designs in red and black; biting the letter is a grotesque stretched across upper margin, outlined in black with details in red. Small initials in red and/or black: ff. 17v, 31r, 35v, etc. Paragraph marks, initial strokes, and lines drawn through text passages written in Greek, all in red.

Some marginalia lost due to trimming and rubbing.

Binding: France, s. xiii [?]. Original sewing (except for the first few gatherings) on three tawed skin, slit straps laced through tunnels in the edge to the outside of quarter sawn [?] oak boards, almost flush, and fastened with rectangular, angled wedges. Blue/green and natural color chevron endbands are sewn on tawed skin cores. There is a strip of tawed skin extending a short distance on the outside of the boards and turned in at head and tail. The boards are edged with white, tawed skin and an outer cover is whip stitched to this edging. There is no adhesive on the spine and the cover is held in place by the endbands. The outer cover probably extended and has been cut off flush. Needle holes along the inner edge of the back board fore-edge turn-in. There are traces of two strap-and-pin fastenings, the pins on the lower board. Hole bored on the tail and fore edge of the front board does not seem to serve any purpose.

Written in Eastern France in the fourth quarter of the 12th century; extensive annotations and hastily drawn sketches in margin indicate it was used for more than a century as a school text. Early inscription of Jacques de Vitry (ca. 1170–1240) states that he purchased the book in Paris, presumably second-hand, since the note is written over an erasure in upper margin, f. 1r: "Iste priçianus est Iakobi de vitriaco emptus parisius [3 *or* 4?] 2 d." Early press-mark (contemporary with binding?) on back turn-in: the number "12" in a diamond with a cross at each point. "609" in ink on upper board and front pastedown. Small rectangular paper label with "41" written in ink, on spine. Round label with saw-toothed edge: "S II 7/ Priscinian [*sic*]/ MS XII/ 4° 75549." Purchased from B. M. Rosenthal (Cat. 1, no. 83, with plate of f. 65r) in 1954 by Thomas E. Marston (bookplate).

secundo folio: Ego ne illam

Bibliography: Faye and Bond, p. 72, no. 67.
The Medieval Book, pp. 95–96, no. 92, with plate of ff. 9v–10r.

Marston MS 69 Northern Italy, s. XIII^{in}
Sermons (in Lat.) Pl. 5

The first 112 sermons in this manuscript (beginning: *Dominica prima de Aduentu domini. Secundum matheum.* In illo tempore. Cum appropinquasset ihesus . . . [Mat. 21.1]. Dominus ac redemptor noster fratres karissimi. qui semper est equalis deo patri. . .") constitute the "Homéliaire italien" as defined and discussed by H. Barré, *Les Homéliaires carolingiens de l'école d'Auxerre*, Studi e Testi 225 (1962), see especially pp. 28–29. Marston MS 69 is, however, missing nos. 31 and 73 and has ten additional sermons at the conclusion for which we give complete incipits and explicits (we thank T. Amos of the Hill Monastic Manuscript Library for his assistance with these texts):

113. ff. 176v–177r *De sancta maria Secundum lucam.* In illo tempore. Missus est angelus gabriel . . . [Luc. 1.26]. *Expositio.* Fratres karissimi multum dilexit nos deus pro quibus tanta facere dignatus est. Scimus quia diabolus per serpentem . . . decoraret uirginitatis excellentiam singularem.

Sermon also found in Paris, B. N. lat. 3576 (a copy of the Italian Homiliary), on f. 107v, and Bibliothèque de l'Arsenal MS 1116 (110 H. L.), part B of a composite manuscript, ff. 55v–56r, where it follows the *Elucidarium* of Honorius Augustodunensis.

114. ff. 177r–178v *Sermo de penitentia.* Deus et misericors fratres karissimi per prophetam nos ammonet ad conpunctionem uel ad penitentiam dicens Conuertamini ad me in toto corde . . . uoluptatibus huius seculi abnegati eternum premium consequi mereamur. . . .

Ps.-Augustine, *Sermo* 66; PL 40.1352–53, cf. G. Morin, ed., CC ser. lat. 104, p. 980. Sermon also found in Basel, Universitätsbibliothek, MS B VIII 6 (a copy of the Italian Homiliary), on f. 71v, with the incipit "Deus misericors. . .".

115. ff. 178v–179v *De penitentia.* Fratres karissimi qui egerit ueraciter penitentiam et solutus fuerit a ligamento [?] quo erat constrictus et christi corpore . . . apropinquare [*corrected from*: apropingquante] designat dicens, Penitentiam agite apropinquabit enim regnum celorum Amen.

116. ff. 179v–180v *Item sermo de penitentia.* Miracula domini nostri ihesu christi fratres karissimi que ipse fecit. amirari et uenerari debemus et qualem . . . audire. ut uitam eternam possimus cum sanctis habere. . . .

Sermon also found in Fermo, Biblioteca Comunale, MS 33 (4 C 1/33), ff. 4r–5r, and edited from this manuscript by S. Prete, *Ordinatio palatii regis Gundafohri dal ms. 33 della Biblioteca Civica di Fermo*, in Miscellanea Giulio Belvederi, coll. Amici d. Catacombe 23 (Vatican City, 1954) p. 512.

117. ff. 180v–181v *Sermo sancti ambrosii in xl.* Ecce nunc tempus acceptabile [*ecce* expunged] adest in quo et peccata uestra confiteri deo et sacerdoti et per ieiunia ... audire a domino. Esuriui enim et dedistis michi manducare sitiui et dedistis michi bibere.

Sermo VII of the Fourteen Homilies from Northern Italy, ed. P. Mercier, *XIV homélies du IXe siècle*, Sources chrétiennes 161 (Paris, 1970) pp. 186–95 (Marston MS 69 not cited).

118. ff. 181v–184v *Sermo in die dominico de lazaro.* Audistis fratres karissimi in hoc sancto euangelio. quomodo saluator noster suscitauerit quatriduanum Lazarum de monumento ... digne ad susceptionem corporis et sanguinis domini possit accedere....

119. ff. 184v–187v *Dominica in Ramis oliuarum.* Cognoscat dilectio uestra amantissimi fratres quod hodie passio christi legitur in ecclesia in qua narratur quomodo ... penitentiam de peccatis uestris dignam facere. et sic deo placere. ut ad eternam gloriam possitis ascendere....

120. ff. 187v–189v *In die Resurrectionis sermo.* Ista solempnitas quam hodie celebramus pascha apellatur. id est transitus quia sicut hodie est transiit christus saluator noster de morte ad uitam ... transeatis de hac uita ad eternam gloriam....

121. ff. 189v–192r *Dominica ii post pascha Secundum lucam* ... Ego sum pastor bonus ... [John 10.11]. Fratres karissimi ihesus christus saluator noster sicut audistis bonus et uerus pastor est quia pascit nos corporaliter ... quia in tribus uirtutibus eleuatur idem fide spe et caritate. Quibus ornatus ... in trinitate perfecta....

122. ff. 192r–193v *Feria ii Secundum iohannem* ... Duo ex discipulis ihesu ibant ... [Luc. 24.13]. Isti duo discipuli de quibus hoc sanctum euangelium narrat non fuerunt ex duodecim apostolis sed ex septuaginta discipulis ... elimosinam. et ceteras uirtutes habere ut ad celi palatium possitis peruenire. Amen.

No. 33 in the Italian Homiliary collection at the beginning of the manuscript, but with the incipit "Duo isti" and with a different explicit. Art. 122 also found in Paris, B. N. lat. 3576, ff. 42v–43r, where it is written as two sermons.

Parchment, ff. i (paper) + i (contemporary parchment) + 193 + i (paper), 234 x 163 (170 x 104) mm. Written in 26 long lines. Double outer and single inner vertical bounding lines. Ruled in lead. Rulings for text often extend through the outer margin. Prominent prickings in upper, lower, and outer margins.

I–XXIII^{8}, XXIV^{10} (–10). Remains of catchwords in lower margin, near gutter, verso. Quires signed with Roman numerals in center of lower margin.

Written in a nice large early gothic script, above top line.

Attractive pen-and-ink drawings throughout the manuscript, in red, though much of manuscript now stained. Folio 1r with a partial border formed of fantastic beasts, dragons and grotesques. Other drawings in margins include a fantastic bird, f. 9r; a dragon with a human head issuing forth stylized scrolls, f. 40v; a scroll inhabited by a fantastic bird, f. 49r; a lizard-like creature, its tail forming a partial border, f. 53r; a grotesque, f. 73v. Several drawings in the lower margin have been trimmed. The style of the decoration is similar to but more modest in design than that appearing in Paris, B. N. lat. 16896, lat. 16894 and lat. 16911, all attributed to Bologna (Avril and Gousset, v. 2, p. 76, no. 93, pl. XLIV; v. 2, p. 74, no. 88, pls. XLII–XLIII; p. 76, no. 92, pl. XLIV). Plain initials in red, some with penwork scrolls or simple flourishing. Headings and underlining of Biblical passages in red.

Binding: Italy [?], s. xix [?]. Brown leather case with title, in ink, on spine: "Homil. in Evangel." Fragment of an unidentified 13th-century Latin document (monastic register?) bound in as second front flyleaf.

Written in Northern Italy at the beginning of the 13th century; provenance unknown. Early inscription in lower margin, f. 193v, erased and illegible. "75" in ink on front pastedown. Purchased from Leo Olschki of Florence in 1956 by L. C. Witten (inv. no. 1320), who sold it the same year to Thomas E. Marston (bookplate).

secundo folio: remissionem

Bibliography: Faye and Bond, p. 72, no. 69.

Marston MS 70 — Northeastern Italy, s. XIV$^{4/4}$

Rudimenta grammatices; Disticha Catonis

1. ff. 1r–11r Ianua sum rudibus primam cupientibus partem [or *artem*?]/ Nec sine me quisquam rite peritus erit/ ... Nam celeri studio discere

multa potes/ [text:] Poeta quae pars est. nomen est. quare est nomen. quia significat . . . uero sunt comunes que posunt preponi et subponi in ordine orationis.

Rudimenta grammatices (*Grammatica latina secundum Donatum*); GKW, v. 7, nos. 8987–9017 (8988, 8991–92, 8995–9000, 9002–04, 9006–11 and 9013–16 also contain the *Disticha Catonis*; cf. art. 2). Bursill-Hall, *Census*, p. 319; Marston MS 70 not listed. For a discussion of the text see W. Schmitt, *Die Ianua (Donatus), ein Beitrag zur lateinischen Schulgrammatik des Mittelalters und der Renaissance*, Beiträge zur Inkunabelkunde, 3, Folge 4, Akademie-Verlag (Berlin, 1969) pp. 43–80, with the text based on GKW 8998 printed on pp. 74–80; Marston MS 70 not cited.

2. ff. 11r–15v [No heading; Epistula begins:] Cum animaduerterem quam plurimos homines errare in uia morum succurendum et consulendum oppinioni eorum fore existimaui . . . et non intelligere neglegere est. [*breves sententiae*:] Itaque deo suplica/ Parentes ama/ . . . ius iurandum serua/ [text, f. 11v:] Si deus est animus nobis ut carmina dicunt/ hic tibi precipue sit pura mente colendus/ . . . Hos breuitas sensus fecit me iungere binos/ Deo. Gratias. Amen. f. 16r-v blank except for later notes

Disticha Catonis; M. Boas, ed. (Amsterdam, 1952). *Breves sententiae* in the following order with nos. referring to Boas, *op. cit.*, pp. 11–30: 1–5, 16–17, 6–11, 29, 35–37, 40, 51, 18, Rumores fuge, 13–15, 20, 28, 26–27, 30–32, 34 (*bis*), 33, 44, 49–50 (*bis*), 52, 54, 25, 41–42, 22–23, 12, 43, 19, 46–47, 39, 45, 55, 21. Distichs in the following order (Boas, *op. cit*, pp. 31–263): I.1–20, 21 (first line of distich repeated at end), 22–40; II.Prefatio, 1–31; III.Prefatio (lines 1–2), 1, Prefatio (lines 3–4), 2–24; IV.Prefatio, 1, 2 (Comoda . . . / Si contentus . . .), 3–15, 17–29, 30 (2 verses compressed into 1), 31–49.

Parchment, ff. i (modern parchment) + 16 + i (parchment; palimpsest), 256 x 181 (192 x ca. 128) mm. 36 long lines and lines of verse. Single vertical bounding lines, ruled in lead. Rulings for text in light brown ink.

Two gatherings of eight leaves.

Written in round gothic bookhand by a single scribe.

Historiated initial, f. 1r, 11-line, pink against blue ground with a half-length portrait in profile of the author, dressed in red and green robes and a red hat against parchment ground with brown penwork. Foliage serifs, green, blue and red extending into inner and upper margin to form partial border. In center of lower margin, blank shield for coat of arms, flanked by stylized foliage, blue and red. In outer margin, small patch of green with boy or man sitting under a tree (visible under ultra-violet light). One illuminated initial on f. 11r, 8-line, pink against blue ground filled with stylized foliage, blue, green, and red. Plain initials in red. Small initials touched with yellow.

The entire manuscript is well worn, affecting the text; f. 1r is badly rubbed and stained.

Binding: England [?], s. xx. Quarter bound in brown, blind-tooled calf over wooden boards.

Written in Northeastern Italy in the fourth quarter of the 14th century; business accounts dated 1482, in Italian, on f. 16v: "tome dal greza dee dar a mi bet. per uno saldo fato cum lui A di 6 de mazo 1482 monete in suma [last portion of text unclear:] 44 q et d 18." Early provenance unknown. "V" with "3" in a circle, in pencil, f. 1r. Purchased from H. P. Kraus in 1955 by Thomas E. Marston (bookplate).

secundo folio: in o naturaliter

Bibliography: Faye and Bond, p. 72, no. 70.

Marston MS 72 — Rome, 1460; Padua [?], s. XV^2

Cicero, De finibus, etc. — Pl. 25

I. 1. ff. 1r–90r *M. T. Ciceronis de finibus bonorum et malorum liber primus incipit foeliciter.* Non eram nescius brute cum que summis ingeniis exquisitaque doctrina phylosophi greco sermone tractauissent . . . Quod cum ille dixisset et satis disputatum uideretur in oppidum ad Pomponium perreximus omnes. *M. T. C. de finibus bonorum et malorum liber v. et ultimus explicit foeliciter. Deo gratias. Finitum Romae XVII Decembris MCCCCLX.* f. 90v ruled, but blank

Cicero, *De finibus bonorum et malorum*; Th. Schiche, ed., Teubner fasc. 43 (1915) pp. 1–203. There are some contemporary interlinear glosses by Scribe 2 that record variant readings or emendations to the text; in addition, the same hand has written in the margins numerous parts of the text left out by the original scribe. Greek words are usually written in Roman letters; occasionally, however, a space is left blank, or the Greek letters are used.

II. 2. ff. 91r–106r *Caroli Aretini ad Cosmum et Laurentium de medicis de matris obitu consolatoria incipit.* Nuper viri mihi amicissimi cum in matris uestre sanctissime atque honestissime femine funere adessem . . . tamen hoc opusculum nostro ingeniolo Lucubratum summa cum uoluptate uos Lecturos existimo. Valete viri prestantissimi ac iterum bene ualete. *Caroli aretini oratoris eximij ad Cosmum et Laurentium de Medicis ciues florentinos uiros clarissimos de matris obitu consolatoria explicit. Deo gratias*. f. 106v blank

Carlo Aretino Marsuppini, *Oratio ad Cosimum et Laurentium de Medicis de matris obitu*; P. G. Ricci, "Una consolatoria inedita del Marsuppini," *La Rinascita* 3 (1940) pp. 363–433; Marston MS 72 not listed.

3. ff. 107r–132v *Bernardi Iustiniani veneti patritij Leonardi filij de laudibus francisci foscari Ducis venetiarum funebris oratio incipit feliciter.* Cum egregia quedam pietatis officia humanissime princeps posterior etas a maioribus accepisset que deinde paulatim exoleuere [*sic*] ... cum omnium principum populorumque beneuolentia perfrui liceat quam in iusto bello petita iustis armis defendere necesse sit. *Bernardi Iustiniani Veneti patritij Oratoris eximij de Laudibus francisci foscari Ducis Venetiarum funebris et elegantissima oratio. Explicit.*

   Bernardo Giustiniani, *Oratio funebris habita in obitu Francesco Foscari Ducis* (d. 1457); published in *Orazioni, elogi e vite scritte da letterati veneti patrizj in lode di doge, ed altri illustri soggetti* (Venice, 1787) v. 1, pp. 21–59.

4. f. 132v *Epitaphium dicti francisci.* Post mare perdomitum post urbes marte subactas/ Florentem populum longeuus pace reliqui.

   Epitaph of Francesco Foscari, Doge of Venice (d. 1457).

5. f. 132v [Added later by the same scribe:] *Franciscus Fosc. Venetorum Dux.* Reip. cura. eloquentia animi magnitudine rerum gestarum gloria omnium Principum ... splendorem immortalem relinquens. Anno salutis Mcccclvij. Ducatus xxxiiij. etatis Lxxxij Kl. Nouembr.

   7-line account, in prose, summarizing the accomplishments and life of Francesco Foscari (see also arts. 3–4).

6. ff. 133r–152r *Petri Balbi Pisani ad R. in chrysto patrem d. Nicolaum de Cusza tituli Sancti petri ad uincula S. R. E. presbiterum Cardinalem uirum eruditissimum in Epitoma Alcinoj disciplinarum platonis de Greco in Latinum conuersum. prefatio Incipit feliciter. Praefatio.* Cum te intelligam sapientissime atque optime patrum tum Aristotelis acutissimam doctrinam ceterorumque priscorum phylosophorum ... [text, f. 133v:] *Epitoma Alcinoi disciplinarum Platonis Incipit.* Que sint proprijssima Platonis documenta queue doctrina probre

inter hinc ordiemur ... Ab his tamen que diximus speculantes et perquirentes cetera platonis precepta consequi possunt. *Epitoma Alcinoi disciplinarum Platonis explicit. Deo gratias.*

Alcinous, *Epitoma disciplinarum Platonis*, translated into Latin by Pietro Balbi; GKW, v. 1, no. 806. The date (1460 or earlier) and circumstances of the translation are discussed in H.-D. Saffrey, "Pietro Balbi et la première traduction latine de la *Théologie platonicienne* de Proclus," *Miscellanea codicologica F. Masai dicata*, ed. P. Cockshaw, et al. (Gand, 1979) pp. 425–37, with the dedicatory preface to Nicholas of Cusa.

7. ff. 152r–157v *Bernardi Iustiniani Veneti legati sue ciuitatis ad Sixtum IIII Ro. Pont. oratio habita.* Si unquam antea sanctissime et beatissime pater diuine prouidentie lumen humanis laboribus affulsit ... sed presenti animo constantique fide semper erunt re atque opere quam uerbo et oratione ueriores.

   Bernardo Giustiniani, *Oratio apud Sixtum IV Pontificem Maximum habita*, delivered at Rome in December 1471; published in his *Orationes, nonnullae epistolae, traductio in Isocratis Libellum ... Leonardi Justiniani epistolae* (Venice, 1493) ff. Gv–G6r.

Part I: ff. 1–90. Parchment, ff. i (paper) + 90, 250 x 177 mm. Remains of prickings in upper and lower margins. Other details of page format are different for the two scribes who copied the text. Scribe 1: ff. 1r–38v (conclusion of quire IV), written space is 168 x 103 mm.; 28 long lines. Double vertical bounding lines ruled in hard point on hair side (Derolez 13.31). Written in a well formed round humanistic script, below top line and sometimes not using the final line ruled for text. Scribe 2: ff. 39r–90r, written space is 165 x 100 mm.; 28 long lines. Double vertical bounding lines ruled in crayon (Derolez 13.31); lines for text ruled faintly in ink. Single pricking in outer margins, 5 mm. above top line (Derolez 18.3). Written in a smaller and less calligraphic humanistic script with cursive features by Stefano Guarnieri, below top line. I^{8}, $II–VIII^{10}$, IX^{12}. Catchwords throughout Part I are perpendicular to text between inner bounding lines (Derolez 12.5) and were added by Scribe 2; many trimmed. 5 illuminated initials, 6- to 4-line, yellow and ochre on blue, green and deep red ground with white vine-stem ornament, sometimes extending into the margins to form partial borders. Headings in red majuscules written by Scribe 2.

Part II: ff. 91–157. Paper (watermarks: Briquet Ciseaux 3668) + i (paper), 250 x 177 (165 x 110) mm. 31 long lines. Frame-ruled in crayon;

text rulings in hard point [?]. I-II^{12}, III^{18}, IV^{24}. Remains of horizontal catchwords along lower edge near gutter, verso (Derolez 12.4). Copied by Scribe 2 of Part I: arts. 2-6 in italic, above top line; art. 7 added later, disregards bounding lines of written space. 4 illuminated initials, 6-line, dark yellow on irregular grounds of blue, green and pink with white vine-stem ornament, shaded with grey; white dots on blue, pale yellow on green, and blue on pink. Headings in red.

Binding: Italy, s. xix. Brick red goatskin, blind-tooled. Bound in the same bindery for the Guarnieri-Balleani library (Iesi) as MS 450 and Marston MSS 86, 212, 181, 182, with the first three probably by the same binder. Title, in ink, on tail edge: "C. DE. FI. BO. ET MA."

Part I was copied in Rome in 1460 (see colophon, art. 1) by two scribes; the second scribe, who completed the work of the first, I have identified as the humanist Stefano Guarnieri (d. 1495; U. Nicolini, "Stefano Guarnieri da Osimo cancelliere a Perugia dal 1466 al 1488," *L'umanesimo umbro: atti del IX convegno di studi umbri - Gubbio 22–23 settembre 1974* [Perugia, 1977] pp. 307–23). Arts. 2–6 of Part II were written in the third quarter of the 15th century after ca. 1460 (see art. 6); art. 7 was added after 1471, the date the oration was delivered; all of Part II was also copied by Stefano Guarnieri, though in a less formal hand than was used in Part I; the decoration in Part II seems characteristic of Padua. For other Beinecke manuscripts either copied, annotated or owned by Guarnieri, see catalogue entries for MS 450, Index V of this volume under Guarnieri-Balleani Library, as well as C. Annibaldi, *L'Agricola e la Germania di Cornelio Tacito* (Iesi, 1907) pp. 4–10. From the Guarnieri-Balleani Library at Iesi (characteristic binding and remains of paper labels on spine). Purchased from Lathrop Harper by Thomas E. Marston (bookplate and note on front pastedown: "Purchased through Lathrop Harper Inc. from Ct. Balleani–Nov. 1953").

secundo folio: [f. 2:] [antio]pam pacuuij
[f. 92:] Morte

Bibliography: Faye and Bond, p. 72, no. 72.

Marston MS 73 Italy, s. XV$^{3/4}$
Diodorus Siculus, Bibliotheca Historica, It. tr. Pl. 58

ff. 1r–126v [Preface:] Meritamente sono obligati gli huomini di douere rendere grandissime gratie agli scriptori ... antichi tenpi discriuerremo.

[text, f. 5v:] [L]a prima generatione degli huomini apresso a doctissimi et prestantissimi philosophi . . . e scripse molte altre cose d'india delle quali innançi non sera auto cognitione alcuna. ff. 127r–129v ruled, but blank

Diodorus Siculus, *Bibliotheca Historica*, Books I (parts 1 and 2)–II, in an unidentified and freely adapted Italian translation (e.g., the opening portion of Book II is greatly abbreviated). Corrections and additions were carefully made by the scribe over erasures or in gaps. According to J. Monfasani (letter on file), Florence, Bibl. Naz., MS Magl. XXIII, 46 contains the same anonymous Italian translation, but with Latin marginalia and comments on the Greek original. This Italian translation was compared with the Greek text in F. Vogel, ed., Teubner (1887) pp. 2–226.

Parchment, ff. i (contemporary parchment) + 129, 213 x 141 (151 x 84) mm. Written in 29 long lines. ff. 1–70: double vertical bounding lines (Derolez 13.31), ruled in ink, single prickings in outer margin 5 mm. below bottom ruling for text; ff. 71–129: double vertical and horizontal bounding lines (Derolez 13.36), ruled in hard point on hair side.

I–XII^{10}, XIII^{10} (–10, blank). Vertical catchwords with dots and flourishes before and after, between inner bounding lines (Derolez 12.5), verso.

Written in an elegant, upright *mercantesca* script by a single scribe, below top line.

Spaces for headings and decorative initials remain unfilled. Initial on f. 1r later addition.

Binding: Italy. s. xv. Sewn on four tawed skin, slit straps nailed in channels on the outside of wooden boards. Yellow edges. Pink, green, and cream endbands sewn on five cores.

Covered in dark red goatskin with corner tongues, blind-tooled with a central ornament in a panel bordered with rope interlace in concentric frames. Two fastenings, leaf-shaped catches on the lower board and the upper board cut in for the clasp straps. Rebacked twice.

Written in Italy in the third quarter of the 15th century; early provenance unknown. Belonged to Cardinal Giuseppe Renato Imperiali (1651–1737; bookstamp on f. 1r; C. Eubel, et al., eds., *Hierarchia catholica medii et recentioris aevi* [Regensburg, 1925; reprinted Padua, 1952] v. 5, p. 17). Marston MS 73 cited in G. Fontanini, *Bibliotheca Josephi Renati Imperialis* . . . (Rome, 1711) p. 155. Unidentified shelf-marks or price codes include "73" in ink on front pastedown; "ΔΔΔ/ III/ S [or 5?] 7" in ink on f. i recto (a similar shelf-mark occurs in Beinecke MS 156); and "871" in pencil on f. i recto. Acquired through the Anderson Auction Company, New York (12–13 April 1915, no. 168) by the medical historian Dr. Edward

Clark Streeter (1874–1947; note, in ink, on front pastedown: "40. N. Y. '15"). Purchased from L. C. Witten in 1955 by Thomas E. Marston (bookplate).

secundo folio: gloria

Bibliography: Faye and Bond, pp. 72–73, no. 73.

Marston MS 74 Southern Germany or Austria, s. XV^2
Jacobus de Vitriaco, Historia Hierosolymitana

ff. 1r–151v [Prologue:] Postquam diuine propiciationis munificencia exercitus christianj longa in [?]itatem et pacienciam clementer respiciens. et eiusdem diuturnos ... manifeste poterit perpendere Explicit prologus *Explicit Prologus*. [table of contents, f. 3r:] *Incipiunt Capitula*. Cur dominus terram sanctam varijs flagellis et subalterius casibus exposuit. *Capitulum secundum*. De varijs [*hon* crossed out] generibus hominum bonorum et malorum ... [text, f. 5v:] Terra sancta promissionis deo amabilis et sanctis angelis uenerabilis. et vniuerso mundo ... et a sancta Romana ecclesia consolationem et subsidium de die in diem expectantes. ff. 152r–156r ruled but blank (ff. 156–157 pasted together); f. 157v: bookplates.

Jacobus de Vitriaco, *Historia Hierosolymitana Abbreviata*, book 1 (the "Historia Orientalis"), ed. J. Bongars, *Gesta Dei per Francos* (Hannover, 1611) v. 1, 1047–1124; for the edition of book 2 (the "Historia Occidentalis") and for a study of the life and writings of the author see J. F. Hinnebusch, *The Historia Occidentalis of Jacques de Vitry*, Spicilegium Friburgense 17 (Fribourg, 1972), with bibliography. In the present manuscript later hands have added chapter headings and running headlines; some marginal annotations, s. xviii.

Paper (watermarks: Piccard Ochsenkopf XII.749, XIII.771, and similar to XI.226), ff. ii (paper) + 156, 215 x 155 (138 x 90) mm. Written in 29 long lines. Double outer and single inner vertical bounding lines; single horizontal bounding lines. Ruled in lead or crayon. Prickings in upper, lower, and outer margins.

I–XIII^{12}. Catchwords (often trimmed) along lower edge near gutter, verso.

Written in a well formed hybrida script by a single scribe.

One illuminated initial, f. 1r, 18-line, dark green with stylized foliage in light green with yellow shading against red with gold filigree and gold ground edged dark and light grey. Foliage serifs, blue, green, pink, red, and grey with gold balls and gold accents extending into the upper, inner, and outer margins to form a partial border of attenuated and stylized curling leaves. One flourished initial, 5-line, blue with red penwork, f. 5v. Plain initials alternate red and blue. Headings in red for table and a few chapters; most spaces left unfilled by rubricator.

Binding: Southern Germany or Austria, s. xv. Original wound sewing on three tawed skin, slit straps laced through tunnels in the edges to channels on the outside of flush beech boards and pegged twice. The spine is lined with vellum between supports.

Covered in brown calf, blind-tooled with a rope-work flower in a central panel which is divided in three, the upper and lower sections divided into triangles; the whole panel within a rope interlace border. Spine: bands outlined with triple fillets. Two fastenings, now wanting, the lower board cut in to accommodate them.

Written in Southern Germany or Austria in the second half of the 15th century. Early 18th-century inscription of Samuel Schoeneck on front pastedown: "Donum ornatissimae foeminae Knolliae 1708. D. 26. Sept. Samuel Schoeneck." Bookplate with initials "H. S." and dated "1780" was identified by T. E. Marston as that of Hieronymus Schultz (attribution unverified). Armorial bookplate with motto "Ars longa vita brevis" of Conde de Mansilla. Belonged to the Honorable William Robertson, "One of the Senators of the College of Justice" (bookplate; 1753–1835; DNB, v. 16, p. 1315). From the collection of Nicholas Toke, of the Toke family of Godinton (bookplate with motto "Militia mea multiplex"; for the family see J. Burke, *Genealogical and Heraldic Dictionary of the Landed Gentry of Great Britain and Ireland* [London, 1846] v. 2, pp. 1401–02). Belonged to the lawyer and legal historian Eyre Lloyd (d. 1895; *Alumni Cantabrigienses*, Pt. 2, v. 4, p. 187). Miscellaneous notes on front pastedown and f. i recto. Purchased from C. A. Stonehill (inv. no. 3039) in 1954 by Thomas E. Marston (bookplate).

secundo folio: quam futurorum

Bibliography: Faye and Bond, p. 73, no. 74.

Marston MS 76 — Northern Italy, s. $XV^{3/4}$

Pomponius Mela; Vibius Sequester; Dares, etc.

I. 1. ff. 1r–38v *Pomponii mellae de cosmographia liber primus incipit feliciter.* Orbis situm dicere ag[*g* added above]redior Impeditum opus: et facundie minime capax ... et donec effossa repleantur euenniunt hominum pars siluas frequentat minus quam quo [*sic*]// ff. 39–40 wanting

Pomponius Mela, *De chorographia libri tres*, ending abruptly in III.107; P. Parroni, ed., *Pomponii Melae De chorographia libri tres* (Rome, 1984) text: pp. 111–72; Marston MS 76 cited on p. 70, no. 59. Text has been corrected by one hand in a different shade of ink; rubrics in margins by another hand.

II. 2. ff. 41r–47v *Virbius* [sic] *Sequester Virgiliano filio salutem pl. d.* Quanto ingenio ac studio filj [?] carissime apud plerosque poetas fluminum mentio habita sit: tanto labore sum secutus ... [conclusion of *gentes*, f. 47v:] Thessali macedones europae L. [?] vi/ Volsci Italici europe Ae. vii. G. ii.

Vibius Sequester, *De fluminibus, fontibus, lacubus, nemoribus, paludibus, montibus, gentibus*; R. Gelsomino, ed., Teubner (1967) pp. 1–54. Many of the entries are followed by brief notes giving the source of the name (e.g., Ae. or Ene. = *Aeneid*; G. = *Georgics*; Luc. = Lucan).

3. ff. 47v–50r [Heading:] De prouinciis et regionibus. [text:] Bugdunum desyderatum mortem a romoriante [?] mari et ideo In omni mari ... [concludes in section *Prouinciae Alpium Maritimarum ci. viii*:] Ciuitas Vinsicensium id est Ventio. [explicit:] Finit sequester virbius [*sic*; followed by drawing of a heart pierced by an arrow, surmounted by a crown]. f. 50v blank

Unidentified text(s) on the names of the Roman provinces and their regions (ff. 47v–48v) and the names of the cities in the provinces (ff. 48v–50r).

III. 4. ff. 51r–70v *Incipit Historia Daretis Frigii de Exitio Troiae.* [prologue:] Cornelius Nepos Salustio Crispo suo salutem. Cum multa athenis curiosus agerem. inueni historiam daretis Frigij ipsius manu scriptam ut titulus indicat ... nunc ad pollicendum reuertamur. [text:] Pelias Rex in poloponense [*sic*] hesonnem fratrem habuit hesonis filius erat iason uirtute prestans ... cum suis patria protinus excedere iubet. Aeneas cum// catchwords: omnibus suis na. f. 71, and perhaps a quire, wanting

Dares Phrygius, *De excidio troiae historia*, ending abruptly and missing f. 54 ("... Et antenorem ab eis nihil impetrasse. Verum // conclamauit moram non esse..."); F. Meister, ed., Teubner (1878) pp. 1-51, line 18.

Arts. 5–9, a series of *exordia*, appear to be school exercises in

Latin prose composition, all poorly written and heavily corrected. They follow approximately the text of Justinus' *Epitoma*, but are much abbreviated; the Latin is often incomprehensible without a prior knowledge of the historical narrative (e.g., *scythae* has been corrupted to *exitae*).

IV. 5. ff. 72r–73r *Incipit Exordium Regis asiriorum qui primi regnauerunt In terram.* [sic] *Exordium Ninj.* Ninus rex asyriorum primus bella Intulit ad quae regna primus imperauit ... uindicato regum [?] cum auctoritate tenuit.

Exordium on Ninus.

6. ff. 73r–74r [Heading:] Exordium Amazonum que exite [i. e. scythae] et ipse fuerunt. [text:] Apud exitas fuerunt aliquando duos reges iuuenes. qui occupauerunt cemerinus [*sic*] campus Iuxta amnem ... et sic ferunt quod usque ad iulio caesare [*sic*] perdurauerant. Finit.

Exordium on the Amazons.

7. f. 74r Darius rex persarum In exitis bellum intulit cum armatis ... et Lacedemonijs uictoria facta domus suas triumphauerunt. Finit.

Exordium on Darius.

8. f. 74v Bellum Iulij Caesaris: quod gessit super regnum cum germanis In quo prelio romani grauiter pugnauerunt ... qui pacem federatam cum eum fecerunt.

Exordium on Julius Caesar and Augustus.

9. ff. 74v–76r [Heading, f. 74v:] De exordia exitarum. [text, f. 75r:] Exiti antiquioris populus hominibus in terre nulli finis: et interclusa est sicut: et gothia: qui primus eam regionem magog ... Et mater eius olympiades nuncupatur.

Exordium on the Scythians, concluding with Alexander the Great and Philip of Macedon.

10. f. 76v [Heading:] Panormus id est comoda cunctis Natio. [text:] Theopompus xuij Epirotarum gentes esse refert ... Lxx igitur epirotarum urbes a Paulo emilio imperatore funditus ... redacta.

Short unidentified passages on Epirus.

The manuscript is composed of four parts of similar size, 220 x 150 mm.; i (paper) + 72 + i (paper); patterns of stains suggest that the parts were originally separate booklets.

Part I: ff. 1–38 (ff. 39–40 wanting), paper (watermarks, in gutter: similar to Briquet Ciseaux 3685). Written space 158 x 84 mm. Ca. 29 long lines. Frame-ruled in crayon; remains of prickings in outer margins. I^{12}, II^{10}, III^{12}, IV^{6} (–5, 6, with loss of text). Horizontal catchwords to left of inner bounding line (Derolez 12.2); vertical catchwords for third quire (Derolez 12.5). Written by multiple scribes in humanistic cursive script, above top line. Plain red initials, 5- to 1-line. Epigraphic heading on f. 1r; other headings in humanistic bookhand, in red.

Part II: ff. 41–50, paper (watermarks, in gutter: similar to Briquet Lettre T 9129). Written space 160 x 95 mm. 30 long lines. Impressed on a ruling board. A single gathering of 10 leaves. Written by several scribes in humanistic cursive, above top line. Epigraphic headings and plain initials, 3- to 1-line, in black.

Part III: ff. 51–70 (ff. 54, 71 wanting), paper (watermarks, in gutter: similar to Briquet Fleur 6654, 6655). Written space 150 x 87 mm. 26 long lines. Impressed on a ruling board. I^{10} (–4, loss of text), II^{10} (–10, loss of text). Vertical catchwords (Derolez 12.5). Written by several scribes in varying styles of humanistic cursive, above top line. Epigraphic heading, f. 51r, and plain initials in black. Parchment binding stays along outer bifolia.

Part IV: ff. 72–76, paper (watermarks, in gutter: similar to Briquet Fleur 6654, 6655). Written space 152 x 105 mm. Ca. 25 long lines. No discernible rulings. A single gathering of four leaves, + 1 leaf added at end. ff. 72r–76r written by a single [?] scribe in humanistic cursive script; text on f. 76v added in a similar contemporary hand. Heading on f. 72r in red.

Binding: Italy, s. xviii. Paper case, once white.

All four parts appear to have been written in Northern Italy in the third quarter of the 15th century; probably used as school texts given the nature of Part IV and the irregular orthography throughout. Early provenance otherwise unknown. Unidentified notes include: "Nu g b" in pencil on front pastedown; "448" enclosed in square in pencil, f. i recto; round paper label with "102" in ink on spine; "115" in pencil on f. 1r. Inscription, s. xviii, in lower margin of f. 1r: "Est Pauli Deod^{ti} Velli Subleu [?]"; the foliation seems to have been added in the same hand as the inscription. Belonged to Henry Allen (acquired ca. 1800; bookplate with "13" within square, in pencil); Samuel Allen sale (Sotheby's, 30 January 1920, no. 91). Purchased from C. A. Stonehill (CAS 1996/#10866) in 1954 by Thomas E. Marston (bookplate).

secundo folio: Tribus

Bibliography: Faye and Bond, p. 73, no. 76.

Marston MS 77

Tyrol [?], s. XV/XVI

Pietro della Vigna, Epistolae

1. f. 1r [Title page, damaged:] Epistole Magistri Petri de Vineis. quas Fridericus primus Imperator in controuersia sua cum L[?]edis et sede apostolica ad diuersos mundi [?]s et principes misit. de exemplo [?]ctuoso et multum in correcto depicte p[?]is quam scripte. [second paragraph added by same hand that wrote art. 2:] De illo petro de Vineis facit mensionem [*sic*] Antoninus Archiepiscopus Florentinus in Cronica sua parte in Titulo xix ... ac ibi mortuus. f. 1v blank

2. ff. 2r–5r Querimonia friderici Imperatoris super deposicione sua contra Papam et Cardinales fo. 1./ Fridericus item Regibus et principibus mundi ... Capitulum Capuanum regraciatur magistro pietro de Vineis Et recomendat se sibi. fo. 131. f. 5v blank

   Table of Contents for art. 3.

3. ff. 6r–136v *Incipit dictamina magistri Petri de Vineis de gestis friderici Imperatoris Et primo querimonia ipsius super deposicione sua Contra Papam et Cardinales.* Collegerunt pontifices et pharisei consilium et in vnum aduersus principem et christum deum conuenerunt. Quid facimus inquiunt: quia hic homo de hostibus ... vos in sacramentis ecclesiasticis vbera lactauerunt [Bk. III.43]. ff. 131r–134v and 137r–154v blank

   Collection of ca. 110 items, with no book divisions and with rubrics entered sporadically by the original scribe and a second hand. The text here follows the normal cycle of published editions for Bk. I (cf. Basel, 1566) up to f. 38v where it deviates after letter 20. The manuscript seems to be incomplete at end since there are a large number of blank leaves. Only the beginning of the manuscript has many marginal annotations. For the life and works of the author see A. Huillard-Bréholles, *Vie et correspondance de Pierre de la Vigne* ... (Paris, 1865) and E. J. Polak, *Medieval and Renaissance Letter Treatises and Form Letters: A Census of Manuscripts found in Eastern Europe and the U.S.S.R.* in Davis Medieval Texts and Studies 8 (1990) pp. 28–29.
   On ff. 120v–130v, mixed in with the letters of Pietro della Vigna, is an incomplete text of Thomas of Capua, *Summa dictaminis*, composed of a few models without the *Ars dictandi* which sometimes precedes the collection ("Miranda tuis sensibus nostra venit epistola [I.1] ... venia non haberet [VII.88]"). For bibliography on Thomas of Capua see Polak, *op. cit.*, pp. 19–20.

Paper (watermarks: similar to Piccard Anker VII.181–83, Briquet Monts

11813, and Briquet Indéterminés 16061–63; unidentified letter *P* with forked descender), ff. 154 (contemporary foliation in Arabic numerals for art. 3 only, 1–131), 203 x 155 (152 x 75) mm. 24 long lines. Leaves folded lengthwise to delineate text space. Prickings at corners of written space.

I^{10} (1 = front pastedown; -3, 8 through 10), II^{10} (-1), III–XVI^{10}.

Written in humanistic cursive script with gothic features.

Headings and some marginalia in red (often faded), by two hands, the second of which ruled two parallel lines in lead for each line of headings that were added in a more upright gothic text hand.

Binding: Northern Italy, s. xv/xvi. Original sewing on three tawed skin, slit straps reinforced with fragments of a parchment manuscript (Lectionary?) set in channels on the outside of beech boards. The spine is lined with pieces of parchment manuscript, extending inside the boards between supports.

Quarter bound in reddish brown leather with a blind-tooled floral roll along the edges [later but early?]. Spine: multiple fillets at head, tail and outlining supports on the spine. Panels tooled with *X*'s with fleurons around them and floral tools in squares on their points in the outer panels. Traces of two fastenings, the catches on the upper board. The lower board is cut in for straps. Title in ink near the head of the upper board ("Epistole Petr. de Vineis de gestis Friderici Romanorum Imperatoris II **") which is cracked and has been repaired.

Written at the end of the 15th or beginning of the 16th century, probably in the Tyrol given the distinctive design of watermarks. Inscription on front pastedown: "Waldaufficae fundationis Anno 1596." Unidentified stamp of French [?] library, blue elongated oval with pointed ends, washed and illegible, in outer margin of f. 1r. Remains of square label with title in upper register of spine. Purchased from B. M. Rosenthal in 1954 by Thomas E. Marston (bookplate).

secundo folio: [table:] De armata
[text:] [furo]re refugis

Bibliography: Faye and Bond, p. 73, no. 77.
The Medieval Book, p. 17, no. 16.

Marston MS 78 Florence, ca. 1440–50
Plato, Phaedo, Lat. tr. Leonardo Bruni, etc. Pl. 17

1. ff. 1r–59v [Letter:] *Leonardi aretini prefatio in phedonem Platonis ad Innocentium.* Qui laudant santitatem tuam beatissime pater opus certe

bonum ac pium agere pergunt ... [text, f. 2v:] *Phaedon platonis incipit.* Ipse affuisti o phaedon ea die qua socrates uenenum bibit in carcere ... sumus optimi et preterea sapientissimi atque iustissimi. Deo gratias. Explicit feliciter.

Plato, *Phaedo*, translated into Latin by Leonardo Bruni and preceded by his prefatory letter to Pope Innocent VII; Baron, pp. 3–4 for letter and p. 161 for text. There are layers of notes on the text, including some contemporary Greek notes in the margins; the names of the interlocutors are written in red until f. 18r. On the translation see E. Berti, "La traduzione di Leonardo Bruni del Fedone di Platone ed un codice greco della Bibliotheca Bodmeriana," *Museum Helveticum* 35 (1978) pp. 125–48. J. Hankins, *Plato in the Early Italian Renaissance* (Leiden, forthcoming) v. 2, Cat. A, no. 196.

2. ff. 60r–77v [Letter:] Ad *Nicolaum Nicolum.* Leonardi arretini in *zenophantis tirannum.* Zenophontis philosophi quemdam libellum quem ego ingenij exercendi gratia e greco sermone ... [text, f. 61v:] Cum ad hieronem tyrannum Simonides poeta aliquando uenisset essentque ambo otiosi sic illum affari coepit simonides ... felix enim cum sis nemo tibi inuidebit. *Xenophontis tyrannus finit.*

Xenophon, *Hiero (Tyrannus)*, translated into Latin by Leonardo Bruni and preceded by his prefatory letter to Niccolò Niccoli; Baron, pp. 100–101 for letter and p. 161 for text.

Parchment, ff. i (paper) + 77 + i (paper), 225 x 152 (148 x 85) mm. 30 long lines. Double vertical bounding lines full length (Derolez 13.31), ruled in hard point; rulings for text in ink. Remains of prickings in lower margin and a single pricking along outer edge, 3–4 mm. below upper horizontal ruling (e.g., f. 48; Derolez 18.3).

I–V^{10}, VI^{10} (–10, blank), VII^{10}, VIII^{8}. Catchwords between inner vertical bounding lines, perpendicular to text (Derolez 12.5).

Written by a single scribe in a somewhat angular humanistic bookhand.

Decorated in the early style of Gioacchino de' Gigantibus (we thank A. C. de la Mare for this information). On f. 1r a partial border in upper, lower and inner margins, white vine-stem ornament on blue, green and dark pink with grey dots on blue grounds, blue dots on pink grounds, and gold balls. In lower border, medallion framed by gold interlace bands and supported by two putti wearing red necklaces, with a coat of arms, now erased, on green ground. Four illuminated initials, 7- to 5-line, in gold, framed in yellow, on blue, green and red grounds, with dots as above. Initial on f. 1r, inhabited by standing putto wearing a red necklace, is joined to the border. Other initials have vine-stem decoration extending into the margins and terminating with groups of three gold balls. Headings and names of interlocutors (see art. 1) in red.

Binding: Italy, s. xix in. Rigid vellum case with the title gold-tooled on a label on the spine: "Leon. Aret. Opus." Gilt edges and faint lettering on the head edge.

Written in Florence in the 1440s. Although the arms (f. 1r) of the original owner have been effaced, A. C. de la Mare suggests that the manuscript may have been produced for Alfonso V, King of Aragon and Naples. Early modern provenance unknown. Belonged to Charles Fairfax Murray (1849–1919; booklabel). Purchased from L. C. Witten in 1954 by Thomas E. Marston (bookplate).

secundo folio: dei confirmationem

Bibliography: Faye and Bond, p. 73, no. 78.

Marston MS 79 Lombardy, s. XV^{med}
Poggio Bracciolini, Facetiae

ff. 1r–36v Multos futuros esse arbitror qui has nostras confabulationes tum ut res leues et uiro graui indignas reprendant ... Misera eorum condicio quibus non ratio sed fortuna opitulatur. finis. [added by a later hand, s. xvii:] Virtus beatos efficit. Diuitiae nec enim nec multa peritia rerum, Sed nos felices mens sine labe facit. f. 37r-v blank

E. Garin and M. Ciccuto, eds., *Poggio Bracciolini, Facezie* (Milan, 1983); the text of Marston MS 79 appears in the following order, with numbers corresponding to the chapters in the printed text: Introduction, 1–5; text missing after f. 3 ("... et haud multum prudens // non diuertit episcopus. at ille..."); 7–41; text missing after f. 11 ("... cum non amplius quam unicum sextarium possis emere // Interim primo inter florentinos ducemque..."); 81; 50–62; text missing after f. 14 ("... Erat in oppido nostro terre Noue uir nomine Guilielmus // commotus. Bisbinam [*sic*] quoque perusinum..."); 74–80, 82–95, 100–108, 111; text missing after f. 22 ("... sepius ob rei nouitatem quid agis mi uir // incidit. ut pluribus diebus..."); 114–31, 133–35, 137–41; text missing after f. 28 ("... ille incantatione que inducet multas uariasque // quidnam ageret relinquentes dormitum iere..."); 144–46, 148, 204, 149; text missing after f. 29 ("... nullo factionis discrimine bona omnium direpta. // hortabatur sepius. ut acriter inueheret..."); 158–59, 161–65, 170; text missing after f. 31

("... quendam domi fieri presentiret abeundi cupidus et // nocitura. Mediolanensis quidam siue stultus...."); 175–77, 180, 179, 178, 183, 185, 191–96, 200–02, 205–06, 198, 203.

Paper (watermarks: similar to Briquet Lettre S 9050; watermark on back pastedown similar to Briquet Fleur 6596–97, 6599 and 6602), ff. ii (contemporary paper) + 37, 226 x 157 (147 x 95) mm. 28 long lines. Double vertical bounding lines (Derolez 13.31), ruled in lead; rulings for text in ink.

I^{10} (1 = second flyleaf). Collation of the rest is difficult due to extensive repairs. Catchwords (ff. 9v, 15v, 24v) accompanied by four symmetrical flourishes, perpendicular to text between inner bounding lines (Derolez 12.5).

Written in a round humanistic bookhand by a single scribe, below top line.

One illuminated initial on f. 1r, 6-line, gold against deep red, green, and blue cusped ground with white filigree and white dots. From left corners penwork sprays issuing forth into inner margin, with blue and red blossoms and green leaves. Plain initials, placed between vertical rulings, alternate blue and red, some omitted.

Binding: Italy, s. xvi. Backs of quires cut in *V*'s. Brown goatskin case faintly blind-tooled with concentric frames and spiralling dragon motifs that incorporate flowers and long beaked birds. Rebacked.

Written in Lombardy in the middle of the 15th century; early provenance unknown. Belonged to the Benedictine house of St. Laumer [Launomar], Blois, of the Congregation of St. Maur, after 1627; inscription, s. xvii–xviii, in upper margin of f. 1r: "Ex lib. Monasterii S. Laun. bles. cong. S. Mauri." Various modern notes of booksellers and/or owners include 142-5467, 217, 1k, 79, all on front pastedown; 21647 on back pastedown. Belonged to James P. R. Lyell (bookplate); Lyell's note on front pastedown: "D o O [?] 30/12/42 D. V. V. + Repairs E V./ D. E. V." indicates that he purchased the manuscript from Davis and Orioli on 30 Dec. 1942. Bought from the Lyell estate by Bernard Quaritch in 1951 (see *Lyell Cat.*, p. xxix). Purchased in 1952 from C. A. Stonehill (inv. no. 1625) by Thomas E. Marston (bookplate).

secundo folio: affuisse

Bibliography: Faye and Bond, p. 73, no. 79.

Marston MS 80 Northern Italy, s. $XV^{1/4}$
Virtues and Vices, exempla

1. ff. 1r–33r *//Declamatio. 3 a. lex. Incesta saxo deiciatur. Cassus.* Incesta id est poluta a consanguineo uel ab allio saxo deiciatur id est proiciatur de ymo saxo ... utilitate et honore spiritualli pro exaltanda anima. f. 33v: short unidentified texts

   Commentary on selections from Seneca the Elder, *Controversiae*, beginning imperfectly in I.3; M. Winterbottom, ed. and tr., *The Elder Seneca: Declamations*, 2 vols., Loeb ser. (Cambridge, 1974). Selections in the following order: Bk. I: ff. 1r–5v (I.3–8); Bk. II: ff. 6r–14v (II.1–2, 4, 3, 5–7); Bk. III: ff. 14v–23v (III.1–9); Bk. IV: ff. 24r–27r (IV.1, 6–8); Bk. V: ff. 27v–32r (V.1–5, 7–8, with 7 followed by two quotes from Valerius Maximus); Bk. VI: ff. 32v–33r (VI.4,3, continued on f. 32r). After each *lex*, given in red in the heading, there follows a brief discussion of the selection with sections labelled: *cassus, exemplum, questio*, and/or *determinatio.*

2. ff. 34r–73v *Incipiunt exempla ad diuersas materias recolecta ex diuersis libbris. et primo de uana gloria mundi. millesimo cccc°. x°. 28° madij. Vbi* primo de potentia magna alexandri quem sibi totum mundum subiecit ... nichil satis est eque mallum in magistratibus iudicans [?] inopiam et auariciam. *Nota superius exempla ccc^ta^.*

   300 exempla from various sources, including Jerome, Ovid, Solinus, Isidore, Valerius Maximus, *Gesta Romanorum*, Macrobius, Peter Comestor, Josephus, Albertus Magnus, Ambrose, Suetonius, Seneca, Cicero, Boethius, Augustine, Frontinus, Anselm, Remigius, Fulgentius, Pliny, Benedict, Pompeius Trogus, Aulus Gellius, Vegetius. Text incomplete: five leaves missing between ff. 56–57. Two types of rubrics help to order the text: the first are headings in the text for the main topics, the second are in the margins to subdivide the major headings (e.g., f. 38v: *De fidelitate*, followed by *de medico, de cane, de seruis, de cane* [bis]; f. 59v: *De humilitate*, followed by *de capra, de corona, de vulpe*). The compiler has marked the conclusion of each 100 exempla with a rubric. On f. 37v, an unidentified sonnet in Italian, 14-lines: "Questa e quella uerita che tuto uince/ che Iullio cessar fece esser si grande/ ... Sotto tal ducca e millitar legreçça/ che ama la uita altrui piu che soa alteçça."

3. ff. 74r–87v *Incipit liber esopi.* [first fable:] *De gallo et Iaspide.* Dum rigido, fodit, ore fymum, dum queritat escam/ dum stupet, inuenta, iaspide, gallus ait/ ... tu gallo stollidum, tu Iaspide, pulcra sophye/ Dona noctes, stolido, nil sapit ista segges. [prose commentary:] *Nota*

fabullam. Ccum [*sic*] gallus, quadam uice, peteret escam in fymo, inuenit margaritam, ualde lucidam et preclaram, et stupens ait ... Dicit auctor quod per gallum debes intelligere stultum qui spernit diligenda ... set pocius a sapiente ... [final fable, f. 87v:] *De muliere que fuit priuata uiro.* Erant uir et uxor qui se inuicem adeo ... ipsa mullier ligauit// [catchwords: capistrum ad collum eius]

Gualterus Anglicus, *Fabulae* 1–18, 24–25, 59, 19, 21–22, 20, 23, 26–33, 60, 34–42, 45–46, 43–44, 65 (ending imperfectly); K. McKenzie and W. A. Oldfather, eds., *Ysopet-Avionnet: The Latin and French Texts* in *University of Illinois Studies in Language and Literature* 5 (1919). For the first two fables the poem is followed by a prose commentary; for the remaining fables there is only the prose commentary which usually incorporates quotes from the fable and concludes with the *moralitas.*

4. ff. 88r–106v *Incipiunt aliqua miraculla gloriosse uirginis marie. De aue maria.* Legitur quod fuit quidam monachus ellectus episcopus qui uadens ad curiam ... et ecce quedam arbor nata est ad capud sepulcri sui, in cuius follijs erat ipsam salutatio descripta .s. aue maria.

More than 100 extracts about the Virgin Mary, and other topics, with rubrics running: *De aue maria; qualiter beata uirgo liberauit seruum suum ... ; quomodo beata uirgo liberauit fideles a saracenis; de aue maria ... de saccullo peccatorum; de arbore nata cum follijs ubi erat aue maria.* Sources quoted include: Petrus Alphonsus, Augustine, Jerome, Valerius Maximus, Ovid, Seneca, Jacobus de Vitriaco.

5. ff. 107r–126v *Incipiunt aliqua exempla extracta de libbris dyalogorum. De abstinencia.* Uenantij quondam patricij, in saroie [*sic*] partibus, villa fuit, in qua collonus eius fillium honoratum nomine habuit ... [concludes in extract *de iudicantibus que recta non sunt*:] defectus et uitam mallam meruerunt, commendabuntur et iustifficabuntur.

Extracts about virtues and vices derived primarily from Gregory the Great, *Dialogi* (ff. 107r–117r), but supplemented with later material (e.g., selections about the life of St. Francis, ff. 120r–121r). A. de Vogüé, ed., *Grégoire le Grand: Dialogues* in *Sources chrétiennes* Introduction = 251 (1978); Libri I–III = 160 (1979); Liber IV, Index, Tables = 265 (1980). The extracts from Gregory begin in the following order, with rubrics cited from manuscript and page references from v. 2 of printed text: f. 107r, I.1.1–2 *De abstinencia* (pp. 18–20); f. 107r-v, I.3.2–4 *De obbedientia serpentis* (pp. 34–36); f. 107v, I.4.7 *De monialli que comedit latucam* (pp. 42–44); f. 107v, I.4.8 *De uerbo dei* (p. 44); f. 107v, I.5.2 *De lampadibus plenis aqua* (pp. 58–60). ...

6. ff. 127r–132r *Infrascripte sunt alique extractiones de moribus et uita phylosophorum.* Fertur quod talles phylosophus assianus dum semel nocte quadam duceretur extra domum a uetulla ut asstra conscideraret . . . [concludes in life of Secundus:] quid est quod amarum dulce facit, ait, fames. quid est quod hominem lapssum fieri non sinit, ait, lucrum.

   Exempla drawn from Walter Burley, *De vita et moribus philosophorum,* including direct quotations, paraphrases and explanations; H. Knust, ed., *Bibliothek des litterarischen Vereins in Stuttgart* 177 (Tübingen, 1886) pp. 2–395 (the extracts occur in the following order of the printed text: 1–8, 10–12, 17–20, 22, 30, 37, 50, 90, 94–96, 100, 104–105, 108, 110–111, 115, 117–18, 121–22). Marston MS 80 listed in J. Prelog, "Die Handschriften und Drucker von Walter Burley *Liber de vita et moribus philosophorum,*" *Codices manuscripti* 9 (1983) p. 7, no. 134.
   The section devoted to each philosopher or group of philosophers is usually introduced by a descriptive rubric (e.g., Thales: *De gratia reffe-rente*; Chilon: *De amicicia*; Bias: *De prudencia*; Epimenides: *De dormitione*; Crates: *De divicijs despicientibus*; Diogenes, *De paupertate*).

7. ff. 132v–150v Additional exempla arranged thematically (e.g., *De fortuna, De sagacitate pugne, De fortitudine,* etc.) drawn from Leo, Augustine, Ambrose, *Vitae patrum,* Gregory, Bede, Valerius Maximus, Boethius, Jerome, Walter Burley, Cicero.

8. f. 151r [Heading:] Versus e [leaf torn]/ [epitaph:] Helpes dicta fui, siculle regionis alump[na]./ Porticibus sacris iam nunc peregrina quiesco/ Iudicis eterni testifficata tronum.

   3-line epitaph; Walther, *Initia,* no. 7695 (cf. 5352).

9. f. 151r Hac sunt in fossa, bede uenerabilli ossa.

   Epitaphium Bedae; Bertalot, no. 2038; cf. Walther, *Initia,* no. 7438.

10. f. 151r [Heading:] Epitaphium supra sepulcrum gloriossi geronimi/ [epitaph:] Hic dux doctorum, iacet et flos presbiterorum/ Sanctus geronimus, set ei locus, est nimis ymmus/ Hic tu discrete catholice, sine facete/ Dic ueniens aue, desuper ire caue/

    4-line epitaph for St. Jerome.

11. f. 151r [Heading:] epitaphium pro. Io./ [epitaph:] Curia, conscilium, tunc ciuem, tera [*sic*] fidelem/ Amisisse suum, et doluit numerossa parentem/ . . . Bis sex adiunctis, rapit cum uita Iohanni/ Sambuco cupiens, meliores pergere in auras.

    8-line epitaph for Johannes Sambucus [?].

12. f. 151r [Heading:] epitaphium domini nicolai episcopi et comitis tergesti ordinis minorum/ [epitaph:] Heu memorande pater fatum Nicolae luisti./ Presule quo digno, claruit hec patria/ . . . ** ue sumus alme pater, pro nobis ora beatis/ Precibus afficimur ad tua sacra Vale, amen./ [colophon:] Mileximo quatrigentesimo. sextodecimo, Die lune 13°. mensis [?] ** in die octauo epiphanie hora sexta. migrauit ad dominum.

10-line epitaph for Nicolaus de Tergesto, O. F. M. (d. 1416), bp. of Trieste; see Eubel, v. 1, p. 477.

13. f. 151v [Heading damaged:] ****arce./* [epitaph:] Frigida francisci lapis, hic tegit ossa petrarce/ Suscipe uirgo parens animam o sate uirgine parce/ Fessaque iam terris, celli, requiescat in arce.

3-line epitaph for Francesco Petrarch; A. Solerti, ed., *Le vite di Dante, Petrarca e Boccaccio scritte fino al secolo decimosesto* (Milan, 1904) pp. 297, 319, 326, 355.

14. f. 151v *Epitaphium senecce.* Cura labor, meritum sumpti, pro munere honores/ Ite post hac allias solicitate animas/ Me. procul a nobis deus euocat illicet actis/ Rebus terenis, hospita tera ualle.

4-line epitaph for Seneca; A. Riese, ed., *Anthologia latina* (Leipzig, 1906) v. 2, p. 138, no. 667.

15. f. 151v [Heading:] Franciscus petrarcha in de remedijs utriusque fortune. [text:] Mors exillium luctus et dollor non sunt suplicia. Set tributa viuendi.

Although the heading states that this quotation is from Petrarch, *De remediis utriusque fortunae*, we have been unable to locate it in that text.

16. f. 151v [No heading, text begins:] O tu qui transsis dominum rogitare memento/ Pro me qui iaceo, tumullatus in hoc monumento/ Tu qui tumullum cernis, cur non mortallia spernis/ Quod tu es fui, et quod sum in posterum eris/ Talli namque domo, clauditur omnis homo.

Unidentified 5-line epitaph.

17. f. 151v [Heading:] Epitaffium dantis. [text:] Iura monarchie, superos, flagetonta, lacusque/ lustrando. cecini, uoluerunt fata, quousque/ . . . hic claudor dantes, patrijs exterus ab oris/ Quem genuit parui, florencia mater amoris.

Bernardo di Canaccio Scannabecchi [?], 6-line epitaph for Dante; *Enciclopedia dantesca*, v. 2, p. 711; G. P. Marchi, "Per l'attribuzione a

Rinaldo da Villafranca dell'epitafio di Dante 'Iura monarchie'," *Vestigia: Studi in onore di G. Billanovich* (Rome, 1984) v. 2, pp. 417–28.

18. f. 151v [Heading, damaged:] epitaffium uer[gi]llij. [text:] Mantua me genuit, calabri rapuere tenent [remainder of leaf damaged]/ Nunc tenore cecini pascua rura duces/ Ac ne missa [?]. carens uicijs eneydos esset./ Inuidia celleri, fata tullere neque.

4-line epitaph for Vergil; verses 1–2 printed in C. Hardie, ed., *Vitae vergilianae antiquae* (Oxford, 1957) p. 14.

Paper (coarse, thick; watermarks, in gutter: similar to Briquet Monts 11854 and unidentified mountain?), i (paper) + 151 (foliation by scribe in red: *.Carta. 3a.* - *.Carta. 190 a.*, but with leaves 1–2, 59–64, 96–127 missing and no foliation present on f. 191; modern pencil foliation 1–151) + i (paper), 216 x 145 (165 x 100–115) mm. 42–48 long lines or lines of verse. Frame-ruled in lead or ink; prickings at corners of written space.

I^{16} (-1, 2, 3), $II\text{-}III^{16}$, IV^{16} (-12 through 16 between ff. 56–57; original foliation skips from 58 to 65), V^{16} (-1), VI^{16} (two? quires missing between ff. 87–88; original foliation skips from 95 to 128), $VII\text{-}X^{16}$. Horizontal catchwords, in decorated rectangular brackets, in black and/or red, center of lower margin, verso.

Written by a single scribe in semi-cursive gothic bookhand, above top line. Arts. 8–18 added by one or more contemporary hands.

2-line plain initials, paragraph marks and headings, in red, throughout; some marginalia in red.

Folio 151 damaged, with loss of text.

Binding: Italy [?], s. xix. Limp vellum case made from a document; text not legible, but docketing note visible under ultra-violet light on upper cover: "N. 167."

Written in Northern Italy in the first quarter of the 15th century, probably ca. 1410 (the date given on f. 34r, art. 2) to 1416 (when the miscellaneous texts on f. 151r-v may have been added; cf. art. 12). The codex appears to have been owner-produced for an individual interested in a wide range of exempla on virtues and vices. Early provenance otherwise unknown. Unidentified "5" in a circle and "7," both in pencil, on front pastedown. Purchased from C. A. Stonehill (nos. "10867" and "1984" on front and rear pastedowns) in 1953 by Thomas E. Marston (bookplate).

secundo folio: Deffenssio

Bibliography: Faye and Bond, pp. 73, no. 80.
Ullman, p. 456, no. 50.
Dutschke, pp. 176–77, no. 70.

Marston MS 81 Rome, ca. 1460–70
Lorenzo Valla, Confutationes

1. ff. 1r–95r [Heading added in a later hand:] Laurentij Vall. confutationis liber in pogium florentinum. [text:] Non eram nescius iam inde ab initio cum de lingue latine elegantia componebam fore ut quantum fauoris ... Quanti non quantum siue quantulum sunt mea extimanda dicere debuisti. Finis.

   Antidotum in Poggium, Books I–III; *Opera omnia* (Basel, 1540; reprinted Turin, 1962) v. 1, pp. 253–325: Book I on ff. 1r–27v, Book II on ff. 28r–62r, Book III on ff. 62r–95r. Marston MS 81 corresponds closely to this text, but offers numerous variant readings. Greek words and passages are normally omitted in the manuscript (e.g., 54r), sometimes with no space left for their insertion; occasionally the Greek word is written in Roman letters.

2. ff. 95r–147v Seundum [*sic*] antidotum. Tandem aliquando podii altera in nos inuectiua in manus uenit plane serpentina non sententiis sed uenenis ... et una cum illa te clerus omnis elata uoce comprecetur. Sancte podi et sancta flora orate pro nobis. *Finis.*

   Antidotum in Poggium, Book IV; op. cit., pp. 325–66; the manuscript on f. 137v abruptly skips from "... decem ne alia dicam nouem a me donatus est" to "superest unum cui respondendum est..." (p. 355, line 15 to p. 362, line 13 of printed text) and has an additional passage on ff. 142v–146v not located in the printed text ("Quare satius est ut aliquas ad faciendam ... est ludi floraria si hoc non est.").

3. ff. 148r–159v [Heading added in a later hand:] Dialogi Laurentij in podium prohemium incipit. [preface:] Audio Podium alterum in me composuisse inuectiuam longe priore acerbiorem in qua nihil ad me de iure ... hoste superato talem nos agere triumphum. [text, f. 149r:] Incipientes ab epistolis ad Nicolaum nicoli missis. sed quo res sit iocundior ... Po. Notet si uolet. summat alios quoscunque a meis libros. G. placet. L. fiat. *Finis.*

   Dialogus in Poggium, Book I; *op. cit.*, pp. 366–74. The letters (in red) *L, G, P, Pa, D,* and *Di* are used for the interlocutors Laurentius, Guarino, Poggio, Parmeno, Dromo, and Dionysius.

4. ff. 159v–174v *Laurentii Vallensis confutatio in benedictum morandum. Vtrum* de me peius mereantur an melius inimici et hostes mei ... et mentionem facere famosi libelli. Finis.

   Confutatio prior in Benedictum Morandum; op. cit., pp. 445–55.

Parchment, ff. ii (paper) + 174 + ii (paper), 213 x 133 (141 x 87) mm. 28 long lines. Single vertical bounding lines, full length (Derolez 13.11). Prickings in upper and lower margins; two single prickings in outer margin near first and last text rulings. Method of ruling varies from hard point to crayon and lead.

I–IX^{10}, X^{8}, XI–XIV^{10}, XV^{8}, XVI^{10}, XVII^{8}, XVIII^{10}. Catchwords perpendicular to text along inner bounding line, verso. Quire and leaf signatures (e.g., a1, a2, a3, etc.) in lower right corner, recto.

Written in a round humanistic script by a single scribe, above top line.

Illuminated page (f. 1r) with partial border in outer and lower margins, white vine-stem ornament on predominantly green and red ground, with some blue and white dots, framed by thin gold bars. In lower border, unidentified mutilated coat of arms, against blue ground. Seven illuminated initials, 4- to 2-line, gold, against blue, green and red grounds with white vine-stem ornament and white dots. Headings and marginal annotations in pale red.

Binding: England, s. xix/xx. Red goatskin case with gold-tooled title "Valla In Poggium MS" and turn-ins. Gilt edges. Bound by Zaehnsdorf (London, 1842–1930).

Written in Rome ca. 1460–70 by the same scribe who copied London, B. L. Harl. 4995 (a. 1470?; Watson, *B. L.* pl. 740), a manuscript which descends from Lorenzo Valla's annotated Quintilian (we thank A. C. de la Mare for this information). There are at least two layers of contemporary annotations in Beinecke MS 81. The scribe of the text has underlined passages from Poggio in either red or the same shade of brown ink as the text, and added key words and names (e.g., varro, T. liuius, quintilianus, etc.) in the outer margins, as well as corrections to the text, in both red and brown ink. A second hand has written more extensive marginalia in a paler shade of brown ink, often glossing the notes of the first scribe and making further corrections to the text; he also added running headlines. Acquired in 1954 from C. A. Stonehill by Thomas E. Marston (bookplate).

secundo folio: apertam accusationem

Bibliography: Faye and Bond, pp. 73–74, no. 81.

Marston MS 82 Italy, s. XV^{2}
Varro, De lingua latina

ff. 1r–94v Quemadmodum uocabula essent imposita rebus in lingua latina sex libris exponere institui. De his tris ante hunc feci . . . et id genus que item et ex parte et uniuersa nominamus nom [with abbreviation stroke]. opus fuit ut in seruis.

Varro, *De lingua latina*; G. Goetz and F. Schoell, eds., *M. Terenti Varronis De lingua latina quae supersunt*, Teubner (1910) pp. 4–191. The scribe of Marston MS 82 carefully recorded in the margins the lacunae by giving the number of missing leaves in the exemplar (e.g., f. 39r: "In exemplari deficit folium unum in quo est principium libri v"); cf. Goetz and Schoell, *op. cit.*, p. xxii. Key words and proper names in margins, some in red. Variant readings and corrections added by at least one contemporary hand. Greek words entered by scribe in text and by a second contemporary hand in margins throughout.

Paper (coarse, some deckle edges; watermarks, in gutter: similar to Briquet Chapeau 3373, Main 10637; unidentified mountain surmounted by a cross and five-pointed star in a circle), ff. i (original parchment flyleaf?) + 94 (foliation by scribe in red, 1–30, in brown 31–52; modern foliation in pencil thereafter) + i (original parchment flyleaf?), 216 x 147 (140 x 75) mm. 27 long lines. Double vertical bounding lines, full length (Derolez 13.31); lines impressed on a ruling board.

I–IX^{10}, X^4. Vertical catchwords between inner bounding lines, verso (Derolez 12.5); remains of quire and leaf signatures (e.g., g 4), recto.

Written in humanistic cursive script, above top line, by a single scribe who added marginalia, foliation (1–52 only), and Roman numerals for running headlines (ff. 1–30).

Plain blue initial, 3-line, on f. 1r; plain red initials, 2-line, at beginning of books; headings in red, ff. 25r, 83v only. Remains of guide letters for rubricator.

Binding: Italy, s. xv. Parchment stays adhered to inner and outer conjugate leaves of quires. Original sewing on three tawed skin, slit straps laid in channels on the outside of boards and nailed. Plain wound, natural color endbands are sewn on tawed skin cores laid in grooves on the outside of the boards and are tied down over strips of green tawed skin.

Quarter bound in dark brown leather over beech boards with a leather strip nailed along the edge. One fastening, the leaf-shaped catch on the lower board, the upper board cut in for the clasp strap. Title, in ink, on fore edge: "Marcus Varo. De Lingua Latina."

Written in Italy in the second half of the 15th century; the manuscript was probably owner-produced since the inscription on f. i recto (".A./ Antonii andree andree clementis stephani") appears to be in the same hand as the text. Unidentified shelf-marks include: "XL: Terentius Varro de lingua latina," s. xvi, on verso of back flyleaf and the modern notation "41.3.8" in pencil on f. i recto. Remains of square white paper label on spine with author's name and title. Belonged to the library of the Princes of Liechtenstein (bookplate). Purchased from H. P. Kraus in 1955 by Thomas E. Marston (bookplate).

secundo folio: quo grammatica

Bibliography: Faye and Bond, p. 74, no. 82.

Marston MS 83 — Venice [?], s. $XV^{1/3}$ and XV^2

Aulus Gellius, Noctes Atticae (abridged)

ff. 1r–91v *Incipit liber agellij noctium acticarum.* Tanta pedis herculei qua idem olimpium stadium apud pisas sexcentarum numero mensus fuit ... emere uelit empturum sese negare prope competitores emptionis// ff. 92r–100v ruled, but blank

For the complete text of Aulus Gellius see P. K. Marshall, ed., OCT (1968) 2 vols.; regarding the manuscript tradition see the article by Marshall in *Texts and Transmission*, pp. 176–80. The abridged text in Marston MS 83 appears in the following order: Books I–V, VII, VI, IX–XII.2 (ending abruptly; the scribe has stopped copying, although there are several blank leaves ruled and ready to be filled). Chapter lists for each book, except for I and XI which are absent, precede the text of the book. The scribe made an error while copying so that the text on f. 50 belongs after f. 46; he added catchwords on ff. 46–50 to assist the reader in determining the correct sequence of the text. As in Marston MS 167 all passages containing Greek have been omitted. Books I and II are heavily abridged; beginning, however, with Bk. III fewer passages are deleted. This trend continues, until in Bks. IX–XII.12 the text is complete (always excepting the portions in Greek). According to P. K. Marshall (in unpublished correspondence) Marston MS 83 exhibits the same abbreviated text as the following 15th-century manuscripts: Oxford, Bodleian Library, Canon. Lat. 307; Paris, B. N. lat. 13039 (S. Germ. 1185); Rome, Biblioteca Casanatense D II 5 (679).

Parchment, ff. ii (contemporary parchment bifolium, i = front pastedown) + 100 + ii (contemporary parchment bifolium, ii = back pastedown), 233 x 140 (174 x 94) mm. Ruled in 31 long lines. Physical format is inconsistent. Folios 1–70: upper horizontal bounding line full across (Derolez 13.12), ruled in hard point on hair side; text rulings in hard point and vertical bounding lines in lead. Prickings in upper and lower margins and a single pricking in outer margin, 35 mm. below top line (for ff. 1–11 only). Full row of prickings in outer margin for remainder of codex. Folios 71–80: single vertical bounding lines, in lead (Derolez 13.11); folios 81–100: upper horizontal bounding line, in hard point, extends through inner margin and gutter (Derolez 13.17).

I–X^{10}. Catchwords, often with pen flourishes on all sides, in red, in center of lower margin, verso (Derolez 12.1).

Written in fere-humanistic script by a single scribe, below top line.

Folio 1r with partial border in inner and lower margin (rubbed). Inner margin has scrolling vine, yellow, on parchment ground with red dots, with stylized foliage, flowers and fruit in green, red, purple and dove grey. Illuminated initial, 3-line, purple on dark green ground, is incorporated into border. In lower margin, wreathed medallion (unidentified mutilated arms: per pale, or and sable?) on pink ground, supported by two heraldic dragons, parchment colored (unfinished) against red ground. All of this decoration appears to be a later addition. Plain initials and headings in red.

Binding: Italy, s. xv. Sewn on three tawed skin, kermes pink slit straps nailed in channels on the outside of the wooden boards. Yellow edges. The plain wound endbands may have been resewn. The spine is lined with cloth.

Covered in brown, originally tan, sheepskin with corner tongues. Blind-tooled with two rope interlace stars in a central panel bordered with concentric frames. Spine: bands outlined with double fillets; panels diapered with triple fillets. Two truncated diamond fastenings, the catches on the lower board (one wanting), the upper board cut in for straps attached with star-headed nails.

Written probably in Venice in the first third of the 15th century with decoration added in the second half of the century; early modern provenance unknown. Unidentified shelf-mark, in ink, on f. 1 verso: "D. 3." with an erasure below. Purchased from C. A. Stonehill in 1955 by Thomas E. Marston (bookplate).

secundo folio: amico

Bibliography: Faye and Bond, p. 74, no. 83.

Marston MS 85 Rome [?], s. $XV^{2/4\text{-med}}$
Leonardo Bruni, Commentaria rerum graecarum Pl. 24

ff. 1r–26v [Letter:] Animaduerti nonnumquam o angele te admirari solere meam ut ita dixerim cunctationem ac tarditatem ... [text, f. 2r:] Athenienses simulo ac mithylenam obsideri a lacedemoniis nuntiatum est ferre auxilium properantes ... ad thebanos mirabili fortune conuersione deuenit. finis.

Leonardo Bruni, *Commentaria rerum graecarum (De principatu Graeciae)*, preceded by Bruni's letter to Angelo Acciaiuolo; Baron, pp. 146–47 for letter, p. 176 for text reference. J. Gronovius, ed., *Thesaurus graecarum antiquitatum* (Venice, 1735) v. 6, cols. 3389–418.

Parchment, iii (paper) + i (contemporary parchment) + 26 (modern foliation, lower right corner, in pencil: on 21, 31, 41, 46 only) + i (contemporary parchment) + iii (paper), 258 x 184 mm. Ruled faintly in hard point; double vertical bounding lines full length (Derolez 13.31).

I–II^{10}, III^{6}.

Written in round humanistic bookhand by two scribes who use somewhat different physical formats. Scribe I: ff. 1r–16r, written above top line, with initials for paragraphs set apart from the text between outer vertical bounding lines; written space (169 x 114) mm. Scribe 2: ff. 16v–26v, written below top line and leaving blank the final line of written space (176 x 114) mm.

Two illuminated initials on ff. 1r and 2r, 5-line and 3-line, gold on blue, green and pale mauve ground with white vine-stem ornament and grey-green dots. On f. 1r vine-stem ornament on blue ground extends into inner margin (3-lines) to form partial border. Possibly by the same artist who executed the initials in Marston MS 257.

Binding: Italy, s. xx. Rigid vellum case with a green, gold-tooled label on spine: "L. Bruni De principatu graeciae. Sec. XV."

Written probably in Rome in the second quarter or middle of the 15th century; early modern provenance unknown. Formerly part of a larger volume as indicated by modern foliation (21–46); it is possible that Marston MS 85 (composed of 20 folios) comprised the other part of Marston MS 257 which was referred to as "De principatu graeciae" in the modern German note pasted to a front flyleaf of that manuscript. Although the two manuscripts were not written by the same scribe, they are of a similar size and contain decorative initials that may be by the same artist. (See also entry for Marston MS 257.) Unidentified "128" in pencil on f. iv recto, with contemporary notation in ink "cxxx." "B" enclosed by circle, in pencil, on f. i recto. Hoepli sale cat., 1955, no. 7 (pl. VI, in color). Purchased from Hoepli of Milan in 1955 by L. C. Witten (inv. no. 919), who sold it the same year to Thomas E. Marston (bookplate).

Bibliography: Faye and Bond, p. 74, no. 85.

Marston MS 86 — France, s. $XII^{3/4}$

Victorinus, Commentarius in Ciceronis De inventione, etc.

1. ff. 1r–47v Omnis quicumque incipit alicuius generis. orationem hec tria in principiis adibere debet. ut auditores faciat attentos. beniuolos. dociles ... que demonstratura partes habet .ii. laudem et uituperationem. Vtrumque tamen ex atributis persone tractatur.

   Victorinus, *Commentarius in Ciceronis De inventione (Explanationes in Ciceronis Rhetoricam)*; C. Halm, ed., *Rhetores latini minores* (Leipzig, 1863) pp. 155–304; text accompanied by a few contemporary and later marginal notes.

2. ff. 47v–49v Cum sint .ix. attributa persone. quibus appropriatur cuiusque persona. nomen nominis certis suis designatis et sanguinem et hominem ... Non ex ipsis rebus. Sed has res ipsas quadam gestione proueniunt. *Explicit.* f. 49v notes (see provenance)

   Anonymous commentary on Cicero, *De inventione* I. 24–28; C. Halm, *op. cit.*, pp. 305–10.

Parchment (warped), ff. i (paper) + 49 + i (paper), 195 x 135 (170 x 103) mm. 42 long lines. Single vertical and widely spaced double horizontal bounding lines. Ruled in hard point on the hair side before folding, or in lead. Prominent prickings in outer margin.

I^8, II^8 (–8, loss of text), $III–IV^8$, V^8 (–5, loss of text), VI^{12} (–12). Quires signed with Roman numerals, center of lower margin, recto. Quire and leaf signatures added, s. xv (e.g., c 1, c 2, etc.)

Written by multiple scribes in cramped early gothic bookhand, above top line. Marginalia by several contemporary and later hands.

Seven illuminated initials are later addition (Italy, s. xv^2): 4- to 3-line, gold on blue, red and green ground with white filigree. Black inkspray with gold leaves and balls extending into margins; f. 1r with blue and red flowers. Guide letters for decorator in margins.

Binding: Italy. s. xix. Brick red goatskin, blind-tooled. Bound in the same bindery for the Guarnieri-Balleani family (Iesi) as MS 450 and Marston MSS 72, 181, 182, and 212.

Written in France in the third quarter of the 12th century; contemporary accounts on f. 49v refer to one Jordanus de Walchelina, and to Rotbertus, Liulfus and Leofric. Partially effaced inscription on f. 49v indicates that Stefano Guarnieri (d. 1495) bought the manuscript in Rome in 1465 (see U. Nicolini, "Stefano Guarnieri da Osimo cancielliere a Perugia dal 1466 al 1488," *L'umanesimo umbro: atti del XI convegno di studi umbri-Gubbio 22–23 settembre 1974* [Perugia, 1977] pp. 307–23). Guarnieri's annotations in humanistic script appear sporadically in the text; it is possible that the illuminated initials, s. xv^2, were added for him. For other Beinecke manuscripts either copied, annotated or owned by Guarnieri, see catalogue entries for MS 450, Index V of this volume under Guarnieri-Balleani Library, as well as C. Annibaldi, *L'Agricola e la Germania di Cornelio Tacito* (Iesi, 1907) pp. 4–10. From the Guarnieri-Balleani Library at Iesi (characteristic binding and remains of paper labels on spine). Purchased from Lathrop Harper in 1953 by Thomas E. Marston (bookplate).

secundo folio: [maxi]marum ciuitatum

Bibliography: Faye and Bond, p. 74, no. 86.

Marston MS 87 Northern Italy, s. XV^{med}
Albertano da Brescia, Opera varia, etc.

Arts. 1-3 also appear together in Beinecke MS 102.

1. ff. 1r–6v *Incipit liber de scientia loquendi et tacendi.* Initio medio ac fine mei tractatus adsit gratia sancti spiritus quoniam in dicendo multi errant . . . Deum insuper exora qui mihi donauit predicta tibi narrare ut ad eterna gaudia nos faciat peruenire. *Explicit liber de doctrina dicendi et tacendi.*

   Albertano da Brescia, *Liber de doctrina dicendi et tacendi*; GKW, v. 1, nos. 531–63; T. Sundby, ed., *Della vita e delle opere di Brunetto Latini* (Florence, 1884) pp. 479–506.

2. ff. 7r–28r *Albertani. Incipit liber secundus de conscilio et consolatione. Rubrica.* Quoniam multi sunt qui in aduersitatibus et tribulationibus taliter affliguntur et deprimuntur . . . Ite in pace et amplius nolite peccare et ita utraque pars cum gaudio et leticia recesserunt. *Explicit liber consolationis et conscilij quem albertanus cau* [sic] *causidicus brisiensis*

de ora sancte agate compilauit. Sub annis domini M°. cc° de mesibus aprilis et madij.

Albertano da Brescia, *Liber consolationis et consilii*; T. Sundby, ed., *Albertano Brixiensis Liber consolationis et consilii* ... (London, 1873) pp. 1–127.

3. ff. 28r–78v *Incipit liber de amore et dilectione dei et proximi et aliarum rerum et de formula honeste uite liber primus. Rubrica.* Initium mei tractatus sit in nomine domini a quo cuncta bona procedunt ... [f. 78v:] peruenire ad quod ille nos perducat qui sine fine uiuit et regnat. Explicit liber de amore et dilectione dei et proximi et aliarum rerum et forma uite quem albertanus causidicus brisiensiensis [*sic*] de ora ... quo obsidebatur ciuitas brisie per eundem imperatorem Indictione xj[a].

   Albertano da Brescia, *De amore et dilectione Dei.*

4. ff. 78v–82r *Hic est sermo quem albertanus causidicus brisiensis de sancta agatha composuit et edidit....* Congregatio nostra sit in nomine domini a quo omne datum optimum et omne donum perfectum de sursum est descendens a patre ... Licet a sapiente dictum sit Inter sapientes non adicias loqui ... habeamus itaque in ore salem sapientie qui nobis proficiat ad uitam eternam ad quam ille nos perducat ... amen.

   Albertano da Brescia, *Sermo*; Schneyer, v. 1, p. 85 (1).

5. ff. 82r–85v [No heading; text:] Orate deum fratres ut ministerio sue sanctitatis per me seruum suum inutilem atque indignum ministret nobis hodie aliquid utilitatis fratres minores ... poterimus refici ad mensam christi in regno dei ad quod ipse nos perducat qui sine fine....

   Albertano da Brescia, *Sermo*; Schneyer, v. 1, p. 85 (2).

6. ff. 85v–89r [No heading; text:] In nomine domini amen. fratres mei ad honorem dei et refectionem pauperum more solito congregati sumus ... Venite benedicti patris mei et percipite regnum quod paratum est uobis ab origine mundi....

   Albertano da Brescia, *Sermo*; Schneyer, v. 1, p. 85 (3).

7. ff. 89r–93r *Sermo factus ad cognoscendum que sunt necessaria in conuiuio et quomodo debeamus intelligere ... qui intelligit super egenum et pauperem.* Domine labia mea ... [Ps. 50.17]. Congregatio sit in nomine domini qui ait. Vbicumque duo uel tres congregati fuerint in nomine meo ... Venite benedicti patris mei percipite regnum quod paratum est uobis ab origine mundi....

   Albertano da Brescia, *Sermo*; Schneyer, v. 1, p. 85 (4).

8. ff. 93r–95r *Hic est sermo quem albertanus causidicus de sancta agatha composuit et edidit inter causidicos brisienses apud fratres minores ... Sermo albertani super doctrina timoris domini.* Rogate deum fratres ut ministerio sue sanctitatis tribuat michi seruo suo inutilius dicere inter uos hodie aliquid utilitatis ... qui omnes gradus procedunt a timore domini ualeamus scandere ad regnum dei....

Albertano da Brescia, *Sermo*; Schneyer, v. 1, p. 85 (5).

9. f. 95r-v [1] Episcopi attendite dei uerba discernite. vobis precepit deus pro uestris mori ouibus. si bona que loquimini operibus feceritis exempla bona dabitis uestris comissis filijs. [2] Presbiteri diaconi qui fertis [corrected from *feritis*] uasa domini estote semper nitidi ... [39] Qui uiuitis in seculo omnes seruite domino. Vt iusti sua dextra regentis super etheria.

Albertano da Brescia [?], *De omnibus ordinibus omnium hominum*: 39 short precepts, ranging in length from 1/2 to 3 lines; each precept preceded by a paragraph mark. Classes of individuals addressed include *episcopi, presbiteri, plebani, magister, scriptores, abbates, monachus ... miles, puelle, meretrices*, etc.

10. ff. 95v–98v Mundalis machine fabricator primum hominis de limo ad ymaginem et similitudinem suam ut absque omni specie coruptionis immortalis formauit ... et statim uolare ualet et comedere potest.

13 short passages, unidentified, the final 4 on the Psalms.

11. f. 99r Virtus est habitus mentis bene constitute et deriuatus a meis. et est sciendum quod socrates nos uocat scientias uirtutes ... Nam supersticio ultra facit quam religio expectat.

Unidentified definitions of *virtus* and *vitium*, followed by a diagram of the cardinal virtues *Iusticia, Prudentia, Fortitudo, Temperantia.*

12. f. 99v Iusticia est habitus animi communi utilitate seruata suam unicuique tribuens dignitatem. Seueritas est uirtus debito supplicio cohercens inuriam [*sic*]. Benignitas.... [concluding with definitions for Sobrietas, Pudicicia].

Unidentified definitions of virtues, followed on f. 100r-v by a diagram of the seven capital sins: *Inanis gloria, Ira, Inuidia, Auaricia, Accidia, Castrimargia, Luxuria.*

13. f. 101r-v Inanis gloria est inordinatus animi motus quo aliquis propriam delet excelentiam ut alios honore precellet. Ira est subiecti animi tempestas ... Struprum [*sic*] proire uirginis est.

Unidentified definitions of vices.

14. ff. 101v–103r Auxilia humilia firma consensus facit. Aut amat aut odit mulier nil est medium. Aspicere opportet quod possis perdere ... Çelum de deo tantum habeas non contra homines. Çelari autem hominibus inuidiosum est.

Ps.-Seneca, *Proverbia*; E. Wölfflin, ed., *Publilii Syri sententiae* (Leipzig, 1869) pp. 65–113.

15. ff. 103r–104r [1] Oratio est theodorica uerborum series cum ornatu et pondere ... [2] Argumentum est inuentio per quam res aliena uel probabiliter ... [5] Demus beneficium non feneremus. [6] Dignus est decipi ... et uiro digna non implere corpus nec saginare sed perturbatione carere. Explicit notabili [followed by erasure] senece de beneficijs. f. 104v blank

Seneca, *De beneficiis* (extracts), etc.

Parchment. ff. i (paper) + 104 + i (paper), 227 x 156 (155 x 100) mm. Ca. 36 long lines. Frame-ruled in lead or ink, remains of prickings in outer margins.

I–VI^{8}, VII–IX^{10}, X–XI^{8}, XII^{10}. Horizontal catchwords, some with modest red flourishes, near gutter (Derolez 12.4). Remains of leaf signatures (e.g., aa, bb, cc, etc.).

Written by a single scribe in an informal gothic bookhand, below top line.

Initials for major text divisions in red with designs on parchment ground, 18- to 4-line, and some (e.g., f. 28r) with modest penwork designs in red and/or black. Small plain initials, 3- to 1-line, rubrics, and paragraph marks, in red.

Binding: Italy, s. xix. Quarter bound in tan paper with semi-limp paper sides. Written, in ink, on spine: "De Scientia/ Loquendi/ Tacendi/ Manos" and "Albertani/ Pergomena." On parchment leaves at front and rear: rust stains from five bosses and 2 fore-edge fastenings of an earlier binding.

Written in Northern Italy in the middle of the 15th century; early provenance unknown. Notes, in Italian, and shelf-mark ("Cod: xxviii") of owner, s. xix, on f. 1r. "Prezioso" in blue ink, s. xix, on upper cover; "Manuscrit du xive siècle" in ink on back cover. Belonged to Professor Hermann Suchier (1848–1914; bookplate). Purchased in 1954 from B. Rosenthal (Cat. 1, no. 1) by Thomas E. Marston (bookplate).

secundo folio: dubium

Bibliography: Faye and Bond, p. 74, no. 87.

Marston MS 88 — Northern France, s. $XIII^{2/4}$
Aristotle, Opera varia, in Lat. tr. — Pl. 43

1. ff. 1r–31r *Primum oportet* dicere circa quid et de quo est intencio. quoniam circa demonstracionem ... cui autem b. a. omni et non pluribus sed convertitur si autem non: non erit unum vnius signum. Explicit liber priorvm analeticorum [followed by a diagram]. f. 31v blank

   Aristotle, *Priora analytica*, Lat. tr. Boethius. L. Minio-Paluello, ed., *Analytica priora: Aristoteles latinus* v. III, 1–4 (Bruges-Paris, 1962) pp. 5–139 (this manuscript cited on p. xxxvii, no. 265); translation identified by the editor (*Intro.*, p. liii) as a mixture of the *recensio Florentina* and the *recensio Carnutensis*. Text is accompanied by extensive marginalia.

2. ff. 32r–51r *Omnis doctrina* et omnis disciplina intellectiua ex preexistenti fit cognicione ... utique erit intellectus scientie principiorum et principium principiis. hoc autem omne similiter se habet ad omne genus rerum. Explicit liber posteriorum analeticorum. f. 51v blank

   Aristotle, *Posteriora analytica*, Lat. tr. Jacobus Veneticus (ca. 1130–40). L. Minio-Paluello and B. G. Dod, eds., *Analytica posteriora: Aristoteles latinus* v. IV, 1–4 (Bruges-Paris, 1968) pp. 5–107 (this manuscript cited on p. xxxiii, no. 287). Text is accompanied by extensive marginalia.

3. ff. 52r–66r [Part I:] *Omnis ars et omnis* doctrina. Similiter autem et operacio et proheresis boni alicuius operatrix esse uidetur ... [f. 57r:] habitum autem eos qui laudabiles uirtutes dicimus intellectuales. [Part II, beginning on line 8:] Duplici autem uirtute existente hac quidem intellectuali illa uero consuetudinali ... [f. 66r, line 20:] nomen autem incontinencie et ad puerilia peccata transferimus. [Additional paragraph, beginning with line 21:] habet enim simile ... de castitate in tantum dictum sit. Explicit liber ethicorum.

   Although written as a single work in this manuscript, the text consists of two distinct parts. Part I is the "Ethica nova" (Bk. I of the *Ethica Nicomachea*) in an anonymous translation produced s. XIII^{in}; R. A. Gauthier, ed., *Ethica Nicomachea: Aristoteles latinus* v. XXVI, 1–3.2 (Leiden, 1972) text: pp. 65–95; detailed analysis of Marston MS 88, which was used to establish this edition, on pp. lxxi–lxxv.

Part II is the "Ethica vetus, editio longior" (Bks. II and III of the *Ethica Nicomachea*) in an anonymous translation produced s. XII^{ex}. Gauthier, *op. cit.*, text: pp. 5–48, 130–131; Marston MS 88 discussed on pp. xx, xxxvii–xxxviii, xlii. The text in this manuscript is called the "editio longior" because of the additional paragraph at the conclusion (cf. Gauthier, *op.cit.*, Appendix on pp. cxlvii–cli). Text is accompanied by extensive marginalia; in addition, a long continuous text on the ontological structure of forms was written into the margins of ff. 56v–66r.

4. ff. 66v–84r [In upper margin:] *Incipit liber de anima.* [text:] *Bonorum et honorabilium* notitiam opinantes magis autem alteram altera que est secundum certitudinem aut ex eo quod meliorum ... auditum autem ut significet aliquid sibi ipsi linguam uero quatenus significet aliquid alteri.

   Aristotle, *De anima*, Lat. tr. Jacobus Veneticus as identified by L. Minio-Paluello, "Le texte du *De anima* d'Aristote: la tradition latine avant 1500," *Autour d'Aristote: Recueil d'études ... offert à Mons. A. Mansion* (Louvain, 1955) pp. 217–43. The text is accompanied by extensive marginalia.

5. ff. 84r–86r Reliquorum autem primo considerandum de memoria et memorari quid est et propter quas fit et cui anime ... memorantur animalia et de reminisci quidem et quo modo fit et propter quas causas dictum est. f. 86v blank

   Aristotle, *De anima* (Περὶ μνήμης καὶ ἀναμνήσεως from the *Parva naturalia*), Lat. tr. Jacobus Veneticus; this treatise follows art. 4 directly without break or rubric. See L. Minio-Paluello, "Jacobus Veneticus Grecus: Canonist and Translator of Aristotle," *Traditio* 8 (1952) pp. 265–304.

Parchment (thin, pliable), ff. i (paper) + 86 + i (paper), 202 x 150 (117 x 80) mm. Ca. 32 long lines. Single vertical and double horizontal bounding lines; ruled faintly in lead.

I–II^{8}, III^{8} (–7, no loss of text), IV–VII^{8}, VIII^{10}, IX–X^{8}, XI^{8} (–6 through 8, blanks, stubs remain). Faint traces of catchwords, lower edge near gutter.

Written in a small neat gothic text script, above top line and with uncrossed tironian *et*. Marginal and interlinear annotations, contemporary or slightly later, in a variety of scholarly hands; annotations written in ink, crayon and lead, some very faded and barely legible.

Attractive flourished initials, red and blue divided with penwork designs in the same colors, mark the beginning of arts. 1–4; first few words of each of these texts written in red and blue alternating majuscules. For minor text divisions 2-line initials red or blue with designs in the opposite color. Paragraph marks in red (or sometimes alternating red and blue). Headings and instructions to rubricator in red.

Binding: Germany, s. xix. Parchment case binding made from a bifolium of a missal (Germany, s. XV) containing text for the end of the Secret for the 11th Sunday after Pentecost through part of the Gospel reading for the 12th Sunday. Remains of title, in ink, on spine. Pink (faded red?) edges.

Written in Northern France in the second quarter of the 13th century; given the extensive contemporary annotations, it was probably produced as a school text. Contemporary inscription on f. 86v: "pro duodecim sol. emptus fuit"; remainder illegible. Belonged in the 18th century to the library of the Benedictine monastery of St. Georgenberg, now Fiecht, in Austria (inscription in upper margin, f. 1r: "Bibliothecae Montis Sancti Georgij. II. 68"); Gauthier, *op.cit.*, p. xx (Marston MS 88 listed incorrectly as Marston MS 11 and assigned to Germany, s. XIII^{ex}). For a brief history of this monastery, pertinent bibliography, and a catalogue of its present holdings see P. Jeffery and D. Yates, *Descriptive Inventories of Manuscripts Microfilmed for the Hill Monastic Manuscript Library*, Austrian Libraries, Vol. II: St. Georgenberg-Fiecht (Collegeville, Minn., 1985). Traces of large bookplate, now missing, on front pastedown. Pencil notes on front pastedown and front flyleaf: "II c. 20" and "M. II. c. 20"; in ink on front flyleaf: "14." Clipping, in German, from unidentified sale catalogue glued to front pastedown. Two modern pencil notes on back pastedown: "66 fl [?]W" and "M. Z. Sanders." Purchased from C. A. Stonehill (inv. no. 3034) in 1954 by Thomas E. Marston (bookplate).

secundo folio: non album

Bibliography: Faye and Bond, p. 74, no. 88.

Marston MS 89 — Northern France, s. XII^1
Boethius, De arithmetica

ff. 1r–37r //inchoans equaliter que disterminans [?]. Idem autem dico numerat quod metitur. Si igitur bis maiorem numerum solum minor numerus metiatur ... sola est epigdous [corrected from *epigdoun*?] differentia. Huius descriptionis subter exemplar adiecimus [added in a later hand: *et omnis*]. f. 37v contains the "exemplaria" promised at the conclusion of the text in a full-page illustration (with later additions).

G. Friedlein, ed., *Boetii De institutione arithmetica libri duo* Teubner (1867) pp. 47.14–173. Text begins imperfectly in Bk. I, ch. 23, missing perhaps two gatherings of eight leaves; loss of one leaf with text between ff. 29–30 in Bk. 2, ch. 44–46 ("... in terminis ut subita descriptio monet [followed by diagram] // tercium. Sin uero fuerint cybi duas...") . Bk. 2 begins on f. 8v without table of *capitula* and without indication that one book has ended and the next begun. Some contemporary corrections and annotations. On f. 37r a later hand, s. xiii, added accounts in the lower half of the page.

Parchment (poor quality; end pieces), ff. 37, 210 x 140 (155 x 90) mm. 29 long lines. Single vertical bounding lines, full length; some horizontal bounding lines, full width. Ruled in lead or in hard point on hair side. Prickings prominent in upper, lower and outer margins.

I–III^{8}, IV^{8} (–6), V^{6}.

Written by multiple scribes (some copying or correcting only brief portions of text) in late caroline minuscule.

Plain initials, 6- to 2-line, red, blue or black, occasionally with modest pen design in red (e.g., ff. 27v–28r). Numerous diagrams and charts throughout.

Parchment stained and warped by damp.

Binding: Eastern Europe [?], s. xiv or xv. The back pastedown consists of a portion of a Latin parchment document dated 1374 (see also provenance below). Front pastedown removed and preserved as Marston MS 89A (see catalogue entry below). Sewn on three supports laced into thick oak boards and wedged. Plain wound endbands on alum-tawed cores originally laced into the boards.

Covered with parchment with irregularly serrated turn-ins, with a strap-and-pin fastening, the pin on the upper board. The codex has been so tightly rebacked that it is difficult to open.

Written in Northern France in the first half of the 12th century, to judge from the script. Bound in the 14th or 15th century, probably in Eastern Europe, since the parchment document serving as back pastedown was executed in "Camyn" (with abbreviation stroke) and contains the following proper names: Nicolaus Zagentzen de Jasdowe (or Iasdow), Nicolaus Colver de Warsecowe, and Wyscau. Purchased from G. Heilbrun of Paris in 1951 by L. C. Witten (inv. no. 134) who sold it in 1953 to Thomas E. Marston (bookplate).

Bibliography: Faye and Bond, p. 74, no. 89.

Marston MS 89A — France, s. XII
Drawings

A single parchment folio (damaged) removed from Marston MS 89 where it was used as a front pastedown. The one side has fine drawings of a king and queen (with falcon) in elaborate robes. Beside them is a foot soldier in armor; below, a warrior on horseback, in armor, pursued by an archer, without armor. Above is a centaur (Chiron?) shooting an arrow at a flying bird, a second bird on the ground. On the other side (much affected by paste) three warriors storm a tower. See also catalogue entry for Marston MS 89.

Marston MS 90 — Florence or Rome, s. $XV^{3/4}$
Leonardo Bruni, De primo bello punico

ff. 1r–58v *Leonardi Arretini commentariorum primi belli punici liber primus incipit. Prefatio.* Vereor ne qui me putent antiqua nimium consectari si commentaria primj punicj belli ... *Finis proemii.* [text, f. 1v:] *Incipit liber primus.* Origo primj punicj belli quod populus romanus aduersum carthaginenses terra marique ... pauca loca excedere iussi sunt. Finis. Gratis deo. Amen.

Leonardo Bruni, *De primo bello punico,* compiled largely from Polybius; text is defective, missing two leaves between 30 and 31 ("... suspicatj quinquaginta [catchword: nauibus] // stigio quadriremes premere abeuntem...") and two more between 36 and 37 ("... non dubitauit hoc // receperunt. Consul post prelium cum..."). GKW, v. 5, no. 5603 (Brescia: Jacobus Britannicus, 24 October 1498) and thereafter; text of Preface edited by Baron, pp. 122–23. Marginal notes and rubrics by several hands, s. xv–xvi.

Parchment (poor quality), ii (paper) + i (original parchment flyleaf or wrapper?) + 58 (early foliation, 1–30, 33–38, 41–62, before leaves were lost) + i (original parchment flyleaf or wrapper?) + ii (paper), 220 x 141 (151 x 80) mm. 28 long lines ruled in hard point. Double vertical bounding lines, full length (Derolez 13.31).

I–III^{10}, IV^{10} (-1, 2, 9, 10), V–VI^{10}, VII^{4} (-3, 4, blank). Catchwords in gutter near lower edge, perpendicular to text (Derolez 12.7).

Text written by a single scribe in humanistic cursive script, above top line. Marginal notes (mostly proper names and events) added by at least two hands, s. xv–xvi, with one set added throughout in red by a scribe who also placed Roman numerals for each book in upper margin.

One large illuminated initial, 4-line, gold on blue, light green and pink ground with white vine-stem ornament. Initial joined to partial border, white vine-stem ornament on blue, light green and pink ground with white dots and gold balls with penwork extensions in brown ink. Two smaller initials on ff. 23v and 38r, 4-line, gold, outlined in yellow on blue grounds with white highlights. Plain initial, f. 1v, and headings in pale red.

Binding: England [?], s. xix. Quarter bound in red, hard-grained goatskin, gold-tooled, with printed marbled paper sides. Edges spattered yellow and black. Title on spine: "Leonardi Aretini, Commentarii. MS. in membranis."

Written in Florence or Rome in the third quarter of the 15th century to judge from the styles of script and decoration; the manuscript has an owner-produced appearance and was presumably copied for personal use. Unidentified armorial bookplate inside front cover, with motto "Excelsior." Ex libris of John A. Murphy inside front cover. Purchased from Maggs Bros., London, in 1955 by L. C. Witten (inv. no. 655), who sold it the same year to Thomas E. Marston (bookplate).

secundo folio: [eni]xissime gessit

Bibliography: Faye and Bond, pp. 74–75, no. 90.

Marston MS 91 Milan [?], s. XV$^{\text{med or } 3/4}$

Walter Burley, De vita et moribus philosophorum, etc. Pl. 31

1. ff. 1r–129r [Title:] De uita et moribus philosophorum ueterum tractaturus multa que ab antiquis Auctoribus in diuersis libris ... consolacionem et morum informacionem conferre ualebunt. [text:] Talles [*sic*] philosophus asianus vt ait laercius in libro de uita philosophum ... Scripsit insuper librum de naturalibus questionibus ad Cosdroe [*sic*] regem persarum. Deo gratias Amen. Amen. Qui scripsit scribat. Semper cum domino viuat. [added later:] Ad quam nos perducat ille. ff. 129v–130v ruled, but blank

Walter Burley, *De vita et moribus philosophorum*; H. Knust, ed., *Bibliothek des litterarischen Vereins in Stuttgart* 176 (Tübingen, 1886) pp. 2–395; listed in J. Prelog, "Die Handschriften und Drucke von Walter Burleys Liber de vita et moribus philosophorum," *Codices manuscripti* 9 (1983) p. 7, no. 135, and R. Wedler, *Walter Burleys "Liber de vita et moribus philosophorum poetarumque veterum" in zwei deutschen Bearbeitungen des Spätmittelalters*, Ph. D. Thesis (Heidelberg, 1969) p. 23. Beinecke MS 91 contains 130 lives in approximately the same order as the edition by Knust, with two major differences: [i.] A misplacement of a block of material: within the life of Bias (f. 11r) the scribe begins to copy without interruption the middle of the life of Zoroastes; the remainder of the life of Bias, as well as the lives of Cleobulus, Periander and the first lines of the life of Zoroastes, are inserted into the life of Misosternon on f. 13r. Then on f. 15v, having completed the life of Zoroastes up to the point where he had started on f. 11r, the scribe finished with the concluding four lines of Misosternon. [ii.] After the life of Seneca on ff. 111v–117r is the complete text of Ps.-Seneca, *De remediis fortuitorum liber* (F. Haase, ed., Teubner, v. 3 [1872] pp. 446–57).

2. ff. 131r–165r [C]um decertarent inter se aliquando superiora simul atque inferiora mundi corpora iactaretque unumquodque uim et pulcritudinem suam placuit . . . non expectata etiam ulla iudicis snia [*for* sententia] manifeste declarauit.

   Mapheius Vegius, *Declamatio seu disputatio inter solem, terram et aurum; Maxima Bibliotheca veterum patrum et antiquorum scriptorum ecclesiasticorum* v. 26 (Leiden, 1677) pp. 777–87.

3. ff. 165r–174v [A]dmirari nonnunquam soleo cum alia permulta diuinitus apud homerum scripta . . . repellas non tamen par gratia atque honor tibi erit. Finis. Ad laudem dei. ff. 175r–176v ruled, but blank

   Selected speeches from Homer, *Iliad IX* (*Oratio Ulixis, Responsio Achillis, Oratio Phoenicis*) translated into Latin and with a preface by Leonardo Bruni; Baron, p. 172. D. Mansi, ed., *Stephani Baluzii tutelensis Miscellanea novo ordine* . . . (Lucca, 1762) v. 3, pp. 151–54; preface only in Baron, pp. 132–34.

Paper (highly polished; watermarks: unidentified crown over five-pointed star in upper margin, trimmed), ff. ii (modern paper) + i (contemporary paper) + 176 (ff. 1 and 10 parchment) + ii (modern paper), 216 x 150 (120 x 70) mm. 22 long lines, with single vertical bounding lines full length in lead and rulings for text in ink (Derolez 13.11). Single pricking in outer margin, 8 mm. above top line (Derolez 18.3).

$I–XVII^{10}$, XVIII^{6}. Catchwords perpendicular to text on inner bounding line (Derolez 12.6).

Written by a single scribe in humanistic cursive script with gothic features, above top line.

The decoration consists of an elaborately illuminated page (f. 1r) in a style influenced by the "Master of the Vitae Imperatorum" who was active in Milan in the second quarter of the 15th century. Included in the full border of curling inkspray with heart-shaped and trefoil leaves in green, flowers in blue, red, pink and mauve, a strawberry, and gold balls is a standing figure of a naked boy holding a scroll inscribed with the motto "Seul e la fin." At the corners four quatrefoil medallions bordered in gold with portraits of philosophers against blue grounds with gold filigree. In lower border unidentified arms (quarterly, 1 and 4 or a millrind gules, 2 and 3 or a lion azure; with a bishop's mitre and crozier); in upper border a scroll with same motto as above. One historiated initial, f. 1r, 7-line, formed of acanthus leaves, mauve and red on gold ground, containing a portrait of the author against blue ground with gold filigree. One illuminated initial, 6-line, in mauve on gold ground with stylized foliage in green and blue with yellow highlights. In the text blank spaces for headings and initials.

Binding: England, s. xix. Straight-grained brown leather, gold tooled. Edges gilt. Bound by F. & T. Aitken. Title on spine: "Diogenis Laertii Philosophorum Vita et Dicta. Codex MS. Saec. XV."

Written in Northwestern Italy, probably in Milan, in the middle or third quarter of the 15th century, to judge by the decoration; owned by an unidentified cleric whose arms appear on f. 1r. The manuscript was annotated by several contemporary or slightly later hands. Early modern provenance unknown. Note, s. xviii, on f. iii verso, incorrectly attributes the text to Diogenes Laertius: "Continet codex iste saec. XV. Diogenis Laertij Philosophorum vitas et Dogmata. Versio hec anonymi e Greco facta plurimum distat a versionibus editis, et quasi ceterarum compendium est. Notande sunt in fronte Codicis quinque Philosophorum effigies egregia manu depicte. Extat in fine aliud Opusculum singulare usque adeo mihi ignotum." Purchased from E. P. Goldschmidt of London in 1955 by L. C. Witten (inv. no. 804), who sold it the same year to Thomas E. Marston (bookplate).

secundo folio: dandam qui

Bibliography: Faye and Bond, p. 75, no. 91.

C. E. Lutz, "Walter Burley's De Vita et moribus philosophorum," *Gazette* 46 (1972) pp. 247–52; reprinted in her *Essays on Manuscripts and Rare Books* (Hamden, Conn., 1975) pp. 51–56, with pl. 3 of f. 1r.

Marston MS 92 Northern Italy, s. XV^2
Ps.-Cicero, Synonyma

1. f. 1r Early (s. xvi?) cartoon drawing, traced over, of a man on the left standing in front of a cask filling a container; on the right another man drinking (?). Captions visible under ultra-violet light indicate that "Rico" (left) and "Boto" are both labelled "canauaro" (tavernkeeper) and that the cask is designated "la bota de la maluasia." A second cartoon (obscene) visible under ultra-violet light. f. 1v blank

2. ff. 2r–23r *.M. T. Ciceronis. ad .L. Veturium Sinonimorum. Liber Incipit per alfabetum.* Cicero. lucio uecturio suo salutem. Collegi ea que pluribus modis dicerentur, quo uberior promptiorque esset oratio ... *Vitare/* Declinare/ Cauere/ Subterfugere/ [bracketed:] Operitur/ Prestolatur/ Expectat/ Sustinet/ Deo gratias Amen. ff. 23v–25v ruled, but blank

Ps.-Cicero, *Synonyma*; GKW, v. 6, nos. 7031–40.

Parchment (palimpsest throughout from text manuscripts and accounts; remains of rulings and prickings, e. g., lower margin of f. 16), ff. i (modern parchment) + i (contemporary parchment, f. 1) + 24 (ff. 2–25) + i (modern parchment), 205 x 144 (156 x 80) mm. 4 columns of 36 lines, with the first column written outside of ruled space. Single vertical bounding lines ruled in lead; text lines ruled in ink.

I–III^8. Horizontal catchwords centered below written space, verso (Derolez 12.1).

Written in a well formed round gothic bookhand by a single scribe.

Initials, 5-line, at beginning of text: red with delicate black penwork designs. Heading and each *verbum* in red; synonyms connected by a curving red line.

Binding: Italy, s. xix. Original sewing on three slit straps.

Quarter bound in white sheepskin. The beech boards are early, s. xv, with title written twice on front and once on back (see also below). A leaf-shaped catch on the lower board, the upper one cut in for a clasp strap. Spine covering and clasp strap are recent additions.

Written in Northern Italy in the second half of the 15th century and possibly used as a school text given the cartoons on f. 1r. The text of the *Synonyma* was formerly bound with Agostino Dati's *Elegantiolae*, since the early title on the back cover reads: "Sinonima/ Aug Dati Eleganziole." Belonged in the 16th century to Camillo Capilupi, presumably a member of the Mantuan family of that name; inscription visible under ultra-violet light on f. 1v: "Camillus Capilupus iuuenis"; a second inscription written below in the same hand reads: "amasius musarum." It is unclear whether these are the inscriptions of the father by that name (1504–48; Cosenza, v. 1, 840–41) or of his son (1531–1603; *Dizionario biografico degli italiani*, v. 18, pp. 531–35). Belonged to Giuseppe (Joseph) Martini of Lugano (his note on front pastedown). Purchased from H. P. Kraus in 1955 by Thomas E. Marston (bookplate).

secundo folio: *Audacia*

Bibliography: Faye and Bond, p. 75, no. 92.

Marston MS 93 — Florence, s. $XV^{3/4}$
George of Trebizond, Isagoge dialectica, etc. — Pl. 59

1. front pastedown: σοφοκλεῖ τὲ μὴ ἀπιστεῖν· μόνοις οὐ γίνεται θεοῖς γῆρας . . . ὁ δεῖνα τοῦ δεῖνος ἔχων οὐκ ἔχει.

   Passage from Philostratus, *Vita Apollonii*, 8, 7, 56; A. Westermann, ed. (Paris, 1849).

2. ff. 1r–30v Clarissimi et doctissimi uiri georgii trapezuntii dialecticorum opus ad artem dicendi attinens. [preface:] Multa sunt mi petre. que faciunt vt omni cura omnique diligentia cogitem . . . Quod si facies nec te preceptionis nostre nec me mei laboris poenitebit. [text, f. 1v:] *Dialectica*. Dialectica igitur est diligens disserendi ratio: disserere uero nemo poterit diligenter . . . et maiorum scientia rerum non abiecta uere doctus sis et uidearis. Vale. *Doctissimi et latinarum graecarumque litterarum peritissimi georgii trabezuntii de dialecticis opus explicitum est.* τέλος.

   George of Trebizond, *Isagoge dialectica*, with his preface to Petrus Gambacurta; J. Monfasani, ed., *Collectanea Trapezuntiana: Texts, Documents, and Bibliographies of George of Trebizond*, Medieval and Renaissance Texts and Studies 25 (Binghamton, 1984) pp. 309–11 (preface) and pp. 473–77 (list of 55 manuscripts and printed editions including Marston MS 93 [no. 12], which is also described on p. 37).

3. ff. 31r–37r *De locis sophisticis ex aristotele excerptio*. Disputatio est inter duos contentio per ratiocinationem ad propositum obtinendum . . . questio que est multiplex. fallacie uero causa est multiplex interogatio. *Compendium* [corrected from *Compennium*] *de sophisticis locis explicitum est.* δόξα τῷ θεῷ μοῦ.

   Extracts from Aristotle, *De sophisticis elenchis*, in an unidentified Latin translation.

4. f. 37v Full-page diagram in red, with inscriptions in black, of *A, E, I, O* syllogisms.

5. ff. 38r–40r *De inuentione medii termini erga qualemcumque conclusionem.* Ad unamquamque conclusionem syllogizandam opus est adhibere medium terminum ... Ex his patet particularem negatiuam posse syllogizari secundum omnes figuras. Finis.

6. f. 40r Sciendum quod in prima figura ubi conluditur particularis ... ergo aliquod rudibile est homo. ff. 40v–41v blank

Unidentified paragraph on logic, followed by a diagram, in red and black, of *contraria* and *contradictoria.*

7. f. 42r Diuo principi federico monpheltrio m. philethicus. Nulla tuum nomen poterit delere uetustas/ Belligeri Princeps martis Alumne dei/ ... Sed quia ditasti multos federice poetas/ Incipe praxiteles iamque beare viros.

Martinus Philеticus (ca. 1430–ca. 1490), 14-line poem to Federico da Montefeltro of Urbino, written in the hand of the author; not listed in Bertalot.

Parchment (speckled), ff. iv (two contemporary parchment bifolia; i = front pastedown) + 40 + iv (including ff. 41–42; two contemporary parchment bifolia; iii is missing, iv = back pastedown), 196 x 133 (128 x 83) mm. 28 long lines. Single vertical bounding lines full length (Derolez 13.11). Ruled in hard point on the flesh side; two additional rulings for catchwords.

I–IV^{10}. Horizontal catchwords near gutter (Derolez 12.4).

Art. 1 in a small and regular Greek minuscule script; arts. 2–6 in humanistic cursive script, below top line, by a single scribe who also added marginalia; art. 7 in humanistic cursive by a different scribe.

One illuminated initial of poor quality, gold, 3-line, on blue, green, and pink ground. Rubrics and marginal key words (for ff. 1r–6r, 31r only; e.g., *nomen, uerbum,* etc.) in pale red. Plain blue initials in art. 2; red or blue elsewhere.

Binding: Italy, s. xv (attributed to Florence or Tuscany by De Marinis, *La legatura,* v. 1, p. 102, no. 1021). Original sewing on three tawed skin, slit straps laid in channels on the outside of wooden boards and nailed. The spine is lined with leather between sewing supports.

Covered in brown sheepskin with corner tongues and blind-tooled with concentric frames, one filled with rope interlace, and a rope interlace square on a point in the central panel. Annular dots are colored with gold or copper, now green. Spine: very faint diapering with triple fillets. There are five round bosses on each board and two fastenings, leaf-shaped catches on the lower board and the upper one cut in for fabric straps. The front board is detached; one boss wanting.

Written in Florence in the third quarter of the 15th century; according to A. C. de la Mare art. 7 is in the hand of Martinus Phileticus, who accompanied his student Battista Sforza to Urbino when she married Federico da Montefeltro (see art. 7); art. 1 on the front pastedown and a few marginal annotations in Greek were added by the same scribe who copied portions of Munich, Bayerische Staatsbibliothek, Monac. graec. 537 (see Monfasani, *op. cit.*, pl. V, lines 2–9) and of El Escorial Σ–III–1. Ownership inscriptions in two different hands on f. ii recto: "A. Nicolao thermio Archipresbitero balneoregiensi [Bagnorea] Hic Dialecticorum Liber de dicendi Arte pro .xxx.[ta] carlenorum pretio: emptus est. Anno domini M° cccc Lxxxxvj. xv° Kalendas decembris Alexandri vj. pontificis maximj." and "Ex dono auctoris A. D. MCCCCXCVII Jacobus Macchiauellius." Notes, in French, on f. iii recto and verso concerning George of Trebizond, with citations from "Morery Diet. Edit. 1702" and Leone Allacci (1586–1669), Paolo Giovio (1483–1552), Vossius. Unidentified "4" in pencil on f. ii recto. Purchased from C. A. Stonehill (inv. no. 11386) in 1955 by Thomas E. Marston (bookplate).

secundo folio: elementa sunt

Bibliography: Faye and Bond, p. 75, no. 93.

Marston MS 94

Lexicon Greco-Latinum, etc.

Verona, ca. 1460
Pl. 28

1. ff. 1r–198r ʽΕρανον λέξεων ἑλληνικῶν λατινικῶς ἑρμηνευθέντων. Αατος. Insatiabilis. illaesus. innocens dicitur etiam ἄτος. / ʽΑάατος pro ἄατος illaesus/ ... ἄαπτος intangibilis/ ἀαγές infrangibile/ ... ὠχρίας pallidus/ ἡ ὤχρα ille color qui teritur a pictoribus/ ἡ ὤψ τῆς ὠπός uultus. ΤΕΛΟΣ. f. 198v ruled, but blank

   Unidentified Greek-Latin lexicon. The text is arranged for the most part in two columns, with the first letter of each Greek word placed between bounding lines. In several longer entries (e. g., ἄγω, ἡγοῦμαι) the Latin equivalents extend the width of the written space for several lines. For a similar lexicon, see Beinecke MS 277, art. 1.

2. ff. 199r–202v *De aspiratione graecarum dictionum. Guarinus Veronensis Francisco Barbaro Patritio Veneto. S.* Cum amorem tuum erga me beneficiaque francisce recenseo grande tecum ... in principio sicut verbi gratia οἶνος φίλοινος, nec scribendum est φιλόινος. [text:] περὶ δασείας καὶ ψιλῆς. Πόσα πνεύματα; δύο ἡ δασεῖα καὶ ἡ ψιλή. πᾶσα λέξις ... ἀπὸ τῆς οὗτος ἀντωνυμίας δασύνονται.

Anonymous treatise on breathing marks in Greek; printed in Milan, 1476, by Dionysius Paravisinus and entitled Περὶ πνευμάτων (British Museum, XV cent., v. 6, p. 731). Preceded by the letter of Guarino of Verona to Francesco Barbaro; R. Sabbadini, ed., *Epistolario di Guarino Veronese* in *Miscellanea di storia veneta,* ser. 3, v. 8 (1915) letter 195, pp. 310–11.

3. ff. 203r–205r *De formationibus temporum uerborum graecorum.* Tempus omne in tres partes diuisum est εἰς ἐνεστῶτα, εἰς παρακείμενον καὶ εἰς μέλλοντα. id est in praesens. in praeteritum et in futurum ... ὄπτομαι uideo ὁ μέλλ. ὄψομαι ὄψει τέλος.

4. f. 205v *De praepositionum significatione et constructione.* ἘΝ in sed in compositione cum verbo intus significat et construitur semper cum datiuo ... [for ὑπέρ] et supra cum accusatiuo et super.

5. f. 206r-v *De numeris.* Εἷς μία ἕν. unus una unum./ δύο duo/ ... χιλιοστός millesimus. Followed by a table with Greek numerals and their Arabic equivalents. f. 207r-v ruled, but blank

Parchment, ff. i (contemporary parchment bifolium; i = front pastedown) + 207, 190 x 110 (137 x ca. 63) mm. 2 columns, 44 lines. Double or single vertical bounding lines ruled in crayon (Derolez 13.31); additional vertical ruling to delineate the written space for Latin equivalents of Greek words; horizontal rulings for text in light brown ink. Prickings in upper and lower margins; single pricking along outer edge, 2 mm. above top line.

I–XX^{10}, XXI^{10} (–8, 9; 10 = back pastedown). Two sets of quire signatures on verso: Arabic numerals in lower left corner and Greek numerals in lower right. Remains of quire and leaf signatures (e. g., b1, b2, b3, etc.) in lower right corner, recto, mostly trimmed.

The decoration consists of an illuminated title page, with full border, thin white vine-stem ornament with stylized foliage in red, pink, blue against blue, green and pink ground with white dots and gold balls. In outer border two vases, blue with white highlights, and three roundels framed in red, green or pink with Roman profile heads wearing fillets against blue or gold ground. In inner border foliage curling around a thin gold bar. The upper border consists of a garland, green with gold highlights, tied with red ribbons against a blue and gold ground with two masks, one spouting water. Unidentified arms (palm? tree on red ground) in center of lower border. Large illuminated initial, 12-line, gold against a predominantly blue ground with some green, pink, red and gold, and sprouting vine-stem ornament, white with pale brown shading and stylized foliage in red, pink and light brown. 25 illuminated initials for letters of Greek alphabet B to Ω, 6- to 5-line, gold, against blue, green and dark pink grounds with stylized white vine-stem ornament or white stylized foliage. 2 small illuminated initials (ff. 205v and 206r), 3-line, gold against blue, red and green ground with pale yellow and white dots and white filigree. The initials are similar in style to Harvard, Houghton Library, Typ 447, signed by Biagio Saraceni of Vicenza in 1460 at Verona. Heading on f. 1r in blue; others in red. Plain initials in red.

Binding: Italy, s. xv/xvi. Original sewing on three tawed skin, slit straps laid in channels on the outside of wooden boards. Gilt edges. The secondary, beaded endband is cream and green.

Covered in reddish brown goatskin, blind-tooled with a floral border and fleurons in a central panel. Name of owner is gold-tooled on side in Roman letters that have been modified to form Greek letters: ΙΟΥΛΙΟΣ ΦΟΝΤΑΝΑ. Spine: triple fillets at head and tail; single fillet diapering in the panels. Gold tooling added later. Traces of two fastenings, the catches on the lower board; the upper board heavily cut in for clasps. Modern title on spine: "Guarini Lexicon Ineditum. MS. in membranis." Described and illustrated in Walters Art Gallery, *Bookbinding*, p. 94, no. 211, pl. XLIV.

Written in Verona ca. 1460 for an individual whose unidentified arms appear on f. 1r. Contemporary inscription, partially visible under ultraviolet light, on rear pastedown: "Iulio Spolnetino [?]." Belonged to Giulio Fontana of Vicenza, s. xvi; his name is stamped on the upper cover and his inscription appears on f. i recto: "De Giulio Fontana vicentino et de gl'Amici." From the collection of Bernardo Nani of Venice (b. 1712; armorial bookplate inside front cover: "Bernardus Nanius Nob. Ven. Ant. Fil."). Purchased from Payne by the Rev. Henry Drury (1778–1841); his inscription on f. 1 recto: "An inedited MS. Greek Lexicon (most beautifully written) by Guarini - bought of Payne for ten Guineas. Henry Drury. Illuminated Capitals. The binding is contemporary." Drury sale (Evans, 3 March 1827; information not verified). Belonged to Sir Thomas Phillipps (no. 3384; tag on spine and pencil note on front pastedown). Unidentified "1686" in pencil on front pastedown. Purchased in 1956 from L. C. Witten by Thomas E. Marston (bookplate).

Bibliography: Faye and Bond, p. 75, no. 94.

Marston MS 95
Vincent Ferrer, Sermones

Spain, s. XV²

For the following collection of sermons we list *incipits* for the first and last items in the volume. In this version of the sermons the text begins in Latin, presents the main points of the sermon in Spanish, and then returns to the body of the text in Latin.

1. ff. i recto–ii recto *Ista est tabulla sermonum qui continentur in isto libro.* In die resurrectionis. sermo. Surrexit non est hic. folio *iij°./ Feria secunda. sermo surrexit dominus vere. et aparuit. folio. primo./* ... Item quidam sermo de humillitate. Incuruabitur sublimjtas et cetera. folio. *cclxxxij°./* Explicit deo gracias Amen. f. ii verso ruled, but blank

   Table of contents for art. 2; entries alternate in black and red with paragraph marks and margin guides to the text in the opposite color.

2. ff. 1r–293v *In resurrectione dominj sermo.* Surrexit dominus vere et apparuit ... [Luc. 24.34]. Sermo erit de vno mirabili opere quod christus fecit discipulis duobus discipulis in die resurrectionis de quo loquitur euuangelium hodiernum ... ; [f. 3r:] *In die resurrectionjs dominj.* Surrexit non est hic [Mark 16.6]. Volens predicare de christi resurrectione ut hec alta materia sit ad honorem dei ... ; [f. 5v:] *Feria secunda in resurrectione dominj.* Mane vobiscum domine quoniam ... [Luc. 24.29]. Pro declaracione thematis sciendum quod in sacra scriptura christus uocatur sol Ratio et auctoritas quia sol naturalis ...; [f. 7v:] Item *In feria secunda.* Tu solus peregrinus es ... [Luc. 24.18]. Verba sunt cleophe vnjus uidelicet de illis duobus quibus apparuit dominus in die resurrectionjs ... ; [f. 8v:] *Feria tertia sermo.* Aperuit illis sensum ut intelligerent ... [Luc. 24.45]. Sciendum quod inter omnes veritates et difficultates fidei christiane articulo ... [f. 288r:] *Domjnjca ante aduentum sermo de epistola.* Faciet iudicium et iusticiam jn terra [Ier. 33.15]. Habetur uerbum istud originaliter in libro jeronime prophete ca. 23. et recitatiue In epistola currentis dominice. sermo noster erit de defunctis. sed ut sermo sit deo acceptabilis ... ; [f. 289v:] *Domjnjca ante aduentum sermo de epistola.* Ecce dies ueniunt dicit dominus ... [Ier. 23.5]. Et recitatiue In epistola currentis domjnjce verbum propositum pro themate et fundamento ... ; [f. 292r:] *Sermo de humilitate et cetera.* Incuruabitur sublimitas hominum et humiliabitur altitudo ... [Is. 2.17]. In verbis per thema preassumptis et vestre reuerencie ... et finaliter gloriam consequamur quam nobis prestare dignetur et cetera. Explicit deo gracias. f. 294r beginning of table of contents, similar to that in art. 1, but incomplete; f. 294v blank

Paper (sized; watermarks: similar in design to Briquet Ciseaux 3694–3702, and unidentified cross bow in a circle), ff. ii (contemporary table of contents) + 284 (contemporary foliation in red: *i–cclxxxij*; modern foliation, in pencil, incorrectly runs 1–179, 190–294), 414 x 290 (282 x 205) mm. 2 columns, 48 lines. Frame-ruled in lead or ink. Prickings in upper, lower, and outer margins.

I^{6} (–1 through 4, ff. i–ii = 5, 6), $II–XXIV^{12}$, XXV^{8} [structure uncertain, + 3 stubs at end]. Catchwords for gatherings and usually the first six leaves of each gathering, verso. Quire and leaf signatures (e. g., p. iij, p. iiij, etc.) in lower right corner, recto.

Written in gothic cursive script, above top line.

Plain red initials for each sermon; headings, foliation and paragraph marks in red. First words of each sermon in large gothic bookhand for display script.

Binding: Spain, s. xv/xvi. Wound sewing on four tawed skin, slit straps or double cords laced into the wooden boards. Plain wound natural color endbands, caught up on the spine, are sewn on cores laced into the boards and pegged. They are tied down around a strip of tawed skin. There is a coarse cloth spine lining. Back pastedown is part of a bifolium from a liturgical manuscript with Aquitanian musical notation similar to that in three manuscripts also from the monastery of Santo Domingo de Silos: Paris, B. N. n. a. l. 2171, 2193, 2194 (we thank M. Huglo for this information; see provenance below).

Covered with reddish-brown sheepskin, blind-tooled with a rope interlace tool, fleurs de lis and annular dots. Spine: supports outlined with double fillets; panels diapered with double fillets with annular dots at the intersections. There are traces of two fastenings, the catches on the lower board, and traces of five round bosses on each board. Damage from a chain attachment [?] near the tail of the upper board; remains of a paper or vellum label near the head.

Written in Spain in the second half of the 15th century. Belonged to the monastery of Santo Domingo de Silos near Burgos (shelf-mark "Caj 12" on f. i recto; listed [item 49] in the unpublished index of books compiled by P. Gregorio Hernández in 1772). Purchased from Maurice Chaminal of Paris in 1957 by L. C. Witten (inv. no. 1743), who sold it in 1958 to Thomas E. Marston (bookplate).

secundo folio: [table, f. ii] Item sermo
[text, f. 2] et ipse facit

Bibliography: Faye and Bond, p. 75, no. 95.

Marston MS 96 France, s. $XVI^{1/4}$
Ovid, Heroides, in Lat. and Fr.

1. f. 1r blank; ff. 1v–35v [Latin text, on versos only, heading:] *Paris helenae Epistola Ouidii./* [text:] Hanc tibi Priamides mitto Ledaea salutem/ . . . Exige cum plena munera pacta fide. Finis.

   Heroides 16 (Paris to Helen) 1–38, 145–378, with the two verses "Cum Venus et Iuno Pallasque in vallibus idque/ Corpora iudicio supposuere meo/" added after v. 168 on f. 9v. H. Dörrie, ed., *P. Ovidii Nasonis Epistulae heroidum* (Berlin, 1971) pp. 193–213. Latin text, which is written only on the verso of each leaf, faces the French translation, which is written on the recto of each leaf (cf. art. 2).

2. ff. 2r–36r [French translation on rectos only, heading:] *Paris A helayne Epistre D'Ouide.* [text:] Paris le filz de Priam Roy de Troye/ L'heur et salut fille A ledi t'enuoye/ Qui par toy seulle estre luy peult donne/ Doy Je parler. et en stille ordonne/ . . . Partir d'icy seullement delibere/ En seur espoir de fortune prospere/ Ny d'autre chose au surplus te souuienne/ Fors de sommer que promesse on te tienne. Fin. f. 36v blank

   Unidentified French translation of art. 1; not located in R. H. Lucas, "Medieval French Translations of the Latin Classics to 1500," *Speculum* 45 (1970) pp. 225–53, or J. Monfrin, "Humanisme et traductions au moyen âge," *Journal des savants* (1963) pp. 161–90.

Parchment, ff. i (paper) + ii (modern? parchment, only stubs remain) + 36 + ii (modern? parchment) + ii (paper), 211 x 142 (148 x 95) mm. Ruled for 18 lines of verse, not all utilized on each page. Single vertical and horizontal bounding lines, full across. Ruled in red ink. Remains of prickings in upper and lower margins.

I–IV^8, V^4. No trace of quire marks or catchwords.

Latin text written in a round humanistic script much influenced by printing; Scribe 1: ff. 1v–21v and Scribe 2: ff. 21v–35v. French text written in upright bâtarde; Scribe 1: ff. 2r–22r and Scribe 2: ff. 22r–36r (a more flamboyant style of script).

Two initials, one at beginning of art. 1 (2-line), the other at the beginning of art. 2 (3-line), respectively gold on blue square ground with gold filigree and gold on dark red square ground with gold filigree. Most stanzas introduced by paragraph marks in gold on blue or red alternating grounds, with gold filigree. First letter of each verse stroked with yellow, as are usually majuscules in text. Headings on ff. 1v and 2r in red.

Binding: France [?], s. xvii. Bound in red goatskin, gold-tooled. Gilt edges. Title, much worn, on spine.

Written in France, probably in the first quarter of the 16th century; early provenance unknown. Printed material (catalogue descriptions?) pasted on back flyleaf and pastedown now removed. Bookplate of Thomas Wallis, Esquire, s. xviii, on front pastedown. Belonged to Richard Bull, Esquire, of Ongar in Essex (1725–1806; bookplate); his inscription, f. i verso: "R. Bull Aulae Trinitatis Canta: Anno 1742." Unidentified notes, in ink and pencil, on f. i verso. Purchased from C. A. Stonehill (inv. no. 11737) in 1956 by Thomas E. Marston (bookplate).

secundo folio: Paris

Bibliography: Faye and Bond, p. 75, no. 96.

Marston MS 97 — Italy, s. XV^2

Paulus Venetus, Logica parva, etc.

1. ff. 1r–44r [Prologue:] *Conspiciens in* circuitu librorum magnitudinem studentium constituentem in animo nec non aliorum nimiam breuitatem quibus fere nulla est annessa [*sic*] doctrina ... ideo tractatus primus sic diffiniens incipit a priori. [text:] *Incipit primo de terminis.* Terminus est signum orationis constitutiuum. ut pars propinqua eiusdem sicut li homo et li animal ... sed partim secundum intencionem aliorum ut Iuuenes incipientes adiscere facilius introducantur.

   Paulus Venetus (Nicoletti d'Udine, d. 1429), *Logica parva*, with diagrams. Many manuscripts and early printed editions; see C. H. Lohr, "A Note on Manuscripts of Paulus Venetus, Logica," *Manuscripta* 17 (1973) pp. 35–36, reprinted in *Bulletin de philosophie médiévale* 15 (1973) pp. 145–46 (Marston MS 97 not listed). Some contemporary corrections and marginal annotations.

2. ff. 44r–45v Incipiunt objectiones contra supradicta videlicet [?]. *Vt summularum* noticia ad memoriam reducatur ponende sunt quedam obiectiones contra quasdam regulas ... sedillius nullus homo curit et cetera. [I]*n materia figurarum//* ff. 46r–54v ruled, but blank

   Paulus Pergulensis (d. 1451), *Obiectiones contra primum tractatum*, ending imperfectly; this treatise occurs immediately following Paulus Venetus' *Logica* in early printed editions, also without indication of the author (e.g., C. Valdarfer: Milan, 1484).

3. ff. 55r–59r [Title, in upper margin:] Tractatus de sensu composito et diuso [*sic*] secundum paulum pergulensem et cetera. [prologue:] *Cum sepe numero* cogitarem non mediocrem iuuenibus fructum affere si compositionis et diuisionis materiam clarissime intelligerent . . . primum dissolutas videbis. [text:] *Septem modis* committitur fallacia composicionis et diuisionis de quibus per ordinem videamus . . . non tamen sentirent quid dicatur in hac materia perfecte et cetera finis amen. Explicit tractatus de sensu composito et diuiso recolectuus [*sic*] in breui per famosissimum artium doctorem magistrum paulum pergulensem et cetera. finis.

Paulus Pergulensis, *Tractatus de sensu composito et diviso*; published in early printed editions under the title *Tractatus de modis composito et diviso*. M. A. Brown, ed., *Paul of Pergula: Logica and Tractatus de sensu composito et diviso* (St. Bonaventure, 1961) pp. 149–58 (Marston MS 97 not cited in list of manuscripts on pp. x–xi).

4. ff. 59v–60r [1] Nota quod in quolibet sillogismo sunt due propositiones . . . ; [2] Et si obiciatur quod sunt 4 or termini quia est ibi est . . . ; [9] Si autem est sillogismus negatiuus requiritur quod habet principium . . . ; [10] Nota quod hunc verbum est quando ponitur inter duos nominatiuos sub tempore presenti . . . factus senex erat puer.

10 short paragraphs on logic, followed by diagram on f. 60r.

5. f. 60v Cului che bate non conta le bote/ Si como fa cului che le rezeue/ . . . Inpero chi percote tute [?] e non li mete cura/ Spesse volte le sole prestare nixuna.

Unidentified 14-line poem, in Italian; also in Vatican City, Biblioteca Apostolica Vaticana, Chigi M VII 154, f. 57r, and Florence, Biblioteca Riccardiana 1156, f. 15.

Paper (watermarks, in gutter and obscured by parchment binding stays: unidentified mountain and animal [?]), ff. 60, 209 x 154 (135 x 98) mm. 2 columns, ca. 29–36 lines. Single vertical and horizontal bounding lines, full across. Ruled in lead; remains of prickings in upper, lower and outer margins.

I^{12}, (1 + 2 = front pastedown), II^{10} (–9, no loss of text), III^{12}, $IV–V^{10}$, VI^{10} (10 = back pastedown). Vertical catchwords along inner bounding line or near gutter, verso.

Written by several scribes in a humanistic bookhand that exhibits various gothic and cursive features, above top line.

Red or blue initials, poor quality, 7- to 3-lines, with penwork designs in red, blue, and/or black. Headings, paragraph marks and line divisions between segments of text, in red.

Binding: Italy, s. xvi? Stays made from parchment manuscripts adhered inside of quires and outside of first and last ones, the pastedowns included. Original, wound sewing on three tawed skin, kermes pink, slit straps laced into paste boards. The endbands, caught up on the spine, are sewn on tawed skin cores laced into the boards.

Covered on greenish tan tawed skin (sheep?) with corner tongues and the remains of two tawed skin ties. Remains of title scratched on upper cover "Logica Paul*."

Written in Italy in the second half of the 15th century before 1497 when Brother Iohannes Andreas added a note on f. 60v that suggests the codex was used in a religious house: "mihi placet. 1497 a di 10 Februaro morite [*sic*] mastro ant[oni]o da la ****** mia/ mia barba Carissima et ego Fr. Ioannes andreas uolo Singulis annis tali die facere unam pietantiam toti Conuentui." Contemporary inscription written on a scroll drawn and shaded in red on front pastedown: "Cane che lecha cenere non le fidare farina"; A. Arthaber, *Dizionario comparato di proverbi e modi proverbiali in sette lingue* (Milan, 1981) p. 108, no. 205. Various early pentrials and accounts on f. 60r and back pastedown. Early shelf-mark, in ink, in upper left corner of upper cover: "163" and title (in same hand?) on front pastedown: "Pauli Veneti Logica." Modern notations in pencil on front pastedown "L. 13. 12272," "A 5," and "U/1/C"; other pencil notes erased. Purchased from E. P. Goldschmidt of London in 1955 by L. C. Witten (inv. no. 802), who sold it the same year to Thomas E. Marston (bookplate).

secundo folio: [propositio]nes non obstante

Bibliography: Faye and Bond, p. 75, no. 97.

Marston MS 98 — Northern Italy, 1473

Prudentius; Fortunatus; Sedulius, etc.

1. f. 1r-v [Per] Quinquennia iam decem ni fallor fuimus/ Septimus insuper annum cardo rotat/ Dum fruimur sole uolubili. Instat terminus/ ... Carmen martyribus deuoueat laudet apostolos./ [colophon:] Hec dum scribo uel eloquor: uinclis nec utinam corporis emicem: Liber/ Quo tullerit lingua sono mobilis ultimo.

   Prudentius, *Praefatio*; M. P. Cunningham, ed., CC ser. lat. 126 (1966) pp. 1–2.

2. ff. 1v–19v [Preface:] Senex fidelis prima credendi uia est/ Abraam beati seminis serus pater/ Adiecta cuius nomen anxit [*sic*] syllaba/ ... herede digno patris imolebit domum./ [text, f. 2v:] Christe graues hominum semper myserate labores/ Qui patria uirtute cluis propriaque sed una/ ... Ornamenta anime quibus oblectata decoro/ Eternum solio diues sapientia regnet. [colophon:] Finis prudentii 9° kalendas maias. 1473.

   Prudentius, *Psychomachia*; Cunningham, *op. cit.*, pp. 149–81.

3. f. 20r Vnum crede deum qui cuncta potestque creatque/ Quemque deus genuit maria de uirgine nullo/ Semine conceptum nam semen spiritus ipse/ ... Hec si credideris simul egeris: error euntem/ Impediet nullus propereque frueris olympo/ Explicit symbolus philelphi poete.

   Final verses from Francesco Filelfo, *Satyrarum hecatostichon septima decas, hecatosticha quinta*; the satires were published in Milan in 1476 by Christoph Valdarfer (Hain 12917) and thereafter. Bertalot, *Initia*, no. 6466, citing this manuscript in F. Roediger, *Catalogue des livres manuscrits et imprimés composant la bibliothèque de M. Horace de Landau* (Florence, 1885–90) v. 2, 104; A. Calderini, "I codici milanesi delle opere di Francesco Filelfo," *Archivio storico lombardo* 42 (1915) citing Milan, Biblioteca Ambrosiana J. 86 sup. on p. 341.

4. ff. 20v–21v Inclita que radiis illustras sydera uirgo/ Cuncta tuis ornasque polos maiore sereno/ Luce replens superi stellatum cardinis axem/ ... Erige: et a tantis seruet tua dextra periclis/ Me tantis neu linque malis miserere tuorum./ Explicit supplicatio ad uirginem Mariam.

   Franciscus de Fiano, *Deprecacio pulcherrima ad gloriosissimam matrem*; Kristeller, *Iter Italicum*, v. 3, p. 44; RH, v. 1, no. 8820; Walther, *Initia*, no. 9225

5. ff. 21v–23r [Heading:] Lactantius ad pasca [*sic*] felicitatem d. [text:] Salue festa dies toto uenerabilis euo/ Qua deus infernum uicit et astra tenet/ Tempora florigero rutilant distincta sereno/ Et maiore poli lumine porpa [*sic*] patet/ ... Quo prius eua nocens inferret et hoc modo reddit/ Ecclesie pastus ubere lacte sinu./ Finis/ [colophon:] Quisquis aues lector scriptoris noscere nomen/ Cisterciensis monachus ipse fuit.

   Fortunatus, selected verses from *Carmina* III.9.1 (*Ad Felicem episcopum de pascha*) in the following order: 39–40, 1–38, 41–100. F. Leo, ed., MGH AA 4,1 (1881) pp. 59–62.

6. ff. 23r–58v [Preface:] Paschales quicumque dapes conuiua requiris/ Dignatus nostris accubitare thoris/ ... Rubra quod appositum testa ministrat olus./ [heading, f. 23v:] Argumentum/ [text:] Cum sua gentiles studeant figmenta poete/ Grandisonis pompare modis tragicoque uoatu [*sic*]/ ... Facta redemptoris nec totus cingere mundus/ Sufficeret densos per tanta uolumina libros.

   Sedulius, *Carmen paschale*; J. Hümer, ed., CSEL 10 (1885) pp. 14–146; rubrics and divisions for books entered sporadically.

7. ff. 58v–61r Cantemus socii domino cantemus honorem/ Dulcis amor christi personet ore pio/ ... Gloria magna patri semper tibi gloria nate/ Cum sancto spiritu gloria magna patri./ Amen.

   Sedulius, *Hymnus* I; Hümer, *op. cit.*, pp. 155–62.

8. f. 61r-v [Poem, 8-lines:] Ista tibi antoni rocalis [*sic*] stirpis alumne/ Perscripsit currente manu et inculte benignus/ ... et per sacratam que cingit tempora cleram/ Carmine diuino uolitabis in ora tonantis. [Poem, 30-lines:] Continet ista gradus benedicti carta beati/ Quis humilis monacus discat et antonius/ ... Antoni gradibus his pergas ducque benignum/ Scandere quos possis annuat omnipotens. f. 62 = stub; ff. 63r–64v blank, except for notes on provenance and pen trials

   Two unidentified poems; Walther, *Initia*, nos. 9607 and 3264, citing this manuscript.

Paper (coarse; watermarks, in gutter: similar to Briquet Lettres Assemblées 9607; similar to Piccard Blume II.900, but with prominent stitching holes), ff. i (paper) + 61 (contemporary foliation, in ink, in upper right corner skips from 4 to 6; correct modern foliation, lower right, in pencil) + i (paper), 186 x 137 (146 x 90) mm. Ca. 27 lines of verse. Frame-ruled in hard point.

I–III^{12}, IV^{10}, V^{12}, VI^{6} (-4, numbered 62, blank). Horizontal catchwords, with dots and flourishes, to right of center in lower margin, verso (Derolez 12.2).

Written in humanistic bookhand with gothic features by a single scribe, above top line.

Some headings, in red, for art. 6 only.

Binding: Italy [?], s. xix. Bound in tan sheepskin, over wooden boards. Bluish green edges. "Prudentii" scratched on leather of upper board.

Written in Northern Italy in 1473 (colophon, art. 2) by a Cistercian monk (colophon, art. 5), perhaps by the Antonius mentioned in art. 8; contemporary ownership inscription of the Cistercian abbey of Chiaravalle in Milan on f. 64v: "Iste liber est Monasterii Careuallis [*sic*] mediolani." The same inscription (effaced, but visible under ultra-violet light) appears in Marston MS 233. Miscellaneous notes and pen trials (including "Ermitage du gaudiceur"), s. xvi, on f. 64v. Inscription, f. 61v: "Gio[vanni] Batt[ist]a Montalti," with date "1809" on ff. 62v and 63r in the same hand as the inscription. Belonged to Gustavo Cammillo Galletti of Florence (1805–68; bookstamp on f. 1r). Collection of Baron Horace de Landau (1824–1903; bookplate stamped with numbers "319" and "329" on front pastedown; see his *Catalogue des livres manuscrits et imprimés composant la bibliothèque de M. Horace de Landau* [Florence, 1890] v. 2, 104); the collection was maintained by his niece Madame Finaly, of Florence (d. 1938). Purchased in 1956 from L. C. Witten by Thomas E. Marston (bookplate).

secundo folio: frangit

Bibliography: Faye and Bond, pp. 75–76, no. 98.

Marston MS 99 — Italy, s. $XV^{1/4}$

Petrarch, Rerum vulgarium fragmenta, etc.

1. f. 1r [Title page, in later hand:] Le Rime di M. Francesco Petrarca; ff. 1v–131v Voi che Ascoltate In rime sparse el suono/ . . . Ch'accolga 'l mio spirto vltimo in pace. Francisci petrarche Laureati poete rerum vulgarium fragmenta Expliciunt. Deo Gratias Amen.

   Francesco Petrarca, *Rerum vulgarium fragmenta*; nos. 1, 3, 2, 4–23, 25, 26, 24 (vv. 1–13), 27–61, 66, 67, 62–65, 68–71, 72 (vv. 1–37, [vv. 16–72 of no. 73 interpolated], vv. 38–78), 73 (vv. 1–15, [vv. 16–72 in no. 72], vv. 73–93), 74–79, 81, 82, 80, 83–210, 212–336, 350, 355, 337–349, 356–359, 360 (vv. 1–47), 352 (vv. 9–14), 354, 353, 366. G. Contini, ed., *Il Canzoniere di Francesco Petrarca* (Turin, 1964). Order of verses in nos. 22 and 30 (each a *sestina*) garbled.

2. f. 132r-v [Heading:] Magistri Antonij de monte alCino et cetera. [text:] O fiero mio destino o crude stelle/ O sorte mia damor turbata in celo/ . . . O che mai pace impetre piu dal cielo. finis.

   Unidentified Italian *sestina*, here attributed to Antonius de Monte Alcino.

3. f. 132v Sja maledecto mille volte Amore/ Crudele acerbo despiatato: e rio/ . . . poi che me lassi: in si crudel[*e* erased] tormento. ff. 133r–134r ruled, but blank

Unidentified Italian sonnet.

4. f. 134v [L]a nocte che segui l'orribel caso/ ... Ançe che giorno gia uicin n'agiunga.

Francesco Petrarca, *Triumphi*, *Triumphus mortis* II, vv. 1–27; F. Neri, ed., *Rime, Trionfi, e poesie latine* (Milan and Naples, 1951) pp. 523–24.

5. f. 135r Deuoto mio la tua ingratitudine/ Tor non porria giu la tua cançone/ ... non parolette non mençogne o versi. finis.

Unidentified poem [last stanza of a *canzone*?].

6. ff. 135r-136r [Heading:] Romanus. [text:] [S]e'l canpo bianco quale el corpo mio/ Piu uolte lasso di pensier se scese/ ... Ch'io ueggio l'altre assai per essa inuito; [heading:] uituperium mulieris. [text:] Femineo sesso d'ogne mal radice/ Lupina stirpe animal sença freno/ ... Sença pudore di uituperio amica; [heading:] Romanus missum [?] [text:] Tva fama a me assai piu che altra e nota/ Spirata in te da quelle Antiche muse/ ... Dentro alla calla sorto y tuoy capellj/ Di poetichi vcellj/ Mispandi el canto e la dolce armonia/ In etica morale o poesia. ff. 136v–142v ruled, but blank

Unidentified Italian sonnets.

Paper (unidentified watermarks in gutter), ff. iv (paper) + i (parchment; early wrapper?) + 142 (early pagination 1–11, replaced by early pagination 1–128 [leaves 129–131 missing], 132–134; modern foliation in lower right corner, 1–142) + i (parchment: early wrapper?) + iv (paper), 212 x 144 (written space varies considerably, ca. 155–150 x 95–90) mm. Ca 27–30 lines of verse. Double vertical bounding lines; ruled in lead or crayon. Remains of prickings in upper, lower, and outer margins.

Precise collation impossible due to tight binding. Perhaps: I^{12}, $II\text{-}III^{16}$, $IV\text{-}X^{12}$, XI^{6}, XII^{8}. Horizontal catchwords with simple penwork flourishes on all sides, center of lower margin, verso.

Written by multiple scribes in various scripts ranging from cancelleresca to gothic bookhand.

One historiated initial, rubbed and of poor quality, f. 1v, 6-line, green and red with foliage serifs. The body of initials is formed from a dragon and filled with a portrait of Petrarch seated at a writing table, against parchment ground. Spaces left blank for initials remain unfilled; guide letters for decorator. Opening initial for each verse set apart between vertical bounding lines.

Binding: England, s. xx. Dark brown goatskin with a gold-tooled title "Petrarca Francesco Le Rime. Italy Circa 1400." Bound by Sangorski and Sutcliffe of London.

Written in Italy in the first quarter of the 15th century; according to E. Pasquini, the language of the manuscript is generically Tuscan; provenance unknown. "No 77 [?]" in ink on f. 1r. Purchased from C. A. Stonehill in 1956 by Thomas E. Marston (bookplate).

secundo folio: [P]er fare

Bibliography: Faye and Bond, p. 76, no. 99.
Ullman, no. 47.
Dutschke, pp. 178–79, no. 71.

Marston MS 100 Milan, s. $XV^{3/4}$
Phalaris, Epistolae, etc.

1. ff. 1r–76r *Francisci Aretini in Phalaridis tyramni* [sic] *agrigentini epistolas ad Ill. Principem Malatestam Nouellum Praefacio.* Vellem Malatesta nouelle Princeps Illustris tantam mihi dicendi facultatem dari ut uel prestantie tue . . . [text, f. 5r:] *Phalaris Alciboo.* Policletus messenius quem proditionis apud ciues tuos insimulas morbo me incurabili liberauit . . . qui miserit laudem consecuturam. τελωσ.

   Phalaris, *Epistolae*, translated into Latin by Francesco Griffolini of Arezzo and dedicated to Malatesta Novella of Cesena. The text is complete and corresponds to that printed by Gerardus de Lisa at Treviso in 1471 (Hain 12892), except that this manuscript does not contain the extra letters "discovered later" which appear at the end of the printed text.

2. f. 76v Carminis iliaci libros consumpsit asellus/ O fatum troie: aut equus aut asinus.

   Anthologia Latina, no. 222.

3. ff. 77r–96v *Renucii Florentini in M. Bruti epistolas ad Nicolaum Quintum Summum Pontificem. Praefacio. Solent* beatissime pater qui inuigilant alicui operi quod ad mores hominum spectet . . . [text, f. 78v:] *Methridates Regi Methridati anepsio. s.* Bruti epistolas iterum admiratus non ui dum taxat et breuitas gratia . . . quod exhibere nequeunt id eos denegare necesse est. τελωσ.

   Ps.-Brutus, *Epistolae*, translated by Rinuccio Aretino and dedicated to Pope Nicholas V; printed by Antonius Franciscus Venetus (Florence, 1487). For manuscripts and editions see D. P. Lockwood, "De Rinucio Aretino Graecarum Litterarum Interprete," *Harvard Studies in Classical*

Philology 24 (1913) pp. 78–83, with text of preface on pp. 82–83. Rubrics occur only on ff. 77r, 78v, as noted above.

4. f. 97r–v Plutarcus Traiano Imperatori salutem dicit. Modestiam tuam noueram non appetere principatum quem semper morum elegantia mereri studuisti . . . non pergis auctore plutarco.

Ps.-Plutarch, *Epistola ad Traianum*; L. Bertalot, "Uno zibaldone umanistico latino del Quattrocento a Parma," *La Bibliofilia* 38 (1936) p. 79, no. 18; article reprinted in P. O. Kristeller, ed., *Studien zum italienischen und deutschen Humanismus* II (Rome, 1975) pp. 241–64.

5. f. 97v Philippus Macedonum Rex. Aristoteli philosopho salutem dicit. Filium mihi genitum scito quo equidem dijs habeo gratiam . . . istarum susceptione. Vale.

Ps.-Philip of Macedon, *Epistola ad Aristotelem*; Bertalot, *op. cit.*, p. 78, no. 15.

6. ff. 97v–98r C. Fabritius et Q. Emulus consules Pirrho Regi salutem. Neque amicorum neque hostium fortunatus existimator esse uideris . . . nequiremus te superare dolo contendisse.

Plutarch, *Pyrrhus* (extract), Lat. tr. of Leonardo Bruni; Bertalot, *op. cit.*, pp. 78–79, no. 17.

7. f. 98r–v Caesar Imperator salutem dicit Ciceroni imperatori. Etsi te nihil temere nihil imprudenter facturum iudicarem. Tamen permotus hominum fama . . . ab omni contentione abesse. Vale xv° Kall. Maias ex itinere.

Ps.-Caesar, *Epistola ad Ciceronem* = Cicero, *Epistola ad Atticum*, X. 8. B.

Arts. 8–11 are excerpts from an 11th- or early 12th-century supplement to Curtius Rufus, *Historia Alexandri Magni*; see E. R. Smits, "A Medieval Supplement to the Beginning of Curtius Rufus's Historia Alexandri: An Edition with Introduction," *Viator* 18 (1987) pp. 100–12. These texts are often falsely attributed to Leonardo Bruni.

8. f. 99r *Heschines.* Remeniscor [*sic*] Athenienses alexandrum hac nostra in urbe liberalibus artibus instructum . . . paratosque inuenerit.

Oratio Aeschinis; R. Sabbadini, "Antonio da Romagno e Pietro Marcello," *Nuovo Archivio Veneto* 30 (1915) p. 241.

9. f. 99r–v Demas. Admirans uehementer admiror Athenienses quonam modo timiditatem nobis incutiens Heschines . . . et consilijs vacuam facilius diripiat.

Oratio Demadis; Sabbadini, *op. cit.*, pp. 241–42.

10. f. 100r–v *Oratio demosthenis contra Demadem ... Alexandro pareant.* Apud vos in questione uerti uideor uidere utrum sint contra Alexandrum ... Philippo ne similes simus Thebanis.

Oratio Demosthenis contra Demadem; Sabbadini, *op. cit.*, p. 242.

11. ff. 101r–103v *Oratio Demosthenis ad Alexandrum traducta ... per leonardum Aretinum....* Nihil habet Rex Alexander uel fortuna tua maius quam ut possis ... quam hodierno die cum haec feceris consecuturus es. Vale. *Phalaridis et Brut.*

Oratio Demosthenis ad Alexandrum; Sabbadini, *op. cit.*, pp. 243–44; Baron, p. 179.

12. ff. 103v–104v Phalaris Demoteli Salutem. Monitus tuos Demoteles non egre tuli. Imperator N nunquam factus principatum consulis deponere ... uel hanc dignitatem cum uita relinquam. Vale.

Ps.-Phalaris, *Epistola ad Demotelem*, Lat. tr. Giovanni Aurispa. See R. Sabbadini, *Carteggio di Giovanni Aurispa* (Rome, 1931) p. 176.

13. f. 104v Extra Pattauium in Sacello Ronchoni. Villicus aerarii quondam nunc cultor agelli/ hec tibi perspectus templa Priape dico/ ... Improbus vt si quis nostrum uiolabit agellum/ hunc tu sed tento. Scis puto quod sequitur.

Priapea I, often published with the poems of Tibullus; F. W. Lenz and G. C. Galinsky, eds., *Albii Tibulli aliorumque carminum libri tres* (Leiden, 1971) pp. 172–73.

Paper (watermarks: similar in design to Briquet Fleur 6597, 6601), ff. ii (paper: i = uncertain date; ii = contemporary) + 104 + ii (paper: i = contemporary; ii = uncertain date), 200 x 144 (130 x 78) mm. 21 long lines. Double vertical bounding lines (Derolez 13.31); ruled in hard point on versos. No visible remains of prickings.

I-XIII^8. Catchwords with symmetrical pen flourishes, perpendicular to text between inner bounding lines (Derolez 12.5). Remains of quire and leaf signatures (e. g., aj, aij, aiij, etc.) in lower right corner, recto.

Arts. 1 and 3–12 written in humanistic cursive by a single scribe, above top line; arts. 2 and 13 added in a more flamboyant style of humanistic cursive.

Two illuminated initials, 4-line, gold against blue, green and dark red grounds with white vine-stem ornament and white dots. From the corners issue penwork inkspray with leaves, green with yellow or gold highlights, and blue or red blossoms, extending into margins to form partial border. Plain initials alternate in blue and red. Headings in pale red.

Binding: Italy [?], date uncertain. Sewn through pieces of vellum. Limp vellum case with title in ink on spine: "Phalaridis Epistole." Badly worm eaten.

Arts. 1 and 3–12 written in Milan in the third quarter of the 15th century; according to A. C. de la Mare the style of writing in arts. 2 and 13 is characteristic of Northeastern Italy, especially Padua, in the 1460s and later. Contemporary inscription on f. ii recto: "Philippini Laudensis." Added below, in a later hand: "Libri quattro datimi dal signore [name illegible]." Purchased from C. A. Stonehill in 1955 by Thomas E. Marston (bookplate).

secundo folio: soboles nulla

Bibliography: Faye and Bond, p. 76, no. 100.

Marston MS 102 — Flanders or Northern France, s. XV^2
Vegetius, Epitome rei militaris

ff. 1r–74r *Flauij uegecij Renati Comitis epythoma institutorum rei militaris de commentarijs augusti incipit.* [table of chapters for Bk. 1:] Primus liber electionem edocet Iuniorum ex quibus locis vel quales milites . . . xxviij. De adhortatione rei militaris romaneque uirtutis. [f. 1v:] *Prologus.* Antiquis temporibus mos fuit bonarum artium studia . . . credis inuenias. [text, f. 2r:] *Romanos omnes gentes sola armorum exercitatione uicisse.* j. Nulla enim alia re videmus populum romanum orbem subegisse . . . uetus doctrina monstrauerat. Flauij uegecij Renati Comitis de uiris illustribus explicit Ephitoma. Laus deo *Qui est in euo.* f. 74v blank, except for note on provenance

C. Lang, ed., Teubner (Leipzig, 1885, 2nd ed.) pp. 1–165; each book is preceded by a table of chapters.

Parchment, ff. iii (paper) + i (contemporary parchment) + 74 + i (contemporary parchment) + iii (paper), 146 x 98 (86 x 69) mm. 24 long lines. Single vertical bounding lines. Ruled in crayon.

$I–IX^8$, X^2 *or* $I–VIII^8$, IX^{10} [structure of final two quires uncertain due to tight binding]. Remains of catchwords along lower edge near gutter, verso. Traces of quire and leaf signatures (e.g., c.1., etc.) lower right corner, recto.

Written in small gothic bookhand by a single scribe.

Three illuminated initials, 3-line, at the beginning of the Prologue (f. 1v), Bk. 3 (f. 29v), Bk. 4 (f. 58r), blue or mauve with white filigree against gold ground thinly edged in black. Initials filled with stylized leaves, blue and mauve with white filigree. Black inkspray with spiky gold leaves and small blossoms in pink or blue extend into the margins to form partial borders. Numerous small initials, 2-line, gold, on mauve and blue ground with white filigree. Running headlines in red and blue; headings in red. Paragraph marks alternate red and blue. Initials stroked with pale yellow.

Binding: England or France, s. xviii. Bound in olive-green goatskin gold-tooled with a "broken cable" border and decorated board edges. Probably bound by Richard Wier (active in London and Toulouse to ca. 1792); for the broken cable roll see C. Ramsden, "Richard Wier and Count MacCarthy-Reagh," *The Book Collector* 2 (1953) pp. 247–57; Breslauer Cat. 104 (n. d.) p. 134, with pl. on p. 135; J. Greenfield, "Notable Bindings II, MS 497," *Gazette* 65 (1990) pp. 43–44. Decorated edges. Title on spine: "Vegetius De Viris Il."

Written in Northern France or Flanders in the second half of the 15th century. Contemporary inscription, f. 74v, "Busleidianus," probably to be identified with the classicist and collector of manuscripts, Jerome Busleiden (fl. 1490s). Belonged to James P. R. Lyell (1871–1943; bookplate); Lyell's note on front pastedown, "C. Z. V. 4/9/42," indicates that he bought the manuscript in 1942. For further information on his manuscripts see *Lyell Cat.*, pp. xv–xxix. Bought from the Lyell estate by Bernard Quaritch in 1951 and sold in 1952 (cat. 699, no. 141). Miscellaneous notes, in pencil, on f. i verso: "189," 191," and "336/713." Comments about the author, in purple ink, f. ii recto. Purchased from C. A. Stonehill (inv. no. 10790) in 1953 by Thomas E. Marston (bookplate).

secundo folio: libenter

Bibliography: Faye and Bond, p. 76, no. 102.

Marston MS 104 — Italy, s. XIV^2
Gualterus Anglicus, Fabulae

ff. 1r–8v [Prologue:] [U]t iuuet et prosit conatur pagina presens./ Dulcius arrident seria pieta iocis./ . . . Verborum leuitas morum fert podus [*sic*] honestum./ Et nucleum celat arrida testa bonum. [Fabula 1:] *De gallo qui inuenit in aspidem* [*sic*]. [D]um rigido fodit ore fimum dum queritat escam./ Dum stupet inueta [*sic*] iaspide gallus ait./ . . . [conclusion of

Fable 36, beginning of 37:] Verba solent odium ligua [*sic*] fidemque parit/ [R]espondere lupo de furti labe tenetur//

Text ends imperfectly; K. McKenzie and W. A. Oldfather, eds., *Ysopet-Avionnet: The Latin and French Texts*, in *University of Illinois Studies in Language and Literature* 6 (1919). Order of the fables: Prologue, 1–18, 24–25, 59, 19, 21–22, 20, 23, 26–33, 60, 34–37.

Parchment, ff. iii (paper) + 8 (old foliation begins with 8 on f. 1r) + iii (paper), 206 x 146 (143 x 93) mm. 34 lines of verse. Single or double vertical bounding lines on left, single on right (f. 1r ruled for 2 cols.). Ruled in hard point. Prickings at four corners of written space and in outer margin; additional two prickings in upper and lower margins indicate format was originally for 2 cols.

A single gathering of 8 leaves.

Written in gothic bookhand by a single scribe, below top line.

Rubrics on ff. 2r–6v by same scribe who copied text; another hand added rubrics on f. 1r–v. Spaces for initials left unfilled; guide letters for decorator.

Binding: Place uncertain, s. xix–xx. Greyish green paper case with a black gold-tooled label: "Aesopus. Sec. XIV."

Written in Italy in the second half of the 14th century as part of a larger codex (ff. 8–15); early provenance unknown. Collection of Baron Horace de Landau (1824–1903; bookplate stamped with no. "287" on front pastedown; *Catalogue des livres manuscrits et imprimés composant la bibliothèque de M. Horace de Landau* [Florence, 1890], precise reference unverified); the collection was maintained by his niece Madame Finaly, of Florence (d. 1938). Purchased from C. A. Stonehill (inv. no. 1295) in 1952 by Thomas E. Marston (bookplate).

Bibliography: Faye and Bond, p. 76, no. 104.

Marston MS 105 — Rome, s. XV²

Basil, De legendis libris gentilium, Lat. tr. Leonardo Bruni, etc. — Pl. 26

I. 1. ff. 1r–16r [Preface:] Ego tibi hunc librum Coluci ex media ut aiut [*sic*] grecia delegi ubi eiusmodi rerum magna est copia et infinita ... [text, f. 2r:] *Diui basilij magni libellus incipit.* Multa sunt filij que hortantur me ad ea uobis consulenda que optima esse ... quod uos non putemini recta conscilia non aspernentes. Amen. Laus Deo.

Basil the Great, *De legendis libris gentilium*, translated into Lat. by Leonardo Bruni and with his dedicatory preface to Coluccio Salutati. Baron, pp. 99–100 for preface; pp. 160–61 for text.

2. f. 16r Morte sua uitam tribuit mortalibus inde/ Nomine hoc yhesu flectitur omne genus/ flecte redente genu nomen ueneratur id ipsum/ Aer et vnda maris tartara terra polus.

   Unidentified poem, 4 lines, not listed in Bertalot.

3. ff. 16v–17r Versus doctissimi atque elegantissimi prestantissimoque ingenio viri Benedicti cingulani vatis clarissimi. [poem, 10 lines:] Auctorem fecere suum tua carmina clarum/ non me quem laudas marce suprameritum/ ... At si yota locum quem possidet alpha Bibit/ quem bene conueniens tunc tibi nomen erit. [second heading:] quidem Iuuenis Iocunditatis gratia cum coronis de lauro ... quos versus vir doctissimus et clarissimus vates benedictus de cingulo depromerat. [poem, 30 lines:] Salue pulchra cohors specimen memorabile forme/ Salue carminibus digna corona sacris/ ... Et iam pegasidum sacris amitteris vndis/ Queque nouem fuerant iam facis ipsa decem. [added by a later hand:] Nota quod istud opusculum fuit translatum ab egregio uiro Leonardo Arretino de greco in latinum. f. 17v ruled, but blank

   Benedictus Cingulanus (Benedetto da Cingoli), *Carmina*; not listed in Bertalot.

II. 4. ff. 18r–25v Hunc librum composuit Seneca nobilissimus orator ad Gallionem amicum suum contra omnes impetus et machinamenta fortune. Fecit autem illum ... Incipit liber Senece de Remedijs Fortuitorum. Licet cunctorum Poetarum carmina gremium tuum semper illustrent aliquando deliberans hoc tibi opusculum ... Vides autem quam rara domi sit ista foelicitas. Annei Lucij senece de Remedijs fortuitorum. liber explicit.

   Ps.-Seneca, *De remediis fortuitorum*; F. Haase, ed., Teubner (1872) v. 3, pp. 446–57. The text is divided into sections and provided with headings and assignments of parts of the "dialogue" to *Sensus* (S) and *Ratio* (R).

Composed of two parts with distinctive physical formats:

Part I: Parchment, ff. 17, 185 x 125 (113 x 70) mm. 20 long lines. Double vertical and single horizontal bounding lines, full length and full width (Derolez 13.33). Ruled either in hard point on hair side or traced over (e.g., f. 8v) in lead or ink. Remains of prickings in outer margin. I^{10}, II^{10} (-8, 9, 10, blanks). Quire and leaf signatures (e.g., a 1, a 2, etc.) in lower right corner, recto. Art. 1 written in a humanistic bookhand characterized by tall ascenders, above top line; arts. 2–3 added later in a less expert hand. Decoration consists of one illuminated full border, f. 2r, white vine-stem ornament with pale yellow shading on vibrant blue ground, green and deep purplish red and gold ground with white dots on blue, pale yellow dots on green and red. In lower border, medallion, framed by a wreath, with mutilated coat of arms. Illuminated initial, 4-line, gold, framed in pale yellow, on blue, green and red ground with yellow and white filigree, joined to the border. One large illuminated initial, f. 1r, gold on blue, green and red ground with white vine-stem ornament, extending into the upper and inner margin to form partial border. Small initial, 2-line, gold, framed in yellow, on red, blue and green ground with yellow filigree, f. 3r. Headings in red.

Part II: Paper (watermarks: unidentified basilisk buried in gutter), ff. 18–25 (contemporary foliation 169–176), 184 x 128 (141 x 80) mm. 26 long lines. Double vertical and single horizontal bounding lines, full length and full across (Derolez 13.33); ruled faintly in hard point. A single gathering of eight leaves. Written in humanistic cursive script by one scribe, above top line. Initials for paragraphs set apart from written space between vertical bounding lines. Stained throughout.

Binding: Italy, s. xvi. Front and rear pastedowns from an unidentified moral treatise (Italy, s. XV ^{med}): Parchment, 2 columns with individual column measuring 72 mm. wide. Ruled in lead; single outer vertical bounding lines and additional ruling between columns. Portion of text on front pastedown reads: "*De apostaticis et reiterantibus baptismum.* Preterea. Nota quod ecclesia non defendit clericos in criminibus comprehensos et detentos." Sewn on three supports set in grooves on the outside of wooden boards. Plain wound endbands. The spine is round.

Covered in brown calf, blind-tooled with an arabesque border and a central diamond with assorted fleurons. Aldine leaves and acorns dotted about. Spine: four fillets at head and tail and outlining the bands. There are five large, round bosses on each board and two fastenings, the catches on the upper board and the lower one cut in for the straps, one of which is wanting.

Written in Rome in the second half of the 15th century probably for the individual whose arms appear on f. 2r. Part II was once ff. 169–76 of another manuscript; Parts I and II were apparently joined in the 16th century, the date of the present binding. Contemporary inscription on front pastedown: "tanto che tuti dii francescho Patrianuzi [or Patriarchi?]." Purchased from the Florence dealer Olschki by H. P. Kraus, who sold it in 1955 to Thomas E. Marston (bookplate).

secundo folio: [f. 2:] Sed id dum
[f. 19:] [super]uacuus est

Bibliography: Faye and Bond, p. 76, no. 105.

Marston MS 106 — Northern Italy, s. XV²
Lexicon Latino-Grecum

1. f. 1r Qui semel offendit, numquam contentus erit, offendisse fat [?] ff. 1v–3v blank, except for notes on provenance (see below)

2. f. 4r *Epigramma Hubertini Crescentinatis./ Cui preceptor abest. cui greca uolumina desunt/ Huic. ut graia sonet: uerba magister ero.*

   Hubertinus Clericus (Hubertinus de Crescentino), Professor of Rhetoric at Pavia and Milan (Cozenza, v. 2, 1024–27).

3. ff. 4r–158v Ab ἀπὸ/ Abactor/ Abactus/ Abacus ἄβαξ ὁ/ Abalieno ἀπαλλοτριόω/ Abauia ἀπόμαμμα ἡ/ Abauus ἀπόπαππος ὁ/ . . . Zelus ζῆλος/ Zephyrus ζέφυρος/ Zona ζώνη./ Finis. ff. 159r–161v blank

   The text follows in general the lexicon compiled by Giovanni Crastoni, published in Milan by Bonus Accursius ca. 1480, and thereafter (GKW, v. 7, nos. 7816–18); there are, however, such significant differences between the manuscript and printed edition as to question T. E. Marston's previous attribution to Crastoni (Faye and Bond, p. 76, no. 106). Not all Latin words have Greek equivalents; some entries added in margins.

Paper (watermarks, in gutter: similar in general design to Briquet Couronne 4659; two unidentified serpents), ff. iii (contemporary paper) + 161, 203 x 143 (142 x 90) mm. 24 long lines divided into 2 columns, the one for Latin words, the other for Greek equivalents. Double vertical bounding lines (Derolez 13.31); single vertical ruling, often added within text space in lead, to delineate second column.

I^4 (1 = front pastedown), $II–XVI^{10}$, XVII^{10} (–9, 10, blank). Remains of quire and leaf signatures (e.g., m1, m2, m3, m4, m5, x, etc.) lower right corner, recto.

Latin words written in humanistic bookhand; Greek words in a neat minuscule.

First initial for each letter of the Roman alphabet: plain red or blue majuscules, 4- to 2-line. On recto, all Latin words begin with bright blue 1-line initials, on verso all begin with bright red; color scheme reverses on f. 7v to end. Art. 2, f. 1r, in pale red.

Binding: Italy [Italo-Greek?], s. xvi. Parchment stays adhered to inner and outer conjugate leaves of quires. Own endleaves. Unusual sewing through three spine linings, the central one paper. An endband of two joined lines of chain stitching is sewn on a largely exposed leather core. The flush paste boards are held on by the cloth spine linings which extend on either side of them and are glued to them.

Covered in brown goatskin with rope interlace crosses and random small tools. Traces of four ribbon ties.

Written in Northern Italy in the second half of the 15th century; inscriptions, s. xvi, on f. 3v, the first mostly illegible due to erasure and hole in paper: "Iste liber est mei Alexandri S[ca. 4 letters missing]uini bon"; name added above erasure: "Aluisi Odescalchi" and ex libris beneath: "Iste liber est mei Aluisi odeschachi [*sic*]." Aloisius Odescalchi may perhaps be identified as the Jesuit teacher of Mathematics and Philosophy who was born at Como in 1547 and died in Naples at the end of the century. Square paper label with blue border (shelf-mark or inv. no. erased) on f. 1r. Jacques Rosenthal, cat. 90 (Munich, 1928) no. 200. Purchased from B. Rosenthal (Cat. 1, no. 96) in 1955 by Thomas E. Marston (bookplate).

secundo folio: Abrumpo

Bibliography: Faye and Bond, p. 76, no. 106.

Marston MS 107 — Northeastern Italy, s. XV^2
Agostino Dati, Elegantiolae, etc.

I. 1. ff. 1r–43r Credimus Iamdudum a plerisque uiris etiam disertissimis persuasum [added above: *esse*]. tum demum artem quempiam in dicendo nonnullam adipisci . . . Atque in dies assequere: Exercitationi acomoda. Τελος· τελος. [added in a contemporary or slightly later hand, f. 43v:] Irrita uentose rapuerunt uerba procelle. Sex nonas maiius october iulius et mars/ Quatuor at reliqui, tenet idus quilibet octo [Walther, *Initia*, 17607]. ff. 44r–48v ruled, but blank.

Agostino Dati (1420–78), *Elegantiolae*; published in Ferrara by Andreas Belfortis in 1471, and thereafter (GKW, v. 7, nos. 8032–

138). Marston MS 107 not listed in Bursill-Hall, *Census*, p. 306. Brief marginal notes containing proper names and topics (e.g. *Talis et qualis*) added by scribe on ff. 1r–38v; marginal annotations by several contemporary hands throughout.

II. 2. ff. 49r–77r [Preface:] Franciscus senior auus tuus cuius extant plurime res magnifice geste ita ut multa passim sapienter ab eo dicta memoranter ... aut illiberabus [*sic*] implicare negocii [?]. [text, f. 51r:] Omnino autem liberalis ingenij primum argumentum est studio laudis excitari ... nichil tibi, nisi te ipsum uideri, deffuisse. finis. f. 77v blank

Pier Paolo Vergerio, *De ingenuis moribus*; A. Gnessotto, ed., *Atti e memorie della R. Accademia di scienze, lettere ed arti in Padova*, N. S. 34 (1917–18) pp. 95–156; 37 (1920–21) pp. 45–57.

Composed of two distinct parts, ff. i (paper) + 77 + i (paper), now trimmed to 203 x 142 mm. The codex is too tightly bound for accurate collation.

Part I: ff. 1–48, paper (watermarks, in gutter: similar in design to Piccard Waage VII.261–66 and similar to Piccard Werkzeug IV.1162–63; unidentified crossed arrows and balance within a circle), written space: 132 x 74 mm. ff. 1–41: single vertical bounding lines ruled in lead, with rulings for text in ink or lead (Derolez 13.11); ff. 42–48: single vertical and horizontal bounding lines and rulings for text, all in lead (Derolez 13.13). Single pricking in upper outer margin for ff. 1–32; prickings in upper, lower, and outer margins (ff. 33–48). Catchwords and some final words on each folio written perpendicular to text, both recto and verso. Written in humanistic bookhand, below top line. 3-line red initial, f. 1r, with penwork designs extending length of inner margin. Headings, marginalia, paragraph marks, initial strokes, in red, through f. 39r only.

Part II: ff. 49–77 (watermarks, in gutter: similar to Piccard Waage V.378 and similar in design to Piccard Waage VII.261–66 [cf. Part I]; unidentified bull's head and same unidentified balance in a circle as in Part I), written space varies: 134 x 90 to 151 x 92 mm. ff. 49–59: double horizontal bounding lines (Derolez 13.31); ff. 60–77: single horizontal and vertical bounding lines (Derolez 13.13). Ruled in hard point. Horizontal catchwords on every verso, center of lower margin, ff. 49v–57v (Derolez 12.1). Written by multiple scribes in different styles of humanistic bookhand.

Binding: France, s. xviii. Tan, mottled sheepskin; gold-tooled spine and red label with title: "Passio/ M. S. XIII. S."

Parts I and II were both written in Northeastern Italy in the second half (third quarter?) of the 15th century. It is unclear whether or not they were formerly bound together; however, the fact that some of the same watermarks appear in both parts suggests a common place of origin. Belonged in the 16th century to the Jesuit College at Agen (inscription in upper margin, f. 1r: "Colleg. Agen. Socie. Iesu Catal. Inscrip. 1520"). For additional information on manuscripts from Agen see N. Mann, "Petrarch Manuscripts in the British Isles," *Italia medioevale e umanistica* 18 (1975) p. 273, note 1. Notes, s. xvii–xviii, f. 1r: "Explicatio verborum dictionum et passionum hominum" and "Passiones M. S. XIII S." [cf. title on spine]. Belonged to Abate Luigi Celotti (ca. 1768–ca. 1846; remains of paper label on spine with "IX. [4]25" in ink); his sale to Sir Thomas Phillipps (no. 1010, tag on spine; *Phillipps Studies*, v. 3, pp. 50–51, 147). Unidentified notations include: "15" within a circle and "11554" in pencil on front pastedown; "a56. 2326" in pencil beneath Phillipps' stamp; "S 12/49" in pencil on back pastedown. Purchased from C. A. Stonehill (inv. no. 3255) in 1955 by Thomas E. Marston (bookplate).

secundo folio: [Part I, f. 2:] potius
[Part II, f. 50:] Tenuit

Bibliography: Faye and Bond, pp. 76–77, no. 107.

Marston MS 111 — Florence, ca. 1460s [?]
Grammatica latina — Pl. 21

ff. 1r–76r Litera est uox que scribi potest indiuidua vel nota elementi et ueluti imago quedam uocis litera . . . Noceo. Valeo. Placeo. Careo. Pateo. Liceo. Oleo. Taceo. Pareo. Doleo. etc. τέλος. f. 76v blank, except for note (see provenance).

Anonymous Latin grammar; Bursill-Hall, *Census*, lists twelve other copies of this text; Marston MS 111 not recorded. The scribe has often added Italian equivalents or examples in the margins (e.g., f. 53v: Buono, Tristo, Grande, Picholo, Destro, Sinistro, corresponding to a list of irregular Latin comparative and superlative forms of adjectives).

Parchment, ff. ii (modern parchment bifolium, i = front pastedown) + 76 + ii (modern parchment bifolium, ii = back pastedown), 165 x 115 (105 x 58) mm. 21 long lines. Double vertical and horizontal bounding lines, full across and full length (Derolez 13.36); ruled in hard point on hair side. Prickings in upper, lower and outer margins (Derolez 18.1).

$I–VI^{10}$, VII^{6}. Catchwords perpendicular to text between inner vertical bounding lines (Derolez 12.5).

Written by a single scribe in careful humanistic cursive, above top line; A. C. de la Mare has identified this writer as the "Scribe of the former Yates Thompson Petrarch" (see de la Mare, *New Research*, v. 1, pp. 553–54).

Folio 1r illuminated by Francesco d'Antonio del Chierico who was active in Florence from the mid-15th century to 1484 (see Garzelli, *Miniatura fiorentina*, p. 99 and *passim*). Full border, partially rubbed, of white vine-stem ornament curling around a thin gold bar against blue, green and pink ground. In outer border, a medallion, framed in gold, with profile of a young man against blue ground. In lower border a wreathed medallion, framed by two circles of gold with partially erased arms. Medallion supported by six green-and-red winged putti. The entire border inhabited by a large number of putti playing among the vine stem, various birds and three does. Illuminated initial, 3-line, joined to the border, gold against blue, green and pink ground with white vine-stem ornament inhabited by a seated putto. One small illuminated initial, f. 1v, 2-line, gold against blue and pink ground with white filigree (partly rubbed). Plain initials alternate in red and blue. Guide letters for initials.

Binding: Italy [?], s. xix. Semi-limp vellum case.

Written in Florence probably in the 1460s, perhaps for the young man whose portrait and arms (effaced) appear on f. 1r. Inscription, s. xvii, on f. 76r: "Ad istantia di Antonio Cialderotti da s[an]to g[?]no"; inscriptions (date?) on f. 76v: "Camillo An[t?]onini [?] dase [?]," and "di camillo di piero Gra [?]." Purchased from C. A. Stonehill in 1956 by Thomas E. Marston (bookplate).

secundo folio: et hec aduena

Bibliography: Faye and Bond, p. 77, no. 111.

Marston MS 112 — Southern Italy, s. XII[1]

Honorius Augustodunensis, Elucidarium, etc. — Pl. 4

1. ff. 1r–68v [Upper margin damaged; prologue begins in third line of text space:] Sepius rogatus a condispulis [*sic*] quosdam [?] questiunculas enodare . . . [text, f. 1v:] Gloriose magister rogo ut ad inquisita mihi [?] ne pigriteris respondere . . . et uideas bona hierusalem omnibus diebus. uite tue. *M. Amen.*

   Honorius Augustodunensis, *Elucidarium*; Y. Lefèvre, ed., *L'Elucidarium et les Lucidaires*, Bibliothèque des Écoles Françaises d'Athènes et de

Rome 180 (Paris, 1954) pp. 361–477. Chapter lists added in the margin, f. 1v, by the same hand who retraced the faded text and wrote marginal notes throughout. The first two lines of text on f. 1r appear to be the conclusion of a poem: "//vax rex arabum legit**/ Qui post augustinum regn***." This manuscript listed by H. Düwell, "Noch nicht untersuchte Handschriften des *Elucidarium* von Honorius Augustodunensis," *Scriptorium* 26 (1962) p. 341, no. 78, cited incorrectly as Yale University Library, 112 (Marston 7).

2. ff. 68v–71v Fratres in domo domini cum consensu ambulantes ... quo modo malum elegisse affirmetur//

Honorius Augustodunensis, *Inevitabile*, beginning of the first version (see Lefèvre, *op. cit.*, passim).

3. ff. 71v–72v Quattuor sunt que adiuuant homines post mortem ... [conclusion on f. 72v damaged]//

Moral sentences similar to those appearing in Paris, Bibliothèque Nationale lat. 2878 (see Lefèvre, *op.cit.*, p. 26 and *passim*).

Parchment (thick, end pieces; ff. 7v–8v palimpsest), ff. i (paper) + 72 + i (paper), 160 x 105 (132 x 79) mm. Text space for ff. 1r–7r ca. 125 x 75 mm. 23 long lines. Inconsistent pattern of rulings. Ruled in hard point. Prickings prominent in upper, lower and outer margins.

I–IX^{8}. Catchwords (some trimmed) right of center near inner bounding line, verso.

Folios 1r–7r written in late caroline minuscule (portions of text retraced); the underscript of the palimpsest on ff. 7v–8v was also written in caroline minuscule. Folios 7v–72v written in inelegant Beneventan script.

Plain red initials, f. 1r-v; modest black initials filled with red, ff. 24v, 48r, 68v, 71v. Majuscules touched with red throughout.

Upper edge of book block damaged, with some loss of text.

Binding: Italy, s. xviii–xix. Rigid vellum case with traces of title (upside down) on spine. Edges daubed red and green.

Written in Southern Italy in the first half of the 12th century; early provenance unknown. It is likely that the codex contained at least one other work at the beginning, given the 2 lines of verse that precede art. 1 on f. 1r. "46" and "19" written in ink upside down at head of spine; "297/4" in ink on small round paper label on spine. Belonged to Sir Thomas Phillipps (no. 24783; bookstamp). In pencil on front pastedown: "a54. 594." Purchased from W. H. Robinson Ltd. of London in 1956 by L. C. Witten (inv. no. 1170), who sold it the same year to Thomas E. Marston (bookplate).

Bibliography: Faye and Bond, p. 77, no. 112.
E. A. Lowe, rev. ed. by V. Brown, *The Beneventan Script: A History of the South Italian Minuscule* in Sussidi Eruditi 34 (1980) p. 107.
F. Newton, "One Scriptorium, Two Scripts: Beneventan, Caroline, and the Problem of Marston 112," ed. R. Babcock, *Gazette*, supplement to v. 66 entitled *Beinecke Studies in Early Manuscripts* (forthcoming 1991).

Marston MS 113 Northeastern Italy, s. XVI$^{1/4}$
Battista Guarino, Epistola ad Iohannem Bertuccium

ff. 1r–9v *Baptista Guarinus Affini suo carissimo Ioanni Bertucio sal. plu. d.* Nuper cum apud te coenaremus ac uarijs de rebus (ut sit) colloqueremur, aetatis nostrae Poetarum orta mentione cum ego Ianum Pannonium ... conferri aequarique possit. Vale Ferrariae Nonis Aprilibus Anno Christi M° cccc° Lxvij.

Battista Guarino (1434–1513), *Epistola ad Iohannem Bertuccium*, dated 1467 in Ferrara.

Parchment, ff. iii (paper) + 9 (modern pagination, partially trimmed, upper right: 1–18; modern foliation, lower right) + iii (paper), 183 x 120 (125 x 80) mm. 21 long lines. Single vertical bounding lines (Derolez 13.11, with f. 1r Derolez 13.12).

A single gathering of 8 leaves, with one leaf tipped in at end.

Written in a stylized humanistic cursive script much influenced by printing, below top line; heading in humanistic bookhand.

Plain 1-line initial, f. 1r, in blue. Heading in red.

Binding: Paris, s. xix. Light brown goatskin with a gold-tooled title ("B. Gua./ Episto.") and doublures. Edges gilt. Bound by Chambolle-Duru (Paris, 1863–1915).

Written in the first quarter of the 16th century, perhaps in Northeastern Italy to judge from the script; early provenance unknown. Unidentified notations: "860" in pencil, f. 9v; "LNG [or 9?]" and "8242" on final flyleaf, recto. Purchased from Lathrop C. Harper, Inc., in 1956 by Thomas E. Marston (bookplate).

secundo folio: Disciplinarum

Bibliography: Faye and Bond, p. 77, no. 113.

Marston MS 114 Padua or Bergamo, 1460s
Walter Burley, De vita et moribus philosophorum, It. abridgement

ff. 1r–59r Tales philosofo fu de Asia, fu el primo de sete sapienti di grecia et habitaua nelo studio di Athene ... che non lascie strachare luomo. Il guadagno visse al tempo de Adriano. f. 59v ruled, but blank

Walter Burley, *De vita et moribus philosophorum*; an abridged version in Italian that contains only 77 lives; the Italian text corresponds to the version printed in *Vite de Philosophi moralissime. Et delle loro elegantissime sententie. Estratte da Laertio et altri antichissimi auttori* ... (Venice, 1525) where it is said to have been drawn from Diogenes Laertius and others. When the Italian text is compared with the Latin text of Walter Burley (H. Knust, ed., Tübingen, 1886, pp. 2–395), it is clear that the Italian text is actually an abridgement of his Latin and that Marston MS 114 omits many lives. For example, after the second life of Zeno on f. 54r, chapters 79–110 in the printed text are lacking; the manuscript concludes abruptly with the life of Secundus (ch. 122). In addition, all of Italian entries are shorter than the original Latin ones.

Parchment (hair side yellow and speckled), ff. ii (paper) + 59 + i (parchment) + ii (paper), 162 x 115 (116 x 69) mm. 25 long lines. Double vertical bounding lines full length (Derolez 13.31); remains of prickings in upper, lower and outer margins (Derolez 18.1). Ruled in hard point on the hair side for gatherings I–V and VIII; ruled two leaves at a time on the flesh side for gatherings VI–VII.

I–VII^{8}, VIII^{4} (–4, blank). Catchwords perpendicular to text between inner vertical bounding lines (Derolez 12.5).

Written in a humanistic hand both above and below top line by a scribe who would sometimes complete the final word of the final line of text (recto only) by writing the letters down between the outer vertical bounding lines.

Space left for decorative initial on f. 1r later filled with plain initial and a stylized sprig of flowers, in turquoise. Plain initials throughout text alternate in red and blue.

Binding: Italy, s. xix. Tan calf, blind- and gold-tooled. Head and fore edge bluish green; lettering on tail edge. In panels on spine: "Detti de' filosofi/ MSS. in Perg./ Sec. XV."

Written by Johannes Nydenna de Confluentia who was active in Padua and/or Bergamo in the 1460s and '70s; to judge from the script of Marston MS 114 it was produced during the 1460s in the early part of his career (we thank A. C. de la Mare for providing xeroxes of manuscripts which made a comparison of scripts possible); early modern provenance unknown. Belonged to Giuseppe (Joseph) Martini from whom it was acquired by H. P. Kraus, who sold it in 1956 to Thomas E. Marston (bookplate).

secundo folio: [con]siderar il ciclo

Bibliography: Faye and Bond, p. 77, no. 114.

Marston MS 116 — Northeastern Italy, s. XV²
Cicero, De natura deorum

ff. 1r–106r [Heading, in a later hand:] M. T. C. de natura deorum L P [?]. [text:] [C]um multe res in philosophia nequaquam satis adhuc explicate sint tum perdifficilis brute et obscura questio est de natura . . . [final folio defective:] ut ueleio cotte disputati[o] uerior mihi balb[i] ad ueritatis simil[i]tudinem uideret[ur] esse propensior. f. 106v ruled, but blank

Cicero, *De natura deorum*; O. Plasberg, ed. (iterum edidit appendicem adiecit W. Ax) Teubner fasc. 45 (1933) pp. 1–160. The scribe was apparently copying from a defective or misbound exemplar for Book II: he skips, with interruption in the text, on f. 38r from " . . . quid potius dixeris quam deum" (Teubner, p. 55, line 17) to "largitate fundit ea ferarum ne an hominum causa gignere uidetur" (Teubner, p. 113, 15) and copies only this single phrase; he then resumes copying, without interruption, with "perfectiones habere naturas quam ea" (Teubner, p. 83, 14) until f. 58r where he concludes copying with "frugibus et uario leguminum genera" (Teubner, p. 113, 14); without interruption he returns to "Etenim si dii non sunt" (Teubner, p. 55, 17 where he had originally stopped on f. 38r) and continues copying the text until f. 76v, "non intelligat ea . . . aliquid" (Teubner, p. 83, 13); he copies for a second time the phrase "largitate fundi [*sic*] ea ferarum ne an hominum causa gignere uidetur" and then writes the remainder of the text without similar disruptions. There are no breaks, divisions, or punctuation within the text to indicate that the scribe was aware of textual problems; a modern reader has noted, in pencil, the breaks in the outer margins. The text has been erased and corrected by at least one contemporary hand (see also provenance). Marginalia, also by this main hand, include: 1. proper names extracted from the text; 2. Greek words written in Greek letters (and also transliterated in the text into Roman letters); 3. running headlines; 4. extracts on shells and other aspects of natural history as follow: f. 48r Pliny the Elder, *Naturalis historia*, bk. 9, ch. 42, sec. 142 (C. Mayhoff, ed., Teubner, v. 2 [1967] p. 203, lines 17–20); f. 48v Aristotle, *Historia animalium*, in an unidentified Latin translation, ix.10, 614b26–30 (P. Louis, ed., Budé, v. 3 [1969] p. 84), followed by viii.12, 597a10–11 (ibid., p. 28); f. 49v Pliny the Elder, *Naturalis historia*, bk. 8, ch. 15, sec. 40 (Mayhoff, *op. cit.*, p. 91, lines 6–11); f. 50r Pliny the Elder, bk. 9, ch. 10, sec. 37 followed by bk. 8, ch. 25, sec. 89 (Mayhoff, *op. cit.*, p. 170, lines 4–7, and p. 108, lines 13–15).

Parchment, ff. i (paper) + 106 + i (paper), 160 x 116 (113 x 76) mm. 26 long lines. Single horizontal and vertical bounding lines (Derolez 13.13), with horizontal bounding lines not always extending into outer margins. Ruled in hard point, on versos.

I-VIII^{10}, IX-X^{8}, XI^{10}. Catchwords perpendicular to text along inner vertical bounding line.

Written by a single scribe in round humanistic bookhand, below top line.

Spaces for decorative initials left unfilled.

Binding: Italy, s. xviii–xix. Rigid vellum case with title, in ink, on spine: "Ciceronis de Natura Deorum M. S." Gilt edges.

Written in Northeastern Italy in the second half of the 15th century; corrected and annotated mostly by the same unidentified humanistic scholar who annotated Marston MS 212. Belonged to Henry Allen (acquired ca. 1800; bookplate); Samuel Allen sale (signature, in pencil, but partially erased, on f. i recto; Sotheby's, 30 January 1920, no. 29). Unidentified modern notations, in pencil, on front pastedown: "3448" and "106"; rectangular white paper tag with blue border along left edge, with "39" written in ink. On f. i recto: 23/2/3, 5116, gis/KO5, and many pencil notes, now erased. On rear pastedown in ink: bfs [?]. Acquired in 1953 from C. A. Stonehill (inv. no. 9600) by Thomas E. Marston (bookplate).

secundo folio: uolunt

Bibliography: Faye and Bond, p. 77, no. 116.

Marston MS 117 — England, s. XIII$^{3/4}$
Boethius, De topicis differentiis — Pl. 52

f. 1r [Title, added by a later hand:] Severini Boetii de differentijs Topicis libri quatuor. ff. 1v–30v Omnis ratio disserendi quam logicen peripatecici ueteres appellauerunt in duas distribuitur partes . . . Quo autem modo de hiis dialeticis rationibus disputetum [*sic*] in hiis commentariis quos in aristotilis topica a nobis translata conscripsimus. expeditum est.

PL 64.1173–1216. For an English translation, notes and essays on the text see E. Stump, *Boethius' De topicis differentiis* (Ithaca, N. Y., 1978).

Parchment, ff. 30, 132 x 100 (115 x 78) mm. 26 long lines. Single or double vertical bounding lines. Ruled in lead. On most leaves a single pricking in lower margin, 10 mm. below bottom line.

Collation impossible: each leaf trimmed and mounted on stubs.

Written in compact gothic bookhand by a single scribe, below top line.

According to N. Morgan the decoration was executed in a workshop active between 1250–70, probably at Oxford; for a discussion of the workshop and a list of manuscripts attributed to it see his *Early Gothic Manuscripts* (London, 1988) v. 2, pp. 124–25. One historiated initial, f. 1v, blue with white filigree and highlights against a square reddish brown ground with white filigree, showing Boethius as a monk in a blue robe seated on a chair and holding a scroll inscribed with his name, and a student, dressed in a red robe and holding a book inscribed with the opening words of the text proper, both figures against a grey ground with white filigree. Three illuminated initials, ff. 7v, 16v, 23r, 6- to 4-line (without ascenders or descenders), blue with white filigree against reddish brown ground with white filigree or reddish brown against blue ground with white filigree. The initials are filled with scrolling vines blue or reddish brown with white highlights, with stylized leaves, ending in dragons' heads against reddish brown or blue grounds. Descender, f. 16v, in form of a dragon, reddish brown against blue ground. The style of the initials is similar to Oxford, Bodleian Library, Bodley 356 (Pächt and Alexander, v. 3, no. 414). Flourished initials, 2-line, and paragraph marks alternate red and blue.

Binding: Place and date uncertain. Limp vellum case with title, in ink, on spine: "Topica boetij."

Produced in England, probably at Oxford, between 1250 and 1270 (Morgan, *op. cit.*); the manuscript has been drastically trimmed from an original format that would have accommodated marginal annotations, some of which, in lead, are partially visible in the margins. Provenance unknown; effaced inscription [?] on front turn-in. Purchased from C. A. Stonehill (inv. nos. 3192 and 11300) in 1955 by Thomas E. Marston (bookplate).

Bibliography: Faye and Bond, pp. 77–78, no. 117.

Marston MS 118 England, s. XIV^{med}
Hugo Ripelin, Compendium theologicae veritatis

pp. 1–205 [Prologue:] Ueritatis theologice sublimacio cum superni sit splendoris radius illuminans intellectum ... opusculum compilaui. [text:] *Quod deus est.* Deum esse multis modis ostenditur. hoc enim fides testatur ... sed merita recipiet sine fine. *Explicit liber .7.* pp. 206–8 contain numerous notes, mostly illegible

Composed by Hugo Ripelin (Hugh of Strassburg), this text has been sometimes erroneously attributed to Albertus Magnus, Bonaventure or Thomas Aquinas; for numerous manuscripts and printed editions see Bloomfield, *Virtues and Vices*, 6399 (Marston MS 118 cited on p. 551). Text edited by S. Borgnet, *Alberti Magni ... opera omnia* v. 34 (Paris, 1895) pp. 1–261. Marston MS 118 has been annotated throughout by at least two contemporary hands.

Parchment (poor quality), ff. vii (paper) + ii (contemporary parchment) + 104 (medieval pagination 1–208) + vii (paper), 168 x 110 (130 x 81) mm. 34 long lines. Single inner and double outer vertical bounding lines, full length; additional vertical ruling in outer margin. Ruled in crayon. Prickings in upper and lower margins.

$I–VIII^{12}$, IX^{12} (–9 through 12). Horizontal catchwords right of center along lower edge, verso.

Written in small gothic bookhand, below top line. Marginal notes in anglicana scripts.

Flourished initials, 14– to 5–line, primarily blue with red and/or parchment designs (including circles), mark beginning of each book. Many blue initials with modest red penwork designs, 5– to 2–line. Headings in red. Paragraph marks alternate red and blue. Guide letters for decorator.

Binding: England, s. xix^{in}. Brown, diced calf, gold-tooled. Rebacked.

Written in England in the middle of the 14th century. Belonged to the Carmelite convent in Stamford, England (ownership inscriptions, now erased, but partially visible under ultra-violet light; press-mark "H 30"); table of contents on original front flyleaf suggests codex may have originally contained additional texts: "Thomas de veritatibus/ Cum alijs paruis cronicis de creatione mundi/ Cum tractatu fundacionis religionis/ Cum alijs." See N. R. Ker, *Medieval Libraries of Great Britain*, 2nd ed. (London, 1964) p. 182, and A. G. Watson, Supplement to the second edition (London, 1987) p. 64. Belonged to Radulph Sneyd (d. 1703); inscription on original front flyleaf: "Liber Radulphi Sneydo [?] Iuris Vtriusque

Doctoris pro quo Libro soluit ij^d." From the collection of the Rev. Walter Sneyd; his sale (Sotheby's, 19 Dec. 1903, no. 777). Inscription and shelf-mark of E. H. W. Meyerstein, Esq., who acquired the manuscript from Leighton in 1925; Meyerstein sale (Sotheby's, 15 Dec. 1952, no. 20). Miscellaneous modern pencil notes concerning the attribution of the text, etc., on f. ii recto. Acquired from C. A. Stonehill (inv. nos. 10644 and 1931) in 1952 by Thomas E. Marston (bookplate).

secundo folio: caracteribus

Bibliography: Faye and Bond, p. 78, no. 118.

Marston MS 119 Northern Italy, s. XIII^2
Aegidius Beneventanus, Florilegium

1. ff. 1r–2r [Rubric erased, text begins:] Si sapientes moderni temporis antiquorum philosoforum doctrinis dignantur attendere quibus nobis eorum posteris mandando suggerentur [?] et suggerendo mandatur ut cum defecerimus . . . [f. 1v:] Ego quidem Egidius Beneventanus scriptor in penitentiaria domini pape. minimus introducendorum in huiusmodi thalamum cum extra clamantibus et pulsantibus . . . Vt autem in presenti opusculo celerius occurrat desideranti quod petit materias quaslibet de quibus hic agi contingerit sub certis capitulis seu rubricis capitulationem sub certis particulis collocaui.

   Prologue to art. 3 by the author, Aegidius Beneventanus, papal secretary who remains unidentified.

2. ff. 2v–29v [column 1] Primus quaternus/ .53. Auctoritates/ [column 2] In folio xxx°/ Nota contra otiosum pigrum et sompnolentum/ [column 3] .20. Actores. [followed by list of authors and/or texts cited] . . . [column 1] Auctoritates [column 2] Nota quedam argumenta cum plures diuerseque [?] probitates. et gratie in una eademque persona concurrerunt. [column 3] Actores//

   Table of contents for art. 3 arranged in three columns, with the topics listed in the order in which they appear in the text, followed by folio references in the second column, and a list of authors and/or texts cited for each topic in the third column. The table is incomplete: folio references to text cease on f. 25v (note that "Amplius deficit" at this point and the end of the folio references correspond to the conclusion of Part I in art. 3; the remaining entries in this table do *not* correspond to the topics discussed in Parts II and III), and there are no authorities cited in the final entry.

3. ff. 30r–167v *Nota contra otiosum pigrum et sompnolentum.* Plus uigila semper ne sompno deditus esto. Nam diuturna quies uitijs aumenta ministrat. Segnitiem fugito que uite ignauia fertur. Otia nullus amet ... [secunda pars, f. 141r:] *Incipit Secunda pars.* [I]n hec secunda parcicula [*sic*] huius libri agitur de ciuitatum. et castrorum ac plurium famosorum locorum fundatoribus primis seu ampliatoribus ... [tertia pars, f. 158r:] [T]ertia huius operis particula que quidem ultima est continet quasdam explorationes seu excerpta. ex pantheon. Speculo regum anselmo solino de mirabilibus mundi. et ysidoro ethimologiarum. per que legentibus constare poterit de successione ac quibusdam regum. et Imperatorum actubus a tempore diluuij usque fere ad tempus frederici Imperatoris ... Africa a meridie usque ad occidentem extenditur.

   Collection of extracts on moral subjects (Part I), and historical, genealogical and geographical subjects (Parts II and III) drawn from classical, Biblical and medieval texts. Rubrics in Part I include: *Nota contra otiosum pigrum et sompnolentum, Nota frenandam esse linguam et loquendum cum discretione, Contra detractores et aliud loquentes quam corde gerant, Nota quod promissum non debet differri, Nota filij debent erudiri et corrigi ab infancia*; Part II: *De egypto et a quo sic uocata est primo. et perconsequens, De armenia. et a quo primum sic uocata est, De thebis egiptijs, Quando incipit regnum egiptiorum*; Parts I and II frequently have spaces left for rubrics that remain unfilled; no rubrics in Part III. Authors and texts cited include: the Bible, Cato, Cassiodorus, Vergil, Sallust, Ovid, Seneca, Boethius, Socrates, Bernard, Juvenal, Hrabanus Maurus, Cicero, Claudian, Jerome, Augustine, Isidore, Lucan, Ambrose, Symmachus, Horace, Arator, Pamphilus, Origen, Anselm, Solinus. In Part I only the names of the authors (and sometimes the title of a specific work) are written in the margins next to the quotations.

4. ff. 167v–175v Amititia [*sic*] uera est. ad quam fertur homo sine ulla utilitatis causa./ Amititia est idem uelle. et idem nolle in honestate./ Amor rationalis est uita nobilissima. et postmodo [?] scientia./ Amor secundum spiritum est concupiscentia uitalis secundum animam et rationem/ Amor secundum corpus est concupiscentia coitus/ ... Yris est celestis arcus./ Yrtosus est cui os olet./ .Z.//

   Alphabetical list of figurative meanings, ending with Z, for which there are no entries.

5. ff. 176r–177v [S]ecula generationibus constant et inde secula quod sequantur. abscendentibus enim alijs alij succedunt. Prima etas mundi est ab adam usque ad noe. Secundum a noe usque ad habraam. Tertia ab abraam usque ad dauid ... [table begins:] Adam habens annos 2.30.

genuit Seth. a quo filij dei./ Seth in anno 3.0 5. genuit Enos. qui cepit inuocare nomen domini./ Enos anno .160. genuit Caynan./ . . . Mauritius annos .2.1 Gothi catholici efficiuntur/ Focas. annos .7. Romani ceduntur a persis.

Biblical and classical genealogy, in tabular format.

6. ff. 177v–183r [O]mnibus animantibus. Adam primum uocabula indidit appellans unicuique nomen iuxta conditionem nature cui seruiret. Gentes autem unicuique animalium . . . Gurgulio dicitur quia fere nil est aliud nisi guttur.

Bestiary, extracts from Isidore, *Etymologiae*, Bk. 12.1.1–12.8.17.

7. f. 183r-v [P]hilosofi grece latine amatores sapientie interpretantur. Nomen philosophorum primo a pictagora fertur exortum [corrected from *ortum*]. Nam iste interrogatus quid profiteretur . . . [P]oete immo sint dicti sicut ait Tranquillus cum primum homines exuta . . . et copia plurium uerborum . . . [S]ocrates hic primus ad corrigendos componendosque mores . . . [list of philosophers and poets follows:] Pithagoras Seneca. Carmentis Anaxagoras . . . Terentius. Celsus. Iulius.

Extracts from Isidore, *Etymologiae*, Bks. 8 and 2.

8. ff. 183v–184r *De aquis et earum ueritate ac uirtutibus*. qua dicta quod superficies eius equalis sit. Ignis uero et aqua sunt duo ualidissima helementa uite humane . . . ultra modum crescunt. aliqua futura significant.

9. ff. 184v–186r Unidentified table, damaged at the top of each folio and with text missing at beginning; explicit: " . . . Vnusquisque non tantum a proximis dissenset plerumque [?] etiam a se ipso. Amen." [Text followed by miscellaneous extracts and pen trials.] f. 186v covered by paper glued to parchment surface; originally blank?

Parchment, ff. 186 (contemporary foliation, upper right i-clxxxv, the last few numerals lost due to damaged leaves; modern foliation, lower right corner 46–186, begins with error on the first of two leaves numbered f. xlvi), 235 x 161 (156 x 96) mm. 24–42 long lines. Single vertical and horizontal bounding lines. Two additional vertical rulings in center of page for ff. 2r–30v, rulings for text often extend through inner and outer margins. Ruled sporadically, in lead, hard point and ink. Prickings in upper, lower and outer margins. Folios 94–101 (quire XIII) have two rows of prickings in outer margin.

I-III^{8}, IV^{4} (+ 1 leaf at end), V-XIV^{8}, XV^{4} (+ 1 leaf at end), XVI-XVIII^{8},

XIX^{10}, XX–XXIII^{8}, XXIV^{6}. Remains of catchwords in lower margin, right of center, verso. Most leaves signed faintly with letters of alphabet for each quire (i.e., m, m, . . . m) in upper left corner, verso.

Written by several scribes in uneven gothic bookhand.

Two attractive illuminated initials, 4-line, with partial borders. Folio 1r, initial constructed of a winged dragon, pale yellow with white highlights and red contouring strokes against a blue ground. Tail of dragon extends down the inner margin to form a partial bar border, blue, red, pale yellow with beads in red, blue, and yellow and small stylized leaves, blue and pale yellow swirling around bar. Border ends in lower margin in stylized scroll inhabited by a bird, outlined in red and brown ink, and a fowler, pointing a bow and arrow. Folio 30r, initial, red and pale yellow against blue ground with white filigree, filled with a grotesque and a dragon. Descender of initial extends into margin to form a partial bar border, same as above; border terminates in lower margin in a stylized scroll, ending in a dragon's head. The style of the decoration is similar to that in Oxford, Bod. Lib., Canon. Misc. 473 (Pächt and Alexander, v. 2, no. 94) and Paris, B. N. fr. 12599 (Avril and Gousset, no. 19, pl. IX). Several flourished initials of good quality, 3-line, blue or red with penwork in the opposite color, extending the entire length of the text column (e.g., f. 45v). Other pen-and-ink initials, red with crude penwork in brown ink. Plain initials and headings in red. Paragraph marks primarily in red. Instructions to rubricator throughout; remains of guide letters. Spaces left unfilled for some initials.

Binding: France [?], s. xix–xx. Quarter bound in blind-tooled brown calf over oak boards by the same binder as Marston MSS 214, 216 and 236.

Written in Northern Italy in the second half of the 13th century to judge from the style of decoration; rubric and early inscription erased in upper margin, f. 1r. Provenance otherwise unknown. Modern "133" in ink, upper margin, f. 1r; "-visss-" in pencil on back pastedown. Unidentified handwritten description of manuscript, in French, in library files. Purchased from Nicolas Rauch S. A. of Geneva in 1958 by L. C. Witten (inv. no. 2091), who sold it the same year to Thomas E. Marston (bookplate).

secundo folio: distinctionem

Bibliography: Faye and Bond, p. 78, no. 119.

Marston MS 122 Southern France, s. XIII/XIV
Bernard of Clairvaux, Opera varia, etc.

1. ff. 1r–6v *Incipit prologus domini .Bernardi. abbatis clareuallis de diligendo deo.* [Prologue:] Uiro illustri domino. ameruco [?] ecclesie Romane diachono cardinali ... Reliqua diligentioribus reseruate. *Explicit prologus. Incipit liber.* Uultis ergo a me audire quare et quo modo diligendus sit deus. et ego causa diligendi ... profectus [*sic*] esse poterit miserationis affectu.

   Bernard of Clairvaux, *De diligendo Deo*; J. Leclercq, H. M. Rochais, C. H. Talbot, eds., *S. Bernardi Opera* (Rome, 1957–) v. 3, pp. 119–54 (hereafter referred to as *Opera*).

2. ff. 6v–13v *Incipit prefacio sancti bernardi abbatis in laudibus uirginis matris domini.* Scribere me aliquid et deuotio iubet ... si proprie satisfacio deuotioni. *Explicit prefacio incipit homilia prima.* Missus est angelus gabriel ... [Luc. 1.26]. *homelia lectionis eiusdem beati bernardi abbatis.* Quid sibi uoluit euangelista tot propria nomina rerum in hoc loco ... [f. 7v:] *Explicit homelia prima. Incipit secunda.* Nouum quidem canticum. illud quod solis dabitur in regno dei cantare uirginibus ... [f. 10r, rubric misplaced on f. 10v:] Libenter ubi mihi congruere uideo uerba sanctorum assumo ... [f. 11v:] *explicit .iii. Incipit .iiij.* Non est dubium quicquid in laudibus nostris proferimus ad filium pertinere ... cui hoc meum qualecumque opus domini deuotissime destinaui.

   Bernard of Clairvaux, *Homiliae IV in laudibus virginis matris domini*; Schneyer, v. 1, p. 442 (9–12); *Opera* 4.13–58.

3. ff. 13v–28v *Incipit tractatus eiusdem .bernardi. de consideratione ad eugenium papam epistola primi libri.* [table of contents for *Libri I–V*, f. 14r:] *i.* Quod non presumptorie sed ex sincera dilectione ei scribit ... *x.* Quod non in cognitione dei sed ... contemplationis. *Incipit tractus* [sic]. *.bernardi. clareuallis ad eugenium papam de consideratione.* Subit animum dictare aliquid quod te beatissime eugenii uel edificet uel delectet uel consoletur ... finis libri sed non finis querendi.

   Bernard of Clairvaux, *De consideratione libri quinque ad Eugenium III*; *Opera* 3.393–493. The divisions for each book noted in the table of contents at the beginning of the work do not appear as headings in the text.

4. ff. 28v–32v *Incipit apologia beatissimi Bernardi abbatis clareuallis.* Uenerabili patri .Guillelmo. frater Bernardus. fratrum qui in claraualle sunt inutilis seruus. salutem in domino. Vsque modo si qua me scriptitare

iussistis. aut invitus, aut nullatenus acquieui ... quod nobis semper fiat omnino precor et supplico explicit apologia beati bernardi clareuallensis abbatis.

Bernard of Clairvaux, *Apologia ad Guillelmum S. Theodorici abbatem*; *Opera* 3.81–108.

5. ff. 32v–40r *Incipit prologus dompni bernardi abbatis clareuallis in libro De Dispensacione et precepto.* [preface:] Domino abbati columbensi frater .Bernardus. abbas dictus de clarasualle. ualere in domino semper. Rescriptum meum ad epistolas ... congruentius uideatur. [text, f. 33r:] *Incipit liber.* Qua mente iam tacebo qua fronte tamen loquar Crebis [*sic*] epistolis ... quod studui satisfacere uoluntati.

   Bernard of Clairvaux, *De precepto et dispensatione*, preceded by a letter to the abbot of Coulombs; *Opera* 3.253–94.

6. ff. 40r–42r *Sermo beati bernardi de passione domini.* Uigilate animo fratres. ne infructuose pertranseant uos huius temporis sacramenta copiosa est ... passiones. propter iusticiam sustinendo// Explicit sermo beati bernardi abbatis de passione domini.

   Bernard of Clairvaux, *Sermo de passione domini*, ending imperfectly; Schneyer, v. 1, pp. 445–46 (64); *Opera* 5.56–66 (line 25).

7. ff. 42r–43v *Hic incipit contemplatio sancti augustini episcopi de passione beate marie uirginis in passione unigeniti filii sui.* Quis dabit capiti meo aquam et occulis meis fontem lacrimarum ut possim flere per diem et noctem donec sermo [?] ergo dominus ihesus appareat uisu uel sompno consolans animam meam ... omnia sit benedictus filius eius ihesus christus dominus noster Qui ... Explicut [*sic*] contemplatio sancti augustini episcopi de compassione beate uirginis....

   Ogerius de Lucedio, *Planctus Beatae Virginis Mariae* (an extract from his *De laudibus sanctae Dei Genitrix*); G. Penco, "Ogerio di Lucedio e il *Planctus Mariae*," *Benedictina* 16 (1969) pp. 126–28; M. Capelleno, "Codici delle opere del beato Ogerio di Lucedio," *Bolletino storico vercellese* 18 (1982) pp. 177–83. This work had been attributed previously to Bernard, Augustine, et al.

8. ff. 43v–110v *Liber iste incipitur ad collationem adlegens in die cene ... a quodam dyachono et cantore premonito.* [begins with quotation from John 13.1–26; followed by, f. 44r:] *Sermo sancti bernardi abbatis de euangelio in crastino pasche ibant duo ex discipulis et cetera.* [Luc. 24.13]. [1] Cconuertere [*sic*] anima mea. in requiem tuam [Ps. 114.7] quia christus resurrexit a mortuis ... [2] Duo ex discipulis ... [Luc. 24.13]. Considerata

lectionis huius mira suauitas totas inebriat medullas anime . . . esurientem. et salutaribus reparat alimentis.

Bernard of Clairvaux, *Sermones ad collationes*, some lacking tituli and/or Biblical readings. The sermons are arranged in the following order with numbers in parentheses referring to those in Schneyer, v. 1, pp. 442–55; incipits are provided for texts as yet unidentified or for those not located in either Schneyer or *Opera*: f. 48r (99); f. 49v (for the Annunciation: "Missus est angelus . . . [Luc. 1.26]. Gabriel missus est ad mariam . . . "; also in Paris, B. N. lat. 2914, cited as anonymous in Schneyer, v. 9, p. 102 [1]); f. 49v (92); f. 50r (93); f. 50v (108); f. 51v (177); f. 51v (Petrus Venerabilis [?], sermon for the Assumption: "Ad interrogata de uirginis et matris domini resolutione temporali . . . "; also in Paris, B. N. lat. 12410, f. 42v); f. 52r (sermon for the Assumption variously attributed to Paschasius Radbertus, Augustine, Jerome, Anselm: "Quia profundissime et sui dignitate altissime sum responsurus. . ."); f. 53v (for the Nativity of the Virgin Mary: "Celebritas hodierne diei nos ammouet. . ."); f. 54r (176); f. 55r (6); f. 55v (*Opera*, 6.9–20); f. 57v (7); f. 59v (16); ff. 60v–64r (20–24); f. 64r (26); f. 64v (25); ff. 65v–68v (30–33); f. 68v (89); f. 70r (34); f. 71r (36); ff. 71v–73v (37–39); f. 73v ("*Sermo in ramis palmarum de euuangelica lectione. Dixit ihesus discipulis suis. Ite in castellum* . . . [Mat. 21.2]. Mundus est castellum cuius. uallum superbia . . . "; cited as anonymous in Schneyer, v. 9, p. 102 (10) from Paris, B. N. lat. 2914); f. 75r (61); f. 76r ("*Sermo in die pasce*. Hec est dies quem [*sic*] fecit dominus exultemus et letemur . . . [Ps. 117.24]. Ista dies est non dies mundi . . . "; cited as anonymous in Schneyer, v. 9, p. 102 (2) from Paris, B. N. lat. 2914); ff. 77v–79r (69–71); f. 79r ("*Sermo in ascencione domini*. In hac domini ascensione multa nobis beneficia sunt collata . . . "; cited as anonymous in Schneyer, v. 9, p. 102 [9] from Paris, B. N., lat. 2914); ff. 79v–82r (72–74); f. 82r (174); ff. 82v–84v (78–79); f. 84v ("*Sermo in festiuitate sancti iohannis baptiste* . . . In sancti cuiuslibet sollempnitate tria sunt memorie nostre comendanda . . ."); ff. 86v–89v (100–102); f. 89v (108); f. 90v (177); ff. 91r–92v (111–12); ff. 92v–96v (114–17); ff. 96v–100r (120–21); ff. 100r–102r (126–28); f. 102r (130); ff. 103v–106v (122–24); f. 106v (156); ff. 107v–108v (82–83); f. 108v (132); f. 110r (145).

9. f. 111r-v Index for sermons, arranged according to *sermones de tempore, sermones de sanctis, sermones de communi sanctorum et de occasionibus*; unrubricated. A contemporary hand gives folio references in margins.

10. f. 112r-v Index for sermons, arranged according to Biblical readings; rubricated. Contemporary hands have added folio references and

another indexing system using letters of the alphabet.

11. ff. 112v–167v *Incipit sermo de aduentu domini et vj. circumstancijs.* Hodie fratres celebramus aduentus initium. cuius utique sicut et ceterarum [?] sollempnitatum ... prouideat ut ad penitenciam adducatur. *Expliciunt sermo* [sic] *de tempore.*

Bernard of Clairvaux, *Sermones de tempore*. The sermons are arranged in the following order with numbers in parentheses referring to those in Schneyer, v. 1, pp. 442–55: ff. 112v–117r (1–5); ff. 117r–118v (13–14); ff. 118v–122r (17–19); ff. 122r–125v (27–29); f. 125v (35); f. 125v (40); f. 126v (42; with Biblical reading: Obsecramus tamquam aduenas. et peregrinos, abstinere ...); ff. 127r–129r (43–44); ff. 129r–141r (47–55, but with irregular text divisions in 48 and 49); ff. 141r–145r (57–60); ff. 145r–146v (62–63); ff. 146v–152r (65–68); f. 152r (175); ff. 152v–158r (74–77); ff. 158r–159r (80–81); f. 159r (83); f. 160r (167); ff. 160v–161v (169–170); f. 161v (168); f. 162v (166); f. 163v (84 + 85 written as a single sermon); f. 164v (86); f. 165r (87); f. 166r (88).

12. ff. 167v–190r *Incipiunt sermones de sanctis et primo* [sic] *de sancto stephano.* Benedictus qui uenit in nomine domini [Ps. 117.26]. Benedictum nomen glorie eius quod est sanctum ... suffragia uoluit non deesse.

Bernard of Clairvaux, *Sermones de sanctis*. The sermons are arranged in the following order with numbers in parentheses referring to those in Schneyer, v. 1, pp. 442–55: f. 167v (24); f. 168r (91); ff. 168v–173v (96–98); ff. 173v–177r (103–106); f. 177r (*Opera*, 5.250–60: *Sermo V in Assumptione*); f. 179r (107); ff. 180r–185r (109–110); f. 185r (113); f. 187v (129); f. 188v (118).

13. ff. 190r–197v *Incipit prologus sancti bernardi abbatis in libro xij*[m]*. graduum humilitatis.* In hoc opusculo cum illud de euuangelio quod dominus ait ... opusculi ipse breuiter intimare curauj. *Explicit prologus.* [table:] Duodecimus corde et corpore semper humilitatem ostendere ... et asperis pacienciam amplecti. [text:] Rogasti me frater guilbertus quatenus ea que de gradibus humilitatis coram fratribus ... tu in tuo corde quam in meo codice leges. *Explicit.*

Bernard of Clairvaux, *De gradibus humilitatis et superbiae*; *Opera* 3.13–59. Table for *Duodecim gradus humilitatis* only, thus lacking lines 15–20 in printed text.

14. ff. 197v–204r *Incipit prologus sancti bernardi abbatis de gracia et libero* [sic] *directus ad dominum hugonem de sancto uictore.* [prologue:] Opuscu-

lum de gracia et libero arbitrio quod illa qua scitis occasione ... uitam eternam habebsit [*sic*]. *Incipit liber sancti bernardi* ... Loquente me coram aliquo et dei graciam in me commendante ... non quos iustos inuenit. hos et magnificauit.

Bernard of Clairvaux, *De gratia et libero arbitrio*; *Opera* 3.165–203.

15. ff. 204r–208v [No rubric, prologue:] Hugoni militi christi et magistro milicie christi. Bernardus Clareuallis solo nomine abbas. bonum certamen certare. Semel. et secundo. et tercio nisi fallor ... non defui voluntati. [capitula, f. 204v:] Exortatio. Ad milites templi ... De bethpage. De bethania. [text:] Nouum milicie genus nuper ortum auditur in terris quam olim in carne ... ad prelium et digitos uestros ad bellum. Amen.

Bernard of Clairvaux, *Liber ad milites templi de laude novae militiae*; *Opera* 3.213–239.

16. ff. 208v–217v *Tractatus sancti Bernardi*. Securum habes aditum. ad deum o homo habes filium autem patrem matrem autem filium. filius ostendit patri latus et uulnera. Mater ostendit filio pectus et ubera ... dedignari parentes. *Explicit tractatus sancti Bernardi*. [short paragraph:] Nullum sacrificium magis deo placet quam zelus animarum ... si mercedis nil agimus quantum possumus.

Auctoritates Bernardi.

17. ff. 217v–218v *Dictatus domini bernardi abbatis de conflictu babilone et iersulem* ... Inter babylonem et ierusalem nulla pax est. sed guerra continua ... timoris [*ille* crossed out] mille et a dextris caritatis decem milia.

Bernard of Clairvaux, *Parabola II de conflictu duorum regum*; *Opera* 6 (2).267–273.

18. ff. 218v–219v *De obuiatione et misericordie et ueritatis opusculo iusticie et pacis*. Misericordia et ueritas obuiauerunt ... [Ps. 84.11]. Iste quattuor uirtutes et ut ita dicam sorores filie ... est honor et gloria....

This text also occurs in the collected works of St. Bernard in Stuttgart, Hofbibliothek VII 55, ff. 40r–42v; J. Autenrieth, ed., *Die Handschriften der ehemaligen Hofbibliothek Stuttgart* (Wiesbaden, 1963) II, 3, p. 203.

19. f. 219v [Heading:] *Quidam monachus erat in burgundia qui salutare consueuerat ... Dominus dans istos quinque uersus dixit sic me salutare curabis*. Aue domine ihesu christe uerbum patris filius uirginis agnus dei salus mundi hostia sacra....

Hymnus ad dominum Iesum Christum; Wilmart 412–13.

20. ff. 219v–221v *Opus beati bernardi de forma uiuendi in religione.* Primo semper debes considerare qua re ueneris ad quid ueneris et propter quid ueneris nisi solum modo propter deum ... Statim uolunt de hac disputare ut uideantur et ipsi aliquid// *Explicit iste liber. Explicit opus beati bernardi de forma uiuendi in religione.*

David of Augsburg, O. F. M., *Formula novitiorum*, ending imperfectly; PL 184.1189–98, where the text is attributed to Ps.-Bernard; Bloomfield, *Virtues and Vices*, no. 4155 (Marston MS 122 not listed).

21. ff. 221v–222v *Item de religiosis. Item alio modo in religione.* Si quis inter nos emendatioris uite desiderio actus intrinsecus cogitationum ... ymo sic se estimet quasi solus ipse et deus pater// amen.

Arnulfus de Boeriis, *Speculum monasticum*, ending imperfectly; PL 184.1175–78, where the text is attributed to Ps.-Bernard.

22. ff. 222v–236v *Incipit prologus in lucidario.* [prologue:] Sepius rogatus a discipulis quasdam questiunculas enodare ... solers subtilitas. [text:] *Incipit primus liber in lucide* [?] *diuinis rebus. I. D.* Gloriose magister rogo te ut ad inquisita michi ne pigriteris respondere ad honorem diei. *M.* Equidem faciam quantum uires ipse michi dabit ... et uideas bona iherusalem omnibus diebus uite tue. *Amen.* Explicit lucidarius. [f. 236r:] Incipit tabula de diuinis rebus .I./ De creatione mundi .ij./ De elementis .iij./ ... De honore sanctorum [*De pleno gaudio sanctorum* crossed out] .cxlvi./ De pleno gaudio sanctorum .cxlvij.

Honorius Augustodunensis, *Elucidarium*; Y. Lefèvre, ed., *L'Elucidarium et les Lucidaires*, Bibliothèque des Écoles Françaises d'Athènes et de Rome 180 (Paris, 1954) pp. 359–477. Chapters numbered (some missing) in Roman numerals, i-clxix; numbers in text do not always correspond to those given in the table on f. 236r-v. Initials *M*[agister] and *D*[iscipulus] for interlocutors, in red, throughout.

23. ff. 236v–263v *Item bernardus ad dominum papam eugenium* ... Tempus est ut ego scribam non iam pro episcopo sed ... quibus abiectus bibet cum illo calicem dolore.

Bernard of Clairvaux, *Epistolae*; the letters appear in the following order, with numbers referring to *Opera*, vols. 7–8; in the manuscript the letters are numbered, often carelessly, cxxvij–cccxliiij (ending on f. 255r): 246, 256, 248–52, 122–23, 257–66, 268–71, 267, 272–84, 289, 285, 288, 253, 290, 374, 310, 365, 382, 395, 400, 339, 414, 318, 349, 367, 386, 291–96, 286–87, 297–307, 362, 368, 345, 390, 341, 356–57,

324–25, 401–03, 385, 383–84, 315, 404–05, 391, 407–09 [followed by a series of letters about Abelard:] 190, 189, 188, 187, 191 [the *capitula de erroribus Abelardi* on f. 260v in the following order: 1–7, 17, 8–16, 18–19], 194, Ad dominum papam. Dei omnipotentis qui iudicat equitatem graciam roborati et in nostri . . . , 236, Papa ad abbatem clarauallis. Litteras uestras de electione eboracensis ecclesie nobis transmissas . . . , 239, Ad Eugenium papam. Cum multi sunt uocati pauci uero electi. Non est magnum . . . , 363, Gracioso et felici militi Raymundo domino castri anbrosij. Bernardus in senium te ductus saluum totis petis. . . .

24. f. 263v Reference to the assassination of Louis d'Orléans in 1407 added by a contemporary hand.

Parchment (palimpsests of ecclesiastical documents, many leaves pieced and patched), ff. ii (paper) + 263 (remains of contemporary foliation 1–263) + ii (paper), 332 x 230 (252 x 168) mm. 2 columns, 50 lines. Ruling format varies. Ruled in lead or crayon; some traces of prickings.

I–X^{10}, XI^{10} (+ 1 leaf at end, f. 111), XII–XIX^{10}, XX^{6}, XXI–XXIII^{10}, XXIV^{8}, XXV–XXVI^{10}, XXVII^{6} (+ 2 leaves at end). Catchwords, decorated with red and/or black designs, center of lower margin, verso.

Written by multiple scribes in small rounded gothic bookhand, below top line.

Folios 1–50 have flourished initials, 3- to 2-line, alternating blue with red penwork designs and red with purple; two initials of better quality, divided red and blue, with red and purple flourishes (ff. 42r, 43v); many initials have harping designs. For remainder of manuscript uninspired red initials, either plain or with harping designs in brown ink. Rubrics, underlining and initial strokes, in red, throughout. Running headlines, in red, on ff. 1r–83r. Notes to rubricator in margins. Paragraph marks, red or blue.

Binding: France, s. xviii. Greenish brown goatskin gold-tooled. Gold-tooled panels and dark red gold-tooled label (damaged) on spine. Red edges.

Written at the end of the 13th or beginning of the 14th century in Southern France, most probably near Avignon since one of the ecclesiastical documents used as a palimpsest (f. 65r) was executed at Villeneuve-les-Avignon (name visible under ultra-violet light). Early provenance otherwise unknown; contemporary note in lower margin, f. 1v: "Bf. Consignatus est." From the library of Acton Griscom of High Point, New Jersey (De Ricci, v. 2, p. 1162, no. 8). Purchased from Lathrop C. Harper in 1957 by Thomas E. Marston (bookplate).

secundo folio: floribus

Bibliography: Faye and Bond, p. 78, no. 122.
Leclercq, 1961, p. 164.

Marston MS 123 Bohemia, s. XV^{med}
Isidore of Seville, Etymologiae, etc.

1. f. 1r-v blank; ff. 2r–4r *Epistola Esydori* [sic] *Episcopi Ad broulionem* [sic] *episcopum*. Domino meo et dei seruo Broulyoni Episcopo ysidorus Omni desiderio desideraui nunc videre faciem tuam . . . ; *Epistola Broulionis ad ysidorum*. Domino meo et vere domino christique electo ysidoro Episcopo summo Broulio seruus inutilis seruorum dei. O pie domine et virorum prestantissime . . . ; *Epistola ysidori ad Broulionem*. Domino meo et dei seruo Broulioni Episcopo ysidorus quia te incolumem cognoui . . . ; *Epistola Broulionis ad ysidorum*. Domino me [*sic*] et vere domino christique electo ysidorum [*sic*] Episcoporum summo Braulio seruus invtilis sanctorum dei. Solet repleri liticia [*sic*] homo interior . . . ; *Epistola ysidori Braulioni Episcopo*. Domino meo et dei seruo Braulioni Episcopo ysidorus tue sanctitatis epistole me in vrbe Tolletana invenerunt . . . ; *Item ysidorus Braulioni*. Domino meo et dei serui Braulioni episcopo ysidorus In [?] tibi sicut pollicitus sicut misi opus de origine quarundam rerum . . . stilo maiorum. *Incipiunt libri ysidori In moris Spalensis Episcopi ad Braulionem cesarem Augustam Episcopum vel Ad Sizebutum . . . conditor huius codicis disputauit* [followed by a list of subjects].

   Epistolae of Isidore, Braulio and Sisibutus, which serve as an introduction to art. 2; J. Madoz, ed., *Epistolario de S. Braulio de Zaragoza* (Madrid, 1941) pp. 74–89, here in the order VIII, III–VII. Running headline in upper margins: *Prologus*.

2. ff. 4r–203v [Chapter list for Book 1:] *Incipiuntur capitula primi libri. 1.* De dissciplina [*sic*] et arte. *2.* de septem liberalibus artibus . . . *28.* de generibus hystorie. [text:] *Incipit liber primus Ethymoloyarum* [sic]. Disciplina a discendo nomen accepit vnde et scientia dici potest . . . quod interdum pro signo interdum pro cura adhibetur Vt vis morbi ignis ardore siccetur et cetera. Pro quo deus gloriosus sit benedictus in secula seculorum Amen. [colophon:] *Iste liber reportatus est per Iacobum de Tacho et cetera*.

   Isidore of Seville, *Etymologiae*; M. Díaz y Díaz, et al., eds. (Madrid, 1982)

2 vols. For an extensive list of manuscripts of Isidore in European libraries see J. M. Fernandez Caton, *Las Etimologias en la tradición manuscrita medieval estudiada por el Prof. Dr. Anspach* (León, 1966).

3. ff. 203v–209r In uirtute sancte crucis et sacramento Altaris magna est conveniencia et magna efficacia ... Diximus de tantis sacramentis non ut debuimus sed ut potuimus cuius finis iam restat. Pro quo deus gloriosus sit benedictus in secula seculorum. Amen. [colophon, crossed out:] *Iste liber reportatus est per Iacobum de Tacho.*

   Richardus de Wedinghausen (Richardus Praemonstratensis), *Expositio missae*; PL 177.455–70 (formerly attributed to Hugh of St. Victor, Thomas Aquinas and Joannes Cornubiensis). For a list of manuscripts of this text see G. Macey, "A Bibliographical Note on Richardus Praemonstratensis," *Analecta Praemonstratensia* 52 (1976) pp. 64–69 (this manuscript not listed).

4. ff. 209r–214r Signum magnum apparuit in celo et cetera [Apoc. 12.1]. Si celum sumatur pro ecclesia triumphante tunc thema est de assumpcione beate virginis ... mater est huius igitur beatissime matris intercessio nos perducat ad celi palacia ... Amen. Sermo fratris Boneuenture [*sic*] ... ad vniuersitatem Parisiensem ... et cetera.

   Bonaventure, *Sermo VI de assumptione Beatae Virginis Mariae*; *Opera omnia S. Bonaventurae* (Quaracchi, 1901) v. 9, pp. 700–06.

5. ff. 214r–215r [In upper margin, partially trimmed:] Studio diuinarum scripturarum de sancto uictore. Hugo didascolicon libro 4°. Que scripture sunt autentice. [text:] De nostris aput grecos Oriens in scripturarum labore tam grecos quam latinos ... errore defecerunt et cetera.

   Extract from Hugh of St. Victor, *Didascalicon* IV.14; PL 176.786.

6. f. 215r-v Item de sortilegijs et diuinationibus. Omnis diuinatio est prohibita et maledicta a deo et sancta Ecclesia ... [at conclusion of list:] Hec omnia sunt interdicta ab Ecclesia.

   List of forbidden magical arts, including *Geomancia, Pyromancia, Ydromancia ... Augurium, Interpretacio sompniorum.*

7. ff. 215v–216v Excerpts on various subjects from Jacobus de Voragine, Hugo Ripelin, Ps.-Augustine, *De triplici habitaculo, Liber Sextus Decretalium*; list of books in the Old Testament and the number of chapters in each book.

Paper (watermarks for both end papers and text: Piccard, Ochsenkopf

XII.685, Nuremberg 1430). ff. iv (i = front pastedown) + 216 + iii (iii = rear pastedown), 300 x 211 (238 x 160) mm. 2 columns, 43 lines. Frame-ruled in ink. Remains of prickings in upper, lower and outer margins.

I–XVIII^{12}. Traces of catchwords along lower edge near gutter, verso.

Written by a single scribe in running hybrida script.

Unattractive initials in red (or red and black divided) with penwork designs, dots, knobs and/or heart-shaped appendages, all in red and black. Numerous plain red initials of similar design. Headings, running headlines, chapter numbers and initial strokes in red. T-O map of the world on f. 131v in red.

Binding: Bohemia, s. xv–xvi. Stays from 15th-century parchment manuscript. Original sewing on three double supports attached to flush, sharply bevelled wooden boards. Spine leather originally sewn around endbands.

Covered in cream colored suede-like skin with very faint traces of a blind-tooled *X* in an outer frame. Spine: double fillets at head and tail; a neat, sewn mend near the head. Pink paper place marks on the fore edge. Two strap-and-pin fastenings, the pins on the upper board and stubs of kermes pink straps attached to lower one with flower-shaped plates. Trace of a chain attachment near head of lower board; title (mostly effaced) in gothic bookhand near head of upper board.

Written in Bohemia in the middle of the 15th century by Jacobus de Tacho (Tachau?; see colophons, arts. 2–3). Table of contents, s. xvi, on f. i recto: "Contenta huius libri./ Ethimologiarum libri Isidori episcopi./ misse declaracio/ ... librorum veteris testamenti Capitula." In ink on front pastedown: "Isidorus." Large paper label on spine with contents in ink and manuscript number scratched out. Signature on f. 1r: "Wilhalm Klopffur Dockhtor." Modern notes on front pastedown: "396" and "80/121." Rectangular white paper tag with blue border ("MS II 40" in pencil) on front pastedown covers another shelf-mark, in ink. Purchased from H. Rosenthal in 1946 by H. P. Kraus (Cat. 80, no. 121; reproduction of T-O map) who sold it in 1957 to Thomas E. Marston (bookplate).

secundo folio: quia

Bibliography: Faye and Bond, p. 78, no. 123.

Marston MS 124 — Rome [?], ca. 1455–65
Ambrose, Opera varia

1. ff. 1r–50v *Beati ambrosii episcopi de virginibus ad marcellinam sororem liber primus incipit. Si iuxta celestis* sententiam ueritatis uerbi totius

quodcumque otiosum fuerimus locuti habemus prestare rationem ... Denique cum caetera poenarum genera uicisset gladium quem querebat inuenit. *Finis libri tertii.*

Ambrose, *De virginibus*; O. Faller, ed., *S. Ambrosii De virginibus*, Florilegium patristicum tam veteris quam medii aevi auctores complectens, fasc. 31 (Bonn, 1933) pp. 18–78.

2. ff. 50v–93v *Principium quarti libri.* Nobile apud veteres salomonis illud fertur fuisse iuditium cum a duabus litigantibus mulieribus interpellatus esset ... quia mundum descripsit in isto quia mundum ignorauit. *Finis libri quarti de laudibus virginum.*

   Ambrose, *De virginitate*; PL 16.265–302 and M. Salvati, ed., *Scritti sulla verginità*, Corona patrum salesiana, ser. lat. 6 (Turin, 1955) pp. 168–297.

3. ff. 93v–105r *Incipit eiusdem de lapsu virginis. Quid taces anima* quid cogitationibus estuas quid non erumpis ... dummodo illum nec illas poenas aeterni ignis incurrerent. *Finis libri de lapsu virginis.*

   Ps.-Ambrose, *De lapsu virginis consecratae*, also attributed incorrectly to Jerome; CPL, no. 651. Salvati, *op. cit.*, pp. 504–37. Text in the manuscript ends in ch. 38.

4. ff. 105r–137v *Beati ambrosii episcopi de viduis liber incipit. Bene accidit fratres* ut quoniam tribus libris superioribus de uirginum laudibus disseruimus uiduarum tractatus ... ne gratia nuptiarum tenere nequeatis et molestias augeatis. Finis libri de viduis. laus deo.

   Ambrose, *De viduis*; PL 16.233–62.

5. ff. 138r–169r *Incipit liber sancti ambrosii archiepiscopi de virginitate sancte marie virginis.* Commendas mihi pignus tuum quod eque est meum ... per illam uenerabilem gloriam trinitatis cui est honor et gloria.... Amen. *Finit feliciter deo gratias.*

   Ambrose, *De institutione virginis*; PL 16.305–34 and Salvati, *op. cit.*, pp. 302–97.

6. ff. 169r–203v *Incipit liber sancti ambrosii archiepiscopi de ieiunio.* Diuinum ad patres resultauit oraculum ut cum egrederentur ad bellum ... oblatione prelatus meruit insigni pietatis laudari oraculo.

   Ambrose, *De Helia et ieiunio*; C. Schenkl, ed., CSEL, v. 32 (1897) pp. 411–65.

7. ff. 204r–220v *Tractatus sancti ambrosii archiepiscopi de penitentia incipit*

liber primus. Si virtutum finis ille est maximus qui plurimorum spectat profectum ... [f. 219v:] omnes tamen meritorum ordine suscitantur// f. 220r-v illegible except for running title and catchword: adhuc

Ambrose, *De penitentia*; O. Faller, ed., CSEL, v. 73 (1955) pp. 119–36; on f. 215r the manuscript inserts Ambrose, *De excessu fratris*, sections 106–16 ("Sed adversus spiritalia nequitie quae sunt in caelestibus non carnalia ... "; Faller, *op. cit.*, pp. 307–15).

Parchment, ff. i (parchment) + 220 (contemporary foliation, red Roman numerals in upper right corner skip [no text missing] from xx to xxxi and from cxv to cxxvi) + i (parchment), 222 x 133 (141 x 77) mm. 24 long lines. Double vertical bounding lines (Derolez 13.31); ruled in hard point on flesh side, probably on a ruling frame though no distinctive prickings remain.

I–XXII^{10}. Horizontal catchwords in center or right of center in lower margin (Derolez 12.1 or 2). Remains of quire and leaf signatures (e.g., k 4, k 5, X, etc.) in lower right corner, recto.

Written in bold humanistic cursive script that slopes toward the right by a single scribe, above top line.

The illumination may, according to A. C. de la Mare, be in the early style of Andrea da Firenze. Illuminated title page, severely rubbed and stained, with full border, white vine-stem ornament on red, blue, green and gold ground with white dots, in inner border with ribbon interlace. In lower border wreathed medallion within narrow gold bands, supported by two haloed angels, one dressed in green, the other in red; central shield of medallion blank. Included in border are a standing and a seated putto. Historiated initial, 6–line, gold, with a portrait of St. Ambrose seated at a lectern and reading, against a blue sky. 8 illuminated initials, 5–line, in gold against blue, green and red grounds with white dots and white vine-stem ornament extending into the margins to form partial borders. Headings, running titles and foliation (Roman numerals), in red.

Many pages stained with some loss of text; f. 220r-v mostly illegible.

Binding: France, s. xix. Brown goatskin with the arms of comte Chandon de Briailles gold-tooled on both sides. Edges, headcaps, and doublures also gold-tooled.

Written probably in Rome ca. 1455–65; early modern provenance unknown. Bookplate (with "Mss. 63" in ink) and armorial binding of comte Chandon de Briailles. Unidentified notation, in pencil: "C 44" on front pastedown. Acquired from Rousseau-Girard (Frères) of Paris in 1956 by L. C. Witten (inv. no. 1246), who sold it in 1957 to Thomas E. Marston (bookplate).

secundo folio: [corporali]bus exuatur

Bibliography: Faye and Bond, p. 78, no. 124.

Marston MS 125 Hautecombe [?], s. XII[1], etc.
Gregory the Great, Regula pastoralis, etc.

I. 1. ff. 1r–80r Pastoralis cure me pondera fugere delitistendo [*sic*] uoluisse benigna frater karissime acque humillima intentione reprehendis ... Sed in huius queso uite naufragio. orationis tue me tabula sustineat. utque pondus proprium deprimit. tum me meriti manus leuet. *Explicit liber. pastoralis cyre. beati gregorii pape.*

Gregory the Great, *Liber regulae pastoralis*; PL 77.13–128.

2. f. 80r Hilarius gallus episcopus pictauensis eloquentia conspicuus. hymnorum carmine floruit primus. Post quem ambrosius mediolanensis episcopus. uir magne glorie in christo. et in ecclesia clarissimus doctor ... Carmina autem quecumque ad laudem canuntur. hymni uocantur.

Unidentified passage, added in a later hand, dealing with hymns.

3. f. 80r caspar baltasar melchion [*sic*];/ appelius amerus damascus;/ madalat galgalat seracim;
Names of the Three Wise Men, in Latin, Hebrew and Greek; *Dictionnaire d'Archéologie chrétienne et de Liturgie* v. 10, s.v. "Mages."

4. f. 80r Confueris rome. romano uiuito more/ Confueris alibi. uiuito sicut ibi.
Walther, *Sprichwörter*, vol. 1, no. 4176.

5. f. 80v *contra tempestatem*. Adiuro uos o maligni spiritus et omnes angeli sathane per deum principem omnipotentem qui in principio cuncta creauit ... et abite in illum locum ubi nec signum sonat. nec auis uolat. nec arator arat.

Adiuratio against evil spirits, calling upon God, Christ, the Holy Spirit, the Blessed Mary, the nine orders of angels, etc., so that the evil spirits will depart from homes and fields, and will have no power to work harm.

II. Arts. 6–36 contain the *Sermones in Cantica Canticorum* XVIII–XLVIII of Gilbert of Hoyland; all references are to PL 184. For a list of manuscripts and early printed editions see E. Mikkers, *Cîteaux commentarii cistercienses* 14 (1963) pp. 266–72 (Marston MS 125 not cited).

6. ff. 81r–82r Lignis libani. incorruptio carnis. et mundicie uobis est candor expressus. Bona quidem est castitas, sed quod non est ex fide . . . uelut ornamento quodam caritate constrata dicuntur. propter filias iherusalem.

   Sermo XVIII; 92–96.

7. ff. 82r–83v Nouum aliquid uultis audire. sed ego . . . Totus enim amabilis est dilectus uester christus ihesus. . . .

   Sermo XIX; 96–102.

8. ff. 83v–84v Audistis quo inuitate sint filie syon . . . et in die leticie cordis tui.

   Sermo XX; 102–109.

9. ff. 85r–86r Et uos audeo confidenter ad uisionis huius inuitare leticiam . . . cum deo patre et spiritu sancto. . . .

   Sermo XXI; 109–113.

10. ff. 86r–87v Non ueretur ne suis intumescat laudibus . . . Cuius plenitudo uitam nobis eternam conferat. per ihesum. . . .

    Sermo XXII; 113–118.

11. ff. 87v–89v Ecclesie ut bene nostis hec blandimenta dicuntur . . . ut cognoscant te uerum deum. et quem misisti ihesum. . . .

    Sermo XXIII; 118–125.

12. ff. 89v–90v Audistis precedenti commendatos sermone sponse dentes . . . et est uerbum eternum. Quod cum patre. . . .

    Sermo XXIV; 125–129.

13. f. 91r–v Quam suaues sunt putas sponse gene . . . quod ipse dauid dederit auctor eius et tutor. christus. . . .

    Sermo XXV; 129–133.

14. ff. 91v–93r Nam fortia ad sponsam et de sponsa loquitur . . . prestante copiam. qui prestat affectum christo. . . .

    Sermo XXVI; 133–139.

15. ff. 93r–94r Videtis fratres. quomodo nec ubera sponse laude priuantur . . . qui pascuntur in liliis donec aspiret dies de die. . . .

Sermo XXVII; 139–145.

16. ff. 94r–95r Ubera inquit tua sicut hinnuli capree gemelli ... iudex iustus et dulcis sponsus christus....

Sermo XXVIII; 145–149.

17. ff. 95r–96r Tota pulcra es amica mea ... [Cant. 4.7]. Quis mihi dabit istud trium ... ad coronam christus ihesus sponsus eius qui est deus benedictus....

Sermo XXIX; 149–155.

18. ff. 96v–97v O [?] cor durum et male durum in quo uerba ista uulnera ... quoniam in hac unitate mandas benedictionem et uitam...

Sermo XXX; 155–160.

19. ff. 97v–98r Leniter sunt a nobis perstringenda nunc ubera sponse ... qui uberum et unguentorum sponse sue et commendator est et dator....

Sermo XXXI; 160–165.

20. ff. 98r–99r Exiguum est mihi olei et unguenti fratres ... et odoris huius fumus ascendat de cordibus nostris in secula....

Sermo XXXII; 165–171.

21. ff. 99v–100v Dies ista dominice resurrectionis annua [*sol* deleted] celebritate sollempnis....

Sermo XXXIII; 171–177.

22. ff. 100v–101v Fauus distillans labia tua ... [Cant. 4.11]. Vehementer dulcia sunt que nunc dicta sunt ... qui necdum in sponsarum sortem meruit acisci a domino....

Sermo XXXIV; 177–183.

23. ff. 101v–102v Ortus conclusus es. soror ... [Cant. 4.12]. Primo ex uerbis suis. laudatoris ... in oram uestimenti ab ipso capite christo....

Sermo XXXV; 183–187.

24. ff. 102v–103v Emissiones tue paradisus ... [Cant. 4.13]. A cipro incipiendum est nam ibi ... et sponse sue applaudit muneribus....

Sermo XXXVI; 187–192.

25. ff. 103v–104v Fons ortorum puteus ... [Cant. 4.15]. In prin-

cipio capituli istius. fons dicta est sponsa ... aliquo separantur obstaculo a caritate dei que est in christo. ...

Sermo XXXVII; 192–198.

26. ff. 104v–105r Affectiones dulces et sancte. sunt sponse aromata ... et te flante. non deficient eius aromata Qui. ...

Sermo XXXVIII; 198–203.

27. f. 105r–v Exple ihesu bone quid iubes ... ad mutuas inuitores sponsi et sponse transibit. si gratiam nobis. ...

Sermo XXXIX; 203–207.

28. ff. 105v–106v Quam longe fratres a conuersatione mea sunt uerba ... noue resurrectionis degustes dulcedinem. ...

Sermo XL; 207–214.

29. ff. 106v–108r Messui mirram meam ... [Cant. 5.1]. Putate fratres uocationem hanc ad seculi finem ... uigilanter intelligere. et uobis audire. ...

Sermo XLI; 214–219.

30. ff. 108r–109r Ego dormio et cor meum uigilat [Cant. 5.2]. Post hesternum capitulum ... sed tamen ad dilecti tui uocem assurge. ...

Sermo XLII; 219–225.

31. ff. 109r–110r Superiore sermone hunc locum ita discussimus ... qui habet clauem dauid. sine qua nemo aperit. ...

Sermo XLIII; 225–231.

32. ff. 110r–111r Hodie uobis fratres de apertione ostij ... ad loquelam dilecti sui christi. ...

Sermo XLIV; 231–236.

33. ff. 111r–112r Cum tibi fuerit dilectus tuus elapsus ... ihesu regi et sponso celesti per infinita secula.

Sermo XLV; 236–241.

34. ff. 112r–113r Ordo conueniens post exhortationem doctorum ... sponsi ecclesie et anime sancte. qui uiuit. ...

Sermo XLVI; 242–245.

35. ff. 113r–114r Qualis est dilectus tuus ex dilecto ... [Cant. 5.9].

Magno profuse uidentur . . . Sed iam ipsa dilecti sui laudes retexat.

Sermo XLVII; 245–250.

36. f. 114r Dilectus meus candidus . . . [Cant. 5.10]. Studium querendi dilectum. intermittit . . . Nam ipse sicut serenandi. ita et succendendi uim habet. Qui approximat illi. approximat igni. f. 114v blank

Sermo XLVIII; 250–252.

III. 37. ff. 115r–121r [Preface:] Que de libro [corrected from *lilibro*] salomonis qui ecclesiastes dicitur nuper uobis coram disserui. breuiter nunc perstringens . . . sed a uobis intellecta gaudeatis. [text:] Verba ecclesiastes filii dauid regis ierusalem. Titulus est libri iste in quo breuiter. et qualitas exprimitur sequentis operis . . . aut infirmus inuentus est ut in manibus eius bona illa materia deterior efficeretur? absit. Imo uero meliorem te fecit quam illud fecit fuerat// f. 121v blank

Hugh of St. Victor, *Homilia prima in Salomonis Ecclesiasten*; PL 175.113–132A.

Composed of three distinct sections that now all measure 235 x 161 mm., ff. i (paper) + 121 + i (paper).

Part I: ff. 1–80, parchment and paper (ff. 2–7; watermarks: unidentified column [?] in an asymmetrical composition). Format of the first gathering (I^8) is inconsistent and the leaves were written by several scribes in different styles of gothic bookhand and bâtarde. For ff. 9–80: 26 long lines, written space: 177 x 102 mm. Double vertical bounding lines. Quires II–III ruled in hard point on hair side; the remainder in lead or crayon. Remains of prickings in upper and lower margins. II–X^8. Written by a single scribe in a well formed late caroline calligraphic minuscule; arts. 2–4 in similar nearly contemporary scripts; art. 5 in a later gothic bookhand. Decorative initials, 3- to 2-line, in black, with simple pen designs and small "pearls" on the thin parts of the letters, on irregular grounds of pale yellow wash. Initial strokes and plain line-fillers in pale yellow (initial strokes in red on f. 9r presumably added by the rubricator of ff. 1–8). A series of red dots (also a later addition?) outline the ground of initial on f. 18v. Explicit on f. 80r brushed with yellow wash.

Part II: ff. 81–114, parchment, written space: ca. 198 x 132 mm. 42 long lines. Single vertical bounding lines; ruled in lead. Remains of prickings in all four margins. I–II^5 (original structure uncertain; 1 stub precedes f. 81 and 1 stub follows f. 90), III–IV^8, V^{10} (-3, 10; no loss of text). Remains of catchwords along lower edge, f. 98v. Written by multiple scribes in small highly abbreviated noting hands, above top line. Plain monochrome initials, 3- to 2-line, in red or blue. Spaces for rubrics left unfilled; guide letters.

Part III: ff. 115–121, parchment, written space: 185 x 127 mm. 2 columns, 35 lines. Single vertical bounding lines; ruled in crayon or lead, including space between columns. Prickings in upper margin. I^8 (-8; no loss of text). Written by a single scribe in gothic bookhand, above top line. Plain initials, 3- to 2-line, in red. Guide letters.

Binding: Italy, s. xix^{in}. Half bound in brown calf with bright pink paper sides and edges spattered bluish green. Two green, gold-tooled labels: "Gregorii. M/ Pastoralis/ Manuscrip" and "Saecul XII." Bound in the same distinctive style as Marston MSS 50, 128, 135, 151, 153, 158, 159, and 197, also from the Cistercian abbey of Hautecombe.

Folios 9–80 of Part I were written in Germany or Switzerland in the first half of the 12th century; leaves 1–8 were added in the 15th century to replace the damaged first quire (the scribe of these leaves even copied the catchword from the exemplar as if it were part of the text). The short texts in arts. 2–4 are roughly contemporary additions to Part I, whereas art. 5 was added in the 14th century. Part II was written perhaps in France or Switzerland in the last quarter of the 12th century and appears to have existed as a booklet separate from Part I given the pattern of stains and wear on ff. 80v and 81r. Part III was written in France or Switzerland in the first quarter of the 13th century. It is unclear precisely when and where the three parts were bound together, though this may have occurred at the Cistercian abbey of Hautecombe in the 13th century when the ex libris "Liber sancte marie [followed by erasure]" was written on f. 121r; it is also possible that one or more parts were produced at Hautecombe, which is located in the ancient diocese of Geneva and was founded toward the beginning of the 12th century by monks from the abbey of Aulps (see R. Clair, "Les origines de l'abbaye d'Hautecombe," *Mélanges à la mémoire du Père Anselme Dimier* [Arbois, 1982–87] tome II, v. 4, pp. 615–27). Marston MS 125 has the characteristic bright pink binding of the books of Monseigneur Hyacinthe della Torre who acquired and rebound a group of twelve manuscripts from Hautecombe at the beginning of the 19th century (see Leclercq, 1951, p. 75). Belonged to the Biblioteca del Seminario Metropolitano in Turin (Leclercq, *op. cit.*, p. 75, no. 7). Acquired from Maggs Bros. of London in 1957 by L. C. Witten (inv. no. 1597), who sold it the same year to Thomas E. Marston (bookplate).

secundo folio: [Part I, f. 2:] summi

[Part II, f. 82:] in memoriam
[Part III, f. 116:] conteplationis [*sic*]

Bibliography: Faye and Bond, pp. 78–79, no. 125.

Marston MS 127 Italy or Southern France, s. XIII^{med}
Raymundus de Pennaforte,
Summa de poenitentia et matrimonio, etc.

1. front flyleaf, verso: recipe for a digestive; list of bodily parts where food is digested; recipe for an upset stomach; texts written primarily in Latin with some Italian interspersed.

2. ff. 1r–129r *Incipit summam magister R. de penitentia.* [prologue:] Quoniam ut ait ieronimus secunda post naufragium tabula est culpam simpliciter [*con* erased ?]fiteri ... [list of chapters:] De simonia ... de sepulturis. [text, f. 1v:] *de symonia.* Quoniam inter crimina ecclesiastica symoniaca heresis obtinet primum locum ... id est voluptarias uero perdit sicut ibi dicitur. [one line erased]

   Raymundus de Pennaforte, *Summa de poenitentia et matrimonio* (Libri I–IV). For preface see Jerome, *Epistola 84 Pammachio et Oceano*; PL 22.748. For text see *Raymundus de Peniafort, Summa de poenitentia et matrimonio cum glossis Ioannis de Friburgo* (Rome, 1603; repr. Farnborough, 1967) pp. 1–502, an edition closer to the medieval text than S. Raimundus de Pennaforte, *Summa de Paenitentia*, ed. X. Ochoa et A. Diez (Rome, 1976). Each book preceded by a list of chapters; a later hand has added notes and some subject headings in upper right corner.

3. ff. 129r–132v [Heading erased.] Gregorius viijjus [?]. [1.6.49] Cum in magistrum ...; [1.6.59] Si alicuius ...; [1.11.16] Consultationi tue ...; [1.11.17] Quesitum est ... [5.27.10] Si quem sub ...; [5.36.60] Pueris qui ... rigor sit mansuetudine temperandus.

   61 selections from the *Decretales* of Gregory IX compiled by Raymundus de Pennaforte; H. Boese, "Über die kleine Sammlung Gregorianischer Dekretalen des Raymundus de Penyafort O. P.," *Archivum Fratrum Praedicatorum* 42 (1972) pp. 69–80 (Marston MS 127 = Y).

4. ff. 132v–135v *De excommunicatione qualiter fieri debeatur.* Scis uel credis uel fama est. episcopum uel aliquem clericum ciuitatis uel dyocesis fecisse ...; *De tribus modis eligendi.* Tres sunt forme que sunt in electionibus obseruande....

   Unidentified text[s?] on canon law.

5. ff. 135v–138v *De quibusdam dubitabilibus*. Dilectis in christo fratribus I. priori de ordine fratrum predicatorum ... Postulastis per sedem apostolicam edoceri. quid in subsequentibus tenere articulis debeatis ... ut insoluatur precium emptetrice ad opus cymiterii. Deo gracias.

   Raymundus de Pennaforte, *Dubitalia cum responsionibus (Responsio canonica)*; S. Kuttner, *Repertorium der Kanonistik (1140–1234)* Studi e Testi 71 (Vatican City, 1937) pp. 446–47.

6. f. 138v De negligentiis uel omissionibus que circa missam solent contingere qualiter de hiis sit agendum ...; Si uinum non miscetur ...; Si musca uel aranea in calicem ceciderit ...; [concluding:] Si sanguis in calice congeletur ... non ualet solidum transglutire. Explicit. deo gracias. Amen. Summe scriptorem. benedic rogo te creatorem.

   Unidentified text dealing primarily with defects in the performance of the mass.

Parchment, ff. i (early parchment flyleaf) + 138 (medieval foliation *i–l* begins on f. 2), 168 x 114 (120 x 75) mm. 2 columns, 40 lines. Double outer and single inner vertical bounding lines with an additional ruling between columns. Single upper horizontal ruling. Ruled in lead or crayon. Remains of prickings in upper, lower and outer margins.

I–VIII^{12}, IX^{16}, X–XI^{12}, XII^{2}. Remains of catchwords along lower edge, verso.

Written in small gothic bookhand, below top line.

Fine flourished initial, 5-line, divided red and blue, with penwork designs in both colors and long marginal tail of letter *Q*, f. 1r. Smaller flourished initials incorporating the heads of bird-like grotesques and cross-hatching designs. 1-line initials alternate red and blue for chapter lists. Paragraph marks and running headlines in red and blue. Rubrics throughout; instructions for rubricator along outer edges of leaves, some perpendicular to text.

Binding: Place and date uncertain. The covers are wanting but were probably of limp vellum. Original sewing on twisted tawed skin, slit ribbons, the sewing beaded in the center. A fragment of a parchment bifolium from a 14th-century breviary (the outer part of the leaf that was against the binding now rubbed and illegible; the inner portion contains text of the office for Saturdays at matins according to Roman use) is glued to the spine and cut out for the sewing supports; a portion of the fragment extends along the front and back of the text block.

Written in Italy or Southern France in the middle of the 13th century;

provenance otherwise unknown. Purchased from Enzo Ferrajoli in Geneva in 1957 by L. C. Witten (inv. no. 1626), who sold it the same year to Thomas E. Marston (bookplate).

secundo folio: cautio

Bibliography: Faye and Bond, p. 79, no. 127.

Marston MS 128 Hautecombe [?], s. XIII$^{2/4}$
Sermons (in Lat.)

Arts. 1–148 constitute a collection of anonymous sermons, most of which are also found in Pavia, Biblioteca Universitaria 173 III, and Paris, B. N. lat. 14520; the Schneyer references for these two manuscripts are noted for each sermon together with the rubric as it appears in Marston MS 128. Complete incipits are given only for those items as yet unidentified or for sermons not found in the two manuscripts with similar contents.

1. p. 1 *De testimoniis incarnationis. que in lege reperiuntur. Sermo primus.* Schneyer, 9.178 (1); 9.294 (1).

2. pp. 1–2 *De incarnatione Sermo ij^{us}*. Schneyer, 9.178 (3); 9.294 (3).

3. pp. 2–3 *Sermo iii^{us}*. Schneyer, 9.178 (4); 9.294 (4).

4. pp. 3–4 [No rubric]. Schneyer, 9.178 (5); 9.294 (5).

5. p. 4 *Sermo v^{us}*. Schneyer, 9.178 (7); 9.294 (6).

6. pp. 4–6 *Sermo vi^{us}*. Schneyer, 9.178 (8); 9.294 (7).

7. pp. 6–7 *Sermo viii^{us}* [*sic*]. Schneyer, 9.178 (9); 9.294 (8).

8. pp. 7–8 *Sermo ix^{us}*. Schneyer, 9.178 (10); 9.295 (9).

9. pp. 8–9 *Sermo x^{us}*. Schneyer 9.178 (11); 9.295 (10).

10. pp. 9–11 *Sermo xi^{us}*. Schneyer, 9.178 (12); 9.295 (11).

11. pp. 11–12 *De testimoniis prophetarum Sermo .j^{us}*. Schneyer, 9.178 (13); 9.295 (12).

12. pp. 12–13 *Sermo. ij^{us}*. Schneyer, 9.178 (14); 9.295 (13) + (14).

13. pp. 13–14 *Sermo iij^{us}*. Schneyer, 9.178 (15); 9.295 (15).

14. pp. 14–18 *De aduentu*. Schneyer, 9.178 (16); 9.295 (16).

15. pp. 18–19 *De incarnatione*. Schneyer, 9.178 (17); 9.295 (17).

16. pp. 19–20 *De incarnatione*. Schneyer, 9.178 (18); 9.295 (18).

17. pp. 20–21 *De incarnatione*. Schneyer, 9.178 (19); 9.295 (19).

18. pp. 21–22 *De incarnatione*. Schneyer, 9.178 (20); 9.295 (20).

19. pp. 22–24 *De aduentu*. Schneyer, 9.179 (21); 9.295 (21).

20. p. 24 *De incarnatione*. Schneyer, 9.179 (22); 9.295 (22).

21. pp. 24–25 *De incarnatione*. Schneyer, 9.179 (23); 9.296 (23).

22. p. 25 *De incarnatione*. Ecce uir species cuius quasi species eris ... [Ezek. 40.3]. Nomine eris quod est metallum durabile....

23. pp. 25–26 *De incarnacione*. Schneyer, 9.179 (24); 9.296 (24).

24. pp. 26–27 *De incarnatione*. Schneyer, 9.179 (25); 9.296 (25).

25. pp. 27–29 *De aduentu domini*. Schneyer, 9. 179 (26); 9.296 (26).

26. p. 29 *De incarnatione*. Schneyer, 9.179 (27); 9.296 (27).

27. pp. 29–30 *De incarnatione*. Ecce dies ueniunt dicit dominus ... [Amos 9.13]. Sicut enim in autumno ad literam accepta [?] est.... Sermon also found in Paris, Bibliothèque Nationale lat. 2295, f. 92v.

28. pp. 30–31 *De incarnatione*. Schneyer, 9.179 (28); 9.296 (28).

29. pp. 31–32 *Item vnum supra*. Schneyer, 9.179 (29); 9.296 (29).

30. pp. 32–33 *De incarnatione*. Schneyer, 9.179 (30); 9.296 (30).

31. pp. 33–34 *De incarnatione*. Schneyer, 9.179 (31); 9.296 (31).

32. p. 34 *De incarnatione*. Mulierem forcem quis inuenit procul ... [Prov. 31.10]. Primo commendat sanctam ecclesiam [?] uel beatam uirginem ... In muliere commendabilia sunt fecunditas....

33. pp. 34–35 *De incarnatione*. Schneyer, 9.179 (32); 9.296 (32).

34. pp. 35–36 *Item de incarnatione*. Schneyer, 9.179 (33); 9.296 (33).

35. pp. 36–37 *De incarnatione*. Schneyer, 9.179 (34); 9.296 (34).

36. pp. 37–38 *De sacramento incarnationis*. Schneyer, 9.179 (35); 9.296 (35).

37. pp. 38–39 *De incarnatione*. Schneyer, 9.179 (36); 9.296 (36).

38. pp. 39–40 *De incarnatione*. Schneyer, 9.179 (37); 9.297 (37).

39. pp. 40–41 *De incarnatione*. Schneyer, 9.179 (38); 9.297 (38).

40. pp. 41–42 *Item de incarnatione. De incarnatione.* Schneyer, 9.179 (39); 9.297 (39).

41. pp. 42–44 *De incarnatione.* Schneyer, 9.179 (40); 9.297 (40).

42. pp. 44–45 *De incarnatione.* Schneyer, 9.180 (41); 9.297 (41).

43. p. 45 *De incarnatione.* Schneyer, 9.180 (42); 9.297 (42).

44. pp. 45–47 *De natiuitate.* Consummata partem huius operis. circa testimonia incarnationis. transeundum est ad testimonia natiuitatis. Schneyer, 9.180 (43); 9.297 (43).

45. pp. 47–48 *De natiuitate.* Schneyer, 9.180 (44); 9.297 (44).

46. pp. 48–49 *Sermo de natiuitate domini.* Schneyer, 9.180 (45); 9.297 (46).

47. pp. 49–50 *De eadem.* Schneyer, 9.180 (46); 9.297 (45).

48. pp. 50–51 *Sermo de circumcisione.* Schneyer, 9.180 (47); 9.297 (47).

49. pp. 51–52 *De circumcisione.* Schneyer, 9.180 (48); 9.297 (48).

50. pp. 52–53 *De apparitione.* Schneyer, 9.180 (49); 9.297 (49).

51. pp. 53–54 *De apparitione.* Schneyer, 9.180 (50); 9.298 (50).

52. pp. 54–56 *De apparitione.* Schneyer, 9.180 (51); 9.298 (51).

53. pp. 56–57 *Sermo In septuagesima.* Schneyer, 9.180 (52); 9.298 (52).

54. pp. 57–58 *Sermo in lx.* Schneyer, 9.180 (53); 9.298 (53).

55. pp. 58–59 *In xl.* Schneyer, 9.180 (54); 9.298 (54).

56. pp. 59–61 *De penitentia.* Schneyer, 9.180 (55); 9.298 (55).

57. pp. 61–62 *De penitentia.* Schneyer, 9.180 (56); 9.298 (56).

58. pp. 62–63 *De passione.* Schneyer, 9.180 (57); 9.298 (57).

59. p. 63 *Item de passione.* Schneyer, 9.180 (58); 9.298 (58).

60. pp. 63–64 *De passione.* Schneyer, 9.180 (59); 9.298 (59).

61. pp. 64–65 *De passione.* Schneyer, 9.180 (60); 9.298 (60).

62. pp. 65–66 *De passione domini.* Schneyer, 9.181 (61); 9.298 (61).

63. pp. 66–67 *De resurrectione.* Schneyer, 9.181 (62); 9.298 (62).

64. pp. 67–68 *De resurrectione.* Schneyer, 9.181 (63); 9.299 (63).

65. pp. 68–69 *De resurrectione.* Schneyer, 9.181 (64); 9.299 (64).

66. pp. 69–70 *Sermo de resurrectione*. Schneyer, 9.181 (65); 9.299 (65).

67. pp. 70–71 *De passione. resurrectione*. Schneyer, 9.181 (66); 9.299 (66).

68. pp. 71–72 *De ascensione domini*. Schneyer, 9.181 (67); 9.299 (67).

69. pp. 72–73 *De ascensione*. Schneyer, 9.299 (68).

70. pp. 73–74 *De ascensione*. Schneyer, 9.181 (68); 9.299 (69).

71. pp. 74–75 [Rubric effaced]. Schneyer, 9.299 (70).

72. pp. 75–76 *De spiritu sancto*. Schneyer, 9.181 (70); 9.299 (72).

73. pp. 76–77 *De spiritu sancto*. Schneyer, 9.181 (71); 9.299 (73).

74. pp. 77–79 *De spiritu sancto*. Schneyer, 9.181 (72); 9.299 (74).

75. pp. 79–80 *De spiritu sancto*. Schneyer, 9.181 (73); 9.299 (75).

76. pp. 80–81 *De spiritu sancto*. Schneyer, 9.181 (74); 9.299 (76).

77. pp. 81–84 *De die iudicii*. Schneyer, 9.181 (75); 9.300 (77).

78. pp. 84–85 *De beata maria uirgine*. Schneyer, 9.181 (76); 9.300 (78).

79. pp. 85–86 *De annuntiatione*. Schneyer, 9.181 (77); 9.300 (79).

80. pp. 86–87 *De beata maria virgine*. Schneyer, 9.181 (78); 9.300 (80).

81. pp. 87–88 *De beata maria virgine*. Schneyer, 9.181 (79); 9.300 (81).

82. pp. 88–89 *De assumptione virginis*. Schneyer, 9.181 (80); 9.300 (82).

83. pp. 89–90 *De assumptione virginis*. Schneyer, 9.182 (81); 9.300 (83).

84. pp. 90–91 *De assumptione virginis*. Schneyer, 9.182 (82); 9.300 (84).

85. pp. 91–93 *De beate marie virginis* [*sic*]. Schneyer, 9.182 (83); 9.300 (85).

86. pp. 93–94 *Item de beata uirgine*. Schneyer, 9.182 (84); 9.300 (86).

87. pp. 94–95 *De beata magdalena*. Schneyer, 9.182 (85); 9.300 (87).

88. pp. 95–96 *De sancto michaele*. Schneyer, 9. 182 (86); 9.300 (88).

89. pp. 96–98 *De angelis*. Schneyer, 9.182 (87); 9.300 (89).

90. pp. 98–99 *De sancto micha*. Schneyer, 9.182 (88); 9.300 (90).

91. pp. 99–101 *De angelis*. Schneyer, 9.182 (89); 9.301 (91).

92. pp. 101–102 *De officio angelorum*. Schneyer, 9.182 (90); 9.301 (92).

93. pp. 102–103 *De Iohanne batis-* [*sic*]. Schneyer, 9.182 (91); 9.301 (93).

94. pp. 103–104 *De Iohanne baptista.* Schneyer, 9.182 (92); 9.301 (94).

95. pp. 104–105 *De sancto Iohanne baptista.* Schneyer, 9.182 (93); 9.301 (95).

96. pp. 105–107 *De Iohanne baptista.* Schneyer, 9.182 (94); 9.301 (96).

97. pp. 107–108 *De apostolis.* Schneyer, 9.182 (95); 9.301 (97).

98. p. 108 *In hiis locis predicauerunt apostoli.* Notandum quod thomas in india maiori predicauit. bartolomeus in india minori ... petrus et paulus deinde in ytalia.

99. pp. 108–110 *De apostolis.* Schneyer, 9.182 (96); 9.301 (98).

100. pp. 110–111 *De apostolis.* Schneyer, 9.182 (97); 9.301 (99).

101. pp. 111–112 *De apostolis.* Schneyer, 9.182 (98); 9.301 (100).

102. pp. 112–113 *Ad uincula sancti petri.* Schneyer, 9.183 (100). Sermon ends imperfectly; one leaf of text missing after p. 112.

103. pp. 113–114 *De sancto paulo.* Schneyer, 9.183 (103); 9.302 (103).

104. pp. 114–115 *De apostolis.* Schneyer, 9.183 (104); 9.302 (104).

105. pp. 115–116 *De beato matheo.* Schneyer, 9.183 (105); 9.302 (105).

106. pp. 116–117 *De apostolis.* Schneyer, 9.183 (99); 9.301 (101).

107. pp. 117–118 *De euangelistis.* Schneyer, 9.183 (106); 9.302 (106).

108. pp. 118–119 *De beato stephano.* Schneyer, 9.183 (107); 9.302 (107).

109. pp. 119–120 *De martire quouis.* Schneyer, 9.183 (108); 9.302 (108).

110. pp. 120–121 *De beato laurentio.* Schneyer 9.183 (109); 9.302 (109).

111. pp. 121–122 *De martire quouis.* Schneyer, 9.302 (110).

112. pp. 122–123 *De sanctis martiribus.* Schneyer, 9.183 (110); 9.302 (111).

113. pp. 123–124 *De martiribus.* Schneyer, 9.183 (111); 9.302 (112).

114. pp. 124–125 *De martiribus.* Schneyer, 9.183 (112); 9.302 (113) ascribed to Odo de Castro Radulpho, Schneyer, 4.459 (805).

115. pp. 126–127 *De martiribus.* Schneyer, 9.183 (113); 9.302 (114).

116. pp. 127–128 *De uno confessore.* Schneyer, 9.183 (114); 9.302 (115).

117. pp. 128–129 *De ascensione.* Schneyer, 9.183 (115).

118. pp. 129–130 *De confesore episcopo.* Schneyer, 9.183 (116); 9.303 (116).

119. pp. 130–134 *De beato benedicto.* Schneyer, 9.183 (117).

120. pp. 134–135 *De confesore episcopo.* Schneyer, 9.184 (118); 9.303 (117).

121. pp. 135–136 *De confesore.* Schneyer, 9.184 (119); 9.303 (118).

122. pp. 136–137 *Sermo i^us^ de virginibus.* Schneyer, 9.184 (120); 9.303 (119).

123. p. 137 *De uirginibus.* Schneyer, 9.184 (121); 9.303 (120).

124. pp. 137–138 *De virginibus.* Schneyer, 9.184 (122); 9.303 (121).

125. pp. 138–139 *De beata magdalena.* Schneyer, 9.184 (123); 9.303 (122).

126. pp. 139–140 *De maria magdalena.* Schneyer, 9.184 (124); 9.303 (123).

127. p. 140 *De omnibus sanctis.* Schneyer, 9.184 (125); 9.303 (124).

128. pp. 140–141 *Item de omnibus sanctis.* Schneyer, 9.184 (126); 9.303 (125).

129. p. 141 *In dedicatione ecclesie.* Schneyer, 9.184 (127); 9.303 (126).

130. p. 142 *De omnibus sanctis.* Schneyer, 9.184 (128); 9.303 (127).

131. pp. 142–146 *Item de omnibus sanctis.* Schneyer, 9.184 (129); 9.303 (128).

132. pp. 146–147 *De omnibus sanctis.* Schneyer, 9.184 (130); 9.304 (129). Sermon ends complete, but with one leaf missing between pp. 146–147.

133. p. 147 Conclusion of unidentified sermon: //citur ad laborem sicut auis ad uolandum. recolit diem ... ut requiescat in septima. et resurgat in octaua....

134. pp. 147–148 *De dedicatione ecclesie.* Schneyer, 9.184 (135); 9.304 (134).

135. p. 148 *In dedicatione ecclesie.* Schneyer, 9.184 (136).

136. pp. 148–152 *Sermo ad sacerdotes.* Schneyer, 9.184 (137); 9.304 (135).

137. pp. 152–155 *Ad sacerdotes.* Schneyer, 9.184 (138).

138. pp. 155–156 *De apostolis.* Schneyer, 9.184 (139); 9.304 (136).

139. pp. 156–157 *Contra prelatos ecclesie.* Schneyer, 9.184 (140); 9.304 (137).

140. p. 157 *Contra prelatos uel sacerdotes.* Vbi boues non sunt presepe uacuum ... [Prov. 14.4]. Verus salomon in parabolis in una locucione duo ostendit. et quod detrimentum sustineat ex absencia.... Text also found, without rubric, in Paris, Bibliothèque Nationale lat. 14520, ff. 204v–205r (not cited by Schneyer).

141. pp. 157–158 *Ad sacerdotes. uel prelatos.* Schneyer, 9.185 (141); 9.304 (138).

142. pp. 158–159 *De prelatos* [*sic*]. Schneyer, 9.185 (142); 9.304 (139).

143. pp. 159–160 *De sacerdotibus.* Schneyer, 9.304 (140).

144. pp. 160–161 *De sacerdotibus.* Schneyer, 9.185 (144); 9.304 (141).

145. p. 161 *Item de sacerdotibus uel prela* [*sic*]. Schneyer, 9.185 (145).

146. pp. 161–162 *De sacerdotibus.* Aaron ac filios eius applicabis ad hostium ... [Ex. 29.4]. His uerbis que proponit legislator in exodo. insinuat et locum quo suscipienda sunt sacramenta.... Text also found, without rubric, in Paris, Bibliothèque Nationale lat. 14520, f. 207r (not cited by Schneyer).

147. pp. 162–163 *De sacerdotibus.* Schneyer, 9.185 (146).

148. p. 163 *De sacerdotibus.* Schneyer, 9.185 (147).

149. pp. 163–164 *Item de sacerdotibus.* Abicite deos alienas ... [Gen. 35.2]. In uerbis istis quattuor insinuantur. Ad que spiritualiter ... ut de militanti ecclesia assumamur ad trihumphantem [*sic*]....

150. pp. 164–165 *Ad contemplatiuos.* Deus hebreorum uocauit nos ibimus ... [Ex. 3.18]. Hec sunt uerba que contemplatiuis conueniunt. In quibus [added in margin:] tria notantur ... in proprium eius reuertentes. ut glorie efficiamur consortes....

151. p. 165 *Ad sacerdotes.* Quicquid ignem sustinere non potest aqua expiationis ... [Num. 31.23]. Oleum super enatat et miserationes domini super omnia opera eius ... misericordes ergo simus. ut miseriam consequi ualeamus....

152. pp. 165–166 *De contemplatiuis.* Lia erat lippa oculis rachel ... [Gen. 29.17]. Contemplatiua uita quam elegistis his uerbis commendatur. Collectiue. et absolute ... ut de contemplatione enigmatica ueniamus ad comprehensiuam....

153. pp. 166–167 *De penitentia.* Nolite uocare me noemi [?] ... [Ruth 1.20]. Verba ista fundamentum hunc hystorie. ex libro ruth elimeleech e mortuo ... et enim hostiis promeretur deus. ad cuius uisionem peruenire ualeamus....

154. p. 167 *De beata uirgine maria.* Mulierem forte [*sic*] quis inueniet. procul et de ultimis finibus ... [Prov. 31.10]. Hec verba salomonis laudem uestram resonant. In quibus et raritas mulierum forcium osten-

ditur ... ergo ad complexus uestri mariti ut sciamini eius uisione....

155. p. 168 *De pace*. Rogate que ad pacem sunt ierusalem [Ps. 121.6]. Dauid propheta spiritu dei confortatus quem nec prosperitas eneruauit nec aduersitas fregit ... hic uero pacem pectoris. hic det nobis et in futuro pacem eternitatis....

156. pp. 168–169 *De oratione*. Pluet super peccatores laqueos ignis ... [Ps. 10.7]. Sicut preceptum est ut primo queramus regnum dei. ita debemus primo orare ... rex et dominus omnia disponit et gubernat....

157. p. 169 *De abstinentia*. Adhuc esce eorum erant in ore ... [Ps. 77.30]. Verbum istud terribile est et cum tremore et reuerentia. ipsum debetis suscipere ... enim cum apparuerit gloria eius qui uenturus est....

158. pp. 169–170 *De fide*. Fides sine operibus mortua est ... [Jac. 20.26]. Duo perfectioni christiane necessarie comprehendit iacobus his uerbis. fidem ... cum bonis operibus de ipsa fide ad spem uenietis....

159. pp. 170–172 *De omnibus defunctis*. Beati mortui qui in domino moriuntur [Apoc. 14.13]. Omnium fidelium defunctorum memoriam sancta ecclesia recolit ... et omnium sanctorum dei nobis prestare dignetur....

160. pp. 173–178 *Sermo*. Ecce concipies in utero. et ... [Luc. 1.31]. In his uerbis dictis ab angelo ad mariam. tria considerari possunt. primum est concipientis et concepti ... predestinari ad uitam populi saluatione. per infinita secula seculorum amen.

161. pp. 178–179 *De annuntiatione*. Aue gratia plena ... [Luc. 1.28]. In uerbo isto commendatur beata tripliciter. primo ab omni peccato uacua esse ostenditur ... mereamur in futuro sociari in eterna gloria....

162. pp. 179–181 *De annuntiatione*. Ecce uideo nebulam totam.... Verba ista in nocte ad uigilias sunt cantata. et significant aduentum christi in carnem ... Nobis confusio faciei tibi....

Arts. 163–171 have been attributed variously to Petrus de Remis (cf. Kaeppeli, SOPMA, v. 3, no. 3326, for a list of manuscripts), Graeculus, Alexander of Hales, and others.

163. pp. 181–183 *De apostolis*. Qui sunt isti qui ut nubes ... [Is. 60.8]. Profectus apostolorum uolatui nubium et columbarum comparatur merito ... Tercij qui perfecti sunt omnino....

Schneyer, v. 4, p. 753 (462: Petrus de Remis).

164. pp. 183–184 *Sermo de apostolis*. Nimis bone [?] amici tui ... [Ps. 138.17]. Amici dei dicuntur apostoli propter tria que pertinent ad ueros

amicos ... quando eis cum cum [*sic*] christo potestas iudiciaria confertur.

Schneyer, v. 9, p. 128 (38); v. 4, p. 753 (464: Petrus de Remis).

165. pp. 184–185 *De apostolis*. Posui uos ut eatis ... [John 15.16]. In hac duplici missione tota uita apostolorum signatur ... in sepulcro carnales et infructuosi. predicatoribus ergo dicitur.

166. pp. 185–187 *De apostolis*. Posui uos ... [John 15.16]. Quid est circa eos qui officio predicationis propria auctus [?] se ingerunt et imponunt non expectantes ... et sustentant scilicet dilectio dei et proximi.

167. pp. 187–188 *De apostolis*. Estote prudentes sicut serpentes ... [Mat. 10.16]. Duos hostes habuerunt apostoli. hereticos et tirranos. Duo ergo erant eis necessaria ... Nota quomodo hec triplex simplicitas conuenit.

Schneyer, v. 2, p. 235 (372: Graeculus); v. 4, p. 38 (337: Petrus de Remis); v. 9, p. 128 (40).

168. pp. 188–190 *De apostolis*. Hoc est preceptum meum ... [John 15.11]. Nota precepit dominus amorem plusquam mandatum aliud. primo ut dilectio ... Ego plantaui te uineam electam....

Schneyer, v. 4, p. 753 (467: Petrus de Remis).

169. p. 190 *De apostolis*. Uos amici mei estis ... [John 15.14]. Nota iii in presenti euuangelio. assignantur tria in quibus consistit perfecta dilectio ... secundum ad proficientes. tercium ad perfectos.

Cf. Schneyer, v. 9, p. 128 (39); v. 4, p. 753 (468: Petrus de Remis).

170. pp. 190–192 *De apostolis*. Tollite iugum meum super uos ... [Matt. 11.29]. None boues sunt apostoli. numquid de bobus cura est deo. boues quidam sunt ... inportabile notatur de pharaone.

Schneyer, v. 4, p. 753 (469: Petrus de Remis).

171. p. 192 *De confessore*. Ecce nos reliquimus omnia ... [Matt. 19.27]. Vẹre in hoc uerbo uir obediens. id est simon locutus est uictorias ... ujlia sustinujt ut sustinenda doceret....

Schneyer, v. 2, p. 235 (373: Graeculus); v. 4, p. 753 (470: Petrus de Remis).

172. p. 193 [E]go rogabo patrem ... [John 14.16]. Hec uerba referente beato iohanne in euangelio suo. locutus est dominus pridie quam pateretur ad discipulos suos. In quibus uerbis tria nobis consideranda ... descendens a patre lumjnum....

Cf. art. 173 below.

173. pp. 194–198 *De spiritu sancto.* Ego rogabo patrem ... [John 14.16]. Hec uerba referente beato Iohanne in euuangelio suo. xiiii. e. locutus est deus ad discipulos suos ... et omnis ueritatis doctorem mereamur accipere....

Cf. art. 172 above.

174. p. 198 *Hoc non est de sermone isto.* Est enim spiritus malignus. Est spiritus humanus. Est spiritus diuinus. primus impedit. Secundus currit. Tertius dirigit. Impedit errore. Currit amore. dirigit splendore ... ad ostendedam [*sic*] et cet.

Unidentified text.

Parchment (poor quality: heavily speckled, thick, holes, end pieces), ff. i (paper) + 99 (paginated 1–198) + i (paper), 173 x 137 (140 x 105) mm. 2 columns, 38 lines. Single vertical and horizontal (sometimes double) bounding lines, ruled in lead. Remains of prickings in upper, lower and outer margins.

I^{12}, II^{10}, III^{12}, IV^{8}, V^{12}, VI^{10} (–3 between pp. 112–113; loss of text), VII^{10}, VIII^{10} (– 1 between pp. 146–147; loss of text), IX^{4}, X^{12} (+ 1 leaf added at end).

Written by multiple scribes in cramped and highly abbreviated gothic bookhand, above top line.

Crude initials, 5- to 2-line, red with uninspired penwork designs in black and/or red. Rubrics and notes for rubricator. Paragraph marks in red or stroked with red.

Binding: Italy, s. xix^{in}. Half bound in brown calf with bright pink paper sides and a green gold-tooled label: "Sermones de Incarn. Uarii Manuscript." A second label covered by a paper one. Edges spattered blue-green. The same distinctive bindings also found on Marston MSS 50, 125, 135, 151, 153, 158, 159, and 197, all of Hautecombe provenance.

Written in the second quarter of the 13th century, perhaps at the Cistercian abbey of Hautecombe, located in the ancient diocese of Geneva and founded toward the beginning of the 12th century by monks from the abbey of Aulps (see R. Clair, "Les origines de l'abbaye d'Hautecombe," *Mélanges à la mémoire du Père Anselme Dimier* [Arbois, 1982–87] tome II, v. 4, pp. 615–27). Although there is no ex libris, the volume exhibits the characteristic pink binding of the books of Monseigneur Hyacinthe della Torre who acquired and rebound a group of twelve manuscripts from this monastery at the beginning of the 19th century (see Leclercq, 1951, p. 75).

Belonged to the Biblioteca del Seminario Metropolitano in Turin (Leclercq, *op. cit.*, p. 77). Purchased in 1957 from C. A. Stonehill by Thomas E. Marston (bookplate).

secundo folio: dicitur [? folio damaged]

Bibliography: Faye and Bond, p. 79, no. 128.

Marston MS 129 Florence, ca. 1476–78
Naldo Naldi, Oratio

ff. 1r–18v *Naldi Naldi Florentini oratio de laudibus urbis venete atque eius principis ad clarissimum andream venderminum illustrissimum venetorum ducem.* [text:] Etsi scio me onus aethna grauius subiturum illustrissime Princeps qui nulla [added above: *fere*] dicendi arte aut exercitatione ingrediar intra tam angustos ... tum in republica domi atque foris ut ipsi quidem facitis sanctissime administranda. τέλοσ. f. 19r–v ruled, but blank

Naldo Naldi, *Oratio ad Andream Vendraminium* (doge of Venice 1476–78). This manuscript is cited by W. L. Grant, "The Life of Naldo Naldi," *Studies in Philology* 60 (1963) pp. 613–14, note 33; others are noted in Cosenza, v. 3, p. 2410, card 31.

Parchment, ff. 19, 210 x 127 (122 x 57) mm. 20 long lines. Double vertical and horizontal bounding lines (Derolez 13.36); ruled in hard point on hair side. Prickings in upper and lower margins (Derolez 18.2).

I–II^8, III^4 (–4 blank). Catchwords perpendicular to text along innermost bounding line (Derolez 12.6), near lower edge.

Written in a round humanistic hand by a single scribe, below top line.

One illuminated initial of average quality, 3-line, gold against blue ground with gold filigree. Filled with half-length portrait of the doge dressed in red robes and a red hat against green ground. Dedication, 5 lines, in alternating lines of gold and blue majuscules followed by the first three lines of text in red majuscules.

The margins of f. 1 have been trimmed away from the written space, which was then mounted on another piece of parchment conjugate to the front pastedown; hence, any marginal decoration, which may have included a coat of arms, is now lost.

Binding: Italy, s. xv–xvi. Sewn on three tawed skin, slit straps laced through tunnels in the edge of beech boards to channels on the outside and nailed. Gilt edges. Fragment of head endband. The spine is lined with tawed skin between supports.

Covered in red silk with traces of four fastenings on each board.

Copied by the poet Tommaso Baldinotti of Pistoia (1451–1511), who was active in Florence ca. 1473–85 (regarding this scribe see A. C. de la Mare, "The Frontispiece," in *Boethius: His Life, Thought and Influence*, ed. M. Gibson [Oxford, 1981] pp. xvii–xix and J. F. Preston, "An Italian Horae," *Princeton University Library Chronicle* 50, 1 [1988] pp. 74–75). The manuscript must date from 1476 or slightly later; it appears to be the presentation copy to Andrea Vendramin who was elected doge of Venice 5 March 1476 and died 6 May 1478. Early modern provenance unknown. Shelf mark, s. xviii, in ink on front pastedown: "Ms/ No/ 220/," and paper tag with "220" on spine. Unidentified modern notes, in pencil, on front pastedown: "H/ 4/ c" and "IL/ 213". Belonged to the Mostyn family library, Mostyn Hall, Cheshire (Sotheby's, 13 July 1920, no. 85). Purchased from H. P. Kraus (Cat. 85, no. 85) in 1957 by Thomas E. Marston (bookplate).

secundo folio: cupiditate

Bibliography: Faye and Bond, p. 79, no. 129.

Marston MS 130 Italy, s. XV²

Henry Suso, Horologium sapientiae, It. tr., etc.

1. front pastedown: Four sets of numbered similes likening repentance in a man's soul to a boat: Nota che la penitentia e asimigliata a la naue per quatro cose a le quali la naue e ordinata. Et prima e fatta la naue: primo, per fuggir e scanpar le [*sic*] tenpesta del mare, E questo sie el mondo . . . ; Nota sette homini e quali anno a lauorar ne la naue e cosi ne la penitentia: El primo sempre sgraua la naue, E questa e la pouerta . . . ; Nota quattro venti contrarij a la penitentia: El primo e australe ed e caldo, E questo sie la maledecta Superbia . . . ; Nota sette ausilii che liberano la naue e cosi l'anima: El primo chiama e dice a dio, Signor credo che possi me liberare, E questa e la fede. . . .

2. ff. 1r–2v [A] Conseruar el tempo deinducono [*sic*?] tre raxone, l'una e la sua breuita. Vnde conç[i]osia cosa che la uia sia longa e lo tempo breue e li debiti molti, non e da perderlo in otiosita . . . peroche maçor honor farebono a dio et al suo officio se il seguisseno in solicitudine e in fatica che non fano stando ociosi che se maçor nobilita fossi pur mançar e non far nulla piuj [*sic*] nobel seria lo porco che lo homo.

   Citing Seneca, St. Bernard, Hugh of St. Victor and St. Paul against laziness and waste of time particularly on the part of the clergy.

3. f. 3r Quando yhesus nominatur/ et maria memoratur/ ... Semique ter flectatur/ dies confert totidem.

Indulgence in four 4-line strophes, conceded by a "Pope John" for 40 days.

4. f. 3r Incomenza el modo de la contemplation de tucte le cose. Deus: potentia, Sapiencia, Perfectio, Bonitas ... Infernus: videre diabolos Ignis inextinguibilis. Frigus intolerabile. Priuatio dei Et omnis boni.

List of 12 topics for meditation, each followed by 4 subdivisions of the topic.

5. f. 3v Questo libro .e. delle done done [*sic*] de sancta. chiara de muran. a chi sera prestado per charita presto lo remande indriedo.

6. ff. 4r–237v [Prologue:] *Incominciasi il prolagho nel libro il quale si chiama Oriuolo della sapientia A llause* [sic] *christi*. Sentite del signiore in bonitade. et con sinplicita di chuore cierchate per lui ... comando che queste cose fossono comunicate et participate, ch'en tuttj coloro ch'amano iddio. [f. 10r, book 1, chapter list:] La materia di questo primo libro e la pretiosissima passione di cristo ... Come alquantj electj. et preuenutj dalla diuina gratia. sono tractj marauigliosamente a dio. Et spetialmente come alcuno giouane fu tracto et tirato a dio. *Capitolo primo*. Come la passione de dio et [*sic*, as tironian *et*] messaggiera alla chognitione della diuinitade e qual forma christo trasse della crudelta della passione. *Capitoli ij* ... et del dolore ch'ell'ebbe nella passione di christo. *Chapitolo xvi*. [f. 11r, book 1:] *Come alquantj elettj preuenutj dalla diuina gratia sono tractj a ddio. Et come alchuno fu tracto. Capitolo j*. La Sapientia io amai. et per lei cierchai infino da giouaneçça ... et sieno menatj con allegreçça a quella cielestiale gierusalem. [f. 150v, book 2, chapter list:] Della diuersita marauigliosa delle dottrine de disciepoli. *Capitolo j*. Della scientia utilissima all'uomo la quale e sapere morite. *Capitolo ij* ... la quale i disciepoli della diuina sapientia meritano. *Chapitolo viij*. [f. 151r, book 2:] *Della diuersita delle dottrine. Capitolo primo*. Alchuno desideroso disciepolo della sapientia cierchaua la sapientia di tuttj li antichi ... Chontenplando te re di gloria e signore delle virtudi nella tua belleçça giesu christo signore nostro Il quale col padre et chol filio et collo spirito santo viuj e regnia per infinita secula seculorum amen.

Henry Suso, *Horologium Sapientiae*, in It.; Kaeppeli, SOPMA, v. 2, no. 1852; P. Künzle, O. P., *Heinrich Seuses Horologium Sapientie* (Freiburg,

1977) pp. 263–67 (Marston MS 130 cited incorrectly as two manuscripts, nos. 16 and 17).

7. ff. 238r–244r Chiunque desidera di farsi amico et dimestico della diuinia sapientia dee queste ore continuamente leggiere et dire. Salutem mentis in [*sic*] corporis donet nobis yhesus sapientia patris ... Et tibi summo bono ardenti desiderio iugiter ardere [*sic*] per christum dominum nostrum. Benedicamus domino. Deo gratias. Etterna sapientia benedicat et custodiat chorda et corpora nostra amen. Amen.

   Office of Eternal Wisdom (*Cursus de aeterna sapientia*), composed by Henry Suso, as printed by Künzle, *op.cit.*, pp. 606–18.

8. ff. 244r–251r *Queste sono ciento meditationi con ciento petioni* [sic] *della passione di christo le quali si uogliono dire ogni di con ciento gienue. E tosto sentira* [sic?] *il dolore di christo crucifisso* Domine yhesu christe qui permessisti a [*sic*] maria madalena sanctos pedes tuos lacrimis deuotionis lauari. et unguento ungni [*sic*]. Unge et compunge cor meum tua santissima passione. Domine yhesu christe qui disisti [*sic*] pauperes senper abetis uobiscum me autem non senper abebitis. fac me pauperem spiritu. ut abere merear regnum cielorum ... Domine yhesu christe qui tertia die ad [*sic*] mortuis resuscitastj resuscitat [*sic*] uiuifica animam meam ut in ueritate te ualeam inuenire. In nomine Patrj [*sic*]. et Filij et Spiritus sancti Amen. Amen. *Finito L'oriuolo della sapientia A llaude di christo crucifisso E di maria dolcie.*

   Brief meditations (98, not the 100 announced in the rubric) and petitions on the passion of Christ; they are not the same as those printed in the 1511 edition.

9. ff. 251r–252v Santo ylario ch'e uesco [*sic*] de parise si troua in le scrite de sancto chimento [*sic*] papa da po sancto piero e fo so discipolo. E questo sancto clemento si trouo in le scripte de so maistro çoe san piero queste socto scripte cose. Quando alguna persona uuol pregar lo nostro signor dolzemente e deuotamente. si diga de buon cuor auanti la crose vij fiade questj iij salmi. Usquequo domine. Ad te domine leuaui. Deus deus meus respice in me ... [other psalms specified for:] Quando alguna persona e in gran tribulation ..., Quando alguna persona uolese andar in uiaço ..., Quando alguna persona se leua de lecto la matina ..., Quando alguna persona fosse in aduersita ..., Quando alguno fosse incolpado de peccado ..., Quando sente le tentatione del demonio ..., Quando alguno uol començar alguna cosa ..., Quando sei in aduersita de questo mondo ..., Quando hai alguno dolore o tristitia de cuore ..., Quando tu sei in grande tribulation e tristitia de

cuore . . . , Quando algun uuol recorere a la misericordia de dio et compire el so desiderio . . . , Quando alguno uuol mostrar perfectamente el so dolore e presentare dinanti da dio. . . .

Thirteen occasions of special need with the psalms to be recited for invoking the help of God; similar texts in Latin and in Middle English may be found respectively in Edinburgh, University Library, MS 57, f. 16r and in San Marino, Huntington Library, HM 140, f. 169v.

10. f. 252v and back pastedown: Nesuno piu integramente puo mustrar le soe tribulatione ai sancti c'al nostro signor misser yhesu christo tucti li psalmi che son da Beati immaculati perfina ad dominum cum tribularer.

Promise of receiving the mercy of God, in reciting Ps. 118 (broken down into sections, each of which is referred to as a psalm.)

11. back pastedown [in a later, noting hand:] fo sagin el primo di zugno fa sag// sie altar a quel nobel monesti// misier sen [*sic*] zacharia per ogno a// xxxx di [followed by an erasure].

Written in two different formats, both on parchment 185 x 125 mm.

Folios 1–3, written space 110 x 72 mm. 27 long lines. A single gathering of four leaves, the first missing. Art. 2 frame-ruled in ink and written by a single scribe in humanistic bookhand with gothic features, above top line; space for initial on f. 1r left unfilled, but with guide letter. Arts. 3 and 5 in round gothic bookhand; art. 4 in poorly formed bookhand. Folio 3r fully ruled in lead for 30 lines of text; f. 3v unruled.

Folios 4–252, written space 116 x 75 mm. 24 long lines. Double upper and single (sometimes double) lower horizontal bounding lines; single vertical bounding lines, all full across. Ruled in lead or crayon; prickings in upper, lower and outer margins. I–XXV^{10} (final folio = back pastedown). Decorated horizontal catchwords in center of lower margin, verso. Written in gothic bookhand, below top line. Arts. 9 and 10 in round gothic bookhand of a larger module. For main text divisions good blue initials with plain parchment designs and red penwork flourishes; elsewhere 2-line initials alternate red with blue harping designs and blue with red. On f. 11r red rectangular page filler at bottom of text space. Small plain 1-line initials alternate red and blue. Headings and paragraph marks in red. Majuscules stroked with yellow. Remains of guide letters.

Binding: Italy, s. xv. Original sewing on four tawed skin, kermes pink slit straps laced through tunnels in the edge of wooden boards to channels on the outside and nailed. A tawed skin endband core is laid in grooves and covered with plain, wound primary and red secondary embroidery. Spine: supports outlined and panels diapered with triple fillets.

Covered in light brown goatskin with corner tongues, and decorated with interlace squares on their points within concentric frames. Trace of one fastening, the catch on the lower board and the upper one cut in for a red fabric strap attached with star-headed nails. The cover has been varnished.

Written in Italy in the second half of the 15th century, with the texts of arts. 2–5 probably added somewhat later to what were originally blank flyleaves. Belonged, according to early ownership inscription (art. 5), to the Franciscan house of nuns of Santa Chiara on the island of Murano in the Venetian lagoon (house founded in 1439; suppressed in 1826). Notes on the back pastedown (art. 11) presumably refer to the famous Venetian monastery for Benedictine nuns, San Zaccaria (suppressed in 1810). Belonged to T. Henry Foster of Ottumwa, Iowa; his sale (Parke-Bernet, March 1957). H. P. Kraus (*List 189*, no. 173, where it is said to be from the collections of Lord Vernon and Giuseppe [Joseph] Martini). Purchased from B. M. Rosenthal of New York in 1957 by L. C. Witten (inv. no. 1588), who sold it the same year to Thomas E. Marston (bookplate).

secundo folio: [f. 2] li cristiani
[f. 5] si a cosa

Bibliography: De Ricci, v. 1, p. 723, no. 4 (when in Foster collection); Faye and Bond, p. 79, no. 130.

Marston MS 131 — Germany, s. XVI

Ps.-Dionysius the Areopagite, De ecclesiastica hierarchia, Lat. tr. John the Scot

1. f. 1r ruled, but blank; ff. 1v–39r *Epigramma in beatum Dionysium. et hoc de ecclesiastica hierarchia duobus versibus exametris apud grecos comprehensum.* Simbola [corrected from *symbola*] diuinorum mirabilium sacrorum vniformi ratione ad singularitatem resoluisti vnius luminis vnam claritatem. *Dionysij areopagite episcopi athenarum ad timotheum ... Dionysius presbyter.* [list of *capitula* i–vii follows:] [R]ecumbentium capitulorum doctrinam secundum duplicem perficit modum. Primum exponit hoc quomodo perficitur mysterium capituli ... [text:] Capitulum primum. *Que sit ecclesiastice hierarchie traditio. et que eiusdem speculatio.* [Q]uia quidem secundum nos hierarchia diuinorum principiorum sacratissime intenta atque diuina. habetur deifica scientia ... Confido enim ex his que dicta sunt ego repositos in te diuini ignis accendens usque uapores. *Magni dionysij Areopagite liber de ecclesiastica hierarchia finit.* ff. 39v–40v ruled, but blank

Dionysiaca: recueil donnant l'ensemble des traductions latines des ouvrages attribués au Denys de l'Areopage (Paris, Bruges, 1937) v. 1, pp. xxi–lxiv for numerous printed texts; v. 2, pp. 1071–476 for text.

Paper (unidentified watermarks along upper edge), ff. i (paper) + 40 + i (paper), 180 x 115 (113 x 80) mm. 30 long lines. Single vertical bounding lines ruled in lead or crayon; every third text line ruled in ink.

Accurate collation impossible due to tight binding.

Written by a single scribe in a stylized gothic script.

Spaces for decorative initials left unfilled. Headings, paragraph marks and running headlines in red.

Binding: Place uncertain, s. xix. Quarter bound in brown leather with olive green paper sides. Parts of edges daubed bluish-green.

Copied probably in Germany in the 16th century, perhaps from a printed book. Belonged to T. Henry Foster of Ottumwa, Iowa; his sale (Parke-Bernet, March 1957). Purchased from C. A. Stonehill in 1957 by Thomas E. Marston (bookplate).

secundo folio: *Que sit*

Bibliography: De Ricci, v. 1, p. 723, no. 2 (when in Foster collection); Faye and Bond, p. 79, no. 131.

Marston MS 132 — Italy, s. XV[2]

Pius II, Bulla Ezechielis, It. tr.

ff. 1r–6v Pio vescouo seruo de li serui dedio. Ad tucti et ad ciaschuno . . . et apostolica benedictione. Sententia e del grande propheta ecechiele. Selu speculatore. cio pastore non annuntiara . . . in secula seculorum. Dato a roma apresso a sancto pietro nel anno de la incarnatione de signore mille. cccc°. Lxiij. ad xi Kalende de Nouembre cioe a xxij. di doctobra nel sexto anno del nostro pontificato. Laus Deo Amen. f. 7r–v ruled, but blank

Papal bull dated 22 October 1463 in unidentified It. tr., announcing the adherence of Pope Pius II to the Hungarian-Venetian league. *Opera omnia* (Basel, 1551) Epistle 412 on pp. 914–23 for the Latin text.

Paper (watermarks: unidentified horn in gutter), ff. i (paper) + 7 + i (paper), 187 x 130 (175 x 114) mm. Ca. 40 long lines. Single vertical and horizontal bounding lines. Ruled in hard point or lead.

Collation impossible due to repairs. Folios 4–5 are conjugate leaves.
Written in upright *mercantesca* bookhand (no loops).
One initial, 4-line, in black ink on f. 1r.
Binding: Place uncertain, s. xix. Rigid vellum case.

Written in Italy in the second half of the 15th century, in 1463 or thereafter, given the date of the bull. Provenance unknown. Traces of notes, in pencil but erased or covered by bookplate, on front pastedown. Purchased from B. M. Rosenthal (Cat. 1, no. 81) in 1957 by Thomas E. Marston (bookplate).

secundo folio: Ecco

Bibliography: Faye and Bond, p. 79, no. 132.

Marston MS 134 — Northern Italy, s. XV/XVI
Boniohannes de Messana, Quadripartitus figurarum moralium

ff. 1r–92r *Quadripartitus Apologus Cyrilli Episcopi* [*Hierusalem* crossed out] *poete in quo Speculum omnis sapientie relucet.* [prologue:] Secundum Aristotelis sententiam in problematibus suis: Quamquam Exemplis in ostendendo gaudeant omnes in disciplinis moralibus . . . per somnium feriamus. [table, f. 2r:] *Capitula prime partis.* [chapter numbers and folio references are contemporary additions:] 1. Semper disce et in extremis horis sapientie magis stude. fo 3/ 2. Nihil sibi homo est sine sapientia f. 4/ . . . 27 In bono nomine uirtutum, tetragono semper uige. fo 26/ [text, f. 2v:] *Semper disce et in extremis horis magis stude. Liber primus.* Vulpes decrepita ardens cupidine plus sciendi, querendo magistrum membris grauioribus sui corporis itineris adijt graue pondus . . . et dementius tanto facit, quanto letalius se perdit. Quibus dictis libidinosissimum passerem reliquit. *Explicit quatripartitus* [sic] *apologus cyrilli poete laureati.* f. 92v blank

Boniohannes de Messana (previously attributed to Ps.-Cyrillus), *Quadripartitus figurarum moralium*, with a table of contents preceding each book; Kaeppeli, SOPMA, v. 1, no. 699 (Marston MS 134 listed on p. 252 as Yale University, Reinecke [*sic*] Library Marston 67); Bloomfield, *Virtues and Vices*, no. 5372. Text printed by J. G. T. Graesse, *Bibliothek des litterarischen Vereins in Stuttgart* 148 (1880) pp. 3–118.

Paper (watermarks, in gutter: similar to Piccard Waage VI.29–31; unidentified anchor in a circle with linking ring at top, the whole surmounted by a star), ff. i (paper) + 93 (ii, 1–92) + i (paper), 202 x 148 (140 x 100)

mm. Ca. 21–23 long lines. Frame-ruled in pale ink or lead.

I^{12} (–1, 2; 3 = ii, –4; all missing leaves precede beginning of text on f. 1), II–III^{12}, IV (–9; no loss of text), V–VIII^{12} (+ 1 leaf tipped in at end). Quires signed with letters of alphabet (A-H) in lower right corner, recto.

Written by a single scribe in neat, even humanistic cursive.

Plain initials, 3- to 1-line, and headings in red.

Binding: Italy, s. xix. "Alla rustica" paper case.

Written in Northern Italy at the end of the 15th or beginning of the 16th century. Partially effaced inscription in lower margin, f. 1r, indicates it belonged (s. xvi?) to the monastery of San Salvatore in Pavia (Cottineau, v. 2, cols. 2237–38). Provenance otherwise unknown. Purchased from Renzo Rizzi of Milan in 1957 by L. C. Witten (inv. no. 1702), who sold it the same year to Thomas E. Marston (bookplate).

secundo folio: luxurie

Bibliography: Faye and Bond, p. 79, no. 134.

Marston MS 135 — Hautecombe [?], s. XII^{med}

Sermons (in Lat.)

Similar collections of sermons, often with individual items unattributed, also occur in Olomouc, Statni Archiv C. O. 24; Engelberg, Bib. Abbat. 33; Zurich, Zentralbibliothek, Rheinau 68; Heiligenkreuz, Bibl. mon. 192. A number of the sermons listed below remain unidentified.

Vol. I:

1. ff. 1r–2v Missus est angelus gabriel ad mariam. *de aduentu dei.* id est predicator diuini [*sic*] ad peccatorem ... sed quia iusticie solent esse impedimenta. sed propter quosdam qui ex ypocrisi. hoc faciunt. additur propter iusticiam.

   Bernard of Clairvaux, *Sermo de adventu*; J. Leclercq, "Études sur S. Bernard et le texte de ses écrits," *Analecta Sacri Ordinis Cisterciensis* 9.1–2 (1953) pp. 57–58.

2. ff. 2v–6r Excutere de puluere. consurge sede ... [Is. 52.2]. Audite fratres karissimi. quam dulciter quam affectuose celestis sponsus sibi iussit reconciliare ecclesiam ... surgite rumpite uincula peccatorum. et malorum operum. ut mereamini dominum deum uidere in terra uiuentium. Qui uiuit....

Geoffroi Babion, *Sermo*; Schneyer, v. 2, p. 151 (13).

3. ff. 6r–8v Noli emulari in malignantibus ... [Ps. 36.1]. Multi sunt in mundo fratres karissimi. qui cum uideant huius mundi homines florere. et omnibus bonis habundare. quantum libet peccatores. quantum libet scelerosos ... Deus autem pacis qui uos a morte redemit. aptet uos in omni opere bono. ut faciatis eius uoluntatem cui est honor et....

Geoffroi Babion, *Sermo*; Schneyer, v. 2, p. 151 (14).

4. ff. 8v–13r Dicite filie syon ecce rex tuus uenit tibi mansuetus ... [Mat. 21.5]. Mandat uobis rex celestis fratres karissimi per zachariam prophetam gaudium sui aduentus. Uenit ad recordationem dominus. qui pro peccato primi parentis ... nullus accedat uacuus ante dominum. ut mereantur omnes equitari et ut eos super sedens ducere dominus et regere....

Geoffroi Babion, *Sermo*; Schneyer, v. 2, pp. 151–52 (15).

5. ff. 13r–15v Salomon edificauit domum domini in iherusalem. vii. annis. et dedicauerunt eam ... [2 Chron. 6.7]. Omnia fratres karissimi facta antique legis sunt figura noue. et propter nos memorie commendata. Templum autem domini ab antiquis ... Pensate fratres pensate. fideles sanctos dei intercessores habete. et preciosum confessorem nicholaum ut eius meritis eternam patriam mereri possitis....

Geoffroi Babion, *Sermo*; Schneyer, v. 2, p. 154 (49).

6. ff. 15v–18v Fundamenta eius in montibus sanctis ... [Ps. 86.1]. Gloriosam fratres karissimi ciuitatem cepit ab inicio mundi dominus edificare. nec dum tamen consummata est. Uoluit enim ... Qui locuntur pacem cum proximo suo. mala autem in cordibus eorum [Ps. 27.3].

Geoffroi Babion, *Sermo*; Schneyer, v. 2, p. 154 (48).

7. ff. 18v–20v Montes israel audite uerbum domini. Hec dicit ... [Ezech. 6.3]. Fratres attendat caritas uestra quid spiritus sanctus in ezechiele uobis proponat. Sacra mater ecclesia que ciuitas uestra ... sedem in tuto collocare mereamur....

Jacobus Berengarius, *Sermo*; Schneyer, v. 3, p. 880 (45).

8. ff. 20v–21r Nemo uestrum dubitet karissimi duos esse nostri redemptoris aduentus. Quorum primum iam prececisse alterum adhuc futurum esse fide cognoscimus ... Beati enim misericordes. quoniam ipsi miseriam consequentur....

Jacobus Berengarius, *Sermo*; Schneyer, v. 3, p. 880 (46).

9. ff. 21r–22r Penitentiam agite. appropinquabit enim regnum celorum

... [Mt. 3.2, 4.17]. Euangelice tuba lectionis fratres karissimi meo uestris auribus [*uestris* crossed out] insonuit. ut si regna celestia adipisci uolumus ... Penitentiam ergo agite. dum fructuosa est et utilis. inuenire miseriam. quia appropinquauit regnum celorum.

10. ff. 22r–23r Quanti sit elemosinam facere. sententiam domini in euangelio fratres aduertite. Date inquit elemosinam. et ecce omnia munda sunt uobis ... de quibus in euangelio dominus. Dimittite inquit et dimittemini. date et dabitur uobis.

Jacobus Berengarius, *Sermo*; Schneyer, v. 3, p. 880 (47).

11. ff. 23r–24r Populus et oues pascue eius. introite portas eius ... [Ps. 99.3]. Duas esse confessiones bonas et deo acceptabiles sancta nobis fratres karissimi declarat auctoritas ... Aperite mihi portas. et ingressus in eas confitebor domino hec porta domini iusti intrabunt in eam....

Jacobus Berengarius, *Sermo*; Schneyer, v. 3, p. 880 (48, but ending differently).

12. f. 24r–v Audistis fratres karissimi in sancto euangelio terribilem ac desiderabilem uocem metuendam pariterque delectabilem sententiam ... et peregrinis erogemus. ut et peccata nostra redimamus. et de illis bonis operibus....

Unidentified sermon.

13. f. 25r–v "Adorna thalamum tuum syon. et suscipe regem christum" [Antiph. in festo Purificationis b. Mariae]. Que est ista syon que thalamum suum precipitur adornare. nisi sancta ecclesia uel unaqueque fidelis anima ... et fide et bonis operibus uos met [*sic*] ipsos cotidie hostiam uiuam et immaculatam domino offeratis....

Anonymous sermon; see Schneyer, v. 8, p. 605 (96) and p. 710 (58).

14. ff. 25v–27r Hodie mater ecclesia filios suos in quibus detrimentum se sensisse cognoscit paterna seueritate corripit ... quia hic rubor sequestrationis fit uobis ad interitum carnis. ut spiritus saluus sit in die [*iudicij* crossed out]. uestre resurrectionis.

Ivo of Chartres, *Sermo XIII*; PL 162.579–81.

15. ff. 27r–28r Qui uult hominem exhibere perfectum in christo reperiet omnia documenta uirtutum ... ut sitis filii patris uestri qui in celis est. Si autem filii et heredes. Heredes quidem dei. coheredes autem christi. Ivo of Chartres, *Sermo XVI*; PL 162.586–88.

16. ff. 28r–29r Cum cetere festiuitates in recordatione rerum gestarum

leticia spirituali fidelium ... uerum pascha celebremus. id est ut de imis ad superna celorum gaudia toto desiderio transeamus.

Ivo of Chartres, *Sermo XVIII*; PL 162.589–91.

17. ff. 29r–30r Hodie fratres uictoria christi completa est. hodie triumphalia [*eius* added above] uexilla eriguntur. despoliatione sua dolet ... donec inmarcessibilem ab imperatore suo completo agone percipiant coronam.

Ivo of Chartres, *Sermo XIX*; PL 162.591–92.

18. ff. 30r–31r Dies pentecostes sacratus in lege et in euangelio. In lege. quia die quinquagesimo a die quo egiptus spoliata est ... hec omnia operatus unus [*quisque* deleted] atque idem spiritus diuidens singulis prout uult.

Ivo of Chartres, *Sermo XX*; PL 162.592–95.

19. ff. 31r–33r Labia sacerdotis custodiunt scientiam ... [Mal. 2.7]. Iacet fratres karissimi propheticum istud in capite nostro sumo [*sic*] sacerdote impletum esse constet. in nobis tamen qui sacerdotalis professionis ... auditurus illud ultimum euge serue bone et fidelis quia in pauca fuisti fidelis....

20. ff. 33r–35v Deus iudicium tuum regi da. et iusticiam ... [Ps. 71.2]. Omnis potestas a deo data est. que autem a deo data sunt. ordinata sunt. Qui uero resistit potestati ... Glorificate igitur fratres karissimi hanc personam quam deus in oculis uestris glorificat.

Jacobus Berengarius, *Sermo*, Schneyer, v. 3, p. 880 (50).

21. ff. 35v–37r Scitis ut ait apostolus fratres karissimi gratiam domini nostri ihesu christi quoniam propter nos egenus factus est cum diues esset. ut uos inopia illius diuites essetis ... ut ipse dixit. gaudium est in celo super uno peccatore penitentiam agente. Seruite ergo domino in timore....

Jacobus Berengarius, *Sermo*; Schneyer, v. 3, p. 880 (51).

22. ff. 37r–39r Assumpta est maria in celum. gaudent angeli laudantes benedicunt dominum [*Versic. Grad. Missae*]. Sicut regina nostra uirgo maria incomparabilis est ceteris uirginibus ... si tales fuerimus de massa perditorum assumpti sumus....

Jacobus Berengarius, *Sermo*; Schneyer, v. 3, p. 880 (52).

23. ff. 39r–41v Paradisi porta per euam cunctis clausa est ... [Resp. in Assumptione Sancte Marie]. Sicut dolendum est de conditione tempora-

lis miserie et dampnationis eterne quam per euam incurrimus ... ut mereamur diujcias regni celestis possidere....

Jacobus Berengarius, *Sermo*; Schneyer, v. 3, p. 880 (53).

24. ff. 41v–43v Tu es petrus. et super hanc petram ... [Mt. 16.18]. Sicut filij israel qui per moysen transiordanem [*sic*] acceperunt hereditatem. tamen cum fratribus ut et ipsi hereditatem acciperent. perrexerunt armati ... Sic et nos ut peracta penitentia dicamus cum propheta. Ut cantet tibi gloria mea et non compungar....

Jacobus Berengarius, *Sermo*; Schneyer, v. 3, p. 880 (54).

25. ff. 43v–45r Dum medium silentium tenerent omnia [Sap. 18.14]. Tria sunt silentia. primum ignorantia languoris. Secundum desperatio curacionis. Tercium silentium est adeptio sanitatis ... sed a sedibus regalibus uenire debuit. quia regnum ad quod uocantur electi dei preparatum est ab inicio seculi amen.

Hugh of St. Victor, *De verbo incarnato, Collationes seu disputationes tres: Collatio I*; PL 177.315–18.

26. ff. 45r–46r In illo tempore. Dixit ihesus discipulis suis. Hoc est preceptum meum ... [Io. 13.34]. Saluator noster fratres karissimi in principio hominem fecit adam de terra uirgine. et ex costa eius formauit euam ... ut consequamini gaudia regni celorum ad quod ipse nos perducat qui in trinitate perfecta....

27. ff. 46r–48v [E]cce quam bonum et quam iocundum habitare ... [Ps. 132.1]. Sic fratres dauid propheta fraternitati uestre et conuentus uestros quos per spiritum de longinquo preuidebat magna exultatione collaudat ... sicut dignum est emendetur. Et pax dei que exuperat omnem sensum....

Geoffroi Babion, *Sermo*; Schneyer, v. 2, p. 152 (37).

28. ff. 49r–52v Populе meus quid feci tibi ... [Mich. 6.3]. Diu fratres R. tolerauit nos dominus. diu distulit penam inuitans nos ad penitentiam ... ubi in eternum floreatis [corrected from *floretatis*] ubi in eternum [*flor* excised] gaudeatis....

Geoffroi Babion, *Sermo*; Schneyer, v. 2, p. 152 (24).

29. ff. 52v–54v Locutus est dominus ad moysem dicens ... [Lev. 13.44]. Fratres karissimi timeo ne quosdam uestrum tangat hec sententia. timeo ne aliquos uestrum contaminet ... ut ab hac lepra abstineatis. ne similes supradictis eandem dampnationem incurratis.

Geoffroi Babion, *Sermo*; Schneyer, v. 2, p. 153 (43).

30. ff. 54v–57r Locutus est dominus ad moysen dicens ... [Lev. 21.16; 22.4]. Fratres karissimi que in ueteri lege de sacerdocio iubentur. ad uestrum sacerdocium spiritualiter intellecta pertinere uidentur ... cauete ne pro omnibus istis dignitate officii inueniamini indigni.

Geoffroi Babion, *Sermo*; Schneyer, v. 2, p. 154 (44).

31. ff. 57r–59v Exite popule meus de babylonia et ... [Apoc. 18.4]. Sunt fratres karissimi in mundo duo regna. duo principes. due familie alterum enim est regnum dei ... qui habitat in iherusalem mittat uobis auxilium de sancto. et de syon tueatur uos. Qui uiuit.

Geoffroi Babion, *Sermo*; Schneyer, v. 2, p. 154 (53).

32. ff. 59v–62r Conuertimini et agite penitentiam ab omnibus ... [Ezech. 18.30]. Audite fratres quante misericordie. quante pacientie est redemptor noster. qui nos cotidie cadentes ... confirmet uos in omni opere bono. ut spiritus sit saluus in die domini. ...

Geoffroi Babion, *Sermo*; Schneyer, v. 2, p. 155 (59).

33. ff. 62r–65r Filij hominum usque quo graui corde ... [Ps. 4.3]. Fratres karissimi si filij dei estis audite patienter correctionem patris. Increpat uos dominus. sed qui increpat correctionem uestram desiderat ... facit deus pauperes ut probet diujtes. alij dant se ipsos ut martyres sicut sanctus laurentius.

Geoffroi Babion, *Sermo*; Schneyer, v. 2, p. 155 (61).

34. ff. 65r–67r Surge qui dormis. et exurge a mortuis ... [Eph. 5.14]. Huc usque fratres karissimi satis obdormistis. huc usque [*peregrinati* crossed out] pigritati estis ... nisi excommunicato participare? Quid est ab ea inquinari. nisi cum eo excommunicari?

Geoffroi Babion, *Sermo*; Schneyer, v. 2, p. 155 (62).

35. ff. 67r–69v Uerbum crucis pereuntibus quidem ... [1 Cor. 1.18]. Fratres karissimi quia fidelibus locuturi de misterio crucis sumus. ideo non credimus uobis stulticiam uideri deum predicare crucifixum ... eam exaltemus in omnibus ecclesiis. ut nobis sit communiter salus. ...

Geoffroi Babion, *Sermo*; Schneyer, v. 2, p. 152 (28).

36. ff. 69v–72r Verbo domini celi ... [Ps. 31.6]. Fratres karissimi scire debetis que et quanta sit sollempnitas ista. et quare per omnes ecclesias uniuersaliter celebrata hodie ... uirtutibus ornemus a uicijs inundemur. ut eum suscipere mereamur. ...

Geoffroi Babion, *Sermo*; Schneyer, v. 2, p. 153 (32).

37. ff. 72r–73v Super muros tuos iherusalem constitui ... [Is. 62.2]. Iherusalem fratres super muros cuius dominum custodes posuisse propheta testatur. sancta ecclesia est que munita fidei et caritatis muro ... ut hac pugna cum grege nobis commisso amalech et principes eius mereamur superare....

Hauréau, *Initia*, v. 6, 208.

38. ff. 73v–74v Ecce ego super pastores requiram gregem meum ... [Ezech. 34.10]. Quam graue sit fratres [*mei* deleted] magisterij pondus appetere. et quam graue sit pastoralem curam assumere ... vigilanti cura aperiant. Unde ad ezechielem dicitur. Sume tibi laterem.

Jacobus Berengarius, *Sermo*; Schneyer, v. 3, p. 881 (56).

39. ff. 74v–75v De cunctis hominum generibus fratres karissimi tres tantummodo uiri perhibentur. qui soli de sententia districti ex animis in fine in fine [*sic*] liberentur. id est noe. daniel. et iob ... in quo repertus fuerit in fine ad electorum societatem mereamur peruenire....

Jacobus Berengarius, *Sermo*; Schneyer, v. 3, p. 881 (57).

40. ff. 75v–77r Oportet fratres karissimi ut tota mentis intentione inquirere uel intelligere studeamus quare christiani sumus. et quare crucem christi in fronte portamus ... quod dicimus. et nobis concedat uobiscum implere posse quod predicamus adiuuante domino.

Jacobus Berengarius, *Sermo*; Schneyer, v. 3, p. 881 (58).

41. ff. 77r–79r Designauit dominus et alios ... [Luc. 10.1]. Elegit sibi fratres karissimi dominus in primitiua ecclesia duodecim apostolos qui alios conuerterent ... quo iudex ueniet. et racionem cum seruis suis quibus talenta tradidit ponet....

Geoffroi Babion, *Sermo*; Schneyer, v. 2, p. 154 (54).

42. ff. 79r–81v Ve [corrected from *De*] pastoribus qui dispergunt ... [Jer. 33.1]. Audite fratres super uos sententiam domini terribilem. increpantem. comminantem ... ut qui nomen accepistis sacerdotis. rem nominis studeatis retinere ...

Geoffroi Babion, *Sermo*; Schneyer, v. 2, p. 154 (55).

43. ff. 81v–84r Dum egrederetur loth de sodomis ... [Gen. 19.17]. Nostis fratres quod loth nepos abrahe inter pessimos in sodoma et gomorra commoratus est ... totus pendet in uoluntate patris iubentis. et ideo maiorem gloriam pre ceteris sortitus est.

Geoffroi Babion, *Sermo*, Schneyer, v. 2, p. 153 (36).

44. ff. 84r–86r Nemo mjttit ujnum nouellum ... [Marc. 2.22]. Dominus ihesus christus fratres karissimi loquens hominibus aliquando per similitudines. aliquando per figuras. aliquando aperte uerbum uite seminauit ... Audite quantam misericordiam dominus filijs israel in samaria obsessis contulit.

Geoffroi Babion [?], *Sermo*.

45. ff. 86r–88v Dicite pusillanimes confortamini ... [Is. 35.4]. Ante aduentum domini fratres karissimi in tanta caligine totum genus hominum uoluebatur ... ornate ergo uirtutibus corda uestra ut digne recipiatis regem// [end of Vol. I]

Geoffroi Babion, *Sermo*, ending imperfectly; Schneyer, v. 2, p. 150 (1).

Vol. II:

46. f. 89r–v //qui ab utero matris dominum recognouit. qui per eundem angelum gabrielem ... preparemus habitacula peccatorum contra talem imperatorem. ut dignetur nos recipere in celesti iherusalem.

Geoffroi Babion, *Sermo*, beginning imperfectly; Schneyer, v. 2, p. 151 (3).

47. ff. 89v–91r Diligite inimicos uestros ... [Mat. 5.44]. Dominus ac redemptor noster fratres karissimi uenerat in mundum ex sola dilectione. et ideo uoluit suos in dilectione confirmare ... deus autem qui prior dilexit nos. ipse inspiret eam in cordibus nostris. ...

Geoffroi Babion, *Sermo*; Schneyer, v. 2, p. 151 (4).

48. ff. 91r–93v Cum natus esset ihesus in bethleem ... [Mat. 2.1]. Cum creator omnium fratres karissimi formam serui pro seruis accipiens latenter in mundum uenisset ... uoluit in mundo descendere per incrementum uirtutum ad celestem curiam [added: *vos faciat*] ascendere. ...

Geoffroi Babion, *Sermo*; Schneyer, v. 2, p. 151 (6).

49. ff. 93v–96r Cum descendisset ihesus de monte ... [Mat. 8.1]. Quoniam christus fratres karissimi uoluit inter homines habitare. et miraculis potentiam ... ut recipiant uos in futuro in eterna tabernacula. ...

Geoffroi Babion, *Sermo*; Schneyer, v. 2, p. 151 (7).

50. ff. 96r–99v Postquam impleti sunt dies ... [Luc. 2.22]. Consuetudo erat fratres karissimi in ueteri lege. ut si mulier masculum peperisset ... quia uiderunt oculi mei salutare tuum. ...

Geoffroi Babion, *Sermo*; Schneyer, v. 2, p. 151 (8).

51. ff. 99v–102r Audi israel mandata uite.... [Bar. 3.9]. Ammonet uos dominus noster fratres karissimi per iheremiam prophetam. Vt audiatis mandata eius increpat uos ... recipere puro corde in die resurrectionis. et gaudere cum eo in celis....

Geoffroi Babion, *Sermo*; Schneyer, v. 2, p. 151 (9).

52. ff. 102r–105v Si quis diligit me sermones meos ... [John 14.23]. Vnde psalmista. Furor illis secundum similitudinem serpentis. et cetera. et ecce sermones eius dicentis per ysaiam ... In hac quadragesima [*sic*] precipue parate uiam domino uenienti. ut digne possitis....

Geoffroi Babion, *Sermo*; Schneyer, v. 2, p. 151 (10).

53. ff. 105v–108v Maria soror moysi peccauit murmurando.... Ultiones fratres karissimi ueteris testamenti ad correctionem hominum illius temporis facte sunt ... Seminate ergo in lacrimis penitentes. ut mereamini in domum domini [*intrare* added above] gaudentes. cooperante domino....

Geoffroi Babion, *Sermo*; Schneyer, v. 2, p. 151 (11).

54. ff. 108v–111v Nolite diligere mundum neque ea ... [1 John 2.16]. Est quidam specialis inimicus. qui genus humanum excecat. Fratres karissimi et falsis bonis allicit ... et qui non mortem peccatoris uult. sed uitam uobis ipse gratia penitentie inspiret....

Geoffroi Babion, *Sermo*; Schneyer, v. 2, p. 151 (12).

55. ff. 111v–113r Postquam de paradisi gaudiis culpa exhigente pulsus est primus humani generis parens ... quia salutari hostia post mortem non indigebimus. si ante mortem deo hostia ipsi fuerimus.

Gregory the Great, selections (Book IV.1–5, 59–62) from *Dialogi*; A. de Vogüé, ed., *Grégoire le Grand: Dialogues* in *Sources chrétiennes*, Liber IV = 265 (1980) pp. 18–22, 200–06.

56. ff. 113v–116r Dominus noster ihesus christus ut sanctificaret ... [Hebr. 13.12]. Satis fratres karissimi audistis ordinem redemptionis nostre. sed dignum est tamen multociens beneficium memorare ... Quod est ualde magnum peccatum. ut ait gregorius in dialogo.

Geoffroi Babion, *Sermo*; Schneyer, v. 2, p. 152 (16).

57. ff. 116r–119v Scitote fratres karissimi quia uetus ... [Rom. 6.6]. Letum nuntium affert nobis fratres karissimi apostolus. et quia est [*omne* crossed out] commune bonum ... ut anima nostra in uirtutibus resurgat....

Geoffroi Babion, *Sermo*; Schneyer, v. 2, p. 152 (17).

58. ff. 119v–122v Ecce odor filij mei sicut odor ... [Gen. 27.27]. Aggratulatur nobis pater celestis quia sibi ut filij karissimi cum tanto gaudio cum tot floribus cum tot palmis ... et non uult mortem peccatoris sed ut conuertatur et uiuat. et uobis [*condonare* added above] peccata dignetur....

Geoffroi Babion, *Sermo*; Schneyer, v. 2, p. 152 (18).

59. ff. 122v–126r Dominus noster ihesus christus in qua nocte ... [1 Cor. 11.23]. Inminente fratres karissimi domini[*ce* added above] passionis articulo. quando iam pene erat in ipsa traditione ... sed etiam diligendus est amicus in deo. et inimicus propter deum.

Geoffroi Babion, *Sermo*; Schneyer, v. 2, p. 152 (19).

60. ff. 126r–129r Uenite filij audite me. timorem domini ... [Ps. 33.12]. Audite fratres karissimi quam dulci uoce. quali affectu reuocat nos mitissimus pater ... gaudeant de capitis resurrectione et possint per resurrectionem huius sollempnitatis ad superna gaudia peruenire....

Geoffroi Babion, *Sermo*; Schneyer, v. 2, p. 152 (23).

61. ff. 129r–132r Estote imitatores dei sicut filij karissimi ... [Eph. 5.1]. Admonet uos apostolus fratres karissimi. ut sicut filij dei estis. non a tanto patre degeneretis ... et pacem det uobis ueram. ut per eam possitis consequi sempiternam....

Geoffroi Babion, *Sermo*; Schneyer, v. 2, p. 152 (20).

62. ff. 132r–134v [Added by a later hand:] In die sancto pasce. [text:] Paulus apostolus ait. Etenim pascha nostrum inmolatus est christus ... [1 Cor. 5.7]. Si ergo pascha nostrum christus. pensandum nobis est quid de pascha lex loquitur ... Si ad amorem dei pigri non sumus. adiuuat ipse quem amamus ihesus christus....

Geoffroi Babion, *Sermo*; Schneyer, v. 2, p. 152 (25).

63. ff. 134v–137r [Added by a later hand:] In Rogationibus sermo. [text:] Confitemini alterutrum peccata uestra ... [Jac. 5.16]. Cum in alijs diebus fratres karissimi ad confessionem et ad penitentiam debeatis inuitari. in ieiunijs precipue que peccatorum ... seminat de benedictionibus et metet in presenti de mundanis....

Geoffroi Babion, *Sermo*; Schneyer, v. 2, p. 153 (30).

64. ff. 137r–139v [Added by a later hand:] In Rogationibus sermo. [text:] Quis uestrum habebit amicum et ibit ad illum ... [Luc. 11.5]. Modo

sunt dies fratres rogationum [*et oracionum* added above] et ideo dignum duximus ... et pro ceteris necessitatibus ut lacrimis uestris et oracionibus dei pietas commoueatur....

Geoffroi Babion, *Sermo*; Schneyer, v. 2, p. 152 (29).

65. ff. 139v–141v Eleuatus est sol in celum ... [Habac. 3.11]. Hodie fratres karissimi est ascensionis domini iocunda festiuitas. hodie destructa est humani generis captiuitas ... Laboremus ergo fratres ut sicut sumus eodem sanguine redempti. ita eo[*dem* added above; *quod* crossed out] premio ascensionis simus [corrected from *sumus*] remunerati....

Geoffroi Babion, *Sermo*; Schneyer, v. 2, p. 153 (31).

66. ff. 141v–144r Fecit deus duo magna luminaria ... [Gen. 1.16]. Sic uoluit dominus fratres facere creaturas mundi [*ut* added above] in modo creationis aliquid nobis significet ministerij ... ego sum. pastor bonus pastores suos et greges suos conseruet....

Geoffroi Babion, *Sermo*; Schneyer, v. 2, p. 155 (63).

67. ff. 144r–146r [Added by a later hand:] In die sancto pentecostes. [text:] Dum complerentur dies pentecostes ... [Acts 2.1]. Congruum est fratres karissimi ut his diebus conuentum in domum domini faciatis ... et custodita multiplicet. ut nos in eterno suo regno de labore uestro remuneret....

Geoffroi Babion, *Sermo*; Schneyer, v. 2, p. 153 (33).

68. ff. 146r–147v [Added by later hand:] de Sancto Iohanne baptista. [text:] Vbi uenit plenitudo temporis misit deus filium suum ... [Gal. 4.4]. Fratres karissimi, magna dispensatione uoluit deus ... conferat morbos repellat. tempestates dimoueat. fructuum copiam tribuat....

Geoffroi Babion, *Sermo*; Schneyer, v. 2, p. 153 (34).

69. ff. 147v–149r [Added by later hand:] de Assumpcione beate marie. [text:] Ab inicio et ante secula creata sum ... [Ecclus. 24.14]. Quam uenerabilis [*sit* added above] fratres sollempnitas gloriose uirginis marie ex uerbis ipsius domini ... imploremus eam precibus ut ipsa pro nobis intercedere dignetur apud filium eius dominum nostrum ihesum christum.

Jacobus Berengarius, *Sermo*; Schneyer, v. 3, p. 880 (44).

70. ff. 149r–150r Facta sunt encenia ... [John 10.22]. Fratres karissimi edificauit salomon templum domini in iherusalem. quod multum aureo opere ditauit ... uellebant et manducabant. Scriptum est enim. Abiit dominus per sata sabbato.

Geoffroi Babion, *Sermo*; Schneyer, v. 2, p. 154 (47).

71. ff. 150r–153v Homo quidam peregre proficiscens uocauit ... [Matt. 25.14]. Hec parabola fratres karissimi dicta a domino discipulis non solum prioribus pertinet ... ut seruos in commissa pecunia fideles in celos cum alijs remuneret. ...

Geoffroi Babion, *Sermo*; Schneyer, v. 2, p. 153 (42).

72. ff. 153v–156r Simile est regnum celorum homini qui seminauit ... [Matt. 13.24]. Dominus ihesus christus fratres karissimi inter homines habitans et tenebras mundi predicationis sue luce illuminans sedebat ... in eterna uisione contemplari mereamini. ...

Geoffroi Babion, *Sermo*; Schneyer, v. 2, p. 155 (64).

73. ff. 156r–158r Harborem fici habebat quidam ... [Luc. 13.6]. Dominus et redemptor noster fratres karissimi aliquando per similitudinem uobis loquitur. ut melius rudibus per rem ... ibi eritis socij angelorum. heredes dei. coheredes christi. ...

Geoffroi Babion, *Sermo*; Schneyer, v. 2, p. 155 (65).

74. f. 158r–v [N]atalis domini diem hodie celebremus octauum in quo puer ihesus a parentibus carnis sue carnale circumcisionis accepit sacramentum ... [verso mostly illegible].

Sermo de nativitate Christi; Hauréau, v. 4, 120; added by a slightly later hand.

Parchment (thick, holes, end pieces), vol. I: i (paper) + 88 + i (paper), vol. II: i (paper) + 70 (ff. 89–158) + i (paper), 219 x 152 (171 x 104) mm. 26 long lines. Single vertical bounding lines; double upper and single or double lower horizontal bounding lines. Ruled in lead. Remains of prickings in upper, lower and outer margins.

Vol. I: $I–VII^8$, VIII^6, $IX–XI^8$, XII^2 [with loss of text between volumes]; Vol. II: I^2, $II–VIII^8$, IX^4.

Written in late caroline minuscule by several scribes, above top line.

Plain red initials, 4- to 2-line, some with small pearls added to the body of the letter. Spaces for rubrics remain unfilled.

Folios 1r and 158v stained with loss of text.

Binding: Italy, s. xix. Backs of quires of both volumes cut in at sewing stations. Sewn on three cords. Paper lining between supports on spine. Red edges.

Both volumes half bound in brown mottled calf with bright pink paper sides and two red gold-tooled labels on each volume: "Manuscr. Homiliae

Caes. Max. Cod. I [and II]" and "Saecul. XIII." Bound in the same distinctive style as Marston MSS 50, 125, 128, 151, 153, 158, 159 and 197, all of Hautecombe provenance (see below).

Written in the middle of the 12th century, perhaps at the Cistercian abbey of Hautecombe to which it belonged. Located in the ancient diocese of Geneva, the abbey was founded toward the beginning of the 12th century by monks from the abbey of Aulps (see R. Clair, "Les origines de l'abbaye d'Hautecombe," *Mélanges à la mémoire du Père Anselme Dimier* [Arbois, 1982–87] tome II, v. 4, pp. 615–27). Marston MS 135 has the characteristic bright pink binding of the books of Monseigneur Hyacinthe della Torre who acquired and rebound a group of twelve manuscripts from Hautecombe at the beginning of the 19th century (see Leclercq, 1951, p. 75). The manuscript may have been a single volume before his rebinding. Belonged to the Biblioteca del Seminario Metropolitano in Turin (Leclercq, 1961, p. 183, no. 4: number in red crayon on front pastedown of Vol. I). Acquired from C. A. Stonehill in 1957 by Thomas E. Marston (bookplate).

secundo folio: Sed memoria

Bibliography: Faye and Bond, p. 79, no. 135.

Marston MS 138 — Western France, s. $IX^{2/3-3/3}$
Priscian, Institutiones (fragment)

ff. 1r–2v //Plautus in rudente: homunculi quanti estis eiecti ut natant ... preterea haec beta malua hic betaceus. maluaceus. *Explicit liber tertius artis prisciani gramatici caesarensis. Incipit liber quatus* [sic] *de denominativo.*// ff. 3r–4v //do. ut dulcis. dulcedo. acris. acredo. sin a uerbis secundarum terminationes personarum ... obseruare ut supradictum est. Vnde liber libertas.//

Two bifolia containing the conclusion of Bk. III (chs. 34–44) and part of Bk. IV (chs. 9–20); H. Keil, ed., *Grammatici latini* (Leipzig, 1855–80) v. 1, 109.1–116.2 and 122.18–128.16. Marston MS 138 cited by M. Gibson, "Priscian, *Institutiones grammaticae*: A Handlist of Manuscripts," *Scriptorium* 26 (1972) p. 116, and M. Passalacqua, *I codici di Prisciano* (Rome, 1978) p. 193, no. 431. The text here is accompanied by modest contemporary interlinear glosses, primarily in Latin with a few in Breton. Notes in outer margins, trimmed.

Parchment (thick), ff. 4 (two bifolia), 315 x 215 (260 x 168) mm. 31

long lines. Single vertical and horizontal bounding lines; ruled in hard point with a blunt instrument.

Perhaps originally a quire of 6 leaves, with the inner bifolium now wanting.

Written in elegant caroline minuscule script. Heading on f. 2v in rustic capitals.

Heading touched with red and enclosed in a red rectangle. Initial letters stroked with red or yellow (faded).

Leaves stained and affected by pen trials.

Unbound; boxed. Two disbound bifolia originally cut in at five supports and kettle stitches. Discoloration from turn-ins and traces of boss attachments.

Written in Western France in the second or final third of the 9th century according to B. Bischoff (letter on file); leaves removed from unidentified binding. Purchased from B. M. Rosenthal in 1957 by Thomas E. Marston.

Bibliography: Faye and Bond, p. 80, no. 138.

Marston MS 139 — France, s. XIV$^{1/4}$

Aegidius Romanus, De regimine principum

ff. 1r–179v *Incipit liber de regimine principum editus a fratre egydio romano ordinis fratrum heremitarum sancti augustini.* Ex regia ac sanctissima prosapia oriundo ... ut nostra reuerenda nobilitas requisiuit. [table of chapters, Bk. I, part 1:] *Incipiunt capitula prime* [sic] *prime partis primi libri de regimine principum.* Quis sit modus procedendi in regimine principum. Quis sit ordo dicendorum ... Quantum sit premium regis bene regentis populum sibi commissum. [text, f. 1v:] *Capitulum .i. quis sit modus procedendi in regimine principum.* Oportet ut latitudo sermonis ... deus ipse suis promisit fidelibus qui est benedictus in secula seculorum. Amen.

Many manuscripts and early printed editions; Glorieux, no. 400q; Zumkeller, no. 54; G. Bruni, *Le Opere di Egidio Romano* (Florence, 1936), with list of manuscripts on pp. 83–90 (Marston MS 139 not identified). Table of chapters, numbered in Arabic numerals in margins, precedes each part of each book. One leaf missing between ff. 88–89 with portions of chs. 9–10 of Bk. II, part 2 ("... ut sit memor prouidus. cautus. et circumspectus // heres essent depicte uel sculpte...").

Parchment (poor quality, pieced), ff. iii (paper) + i (contemporary parchment flyleaf) + 179 + iii (paper), 175 x 130 (125 x 88) mm. 2 columns, 34 lines. Double vertical bounding lines, single rulings between columns, single upper horizontal bounding line, all full across. Pairs of rulings in upper, outer and lower margins, the first pair for running titles, the last for catchwords. Ruled in lead. Prickings in upper, lower, and outer margins.

I-V^{12}, VI^{10}, VII^{12}, VIII^{10} (-7), IX-X^{10}, XI^{12}, XII^{14}, XIII-XV^{12}, XVI^{6}. Remains of quire and leaf signatures (e.g., a i, a ij, a iij, etc.) in lower margin, recto, lightly written in red or black. Catchwords below inner column, verso, between rulings.

Written by multiple scribes in small gothic bookhand.

Divided initials, red and blue, 6- to 5-line, with pen flourishes in red and blue, mark major text divisions; initial on f. 1r has simple border extending down inner margin. Small initials, 3- to 2-line, alternate red and blue, with penwork flourishes in opposite color. Headings (some missing) and running headlines in red. Paragraph marks alternate red and blue. Notes to rubricator.

Binding: France, s. xix. Black goatskin, blind-tooled, with gold-tooled doublures. Bound by L. Magnin, Lyon. Stains from fore-edge clasps of earlier binding on early parchment flyleaf.

Written in France in the first quarter of the 14th century. Two early ownership inscriptions on f. iv verso, one written over the other. The later one, partially visible under ultra-violet light, states that Brother Jacobus de Arigonis purchased the volume from Bartolomeus Baraterius, 25 May 1396, for eight [?] gold florins ("Iste liber est fratris Iacobi de arigonis [*landii* or *bandii*?] quem emit a bartolameo baraterio *** mccclxxxxvj die xxv madij precio flor. uiij [?] auri"). Early shelf-mark in ink on f. iv recto "+ xxxij" followed by a brief later note, s. xvi, on the author and the text which paraphrases Johannes Trithemius, *De scriptoribus ecclesiasticis*, from the Paris edition of 1512 (ff. 109v–110r). Unidentified modern notation on recto of final flyleaf, in pencil: "5414–E." Purchased from Emile Rossignol of Paris in 1958 by L. C. Witten (inv. no. 2158), who sold it in 1959 to Thomas E. Marston (bookplate).

secundo folio: morali

Bibliography: Faye and Bond, p. 80, no. 139.

Marston MS 140 — Southern Austria, ca. 1441

Jacobus de Voragine, Legenda aurea, etc.

I. 1. f. 1r Quotation from Jacobus de Voragine, *Legenda aurea*, Ch. X.1 "De innocentibus"; Th. Graesse, ed., *Jacobi a Voragine Legenda aurea* (Leipzig, 1846) p. 63. f. 1v blank

2. f. 2r Quingentos decies et bis centum annos [*sic* for "minus"] uno/ Annos dic ab adam donec verbum dei caro factum est [verses on the span of time between Adam and Christ; Walther, *Initia* 16015a]; Notandum decies decem faciunt centum . . . Decem turbe angelorum lapse sunt de celo [list of 14 collective nouns, each multiplied by 10 to arrive at number of fallen angels]; Post inuoca post penthen post crucis postque lucie/ Seruant ieiuna sequens feria quarta [verses on the Wednesday fast for the Ember days of spring ("Inuocabit," the incipit of the introit for the mass of the first Sunday in Lent), summer (Pentecost), fall (Invention of the Holy Cross, 14 September), and winter (feast of St. Lucia, 13 December)]. f. 2v blank

3. ff. 3r–9r Calendar with extensive computistical information including columns for the cycles of conjunctions and oppositions of the sun and the moon (each subdivided for the Golden Numbers, the hour, the minute, the distinction of day or night), the numerical calendar day, the dominical letter, the Roman calendar day (with respect to nones, ides and kalends, the saints, the zodiac (with the degree of the sun and the 27-letter distinction for the 27-day lunar month; the letters are the alphabet including *k*, tall *s*, round *s*, tironian *et*, the *cum* abbreviation, and the *-tur* abbreviation), the quantity of the day (in hours and minutes), sunrise and sunset (each with hour and minute), and the outer column with the indication of the bad luck days (according to the "Egyptian" system of two days per month), and the name of the zodiacal sign; the *claves terminorum* are signalled in either of the margins or in the space for the saints (7 January, 28 January, 11 March as normal, but here 14 and 30 April for the keys of the Rogationtide and Pentecost). Among the saints, pointing to Salzburg and to Benedictine interests, are: Valentinus, bishop of Passau (7 January); Erhard, bishop of Ratisbon (8 January); Translation of Vigilius, bishop of Trent, and companions (31 January); Scholastica (10 February); Walpurgis (25 February); Chunegundis Empress (3 March); Benedict (21 March); Rupert, bishop of Salzburg (27 March); Trudpertus martyr (26 April); Sigismund king (2 May); Florian (4 May); Gothard, bishop of Hildesheim (5 May); Udalric, bishop of Augusta in Bavaria (4 July); Willibald, bishop of Eistetten (7 July); Translation of Nicholas of Bari/of Myra (7 July, in Salzburg only); Translation of Benedict (11 July); Henry Emperor (13 July); "Divisio apostolorum" (15 July); Translation of Valenti-

nus, bishop of Passau (4 August); Oswald king (5 August); Translation of Rupert, bishop of Salzburg (24 September); Dedication of the cathedral of Salzburg (25 September); Translation of Virgilius, bishop of Salzburg (26 September); Maximilianus, bishop of Lorch (12 October); Colomannus martyr (13 October); Gallus abbot (16 October); Amandus, bishop of Strasbourg (26 October); Narcissus, bishop of Jerusalem (29 October); Wolfgang, bishop of Ratisbon (31 October); Othmar abbot (16 November); Virgilius, bishop of Salzburg (27 November); Odilia (13 December); Translation of Ignatius, bishop of Antioch (17 December).

4. f. 9v Table combining the Golden Numbers, the 27 lunar letters, and the signs of the zodiac to locate the position of the moon in the zodiac with auspices (good, bad, indifferent) for consultation before major undertakings.

5. ff. 9v–10r Si scire desideras in quo signo zodiaci et quotto gradu ipsius sit sol quocumque die anni . . . ; Si scire volueris quocumque die anni in quo signo sit luna . . . [explanations for locating the position of the sun and of the moon in the zodiac according to the calendar on ff. 3r–9r (respectively in the first and second columns to the right after the saints), and, for the moon, also according to the table on f. 9v].

6. f. 10r Ad habendum autem bonum tempus seu malum pro flebothomia seu minucione notanda sunt proprietates duodecim signorum et membra corporis humani que signa illa 12 respiciunt. Si sanguis fuerit sposus [?] trahens male habet circa pectus . . . ; Prima dies vene gaudet moderamine cene/ Altera leta dies quam tercia tota quies . . . Dies octava ludet//

   Walther, *Initia* 14570. Note on correlation between zodiacal signs and parts of the body; short paragraph on colors and viscosity of the blood for diagnosis of illness; verses, here ending incomplete, on activities for each day of the week.

7. ff. 10v–11r Diagram and explanation for determining the Golden Number and the "claves terminorum"; diagram and explanation for determining the dominical letter; both diagrams begin with the year 1435 as 0, thus 1436 as the first entry, etc.

8. f. 11r Diagram and explanation for determining the Concurrent (i.e. the interval in days between the last Sunday of December and the first day of January).

9. f. 11r-v Explanation for determining the moveable feasts of

Septuagesima Sunday, Quadragesima Sunday, Easter, summer Ember days, and Pentecost by means of the "claves terminorum" marked on the calendar and the first table on f. 10v, with the verses "In Iano prima supremaque marte secunda. Aprilis trina ergo [?] anno serat et ultima" and "Terminus et festum numquam celebratur ibidem/ Proxima sed post hunc diem lux dat tibi festum."

10. ff. 11v–12r Explanation for determining conjunctions (new moon) and oppositions (full moon) of the sun and the moon according to the first 8 columns in the calendar, beginning with the year 1436, followed by another rule, given in the first person (*ego posui; sum expertus; obmitto*), for arriving at a more precise determination of the duration of the conjunction or opposition.

11. ff. 12v–13v Table for the years 1441–62 (but skipping some, and doubling or tripling other years) with phases of the moon on certain days, specifying the length or the conjunction or opposition.

II. 12. ff. 14r–138v [Prologue:] Uniuersum tempus presentis vite in quattuor distigwuntur [?] . . . Quedam sub tempore peregrinatorum. [text:] Aduentus domini per quatuor septimas agitur ad significandum . . . [concludes in chapter on John the Baptist:] Magna enim mirabilia mel siluestre et locustas edere pilos cameli induere et huius modi et cetera.

T. Graesse, ed., *Jacobi a Voragine Legenda aurea* (Leipzig, 1846). The legends in the manuscript occur in the following order (with numbers corresponding to Roman numerals in Graesse); many sections lack rubrics. 1, 6 (f. 22r, beginning "Natiuitas domini nostri ihesu christi secundum carnem ut quid fuit. . ."), 13–14, 31–35, 53–54, 70, 72–73, 37, 51, 99, 131, 145, 162–63, 182, 86.

III. 13. ff. 139r–171r *Incipit Tractatus sew epistola missa a quodam doctori Iohanni huss eum corripiendo ut desisteret.* Eloquenti viro domino Iohanni verbi dei seminatori in praga. hec epistola detur fratri suo in christo dilecto pro saluacione in christo ihesu domino nostro. dileccione fraterna in caritate non ficta ante omnia preporrecta . . . et desiderans salutem anime mee et anime tue et omnium animarum christianorum. Amen. [colophon:] *Explicit epistola pulcra missa magistro Iohanni huss finita anno 1439°* [*11°* crossed out?] *feria secunda post ascensionem Et 18 die mensis maij.*

Anonymous letter to John Huss written after the Council of Constance; published by H. von der Hardt, ed., *Rerum Concilii Oecumenici Constantiensis* v. 3 (Frankfurt and Leipzig, 1698) pp. 338–91.

14. ff. 171r–173v *Secuntur errores Grecorum.* Nouerunt vniuersi christiani et presertim sedis [?] apostolice domini nostri pape Eugenij beatissimi ... Primus articulus et error grecorum est iste quod in ista comprehensibilitate trinitate et sanctissima Spiritus sanctus ... Tricesimus quintus Quod sacrificie eliemosyne orationes non prosunt defunctis ... seculo merentur.

35 articles of erroneous dogmatic teaching of the Greek church, written in the circle of the papal court during the endeavor to reconcile the Greek and Roman Churches at the Council of Ferrara and Florence (1437–39).

IV. 15. ff. 174r–235r Abba sicut dicit glosa id est deus pater/ Abissus abgrunt/ Abissis abseÿten/ Absida idem significat/ Absintheum bermut/ ... zonolarius gürtlär/ zodiacus est arculus in celo. Et sic est finis nominum/ Sequitur nunc de verbis.

Latin-German vocabulary, primarily for nouns, beginning imperfectly [?]. Marston MS 140 not listed in vols. 1–3 of K. Grubmüller, et al., "*Vocabularius Ex quo:*" *Überlieferungsgeschichtliche Ausgabe* in Texte und Textgeschichte. Würzburger Forschungen 22–24 (Tübingen, 1988).

16. ff. 235v–268r [A]bbreuiare churczen/ [A]bibere abtrincken/ [A]bicere abwerffen/ [A]bdelere abtuen/ ... zimare sweren/ Zunare vrhab seczen oder feueren. [colophon:] Deo gramaczi/ Finitum per me Georium diechercz [?] De falle Iunensj [?] partibus Karinthie.

Latin-German vocabulary, for verbs; cf. art. 9.

17. ff. 268v–269r Ebrietas est impedimentum virtutum multiplicando scelerum aufferens memoriam dissipans intelectum ... *Virtutes misse.*

Short notes on drunkenness, the virtues of the mass, etc.

18. f. 269v Ad arcem igitur scriptorie pertractanda breviter accedam obligacio circa cognicionem scripturarum quod conueniat scriptoibus [*sic*] succinte declarabo....

Brief passage, 9-lines, giving instructions on copying; poorly composed and written [!].

Composed of four parts, all written on paper, 208 x 145 mm.

Part I: ff. 1–13 (watermarks: unidentified mountain in gutter), different formats to accommodate each text, e.g., a row of prickings along upper and lower margins and multiple horizontal rulings full length of page for calendar. A single gathering of ten leaves (ff. 4–13) preceded by three single leaves. Written by one scribe in hybrida with loops. *KL* in calendar in blue; other charts and diagrams in shades of red and black. Small plain initials, headings, initial strokes and underlining in red.

Part II: ff. 14–138, written space 150 x 100 mm. 2 columns, 32 lines. Frame-ruled in ink. I-X^{12}, XI^{12} (-7 through 12, blanks?). Quires signed with Arabic numerals (1–10) in center of lower margin, verso; catchwords just below written space near gutter. Written in hybrida script (no loops). Red or blue initials, 4- to 3-line, some with simple designs. Headings, paragraph marks, initial strokes, underlining in red. Guide letters for decorator.

Part III: ff. 139–173, written space 146 x 100 mm. 31 long lines. Frame-ruled in ink: prickings in upper, lower and outer margins. I-II ^{12}, III^{12} (-11, 12, blanks?). Catchwords along lower edge near gutter, verso. Written by a single scribe in hybrida script (with loops). Same style of decoration as in Part II.

Part IV: ff. 174–269, written space 151 x 100 mm. Frame-ruled in ink for long lines, but the beginning of art. 15 written in 2 columns, ca. 37 lines. Remains of prickings in upper, lower and outer margins. I–VIII^{12}. Traces of catchwords along lower edge to right of center, verso. Arts. 15–16 written by a single scribe in hybrida (with loops); arts. 17–18 added by less skilled scribes. Plain initials, and initial strokes, in red, for ff. 174r–176r; headings in red.

Binding: Austria, s. xv/xvi [?]. Parchment stays from early manuscripts in center of quires. Original [?] sewing on three tawed skin, double, twisted sewing supports laced into grooves in flush wooden boards and fastened with square pegs. The grooves are filled in with glue. The spine is rounded and backed (naturally?) and back bevelled. A plain, wound endband is sewn on a tawed skin core and also laced and pegged. The spine is lined with coarse cloth in the center and vellum at the ends, extending on the outside.

Covered in plain, kermes pink, tawed skin (sheep?), possibly a later addition. Trace of one fastening, the catch on the upper board. There may have been a chain attachment at the head of the lower board. The insides of the boards have been varnished; off-set impressions of pastedowns from early manuscripts on both boards.

Parts I–IV all written in Southern Austria, probably ca. 1441 given the contents of art. 11. The list of saints in art. 3 suggests Benedictine interests and a possible connection to Salzburg. Part IV signed by the scribe Georgius Diechercz [?] of Jauntal in Carinthia (colophon in art. 16). The various parts were bound together at the end of the 15th or beginning of the 16th century. Ownership inscription, s. xv, on f. 269v: "Fr. Oswaldus sant [?] ***." Purchased from H. Rosenthal in 1946 by H. P. Kraus who sold it in 1957 to Thomas E. Marston (bookplate).

secundo folio: Ciclus

Bibliography: Faye and Bond, p. 80, no. 140.

Marston MS 141 Southern Germany, 1444
Nicolaus de Dinkelsbühl; Johannes Herolt, etc. Pl. 63

1. f. 1r blank; f. 1v [Heading:] De modo concludendi collectas. [text:] Per dominum dicas si patrem prespiter oras/ Cum loqueris nato qui uiuus dicere debes/ ... Cum memoras flamen eiusdem dic prope finem.

   Five lines of verse on the proper formulaic conclusion to prayers addressed to members of the Trinity.

2. ff. 2r–12r Secundum magistrem [*sic*] et doctores In quarto [libro Sentenciarum] distincione 16ª tres sunt partes vere penitentie ... benefactoribus suis viuis et defunctis preces fundere neglexerit et cetera est finis. Explicit summa viciorum mortalium magistri Nicolaij de dinkelspuhl congregatii [?] doctoris.

   Nicolaus de Dinkelsbühl, *De septem peccatis capitalibus* (*Confessionale*); A. Madre, *Nikolaus von Dinkelsbühl: Leben und Schriften. Ein Beitrag zur theologischen Literaturgeschichte.* Beiträge zur Geschichte der Philosophie und Theologie des Mittelalters. Texte und Untersuchungen. Band 40, Heft 4 (Münster Westfalen, 1965) pp. 199–202 (with reference to Marston MS 141 on p. 201).

3. ff. 12v–13r Latin and German names of the books of the Bible; Latin and German names of Aristotle's principal works; Latin names of the Minor Prophets; list of "The 14 Holy Helpers"; list of short questions and answers on theological subjects, beginning: "Que lux fuit ante solem et lunam/ lux angelica que est in principio hec est in fine...". ff. 13v–14v blank

4. ff. 15r–239r [Prologue:] Ad honorem dei et beate marie virginis et omnium sanctorum et vtilitatem ... invocari veni sancte spiritus et cetera. [text, f. 15v:] Ecce rex tuus venit tibi ... [Zach. 9.9; Mat. 21.5]. hodie mater ecclesia jncipit tempus aduentus christi sicut incarnatus est et descendit de celis ... ad quintum uel sextum chorum angelorum peruenire poterimus et sic est finis huius operis et cetera. [colophon:]

Explicit manuale sermonum discipuli collectum ex sermonibus euisdem discipuli de tempore Anno 1444°. Amen.

Johannes Herolt ("Discipulus"), *Sermones dominicales*, with one sermon selected from his *Sermones de tempore* for each Sunday; in some instances the exordium of the sermon has been abridged. Many manuscripts and early printed editions. Beginning on f. 167v sermons are numbered sporadically, 48–66, in Arabic numerals by contemporary hands.

5. ff. 239v–240r Inter natos mulierum non surrexit ... [Mat. 11.11]. Dilectissimi In hijs verbis christus exprimit excellenciam sancti iohannis baptiste cum dicit inter natos ... ut inter viscera materna iam posset cognoscere creatorem suum// ff. 240v–247v blank

Johannes Herolt, *Sermo in festo Iohannis Baptiste* from his *Sermones de Sanctis*, ending imperfectly; many manuscripts and early printed editions.

Paper (thick; watermarks, in gutter: similar to Briquet Monts 11786 and unidentified bull's head), ff. i (f. 1) + 246, 208 x 145 mm. Size of written space varies as does the number of long lines of text. Frame-ruled in ink or hard point; remains of prickings in upper, outer, inner margins.

I–IX^{12}, X^{16} (ff. 110–125), XI–XII^{12}, XIII^{16}, XIV–XIX^{12}, XX^{10}. Quires II–IX signed on verso with Arabic numerals 1–8, some trimmed; remainder of quires have catchwords, also trimmed.

Written by multiple scribes in varying styles of gothic hybrida and bookhand scripts.

Crude red initials, 3- to 2-line, throughout; ff. 33v–38r, 113v–114v and 166r–203r rubricated.

Binding: Germany, s. xv. The backs of the quires are cut in. Original sewing on three double supports is laced into almost flush wooden boards, and the tawed skin cores of braided endbands, sewn through the cover, are also laced. The spine is back cornered with lining extending between supports on the outside of the boards. Large vermilion and sepia roses are painted on each edge (see also provenance). Back pastedown (and perhaps the inner front pastedown, covered by paper) consists of a parchment bifolium (Germany, s. XIII^{1}) containing the *Sermones de tempore* of Johannes Halgrinus de Abbatisvilla (Schneyer, v. 3, p. 512, nos. 26–27). Ca. 31 long lines, written space ca. 150 x 90 mm. Written in small neat early gothic bookhand, above top line. Binding stays from this and other parchment manuscripts, s. xiii–xiv.

Covered in kermes pink skin blind-tooled with an *X* in a frame on the front board, tying-up marks on the spine, and a frame on the lower one.

Five round, brass bosses on each board and one fastening, the catch inset on the upper board, the lower one cut in for the strap.

Written in Southern Germany in 1444 (see colophon, art. 4). Perhaps produced and/or owned by the Benedictine abbey of Amorbach in Bavaria (Cottineau, v. 1, 88–89). According to A. Derolez (letter on file) the same roses that are painted on the edges of Marston MS 141 also occur (but on a larger scale) on the edges of the three volumes of the following printed book in the University Library, Ghent: *Biblia latina glosata* (Strasbourg: Adolf Rusch, ca. 1481; GKW 4282). These volumes are blind-stamped with the text-stamp "Amorbach" and contain the ownership mark of this abbey; the roses are not, however, mentioned as characteristic of the Amorbach books in P. Lehmann, "Die Bibliothek des Klosters Amorbach," *Erforschung des Mittelalters*, v. 3 (Stuttgart, 1960) pp. 76–109. Purchased in 1946 from H. Rosenthal by H. P. Kraus ("4055/UZR"), who sold it in 1957 to Thomas E. Marston (bookplate).

secundo folio: Cum ergo

Bibliography: Faye and Bond, p. 80, no. 141.
The Medieval Book, p. 60, no. 59 (with reproduction of binding).

Marston MS 142 — Italy, s. XV²
Servius, De centum metris, etc.

1. ff. 1r–14v Abdera ciuitas/ Abyssus/ Abaris/ Achademia/ Acesnius. flu./ Acropolis/ Achelous/ Acheolus. flu./ ... d. Zeb[*a* deleted] edaeus/ d. Zacchaeus/ Zutus uel Zutj.

   Word list from *a* through *z* primarily of proper names; some entries preceded by the letter *d* or *y*.

2. ff. 14v–15r Acutus accentus est uero per obliquum ascendens in dextram partem [followed by drawing of acute accent]. Grauis ad dextram partem a summo descendens [followed by drawing of grave accent] ... Sponte ultro uoluntarie voluntario. uolontariosamente.

   Brief notes on accents followed by Latin word list with Italian equivalents.

3. ff. 15v–16v Clarissimo uiro albino maurus seruius grammaticus salutem. tibi hunc libellum protextatorum et cetera usque uale tu licet audacter non tamen indignanter ... ducit voluntas. [text:] Metra iambi-

ca locis imparibus quinque recipere possunt pedes ... Eurapalicus versus est cum verba prout secuntur per sillabas crescunt ut est Rem tibi confeci doctiss[imorum, end of word covered by tape] dulcisonorum. Amen.

Servius, *De centum metris*; H. Keil, ed., *Grammatici latini* (Leipzig, 1855–80) v. 4, pp. 456–67.

Paper (watermarks: unidentified quadruped in gutter), ff. i (paper) + 16 + i (paper), 2 columns, ca. 44 lines. Frame-ruled in lead or crayon for two columns throughout, but art. 3 written in long lines. Prickings in upper, lower and outer margins.

Two gatherings of eight leaves.

Written in humanistic cursive script with gothic features.

Binding: Place uncertain, s. xix. Vellum stays outside the quires. Pastepaper case in shades of deep purple.

Written in Italy in the second half of the 15th century as part of a longer codex (ff. 141–156; traces of earlier foliation, in lead); early provenance unknown. Rectangular white paper label on spine, blank; round white paper label with scalloped edge on spine: "75102" in pen, "III IV" in pencil. On front pastedown: "II L/ 243"; on back pastedown: "5481/LSR," and "R." Purchased from H. P. Kraus (notes on front pastedown and paper tipped into back cover) in 1957 by Thomas E. Marston (bookplate).

Bibliography: Faye and Bond, p. 80, no. 142.

Marston MS 144 — Crete, s. XIII–XV
Legal documents, in Lat. and It.

Collection of original documents, copies, translations (from Greek and Turkish) of other documents of the Venetian doges of Candia, dated between 1299 and 1472, mostly in Latin with some later documents in Venetian dialect. For a discussion of specific documents in the manuscript see E. Zachariadou, "Sept traités inédits entre Venise et les émirats d'Aydin et de Mentese (1331–1407)," in *Studi preottomani e ottomani: Atti del Convegno di Napoli (24–26 settembre 1974)* pp. 229–40. Zachariadou indicates (*op. cit.*, p. 229) that Venice, Museo Civico Correr MS P. D. 675 is a 16th-century copy of Marston MS 144. Many of the leaves are illegible due to severe water damage and damp rot throughout; the codex emits a foul odor.

Parchment (thick, repaired), ff. ii (paper) + 148 + ii (paper). Leaves of varying sizes and formats. Codex measures 340 x 250 mm. Written throughout by multiple scribes in *mercantesca* scripts.

Binding: Italy, s. xviii/xix. Brown goatskin, blind-tooled with a gold-tooled red label on spine: "Monum. di Cand. Sotto il Dom. Ven. Cod. Memb."

From the archive of the Cretan noble family Callerghi (see Zachariadou, *op. cit.*); most of the documents date to the 14th and 15th centuries. Belonged to Frederick North, 5th Earl of Guilford (1766–1827; no. 227 in his sale catalogue; number recorded on f. ii verso); sold to Bohn. Acquired by Sir Thomas Phillipps (no. 11868, tag on spine and note with stamp on f. i recto). Purchased from H. P. Kraus in 1959 by Thomas E. Marston (bookplate).

Bibliography: Faye and Bond, p. 80, no. 144.

Marston MS 145 — France, s. XV^{med}

Henry Suso, Horologium sapientiae, in Fr.

1. ff. 1r–2v [Table of contents:] Vous deues sauoir que le volume de cest present contient en soy deux liures des quelx deux le premier si contient en soy xvi chappitres cy apres nommez et declairez. Et le second liure si contient en soy .viij. chappitres nommez et declairez apres ensuiuant aussi somme xxiiij. chappitres que les deux liures contiennent sans le prologue de l'acteur qui se commance *Salemon* et cetera qui n'est point du nombre. Le premier chappitre du premier liure se commance ainsi *Hanc amaui* et est escrit ou *cinquieme* feullet au commancement de cest present liure lequel parle comment la diuine sapience par merueilleuse maniere trait ses amis a soy . . . Le huitiesme et derrenier chappitre se commence *Cum enim aurora.* Et escript ou [blank space] feullet lequel parle des grans et espirituelz fruis qui viennent de la beneicon que Recoiuent ceulx qui ont espouse sapience.

2. ff. 3r–180v *Cy commance le liure nomme l'aurloge de sapience ou quel est parfautement* [? word rubbed] *contenue la propre voye et maniere de arguer et* [?] *le salut de son ame. Et tout premierement commance le prologue.* [prologue:] Salemon en son liure de sapience ou premier chappitre dit: *Sentite de domino in bonitate et simplicitate* . . . [f. 7v:] Ilz commanderent que ce liure cy feust publie et de [?] a toutes deuotes personnes qui ayment et seruent nostre seigneur et oyent bien dire voulentiers et

Racompter bonnes exemples. [text:] *Cy endroit commance le premier chappitre du premier liure de cest present volume ou quel parle l'acteur comme les esleuz de la diuine sapience sont traiz et approuchiez a dieu par merueilleuse maniere et comment l'acteur mesme des sa Ieunesse y feust tout adonnez. Hanc amavi* ... Ces paroles cy sont les paroles de salemon en son liure de sapience en le huitiesme chappitre ... dieu mon pere et dieu le saint esperit qui sommez troys personnez en vne deite en vne essence et en vne mesme voulente des siecles en sieclez pardurablement. Amen.

The *Horloge de Sapience* is a loose translation and adaptation into French of Henry Suso, *Horologium sapientiae*; 48 manuscripts of the French text are cited in J. Ancelet-Hustache, "Quelques indications sur les manuscrits de l'Horloge de sapience," *Heinrich Seuse: Studien zum 600. Todestag, 1366–1966*, ed. E. Filthaut (Cologne, 1966) pp. 161–70 (Marston MS 145 not cited) and 15 additional manuscripts listed in P. Künzle O. P., *Heinrich Seuses Horologium Sapientie* (Freiburg, 1977) pp. 253–54 (Marston MS 145 cited incorrectly as two manuscripts, nos. 8 and 9). We have not seen the recent edition by M.-F. Ajdnik, *Édition critique de "L'Orloge de Sapience," Livre I* ..., Thèse 3ème cycle, nouveau régime, Université de Nancy-II (1984). The scribe of Marston MS 145 adds marginal comments throughout to help explain and summarize the contents and individual sections; some loss of marginalia due to trimming.

3. ff. 180v–181r Ceste doctrine couronnee/ ffut premierement ordonnee/ Du saint esperit et fut ditte/ A un homme de grant merite/ Saige et de grant perfection/ Proffez en la Religion/ Du glorieux Saint dominique/ Nez fut de terre alematique/ ffrere Iehan dit de souhaube/ ... Se plaisir vous vient vous direz/ Ou nom de saint Iehan l'appostre/ Pour moy vne patenostre/ Disont en la derniere Roye/ Amen amen que dieu l'ottroye/ Amen. f. 181v ruled, but blank

Colophon, in French verse, stating that the translation was made by a French Franciscan master of theology at Neufchâteau in 1389; Ancelet-Hustache, *op.cit.*, pp. 167–69.

Parchment, ff. ii (paper) + i (original parchment pastedown) + 181 (contemporary foliation in red Roman numerals, I–Clxxviiij, begins on f. 3r for text, upper right corner) + ii (paper), 324 x 222 (228 x 140) mm. 2 columns, 38 lines. Single vertical and double or triple horizontal bounding lines. Ruled in lead.

Precise collation impossible due to tight binding: I^{10} [or I^{2} and II^{8}?], II–XI^{8}, XII^{6}, XIII–XV^{8}, XVI^{7} [?], XVII–XXI^{8}, XXII^{8} [?], XXIII^{6} [?]. Horizontal catchwords under inner column.

Written in bâtarde script, below top line.

Plain initials, 4- to 1-line, headings, paragraph marks, initial strokes, foliation and underlining, all in red.

Binding: France, s. xix^{in}. Diced brown calf, blind-and gold-tooled. Edges gilt. Stains from turn-ins of early binding on original front parchment pastedown. Rebacked.

Written in France in the middle of the 15th century; early provenance unknown. Unidentified 15th-century text, in French verse, on original front pastedown (9 lines). Bookplate of marquis de Queux de St. Hilaire. Miscellaneous modern pencil notations on first front paper flyleaf, verso. Purchased from Maggs Bros. of London in 1955 by L. C. Witten (inv. no. 661), who sold it in 1957 to Thomas E. Marston (bookplate).

secundo folio: [table, f. 2] Le quatorziesme
[text, f. 4] mon langaige

Bibliography: Faye and Bond, p. 80, no. 145.

C. E. Lutz, "The Clock of Eternal Wisdom," *Gazette* 52 (1978) pp. 79–85, reprinted in her book *The Oldest Library Motto and Other Library Essays* (Hamden, Ct., 1979) pp. 25–31.

Marston MS 147 — Northeastern Italy, s. $XV^{2/4}$
Eutropius, Breviarium, etc.

1. ff. 1r–59v *Liber Eutropii de Regibus Romanorum et de origine imperii feliciter incipit.* [P]rimus qui in italia ut quibusdam placet regnauit Ianus. deinde Saturnus iouem filium ... qui iam ultra x. annos regnauerat interfecit. vniuersamque Italiam ad rei publicae iura perduxit. *Finit Eutropii Historia laus deo.* f. 60r-v blank

   Eutropius, *Breviarium*, H. Droysen, ed., MGH AA 2 (1879) pp. 8–18, and C. Santini. ed., Teubner (1979) pp. 3–71, with the insertions and addition of the final six books by Paul the Deacon, A. Crivellucci, ed., *Pauli Diaconi Historia Romana* (Rome, 1914) pp. 5–239. Proper names and brief notes in outer and inner margins throughout; text not divided into numbered books (except for "Liber secundus" in margin, f. 6r).

2. ff. 61r–65r *Franciscus Patritius* Achilli petrucio. S. P. Dicit. Quamquam tibi plurimum cum adessem coram gratulatus fuerim. adiecerimque. nonnulla. que ad hunc tuum precellentissimum ... uolumus et optamus. Vale et communes amicos nostros omni studio tueare. Iterum uale. ex corsinio [?] Idibus Ianuarijs.

Francesco Patrizi of Siena (1412–94), *Epistula Achilli Petrucio de regendo magistratu*; the same letter is listed as anonymous by Kristeller, *Iter italicum*, v. 1, p. 333, citing Milan, Biblioteca Ambrosiana L. 69 sup.; v. 2, p. 383, citing Vatican, Biblioteca Apostolica Vaticana Vat. lat. 7179. See also L. F. Smith, "A Notice on the Epigrammata of Francesco Patrizi, Bishop of Gaeta," *Studies in the Renaissance* 15 (1968) pp. 92–143.

3. f. 65r Quintilianus institutionum oratoriarum libro. primo. Plura de officijs docentium locutus. discipulos in unum interim moneo. ut preceptores suos . . . accipientisque concordia. ff. 65v–70v blank

Extract from Quintilian, *Institutio oratoria* 2.9.1.

Paper (watermarks: two different unidentified ladders, the one on ff. 1–60, the other on ff. 61–70), ff. i (fragment of 12th-century missal, containing the masses of Sebastian, 20 January; Agnes, 21 January; Vincent of Saragossa, 22 January; the Conversion of Paul, 25 January) + 70 + i (fragment from the same 12th-century missal, containing masses of the Annunciation, 25 March; Tiburtius and Valerianus, 14 April; George, 23 April; and the Three Youths in the Furnace, Sidrach, Misach and Abdenago), 286 x 214 (190 x 110) mm. Ca. 30–34 long lines (art. 1), 33–34 long lines (art. 2). The leaves have been folded in quarters lengthwise to delineate the written space.

I–VII^{10}. Horizontal catchwords centered in middle of lower margin, verso (Derolez 12.1).

Written by a single scribe in a sloping humanistic bookhand.

Spaces for decorative initials in art. 1 are unfilled; remains of guide letters. Headings and first word(s) in text divisions in epigraphic majuscules.

Binding: Italy, s. xix. Yellow marbled paper case with title written in ink on narrow paper label on spine: "Liber Eutropii de Regibus Rom. et de Orig. Imperii."

Written in Northeastern Italy, perhaps as early as the second quarter of the 15th century according to A. C. de la Mare; early provenance unknown. Inscription, s. xviii [?], in upper margin of front flyleaf: "Decano Sebastiano Zucchetti." Acquired by James P. R. Lyell in 1936 (1871–1943; bookplate and note on front pastedown, "E.V.V. 31/7/36," and again on a description, typed in red and black, pasted inside back cover. For further information on his manuscripts see *Lyell Cat.*, pp. xv–xxix. Bought from the Lyell estate by Bernard Quaritch in 1951 and sold in 1952 (Cat. 699, no. 60, description from this catalogue pasted inside front cover). Unidentified modern notes, all in pencil, on front pastedown: "250" and "No.

55" each within a circle, "M" in a circle with "4" below; on back pastedown, "21553" in pencil. Purchased from H. P. Kraus (notes on back pastedown) in 1957 by Thomas E. Marston (bookplate).

secundo folio: [tem]poribus homerus

Bibliography: Faye and Bond, p. 81, no. 147.

°

Marston MS 149 Italy, s. $XV^{2/4}$
Leonardo Bruni, De prima guerra punica, It. tr., etc.

1. ff. 1r–51v [Preface:] *De la prima guerra punica Il primo Libro comincia felicemente opera compilata per meser Leonardo Aretino Prohemio.* Parera forse a molti che io uada dietro a cose troppo antiche hauendo per materia preso a scriuere ... primamente ebbero nauili, primamente combattero per mare. [text, f. 1v:] *Incomincia el primo libro de la prima guerra punica.* La prima guerra punica, cioe la prima guerra ... Et non molto di puoi tolte loro possessione constretti fuoro in gran parte abandonare il paese. Deo gratias.

   Leonardo Bruni, *La prima guerra punica*, in an anonymous It. tr.; GKW, v. 5, no. 5604; A. Ceruti, ed. (Bologna, 1878) pp. 1–246.

2. ff. 51v–56v *Incomincia el libro de la uita e studij e costumi de dante e de meser francesco petrarcha poeti chiarissimi composto e ordinato per decto meser leonardo.* [Preface:] Avendo in questi giornj posto fine a una opera asaj longa me uenne appetito de uolere ... Veniamo adenqua a la citta di dante. [text, f. 52r:] *Incomincia la uita de dante.* I magior de dante forono in firenze de molto antica stirpe intanto che lui per uolere in alcun luoco ... e cosi la fortuna questo mondo gira e permuta gli abitatorj con uolgere de sue rote. Amen.

   Leonardo Bruni, *Vita di Dante*; Baron, pp. 50–63; A. Solerti, ed., *Vite di Dante, Petrarca e Boccaccio scritte fino al secolo decimosesto* (Milan, 1904) pp. 97–107.

3. ff. 57r–59v *Incomincia la uita de meser francesco petrarcha ordinato como di sopra.* Francescho petrarcha homo de grande ingegno e non di minore uirtu naque in arezo ... cosi a chi non merita como a chi merita dare se puote. finis. *Deo gratias Amen.* f. 60r–v blank

   Leonardo Bruni, *Vita di Francesco Petrarca*; Baron, pp. 63–69; Solerti, *op. cit.*, pp. 288–93.

Paper (watermarks: similar to Briquet Monts 11684), ff. ii (paper) + 60

+ ii (paper), 288 x 213 (190 x 115) mm. Ca. 35–38 long lines. Single horizontal and vertical bounding lines (Derolez 13.13). Ruled in hard point, except for ff. 52v–59v which are ruled in lead or crayon, with written space larger (198 x 157 mm.) than on preceding leaves.

I–V^{10}, VI^{10} (10 = replacement leaf). Horizontal catchwords centered below text, verso (Derolez 12.1).

Written by two scribes: ff. 1r–51v in humanistic semi-cursive script, above top line; ff. 51v–59v in fere-humanistic script, above top line.

Decoration of poor quality: 12-line divided initial in red and blue, f. 1r; 5-line blue initial with red penwork decoration, f. 51v; 5-line divided initial red and blue, f. 51r. Plain red and blue initials, 4- to 3-line, alternate throughout. Headings in bright red.

Binding: England [?], s. xx. Hard-grained, brown leather case. Gold-tooled title and date on spine: "L. Bruni Guerra Punica/ Vite di Dante e Petrarca/ MS. Sec. XV." Bright blue marbled edges.

Written probably in Central or Southern Italy in the second quarter of the 15th century according to A. C. de la Mare; early provenance unknown. Stamp on f. 1r, lower margin: egg-shaped circle enclosing a cross between the letters *S* and *A*. Belonged to Karl W. Hiersemann of Leipzig from whom it was purchased in 1920 by the bookdealer Giuseppe (Joseph) Martini of Lugano (note in library files). Description in English from unidentified sale catalogue in library files. Modern shelf-marks and notes, in pencil: "44/10 (MS)" on front pastedown; "ARI^{56}" and "M" in a circle with "3" below, both on f. 1r; "M-P" and "401" in a circle with "LSZ," on rear pastedown. Purchased from H. P. Kraus in 1957 by Thomas E. Marston (bookplate),

secundo folio: [ri]paro

Bibliography: Faye and Bond, p. 81, no. 149.
Ullman, p. 456, no. 48.
Dutschke, no. 72, pp. 179–80.

Marston MS 150 — Northern Italy or Southern France, s. XV^2
Nicolas Trevet, Commentarius in tragoedias Senecae — Pl. 2

1. leaf inserted before f. 1r: recto, unidentified passage on the genre of tragedy; verso blank

2. ff. 1r–254r [Preface:] Tria genera theologie distingui a Varone narrat augustinus libro sexto de ciuitate dei . . . per exempla hic posita. Et hec

sufficiunt quantum ad prohemium. [text, f. 1v:] Soror tonantis hoc ... [text:] Ista prima tragidia [*sic*] senece cuius materia est furia herculis in qua quinque actus continentur. Quorum primus est querimonia ... liberet nobis dominus ihesus christus qui est honor et honor [*sic*] et gloria in seculorum secula. Amen. *Explicit liber marci senecae tragediarum. Inepte igitur quidam dicere uidentur lucium anneum moralem philosophum stoicum hoc opus edidisse. hoc opus* [*comenti* added above] *frater nicholaus treuetus edidit.* f. 254v ruled, but blank

Nicolas Trevet's commentary on the tragedies of Seneca, each designated by a Roman numeral in the upper right margin, recto: I. *Hercules furens* (f. 1v); II. *Thyestes* (f. 34r); III. *Phoenissae* (= *Thebais* in manuscript, f. 57r); IV. *Phaedra* (= *Hippolytus* in manuscript, f. 71r); V. *Oedipus* (f. 98v); VI. *Troades* (= *Troas* in manuscript, f. 120v); VII. *Medea* (f. 146r); VIII. *Agamemnon* (f. 170r); IX. *Octavia* (f. 191v); X. *Hercules Oetaeus* (f. 213v). Marston MS 150 noted by M. Palma, ed., *Nicola Trevet Commento alla "Troades" di Seneca* (Rome, 1977) pp. xxxi, xlvii–ix.

Paper (watermarks: similar to Briquet Tête de boeuf 14330, 14338, Piccard Ochsenkopf I.701, Briquet Main 11092), ff. ii (modern insertion) + i (contemporary paper) + 254, 282 x 206 (183 x 135) mm. 40 long lines. Single vertical bounding lines in hard point or ink; text rulings in ink.

I^{12}, II^{14}, $III–IV^{12}$, V^{10}, $VI–XXI^{12}$ (+ 2 leaves at end). Horizontal catchwords on most leaves, verso (Derolez 12.2).

Written in semi-gothic cursive script by a single scribe, above top line; headings in gothic bookhand.

Red and/or deep aquamarine blue initials, 10- to 5-line, with penwork flourishes in same color(s), mark beginning of each play. On f. 1r head of bearded man peeps out from behind foliage in interior of letter; on other initials penwork designs extend into margins to form borders (e. g., 170r). Plain initials, 5- to 2-line, paragraph marks, headings, in red.

Many leaves stained and crumbling along edges; no loss of text.

Binding: Italy or France?, uncertain date. The backs of the quires are cut in, some in a *W* shape. Resewn on two tawed skin, slit straps. Endband sewn on a tawed skin core laid in grooves on the outside of the boards and nailed. The back oak board was previously covered with leather; front board is of unidentified wood. This seems to be a patched together binding using boards from different, possibly s. xv, books.

Presently quarter bound with brown sheepskin, blind-tooled, with radiant *IHS* in circles. Spine: supports defined with triple [?] fillets; an *X* with a central cross bar in the panels. Two fastenings, with the catches on the lower board. The upper board cut in for straps fastened with star-headed nails. Remains of title, in ink, on tail edge.

Produced in Northern Italy or Southern France in the second half of the 15th century given the watermarks, style of script and decoration; early provenance unknown. Unidentified "1586" and "2 T. M." in pencil on f. i recto and "6061/ VLSZ" on back pastedown. Belonged to Federico Patetta (1867–1945), Professor of the History of Law at the University of Turin at the beginning of the 20th century, whose notes on the life and works of Nicolas Trevet occur on f. i recto. Purchased from the Turin dealer Bourlot by H. P. Kraus, who sold it in 1957 to Thomas E. Marston (bookplate).

secundo folio: ex cuius

Bibliography: Faye and Bond, p. 81, no. 150.

Marston MS 151 Northern Italy, s. IX/X
Paul the Deacon, Homiliarium, pars hiemalis Pl. 2

All bibliographical citations refer to R. Grégoire, *Homéliaires liturgiques médiévaux: Analyse de manuscrits* (Spoleto, 1980), where there is additional information for each text.

1. ff. 1r–2v //posset non dixit. sed angelo dicendum reseruauit. Respondens autem angelus dixit ei ... ad profundam hanc conuallem lacrimarum descendere dignatus est ...

   For the Wednesday before Christmas; Bede, *Homilia* I. 3, here beginning imperfectly; Grégoire, p. 432, no. 11.

2. ff. 2v–7v *Lectio sancti euangelii secundum Lucam.* In illo tempore. Exsurgens [*autem* added above] maria habiit in montana ... [Luc 1.39]. *Omelia eiusdem beati bede presbyteri de eadem lectionem* [*sic*]. Lectio quam audiuimus sancti euuangelii. et redemptionis nostre ... de stirpe abrahe ad nos uenire dignatus est.//

   For the Friday before Christmas; Bede, *Homilia* I.4, here ending imperfectly; Grégoire, p. 432, no. 12.

3. ff. 8r–9v // [des]speratione soluantur. Quos autem per oliuam nisi misericordes accipimus? quia grece oleos misericordia uocatur ... iam sanatos aspicimus. quid aliud quam superne misericordiae pignus tenemus. [added by another hand:] Ipso adiuuante qui cum patre ... Amen.

   Gregory, *Homiliae in Euangelia* I.20; here beginning imperfectly; Grégoire, p. 432, no. 13.

4. ff. 9v–11r [No heading, text begins:] Letitia quanta sit. quantusque concursus. cum imperatoris mundi istius natalis celebrandus est ... ut fiat oblatio uestra accepta sanctificata in spiritu sancto.

Maximus Taurinensis, *Sermo* 60; Grégoire, p. 432, no. 14.

5. ff. 11r–15v *Lectio sancti euangelii secundum matheum.* In illo tempore. Cum esset desponsata mater ihesu maria ... [Mat. 1.18]. Cum desponsata esset mater eius maria ioseph. que fuit necessitas ut desponsata esset ... Ecce ego uobiscum sum omnibus diebus usque ad consumationem qui ... amen.

For Christmas Eve, at none; Ps.-Origen, *Homilia 1 in Mat.* l. 18–25; Grégoire, pp. 432–33, no. 15.

6. ff. 15v–16r [No heading.] Natalis domini dies ea de causa a patribus uotiue sollemnitatis institutus est ... quod natus est ihesus christus ... amen.

For Christmas; Isidore of Seville, *De ecclesiasticis officiis* I. 26; Grégoire, p. 433, no. 16.

7. ff. 16r–17r [No heading.] Saluator noster dilectissimi hodie natus est. gaudeamus. Neque enim ... qui ueritate te iudicabit. qui misericordia te redemit christus dominus noster.

Leo, *Sermo* 21; Grégoire, p. 433, no. 17.

8. ff. 17r–19r [No heading.] Exultemus in domino dilectissimi et spiritali iocunditate letemur. quia inluxit dies ... ut eum uidere mereamini deum gloriae in sua magestate [*sic*] regnantem. cum deo ... amen.

Leo, *Sermo* 22; Grégoire, p. 433, no. 18.

9. ff. 19r–21v [No heading.] Cupientes aliquid de huius diei sollempnitate narrare. simulque considerantes illud unum uerbum ... et pace perducat populumque suum in fide et caritate custodiat ... amen.

Fulgentius, *Sermo* 2; Grégoire, p. 433, no. 19.

10. ff. 21v–23v [No heading.] Iustissime fratres festiuitate presentis diei in omne se gaudium totus ... honore debito mysteria semper christi uirtutes que laudaemus [*sic*].

Ps.-Maximus Taurinensis, *Homilia* 11; Grégoire, p. 434, no. 20.

11. ff. 23v–24v [No heading.] Hodie fratres karissimi. christus natus est nos renati. Hodie saluator mundi per matrem nascendi tempus accepit ... inoffensam teneamus celestis fidei ueritatem.

Ps.-Maximus Taurinensis, *Homilia* 10; Grégoire, p. 434, no. 21.

12. ff. 25r–26r [No heading.] In aduentu dominico fratres karissimi solutus est omnis paterne preuaricationis metus . . . ut ueritatem predicans uniuersam mundi faciem dampnata iniquitate purgaret.

Ps.-Augustine, *Sermo* 122 (Ps.-Maximus Taurinensis, *Homilia* 12); Grégoire, p. 434, no. 22.

13. ff. 26r–27r [No heading.] Hodierni [added above: *misterii*] sacramentum fratres karissimi sicut credidistis semper et creditis . . . et natum hominem credas. et deum esse dubitare non possis.

Ps.-Maximus Taurinensis, *Homilia* 13; Grégoire, p. 434, no. 23.

14. ff. 27r–28r *Lectio sancti euangelii secundum Lucam.* In illo tempore. Exiit edictum a caesare augusto . . . [Luc. 2.1]. Quia largiente domino missarum sollempnia ter hodie caelebraturi sumus . . . quia propter te factus est deus homo.

Gregory, *Homiliae in Evangelia* I.8; Grégoire, p. 434, no. 24.

15. ff. 28r–31r *Lectio sancti euangelii secundum Lucam.* In illo tempore. Pastores loquebantur ad inuicem . . . [Luc. 2.15]. Nato in bethleem domino saluatore sicut sacra euangelii testatur historia . . . et laudemus ipsum deum. ac dominum nostrum ihesum christum . . . amen.

Bede, *Homilia* I.7; Grégoire, p. 435, no. 25.

16. ff. 31r–36r *Lectio sancti euangelii secundum iohannem.* In principio erat uerbum et uerbum erat . . . [John 1.1]. Quia temporalem mediatoris dei et hominum. hominis ihesu christi natiuitatem . . . sue diuine maiestatis ostenderet . . . amen.

Bede, *Homilia* I.8; Grégoire, p. 435, no. 26.

17. ff. 36r–38v [No heading.] Heri celebrauimus temporalem sempiterni regis nostri natalem hodie celebramus triumphalem militis passionem . . . ut ad premia aeterna peruenire possitis. adiuncti gratia christi domini saluatoris.

For the feast of Stephen (26 December); Fulgentius, *Sermo* 3; Grégoire, p. 435, no. 27.

18. ff. 38v–40v [Added in outer margin:] In octaua Sancti Stephani. [added in column:] Hic legitur in octaua Sancti Stephani. [text:] Lectio actuum apostolorum quae nobis hodie lecta est . . . Quam rem orantibus uobis ipse prestare dignetur . . . amen.

For the octave of Stephen (2 January); Caesarius, *Sermo* 219; Grégoire, p. 435, no. 28.

19. ff. 40v–43v [No heading.] Ad aquas tibilitanas episcopo afferente protomartyris gloriosissimi stephani memoriam ueniebant ... Quia et ipsi martyres huius fidei martyres idem huius fidei testes fuerunt.

On the miracles of Stephen; Augustine, *De civitate Dei* XXII.8–9; Grégoire, p. 435, no. 29.

20. ff. 43v–45r *Lectio sancti euangelii secundum matheum.* In illo tempore. Dicebat ihesus turbis iudeorum et principibus sacerdotum. Ecce ego mitto ad uos ... [Mat. 23.34]. Ecce ego mitto ad uos prophetas et sapientes ... Hoc quod antea dixeram uos implete mensuram patrum uestrorum ... benedictus qui uenit in nomine domini nostri et christi ora conspicient.

Jerome, *Commentarius in Evangelium Matthaei* IV.23.34–39; Grégoire, p. 435, no. 30.

21. f. 45r–v [No heading.] Iohannes apostolus et euuangelista filius zebedei fratrer [*sic*] iacobi. uirgo electus a domino ... ad superiora puluis ebulliat.

For the feast of John the Evangelist (27 December); Isidore of Seville, *De ortu et obitu Patrum*, 72; Grégoire, p. 436, no. 31.

22. ff. 45v–47r [Added later:] Hic legitur in notaua [*sic*] sancti Iohannis euangeliste. [text:] Audi fabulam non fabulam. sed rem gestam de iohanne apostolo ... in eo resurrectionis ostendens.

For the octave of John the Evangelist (3 January); Eusebius, *Historia ecclesiastica*, I.3.23, 6–19, Lat tr. Rufinus; Grégoire, p. 436, no. 32.

23. ff. 47r–50r *Lectio sancti euangelii secundum Iohannem.* In illo tempore. Dixit ihesus petro sequere me ... [John 21.19]. Lectio sancti euangelii que nobis lecta est fratres mei tanto maiori a nobis intentione debet ... ad dona sempiterna que promisit peruenire ... amen.

Bede, *Homilia* I.9; Grégoire, p. 436, no. 33. Text missing between ff. 48–49 (" ... de illo futurum predixit. Et psalmista ait // monachis. sed et cuncto ut diximus...").

24. ff. 50r–51v [no heading.] Zelus quo tendat quo prosiliat liuor. inuidia quo feratur ... de morte uitam non uirtutis humane sed muneris est diuin[final letter corrected and/or erased?].

For the feast of the Holy Innocents (28 December); Petrus Chrysologus,

Sermo 152; Grégoire, p. 436, no. 34.

25. ff. 51v–52v [Later addition, partially trimmed, in outer margin:] [Hi]c legitur notaua [*sic*] [inno]centium. [text:] Dedicatur nouus ab infantibus sermo sanctis laudibus christi ... cadendos urgitur uictoria per interitum comparatur.

For the octave of the Holy Innocents (4 January); author uncertain, though formerly attributed to John Chrysostom; Grégoire, pp. 436–37, no. 35. Folios 51v–52r have been heavily traced over in black ink, thus rendering portions of the text difficult to read.

26. ff. 52v–55r *Lectio sancti euangelii secundum matheum.* In illo tempore. Angelus domini apparuit in somnis ... [Mat.2.13]. De morte preciosa martyrum christi innocentium sacra nobis est fratres karissimi ... et salutis eterne in tabernaculis iustorum ... seculorum.

Bede, *Homilia* 1.10; Grégoire, p. 437, no. 36.

27. ff. 55v–56v *In octauas domini.* Quamquam non dubitem uos karissimi. per paternae solicitudinis [?] instructionem diuini sermonis edoctos ... et iudex doctrine sue fructum paulus inueniat.

For the octave of Christmas (1 January); Ps. Maximus Taurinensis, *Homilia* 16; Grégoire, p. 437, no. 37; large portions of text traced over.

28. f. 56v [No heading.] Quod mortuus est christus peccato[r *erased*?] mortuus est. Non quia ipse//

For the feast of the Circumcision (1 January); Origen, Lat. tr. Jerome, *In Lucam, Homilia* 14, the beginning lines only; Grégoire, p. 437, no. 38.

29. ff. 57r–59v // populos appeccatorum [*sic*] sorde lauari uoluit ipse non necessitatis. sed exempli causa subiit ... ita et nos in nouitate uite ambulemus. Prestante....

Bede, *Homilia* 1.11, here beginning imperfectly; Grégoire, p. 437, no. 40.

30. ff. 59v–60v *Dominica 1. post natale domini.* Lectio sancti euangelii secundum lucam. In illo tempore. Erant pater ihesu et mater ... [Luc. 2.33]. Congregemus in unum ea que in ortu ihesu dicta scripta sunt de eo ... coeperunt uidere male. Et aspectum//

For the first Sunday after Christmas; Origen, Lat. tr. Jerome, *In Lucam, Homilia* 16, here ending imperfectly; Grégoire, p. 438, no. 41.

31. f. 61r–v // non uidebam et qui mihi postea reserati sunt. Quam post

inobedientiam et adam et eue oculi sunt aperti de quibus superiore sermone tractauimus ... peccatum meum notum tibi feci. et iniquitatem meam non abscondi.//

Leaf from unidentified sermon, previously detached and laid in.

Parchment (thick, worn, repaired), ff. i (paper) + 61 + i (paper), 294 x 235 (235 x 190, with the text space of the inner column often wider than that of the outer) mm. 2 columns, 29 lines. Double outer and single inner vertical bounding lines; single horizontal bounding lines. Ruled in hard point on hair side. Prickings (slashes) in upper and lower margins.

I^8 (-1, 2), II^2 (bifolium), III–VII^8, VIII^8 (-1), IX^6 (structure uncertain, leaves with text missing after ff. 56 and 60; f. 61 probably does not belong to quire).

Written by several scribes in well formed early caroline minuscule. Headings in majuscules, some in red rustic capitals (e.g., f. 11r); many omitted. A modern hand has often added names of authors. Plain 2-line initials in red or black.

Binding: Italy. s. xix. Half bound in brown calf with bright pink paper sides and red edges. There are three blackish green, gold-tooled labels on the spine: "Homeliae Usq./ Ad Domi. Post Natale/ Manuscr. Saecul. IX." Bound by the binder of Marston MSS 50, 125, 128, 135, 153, 158, 159 and 197, all of Hautecombe provenance.

Written probably in Northern Italy at the end of the 9th or beginning of the 10th century according to B. Bischoff (letter on file). Other leaves from the homiliary include: Bloomington, Indiana, University of Indiana, Lilly Libr. MS 38 (George A. Poole Collection MS 259); Detroit, Michigan, The Detroit Public Library, MS 1; Los Angeles, University of California, Research Library MS **170/ 403 (2/ IX/ Ita/ 1). Belonged to the Cistercian monastery of Hautecombe in the ancient diocese of Geneva, which was founded toward the beginning of the 12th century by monks from the abbey of Aulps (see R. Clair, "Les origines de l'abbaye d'Hautecombe," *Mélanges à la mémoire du Père Anselme Dimier* [Arbois, 1982–87] tome II, v. 4, pp. 615–27). Although there is no ex libris, the volume exhibits the characteristic pink binding of the books of Monseigneur Hyacinthe della Torre who acquired and rebound a group of twelve manuscripts from this monastery at the beginning of the 19th century (see Leclercq, 1951, p. 76). Belonged to the Biblioteca del Seminario Metropolitano in Turin (Leclercq, *op.cit.*, p. 76 and Leclercq, 1961, p. 183). Purchased from Maggs Bros. of London in 1957 by L. C. Witten (inv. no. 1596), who sold it the same year to Thomas E. Marston (bookplate).

Bibliography: Faye and Bond, p. 81, no. 151.
Exhibition Catalogue, pp. 181–82, no. 6.
C. E. Lutz, "A Manuscript of Charlemagne's *Homiliarium*," *Gazette* 47 (1972) pp. 100–02; reprinted in her *Essays on Manuscripts and Rare Books* (Hamden, Conn., 1975) pp. 24–27.

Marston MS 152 France, s. XII^{med}
Pauline Epistles, with commentary of Gilbert de la Porrée Pl. 40

1. ff. 1r–165v //legem consummans te qui per litteram et circumcisionem preuaricator legis es? Non enim qui in manifesto ... aciem gladij conualuerunt de infirmitate//

   Pauline Epistles, written only in the inner column of each page and beginning and ending imperfectly (*Epistola ad Romanos* 2.27 through *Epistola ad Hebreos* 11.34). Leaves with text lost between ff. 95–96 (Gal. 4.25–5.4), ff. 119–120 (Col. 3.11–4.6).

2. ff. 1r–165v //nonne iudicabit id est comparatione sui iudicabilem ostendet te qui non modo per naturam uerum etiam per litteram ... exercitus armatorum. ut iosue. samson. dauid. et alij multi. conualuerunt de infirmitate.//

   Commentary of Gilbert de la Porrée written only in the outer column of each page in a smaller script than that in art. 1. Beginning and ending imperfectly; Biblical passages underlined. Stegmüller, v. 2, 2515–28. On the author of this work and its date see H. C. van Elswijk, *Gilbert Porreta. Sa vie, son oeuvre, sa pensée* (Louvain, 1966) pp. 54–58 (Marston MS 152 not cited).

3. [*Argumenta*, later additions, as follow; f. 69r:] *Incipit argumentum epistole ad corinthios*. Post actam penitenciam consolatoriam scribit eis a troade ... ostendens. Explicit argumentum. [f. 86r:] *Incipit argumentum epistole ad galatas*. Galate sunt greci hi verbum ueritatis ab apostolo primum acceperunt ... scribens eis ab epheso. Explicit argumentum. [f. 110r:] Incipit argumentum. Philippenses sunt macedones hi[*c* deleted] accepto uerbo ueritatis perstiterunt in fide ... per afroditum. Explicit argumentum. [f. 115v:] Incipit argumentum. Colosenses et hi sicut laodicenses sunt asiani. et ipsi preuenti erant ... ab urbe roma. Explicit argumentum. [f. 120r:] Thesalonicenses sunt macedones in christo ihesu qui accepto uerbo ueritatis ... acolitum. Explicit argumentum.

   Stegmüller, v. 1, nos. 699, 707, 728, 736, 747; all attributed to Hugo de Sancto Caro or Peter Lombard.

Parchment, ff. iii (paper) + 165 + iii (paper), 293 x 215 (215 x 150) mm. 2 columns, 21 lines for text, 46 lines for commentary. Single vertical bounding lines for inner margin and space between columns; double vertical bounding lines for outer margin of outer column. Rulings for commentary drawn in hard point; rulings for main text drawn faintly in lead or crayon. Ruling format for each leaf tailored to specific contents. Prickings in upper, lower, and outer margins.

I-XI^{8}, XII^{8} (-8), XIII-XV^{8}, XVI^{8} (-1), XVII-XX^{8}, XXI^{8} (-8). Quires signed with letters of the alphabet (*A* through *Y*), later additions, lower margin near gutter on recto.

Written in fine early gothic bookhand in two sizes of script, above top line.

Three illuminated initials at beginning of first three Epistles, of excellent quality, ff. 34v, 69v, 86v, 8- to 5-line, with descenders extending into margins, red, blue, green and beige against gold ground. Bodies of initials filled with stylized scrolling foliage, bright blue, red, green, orange, silver and yellow with white highlights against gold ground. Descenders serve as a trellis for similar scrolls, some ending in biting animals' heads or fantastic birds. Scrolling foliage, f. 86v, inhabited by beasts of a canine variety, white with red shading. The decoration of manuscript is unfinished; f. 99r pen and ink underdrawing for an initial as above, with only touches of red added; blank spaces left for initials for remaining Epistles. Small initials, 3-line, gold with red penwork, for beginning of commentary for each Epistle. Headings in red or alternating red and blue majuscules. Plain initials touched with red. Running titles, later addition, in red.

Binding: United States?, s. xx. Half bound in dark red goatskin with gold-tooled lettering on the spine ("St. Paul/ Epistulae cum commento/ MS. 12th Cent."), marbled paper sides, and yellow edges.

Written in France in the middle of the 12th century; early provenance unknown. Entry from unidentified sale catalogue (with pl.), in French, in library files. Purchased from L. C. Witten in 1957 by Thomas E. Marston (bookplate).

Bibliography: Faye and Bond, p. 81, no. 152.

Exhibition Catalogue, pp. 187–88, no. 15, pl. 5 of f. 34v.

The Medieval Book, p. 18. no. 18 (with plate of f. 86v and drawing of page format).

C. de Hamel, *Glossed Books of the Bible and the Origins of the Paris Book Trade* (Suffolk, 1984) pp. 20, n. 33; 34, n. 45.

Marston MS 153 Hautecombe [?], s. $XII^{2/4}$
Ambrose, De paradiso, De Cain et Abel, etc.

1. ff. 1r–28r *Incipit liber beati ambrosii mediolanensis episcopi. De paradiso.* Et plantauit deus paradisum in eden secundum orientem; et posuit ibi hominem quem finxit. De paradiso adoriundus sermo. non mediocrem estum nobis uidetur incutere ... Si uero spiritualia seminauerimus. ea que sunt spiritualia metemus. f. 28v ruled, but blank

   Ambrose, *De paradiso*; C. Schenkl, ed., CSEL, vol. 32, 1 (1896) pp. 263–326 (f. 9 *bis* contains 6.31–32 of the printed text [p. 288, line 3 - p. 289, line 21], a passage omitted by the original scribe and added on the inserted leaf by a slightly later hand).

2. ff. 29r–56r *Explicit de paradiso. Incipit de cain et abel.* De paradiso in superioribus pro captu nostro ut potuimus quod dominus infudit. sensus inuenit digessimus. in quibus adam atque eue lapsus est comprehensus ... quod se redemisset uel sera actione penitentie. nisi eum prematura pena rapuisset. *Explicit.*

   Ambrose, *De Cain et Abel*; Schenkl, *op. cit.*, pp. 337–409.

3. ff. 56r–70r *Incipit adhortatio uirginitatis sancti ambrosii episcopi.* Qui ad conuiuium magnum inuitantur. apoforeta secum deferre [corrected from *referre*] consuerunt. Ego ad bononiense inuitatus conuiuium ... christo domino placentes. et integrum spiritum earum animam et corpus sine querele loco. usque in diem domini nostri ihesu christi filii tui seruare digneris. amen.

   Ambrose, *Exhortatio virginitatis*; PL 16.335–64.

4. ff. 70r–83r *Incipit liber beati ambrosii de uirginitate ad ambrosium.* Commendas michi pignus tuum quod eque est meum ambrosi. domini sacram. et pio affectu eius tibi asseris ... per illam uenerabilem gloriam trinitatis. cui est honor et gloria. perpetuitas patri deo et filio. et spiritui sancto. a seculis et nunc et semper et in omnia secula seculorum. Amen.

   Ambrose, *De institutione virginis*; PL 16.305–34 and M. Salvati, ed., *Scritti sulla verginità, Corona patrum salesiana, ser. lat.* 6 (Turin, 1955) pp. 168–297.

5. f. 83r–v Various notes including: Nulla Dies habeat quin lignea ducta supersit/ Non decet ignauium preteriisse diem. [Walther, *Sprichwörter*, no. 18894].

Parchment, ff. iii (paper) + 84 (1–83; f. 9 *bis* is a near contemporary insertion) + iii (paper), 330 x 235 (ff. 1–28: 250 x 175; ff. 29–83: 270–265 x 185–180) mm. 2 columns, ca. 31 lines. Single vertical bounding lines, ruled in hard point on hair side. Remains of prickings in upper, lower and outer margins.

I^8, II^8 (+ 1 leaf, 9 *bis*), $III-IV^6$, $V-X^8$, XI^8 (–7, no loss of text). Scribe 1 (see below) places catchwords along lower edge under inner column.

Written by two scribes in late caroline minuscule. Scribe 1 (ff. 1r–61r): preference for uncial *d*, angular abbreviation strokes, and a slightly larger module of script than that used by Scribe 2 (ff. 61r–83r).

Plain red initials, 6- to 4-line, with small "pearls" on the thin strokes of the letters, introduce each text. Headings in red. Instructions to rubricator and guide letters.

Heavily stained but with no loss of text.

Binding: Italy, s. xix^{in}. Half bound with a brown calf spine and goatskin corners, bright pink paper sides and red edges. Three green, gold-tooled labels on the spine: "Manuscri," "S Ambrosi de Cain" and "Seculi XII." Bound in the same distinctive style as Marston MSS 50, 125, 128, 135, 151, 158, 159 and 197, all of Hautecombe provenance.

Written in the second quarter of the 12th century, perhaps at the Cistercian abbey of Hautecombe to which it belonged; early ex libris, s. XII–XIII, on f. 83r: "liber sancte marie [with later addition, much damaged and faded written over erasure:] Altecumbee in Sabaudia Monasterii Ord. Cisterciensium emptus fuit a canonico Taurinensi presbitero cardinalis [?] titulis [?] s. Maximi in quinto Philippo Amadeo Millo anno Domini 1766 [this information not verified]." Additional notes, s. xvi–xvii, on f. 83r-v, record the entry of monks into the abbey of Hautecombe; another ex libris, s. xvi–xvii, written on f. 83v. Located in the ancient diocese of Geneva, the abbey was founded toward the beginning of the 12th century by monks from the abbey of Aulps (see R. Clair, "Les origines de l'abbaye d'Hautecombe," *Mélanges à la mémoire du Père Anselme Dimier* [Arbois, 1982–87] tome II, v. 4, pp. 615–27). Marston MS 153 has the characteristic bright pink binding of the books of Monseigneur Hyacinthe della Torre who acquired and rebound a group of twelve manuscripts from Hautecombe at the beginning of the 19th century (see Leclercq, 1951, p. 75). Belonged to the Biblioteca del Seminario Metropolitano in Turin (Leclercq, *op. cit.*, p. 76, no. 13: number in red crayon on front pastedown). Acquired from Maggs Bros. of London in 1957 by L. C. Witten (inv. no. 1598), who sold it the same year to Thomas E. Marston (bookplate).

secundo folio: que multiplicat

Bibliography: Faye and Bond, p. 81, no. 153.

Marston MS 154 — Paris, s. $XIV^{1/4}$
William of Melitona, Commentarius in Ecclesiasticum — Pl. 46

1. ff. 1r–9v Abicere 164/ abiectio 243/ abisac 145/ . . . zelare mulierem 44/ zelare gloriam 47/ zmaragdus. 188. f. 10r-v ruled but blank

   Alphabetical index for art. 2 with folio references entered in red; this index is a 15th-century addition on a complete gathering inserted at the beginning of the volume.

2. ff. 1r–293v [medieval foliation] *Sapiencia edificauit sibi domum* . . . [Prov. 9.1]. Sicut eternus artifex sua potentia spiritum rationale de nihilo produxit in esse . . . [f. 2v:] *Multorum nobis et cetera.* operi principali duo prohemia siue prologi proponuntur . . . et dabit uobis mercedem in tempore suo. quam nobis prestare dignetur . . . amen. Explicit super ecclesiasticum.

   Stegmüller no. 2938.

3. ff. 293v–295r Abstinendum est a multis. fo. ccxvi. co. ij./ accedit quis ad deum duplici cordis cur [?]. fo. 9. co. 4./ . . . christus comparatur nebule. fo. cxxviij. col. ij./ christus columpna. propter. virtutem fo. cxxviij. co. iij. f. 295v blank (contemporary parchment flyleaf)

   Alphabetical index for art. 2 with folio and column references; the entries correspond to key phrases entered in the margins of the text.

Parchment (poor quality, yellow and speckled on hair side), ff. 304 (medieval foliation for art. 2, 1–293) + ii (contemporary parchment bifolium; ii = back pastedown), 325 x 208 (240 x 146) mm. 2 columns, 48 lines. Single vertical and single upper horizontal bounding lines. Two additional rulings in upper, lower and outer margins; one additional ruling in inner margin. Remains of prickings in all margins for bounding lines only.

I^{10} (art. 1; later addition), $II–XII^{12}$, XIII^{14}, $XIV–XXV^{12}$, XXVI^{4}. Catchwords, in rectangular red frames, lower margin near gutter, verso. Leaf signatures, perhaps written in two stages: the one in Roman numerals, in black; the other letters of the alphabet, in red, both in lower right corner, recto.

Written in neat gothic bookhand for arts. 1 and 2; art. 3 written in inelegant gothic text hands.

One historiated initial of fine quality on f. 11r, 9-line, reddish brown with white filigree against blue ground with white filigree, edged in gold, showing the author and three companions, presenting a book to a seated monarch dressed in a blue robe against a reddish ground with geometric designs in blue, black and red. Terminals of initial extend as a bar border into inner margin, blue and reddish brown against reddish-brown and blue grounds with white filigree and touches of gold. Border terminates in lower margin in a spray of spiky ivy, blue with gold leaves. The decoration and figure style is representative of Parisian work of the first quarter of the 14th century and can be compared to Paris, B. N. lat. 14563 (cf. C. de Hamel, *A History of Illuminated Manuscripts* [Boston, 1986] p. 123, pl. 117); it also resembles the early work of Jean Pucelle, in such manuscripts as the Bible of Robert de Billyng (Paris, B. N. lat. 11935) dated 1327 (see H. Martin, *La miniature française du XIIIe au XVe siècle* [Paris, 1923] pl. 34, fig. XLIII). Flourished initials, 6– to 3–line, blue or red with red and/or blue penwork designs, often extending the entire length of the text column. Running titles in red and blue. Paragraph marks alternate red and blue. Biblical passages underlined in red. Initials touched with red. Remains of instructions to rubricator.

Binding: Spain, s. xv. Early [?] resewing on four tawed skin, slit straps or double cords laced into grooves in wooden boards. Beaded, red, green and natural color secondary endbands are sewn on tawed skin cores laced into the boards. The spine is lined with vellum between supports. Front and back (mostly concealed by another parchment leaf) pastedowns from a liturgical manuscript with neumes (Spain, s. XII). Remains of contemporary rectangular label on lower board: "Holcot super eccl***/ cum."

Covered in brown sheepskin, blind-tooled with a central panel and alternate concentric frames filled with rope interlace with red bordering fillets. Spine: supports defined with double fillets on the spine and an *X* with a central cross-bar in the panels. There are four fastenings, the catches on the lower board, the clasp straps fastened with star-headed nails.

Written in Paris in the first quarter of the 14th century, from a stationer's exemplum *secundum pecias*. The pecia notation runs as follows (we give the numbers of those marks visible in margins or those that can be reconstructed with reasonable certainty): f. 43r 13; f. 47r 14; f. 51r 15; f. 54r 16; f. 58v 17; f. 62v 18; f. 66v 19; f. 78r 22; f. 105r 29; f. 109r 30; f. 113r 31; f. 132r 36; f. 135v 37; f. 143r 39; f. 150v 41; f. 154v 42; f. 165v 45; f. 169r 46; f. 172v 47; f. 175v 48; f. 179r 49; f. 183r 60 [*sic*]; f. 187r 51; f. 191r 52; f. 195r 53; f. 210r 57; f. 236r 64; f. 251r 68; f. 261v 71; f. 269r 73; f. 272v 74; f. 280r 76; f. 283v 77; f. 287v 78 [?]. Early ownership inscription, s. xiv–xv, of the bishop of Saragossa, visible under ultra-violet light on verso of rear flyleaf: "Iste liber est episcopi Ces. ag." The manuscript was probably rebound while at Saragossa in the 15th century. Purchased from C. A. Stonehill in 1957 by Thomas E. Marston (bookplate).

secundo folio: [table, f. 2:] caro
[text, f. 2:] uidemus

Bibliography: Faye and Bond, p. 81, no. 154.

Marston MS 155 — Bologna, ca. 1325
Boniface VIII, Sextus Liber Decretalium, etc. — Pl. 6

1. ff. 1r–96v [Main text in center of page:] Bonifacius episcopus seruus seruorum dei dilectus filijs doctoribus et scolaribus uniuersis ... benedictionem. [prologue:] Sacrosancte romane ecclesie quam imperscrutabilis diuine prouidentie ... pro decretalibus habituri. [text; f. 2r:] *De summa trinitate et fide catholica. Rubrica.* Fideli ac deuota professione fatemur ... Certum est quod is committit in legem qui legis uerba complectens contra legis nititur uoluntatem. [colophon:] Data rome apud sanctum petrum quinto nonas martij pontificatus nostri anno iiij. Deo Gracias.

   Boniface VIII, *Sextus liber decretalium*, missing several leaves (see collation) and with final leaf (now foliated 96) misbound between ff. 93–94. E. Friedberg, ed., *Corpus iuris canonici*, Pars secunda, Decretalium Collectiones (Leipzig, 1922) v. 2, cols. 933–1124. Text of arts. 1 and 2 accompanied by interlinear and marginal glosses in one main hand.

2. ff. 1r–96v [Commentary surrounding text; rubric in later hand, s. xv, written around decorative initial:] *Iohannis Andree Doctoris Apparatus super 6º libro Decretalium.* [text:] Quia preposterus est ordo prius humana subsidia petere ut illis ... labores meos offeram. iam licet nouiter inchoactos. Io. [colophon on f. 96v, see art. 1 above:] Explicit apparatus domini johannis. Amen. Andree super sexto libro decretalium. Quis scripsit scribat sempper [?] cum domino uiuat. viuat in celis in nomine felix.

   Commentary of Joannes Andreae on art. 1; numerous printed editions, GKW, v. 4, nos. 4848–87 and thereafter.

3. ff. 1r–22r [New foliation; preface:] Iohannes episcopus seruus seruorum dei dilectis filijs doctoribus et scolaribus vniuersis bononie commorantibus salutem et apostolicam benedictionem. Quoniam nulla iuris sanctio ... usuri de cetero in iudiciis et in scolis. Data auinione. kalendas. nouembris pontificatus nostri anno secundo. [text:] *De summa trinitate et fide catholica.* Clemens quintus in concilio vienensi. Fidei catholice fundamento preter quod teste apostolo ... non erit processus

propter hoc irritus nec eciam irritandus. [colophon:] Expliciunt constitutiones domini pape clementis. v. edite in concilio vianenci [*sic*]. amen.

Clemens V, *Constitutiones*, with preface of John XXII; Friedberg, *op. cit.*, cols. 1129–1200. Text accompanied by modest interlinear and marginal notes.

4. f. 22v [I]ohannes episcopus seruus seruorum dei ... memoriam. quia nonnumquam quod coniectura profuturum credidit subsequens experiencia ... et patulo iuditio publicabunt. Data Auinione kalendas Aprilis pontificatus nostri Anno sexto.

John XXII, "Quia nonnunquam"; J. Tarrant, ed., *Extravagantes Iohannis XXII*, Monumenta iuris canonici, Series B: Corpus collectionum, v. 6 (Vatican City, 1983) pp. 217–21.

Parchment, ff. i (paper) + 118 (modern foliation 1–96, 1–22) + i (paper), 450 x 275 (written space: 415 x 235 mm. for ff. 1r–96v with gloss, ca. 260 x 175 mm. for ff. 97r–114v). Art. 1 written in two columns with a maximum of 47 lines of text and with 88 lines of gloss; art. 2 written in 2 columns of 33–55 lines. Double vertical and horizontal bounding lines full across for gloss, single bounding lines for text. Ruled in hard point, ink and lead.

I–II^{10}, III^{10} (-9), IV–VIII^{10}, IX^{8} (quire X missing), XI^{8} (+ 1 leaf, f. 96, misbound between ff. 93–94), XII–XIII^{10}, XIV^{2}. Quire signatures, Arabic numerals, in upper left corner, recto. Remains of decorated catchwords, lower edge near gutter, verso.

Folios 1–96 written in *littera bononiensis*; ff. 1–22 written in a less formal Gothic bookhand. Numerous annotations in the margins by contemporary and later hands.

Two miniatures, f. 1r, an enthroned pope holding an open book and symmetrically flanked by ecclesiastical and secular parties, and f. 96r, a Franciscan monk presenting a book to an enthroned pope with clerical and lay attendants. A similar composition to f. 1r is frequently encountered in Bolognese manuscripts of canon law (see *Exhibition Catalogue*, p. 204, no. 30). Full border for text on f. 1r, constructed of solid panels, gold and red with white filigree, filled with two karyatid figures, a cleric, and a man in a blue robe. Partial border in lower margin, 3 medallions in blue, pink and red, with a papal portrait in half length, an angel, and a third subject now effaced. The medallions are connected by lozenges, green, blue and red with scrolling vines in blue, red, and green with white filigree and gold dots (cf. G. Canova, "Nuovi contributi alle serie liturgica degli antifonari de S. Domenico in Bologna," *La miniatura italiana in età romanica e gotica* [Atti del I Congresso di storia della miniatura italiana, Cortona, 26–28 March 1978], figs. 1–3). 32 marginal figures in various costumes, among them several clerics, knights and an angel, often in animated poses. Numerous illuminated initials, 6- to 3-line, in pink, blue or grey on blue, red, pink and gold grounds with white filigree. Foliage serifs in pink, red, grey and blue with white highlights. 39 initials with bust-length figures. Remaining initials in pink and red with white filigree (cf. S. Pettenti, "Alcuni codici Bolognese del XIII secolo della Biblioteca Nazionale di Torino," *op. cit.*, pp. 327–42, fig. 2). The style of the decoration is characteristic for Bologna in the early 14th century and can be compared to Rome, Vat. lat. 1375, ascribed to Jacopino da Reggio, and a group of canon law manuscripts, among them Naples, Biblioteca Nazionale XII. A. I. Calligraphic initials, alternating in red and blue with blue and red penwork scrolls. Plain initials and paragraph marks alternate in red and blue.

Binding: Italy, s. xv [?]. Limp vellum case, restored.

Written in Bologna ca. 1325; early provenance unknown. Belonged to Sir Thomas Phillipps (no. 13625; tag on spine, number written in pencil on front pastedown and flyleaf); his acquisition from Boone in 1853 (pencil note). Purchased in 1957 from H. P. Kraus (pencil notes on back pastedown) by Thomas E. Marston (bookplate).

secundo folio: [du]bia deciduntur

Bibliography: Faye and Bond, p. 81, no. 155.
Exhibition Catalogue, p. 204, no. 30.
The Medieval Book, pp. 30, 34, no. 31 with pl. of f. 70v.

Marston MS 156 — Germany, s. XIV^1

Ps.-John Chrysostom; Martinus Strepus, etc.

1. ff. 1r–52r, 57r–86v [Prologue:] Sicut referunt mathaeum conscribere euuangelium causa compulit talis. Cum facta fuisset persecutio grauis in palestina ita ut periclitarentur ... hec commutatio dextere excelsi [Ps. 76.11]. *Capitulum primum.* [table of contents:] Liber generationis ihesu christi filii dauid filii abraheo/ Cum esset desponsata mater eius maria ioseph./ Cum natus esset ihesus in bethleem iude/ ... Ideo ecce ego mitto ad uos prophetas et sapientes et scribas et ipsos occidetis. [Sermo I, f. 1v:] Liber generationis ihesus christi fili dauid. filii abrahe. Liber quasi apotheca gratiarum. Sicut in apotheca diuitis alicuius omnis homo quod desiderat inuenit ... [concludes imperfectly:] putat imple-

tum qui in actibus apostolorum leguntur// ff. 54v–56v ruled, but blank

Ps.-John Chrysostom, *Opus imperfectum in Mathaeum*; the sermons, labelled in the manuscript according to Biblical chapters 1–8 (ff. 1r–52r) and 19–23 (ff. 57r–86v), correspond to sermons nos. 1–22 and 32–46 in PG 56.611–754, 798–897. One leaf, with text in Sermons 44–45, missing between ff. 83–84 ("... lauanda sunt aquis sed conscientie precibus // uestrorum prophetat illis uenturum..."). See Stegmüller, v. 3, no. 4350, for manuscripts, early printed editions and bibliography. The scribe left blank ff. 52–56 to accommodate the missing sermons; a slightly later hand added arts. 2–3 on some of these leaves.

2. ff. 52r–53 [Instructions to rubricator in inner margin:] *De cordis stabilitate.* [text:] [P]ost tractatum de apericione [*sic*] cordis sub multiplici diuisione diffusum ad tractandum de ipsius cordis stabilitate accedamus. Cordis stabilitatem commendat apostolus dicens ... [text missing since lower half of f. 53 has been excised].

   Hugo de Sancto Caro, *De doctrina cordis*; see G. Hendrix, "Hugh of St. Cher OP Author of Two Texts Attributed to the 13th-century Cistercian Gerard of Liège," *Cîteaux* 31 (1980) pp. 343–56 (A. Wilmart, "Gérard de Liège: un traité inédit de l'amour de Dieu," *Revue d'ascétique et de mystique* 12 [1931] pp. 370–73). It is possible that arts. 2 and 3 are parts of the same text.

3. ff. 53–54r [Beginning missing?] //hec sunt puncta fidei tue detur o christiane qui puncta cridenciorum [?] in ictu oculi bene scis numerare puncta vero fidei tue si nosti etiam inplitice [?] numerare. Expliciunt articuli fidei.

   Unidentified *articuli fidei*; see art. 2 above.

4. ff. 86v–127v *Incipit cronica fratris martini penitenciarii domini pape et capellani.* [prologue:] Quoniam scire tempora summorum pontificum romanorum ac imperatorum ... Quinto de rectoribus et regimine quo profecit. [text:] *De iiij*^{or} *regnis maioribus regibus de quibus romanum ultimus fuit.* Sicut ergo dicit orosius ad beatum augustinum scribens a mundi creacione usque ad urbem conditam ... qui infirmus de affrica processerat in syciliam veniens est defunctus. *Explicit.*

   Martinus Strepus, *Chronicon pontificum et imperatorum*, concluding with "Ludovicus rex francie" in 1270; Kaeppeli, SOPMA no. 2974, citing Marston MS 248 [156]. L. Wieland, ed., MGH Scriptores (1872) v. 22, pp. 397–474; Marston MS 156 conflates the pope and emperor lists, includes the narration for the four reigns after the prologue, but lacks the interpolation for St. Joan.

Parchment (thick), ff. ii (paper) + i (early parchment reinforced with paper on recto) + 127 + i (f. 128, early parchment reinforced with paper on verso) + iii (paper), 346 x 250 (272 x 196) mm. 2 columns, 45–46 lines. Single vertical and single (sometimes double) horizontal lines, full across. Ruled in lead before folding since text rulings extend through gutter. Remains of prickings in upper, lower and outer margins.

I-IV^{12}, V^{8} (lower half of 5 excised), VI-VII^{12}, VIII^{12} (-4), IX-XI^{12}. Catchwords, enclosed in rectangular frame and flourishes, center of lower margin, verso.

Written in good quality gothic bookhand.

Red and blue divided initials, f. 1r (10-line) and f. 86v (9-line), with floral and linear motifs in parchment. Running titles, headings in red. Plain initials, 3- to 2-line, alternate red and blue. Red and blue 1-line initials alternate in table of contents. Majuscules stroked with yellow. Remains of notes for rubricator.

Binding: U. S. A., s. xx. Half-bound in red goatskin with gold-tooled title on spine ("Martinus Polonus/ Chronicon/ MS c. 1300") and marbled paper sides. By the same binder as Marston MS 152.

Written in Germany in the first half of the 14th century to judge from the script; early provenance unknown. Folio references added, s. xvi, to the table in art. 1 and the corresponding sermon numbers and folio references added in the upper margin on ff. 1–51 (14 and 24 *bis*); table of contents in French, s. xix, on f. iv verso. Purchased from E. P. Goldschmidt of London in 1957 by L. C. Witten (inv. no. 810), who sold it the same year to Thomas E. Marston (bookplate).

secundo folio: quicumque

Bibliography: Faye and Bond, p. 82, no. 156.

Marston MS 157 Northern France, s. XII$^{2/4}$
Augustine, Confessiones Pl. 38

ff. 1r–76v [cor]//dis mei ut uoluntati pateretur. nec ualerem que uolebam omnia. nec quibus uolebam omnibus; pensabam memoria cum ipsi appellabant rem aliquam ... ad te pulsetur. Sic sic accipietur. sic inuenietvr. sic aperietur. Amen. *Explicit tractatus sancti augustini de confessionibus. libri numero tredeci* [sic].

L. Verheijen, ed., CC ser. lat. 27 (1981) pp. 7–273. Text is defective: two leaves missing at beginning (text begins in I.8.13); one leaf missing between ff. 30–31 (VII.21.27–VIII.2.3; "... mentis sue. et se captiuum ducente // tot annos ore terricrepo..."); one leaf missing between ff. 53–54 (X.43.69–XI.3.5; "... Qui filio tuo unico non peper- // intus in domicilio cogitationis..."). Corrections made by scribe on ruled lines in outer and lower margins, and linked to the text with tie marks; extensive contemporary signs, added in lead, indicate problem areas in the text and corrections made to the text; "nota" signs in ink. The text has also been marked in the margins for readings at the beginning of several books. Running headlines added, s. xv.

Parchment (thick and furry, numerous imperfections, some repaired), ff. i (paper) + i (contemporary parchment) + i (modern parchment?) + 76 + i (paper), 302 x 210 (226 x 150) mm. 2 columns, 39 lines. Single vertical and horizontal bounding lines; additional horizontal ruling through center of page. Ruled in lead. Prickings in all margins, including inner.

I^8 (–1, 2), II–IV^8, V^8 (–1), VI–VII^8, VIII^8 (–1), IX–X^8. Quires signed with Roman numerals (e.g., i, ii, iii) in center of lower margin, verso.

Ten illuminated initials of good quality, 19- to 6-line, drawn in brown ink against medium blue, reddish orange and/or ochre grounds. The initials are constructed of scrolling vines with stylized foliage and/or winged dragons, with vines issuing from their mouths, accentuated or shaded in red. Some initials inhabited by winged dragons, f. 10v with grotesque (outlined by prickings), f. 25r with a nude male figure. Headings in red.

Binding: France, s. xix. Brown, diced calf with a gold-tooled spine and title: "Confescion/ Santti/ Augustini" and "Manuscrit/ du 12e siécle."

Written in the second quarter of the 12th century, probably in Northern France according to W. Cahn. The precise origin, however, is problematic. According to J. J. G. Alexander some features of the decoration, most notably the Anglo-Norman design of the initial *A* on f. 15r (cf. Pächt and Alexander, v. 3, no. 70), are similar to those from south English monastic houses such as Canterbury. From the library of Dr. Lucien-Graux (ca. 1878–1944; booklabel inside front cover; *Dictionnaire de Biographie Française*, v. 16, col. 1098). No. 4 in an unidentified French sale catalogue (description pasted to first flyleaf). Purchased from Lucien Scheler of Paris in 1957 by L. C. Witten (inv. no. 1580), who sold it the same year to Thomas E. Marston (bookplate).

Bibliography: Faye and Bond, p. 82, no. 157.

The Medieval Book, pp. 28–29, no. 29, with fig. of initial on f. 19v.

Marston MS 158 Northern Italy, s. XI/XII
Ambrose, Expositio Evangelii secundum Lucam Pl. 3

1. f. 1r *Decretum urbani pape.* Anno dominice incarnationis milesimo x. c. v.^{to}. Indictione iii. celebrata est placentie sinodus presidente domino urbano papa ... Tercium uero et quartum in septembri et decembri more solito Fiat.

Acts of the synod of Piacenza, March 1095 (Urban II), chs. 1–14; J. D. Mansi, ed., *Sacrorum conciliorum nova et amplissima collectio* ... (Venice, 1775) v. 20, cols. 804–06; C. J. Hefele and H. Leclercq, *Histoire des conciles* 5,1 (Paris, 1912) p. 388, n. 2.

2. ff. 1v–136v *In isto codice Sunt Sancti ambrosii expositi Sancti euagelii* [sic] *secundum lucam libri x. Scripturi in euangelii librum quem* lucas sanctus. pleniore quadam rerum dominicarum distinctione digessit. stilum ipsum prius exponendum putamus ... Nam quod tangitur corpus est. quod palpatur. corpus est. in corpore autem resurgimus. Seminatur enim corpus animale. surgit// quire signature: R

Ambrose, *Expositio Evangelii secundum Lucam*; M. Adriaen, ed., CC 14 (1957) pp. 1–400. The text breaks off at p. 394, line 1601, in the printed text and is therefore lacking the concluding 179 lines. The manuscript has been carefully corrected by several contemporary hands.

Parchment, ff. i (paper) + 136 + i (paper), 343 x 230 (255 x 163) mm. 2 columns, 35 lines. Double vertical bounding lines, with an additional ruling between columns. Three upper horizontal bounding lines; usually three, sometimes two, lower horizontal bounding lines. Ruled in hard point on hair side before folding. Prickings (small slashes) in upper, lower and outer margins.

I–XVII^{8}. Quire signatures (e.g., A, B, C, etc.) with symmetrically arranged dots and lines on four sides in center of lower margin, verso.

Numerous pen and ink initials of good quality, 8- to 3-line, drawn in red. The initials are constructed of thick vine stems, divided in half and swelling at the ends, issuing sprouts of intertwining stylized foliage. On f. 10v the letter *E* is formed from a bird and its extended wing; on ff. 75r and 103r the initials terminate in animal heads. The most important initials, ff. 1v, 13r, 36v, 62r, 75r, 114r, 115v and 119v, are touched with patches of ochre and summary modelling in the same color. The overall design owes its inspiration to Ottonian art, especially the style of St. Gall and Reichenau (see *Exhibition Catalogue*, p. 184, no. 10). Similar initials appear in Oxford, Bodleian Library, Canon. Pat. Lat. 227 (see Pächt and Alexander, vol. 2, no. 14) and Paris, B. N. lat. 4450 (see Avril and Zaluska, p. 66, no. 112, pls. XLV–XLVI), all assigned to Northern Italy and tentatively dated to the end of the eleventh or beginning of the twelfth century. On f. 1v the continuation capitals are filled in with red and ochre (cf. Abbey MS J. A. 7350 in *Abbey MSS*, pp. 3–6, no. 1, pls. I–IIa). Plain initials and headings in red. Remains of instructions to the rubricator along outer edge perpendicular to text (e.g., ff. 119v, 120v).

Binding: Italy, s. xix^{in}. Half bound in brown calf with bright pink paper sides that have been covered with tan paper; edges spattered blue-green. Two gold-tooled labels on spine, the first left blank and the lower one reading "Saecul XII." Bound in the same distinctive style as Marston MSS 50, 125, 128, 135, 151, 153, 159, and 197, also from the Cistercian abbey of Hautecombe (see provenance).

Written in Northern Italy at the end of the 11th or the beginning of the 12th century; the manuscript was owned by the Cistercian abbey of Hautecombe soon thereafter when its ex libris ("liber sancte marie altecumbe"), s. xii–xiii, was added in the lower margin of f. 136v, thus indicating that the manuscript was already incomplete at this early date. A second ex libris was added in the 15th century: "Liber sancte marie de alta comba." Marston MS 158 has the characteristic bright pink binding of the books of Monseigneur Hyacinthe della Torre who acquired and rebound a group of twelve manuscripts from Hautecombe at the beginning of the 19th century (see Leclercq, 1951, p. 75). Belonged to the Biblioteca del Seminario Metropolitano in Turin (Leclercq, 1961, p. 183). Purchased from Arthur Rau of Paris in 1957 by L. C. Witten (inv. no. 1447), who sold it the same year to Thomas E. Marston (bookplate).

secundo folio: edidit

Bibliography: Faye and Bond, p. 82, no. 158.
Exhibition Catalogue, p. 184, no. 10.

Marston MS 159 — Hautecombe [?], s. XII^{med}

Gregory the Great, Homeliae in Hiezechielem prophetam

ff. 1r–105v [Preface:] [Dilectissimo fratri] martino episcopo. Gregorius episcope [?]. seruus seruorum dei. Homelias que in beato ezechiele propheta. ita ut coram populo loquebar excepte sunt . . . epulas auidius redeatur. [text, f. 1r:] [Dei omnipotentis] adspiracione. de ezechiele propheta locuturus. Prius debeo tempora et modos aperire prophecie ... qui necdum a malo declinauit? Et sunt quidam qui sicut dictum est ab alimentis abstinent.//

M. Adriaen, ed., CC ser. lat. 142 (1971) pp. 3–308 (l. 453); Marston MS 159 listed on p. xviii. The manuscript ends imperfectly in Book II, *Homilia* 6, and contains the following irregularities. The third quire, originally of eight leaves, is defective, with leaves 2 and 3 missing after f. 17 (Book I, *Homilia* 5.2–12: "... ad largitatem misericordie ad inte- // -diens suauitatis dei memoria pascitur...."); in addition, leaves have been misplaced, presumably in rebinding, so that the text must now be read: ff. 17 (–2 leaves), 20, 21, 18, 19, 22. Also, a portion of the text has been omitted on f. 79r (Book II, *Homilia* 2.3–4: "... de his [added in margin:] ad que rapta est extollatur // patriam reuiuescant. uerba uite audire...").

Parchment (poor quality: thick, holes, ends, repairs), ff. ii (paper) + 105 + ii (paper), 300 x 220 mm., greatly trimmed. Size of written space and format of leaves vary considerably, but most leaves ruled in hard point with single vertical and sometimes single horizontal bounding lines. Remains of prickings in lower margins.

I–II^{8}, III^{8} (misbound; 2 leaves missing; see text above), IV–X^{8}, XI^{4}, XII^{6}, XIII^{10} (–10). Quires signed i–vii only, center of lower margin, recto, first leaf of gathering.

Written by multiple scribes in spiky early gothic bookhand.

Spaces left unfilled, f. 1r, for initials and headings at beginning of prologue and text. Decorative monochrome initials and headings, which extend the width of columns, of modest quality, in red (many oxidized). Minor initials, 5- to 2-line, some with simple penwork designs, headings, initial strokes in red.

Many leaves damaged along outer edges, now repaired, but with loss of text; stained throughout.

Binding: Italy, s. xix^{in}. Half bound in mottled brown calf with bright pink paper sides. Two gold-tooled, brick red labels on spine: "Greg. Pape. in Ezechiel." and "Saecul. XIII." Red edges. Bound in the same distinctive style as Marston MSS 50, 125, 128, 135, 151, 153, 158, 197, also from the Cistercian abbey of Hautecombe (see provenance).

Written in the middle of the 12th century, perhaps at the Cistercian abbey of Hautecombe to which it belonged; early ex libris visible under ultraviolet light in lower margin, f. 105v: ":liber sancte marie altecumbe:". Located in the ancient diocese of Geneva, the abbey was founded toward the beginning of the 12th century by monks from the abbey of Aulps (see

R. Clair, "Les origines de l'abbaye d'Hautecombe," *Mélanges à la mémoire du Père Anselme Dimier* [Arbois, 1982–87] tome II, v. 4, pp. 615–27). Marston MS 159 has the characteristic bright pink binding of the books of Monseigneur Hyacinthe della Torre who acquired and rebound a group of twelve manuscripts from this monastery at the beginning of the 19th century (see Leclercq, 1951, p. 75). Belonged to the Biblioteca del Seminario Metropolitano in Turin (Leclercq, *op. cit.*, p. 76, no. 16). Acquired from C. A. Stonehill in 1957 by Thomas E. Marston (bookplate).

secundo folio: [somp]nium. A sompnio

Bibliography: Faye and Bond, p. 82, no. 159.

Marston MS 160 — Central [?] Italy, s. XV$^{3/4}$

John Chrysostom, Sermo de dignitate humanae originis, Lat. tr. Ambrogio Traversari

ff. 1r–51v [Letter:] *Incipit tractatus gloriosissimi doctoris sanctissimique uiri Iohannis os auri Ad Stagirium sanctissimum monacum singularissimum eius amicum arreptum a demone. de remedio omnis mestitie diuisus in tres libros. In primis incipit epistola famosissimi uiri religiosi fratris anbrosij* [sic] *de florentia generalis ordinis camaldulensis. Ad excellentissimum principem Rainerium regem. Secundo idus octubris. Sunt quidem plurima que in te laudari merito possint princeps inclite* ... [text, f. 2r:] *Incipit liber primus supradicti sanctissimi uiri Iohannis crisostomi ad predictum stagirum monacum correptum a demone super id consolatorius.* Oportuerat quidem o mi amantissime omnium stagiri fueratque sane ... Nobis autem confusio satis et regibus nostris et patribus nostris quia peccauimus tibi domine// f. 52r-v ruled, but blank except for title written on f. 52r in a later hand (same hand wrote title on spine) and the offset impression of a seal or a pilgrim's badge on the verso

The text is preceded by a dedicatory letter, here directed to René d'Anjou (King of Sicily and Naples, 1435–42); in other manuscripts and early printed books it is directed either to Pietro, duke of Coimbra, or to the Emperor Sigismund. Printed in Alost, 1487, and thereafter. Guides to subject matter of text appear in the outer margins of the manuscript, preceded by paragraph marks in red.

Parchment, ff. 51 + i (contemporary parchment, f. 52), 194 x 105 (135 x 65) mm. 34 long lines. Single vertical bounding lines, full length (Derolez 13.11), ruled in hard point on hair side; guide lines for text in pale brown ink. Prickings in upper and lower margins, with a single pricking in outer margin, 2 mm. above top line.

I^{10}, II–V^{8}, VI^{10} (–10). Horizontal catchwords in lower margin, left of inner vertical bounding line (Derolez 12.2). Quire and leaf signatures (e.g., b.1, b.2, etc.) in lower right corner, recto.

Written by a single scribe in humanistic cursive script, below top line.

3 large initials of modest quality, 8- to 7-line, gold on blue or blue and red grounds with white dots and white vine-stem ornament. 1 smaller initial, 3-line, gold on red and blue ground with white dots. Plain initials in blue and red, one in gold, some with penwork flourishes in red. Rubrics throughout. Paragraph marks in red or blue. Guide letters for initials.

Binding: Italy, s. xv. Original sewing on three tawed skin, slit straps laced through tunnels in the edge to channels on the outside of beech boards and nailed. Beige and white chevron endbands are sewn on tawed skin cores laid in grooves on the outside of the boards. The spine is lined with green tawed skin between supports.

Covered in brown, originally tan, calf with corner tongues, blind-tooled with a triple cross in a border of rope interlace. Spine: sewing bands defined and panels diapered with triple fillets. Two truncated diamond catches with a flower in a circle on the lower board, the upper one cut in for the red fabric straps attached with star-headed nails.

Written in Central [?] Italy in the third quarter of the 15th century according to A. C. de la Mare. Unidentified shelf mark on f. 52r "I. [?] s. O. 2." "T. B. N" in pencil on front pastedown; "J" enclosed by a circle, in pencil, in upper margin of f. 1r. On inside of back cover, in pencil: "M-EO-21/ Sl [?] EHS." Purchased from Giuseppe (Joseph) Martini of Lugano by H. P. Kraus, who sold it in 1957 to Thomas E. Marston (bookplate).

secundo folio: Inherebit memorie

Bibliography: Faye and Bond, p. 82, no. 160.

Marston MS 161 — Northeastern Italy, ca. 1493–97

Quintus Aemilianus Cimbriacus, Carmina

1. f. 1r ruled, but blank; f. 1v *Cimbriacus poe. ad suum libel.* Dum tantum properas exire ingrate libelle/ Teque putas doctis posse placere viris/ ... Quod si nos audis: patriarche tecta subito:/ Illic: aut nusquam: tutior esse potes. Finis [with the illuminated arms of Niccolò Donati occupying lower half of page].

The author, Quintus Aemilianus Cimbriacus (1449–1499) of Vicenza, speaking to his book of poetry, 6 lines; for information about the life and works of Emiliano Cimbriaco see A. Benedetti, *L'attività educativa e poetica del Cimbriaco (1449–1499) e la sua influenza nel diffondersi della cultura umanistica in Friuli* (Udine, 1963); this text published on p. 90.

2. f. 2r–v Quintii Haemyliani Cimbriaci poe. ac comitis pal. ode dicolos tetrastrophos ad Nic. Don. Aq. Patr. Encomiasticos. Antistes fidei nobilis arbiter/ Qui sic ab venetis ducis originem:/ ... Cum possim melius perdere tempora/ Et qui non redeunt dies. Finis.

   28-line encomium dedicated to Niccolò Donati, Patriarch of Aquileia, 1493–97 (see also the encomium in art. 5); Benedetti, *op. cit.*, pp. 90–91.

3. ff. 2v–4v *De Vet. Aq. Claritud. Q. Haemyl. Cimbr. Poe. Et. Com. Pal. Rhapsodiarum liber III ad Nic. Don. Aq. Patr.* Presul honorate blandissima gloria gentis./ Et uere antique fama suprema domus/ ... Teque colant gentes: cineresque uel ossa recondant:/ Vnde sibi querat credulus eger opem./ Finis.

   Rhapsodia I, 78 lines; Benedetti, *op. cit.*, pp. 91–93.

4. ff. 5r–7r *Rhapsodia Secunda De Aq. Diocesi.* Anne tibi gratum fiat si carmine fabor/ Antistes solio debita iura tuo/ ... Cui sic castalius lucus: blanditur et antrum/ Dirceusque liquor coryciusque furor./ Finis.

   Rhapsodia II, 92 lines.

5. ff. 7v–9r *Rhapsodia III Encomiasticos.* Cum te multiplici certatim munere honorent:/ Et variis studeat quisque placere modis:/ ... Ni subeant uotis contraria fata secundis:/ Aut mea pierius deserat ora calor./ Finis.

   Rhapsodia III, 74 lines; see art. 2 above.

6. ff. 9v–11r *Rhapsodia. IIII. De Conceptione Virginis.* Qui mariam ueterum maculam traxisse parentum/ Credidit ah nimium credulus ille fuit./ ... Angelicosque choros: solio uel proxima nati/ Aspectu frueris liberiore dei./ Finis.

   Rhapsodia IV, 68 lines.

7. ff. 11r–12v *Rhapsodia .V. de Annuntiatione. Virg.* Sic iubet antistes celebrator uirginis inquam/ Preterite noctis conscius esto procul/ ... Ergo qum [*sic*] nouies sibi luna relegerit ignes:/ Mater eris salua uirginitate dei. Finis.

Rhapsodia V, 56 lines, with 12 lines erased at end.

8. ff. 13r–15r [Most of rubric erased and illegible.] *[M]ysteriis [chris]tianis.* Si quis forte petat: quanto sit honore sacerdos:/ Et quantum in nostra relligione [*sic*] decuș./ . . . Vnde sacerdotes summos fateamur honores:/ Et uerum nostra [?] secula habere deum.

   De mysteriis christianis, 90 lines; f. 15r badly rubbed.

9. f. 15v *Cimbr. Poe. Hendecasyl. Epos ad Angelum Padavinum.* Si tantum datur otium padaui:/ Vt possis et ineptiis vacare/ . . . Tam casti domini pudens minister/ Quicquid calfacit ignibus medullas./ Finis.

   17-line poem to Angelus Padavinus (see also art. 10).

10. f. 16r *Ad Eundem.* Pierii cultor nemoris facunde padaui:/ Qui potes orpheam sollicitare lyram:/ . . . Quod sperare licet: meritis si premia dentur/ Aequa: nec ignauum qualia uulgus amat./ Finis. f. 16v ruled, but blank

    12-line poem to Angelus Padavinus (see also art. 9).

Parchment, ff. 16, 190 x 134 (114 x 81) mm. 21 long lines. Double and single vertical bounding lines ruled in hard point or lead; text rulings in ink. Prickings in upper and lower margins.

I–IV^4. Remains of quire and leaf signatures (e.g., A. ii, C. i, etc.).

Written in a well-formed upright humanistic bookhand.

Half-page coat of arms (argent [oxidized], a chief with 3 roses gules above 2 bars gules; crest: bishop's mitre surmounted by gold cross) enclosed by a wreath with flowers and fruit and four ribbons, f. 1v. Plain gold majuscules outlined in black, 4- to 2-line, mark beginning of arts. 2–8; headings for each poem in black epigraphic square capitals.

Binding: Italy, date? Tacketed to a limp vellum wrapper made from a parchment document: Agostino Barbarigo, doge of Venice (1486–1501), writes on behalf of the secretary Joannes B[remainder of name missing due to hole in parchment], dated Venice, 5 May 14[8?]8. Filing notes on upper cover. Title in majuscules on upper cover: "Quintii Haemiliani Cimbriaci Vti [for Vincentinus?]."

Written in Northeastern Italy between 1493 and 1497 when Niccolò Donati was Patriarch of Aquileia; perhaps the poet's dedication copy to Donati, since the latter's arms appear on f. 1v. The inscription on upper cover, s. xvi^1, "Domini Palladij" [followed by illegible word or abbreviation], which also occurs on the cover of Marston MS 188, suggests that Marston MS 161 may be the manuscript owned by Alexandrus Palladius of

Udine (as noted by Benedetti, *op. cit.*, p. 97). Unidentified handwritten notes of a French bookdealer in library files. Purchased from Nicolas Rauch of Geneva in 1958 by L. C. Witten (inv. no. 2088), who sold it the same year to Thomas E. Marston (bookplate).

secundo folio: Quintii

Bibliography: Faye and Bond, p. 82, no. 161.

Marston MS 162 Northern Italy, s. XV^2
Albertus Magnus, Ethica

1. ff. 1r–4v *De litteris incipientibus ab a.* De titulo et auctore libro primo tractatu primo capitulo vij^o./ Quod omnis actus quoddam bonum appetere uidetur. libro 1. tractatu 3. capitulo iiij^{to}/ ... Quod talis vita preciosissima [?] est et nobilissima. libro x. tractatu .j. capitulo iij. et cetera.

   Alphabetical subject index to art. 2.

2. ff. 5r–215r *Incipit ethica fratris Alberti cuius primus tractatus est de communibus quae oportet sciri ante scientiam capitulum primum de nobilitate huius scientie.* Cum omnis scientia sit de numero bonorum et honorabilium tamen quando comperatur ad alteram una alia melior est et honorabilior ... et quibus legibus et quibus consuetudinibus sit utendum. Ad hoc ergo aliud principium facientes dicamus incipientes. *Explicit liber ethicorum compilatus a fratre alberto theutonico de ordine fratrum predicatorum.* f. 215v ruled, but blank

   S. Borgnet, ed., *B. Alberti Magni ... opera omnia*, v. 7 (Paris, 1891) pp. 1-641.

Paper (watermarks: similar in design to Piccard Armbrust XI.2234, and unidentified cardinal's hat), ff. i (paper) + 215 + ii (paper), 333 x 230 (218 x 147) mm. 2 columns, 50 lines. Single vertical bounding lines; ruled in ink. Single prickings in outer margin near lower right corner of written space and in upper and lower margins near gutter.

I^4, II-XI^{10}, XII^{10} (-10, with note on f. 113v "hic nichil deficit"), XIII-XV^{10}, XVI^{14}, XVII-XXI^{10}, XXII^{10} (-9, 10). Vertical catchwords along inner bounding line, f. 14v; horizontal catchwords along lower edge (trimmed), verso. Remains of quire and leaf signatures (e.g., a 2, etc.), lower edge, recto.

Written by multiple scribes in small gothic bookhand with varying degrees of humanistic influence.

One illuminated initial, 9-line, and border decoration, on f. 5r: blue with yellow highlights on gold ground edged in black; interior and exterior leaf designs in pink and blue on green ground with yellow highlights; gold balls and penwork designs in inner margin. In lower margin, foliage and gold balls support and surround coat of arms in pen and ink (incomplete and later addition?). For major text divisions, blue initials, 8- to 6-line, with tightly executed penwork designs in red and/or blue; numerous flourished initials, blue with red alternate red with purple, most with harping. Headings in red preceded by paragraph marks in blue. Paragraph marks in art. 1 alternate red and blue.

Binding: Northern Italy or Austria, s. xvi [?]. Sewn on five supports attached to wooden boards. Yellow edges. The beaded endbands are sewn on tawed skin, slit straps.

Covered in brown sheepskin blind-tooled with concentric frames, the central panel divided in three; the upper and lower sections filled with a leafy staff design; a circular ornament in the central section. Spine: multiple fillets at head and tail; supports defined; leafy staff or fleurons in panels. Faint traces of four catches on upper board, the lower one cut in for fabric straps which are attached with star-headed nails. Entire binding is heavily restored.

Written in Northern Italy in the second half of the 15th century and then bound in either Northern Italy or Austria, probably in the 16th century. Provenance unknown. Purchased from Libreria Mediolanum of Milan (Dr. E. Pozzi) in 1957 by L. C. Witten (inv. no. 1701), who sold it in 1958 to Thomas E. Marston (bookplate).

secundo folio: [index, f. 2:] libro
[text, f. 6:] est quoddam

Bibliography: Faye and Bond, p. 82, no. 162.

Marston MS 163 — Northern Italy, s. $XV^{3/4}$
St. Antoninus, Summa moralis

1. ff. Ir-IIr [Preface:] *Incipit prohemium super presenti opere.* Quam magnificata sunt opera tua domine omnia in sapientia fecisti impleta est terra . . . [Ps. 91.6]. Contemplatus propheta in excelsu mentis positus diuinam maiestatem . . . frequenter non curaui nominare.

 Preface to St. Antoninus of Florence, *Summa moralis*; Bloomfield, *Virtues and Vices*, no. 4355; see also art. 3.

2. ff. IIv–Vr *Incipit tabula super prima parte presentis operis que est de peccatis in genere contentiua titulorum. Capitulorum. et cet.* Prima pars presentis operis habet titulos quattuor. Primus est de legibus qui habet Capitula octo. 1. De diffinicione legis et de lege eterna/ 2. De lege naturali./ ... 6. *De decimis. Tabula super secunda parte que est de peccatis in specie.* Secunda pars presentis operis habet titulos duodicim [*sic*]. Primus est de auaricia qui habet capitula 23. 1. De symonia/ 2. De usuris./ ... De mercatoribus et alijs artificibus. [f. IIIr:] *Tertia tabula super parte. que est de statibus hominum.* Tercia pars huius operis que est de quibusdam statibus hominum habet titulos xij. Primus de coniugatis qui habet capitula. x. 1. De ipso matrimonio quo ad eius diffinicionem./ ... De summo pontifice siue de papa. [f. IVr:] *Tabula quarta super parte. que est de censuris.* Quarta pars presentis operis. que est de censuris./ ... Sextus titulus est de peccatis in genere. qui tantum habet vnum capitulum. Explicit tabula super toto opere. f. V verso ruled, but blank

Four tables, the first two of which have folio references to art. 3 added by a contemporary hand. Tables III and IV may refer to a second volume, never completed or now missing.

3. ff. 1r–250r *Incipit prima pars presentis operis intitulata de peccatis in generali. Rubrica. titulus primus de legibus.* Quia peccatum est debitum uel factum uel concupitum contra legem eternum. et ambrosius dicit quod peccatum est transgressio legis diuine ... Et sic est finis prime partis. [f. 56r:] *Incipit secunda pars. titulus primus. Sermo predicabilis de symonia editus a uenerabili patre fratre Antonio de florentia.* Deus deorum dominus locutus est. et uocauit eram. Ps. deus deorum dominus. est uerus deus qui est dominus sanctorum ... [f. 249r:] ut bestialiter uiuentes aliquando etiam bestialiter moriantur. Et sic est finis huius secunde partis. [colophon:] *Explicit secunda pars presentis operis per me Iohannem ardellum de stauolis Laudetur deus.* [followed by a passage omitted from f. 155v] ff. 250v–251v ruled, but blank

St. Antoninus of Florence, *Summa moralis* (extracts on sins, virtues and vices arranged thematically, e.g., in *Pars secunda, titulus primus*: De symonia, De usuris, De uariis [for *denariis*] montis florencie, De rapina, De furto ... De inhumanitate, De auaricia mentis, De prodigalitate); Kaeppeli, SOPMA, v. 1, no. 239 (listed as "New Haven, Yale Univ. Libr., Reinecke [*sic*] Libr., Marston 163 [xv]: compendium part. I [?]").

Paper (watermarks, buried in tight binding: unidentified flower), ff. 256 (first five leaves: modern foliation, I–V; art. 3: contemporary foliation 1–250; f. 251 unfoliated) + 28 (modern paper; see binding below), 233 x 165

(189 x 110) mm. 2 columns, 48 lines. Single vertical bounding lines, ruled in lead; text rulings drawn faintly in ink (Derolez 13.41). Single pricking in outer margin, 44–46 mm. below top line.

I-XXV^{10} (ff. I-V, 1-245), XXVI^{6} [?]. Horizontal catchwords, some in upright humanistic script, in lower margin under second column, for quires I-XVII; remaining quires have vertical catchwords, with dots and flourishes, along inner bounding line.

Written by multiple scribes in small informal styles of gothic bookhand with humanistic features, below top line.

Decorative initials, 9- to 5-line, for main text divisions, blue with red penwork designs (red much faded); headings, initials (5- to 3-line), paragraph marks in bright red; initial strokes in yellow.

Binding: Northern Italy, s. xvii–xviii. Resewn and bound in alum tawed pigskin, blind-tooled. Lower board cut in for the strap. The boards and cover are probably early (s. xv) and reworked and reshaped to fit the text block, given the large number of later blank leaves inserted at end of text and the way the text block appears to have been trimmed at the tail and the new endbands added. In addition, the title written twice, s. xv, on upper cover ("Rationale diuinorum offitiorum" of Guilielmus Durandus) does not correspond to the present text. Title, written in ink, on a square paper label on spine mutilated and largely illegible. Strip of liturgical manuscript with musical notation, s. xv?, used as spine lining.

Written in Northern Italy in the third quarter of the 15th century probably as the first of a two-volume set (see art. 2); signed by the scribe, Johannes Ardellus de Stavolis (colophon, art. 3), who remains unidentified. Contemporary inscription in upper margin of f. 1r reveals that the manuscript was given by Benignus of Genoa for the use of Sanctus of Milan at the convent of Santa Maria Incoronata in Milan: "Sancte Marie Incoronate Mediolani ad usum fratris Sancti de Mediolano, frater B[enignus] de I[anua] V[icarius] G[eneralis]." (We thank M. Ferrari for her assistance with this early provenance.) Benignus de Ianua, as Vicar General OESA Lom., was in Milan in 1471 (see document edited by M. L. Gatti Perer, "Umanesimo a Milano: L'osservanza agostiniana all'Incoronata," *Arte Lombarda* N. S. 53–54 [1980] pp. 106, 166); other manuscripts given *ad usum* by him include Milan, Biblioteca Ambrosiana G 35 sup., H 19 sup., M 39 sup., and Cremona, Gov. 182 (see M. Ferrari, "Un bibliotecaio milanese del Quattrocento," *Ricerche storiche sulla Chiesa Ambrosiana* 10 [1981] p. 243). Two documents list Frater Sanctus de Mediolano among the chapter members in the convent of Santa Maria Incoronata in 1471 and 1474 (Gatti Perer, *op. cit.*, pp. 166, 173). Belonged to the Franciscan convent at Bolzano in the Italian Alps where it was presumably rebound

(s. xvii–xviii; see binding description); bookplate of the convent pasted inside front cover; oval paper label on spine: "Z/ 210/ (1494)." Unidentified notes on front pastedown include: "Q-G. 86" (inscription contemporary with binding?) in ink; "Br 18/10/39 W. V." in pencil; "No 26" in pencil. Unidentified description, in English, from sale catalogue (lot 431) pasted inside front cover. Purchased in 1958 from C. A. Stonehill (inv. no. 21582) by Thomas E. Marston (bookplate).

secundo folio: omnia doctores

Bibliography: Faye and Bond, p. 82, no. 163.

Marston MS 164 — Northern Italy or Switzerland [?], s. XV^2
Aristotle, Ethica Nicomachea, Lat. tr. Leonardo Bruni

ff. 1r–98r [O]mnis ars omnisque doctrina similiter autem et actus et electio bonum quoddam appetere videtur. Qua propter bene ostenderunt summum bonum quod omnia appetunt . . . si quomodo vnaqueque res publica constituta sit. et quibus legibus et moribus. deo gracias. amen. expliciunt X. libri ethicorum. ff. 98v–101v ruled, but blank; unidentified quotations in a contemporary hand on front and back pastedowns

Latin translation of Aristotle's *Ethica Nicomachea* by Leonardo Bruni (GKW, v. 2, nos. 2367–80), but lacking Bruni's prefatory and concluding remarks (Baron, pp. 75–81); the manuscript text is divided into ten books, not always distinguished by scribe or rubricator, but sometimes indicated by running headlines; extensive marginalia and interlinear glosses in at least two hands. There are often references to the commentary of St. Thomas Aquinas (e.g., ff. 93v–94r) and to Boethius, *De consolatione philosophiae* (e.g., f. 95v). A comparison of this manuscript with the text printed by Johann Mentelin in Strassburg ca. 1469 indicates two major irregularities in the manuscript, probably as a result of copying from a defective exemplar. On f. 1v (col. 1, line 4) a block of text, which belongs on f. 3r, has been misplaced and inserted between syllables of the word "diui//nus"; the error has been noted by contemporary symbols in the margins. On f. 39r ca. 40 lines of text are omitted (line 15: " . . . Tres igitur supradicte mediocritates sunt omnes // et potenciis et habitibus. nam potencia. . ."); the missing passage was copied into the margins of ff. 40v–41r and keyed to the text on f. 40v. For a discussion of this translation see E. Franceschini, "Leonardo Bruni e il 'Vetus Interpres' dell'Etica a Nicomaco," *Medioevo e Rinascimento: Studi in onore di Bruno Nardi* (Florence, 1955) v. 1, pp. 299–319.

Paper (sized; watermarks: quires I–III similar in design to Briquet Anneau 689; remainder of manuscript, including end leaves, similar in type to Piccard Ochsenkopf I.341–55 and Briquet Tête de boeuf 14335), ff. ii (contemporary paper; i = pastedown; ii = flyleaf) + 101 (101 = back pastedown), 302 x 220 (218 x 140) mm. Format varies throughout: ff. 1-36, 2 columns, 27 lines; ff. 37–98, ca. 22–30 long lines. Ruled either in hard point or crudely in lead; some leaves frame-ruled. Remains of prickings in upper, lower, and outer margins.

I-VI^{12}, VII^{12} (-12, no loss of text), VIII^{14}, IX^{4} (= ff. 98–101 + rear pastedown). Remains of quire and leaf signatures in lower right corner, recto (e.g., a1, a2, etc.). Catchwords for each leaf, quires I–III, below written space, verso; some erased.

Written in various styles of informal gothic bookhand by multiple scribes and annotators.

Plain 3- to 1-line letters, of poor quality, headings, and paragraph marks, in red, sporadically throughout.

The ink on many leaves has seeped through to the other side, thus rendering portions of text illegible.

Binding: Spain, s. xv. Endleaves and pastedowns sewn with book. On rear pastedown an undeciphered Hebrew [?] inscription. Sewn on four double, twisted, tawed skin supports laced into grooves in wooden boards and wedged. The spine is lined with coarse cloth between supports (Moorish influence). A strip of parchment extends inside the boards under the pastedowns. Green and gold, five core [?] endbands are sewn on tawed skin cores laced into the boards and pegged.

Covered in blue tawed skin with two fastenings, the catches on the lower board.

Produced in the second half of the 15th century, perhaps in Northern Italy or Switzerland. The precise origin of the manuscript is problematic. The watermarks, style of decorative initials and scripts suggest an area under German, Italian and French influence. The binding, however, indicates an early Spanish provenance. The manuscript can probably be identified with a volume formerly in the Library of the Santa Iglesia del Pilar and Biblioteca del Cabildo (no. 19.88) in Saragossa. (Cf. also binding description for Marston MS 265 which definitely came from Saragossa.) Purchased from Enzo Ferrajoli through Nicolas Rauch of Geneva in 1958 by L. C. Witten (inv. no. 2012), who sold it the same year to Thomas E. Marston (bookplate).

secundo folio: [diui]nius

Bibliography: Faye and Bond, p. 82, no. 164.

Marston MS 166 Northern Italy, s. XII/XIII
Augustine, De doctrina christiana, etc.

1. f. 1r [Heading, added s. xv–xvi:] Retractatio Beatissimi Augustini In libros De doctrina christiana. [text:] Libros de doctrina christiana cum imperfecos [*sic*] comperissem. perficere malui. quam eis ... quem de sacramentis siue de philosophia scripsit. Hoc opus sic incipit. Sunt precepta quedam.

   Augustine, *Rectractatio XXV*; A. Mutzenbecher, ed., CC ser. lat. 57 (1984) pp. 92–93.

2. ff. 1r–67r [Heading, added s. xv–xvi:] De Doctrina christiana liber eiusdem Incipit. [prologue:] Sunt precepta quedam tractandarum scripturarum. que studiosis earum uideo non incommode posse tradi ... tale nobis occurrit exordium. [text, f. 3v:] Due sunt res quibus nititur omnis tractatio scripturarum. Modus inueniendi que intellegenda sunt ... sed aliis etiam laborare studet. quantulacumque potui faccultate disseruj. [added later:] Omnis uirtutes ipsa primis inuenies si adeo me.

   Augustine, *De doctrina christiana*; J. Martin, ed., CC ser. lat. 32 (1962) pp. 1–167. The text on f. 67r written in a later hand, s. xiv.

3. f. 67v Aristoteles V topica. [brief quote from Aristotle, *Topica* 5.129, *Translatio Vetus*; followed by list of 8 pairs of friends:] Achilles/ Patroclus ... Scipio/Lelius.

4. Rear pastedown: two brief quotations from Ecclesiasticus 4.31 and 5.8.

Parchment (speckled), ff. ii (i = pastedown, ii = flyleaf) + 67 + ii (i = flyleaf, ii = pastedown), 162 x 106 (122 x 68) mm. 30 long lines. Double vertical bounding lines, full length and single or double horizontal bounding lines. Rulings for text often extend through gutter. Ruled in hard point on hair side. Prickings in upper, lower, and outer margins.

I–VIII^{8}, IX^{4} (–3). Horizontal catchwords enclosed by rectangle in lower margin, verso (later additions, s. xiv). Original quire signature (V) on f. 40v.

Written in late caroline minuscule.

Plain initials with foliage motifs, in red, 6- to 5-line, on ff. 1r, 13r; initial, 5-line, red and deep purple, f. 31r; similar initial in deep purple and black, f. 45v. Allegorical diagram of the cross, in outer margin, f. 31r: "altitudo, latitudo, longitudo, profundum."

Binding: Italy, s. xv. Original wound sewing on three tawed skin, slit straps laid in channels on the outside of wooden boards and pegged. A three-core, red and green secondary endband is sewn on a core of twisted, tawed skin laid in a groove and pegged.

Covered in brown calf with corner tongues and blind-tooled with a concentric frame pattern alternating multiple fillets, the Visconti serpent device (*piccola biscia*) in a square on its point, and two different dotted ribbon tools. For the *biscia* device see De Marinis, *La legatura*, v. 3, pl. CCCCXXV. Annular dots in blank areas, possibly originally gilt. This binding discussed and illustrated in A. Hobson, *Humanists and Bookbinders: The Origins and Diffusion of the Humanistic Bookbinding 1459–1559 ...* (Cambridge, 1989) p. 13, pl. 8.

Written in Northern Italy at the end of the 12th or beginning of the 13th century; brief notes by several Italian hands, s. xiv–xv. Belonged to the Visconti family of Milan for whom it was bound in the first half of the 15th century (see binding above); the manuscript can probably be identified as no. 511 in the 1426 Pavia inventory (E. Pellegrin, *La Bibliothèque des Visconti et des Sforza ducs de Milan au XVe siècle* [Paris, 1955] p. 187). Unidentified signature, s. xv, along lower edge, verso, of rear flyleaf: "Geruasius" or "Çeruasius." Purchased from H. P. Kraus in 1957 by L. C. Witten (inv. no. 1540), who sold it in 1958 to Thomas E. Marston (bookplate).

secundo folio: possum

Bibliography: Faye and Bond, p. 83, no. 166.

Marston MS 167 Northwestern Italy, 1443
Aulus Gellius, Noctes Atticae (abridged) Pl. 30

1. f. 1r blank; f. 1v 12-line note (s. xvii), in Italian, giving a list of bibliographical citations

2. ff. 2r–61v *Super enthimemate T. C. de debitione pecunie et gratie*. Antonius Julianus rhetor per quam fuit honesti atque ameni ingenij doctrina quoque ... eo titulos quoque ad eam sententiam exquisitissimos indiderunt. τελος. [colophon, enclosed by red design:] Explicit A. Gelii Breviator [Greek phrase added, s. xvi?, over an erasure that is partially visible under ultra-violet light: Porcelli***verius] XVI. Kl. Ianua. M. CCCC. XLIII. [final line written in cipher that can be transcribed as:] Iohannes de sangans scripsit. f. 62r title at top of page: Auli gelij Abbreuiator; f. 62v blank

For the complete text of Aulus Gellius see P. K. Marshall, ed., OCT

(1968) 2 vols. The abridged text in this manuscript appears in the following order: Books I–V, VII, VI, IX–XX, Preface; the following chapters are omitted: I.1–3, 8; II.8, 23, 28, 30; III.1, 5, 7, 10, 13, 17; IV.3, 8, 10, 14; V.1, 3, 5, 10, 11, 13, 15–17; VI.3, 5, 16–19; VII.1–2, 9, 10, 13–16; IX.6, 15–16; X.3, 6, 13, 15, 19, 20, 22; XI.3–5, 10; XII.2, 4-5, 7, 15; XIII.4, 15, 18–19, 24, 26, 28; XIV.1–2, 5–6, 8; XV.2, 14, 19, 22–23, 26–27; XVI.3, 18–19; XVII. 3–7, 11–15, 20; XVIII. 8; XIX.3, 6, 10, 11; XX.2–5, 10.

The author of the abridgement has deleted all passages containing Greek; in addition, he has compressed, revised, and paraphrased large portions of the text. The name of the abbreviator has been erased from the colophon (art. 2).

Parchment (palimpsest throughout, primarily from documents that had been folded), i (paper) + i (parchment) + 62 + i (parchment) + i (paper), 240 x 156 (154 x 98) mm. 27 long lines. Ruled in hard point on flesh side one bifolium at a time; double vertical and single horizontal bounding lines (Derolez 13.33). Prickings prominent in upper, lower and outer margins.

I–VI^{10} (+ 2 leaves at end?, ff. 61–62). Horizontal catchwords in lower margin near gutter (Derolez 12.4).

Written by a single scribe in formal humanistic script, above top line, with first word or phrase of each section in majuscules.

Plain initials, 4- to 2-line, alternate red and blue (guide letters remain). Headings in red throughout.

Binding: England, s. xix. Brown calf blind-tooled with gold-tooled title on the spine. Gilt edges. Discoloration from turn-ins and fastenings [?] on first and last parchment leaves. Bound by Charles Lewis (London, 1807–36).

Written in Northwestern Italy in 1443 by the scribe Iohannes de Sangans whose name appears in code in the colophon and who also copied Florence, Biblioteca Marucelliana MS. B. V. 9 (signed and dated 1464); early modern provenance unknown. Belonged to the Rev. Henry Drury (1778–1841); his sale (Evans, 1827; information not verified). According to his note on f. i recto the manuscript was bound for him by C. Lewis. From the collection of Sir Thomas Phillipps (no. 3368; tag on spine and note in pencil on front pastedown). Acquired from L. C. Witten in 1958 by Thomas E. Marston (bookplate).

secundo folio: Reprehenditur

Bibliography: Faye and Bond, p. 83, no. 167.

Marston MS 168 Northern Italy, s. XV^{med}
Gasparino Barzizza, Commentarii in epistolas Senecae

ff. 1r–338r Avisti [*sic*] heri nobiscum et cet. hec est 65a epistola que sic potest ad precedentem epistolam continuari. Postquam superius nactus occasionem . . . honestissimis actibus et pulcherrimis sapientissimorum hominum. Sed ante omnes huius amplissimi et sanctissimi viri Senece fluxit. etc. Expliciunt commentarij Gasparini pergamensis in epistolas senece etc. ff. 338v–340v blank

Gasparino Barzizza, Commentary on *Epistolae morales ad Lucilium*, 65–124 only; f. 272v (in Epistle 115) blank with note "uacat." Marston MS 168 not discussed in L. A. Panizza, "Gasparino Barzizza's Commentaries on Seneca's Letters," *Traditio* 33 (1977) pp. 297–358.

Paper (polished; watermarks: similar to Briquet Tour 15909 and Piccard Turm II.617), ff. ii (contemporary paper; watermarks: Briquet Lettre T 9120) + 340 + ii (same paper as front flyleaves), 335 x 230 (205 x 123) mm. 43 long lines. Single vertical bounding lines (Derolez 13.11), ruled in crayon or lead. Rulings for text in lead. Prickings in upper and lower margins; two additional prickings in outer margin below top and just above bottom lines of written space.

I–XXXIV^{10}. Catchwords, mostly trimmed, along edge of lower margin near gutter, verso (Derolez 12.4). Remains of quire and leaf signatures (e.g., a 1, a 2, a 3, etc.) in lower right corner, recto.

Written in gothic cursive with humanistic features by a single scribe, above top line.

Illuminated initial, f. 1r, 8-line, blue with white highlights and burnished gold on gold ground with stylized foliage in green and dark red with yellow highlights. Terminals ending in foliage serifs, red, green with yellow highlights, and gold balls with hairline extensions. Numerous pen and ink initials, 3-line, alternate red and bright blue with penwork designs of the other color extending along margin.

Binding: Italy, s. xv. Parchment stays are adhered to inner and outer conjugate leaves of quires. Original wound sewing on three tawed skin, slit straps laid in channels on the outside of beech boards. The endbands, which are wanting, were sewn on tawed skin cores laid in grooves and nailed or held in place by the bosses; they were tied down through a tawed skin spine lining.

Covered in sheepskin, originally brick red, with the surface now badly rubbed and shedding. Corner tongues. Blind-tooled with an *X* in concentric frames. Four leaf-shaped catches with three flowers on each on the lower board, one wanting; the upper board cut in for two kermes pink straps attached with star-headed nails. Five flower-shaped bosses on each board and the trace of a chain attachment at the tail of the lower one.

Written in Northern Italy in the middle of the 15th century, probably as the second part of a two-volume set: the text begins with Epistle 65 and contains none of the introductory material generally found in Barzizza's *Commentaries* on Seneca. Customs declaration, s. xv^2, on back pastedown: "Aquesti libro de mosser Nicolau roujra Vicario de Munjesa. ha de pagar de port de Roma aqui vn florjn e medio." Paper label, ca. 1800–1830, of the hatseller [!] Francisco Tolrrá of Madrid (we thank S. Sider of the Hispanic Society of America for helping with the provenance of this manuscript). Bookplate of the literary scholar Feliciano Ramírez de Arellano, Marqués de la Fuensanta del Valle (s. xix^2). Unidentified notes in pencil on back pastedown, including "MS–XIV/ A.–1 vol."; unidentified bookplate on front pastedown superimposed on the Tolrrá ticket: Greek cross within concentric circles. According to P. Kristeller (*Iter Italicum*, v. 5, p. 287, no. 168), this manuscript was formerly "31–17" in the Capitular library at Zaragoza. Purchased from Enzo Ferrajoli through Nicolas Rauch of Geneva in 1958 by L. C. Witten (inv. no. 2149), who sold it the same year to Thomas E. Marston (bookplate).

secundo folio: qui non seruit

Bibliography: Faye and Bond, p. 83, no. 168.

Marston MS 169 — Roccacontrada, s. XV^2
Gasparino Barzizza, Epistolae ad exercitationem accommodatae — Pl. 37

ff. 1r–83v *Incipiunt Epistole Gasparinj*. [G]audeo plurimum atque letor in ea te sententia esse ut nihil a me sine causa fieri potes. Ego uero si multorum verebar suspitionem ... Tu me admonebis quibus adiumentis opus tibi fiet Et ego neque pecunia mea neque consilio tibi deero. Vale. Vale. Et Deo Gratias. [colophon:] *Expliciunt Epistole Gasparinj Scripte per me Valerium Rochensem Zitellum In Rocha contrata*. f. 84r ruled, but blank; f. 84v blank

Gasparino Barzizza (1360–1431), *Epistolae ad exercitationem accommodatae* (a collection of model addresses and letters); G. A. Furietti, ed., *Gasparini Barzizii Bergomatis et Guiniforti filii opera* (Rome, 1723) pars 1, pp. 220–332. See also E. J. Polak, *Medieval and Renaissance Letter Treatises and Form Letters: A Census of Manuscripts found in Eastern Europe and the U.S.S.R*, in

Davis Medieval Texts and Studies 8 (1990) pp. 12, 124. For certain letters the scribe has written rhetorical terms in the margins: *exordium, confirmatio, confutatio, conclusio, narratio confirmatiua, metafora*, etc.

The order of the letters is as follows:

1. f. 1r [G]audeo plurimum atque letor . . . ;
2. f. 1r–v [S]et si antea literis et sermone . . . ;
3. ff. 1v–2r [M]erito amo te quia (non ut . . . ;
4. f. 2r–v [Q]uod tiberio claudio non . . . ;
5. ff. 2v–3r [E]tsi de tuo in me animo . . . ;
6. f. 3r–v [B]ene habet quod ut soles . . . ;
7. f. 3v [M]agnas habeo nature tue glorias . . . ;
8. ff. 3v–4r [S]i Adiumentis de quibus ad me . . . ;
9. f. 4r–v [N]isi scirem de qua re et apud . . . ;
10. f. 4v [S]i a nostris Legibus . . . ;
11. ff. 4v–5v [M]axima causa me inpulit . . . ;
12. ff. 5v–6r [Q]uantam molestiam ipse perceperem [for *perceperim*?] cognita . . . ;
13. f. 6r–v [N]on parua res est neque vsitata . . . ;
14. ff. 6v–7r [Q]uamquam maxime in cursu eram . . . ;
15. f. 7r–v [Q]uod ad te scribo tale est ut id . . . ;
16. f. 7v [S]i meo aliquo offitio poterit sedarj . . . ;
17. f. 8r–v [N]on de re vulgari aut negligenda . . . ;
18. ff. 8v–9v [Q]uantum cupiam nostram rem publicam . . . ;
19. ff. 9v–10r [Q]uid de me sentias facile . . . ;
20. f. 10r–v [S]atis spectata est mihi . . . ;
21. ff. 10v–11r [S]i tibi non satis prospectus . . . ;
22. f. 11r–v [E]tsi admonitione non egebam . . . ;
23. ff. 11v–12v [Q]ua vita sit aut quibus moribus . . . ;
24. ff. 12v–14r [Q]uod me de natura et moribus . . . ;
25. f. 14r–v [N]on vereor tacitum iudicium tuum . . . ;
26. ff. 14v–15v [Q]uamquam nunquam de tuo in me studio . . . ;
27. ff. 15v–16r [S]cribo ad te de concordia . . . ;
28. f. 16r–v [R]em mihi nuntias gratissimam . . . ;
29. f. 16v [M]agni honores his diebus delati . . . ;
30. f. 17r [N]ulla re scito nos multis annis . . . ;
31. f. 17r–v [G]ratulor illud tibi ex summa optimorum uirorum . . . ;
32. ff. 17v–18r [Q]uominus litere tue expectat de mea . . . ;
33. f. 18r–v [N]ulla res est que te perturbare . . . ;
34. ff. 18v–19r [N]on ignoro de pace . . . ;
35. f. 19r–v [S]i optas ex me scire . . . ;
36. ff. 19v–20r [L]ittere tue magnam mihi attulerunt . . . ;
37. f. 20r–v [N]on putaui id laturum tam . . . ;

38. ff. 20v–21r [Q]uod in me fueris equo animo . . . ;
39. f. 21r [C]upis ex me scire quo in statu . . . ;
40. ff. 21r–22r [E]tsi rumor sinister de uestris rebus . . . ;
41. f. 22r–v [N]e desiderium tuum differam . . . ;
42. f. 22v [H]abeo tibi gratias et magnas . . . ;
43. ff. 22v–23r [Q]uid de te sentiant omnes . . . ;
44. f. 23r [Q]uod modestiam a me desiderari . . . ;
45. ff. 23r–24r [Q]uamquam alias de maioribus . . . ;
46. ff. 24r–25r [P]riusquam literas tuas recepissem . . . ;
47. f. 25r–v [S]i ullo tempore de rebus . . . ;
48. ff. 25v–26v [L]ittere tue tantam actulerunt . . . ;
49. ff. 26v–27r [M]aximam omnem laudem hodierna die . . . ;
50. ff. 27r–28r [Q]uominus expectatum a me fuerit . . . ;
51. f. 28r–v [N]ihil enim est quod libentius faciam . . . ;
52. ff. 28v–29r [D]e his que ad me scripsisti . . ;
53. f. 29r–v [S]cio te rerum nouarum cupidum . . . ;
54. ff. 29v–30r [N]on puto dubitandum ex his . . . ;
55. f. 30r–v [M]ulta ex finitissimis cotidie noua . . . ;
56. ff. 30v–31v [B]ellum mihi significes magno . . . ;
57. ff. 31v–32r [N]ouissima res his diebus nobis accedit . . . ;
58. ff. 32v–33r [S]ulpitii magnum in rem . . . ;
59. ff. 33r–34r [S]i te noua delectant habeo . . . ;
60. f. 34r–v [E]pistolam tuam plenam rerum nouarum accepi . . . ;
61. ff. 34v–35v [E]tsi ea de quibus ad te scribo . . . ;
62. ff. 35v–36r [I]dibus Februarijs reddite sunt . . . ;
63. ff. 36r–37r [C]um de rebus inusitatis ad te scribo . . . ;
64. f. 37r–v [R]ecte uobis accidit . . . ;
65. ff. 37v–38r [T]andem ex magna sollicitudine . . . ;
66. f. 38r–v [Q]uod humanissime predones . . . ;
67. ff. 38v–39r [R]em non consuetam ad te scribo . . . ;
68. f. 39r–v [G]aium lutium donatum esse . . . ;
69. ff. 39v–40r [N]on de priuatis comedis . . . ;
70. f. 40r–v [S]i ea in me esset uel autoritas . . . ;
71. ff. 40v–41r [Q]uis si nostre ciuitatis status . . . ;
72. f. 41r [?]u qui optima re publica utaminj . . . ;
73. ff. 41r–42r [Q]uid de publica utilitate nostrorum ciuium . . . ;
74. f. 42r–v [N]isi res de qua ad me scribis . . . ;
75. ff. 42v–43r [S]i de tua re publica liberius ad te . . . ;
76. f. 43r–v [C]um tue littere de statu . . . ;
77. ff. 43v–44r [N]isi rebus tuis caues inplicabis . . . ;
78. f. 44r [N]isi rebus tuis caueas tale incomodum . . . ;
79. ff. 44v–45r [G]aij uicturii consilijs maxime utor . . . ;

80. f. 45r–v [S]pero me animo perspexisse . . . ;
81. ff. 45v–46r [N]on dubito omnes amicos de iniquitate . . . ;
82. f. 46r [T]ua res in tuto est . . . ;
83. f. 46r–v [N]ullum officium est quod magis necessarium dicam . . . ;
84. ff. 46v–47r [S]cito me omnibus . . . ;
85. f. 47r–v [N]ihil ad hanc tuam sollicitudinem . . . ;
86. ff. 47v–48v [C]upis ex me scire quid ad bene uiuendum . . . ;
87. ff. 48v–49r [S]atisfeceras desiderio meo . . . ;
88. f. 49r–v [C]um ad te literas meas dare constituissem . . . ;
89. ff. 49v–50r [L]ibrum basilij nostri perlegi . . . ;
90. ff. 50r–51r [Q]uod ad te scribo maxime . . . ;
91. f. 51r–v [E]t religionem probo . . . ;
92. ff. 51v–52r [S]cribo ad te de religione . . . ;
93. f. 52v [L]ittere tue incredibili uoluntate . . . ;
94. f. 53r–v [S]i quid est quod ullo tempore . . . ;
95. ff. 53v–54r [T]abellarius tuus nuper ad me . . . ;
96. f. 54r–v [N]ihil est quod a te gratius . . . ;
97. ff. 54v–55r [Q]uid egerim nemo nouit melius . . . ;
98. f. 55r [S]i ullum apud te locum . . . ;
99. ff. 55v–56r [S]i litteras tuas diligenter perlegi . . . ;
100. f. 56r–v [H]abeo tibi immortales gratias . . . ;
101. ff. 56v–57r [E]tsi intellectus noster satis . . . ;
102. f. 57r [Q]uid adhuc in tua causa . . . ;
103. f. 57r–v [Q]ue de mea causa scribis et hoc . . . ;
104. ff. 57v–58r [S]cripsi de libello conficiendo et de pecuniis . . . ;
105. f. 58r [Q]ue adhuc sunt a te . . . ;
106. ff. 58v–59r [M]ulta sunt de quibus . . . ;
107. f. 59r–v [N]unquam literas tuas lego . . . ;
108. ff. 59v–60r [Q]uantum omnes presentiam atque officium . . . ;
109. f. 60r–v [N]isi rey publice et amicis . . . ;
110. f. 60v [Q]ualem in gerendis magistratibus . . . ;
111. ff. 60v–61r [E]tsi de tuo officio nunquam . . . ;
112. f. 61r–v [Q]uotiens de meo officio scribo . . . ;
113. ff. 61v–62r [C]um in maximis occupationibus . . . ;
114. f. 62r–v [P]ossem ad te de mea constantia . . . ;
115. ff. 62v–63r [N]unquam sperem de meo animo . . . ;
116. f. 63r–v [N]on possum moueri . . . ;
117. f. 63v [Q]uantum sum tuis literis commotus . . . ;
118. ff. 63v–64r [P]lurimum semper nostram rem publicam . . . ;
119. f. 64r–v [S]i in nostram rem publicam . . . ;
120. ff. 64v–65r [D]iispeream [?] nisi res publica . . . ;
121. f. 65r–v [N]on possum dolorem . . . ;

122. ff. 65v–66r [Q]ua res merito esset ... quomodo in periculis ... ;
123. f. 66r–v [G]audeo medius fidius ... ;
124. ff. 66v–67r [Q]ua pietate semper patrem meum ... ;
125. f. 67r–v [N]ihil est quod te perturbare magno opere ... ;
126. ff. 67v–68r [M]atrem meam iam ultime ... ;
127. f. 68r [Q]uamquam de tua pietate ... ;
128. ff. 68r–69r [Q]uo animo in parentes meos ... ;
129. f. 69r–v [E]go de tuo in parentes ac omnes ... ;
130. ff. 69v–70r [O]mnes necessarios meos ex animo ... ;
131. f. 70r [M]agnam ex epistola tua ... ;
132. f. 70r–v [M]ulta sunt que magno a me ... ;
133. ff. 70v–71r [S]i causa pomponij iure ... ;
134. f. 71r [P]ostea quam togam a patre sumpsi ... ;
135. f. 71r–v [?]in [for *cum*?] referenda gratia ...;
136. ff. 71v–72r [E]tsi de meo in tuos ... ;
137. f. 72r–v [P]ridie quem tue litere mihi ... ;
138. ff. 72v–73r [N]umquam futurum putasse ... ;
139. f. 73r–v [N]imis in me officiosus es ... ;
140. f. 73v [C]um te ualde [?] semper amauerim ... ;
141. ff. 73v–74r [S]ollicitudinem tuam ac studium ... ;
142. f. 74r–v [L]ibenter in omnibus negotiis ... ;
143. ff. 74v–75r [Q]ue ad me de tuo amore scribis ... ;
144. f. 75r–v [D?]e meis hodierno die uiuere qui me infortunatior ... ;
145. ff. 75v–76r [T]anto me dolore tue litere affecerunt ... ;
146. f. 76r–v [T]antis incomodis hoc tempore afficior ... ;
147. ff. 76v–77r [M]allem te posse aliquo meo auxilio ... ;
148. f. 77r–v [Q]uo res mee perducte sunt ... ;
149. ff. 77v–78r [E]tsi tuas literas semper attente lego ... ;
150. f. 78r–v [M]aiora sunt iam incomoda ... ;
151. ff. 78v–79r [N]ihil minus quam ut in ista etate ... ;
152. f. 79r–v [G]raue mihi sit in senectute ... ;
153. ff. 79v–80r [Q]uid tibi consilii mandem ... ;
154. f. 80r–v [Q]uo in statu fuerim ... ;
155. ff. 80v–81r [L]egi nuper literas tuas mihi ... ;
156. f. 81r–v [S]i uitio meo quod multis accidere video ... ;
157. ff. 81v–82r [N]on de re noua mihi scribis ... ;
158. f. 82r–v [S]i ullum inopie mee finem ... ;
159. f. 82v [Q]uid ad te scribam nescio ... ;
160. ff. 82v–83r [Q]uo me credis animo esse ... ;
161. f. 83r–v [M]allem incomodis aliorum....

Paper (watermarks, in gutter: similar in design to Briquet Chapeau 3373 [quires I–IV]; Briquet Flèche 6270–71 [quire V]; Briquet Colonne 4411 [quires VIII–IX]; unidentified object in two concentric circles [quires VI–VII]), ff. i (paper) + 84 (early foliation 11–43 only) + i (paper), 218 x 147 (153 x 88) mm. 26 long lines. Single vertical (and sometimes horizontal) bounding lines (Derolez 13.11 and 13). Ruled in lead. Prickings in upper, lower, and outer margins.

I–IV^{8}, V^{10}, VI–VII^{12}, VIII^{10}, IX^{8}. Vertical catchwords perpendicular to text along inner bounding line (Derolez 12.6).

Written in humanistic cursive script by a single scribe, above top line.

Heading on f. 1r and colophon in red. Spaces left for decorative initials remain unfilled; guide letters for the decorator sporadically throughout.

Binding: Place uncertain, s. xix–xx. Rigid vellum case. Title, in ink, on spine: "Gasparini de Barzizza/ Epistolae" and "Ms. Sec. XV."

Written at Roccacontrada, in the province of Ancona, Italy, in the second half of the 15th century by the scribe Valerius Rochensis Zitellus (see colophon); provenance unknown. Purchased in 1959 from L. C. Witten by Thomas E. Marston (bookplate).

secundo folio: semper horum

Bibliography: Faye and Bond, p. 83, no. 169.

Marston MS 171 — Germany, 1493
Antonio Beccadelli, De dictis et factis Alphonsi V, etc.

1. ff. 1r–95v *Anthonij panormite in Alfonsi Regis dicta et facta memoratu digna. Prohemium.* [prologue:] Xenophon is quem greci non [remains of book stamp obscures text: *ab re*?] musam atticam uocant: dictorum aut factorum socratis commentarios edidit ... accendere cantu. [letter of Pius II, f. 2r:] Eneas Episcopus senensis Antonio panormite poete clarissimo. S.P.D. Siluester chimensis antistes cuius consilio in suam me curiam ... uideris esse commentum. [commentary of Pius II, f. 2v:] *In prohemium primi libri.* Alfonsus. tanto est socrate. maior: quanto grauior romanus homo ... [text, Beccadelli:] Orabant et quidem suppliciter Ioanne ... Nam vitam in qua tot populorum uita consistit sine magna causa periculis obiectare nolim. [f. 94r:] *Alfonsi Regis oratio in expeditionem contra turcos inimicos hiesu* [sic] *cristi.* Scio plerosque vestrum demirari patres conscripti. Qui cum totiens de expeditione in turcos uerba fecerimus eam ... sit confestim suscipere. *Alfonsi Regis dicteria atque facta memoratu digna. Expliciunt Anthonius panormita poeta clarissimus compilauit.*

Antonio Beccadelli (Panormita), *De dictis et factis Alphonsi V*, with a letter of Pope Pius II and his commentary on the text. The text of Panormita alternates with the commentary of Pius II throughout. For the works of Panormita (arts. 1 and 3) see *Antonii Panormitae De dictis et factis Alphonsi Regis Aragonum libri quatuor* ... (Basel, 1539); for those of Pope Pius II (arts. 1, 2, 4) see *Aeneas Sylvii Piccolominei ... opera* (Basel, 1551) pp. 472–98.

2. ff. 95v–96r *Eneas*. Oratio a magnanimo Rege atque ipso Alfonso digna, Digitus hic dei est ... et tueri et amplificari poterit. *Expliciunt dicta Enee Siluij Episcopi Senensis ad Anthonium panormitam poetam clarissimum de Serenissimi Alfonsi Aragonum Regis incliti dictis et factis.*

   Pope Pius II, *In orationem pro suscipiendo in Turcos bello.*

3. ff. 96r–102r *Incipit eius Triumphus*. Postea quam Rex Cum Principibus regni decreuerunt conuentum celebrare neapoli relicto beneuento Primum auersam deinde templum diui Anthonij ... aduesperascente perductus est.

   Antonio Beccadelli, *Triumphus Alphonsi regis.*

4. f. 102r–v *Eneas*. Cum rediret Alfonsus subactis turcis. liberata gretia [*sic*] et spolia illa cruenta nephandique mahumeti caput retulerit ... inueniemus quod de tanto rege ad posteros referamus ... ad dicteria tua adijceremus. Tu vale et boni consule. Ex neapoli ... [with text dated 1456].

   Pope Pius II, *Oratio in triumphum Alphonsi.*

5. ff. 103r–105r *Ad gloriosum Principem Alfonsum Arroganie* [sic] *Regem Enee Senensis episcopi Oratio incipit.* Modestius fortasse fuerit Rex maxime ac pijssime Audito Iohanne solerij apostolico legato patre optimo ac doctissimo diuina re diutius protracta: fugiente iam die ... bernardinus haud dubie impetrabunt Amen. [colophon:] *Laus deo. finitus est liber vicesima die Iunij Anno et cetera .93.* ff. 105v–110v ruled, but blank

   Pope Pius II, *Oratio ad Alphonsum Aragoniae.*

Paper (watermarks: unidentified Tête de boeuf, plainly visible but not located in Briquet or Piccard), ff. i (paper) + 110 + i (paper), 205 x 157 (142 x 87) mm. 27 long lines. Single vertical and horizontal bounding lines; ruled in hard point.

I–XI^{10}. Quires signed in ink with Arabic numerals, upper right corner, recto.

Written in small gothic bookhand by a single scribe; first word(s) of each major section of text written in majuscules.

Red initial outlined in black ink, 3-line, on f. 1r. Plain red initials, with either decorative dots or knobs, 2- to 1-line, throughout. Headings in red.

Binding: Place and date uncertain. A pieced-together binding with a brown sheepskin spine and early wooden boards covered with suede-like skin. Traces of one fastening, the catch on the upper board. Wormholes in text block repaired. Residue of rectangular label on upper board.

Written in Germany in 1493 (colophon, art. 5); contemporary table of contents, presumably removed from original paper flyleaf or wrapper, pasted inside front cover: "Alphonsi Regis dicteria atque facta memoratu. digna per Antho. penormitam [*sic*] compillata et Eneam siluium Episcopum Senensem [*compil* crossed out] appostillata [*sic*]." Purchased in 1957 from Leo S. Olschki of Florence by L. C. Witten (inv. no. 1663), who sold it in 1958 to Thomas E. Marston (bookplate).

secundo folio: excitabo

Bibliography: Faye and Bond, p. 83, no. 171.

Marston MS 172 Northern Italy, s. $XII^{1/4}$
Homiliary (in Lat.)

1. p. 1 //dominus ihesus yerosolimis. et uenisset bethfage ad montem olиueti. tunc misit duos discipulos ... et statim inuenietis asinam alligatam et pullum cum ea. soluite et adducite mihi. et reliqua.

   Matthew 21.1–2, imperfect at beginning.

2. pp. 1–7 *Omelia bede.* Mediator dei et hominum homo christus ihesus. qui pro humani generis salute ... et celestium gaudiorum pignus dare dignatus est. Ihesus christus dominus noster. qui ... amen.

   Bede, *Homelia Evangelii* II.3; D. Hurst, ed., CC ser. lat. 122 (1955) pp. 200–206.

3. pp. 7–11 *Feria .ii. in autentica extractus sancti augustini in iohannem.* Hesternam lectionem sancti euangelii de qua locuti sumus quod dominus dedit ... Quo decedente et alio succedente. et suppleta est apostolica ueritas. et numeri permansit integritas.

   Augustine, *In Iohannis Evangelium tractatus* 50.1–10 (continues in art. 4); R. Willems, ed., CC ser. lat. 36 (1954) pp. 433–37.

4. pp. 11–15 *Feria .iii. in autentica.* Iuda decedente. et mathia succedente. suppleta est apostolica ueritas. et numeri permansit integritas. Quid ergo uoluit dominus noster ihesus fratres mei. admonere ecclesiam suam ... Et lazarum mortuum et se ipsum suscitauit occisum.

Augustine, *In Iohannis Evangelium tractatus* 50.10–14; Willems, *op. cit.*, pp. 437–39.

5. pp. 15–19 *Feria .iiii. in autentica tractatus sancti augustini in iohannem.* Postea quam dominus quatriduanum mortuum suscitauit. stupentibus iudeis ... Petro autem dixit. significans qua morte glarificaturus [*sic*] esset deum.

Augustine, *In Iohannis Evangelium tractatus* 51.1–10; Willems, *op. cit.*, pp. 439–43.

6. pp. 19–24 *Feria .v. commentario yeronimi in matheo.* Prima die azimorum accesserunt discipuli ad ihesum dicentes ... Prima azimorum. quarta decima die mensis primi est. quando agnus immolatur et luna plenissima est ... Vigilate et orate ne intretis in temptationem.

Jerome, *Commentariorum in Matheum liber IV.* 26.17–41; D. Hurst and M. Adriaen, eds., CC ser. lat. 77 (1969) pp. 248–55.

7. pp. 24–30 *Feria .vi. euangelium secundum matheum.* Mane facto consilium inierunt omnes principes sacerdotum ... Non solum ad pilatum. sed etiam ad herodem ductus est. ut uterque domino illuderet ... Surge qui dormis et exurge a mortuis. et illuminabit te christus.

Jerome, *Commentariorum in Matheum liber IV.* 27.1–33; Hurst and Adriaen, *op. cit.*, pp. 263–70.

8. pp. 30–35 *Passio domini ihesu christi secundum matheum* [sic]. Prima die azimorum. quando pascha immolabant ... qui et ipse erat. expectans regnum dei.

Mark 14.1–15.43.

9. pp. 35–40 *Passio domini nostri ihesu christi euangelium secundum lucam.* Appropinquabat dies festus azimorum. qui dicitur pascha ... et sabbato quidem siluerunt secundum mandatum.

Luke 22.1–23.56.

10. pp. 41–47 *Passio domini nostri ihesu christi secundum iohannem.* Ante diem festum pasche. sciens ihesus quia uenit eius hora ... quia iuxta erat monumentum posuerunt corpus ihesu. Tu autem domine miserere nobis. p. 48 ruled, but blank

John 13.1–14.6; 18.1–19.42, followed by prayer of final sentence.

Parchment, ff. iii (paper) + 24 (old foliation, in ink: cliiij-clxxvij; modern pagination, in pencil, 1–48) + iii (paper), 321 x 232 (240 x 165) mm. 2 columns, 30 lines. Format varies: single vertical and two to four upper and one to two lower horizontal bounding lines; space between columns ruled. Ruled in hard point on hair side. Prickings in upper, lower and outer margins.

I–III^8. Remains of catchwords along lower edge, verso.

Written by a single scribe in a late caroline minuscule.

Plain initials, 2-line, in red and/or brown. Headings in red. Instructions for rubricator and guide letters.

Binding: Place uncertain, s. xx. Half bound in black goatskin with black cloth sides and gold tooling on the spine, including: "Omelie" and "MS. Saec. XI."

Written in Northern Italy in the first quarter of the 12th century as part (ff. 154–177) of a codex intended for recitation: a series of accents added in a contemporary hand acts as an aid for pronunciation (see especially art. 10). According to the notes of Thomas Marston (in library files) the manuscript belonged to the Cistercian abbey of Hautecombe in Savoy; it does not, however, have either an ex libris or the distinctive pink binding which indicates it was owned at the beginning of the 19th century by Monseigneur Hyacinthe della Torre (see Leclercq 1951, p. 75) who acquired and rebound a number of manuscripts from this abbey. (See also catalogue entries for Marston MSS 50, 125, 128, 135, 151, 153, 158, 159, 197). Purchased in 1956 from Arthur Rau of Paris by L. C. Witten (inv. no. 1241), who sold it in 1958 to Thomas E. Marston (bookplate).

Bibliography: Faye and Bond, p. 83, no. 172.

Marston MS 174 — Italy, s. XV

Giovanni Boccaccio, Lettera consolatoria a Messer Pino de' Rossi

f. i recto blank; f. i verso [Title in a later? hand, written between lines ruled in lead:] Epistola di Messere Giovanni Boccacio da Certaldo mandata a Mes. Pino de Rossi. ff. 1r–24v [Heading, in upper margin:] Epistola di messere giovannj di bochaccio da certaldo mandata a messer pino de rossi. [text:] [I]o stimo messer pino che non solamente sia utile . . . che non solamente nelle fatiche sostenghono i mo// 4 leaves missing

N. Bruscoli, ed., *L'Ameto, Lettere, il Corbaccio* (Bari, 1940) pp. 159–82.

Marston MS 174 does not have the interpolation "Lucio quinto cincinnato" shared by the majority of manuscripts (see Bruscoli, *op. cit.*, pp. 283–84). Cited by V. Branca in "Un nuovo elenco di codici," *Studi sul Boccaccio* 1 (1963) p. 20; "Un quarto elenco di codici," *op. cit.*, 9 (1975–76) p. 10; D. Dutschke, "Un quinto elenco di codici," *op. cit.*, 13 (1981–82) p. 8.

Parchment, i (paper) + i (original parchment wrapper?, f. i) + 24 (remains of old foliation in Arabic numerals in ink) + i (paper), 165 x 120 (112 x 88) mm. Ca. 18 long lines. Frame-ruled lightly in crayon, with prickings at intersections of vertical and horizontal rulings.

I–III^{8} (+ 1 leaf, f. i, tipped in at beginning).

Written by a single scribe in an inelegant *mercantesca* script.

Spaces for decorative initials left unfilled. Some guide letters visible in gutter.

Binding: Italy, s. xix. Marbled paper case with two labels on spine; the upper one wanting, the lower one in green with gold-tooled legend: "M.S. Membra. Sec. XV." Traces of an earlier quarter binding on the first and last parchment leaves.

Written in Italy in the 15th century; early provenance unknown. Unidentified shelf-marks include mutilated round paper labels on spine and on upper cover, the latter with "14[remainder of number wanting]" written in ink. Modern pencil notation on front flyleaf, recto: "Mancano le ultime 4 cc. Raffaello Uccelli Firenze Giugno, 1925." Belonged to Giuseppe (Joseph) Martini of Lugano; his [?] notes on f. 24v ("4 carte mancanti"), on modern back flyleaf ("Mancano le ultime quattro carte, cioè da: [rtali: ma ad esse volontariamente sottentrare ne gli fanno, siccome noi manifestamente veggiamo. . . .] alla fine"), and on rear pastedown ("20"). Purchased from Martini by H. P. Kraus (collation notes on rear pastedown), who sold it in 1958 to Thomas E. Marston (bookplate).

secundo folio: [Non dim]eno si

Bibliography: Faye and Bond, p. 84, no. 174.

Marston MS 175 — Bologna [?], s. XIII$^{4/4}$

Bonaventure, Commentarius in Librum IV Sententiarum Petri Lombardi

1. ff. 1r–149r Unguentarius faciet pigmenta suauitatis . . . [Eccli. 38.7]. Verbum istud scribitur. ecc. xxxviij. in quo diligentius considerato

explicatur et commendatur. materia. quarti libri Sententiarum ... Ad quam nos perducat pontifex. et precursor noster ihesus christus. filius dei et beate marie. domine et adiutricis nostre. sua pia mia [*sic*] cui est benedictio ... secula seculorum. Amen.

Stegmüller, *Rep. Sent.* 111; *Opera omnia S. Bonaventurae* (Quaracchi, 1889) v. 4.

2. ff. 149r–156r Introitus in quartum librum. Vtrum sacramenta debuerint instui [*sic*]. Vtrum significatis sit de essentia sacramenti et utrum sacramentum sit signum ... de pedibus sedentis et cetera. finito libro referamus gratia [*sic*] christi. f. 156v blank

List of *distinctiones* and *articuli* for art. 1. Three sets of numbering, all early; the first, in red, is incomplete and incorrect, the second includes Dist. 2–30, notes a *lacuna*, and then stops; the third picks up with 34 and continues to the end.

Parchment, ff. i (paper) + 156 + i (paper), 229 x 180 (168 x 130) mm. 2 columns, 43–44 lines. Single vertical bounding lines; double horizontal rulings in upper margin for running headlines; ruled in lead or crayon. Remains of prickings in upper margin.

I-XIII^{12}. No remains of catchwords or signatures.

Written by several scribes in small gothic bookhand.

One historiated initial, f. 1r, 6-line, beige with foliage serif, red, against blue ground with white filigree, containing an apothecary (*unguentarius*) mixing ingredients in a mortar with two pestles. Numerous flourished initials, 3- to 2-line, alternate in red with blue, and vice versa, or often plain initials in red or blue. Running headlines in red and blue. Paragraph marks, alternating red and blue, appear sporadically (ff. 1r–36v).

Binding: Germany, s. xviii. Cream colored pigskin, blind-tooled. Gilt edges. Green and cream endbands. Title on spine: "De septem/ Sacrament. Tract. Mst."

Written in the fourth quarter of the 13th century, probably in Bologna to judge from the decoration; bound in Germany in the 18th century. Belonged to Eucharius Gottlieb Rinck (1670–1745), a member of the Imperial Council and head of the Academy at Altdorf. Upon his death his son-in-law, Adam Friedrich Glafey, catalogued his collection for sale (*Bibliotheca Rinckiana, seu supellex librorum ... quos collegit E. G. Rinck* [Leipzig, 1747]); Marston MS 175 can be identified as no. 8570 (traces of number on spine and note on front flyleaf) which was described as *Dogmata Theologica*. Inscription on front pastedown, erased but partially visible under ultra-violet light: "876 28 May N***" and "A. M. Taylor"; to the right "T. Price, [one word unclear], 1839." Purchased from C. A. Stonehill in 1958 by Thomas E. Marston (bookplate).

secundo folio: facientis

Bibliography: Faye and Bond, p. 84, no. 175.

Marston MS 176 — France, s. $XIV^{2/4}$

Boniface VIII, Sextus Liber Decretalium, etc. — Pl. 48

1. ff. 1r–107v [Text in center of page:] *Incipit liber. vj. decretalium.* Bonifacius episcopus seruus seruorum dei dilectis filiis doctoribus et scolaribus ... apostolicam benedictionem. [prologue:] Sacrosancte romane ecclesie quam inperscrutabilis diuine prouidencie ... recepturi ulterius aut pro decretalibus habituri. [text, f. 2v:] Gregorius x in generalibus concilio lugdunensi. *De summa trinitate et fide catholica.* Fideli ac deuota professione fatemur quod spiritus sanctus eternaliter ... Certum est quod is committit in legem qui legis uerba complectentes contra legis nititur uoluntatem. Explicit textus. vj. libri [?] decretalium deo gratias.

   Boniface VIII, *Sextus liber decretalium*; E. Friedberg, ed., *Corpus iuris canonici*, Pars secunda, Decretalium Collectiones (Leipzig, 1922) v. 2, cols. 933–1124. Arts. 1 and 2 accompanied by some interlinear and marginal glosses; running headlines (chapter titles) in upper margins also added by later hand.

2. ff. 1r–107v [Commentary in margins:] In dei nomine amen. [prologue:] secundum phylosofum scire est rem per causam cognoscere. xxiij ... [text:] Bonifacius. hoc prohemium diuiditur in duas partes. primo premittit [?] salutationem ... quanto. et decima quarta. questione. tercia plerique. Explicit apparatus sexti libri decretalium. Deo gracias. amen.

   Johannes Monachus, *Apparatus in Librum Sextum*; edition: *Glosa aurea* (Paris, 1535; repr. Aalen, 1968).

Parchment, ff. 107, 420 x 260 (357 x 222) mm. 2 columns, 4–45 lines of text surrounded by a maximum of 94 lines of commentary. Single or double vertical bounding lines. Ruled in lead and crayon. Prickings in upper and lower margins; additional single prickings in outer and inner margins for horizontal ruling for top of text space in art. 1.

I–II^{12}, III^{12} (–10), IV–IX^{12}. Catchwords, some decorated, to right of center in lower margin, verso.

Written in gothic bookhand, below top line; larger module of script for art. 1.

Folio 1r, small initial of poor quality, 10-line, framed in gold and blue with white highlights, depicting Cardinal Johannes Monachus, accompanied by two clerics, presenting a copy of his commentary to Pope Boniface VIII; miniature is against deep pink ground with white filigree. One illuminated initial, 7-line, pink with white filigree on blue ground with white filigree; initial filled with stylized leaves, blue, pink and white against gold ground. Foliage serifs, pink and blue with white shading. Numerous flourished initials, 18- to 2-line, red and/or blue (some divided in both colors) with red and/or blue penwork. Headings (many omitted) in red. Running titles in red and blue. Paragraph marks alternate red and blue. Notes to rubricator.

Binding: France, s. xiv [?]. Original wound sewing on seven tawed skin, twisted, double supports laced into grooves in beech boards and pegged. A plain wound, natural color endband is sewn through the vellum spine lining and on a tawed skin core laced into the boards and pegged.

Covered in orange tawed skin, mostly wanting. Two fastenings, the catches on the lower board. Off-set impression from text of manuscript formerly used as front pastedown.

Written in France in the second quarter of the 14th century; provenance unknown. Purchased from C. A. Stonehill in 1958 by Thomas E. Marston (bookplate).

secundo folio: contrarie

Bibliography: Faye and Bond, p. 84, no. 176.

Marston MS 179 — Naples, s. XV^2

Caesar, Bellum Gallicum, It. tr. Pier Candido Decembrio — Pl. 27

1. ff. 1r–2r [Rubric lacking, letter begins:] Molti sono gia stati Serenissimo Princip[*e* partially erased] li quali o per poca noticia deglistorie antique ... e di magiori anchora pienissima autoritate noticia e fede a luy daranno.

   Dedication of the translation of Pier Candido Decembrio to Filippo Maria Visconti, Duke of Milan. See C. Frati, "Il volgarizzamento dei Commentarii di G. Cesare fatto da Pier Candido Decembrio," *Archivum Romanicum* 5 (1921) pp. 74–80.

2. f. 2v [Full-page title within decorative wreath:] Incomincia listoria di

Caio Iulio Cesare impeatore [*sic*] maximo continuo consulo et prpetuo [*sic*] dictatore de le battaglia di Gallia da luy proprio descripte e in libri ordinate libro primo.

3. ff. 3r–179v *Tutta la Gallia in tre parte e diuisa de le* quale luna e habitata dali Belgi laltra dagli Equitani . . . per sue littere le processione per trenta giorni dal senato ordinate fureno. *Finisce el Septimo e lultimo libro delistoria di Caio Iulio Cesare . . . da luy proprio descripte e da p. Candido in Vulgari traducte felicemente.* f. 180r-v ruled, but blank

Caesar, *Bellum Gallicum*, translated into Italian by Pier Candido Decembrio in 1438.

Parchment, ff. ii (parchment bifolium; i = front pastedown) + 180 + ii (parchment bifolium, ii = back pastedown), 279 x 198 (183 x 105) mm. 25 long lines. Double vertical and horizontal bounding lines, full length and full across (Derolez 13.36); ruled in hard point on hair side. Prickings in upper, lower and outer margins, with an additional pricking in the outer margin to mark the first of the two lower horizontal bounding lines.

I–XXI^{8}, XXII–XXIII^{6}. Vertical catchwords with penwork designs to left and right perpendicular to text between inner vertical bounding lines (Derolez 12.5). Remains of quire and leaf signatures (e.g., a. 3., etc.) in lower right corner, recto.

Written below top line in a bold round humanistic hand by a single scribe who added extra rulings in outer margins for headings, annotations, etc., in red. Additional annotations in humanistic cursive, in a brighter shade of red.

Elegant illuminated title page (f. 2v) with the title, written in blue over an erasure, in a circular wreath, green with gold flowers, and framed by narrow gold bands with fillets and inkspray issuing from the top and bottom with blue and deep red flowers, green leaves and gold balls. Full border, f. 1r, white vine-stem ornament on blue, green, deep red and gold ground between thin gold frames. In lower border, medallion, blank, framed by wreath, green with yellow highlights and narrow deep red frame. Partial border, f. 3r, white vine-stem ornament on blue, green and deep red ground between narrow gold frames, enlarged to elongated dots at terminals; white vine-stem ornament extends into upper (trimmed) and lower margins, with single gold balls with hair-line strokes. 8 large initials, 11- to 3-line, gold on blue, green, gold and deep red ground with white vine-stem ornament shaded with pale pink. First few words of each book in gold; incipits, explicits and marginalia in red.

Binding: Italy, date uncertain. Vellum case with title in ink on spine: "Cesare Comment." Gilt, gauffered edges and gold and cream silk endbands. Fragments of a printed service book with musical notation partially visible under pastedowns.

Written in Naples in the second half of the 15th century, probably in the mature to late style of the scribe Giovanmarco Cinico of Parma (we thank A. C. de la Mare for this information); owned by an unidentified Italian humanist who added marginal notes in humanistic cursive in a bright shade of red. Inscription on f. 2r [s. xvii?], erased but partially visible under ultra-violet light: "Ex libris [P or R?]*luninij [remainder illegible]"; f. 180v: "D. Surgente" and an erased inscription. Unidentified "F. F. 24." handwritten in ink on front pastedown; "M" and "2" in a circle, in pencil, on f. 1r; "1N. N1. [?]" on f. i verso. Hoepli Cat. 1955, no. 8, with pl. VII in color of title page. Purchased from C. A. Stonehill (inv. no. 1368) in 1958 by Thomas E. Marston (bookplate).

secundo folio: essendo data

Bibliography: Faye and Bond, p. 84, no. 179.

Marston MS 180 — France, 1410–13
Historical roll chronicle, in French

Column I:

Cy sensuiuent les papes qui ont este a Romme depuis nostre saulueur Ihesucrist Iusques au pape alixandre qui regna en l'an M.iiii.^c. et ix. Nostre sauueur ihesucrist qui est sans fin et sans comencement premier tressaint pere fist en humanite en cest monde ... Urbain qui estoit arceuesque de saint nicholas de bar fut pape l'an M.iii^{c} lxxviii et fut sacre le Iour de pasques en la cite de rome a tres grant solemnite. Et apres sy commenca la diuision en saincte eglise de quoy ce fu dommaige et pitie pour toute chretiente.

Chronology of the popes from Peter to the antipope John XXIII. The text ends with Urban VI (1378–89), the last Pope elected before the Great Schism, and the diagram ends with John XXIII (antipope 1410–15). However, the rubric cites Alexander V (1409–10) as the last pope of the list.

Column II:

Cy sensuiuent les empereurs qui ont regne a Romme depuis Iulles cesar Iusques a loys de bauiere qui fut empereur en l'an M.iii^{c} .xxviii. et combien que chascung a *regne et leur mort.* Othouian auguste fut empereur Et fut auant nostre seigneur xiiij. ans Et depuis l'aduenement de nostre seigneur. xv. ans se Dient aucunes croniques et . . . Et apres regna loys de bauiere et lors les romains firent vng antipape. Cy ne parle plus des empereurs.

Chronology of the rulers of the Empire from Augustus to Louis of Bavaria, Holy Roman Emperor from 1328–47.

Column III:

Cy sensuiuent les lignies des Rois de france Et comment les generations sont descendues l'une de l'autre Et comment Ilz sont faillies Et si parle en brief de leurs faiz Et en quel temps ilz ont regne et combien et ou ilz gisent Et quieulx enfans ilz ont eu Et en quel temps la cite de lutesse fut commencie et comment elle fut nommee paris Et comment le royaulme de gaule fut nomme france. Aux nobles qui ayment biaux fais et bonnes hystoires vuelx escripre et enseignier au plaisir de dieu qui soit a mon commencement . . . [The genealogy ends in two paragraphs at the bottom of the roll. The left paragraph begins with the coronation of Charles VI; the right paragraph discusses the reign of Charles V.] [on left:] l'an M. iii^{c} iiii^{xx} le dimenche $iiij^{e}$ iour de nouembre fut couronne Charles vi^{e} . . . Si furent les corps dez Iiufs ramenez et aucuns des biens maiz ce fut poix. [on right:] Charles qui estoit regent et duc de normendie fut couronne l'an M. iij^{c}. lxiiii . . . Et tant fist a l'ayde de dieu et de ses freres que il mist le royaume en bon point et fut preudomme et saige et bien gouuerna son royaulme tant comme il vesquist.

Chronology of the Monarchs of France, beginning with the Trojan nobles and concluding with Charles VI, king from 1380–1422.

Column IV:

Cy sensuit les Rois qui ont regne en engleterre depuis Ihesucrist et depuis le temps Iulles cesar Iusques au Roy richart Et combien que chascung a regne Iusques a l'an M.iiii^{c} ou environ. Lud fut roy de la grant bretaingne qui de present est nommee engleterre . . . Et apres ce fut renuoye en france la royne d'engleterre que le roy richart auoit eu espousee dame ysabel de france qui depuis fut duchesse d'orleans.

Chronology of the kings of England, from King Lud in the time of Julius Caesar to King Henry IV (d. 1413).

Parchment roll composed of 8 membranes (numbered with contemporary Roman numerals on dorse) overlapping ca. 10 mm. at the seams; 5,660 x 640 mm. Written in 4 columns: double vertical bounding lines and single lower horizontal bounding line. Additional double rulings between text columns for genealogical diagrams. Ruled in lead. Rulings for text in brown ink. Prickings in left and right margins.

Written in bâtarde script by a single scribe.

Text is accompanied by parallel schematic genealogical diagrams in red consisting of connected roundels inscribed with the names of various rulers in succession, between the columns. The genealogical diagrams are periodically interspersed with 58 roundels framed in red with lively pen drawings in brown ink with washes in blue, pink and green, depicting cities and churches whose foundations are ascribed to particular rulers or occurred during their reigns. Each of the genealogical diagrams begins at the top of the text with a roundel, depicting respectively (I) Mount Calvary, (II) Rome, (III) Venice (whose foundation is ascribed to Trojan nobles) and (IV) London. Included are drawings of Constantinople, Hagia Sophia, Santiago de Compostela; the majority of the drawings appear in the chronology of the French monarchs, with depictions of Paris, St. Geneviève, St. Denis, St. Martin-de-Champs, and others. The buildings are all late medieval in character and do not bear resemblance to the monuments themselves. For a similar, though somewhat later French roll chronicle, see New York Public Library MS 124, reproduced in *The Secular Spirit: Life and Art at the End of the Middle Ages*, exhib. cat. (New York: Metropolitan Museum of Art, 1975) p. 166, no. 184; other historical rolls noted by C. Camus, *Notices et extraits des manuscrits* ... v. V, pp. 147–54, and M. François, *Les Trésors des Bibliothèques de France* IV (Paris, 1936) pp. 172–75.

Four illuminated initials, 4-line, at the top of each column, blue with white filigree against gold ground with stylized foliage or geometric patterns in red and blue. At the top of each initial, black inkspray with gold leaves; at the first initial (left column), decoration extends into the left margin to form a partial border. Numerous smaller initials, 2-line, gold on blue and mauve grounds with white filigree. Headings in red.

Unbound.

Written in France, sometime between the elevation of antipope John XXIII in 1410 (cf. Col. I) and the death of King Henry IV in 1413 (cf. Col. IV); provenance unknown. Filing notes on dorse: "7 9eme [?] 1701 Genealogie des Roys et Empereurs." Purchased from Maggs Bros. of London in 1958 by L. C. Witten (inv. no. 2171), who sold it in 1959 to Thomas E. Marston (bookplate).

Bibliography: Faye and Bond, p. 84, no. 180.
Exhibition Catalogue, pp. 218–19, no. 44.
The Medieval Book, pp. 92–95, no. 91, with plate.

Marston MS 181 Rome [?], 1456
Cicero, De divinatione

1. ff. 1r–57r //arbitrati eorum decem interpretes delectos ex ciuitate esse uoluerunt. ex quo genere sepe ariolorum etiam . . . Mihi uero inquit nihil potest esse iucundius. Que quom essent dicta surreximus. Amen. Laus. Deo. Marci Tulij Ciceronis liber de diuinatione explicit. M. ccccIvi.

   Cicero, *De divinatione*; W. Ax, ed., Teubner fasc. 46 (1938) pp. 2–129. First folio excised; only stub remains. Marginalia by a contemporary hand, mostly proper names taken from text for easy reference; a few variant readings (e.g., f. 2r "est" in text, "sit" in margin) and other miscellaneous notes. Spaces left unfilled where Greek words occur.

2. f. 57r–v [List of abbreviations:] A. Aulus. P.C.Q.R. populo Carthaginensi quis resistet. S.P.Q.R. Senatus populusque romanus. C. Caius. R.P. res publica . . . Coss. design. Consules designati. D. Dijs. M. Manibus. S. Sacrum. f. 58r–v ruled, but blank

Parchment (warped and stained by moisture), ff. v (paper) + 58 + i (paper), 193 x 131 (131 x 79) mm. 30 long lines. Double vertical bounding lines in outer margin and single in inner (Derolez 13.21); apparently ruled in hard point on hair side and traced in lead on flesh side. Text rulings in light brown ink. Prickings in upper and lower margins (Derolez 18.2), and two single prickings in outer margin 2 mm. above upper and below lower rulings for text.

I^{10} (–1), II–V^{10}, VI^{10} (–9, blank). Horizontal catchwords in center of lower margin (Derolez 12.1). Remains of leaf signatures (e.g., 1, 2, 3, 4, 5) in lower right corner, recto.

Written in a small humanistic bookhand by a single scribe, above top line. Marginalia added in a contemporary hand.

One illuminated initial, 6-line, on f. 28r, gold against blue, green and deep red ground with white vine-stem ornament, joined to a partial border, white vine-stem ornament curling around a thin gold bar on blue, green and deep red ground with white dots on blue, grey on red and pale yellow on green. Headings and running titles (*L* or *Liber* on verso [for last leaf in gathering only]; Roman numeral for book number on adjacent recto) in red.

Binding: Italy, s. xix. Brick red goatskin, blind-tooled. Bound in the same bindery for the Guarnieri-Balleani library (Iesi) as MS 450 and Marston MSS 72, 86, 182, 212.

Copied in Italy, perhaps in Rome, in 1456 (see colophon in art. 1) by the humanist Stefano Guarnieri probably for his personal use; it is not as attractively produced as some others in his collection (for manuscripts either copied, annotated or owned by him, see catalogue entries for Beinecke MS 450, Index V of this volume under Guarnieri-Balleani Library, as well as C. Annibaldi, *L'Agricola e la Germania di Cornelio Tacito* [Iesi, 1907] pp. 4–10). From the Guarnieri-Balleani Library at Iesi (see binding). Purchased from C. A. Stonehill in 1959 by Thomas E. Marston (bookplate).

secundo folio: arbitrati

Bibliography: Faye and Bond, p. 84, no. 181.

Marston MS 182 — Northern [?] Italy, s. XV^{med}
Cicero, Orator; Orationes

I. 1. ff. 1r–46v *M. T. C. Orator ad Brutum. Vtrum* difficilius an maius esset negare tibi sepius idem roganti an efficere id quod rogares diu multumque Brute dubitam ... tibi roganti uoluerim obsequi uerecundia negandi scribendi me impudentiam suscepisse. ΤΕΛΩΣ ff. 47r–48v ruled, but blank

Cicero, *Orator ad M. Brutum*; P. Reis, ed., Teubner fasc. 5 (1932) pp. 1–92. The text is accompanied by a few contemporary marginal annotations, some trimmed.

II. 2. ff. 49r–62r *Ciceronis Oratio Gn. pom. contra Mitridatem esse Imparatorem* [sic] *eligendum. Quanquam* mihi semper frequens conspectus uester multo iocundissimus. hic autem locus ad agendum amplissimus ad dicendum ornatissimus est uisus ... atque sociorum meis omnibus comodis et rationibus preferre oportere. τελωσ

Cicero, *De imperio Cn. Pompeii*; P. Reis, ed., Teubner v. 6, 1 (1931) pp. 3–34. Some contemporary marginalia, including rhetorical key words.

3. ff. 62v–68v [Heading in another hand in upper margin:] Pro Q. Ligario. [text:] [N]ouum crimen .G. Caesar et ante hunc diem inauditum propinquus meus ad te .Q. Tubero detulit ... Tantum te ipsum admoneo si illi absenti salutem dederis presentibus his omnibus te daturum. finis.

Cicero, *Pro Q. Ligario*; A. Klotz, ed., Teubner v. 8 (1918) pp. 84–100. Contemporary corrections to text throughout.

4. ff. 69r–89r [E]tsi uereor iudices ne turpe sit pro fortissimo uiro dicere incipientem timere minimeque deceat cum T. Annius ipse magis de rei publicae salute ... in iudicibus legendis optimum et sapientissimum quenque legit. finis pro T. Annio Milone.

   Cicero, *Pro T. Annio Milone*; Klotz, *op. cit.*, pp. 13–66. Contemporary marginalia, rhetorical in nature.

5. ff. 89v–96v [C]um in omnibus causis grauioribus .G. Cesar initio dicendi commoueri soleam uehementius quam uideretur uel usus uel etas mea postulare ... quorum alterum optare eorum crudelitatis est alterum conseruare clementie.

   Cicero, *Pro rege Deiotaro*; Klotz, *op. cit.*, pp. 101–19.

6. ff. 96v–102v [S]i quid est in me ingenij Iudices quod sentio quam sit exiguum aut siqua exercitatio dicendi in qua me non mediocriter esse uersatum ... a uobis spero esse in bonam partem accepta ab eo qui iudicium exercet certe scio. Explicit pro .A. Licinio Archia.

   Cicero, *Pro Licinio Archia*; P. Reis, ed., Teubner v. 6, 2 (1932) pp. 165–80. Contemporary marginalia, neatly keyed to the text with gloss marks, of an explanatory nature (e.g., f. 97r, gloss on "humanitatem" is "humanitas est cultus hominis cum ratione factus").

7. ff. 102v–103r [S]i patres conscripti pro nostris immortalibus in me fratremque que [*sic*] meum liberosque ... qua nihil potest esse iocundius quidemque nosmet ipsos nobis reddidistis.// ff. 103v–114v ruled, but blank.

   Cicero, *Oratio cum senatui gratias egit*, incomplete; T. Maslowski, ed., Teubner fasc. 21 (1981) p. 3 (ll. 1–11).

Composed of two distinct parts; f. i (paper) + i (contemporary parchment: palimpsest of unidentified accounts?) + 114.

Part I: ff. 1–48. Paper (watermarks: unidentified hunting horn, in gutter), 210 x 145 (151 x 86) mm. 28 or 29 long lines. Single vertical bounding lines (Derolez 13.11); ruled in hard point. I–IV^{12}. Horizontal catchwords with symmetrical flourishes just below written space near inner vertical bounding line (Derolez 12.2). Written in humanistic cursive by a single scribe, above top line. Plain initials in red or blue; heading on f. 1r in red majuscules.

Part II: ff. 49–114. Paper (watermarks, in gutter: similar in design to Briquet Fruit 7380–81), 210 x 145 (153 x 93) mm. 29 or 30 long lines. Single vertical bounding lines ruled in lead, with rulings for text in ink (Derolez 13.11). Prickings in upper and lower margin and a single pricking in outer margin, 5 mm. above top line. V–IX^{12}, X^{6}. Horizontal catchwords along lower edge near gutter (mostly trimmed). Written in humanistic cursive by a single scribe, above top line. Heading and plain initial, in red, on f. 49r only.

Binding: Italy, s. xix. Brick red goatskin, blind-tooled. Bound for the Guarnieri-Balleani library (Iesi) in the same bindery as MS 450 and Marston MSS 72, 86, 181, 212 and probably by the same binder. Title in ink on the tail edge, mostly illegible.

Written possibly in Northern Italy in the middle of the 15th century. Part II was copied by the humanist Stefano Guarnieri who never completed copying the text (for manuscripts either copied, annotated or owned by him, see catalogue entries for Beinecke MS 450, Index V of this volume under Guarnieri-Balleani Library, as well as C. Annibaldi, *L'Agricola e la Germania di Cornelio Tacito* [Iesi, 1907] pp. 4–10). Contemporary note on f. ii verso: "De perfecto genere dicendi." From the Guarnieri-Balleani Library at Iesi (see binding). Purchased from C. A. Stonehill in 1959 by Thomas E. Marston (bookplate).

secundo folio: [f. 2:] et clari fuerunt
[f. 50:] et subsidia

Bibliography: Faye and Bond, p. 84, no. 182.

Marston MS 184 — Florence, 1431
Cicero, Tusculanae disputationes; De finibus — Pl. 16

1. ff. 1r–78r *.M. T. ullii.* [sic] *Ciceronis. Tusculanarum. disputationum. liber primus incipit feliciter.* Cum defensionum laboribus senatoriisque muneribus aut omnino aut magna ex parte essem aliquando liberatus ... Nostris acerrimis doloribus uariisque undique circumfusis molestiis alia nulla potuit inueniri leuatio. *Explicit feliciter. deo gratias. amen.* [added in a later hand:] Quintus et ultimus liber explicit feliciter. amen. [in original hand:] *Quintus et .ultimus liber. explicit. feliciter.* f. 78v ruled, but blank

   Cicero, *Tusculanae disputationes*; M. Pohlenz, ed., Teubner fasc. 44 (1918) pp. 217–459. Throughout the text the parts of the dialogue are assigned to *M* or *DI*, in red. The scribe who copied the manuscript has carefully entered variant readings (corresponding for the most part to the preferred readings in the Teubner edition) and an occasional note in the margins; a somewhat later hand has added annotations to both arts. 1 and 2.

2. ff. 79r–150v [Rubric missing; text begins:] *Non eram nescius brute cum que* summis ingeniis exquisitaque doctrina phylosophi greco sermone tractauissent . . . Quod cum ille dixisset et satis disputatum uideretur in oppidum ad pomponium porreximus omnes. Finis. [colophon:] Die xxiiii° mensis maij. M.° cccc° xxxi° .manu mei. D.° N.[i] Pollini.

Cicero, *De finibus bonorum et malorum*; Th. Schiche, ed., Teubner fasc. 43 (1915) pp. 1–203. Variant readings are recorded as in art. 1, as well as annotations by the same later hand.

Parchment (hair side speckled), ff. ii (parchment bifolium; i = front pastedown) + 150 + ii (parchment bifolium; ii = back pastedown), 275 x 180 (196 x 114) mm. 32 long lines, above top line. Double vertical bounding lines; single upper horizontal bounding line; pattern of lower horizontal bounding lines varies between zero (Derolez 13.32) and one or two rulings full width (Derolez 13.33). Ruled in hard point on hair side. Prickings in outer margins.

I–IX^8, X^8 (–7, 8, blanks), XI–XIX^8. Horizontal catchwords in center of lower margins, verso.

Written in fine round humanistic script, above top line.

The decoration appears to have been executed in two stages. In the first are eleven illuminated initials of fine quality, 7– to 4–line, gold on blue, green and peach square grounds with white vine-stem ornament and headings in red for art. 1 only. In the second stage: a full border on f. 1r of white vine-stem ornament curling around a thin gold bar on blue, green and pink ground with white dots; in lower border, medallion, framed by a wreath and supported by two putti pushed by clouds, contains unidentified arms (gules, a bend argent; crest an eagle?) on blue ground; inner and outer border inhabited by a stag, a rabbit and two putti, one playing a horn; upper border consists of green garlands suspended between 2 medallions, framed in gold, one with a lectern, the other with a portrait in profile (of Cicero?) on blue ground with white filigree. According to A. C. de la Mare the border may be in the early style of Giovanni Varnucci. Also a later addition is the initial on f. 134v, 5–line, gold on blue and red ground with gold filigree.

Binding: Italy, s. xx. Early brown calf sides (s. xv?) are inset on a modern brown calf binding. Blind-tooled with a circle in a central rectangle within concentric frames. Some tooling added at the time of rebinding. Traces of two fastenings and round corner bosses. Edges gilt.

Written in Florence in 1431 (see colophon, art. 2) by Domenico di Niccolò Pollini (1395–1473) who copied texts primarily for his own use; for other manuscripts in his hand see A. C. de la Mare, *New Research*, Appendix I, pp. 492–93; the full border and unidentified arms on f. 1r appear to be later additions, perhaps by Giovanni Varnucci (1416–57). Belonged to Ambroise Firmin-Didot; see his *Catalogue illustré des livres precieux manuscrits* . . . (Paris, 1882), v. 4, p. 59, no. 37, where the arms are attributed to the Falcone family. Sotheby's sale (London, 12 April 1899, no. 176). J. Rosenthal of Munich (Cat. 27, no. 18). Purchased from J. Rosenthal, 21 June 1901, by Sir Sydney Cockerell (his extensive notes and signature on front pastedown and f. i recto); see S. Cockerell, "Signed Manuscripts in My Collection," *Book Handbook* 2, 1 (1951) pp. 13–14, pl. 8, and C. de Hamel, "Medieval and Renaissance Manuscripts from the Library of Sir Sydney Cockerell (1867–1962)," *The British Library Journal* 13, 2 (1987) pp. 186–210. Cockerell sale at Sotheby's (19 May 1958, no. 123). Purchased from H. P. Kraus (Cat. 88, *Fifty Mediaeval and Renaissance Manuscripts*, p. 91, no. 42) in 1958 by Thomas E. Marston (bookplate).

secundo folio: [homi]nis est intemperate

Bibliography: Faye and Bond, p. 85, no. 184.

Exhibition Catalogue, pp. 226–27, no. 50.

Burlington Fine Arts Club, *Illustrated Catalogue of Illuminated Manuscripts* (London, 1908) no. 187.

J. Ruysschaert, "Miniaturistes 'romains' sous Pie II," in *Enea Silvio Piccolomini. Papa Pio II*, Atti del convegno per il quinto centenario della morte e altri scritti raccolti da Domenico Maffei (Siena, 1968) p. 257, n. 70.

Marston MS 185 — Venice, s. XV^{ex}

Marco Antonio Sabellico, Opera varia

Arts. 1–4 and 7 are later additions.

1. f. i recto Georgius Merula Alexandrinus M. Antonio Coccio, sive Sabellico. Rerum patrie commentarios, quos nuperime scripsisti carptim legimus. Nec non ocium fuit . . . tuis istis comentariis eternitati commendas. Vale.

   Epistola of Georgius Merula to Marco Antonio Coccio Sabellico (1436–1506), printed in Venice ca. 1482–84 by Antonius Avinione (Hain-Copinger 14058) (f. 1 ii recto).

2. f. i verso Index. Librorum De Vetustate Patrie M. Antonii Sabellici. Liber Primus. qui Corographia inscribitur—pag. 1 . . . Index Carminum ad calcem remittitur [f. 102r].

Table of contents for art. 6.

3. f. i verso Cynthius M. Antonio Sabellico. Donec secula colligata fastis/ Extabunt latiis: Forum manebit/ . . . Vivas Nestoreiam precor senectam.

10-line poem to Sabellico; printed by Avinione, *op. cit.*, f. a i verso.

4. f. ii recto-verso M. Antonius Sabellicus: Ioanni Hemo Venetarum copiarum adversus Ferrarie ducem. Provisori Generali Salutem. Multum diuque dubitavi Ioannes Heme vir clarissime debere hos nostros commentarios, quos de vetustate Aquileiensis patrie . . . diis iuvantibus maiora erunt. tuo solius nomine appareant. Vale.

Epistola of Sabellico to Johannes Hemus; printed by Avinione, *op. cit.*, f. a ii recto-verso.

5. f. 1r blank except for date 1490; f. 1v *Ex quibus auctoribus .M. Antonij Sabellici commentarij de Vetustate patriae excerpti sint. Ex Plinio./ Ex Ptolemaeo* [sic]./ *Ex Marone./ . . . Ex Patriarchica historia./ Ex Bernardo Iustiniano Veneto*

This list differs somewhat from that printed by Avinione, *op. cit.*, f. a i verso.

6. ff. 2r-101v *.M. Antonii. Sabellici. De Vetustate Aquileiensis. Patriae. Liber. Primus. Qui. Chorographia inscribitur.* [text:] *Et Si Ex Omni Scriptorum Num*ero qui sunt aut unquam fuerunt nullus uti ego existimo aut certe quam paucissimi reperti sunt . . . unde patriae antiquitatem scribere orsi sumus: consequi non potuerunt. Finis. deo gratias.

Sabellico, *De vetustate Aquileiensis patriae*; the text and marginalia follow closely Avinione, *op. cit.*, ff. a iii recto-f ix verso.

7. f. 102r Carminum Index. In Cupidinem Elegia—pag. 1 . . . In rerum et artium inventores.

A table of contents added by the same hand as arts. 1-4.

8. ff. 102v-103v *M. Antonij Sabellici Elegia. in cupidinem.* [S]i qua deos humana mouent conuicia: si quem/ Turpiter e superis depuduisse potest./ . . . Denique sis qualem coelum propulset et orcus/ Et tua quem nequeat mitis amare parens.

9. ff. 103v-104v *Ad Liburnam Bellunnensem* [sic]. [C]ogar ut insano quum sim modo liber amori/ Cedere: et ingrato subdere colla iugo/ . . . At te si qua mouet nostri pia cura laboris/ Te tantum frustra ne patiare coli.

10. ff. 104v-105v *Queritur de morte Tipulanae comitis Liburnae.* [F]lete

feros casus suspectaque furta Siline/ Naides. indignum dissimulate nefas./ ... Meque dolente doles sic demum moestus uterque/ Cogimur indignam dissimulare uicem.

11. ff. 105v–106r *In primos toros Cynthij Cenetensis et Florae coniugis.* [Q]uum doctus modo Cynthius thalasson/ Florae pro thalamo assidens iugali/ ... Hoc ipsum torus et lucerna dicant/ Et sparsas prope qui nuces legebant.

12. ff. 106r–107r *Ad Philippum thronum de morte matris consolatoria Elegia.* [D]esine maternos lachrymis confundere manes/ Proficit iste nihil magne Philippe dolor./ ... Parce pijs lachrymis: manes te rite sepultae/ Matris: et omnis idem Iulia terra rogat.

13. ff. 107r–108r *Ad Illustrissimum Rubertum Malatestam Ariminensium principem.* [T]am foelix populos et Carnica uiseris arua/ Faustus et in tanto sic precor imperio/ ... Imperiumque tuum tam prospera fata sequantur/ Vt tibi cum Veneto nomine perstet honos.

14. ff. 108r–109r *Ad Diuam gratiarum Virginem.* [O] Patris ueneranda parens: o filia natii:/ Sydus: et astriferi ianua sancta poli/ Haec te diua manent maioraque praemia: sed tu/ Saepius huc adsis rite uocanda tuis.

Elegia tertia decima in laudem B. M. Virginis; Avinione, *op. cit.*, f. n vi recto–n vii recto.

15. ff. 109r–110r *Ad Pomponium praeceptorem suum.* [P]omponi latiae decus mineruae./ Qui priscos sapis et sapis recentes:/ ... Quiuis sic amat et potest amari/ Pomponi latiae decus Mineruae.

16. f. 110r *Ad Vatem Amicum.* [L]anguebam: sed tu uates formose reuinctus/ Flauentes circum candida colla comas./ ... Alternum dedit ille suo olim uiuere Fratri/ Tu mihi perpetuum uiuere et ingenium./ f. 110v blank

17. ff. 111r–114v *M. Antonii Sabellici Carmen In Municionem Sontiacam.* Funditur Illyricis rapidus de montibus amnis/ Hybernis quum creuit aquis. haud peruius ulli/ ... Gens Domitrix rerum: victrix terraque marique/ Romanum transgressa decus Dominabitur orbi.

Sabellico, *Carmen in munitionem Sontiacam*; Avinione, *op. cit.*, ff. g recto–g iii verso.

18. ff. 114v–124r *Poema .M. Antonii Sabellici. In Caedem Sontiacam.* Quo Praeceps Fortuna Ruis? Quo Pergitur ultra/ Oenotrium delere Decus: Sat triste recensque/ ... Scuta uirum: Spoliant multaque in strage

uolutant./ Foedaque destituunt foedos per gramina Truncos.

Sabellico, *Poema in caedem Sontiacam*; Avinione, *op. cit.*, ff. g iii verso–h ii verso.

19. ff. 124r–134r .*M. Antonii Sabellici Carmen in Carnicum Incendium.* Iam Fuscis Prouecta Rotis Nox Atra ruebat/ Oceano. vallesque umbris complexa cruentas/ . . . Sic mensis qui nonus erat numandus [corrected to *numerandus*] ab imbre/ Luctibus et Lachrymis Tristes abiere Calende.

Sabellico, *Poema in Carnicum incendium*; Avinione, *op. cit.*, ff. H ii verso–I verso.

20. ff. 134r–154r .*M. Antonii. Sabellici. In. Vtini. Originem. Carmen. Incipit.* Haec Spatiantis Humi Facies quam Claudit ad Euros/ Sontius ad Boream rursus Zephyrosque tepentes/ . . . Atque exosa uetus quod uox dedit vnnia [*sic*] nomen/ Auctore hemoniam dici se mandet ab hemo./ .Finis./ Laus Deo.

Sabellico, *Poema in Utini originem*; Avinione, *op. cit.*, ff. k iii recto–l ix verso.

21. ff. 154r–160r .*M. Antonij Sabellici Carmen in Fluctuantem Diui Petri Cymbam.* [F]*luctuat. Alma Ratis. medioque eiecta profundo/* Vltima uota facit: gelida dilapsus ab arcto/ . . . Non cadat: immo poli nitidis referatur in astris/ Hemonis ut quondam phamae si credimus argo./ ΤΕΛΟΣ.

Sabellico, *Poema in naufragantem divi Petri Cymbam*; Avinione, *op. cit.*, ff. i ii recto–i vi recto.

22. ff. 160r–166v .*M. Antonij Sabellici Carmen in rerum et artium inuentores.* [I]*nter grata soles studij commercia nostri/* Priscorum laudare frequens monumenta uirorum/ . . . Sistimus ergo gradum placido considere portu/ Me iuuet: emeritam fundetque hic ancora puppim./ ΤΕΛΟΣ.

Sabellico, *De rerum et artium inuentoribus poema*; Avinione, *op. cit.*, ff. i vi recto–k ii verso.

Paper (watermarks, in gutter: similar in design to Piccard, Anker IV.166–69), ff. i (paper) + ii (paper, thick; ruled in ink for arts. 1–4) + 166 (old foliation 1–98, beginning on f. 4; 1–10 for ff. 102–111; modern foliation, in pencil, lower right corner) + i (paper), 206 x 150 (152 x 85) mm. 23 long lines or lines of verse. Double vertical bounding lines (Derolez 13.31). Ruled in hard point from center of quire out.

I^{14}, $II\text{-}XII^{12}$, $XIII\text{-}XIV^{10}$. Vertical catchwords perpendicular to text between inner bounding lines, verso (Derolez 12.5).

Scribe I (ff. 1v–110r, 154r–166v): elegant sloping humanistic bookhand, below top line and leaving the final line blank; catchwords in red. Scribe II (ff. 111r–154r): a similar but less well formed style of script, below top line; catchwords in black. Each scribe rubricated the section he copied, but the heading on f. 134r was written by Scribe I.

Arms of Savorgnan family (argent, a chevron sable) in lower margin, f. 2r, within gold wreath with red ribbons. Plain initials, 2-line, in blue or red; many spaces for initials left unfilled in text copied by Scribe I. Headings and first line or words of text in epigraphic majuscules; headings, marginal notes, all of art. 5, initial strokes for each verse on ff. 111r–166v, in red.

Binding: Italy, s. xviii. Brown sheepskin spattered with black on the outside and striped on the edges and turn-ins of the boards. Modestly blind-tooled on spine.

Written toward the end of the 15th century in Venice for an unidentified member of the Savorgnan family whose arms appear on f. 2r; the date "1490" on f. 1r is consistent with the appearance of the manuscript. Early provenance otherwise unknown. Arts. 1–4 and 7 are later additions (s. xvii?), with 1, 3–4 probably copied from a printed source, since the texts often appear before Sabellico's *De vetustate Aquileiensis patriae* from the 15th century on. Unidentified notes: "32" written twice on f. i recto, in pencil and in fine blue crayon. Purchased from C. A. Stonehill (inv. no. 13710) in 1958 by Thomas E. Marston (bookplate).

secundo folio: *.M. Antonii*

Bibliography: Faye and Bond, p. 85, no. 185.

Marston MS 186 — England, s. $XV^{1/4}$
Guido de Columnis, Historia destructionis Troiae

ff. 1r–94v *Incipit liber primus de bello troiano.* [prologue:] Licet cotidie vetera recentibus obruant. nonnulla tamen iam dudum precesserunt uetera. que sic sui magnitudine viuaci ... ad eius narracionis seriem accedamus. [text, f. 1v:] *De peleo Rege thesalie inducente iasonem vt iter arripiat ad aureum vellus.* In regno Thesalie de predicte scilicet pertinencijs romanie cuius incole mirmidones dicti sunt ... Regem prothenorem [*sic*] et Regem Oschomenum [?]. Epithapheum hectoris. Troihum protector danaum// [text begins again on f. 94r:] Epithapheum Hectoris. Troiphum protector. danaum metus. hic Iacet hector/ ... Condidit et merens. accumulauit humo. Epithapheum achillis. Pelleudes ego sum. Thetidis notissima proles/ ... Me paris hostili. fraude peremit humo. [author's epilogue:] Ego autem Guido de columpnis predictum ditem grecum in omnibus sum secutus ... ffactum est autem presens opus. anno dominice incarnacionis Millesimo ducencesimo Octagesimo Septimo eiusdem prime Indictionis.

N. E. Griffin, ed., *Guido de Columnis Historia destructionis Troiae* (Cambridge, Mass., 1936) pp. 3-276. The text is defective: single leaves missing between ff. 34-35 ("... aura potiti. felici remige // inueniunt rapaci prede velociter..."), between ff. 87-88 ("... Palamides se optulit descensurum [catchwords:] qui discalciatis // quidam filius. uocatus assandrus..."), between ff. 88-89 ("... diomedis uxor postquam ad eius peruenit // purgata uere dici potuit agamenonis..."), between ff. 90-91 ("... ad eas perueniunt tanta earum dulcedine // salie. sic quod ipsum acastus..."); two leaves missing between ff. 91-92 ("... ad litora proiecerunt in quorum spuma // eos ad se uenire mandauit..."). Some corrections and marginal annotations, s. xv-xvi. Chapters numbered and lettered in margins (for indexing?).

Parchment, ff. ii (paper) + 94 (nearly contemporary foliation in Roman numerals on recto, Arabic numerals on verso), 247 x 162 (185 x 101) mm. 2 columns, 40 lines. Single vertical and multiple horizontal bounding lines, full across; ruled carelessly in crayon or lead. Remains of prickings in upper, lower and outer margins.

I-II^{12}, III^{12} (-11), IV-VII^{8}, VIII^{12}, IX^{8}, X^{8} (-1, 3, 6, 8), XI^{8} (-1, 5 through 8). Quire and leaf signatures (e.g., a i, a ii, a iii, etc.) lower margin, recto. Catchwords in lower margin to left of inner vertical ruling, verso.

Written by at least two scribes in anglicana formata script; cf. Watson, *B. L.*, no. 311, Watson, *Oxford*, no. 257, Robinson, *Cambridge*, no. 212.

Inelegant red or blue initials, 5- to 3-line, with crude penwork flourishes in the opposite color, ff. 1-12; for the remainder of the codex, blue initials, 3- to 2-line, with more delicate penwork designs in red. Headings in red, some omitted, others entered in margin.

Binding: England, s. xviii. Brown calf, blind-tooled with gold-tooled spine and edges of boards. Title on spine: "Historia/ Troiana/ M. S." Gilt edges. Varnished.

Written in England in the first quarter of the 15th century; early provenance unknown. Unidentified shelf-mark, s. xvi-xvii, upper margin of f. 1r: "(25)." Belonged to Charles William Hamilton Sotheby (1820-87; armorial bookplate with "Historia Trojana" written in ink); Col. H. G. Sotheby sale (Sotheby's, 25 July 1924, no. 113) to Dobell (cat. 38, Oct. 1924, no. 5). Unidentified notes, in pencil, on front pastedown: "III R/ 141" and "F5806." On back pastedown: "6506/ESZV." From the estate of the New York bookdealer Wilfrid M. Voynich. Purchased from H. P. Kraus (Cat. 86, no. 260) in 1958 by Thomas E. Marston (bookplate).

secundo folio: minus

Bibliography: De Ricci, v. 2, p. 1847, no. 9 (while in the Voynich estate); Faye and Bond, p. 85, no. 186.

Marston MS 187 — Northern France or Flanders, s. $XV^{med\text{-}3/4}$
Exordium magnum cisterciense

1. ff. 1r–3v *Incipiunt capitula tocius uoluminis. Distinctionis prime. Capitulum primum.* Quam dominus ihesus in doctrina sua formam perfecte penitencie tradiderit. *capitulum secundum.* Quam a primitiua ecclesia . . . Recapitulatio finalis eorum que in hoc uolumine continentur [another hand has added:] finis.

   List of chapters for art. 2.

2. ff. 3v–162r *Incipit prologus sequentis operis versifice editus.* [metrical prologue, written as prose:] Quisquis ad eternam cupis [*sic*] pertingere vitam. Currere felicem monachi contendis agonem . . . Illius a manibus procul auolet iste libellus. *Explicit prologus.* [f. 5r:] *In nomine domini nostri ihesu christi. Incipit narracio de inicio cysterciensis ordinis. qualiter scilicet patres nostri de molismensi cenobio propter puritatem . . . Capitulum primum.* Eternus deus eterni dei filius dominus noster ihesus christus creator omnium rerum. redemptor omnium fidelium. dum in diebus humilitatis sue salutem operaretur in medio terre . . . et spiritu sancto viuit et regnat . . . Amen. *Explicit liber de inicio cysterciensis ordinis* [erasure visible under ultra-violet light:] *editus a uenerabili* [?] *magistro petro clyniacensi* [not *dunacensis* as reported by Leclercq, 1961, p. 164]. f. 162v ruled, but blank

   Conradus of Eberbach, *Exordium Magnum Cisterciense*; text of Marston MS 187 belongs to Type 2 as described and edited by B. Griesser, *Series Scriptorum S. Ordinis Cisterciensis* v. 2 (Rome, 1961), Marston MS 187 cited as MS 7 on p. 24. Here the text is divided into six *distinctiones*; initial letter of each verse in metrical prologue stroked with red.

Parchment (end pieces, repaired, mottled), ff. ii (modern parchment) + i (contemporary parchment, ruled but blank) + 162 + ii (modern parchment), 268 x 180 (186 x 120) mm. 2 columns, 37 lines. Single vertical and double horizontal bounding lines. Ruled in crayon or ink. Remains of prickings in upper, lower, and outer margins.

I–V^{8}, VI^{8} (–8, no loss of text), VII–XX^{8}, XXI^{4} (–4). Remains of catchwords along lower edge, verso; quire and leaf signatures (e.g., k1, k2, etc.) in lower right corner, recto.

Written in a well formed hybrida script, without loops.

At the beginning of each *distinctio* flourished initials, 11– to 6–line, divided red and blue with parchment spaces and penwork designs in brown and red. Plain initials, some with parchment designs, alternate red and blue. Headings and running headlines in red. Paragraph marks either alternate red and blue (in art. 1) or are in red (art. 2). Majuscules stroked with red. Guide letters for decorator. Repairs and imperfections in parchment often outlined in red.

Binding: England, s. xix/xx. Blind-tooled olive green goatskin over oak boards; bound by Maltby, Oxford.

Written in Northern France or Flanders in the middle or third quarter of the 15th century; early provenance unknown. Belonged to James P. R. Lyell (bookplate; 1871–1949); 250 medieval manuscripts from his collection were bequeathed to the Bodleian Library (see *Lyell Cat.* for information and bibliography). The remainder of the collection was sold by his executors to Quaritch in 1951; this manuscript sold by Quaritch (cat. 699, 1952, no. 47). Purchased from C. A. Stonehill (inv. no. 21543?) in 1958 by Thomas E. Marston (bookplate).

secundo folio: in sancto

Bibliography: Faye and Bond, p. 85, no. 187.
Leclercq, 1961, p. 164.

Marston MS 188 — Northern Italy, ca. 1454–65
Fanensis [?], Carmina — Pl. 32

The following poems are not listed in L. Bertalot, *Initia*; the identity of the poet, who refers to himself throughout as *Fanensis*, has yet to be determined. According to P. Kristeller (*Iter Italicum*, v. 5, p. 288) the author may be Christophorus Fanensis.

1. f. 1r–v [Title, in later hand:] Carmina Fanensi [?]. [letter:] *Ad reueren-*

dissimum d. dominum Iohannem barocium benemeritum Bergomi sacerdotum principem. Consideranti alias mihi damnatio tua quanta esset. defecit quippe animus ... uel carminulis meis portiunculam gratitudinis et ostensurus sum. [4-line poem:] Accipe fanensis modicum pater optime domum/ ... Atque sue laxorios [?] mitia poma ferunt.

Dedicatory letter and short poem to Giovanni Barozzi, bp. of Bergamo (1449–65), in which the poet expresses gratitude on behalf of "ordini nostro" (Franciscan).

2. ff. 2r–3v *Consultissimo vtriusque iuris doctori. d. Ambrosio de aduocatis amico Lectissimo.* Si vir patricie quicquam conduxeris olim/ Ex me de rebus dum certabamus honestis/ ... Ipse tibi inueniar uel calle recedere sancto.

83-line poem in hexameters in which the poet expresses his gratitude to the addressee for having praised his moral character, then begins a polemic against such vices as vanity, avarice, pride, etc., and an invective against worldliness.

3. ff. 3v–4r *Ad eundem soluta oratiuncula.* Scio circunspectionem tuam vir illustris imperatorias leges maximorumque ... quondam reminiscamur amoris. Vale vir optime et parem pari gratiam referto.

Prose *laudatio* of the addressee in art. 2.

4. f. 4r–v *Epitaphium. M. Ia. de mozanica generalis minorum.* Mozanicus iacet hic Iacobus princepsque minorum/ Vnicus eloquij subrutilantis amor/ ... Infimus iste iacet qui modo maior erat.

Epitaph (26 lines) of Jacobus de Mozzanica (Jacobus Busolinus, d. 1454, in Milan); Wadding, *Supplementum*, v. 2, p. 16.

5. f. 4v *Distichon.* Inuida nex hominum quo non prestantior alter/ Abstulit ex oculis. occuluitque solo.

6. ff. 5r–6v *In quempiam asserentem nihil scire qui grecum nescierit et Inutilem penitus rem metricam fore.* Officij quicquam linguae callere latinae/ Greculus iste negat steterit qui nullus athenis/ ... Posteritas. laudesque sue per saecula viuent.

74 hexameters of invective against a proponent of Greek studies at the expense of Latin and against the preference of this "Graeculus" for prose over poetry.

7. ff. 6v–7r *Ad locupletem Inhumanum.* Si me [?] tibi reris quia gazophilatia gaudes/ Esse dies proprios ... Spiritus indignans nigras rapietur ad umbras.

55 hexameters attacking the stock character of the cruel rich man. Divine retribution after death is stressed, as is the uselessness of wealth hereafter.

8. ff. 7r–9r *Ad Monachum caluum incompositum.* Acaluaster abi ne pollue phana. Quo usque/ Obliquum facinus troculo sub condere nigro/ ... Spernitur attriti. nunquam est conuersio sera.

   88 hexameters condemning the loose morals among monks.

9. ff. 9r–10v *In militem emeritum didimum et seculi conformem.* Abs te scire uelim centaure incredule qui non/ Credis ab imbricibus supra cur solus aberras/ ... Ignibus eternis nec auerna vrentia terrent.

   87 hexameters attempting to justify God's ways to men of the military class by appealing to their Stoic and taciturn mentality.

10. ff. 10v–13r *Fanensis soliloquium Incipit.* Quid fanensis agis? num te suprema dierum/ Excitat? an falsa pellectus imagine mundi/ ... In quibus eternam possis reperire salutem. *Explicit soliloquium.*

   A critical and repentant self-examination (119 hexameters) by the poet who quotes verbatim (ll. 95–102) from a selection of classical authors: Vergil (*Aen.* 1.1; *Ecl.* 1.1); Statius (*Theb.* 1.1; *Achill.* 1.1), Lucan 1.8; Ovid (*Met.* 1.1), Horace (*Ars Poet.* 1); Juvenal (*Sat.* 1.1). The poet advises the reader to pay less attention to the achievements of the ancient Romans and more to those of Christ and the early Christians; he concludes with the statement that salvation is to be found above all in books.

11. ff. 13r–17r *Quod sola Iesuchristi cognitio sit scientia vera.* Desertorem olim contemptoremque superne/ Legis penituit condoluitque diu/ ... Triuit in angusta relligione diem.

   185 1/2 lines in elegiac couplets giving a detailed description of the kind of education the poet received under the tutelage of an unidentified master.

12. ff. 17r–20v *Ad cilonem quendam sirum.* Non erit ostentum si quid tibi scripsero quamuis/ Nulla mihi tecum sit consuetudo nec ullam/ ... A vicio refert uirtus celeberrima tantum.

   188 hexameters in which the poet calls upon a friend to renounce his worldly ways.

13. ff. 20v–22v *Ad Lafranchum militarium secretarium brixiensem.* Quem mihi das Lanfranche mili seu nobilis ille/ Egregij obscuriue laris cui siccet aristas/ ... Altitonans humiles et limpida tollit ad astra.

100 hexameters addressed to one Lanfranc of Brescia in which the poet laments the arrogance, deceitfulness and venality of this world, but concludes with the optimistic note that it is in the power of good people to make this world a better place.

14. ff. 23r–25r *Ad. d. Ioannem de salis iure peritum nubilem.* Non satis admiror stupet os et cetera membra/ Vnde sit alipidem si quis uel comparat edum/ ... Officiumque tuum et rectum seruabis amorem.

108 hexameters outlining the poet's advice to an eligible bachelor on what to look for in a wife, what her duties should be, etc.

15. ff. 25r–26r *Ad semet ipsum auctor.* Qui solus quaecunque potest facit omnia quae uult/ Per moysen mandauit aron sibi notatus [?] / ... Visceris et tabidi fluuidum succinge tumorem.

61 hexameters in which the poet cites Levit. 21.16–20 and interprets it allegorically as referring to those who are deformed in mind or spirit.

16. ff. 26r–28v *Apologia ad quempiam socium modiciensem querentem quod apud se aditum non habuerit.* Accepi nuper tibi limina nostra petenti/ Pulsantique diu non reserauit homo/ ... Vt facias iterum teque iterumque rogo.

104 lines addressed to an unidentified friend from Monza [province of Milan] in which the poet calls down on his own head a series of curses, if it were proved that he knowingly refused to answer the door when the friend came to call.

17. f. 28v *Ad eundem.* Philosophari tecum in presentia non intendo neque ex peregrino aucupio uerba moliri. uerum comice admodum atque paucis meam dicere sententiam ... Bene te ualere opto et constantem mihi beniuolum.

Prose paragraph addressed to the friend in art. 16 on the nature of friendship.

Parchment, ff. i (contemporary paper) + 28, 182 x 137 (127 x 83) mm. Written in 25 long lines or lines of verse. Single vertical bounding lines, ruled in lead; rulings for text in pale brown ink (Derolez 13.11). Single prickings in outer margin, 73 mm. below top line.

I^4, $II\text{–}IV^8$. Catchwords perpendicular to text along inner bounding line, verso (Derolez 12.6).

Written in humanistic bookhand by a single scribe, above top line.

One illuminated initial, f. 1r, gold on blue, green, and deep red ground with loosely curling white vine-stem ornament (cf. Pächt and Alexander, v.

2, no. 531), extending into the margins to form partial border. Initial inhabited by a kneeling putto blowing a gold trumpet. In inner margin a life-size fly, grey with red eyes. In lower margin, arms of the Barozzi family of Venice (argent, a fess azure; surmounted by a mitre) flanked by two putti drawn in pen, standing on a patch of green ground. Plain initials in green, red and blue. Headings in red; paragraph marks in red and blue.

Binding: Italy, uncertain date. Limp vellum wrapper. Traces of two fastenings. Title, in ink, on spine ("Fanensis Poemata") visible under ultra-violet light.

Written in Northern Italy, perhaps in the Veneto according to A. C. de la Mare; the manuscript, presumably the dedication copy from the poet to Giovanni Barozzi whose arms appear on f. 1r, was produced between 1454, the date of the death of Jacobus de Mozzanica (art. 4), and 1465, when Barozzi ceased serving as bishop of Bergamo (dedication in art. 1). The inscription on upper cover, s. xvi[1]: "Domini Palladij [followed by illegible word or abbreviation]," which also occurs on the cover of Marston MS 161, suggests that the manuscript formerly belonged to Alexandrus Palladius of Udine (see also catalogue entry for Marston MS 161). From the collection of Vincenzo Joppi. Purchased from L. C. Witten in 1958 by Thomas E. Marston (bookplate).

secundo folio: *Consultissimo*

Bibliography: Faye and Bond, p. 85, no. 188.

Marston MS 189 — Northeastern Italy, in or after 1434
Land and Property Register of the Marquis of Este

1. ff. 1r–2r Description of house and appurtenances in San Martino (probably San Martino di Venezze on the border of the provinces of Rovigo and Padua, or San Martino di Lupari in the northern part of the province of Padua, near Castelfranco) inhabited by the stewards ("canevari") of the marquis of Este, including a description of the "new" and the "old" land registers, specifying for each book the support, number of leaves, first and final instruments, and binding (the "catasto novo" in 300 leaves of which 147 contain documents, covering 1424–34; the "catasto vechio" in 312 leaves of which 295 contain documents, covering 1396–1424); also mentioned is a book of rents of 100 leaves, identified by its *secundo folio* and by its explicit.

2. f. 2r–v Description of house and appurtenances in Calaone (north of

Este, in the province of Padua) inhabited by the land-agent ("castaldo") of the marquis of Este.

3. ff. 2v–53r for Este and ff. 53r–84v for Montagnana (both towns in the province of Padua): Resumé in 1434 of previous land contracts contained in full in the new and in the old registers (see above, art. 1), or occasionally in notaries' registers, giving name(s) of renter(s), the land boundaries, the amount of the rent, the date due, and the present location of the full document (which register, with folio number); rents are to be paid in cash or in kind (wheat, spelt, fruit, chickens, capons, pheasant, thrush, lamb, kid, salt pork, oil, wine, candles of white wax, spurs, dog collar and leash, hawking gloves or the entire hawking furnishings, "uno bello fornimento da sparavero," f. 71r); payment dates are usually set for the Nativity of the Virgin (8 September), but also for Easter, the Annunciation (25 March), St. Peter's feast (29 June), St. Michael's feast (29 September), harvest time, or Christmas; the method of payment for wheat is often directed to be made specifically "to the granary of the marquis in Este." In the right-hand column, the summary of the main text lists revenue alone; in the left column are updated notices with names of more recent renters, frequently dated 1464, but also as far back as 1444 (f. 71r) or as recent as 1469 (f. 2v). Two folios, ff. 37 and 48, are ruled but blank

4. ff. 84v–86r Résumé of later documents, 1434–1472, added in various hands; ff. 86v–88v ruled but blank

Parchment, ff. 88, 309 x 243 (210 x 125) mm. 41 long lines. Two pairs of vertical bounding lines on both sides of written space, full length. Ruled in brown ink.

$I\text{-}III^{10}, IV^{12}, V^{6}, VI\text{-}IX^{10}$.

Written by multiple scribes in neat *mercantesca* scripts, below top line.

Binding: Italy, date uncertain. Vellum wrapper. Wound sewing on four double supports. The spine is lined with brown leather. Endbands sewn on tawed skin cores and through spine linings. Pink stain from earlier turn-ins on f. 88v. Traces of one tie.

Written in Northeastern Italy in or after 1434, with summaries of some documents dated as late as 1472 at end (art. 4). Miscellaneous titles, s. xviii, on front cover; shelf-marks and notations include: "folio [?] x," "No. 26," "R." Note in upper margin, f. 1r: "No 5 E. del 86." In pencil inside back cover: "282." Purchased from H. P. Kraus in 1958 by Thomas E. Marston (bookplate).

secundo folio: de zinar.

Bibliography: Faye and Bond, p. 85, no. 189.

Marston MS 190 Veneto [?], s. XV^{med}

Bartolomeus Facius, De vitae felicitate, etc.

1. ff. 1r–43r *Ad Alfosum* [sic] *Regem Gloriosissimum Bartolomei Facii In Dialogum De Vite Felicitate Proemium Incipit.* [dedication to Alfonso V:] Humane vite condicionem sepius michi reputanti. Rex clementissime illud maxime mirandum ... a te consecutum existimabo. [text, f. 2v:] *Incipit Dialogus.* Cum Antonius panormita clarus ex singulis poeta iureque consultus ferrariam sese aliquando contulisset ... datum est. [letter, f. 41v:] Adnimauerti [*sic*] vir ornatissime et litteris tuis perbreuibus id quod per hosce dies ... Alterius augere si modo possum uehementer cupio. Vale.

   Bartolomeus Facius (or Fazio), *De vitae felicitate*, composed in 1445 or 1446; a dialogue between Antonius Panormita, Guarino da Verona and Johannes Lamola, dedicated to King Alfonso V of Aragon and with added letter to Roberto Strozzi. Text printed in F. M. Sandeus, *De regibus Siciliae et Apuliae* (Hanover, 1611) pp. 106–48; Facius' letter to Strozzi edited by T. De Marinis, *La biblioteca napoletana dei Re d'Aragona* (Milan, 1952) v. 1, p. 25. For a recent summary of Facius' life and works, as well as bibliography, see E. I. Rao, *Bartolomeo Facio, Invective in Laurentium Vallam* (Naples, 1978) pp. 13–25. Proper names written in red by scribe in margins, many trimmed; names of interlocutors in red.

2. ff. 43v–47v *In Cena domini Oratiuncula.* Quoniam sepe ac multum superioribus annis a maioribus meis de diuinissimo eucaristie sacramento luculenter peroratum est patres optimi ... eterne felicitatis inueniamur epartes [?]. Dixi.

3. ff. 47v–50v [Heading:] De dominica resurectione oratiuncula incipit. [text:] TAn [?] et si pro ingenij mei paruitate rem michi et ut uerius dicam imposibilem impositam fuisse conspexerim ... in hoc mundo quo tandem cum ipso in perpetuum triumphare mereamur in celo. Amen.

Paper (watermarks, in gutter and obscured by reinforcement stays: unidentified mountain), ff. i (paper) + 50 (contemporary foliation, arabic numerals), 214 x 154 (150 x 98) mm. 24 long lines. Frame-ruled in lead.

I–V[10]. Horizontal catchwords in lower margin to left of inner bounding line, verso (Derolez 12.2).

Written in a sloping humanistic bookhand with cursive features, above top line.

Two finely drawn vine-stem initials in pen, unfilled and unpainted; f. 1r, 6-line; f. 2v, 4-line; sketches, in lead, for initials visible beneath. Headings, in red, f. 1r and 1v, and continuation letters for first words of text, f. 1r, in majuscules heavily influenced by Greek models.

Binding: Italy, s. xix. Rigid vellum case with title in ink on spine: "Incerti auctoris manuscriptum De uite felicitate." Edges spattered orange.

Written in the middle of the 15th century, probably in the Veneto according to A. C. de la Mare; early provenance unknown. Purchased in 1958 from C. A. Stonehill (inv. no. 13686) by Thomas E. Marston (bookplate).

secundo folio: in me

Bibliography: Faye and Bond, p. 85, no. 190.

Marston MS 192 — Belgium, s. XII$^{\text{med-3/4}}$
Gregory the Great, Homeliae XL in Evangelia

ff. 1r–167v *In nomine domini nostri ihesu christi atque salvatoris. in hoc uolumine continentur omelie sancti gregorii. numero. xl. in christi nomine incipit epistola domini gregorii pape ad episcopum tauromenitanum.* [preface:] Reuerentissimo et sanctissimo fratri secundino episcopo, Gregorius seruus seruorum dei. Inter sacra missarum sollempnia ex his que diebus certis in hac ecclesia legi ex more solent, sancti euangelij quadraginta lectiones exposui . . . unde in his que emendate sunt certiores fiant. Explicit epistola. [table of contents, f. 1v:] *Incipiunt capitula omeliarum.* Omelia sancti euuangelij secundum Lucam. In illo tempore, Dixit ihesus . . . xx. *Omelia sancti euuangelii secundum Lucam.* Anno xv. imperij tyberij cesaris procurante pontio pilato iudeam. *Expliciunt.* [f. 2r:] *Lectio sancti euuangelii secundum Lucam. capitula. Capitulum. .i.* In illo tempore, Dixit Ihesus discipulis suis. Erunt signa in sole et luna et stellis . . . [Luc. 21.25]. *Omelia lectionis eiusdem beati Gregorij pape. habita ad populum in basilica sancti Petri apostoli.* Dominus ac redemptor noster paratos nos inuenire desiderans. senescentem mundum que mala sequantur denuntiat . . . [f. 72v:] quam superne misericordie pignus tenemus. *Expliciunt omelie euangelorum numero. xx. in prima parte.* [table:] *Incipiunt capitula secunda. Omelia sancti euangelii secundum Marcum. xxi.* In illo tempore. Maria magdalene. et maria iacobi ... *xl.* Dixit ihesus discipulis suis. Homo quidam erat diues et induebatur purpura et. *Secundum Lucam.* [f. 73r:] *Incipiunt omelie que maiores uocantur. numero uiginti. dominica sancta in pascha. Lectio sancti euangelij, secundum marcum. capitulum .i.* In illo tempore, Maria magdalene. et maria iacobi ... [Mark 16.1]. *Omelia lectionis eiusdem beati Gregorii pape, habita ad populum in basilica sancte marie die sancto pasche.* Multis uobis lectionibus fratres karissimi per dictatum loqui consueui, sed quia lassescente stomacho ... [concludes in *Sermo XL*:] Sed hec omnipotens deus que per me in uestris auribus loquitur. per se in uestris mentibus loquatur,// A later hand, s. xvii–xviii, has completed the text by adding the formulaic ending: qui uiuit et regnat cum patre in vnitate spiritus sancti deus. per omnia secula seculorum amen. Explicit omelia.

Gregory the Great, *Homeliae XL in Evangelia*, ending imperfectly and missing text in *Sermo XXVI* (between ff. 138–139): "...quia nonumquam ipsi qui ei per fidem sub- // perceperat. prodige expendit, postquam esurire cepit..."; PL 76.1075–1312.

Parchment, ff. v (paper) + 167 + v (paper), 291 x 187 (214 x 130) mm. Written in 27 long lines. Single vertical and double horizontal (for lines 1, 3, 25, 27) bounding lines. Ruled in lead. Prickings in lower margin.

I-XVII^8, XVIII^8 (-3, 4 between ff. 138–139), XIX-XXI^8, XXII^2 (-2, with loss of text). Quires signed with Roman numerals surrounded by dots and with abbreviation stroke for *-us*, center of lower margin, verso.

Written in an elegant late caroline minuscule script.

One large initial, f. 1r, 8-line, in red ink, filled with stylized scrolls issuing from the mouth of a fantastic bird. 5-line incipit, f. 1r, in rows of majuscules: red, red, black, green, red. Numerous other initials, 7- to 4-line, in blue, red or green, some with stylized leaf terminals and interior arabesque designs on parchment ground. Small initials, 1-line, alternate blue, red, and green for tables of contents. Headings (often crowded into inadequate space left by scribe) and running headlines in red.

Upper corner of f. 75 torn affecting text; many leaves neatly repaired.

Binding: Broadway, Worcestershire, England, 1911, by Katherine Adams (fl. 1901–45; note of Sir Sydney Cockerell on back pastedown). Green goatskin with gold-tooling on the turn-ins and gold-tooled title on spine: "Gregorii/ Magni/ Homiliae/ XL de/ Diuersis/ Evangelii/ Lectionibus" and "MS. Saec. XII."

Written in the middle to third quarter of the 12th century at the Cistercian abbey of Villars, founded in 1146 in the diocese of Liège; although the manuscript was rebound while in the possession of Sir Sydney Cockerell, inscriptions from its earlier binding have been pasted inside the back cover: "Villarie" (s. xvi); "Ad Villarium [remainder illegible]" (s. xvii–xviii); "462" (s. xviii–xix). Marston MS 192 can perhaps be identified with the "Omelie beati Gregorii pape" listed in an early 14th-century catalogue of the abbey published by H. Schuermans, "Bibliothèque de l'Abbaye de Villers," *Annales de la Société archéologique et folklorique de Nivelles* ... 6 (1898) p. 202. The manuscript was still being used during the 15th–16th centuries when certain passages were marked in the margin "In refectorio" and accents were added to the text to aid pronunciation (e.g., f. 20r). Belonged to Sir Thomas Phillipps (no. 6932); Phillipps sale (Sotheby's, 30 April 1903) to Quaritch from whom it was acquired in September 1907 by Sir Sydney Cockerell who then signed and dated it after it was rebound: "Sydney C. Cockerell/ Cambridge/ Aug. 20 1911." When Cockerell bought the volume the Gregory text was bound with Ps.-Origen, *Homilia de lectione Maria stabat monumentum* (6 ff.), in what Cockerell described as a "shabby brown calf of the 18th century with brass rim and clasp lettered HOMELIA D. Gregory" [note on front pastedown]; for a description of the Ps.-Origen manuscript see H. P. Kraus, Cat. 165 *Cimelia,* 1983, no. 36. Sold privately by Cockerell on 21 February 1957 to Dawson's. For more information on Cockerell's collection see C. de Hamel, "Medieval and Renaissance Manuscripts from the Library of Sir Sydney Cockerell (1867–1962)," *The British Library Journal* 13.2 (1987) pp. 186–210 (Marston MS 192 listed on p. 201, no. 53). Purchased in 1958 from C. A. Stonehill (inv. no. 10498) by Thomas E. Marston (bookplate).

secundo folio: In illo

Bibliography: Faye and Bond, p. 86, no. 192.
Leclercq, 1961, pp. 163–64.

Marston MS 194
Gregory IX, Decretales

Low Countries, s. XIV[1]

f. 1 = pastedown, ruled, but blank; ff. 2r–82v [prologue:] [Gregorius] Episcopus seruus seruorum dei dilectis filiis. doctoribus et scolaribus vniuersis parisius commorantibus salutem et apostolicam benedictionem. [R]ex pacificus pia miseratione disposuit sibi subditos ... facere absque auctoritate sedis apostolice speciali. [text:] Innocentius iij. in concilio generali. [F]irmiter credimus et simpliciter confitemur quod vnus solus est uerus deus ... iudicandi seu arbitri. de hac causa cognoscere//

Gregory IX, *Decretales*, ending imperfectly in Bk. I, tit. 41, cap. 9. A. Friedberg, ed., *Corpus iuris canonici*, Pars secunda, Decretalium Collectiones (Leipzig, 1922) v. 2, cols. 1–228. The text is arranged symmetrically in the center of each page, but lacks any rubrics, decorative initials, running headings or commentary as are usually found in similar canon law manuscripts.

Parchment (fuzzy), ff. 82 (modern foliation includes front pastedown), 450 x 307 (212 x 124) mm. 2 columns, 35 long lines. Single vertical bounding lines. Ruled faintly in ink with text rulings in column spaces only. Prickings in upper, lower, and outer margins.

I^{10} (1 = front pastedown), $II–IV^{10}$, V^{12}, $VI–VIII^{10}$. Quires signed with Roman numerals along lower edge, near gutter.

Written in bold gothic bookhand, below top line.

Spaces for decorative initials and rubrics remain unfilled.

Binding: Place uncertain, s. xv. The backs of the quires are cut in to mark the sewing stations. Original sewing on five supports laced through tunnels in the edge to channels on the outside of beech boards, back inside and wedged. The endband cores are laced into the boards and pegged. The boards are flush and square.

Covered in cream colored tawed skin with traces of two strap-and-pin fastenings, the pins on the upper boards. Title written in contemporary hand on upper board: "liber decretalium sine glosa non completus."

Written in the Low Countries in the first half of the 14th century; both the text and decoration of the codex were never finished. Provenance unknown. Remains of three unidentified labels on spine. In pencil on back pastedown: "B/335/S75 = [?]." Purchased in 1956 from A. L. van Gendt of the Netherlands by L. C. Witten (inv. no. 1044), who sold it in 1958 to Thomas E. Marston (bookplate).

secundo folio: sacerdos qui

Bibliography: Faye and Bond, p. 86, no. 194.

Marston MS 196 — Germany, s. XV^2
Johannes Herolt, Sermones de tempore

1. f. 1r notes on provenance; f. 1v blank ff. 2r–21r Indices: alphabetical index to the sermons of Johannes Herolt, *A-Y*, ending *Explicit tabulatura de tempore* (ff. 2v–10v); Nota infra de x preceptis, 7 peccatis et sacra-

mentis (f. 11r-v); Saints and feast days listed in the order of the calendar from *De sancto andrea* through *De Sancta Cruce*, ending *Explicit Registrum de Sanctis* (ff. 12r–14r); *De dedicacione sermones tabule* (f. 14v); *Tabula per Quadragesimam* (ff. 14v–16v); *Tabula siue registrum exemplorum contentorum in sermonibus sequentibus secundum aliqualem ordinem alphabeti Primo de abstinencia .2. exempla*, from *abstinencia* through *yppocrita* (ff. 16v–21r).

Index entries refer to sermons in art. 4 by numbers, and by letters that indicate subdivisions of the text. All sermons are numbered in upper margin and lettered in inner or outer margin, but numbering in text is inconsistent or sometimes absent (cf. comments on art. 4).

2. ff. 21v–23r *Articuli qui repellendi sunt a communione*. Isti infrascripti quos nominabo prohibebo a sacra communione eucaristie nisi contriti et confessi fuerint ... ut ipsi simplices homines addiscant per hoc peccata sua cognoscere et ea confiteri Amen.

   A system of indexing similar to that in art. 1 is used here, but less consistently.

3. f. 23r–v *Inposicio crucis et absolucio* [?]. Modus autem et signum crucis huius modi affugendum quantus affixio ipsa eo conformius in singulis ciuitatibus ... pollicior augmentum In nomine patris et filij ... Amen. ff. 24r–25v ruled, but blank

4. ff. 27r–323v //arma lucis vnum quilibet peccator iam illo tempore sacro debet a peccatis cessare et preterita peccata deplangere ... [Sermo 2, f. 28r:] *Dominica prima aduentus*. Hora est iam nos de sompno ... [Rom. 13.11]. Boetius vnicuique viro bono inserta est naturalis cupiditas boni ... Domine filia mea modo defuncta est ... [Mat. 9.18]. Videtur esse contraictas [?] inter matheum et marcum Marcus enim dicit quod pater dixit ... tunc non audere ad talem virum venire. Sc. *Expliciunt dicta discipuli*.

   Johannes Herolt ("Discipulus"), *Sermones de tempore*, beginning imperfectly; some contemporary annotations throughout. Kaeppeli, SOPMA 2393. See also comments on indexing in art. 1. Three different early hands have numbered the sermons with conflicting sequences.

Paper (watermarks: several bull's heads including Piccard Ochsenkopf V.636 and similar in design to V.305–13), ff. i (modern paper) + 322 (modern foliation, 1–323, omits 26) + i (modern paper), 311 x 215 (225 x 160) mm. 2 columns, ca. 41 lines. Frame-ruled with single vertical (and sometimes upper horizontal) bounding lines. Ruled in lead or ink.

Collation impossible due to tight binding; no quire marks or catchwords.

Written in hybrida script, perhaps by a single scribe.

Plain red initials, 3- to 2-line. Paragraph marks, initial strokes and underlining in red; rubrics added sporadically.

Binding: Germany, s. xv. Sewn on four supports attached to wooden boards. Covers lined with parchment documents; text side pasted down and illegible (see also provenance).

Covered in white tawed skin with two fastenings, the catches on the upper board. Remains of label with title on spine; traces of inscription on upper board. Rebacked.

Written in Germany in the second half of the 15th century. Title and ownership inscription, s. xvi^{in}, on f. 1r indicates that the manuscript was donated to the Charterhouse at Buxheim by Hilprand Brandenberg of Biberach (d. 1514): "Titulus Sermones discipuli de Tempore" and below "Liber Cartusiensis In Buchshaim prope Memingen proueniens a confratre nostri domino hilprando Brandenbergense de Bibraco/ donatus sacerdote/ continens ut supra/ Oretur pro eo et pro quibus desiderauit." The bookplate of Hilprand Brandenberg (hand-colored woodcut of an angel holding a shield representing his arms: an ox passant with a ring in its nose) is pasted below the ownership inscription, to which the shelfmark "CXXXI" was added by a later hand. For other information on this donor and books given by him to Buxheim see P. Ruf, ed., *Mittelalterliche Bibliothekskataloge Deutschlands und der Schweiz* (Munich, 1932; reprinted 1970) v. 3.1, p. 82 (additional bibliography on the Charterhouse listed on pp. 90–91) and P. Needham, "The Books of Hilprand Brandenberg," *Twentieth Report to the Fellows of the Pierpont Morgan Library 1981–1983*, pp. 152–54, 401. Later inscription of Buxheim, s. xvii, in upper margin, f. 2r: "Aulae B. Mariae Virginis." Pen-trials, s. xv–xvi, on back pastedown include the names Hans Jacob von Vadmen and Johannes Schwencz. Buxheim was suppressed in 1803; its books passed to the Count of Ostein and then to the Counts of Waldbott-Bassenheim. Unidentified "421" on large paper tag, on spine. "No 51" in circle and "L. B. 1019" in pencil on front pastedown; "21655" in pencil on back pastedown. Purchased in 1956 from Bernard Quaritch of London by L. C. Witten (inv. no. 1158), who sold it in 1958 to Thomas E. Marston (bookplate).

secundo folio: uolenti

Bibliography: Faye and Bond, p. 86, no. 196.

Marston MS 197 Hautecombe [?], s. XII^{med}
Jerome, Commentaries on the Minor Prophets Pl. 39

Vol. I:

1. ff. 1r–33r *Incipit prologus beati hieronimi presbiteri in explanatione* [corrected from *explatione*] *osee prophete.* Si in explanacionibus omnium prophetarum sancti spiritus indigemus aduentu ... ea que scripta sunt disseramus. *Explicit prologus. Incipit explanatio.* Uerbum domini quod factum est ad Osee filium beeri Septuaginta similiter ... in ruinam et resurrectionem multorum in israel. *Explicit osee propheta.*

   Commentariorum in Osee prophetam libri 3 ad Pammachium; M. Adriaen, CC 76 (1969) pp. 1–158.

2. ff. 33r–43r *Incipit prologus in iohel.* Non idem ordo est .xii.^{cim} prophetarum apud septuaginta interpretes ... in nobis uires consideres sed uoluntatem. *Incipit explanatio.* Verbum domini quod factum est ad iohel filium fathuel. Septuaginta interpretes pro fatuhel ... diligit dominus portas syon super omnia tabernacula iacob. *Explicit iohel propheta.*

   Commentariorum in Ioelem prophetam ad Pammachium liber; Adriaen, *op. cit.*, pp. 159–209.

3. ff. 43r–67v *Incipit prologus in amos.* Amos propheta qui sequitur iohelem. et est tercius duodecim prophetarum ... [prologue concludes at the bottom of f. 43r, col. 2:] Vnde nos ex hebreo uertimus. [Book I begins without any rubric:] Verba amos qui fuit in pastoralibus ... quid mihi uideatur in singulis disseram. *Explicit prologus. Incipit expositio.* [beginning of Book I, section 2, f. 44r:] Et dixit. Dominus de syon rugiet ... cuius promissio lex. natura est. *Explicit amos propheta.*

   Commentariorum in Amos prophetam libri 3; Adriaen, *op. cit.*, pp. 211–348.

4. ff. 67v–72v *Incipit prologus. in explanacione abdie prophete.* Cum essem paruulus. ut paruulus loquebar ut paruulus sapiebam ... ethyopicos fluctus bibit. alter madescit unguentis. *Explicit prologus. Incipit explanatio.* Hunc esse aiunt hebrei. qui sub rege samarie ahab ... Qui ueriora et meliora dixerit. in illius sentenciam transgredere. *Explicit abdias propheta.*

   Commentariorum in Abdiam prophetam liber; Adriaen, *op. cit.*, pp. 349–75.

5. ff. 72v–80v *Incipit prologus in ionam prophetam.* Triennium circiter fluxit. postquam quinque prophetas interpretatus ... nobis christus dei filius soluitur. *Explicit prologus. Incipit explanatio.* Et factum est uerbum

domini ad ionam filium amathi . . . comparantur iumentis insipientibus. et assimilantur eis. *Explicit ionas propheta.*

Commentariorum in Ionam prophetam liber; Adriaen, *op. cit.*, pp. 377–419.

Vol II:

6. f. 80v of Vol. I and ff. 1r–21r in Vol. II: *Incipit prologus in explanatione michee prophete.* Micheas in quem nunc commentarios dictare cupio . . . liberis a parentibus imponuntur. *Explicit prologus. Incipit explanatio.* [Vol. II, f. 1r:] Uerbum igitur [domini] quod factum est ad micheam . . . de luto et paleis egyptias extruat ciuitates. *Explicit micheas propheta.*

   Commentariorum in Michaeam prophetam libri 2; Adriaen, *op cit.*, pp.422–524.

7. ff. 21r–32r *Incipit prologus in explanationem naum.* Iuxta septuaginta interpretes in ordine .xii. prophetarum post ionam naum ponitur . . . ueros assyrios futurus est dominus. *Explicit prologus. Incipit explanatio.* Deus emulator. et ulciscens dominus. Vox prophete . . . irruit quidem sed ingredi non potest. *Explicit naum propheta.*

   Commentariorum in Naum prophetam liber; M. Adriaen, CC 76A (1970) pp. 525–78.

8. ff. 32r–49r *Incipit prologus in abachuc propheta.* Primum chromaci episcoporum doctissime scire nos conuenit . . . propheta scribit que uentura cognoscit. *Explicit prologus. Incipit expositio.* Usquequo domine clamabo et non exaudies . . . cantores ceteros meo carmine superabo. *Explicit abacuc propheta.*

   Commentariorum in Abacuc prophetam ad Chromatium libri 2; *ibid.*, pp. 579–654.

9. ff. 49r–62r *Incipit prologus in sophonia propheta.* Ante quam sophoniam aggrediar qui nonus est in ordine . . . quem iam fragilior sexus inuenerat. *Explicit prologus. Incipit explanatio.* Uerbum domini quod factum est ad sophoniam filium chusi . . . ab eorum translatione discordat. indigere expositione non arbitror. *Explicit sophonias propheta.*

   Commentariorum in Sophoniam prophetam liber; *ibid.*, pp. 655–711.

10. ff. 62r–70r *Incipit prologus beati iheronimi in explanatione aggei prophete.* Secundo anno darii regis. persarum filii hystapis . . . quam prohibentis regis imperium. *Explicit prologus. Incipit explanatio.* In anno secundo darii regis. in mense sexto . . . Dominus dabit [*uerbum* expunged] euangelizantibus uerbum. uirtute multa. *Explicit ageus propheta.*

Commentariorum in Aggaeum prophetam ad Paulam et Eustochium liber; *ibid.*, pp. 713–46.

11. ff. 70r–104v *Incipit prologus in zacharia propheta.* Ultimo iam autunni tempore. frater noster filius tuus sisinnius monachus . . . interpretationis uela pandamus. *Explicit prologus. Incipit explanatio.* In mense octauo. in anno secundo darii. factum est uerbum . . . alienigenum appellari uolunt. quem de domo domini asserunt auferendum. *Explicit zacharias propheta.*

Commentariorum in Zachariam prophetam ad Exsuperium Tolosanum episcopum libri 3; *ibid.*, pp. 747–900.

12. ff. 104v–113v *Incipit prologus malachie prophete.* Ultimum .xii. prophetarum malachi interpretari uolumus . . . interpretationis note dicende sunt. *Explicit prologus. Incipit explanatio.* Onus uerbi domini ad israel in manu malachi . . . et sicut uictima domini. Nec hoc leticie fine contentus est. sed calcabit impios//

Commentariorum in Malachiam prophetam ad Minervium et Alexandrum liber; *ibid.*, pp. 901–40; the text breaks at IV.3, p. 940, line 4, with 68 lines of text missing.

13. f. 114r–v //terra. dracones et omnes abyssi. Dracones circa aquam uersantur. de speluncis procedunt. feruntur in aere. concitatur propter eos aer. Magna quedam sunt animantia dracones maiora non sunt super terram . . . siue inde siue inde//

Unidentified text from another manuscript of similar format, but of slightly earlier date; top and bottom of leaf damaged with loss of text.

Parchment, vol. I: f. ii (paper) + 80 + i (paper); vol. II: ff. ii (paper) + 114 + i (paper), 392 x 275 (301 x 212) mm. 2 columns, 43 lines. Single vertical and one to three horizontal bounding lines, full across; additional ruling between columns and in outer margin along which quotation marks and *Nota* signs have been aligned. Corrections and additions to text on rulings drawn in margins. Ruled in lead; remains of prickings in all four margins.

Vol. I: I–VI^{8}, VII^{8} (2, 7 = single leaves), VIII–X^{8}. Vol. II: I–XIII^{8}, XIV^{10} (–10, loss of text; + 1 leaf added at end from contemporary manuscript).

Written and neatly corrected in early gothic bookhand by several scribes; f. 114 in a similar but somewhat earlier hand.

Fine painted initials, 19- to 5-line, for major text divisions, monochrome red or polychrome in red, bright green, olive green and/or brown, with pale yellow washes. Preliminary sketches in lead often visible underneath; some bows appear to be drawn with compass. Smaller initials of similar design throughout. Initials are characterized by lattice work, acanthus scrolls and decorative empty spaces within initials like those in Cambridge, Mass., Harvard University, Houghton Library MS Richardson 27 (see L. Light, "The Bible in the Twelfth Century," exh. cat. [Cambridge, Mass., 1988] p. 49, pl. 11). The opening initial on f. 1r is executed in red and blue. Headings in red throughout.

Binding: Italy, s. xix in. Half bound in brown calf with bright pink paper sides. Three green gold-tooled labels on the spine of each volume: "Vol. I" or "Vol. II"; "Hieronimi in XII Prophetas Manuscrip"; "Saecul XII." Title on black gold-tooled labels: "Hieronimi in XII Prophetas Manuscrip." Edges spattered blue-green. The same distinctive bindings also found on Marston MSS 50, 125, 128, 135, 151, 153, 158, and 159, all of Hautecombe provenance.

Produced in the mid-12th century, perhaps at the Cistercian abbey of Hautecombe, located in the ancient diocese of Geneva and founded toward the beginning of the 12th century by monks from the abbey of Aulps (see R. Clair, "Les origines de l'abbaye d'Hautecombe," *Mélanges à la mémoire du Père Anselme Dimier* [Arbois, 1982-87] tome II, v. 4, pp. 615-27). Although there is no ex libris, the two volumes exhibit the characteristic pink binding of the books of Monseigneur Hyacinthe della Torre who acquired and rebound a group of twelve manuscripts from this monastery at the beginning of the 19th century (see Leclercq, 1951, p. 75). The script, format, and general design of the decorative initials in this manuscript resemble closely those in Marston MS 50, which also belonged to Hautecombe. Belonged to the Biblioteca del Seminario Metropolitano in Turin (Leclercq, *op. cit.*, p. 77). Acquired from E. Rossignol of Paris in 1958 by L. C. Witten (inv. no. 2036), who sold it the same year to Thomas E. Marston (bookplate).

secundo folio: [vol. I:] Verbum domini
[vol. II:] de samaria

Bibliography: Faye and Bond, p. 86, no. 197.

Marston MS 198 — Northeastern Italy, ca. 1430-40

Jerome, Dialogus contra Pelagianos, etc.

1. ff. 1r-26r *Incipit prefacio sancti Ieronimi in dialogon contra pelagianos hereticos sub nominibus attici et Crithobole. Vbi commendatur gracia dei.*

[prologue:] Scripta iam ad thesiphontem [*sic*] epistola. in qua ad interrogata respondi. . . . [text, f. 1v:] *Incipit dialogus contra eos qui dicebant homini sufficere liberum arbitrium ad salutem.* Atticus. dic michi critobole, verum est quod a te scriptum audio . . . vt cuius in ceteris auctoritate ducimini eciam in hac parte errorem sequamini.

Jerome, *Dialogus contra Pelagianos*, Books I–III; PL 23.495–590.

2. ff. 26r–47r *Incipit liber primus controuersiarum ruffini aduersus Ieronimum.* Relegi al. perlegi scripta aproniane fili karissime que ab amico et fratre bono de oriente ad uirum nobilissimum pammachium missa transtulisti ad me . . . necesse est ecclesie catholice sentenciam. siue aduersus tuos datam.

   Rufinus Tyrannius, *Apologia contra Hieronymum*; M. Simonetti, ed., CC ser. lat. 20 (1961) pp. 37–123.

3. ff. 47r–63r *Incipit liber primus ad pammachium et marcellam pro se contra accusatores defensio.* Ex vestris et multorum litteris didici obici mihi in scola tyrannica lingua . . . quam hostem latentem sub amici nomine sustinere.

   Jerome, *Apologia contra Rufinum*, Books I–II; P. Lardet, ed., CC ser. lat. 79 (1982) pp. 1–72. Marston MS 198 listed on pp. 16* (s. xiv), 137*, 141*.

4. ff. 63r–72r *Incipit liber xi questionum* [?]*icon ad algaudsiam* [sic]. De hac questione in commentarijs mathei plenius diximus. Vnde apparet que hec interrogas . . . postea mendacium id est antichristum suscepturi sint.

   Jerome, *Ad Algasium liber quaestionum undecim* (Letter 121); I. Hilberg, ed., CSEL 56 (1918) pp. 4–55. A 15th-century hand has added in the margin at the beginning of the text: "Proemium huius libri sequitur post xx folia nam ibi replicatus est hic liber non tamen absolutus [art. 8 below]." The original scribe had written in the margin the first *questio* omitted here (incipit: Cur iohannes discipulos . . .), but appearing on f. 84v.

5. ff. 72r–75r *Disputacio de ratione anime.* Cum apud vos celestis eloquencia purissimi fontis et litterarum omnium fluenta redundent . . . Tunc deinde illi idest appollonius. tertulianus. pompeius. arnobius. lactancius. atque appollinaris. qui unam quidem ex nullis subsiscentibus a deo factam esse dicunt . . . [f. 72v:] *Ieronimus.* Beatus itaque Ieronimus tam sanctum victorinum martirem . . . *Augustini testimonium.* Sanctus quoque augustinus hanc opinionem in octo ad modum voluminibus verbis tueri cernitur . . . [followed by a series of alternating extracts from the works

of Jerome and Augustine, labelled with the rubrics Augustinus Ieronimo and Ieronimus Augustino] ... vbertate rigati redundetis fluentis sanctorum.

Anonymous, *Disputatio de ratione anime*; most of the text (ff. 73r–75r) consists of the extracts in a "dialogue" format between Augustine (e.g., selections from *Epistola CXXXI ad Hieronymum*; PL 22.1124–38) and Jerome (*Epistola CXXVI ad Marcellinum et Anapsychiam*; PL 22.1085–86). The text is published in PL 30.261–71 (*Epistola XXXVIII. Dialogus sub nomine Hieronymi et Augustini*).

6. ff. 75r–76v *Planctus seu lamentum origenis translatum a beato Ieronimo presbitero.* In afflictione et dolore animi incipio loqui ad eos qui cogunt me extra asserentem ordinem ... Quia tibi est gloria cum patre et spiritu sancto in secula seculorum.

   Origen [?], translated into Latin by Jerome.

7. ff. 76v–84r *Epistola Ieronimi ad hebidiam de xii questionibus.* Ignota uultu. fidei mihi ardore notissima es. Et de extremis gallie finibus in bethleemitico iure [?] latitantem ... que nostra uel virtute uel uicio et accenduntur et extinguuntur in nobis.

   Jerome, *Ad Hebydiam de quaestionibus duodecim* (Letter 120); I. Hilberg, ed., CSEL 55 (1912) pp. 470–515.

8. ff. 84r–91v *Capitula subscriptionis epistole. i.* Cur iohannes mittit discipulos suos ad dominum.... *Epistola vndecim questionum ad galasiam.* [prologue:] Filius meus apodemius qui interpretationem nominis sui longa ad nos nauigatione signauit ... [text, f. 84v:] *Prima questio.* Cur iohannes discipulos mittit ad dominum ut interrogarent eum. tu es qui uenturus ... et prouincie sue familiarius apostolus vtitur. e quibus exempli gracia pauca ponenda sunt//

   Jerome, *Ad Algasium liber questionum undecim* (Letter 121), ending abruptly in the *tenth questio*; I. Hilberg, ed., CSEL 56 (1918) pp. 4–42. See also art. 4 above.

9. ff. 91v–101v *Incipit Epistola Ieronimi ad demetriadem uirginem. Hanc epistolam notat beda non esse beati Ieronimi. Sed iuliani episcopi de campania qui fuit discipulus pelagii heretici. Et ipse hereticus multa in hac contra graciam dei disseruit.* Si summo ingenio parique fretus scientia officium scribendi facile me inplere posse crederem, tamen tam arduum ... nullum tempus longum uideri debet, quo gloria eternitatis adquiritur.

   Epistola ad Demetriadem de virginitate et vitae perfectione, variously attributed to Pelagius, Julian d'Eclane, Jerome (PL 30.15–45) or Augustine (PL 33.1099–1120).

10. ff. 101v–109v [*E*]*pitaphium sancte paule a beato Ieronimo editum.* Si cuncta mei corporis membra verterentur in linguas et omnes artus humana uoce resonarent nichil dignum sancte ac venerabilis paule virtutibus dicerem . . . Omne tempus uite impleuit annos. lvi. mensibus. viii. diebus. xxi.

Jerome, *Epistola CVIII ad Eustochium virginem*, on St. Paula; PL 22.878–906.

11. f. 109v Lectio ad Augustinum contra hereticos. Multi vno claudicant pede et nec fractis quidem ceruicibus inclinantur . . . et ibi seruitute pereat sempiterna. f. 110r ruled, but blank; for notes on f. 110v see provenance

Jerome, *Epistola CXLII ad Augustinum*; PL 22.1180–81.

Paper (watermarks: similar to Briquet Monts 11895 and 11702; unadorned anvil similar to Harlfinger Enclume 5; unidentified letter (D?) similar in general design to Harlfinger Lettre 14), ff. i (paper) + 110 + (paper), 292 x 215 (198 x 140) mm. 2 columns, 44 lines. Single vertical bounding lines and sometimes a single upper horizontal bounding line, full length and full width; ruled in lead or crayon. Prickings in upper, lower, and outer margins for bounding lines only.

I–XI^{10}. Scribe 1: horizontal catchwords in lower right of inner vertical bounding line, verso (Derolez 12.2). Scribe 2: horizontal catchwords in center of lower margin surrounded by four symmetrical clusters of three dots, verso (Derolez 12.1). Quire and leaf signatures (e.g., b1, b2, b3, b4, b5, x) in lower right corner.

Written by two scribes. Scribe 1 (ff. 1r–76v) in a fere-humanistic hand with features of round humanistic; Scribe 2 (ff. 76v–109v) in a more angular fere-humanistic hand.

One 4-line illuminated initial, f. 1r, shaded pink with red and green acanthus leaves on dark blue with white filigree against a gold ground edged thickly in black. In the upper left corner a red, blue and gold flower with spiralling acanthus in the upper and inner margins, forming a partial border, green, blue, red, brown, the spirals filled with gold or blue with white filigree. Large gold dots with four black spikes. Numerous pen and ink initials, 5– to 1–line, alternating in red and blue with purple or red penwork. Headings in red. Instructions to the rubricator at lower edge, f. 1r.

Binding: Place uncertain, s. xix–xx. Rigid vellum case with the title in ink on the spine: "Dialogi Pelagii et Attici."

Written in Northeastern Italy (perhaps Padua?); the painted and the penwork decoration of the manuscript are strikingly similar to those of Beinecke MS 343 dated 1437 and seem to have been executed in the same workshop (see vol. II, pp. 176–77, pl. 33). Bears evidence of having been read by Lorenzo Valla (1407–57), whose annotations in humanistic bookhand appear throughout the manuscript. Two contemporary ownership inscriptions (s. xv^2) on f. 110v ("Anthonj liso prouincie [?] de mallorca" and immediately below "Bernardus andor secretarius domine Regine") may suggest a link with the Aragonese court at Naples. Lorenzo Valla entered the service of Alfonso d'Aragona in 1435 and in 1445 he wrote the *Historiae Ferdinandi regis Aragoniae*; by 1448 he returned to Rome. Purchased in 1958 from C. A. Stonehill by Thomas E. Marston (bookplate).

secundo folio: dicere. cum

Bibliography: Faye and Bond, pp. 86–87, no. 198.

Marston MS 199 Florence, s. XV$^{3/4}$
Jerome, Epistolae, etc.

1. ff. ii recto–iv verso *Incipiunt tituli siue rubrice epistolarum* [remainder of heading mostly illegible]. *A/ Hieronymus ad Eustochium virginem de virginitate seruanda/* Audi filia et vide et inclina aurem tuam et obliuiscere populum [added above: *tuum*] et domum patris tui et cet. folio 15/ ... [ends in the letter *R*:] *Hieronymus ad pamachium et Marcellam contra suos detractores inuectiua ... de greco in latinum translatis./* folio 267 Rursum orientalibus uos locupleto mercibus et alexandrinas opes.//

   Table of contents arranged alphabetically according to *incipits*; each *incipit* preceded by rubric as it appears in text. Some portions badly stained and illegible; ends defectively.

2. ff. 2r–328v [f. 1 missing; text begins on 2r:] //mariam uxorem tuam. Et rursum. Exsurgens ioseph ... hoc accidisse ab omnibus iudicetur. Mei augustine carissime in tuis orationibus memor esto. *Explicit transitus beati et gloriosi hieronymi cum miraculis eiusdem.*

   A compilation of both genuine and spurious works attributed to Jerome, letters addressed to Jerome, and works by other authors about Jerome. In the following concordance we give the folio reference on which a work begins, with the appropriate citation in B. Lambert, ed., *Bibliotheca Hieronymiana Manuscripta* in Instrumenta Patristica IV

(Steenbrugge, 1969). A text is complete unless otherwise noted. A contemporary hand has entered some variant readings and pointing hands in margins. Spaces usually left unfilled for Greek, often with scribe's note "g" in margin; in those instances where Greek was written out, Latin glosses appear in margin.

[f. 1r] (251); f. 7r (309); f. 9 missing: " . . . in eternam regina // natura quam virgo. . ."; f. 15r (22); f. 24v (107); f. 27v (130); f. 33r (54); f. 36r (123); f. 40v (79); f. 43r (117); f. 45v (122); f. 48v (31, 20 lines omitted: "//armillis in Ezechihele . . . quae bona, bona ualde//"); f. 48v (672); f. 48v (313); f. 53v (125); f. 57r (58); f. 59v (342); f. 60v (69); f. 64v (147); f. 67r (14); f. 69v (52); f. 73v (318, with text in manuscript concluding: " . . . totiens te scias quo pollicitus es esse veniendum."); f. 76r (60); f. 80r (68); f. 80v (118); f. 82v (1); f. 84r (77); f. 86v (66); f. 89r (39); f. 92r (108); f. 100v (127); f. 103r (358, text ending: " . . . Vnde vides. quia sicut peccati contagione maculamur. ita expulsione eius abluimur"; PL 20.1037–41); f. 104v (73); f. 106r (129); f. 108v (64); f. 113r (308); f. 115r (120); f. 124r (121); f. 134v (119, the text is complete, but several sections have been transposed); f. 139r (319); f. 147v (334, conclusion of text in manuscript differs from that printed in PL 30.245–48 [253–56]); f. 148v (307); f. 153r (35); f. 153r (36); f. 156r (206, Prologue to *Interpretatio Homiliarum duarum Origenis in Cantica Canticorum*, followed by *Origenis in Cant. Cant.: Homilia prima, Homilia secunda*); f. 163v (18A); f. 167r (18B); f. 168r (19); f. 168r (20); f. 169r (21); f. 174r (316); f. 175r (317); f. 177r (514); f. 187v (15); f. 188r (16); f. 188r (343); f. 188v (346); f. 188v (347); f. 189r (49); f. 194v (48); f. 195r (50); f. 196v (51); f. 199v (57); f. 203r (83); f. 203r (80); f. 203v (84); f. 206v (124); f. 210v (81); f. 210v (PL 21.623–28: *Apologia quam pro se misit Rufinus Presbyter ad Anastasium*); f. 211v (256); f. 222r (61); f. 223r (109); f. 224r (253); f. 227r (332); f. 228r (138); f. 228v (63); f. 228v (91); f. 229r (87); f. 229r (88); f. 229r (89); f. 229v (90); f. 229v (254); f. 240v (56); f. 242r (67); f. 243r (110); f. 245r (105); f. 245v (104); f. 246v (116); f. 252r (112); f. 256v (115, manuscript includes passage not in printed text: "Si legisti librum explanationum . . . et sine nostro inuicem dolore ludamus."); f. 256v (103); f. 257r (111); f. 257r (131); f. 261v: *Augustini ad hieronymum responsiua de anima.* Scio animam ex opere dei consistere et prorsus opus dei . . . nihil ibi iam metuens respondebo. Ora pro me carissime frater.; f. 261v (132); f. 264v (126); f. 265r (102); f. 265v (143); f. 266r (142); f. 266r (101, 2.2–3); f. 266r (141); f. 266r (134); f. 266v (85); f. 267r (97); f. 267v (27); f. 268r (40); f. 268v (37); f. 268v (24); f. 269v (23); f. 270r (38); f. 270v (46); f. 273r (43, followed by 46.11–12); f. 273v (30); f. 274v (29); f. 276r (28); f.

276v (34); f. 277v (42); f. 278r (41); f. 278v (59); f. 279v (32); f. 279v (303); f. 281r (62); f. 281r (47); f. 281v (357); f. 282v (70); f. 283v (72); f. 284v (74); f. 285v (146); f. 286r (55, manuscript omits part 3: "Tertia id est . . . totus in cunctis."); f. 287r (55.3); f. 287v (71); f. 288v (348); f. 288v (349); f. 289r (99); f. 289r (219, with text ending abruptly in commentary: " . . . comendatrices ad dominum litteras sumpserat.//"); f. 290v (75); f. 291v (76); f. 291v (5); f. 292r (4); f. 292v (145); f. 292v (7); f. 293v (352); f. 293v (2); f. 294r (10); f. 294r (9); f. 294v (6); f. 294v (17); f. 295r (8); f. 295v (12); f. 295v (11); f. 296r (13); f. 296r (311); f. 297r (3); f. 297v (302); f. 299v (640); f. 299r *bis* (903E); f. 313v (903A); f. 316v (903C, with leaf with text missing between ff. 326 and 327: " . . . uidere cogi[tans] // romana urbe. . .").

Parchment, ff. i (paper) + i (modern parchment title page) + iv (contemporary parchment, art. 1) + 328 (contemporary foliation begins in art. 2, 2–299, with leaves 1 and 9 missing; modern foliation 299 *bis*–328) + i (paper). 365 x 254 (242 x 154) mm. 43 long lines. Single vertical bounding lines; ruled in pale brown ink or lead. Double rulings for each line of text ruled in lead. Remains of prickings in upper and lower margins.

I^4 (art. 1; structure uncertain, but one leaf missing at end), II (8 leaves foliated 2–8, 10), $III–XXXIII^{10}$, XXXIV^{10} (ff. 319–328; structure uncertain; leaf lost between 326–327).

Written in an upright humanistic script by a single scribe.

Three illuminated initials, 10- to 6-line, ff. 299r *bis*, 313v, 316v, gold against blue, green and dark red ground with white vine-stem ornament and pale yellow and white dots. Numerous small initials, 4- to 2-line, gold, against blue, green and dark red rectangular grounds with yellow or white filigree. The first leaf of art. 2, which was probably decorated with a border and/or arms, has been excised. A 19th-century title page has been inserted at the beginning: title is displayed in gold letters with black filigree against rectangular grounds of blue, red and ochre with gold filigree and framed by a full bar border, dark blue with geometric interlace, thickly edged in red, accented with gold dots. For art. 1, numerous small flourished initials, alternating red and blue with purple and red penwork. Headings in pale red.

Binding: Italy, s. xix. Brown sheepskin, blind- and gold-tooled. Metal corners and red, gold-tooled label: "Epistolae Divi Hieronimi." Yellow edges. Name, now partially effaced, in gold on upper cover: "P. Paolino."

Written in Florence in the third quarter of the 15th century; early provenance unknown. Various stains and corroded patches of parchment on ff. i–iv suggest early ownership inscriptions have been effaced. Belonged to

P. Paolino, s. xix, whose name appears on upper cover and who presumably rebound the volume and inserted the title page. "T. M." with "1" in a circle, in pencil, on title page. Purchased from Sotheby's through Maggs Bros. of London in 1958 by L. C. Witten (inv. no. 2057), who sold it in the same year to Thomas E. Marston (bookplate).

secundo folio: [table, f. ii:] *Hieronymus*
[text, f. 2:] mariam

Bibliography: Faye and Bond, p. 87, no. 199.

Marston MS 200 Italy, s. XIII/XIV
Honorius Augustodunensis, Expositio in Cantica Canticorum

1. ff. 1r–115v *Incipit prologus honorij in Cantica Canticorum.* Symonj. donum sapientie cum salomone poscenti. honorius a uero pacifico postulata consequi. Quia predecessori tuo beate memorie . . . sententias uero auctoritati sanctorum relinquens. *Quid sit equiuocum.* In principijs librorum tria requiruntur. scilicet auctor. materia. intentio. Auctor. ut noueris nomen scriptoris . . . desiderans dicit. [text, f. 10r:] *Explicit prologus. Incipit expositio in Cantica Canticorum.* Osculetur me osculo . . . compositori et expositorj utriusque operis gracias agamus. *Amen.*

   Stegmüller, no. 3573; PL 172.347–496.

2. f. 116r Instructions for casting bells, in It. f. 116v blank

3. f. 117r Lictera [*sic*] gesta docet/ Quid credas allegoria/ Moralis quid agas/ Quid speres anagia.

   Walther, *Sprichwörter*, no. 13899.

4. f. 117v Portion of a Latin document dated 1325.

Parchment, ff. i (modern parchment) + 117 + i (modern parchment), 205 x 149 (136 x 96) mm. 28 long lines. Double vertical and double or single horizontal bounding lines. Ruled in brown ink. Prickings in lower margin.

I–XIV^{8}, XV^{6} (–5, replaced with portion of 13th-century document pasted to stub, f. 117; –6, stub remains). Catchwords, surrounded by pen flourishes in brown and/or red, in center of lower margin, verso.

Written in round gothic bookhand by a single scribe, below top line.

One illuminated initial of poor quality, f. 1r, 6-line, in form of a snake, mauve, pink and white against blue ground. Partial border in inner margin composed of a green bar with blue and pink leaves framing a coat of arms, effaced, in the lower margin. Numerous flourished initials, 2-line, red with crude penwork designs in light purple. Headings in red. Majuscules touched with red.

Decoration on f. 1r rubbed.

Binding: Italy, s. xx. Backs of quires cut in for original sewing. Semi-limp vellum case made from leaf of a 15th-century choir book, with musical notation. Rust stains on first and last leaves from two fore-edge fastenings.

Written in Italy at the end of the 13th or beginning of the 14th; the dialect of art. 2 suggests an origin in the Southern Marches (we thank E. Pasquini for this information). Belonged to Giuseppe (Joseph) Martini of Lugano (signature inside front cover). Purchased from H. P. Kraus in 1957 by Thomas E. Marston (bookplate).

secundo folio: regnum

Bibliography: Faye and Bond, p. 87, no. 200.

Marston MS 201 — Verona, 1460s
Humanistic Commonplace Book — Pl. 29

1. f. 1r blank; f. 1v [Table of contents, in red, much faded:] *De diuitijs et auri cupiditate; De Muneribus ac liberalitate; De honore preceptoribus habendo; De membrorum validitate ac* ["uel" added above] *infirmitate; De Viuendi luxu atque delitijs; De sedendi Ordine; De aliorum immitatione* [sic]; *Contra loquacitatem et de silentio; De subditorum odio uel benificio* [sic] *in principem et e contra; De his qui damnati sunt in publico magistratu; De loci mutatione; De Varijs poenarum generibus; De coitus continentia uel incontinentia; De his qui parua sua eloquentia magna faciunt; De Coena et compotatione; De contemnenda uita pro glorie cupiditate; De maledictis aduersus alios; De secretis manifestandis uel non; De fide aut perfidia; De magnanimitate; De dignandum non esse ab unoquoque adiscere; De legum obseruantia; De Vicinia; De imperatore exercitus; De Bello et Re militarj; De sui ipsius tutella; De publico magistratu; De Experientia; Quanta sit vis orationis; De facaetijs; De indecora pinguedine* [sic]; *De tyramnide* [sic]; *De edificatione; De Amicitia; De sciendi studio et cupiditate; Quanta sit laus litterarum et dulcedo; De funeris luctu uel consolatione; De his qui sibi manus consciuerunt; Ab initio parua progressu temporis magna esse; De taciturnitate. Vide in primo de officijs Ambr. in principio; De Verecundia et motibus corporis in* [one word

illegible] *Rubrica de Virgine Maria; De Iracundia in eodem exemplum Iacob Rubrica.*

2. ff. 2r–93v *Iovi optimo De diuitijs et auri Cupiditate. Aurum Contempserunt et multi Philosophi* ex quibus unus Crates thebanus. Vt ceteros scileam multarum possessionum precium proiecit in pelagus abite dicens in profundum male cupiditates. Ego uos mergam. ne ipse mergar in uobis. [2nd paragraph:] Diuitie sunt bona huiusmodi que fur capere potest. hostis inuadere ... [concludes in section: *Ab initio parua progressu temporis magna esse*:] Idque frequens peragas grandis cumulatur aceruus. ff. 94r–96v ruled, but blank.

   A collection of extracts primarily on virtues and vices arranged according to the topics listed in art. 1. In most cases the precise source is not cited; there are frequent extracts from Classical Latin authors such as Ovid and Seneca (e. g., the section *Quanta sit Vis orationis* contains many quotations from Cicero, *Brutus*). There are also quotations from Greek authors in unidentified Latin translations.

3. Back cover: Maximam atque optimam rem fortunae tribuere [?] maxima [?] absurdum est [?] ...

   Three short texts, mostly faded.

Paper (watermarks: unidentified letter?, in gutter), ff. 96, 305 x 105 (250 x 62) mm. 46 long lines. Single vertical and upper horizontal bounding lines ruled in crayon. Text rulings in lead (Derolez 13.12). Remains of prickings for bounding lines in upper, lower and outer margins.

I-IX^{10}, X^{6}. Vertical catchwords perpendicular to text along inner bounding line, verso (Derolez 12.6).

Written in a calligraphic and sometimes flamboyant humanistic cursive script by a single scribe, below top line.

Large decorated initial, f. 2r, 16-line. Body of initial formed of intricate interlace bands, yellow and brown washes, against paper and yellow and brown ground. The style of this initial is almost identical to that in Oxford, Bodleian Library, Canon. Ital. 56 (Pächt and Alexander, v. 2, no. 636), except that the initial in Marston MS 201 exhibits strong shading. Display script in red and blue. Rubrics (pale red) in text in humanistic bookhand.

Binding: Italy, s. xv. Strips cut from a parchment manuscript (text washed) are adhered around the fold of each quire. Original sewing on three kermes pink, slit straps. The parchment sides are sewn with the first and last quires. See also provenance below.

Written and decorated by the humanist Felice Feliciano, probably in

Verona in the 1460s, given the remarkable similarity of the script and decorative initial to that in Oxford, Bodleian Library, Canon. Ital. 56, which was written in Verona in 1465 (we thank A. C. de la Mare for this information). It is also possible that the plain parchment binding was the work of Feliciano (cf. G. Mardersteig, "Tre epigrammi de Gian Mario Filelfo a Felice Feliciano," *Classical Medieval and Renaissance Studies in Honor of B. L. Ullman*, ed. C. Henderson, [Rome, 1964], v. 2, pl. 5 of the binding of Verona, Bibl. Com. 2845). Two early inscriptions inside front cover erased and illegible; title written below, perhaps in the same hand: "Excerpta et Varia." Pencil note inside front cover states the codex was in the sale of Thomas Rodd (Sotheby's, 5 February 1850, no. 297). Acquired at the Samuel Allen sale (Sotheby's, 30 January, 1920, no. 63) by Sir Sydney Cockerell (his notes dated "Cambridge Jan. 30 1920" and signature inside front cover); see C. de Hamel, "Medieval and Renaissance Manuscripts from the Library of Sir Sydney Cockerell (1867–1962)," *The British Library Journal* 13, 2 (1987) pp. 186–210 (Marston MS 201 cited on p. 205, no. 87). Cockerell's sale on 18 February 1957 to Pierre Berès. Unidentified "184" and "297" and traces of small round paper label all on lower left corner of front cover; "MSS/413" in pencil inside front cover. Purchased in 1958 from Pierre Berès of Paris by L. C. Witten (inv. no. 2206), who sold it in 1959 to Thomas E. Marston (bookplate).

secundo folio: [f. 3r] domo

Bibliography: Faye and Bond, p. 87, no. 201.

Marston MS 202 — Italy, s. XV[1]

Jacobus Palladinus, Belial, etc.

1. ff. 1r–47v [Prologue:] Uniuersis christi fidelibus atque ortodose Ecclesie fidey cultoribus hoc breue conpennium [*sic*] inspecturis Iacobus de Teramo archidiaconus auersanus et canonicus . . . liberati sumus per infinita secula seculorum amen. [text:] Postquam per scientie lignum duplicem mortem habuimus danpnationem . . . Nam omne datum optimum et omne donum perfectum desursum est. Si quid uero indignum a me. etc. [colophon:] Explicit Liber Bellial scriptus manu dompni Iacobi grassi de Camplo. Deo gratias Amen.

   Jacobus Palladinus de Teramo, *Belial* (also known as *Consolatio peccatorum seu Processus Luciferi contra Iesum Christum*); printed by Johann Schüssler (Augsburg, 1472) and thereafter. Bloomfield, *Virtues and Vices*, pp. 338–39 (Marston MS 202 not listed). The scribe and at least one other contemporary hand have added cues for the reader in outer margin, including pointing hands; one annotator has also corrected the text in a darker shade of ink.

2. f. 48r Quicumque vult saluus esse ante omnia opus est vt teneat catolicam fidem ... saluus esse non poterit. f. 48v blank

Athanasian Creed, added in a different hand.

Parchment, ff. ii (paper) + 48 + ii (paper), 312 x 232 (204 x 142) mm. 55 long lines. Frame-ruled in crayon; prickings in upper, lower, and outer margins.

I–IV^{10}, V^{8} (structure uncertain, 8 = original flyleaf?). Catchwords, some surrounded by designs and small circles in red, centered below written space, verso.

Written in a cramped gothic cursive by a single scribe, above top line; art. 2 added in an awkwardly formed gothic bookhand.

Divided initial, 15–line, in red in f. 1r. Plain initials, 10– to 4–line, initial strokes, and paragraph marks (in outer margin) in red throughout.

Binding: France [?], s. xix. Dark brown, hard-grained goatskin, blind- and gold-tooled. Gilt edges. On spine: "Liber Bellial" and "Codex Ms. Saec. XV."

Written in Italy in the first half of the 15th century by the scribe Jacobus Grassi de Camplo [a village 5 miles N. of Teramo] who signed his name in the colophon (art. 1); early provenance otherwise unknown. According to a note in library files, the manuscript was purchased from B. M. Rosenthal via L. C. Witten (inv. no. 2048) in 1958 by Thomas E. Marston (bookplate).

secundo folio: et prophetis

Bibliography: Faye and Bond, p. 87, no. 202.

Marston MS 203 — England, s. XV^{2}

Jacobus de Esculo, Quaestiones ordinariae, etc.

1. ff. 1r–17v [Q. 1.] Utrum noticia actualis omnium diuinorum ad intra presupponatur in deo patre productioni verbi passiue ...; [f. 3v, Q. 2.] Utrum in produccione verbi diuini actus memorie paterne presupponitur [?] actui sue intelligencie ...; [f. 7v, Q. 3.] Utrum produccioni passiue verbi diuini in patre noticia actualis ...; [f. 12r, Q. 4.] Utrum noticia actualis creature presupponatur in deo noticie habituali eiusdem

...; [f. 14r, Q. 5.] Utrum noticia actualis quam habuit deus de creatura posuerit ipsam ab evo ... non potest esse per se terminus produccionis. [concludes with a list of the 5 quaestiones and the colophon:] *Expliciunt questiones ordinarie Iacobi de esculo.*

Jacobus de Esculo, *Quaestiones ordinariae,* also found in Vatican City, Biblioteca Apostolica Vaticana, Vat. lat. 1012 (ff. 60v–62v), Vat. lat. 4871 (ff. 33r–35v) and Cambridge University Library FF. III. 23 (ff. 127r–131r). We thank S. Dumont for his assistance with the bibliographical citations in arts. 1–3. On the author and his works see T. Yokoyama, "Zwei Questionen des Jacobus de Aesculo über das Esse Obiectivum," in *Wahrheit und Verkündigung. Michael Schmaus zum 70. Geburtstag,* ed. L. Scheffczyk, et al., 2 vols. (Munich, 1967) pp. 31–74, with text of quaestio 5 edited from the three manuscripts cited above published on pp. 37–59; Marston MS 203 not used, but contains readings closest to the Cambridge manuscript. Text omitted from f. 10r added by contemporary hand on f. 9, a single leaf inserted in the middle of quire.

2. ff. 17v–55v [Q. 1.] Utrum simplicitas diuine nature compatitur [?] secum aliquam distinccionem ex natura ...; [f. 22r, Q. 2.] Utrum perfecciones creaturarum virtualiter contente in essentia diuina ...; [f. 24v, Q. 3.] Utrum deus possit facere aliquod compositum ex elementis et substantia forma vitali ...; [f. 25v, Q. 4.] Utrum potentia generandi in deo patre cadit sub omnipotencia ...; [f. 26v, Q. 5.] Utrum intellectus agens sit nobilior intellecto ...; [f. 28v, Q. 6.] Utrum omnis habitudo sit relatio ...; [f. 30v, Q. 7.] Utrum respectus sit de conceptu quid ditatiuo [?] absoluti ...; [f. 31v, Q. 8.] Utrum equalitas fundata super duo equalia puta alba sit alia [?] super eadem alba ...; [f. 33v, Q. 9.] Utrum duo corpora simul esse in eodem loco implicet contradiccionem ...; [f. 36v, Q. 10.] Utrum accidentia in sacramento altaris habeant proprie racionem suppositi ...; [f. 39r, Q. 11.] Utrum potencia que est differencia entis sit potentia subjectiva vel objectiva ...; [f. 41v, Q. 12.] Supposito quod voluntas sit actiua et passiua respectu sui actus queritur utrum ...; [f. 44r, Q. 13.] Utrum actus caritatis elicitus sit nobilior ipso habitu vel non ...; [f. 48r, Q. 14.] Utrum agens particulare habeat aliquem effectum [*per se* added in margin] ...; [f. 49v, Q. 15.] Utrum posito quod possibile obiectum fundetur super aliquid absolutum ...; [f. 53r, Q. 16.] Utrum clericus beneficiatus de licencia stans in studio sine spe proficiendi ...; [f. 53v, Q. 17.] Utrum omnis actus integer sit eiusdem speciei.... ff. 56r–58r blank; f. 58v List of 17 preceding *questiones* hastily added to blank leaf.

Jacobus de Esculo, *Quaestiones quodlibetales*, also found in Vatican City, Biblioteca Apostolica Vaticana, Vat. lat. 1012 (ff. 48r–49r), Vat. lat. 932 (ff. 39v–41v); Cambridge University Library FF. III. 23 (ff. 136v–139v); Florence, Biblioteca Laurenziana, Cod. Plut. 31 dext. n. 8 (ff. 53r–54r). Marston MS 203 contains the order of quaestiones as found in the Cambridge manuscript; see Yokoyama, *op.cit.*, pp. 34–35.

3. ff. 59r–88r [Heading absent.] [Q]uomodo a forma absoluta ... [conclusion illegible]. f. 88v blank

Tabula operum Scoti, usually attributed to Jacobus de Esculo, also found in Assisi 136, ff. 137r–166r. See V. Doucet, O. F. M., *Maîtres franciscains de Paris: Supplément au "Repertoire des maîtres en théologie de Paris au XIIIe siècle" de P. Glorieux* (Florence and Quaracchi, 1935) p. 32 [562].

4. ff. 89r–94v [In margin:] Absoluere. [text:] *Absoluere.* Utrum prelatus subdito cui comisit ... [Quodlibet 1, questio 27]; ... [concluding with section on *ymagina*; colophon:] Explicit tabula quodlibetorum henrici de Gandauo. ff. 95r–96v blank

Tabula quodlibetorum Henrici de Gandavo, usually attributed to Jacobus de Esculo. R. Macken, O. F. M., *Bibliotheca Manuscripta Henrici de Gandavo* (Leiden, 1979) v. 1, contents of Marston MS 203 listed on p. 411; v. 2, pp. 1018–19, with this manuscript noted in 4. C.

Paper, with parchment inner and outer bifolia (watermarks: similar to Briquet Armoiries. Bande 1038-41, similar in general design to Briquet Main 11502 [1477], similar in general design to Briquet Main 11180 [1478], and unidentified unicorn), ff. ii (paper) + 96 + ii (paper), 287 x 201 (written space ranges from 245 x 160 to 240 x 150) mm. 2 columns, ca. 46 lines. Frame-ruled in crayon; prickings in upper, lower, and outer margins.

I^{16} (+1 paper leaf added between 8 and 10 in middle of quire), $II–III^{16}$, IV^{12} (-9 through 11, paper blanks), $V–VI^{16}$, VII^{8} (-5, paper, and 8, parchment, both blanks). Some catchwords under inner column.

Written by several scribes in different styles of gothic cursive scripts, all exhibiting Anglicana features.

Majuscules and paragraph marks in red for arts. 1–2 only.

Binding: England, s. xx. Rigid vellum case with gold-tooled title on spine: "Jacques d'Ascoli - Quaestiones Disputatae - England, XV Cent."

Written in England in the second half of the 15th century to judge from the script and the textual variants in arts. 1–2; provenance unknown. Purchased from C. A. Stonehill on 1958 by Thomas E. Marston (bookplate).

secundo folio: similitudine [?]

Bibliography: Faye and Bond, p. 87, no. 203.

Marston MS 204 — Padua [?], s. XV^{med} (after 1433)
Hieronymus de Alexandria, Carmina

The poems in this manuscript were composed by one Hieronymus de Alexandria in Bologna in 1433 (arts. 1, 5, 7, etc.). Given their date of composition and moralizing quality it is unlikely that they are the work of the humanist Girolamo Squarciafico who flourished in the fourth quarter of the 15th century and who was often called Hieronymus Alexandrinus. Poems not listed in Bertalot, *Initia*.

1. f. 1r [Title page:] Bellua septicornigera donni Ieronimi de Alexandria. Contritioque superbie per humilitatem. Bella creati gestaque cum creatore benigno/ Compatiens viuentibus diuersis erroribus inuolutis. et tramite nullo iure recto ambulantibus. bestialiter et oppinionibus varijs se regentibus et nullam regulam certam positam generi humano sequentibus. scripsi hunc librum vt quilibet disceret viuere certitudine et non oppinione in omnibus casibus et moralitate viuendi secundum deum./ Liber theologie moralis iuris canonici iuditio roboratus. salutis viam prebens cuilibet copiosam. f. 1v blank

2. ff. 2r–6v [Heading:] Expositio septem peccatorum capitalium. primo de superbia. [text:] Bellua septicornigera consumptrix bonitatis./ Dicta superbia, dans dominari cuique superbo./ ... Humilitasque superbia concertamina gerunt./ Humilitate superbia conteritur caritatis.

   Poem (264 lines) on the seven vices and on superstition: *de superbia, de ira, de inuidia, de accidia, de auaritia, de gula, de luxuria, de superstitionibus*.

3. ff. 6v–13v [Heading:] Contritio superbie per humilitatem. [text:] Est contritio belluer [*sic*] facta per humilitatem/ Humilitas bellue contritio vita salubris/ ... Mundus dans infernum penarum crutiatu/ Est fugiendus cunctaque que sua despitiendo.

   Poem (409 lines) in praise of humility and the renunciation of worldly things.

4. ff. 13v–14r [Heading:] Lamentabilis conpassio ecclesie christi collapse. [text:] Ha regnum christi nunc versum parte maligna/ Nam capiti numero cum satagit edere membra/ ... Ergo quod dico fac sodes

corde pudico/ Vt nostrum flamen dicat quoque semper et amen/ Ieronimo libri sit merces gratia christi.

Poem (33 lines): a lament upon the corruption of the Church.

5. ff. 14r–15r [No heading; text begins:] Bella per humana curricula fortia mundi/ dant mortem uel uitam concertantibus alme/ humilitatem qui sequitur. datur quoque vita/ ... bello finito. referatur gratia christo/ Contritaque superbia regnemus in patria/ [colophon:] Ieronimus istum tibi librum versificauit/ Anno mille quatercent trigesimoque trieno/ die prima madij completum dat tibi librum/ bononie scriptus fuit optime conpositusque/ bella creati donent nobis gaudia pacis.

Poem (38 lines) inveighing against the pride which leads to damnation instead of humility which leads to salvation.

6. ff. 15r–19r [No heading, text begins:] Colloquium veri falsi quoque cum ratione/ Cum verum saluet falsum dampnare videtur./ Sum via que et veritas, vita quoque saluatoris./ Est falsitas via cunctorum quoque dampnationis/ ... Viues semper letus iocundus quoque magnus/ Colloquio dicto referatur gratia christo./ Et pro compositore semper orare labora./ Colloquium veri quoque falsi do tibi plenum./ Quod ratio dirigat saluans animas perituras./ bella creati donent nobis gaudia pacis.

Poem (234 lines) in which falsehood and damnation are equated as are truth and salvation, with the world as the seat of falsehood and death, and heaven as the seat of truth and life.

7. ff. 19r–39v [No heading, text begins:] Prelia de mundo tibi dicam carmine recto/ Prelia concertantia mundi fraude ducente./ Non rationem, sed libitumque sequentia semper./ Nullus amor cunctos nisi proprius excitat orbe./ ... Predicta que legat bene semper perficiendo/ Et certamen mundi sibi proderit alte./ [colophon:] Anno milleno [*sic*] quatercent trigesimo trieno/ die februarij quintodecimo tibi ceptum/ Et die vigesimo quarto Iunij tibi factum/ Hieronimus librum dat perfecte bene structum./ Liber theologie moralis, iuris canonici iuditio/ Roboratus. salutis viam prebens cuilibet copiosam. ff. 27v–28v blank and crossed out with the note "nihil deficit."

Poem (1,096 lines) attacking worldly acquisitiveness and dishonesty with frequent use of military metaphors.

8. ff. 40r–46v [No heading, text begins:] Grandis amor gregis facit perire pastorem/ Quo que carentes oues disperguntur a lupis/ Grex multum gaudebat tis [*sic*] regimine fultus/ ... Et secum viues felix in culmine

celi./ [colophon:] Finito libro sit laus et gloria christo/ Ieronimo merces sit christus compilatori./ Liber pastoralis tu recte nominaris./de regimine pastorum tractans copiose./ Continet hic liber duo milia quatuor centum./ Versus octuagintaque Iunctis fert manifeste.

Poem (399 lines) lavishly praising Christ in his avatar of the Good Shepherd.

9. f. 46v [In margin:] donnus Iannes. [text:] Ieronimi scripta mirans veneror benedicta/ Nam florent metro. redolet sententia uero./ Attamen accentu, pedibusue, sedule metrum/ Claudicat, in sensu semper tenet optime verum/ Vnde non metrum spernas referens tibi verum/ Sicuti non verum facit omne vilescere metrum. [in margin:] donnus Ieronimus. [text:] Iannes arguit, excusat [?] se Ieronimusque/ Vtilitas proximi lesit quandoque poesim./ Auctoritas figurata etiam non defuit ei./ Hec duo delicta suppleant caritatis amore./ Vtilitas poesi preponi maxima laus est. f. 47r-v ruled, but blank

Dialogue between the author and one Iannes.

Paper (watermarks: unidentified animal in upper margin), ff. ii (paper) + 47 + ii (paper), 158 x 100 (100 x 65) mm. Ca. 29 lines of verse. Single vertical and horizontal bounding lines frame-ruled in hard point or lead. Prickings in upper, lower, and outer margins.

I-III^{12}, IV^{12} (-12?). Vertical catchwords perpendicular to text along inner bounding line (Derolez 12.6), verso. Remains of quire and leaf signatures (e.g., k 1, k 2, k 3, etc.) in lower right corner, recto.

Written by a single scribe in gothic bookhand with some humanistic features, below top lines.

Two illuminated initials, ff. 2r and 40r, 5- and 7-line, silver (partly oxidized) on gold ground filled with stylized foliage in green and red on blue ground with white filigree. Numerous penwork initials, 2-line, in red and blue with purple and red flourishes (harping). Remains of instructions for rubricator (f. 40r) and guide letters for decorator.

Ink has corroded through paper on some leaves.

Binding: United States, s. xx. Half bound in green goatskin with green cloth sides. Title gold-tooled on spine.

Written in the middle of the 15th century after 1433 (arts. 5, 7) as part of a larger codex since the quire and leaf signatures begin on f. 13r with the letter *I*; probably produced in Padua according to A. C. de la Mare. According to P. Kristeller (*Iter Italicum* v. 5, p. 288, no. 204) this manuscript formerly belonged to the Capitular library in Zaragoza ("17-87"). Purchased from Maggs Bros. of London in 1957 by L. C. Witten (inv. no. 1604), who gave it in 1958 to Thomas E. Marston (bookplate).

Bibliography: Faye and Bond, p. 87, no. 204.

Marston MS 205 Germany, 1425
Pilgrim's Passport (Letter of Conduct), in Lat.

[Heading:] Johannes dei gratia abbas monasterij celle sancte marie in nigra silua ordinis canonicorum regularium Constantie diocesis omnibus presencium [?] inspectoribus subscriptorum noticiam cum salute. [text:] Nouerint uniuersi et singuli quos nosce fuerit opportunum Quod constitutus coram nobis et notario publico ac testibus subscriptis ... testibus ad premissa uocatis specialiter et rogatis. [notary's siglum in second hand followed by:] Et ego Conradus Spiegelberg Capellanus ecclesie parrochialis opidi friburgensis Constantie diocesis publicus Imperiali auctoritate notarius ... rogatus et requisitus.

Notarial document, a pilgrim's passport or letter of conduct written for Johannes de Blumenegk, *armiger* of the diocese of Constance by Johannes, abbot of the Augustinian house of canon regulars of Cella Sancte Marie in Nigra Silua (cf. Cottineau, v. 2, cols. 2908–09 *sub voce* St. Ulrich). This document was written in the presence of Johannes Phul, rector of the parish church of Freiburg-im-Breisgau, and was notarized by the notary Conrad Spiegelberg on 18 July 1425.

Single parchment membrane measuring 227 x 350 mm., originally folded into thirds and then into thirds again, with three slits along lower edge, presumably for seal, now wanting. Written by two scribes, the one who copied the body of the document, the other who notarized it, both in neat chancery scripts. Boxed.

Written in Germany in 1425 for the use of Johannes de Blumenegk; later filing notes, in German, on dorse. Provenance otherwise unknown. Purchased from L. C. Witten in 1958 by Thomas E. Marston.

Bibliography: Faye and Bond, p. 87, no. 205.

Marston MS 208 Spain, s. $XII^{4/4}$
Sermons (in Lat.)

For a discussion of the manuscript and further bibliography see R. Étaix, "Sermon inédit de Saint Augustin sur la Circoncision dans un ancien manuscrit de Saragosse," *Revue des Études Augustiniennes* 26, 1 (1980) pp. 62–87; we give page references for those sermons in the manuscript whose texts are edited here.

1. ff. 1r–2r [In margin: *Leonis pape*] *Sermo de aduentu dominj.* Sanctam et desiderabilem gloriosamque sollemnitatem hoc est natiuitatem domini saluatoris fratres karissimi. deuocione fidelissima suscepturi ... secura conscientia poteritis accedere. et in futuro ad eternam beatitudinem feliciter peruenire ... amen.

   Caesarius, *Sermo* 188; Grégoire (1980) p. 183, no. 85.

2. ff. 2r–3r *Item sermo de aduentu dominj.* Karissimi. christus uenit medicina celestis. nolite desperare languentes. Curate. ut curemini. currite. ut sanemini. Vos nolite necligere ... Letemur ergo et iocundemur in misericordia eius. qui cum deo pecre [*sic*] ... amen.

   Unidentified sermon; Grégoire (1966) p. 180. This text also found in the *Homiliarium Toletanum*, no. add. 1.

3. f. 3r–v *Item de aduentu dominj.* Etsi ego taceam fratres karissimi tempus nos ammonet quod domini nostri ihesu christi natalis in proximo est. Nam predicationem meam ... per quod manibus operamus. et corde mundamur ab omni peccato ... amen.

   Maximus Taurinensis, *Sermo* 61a.

4. f. 4r–v *Item sermo natiuitatis dominj nostri.* Karissimi filij. propitia diuinitate diem domini prope esse iam uobis adnuntiamus. in quo domini et saluatoris nostri ihesu christi natiuitatem uobis desiderantibus cum gaudio celebrari significamus ... ad cuius natiuitatem tam deuotissime preparamur....

   Caesarius, *cento* from sermon 187; Grégoire, p. 294, no. 2. This text also found in the *Homiliarium Toletanum*, no. 2; Étaix, *op.cit.*, pp. 72–73.

5. ff. 4v–5r *Item de aduentu dominj nostri. ihesu christi.* Dominus ihesus christus dilectissimi fratres postquam salutifero aduentu suo mundum istum illustrare dignatus est. intonans uoce celesti tale sicut scriptum est ... et tradidit semed [*sic*] ipsum pro nobis oblationem et hostiam deo in odorem suauitatis ... amen.

Unidentified sermon on Mat. 3.7; Étaix, *op.cit.*, pp. 73–74.

6. ff. 5r–6r *Item sermo de aduentu dominj nostri.* Descendet dominus sicut pluuia in uellus ... [Ps. 71.6]. Hec uerba accepit dauid propheta de libro iudicum in quo inuenimus scriptum quod quidam homo gedeon nomine purgabat ... ieiunij tempore sacrum celebramus aduentum....

   Augustine, *Sermo*; Étaix, *op.cit.*, pp. 74–76.

7. ff. 6r–8v *Item sermo beati Iohannis crisostomj in aduentu dominj.* Prouida mente. et profundo cogitatu. cognosci debent duarum rerum distincta negocia. Idem quantum distat inter bonum et malum. Nec aliunde hec cogitatio. quam a primordio repetenda est ... et implesti penitenciam. atque inde perfectam promerebilis [?] indulgentiam ... amen.

   Ps.-John Chrysostom, *Sermo de poenitentia*, Lat. tr.

8. ff. 8v–9v *Item Sermo de aduentu dominj.* Fratres quid in uobis tanta pigritia est. ut ad domum dei minime uigiletis? Non inmerito apostolus ad galatas ait. Miror quod sic tam cito transferimini ab eo ... Scitote quod si bene uixeritis. uos estis templum dei. et spiritus eius habitat in uobis ... amen.

   Caesarius, fragment of a sermon; Grégoire (1980) p. 310. This text also found in *Homiliarium Toletanum*, no. 79; Étaix, *op.cit.*, pp. 76–77.

9. ff. 9v–10r *Item de aduentu dominj nostri.* Fratres karissimi quam timendus est dies iudicij. in qua dominus proposuit uenire cum flamma et igne. que inflammabat inimicos suos qui faciunt iniquitatem ... ad confessionem recursus. De qua pena nos dominus eripere dignetur ille ... amen.

   Ps.-Augustine, *Sermo* ap. 251.

10. ff. 10r–11r *De natiuitate dominj nostri.* Nazjuitatis [*sic*] dominice sacramentum fratres karissimi quod iuxta apostolum manifestatum est in carne. iustificatum est in spiritu ... Postremo tu illi ut mater temporalis uite ministra substanciam ... amen.

    Cento; cf. Étaix, *op.cit.*, p. 65, no.10, for a discussion and printed texts.

11. ff. 11r–12r *Item sermo de natiujtate christi.* Veritas de terra orta est ... [Ps. 84.12]. Veritas de terra orta est. filius dei de carne processit. Quid est ueritas? filius dei ... et ueniet christus ad te. et ponet in uia gressus tuos. ut te informet in uestigiis tuis ... amen.

    Augustine, *Enarrationes in Ps. 84.13–16* (with some changes).

12. ff. 12r–13r *Item sermo sancti augustini de natiuitate.* Clementissimus pater omnipotens deus. cum doleret seculum cenulentis erroribus inuolutum. hominemque mortiferis criminibus cathenatum ... filia diuinitatis. filia mater humanitatis. quia uerbum caro factum est. et habitauit in nobis ... amen.

Ps.-Augustine, *Sermo*; Grégoire (1980) p. 325, no. 15.

13. ff. 13r–15v *Item beati augustini de natiuitate.* Castissimum marie uirginis uterum. sponse uirginis clausum cubiculum. signatum pudoris cenaculum. merito plenissime collaudarem ... et per meritum uirginitatis ita separatus es a concubitu uxoris ... amen.

Ps.-Augustine, *Sermo* ap. 195; Grégoire (1980) p. 141, no. 5.

14. ff. 15v–17r *Item sermo de natiuitate.* Exortatur nos dominus deus noster dilectissimi fratres. pariter et ammonet dicens. audi israel dominus deus tuus deus ... sed quod terrena et celestia sacra ihesu christi mediatoris ligni interposicione sociaujt. ...

Ps.-Ildefonsus, *Sermo* (13.1–6 in *Sermones Dubii*); Grégoire (1980) p. 294, no. 4 (cf. *Homiliarium Toletanum*, no. 4).

15. ff. 17r–18r *Item sermo natalis dominj.* Gaudeamus fratres karissimi simul in unum omnes populi laudent nomen domini. Iuuenes et uirgines seniores cum iunioribus laudent nomen domini ... Ab omni inquinamento carnis animos nostros emundemus. ut cum capite nostro sine fine regnemus. ...

Homiliarium Toletanum, no. 6; Grégoire (1980) p. 295, no. 6.

16. ff. 18r–19r *Item sermo de natiuitate.* Dilectionem uestram admonemus fratres karissimi. ut presenti diei in qua natale domini a fidelibus celebratur. bonorum operum testimonium quisque uestrum peribere ... adorare eum dum inuitat ut possimus non timere eum cum iudicat ... amen.

Maximus Taurinensis, *Sermo* 61b (with changes).

17. ff. 19r–20v *Item sermo natalis dominj.* Sapientia edificauit [?] sibi domum ... [Prov. 9.1 + Sir. 24.10]. Salomon significatiuus. spiritu ueri salamonis inspiratus ... et gustemus et uideamus. quam magna est multitudo dulcedinis ipsius panis. in quem omnes desiderant fideles prospicere. ...

Unidentified commentary on *Sapientia edificauit* (cf. R. J. Hesbert, *Corpus antiphonalium officii* [Rome, 1968] v. 3, p. 466, no. 4810).

18. ff. 20v–21r *Item sermo de circumcisione christi.* Apparuit benignitas et humanitas . . . [Tit. 3.4]. Dominus noster ihesus christus fratres karissimi non solum nasci dignatus est propter nos. sed etiam octaua die natiuitatis . . . introducemini in cubiculum regis eterni. heredes quidem facti dei. coheredes autem christi. . . .

Unidentified sermon on the Circumcision.

19. ff. 21r–22v *Item sermo de natale dominj.* Saluator noster dilectissimi hodie natus est. gaudeamus. Neque enim locum fas est esse tristicie. ubi natalis est uite . . . quia precium tuum sanguis est christi. quia ueritate te iudicabit. qui misericorditer redemit ihesus christus dominus noster.

Leo, *Sermo* 21; Grégoire (1980) p. 433, no. 17.

20. f. 22v *Item sermo de natale dominj.* Natalis domini eadem causa a patribus uotiue sollempnitatis institutus est. quia in eo christus pro redemptione mundi. nasci corporaliter uoluit . . . debemus. ut ad memoria [*sic*] reuocetur quod natus est christus . . . amen.

Isidore, *De ecclesiasticis officiis* I.26; Grégoire (1980) p. 433, no. 16.

21. ff. 22v–24v *Item sermo de natale dominj.* Exultemus in domino dilectissimi. et spirituali iocunditate letemur. quia illuxit dies redemptionis noue. reparationis antique. felicitatis eterne . . . nascentem. ut eum uidere mereaminj deum glorie in sua maiestate regnantem . . . amen.

Leo, *Sermo* 22; Grégoire (1980) p. 433, no. 18.

22. ff. 24v–25v *Item sermo de natale domini.* In huius diei sollempnitate tota mentis alacritate fratres karissimi exultemus quia terra illa nostra qui in primo parente. corrupta fuerat . . . in illo libertatem accipiamus qui propter nos de terra ortus est in illo celum possideamus. . . .

Augustine, *Sermo* 192 (with some changes).

23. ff. 25v–27r [No rubric.] Legimus et fideliter retinemus. quod sub ipso principio nascentis mundi. in primo homine fecerit nos deus ad ymaginem et similitudinem suam. Ecce in hac die mutata . . . ut mater temporalem ministra substanciam. ut ipse nobis et tibi uitam tribuat sempiternam . . . amen.

Ps.-Augustine, *Sermo* ap. 119; Grégoire (1980) p. 324, no. 14.

24. ff. 27r–30v *Item sermo beati augustini episcopi de natiujtate.* Inter pressuras atque angustias presentis temporis. et nostre seruitutis officia cogimur dilectissimi non tacere cum pocius expediat flere . . . et sic deuota mente dicamus omnes pariter. Gloria in excelsis . . . uirtus et potestas . . . amen.

Quodvultdeus, *Sermo contra Iudaeos, paganos et Arianos de symbolo* (with changes); R. Braun, ed., CC ser. lat. 60 (1961) pp. 227–58; Étaix, *op.cit*, pp. 77–78.

25. ff. 30v–39r *Homilia beati iohannis crissostomi* [sic] *de euangelio in principio est uerbum.* Uox spiritualis aquile. aditum pulsat ecclesie. Exterior sensus transeuntem accipit sonitum. interior animus manentem penetrat intellectum ... mutationis assummit. ita uerbum dei non comutatum caro tamen factum est ut habitaret in nobis ... amen.

Johannes Scotus, *Homilia in Prologum S. Euangelii secundum Ioannem.*

26. ff. 39r–40r [No rubric.] Iustissime fratres festiuitate presentis diei in omne se gaudium totus ubique suscitat mundus. quia hodie promissus a seculis ... tanta de salute letemur. atque angelicis nos uocibus sociantes. honore debito misteria semper christi uirtutesque laudemus.

Ps.-Maximus Taurinensis, *Homilia* 11; Grégoire (1980) p. 434, no. 20.

27. ff. 40v–41v [No rubric.] Huius sollempnitatis expositionem uestris auditibus insinuare desiderio o karissimi. nempe ut auctor omnipotens qui circumcisionem ... ad rectium [?] confessionis callem opitulante deo reducere ualeamus. Crastina die omnes ieiunemus. ut misericordiam a domino consequi mereamur. amen.

Cento also found in the *Homiliarium Toletanum*; Grégoire (1980) p. 295, no. 9.

28. ff. 41v–43r [No rubric.] Dies kalendarum istarum quas ianuarias uocant fratres karissimi. a quodam iano. quodam homine perdito ac sacrilego ... ut et pro uobis et pro illis duplicia uobis a domino repensentur. ...

Caesarius, *Sermo* 192; Grégoire (1980) p. 53, no. 6, p. 326, no. 23.

29. ff. 43r–44r [No rubric.] Fratres karissimi domini nostri ihesu christi sublimitas inuisibilis. humilitas uisibilis facta est. sublimitas eius non habet diem. infirmitas eius suscepit ... Crescat igitur christus in cordibus uestris. proficite et credite ut ad uitam perueniatis eternam. ...

Augustine, *Sermo de circumcisione*; Étaix, *op. cit.*, pp. 70–72.

30. f. 44r–v [No rubric.] Karissimi. Sollepnitas [*sic*] quam hodie celebramus propter manifestationem domini epiphanie nomine gregcum [*sic*] accepit ... et cum habundantia bonorum operum pertingere mereamur. ...

Homiliarium Toletanum, no. 10; Grégoire (1980) p. 296, no. 12.

31. ff. 44v–46r [No rubric.] Dies iste fratres karissimi sancte epiphanie.

id est apparitionis domini per cunctas dei ecclesias ritu katholice traditionjs inpensius celebratur . . . In nobis subiectis misericordes simus ut sacratissime passionis dies. socios nos faciat dominice resurrectionjs.

Homiliarium Toletanum, no. 31; Étaix, *op. cit.*, pp. 79–80.

32. f. 46r–v [No rubric.] Magnum hodie fratres karissimi suscepimus. diem festum. quando dominus noster ihesus christus. quadragesimo post diem resurrectionis aureo uolatu conscendit ad celum . . . quicquid nostra uobis predixerit linqua [*sic*]. aure [?] libenter suscipiat karitas uestra . . . amen.

Ps.-Augustine, *Sermo*; Grégoire (1980) p. 171, no. 25.

33. ff. 46v–47v [No rubric.] Sollempnitas diei presentis. non paruam habet graciam festiuitatis. hoc enim die quadragesimo. post resurrectionem domini. ut audiuit. . . . ut future uite in regno celesti consortes effici et glorie corporis domini mereamur . . . amen.

Chromatius Aquileiensis, *Homilia* 8.

34. ff. 47v–48v [No rubric.] Plantauerat autem dominus deus paradisum uoluptatis a principio . . . [Gen. 2.8]. Paradisus est uita beatorum. ubi est fons sapientie . . . ut omnia que ad christi honorem offerimus. rationis et discretionis sappore condiantur. [colophon:] Finito libro reddatur cena magistro. Sit pax scribenti. [*sit* added above] uita salusque legenti.

Commentary on Gen. 2.18ff.; 34.1–3; Ier. 41.5–7; II Sm. 4.5–6; Lv. 2.11–13.

Parchment (speckled, yellow on hair side), ff. i (paper) + 48 + i (paper), 290 x 195 (215 x 130) mm. 2 columns, 30 lines. Single vertical and double horizontal bounding lines. Ruled in lead. Prominent prickings (punctures) in upper, lower and outer margins, including two prickings for first of two lower horizontal bounding lines.

I–VI^8. Catchwords under inner column, verso.

Written in early gothic bookhand by several scribes, above top line.

Plain monochrome initials in red for ff. 1–18; similar initials, but with simple designs in both parchment and red ink, for remainder of codex. Headings in red, ff. 1r–24v, 27r–30v only. Instructions to rubricator along outer and lower edges.

Some staining at end of volume; no loss of text.

Binding: England [?], s. xx. Quires cut in for sewing. Rigid vellum case with title in ink on spine: "Leo P. P. Sermones."

Written in Spain in the fourth quarter of the 12th century; according to R. Étaix (*op.cit.*, pp. 62–63) Marston MS 208 is the second part of a two-part codex that was formerly designated "17–34" in the archives of La Seo in Saragossa. The first part, constituting ff. 1–132, was sold in London by Dawsons of Pall Mall (Cat. 162, June 1966, no. 46, with plate; Cat. 168, June 1967, no. 333). Another manuscript, dating from the 15th century, from the Library of the Santa Iglesia del Pilar (now Escorial P. III. 5, ff. 83–95), contains a copy of the first nine sermons in Marston MS 208. It is possible that the Beinecke manuscript was produced in or near Saragossa and remained there until at least 1956 when it is known to have been microfilmed. Purchased from C. A. Stonehill in 1958 by Thomas E. Marston (bookplate).

Bibliography: Faye and Bond, p. 88, no. 208.

Marston MS 209 — Northwestern Germany, 1480
Leopold of Austria, Compilatio de astrorum scientia

I. 1. f. Ir-v blank; ff. IIr-Vv *Tabula copulacionis* [sic] *Leupoldi ducis Austrie filij*. Primo de Introductorio libri 1/ De Fitulo libri 1/ De auctore libri 1/ . . . De disposicione membrorum nati et corporis tocius 81. f. VIr-v blank

Table of contents for ff. 1–83 only; the list of topics here does not always correspond to rubrics in art. 2.

2. ff. 1r–83r; f. 83v blank; II. pp. 1–74 *Incipit Astronomia Leupoldi de Austria*. [Prologue:] Gloriosus deus et sublimis qui omnia verbo creauit terram in celi medio collocauit et corpora celestia cui virtutum suarum quas a suo creatore et ordinatore perceperant . . . et stupenda. [text, f. 2r:] *Incipit Tractatus primus de Speris et earum circulis et Motibus et cetera*. Premissa intencione ac tractatuum ordinacione ab hijs ad quos compilacio presens peruenerit. tria peto . . . de signo mobili sciui quod hoc quod signat erant. 5. dies in quibus fieri debet. [colophon:] Et in hoc terminatur tractatus decimus. de intentionibus. Cum dei laude et eius auxilio Completus est liber Leopoldi de Austria cuius anima in pace Requiescat. Amen. H. K. V. 1480. 20 Ianuarij. p. 75 blank

Thorndike and Kibre, 588, etc. (this manuscript not located). Here the first part of the text ends abruptly on f. 83r in the middle of *Tractatus VII* (Mercury). Another scribe repeats the final three lines copied by the first and then resumes copying the text on the following leaf (p. 1 of a new numbering sequence). There are no rubrics or headings on pp. 1–74.

3. p. 76 Miscellaneous quotes from the Bible, in Latin.

Composed of two distinct parts, both written on paper and measuring 220 x 150 mm.

Part I: watermarks: unidentified letter *P* similar in general design to Piccard Buchstabe XIII, ff. I–VI and 1–83 (medieval foliation, Arabic numerals 1–83), written space 150 x 90 mm. 29 long lines. Frame-ruled lightly in hard point. Prickings in upper, lower and outer margins. I^{4} (ff. II–V), $II–IX^{10}$, X^{10} (–5 through 10, stubs of blanks remain). Written in well formed hybrida script. Plain red initials, 3- to 1-line, for major text divisions. Headings, paragraph marks, initial strokes, some punctuation, marginalia keyed to art. 1, all in red.

Part II: watermarks: Briquet Coupe 4586, pp. 1–76 (modern pagination, incorrect, followed by foliation, both written carelessly), written space 142 x 92 mm. 33 long lines. Frame-ruled in hard point. Prickings in outer and lower margins and at lower corner(s) of written space. $I–IV^{8}$, V^{8} (–7, blank). Horizontal catchwords in lower margin near gutter, verso; quire and leaf signatures (e.g., a. 1., a. 2., etc.) lower right corner, recto. Written in a small gothic bookhand with many initial letters of the opening word of each section of the text written in oversize majuscules. Plain initials, 3-line, paragraph marks and initials strokes in red.

Binding: Germany, s. xv. Paper wrapper held by stitching at head and tail of spine and sewing around the edges of sides. Astronomical diagram and title in ink on upper side: "Astronomia Leupoldi ducis Austrie filij et cetera."

Written in Northwestern Germany to judge from the watermarks. Part II, dated 1480 (see colophon in art. 2), was copied to finish the incomplete text of Part I. Although composed of different formats and scripts, the two parts appear to be contemporary, since paper with the same watermark as Part I was used for the back pastedown. The significance of the letters "H. K. V." in the colophon is unknown. Ownership inscription on front pastedown indicates that the book belonged to Philippus Schoen, medical doctor and canon of the church of St. Victor at Xanten, who bequeathed the manuscript together with an astrolabe to the convent of nuns at Sousbeek ("Liber magistri et domini Philippi Schoen Doctoris In Medicinis et Canonici ecclesie sancti Victoris Xancten. quem legauit Conuentui sororum in sousbeech ut oretur pro eo cum astrolabio"). Belonged to Reichsgraf Ferdinand Plettenberg-Nordkirchen (1690–1737; bookplate with handwritten shelf-mark in ink: "Nr. 5228"; same number on paper label, spine). Modern notes on front pastedown: "MSS No 37" in ink; "CB 2849," "B,4," collation notes and the date 1480, all in pencil. Purchased from Nicolas Rauch of Geneva in 1958 by L. C. Witten, who sold it the same year to Thomas E. Marston (bookplate).

secundo folio: [table, f. III:] De radiacione
[text, f. 2:] et quid sit

Bibliography: Faye and Bond, p. 88, no. 209.

Marston MS 210 — Italy, after 1410
Lunario volgare perpetuo, in roll format

Texts occur in the following order:

1. Table to determine precise occurrence of the new moon, arranged in 4 columns per month with the first column of each written in red (letters A-T for the *cyclum decemnovenale*; 20 of the possible 31 days of the month; 20 of the possible 24 hours of the day; number of the possible 1080 "points" of the hour), followed by an explanation in Italian of the method of use of the table, beginning with the knowledge that the year 1410 constituted an "R" in the 19-year cycle ("... Et sappiate ch [*sic*] nel 1410 secondo la chiesa *corse* [italics mine; note past tense] R in questa regula..."), that the new year begins on 1 January, and that the new day begins at sunset. Space reserved for June which was not filled in.

2. Table to determine in which ascendant or descendent sign of the zodiac the moon will be for each day of the month and each month of the year, preceded by the heading: "Quessta sie la ragione ouu[er?]o tauula da trouare in che segno e la llune in ciasschuno mese come qui e scripta et dessegnata."

3. Short passage distributing the signs of the zodiac according to the 4 cardinal directions and the 4 elements (fire, air, earth, water).

4. Twelve short passages on good/bad actions to take while the moon is in a particular sign of the zodiac, usually including encouragements/prohibitions regarding business (e.g., when the moon is in Virgo, "Buono e a cominciare add imprender alcuno mistiero ouero arte per guadagnare et specialmente ogni arte che a scriptura s'apartiene..."), marriage, building, planting, travel, making or wearing new clothes; also given for each sign are the qualities of motion, humor, gender,

temperature, bodily part controlled, instructions on taking medicine. The text continues from the last six lines on the recto (ending with the warning "volta"), through most of the dorse.

5. Short passage on the *dies mali* of each month, and on the 4 dangerous Mondays of the year (the first Monday of April and August; the last Monday of September and December), in which one should in particular avoid eating goose.

Parchment roll composed of a single membrane measuring 645 x 235 mm. Remains of prickings along outer edges. Text lines ruled in hard point; tables drawn in ink. Written in a small gothic bookhand on both sides. Key passages and words (e.g., names of the months) and paragraph marks in red; initials touched with yellow. Worn, stained; minor loss of text due to wormholes and rubbing. Unbound; preserved in a modern case.

Written in Italy, sometime after 1410 (see art. 1); provenance unknown. Purchased from H. P. Kraus in 1958 by Thomas E. Marston.

Bibliography: Faye and Bond, p. 88, no. 210.

Marston MS 211 Italy, s. XV^2
Macer Floridus; Marbode, etc.

1. ff. 1r–36r *Incipit macer de uirtutibus herbarum.* Herbarum quasdam diciturus carmine uires./ Herbarum mater dedit artemisia nomen./ Cui grecus sermo iustum puto ponere primo./ . . . Partibus in geminis. pars admiscere terendo./ Vna diagridij sic apta solutio fiet./ Amen deo gratias.

   Macer Floridus (Odo of Meung), *De virtutibus herbarum*; beginning on f. 4v, the sections are numbered 6–76. L. Choulant, ed., *Macer Floridus de viribus herbarum una cum Walafridi Strabonis* . . . (Leipzig, 1832) pp. 28-123. Thorndike and Kibre, 610.

2. ff. 36r–37r Nunc dicam de uirtutibus trium generum/ Lapidum videlicet de chelidonio. Corallo et de albectorio [*sic*]./ At chelidonius lapis est quem gingit yrundo/ Ventre gerens precium quo digna sit ipsa necari./ . . . Et simul humores conpescere quosque nociuos. [f. 36v:] [C]orallus lapis est dum uiuit in equore nimem [*sic*]./ Retibus auulsus uel cesus acumine ferri./ . . . Introitus prestat faciles. finesque secundos.

[f. 36v:] Ventriculo galli qui testibus est uiduatus./ Cum tribus aut nimium factus spado uixerit annis/ ... [ends, f. 37r:] Comodus uxori que uult fore grata marito./ Vt bona tot prestet. clausus portetur in ore.

Extracts from Marbode, *De gemmarum, lapidumque pretiosorum formis, naturis, atque viribus*: *De chelidonio, De corallo, De allectorio*. J. M. Riddle, ed., *Marbode of Rennes' (1035–1123) De lapidibus, Sudhoffs Archiv. Zeitschrift für Wissenschaftsgeschichte*, Beiheft 20 (1977) pp. 54–55, 59–60, 39–40. The text was collated by a later scholar with the Cologne edition of 1528 (note on f. 37r): variant readings and comments appear in margins.

3. ff. 37v–38r Aries caput. Taurus collum. Gemini brachia. Cancer pectus ... Acquarius tibias. Pisces pedes. Vt sciatur que uena incidatur uel purgetur in hora et die cuiuslibet ... Sol preest in homine cordi quod est callidum membrum ... [followed by *Luna, Mars, Mercurius, Iuppiter, Venus, Saturnus*, concluding, f. 38r:] Nota quod imprescripta [*sic*] tabula potest intelligi xij. signa per que pertransit luna in qualibet lunatione ... de brachijs luna existente in gemini et sic de alijs.

Instructions for bloodletting.

4. ff. 38v–39v [1] Elementum diuinum ad integrandum lumen oculorum ... ; [2] Decoptio ad dolorem et tumorem et obtalmiam oculorum ... ; [3] Aqua ad dolorem oculorum ex materia callida ... ; [8] Puluis ad delendos pannos oculorum ... ; [9] Puluis magistri rainaldi [*sic*] de villa noua ... et teratur et utere in oculo.

Nine short recipes for various eye ailments, in Latin.

5. f. 39v [1] Unguento da occhi buono ... ; [2] Acqua da occhi ... ; [3] Vnguento da occi da trarne [or *trarre*?] omne panno et omne male....

Three short recipes for various eye ailments, in Italian (with some Latin interspersed).

Paper (sized, some deckle edges; watermarks, in gutter: similar to Briquet Chapeau 3373), ff. iii (paper) + 39 (contemporary foliation, in ink, 1–39) + iii (paper), 225 x 147 (151 x 88) mm. 33 long lines or lines of verse. Single vertical and horizontal bounding lines full across (Derolez 13.13); ruled in lead. Prickings in upper, lower and outer margins for all rulings.

I^{14}, II^{16}, III^{14} (–10 through 14). Horizontal catchwords centered below written space, verso (Derolez 12.1).

Arts. 1–2 written in a small gothic script with humanistic features, above top line; arts. 3–5 in less formal scripts in larger module.

Simple initials, 2-line, headings and numbering in art. 1, in red, except for ff. 37v–38r where initials are in black. Guide letters and a few sketches (in lead) for initials.

Binding: Italy, s. xix. Rigid vellum case; brown, gold-tooled label with title: "Macer/ Herbarum."

Written in Italy in the second half of the 15th century; provenance unknown. Purchased in 1956 from Arthur Lauria, Paris, by L. C. Witten (inv. no. 1008), who sold it in 1958 to Thomas E. Marston (bookplate).

secundo folio: Noxia

Bibliography: Faye and Bond, p. 88, no. 211.

Marston MS 212 — Central Italy, s. XV$^{med-3/4}$
Macrobius, Saturnalia

ff. 1r–110r *Liber saturnalium Macrobij de diuersis moribus et consuetudinibus antiquorum et dicitur cena philosophorum incipit feliciter.* [M]ultas variasque res in hac uita nobis Eustachi fili natura conciliauit sed nulla nos magis quam eorum qui e nobis essent procreati ... pari ergo ratione infixum corpori pecudis lunari re [remainder of word smudged] humori. τέλος. *Macrobij theodixij Saturnaliorum liber septimus et ultimus explicit.* f. 110v ruled, but blank

J. Willis, ed., Teubner, v. 1 (1970) pp. 1–461. Numerous contemporary marginalia, including names of classical authors quoted in text. Many Greek passages, but not all, entered by an accomplished contemporary hand that sometimes writes more Greek than that quoted in standard editions of the text (e.g., f. 60r).

Paper (thick; watermarks, in gutter: unidentified mountain; a dragon perhaps similar in design to those produced in Ferrara in 1440s–50s, cf. Piccard Drache II.538–72), ff. i (paper) + ii (contemporary parchment endleaves) + 110 + i (paper), 295 x 216 (210 x 125) mm. 40 long lines. Double vertical and horizontal bounding lines (Derolez 13.36). Ruled in hard point on verso.

I–XI^{10}. Horizontal catchwords in center of lower margin.

Copied in humanistic cursive by a single scribe, above top line.

Headings and some plain initials in red.

Ink has corroded through many leaves; minor loss of text.

Binding: Italy, s. xix. Brick red goatskin, blind-tooled. Bound in the same style as MS 450 and Marston MSS 72, 86, 181, 182 for the Guarnieri-Balleani library (Iesi), with the first three probably by the same binder. Written in ink on tail edge: "MACROB." Two front parchment endleaves, presumably reused from the early binding given the patterns of rust stains and wormholes, consist of undated ecclesiastical records from the diocese of Cesena.

Written in Central Italy in the middle or third quarter of the 15th century, perhaps in the diocese of Cesena to judge from the contents of the parchment flyleaves. Probably owned by the humanist Stefano Guarnieri (d. 1495; U. Nicolini, "Stefano Guarnieri da Osimo cancelliere a Perugia dal 1466 al 1488," *L'Umanesimo umbro: atti del IX convegno di studi umbri – Gubbio 22–23 settembre 1974* [Perugia, 1977] pp. 307–23), since the manuscript bears the characteristic binding of the Guarnieri-Balleani library at Iesi (see above). For other Beinecke manuscripts either copied, annotated and/or owned by Guarnieri, see catalogue entries for MS 450, Index V of this volume under Guarnieri-Balleani library, as well as C. Annibaldi, *L'Agricola e la Germania di Cornelio Tacito* (Iesi, 1907) pp. 4–10. Marston MS 212 has been corrected and annotated by several unidentified contemporary hands, one of which also annotated Marston MS 116. Purchased from C. A. Stonehill in 1956 by Thomas E. Marston (bookplate).

secundo folio: [feri]atum deputant

Bibliography: Faye and Bond, p. 88, no. 212.

Marston MS 213 — Austria, s. XIII$^{3/4-4/4}$
Missal — Pl. 53

I. 1. f. 1r Front pastedown numbered as f. 1; f. 2r noted sequence to Catharine of Alexandria, added in a different hand; three short prayers to Dorothea, added in a different hand.

2. ff. 2v–8r Calendar in red and black, with some liturgical, computistic and zodiacal information supplied in the main hand in red ink (including the red "d" to indicate the *dies mali*); among the feasts are: Severinus, apostle of Noricum (5 January), Valentinus bishop (7 January), Erhard bishop (8 January), Antony abbot (17 January, added), Praejectus (25 January), "hainricus dictus heliz[?]mannus" (6 February, added, then erased), "*Dyabolus cecidit*"

(16 February), "*Hic Adam peccavit*" (18 February), 79 Martyrs (21 February), Cunigundis (3 March), "*Primus dies seculi*" (18 March), Benedict (21 March), "Passio domini" (25 March), Castulus (26 March), "Resurrectio domini" (27 March), Rupert bishop (27 March), "*Diluuium factum est*" (3 April), Ezechiel prophet (10 April), "*Rupti sunt fontes aquarum*" (11 April), Senesius (20 April), "[Dedicacio?] parochialis [ecclesie?] [?]" (28 April; added, then erased), Jeremiah prophet (29 April), "Dedicacio altaris sancti Iohannis in medio ecclesie" (29 April, added), Florian (4 May, in red), "Ascensio domini" (5 May), "Dedicacio cappelle in Singulis diebus dantur Sexcenti dies Criminalium et mille. dc. dies venialium que indulgentia durat annuatim octo dies" (6 May, added), octave of Florian (11 May), Gangulph (13 May), "Adventus spiritus sancti" (15 May), "Erasmi episcopi et Martyris hic habetur in Cappella Indulgentia superius adnotata. videlicet. dc. dies Criminalium et mille dc venialium et datur octo dies" (2 June, added), "Dedicacio Cappelle Sancti Laurencii super danubium site habetur singulis annis in sabbato proximo ante Dominicam in albis. et Sequenti die scilicet. Quasimodo geniti erit dedicacio super Carnarium" (moveable feasts falling on the first Saturday and Sunday after Easter, added in outer margin), Nativity of John the Baptist (24 June), "Nota quod indulgentia supra notata habetur etiam in die isto scilicet Iohannis baptiste in cappella et durat similiter octo dies (24 June, added), Erentrude (30 June), Ulric bishop (4 July), Willibald (7 July), Kilian and companions (8 July), Translation of Nicolas (9 July), Translation of Benedict (11 July), Margaret (12 July, in red), Separation of the Apostles (15 July), Translation of Dorothea (18 July, added), Tertullinus (31 July), Maccabean Martyrs (1 August), Invention of Stephen (3 August, in red), Translation of Valentinus (4 August), Afra (7 August, in red), Laurence (10 August, in red), Arnulph bishop (16 August), Magnus (19 August), Decollation of John the Baptist (29 August), Magnus abbot (6 September), Corbinian (8 September), Translation of Cunigundis (9 September), Emmeram (22 September), Translation of Rupert (24 September), Conception of John the Baptist (24 September), Wenceslas (28 September), Michael archangel (29 September, in red), Francis (4 October), Translation of Wolfgang (7 October), Abraham patriarch (9 October), Justus, Artemius and Honesta (11 October), Maximilian (12 October), Coloman (13 October), Martha widow (17 October), Wolfgang (31 October), Caesarius martyr (1 November), Othmar (16 November), Elisabeth of Thuringia (19 November), Virgilius bishop (27 Novem-

ber), Immaculate Conception (8 December, in red), Odilia (13 December), Zosimas monk (14 December), Ananiah, Azariah and Mishael (16 December), Wunibald (18 December), David King (29 December); added in the lower margin of ff. 7v–8r (for 16 October?), collect, secret and postcommunion for two masses of Hedwig.

3. f. 8v *Ad communionem corporis christi. Oratio beati Ambrosij.* Summe sacerdos et uere pontifex ihesu christe qui te obtulisti deo patri hostiam immaculatam in ara crucis pro nobis peccatoribus . . . ; *Item de eodem oratio brevis.* Omnipotens et misericors deus. ecce accedo ad sacramentum corporis et sanguinis domini nostri ihesu christi vnigeniti filij tui licet peccator. . . .

II. 4. ff. 9r–31v Sung parts of masses, noted in neumes, of the temporale, from the first Sunday in Advent through Trinity Sunday, followed by the mass for the dedication of a church.

5. ff. 31v–39v Sung parts of masses, noted in neumes, of the sanctorale, from Sylvester (31 December) through Lucy (13 December), including masses of Florian, Laurence (with vigil and octave), Nicomedis, Michael archangel; marginal additions regarding masses of Kilian, Margaret, Assumption of the Virgin, Decollation of John the Baptist.

6. ff. 39v–43v Sung parts of masses, noted in neumes, of the temporale, from the first through the 23rd Sunday after Pentecost.

7. ff. 43v–44v Sung parts of masses, noted in neumes, of the common of saints.

8. ff. 44v–45r Three settings of the Kyrie and the Gloria; added material in lower margin of f. 45r: Alleluia. Prophete sancti predicauerunt christum nasciturum de virgine matre maria. Mittit ad virginem non [natum?] quemvis angelum sed fortitudinem suam archangelum amator hominis. Mortem expediat pro nobis nuncium . . . Qui nobis tribuat peccati veniam, reatus diluat, et donet [?] pateram in arce syderum. Amen.

9. ff. 45v–57v Sequences, some with alleluias, some noted with neumes, for major feasts from the first mass of Christmas through Trinity Sunday, including sequences of John the Baptist, Mary Magdalen, Afra, Laurence, Michael archangel, the dedication of a church, Separation of the Apostles; sequences for the common of saints, for the Virgin (7 sequences); sequences for the feast of a martyr added in the lower margins of ff. 54v–55r, and for the An-

nunciation in the upper margin of f. 55v; on f. 57v, added prayer for communion: [S]uscipe sancta trinitas et ob memoriam passionis resurrectionis ascensionis domini nostri ihesu christi et in commemoracione beate Marie semper virginis. beati Iohannis baptiste . . . hanc immaculatam hostiam quam ego indignus famulus tuus offero tibi. . . .

III. 10. ff. 58r–60r Prefaces of the mass.

11. ff. 60r–63v Canon of the mass; on f. 63v, added prayers for communion: Domine sancte pater omnipotens sempiterne deus. da mihi hoc corpus et sanguinem filii tui domini nostri ihesu christi. ita sumere. ut per hoc mereamur remisionem . . . ; Domine ihesu christe filii dei viui. qui ex voluntate patris cooperante spiritu sancto per mortem propriam mundum viuificasti . . . ; Domine non sum dignus. ut intres sub tectum meum . . . ; Percepcio corporis et sanguinis domini nostri ihesu christi quam ego indignus et miserrimus peccator summere [*sic*] presumo [?] . . . ; Corpus domini nostri ihesu christi. quod accepi et calix quem potaui . . . ; added by a different hand from above in the lower margin of f. 63v, prayer for peace: Domine ihesu christe qui dixisti apostolis tuis pacem meam do vobis pacem meam. . . .

12. f. 64r–v Blessing of the candle on Holy Saturday, with neumes; collect, secret and postcommunion added in a different hand for masses of All Saints during Eastertide (on otherwise blank leaf at the end of the quire).

IV. 13. ff. 65r–93r Spoken parts of masses (usually collect, secret and postcommunion only, but more extensive for the greater feasts, especially during Eastertide) of the temporale from the first Sunday in Advent through the 24th Sunday after Pentecost.

14. ff. 93r–118r Spoken parts of masses (usually collect, secret and postcommunion only) of two votive masses of the Virgin, and of the sanctorale, from Thomas of Canterbury (29 December) through Thomas the Apostle (21 December), including masses of Benedict, Florian, John the Baptist (with major initial and four postcommunion prayers), Ulric, Kilian, Translation of Benedict, Margaret, Separation of the Apostles, Mary Magdalen, Anne (added; not present in calendar), Maccabean Martyrs, Sixtus (with a blessing of the grapes between the secret and the postcommunion), vigil of Laurence, Laurence (two masses, "in die sancto mane" and "ad publicam"), octave of Laurence, Decollation of John the Baptist, Nicomedes,

Michael archangel, Denis (9 October), Coloman (16 October; with common set of prayers and rubric corrected to his name over an erasure), Francis (4 October; in original hand, and with proper collect), Catharine of Alexandria.

15. ff. 118r–120v Spoken parts of masses (collect, secret and postcommunion only) of the common of saints; additions by various hands in the margins for arts. 14–15, including masses of Bridget (1 February; of Kildare or of Niedermünster), Perpetua and Felicitas, Rupert, Ambrose, Anne (not present in calendar), Oswald, Wenceslas, Coloman, Barbara, Immaculate Conception (*De Concepcione*, "Deus ineffabilis..."; *Secretum*, "Salutiferus pater omnipotens..."; *Complendum*, "Celestis alimonie vegetati libamine...").

16. ff. 121r–124r Votive masses in full (but lections sometimes by cue only) for the week: Trinity, Wisdom, Holy Spirit, Angels, Charity, Holy Cross, Virgin (with changed office according to the liturgical year).

17. ff. 124r–141r Votive masses, some with full text (but lections often by cue only): *pro salute viuorum, pro peccatis, de patrono* ("sancti N. martyris"), *de sanctis, oratio generalis, in veneratione sanctorum* (those whose relics are in the church), *ad postulanda suffragia sanctorum, pro universis ordinibus, pro papa, omni gradu ecclesie, pro Imperatore, pro se ipso* (2 forms), *pro pace, pro Tribulatione, Contra persecutores, pro lacrimis postulandis, ad postulandam humilitatem, pro recta petitione et vita bona, de sancto spiritu, ad repellendas malas cogitaciones, Contra temptaciones carnis, pro amico, pro Inimicis, pro Confitente peccata, pro peccatis* (2 forms), *pro Tribulatione, pro elemosinas facientibus, pro iter agentibus, pro salute viuorum, ad postulandam pluviam, ad postulandam Serenitatem, ad repellendis* [sic] *tempestates, pro Infirmis, pro Infirmo amico, pro Infirmo* (against fevers, through the intercession of St. Sigismund), *pro quacumque tribulatione, pro pestilentia animalium, pro tribulatione,* [*Oratio*] *Generalis* (2 forms); added in several hands on f. 134r–v, in space originally left blank, a *missa generalis, pro quacumque tribulacione, pro omnibus fidelibus defunctis*; ff. 135r–141r, votive masses for the dead (23 forms); f. 141r, added in another hand, Nicene Creed.

18. ff. 141v–148v Collect, secret and postcommunion for masses of the sanctorale, including All Saints before Advent, Praejectus (25 January), Walpurgis, Cunigundis, Nicomedes, Antony of Padua, Achatius and the 10,000 Soldiers, Mary Magdalen, Pantaleon, Translation of Valentinus bishop of Passau, Oswald, Dominic,

Bernard of Clairvaux, Corbinian, Emmeram, Leodegar, Gereon, Maximilian, 11,000 Virgins, Othmar, Elisabeth of Thuringia, Immaculate Conception, Odilia (13 December); a general mass (with collect, secret and postcommunion only); a full mass, partially noted, of *Corpus Christi*; a sequence for Sundays after Easter, a sequence of the Holy Cross, and, added in another hand on the otherwise blank final verso of the quire (f. 148v), a sequence for the mass of the Virgin.

19. ff. 149r–248v Lections for masses of the temporale, from the first Sunday in Advent through the 24th Sunday after Pentecost, with readings for the 25th Sunday added in a different color ink; the text of the Passion Gospels (ff. 192r–196v, 198r–201v, 202v–206r, 207v–210r) marked with suprascript letters "t" (for Christ's part), "a" (for other speakers), "c" (or rarely "s," for the third person narrator); a red cross in the text marks the return to Gospel tone on ff. 201v, 206r, 209v; occasional neumes on Christ's speaking parts; on f. 150v, added readings for the Visitation.

20. ff. 249r–266r Lections for masses of the sanctorale, from Sylvester (31 December) through Andrew (30 November), including the feasts of the Nativity of John the Baptist, Mary Magdalen, Laurence, Decollation of John the Baptist, Michael archangel; among the material added in the margins are readings for the feast of the Visitation.

21. ff. 266r–276v Lections (sometimes by cue only) for masses of the common of saints, missing one leaf after f. 268r, and ending defectively at the first reading for virgins (Ecclesiasticus 51.1–9); on ff. 275r–276r, between the lections for martyrs and those for evangelists, are three readings for the feast of Benedict: *Benedicti abbatis Lectio Libri Sapiencie.* Rigabo hortum meum plantationum. et inebriabo partus mei fructum ... concordia fratrum. et amor proximorum (Ecclesiasticus 24.42–25.2); *Lectio libri Sapiencie.* Beatus homo qui inuenit sapienciam. et qui affluit prudencia ... et nubes rore concrescunt (Prov. 3.13–20), *Mattheum.* In illo tempore. Dixit ihesus discipulis suis. Vos estis sal terre ... ut uideant uestra bona opera. et glorificent patrem uestrum qui in celis est (Mat. 5.13–16).

Composed of four parts, all on thick parchment of good quality, ff. 276 (f. 1, contemporary [?] parchment flyleaf partially pasted to front board) + i (contemporary [?] parchment flyleaf pasted to back board), 322 x 230 mm.

Part I: ff. 2–8, written space: 206 x 178 mm. Ruled in multiple columns for calendar, in ink; prominent prickings in upper, lower and outer margins. Consists of a single gathering of seven leaves; structure uncertain due to repairs, though 4 and 5 are conjugate. Text of calendar written in gothic bookhand by a single scribe; many later additions in several hands. *KL* monograms, in red, embellished with knobs.

Part II: ff. 9–56 (early foliation in Roman numerals, i–xxxvii, for ff. 9–45, in center of upper margin), written space: 230 x 167 mm. 27 long lines. Double vertical bounding lines and widely spaced double horizontal bounding lines, all full across; ruled in ink; remains of prickings in upper, lower and outer margins. II–VII^{8}. Quires numbered in Roman numerals in center of lower margin, recto; numbering sequence runs from beginning to end of codex. Written in gothic bookhand, with additions in several different hands in less formal styles of writing. Musical notation consists of Austrian adiastematic neumes in the same ink as the text. Eleven large initials, 12- to 6-line, drawn in red and/or brown ink against geometric grounds of blue and lime-green washes. The initials are constructed of dragons and other fantastic animals, or of stylized foliage inhabited by biting beasts and birds. Similar initials can be found in manuscripts from Vorau dated 1270–90 (see P. Buberl, *Beschreibendes Verzeichnis der illuminierten Handschriften in Österreich*, vol. IV.1, pp. 188–89, fig. 185, and pp. 192–93, figs. 189–191). Plain initials in blue, red or lime-green, some with blue and/or red penwork designs, others with knobs. Major headings in majuscules with letters alternating red, black, and sometimes lime green; other headings in red. Instructions to rubricator perpendicular to text. Elegant repairs to parchment sewn with blue and chartreuse thread (e.g., f. 27).

Part III: ff. 57–64, written space for ff. 58–63, 220 x 150 mm. 19 long lines. Double vertical bounding lines in hard point [?]. Double rulings for each line of text, ruled faintly in lead. Remains of prickings in upper, lower, and outer margins. A single gathering of 8 leaves (1 and 8, ff. 57 and 64, appear to have been wrapped around an original quire of six leaves; these two leaves have formats similar to Parts II and IV). Written in large liturgical gothic bookhand. The decoration of the Canon of the Mass consists of a 3/4-page miniature of the crucifixion, f. 60r, framed with a narrow border of olive green, red and blue with white filigree. Christ is shown hanging from a Y-shaped *Astkreuz* flanked by Mary and St. John, against gold ground. The gold ground is largely rubbed and the figures are partly restored (lower part of St. John's robe has been reworked, and flaked paint on the cross and Christ's loin cloth replaced). The depiction is the earliest in a series of Crucifixion miniatures in St. Florian manuscripts with the cross symbolically treated as the Tree of Life (see *Exhibition Catalogue*, pp. 193–95, no. 22, fig. 8). Stylistically and iconographically the miniature can be located between the corresponding depictions in St. Florian, Stiftsbibliothek, cod. III. 209 and cod. XI. 394 (see G. Schmidt, *Die Malerschule von St. Florian: Beiträge zur süddeutschen Malerei zur Ende des 13. und im 14. Jahrhundert* [Linz, 1962], pp. 82–84, no. 39). Marginal illustration of what appears to be a kneeling Augustinian [?] canon dressed in white and red robes, adjoining the *Te igitur* (f. 60v). Three illuminated initials, ff. 58r, 59v, 60v, for the Canon of the Mass, 7- to 5-line, pale mauve with stylized scrolls and green foliage against gold ground edged in blue with white filigree. Similar initials appear in St. Florian, Stiftsbibliothek cod. III. 209 (cf. Schmidt, p. 165, figs, 81, 84–85). *Vere dignum* initials, 3-line, alternate in red and blue with penwork in either blue or red. Most of the leaves of this section have been repaired.

Part IV: ff. 65–276 (early foliation, Roman numerals, in upper margin: i-clxiij for ff. 93–253 only), written space 235 x 150 mm. 26 long lines (exceptions include: ff. 141v–148v, 215 x 150 mm., 25 lines; ff. 149r–276v, 25 or 26 lines). Double vertical and single or double upper vertical bounding lines ruled in pen, all full across. Prickings in upper, lower and outer margins. IX-XVIII^{8}, XIX^{4} (ff. 145–148, unnumbered), XX^{6} (old foliation begins with this quire), XXI-XXVI^{8}, XXVII^{10}, XXVIII-XXXIV^{8}, XXXV^{7} [?], XXXVI^{1} (a single leaf signed with quire signature XXXV). Remains of old series of quire signatures (XIV and XV on ff. 260v, 261r); new series of quire signatures, also Roman numerals but on recto, runs from beginning to end of codex (cf. Part II above). Written in gothic bookhand; several layers of marginalia added in less formal hands. Pen-and-ink initials, 7- to 4-line, of a similar design as in Part II, but lacking the vitality; drawn in brown and/or red ink with stylized foliage and palmettes sometimes touched with blue or red against blue, red and/or lime-green ground. Smaller initials, 4-line, red, blue or green with red and/or green penwork design. Plain initials in red. Headings in red. Instructions for rubricator perpendicular to text.

Binding: England, s. xix. Quarter bound in brown calf over wooden board, with decoration cut in (ciselé). Metal fittings at the head and tail of the leather and two fastenings.

Written in Austria at the end of the third quarter or the beginning of the fourth quarter of the 13th century, probably ca. 1270–80. Although all four parts may be roughly contemporary in execution, they apparently were not assembled together as a book for the mass until the 15th century, at which point the manuscript was annotated and cross-referenced from beginning to end; it is possible that only the lectionary and sacramentary in Part IV were originally intended to be used together. The composite nature of the codex is suggested by the following codicological details: the sequence of the early foliation that was written in three different hands (ff. 9r–45r = i–xxxvii; ff. 93r–249r = i–clix; ff. 250r–253r = clx–clxiii); the presence of two distinct sequences of quire marks, one of which was added when the codex assumed its present configuration in the 15th century; the juxtaposition of somewhat different styles of script and decoration found in the four parts. The entire manuscript has been attributed in the past to the house of Augustinian canons of St. Florian on the basis of the calendar, the physical format of the text, and the iconography of the Crucifixion (see *Exhibition Catalogue*, pp. 193–94, no. 22). This attribution may, however, be problematic: textually, some Augustinian features (such as the feast of Augustine's mother, Monica) are absent, whereas certain Benedictine feasts are included; the script and initials in the Gradual (Part II) seem antiquated and do not fit well within the production of the St. Florian scriptorium (cf. Schmidt, p. 165), but similar initials can be found in manuscripts from neighboring Vorau dated ca. 1270–90; given the variety and style of scripts and decoration present in the manuscript, it is possible that the parts were not all produced in a single place. In conclusion, the evidence suggests that the four parts of the codex, either individually or collectively, were not necessarily executed at St. Florian nor were they originally intended to be used together in a single volume. Further research is required before a definite attribution can be made. A 14th-century addition to the calendar (f. 5r) may refer to the chapel of St. Laurence at Lorch. Two later inscriptions in the upper margin, f. 2r, now crossed out: "MS. 366." and "36." Purchased from H. P. Kraus (Cat. 88, no. 11) in 1959 by Thomas E. Marston (bookplate).

secundo folio: [Part I, f. 3:] *KL Februarius*
[Part II, f. 10:] ambulant
[Part III, f. 59:] *Uere dignum*
[Part IV, f. 66:] Indignos

Bibliography: Faye and Bond, p. 88, no. 213.
Exhibition Catalogue, pp. 193–94, no. 22, pl. 8 of f. 60r (with additional early bibliography).
The Medieval Book, pp. 72, 74–75, no. 76, pl. of f. 60r.

Marston MS 214 — France, s. XIV/XV
Postilla in Apocalypsim

1. ff. 1r–4r Omnes qui. Pie volunt viuere ... [2 Tim. 3.12]. Hunc prologum premittit gilbertus libro Apocalypsis in quo prologo tria principa-

liter tangit. videlicet huius libri: Rem subiectiuam veri tenoris/ Causam motiuam cure scriptoris/ ... Quantum ad primum dicit gilbertus omnes qui pie volunt viuere in christo id est cultum christi tenere est ... patebunt suis locis. Explicit prologus.

Commentary on Gilbert de la Porrée's *Prologue* to the Apocalypse; cf. Stegmüller, no. 839. See H. C. van Elswijk, *Gilbert Porreta: Sa vie, son oeuvre, sa pensée* (Louvain, 1966) pp. 58–59.

2. ff. 4r–120v [A]pocalypsis yhesu christi et cet. [Apoc. 1.1]. Iste liber diuiditur in tres partes principales in prima ponitur prefatio attrahens clericorum. in secunda efficiuntur homines studiosi et attenti ... deo gratia dominj nostrj yhesu christi cum omnibus vobis Amen. Amen. Et hec est terminatio libri totalis deo gratias.

Commentary on the Apocalypse, accompanied by marginal notes, some extensive.

Parchment (end pieces), ff. 120, 241 x 183 (195 x 118) mm. 49 long lines. Frame-ruled in ink; some leaves completely ruled in lead.

I–II^{8}, III^{16}, IV–XIV^{8}. Horizontal catchwords enclosed by rectangles, center of lower margin on verso.

Written in a small gothic cursive, above top line.

One illuminated initial, 3-line, blue with white highlights on gold rectangular ground edged in black; gold leaves and black inkspray extend into upper and inner margins to form modest border. Plain initials, red or blue, 3- to 2-line. A few paragraph marks in red or blue.

Binding: France [?] s. xix–xx. Quarter bound in brown blind-tooled calf over wooden boards by the same binder as Marston MSS 119, 216 and 236.

Written in France at the end of the 14th or beginning of the 15th century; formerly bound with Marston MS 216 (see catalogue entry below). Purchased in 1958 from Nicolas Rauch, Geneva, by L. C. Witten (inv. no. 2089), who sold it the same year to Thomas E. Marston (bookplate).

secundo folio: Ratione

Bibliography: Faye and Bond, pp. 88–89, no. 214.

Marston MS 215 Northern France, s. XIV$^{2/4}$
Nicolaus de Lyra, Postillae in Testamentum Vetus Pl. 47

1. ff. 1r–44v *Primus prologus de commendacione sacre scripture.* Hec omnia liber vite. Ecc. 24. Secundum quod dicit beatus gregorius homelia 35 euangeliorum. Temporalis vita eterne ... et ideo verisimile est quod sperabat resurgere cum christo resurgente. Cui est honor et gloria in secula seculorum. Amen. Explicit apostilla super genesym. f. 45r–v blank

Postilla on Genesis; Stegmüller 5829. Bifolium ff. 43–44 misbound; sequence of text should be read ff. 38, 43, 39–42, 44.

2. ff. 46r–78r Secundum quod dicit ysidorus primo libro ethimorum [*sic*]. lex est nullo priuato commodo [?] verum pro comuni utilitate ... in memoria illa que de istis superius sunt expressa.

Postilla on Exodus; Stegmüller 5830.

3. ff. 78v–94r *Uocauit autem moysem* et cetera. Sicud [*sic*] dictum fuit in principio exodi. Lex diuina que danda est populo aduuato [?] sub cultu ... in littera ultimo recapitulat dicens hec sunt mandata et cetera patent.

Postilla on Leviticus; Stegmüller 5831.

4. ff. 94r–114v Locutusque est dominus. Ex predictis in precedentibus libris patet quod sicud [*sic*] in libro genesis. agitur de fidelis populi eleccione cui lex erat danda ... iudicia. quantum ad iudicialia.

Postilla on Numbers; Stegmüller 5832.

5. ff. 114v–134v Declaracio sermonum tuorum illuminat et intellectum dat paruulis [Ps. 118.130]. Sicud [*sic*] dictum fuit in principio exodi. lex non datur proprie vni persone singulari. sed comunitati ... non sunt facta per alium prophetam in ueteri lege. *Explicit Postilla super deuteronomium. Edita a ffratre N. de Lyra de ordine ffratrum minorum sacre theologie doctore. Deo gracias. Amen.*

Postilla on Deuteronomy; Stegmüller 5833.

6. ff. 135r–147r Introduces eos et plantabis eos in monte hereditatis tue. exo. xv. secundum hebreos a libro josue incipiunt libri prophetales ut patet per Ieronimum in prologo ... non est in hebreo nec in biblijs correctis. *Explicit Postilla Super Librum Iosue Edita A ffratre Nicholao de lyra De ordine ffratrum Minorum.*

Postilla on Joshua, Stegmüller 5834.

7. ff. 147r–161r Suscitauit dominus iudices ... [Jud. 3.2]. Sicut in libro Iosue a quo incipiunt libri hystoriales agitur de terre promissionis ingressu ... quia non ceperunt eas de uoluntate uestra.

Postilla on Judges; Stegmüller 5835.

8. ff. 161r–163v *Incipit hystoria Ruth. primum capitulum.* In diebus unius iudicis. hic consequenter ponitur tercius casus. scilicet ipsius Ruth. et diuiditur in quatuor partes ... sicut dictum est supra secundo capitulo. *Explici* [sic] *hystoria Ruth deo gracias.* as [*sic*].

Postilla on Ruth; Stegmüller 5836.

9. ff. 163v–235r *Incipit primus liber Regum Regiminum* [?]. Per me reges regnant. proverb. octauo. Sicut dictum fuit in principio libri Iudicum populus israel post ingressum ... et disponens omnia suauiter. Cui est honor et gloria in secula seculorum. Amen. *Explicit postilla super libros Regum. Edita A ffratre Nicholao de lyra. de ordine fratrum Minorum. Sacre Theologie Doctore. deo gracias. Explicit iste liber scriptor sit crimine liber. et cetera.* f. 235v blank

Postilla on I-IV Kings; Stegmüller 5837–40.

Parchment, ff. i (paper) + 235, 330 x 240 (258 x 176) mm. 2 columns, 60 lines. Single vertical and double upper horizontal bounding lines. Additional pairs of rulings, only present occasionally, in upper, lower, outer and inner margins. Ruled in lead. Remains of prickings in upper, lower and outer margins; some prickings for text rulings between columns.

I–III^{12}, IV^{10} (misbound, see text above; –9, a blank), V–XI^{12}, XII^{6}, XIII–XVI^{12}, XVII^{10}, XVIII–XX^{12}, XXI^{6}. Catchwords, many decorated in a penwork frame, placed between lower horizontal rulings to right of center, verso. Remains of leaf signatures, red or blue, in lower right corner, recto.

Written by several scribes in gothic bookhand.

19 pen-and-ink drawings with washes in red, green, blue and pale yellow, some inserted into the text column, others up to half-page size dealing with the Tabernacle in the Desert and the Temple of Solomon: the drawings serve to clarify the written text by depicting differences in interpretations between Jewish and Catholic exegesis; contrasting drawings are usually juxtaposed and labelled with the respective source for each. The subjects, as discussed by B. Kaczynski, "Illustrations of the Tabernacle and Temple Implements in the *Postilla in Testamentum Vetus* of Nicolaus de Lyra," *Gazette* 48 (1973) pp. 1–11, are as follow: f. 13r: Noah's Ark (2

versions); f. 67r: Ark of the Covenant (2 versions); f. 67v: Table of the Showbreads (2 versions); f. 68r: Candelabrum (2 versions); f. 68v: Two Curtains of the Tabernacle; f. 69r: Framework of the Tabernacle; f. 70r: Altar of Holocaust (2 versions); f. 71r: High Priest in his Vestments; f. 74v: Tablets of the Law (2 versions); f. 78r: Floorplan of the Sanctuary; f. 95v: Arrangement of the Levite Camps; f. 206v: Floorplan of Solomon's Temple; f. 208r: Cross section of the Hall of the Forest of Lebanon; f. 208v: Floorplan of the Hall of the Forest of Lebanon; f. 209r: Capital Surmounting the Bronze Pillar; f. 209v: other version of Capital; f. 210r: Brazen "Sea" (3 versions); f. 211v: Wheeled Stands and Bronze Basins (2 versions). Many fine flourished initials, red and blue divided, 9- to 3-line, with penwork designs in red, blue and/or purple; somewhat smaller less ambitious initials alternate red and blue with designs in the opposite color. The minor decoration appears inconsistently, with running headlines, rubrics, paragraph marks and underlining of Biblical texts, in various colors or totally absent.

Binding: Place and date uncertain [a modern restoration?]. Limp vellum case with earlier title (mostly illegible) running lengthwise on spine and later title added at top of spine: "Fr. Nicolai de Lyra ord. min. Commentaria in Libro historico Sacrae Scripturae."

Written in Northern France in the second quarter of the 14th century to judge from the script and the decorative initials. Inscription on f. 1r (partially erased: "Iste liber Ecclesie Ravenatis") indicates that it was in Ravenna by the 15th century where presumably it remained at least until the 17th century when a note was added on f. 71r concerning a member of the Guiccioli family ("Actum Die Quarta mensis junij Mill.° sexcent. 3. presente DNO Greg. Guicciolo Domino/ Io. Fran. Christ. Iud."). Belonged to comte Chandon de Briailles (bookplate with "MSS.5" written in ink on front flyleaf) and to Charles Lormier (his sale in 1904, cat. IV, no. 2509). Purchased in 1958 from Emile Rossignol, Paris, by L. C. Witten (inv. no. 2064), who sold it the same year to Thomas E. Marston (bookplate).

secundo folio: et minus [corrected from minis?]

Bibliography: Faye and Bond, p. 89, no. 215.
Exhibition Catalogue, pp. 205–6, no. 32.

Marston MS 216 England [?], s. XIII$^{2/4}$; Northern France, s. XV^{med}
Nicolaus de Lyra, etc.

I. 1. f. 1r blank; ff. 1v–3v [Heading in upper margin, damaged:] Magister Nicholaus de torniaco super cc^{a} Exodi ... [text:] Abissus. l. .iiij./ Accessus ad deum. xix./ Aduocati. ii vi. xx. xxxiij. xlviij./ ... Unanimitas. xliij./ Venter et secessus diaboli. xxx./ Zelus. xliiij.

Alphabetical subject index to art. 2 for use in preaching; folio references in art. 2 appear in upper left corner, verso, and the key word in the margin.

2. ff. 4r–59r *Magister Nicholaus de Torniaco super cc^{a}. Exodi.* Ego indurabo et cetera [Ex. 14.4]. Duplicem plagam infligendam iudeis. notat ysa [*sic*] cum ait. Quare nos errare fecisti ... non tantum a uoluptuosis sed etiam a plerisque utilibus abstinere debere. et solis necessariis esse contemptos. Explicit.

Nicolaus Tornacensis [?], *Commentaria super Exodum 14.4–15.5*; Stegmüller, no. 6007 where it is attributed to Nicolaus Parisiensis. Here the text is attributed to Nicolaus de Tornaco (Tournai). Schematization of topics for sermons occurs in many margins for arts. 2 and 6.

3. f. 59v [S]uper cathedram et cetera et infra auctoritate statuimus et ordinamus eadem ut fratres dictorum ordinum de obuencionibus ... confirmacionem Iura aliqua addiderant et cetera.

Unidentified text on canon law.

4. ff. 59v–60r [V]trum fratres teneantur soluere sacerdotibus parochialis [?] quartam partem de hiis que relinquuntur eis ab illis qui non sepeliuntur apud eos ... sepulture incepissent et [one word unclear] sed persona interdicta et cetera [one word effaced] dottores in Curia.

Unidentified text on canon law, with specific reference to Franciscans.

5. ff. 60v–61v [A]bscondere .i./ Accelerate. xliij./ Admirabiliter. xliij./ ... Uirginitas. x. xi./ Vmbra. xix.

Alphabetical subject index to art. 6; folio references in art. 6 appear in upper left corner, verso, and the key word in the margin. The index entries for the letter *u* are written on a piece of parchment carefully stitched to f. 61v so as not to obscure the rest of the text on f. 61v.

6. ff. 62r–107r *Magister Nicholaus de Torniaco. Ego sum Gabriel et cetera.* [Luc. 1.19]. In hoc natatur quod si quis de propria infirmitate diffidat. de fortitudine dei debet confidere ... et ubi pax. ibi est regnum eius. et e contrario. f. 107v blank

Nicolaus Tornacensis [?], *Commentaria in Lucam 1.19–1.33*; Stegmüller, no. 6007,2 where it is attributed to Nicolaus Parisiensis. Here the text is attributed to Nicolaus de Tornaco (Tournai).

7. ff. 108r–110v Letare sterilis ... [Gal. 4.27]. Discubuerunt ergo uiri ... [John 6.10] ... [text:] Cogitanti mihi qualiter in epistola de ysa [*sic*] sumptum ad euuangelij miraculum ordinetur ... in caritate in fide in castitate.

Philippus Cancellarius, *Sermo de tempore*; Schneyer, v. 4, p. 829 (163).

8. ff. 110v–113r Est puer unus hic ... [John 6.9] ... Sume tibi librum ... [Is. 8.1] ... [text:] Est liber nature et est liber experiencie. et est liber gracie ... exercitacio. operis ad modicum ualet. pietas autem ad omnia absque fermento// f. 113v blank

Philippus Cancellarius, *Sermo de tempore* (ending imperfectly?); Schneyer, v. 4, p. 830 (164).

II. 9. ff. 114r–140v *Introduces eos et plantabis eos* ... [Ex. 15.17]. Secundum hebreos a libro iosue incipiunt libri prophetales ut patet per ieronimum in prologo super libros regum. Secundum vero divisionem ... non est in hebreo nec in libris correctis. Explicit iosue.

Nicolaus de Lyra, *Postilla in Iosuam*; Stegmüller, no. 5834. Text here divided into 14 chapters.

10. ff. 141r–165v *Suscitauit dominus iudices* ... [Jud. 2.16]. Sicut in libro iosue a quo incipiunt libri hystoriales agitur de terre promissionis ingressu vel pocius ... non fecistis quia non ceperunt eas de voluntate vestra. Explicit iudicum.

Nicolaus de Lyra, *Postilla in Iudices*; Stegmüller, no. 5835. Text here divided into 21 chapters.

Composed of two distinct parts both written on parchment, 238 x 182 mm.

Part I: ff. 1–113, written space: 175 x 125 mm. 2 columns, 35 lines. Ruled in crayon or lead. Double vertical outer bounding lines, single inner, with an additional ruling between columns; a pair of rulings in outer margin to delineate column for index entries. Horizontal bounding lines ruled irregularly: usually two widely spaced upper and lower bounding lines and two or three widely spaced horizontal rulings through middle of written space. Prickings prominent in outer and inner margins. I^4 (-4), II–VIII^8, IX^2 (ff. 60–61), X^{10}, XI–XIII^8; remaining leaves of Part I difficult to collate due to tight binding and repairs. Remains of horizontal catchwords under inner column along lower edge, verso. Written by multiple scribes in spiky gothic bookhand, both above and below top line; ff. 59v–60r in a later, less formal gothic script. Poorly executed initials, 3- to 2-line, in blue or red with designs in opposite color; plain red or blue initials for arts. 1 and 5. Headings and underlining for Biblical passages in red.

Part II: ff. 114–165, written space: 177 x 139 mm. 2 columns, 41 lines. Single vertical or double upper and single lower horizontal bounding lines. Ruled in pen. I^8 (half leaf, f. 119, with omitted text), II–V^8, VI^{10} (+ 1 leaf added at end). Catchwords for individual leaves in some quires, center of lower margin, verso. Written in bâtarde script, below top line. Plain initials, 4- to 2-line, headings, paragraph marks, underlining for Biblical passages, initial strokes and punctuation, in red.

Binding: France [?], s. xix–xx. Quarter bound in brown calf, blind-tooled, over oak boards. Bound by the same binder as Marston MSS 119, 214 and 236.

Part I was probably written in England in the second quarter of the 13th century, with the text on ff. 59v–60r added in France in the first half of the 15th century; rust stains on ff. 109–113 indicate that Part I was once bound separately. Part II was written in Northern France in the middle of the 15th century. It is unclear when Parts I and II were joined together; the off-set impression of an initial with border on f. 165v does indicate, however, that at least Part II was formerly bound together with Marston MS 214. Oval book stamp of unidentified French seminary on f. 1r. Miscellaneous modern notes about contents of manuscript on front pastedown. Purchased from L. C. Witten (inv. no. 2090) in 1958 by Thomas E. Marston (bookplate).

secundo folio: [Part I, f. 2, index:] Electio
[f. 5, text:] quod hic
[Part II, f. 115:] timebat:

Bibliography: Faye and Bond, p. 89, no. 216.

Marston MS 217 Florence, s. $XV^{3/4}$
Matteo Palmieri, De temporibus

ff. 1r–100v *Matthei Palmerii Florentini de Temporibus incipit. Et primo proemium ad Petrum Cosme filium Medicem.* Animis nostris innatum esse constat ut prestantes ingenio uiri non solum sue etatis uerum etiam preteriti quoque temporis res gestas scire desiderent ... [f. 1v:] *Finit proemium. Praefatio libri incipit.* Querenti mihi sepenumero quibus temporibus per quos et apud quas gentes res memoratu ... *Finit prefatio. Liber de temporibus feliciter incipit.* [text, f. 3r:] A Principio mundi siue ab adam primo hominum usque ad diluuium quod factum est sub Noe computantur anni ... menstrua illi stipendia pollicentur. Mediolanenses laudem receperunt. *Mathei Palmerii Florentini ad Petrum Medicem Liber de temporibus finit feliciter.*

Matteo Palmieri, *De temporibus*, preceded by his preface to Piero de' Medici; the manuscript corresponds to the text published in the series *Rerum Italicarum scriptores*, v. 26: *Matthei Palmerii Liber de temporibus*, ed. G. Scaramella (Città di Castello, 1906–15) pp. 3–127. The text of the manuscript is arranged in tabular format with two columns to the left of the written space headed *Anni salutis* and *Pontificum* (starting on f. 7v) and two columns to the right headed *Imperatorum* and *Anni mundi* (starting on f. 3v). The manuscript is in such unblemished condition that it looks as if it was never used.

Parchment, ff. ii (modern parchment bifolium; i = front pastedown) + 100 + ii (modern parchment bifolium; ii = back pastedown), 360 x 265 (235 x 140) mm. for ff. 1r–2v; (235 x 102) for ff. 3r–100v. Three widely spaced vertical rulings delineate each side of central text space to form two tabular columns, ruled in hard point or crayon. Horizontal rulings for text all extend full width of conjugate leaves, ruled in hard point on hair side. Remains of prickings in outer margins.

I–X^{10}. Quire and leaf signatures (e.g., A 1, A 2, A 3, etc., with red horizontal line added above) in lower right corner, recto.

Written in a round humanistic script, above top line.

Two illuminated initials of fine quality (ff. 1r, 1v), 6- and 5-line, gold on brilliant blue, green and pink grounds with white vine-stem ornament and white and reddish dots. Headings and Roman numerals in red. Paragraph marks alternate red and blue.

Binding: France, s. xix. Red goatskin, blind- and gold-tooled with unidentified arms on the sides.

Written in Florence in the third quarter of the 15th century by Dominicus

Cassii de Narnia; for a list of manuscripts copied by this scribe see de la Mare, *New Research*, Appendix I, pp. 491–92. Belonged to an unidentified owner whose arms appear on the binding. Purchased from Bernard Rosenthal in 1958 by Thomas E. Marston (bookplate).

secundo folio: [f. 2:] longe perdifficile
[f. 4:] Anni salutis. cognouisset

Bibliography: Faye and Bond, p. 89, no. 217.

Marston MS 218 Switzerland or Northern Italy, s. XV^2
Paul the Deacon, Historia gentis Longobardorum, etc.

1. ff. 1r–76v [Title added in upper margin:] De gestis seu rebus Longobardorum. [chapter list:] *Incipiunt capitula primi libri*. Incipiunt capitula libri primi. Quod septentrionalis plaga quanto ... rege gessit. [text, f. 1v:] Septentrionalis plaga quanto magis ab estu solis remota est et niuali frigore gelida tanto salubrior corporibus ... maxime semper cura francorum Auarumque pacem custodiens. Amen. f. 77r–v ruled, but blank

   Paul the Deacon, *Historia gentis Longobardorum*; L. Bethmann and G. Waitz, eds., *Scriptores rerum germanicarum* v. 27 (1878) pp. 52–242. Here the text is divided into six books, each preceded by a table of chapters.

2. ff. 78r–88v Eo anno nitorium palladij mens tua que et discere cupit immenso sapientie amore succensa ... Vniuersam enim humanam ubique naturam uolumus per nos fieri esse meliorem. Explicit gesta. ff. 89r–90v ruled, but blank (see also provenance)

   Palladius of Helenopolis, *Liber de moribus Brachmanorum*, Lat. tr.; PL 17.1131–46.

Paper (watermarks: similar to Piccard Ochsenkopf I.731–35), ff. ii (paper, ii = modern title page) + 90 + ii (paper), 310 x 215 (188 x 132) mm. 2 columns, 27 lines. Single vertical bounding lines ruled in lead. Text rulings in ink. Prickings in upper, lower and outer margins.

I–II^{12}, III–VIII^{10}, IX^6. Vertical catchwords perpendicular to text along inner bounding line, verso.

Written in a cursive minuscule script, above top line; the first words of each chapter in large gothic bookhand.

One initial, divided red and blue, 5-line, with red penwork flourishes, f. 1r; the initial may have been retouched by a contemporary hand. Plain red initials throughout; spaces for rubrics left unfilled, except for those at beginning of each book. Running headlines in red. Guide letters for decorator.

Binding: Germany, s. xix. Quires cut in for sewing. Rigid vellum case with a red, gold-tooled label: "P. Diacon. De Gest. langobar." Early title in ink on fore edge: "De Gest. Longobardo."

Written in Switzerland or Northern Italy in the second half of the 15th century to judge from the watermarks, script and decoration; inscription of Gionnantonio [*sic*] Zavallo with date "1563" on f. 89r. Signature, s. xix, on f. ii verso of "Gaudenzio Claretta," perhaps to be identified with the historian and author Baron Gaudenzio Giuseppe Luigi Maria Claretta (1835–1902). Unidentified shelf-mark [?] "A Tu" in upper right corner, f. 1r. Purchased from C. A. Stonehill (inv. no. 13685) in 1958 by Thomas E. Marston (bookplate).

secundo folio: quo solis

Bibliography: Faye and Bond, p. 89, no. 218.

Marston MS 219 — England, s. XIII$^{3/4}$

Pierre de Peckham, La lumière as lais

ff. 1r–60v //Ore mey dites si ia auerunt./ Plus de ioye en ciel que ore en dreit vut./ Veyre la sauuacioun de gent./ De lur ioie ert ennoycement [*sic*]./ Pour ceo sunt verreyment./ A titles de garder la gent./ Car checun ad verite./ Vn bon angle a ly assigne./ Pour garder le de mal e de vice./ ... [f. 60v:] Ore couient del enfourmement./ Del confessour dire ensement./ De ceo comeint treiz chosez sauoir:/ ... Qe vray dez pechez eit repentaunce./ Qe a qi humblement se confesse:/ Dieu sez pechez ly Relesse// catchwords: Ceo dit seint bernard.

Manuscript is defective at beginning and end: text begins in Book II, Chapter xxxvij (as numbered by a later hand, s. xiii/xiv) and concludes in Book V, distinctio 5, ch. 2 (*Del enfourmement del confessour*); hence all of Books I and VI, and part of Books II and V are missing. Bottom of f. 1 and top of f. 36 torn with loss of text. In addition, after the text of f. 10r was copied it was discovered that the scribe had failed to copy a section, which was then written on inserted leaves, now ff. 8–9. The correct order of the text is: f. 7v, f. 10r (col. *a*), ff. 8r–9v, f. 10r (col. *b*). The disrupted text is marked by the scribe with the letters *a* and *b*, in red, to guide the reader.

A. Langfors, *Les incipit des poèmes français antérieurs au XVIe siècle* (Paris, ca. 1917) p. 436; P. Meyer reprints portions and discusses the text in "Les manuscrits français de Cambridge," *Romania* 8 (1879) pp. 325–32. See also M. D. Legge, "Pierre de Peckham and his 'Lumière as Lais'," *Modern Language Review* 24 (1929) pp. 37–47, 153–71.

Parchment, ff. 60, 215 x 143 (178 x 113) mm. 2 columns, 34 lines (ff. 8–9 = 27 lines). Single vertical and horizontal bounding lines, full across; text rulings drawn through space between columns. Ruled in lead. Prickings prominent in upper, lower, and outer margins.

I^{12} [?, only stubs remain], II^{13} (structure uncertain, –1, a stub; ff. 8–9 contemporary bifolium inserted between ff. 7 and 10), $III–VI^{12}$. Catchwords along lower edge under inner column, verso.

Written in gothic bookhand, below top line.

Plain initials, 3- to 2-line, alternate red and blue for each chapter. Headings in red. Guide letters for decorator.

Many leaves stained, damaged, but with little loss of text.

Binding: England, s. xiii. Original wound, caught up sewing with heavy thread, on four tawed skin, slit straps laced through tunnels in the edge to channels on the outside of oak boards and wedged. The natural color endbands are sewn on leather cores which are laid in grooves on the outside of the boards and pegged. The spine is back bevelled.

Covered in tawed skin, originally white, but now dark brown on the outside. The turn-ins of the upper board are serrated. Two strap-and-pin fastenings, the pins (traces only) on the lower board, the upper one cut in for the fabric-reinforced leather straps. Some sewing supports broken, one board detached, and some covering leather and straps wanting.

Written in England in the third quarter of the 13th century; text still being read at the end of the thirteenth or beginning of the 14th century when chapter numbers were added throughout. Erasure on f. 9v of short text probably dating s. xiv–xv. Partially legible inscription, s. xv-xvi, on back turn-ins: "Ajourd ***ot of moreson *** morreton of y[?]." Purchased from H. P. Kraus (Cat. 80, no. 9) in 1959 by Thomas E. Marston (bookplate).

Bibliography: Faye and Bond, p. 89, no. 219.

Marston MS 220 — England, s. XIII^{in} and XIV^{1}

Petrus Comestor, Historia scholastica, etc. — Pl. 50

I. 1. ff. 1r–150r *Hic incipiunt scolastice historie a secundo petro edite.* [prologue:] Reuerendo domino et patri suo uuillelmo [*sic*] dei gratia senonensi archiepiscopo petrus seruus christi . . . benedictus deus. Amen. [text:] *Prologus super genesim. Prefacio et. Imperatorie* maiestatis est tres in palacio habere mansiones . . . Translatus est enoch subuectus est helias ascendit ihesus propria. sui uirtute. [Additio 1:] Hanc ultimam processionem post ihesum representat ecclesia dominicis diebus egrediendo de ecclesia . . . Sed multiplicatis solennitatibus [?] sanctorum sublata est solempnitas quinte ferie. et processio translata est ad dominicam.

Petrus Comestor, *Historia scholastica*; Stegmüller, v. 4, nos. 6543–64; PL 198.1053–1644. Leaf with text missing between ff. 126–127. Arts. 1–3 have extensive marginal glosses and schematic drawings written by several hands, s. xiii–xiv, some of which exhibit strong anglicana features; authors quoted include Franciscus de Marone on f. 125r (Francis of Meyronnes, fl. xiv$^{1/4}$), Hugo of Vienna on f. 129r (d. 1355), Nicolaus de Lyra on f. 151r. Later hands have numbered each section with different sequences of Arabic numerals as if for indexing.

2. ff. 150r–171r *Incipit historia actuum apostolorum.* Anno quintodecimo imperii tiberii cesaris adhuc procuratore iudee pilato. qui si legatur . . . et in loco magis honorabili scilicet in cathacumbis.

Petrus Pictaviensis, *Historia actuum apostolorum*; Stegmüller, v. 4, 6565 and 6785; PL 198.1645–1722.

3. ff. 171r–173v *Incipit historia de tito et vaspasiano* [sic]. Sciendum est petrum imminente tempore passionis sue clementem sibi substituisse. Precepit autem clementi per literas . . . Tytus itaque cum tali triumpho iudeorum italiam copiose ditauit. *Explicit historia de tito et vaspasiano.*

Unidentified text about Titus and Vespasian.

II. 4. ff. 174r–192r [Heading written in a different hand:] Incipit prologus beati Augustini de mirabilibus veteris et noui testamenti. [text:] Uenerantissimis urbiumque monasteriorum episcopis et presbiteris maxime cartaginensium . . . monstraretur et ceteri exemplo huius castigarentur.

Augustinus Hibernicus, *De mirabilibus sacrae scripturae*, in the long recension; PL 35.2149–2200.

5. ff. 192r–197v *Exameron ambrosij.* Cum esset moyses in aula educatus regia. maluit tum pro amore . . . virtutum emulatorem cupidum celestium graciarum. *Explicit excepcio exameron ambrosij.*

Extracts from Ambrose, *Exameron*; C. Schenkl, ed., CSEL 32,1 (1897) pp. 3–261.

Composed of two distinct parts both written on parchment 357 x 240 mm., i (paper) + 197 + i (paper).

Part I: ff. 1–173, written space 202 x 117 mm. 2 columns, 46 lines. The intricate page format sometimes varies slightly but usually consists of three vertical bounding lines to left and right of written space and three vertical rulings between the columns; three upper and lower horizontal bounding lines. Two additional pairs of vertical rulings in both inner and outer margins and a single additional ruling along upper, inner and outer perimeter of leaf. Ruled in lead or crayon. Prickings prominent in all margins, including inner. $I–II^{8}$, $III–IV^{10}$, V^{4}, VI^{12}, VII^{6}, $VIII–XIII^{10}$, XIV^{10} (-9), $XV–XVII^{10}$, $XVIII–XIX^{8}$. Catchwords near lower edge, right of center on verso. Quires signed with Arabic numeral in crayon lower right corner, recto. Written in neat gothic bookhand, above top line; glosses added by a variety of hands, some exhibiting anglicana features. Two illuminated initials in parallel positions on f. 1r, beginning mid-page and extending almost to the bottom of the leaf. The first initial composed of a gold trellis edged in black with heads of a grotesque devouring the trellis at top and bottom, and foliage designs in green and white scrolling around the body of the initial against pink interior with white highlight and gold balls. The whole on a rectangular ground tapering to a point at bottom, with white designs. The second initial, somewhat narrower and less ambitious in design, gold edged in black with blue interior and thin white design in center and two rosettes, one at top, the other at bottom, and a third stylized floral motif in center, all on a pink ground in the same shape as the first initial. Also on f. 1r, 7-line initial divided red and blue with interior foliage designs in green and white on parchment ground, and red and blue penwork designs around exterior of letter. For major text divisions, fine medium blue and/or red initials, 9- to 6-line, with intricate penwork flourishes in red and blue, each accompanied by several lines of oversize letters for the first few words of text, with letters either in one color with designs in the other or alternating red and blue. Small penwork initials, red or blue with modest design in the opposite color, throughout. Headings, running headlines and vertical lines within text columns, in red. Remains of instructions to rubricator (some perpendicular to text in gutter) and guide letters for decorator.

Part II: ff. 174–197, written space 206 x 115 mm. 2 columns, 52 lines. Double vertical bounding lines to left and right of written space and three vertical rulings between columns; double upper and single lower horizontal bounding lines. Additional pairs of rulings along upper, inner and outer perimeter of leaf and a single ruling in outer margin near written space to delineate a column for commentary, notes, etc. Ruled in crayon. Prickings (horizontal slits) in all margins, including inner. Two gatherings of twelve leaves. Catchwords for first quire, enclosed by red rectangle and stroked throughout with red. Quires numbered as in Part I. Written in gothic bookhand with some marginalia by contemporary and later hands. One gold initial, 4-line, with purple penwork designs on f. 194r. Blue initials with red penwork, 9- to 2-line, throughout. Headings and initial strokes added, in brown and red, unsophisticated drawings of birds, animals, leaves and grotesques in upper and lower margins.

Binding: England, s. xviii–xix. Brown calf, gold-tooled. Striped turn-ins.

Part I was written in England at the beginning of the 13th century and Part II in the first half of the 14th century. The two parts were together by the 15th century when the quires were numbered consecutively with Arabic numerals. Part I was used and annotated heavily in the 13th and 14th centuries. Provenance unknown. From the estate of Wilfred M. Voynich (De Ricci, *Census*, p. 1848, no. 12; contents listed incompletely). "A 826" in pencil on front pastedown and "6505/ESZV" in pencil on rear pastedown. Purchased in 1959 from H. P. Kraus by Thomas E. Marston (bookplate).

secundo folio: [cla]ritas, sicut lux

Bibliography: De Ricci, *Census*, p. 1848, no. 12 (when in Voynich collection); Faye and Bond, p. 89, no. 220.

Marston MS 222 — England s. $XIII^{3/4}$
Peter Lombard, Sententiarum libri IV

1. f. iii recto blank; f. iii verso *Altissimus creauit de terra medicinam.* Verba ista scripta sunt ecc. 38. In quibus uerbis ponuntur per ordinem .4. notabilia in quibus intelligere possumus ... eius bonitas relucet in opere....

   Commentary on Eccles. 38 that is to serve the reader as a guide to art. 2; not located in Stegmüller, *Rep. Sent.*

2. ff. 1r–208v [Prologue:] Cupientes aliquid de penuria ac tenuitate nostra ... titulos quibus singulorum librorum capitula distinguntur premisimus. [list of chapters:] Omnis doctrina est de rebus uel de signis ... [list ends imperfectly, f. 2v:] Cum deus sit ubique et semper non tamen localis nec loco nec tempore// [text, beginning imperfectly:] Dicimus

illa re nos frui quam diligimus ... per media ad pedes usque via duce peruenit. *Explicit liber sententiarum quartus.* [added by a later hand:] Si male quid feci veniam peto. si bene grates. [miscellaneous contemporary notes on back flyleaf]

Peter Lombard, *Sententiarum libri IV*; 3rd ed. in *Spicilegium Bonaventurianum* 4–5 (Grottaferrata, 1971 and 1981) 2 vols. Text is defective with one leaf missing after f. 2 (beginning of text proper), four leaves missing after f. 99 (Bk. 2, portions of *distinctiones* 32–35), three leaves missing after f. 189 (Bk. 4, portions of *distinctiones* 30–32). Certain leaves of the text (e.g., ff. 64v–76r) have been heavily annotated by a slightly later hand, s. XIII^{ex}, exhibiting strong anglicana features. The annotations at the beginning of Bk. 2 (f. 64v) have the same incipit as Stegmüller, *Rep. Sent.* 756 attributed to Romanus de Roma ("Creationem-Cum per creaturas deueniatur in cognicionem creatoris...").

In Marston MS 222 rubrics appear within the text; in the margins the letter *D* followed by Roman numerals signals the *distinctiones* as introduced by Alexander of Hales; patristic references, when present, were added by another hand. Bk. 2, *distinctio* 27 (f. 93v) begins with the pre-Bonaventure division in the chapter "Hic uidendum est quid sit uirtus," but overall patterns in the arrangement of *distinctiones* suggest the manuscript belongs to the newer arrangement of the text (e.g., the division of Bk. 2 into 48 *distinctiones*); lists of chapters are inserted before Bks. 1, 3 and 4. See I. Brady, "The Distinctions of Lombard's Book of Sentences and Alexander of Hales," *Franciscan Studies* 25 (1965) pp. 90–116, and *idem*, "The Three Editions of the 'Liber Sententiarum' of Master Peter Lombard (1882–1977)," *Archivum Franciscanum Historicum* 70 (1977) pp. 400–411.

Parchment, ff. ii (paper) + i (contemporary parchment) + 208 + i (contemporary parchment) + ii (paper), 345 x 220 (228 x 140) mm. 2 columns, 45 lines. Single vertical and horizontal bounding lines, with an additional vertical ruling between columns. Pair of horizontal rulings in upper and lower margins and a single lower horizontal line near lower and outer edges. Remains of prickings in upper, lower and outer margins.

I^{12} (-3), II–VIII^{12}, IX^{12} (-5 through 8), X–XVI^{12}, XVII^{12} (-3 through 5), XVIII^{12}. Catchwords along lower edge near gutter, verso. First leaves of each gathering signed with letters of the alphabet in lower right corner, recto.

Written in gothic bookhand, below top line; annotations added in less formal, later hands.

Red and blue divided initials, 4- to 3- line, for prologue and beginning of books, with penwork designs in the same colors. For other text divisions, 3- to 2-line initials in red or blue with flourishes in opposite color.

Distinctio numbers and running headlines in red and blue; rubrics in red. Initial letters of each entry in chapter lists alternate red and blue.

Binding: England, 1837. Bound by Gough in London (see provenance below). Dark brown goatskin, blind-tooled with a light brown gold-tooled label with title "Liber Sententiarum."

Written in England in the third quarter of the 13th century and annotated toward the end of the same century; early provenance unknown. Belonged to the Rev. John Francis Shearman (fl. s. xviii^2; bookplate on first front flyleaf). Inscription on front parchment flyleaf of the Rev. Philip Bliss (1787–1857; DNB v. 2, pp. 683–84) states: "Purchased of Dr. Hampson, who procured the MS. in Hertfordshire, for [amount crossed out] Oct. 13 1834, bound 1837 by Gough." Dr. Hampson may perhaps be identified with Edward Hampson of Abbots Langley, Herts. (b. ca. 1786; *Alumni Oxonienses* 1715–1886, v. 2, p. 597). It seems likely that the note on f. i recto: "Bought of J. Waller Fleet St. 12 April 1860" was added by James E. Millard (Fellow of Magdalen College, Oxford, between 1853–65), whose bookplate with this title appears on the front pastedown. Belonged to James P. R. Lyell (bookplate; 1871–1949); 250 medieval manuscripts from his collection were bequeathed to the Bodleian Library (see *Lyell Cat.* for information and bibliography). The remainder of the collection was sold by his executors to Quaritch in 1951; this manuscript offered for sale by Quaritch (cat. 699, 1952, no. 112; cat. 731, no. 376; cat. 767 [1957], no. 20). Pencil notes on front pastedown: "No. 12" in circle, "M26." Purchased in 1957 from Quaritch, London, by L. C. Witten (inv. no. 1751), who sold it in 1959 to Thomas E. Marston (bookplate).

secundo folio: deus caritas

Bibliography: Faye and Bond, p. 89, no. 222.

Marston MS 223 — Italy, s. XIV^1; England [?], s. XIII^{ex}–XIV$^{1/4}$

Haimo of Auxerre; John of Wales, etc.

I. 1. f. 1r–v *Ad romanos.* Ab achaia regione grecorum scripxit [*sic*] apostolus paulus romanis epistolam . . . ; *Ad corinthios. prima.* Precepto saluatoris monitus apostolus uenit corinthum . . . ; *Ad galatas.* Galate sunt in bictinia [for *bythinia*] prouincia grecia. et fuerunt galli . . . ; *Ad ephesios.* Ephesus ciuitas est asie et grecie. inde ephesi . . . ; *Ad philippenses.* Philippenses sunt macedones. id est greci. Grecia a diuersis regibus . . . ; *Ad colosenses.* Colosenses siue laudicenses sunt asiani greci. Laudicio ciuitas est grecie . . . ; *Ad thesalonicenses*. Macedonia prouincia est grecorum in qua est ciuitas metropolis . . . ; *Secunda epistola*. Secundam epistolam missit eis confortans . . . ; *Ad timotheum*. Timotheus fuit grecus et sotius apostoli et ab eo episcopus ordinatus . . . ; *Secunda epistola*. Secundam epistolam scribit ei ab urbe roma . . . ; *Ad titum*. Titum instruit de constitutione . . . ; *Ad philemonem*. Philemoni scribit a roma de carcere . . . ; *Ad hebreos*. Hebreis etiam scribit apostolus ipsis dico iudeis ad fidem . . . superbi forte non recepissent.

Brief prologues to the Pauline Epistles, paraphrasing or extracted from the *argumenta* of Haimo of Auxerre, *Expositio in epistolas Sancti Pauli*; PL 117.361–938 (see also art. 2).

2. ff. 1v–23r *Dominica prima de aduentu*. Scientes quia hora est . . . [Rom. 13.11]. Remigius. *De somno* infidelitatis et uiciorum abque ignorantie. *surgere*. ad bona opera agenda . . . ; *Dominica secunda de aduentu*. Quecumque scripta sunt ad nostram doctrinam . . . [Rom. 15.4]. Remigius. *Quecumque scripta sunt*. scilicet in lege moysi et prophetis et psalmis et reliquis scripturis . . . *Dominica .xxiiij. post pentecosten*. Non cessamus pro uobis orantes . . . [Col. 1.9]. Remigius. *Require.//*

   Notes for sermons arranged according to the liturgical year; text defective. After the rubric and Biblical reading, each text consists of key phrases quoted from or paraphrasing Haimo of Auxerre, *Expositio in epistolas Sancti Pauli* (in this manuscript attributed to Remigius); PL 117.361–938. See also art. 1.

3. ff. 23v–24r *Incipiunt alique auctoritates beati Remigij super epistolas beati pauli apostoli. Et primo super epistulam ad Romanos. Romanos .8. Remigius*. Deus eterne qui absconditorum et futurorum es cognitor . . . [concluding in rubric *Hebreos. 1. Remigius*:] qui non flagellatur. sine dubio non est in numero filiorum. [followed by a short passage added in a later hand: De expositione alleluia].

   Supplementary material for art. 2.

4. f. 24v *Dominica secundum* [?] *pasca*. Expurgate vetus fermentum . . . [1 Cor. 5.7]. [added in margin:] Cor. 5. Remigius. Et quia modicum quid corrumpit et inficit totam massam uirtutum . . . sed maneatis in azimis. et cetera.

II. 5. ff. 25r–52r Qui custodierint iusticiam iuste iudicabuntur . . . [Sap. 6.11]. Quantum ad commendacionem electorum duo tanguntur in uerbis istis . . . pane celesti reficiat; [f. 29r:] Qui habitatis terram austri cum panibus occurite. Fundens. ydriam . . . ; [f. 36v:] Probauit me quasi aurum [Job 23.10]. Hic iiii^or^ exprimuntur. scilicet pacientis bonitas in auro . . . ; [f. 38r:] Fons de domo domini [Joel 3.18]. In uerbis gloriose uirginis marie. . . .

Unidentified sermons. This art. and the following have been marked for indexing: arabic numerals 85–100, 1–35 (in this order) in the upper margin, letters of the alphabet *d* and *e* in upper right corner, and key words and phrases in margin that also appear in the subject index at the conclusion of the codex (see art. 7). The beginning of this text appears to be wanting since early indexing begins with "85" on f. 25.

6. ff. 52v–75r [Title, added in a different hand:] Incipit breuiloquium de uirtutibus antiquorum principum ac philosophorum. [prologue:] Quoniam misericordia et ueritas custodiunt regem. et roboratur clemencia tronus eius . . . [Prov. 20.28]. Ymo iiij or uirtutes cardinales. scilicet prudencia . . . [Ch. 1, heading in a different hand:] Capitulum primum de iusticia in possidendo. [text:] Propterea primo premittantur exemplares narraciones de iusticia . . . vbi uis permanere ego uita. Amen. f. 75v blank

John of Wales, *Breviloquium*; Glorieux, 322b and Bloomfield, *Virtues and Vices*, no. 4971 (Marston MS 223 not listed). For the author's life and works see W. A. Pantin, "John of Wales and Medieval Humanism," *Medieval Studies presented to Aubrey Gwynn, S. J.*, ed. J. A. Watt, J. B. Morrall, F. X. Martin, O. S. A. (Dublin, 1961) pp. 297–319. Indexed in the same manner as art. 5.

7. ff. 76r–77v Abicere .66. c./ Aceruus .j. a./ Accipere spiritum sanctum .24. d/ . . . Christus .7. d./ Christus passus .10. d./ Zelus .45. c. f. 78r–v blank except for notes (see provenance below)

Alphabetical subject index for Part II (see also art. 5).

Composed of two distinct parts: parchment, ff. ii (paper) + 78 + ii (paper, with additions pasted in), 149 x 116 mm.

Part I: ff. 1–24, written space 120 x 80 mm. 2 columns, ca. 31–36 lines. Single vertical and horizontal bounding lines in crayon or lead. Remains of prickings in upper, lower and outer margins. I–II^{12}. Scribe I copied ff. 1r–6v in small gothic bookhand with southern features; Scribe II copied ff. 7r–24r in a somewhat more angular gothic bookhand; additions by different scribes on f. 24r–v. Red initials, 3- to 2-line, with crude harping designs in black; headings and paragraph marks (art. 3) in red. Instructions for rubricator.

Part II: ff. 25–78, written space 124 x 77 mm. 33 long lines. Single vertical and usually horizontal bounding lines full across. Additional pair of rulings in upper and lower margins. Text rulings often extend through gutter. Ruled in lead. III–V^{16}, VI^{6}. Arts. 5–6 copied in small neat gothic bookhand, by a single scribe; some marginalia added in anglicana script (e.g., f. 46v); art. 7 added in a less careful gothic bookhand. Flourished initials, 3- to 2-line, alternate red and blue with penwork designs in the opposite color. Paragraph marks alternate red and blue; headings, often added in margin, in red. Remains of guide letters for decorator.

Binding: England, s. xix. Backs of quires cut in for original sewing. Brown calf case, blind-tooled.

A composite manuscript written in different locations and periods: Part II (ff. d85–d100 and e1–e35 of a larger manuscript) was probably written in England (or Northern France?) at the end of the 13th or during the first quarter of the 14th century; Part I was written in Italy in the first half of the 14th century. The index constituting art. 7 was added on blank leaves in Italy in the 14th century, perhaps at the same time that Parts I and II were joined together to form the present codex. Ownership inscription on f. 75r and repeated twice on f. 78v: "liber fratris Baptiste de Binosuperiori [?] ordinis minorum Sotii prouincie Mediolanensis 1490." Belonged to William A. Cragg of Lincoln College, Oxford (bookplate); his correspondence concerning the manuscript pasted in back of volume, including a letter from Reginald Maxwell Woolley dated 1931 encouraging Cragg to place his collection in the Lincoln Cathedral Library, as well as an index of the contents of the manuscript prepared by Woolley. Description from unidentified sale catalogue pasted to back flyleaf. Purchased from C. A. Stonehill in 1958 by Thomas E. Marston (bookplate).

secundo folio: consolationem

Bibliography: Faye and Bond, pp. 89–90, no. 223.

Marston MS 225 — Southern Germany [?], s. $XIV^{2/4}$

Vaticinia Pontificum, etc. — Endpapers

1. Inside front wrapper: Libri huius principium sibillina continet dicta que nostre fidei consona sunt atque communia configuere autem ymaginum xv. papista appellantur. Ostendunt namque quodam occulto lii. vati-

cinio quis papa sequitur alterum in dignitate ac qualis fuerit moribus nec non quibus occupabitur rebus quod per adiectas significatur figuras De iii. post ymaginum sculpturas earundem sub verborum misterio verbis quoque inusitatis atque profundis prefatum exprimit ymaginum significacionem.

2. ff. 1r–14v *De imperatore.* Incipit sibillarius quem fecit Sibilla filia manasses Regis quando in monte aventino ducta fuit . . . Post hec dominus de celo ueniet ad iudicandum seculum per ignem quod nullus scit hanc horam nec dies nec annos eius et sic erit iudicij signum.

A version of the Tiburtine Oracle with special reference to the history of Sicily. A comparison of the text in Marston 225 with the critical edition by E. Sackur, *Sibyllinische Texte und Forschungen* (Halle, 1898) pp. 177–87, shows extensive differences.

3. ff. 15r–22r Ps.-Joachim da Fiore, *Vaticinia Pontificum*: for information on these 15 visions see H. Grundmann, "Die Papstprophetien des Mittelalters," *Archiv für Kulturgeschichte* 19 (1928) pp. 77–138; M. H. Fleming, "Metaphors of Apocalypse and Revolution in Some Fourteenth-Century Popular Prophecies," *Acta* 7 (1980) pp. 131–45; B. McGinn, " 'Pastor Angelicus': Apocalyptic Myth and Political Hope in the Fourteenth Century," *Santi e Santità nel secolo XIV: Fifteenth International Conference* (Assisi, 1987), Edizioni scientifiche italiane, pp. 221–51; R. E. Lerner, "On the Origins of the Earliest Latin Pope Prophecies: A Reconsideration," *Fälschungen im Mittelalter*, Teil V (Hannover, 1988) pp. 611–35 (Marston MS 225 = Y; pls. III and VII of ff. 15r, 19v). M. H. Fleming is preparing a critical edition of the text (we thank her for her assistance with this manuscript).

For each prophecy we describe the miniature that accompanies it.

[1.] f. 15r: Seuus nequam ursus catulos pascens et in quinque romam sceptris turbatis . . . ad quos ad pusillos quomodo eructabis bonum ciuitati.

[Pope Nicholas III, 1277–80, standing holding a book, flanked by two brown dogs begging, while a third leaps over his head.]

[2.] f. 15v: Secundus est fera aliis uolans serpens ad meridiem . . . tuarum gentium dabis in tempore meti.

[Pope Martin IV (1281–85) standing holding a pennant and a book; on the left, a kneeling figure, and on the right, a palm (?) tree with two ravens on top.]

[3.] f. 16r: Suplicum tercium et enim auis eques ancifera auis et eques corniger sicut multum uelox sicut promptus . . . in te principatum et finis eorum est.

[Pope Honorius IV (1285–87) seated on a throne with a boy on the left at his knees, an eagle perched on his crown and a unicorn resting its front legs on the Pope's right shoulder.]

[4.] f. 16v: Iste collus quartus ab ursa carens gladijs et homo monens incisionem . . . in quo letare multum frustra.

[Three columns, the first with the head of a pope, the central one with a tonsured head, and the last with a hand bearing a scythe: prophecy of Pope Nicholas IV (1288–92)]

[5.] f. 17r: Uide iterum alienum existentis modum falcem magnam et rosam . . . in mundo viuens senex uade in infernum duabus tribulationibus in medio.

[Pope Celestine V (1294) in Franciscan (?) habit, holding a scythe and a flower, with the torso of an angel in the sky at the right.]

[6.] f. 17v: Uac [*sic*] aut quartum et filijs urse pascentis [space: *figura* added in margin] manifestat . . . sublinaberis a gloria et mortuus relinques potentissime potencias.

[Pope Boniface VIII (1294–1303) standing with bull fawning at his feet; two disembodied heads floating in the air on either side.]

[7.] f. 18r: Alia ursa secunda pascens catulos . . . coronas manifestant diuisiones tocius potentie.

[Pope standing with, at his feet, a bear that is nursing two bear cubs.]

[8.] f. 18v: Heu misera sustine passiones ciuitatis miserabilis . . . adulter iniustus sodomita uidebunt ultimum lumen ante oculos.

[A fortified town with gates closed.]

[9.] f. 19r: Uulpinam figurasti amititiam pacienter . . . graciose et brauium [?] accepisti infigere [?] sceptri.

[Pope standing and watching a bounding dog with three pennants emerging from its back.]

[10.] f. 19v: Ue tibi ciuitas septicollis littera laudabiliter in mentibus tuis . . . in barba profunda iuste intuet et maxime uituperaberis.

[A fortified town to the left of which three disembodied hands appear.]

[11.] f. 20r: Et reuelabitur uirtus qualiter pro nomen me [for *nomine*; marginal addition illegible] petram habitans . . . uade in inferiora terre.

[A semi-nude figure sitting on a green mound confronted by a standing figure in a robe on the right.]

[12.] f. 20v: Mortuus nunc et oblitus aspectibus nouerunt ... Idem habebit septicollis imperium.

[Pope standing holding his mitre and a book over a pack of wolves or leaping dogs.]

[13.] f. 21r: Ecce idem homo de primo genere abscondito ... dupplicatorum annorum introit mortuus petram.

[Pope crowned by an angel.]

[14.] f. 21v: Recipe donum ne pigriteris senex se recipiens potentissime ... ambula celeste enim in te principium bonorum et finis.

[Pope seated on a dais flanked by two angels supporting a green cloth of honor behind him.]

[15.] f. 22r: Iona uita inuenisti ab iuge ... ire priuaberis a sorde de super. f. 22v blank

[A haloed Pope holding his mitre and a book.]

4. ff. 23r–43r Twenty-six short prophecies, without illumination.

[1.] ff. 23r–28r De laudato paupere et electo imperatore ... praenomen monachim tria tercia eximius a foramine.

Latin version of the Greek "Anonymous Paraphrase of the Leo Oracles" also known as the "Cento of the True Emperor." Greek text in PG 107.1141–50. According to M. H. Fleming (personal correspondence) the Latin version in Marston MS 225 is the earliest version in Latin and predates any surviving version in Greek.

[2.] f. 28v Post omnium malorum principium feram sine membris utilibus ... perflans imperator apparuit et cetera.

According to Lerner, *op. cit.*, p. 630, note 44, this text is a letter of Arnold of Villanova addressed to a Lady Bartolomea which draws upon, or refers to, the *Horoscopus*.

[3.] ff. 28v–29r Uolavit auis inmunda ... grande uelamen obruet iterum uero talem qui semper ultra procedere tractabit.

[4.] f. 29r Gallina fallocinis [?] uestem induet sub qua silebit ... ita quod absque duce mundus durabit et perseuerabit per annum et amnich [?] et dimidium anni.

[5.] ff. 29v–30r Post hec conuenient discordantes in ciuitate magni pauidis ... Quare tamen erit angusta medietas. et cetera.

[6.] ff. 30r–31r Uir medius non perfectus residebit in solio ... Exibunt de limo spendorem [*sic*] reddent potentissime.

[7.] f. 31r Uirgo ornata uirtutibus sine macula predicabit in mundo ... uelum sine splendore non erit.

[8.] ff. 31r–32r Heu, heu omnis christicole dicere poterunt et cetera. Ciuitas super ciuitatem ... Et sic impius impie terminabit quia iniqum [*sic*] se monstrabit in solio.

[9.] f. 32r Inique non poteris extendere super terram ... ueneno remota cum difficultate et cetera.

[10.] ff. 32r–35r Letatus sum in hijs que dicta sunt michi et cetera. Post tribulacionem longinquam et cetera Pastor egregius ... plurimi concurrendo ad eius miracula sepulture.

[11.] f. 35r–v Idem consimili racione diuine non calliditate humana ... in montem syon animam reddet angelis in altari.

[12.] f. 35v Et erit post sexaginta annos uisitabit dominus ... Tu exspiraberis in V.

[13.] ff. 35v–36r Ecce dominus dissipabit terram et undabit eam ... tu requiesce iam.

[14.] f. 36r Te qui cogitatis inutile et opera ... morte subita morieris in F.

[15.] f. 36r Stulte egisti propter hoc ... uteris et morieris in P.

[16.] f. 36r–v Quia ambulasti in uijs symonis magi ... tu fascinatus morieris in R.

[17.] f. 36v Luxit et defluxit terra ... ex insperato sceptra tenebit.

[18.] ff. 36v–37r In sapientia tua et prudentia fecisti ... et interficient et destruent te. et morieris in A.

[19.] f. 37r Recipe donum desuper ne pigriteris senex ... ad mercedem eorum qua operati sunt.

[20.] ff. 37r–40r Puluis carbonum ante faciem petri ... et pastorum ad caulas fidei redidisse.

[21.] f. 40r Gallorum leuitas germanos iustificabit ... sub quo tunc uana cessabit gloria cleri.

O. Holder-Egger, ed., "Italienische Prophetien des 13. Jahrhunderts," *Neues Archiv der Gesellschaft für ältere deutsche Geschichtskunde* 33 (1907–8) pp. 125–26.

[22.] f. 40r Anno m° ccc° decembis. [*sic*] vij. dabit ether . . . greco testante perito.

[23.] ff. 40v–42r Uniuersis et singulis ad quos littere iste peruenerint . . . et uobis que prediximus que periculosa uidemus ualere.

Letter of Magister Johannes de Davidis Toletanus, known to be circulating in this form no earlier than 1322, with marginal gloss "1349" on f. 40v.

[24.] f. 42r In nomine domini amen. Anno Domini M. ccc. septimo viceno. Mense sexto. Regnante profunda scientia. Petra patietur . . . et una fides et omnes gentes obedient ei.

[25.] f. 42v Uolabit aquila ad fontem uinum et de aqua potabit . . . Heu, heu contraria. F. V. R.

[26.] ff. 42v–43r Et erunt iterum pulli tenentes imperium . . . sedes eius modicum tempus erit.

5. ff. 43v–44v Anno domini Millesimo CCC xl vi. Facta est quedam visio in Claustro. Cisterciensis ordinis. Quidam Monachus celebrabat missam et inter absolucionem et communionem . . . in tanta tranquillitate noua audientur de antichristo. Vigilate Ergo.

A revision of the "Tripoli" prophecy, added by a late fifteenth- or early sixteenth-century hand, here recorded as a vision in a Cistercian monastery in 1346; J. Leclercq, ed., 1961, pp. 166–69 (edited from this manuscript). For the history of the Tripoli prophecy see R. E. Lerner, *The Powers of Prophecy* (Berkeley, 1983).

Parchment, ff. 44 (ff. 45–46, stubs only), 179 x 121 (115 x 70) mm. 23 long lines. Single (and occasionally double upper) horizontal and vertical bounding lines, ruled in brown ink. Guide lines for text in hard point or faintly in lead? Prominent prickings in upper, lower and outer margins.

I–III^{10}, IV^{8}, V^{8} (–7, 8, stubs only remain). Catchwords, with dot on either side, center of lower edge, verso.

Arts. 2–4 written in neat gothic bookhand by a single scribe. Art. 1 in a less formal bookhand and art. 5 in a notarial hand with various flourishes. Two annotators have added in the margins words omitted from the text (blank spaces in text remain); the first annotator (ff. 1r–10v) appears to be the scribe of the text whereas the second annotator (beginning on f. 11r) writes in a different, yet contemporary, hand.

15 small miniatures, 12-line, within narrow ochre frames inserted into text column, one for each prophecy in art. 3, ff. 15r–22r. The miniatures

depict a cycle of Popes and cityscapes with emblematic attributes against pink, blue, and ochre grounds with small white filigree designs along the edges. For a description of each miniature see art. 3 above. The manuscript lacks the captions or mottoes often found in other versions and it does not contain inscriptions identifying the Popes; in addition, the artist depicts what are often bears in other manuscripts as dogs. For the illustrative tradition of these prophecies see L. von Wilckens, "Die Prophetien über die Päpste in deutschen Handschriften," *Wiener Jahrbuch für Kunstgeschichte* 28 (1975) pp. 171–80. According to G. Schmidt (*Exhibition Catalogue*, p. 207) the style of the miniatures can be compared to South German illuminations of the second quarter of the 14th century and anticipates the style of later German World Chronicles such as Fulda, Landesbibliothek Cod. Aa 88 (see H. Jerchel, *Zeitschrift für Kunstgeschichte*, N. F. 2 [1933] pp. 389–90, figs. 15 and 16) and Munich, Staatsbibliothek Cgm. 11 (see *idem*, "Die bayerische Buchmalerei des 14. Jahrhunderts," *Münchner Jahrbuch der bildenden Kunst*, N. F. 10 [1933] pp. 83–84, figs. 16 and 17). Numerous flourished initials, 2-line, alternate in red and blue with purple or red penwork designs. Headings in red. Paragraph marks alternate red and blue.

Binding: Place uncertain, s. xv [?]. Tacketed through a limp vellum (palimpsest?) wrapper to thick leather pads with a basket weave around the sewing threads. Contemporary title in ink, on front: "De imperatore." Backs of quires cut in for sewing.

Written perhaps in Southern Germany in the second quarter of the 14th century to judge from the style of illumination and the dates mentioned in the text (*Exhibition Catalogue*, no. 33, pp. 206–8). On the basis of the internal evidence, however, M. H. Fleming (study in progress) suggests a date between 1327/8 and 1334 during the pontificate of John XXII and an origin in Avignon. It may have been associated with or located near the Cistercian monastery of Himmerod in the diocese of Trier when the vision dated 1346 (art. 5) was added (Leclerq, 1961, pp. 166–69). Inscriptions, s. xv/xvi, of Ernst Pfalzgraf bey Rheyn on remains of f. 45v (back stub) and inside back wrapper. Two erased inscriptions, partially visible under ultraviolet light; inside front wrapper: "Norberti" and lower margin, f. 1r: "Michael." From the collection of Franz Trau; his sale by Gilhofer and Ranschburg in Vienna, 27–28 October 1905, no. 15, with illustration of f. 22r in pl. XII. Included in the 50th anniversary catalogue of Ludwig Rosenthal's Antiquariat in Munich, issued in 1909 (Cat. 130, no. 133, with illustration of the miniature on f. 15r between cat. nos 145–46). Belonged to Baron F. Engel-Gros; his sale by Georges Petit in Paris, 2 June 1921, no. 1. Ex libris of André Hachette (white paper booklabel tipped in between wrapper and f. 1r: monogram "H A" with "Ex libris," both in black, and "22" in red); his sale by Libraire Giraud-Badin in Paris, 16 December 1953, no. 37. Purchased from L. C. Witten in 1959 by Thomas E. Marston (bookplate).

secundo folio: Uixit

Bibliography: Faye and Bond, p. 90, no. 225.

Exhibition Catalogue, no. 33, pp. 206–8, pl. 14 of f. 16r.

M. Reeves, *The Influence of Prophecy in the Later Middle Ages: A Study in Joachimism* (Oxford, 1969) pp. 312 (n. 1), 324, 405, 523.

Idem, "Some Popular Prophecies from the Fourteenth to the Seventeenth Centuries," *Studies in Church History* 8 (1971) p. 119.

A. C. de la Mare, *Lyell Cat.*, p. 88.

M. H. Fleming, "Sibylla: De Imperatore," Ph. D. diss., Boston University, 1975.

Marston MS 226 — Northern Italy, s. XV^2

Silius Italicus, Punica, with commentary

1. ff. 1r–184v //Sarrana prisci barce de gente uetustos/ A belo numerabat auos nanque orba marito/ Cum fugeret dido famulam tiron impia diri/ . . . Nec uero cum te memorat de stirpe deorum/ Prolem tarpei mentitur roma tonantis./ Finis.

   Silius Italicus, *Punica*; J. Delz, ed., Teubner (1987) pp. 1–471, Marston MS 226 = Σ, pp. xlvii–xlviii, where it is cited incorrectly as Marston MS 220. Text is imperfect: one leaf missing at beginning with Book I.1–71; one leaf missing between ff. 106–107 with Book XI.24–85 (. . . Letas res libye: et fortunam in marte secuta // Expulit orantem et nuda capitolia consul . . .); one leaf missing between ff. 143–144 with Book XIV.197–260 (. . . Tum cathane nimium ardenti uicina typheo // Tergemino uenit numero fecunda pan[*t* crossed out]hromos . . .).

2. ff. 1r–181r [In outer margin:] //*Hannibal* filius hamilcaris barce fuit. nam hamilcar cognomine barcha dictus est. [below:] *beli* duo fuerunt hic didus pater cognomen accepit ab antiquo illo belo rege qui regnauit in assyria . . . [marginalia, beginning of Book II, f. 9v:] *iussa* quo ad legatos sed quo ad hannibalem petitiones dicuntur . . . [concluding marginalia on f. 184v, XVII.651, partially illegible:] quia ipse fecit menia et tu conseruasti ipsa et nos omnes qui reppulit senones.

   Marston MS 226 is one of four manuscripts containing the "Anonymous B" commentary discussed by E. L. Bassett, CTC, v. 3, pp. 366–67 (cited incorrectly as Marston MS 220); here beginning imperfectly and with some loss of text in inner margin, f. 1r. The scribe of the main text wrote this commentary in the margins and some of the interlinear glosses; at least two other hands have also contributed annotations and corrections.

Paper (watermarks: similar in design to Piccard Werkzeug und Waffen III.737, 739–42; unidentified horn; mountain smaller in size but similar in design to Briquet Monts 11656), ff. 184, 292 x 222 (220 x 110) mm. Ca. 32 lines of verse. Vertical and horizontal bounding lines, full length, ruled in ink or hard point; text lines ruled in hard point. Additional vertical ruling in outer margin (perhaps through folding?) to delineate column for commentary.

I^{12} (–1), II–VIII^{12}, IX (–12), X–XII^{12}, XIII^{12} (–2), XIV^{12}, XV^{10}, XVI^{10} (–10). Vertical catchwords along bounding line, verso.

Text and main commentary written by a single scribe in two sizes of slanting humanistic cursive.

Spaces for initials and headings left unfilled; marginal rubrics for ff. 72–144 and 166–184 only.

Binding: Italy, s. xv. Parchment binding stays within quires. Original wound sewing on three tawed skin, slit straps, originally pegged.

Covers wanting; the text block now preserved in a rigid paper wrapper, s. xix, with an engraving of Petrarch pasted to the front cover (see provenance below).

Written in Northern Italy in the second half of the 15th century; the manuscript was wrongly attributed to Petrarch's library on the basis of the forged inscription added on f. 184v: "Ioannes Columna Francisco Petrarche Mnemosynon." This attribution was supported by various scholars until the 20th century (pertinent correspondence in library files); see also L. Arrigoni, *Notice historique et bibliographique sur 25 MSS ... ayant fait partie de la bibliothèque de François Pétrarque* (Milan, 1883) pp. 21–23, no. 1; Ullman, no. 49; Dutschke, p. 293, no. 2, with bibliography. Purchased from B. Rosenthal in 1958 by Thomas E. Marston (bookplate).

Bibliography: Faye and Bond, p. 90, no. 226.

Marston MS 227 Germany, s. $XV^{4/4}$
Giovanni Sulpizio, De versuum scansione, etc.

1. f. 1r blank; f. 1v Carmen Sulpicij ad lectores./ Sunt quorum in manibus nostri monumenta laboris/ Vos precor: haec iusta pendere lance Iuuet/ ... Cerbeream rabiem sentiet esse mihi./ [second poem:] Ad Aulum./ Quid Iuuat heroo claudum miscere brocheum/ Vltima communis syllaba semper erit/ ... Temporis immiscent non ratione pedes.

   Two poems, 8- and 6-line.

2. ff. 2r–48r [Contents:] Sulpitij Verulani de versuum scansione ... De pedibus et diuersis generibus carminum precepta. Deque illorum connexionibus obseruationes. [dedication:] Ad cyprianum Omagium fforliniensis Episcopi fratrem. lege foeliciter./ Castalios. latices et amena uireta sororum/ Si peragrare cupis ... cypriane comam./ [text:] Carmen Heroicum exametrum duobus legittime [*sic*] conficitur pedibus Dactylo et spondeo Dactylus ex tribus sillabis ... [f. 48r:] prodesse studui ad musicum studium excitasse: librum hoc carmine finiam. Me duce musarum choreas ingressa Iuuentus/ ... Haec per sulpitium plectra lyramque gero./ ffinis. ff. 48v–58v blank

   Many manuscripts and early printed editions. Here the text concludes with verses in the section *Peroratio*; a few variant readings entered into margin by a contemporary hand.

Paper (watermarks, in gutter: unidentified bull's head; human head perhaps similar in general design to Briquet Tête humaine 15687–88), ff. i (paper) + 58 + i (paper), 210 x 146 (150 x 95) mm. 24 long lines. Single vertical bounding lines ruled in lead or ink.

I^{10} (originally 12?), $II–V^{12}$. Horizontal catchwords right of center along lower edge, verso. Remains of quire and leaf signatures (e.g., b 1, b 2, etc.) lower right corner, recto.

Written in hybrida script by a single scribe.

Plain initials, 3- to 2-line, alternate blue and red; one initial on f. 2r with crude penwork detail in interior. Headings, paragraph marks, initial strokes and some underlining in red. Guide letters for decorator.

Binding: Germany, s. xix. Quarter bound in green diced calf with green paper sides.

Written in Germany in the fourth quarter of the 15th century to judge from the script and watermarks. Belonged to the bookdealer Jacques Rosenthal of Munich (white oval label with scalloped edge: "71198/ III O

[?]" and his pencil notes on front and rear pastedown). Purchased from B. M. Rosenthal in 1958 by Thomas E. Marston (bookplate).

secundo folio: Sulpitij

Bibliography: Faye and Bond, p. 90, no. 227.

Marston MS 228 Northern France, s. XIII/XIV
Tancredus Bononiensis, Ordo iudicarius, in Fr. tr.

1. f. iv verso [Table of contents, s. xvi; heading:] Table des tiltres contenus en l'ordinaire de maistre tancrres chanoine de boulogne. [table:] 1 des juges ordinaires—p. 2/ 2 qui peult estre juge ordinaire—3/ 3 des juges delegues—7 ... [concluding:] 20 des dilations/ 21 des reconuentions/ 22 quel ordre il conuient garder/ 23 des Interrogations.

2. ff. 1r–121v *Ci conmence li ordinaires mestre tancrez chanoine de bouloingne.* Mi conpaignon uos uos estes grant pieca entremis. que ge uos feisse. i. liuret. par quoi li demandierres fust ensingniez comment il doit demander. Et conment li deffendierres se doit deffendre ... [First chapter, f. 1v:] *Cist tytres est des Iuges ordinaires.* Li uns des iuges sont ordinaire [*sic*]. et li autre. de legat et li autre albitre.... Cez choses nos senefient que nos auons dites briefment en ceste oeuure pour entendre les iuges. et denteringue restitucion et des autres articles qui i sont compris. *Ci fenist li ordinaires mestre tancrez chanoine de Bouloingne. Deo gracias.*

   Li ordinaires is a literal French translation of the *Ordo iudicarius* of Tancredus Bononiensis (ca. 1185–1236); some contemporary marginalia, in French.

Parchment, ff. ii (paper) + ii (contemporary parchment flyleaves?) + 121 (pagination, s. xvii, 1–241 [81 *bis*]; modern foliation, lower right corner) + ii (contemporary parchment flyleaves?) + ii (paper), 303 x 205 (205 x 133) mm. 2 columns, 40 lines. Single vertical bounding lines. Additional pair of rulings in outer and lower margins. Ruled in lead or crayon. Prickings in upper and lower margins.

Precise collation difficult due to tight binding: I–VII^{8}, VIII^{10} [?], IX^{8} [?], X^{8}, remainder unclear. Remains of catchwords in lower margin near gutter, verso.

Written in gothic bookhand by a single scribe, below top line.

Three rectangular miniatures of good quality, 11- to 8- line, ff. 1r, 25r and 67r, framed in pink and blue with gold cornerpieces and edged in black. The subjects are: f. 1r [Bk. I] two men presenting a book to a seated judge (slightly rubbed); f. 25r [Bk. II] seated monarch with a sword deciding a dispute between two men; f. 67r [Bk. III] group of men and women before a seated judge. One historiated initial, f. 104v, 11-line, blue with white filigree against pink ground with white filigree and gold balls at the corners, showing a group of men handing to a seated judge a legal document from which a seal hangs; serif, blue with gold balls against pink cusped ground. Numerous flourished initials, alternating red and blue, with designs often extending the length of the text column. Running headlines in red and blue. Headings in red. Paragraph marks alternate red and blue. Letters in text (both majuscules and miniscules) often touched with red.

Binding: France, s. xix. Tan calf, blind- and gold-tooled with a black, gold-tooled label: "Li ordinaire de Mestre Tancres." Bound by J. Thouvenin (Paris, 1790–1834).

Written in Northern France at the end of the 13th or beginning of the 14th century. Early inscriptions: s. xv–xvi^{in}, Jean de La Maison, f. iv recto, and Gilbert Chabrol, f. iv verso; s. xvii–xviii, J. V. [?] de Murat (perhaps a member of the family of magistrates of this name from Carcassonne; see Descadellas, "La bibliothèque municipale de Carcassonne," *Bulletin de la Société des Bibliophiles de Guyenne* 39 [1970] pp. 4–5); s. xvii–xviii, Bruyere. Pagination, running titles, and marginal notes were added by the same individual who wrote an extensive signed and dated note on the first rear flyleaf: "Libri eius authorem vocant tancres qui cap. venerabilis ent. de judic. tancredus vocatur Canonicus Bononiensis, hic praxim suam pro jtalis scripsit et composuit apud Quos maxime jus canonicum viget, unde nihil fere ad usum nostrum forensem vixit circa annum 1227 ut probatur ix. d. cap. venerabilis quod ei ab honorio 3. o pontifice, qui eo anno decessit, qui eum gallico sermoni dedit js per quam vetusto loquitur jdiomate. et quod minus a francis jntelligeretur, jnterpres omnia ad normam latinitatis etiam usque ad jneptias traduxit, antiquus hic autor maxime jntelligitur quod nullos laudet doctores, nec ullam nisi vtriusque juris habeat citationem quarum jtalis multa est copia. jtaque meo judicio piscantur hamo aureo quicumque huic lecturae vellent jncumbere, credant experto, et nulli fere vtilitati hunc librum aestimo, nisi forte conducat adjudicanda capita vtriusque juris et eorum jn rebus de quibus hic agitur conuenientiam; sed haec abunde alibi. habebis etiam hic sed raro. verborum aliquorum quibus utimur originem. Et haec ego jnserui; ne alius tantum quantum ego tempus terat 18 augusti anno domini 1665. Prohest." Unidentified shelf-marks include "No 332" in ink on f. 121v; round paper label with "C/Rés." on front pastedown; "No. 17149" in ink on rectangular label on back pastedown. Purchased in 1955 from Maurice Chamonal, Paris, by L. C. Witten (inv. no. 845), who sold it in 1958 to Thomas E. Marston (bookplate).

secundo folio: dabatre

Bibliography: Faye and Bond, p. 90, no. 228.

Marston MS 229 Northern France, s. XV/XVI
Terence, Comoediae, with commentary Pl. 49

1. f. 1r–v *Incipit argumentum Andrie. Orto* bello athenis Chremes quidam senex propter seditionem relinquens ciuitatem suam ... carino sodali ipsius Pamphili dederunt.

   Conclusion of the *Praefatio Monacensis ad Terentium*; Y.-F. Riou, "Essai sur la tradition manuscrite du *Commentum Brunsianum* des comédies de Térence," *Revue d'histoire des textes* 3 (1973) pp. 109–12 (right hand column). See also art. 3.

2. ff. 1v–7v [Argumentum ad Eunuchum:] *Quo* tempore aut in quo loco hec fabula acta sit minime ostendit cum de alijs manifestet ... licebit uti personis; [Argumentum ad Heautontimorumenon, f. 3v:] *Acta* est id est recitata est ludis megalensibus Lucio Cornelio Lentulo. Lucio Valerio Flacco edilibus curulibus ... emulorum respondet; [Argumentum ad Adelphos, f. 4v:] *Acta* est ista fabula adelphe quam Terentius latine composuit post menandrum ludis funebribus ... Cetera plenius legendo videbuntur; [Argumentum ad Hecyram, f. 5r:] *Hechira* dicta a loco non multum siue longe distante ab athenis potest etiam nominari a socru ... quam peperit philomena; [Argumentum ad Phormionem, f. 6v:] *Argumentum* istius fabule istud est duo senes germani fratres dicuntur fuisse athenis ... sequentia manifestabunt. *Explicit Argumentum Andrie* [sic].

   Argumenta to the plays, extracted from the *Commentum Brunsianum in Terentium*; Riou, *op.cit.*, pp. 79–113 (Marston MS 229 not cited).

3. f. 7v *Incipit Vita Terentij Secundum Paulum Orosium.* f. 8r–v *Terentij vita secundum Paulum Orosium.* [text:] *Terentius* genere extitit affer ciuis vero Cartaginensis. Reuertente autem Scipione Romam deuicta. Cartagine et interfecto hanibale ... Quo tali viro recitante maiorem eius fabule captarent fauorem. Hec prima fabula Andria vocatur eo quod quedam

femina nomine Crisis venerat athenas cum qua et glicerium que et passibula vocabatur venit.

Beginning of the *Praefatio Monacensis ad Terentium*; Riou, *op.cit.*, pp. 106–9 (right hand column). Accompanied here by marginal commentary beginning: "Nota quod in hoc tractatu de uita Terentij aliqua sunt vera et aliqua sunt falsa. Paulus orosius acceptus fuit in nomine.... "

4. f. 8v *Epitaphium Terentij.* Natus in excelsis tectis cartaginis alte/ Romanis ducibus bellica preda fui/ ... hec quicumque legit sic puto cautus erit.

Epitaph, 6 lines; *Anthologia latina* 487c. Accompanied here by marginal commentary on f. 8r beginning: "Istud epitaphium non est de essentia operis terentij tamen has sex comedias rome.... "

5. f. 8v *Argumentum Fabule Andrie.* Sororem falso creditam meretricule/ ... hanc pamphilo dat aliam carino coniugem.

Argumentum to the *Andria*, 12 lines; R. Kauer and W. M. Lindsay, eds., OCT (1926, reprinted with additions 1958). Accompanied here by marginalia beginning: "Hec prima comedia sicut et cetere in quinque actibus partitur. Quorum primus est simulacio nuptiarum ad correctionem pamphili.... " Text of marginalia is similar to that in Vatican City, Biblioteca Apostolica Vaticana, Barb. lat. 82 (VIII.82).

6. ff. 9r–28v *Incipit prologus Andrie.* Poeta cum primum animum ad scribendum appulit ... Spectande sint an exigende sint vobis prius. [f. 9v:] Potius quam istorum oscuram diligentiam [whole line crossed out by later hand]./ *Symo senex. Sosia coquus liberalis.*/ Uos istec intro auferte, abite. sosia/ ... Intus despondebitur intus transigetur/ Siquid est quod restat. Valete caliopius recensui. *Terentij affri Andria. Explicit.*

Terence, *Andria*; Kauer and Lindsay, *op.cit.*, pp. 1–54. Text here accompanied by extensive marginal and interlinear commentary, beginning with notes on the prologue: "In hoc prologo Terentius sub persona caliopii intendit captare beniuolentiam populi romani et primo a persona sui dicendo se scripsisse fabulas.... "

7. ff. 28v–51r *Incipit Eunuchus Comedia Secunda. [A]cta* ludis Megalensibus. Lucio postumio ... Fannio Consulibus. *Argumentum fabule Eunuchi Incipit.* [f. 29r:] Meretrix aduloscentem [*sic*] cuius mutuo amore/ Tenebatur exclusit. eique reuocato ... receptus illuditur. *Aliud Argumentum Fabule Eunuchi.* Sororem falso dictam thaidis ... frater collocat uiciatam ephebo. *Incipit prologus.* Si quisquam est qui placere se studeat bonis ... Vos ualete et plaudite caliopius recensui. *Therentij affri. Eunuchus*

Explicit. Deo gratias. Amen.

Terence, *Eunuchus*; Kauer and Lindsay, *op.cit.*, pp. 111–69. Text here is misbound and should be read in the following order: ff. 28–33, 35, 34, 36–37, 39, 38, 40–51. Extensive interlinear and marginal commentary; at top of f. 30r: "*Atque a thesauris*. Rusticus quidam diues habens filium prodigum timens post mortem suam filius ne cuncta perderet totum aurum. . ."; and at beginning of Act 1, Scene 1: "Incipit primus actus de pacificacione phedrie et Thaidis hec prima pars tendit ad eunuchum hoc modo quia in hac reconsiliacione promittuntur munera hoc thaidi."

8. f. 51v [Written in center of page:] *Incipit heutontumerumenos. Comedia Tertia*; ff. 52r–71v *Incipit heutontumerumenos Comedia Tertia. Acta* Ludis Megalensibus. Lucio Cornelio Lentulo . . . Terentio Sempronio Consulibus. *Argumentum Eiusdem Incipit.* An militiam proficisci gnatum cliniam . . . hanc clinia aliam clitipho vxorem accipit. *Incipit Prologus.* Ne cui vestrum sit mirum cur partes seni . . . *Chr.* fiat. O uos valete, plaudite. Caliopius recensui. Deo gratias. *Terentii affri Explicit.*

Terence, *Heautontimoroumenos*; Kauer and Lindsay, *op.cit.*, pp. 55–110. Extensive marginalia and interlinear commentary as in the previous plays on f. 52r–v only; other hands add notes sporadically for the rest of the text.

9. ff. 72r–90v *Incipit. Adelphoe. Comedia Quarta.* [A]cta ludis funebribus Quinto fabio maximo et Publio cornelio affricano . . . Ancio marco cornelio consulibus. *Argumentum Eiusdem.* Duos cum haberet demea adolescentulos . . . A se uiciatam ciuem athicam uirginem. Vxorem potitur thesipho citharistriam. Exorato suo patre duro demea. *Prologus Eiusdem.* Postquam poeta sensit scripturam suam . . . Ecce me qui id faciam uobis. *Esc.* tibi pater permittimus. Plus scis quid opus facto est. sed de fratre quid fiet de sino habeat in istac finem faciant. *esch.* istuc recte. Valete. plaudite Caliopius recensui. *Terentii affri. Heutontumerumeron* [sic] *Explicit.*

Terence, *Adelphoe*; Kauer and Lindsay, *op.cit.*, pp. 273–323. Extensive annotation in an unruly hand on ff. 72r–76v only which includes the same definition of *argumentum* that appears on f. 52r.

10. ff. 90v–107r *Incipit Eschira* [sic]. *Acta* Ludis romanis. Sexto iulio Cesare Gneio Cornelio edilibus curulibus . . . *Argumentum eiusdem.* Exorem [*sic*] duxit pamphilus philomenam [corrected to: philumenam] . . . Vxorem recipit pamphilus cum filio. *Incipit Prologus Eiusdem.* Hechyra est huic nomen fabule hec cum data est . . . [two prologues followed by text] . . . Sequere me intro [?] parmeno. *par.* sequor equi-

dem plus hodie boni feci imprudens quam sciens ante hunc diem unquam O uos ualete plaudite Caliopius recensui. *Terentij affri. Explicit Echira.*

Terence, *Hecyra*; Kauer and Lindsay, *op.cit.*, pp. 227–72. Only a few corrections and glosses.

11. ff. 107v–127r *Incipit Phormio Comedia Sexta. Acta* Ludis romanis. Lucio postumio Albino Lucio Cornelio Merula edilibus curulibus ... *Incipit Argumentum Eiusdem.* Cremetis frater aberat peregre demipho ... Vxorem retinet antipho a patruo agnitam. *Incipit Prologus.* Postquam poeta vetus poetam non potest ... *Na.* Pol uero uoco. *pho.* eamus intro hinc. *na.* fiat. sed ubi est phedria. Iudex noster. *pho.* iam faxo aderit. V. Vos valete et plaudite. Caliopius recensui. *Terentij affri Poete comici Comedie Et Phormio Ultima feliciter Expliciunt.* f. 127v blank except for notes on provenance (see below).

Terence, *Phormio*; Kauer and Lindsay, *op.cit.*, pp. 171–226. Some interlinear glosses on f. 108r–v only.

Parchment (thin, shiny), ff. i (marbled paper) + ii (modern parchment) + 127 + ii (modern parchment) + i (paper). ff. 1–51: 26 lines; ff. 52–end: 28 lines. Single vertical and horizontal bounding lines. Ruled in pale red ink. Prickings in upper, lower and outer margins.

I–VI^{8}, VII^{4} (–4, blank), VIII–XVI^{8}, XVII^{4}. Catchwords in center of lower margin. Remains of leaf signatures (e.g., a 1, a 2, a 3 ... etc.) in red in lower right corner, recto.

Written in bâtarde script of several sizes.

5 historiated initials of fine quality, 11- to 9-line, blue with gold accents against dark red ground with gold filigree. The subjects, which apparently are not tied closely to the text, are as follow: f. 1r arms of the Terrail de Bayard family (azure, a chief argent with lion rampant erased sable, overall a bendlet or); f. 8r Courtship; f. 52r Marriage; f. 90v Birth of child; f. 107v Adulthood. Spaces for initials on ff. 28v, 72r left unfilled. Each initial with partial floral borders, framed in red, consisting of pink, blue and white flowers, red strawberries and/or gold leaves on green stems, all against compartments of parchment ground, infilled with gold dots with hair-line extensions, or of gold ground. Border, f. 8r, incorporating scrolling acanthus, blue and gold. Numerous illuminated initials, 4-line, gold against alternating red and blue ground with gold filigree. Headings in red and blue. Names of characters and plain initials alternate red and blue.

Binding: France, s. xviii. Brown mottled calf with a gold-tooled spine and a brick-red, gold-tooled label ("Terentii Comm Manuserip [?]"), "MC" in the adjoining panel. Turn-ins striped. Red edges.

Written in Northern France at the end of the 15th or beginning of the 16th century, presumably for Pierre Terrail de Bayard whose arms appear on f. 1r. Two inscriptions, s. xvi, on f. 127v: "Claudius de chauureux" and "Claudius de chauureux est huius libri possessor." The number "567" in a circle in blue crayon on f. i verso; "N. [*or* W] 2251" in pencil on recto of final flyleaf. Purchased from H. P. Kraus in 1958 by Thomas E. Marston (bookplate).

secundo folio: senatorum

Bibliography: Faye and Bond, pp. 90–91, no. 229.

Marston MS 230 Spain, s. XV^{med}

Thomas Anglicus, Quaestiones in primum librum Sententiarum contra Iohannem Scotum

1. ff. 1r–175r *Primus sententiarum Tome Anglici contra primum sententiarum Scoti.* [Duns Scotus, *quaestio* 1:] Utrum homini pro statu isto sit necessarium aliquam doctrinam supernaturaliter inspirari ad quam non possit attingere lumine naturali intellectus . . . [Thomas Anglicus, *impugnatio*, f. 2v:] In ista questione dicuntur aliqua minus bene et ideo contra dicta restat arguere primo autem contra dicta sua in [deleted: *solucione*] positione . . . [Thomas Anglicus, *determinatio*, f. 3v:] In ista questione teneo quod necesse est . . . [Thomas Anglicus, *distinctio* 45, concluding on f. 174r:] et ideo quasi generalius accipitur illa diuisio quantum est de veritate secundum rem tamen [*di* crossed out] eadem diuisio est ista secundum alia. [Duns Scotus, *distinctio* 48, concluding on f. 175r:] sed bonitas voluntatis dependet ab obiecto et ab alijs circumstancijs et potissime a fine ultimo. Deo gracias. Explicit Thomas anglicus contra primum sentenciarum Iohannis Scoti.

   This work, ascribed in manuscripts to Thomas Anglicus, has been variously attributed to Thomas Jorz, Thomas Sutton, and Thomas Wilton; Stegmüller, *Rep. Sent.* no. 842. The texts of Thomas and of Duns Scotus alternate throughout the manuscript.

2. ff. 175r–176r [I]ncipiunt rubrice thome Anglici contra primum sentenciarum Iohannis Scoti. *Prologus./* Vtrum homini pro statu isto . . . *.48.* Vtrum voluntas creata sit bona moraliter quandocumque conformatur

voluntati increate. ff. 176v–179v ruled, but blank

Table of contents for art. 1.

Paper (watermarks: unidentified crown), ff. ii (paper) + 179 + ii (paper), 340 x 235 (218 x 141) mm. 2 columns, 46 lines. Single vertical and horizontal bounding lines, full across; text rulings within columns. Ruled in lead. Remains of prickings for bounding lines only.

I–XVII^{10}, XVIII^{10} (–10). Vertical catchwords perpendicular to text along inner bounding line, verso.

Quire and leaf signatures (e.g., a .1., a .2., a .3., etc.) for first five leaves of each gathering, center of lower margin, recto.

Written by a single scribe in slanted running gothic script with rubrics in humanistic script.

One flourished initial of fine quality, f. 1r: red and blue divided initial, 8-line, with intricate penwork designs in red and purple extending across upper and down inner margins. Spaces for small initials left unfilled. Running headlines and rubrics in pale red.

Binding: U. S. A., s. xx. Half bound in brick-red goatskin with cloth sides. Title on spine "Thomas Anglicus. Questiones contra Duns" and "MS. c. 1400."

Written in Spain in the mid-15th century; Marston MS 230 can be identified as manuscript "8.14" from the Library of the Santa Iglesia del Pilar in Saragossa, Spain. Purchased in 1957 from Enzo Ferrajoli, Geneva, by L. C. Witten (inv. no. 1622), who sold it in 1958 to Thomas E. Marston (bookplate).

secundo folio: Ad ista

Bibliography: Faye and Bond, p. 81, no. 230.

Marston MS 231 Spain, s. XIII/XIV
Thomas Aquinas, Questiones de undecim quodlibet Pl. 55

1. ff. 1r–134r [I] Quesitum est de deo angelo et homine. de deo quesitum est ... [II, f. 14r:] Quesitum est de christo de angelis de hominibus. Circa christum quesita sunt ... [XI, f. 123v:] Questio nostra circa tria versabatur. primo circa ea que pertinent ad naturam ... per prius intendemus christi diuinitati quam humanitati. Explicit quodlibet fratris thome deo gracias.

P. Glorieux, *La Littérature quodlibétique de 1260 à 1320* (Le Saulchoir,

P. Glorieux, *La Littérature quodlibétique de 1260 à 1320* (Le Saulchoir, 1925) pp. 277–88; the order here corresponds to Glorieux I–VII, IX–XI, VIII, with VII ending on f. 97r with *questio* 16 ("... licet inde trahi possit per argumentacoem [*sic*]"). Contemporary annotations throughout.

2. ff. 134v–137v Utrum beatus benedictus quando vidit totum mundum viderit diuinam essentiam/ Utrum in christo sint due ffiliaciones/ ... Utrum beati prius ferantur ad contemplandam christi humanitatem quam eius diuinitatem. ff. 138r–140v blank

Table for art. 1; Glorieux, *ibid.* An early hand has added running headlines, foliated art. 1 with Arabic numerals and numbered each entry in the table with the corresponding folio reference.

Parchment, ff. ii (parchment) + 140 (medieval foliation 1–134 for art. 1), 171 x 127 (122 x 92) mm. 2 columns, 37–40 lines. Single vertical and horizontal bounding lines, full across. Ruled in lead; remains of prickings in upper, lower and outer margins.

I–XVII^{8}, XVIII^{4}. Catchwords, some with decorative flourishes, below inner text column, verso. Remains of quire and leaf signatures, s. xv, lower right corner, recto.

Written in small gothic bookhand, above top line.

Initials divided red and blue, 7-line on f. 1r (for I) and 6-line on f. 87r (for VII), with intricate red and purple penwork designs. Flourished initials, 3-line, red with purple designs (throughout), blue with red (ff. 1r–40v) and purple with red (ff. 41r–134r); penwork designs characterized by spiky extensions on margins. Paragraph marks red, blue and purple. Helical line fillers in red, red and blue, red and purple. Some letters stroked with yellow.

Binding: Spain, s. xv. Wound sewing on three tawed skin, double thongs laced from out to inside beech boards. Yellow edges. Plain wound, natural color endbands are sewn on tawed skin cores laid in grooves on the outside of the boards and tied down over strips of leather.

Covered in brick-red sheepskin, with central panel and one frame filled with rope interlace, another frame with a floral motif. Metallic annular dots. Two fastenings, the catches on the lower board. The straps are blue fabric, attached with star-headed nails; one wanting, as is the spine leather. Traces of chain fastening on lower board.

Written in Spain at the end of the 13th or beginning of the 14th century. Belonged to the Library of the Santa Iglesia del Pilar and the Biblioteca del Cabildo in Saragossa (no. 1299; H. V. Shooner, ed., *Codices manuscripti operum Thomae de Aquino* v. 3 [Montreal and Paris, 1985] p. 33). The bookplate on the front pastedown ("Ex libris Francisci Roux et amicorum") was apparently added in the 1950s (see also provenance for Marston MS 232). Purchased in 1959 from Enzo Ferrajoli through Nicolas Rauch, Geneva, by L. C. Witten (inv. no. 2502), who sold it the same year to Thomas E. Marston (bookplate).

secundo folio: alia qua

Bibliography: Faye and Bond, p. 91, no. 231.

Marston MS 232 — Northern Italy, s. XIII^{ex}
Thomas Aquinas, Summa theologiae, pars I

1. ff. 1r–4r *Incipiunt Rubrice summe theologie fratris thome de aquino ordinis fratrum predicatorum. Questio prima de ipsa scientia theologie. et queruntur x./ .j* Vtrum preter alias scientias theologia sit necessaria./ *ij*. Vtrum sit scientia./ . . . *ij*. Vtrum semen quod humane generationis principium sit de superfluo alimenti. Deo gratias Amen. f. 4v blank

   Table of *questiones* and *articuli* in art. 2.

2. ff. 5r–206r *Incipit prima pars summe fratris Thome de aquino ordinis predicatorum*. Quia catholice ueritatis doctor non solum perfectos debet instruere. sed ad eum etiam pertinet . . . Talis enim partus decebat eum qui est super omnia benedictus in secula Amen. [colophon:] Ego scripsi .ix. sexternos de isto opere. finito libro sic laus et gloria christo. amen. [later addition:] explicit liber primus summe fratris thome de aquino quem incepit ipse componere neapolim et perfecit eum parisius. anno domini .m. cc. lxviij. f. 206v blank except for miscellaneous notes

   Stegmüller, *Rep. Sent.*, 847. Marginal notes in several hands.

Parchment (some end pieces; yellow and speckled on hairside), ff. 206, 326 x 224 (229 x 138) mm. 2 columns, 52 lines. Double outer and single inner vertical bounding lines, full length; double upper and sometimes one or two horizontal bounding lines, full across. Additional pair of rulings in upper (trimmed), lower and outer margins, and pair for running headlines. Ruled in lead or hard point. Remains of prickings in upper, outer and lower margins.

I^{4}, II–VII^{10}, VIII^{8}, IX^{6}, X–XXI^{10}, XXII^{8}. Catchwords, enclosed by simple decorative rectangles, between rulings in lower margin below inner text column, verso.

Written in small gothic bookhand, below top line.

One historiated initial with partial border, of good quality but rubbed, f. 5r: mauve on blue rectangular ground both with white highlights; a kneeling figure in monk's robe, presumably the author, holding a book and pointing to the beginning of the text, on gold ground. A bar border extending down inner margin and across lower margin with beads in pale green, blue, blue-green and gold, and stylized leaves, green and blue swirling around bar. Border ending in lower margin in stylized scroll inhabited by a human figure supporting a cupola [?]; a bird perched on bar beneath inner column. 12-line initial divided red and blue (f. 79r for *questio* 44) with red and blue penwork designs. Many small flourished initials, 3- to 2-line, red with blue penwork designs and vice versa. Paragraph marks alternate red and blue. Running headlines in red or blue. Instructions for decorator. Most rubrics wanting.

Binding: Spain, s. xv. Resewn on three double thongs laced into wooden boards. Yellow edges. Plain wound endbands are sewn through a vellum spine lining which extends inside the boards between supports.

Covered in brick-red goatskin; Catalan multiple-line concentric frames and Moorish overtones. Spine: multiple fillets at head and tail. An *X* with 3 eight-petalled flowers at the intersections and in the 4 compartments. Double fillets outlining the panels. Two fastenings, the catches on the lower board. Damage from a chain attachment and a vellum label with title "Prima pars sancti thome," both on the upper board. The boards do not fit the bookblock.

Written in Northern Italy at the end of the 13th century to judge from the style of decoration. Evidence of early provenance was removed sometime after 1954 when the codex was photographed at the Biblioteca del Cabildo, Saragossa, by the Leonine Commission (H. V. Shooner, ed., *Codices manuscripti operum Thomae de Aquino* v. 3 [Montreal and Paris, 1985] p. 34). Evidence removed includes: 1. 15th-century inscription of an owner or reader along upper edge, f. 4v: "Anno domini m° cccc° xi° madii in die translationis beati dominici domino dante incepi hunc librum" (this same hand wrote marginal notes throughout the volume); 2. inscription on an original front flyleaf that recorded the donation of the codex to the Library of the Santa Iglesia del Pilar in Saragossa and the death of the donor, Petrus de Monflorit, in 1477: "hanc primam partem beati thome de aquino. donarunt bibliothece eclesie sancte marie del pilar venerabiles viri scilicet dominus dominicus burian porcionarius sedis cesaraugustensis et dominus martinus vielo capellanus eiusdem sedis. executores testamenti domini petri de monflorit quondam porcionarij sedis cesaraugustensis ac elemonisarij reuerendissimi jn christo patris domini dalmacii de mur genitricis marie et proffectum studencium in supradicta biblyotheca./ obijt predictus dominus petrus de monflorit XXVIJ mensis septembris. anno natiuitatis domini. M° CCCCLXXVII°." (a similar record of donation also occurs in El Escorial T. I. 16, a copy of the *Prima Secundae*); 3. a modern book label: "Biblioteca del Cabildo Metropolitano de Zaragoza, Armario 12, No. del registro 732, No. de orden 332." The 19th-century bookplates glued to the front pastedown ("del Marques de Ovando" and "Tho. St. George Esquire") were not present in 1954. Purchased in 1959 from Enzo Ferrajoli through Nicolas Rauch, Geneva, by L. C. Witten (inv. no. 2519), who sold it the same year to Thomas E. Marston (bookplate).

secundo folio: [table, f. 2:] *i.* Vtrum
[text, f. 6:] debeas

Bibliography: Faye and Bond, p. 91, no. 232.

Marston MS 233 — Northern Italy, s. XII^{med}
Cistercian Order, Statutes

1. f. 1r–v *De negligentia sacrificij*. Si per negligentiam euenerit ut perlecto canone et peracta consecratione ... alter alterius onera portate.

   J. Leclercq, "Manuscrits cisterciens dans les bibliothèques d'Italie," *Analecta sacri ordinis cisterciensis* 5 (1949) p. 100.

2. ff. 1v–2v Qualiter commemorationes sanctorum agantur per totum annum. In die sancti stephani ... Scolastice uirginis. Quinque prudentes. veniente sponso [followed by erasure].

   Leclercq, *op. cit.*, pp. 98, 101.

3. ff. 2v–111v [List of 122 chapters:] *Incipiunt capitula ecclesiasticorum officiorum. i* De aduentu domini./ *ii* Quomodo per hyemem priuatis diebus ad uigilias diuidantur responsoria./ ... *cxxi* De portario et solatio eius./ *cxxii* De versu refectionis. [text, f. 5r:] *Incipiunt ecclesiastica officia. De aduentu domini. capitulum .i.* In aduentu domini dominica prima ysaias incipiatur ad uigilias ... *hec adbiberes* Largitor omnium bonorum. benedicat potum seruorum suorum. Amen.

   Liber usuum; C. Noschitzka, ed., *Analecta sacri ordinis cisterciensis* 6 (1950) pp. 38–124.

4. f. 112r–v [Text added, s. xiii:] *Quomodo legantur libri ad vigilias*. In prima dominica aduentus domini. Incipitur ad vigilias ysaias propheta.

prima dominica aduentus domini. Incipitur ad vigilias ysaias propheta. et legitur tam priuatis diebus . . . in crastino persoluantur [large portion of concluding lines badly rubbed].

J. Leclercq, *op. cit.*, p. 100.

Parchment (yellow and darkly speckled on hair side), ff. iv (paper) + 112 + vii (paper), 226 x 160 (152 x 105) mm. 23 long lines. Single vertical and upper horizontal bounding lines. Ruled very faintly in hard point. Remains of prickings in all margins except inner.

I–XIV^{8}. Quires signed with Roman numerals center of lower margin, verso, in brown and red with decorative dots and squiggles.

Written in a neat late caroline minuscule; art. 4 added in inelegant gothic bookhand.

Nice initials, 12- to 3-line, in red with simple medium blue designs and vice versa; designs on parchment in body of initials. 1-line initials and initials for list of chapters in art. 3 alternate blue, red and dark yellow. Headings and initials strokes in red.

Binding: England, s. xx. Rigid vellum case with a gold-tooled title on spine: "Liber usuum ordinis cister." Bound by F. E. Stoakley, Cambridge. The brown, blind-tooled calf cover of one early board (much worm eaten) is attached inside back cover. Rust stains from five bosses on f. 112v.

Written in the middle of the 12th century in Northern Italy, possibly at the Cistercian abbey of Chiaravalle in Milan (founded in 1135; Cottineau, v. 1, cols. 768–69) to which it belonged in the 14th century (two inscriptions, erased but visible under ultra-violet light, f. 111v: "Iste est liber de Careualis de sancte marie" and "Item liber iste est Sancte Marie"). Purchased from Lathrop C. Harper in 1958 by Thomas E. Marston (bookplate).

secundo folio: sancti Thome

Bibliography: Faye and Bond, p. 91, no. 233.
Leclercq, 1961, p. 164.

Marston MS 234 Northern Italy, s. XIV^{2}

Valerius Maximus, Facta et dicta memorabilia, with glosses

ff. 1r–74v //inca pecude [legibility of first two words obscured by corrections] maiore ex parte anni ore aperto exalto uentos recipientes sitim suam sedare restituerit . . . similitudinis exempla referamus. Magno pompeio [next word unclear; note in outer margin: *al. vibius*] ingenue stirpis et//

Valerius Maximus, *Factorum et dictorum memorabilium libri novem*; C. Kempf, ed., Teubner 2nd ed. 1888, reprinted 1966, pp. 1–472. Text imperfect at beginning and end (I.8. ext. 18 - IX.14.1) and missing one leaf between ff. 68–69 (IX.2.1 - IX.2. ext. 6): "... quisquam satis [added in margin: *digne*] potest quia dum querit // que odiosos sibi non prorupto uinculo...". Each book preceded by list of chapters; extensive interlinear glosses and marginalia, including variant readings, written by several contemporary and later hands.

Parchment, ff. i (paper) + 74 (early foliation, arabic numerals 9–82, in lower right corner, recto) + i (paper), 273 x 199 (170 x 118) mm. 2 columns, ca. 39–45 lines. Single vertical bounding lines; ruled faintly in lead. Remains of prickings in upper and lower margins.

I [missing], II–III^{8}, IV–V^{10}, VI–IX^{8}, X^{8} (–1, 8, with loss of text). Horizontal catchwords with penwork quatrefoils, touched with yellow, and with flourishes on all sides, center of lower margin, verso.

Written in gothic bookhand. Marginal and interlinear annotations in less formal scripts.

8 large initials, 10- to 7-line, of poor quality, pink against gold ground thickly edged in black, filled with stylized foliage, green, orange, and yellow on blue ground. Foliage serifs, pink, blue, orange and yellow with white filigree extending into margins to form partial borders. Gold balls, thickly edged in black. Numerous small initials, 5- to 3-line, pink against gold ground edged in black, filled with stylized foliage, orange and yellow on blue ground. Numerous flourished initials, 2- to 1-line, alternate in red and blue with brown or red penwork. Headings in red by at least two rubricators. Paragraph marks in blue for chapters in tables preceding each book; in red and blue for text.

Folio 1r damaged with some loss of text. Most of the decoration is badly rubbed and stained.

Binding: Italy, s. xix. Brown leather case, blind- and gold-tooled. Title (citing portion of table of contents for Book II, f. 1r) on spine: "De institutis/ antiquis/ de disciplina/ militari/ de iure" and "Triumphandi."

Written in Northern Italy in the second half of the 14th century; provenance unknown. Paper slip pasted inside back cover but extending above upper edge: "61" stamped in red and "11" stamped in purple. Unidentified modern note in pencil on front pastedown: "CB 2 848." Purchased in 1954 from A. L. van Gendt, Netherlands, by L. C. Witten (inv. no. 571), who sold it in 1958 to Thomas E. Marston (bookplate).

Bibliography: Faye and Bond, p. 91, no. 234.

Marston MS 235 — Southern France, s. XV^{med}

Alfonso de Vargas y Toledo, Lectura super libros Sententiarum

1. ff. 1r–244r Incipit lectura super primum sententiarum edita a magistro alphonso de toleto in sacra pagina professore ordinis fratrum heremitarum sancti augustini. *Ego sum alpha* ... [Apoc. 1.8]. Doctor ille gloriosus ysodorus [*sic*] yspalensis qui inter ceteros yspanie philosophos et doctores ... Amen. prologus. [f. 2r:] *Circa prologum* istius operis queritur primo. Vtrum aliqua notitia euidens de veritatibus theologie ... [*distinctio* 1, f. 50r:] *Ueteris ac Noue* ... Quia magister in ista prima distinctione. principaliter. agit de fruitione et vsu ... eo prestante qui est alpha. et .o. principium et finis in secula seculorum Amen. F[inis] N[omine] D[ei]. Explicit lectura primi libri sententiarum edita a fratre alphonso de toleto ordinis fratrum heremitarum sancti augustini. qui legit parisius anno domini [*m°* crossed out] M° ccc° xlv° deo gracias.

   Stegmüller, *Rep. Sent.* 66; for the life and works of the author see J. Kürzinger, *Alfonsus Vargas Toletanus und seine theologische Einleitungslehre*, in *Beiträge zur Geschichte der Philosophie und Theologie des Mittelalters* XXI, 5–6 (Munster, 1930), with the contents of the text listed on pp. 25–31.

2. f. 244r–v Incipiunt tituli questionum. Vtrum aliqua notitia euidens de veritatibus ... et obiectiones soluuntur. Expliciunt tituli questionum.

   List of *questiones* and *distinctiones* in the order in which they appear in art. 1.

3. ff. 244v–253v In dei nomine. Incipit tabula super primum sententiarum fratris alfonsi de toleto sacre pagine doctorum ordinis fratrum heremitarum sancti Augustini. F[inis] N[omine] D[ei]. Quoniam non eque facile est opera registrare multiplicibus contenta partibus ... [ends in section on "voluntas"] ibidem correlatio 4.9.

   Alphabetical subject index to art. 1.

Paper, with parchment inner and outer bifolia (watermarks: similar to Piccard Ochsenkopf I.217; unidentified bull's head; unidentified hand similar in design to Briquet Main 11080–85, but larger and surmounted by a crown), ff. ii (modern parchment) + 253 + ii (modern parchment), 287 x 205 (202 x 155) mm. 2 columns, 48 lines. Frame-ruled in lead.

I–XIV^{16}, XV^{14}, XVI^{16} (-16). Horizontal catchwords in lower margin under inner column, verso; quires signed with letters of the alphabet (*a–p*) lower right corner, verso, with the final gathering signed *vltimo* on f. 239r.

Written in small, highly abbreviated, cursive minuscule script. First few words of each text division in large round gothic bookhand.

Flourished initials, 5- to 3-line, blue with red penwork and red with purple, incorporating harping, cross-hatching designs and marginal extensions. Red paragraph marks on first few leaves of each gathering only.

Ink has discolored and corroded many paper leaves.

Binding: Italy, s. xix. Elaborately blind-stamped and gold-tooled brown calf case. Gilt edges. Bound by G. Glingler, Rome.

Written in Southern France in the middle of the 15th century to judge from the watermarks and decoration; title and ownership inscription effaced, f. 1r. Large embossed and painted ex-libris, s. xix, on front leather pastedown: "Ex libris Ernesti Pagnoni Mediolanensis." Purchased from C. A. Stonehill in 1958 by Thomas E. Marston (bookplate).

secundo folio: *Circa prologum*

Bibliography: Faye and Bond, p. 91, no. 235.

Marston MS 236 — Central or Southern France, s. XIII^{med}

William of Auxerre, Summa aurea I–IV, etc.

1. ff. 1r–222r *Utrum fides possit uel debeat probari.* Fides est substantia rerum . . . [Hebr. 11.1]. Sicut enim uera dileccione deus diligitur . . . Illa gaudia nobis prestare dignetur ihesus christus dominus . . . Amen. f. 74v (at end of Bk. II) blank

   William of Auxerre, *Summa aurea I–IV*; Glorieux, no. 281. Colophon on f. 74r (conclusion of Bk. II): "Laudo creatorem quia finis pena laborem." The beginning of Bk. III contains some contemporary corrections and annotations.

2. f. 222r–v [O?] Dilecte fili dilige lacrimas noli differre eas . . . [Eccle. 5.5]. Qualis tibi fuit ad peccandum in . . . ne quid legendo respicis uiuendo contempnas.

   Unidentified text.

Parchment, ff. 222, 179 x 125 (131 x 96) mm. 2 columns, 55 lines.

Single vertical and double horizontal bounding lines, full across. Two additional horizontal rulings in upper margin for running headlines and sometimes through middle of written space. Remains of prickings in upper, lower and outer margins. Ruled in lead.

I–III^{16}, IV^{14}, V^{10}, VI^{2} (ff. 73–74), VII–XII^{16}, XIII–XV^{12}, XVI^{16}. Horizontal or vertical catchwords with decorative pen designs in red and/or blue, lower margin, under inner column or near gutter, verso.

Written by multiple scribes in small gothic bookhand, both above (e.g., ff. 75v–90r) and below top line.

Decoration by two distinct hands whose division of work does not necessarily correspond to scribal changes of hand or to quire structure. Hand I executed fine initials, split red and blue, with penwork extensions in both colors the entire length of the page at the beginning of Bks. I (f. 1r), II (f. 24v), IV (f. 171r), and many small flourished initials, 4- to 2-line, with looping ascenders and descenders (ff. 1r–69r, 123r–156v, 195r–221v). Hand II executed more modest initials for both major (Bk. III, f. 75r) and minor (ff. 75r–122v, 171r–194v) text divisions. Spaces for initials remain unfilled on ff. 69r–74r and are either unfilled or filled with plain red initials on ff. 157v–170v, 222r–v. Running headlines in red and blue. Rubrics both within text and in margins. Remains of notes to rubricator, often perpendicular to text along outer margin. Paragraph marks, alternating red and blue, appear sporadically.

Binding: France [?], s. xix–xx. Quarter bound in brown calf over wooden boards by the same binder as Marston MSS 119, 214 and 216.

Written in the middle of the 13th century in Central or Southern France to judge from the script and decoration; provenance otherwise unknown. Purchased in 1958 from Nicolas Rauch, Geneva, by L. C. Witten (inv. no. 2092), who sold it the same year to Thomas E. Marston (bookplate).

secundo folio: [com]positioni uel parti

Bibliography: Faye and Bond, p. 91, no. 236.

Marston MS 239 — Italy s. XV
Laudario

1. f. 1r [Rubric in a later hand, upper margin:] *Laudi christiane*. Si fortemente son tracto d'amore/ . . . ch'el troppo senno sempre ci a ingannato.

Ugo Panziera da Prato (d. 1330); see S. Di Zenzo, *Ugo Panziera e l'auten-*

ticità delle sue laudi (Liguori editore, [1970]) no. 24, pp. 64–68.

2. f. 1r–v O derrata guarda el preçço/ ... quello che sente in quello stato. Amen.

   Jacopone da Todi, Laude no. 48 in the edition by F. Mancini, ed., *Laude* (Rome, 1974) pp. 133–36 (all number references for Jacopone are from this edition).

3. f. 1v Chi e cristian chiamato/ ... e de lancia forato.

   Tenneroni, citing four manuscripts; IUPI with five references (other than Tenneroni).

4. ff. 1v–2r Cristo amor dilecto in te sguardando/ ... che in luj solo sia il nostro uagare. amen.

   IUPI with one reference that leads to Venice, Biblioteca Nazionale Marciana, d. IX, 61.

5. f. 2r–v Hamor diuino amore [false start for art. 7]. Piagni dolente anima predata/ ... da poj c'o perduto lo mio redemptore.

   Jacopone da Todi, Laude no. 52; Mancini, *op. cit.*, pp. 145–46.

6. f. 2v Signor mio io uo languendo per te ritrouare/ ... per amor tuo me perdonj ogne mio peccare.

   Tenneroni, citing 32 manuscripts; IUPI with 13 references. See G. Mazza, *Il laudario jacoponico Δ-VII-15 della Biblioteca Civica "Angelo Maj" di Bergamo* (Bergamo, 1960) no. XLVI, pp. 59–60.

7. ff. 2v–3r Hamor diuino amore amor che non si amato/ ... crepasse affogato. amen.

   Tenneroni citing 36 manuscripts; IUPI with two references. Mazza, *op. cit.*, no. LXXXV, pp. 118–20.

8. f. 3r–v O buono iesu poj che m'ai innamorato/ ... stormento che suona di gran rinouança.

   Tenneroni citing 3 manuscripts; IUPI with 3 references.

9. f. 3v Fiorito e cristo ne la carne pura/ ... fa che tu l'ammanti con uesta de fiorj. amen.

   Tenneroni citing 7 manuscripts; IUPI with 11 references. Di Zenzo, *op. cit.*, no. 27, pp. 74–77.

10. ff. 3v–4r O uergine piu che femina/ ... lo lagremare.

Jacopone da Todi, Laude no. 32; Mancini, *op. cit.*, pp. 85–90. Here the text breaks off in the middle of verse 117 (29 verses missing).

11. f. 4r–v O francesco pouero/ ... ad la fonte inamorato.

Jacopone da Todi, Laude no. 40; Mancini, *op. cit.*, pp. 113–19.

12. ff. 4v–5r O francesco da dio amato/ ... e d'ogne bene sera ditato.

Jacopone da Todi, Laude no. 71; Mancini, *op. cit.*, pp. 206–12.

13. f. 5r–v Que farraj fra giacopone/ ... loco sia lo tuo guiderdone. amen.

Jacopone da Todi, Laude no. 53; Mancini, *op. cit.*, pp. 146–52. Verses 147–54 are missing in Marston MS 239.

14. f. 5v O Papa bonifatio/ ... in questo luoco lassato. amen.

Jacopone da Todi, Laude no. 55; Mancini, *op. cit.*, pp. 154–56.

15. ff. 5v–6r Que faraj pier da morrone ch'or se giunto al paragone/ ... cantaraj mala cançone. amen.

Jacopone da Todi, Laude no. 74; Mancini, *op. cit.*, pp. 218–20.

16. f. 6r Dolce amor de pouertade/ ... chi con cristo uol regnare. amen.

IUPI with 6 references to variations of this poem.

17. f. 6r–v O Amor de pouertade/ ... in spirito de libertade. amen.

Anonymous? Corresponds to poem found in edition of F. Tresatti, *Poesie spirituali del B. Jacopone da Todi frate minore* ... (Venice, 1617) I, 9.1–2, as reported by R. Bettarini in *Jacopone e il Laudario Urbinate* (Florence, 1969) p. 408. See also Tenneroni, p. 165.

18. ff. 6v–7r Nullo se sa ma ben confessare/ ... in fin che e non chiama consumato.

Not listed in IUPI. Mazza, *op. cit.*, no. XLVIII, pp. 63–64.

19. f. 7r–v O Alta penitentia pena in amor tenuta/ ... menate la sperança oue l'amor beato.

Jacopone da Todi, Laude no. 11; Mancini, *op. cit.*, pp. 38–40. The last two stanzas in Marston MS 239 are not in Mancini's edition, nor does he report any other manuscripts with appended stanzas. They begin "Lo uiso se fa pouero deforme et di colorj" and "Da poj ch'el corpo perde de fuorj la delectança [?]."

20. ff. 7v–8r Vjta de yesu christo specchio de ueritade/ ... uento de l'abundança del dolce mio signore.

Jacopone da Todi, Laude no. 51; Mancini, *op. cit.*, pp. 142–45.

21. f. 8r Chi uol trouare amore/ ... tanto salle ad misura quanto descende in giue.

Probably by Ugo Panziera da Prato; Di Zenzo, *op. cit.*, p. 166. Tenneroni citing 10 manuscripts; similar text in *Laude de lo contemplativo ed extatico B. F. Jacopone ...*, printed by B. Benaglio (Venice, 1514) pp. 126–27.

22. f. 8r–v Facciam facti ora facciamo/ ... che solo ce'l danno i facti. amen.

Laude attributed to both Jacopone da Todi and Bernardinus of Siena (1380–1444); see D. Pacetti, *De Sancti Bernardini Senensis operibus* (Florence, 1947) p. 116 and Tenneroni citing 9 manuscripts.

23. ff. 8v–9r Pjagne la chiesa/ ... in ciascuno stato ti uegio affocato.

Jacopone da Todi, Laude no. 35; Mancini, *op. cit.*, pp. 95–97.

24. f. 9r Or se parra chi auera fidança/ ... ad esserne securo stolto pare.

Jacopone da Todi, Laude no. 6; Mancini, *op. cit.*, pp. 27–29.

25. f. 9r Assaj me sforço ad guadagnare/ ... c'appena li posso perdonare.

Jacopone da Todi, Laude no. 75; Mancini, *op. cit.*, pp. 220–21.

26. f. 9r–v Que faj anima predata/ ... prouara l'umiliata.

Jacopone da Todi, Laude no. 37; Mancini, *op. cit.*, pp. 102–6.

27. ff. 9v–10r O Christo pietoso perdona el mio peccato/ ... et nel fuoco el fon gittare. amen.

Tenneroni citing 26 manuscripts; IUPI with 2 references.

28. f. 10r Cinque sensi o messo il pegno/ ... che eterno e il delectare.

Jacopone da Todi, Laude no. 19; Mancini, *op. cit.*, pp. 55–57.

29. f. 10r Guarda che non cagi amico guarda/ ... che de ci guardj.

Jacopone da Todi, Laude no. 20; Mancini, *op. cit.*, pp. 57–59. Marston MS 239 has one extra stanza between (Mancini) ll. 14–15 beginning "Guardate dal cibo et dal poto"; nine stanzas between ll. 26–27 beginning, respectively, "Guardati da li presenti," "Guarda non esser otioso," "Guardate dal molto parlare," "Guardati dal bel parlare," "Per lo buo [*sic*] parlamento," "Per fare altrui utilitade," "Guardate da le spirituali," "In nulla cosa e tanto errore," "Guarda ben guarda e non cessare"; one stanza between ll. 34–35 beginning, "Guardate da le deuote," and one after the last (Mancini) stanza beginning, "Nullo hom per se si puo guardare." In the space between columns a contemporary hand has indicated by the letters a–f a different order for stanzas 14–19; new order would be 17, 18, 19, 14, 15, 16. Mancini reports only as many as nine interpolated stanzas for this poem (p. 506); Rome, Biblioteca Angelica MS 2216 and Vatican City, Biblioteca Apostolica Vaticana MS Vat. lat. 13092 have one interpolated stanza at (Mancini) ll. 14–15, but only one between ll. 26–27, not nine as in Marston MS 239. Three other manuscripts have seven stanzas appended to the end, but no other manuscript reported by Mancini shows twelve interpolated stanzas as here.

30. f. 10r–v Laudiamo yesu figliolo de maria/ . . . denançi da dio.

Anonymous? See Mazza, *op. cit.*, no. CXVI, p. 158; here the text differs from the printed version.

31. ff. 10v–11r Nuouo tempo d'ardore/ . . . de l'angelico amore.

IUPI citing 3 references; see Mazza, *op. cit.*, no. LV, pp. 80–81; second stanza missing in Marston MS 239.

32. f. 11r [Line omitted from text added in upper margin:] de molti il cor s'aregna. [text:] Legitima la fede de li puri figliuolj/ . . . e non ne senton sapore. amen.

Tenneroni citing one manuscript (Florence, Biblioteca Riccardiana, MS 2762); IUPI with one reference (leading to Vatican City, Biblioteca Apostolica Vaticana, Fondo Rossi 424), in both cases attributed to Jacopone da Todi.

33. f. 11r Isti sunt casus qui episcopo reseruantur et a quibus simplex sacerdos neminem absolui potest. Non potest absoluere excommunicatum . . . vel falsarios monetarum ponderum seu misurarum vel hijs similia facientes. f. 11v blank

Sins that require absolution from a bishop.

Paper (brown, coarse; watermarks: unidentified balance [?] along upper edge, trimmed), with parchment for inner bifolium, ff. iii (paper) + 11 + iii (paper), 140 x 106 (106 x 79) mm. 2 columns, 49 lines of verse. Single vertical bounding lines ruled in ink or lead.

I^{10} (+ 1 leaf tipped in at end). Horizontal catchword along lower edge under outer column, verso.

Written in a small gothic bookhand; art. 33 added in a large size gothic bookhand by another scribe.

Plain red initials, 2-line, mark beginning of each poem; opening letter for each stanza washed with yellow. In art. 33 two plain red initials, the second with modest penwork designs also in red; first letter of each sentence stroked with red.

Binding: Place uncertain, s. xix [?]. Red velvet case with impression of a very large ornament at fore edge of upper board. Perhaps covered with used fabric, since other impressions appear in unusual locations on boards. Off-set of script on fabric stays.

Written in Italy in the 15th century; early provenance unknown. Modern pencil notes on f. iii verso list contents of volume, in English. Residue from square label on front pastedown. Purchased in 1960 from Harold Maker [?] by L. C. Witten (inv. no. 3099), who sold it the same year to Thomas E. Marston (bookplate).

secundo folio: [langui]sco amando

Bibliography: Faye and Bond, pp. 91–92, no. 239.

Marston MS 240 — Italy, s. XV[1]
William of Ockham, Summa logicae, etc.

1. ff. 1r–80v [Title, added in later hand:] Loice de ockam [?]. [prologue:] Dvdum me frater et amice carissime tujs litteris studebas jnducere vt aliquas regulas artis loyce [*sic*]. In vnum tractatum colligerem collectumque ... quam theologica demostrando. [text:] *Incipit primum capitulum de termino in generali.* Omnes loyce tractatores. Intendunt astruere quod argumenta ex propositionibus et propositiones ex terminis componuntur ... et ideo propter breuitatem ad presens transeo. [colophon:] Explicit Tractatus de sillogismis ... Reuerendum doctorem fratrem Gulielmum. occham. ordinis fratrum minorum.

   William of Ockham, *Summa logicae, Pars I* through *Pars III, tractatus primus*; chapter 51 of *pars prima* omitted. P. Boehner, G. Gál, S. Brown, eds., *Venerabilis inceptoris Guillelmi de Ockham Summa Logicae* (St. Bonaventure, N. Y., 1974) pp. 5–502; Marston MS 240 assigned to the second family of manuscripts "Primo respondeat" and listed on pp. 17* - 18*, no. 22.

2. ff. 80v–91r *De sillogismo demonstratiuo.* Postquam diccum [*sic*] est de sillogismo in communi. Sequitur ... que sunt hic obmissa in expositione posteriorum aristotelis sum. tractaturus. Explicit liber posteriorum siue secundus tractatus. tertie partis loyce .G. de ocham ordinis fratrum minorum. de Sillogismo demonstratiuo Reuerendi doctoris.

   Pars III, tractatus secundus; P. Boehner, *et al.*, *op. cit.*, pp. 505–84.

3. ff. 91r–94r Incipit tertius tractatus tertie partis de obligacionibus. et insolubilibus. R. d. G. de Ocham ... [text:] *De equipollenciis modorum.* Quia circa propositionum modalium equipollencias et Repugnancias sunt varie difficultates ... totaliter dimitteretur intacta. Explicit tractatus de obligacionibus et insolubilibus tertie partis loyce Reuerendi doccoris .G. de ocham ordinis fratrum minorum.

   Chapters 13–16 of *Pars III, tractatus tertius*, followed immediately by chs. 39–45 (*De Obligationibus*) and ch. 46 (*De Insolubilibus*); P. Boehner, *et al.*, *op. cit.*, pp. 642–49, 731–44, 744–46.

4. ff. 94r–110v *De consequentiis et primo de aliquibus etiam generalibus eiusdem.* Post sillogismum demonstratiuum dicendum est de argumentis et consequentiis que non habent formam sillogisticam ... Sed tales consequentie non sunt formales. nec sunt vsitande. Explicit quartus tractatus de consequentijs tertie partis loyce. R. G. doccoris [*sic*] ordinis fratrum minorum.

   Pars III, tractatus tertius, chs. 1–12, 17–38. P. Boehner, *et al.*, *op. cit.*, pp. 587–642, 649–731.

5. ff. 110v–124r *De ultimo capitulo .scilicet. fallaciarum et primo in generali.* Cum dictum sit de argumentis et speciebus argumentorum. Restat nunc dicere. de defectibus argumentorum ... [f. 124r:] Primo Respondeat ... vt semper est declaratum. [colophon:] Explicit loyca. G. de ocham. Summa doctoris ordinis fratrum minorum Edita et composita per manus. Magistri Antonij francisci de Iohannuzio labore massimo et cetera. Manus scriptoris Saluet deus dignas honores. Quj dedit explerj Antonio det gaudia Celi Amen.

   Pars III, tractatus quartus (*de fallaciis*); P. Boehner, *et al.*, *op. cit.*, pp. 749–849.

6. f. 124v [U]t Iuuenes in quolibet proloblemate [*sic*] disputationes possint esse exercitatj et uelociter ... Et continebit iste libellus quattuor partes. In prima parte ponentur quedam regule ... vobis supponit subiectum. f. 125r–v blank

   Walter Burley, *De puritate artis logicae tractatus brevior*, beginning of text only; P. Boehner, ed., Franciscan Institute Publications, Text Series 1 (St. Bonaventure, N. Y., 1951) pp. 199–202.

Paper (thick, coarse, some deckle edges; watermarks indistinguishable), ff. i (paper) + 125 + i (paper), 222 x 145 (195 x 110) mm. Ca. 36–51 long lines. No visible remains of rulings or prickings.

I–XV^{8}, XVI^{6} (-6, blank). Horizontal catchwords, accompanied by lines and flourishes in black and red, centered in lower margin, verso.

Written by a single scribe in small, cramped and highly abbreviated gothic cursive. Art. 6 added by two different hands.

Crude penwork initials on f. 1r in red and blue, 3-line. The first incorporates a five-pointed star in red, with blue dots, and terminates with a full-length marginal border in inner margin. The second incorporates a fleur-de-lis. Other plain initials in red and/or blue throughout. Headings and strokes on paragraph marks and majuscules in red.

Binding: Italy [?], uncertain date. Backs of quires cut in for sewing. Plain limp vellum case with holes in each cover for two ribbons.

Written in Italy in the first half of the 15th century by the scribe Antonius Franciscus de Iohannuzio; provenance unknown. Purchased from Dawsons of Pall Mall in 1960 by Thomas E. Marston (bookplate).

secundo folio: [*vnum* erased, followed by:] Incomplexum

Bibliography: Faye and Bond, p. 92, no. 240.

Marston MS 241 Aix-en-Provence, 1263
Legal Document, in Latin, in roll format

[Heading:] In nomine domini. amen. Cum multe questiones orte essent et oriri [s]perarentur inter illustrem dominum karolum filium regis [Francie, Andegavie] provincie et forchalcherii comitem et marchionem provincie nomine suo. et nomine domine Beatricis uxoris eius eorundem comitatuum comitisse [et marchionisse] provincie ex una parte. fratrem ferandum de barratio commendatorem hospitalis sancti johannis ierosolem in partibus cismarinis nomine d[icti] hospitalis ex altera. que tales erant. [text:] Petebat enim dominus comes predictus ... et per eum dictum hospitale de dictis mille libris sicut de tribus millibus libris antedictis. Actum aquis in prato palatii domini comitis predicti die veneris post festum beate marie magdalene anno domini .M.CC.lxij. in presentia et testimonio testium infrascriptorum ... Et mei milonis de meldis publici notarii dicti domini comitis qui predictis omnibus interfui. et de mandato dictarum partium hanc cartam scripsi. et hoc meo signo signaui. [*III* inserted] eiusdem tenoris. [siglum of notary followed by:] Et ego Gotfridus sitii publicus notarius in manuasca et in aliis terris prioratus sancti egidii pro hospitali. et notarius in comitatibus provincie et forchalcherii pro domino karolo illustri comite. autenticum seu originale huius exempli vidi et diligenter legi et sicut in eo continetur de verbo ad verbum nichil addendo vel minuendo quod mutet intellectum. ita et in hoc scripsi exemplo quod quidem originale erat bullatum et comunitum sigillo domini karoli illustrissimi comitis provincie et forchalcherii et marchionis provincie. et sigillo domine Beatricis illustrissime dictorum comitatuum comitisse uxoris eiusdem. et hoc feci de mandato fratris Berengarii monachi preceptoris manuasce. Anno domini. M.CC.lxiij. xviij kalendas februarii. et sigillum meum apposui.

Copy dated on January 15, 1263, of an agreement made at Aix-en-Provence on July 28, 1262, between Charles I of Anjou and Féraud de Barras concerning respective rights of the Count and the Knights of St. John of Jerusalem in the area around Manosque. The document therefore was issued during the period between Charles I of Anjou's co-regency–along with his brother Alfonse of Poitiers–during the absence of King Louis IX of France (1252–1257) and Charles' accession to the Kingdom of Sicily in 1265 (June 28). Féraud de Barras was Commander of the Knights of St. John for 1259–1262, and this agreement appears to be his last action in that office (cf. J. Delaville Le Roulx, *Les Hospitaliers en Terre Sainte et à Chypre* [Paris, 1904] p. 415). Among the witnesses cited are the troubadours Bertran d'Alamanon and Sordello. Between the years 1252 and 1265, these two troubadours are witnesses to numerous documents as *milites*. Sordello was also witness to two important treaties between Charles and the Comune of Genoa the week before on July 21 and 22, 1262, at Aix (M. Boni, *Sordello, Le poesie* [Bologna, 1954] p. LXXXIX).

The full text of the original agreement is found in the *Cartulaire général de l'Ordre des hospitaliers de S. Jean de Jérusalem 1100–1310* (J. Delaville Le Roulx, ed. [Paris, 1894]), v. 3, pp. 36–42 no. 3035. Delaville reports that the sealed original is in Marseille (*op. cit.*, p. 36, where he lists other copies) as does R. Sternfeld, *Karl von Anjou als Graf der Provence* (*Historische Untersuchungen* Heft X [Berlin, 1888]) p. 166. Marston MS 241 appears to be the earliest copy of this agreement; another copy not reported by Delaville is listed as 757 no. 7 of the Bibliothèque d'Aix (*Catalogue général des manuscrits des bibliothèques publiques de France*, v. XVI: Aix [Paris, 1894] p. 320).

Parchment roll, composed of three membranes, measuring 1,455 x 201 mm. Text of the document covers most of the roll with little margin. Written in small gothic bookhand. Surface much worn, with some loss of text. Unbound.

Early provenance unknown. Series of filing notes on reverse side, very rubbed. [In a 15th-century hand:] "Composatio [?] concordia et [? word] Inter dominum comitem provincie et forcalquerij et? Religionem sanctj Johannis." [Below, 16th-century hand:] "par s? de comon? et par main ... de? entre le comte de provence e la religion d'ospital de Jerusalem ou le sier? compte donne? a la d[ite?] religion toutz droitz de jury? ... 1262." [Below, 17th- or early 18th-century hand:] "Thoard[?] Extraict de transaction Entre le Roy Charles d'Aniou compte de provence et noble ferand de Barras commandeur de l'hospital de Sainct Jean de H. Jerusalem Juillet 1262. ed.[?] Charles estoit frere de St Louis Roy de france." Purchased from L. C. Witten in 1959 by Thomas E. Marston.

Bibliography: Faye and Bond, p. 92. no. 241.

Marston MS 242 England, ca. 1466-67
Genealogical Roll Chronicle, in Middle English

Column I: [Prologue:] Consideryng the lenght and the hardnesse of holy scripture and nameli of the grund of the lettre historial ... [concludes with Edward IV, and his daughter "Elizabeth princesse:"] Edwarde the fourthe after the conqueste of Englond son and heyr of the most worshepful prynce Richarde late duke of yorke ... And he was crowned kyng at Westmynster in the eight and twenty day of the mone of Iuny in the yere of oure lorde a thowsand foure hundred sexti and on.

Column II: Adam was made in damascene feeld by the hand of god. and put in a place of delites callyd paradise ... Harry the sexte was sone of Harry the fithe. and he was crowned at Westmynster in the yere of our lorde a thousand four hundred twenty and nyne.

Column III: The first age of the world was fro adam un to Noe. The secunde fro Noe vn to abraham ... [text ends when the format become two columns rather than three:] Coylle was kyng after hys fader. a man of gode condicions and of al men he had love. he regned in pece al hys life tyme. and when he died he was buried at yorke.

Parchment, 9.76 m. x 330 mm. Composed of 15 membranes, each measuring ca. 705 mm. in length; the individual membranes are glued together, overlapping ca. 15 mm. Approximately the first half of the roll is written in 3 columns, the third (right column) being considerably more narrow. Remainder of roll in 2 columns. Single vertical bounding lines; ruled in pale brown ink. Prickings in left and right margins.

Written by a single scribe in a somewhat rough textura; the hand of this scribe illustrated in *Lyell Cat.*, pl. VI.

The genealogical diagrams, which are fitted into the empty spaces between the columns of text, begin with a roundel formed of concentric bands of blue, gold and red with a miniature of Adam with Eve, who is being handed an apple by the serpent. According to K. L. Scott, the style of the decoration is very close to that in Copenhagen, Kongelige Bibliothek, Ny Kgl. 1858 fol., a Latin roll perhaps decorated by the same artist as Marston MS 242 (see K. L. Scott, *A Survey of Manuscripts Illuminated in the British Isles: Later Gothic Manuscripts*, gen. ed. J. J. G. Alexander, v. 6, forthcoming 1992; Marston MS 242 is cited under no. 116). From the roundel of Adam and Eve to the Ascension of Christ the successive Biblical names, framed in orange or green squares, are linked by a continuous band in blue, red and gold. The names of the ancestors of the Kings of England, starting with Brutus, appear in red or blue circles, surmounted by gold crowns. Other names are in plain red circles. Linking lines in the genealogies are in red or green. At the appropriate places in the text are inserted schematized diagrams in red and green ink of Noah's Ark, a plan of the Israelite camp in the desert and a plan of the city of Jerusalem. One large illuminated initial for the prologue, 8-line, mauve and blue with white filigree against gold ground thinly edged in black. The initial is filled with a large flower, red, yellow and green, and curling acanthus, orange and green extending into the margin and continued as black inkspray with large leaves, heart-shaped or acanthus, blue, pink, orange, white and green with white filigree, a large orange and gold flower, smaller leaves in gold with blue and pink, gold dots and small green leaves, extending into the upper and left margin to form a partial border. Smaller illuminated initial for the beginning of the main chronicle, 5-line, gold on blue and mauve ground with white filigree. Numerous small initials, 2-line, alternate in gold with blue penwork and blue with red. Paragraph marks alternate in red and blue.

Unbound.

Written in England "not earlier than February 1466 and presumably no later than August 1467" (*Lyell Cat.*, p. 82), since only Elizabeth is included as Edward IV's child; Marston MS 242 is closely related to a number of genealogical chronicles of the English kings that were produced at a workshop in London or Westminster in either roll or codex format. For a discussion of these manuscripts see K. L. Scott, *op. cit.*, and *Lyell Cat.* pp. 82–85 (Marston MS 242 cited on p. 82). These manuscripts are Oxford, Bod. Lib., Lyell 33 and Bodl. e. Mus. 42, Corpus Christi College 207; Copenhagen, Kongelige Bibl. MS Ny Kgl. 1858 fol.; London, B. L., Harl. Rolls C. 9; Cambridge, Trinity College R. 4. 3; London, B. L. Stowe 73; Cambridge, Magdalene College Pepys 2244; London, B. L., Add. 31950; Oxford, Brasenose College 17; London, B. L., Stowe 72; London, B. L., Royal 14. B. viii; Oxford, All Souls 40. Marston MS 242 appears to be the earliest of the *A* type versions. Undeciphered contemporary inscription, mostly erased, at top of roll. On dorse, later inscription: "Authentik Pedigree from Adam to Edward 4. Rex Angl[iae]." Provenance otherwise unknown. In the Sotheby's sale of 15 June 1959, no. 194. Purchased from C. A. Stonehill in 1959 by Thomas E. Marston (bookplate).

Bibliography: Faye and Bond, p. 92, no. 242.

The Medieval Book, p. 92, no. 90, with plate.

A. Alison, "Yorkist Propaganda: Pedigree, Prophecy and the 'British History' in the Reign of Edward IV," in *Patronage, Pedigree and Power in Later Medieval England*, ed. C. Ross (Gloucester, 1979) p. 190, n. 15.

L. M. Matheson, "Historical Prose," in *Middle English Prose: A Critical Guide to Major Authors and Genres*, ed. A. S. G. Edwards (New Brunswick, N. J., 1984) p. 235.

Marston MS 243 — England, s. XV^1
Richard Rolle, etc.

1. f. 1r Hee sunt reliquie que habentur in ecclesia appellatiua [?] in qua requie sit corpus beati Jacobi sebedei. Primo corpus beati Jacobi nepotis virginis marie fratris Johannis apostoli . . . Item vna spinorum corone christi.

   List of relics in an unidentified church of St. James, probably in Spain (at Compostela?), given the Saints listed and the contents of art. 2. Individuals mentioned include James the Greater, Athanasius and his disciple Theodore, bishop Fructuosus, Silvester martyr, Cucufas, James the Less (head and tooth only).

2. f. 1r–v Hee sunt indulgencie concesse a sanctis patribus . . . ad ecclesiam beati Iacobi . . . et si veniendo discesserit omnia sunt ei remissa. [list of indulgences, ending:] veniendo vel redeundo discesserit ab omnibus peccatis sicut penitus absolutus.

Indulgences for various prayers, masses, etc. when visiting the church of St. James (cf. art. 1).

3. ff. 2r–3v We chul vndirstond þ[t] we must leue ȝoure synnes and not delite in hem but bewar of hem and of þ[e] .v. soteltes of þ[e] fend as it chewith in þ[e] last ende of þ[s] boke in þ[e] last lef [cf. art. 9] and vse gede vertuse whech may be conceiued in oure hertes ... and blisse to man for his wel worchinge.

Unidentified Middle English devotional text.

4. f. 3v Dominus Ihesus christus pro sua magna pietate perpetue te absoluat et ego te absoluo autoritate mihi commissa ... Accipe spiritum sanctum et viuas in secula seculorum.

Unidentified prayer, probably a form of absolution related to indulgences in art. 2.

5. ff. 4r–14r *Incipit speculum peccatoris.* Quoniam carissime in huius via vite fugientes sumus. dies nostri sicut umbra pretereunt. necesse est igitur corde solicito memorari ... quomodo sane sapies quomodo recte intelliges et quomodo nouissima tua prudenter prouideas// Explicit speculum peccatoris.

Ps.-Augustine, Ps.-Bernard, etc., and wrongly attributed to Richard Rolle, *Speculum peccatoris,* ending imperfectly. PL 40.983–92; Stegmüller, no. 1481. See also H. E. Allen, *Writings Ascribed to Richard Rolle Hermit of Hampole* (New York and London, 1927) p. 353.

6. ff. 14v–42r Libellus Ricardi heremite de hampole de emendacione peccatoris siue de modo viuendi et vocatur libellus iste Regula perfeccionis qui continet in se xij capitula videlicet. *De emendacione peccatoris. Capitulum I[m].* Ne tardes conuerti ad dominum et ne differas de die in diem [Eccli. 5.8]. Nam subito rapit miseros in clemencia mortis ... et cum ineffabili gloria iubilacione et melodia ipsum eternaliter laudare ... Amen. Explicit Regula perfeccionis. ff. 42v–43v blank

Richard Rolle, *De emendatione vitae*; Bloomfield, *Virtues and Vices,* no. 3191 (Marston MS 243 not cited); Allen, *op. cit.*, pp. 230–45 (this manuscript cited on p. 238, LXIX).

7. ff. 44r–102v [Title in upper margin:] Oleum effusum. [text:] Expulsus a paradiso pro transgressione diuini precepti in pomo vetito. primus parens cum posteritate sua astrictus ... in tua dulcedine te mecum et meis comendo sine fine. Amen. Amen. Explicit Oleum effusum.

Richard Rolle, *Oleum effusum* (final four sections of the *Comment on the*

Canticles); Allen, *op. cit.*, pp. 62–88 (this manuscript cited on p. 66, XIV).

8. ff. 102v–106r [I]gnorancia sacerdotum populum precipitat in foueam erroris et clericorum stulticia uel ruditas ... si puro corde quia [or *quoque*?] animo detrahetur.... [added below:] Versus. Clamat intra polum vox sanguinis vox sodomorum vox oppressorum merces ... retenta laborum.

   John of Peckham, extract from *Constitutiones*; Bloomfield, *Virtues and Vices*, no. 2501.

9. f. 106r–v Kyng pharao had v soteltes or wiles. þ^t he dede to þ^e children of israell þei [?] betokene þ^e wiles of þ^e ffend. This is þ^e first he graunted þ^t goddis peple schuld go ... for þus þei lese al here gode werkes of kynd and þ^e mede þ^t chuld sue of hem. [added later:] Verte iam ad primum folium libri [cf. art. 3].

   A previously unrecorded text of the Middle English *The Five Wiles of the Pharaoh* (we thank A. S. G. Edwards for this identification); see Jolliffe K 7 (a) for other texts.

Parchment (thick), ff. iv (original parchment flyleaves; i = pastedown, now lifted; ff. i, 1–3) + 104 (ff. 4–107; f. 107 = pastedown, now lifted). 171 x 113 mm. Folios 4r–102r: written space 115 x 75 mm.; 25 long lines; single horizontal and vertical bounding lines, full across; ruled in lead. Irregular formats for ff. i, 1–3, 102v–106.

I^4 (ff. i, 1–3), II–XIV^8. Catchwords, lower margin near gutter, verso. Quire and leaf signatures (e.g., a j., a ij., beginning on f. 4) lower margin, recto; some quires also signed with letters of the alphabet, verso.

Arts. 5–7 written by a single scribe in anglicana bookhand (cf. Parkes, *Cursive Book Hands*, pl. 2, ii). Other texts by contemporary scribes in less careful bookhands, with art. 4 in a less formal hand.

Flourished initials of good quality, 4- to 2-line, blue with red penwork designs incorporating leaf motifs and marginal extensions. Headings in red. Paragraph marks in blue.

Binding: England, s. xv. Original, caught up sewing with very heavy thread on four tawed skin, slit straps laced from out to inside beech boards and pegged in channels which are filled with gesso [?]. Green and gold, beaded endbands are sewn on cord cores laid in grooves in the outside of the boards. Spine lined with tawed skin.

Covered in tawed skin, originally pink, with two fastenings, the catches on the lower board, the upper one cut in for brown leather straps. Spine covering disintegrating, thus exposing sewing. Covers much worm eaten.

Written in England in the first half of the 15th century. Belonged in the 15th century to the Augustinian priory of St. Mary Overy in Southwark, Surrey; its ex libris, f. 102v: "liber Sancte Marie Ouerey In Sowthwerke" (see N. R. Ker, *Medieval Libraries of Great Britain*, 2nd ed. [London, 1964] pp. 180–81, and A. G. Watson, *Supplement to the Second Edition* [London, 1987] p. 63). Early inscription on f. i verso indicates that the manuscript was given by William Baldwin to Henry Vesey ("Ex dono Guiliel. Baldwini/ Henr. Vesey"). Sold at Sotheby's, 2 March 1921, no. 275, and bought by Sir Leicester Harmsworth (see Allen, *op. cit.*, p. 238); his sale (Sotheby's, 16 October 1945, no. 2091). Modern notes in pencil on f. i: "29" in a circle (*bis*), "967." Purchased in 1956 from Maggs Bros., London, by L. C. Witten (inv. no. 1099), who sold it in 1959 to Thomas E. Marston (bookplate).

secundo folio: [f. 5r:] qui suum

Bibliography: Faye and Bond, p. 92, no. 243.

Marston MS 245 — Bohemia, s. XV[1]

Proverbs, Ecclesiastes, Song of Songs, Wisdom, Ecclesiasticus — Pls. 54, 62

1. ff. 1r–165r *Incipit prephacio sancti ieronimi presbiteri in parabolas*. Iungat epistola quos iungit sacerdotium. ymmo carta non diuidat . . . seruauerunt. *Explicit prephacio*. [Stegmüller 457; text, f. 2r:] *Incipit liber salomonis parabole. Capitulum*. Parabole salomonis filij dauid regis israel ad sciendam sapientiam . . . opera eius. [f. 42v:] *Incipit prologus beati Ieronimi in librum Ecclesiastes*. Nemini [*sic*; *m* written by rubricator above initial *N*] me ferme hoc quinquennio cum adhuc rome essem . . . consectarer. [Stegmüller 462; text, f. 43r:] *Incipit liber Ecclesiastes. Capitulum primum*. Uerba ecclesiastes filij dauid regis ierusalem. Vanitas vanitatum . . . siue malum sit. [f. 58r:] *Incipit liber Canticorum Salomonis. Capitulum primum*. Osculetur me osculo oris sui . . . aromatum. *Explicit liber canticorum Beati Ieronimi*. [f. 66v:] *Incipit prologus*. Liber sapiencie aput hebreos nusquam est . . . exprimitur. [Stegmüller 468; text:] *Incipit liber sapiencie Capitulum primum*. Diligite iusticiam qui iudicatis terram . . . assistens eis. [f. 96r:] *Incipit prologus Beati Ieronimi super Ecclesiasticum*. Multorum nobis et magnorum. per legem et prophetas . . . vitam agere. [Stegmüller 26; text, f. 97r:] *Incipit liber Ihesu filij Syrach Capitulum primum*. Omnis sapiencia a domino deo est. et cum illo semper . . . mercedem vestram in tempore suo.

   Books of Proverbs, Ecclesiastes, Song of Songs, Wisdom and Ecclesiasticus, preceded by prologues as noted above.

2. f. 165v O bone Iesu O dulcis Iesu O Iesu fili virginis marie plenus misericordia et ueritate ... ne perdat me iniquitas. f. 166r ruled, but blank

   Cf. *Lyell Cat.*, p. 386, no. 246.

3. ff. 166v–167r [S]tabat mater dolorosa iuxta crucem lacrimosa dum pendebat ... paradisi gloria. f. 167v blank

   RH 19416.

Parchment, ff. 166 (i = front flyleaf; modern foliation 1–165) + ii (contemporary parchment, ff. 166–167), 128 x 85 (80 x 50) mm. 2 columns, 25 lines. Single vertical bounding lines; two additional rulings for running headlines in upper margin. Ruled in ink. Prickings in upper, lower and outer margins.

I^{12} (1 = front flyleaf), $II–XII^{12}$, XIII^{16}, XIV^{6}. Remains of catchwords in lower margin near gutter, verso. Quires signed with Arabic numerals, mostly trimmed, center of lower margin, verso.

Written in hybrida script by a single scribe. Arts. 2–3 added by later hands.

For prologues and beginning of each book partial borders constructed of a thin bar, unburnished gold, pink or green with burnished gold balls, terminating in sprays of stylized foliage, green, pink, and blue with gold accents. One large illuminated initial, f. 1r, 13-line, blue with light blue foliage shading against a red and pink ground; foliage serifs in green. 6 smaller illuminated initials, blue, pink, green or gold against blue or pink ground with white or gold filigree and/or gold crosshatching. Numerous pen-and-ink initials, 2-line, alternate in blue with red penwork designs and gold with blue penwork designs. Running titles in red and blue. Headings in red. Initials touched with yellow.

Binding: Bohemia, s. xv. Sewn on three supports, with two half bands near head and tail, fastened to wooden boards. Yellow edges and kermes pink place marks.

Covered in brown calf, blind-tooled with floral designs, with a central and four large corner fittings on each board. Spine: supports defined with double fillets; four leafy flower bud tools pointing inward in the two central panels. Two fastenings, the catches on the upper board and the lower one cut in for tawed skin, cream colored straps (only stubs remain). Small pieces of liturgical manuscript (Northern Italy, s. XIV) used for front and rear pastedowns. Head and tail of spine and the upper joint very unobtrusively repaired.

Written in Bohemia in the first half of the 15th century, given the close similarity of its script, decoration and binding to Oxford, Bodleian Library MS Laud Misc. 516, a New Testament written in Czech (Pächt and Alexander, v. 1, no. 161). 16th-century inscription of Heinrich Schkor von Stranov on verso of front flyleaf: "1542/ diss puechle gehert zu dem Edlen vnd Vesten [?] hainrichen schkor [followed by hole in parchment] von stranoff [Stranov in Bohemia] derzait haubtman zu prukh an der layta [Bruck an der Leitha, Southeast Austria]/ 15 A 47 [*sic*]...". Belonged to the Bibliotecha Thallensis in 1776 (inscription on front flyleaf, verso). Acquired from B. M. Rosenthal in 1959 by Thomas E. Marston (bookplate).

secundo folio: [dog]matum confirmandam

Bibliography: Faye and Bond, p. 92, no. 245.

Marston MS 247 — Florence, s. XV^{med}
Miscellany of Italian *dicerie*

I. 1. f. i recto [List of books, s. XVI:] 1. Libro delle pistole numero primo choperto d'asse; 2. Libro di valerio maximo coperto in asse numero 2; 3. Libro di dante leghato in asse numero 3; 4. Libro di aiolfo in asse numero 4; 5. Libro del petrarcha legato con asse numero 5; 6. Libro de morali de S. Jeronimo con asse numero 6; 7. Libro di Giovanni colombinj in asse numero 7; 8. Libro delle prediche di fra Girolamo in asse numero 8; 9. Libro di ella [*sic*] bibbia in asse numero 9; 10. Libro della prima parte della vita di Plotarcho in Cartone numero 10; 11. Libro della seconda parte del detto libro numero 11; 12. Libro dell'arte della ghuerra di niccolo machiavelli in Carta pecora [remainder of line trimmed]; 13. Libro de discorsi del machiavello in carta pecora numero 13; 14. Libro di appiano alexandrino in Carta pecora numero 14; 15. Libro d'ameto del bochacio in Carta pecora numero 15 [D. Dutschke, "Un Quinto Elenco di Codici," *Studi sul Boccaccio* 13 (1981–82) p. 7]; 16. Libro di storie del machiavello in Carta pecora numero 16; 17. Libro di Comedie in Carta pecora numero 17; 18. Libro del pellegrino in Carta pecora numero 18; 19. Libriccioli del bochaccio in Carta pecora numero 19 [Dutschke, *op.cit.*, p. 7]; 20. Libro di fioretti della bibbia numero 20; 21. Libriccino di S. Doratea numero 21; 22. Libro di Commentarij di Iulio Cieseri numero 22. f. i verso blank

II. Marston MS 247 contains a miscellany of vernacular humanistic prose texts very similar to other manuscripts listed by P. Kristeller, *Marsilio Ficino letterato e le glosse attribuite a lui nel codice Caetani di Dante, Quaderni della Fondazione Camillo Caetani* III (Rome, 1981) Appendix I, pp. 59-62 (with Marston MS 247 cited in no. 13). Beinecke MS 329, a similar humanistic collection, will also be cited in the following identifications; for a description of the manuscript see v. 2 of this catalogue, pp. 147–51.

2. ff. 1r–2v [Heading:] *[T]avola de questo libro.* [table:] *Epistola di Messer Giovanni boccacci mandata a Messer Pino de Rossi quando fu cacciato da firençe Robrica ja . . . Sermone di Aristothele che tratta di giustitia Robrica .Lvj.* ff. 3r–4v ruled, but blank

   Table of contents, in red throughout

3. ff. 5r–19v *[E]pistola. di. Messer. Giovanni. Boccacci. mandata. a. Messer. Pino de Rossi. quando. fu. cacciato. da. Firenze. Robrica Prima. Io extimo messer pino che* sia non solamente utile . . . Et sança piu dire prego idio che consoli voi et loro.

   Giovanni Boccaccio, *Lettera Consolatoria a Messer Pino de' Rossi*; N. Bruscoli, ed., *L'Ameto, Lettere, Il Corbaccio* (Bari, 1940) pp. 159–82. The manuscript has several omissions probably due to scribal error; f. 8r has the interpolation "Lucio quinto cincinnato" which is found in the majority of manuscripts (see Bruscoli, *op. cit.*, pp. 283–84).

4. ff. 19v–26r *Epistola di messer francesco petracca* [sic] *fiorentino mandata al famosissimo huomo Messer Niccola acciaiuoli gran siniscalco sopra la incoronatione del Re Luixi, Robrica ij.* Nell'ultimo o huomo famosissimo la fede ha vinto la perfidia . . . secondo che Tullio scrive volera alle sedie del cielo. Vale honore della patria et di noi.

   Petrarch, translation of *Rerum familiarum* XII.2. A different translation of this letter was published by G. Orti, *Volgarizzamento d'una pistola del Petrarca a N. Acciaiuoli siniscalco del Regno di Puglia* (Verona, 1834). The translation in Marston MS 247 is also found in Chapel Hill, University of North Carolina, MS 12 (Dutschke, no. 26, pp. 92–93); Florence, Biblioteca Riccardiana MSS 1073, 1074, 1080; Florence, Biblioteca Nazionale Centrale, Palatino 598; New Haven, Beinecke MS 329.

5. ff. 26v–27r *Risposta di Messere Stephano de porcari da Roma electo capitano del popolo di firençe agli electionari quando gli dierono la electione del capitanato. Robrica iij.* Io cognosco magnifici electionarii della inclita et famosa cicta di firençe . . . et promecto pienamente adempiere et observare.

Stefano Porcari, ed. G. B. C. Giuliari, *Prose del Giovane Buonaccorso da Montemagno* (Bologna, 1874) pp. 85–87. The text of Marston MS 247 is close to that of Beinecke MS 329 (ff. 42v–43r) which contains twelve Porcari orations. The same sixteen orations (here arts. 5–20) are found in Florence, Biblioteca Riccardiana 1074 and 1080; Florence, Biblioteca Nazionale Centrale, Palatino 598 (*I manoscritti della Biblioteca Nazionale di Firenze, Sezione Palatina* pp. 169–72); Siena, Biblioteca Comunale J VI 25 (Kristeller, *Iter Italicum*, v. 2, p. 167).

6. f. 27r–v *Risposta facta per decto messere stephano in sancta maria del fiore quando gli fu dato il giuramento nella sua venuta. Robrica iiij.* Io ho udito magnifici et excelsi signor miei quanto per lo vostro egregio et doctissimo cancelliere . . . et di questo florentissimo popolo.

   Stefano Porcari; Giuliari, *op. cit.*, pp. 75–77.

7. ff. 27v–28v *Risposta facta per decto Messer Stephano a Signori quando gli dierono la bacchecta. Robrica .v.* Beatus su[m] in hiis que dicta sunt mihi. Magnifici et gloriosi signor miei. Io debbo meritamente usare le predecte parole del psalmista . . . populo fiorentino.

   Stefano Porcari; Giuliari, *op. cit.*, pp. 88–90.

8. ff. 28v–29v *Risposta facta per decto Messer Stephano a uno protesto facto per la signoria a Rectori. Robrica .vj.* Magnifici et prestantissimi Signor miei, et prudentissimi et venerabili collegi. Rivolgendomi io spesso nella mente . . . allo extremo della humanita nostra perdurre. Custodiam legem tuam semper in seculum seculi.

   Stefano Porcari; Giuliari, *op. cit.*, pp. 102–5.

9. ff. 29v–31v *Risposta facta per decto Messer Stephano a un altro protesto facta per la Signoria a Rectori. Robrica .vij.* Piu volte ho in me medesimo considerato . . . certamente conservare et amplificare. Qui est benedictus in secula seculorum Amen.

   Stefano Porcari; Giuliari, *op. cit.*, pp. 106–11.

10. ff. 31v–33r *Oratione del decto Messer Stephano a Signori et collegi essendo rifermo capitano dove lascia la risposta del protesto et rende gratie della riferma. Robrica .viij.* Quando io considero magnifici et potentissimi signori miei la grandeça di tanti vostri inverso di me comulatissimi benificij . . . et constanti convenientemente meritare.

    Stefano Porcari; Giuliari, *op. cit.*, pp. 69–74.

11. ff. 33r–34r *Risposta facta per decto Messer Stephano a uno protesto facto per la Signoria a rectori. Robrica .viiij.* In mandatis tuis exercebor et considerabo vias tuas in iustificationibus tuis meditabor non obliviscar sermones tuos. Gloriosi et excelsi Signor miei secondo el mio piccolo giudicio Ad me pare . . . et pace del vostro felicissimo populo.

Stefano Porcari; Giuliari, *op. cit.*, pp. 91–94.

12. ff. 34r–36v *Risposta per decto Messer Stefano a un altro protesto. Robrica .x.* Beatus homo quem tu erudieris, et de lege tua docueris eum. psalmo nonagesimo secundo. Rivolgendo alla vostra excellentia le parole . . . et giustissima Republica per infinita secula seculorum.

Stefano Porcari; Giuliari, *op. cit.*, pp. 95–101.

13. ff. 36v–37v *Risposta di decto messer Stephano a un altro protesto. Robrica .xj.* Quanto piu considero illustri et excelsi Signor miei, i decreti ordini . . . partendo dalle parole proposte. Custodiam legem tuam.

Stefano Porcari; Giuliari, *op. cit.*, pp. 81–84.

14. ff. 37v–40r *Oratione prima facta per Messere Stephano de porcari da roma capitano predecto et decta in su la ringhiera del palagio della cicta di firençe all'entrata de signori. Robrica .xij.* Quante volte io riguardo e dignissimi et giocondissimi conspecti vostri . . . et riposo di questa florentissima Republica ne seguira.

Stefano Porcari; Giuliari, *op. cit.*, pp. 1–11.

15. ff. 40v–45v *Oratione seconda facta per decto messer Stephano in su la ringhiera all'entrare de nuovi Signori. Robrica .xiij.* Io mi ricordo Magnifici Signori Venerabili collegi et prudentissimi cictadini altra volta . . . et gratia si come negli amplissimi et singulari vostri ingegni.

Stefano Porcari; Giuliari, *op. cit.*, pp. 12–27.

16. ff. 45v–52v *Oratione terça facta pel decto Messer Stephano in su la ringhiera all'entrata de nuovi Signori. Robrica .xiiij.* [f. 46r] Se alcuna volta e stato smarrito el mio piccolo ingegno . . . cha la ymagine de vostri benifici fixa nella memoria si serba.

Stefano Porcari; Giuliari, *op. cit.*, pp. 28–49.

17. ff. 52v–56r *Oratione facta per decto Messer Stephano in su la ringhi-*

era del palagio all'entrare de nuoui Signori. Robrica .xv. Molte considerationi m'occorrono all'animo Magnifici et potenti Signori ... la qual cosa fare vi conceda. Qui benedictus est in secula seculorum Amen.

Stefano Porcari; Giuliari, *op. cit.*, pp. 50–60.

18. f. 56r–v *Oratione facta per decto Messer Stephano quando rende la bacchetta. Robrica .xvj.* Questo di Illustri Signor miei finisce la mia administratione ... vi rassegno le insegne del mio magistrato da voi ricevuto.

Stefano Porcari; Giuliari, *op. cit.*, pp. 61–63.

19. ff. 56v–58r *Oratione facta per decto Messer Stephano quando pre* [sic] *licentia da Signori. Robrica .xvij.* Se mai per alcun tempo ho desiderato alcuna vivacita d'ingegno ... ma mai mentre mi durera la vita i lassero d'amare. Son tutto vostro.

Stefano Porcari; Giuliari, *op. cit.*, pp. 64–68.

20. ff. 58v–59r *Oratione facta per decto Messer Stephano a papa Martino quando ritorno a roma. Robrica .xviij.* Se mai nel corso di mia vita l'ardente desiderio mio ... a i piedi della quale l'humile creatura vostra racomando.

Stefano Porcari; Giuliari, *op. cit.*, pp. 78–80.

21. ff. 59r–61r *Oratione di messer francesco philelpho facta nel principio della lectione et dispositione di dante in sancta Maria del fiore. Robrica .xviiij.* Se lo splendido et il campeggiante [*sic*] fulgore de nostri animi ... et deboleça del mio povero ingegno o vero doctrina.

Francesco Filelfo, oration on Dante published by G. Benaducci, "Prose e poesie volgari di Francesco Filelfo," *Atti e memorie della R. Deputazione di storia patria per le province delle Marche* 5 (1901) pp. 1–5.

22. ff. 61r–63r *Sermone di Messer francesco philelpho che tratta della liberta. Robrica .xx.* Pavendo gia piu et piu volte magnifici et egregi cictadini ... insieme alla morte come veri amici sguardarvi.

Francesco Filelfo, oration on freedom; Benaducci, *op. cit.*, pp. 37–39.

23. ff. 63r–65v *Sermone facto per Messer francesco philelpho trattando di giustitia. Robrica .xxj.* Euripide poeta huomo non solo di eloquen-

tia singulare ... idio somma retributione et gratia sempiterna.

Francesco Filelfo, oration on justice; Benaducci, *op. cit.*, pp. 40–44.

24. ff. 65v–68r *Sermone facto per Messer francesco philelpho trattando di liberalita. Robrica .xxij.* Non piccolo spavento al presente nel mio animo tutto affannato ... et divina gloria sempre acquisterete.

Ps.-Leonardo Bruni, *De liberalitate*; Baron, pp. 186–87. According to J. Hankins, this work was probably composed by a student of Filelfo. Text published by E. Santini, "La 'protestatio de iustitia' a Firenze" *Rinascimento* 10 (1959) pp. 93–96; also Benaducci, *op. cit.*, pp. 33–36.

25. ff. 68r–70r *Oratione facta per uno scolare forestiero in sancta Maria del fiore di firençe confortando e cictadini fiorentini a mantenere et acrescere lo studio delle discipline et arte liberali. Robrica .xxiij.* Quando la magnifica et la observantissima moltitudine ... possiate et prestissimamente conseguitare.

Italian oration allegedly by a foreign scholar to encourage the Florentines to maintain the study of the liberal arts. Also found in Beinecke MS 329 (ff. 67r–69v); Florence, Biblioteca Nazionale Centrale, Palatino 598 (*op. cit.*, p. 171, no. VI).

26. ff. 70v–75r *Copia d'una epistola mandata a uno sanato d'una gravissima infermita. Robrica .xxiiij.* Onde nasce dilectissimo mio tanto spirito et tanta sanctimonia di tua vita quanto io veggo ... Et onde questo nasca tu stesso lo giudica. Nec plura vale cum domino.

Copy of a letter sent to an individual cured from a serious illness. Also found in Florence, Biblioteca Nazionale Centrale, Palatino 598 (*op. cit.*, p. 172, no. IX).

27. ff. 75v–81v *Protesto facto per lo spectabile cavaliere Messer giannoço Manecti a Rectori di firençe in palagio dinançi a Signori et a essi Rectori. Robrica .xxv.* Volendo e nostri magnifici et excelsi Signori seguitare gli ordini ... di tale protestatione voi Ser Zanobi a chui s'aspecta ne sarete rogato.

Giannozzo Manetti, oration still unpublished but discussed along with its manuscript tradition by H. Wittschier, *Giannozzo Manetti, Das Corpus der Orationes* (Köln, 1968) pp. 66–69. Also found in Beinecke MS 329 (ff. 83v–89r); Florence, Biblioteca Nazionale Centrale, Palatino 598.

28. ff. 82r–98v *Oratione di Messer Giannoço Manecti et di Bernardo de medici commessari generali del felice campo del Magnifico populo fiorentino, facta in domenica a di .xxx. di septembre nel .MccccLiij. quano* [sic] *e dierono l'auctorita del governo et il bastone alla presentia di tutto l'exercito presso alla terra di Vada al Magnifico Signore et strenuo capitano Signor Messer Gismondo Pandolpho de Malatesti. Robrica .xxvj.* E' puo essere noto alle Magnificentie vostre Magnifici Signori et voi altri strenui condoctieri ... et della vostra magnifica et illustre persona et cosi piaccia a dio che sia.

Giannozzo Manetti, oration printed in *Collezione di opere inedite o rare dei primi tre secoli della lingua,* published by the R. Commissione pe' testi di lingua nelle provincie dell'Emilia, v. 2 *Commentario della Vita di Messer Giannozzo Manetti scritto da Vespasiano Bisticci aggiuntevi altre vite inedite del medesimo e certe cose volgari di esso Giannozzo,* edited by P. Fanfani, pp. 203–28. The oration is discussed with reference to manuscripts in Wittschier, *op. cit.*, pp. 127–33. Here key topics and proper names appear in margins, in red.

29. ff. 98v–101v *Sermone focto* [sic] *per messer Lionardo d'areço Al magnifico capitano niccolo da tolentino capitano di guera del comune di firençe quando ricevecte il bastone in su la ringhiera de' signori la mattina di sancto Giovani baptista. Robrica .xxvij.* Di tutti gli exercitij humani magnifico et prestantissimo capitano che sono ... a perpetua exaltatione et gloria della cicta nostra et fama immortale di voi Magnifico Capitano Amen.

Leonardo Bruni, *De laudibus exercitii armorum*; Baron, p. 175. O. Gamurrini, ed., *Orazione di Leonardo Bruni Aretino detta a Nicolò da Tolentino* (Florence, 1877).

30. f. 102r–v *Lectera composta per messer Lionardo d'areço in nome della Magnifica signoria di firençe Mandata al poplo della cicta di volterra tornati che furono alla divotione del comune di firençe. Robrica .xxviij.* Nobiles viri amici karissimi. Le cose humane secondo che ne monstra la experientia ... come veri figliuoli di questa Signoria. Data florentie die .xxx. ottobrio Mccccxxxi. Priores artium et Vixillifer iustitie populi et comunis florentie.

Leonardo Bruni, letter to the city of Volterra; L. A. Cecina and F. Dal Borgo, eds., *Notizie istoriche della città di Volterra* (Pisa, 1758) p. 229.

31. ff. 102v–103v *Oratione composta per messer Lionardo d'areço quan-*

do Messer giuliano davançati ando ambasciadore al Re di Ragona. Robrica .xxviiij. Se ad altro principe che ad te venissimo gloriosissimo Re . . . quando el tempo el luogo ci fia dato quelle referiremo.

Leonardo Bruni, *Oratio domini Leonardi coram Alphonso Aragonum rege*, anonymous It. tr.; Latin text edited by E. Santini, "Leonardo Bruni Aretino e i suoi 'Historiarum Florentini populi libri XII'," *Annali della R. Scuola Normale Superiore* 22 (1910) p.167. Baron, pp. 177–78.

32. ff. 103v–112v *Epistola di Messer Lionardo d'areço mandata al Signore di manthova trattando della orrigine* [sic] *di Mantoa. Robrica .xxx.* Non e ignoto generosissimo Signore questa essere consuetudine degli huomini licterati . . . gente di ytalia accio che io sança invidia parli in feruore.

Leonardo Bruni, Epistle X.25 (IV.13), anonymous It. tr. Text also found in Florence, Biblioteca Riccardiana 1074 (Morpurgo, *op.cit.*, p. 62, no. IV, no. 2).

33. ff. 112v–114r *Epistola di Don Giovanni delle celle di valle ombrosa a Guido di Messer Tomaso confortandolo della morte del figliuolo. Robrica .xxxj.* Al venerabile in Christo caro divoto Guido Don Giovanni patientia nelle tribulationi. Pensando io alcuna volta di scriverti . . . del mondo della carne et delle demonia. Mandata a Guido a di .ij. di novembre MccсLxxxviij.

Don Giovanni delle Celle, Letter; A. Levasti, ed., *Mistici del Duecento e del Trecento* (Milan, 1960) pp. 792–95, where it is dated December 2, 1388.

34. ff. 114r–115v *Epistola di Guido di Messer Tomaso mandata a don Giovanni delle celle risposta a questa di sopra. Robrica .xxxij.* Venerabile et devotissimo padre carissimo. Ricevecti vostra lectera la quale piu tosto et meglio si dee chiamare epistola . . . con quegli che ci amano ci possiamo trovare. Data in firençe a di iiij d'ottobre [*sic*] .M.cccLxxxviij. perdonatemi se io vi tedio con troppo scrivere.

Guido di Messer Tommaso del Palagio, Letter responding to that in art. 33 above. Text also found in Florence, Biblioteca Riccardiana 1074 (Morpurgo, *op.cit.*, p. 67, no. XXXIII).

35. ff. 115v–125v *Epistola di Marsilio fecino mandata a Cherubino Agnola Daniello Anselmo Beatrice. Robrica .xxxiij.* Perche l'opera del buono fratelli dilectissimi e ben fare . . . fruiranno la divina essentia possedendo infinita et sempiterna gloria.

Marsilio Ficino, *Epistola ad fratres vulgaris*; P. Kristeller, ed., *Supplementum Ficinianum* II (Florence, 1937) pp. 109–28.

36. ff. 125v–135r *Marsilio fecino di dio et d'anima et prima di dio. Robrica .xxxiiij.* La nostra singulare amicitia richiede che non manchi in alcuna cosa . . . che chi piu ne cerca spesse volte pare che piu ne rimanga confuso.

Marsilio Ficino, *Treatise on God and the Soul*, in It.; Kristeller, *op. cit.*, pp. 128–58 (but here text breaks off on p. 141, continues in art. 37 below). In other manuscripts, this text is addressed to Francesco Capponi and dated 24 January 1457.

37. ff. 135r–139r *E ssi decto in fino a qui di dio, hora dice fecino de anima. Robrica .xxxv.* Di tutti e philosophi nessuno dixe l'anima essere nulla . . . quella della quale tu se piu lungo tempo stato amico.

Continuation of art. 36.

38. ff. 139r–140v *Epistola di Marsilio fecino dello appitito mandata a [blank]. Robrica .xxxvj.* A una tua epistola nella quale dimandi onde venga nell'animo lo appitito . . . La qual cosa tu conseguiterai se l'animo tuo possedera l'appitito et non sara dallo appetito posseduto.

Marsilio Ficino, *Epistola de appetitu vulgaris*; Kristeller, *op. cit.*, pp. 158–61. In other manuscripts this text is addressed to Lionardo di Tone Pagni and dated 25 March 1460.

39. ff. 141r–142v [No title; blank lines are unfilled.] *Robrica .xxxvij.* A rimuovere o in altro modo rimediare alle cose future . . . Tutto questo faremo se s'acordera in noi. potentia. sapientia. et volunta. *Vale.*

Marsilio Ficino, *Epistola de fortuna vulgaris*; Kristeller, *op. cit.*, pp. 169–73; also published by A. Perosa, *Giovanni Rucellai ed il suo "Zibaldone"* (London, 1960) p. 196 (with two more manuscripts cited than are used in Kristeller).

40. ff. 142v–145v [No title; blank lines are unfilled.] *Robrica .xxxviij.* E nell'altra vita passare spesse volte in sogno . . . sarete ben governati quando crederrete che lui governi bene.

Marsilio Ficino, *Visione de Anselmo Ficino*; Kristeller, *op. cit.*, pp. 162–67.

41. ff. 145v–148r *Epistola di san Bernardo mandata al cavaliere Messer Ramondo del castello di sancto ambruogio sopra el governo familiare. Robrica .xxxviiij.* Al gratioso et felice kavaliere messer Ramondo signore del castello ambruoscio. Bernardo divoto in sospiri salute. Admaestrato domandi essere . . . Al quale lei producano e meriti della sua laudabile vecchieça.

Ps.-Bernard of Clairvaux, *Epistola (De gubernatione rei familiaris)*, in It. tr.; this is a different translation from that published by U. Amico, *Epistola di S. Bernardo a Raimondo volgarizzamento del buon secolo* (Bologna, 1866). A similar version appears in Florence, Biblioteca Riccardiana 1074 (Morpurgo, *op.cit.*, p. 62, no. V) and other manuscripts, but Marston MS 247 alone has the explicit "laudabile vecchieça" rather than "dannabile vecchieça."

42. f. 148r–v *Lectera scricta per Lentulo officiale romano in giudea de l'advenimento di christo yhesu. Robrica .xl.* Al tempo di Ottauiano Cesare con cio fussi cosa che di diverse parti del mondo si si scrivessi . . . grave raro et modesto et spatioso intra figliuoli degli huomini.

Ps.-Lentulus, *Epistola de conditione Domini nostri Iesu Christi*, anonymous It. tr.; cf. Marston MS 49, art. 5, for additional bibliography. Text edited by G. Manzi, *Testi di lingua inediti tratti da' codici della Biblioteca Vaticana* (Rome, 1816) pp. 80–81.

43. ff. 148v–154r *Oratione del Re agrippa la quale fece a giudei per sconfortargli della guerra che e volevano muovere contro a romani et rubellarsi da loro per le ingiurie ricevute da Cestio floro el quale era suto mandato da romani al governo della giudea. Robrica .xlj.* Se io non vi vedessi tutti commossi et incitati a fare guerra co romani . . . Impero che io non intendo di seguitarvi a si facte imprese.

Josephus, *De bello iudaico* II.345–401 (Loeb Classical Library [Cambridge, Mass., 1927]), anonymous Italian translation. Text also found in Florence, Biblioteca Riccardiana 1074 (Morpurgo, *op.cit.*, p. 63, no. XI).

44. ff. 154v–155v *Oratione di Marco Cato contro a congiurati di catellina. Robrica .xlij.* Padri conscripti quando io raguardo la congiuratione et pericoli et contrapeso in me medesimo . . . Voi gli vedrete venire fieri et crudelmente contro ad voi.

Sallust, *Catilinae Coniuratio* 52.2–36, It. tr.; Lat. text in A. Kurfess, ed., 3rd ed. (Leipzig, 1957). This is a freer and possibly earlier translation than art. 45 below, and appears to be the same as that in Florence, Biblioteca Riccardiana 1080 (Morpurgo, *op.cit.*, p. 74, no. IX, no. 2).

45. ff. 155v–158r *Oratione di Marco catone in senato sopra a congiurati di catellina. Robrica .xliij.* Molto et in tutto e svariata la mente mia ... che sieno condannati a morte secondo l'usança de nostri maggiori.

Sallust, *Catilinae Coniuratio* 52.2–36, It. tr. This text approximates, but is not identical to, the translation by Frate Bartolommeo da San Concordio (B. Puoti, ed., *Il Catilinario ed il Giugurtino libri due di C. Crispo Sallustio volgarizzati per Frate Bartolommeo da San Concordio* [Naples, 1843]).

46. f. 158r *Prohemio di Ser Brunecto latino nella oratione di Julio Cesare contro a congiurati di Catellina. Robrica .xliiij.* Nel tempo che Cathellina fece la grandissima congiuratione ... parlo coperto et admaestratamente in questa forma dicendo.

Introduction, attributed to Brunetto Latini, to the Italian translation of Sallust (cf. art. 47 below). This appears to be the same prologue as that in Florence, Biblioteca Riccardiana 1080 (Morpurgo, *op.cit.*, p. 74, no. IX, no. 1).

47. ff. 158r–160v *Oratione di Giulio Cesare contro a congiurati di cathellina. Robrica .xlv.* Tucti coloro padri conscripti che vogliono directamente consigliare ... et chi facessi contro ad cio sia messo in prigione con loro insieme.

Sallust, *Catilinae Coniuratio* 51, It. tr. This text does not correspond to the translation of Frate Bartolommeo da San Concordio (see art. 45 above), but appears to be the same as that in Florence, Biblioteca Riccardiana 1080 (Morpurgo, *op.cit.*, p. 74, no. IX, no. 1).

48. ff. 160v–161r *Differentia intra le virtu di Iulio Cesare et quelle di Marco Cato secondo che Salustio ne scrive. Robrica .xlvj.* Marco Cato et Giulio Cesare furono in molte cose ... et pero quanto meno desiderava lode et pregio piu n'avea.

Sallust, *Catilinae Coniuratio* 53.6–54, It. tr. This text appears to be the same as that in Florence, Biblioteca Riccardiana 1080 (Morpurgo, *op.cit.*, p. 74, no. XII).

49. f. 161r–v *Oratione che fece Catellina a suoi cavalieri havendo facte le schiere per prende* [sic] *la battaglia contro a romani. Robrica .xlvij.*

Signori cavalieri io ho provato assai che le parole non danno virtu ... e vostri nimici possano piangere il loro danno gia fussi ben cosa che fussi voi vinti.

Sallust, *Catilinae Coniuratio* 58, It. tr. This is a freer and possibly earlier translation than art. 50 below, and appears to be the same as that in Florence, Biblioteca Riccardiana 1080 (Morpurgo, *op.cit.*, p. 74, no. IX, no. 3) but with a different explicit.

50. f. 162r–v *Oratione di Catellina al suo exercito. Robrica .xlviij.* Io ho provato o Militi che le parole non acrescono la força ne la virtu et che l'exercito non diventa ... a guisa d'huomini voi lasciate sanguinosa et dolorosa victoria a nimici.

Sallust, *Catilinae Coniuratio* 58, It. tr. This very accurate translation does not appear to be that of Frate Bartolommeo da San Concordio (see art. 45 above) or that in Florence, Biblioteca Riccardiana 1080 (see art. 49 above).

51. ff. 162v–163r *Oratione che fece Marco Antonio a suoi cavalieri havendo ordinato le schiere per combattere contro a catellina. Robrica .xlviiij.* Signori ricordivi dello honore et dello stato di roma ... et ho havute grande victorie con molti di quegli ch'io veggio qui.

Oration based on Sallust, *Catilinae Coniuratio* 59.5–6, It. tr. The text appears to be the same as that in Florence, Biblioteca Riccardiana 1080 (Morpurgo, *op.cit.*, p. 74, no. X, where it is wrongly attributed to Marcus Petreius).

52. ff. 163r–164v *Exordium Salustii Iucurtini operis. Robrica L.* A Torto si lamentano gli huomini della loro natura ... Certo io sono andato piu libero et piu altamente che mi rincresce et pesa assai de costumi et de modi della cicta. Ora ritornero al mio proponimento.

Sallust, *Bellum Jugurthinum* 1–4, It. tr.; Puoti, *op. cit.*, pp. 119–25, but text differs significantly.

53. ff. 164v–167v *Gaio Mario contro al nobile Salustio. Robrica .Lj.* Io so Quiriti che molti hanno domandato l'imperio da voi non con quelle arti medesime ... se a temorosi le parole adgiungessimo virtu che a savi et a valorosi io credo havere decto assai.

Sallust, *Bellum Jugurthinum* 85, It. tr.; Puoti, *op. cit.*, pp. 249–57, but text differs significantly.

54. ff. 167v–168r *Oratio Micisse in fine uite sue. Robrica .Lij.* Io ti ricevetti piccolo o Iucurta nel mio regno habiendo tu perduto tuo

padre ... che non paia che io habbia preso et ricevuto migliore figliuolo che quegli ch'io ho generati.

Sallust, *Bellum Jugurthinum* 10, It. tr.; Puoti, *op. cit.*, pp. 132–34, but text differs significantly.

55. f. 168r–v *Preambolo facto a una oratione che Marco Tullio Cicerone fece a Cesare nel quale si mostra la cagione perche. Robrica .Liij.* Dopo le battaglie civili essendo rimaso vincitore delle battaglie Caio Cesare molti nobili cictadini ... el quale levato in pie fece la presente oratione al decto Cesare.

The text appears to be the same as that in Florence, Biblioteca Riccardiana 1080 (Morpurgo, *op. cit.*, p. 73, no. VIII, no. 1) where the prologue is ascribed to Leonardo Bruni.

56. ff. 168v–175v *Oratione facta per M. T. Cicerone per comissione de senato a C. Iulio Cesare. Robrica Liiij.* Al lungo silentio padri conscripti el quale io a questi tempi ho usato ... che tu havevi facto inançi verso di me e stato adgiunto grandissimo acrescimento.

Cicero, *Pro M. Marcello Oratio*, It. tr. Brunetto Latini; Latin text, A. C. Clark, ed., OCT (1900). The text appears to be the same as that in Florence, Biblioteca Riccardiana 1080 (Morpurgo, *op.cit.*, p. 73, no. VIII, no.1) where it is ascribed to Leonardo Bruni.

57. ff. 175v–187v *Epistola mandata da Marco Tullio Cicerone a Quinto Cicerone suo fratello stato proconsolo d'asia due anni essendovi contro al suo volere electo et rifermo il terço anno. Robrica .Lv.* Advenga che io non dubitassi che questa epistola molti messi ... essere sani diligen[t]issimamente tu servi et proveghi.

Cicero, *Epistula ad Quintum Fratrem*, It. tr. The text appears to be the same as that in Florence, Biblioteca Riccardiana 1080 (Morpurgo, *op.cit.*, p. 73, no. VIII, no. 2).

58. ff. 187v–188r *Sermone di Aristothele che tratta di giustitia. Robrica .Lvj.* [L]a giustitia e congiugnimento trovato in aiutorio di molti ... ma di molti usi la forma d'essa virtu della giustitia di meço secondo diverse qualita di luoghi di tempi et di persone. ff. 188v–191v blank

Italian discourse on justice based on Aristotle's *Ethics* and/or Brunetto Latini's *Tresor*. The Marston text corresponds to that printed in *L'ethica d'Aristotile ridotta in compendio da ser Brunetto Latini, et altre traduttioni e scritti di quei tempi* (Lyon, 1568) pp. 62–

64, but with a large section not present in Marston MS 247. The missing section corresponds to Latini's *Li Livres dou Tresor*, II.91.4–7 and II.112 (F. Carmody, ed. [Berkeley-Los Angeles, 1948]) or the Italian translation of the same by Bono Giamboni, chapters XLIII and LXIV, ed. L. Gaiter (*Il Tesoro di Brunetto Latini volgarizzato da Bono Giamboni* [Bologna, 1878]).

Paper (watermarks: Briquet Fleur 6655, Échelle 5908, 5910, and similar to Briquet Chapeau 3370). ff. ii (contemporary parchment bifolium; i = front pastedown), + 191 + ii (contemporary parchment bifolium; i = back pastedown) 293 x 217 (180 x 115) mm. 29 long lines. Double vertical (ff. 1–24) and horizontal (ff. 25–191) bounding lines; ruled partly in ink (ff. 1–24) but mostly in hard point. The asymmetrical placement of single prickings in margins of ff. 1–24 suggests text lines may have been drawn with a ruling device.

I^4, $II\text{-}IX^{10}$, X^{12}, XI^8, $XII\text{-}XIX^{10}$, XX^8 (-8). Vertical catchwords perpendicular to written space between inner bounding lines, verso. Remains of quire and leaf signatures (e.g., c1, c2, c3, etc.) in lower right corner, recto.

Written in neat humanistic cursive by a single scribe, below top line.

Three-quarter border, f. 5r, white vine-stem ornament on blue, red and green ground with grey and yellow dots. In lower border, vine-stem turning into a floral border and brown penwork scrolls with pink, blue and green flowers and gold dots. Illuminated initial, 6-line, gold on blue, green and red ground with white vine-stem ornament joined to inner border. Headings in red. Plain 3-line initials in blue mark text divisions. Guide letters in margins.

Binding: Italy, s. xv. Vellum stays adhered inside the quires. Original sewing on four tawed skin, slit straps laid in channels on the outside of wooden boards and nailed. Edges yellow ochre. A green and natural color, beaded endband is sewn on five cores. The primary one laid in grooves on the outside of the boards. The spine is lined with tawed skin or vellum extending onto the edge of the boards between supports.

Covered in tan leather blind-tooled with a potented cross in a central square with rope interlace panels above and below, and a border also filled with rope interlace. Spine: supports defined with double fillets and the panels diapered. Traces of five bosses on each board. Two ivy leaf fastenings, the catches on the lower board, the upper one cut in for green fabric straps attached with star-headed nails. Binding is heavily overoiled.

Written in Florence in the middle of the 15th century, probably ca. 1460–65, by an anonymous scribe who copied a number of vernacular texts, among them Beinecke MS 151 (v. 1, pp. 202–3) and Marston MS 9; he has been named by A. C. de la Mare the "Scribe of Florence, Biblioteca Laurenziana, San Marco 384" (see *New Research*, Appendix I, p. 548, no. 90, for other manuscripts by this scribe). Contemporary Hebrew [?] notes on ff. 21v, 135r, back flyleaf (recto and verso) and pastedown; on verso of back flyleaf: "Se amor non e che dunque e quel che io sente [*sic*]/ E segl e Amor per dio che cosa e tale [*sic*; Petrarch, *Canzoniere* CXXXII]; on back pastedown: "non son non son gia quel che in vista [. . . ?]." Owned by an unidentified Italian humanist, s. xvi, whose book list appears on f. i recto (art. 1); a 16th-century [?] library press mark "M [?] 34" on front pastedown. On f. 191r the inscription, s. xvi/xvii: "Al molto [magnifico signor] Zanobi carissimo" which is repeated on back flyleaf together with pen trials. On f. 1r, two oval library stamps in lower margin, one with "1263" written in ink below, both now effaced. Oval paper label with "6" in ink on spine. Purchased from B. M. Rosenthal in 1959 by Thomas E. Marston (bookplate).

secundo folio: [table, f. 2:] *Sermone*
[text, f. 6:] e nelle medesime

Bibliography: Faye and Bond, p. 93, no. 247.
The Medieval Book, p. 57, no. 57.
Ullman, no. 53.
Dutschke, no. 74.

Marston MS 248 Northern France, s. XIII/XIV
Hugh of St. Victor, Opera varia, etc.

We thank H. Feiss O.S.B. for his assistance with the texts of this manuscript.

1. ff. 1r–141v *Incipit prologus Hugonis in Librum De Sacramentis. Que sunt dicenda ante principium.* Quisquis ad diuinarum scripturarum lectionem erudiendus accedit . . . ueritatem siue profunditatem prospiciet. *Que sit materia diuinarum scripturarum.* Materia diuinarum scripturarum omnium sunt opera restaurationis . . . manifestius quia tractando extendunt. *Explicit prologus.* [text, f. 1v:] *Incipit liber Hugonis de sacramentis* . . . Arduum profecto et laboriosum opus crebra uestra precatione . . . Ecce quod erit in fine sine fine. *Explicit.*

De sacramentis christianae fidei; PL 176.173–618. Bk. 2 preceded by list of chapters; prefatory material for both books differs somewhat from that published in PL. R. Goy, *Die Überlieferung der Werke Hugos von St. Viktor* (Stuttgart, 1976) pp. 133–72.

2. ff. 141v–149r *Archa Noe.* Primum in planicie. ubi archam depinguere uolo medium centrum ... Hoc interim exemplari affectum suum prouocet. Sit deus benedictus per cuncta seculorum secula. Amen.

   De arca Noe mystica; PL 176.681–704. P. Sicard is producing a new edition and critical study of this text and that in art. 3. No chapter headings. Goy, *op.cit.*, pp. 237–45.

3. ff. 149r–169v *De archa noe pro archa sapiencie cum arcu ecclesie et arca matris gracie.* Cum sederem aliquando in conuentu fratrum ... in corde tuo expresseris domum dei in te edificatam esse leteris.

   De arca Noe morali; PL 176.617–80. See art. 2 above. Chapter headings differ from those in PL or are lacking. Goy, *op.cit.*, pp. 212–37.

4. ff. 169v–178v *De institutione nouitiorum.* Quia fratres largiente domino de uana conuersatione huius seculi per desiderium sanctum conversi estis ... Hec uobis fratres de scientia et disciplina. interni nos diximus. Bonitatem uero orate. ut uobis det deus. *Amen. Explicit.*

   De institutione novitiorum; PL 176.925–52. Goy, *op.cit.*, pp. 340–67.

5. ff. 178v–179v *Hugo Ranulfo de Mauriaco.* Feruor[e *expunged*] caritatis tue pondus questionum nobis inuexit. Postulas ... sed ab his qui renouandi sunt denuo recuperari potest ut eo recuperato amisisse dampnabile non sit.

   Epistola 2. Ad Ranulphum de Mauriaco; PL 176.1011–14 (= *Miscellanea* 1.200: PL 177.588). Goy, *op.cit.*, pp. 450–52.

6. ff. 179v–202v *Incipit prologus in didasculon hugonis. Due* precipue res sunt. quibus quisque ad scienciam instruitur ... et sic secunda quoque pars finem accipit. *Didascalicon hugonis de studio legendi. Primus liber de origine artium.* Omnium expectendorum prior est sapiencia ... Aruspicinam tages primus etruscis tradidit. Ydroma ima primum a persis uenit. *Explicit sextus liber de archa noe.*

   Didascalicon; PL 176.739–812 and C. H. Buttimer, ed., *Didascalicon. De studio legendi*, The Catholic University of America Studies in Medieval and Renaissance Latin 10 (Washington, D. C., 1939).

7. ff. 203r–220r [Heading in upper margin:] *Prologus in librum de religione.* Ut ait propheta. querite dominum et uiuet anima vestra. Quidem querunt deum. sed non inueniunt ... quia non senciunt retro impellentem. ut precipitentur. *Prologus in librum de religione de claustro materiali de claustro anime et de contemplatione.* Sepe et multum rogatus a fratribus nobiscum commorantibus ... corporis castitatem. et mentis

pudiciciam muniat propensius. [text, f. 203v:] *Liber primus de religione. quid sit.* Religio iusticie species. est. uirtus ius suum reddens ... est in celis peruenire festinamus.

Hugo de Folieto, *De claustrum animae*; text corresponds for the most part with Bks. 1–3 as printed in PL 176.1017–1130, except for the prologue and Bk. 1.1–3. Goy, *op.cit.*, pp. 491–92.

8. f. 220r [No rubric.] Scala mistica iacob. xiij. gradus habet inter duo latera ... ad libitum domini moueri.

Scala mistica; R. Baron, "Textes spirituels inédits de Hugues de Saint-Victor," *Mélanges de science religieuse* 13 (1956) p. 177 [15]. For the collection of *miscellanea* from which arts. 8–11 are taken, see D. van den Eynde, *Essai sur la succession et la date des écrits de Hugues de Saint-Victor*, Spicilegium Pontificii Athenaei Antoniani 13 (Rome, 1960) p. 11.

9. f. 220r [No rubric.] Est unitas naturalis ... principalis. in trinitate.

Est unitas naturalis; Baron, *op.cit.*, p. 177 [16]. See also art. 8.

10. f. 220r [No rubric.] Ecce quam bonum ... expellitur humilitate. simulatio. caritate.

Ecce quam bonum; Baron, *op.cit.*, p. 177 [17]. See also art. 8.

11. f. 220r [No rubric.] Triplex est diluuium ... per arcam sapiencie summi boni delectatio.

Triplex est diluvium; Baron, *op.cit.*, p. 177 [18].

12. ff. 220r–227v *De contemplatione et eius speciebus. Et primum de meditatione* ... Iuxta primarias ueterum auctoritates. contemplatio est ... Si non potes solem contemplari in rota. intuere ipsum in salomonis fenestra.

De contemplatione et eius speciebus; B. Hauréau, *Hugues de Saint-Victor, Nouvel examen de l'édition de ses oeuvres* (Paris, 1959) pp. 177–210; R. Baron, ed., *La contemplation et ses espèces*, Monumenta Christiana Selecta 2 (Tournai, 1955).

13. ff. 227v–229v *Incipit liber De tribus maximis circumstancijs gestorum.* Fili sapiencia thesaurus est ... Et cetera sicut subter sequuntur secundum hebraicam ueritatem dispositi. *Explicit liber. De claustro anime.*

Chronica; for partial editions see W. H. Green, "De tribus maximis circumstantiis," *Speculum* 18 (1943) pp. 488–92, and G. Waitz, ed., "Chronica quae dicitur Hugonis de Sancto Victore," MGH SS 24 (1879) pp. 88–97. Goy, *op.cit.*, pp. 36–43. This text continues in art. 21 below.

14. ff. 229v–272v *Incipit tractatus hugonis in expositionem ecclesiastes.* Que de libro salomonis qui ecclesiastes dicitur ... aliis post se pro futura sint ignorant. *Explicit liber ecclesiastes.*

Homiliae in Ecclesiasten; PL 175.113–254 (new critical edition in preparation by H. Feiss). Goy, *op.cit.*, pp. 329–40.

15. ff. 272v–279r *De virginitate beate Marie.* [prologue:] Sancto pontifici. G. H. Seruus uestre beatitudinis. Narrastis michi de beate marie uirginitate ... stilo signans uobis legenda transmisi. Vale. *Explicit prologus.* [text:] *Incipit liber.* De incorrupta virginitate matris domini. hoc fides ... in eodem quoque sexu utrobique non simili ueritate sanciatur.

De Beatae Mariae virginitate; PL 176.858–76. Goy, *op.cit.*, pp. 116–23.

16. f. 279r–v *Incipit expositio super prologum ieronimi in pentateuchum quem dirigit ad desiderium ... in latinum transtulit.* Desiderius proprium nomen est hinc desiderij mei ... greca quam latina et hebraea quam graeca.

Adnotationes elucidatoriae in Pentateuchon, ch. 1; PL 175.29A–32B. Goy, *op.cit.*, pp. 48–53.

17. ff. 279v–284r *Que scripture merito diuine appellari debent.* Lectorem diuinarum scripturarum primum instruere oportet ... vt ab edom. idumei a leui leuite. a iuda iudei.

De scripturis et scriptoribus, chs. 1–17; PL 175.9–24D.

18. ff. 284r–299r *De nuncupatione genesis.* Liber iste qui primus est diuinorum uoluminum ... filij post eam nascerentur. non oportebat redimi.

Adnotationes elucidatoriae in Pentateuchon, chs. 2–13 (Genesis-Leviticus); PL 175.62B–84C.

19. ff. 299r–301v *Incipit liber iudicum.* Liber iudicum qui hebraice sophthim dicitur ... Hic booz ergo qui propinquus erat dixit alteri qui ei credebat. Tolle calciamentum.

Adnotatiunculae elucidatoriae in librum Iudicum; PL 175.87A–96C.

20. ff. 301v–308r *Incipit liber regum.* Liber regum apud nos quatuor distinctionibus clauditur ... et maius desiderari potest in hoc seculo.

Adnotationes elucidatoriae in libros Regum; PL 175.95D–112D, with the concluding text of the manuscript differing from that printed.

21. ff. 308r–309v [No rubric.] Presens seculum distinguitur in duos status siue in tria tempora. Primus status qui dicitur uetus ... Sub hoc

decem tribus a salmanasar ... finem accepit.

Chronica, unpublished continuation of art. 13. This text often found associated with art. 22 in other manuscripts; see R. Baron, "La chronique de Hugues de Saint-Victor," *Studia Gratiana* 12 (1967) pp. 169–70.

22. ff. 309v–310v [No rubric.] Multa in scriptura occurrunt. que rerum gestarum seriem ignorantibus ... Secundus patruus qui iacobum interfecit.

De scripturis et scriptoribus, ch. 18; PL 175.25A–28D. See art. 21 above.

23. ff. 310v–311v [No rubric.] Proportiones rerum in ponderibus et mensuris considerantur. Principium ... Leuga. Miliare et dimidium.

De ponderibus et mensuris; R. Baron, ed., "Hugues de Saint-Victor lexicographe," *Cultura Neolatina* 16 (1956) pp. 132–37. Goy, *op.cit.*, pp. 478–79.

24. f. 311v [No rubric.] Doloris in affectum bone presumptionis. Recurrens aio ... in ara cordis adoletur.

De modo orandi, concluding lines only; PL 176.988A.

25. ff. 311v–321v [1.3:] *Quod omne cor pronum est* ... Fabula dicit. Omnes bestias ... sensum suum commendare non erubescat ... [1.75:] Cathedra doctoris sacra scriptura est ... que futura sunt non uidentur. Explicit liber.

Miscellanea, with text in the following order: 1.3–18, 20, 19, 21–30 [followed by "In pater [*sic*] corroboramur ad spem ... erudimur ad petitionem"; R. Baron, "Textes spirituels inédits de Hugues de Saint-Victor," *Mélanges de science religieuse* 13 (1956) p. 177], 1.31–41, 2.60, 1.42–56, 2.63, 1.57–59, 1.63–68, 2.80, 1.69–71, 2.55, 1.72–75. PL 177.481-632; Goy, *op.cit.*, pp. 452–57. See also arts. 29 and 35 below.

26. ff. 321v–323v *Incipit prologus de laude caritatis*. Seruo christi petro. h. gustare et uidere quam suauis ... dilectio quod recompensatur. *Explicit prologus. Incipit tractatus*. Tam multos iam laudatores caritas habuisse ... et mansionem in nobis facere. Qui cum eodem patre ... seculorum. Amen.

De laude caritatis; PL 176.969D–976D; critical edition by P. Sicard forthcoming. Goy, *op.cit.*, 253–67.

27. ff. 323v–324r *Incipit de substancia dilectionis*. Cotidianum de dilectione sermonem. ... sed inordinata cupiditas.

De substantia dilectionis; PL 176.14A–18B; R. Baron, ed., *Six opuscules spirituels*, Sources chrétiennes 155 (Paris, 1969) pp. 82–93. Goy, *op.cit.*, 392–99

28. ff. 324r–327v *Incipit prologus*. Domino [?] et patri th. h. munusculum ... donum impendere debetis. Valete. *De uirtute orandi*. Quo studio et quo affectu a nobis.... in ara cordis adoletur.

De virtute orandi; PL 176.977A–988A; critical edition by H. Feiss forthcoming. Goy, *op.cit.*, 404–38.

29. ff. 327v–330r [No rubric. 1.76:] Sapiencia uincit maliciam. attingit ergo a fine.... et iudicium cum ratione exhibet ... [1.80:] Iohanni quondam hispalensi archiepiscopo. Hugo seruus crucis christi. Quid frater karissime.... Non potes euadere confusionem. nisi ostendas confesionem [*sic*].

Miscellanea 1.76–80; PL 177.511A–516A and 176.1014B–1018A. Goy, *op.cit.*, pp. 446–48. See also art. 25 above and art. 35 below.

30. ff. 330r–338v *Incipit liber de tribus diebus pro ea que in meditatione constat speculatio rerum et post lectionem secunda*. Verbum bonum et uita sapiens. que mundum fecit ... octauus pertinet ad resurrectionem. Explicit de tribus diebus. *Explicit de tribus diebus* [sic].

De tribus diebus; PL 176.811B–838D. Goy, *op.cit.*, pp. 98–115.

31. ff. 338v–344r *Incipit prologus in soliloquium de arra anime*. Dilecto fratri. G ... conscribi exopto. Vale. *Incipit soliloquium de arra anime*. Loquar secreto anime mee et amica ... hoc totis precordijs concupisco.

Soliloquium de arra animae; PL 176.951–70; Müller, ed. *Soliloquium de arrha animae und De vanitate mundi*, Kleine Texte für Vorlesungen und Übungen 123 (Bonn 1913) pp. 3–25; Feiss, forthcoming. Goy, *op.cit.*, pp. 277–329.

32. ff. 344r–347v *Incipit tractatus de sapiencia christi et sapiencia christi prologus*. Prudenti ac religioso uerbi diuini inter ceteros ... quam cor peruersum. *De anima christi*. Queritis de anima christi. id est de illo rationali spiritu ... non arroganter presumere. Vale.

De sapientia animae Christi; PL 176.845C–856D. Goy, *op.cit.*, pp. 124–33.

33. ff. 347v–348r [No rubric:] Dum medium silencium tenerent omnia. [Sap. 18.14] Tria sunt silencia ... preparatum est ab initio seculi. Amen.

De verbo incarnato, collatio prima; PL 177.315D–318C. Goy, *op.cit.*, pp. 81–91.

34. ff. 348r–349v [No rubric.] Quod natum est ex carne caro est.... deorsum informans rationem scienciam facit.

De unione spiritus et corporis; PL 177.285A–289A; A. M. Piazzoni, ed., "Il De unione spiritus et corporis di Ugo di San Vittore," *Studi Medievali* 21 (1980) pp. 861–68; new edition with wider manuscript base in preparation by H. Feiss. Goy, *op.cit.*, pp. 95–98.

35. ff. 349v–355r [No rubric. I.81:] Cum esset Iesus annorum xij et cetera. Sicut mundus iste.... sacri uerbi doctoribus ueritas cognoscitur ... [I.102:] Nisi ego abiero paraclitus non ueniet. christus discipulis corporalem.... mentem suam per intentionem effundant. *Explicit liber.* f. 355v blank

Miscellanea, with text in the following order: I. 81–91, 106, 92 [followed by "In peccato duo sunt. vicium et culpa ... culpa contra pietatem"; R. Baron, "Textes spirituels inédits de Hugues de Saint-Victor," *Mélanges de science religieuse* 13 (1956) p. 177], I.93–96, 99, 97–98, 100–102. PL 177.516–36. Marston MS 248 has a shortened and garbled version of I.106, with the beginning and end being identical with 5.13. See also arts. 25 and 29 above.

Parchment (fine; leaves repaired before pricking and ruling), ff. i (contemporary parchment) + 355 (all leaves except the last are numbered with Roman numerals, in red, in upper left corner, verso), 375 x 253 (253 x 166) mm. 2 columns, 53 lines. Double outer and single inner vertical bounding lines; double upper horizontal bounding lines. Additional pair of horizontal rulings, full width, in upper margin for folio numbers and running headlines. Prickings in upper, lower and sometimes outer margins; prickings in inner margins for double upper horizontal bounding lines only.

I-XXIX^{12}, XXX^{7} (structure uncertain). Catchwords in lower margin near gutter, verso.

Written in uniform gothic bookhand throughout; contemporary marginal notes in several less formal hands.

8-line illuminated initial (f. 1r), blue with white highlights on square ground, magenta with blue and white highlights; interior of initial inhabited by scrolling vines, rabbit and two animal heads on gold and blue ground; tail of letter extends down inner margin. 11- to 7-line red and blue initials divided by a zig-zag line in parchment and with interior red and blue flourishes resembling the design on a peacock's tail feathers, mostly in red with small blue circles. This style of initial accompanied by long penwork extensions in red and blue *I* designs and with small spirals, circles, flourishes (cf. *L'enluminure de Charlemagne à François Ier, Manuscrits de la Bibliothèque publique et universitaire de Genève* [Geneva, 1976] p. 43). Small 3-line initials alternate red and blue with penwork flourishes in the opposite color. 1-line plain initials alternate red and blue for chapter lists. Remains of guide letters for decorator. Headings, running titles (often incorrect), deletions (single horiztonal red line) and initial strokes in red.

Binding: France [?], s. xix. Brown calf, elaborately blind-stamped with figure of Christ giving a blessing with his right hand, while his left hand holds a book with alpha and omega displayed on the open pages. Original endbands (and therefore sewing?) and yellow edges.

Written in Northern France at the end of the 13th or beginning of the 14th century. According to H. Feiss the canons regular of St. Victor in Paris prepared or had prepared in the early 13th century a series of large-format, comprehensive manuscripts of Hugh's works, including Paris, Bibliothèque Mazarine 717, Paris B. N. lat. 14303 and 14506. Marston MS 248 appears to be descended from these three Victorine manuscripts. Two contemporary inscriptions, effaced and only partially legible under ultra-violet light: on blank parchment leaf pasted to front pastedown: "Iste liber est * * * fratrum p [?]"; on the verso of pastedown, now lifted: "Egidius familiaris d[o]mi Formulien[sis]." If the second reading is accurate, Egidius may have been a member or associate of the canons regular of the monastery of Sainte-Marie at Voormezele in West Flanders. Belonged to Thomas Philip Earle de Grey of Wrest Park (1781–1859; bookplate) and to Juan M. Sanchez (b. 1874; bookplate). Purchased from L. C. Witten in 1960 by Thomas E. Marston (bookplate).

secundo folio: sed exponendo

Bibliography: Faye and Bond, p. 93, no. 248.

Marston MS 249 — Northern Italy, s. XV^2
De orthographia

ff. 1r–16v [V]ocum alia literata alia inliterata uox licterata est illa que scribi potest licteris ut deus et hec est duplex ... ne quamquam potest saltem in latinis dictionibus. Finit uocalis aut .n.r.z. sequente. Ortho completa iam sistat penna graphia. Finis Fit Orthographia.

Anonymous work on orthography; other manuscripts with this text given in Bursill-Hall, *Census*, p. 359 (Marston MS 249 not listed).

Paper (watermarks, in gutter: unidentified mountain), ff. i (paper) + 16

+ i (original parchment flyleaf or wrapper) + i (paper), 218 x 142 (138 x 79) mm. 20 long lines. Single vertical bounding lines, full length; single upper horizontal bounding line, full across (Derolez 13.2). Ruled in lead; remains of prickings in upper, lower, and outer margins.

I–II^8. Horizontal catchwords to right of center in lower margin, verso (Derolez 12.2).

Written by a single scribe in fere-humanistic script, below top line.

Binding: Germany [?], s. xix. Greenish brown paste-paper case with paper labels wrapped around spine. The same paste paper was used for Marston MS 284. Parchment stays adhered to outer conjugate leaves of quires.

Written in Northern Italy in the second half of the 15th century; early provenance unknown. Round paper label with scalloped edge on spine: "75650a" in ink and "III [?]. M." added below in pencil. Unidentified notations: "103" in circle and "MS. 74," both in pencil, inside front cover; "T. M./ 7" in a circle and "437" on f. 1r. Purchased in 1959 from Bernard M. Rosenthal by Thomas E. Marston (bookplate).

secundo folio: sonant

Bibliography: Faye and Bond, p. 93, no. 249.

Marston MS 250 — Lucca, 1435, 1436
Francesco Barbaro, De re uxoria, etc.

1. ff. 1r–44r *Francesci barbari Veneti ad Insignem Laurentium de medicis florentinum de re uxoria liber incipit feliciter. Prologus.* Maiores nostri Laurenti carissime beniuolentia uel necessitate [in margin: al. necessitudine] sibi coniünctos in nuptiis sibi donare consueuerunt ... [f. 2v:] *De coniugio. C. i.* Antequam de delectu uxoris et officio dicere incipio de ipso coniugio prius pauca mihi dicenda sunt ... ab optima fide ac animo certe tibi deditissimo certe proficiscitur. [colophon:] Expletus scribi per me Guilliel-mum Rustichellium [?] Pisis Luce D. Ia. mccccxxxiiij Indictione xij. pridie Nonas Nouembris.

   Francesco Barbaro, *De re uxoria,* with his dedicatory preface to Lorenzo di Giovanni de' Medici; A. Gnesotto, ed., *Atti e Memorie della R. Accademia di scienze, lettere ed arti in Padova* n. s. 32 (1915–16) pp. 23–100. Proper nouns, extracted from text, are noted in margins along with brief notes in several hands (e.g., f. 5v: Quot In uxorem spectanda: mores, virtus, etas, genus, forma, opes). Chapters numbered i–xvi (last two partially erased).

2. ff. 44v–49r *Oratio Leonardi Aretini in qua Heliogabalus Augustus ad matronas Romanas orat ad meretriciam inuitans. Prohemium.* Heliogabalus Augustus Inter caetera notate lasciuie flagitia.... *Oratio.* Incredibilis me libido habet conmilitones et uehementem in me ardorem concitari sentio ... in hac cupidinis militia dona magnifica reportabit. dixi/ Leonardus Aretinus recreandi ingenij causa ludens ridensque dictauit ... ne esserant. [colophon:] Scripta oratio Heliogabali per me Guilliel-mum Rustichellum a pisis. Luce die xxviij Iunij. mccccxxxv more Pisanorum.

Leonardo Bruni, *Oratio Heliogabali ad meretrices*; Baron, p. 162; M. Z. Boxhorn, *Historiae Augustae scriptorum latinorum minorum* (Leiden, 1632) p. 97.

3. ff. 49v–59r *Dialogus Platonis cur Socrates a carcere fugere recusarit cum capitaliter damnatus foret E grais in latinas uersus litteras a Leonardo Aretino Incipit. So.* Quid huc aduenisti o Crito? an non adhuc summum est mane ... ipse reboat sonitus. facitque ut audire queam alios. *Explicit dialogus Platonis cur Socrates aufugere recusarit cum capitaliter damnatus foret. E greco in latinum translatatus* [sic] *per Lenardum* [sic] *Aretinum.*

Plato, *Crito*, the first version of the Latin translation by Leonardo Bruni (1420s); Baron, pp. 173–74. A. Carosini, ed., *Il Critone latino di Leonardo Bruni e di Rinuccio Aretino*, Accademia toscana di scienze e lettere "La Colombaria" Studi 62 (Florence, 1983) pp. 165–83; Marston MS 250 not cited.

4. ff. 59r–63v *Incipit Apologia Socratis de greco in latinum translatata* [sic] *per Leonardum Aretinum.* Socratis quoque dignum mihi uidetur memi-nisse. Cum in iudicium uocatus fuit ... quam Socrates usus est illum ego uirum felicissimum duco. *Explicit Apologia Socrates per Aretinum translata.*

Xenophon, *Apologia Socratis*, translated into Latin by Leonardo Bruni; Baron, p. 187.

5. f. 64r *Epistola Virgilij ad Mecenatem.* Virgilius Mecenati salutem. Ruf-fum Pomponium libertum tuum nouelle uidi ... sat tenuit Philelphum reconciliet siuis [?] est. Vale. f. 64v blank

The ps.-Virgilian *Epistola Virgilii ad Maecenatem* written by Pier Candido Decembrio as a young man in 1426; he had difficulty convincing his contemporaries that it was not genuine. See text and note published by L. Barozzi and R. Sabbadini, *Studi sul Panormita e sul Valla* (Florence, 1871) pp. 23–24, n. 10; see also R. Sabbadini, *Le scoperte dei codici latini codici latini e greci ne' secoli XIV e XV* (Florence, 1967) p. 176.

Parchment (most leaves palimpsests from several different manuscripts and parchment previously ruled with lines perpendicular to current written space), ff. i (paper) + 64 (modern pagination in pencil 1–127) + i (paper), 212 x 142 (142 x 76) mm. 28–31 long lines. Double vertical bounding lines, full length (Derolez 13.31); some single horizontal bounding lines (Derolez 13.13); all rulings in ink. Remains of prickings in upper margin.

I–VIII^8. Horizontal catchwords to right of center in lower margin, verso (Derolez 12.2).

Written in humanistic bookhand by a single scribe, above top line.

Illuminated initial of poor quality, f. 1r, 7-line, gold (almost completely rubbed), with red penwork filigree and small stylized leaves, with some touches of gold. At the top of the page, beneath rubric, arms of the Rustichelli family (per pale, or, a lion rampant sable; or, 4 bars nebuly sable), surrounded by red penwork. Plain initials in red and blue. Headings in red. Some small initials touched with yellow.

Off-set impression of eyeglasses on ff. 33v–34r.

Binding: Germany [?], s. xix–xx. Case bound with leaves from a parchment manuscript (Breviary, France, s. xiii^2). On the front pastedown: rubrics for the major feasts and their octaves occurring in late June (John the Baptist, 24 June) through mid-August (Assumption, 15 August), and the beginning of the lessons to be read within the octave of the feast of John the Baptist; on the back pastedown: end of the lessons for Hilarianus of Arezzo (7 August) and beginning of the second lesson for Cyriacus, Largus and Smaragdus (8 August).

Written in Lucca in 1435 (colophon, art. 1) and 1436 (colophon, art. 2) by Guillielmus Rustichellus of Pisa whose arms appear on f. 1r and who dated the manuscript "more pisanorum" (see A Cappelli, *Cronologia, cronografia e calendario perpetuo* pp. 9–10, 11, 14). He also copied another manuscript in Lucca in "1434–35" (*Colophons*, v. 2, no. 6058; A. Mancini, "Index codicum latinorum Publicae Bybliothecae Lucensis," *Studi italiani di filologia classica* 8 [1900] pp. 213–14). Provenance otherwise unknown. Purchased in 1957 from H. P. Kraus by L. C. Witten (inv. no. 1538) who sold it in 1959 to Thomas E. Marston (bookplate).

secundo folio: es exempla

Bibliography: Faye and Bond, p. 93, no. 250.

Marston MS 251 Northern Italy [?], s. XIV/XV
Isidore, Synonyma

1. notes on front pastedown (now lifted): Senecha tragediarum/ Iniqua rare maximis virtutibus fortuna parcit/. Quare multa bonis uiris aduersa eueniunt/ nichil accedere bono uiro mali potest. [followed by:] Isidorus ethimologiarum/ Omnino enim fingendi locus vachat ubi ueritas cessat.

   Extracts here attributed to Seneca and Isidore, *Etymologiae*.

2. ff. 1r–64r *Incipit prologus synonime sancti ysidori archiepiscopi yspaniensis.* [prologue:] In subsequenti hoc libro qui nuncupatur synonima id est multa uerba in unam significationem coeuntia. sancte recordationis ysidorus archiepiscopus ex yspania introduxit ... *Explicit prologus. Prefatio sancti ysidori. ysidorus lectori salutem.* [text, f. 2r:] Uenit nuper ad manus meas quedam cedula quam synonimam dicunt. Cuius formula persuasit ... tu mihi supra omnia in uita mea places. *Explitiunt* [sic] *synonima sancti ysidori.* [followed by the plea to the reader to read and profit from books rather than merely to collect them, f. 63r:] In cuiuscumque manibus libellus iste uenerit. rogo et cum grandi humilitate supplico ... sed magis de assidua predicatione eternum premium mereantur accipere. *La pe ra* [sic]. f. 64v ruled, but blank

   Isidore of Seville, *Synonyma de lamentatione animae peccatricis*; PL 83.827–68.

Parchment, ff. i (original parchment pastedown) + 64, 156 x 118 (91 x 68) mm. 18 long lines. Single vertical and double horizontal bounding lines; ruled in lead. Remains of prickings in upper, lower and outer margins for all rulings, with some double prickings for the first of the lower horizontal bounding lines.

I–VIII^{8}. Horizontal catchwords centered below text space and written between lead rulings, verso.

Main text written by a single scribe in round gothic bookhand; art. 1 added in a *mercantesca* script.

Plain letters, 5- to 2-line, in red, mark text divisions. Headings, initial strokes, a few pointing hands, in red. Guide letters for initials.

Binding: Italy, s. xv. Original wound sewing on three tawed skin, slit straps laced through tunnels in the edge to channels on the outside of wooden boards and nailed. Primary endbands caught up on the spine. Red, cream and green chevron endbands are sewn on tawed skin cores which are laid in grooves on the outside of the boards and nailed. Spine lined with leather between supports. Modern parchment addition pasted around spine, much wormeaten. Off-set impression of liturgical manuscript (s. xii?) with neumes, inside front board.

Covered in kermes pink, tawed sheep with corner tongues. Blind-tooled with diagonal and quartering triple fillets. One fastening, the catch on the lower board, the upper one cut in for the strap which is attached with star-headed nails. Five flower-shaped bosses on each board (two wanting on each).

Written perhaps in Northern Italy at the end of the 14th or beginning of the 15th century; early provenance unknown. Unidentified notes, s. xix–xx: "34" in pencil on parchment addition to spine; "Isidorus - 14th–15th century" and "40921" in pencil on front pastedown. Purchased from B. M. Rosenthal in 1959 by Thomas E. Marston (bookplate).

secundo folio: Uenit nuper

Bibliography: Faye and Bond, p. 94, no. 251.

Marston MS 252 England, s. XIII$^{1/3}$, XV
Gautier de Châtillon, Gesta Alexandri Magni, etc.

Part I consists of short aphorisms, prayers, recipes, etc. added in the 15th century, including but not limited to the following texts.

I. 1. f. i recto [a] Quidquid agat dominus regnet benedictus . . . [Walther, *Sprichwörter* 25246]; [b] Inconsulta temeritas nescit consilium expectare . . . ; [c] ffor the ffassion of an hors. Take a grete handfull of Betayn and bray hit Well yn a morter . . . Quod hodys [?] bok; [d] Consilium Iuuenum/ Latens [?] odium . . . [cf. Walther, *Sprichwörter* 3166a]; [e] O rex. si rex es. rege te. vel eris . . . [Walther, *Sprichwörter* 19575]; f. i verso [Title:] Gauterus gallicus de gestis Alexandri magni. [a] Virginis ecce pie species nati que Marie/ hic si transire speras prosper que redire/ . . . Aliter in duobus rotulis. Ad Ihesum genitrix mea prospera sis mediatrix/ . . . ; [b] Lux laus. Regina. Rethores Rote que ruina./ Lac oleum Syna. te glorificant Katerina; [c] references to Phil. 2.9–10 and Acts 4.12; f. ii recto [a] drawing of a heart with the words "Credo quod" and extending upwards three quotes from Job 19.25–26: "Redemptor meus viuit/ De terra surrecturus sum/ In carne mea videbo deum saluatorem meum"; [b] quotation from Ps.-Boethius, *De disciplina scholarium*; [c] paraphrase of Cicero, *De officiis* 2.64.

2. f. ii verso O fragilis nimiumque breuis terrena potestas/ Spes que hominum fallax et vita simillima vento/ ... Si queres rectum, si te prestabis honesto/ Quamque ego pugnando, tu tantum pace valebis.

   Latin poem, 24 lines, in which a victorious king, now deceased, speaks against the vanity of human ambition and glory.

3. f. iii recto [Heading:] Epistola Abgari Ad Ihesum. [text:] Abgarus Euchamae filius toparcha. Ihesu saluatori bono qui apparuit in locis hierosolimorum salutem. Auditum michi est et de te et de sanitatibus ... Est autem ciuitas michi parua quidem sed honesta. que sufficiat vtrisque. [followed by statistics for English towns and churches, e.g., "Et sunt 45. mill. et .11. ecclesie parochiales"]

   Apocryphal correspondence of Abgarus, king of Edessa, with Christ.

4. f. iii verso [a] Extract from John Chrystostom; [b] Aphorisms, including: Mutua dando vice sunt filia, mater amice [Walther, *Sprichwörter* 15815]; Stulti mirantur, prudentes vnde regantur [Walther, *Sprichwörter* 30394]; Hic et in hispanis pigro deest copia panis [Walther, *Sprichwörter* 10841]; Nulla fames vrget, vbi panis copia surget [Walther, *Sprichwörter* 18906]; Parua necat morsu spaciosum vipera taurum/ ... [Walther, *Sprichwörter* 20767]; fforma pudicie rara, sed apta comes.

5. f. iv recto [a] Extract from Ovid, *Remedia amoris* (807–8); [b] Aphorisms, including: Vinum moderate sumptum acuit ingenium, immoderate corrumpit; Nescit abesse deus in se sperantibus egros/ ... [Walther, *Sprichwörter* 16547]; Spiritus excludit vicium carnale, propinat/ ... [Walther, *Sprichwörter* 30233]; Venditur arbitrium dum viuitur ex alieno/ ... [Walther, *Sprichwörter* 32982]; Est sine melle fauus, sine messe seges, sine fructu/ ... [Walther, *Sprichwörter* 7913]; Dulcis amicorum redolet congressus, amicos/ ... [Walther, *Sprichwörter* 6390]; Pessimus in dubia sorte propheta timor/ ... [Walther, *Sprichwörter* 21442].

6. f. iv verso [Prologue to art. 7, added in the 15th century:] Moris est vsitati cum in auribus multitudinis ... Et ad hoc respectu discant//

   Prologue to Gautier de Châtillon, *Alexandreis*, written as prose and ending imperfectly (stub between ff. iv verso and f. 1r). A 13th-century leaf, containing the complete text of the prologue and probably the original first folio of this manuscript, now serves as front pastedown.

II. 7. ff. 1r–70v and III. ff. 71r–86v: [Capitula primi libri:] Primus aristotilis [*sic*] inbutum nectare sacro/ Scribit alexandrum septrisque [*sic*] insignit et armis/ cicropidas regi rursus consederat arces/ . . . Pergama miratur et sompnia uisa retractat. [text:] Gesta ducis macedum totum digesta per orbem/ Quam large dispersit opes quo milite porum/ Vicerit et darium. quo principe grecia uictrix/ . . . nullum moritura per euum. Explicit. f. 87r blank

Gautier de Châtillon, *Alexandreis*, with Bks. I–VIII.307 (ff. 1–70) written by a 13th-century scribe and the remainder of the text copied in the 15th century. Loss of considerable text from f. 56 to end due to severe rodent damage. M. L. Colker, ed., *Galteri de Castellione Alexandreis* (Padua, 1978) pp. 3–274 (this manuscript not cited). For a detailed analysis of the text of Marston MS 252 see T. Pritchard, "Notes on a Manuscript of Walter of Châtillon's Alexandreis from an Illustrious Welsh Library," *Scriptorium* 41.1 (1987) pp. 107–13. Some contemporary marginal and interlinear notes in pen and crayon, including a reference to Peter of Blois on f. 19v.

8. ff. 87v–88v Short texts in Latin and Middle English similar to those in arts. 1, 4–5; leaves mostly eaten by rodents.

f. i (modern paper) + iv (15th-century parchment additions that compose Part I) + 70 (13th-century parchment: Part II) + 18 (15th-century parchment additions: Part III) + i (modern paper).

Part I: ff. i recto–iv verso do not have a consistent format and are written by several cursive hands of a decidedly English character. At the beginning of art. 6, text begins with blue 3-line initial with red herringbone penwork designs and the additional letters *R* and *N*, in blue, whose significance is unclear.

Part II: ff. 1–70, 157 x 111 (101 x 51) mm. 31 lines of verse. Double or triple vertical bounding lines ruled in hard point or crayon (more common). Collation impossible due to tight binding. Written in early gothic bookhand, above top line. Divided initials red and black with simple penwork designs in one or both colors for major text divisions; plain red initials elsewhere. First letter of each verse separated from text between bounding lines and stroked with red; paragraph marks in black. T–O map of the world, f. 7v.

Part III: ff. 71–88, precise measurement of leaves unknown due to damage, written space 100 x 74 mm. 23 lines of verse. Leaves frame-ruled in crayon. Remains of decorated catchwords, f. 84v, and quire and leaf signatures (e.g. l iiii, l v, etc.) in lower right corner, recto. Written in well-formed English cursive script. Texts in art. 8 in a variety of cursive hands. Decorative initials similar to those in Part I.

Binding: England, s. xv. Covered first with thin, white tawed skin, second with a tawed skin chemise, third with heavy tawed skin originally sewn to the chemise. One fastening, the catch on the lower board, the upper one cut in for the strap which is wanting. Sewn on three supports attached to oak boards and pegged with wedges set at an angle. The spine is back beveled. Later additions include title, in ink, near head of upper board: "Gesta Alexandri Magni M.S." Repaired at head and tail of spine; rebacked. Parchment leaf for front pastedown (cf. art. 6 and provenance).

Part II, the oldest part of the codex, was written in England in the first third of the 13th century. In the 15th century the Prologue (art. 6) was rewritten as was the conclusion of the text (Part III); when the manuscript was rebound, the old Prologue was presumably used as the front pastedown. Miscellaneous texts in arts. 1–5 and 8 were added in the 15th century. Belonged to the Gwysaney Library of Wales, a collection of manuscripts formed by the Welsh antiquary and naturalist Robert Davies of Llannerch (1684–1728); cf. H. D. Emanuel, "The Gwysaney MSS," *The National Library of Wales Journal* 7 (1951–52) pp. 326–43; J. C. Jeaffreson, *Sixth Report of the Royal Commission on Historical Manuscripts*, Part I (1877–78) pp. 418–21. The codex remained in the Davies family until its sale by Lt. Col. P. R. Davies-Cooke (Sotheby's, 15 June 1959, no. 207). Unidentified shelf-marks include "No 39" written in ink on front cover and "74" in ink on a square white paper label on spine. Purchased from C.A. Stonehill in 1959 by Thomas E. Marston (bookplate).

secundo folio: Cornibus

Bibliography: Faye and Bond, p. 94, no. 252.

Marston MS 253 — Northeastern Spain, s. XIII$^{3/3}$
Gautier de Châtillon, Gesta Alexandri Magni

f. 1r Modern title-page: "Philippi Galtheri Alexandreidos libri decem"; ff. 1v–4v modern flyleaves, blank; ff. 5r–128v // Quod solem galeis equites clipeisque retundant./ Nec te terruit numerus. si molliter illos/ ... Ad maiora uocor. et me uocat ardus heternus [?]/ Vt solium regni et sedem sortitus in astris.// ff. 129r–130v blank

Text (I.135–X.407) is defective at beginning and end; in addition, the following leaves containing text (now replaced by foliated blanks) have been lost: ff. 14–18, containing I.494–II.199 ("... Non uos excutiat cepto gens prouida bello// Sola mobilitas stabilem facit. hec ubi dicta..."); ff. 32–33, containing III.198–282 ("... Ne capiti afigit. cerebrum tamen ossa tuentur.// Que lapidum ualeant refugos elidere iactus..."); ff. 65-66, containing V.466–VI.20 ("... Barbarico nequeunt insolitos sufferre paratus.// Moribus illius. nichil est instructius illis..."); f. 80, containing VII.12–53 ("... Humanes [?] cum sole labor. sed pena manebat// Antropos incissum maturat scindere filum..."); ff. 122–125, containing X.83–286 ("... Quo d[*sic*] conspecto. scelerum pater jnquit et ultor dea.// Sangujnis inpenssa macedum certamina nondum..."). M. L. Colker, ed., *Galteri de Castellione Alexandreis* (Padua, 1978) pp. 3–274 (this manuscript not cited). The manuscript has been heavily annotated in both Latin and Catalan and exhibits evidence of use as a school text; proverbial expressions are sometimes underlined and the reader has used letters of the alphabet to indicate the order in which words should be translated.

Paper (heavy, coarse, brown), ff. 130 (combination of original leaves and modern insertions, all foliated by a modern hand, probably by the same person who added the title to f. 1r) + i (paper), 193 x 148 (140 x 70) mm. 21 lines of verse. Precise format unclear due to condition of manuscript.

Accurate collation impossible: many leaves missing, damaged and/or repaired, or mounted on stubs. Remains of catchwords in lower margin to right of center, verso. A later hand has signed gatherings with letters of the alphabet, lower right corner, recto.

Written by a single scribe in a small gothic minuscule; annotations in several contemporary cursive hands.

Inelegant red initials with modest penwork designs in red and/or black mark major text divisions. First letter of each verse stroked with red. Paragraph marks in black and red.

Binding: Place uncertain, s. xviii–xix. Limp vellum case with traces of title written in ink on spine; stubs of two tawed skin, ribbon ties.

Written in Northeastern Spain in the last third of the 13th century; early provenance unknown. Traces of a square paper label on spine; "62" in pencil on first front flyleaf, recto. Purchased from C. A. Stonehill in 1959 by Thomas E. Marston (bookplate).

Bibliography: Faye and Bond, p. 94, no. 253.

Marston MS 254 — Alsace, s. XIII [?]
Legal document, in Middle High German, in roll format

[First article:] Ein vogt ze blixberg sol och alle iâr ze dinge sin ze ongersheim an deme nehisten mantage nach sancte martins tage ... ; [second article:] er sol och hie sin alle iâr an deme mantage, nâch der liehtemes, vnd an deme abende ... ; [last article:] der hof sol och gâben, deme dorfen einen pfeh rem [?] und ein eber.

Constitution for the *dinghof* or *colonge* of Ingersheim in Alsace, consisting of 16 articles. A later French translation of this text is edited by M. L'Abbé Hanauer, *Les constitutions des campagnes de l'Alsace au moyen-âge* (Paris-Strasbourg, 1865) pp. 349–54. It is possible that some text has been lost at the beginning.

Parchment roll consisting of 2 irregularly trimmed membranes stitched together, the whole measuring 1250 x 155 (widest part)–118 (narrowest part) mm. Written in neat gothic hand by a single scribe who placed a paragraph mark before each article. Roll shows considerable use. Boxed.

Written in Alsace probably in the 13th century; provenance unknown. Purchased in 1958 from Roux-Devillas, Paris, by L. C. Witten (inv. no. 2125), who sold it in 1959 to Thomas E. Marston.

Bibliography: Faye and Bond, p. 94, no. 254.

Marston MS 255 — England, s. XV^{med}
Nicholas Upton, De officio militari

1. ff. 1r–46v [Prologue:] Summum opificem alpha et oo [*sic*] in essentia vnum et trinum in personis invocans ipsum clementissime exoro ... libellus de militari offitio. *Incipit primum capitulum prime partis huius libri de officio militari.* Famosissimus ille pater legum et doctor eximius dominus Bartholus de saxo ferrato ... et que corrigendo viderint animo violenti animo sed benigno corrigant et emendant. *Et hic est finis deo gratias.* ff. 47r–48v blank

   Nicholas Upton (d. 1457), *De officio militari libri IV*; E. Bysshe [Bissaeus], ed. (London, 1654) pp. 1–259. Manuscript is defective in Book IV: missing text between ff. 24–25 (" ... ab incarnatione domini quingentesimo [catchwords:] xl v to // Iohannis portare pro eo. . ."); between ff. 39–40 (" ... in campo asorio ut hic quo quidem // tunc vocantur in gallico. . ."); between ff. 43–44 (". . . cum vno simplici scuto // talentis is eodem Et gallice. . ."). Books I and II have chapters numbered with Roman numerals; Book IV contains a series of painted coats of arms numbered consecutively with the same number entered next to the corresponding text.

2. ff. 49r–61v *Summaria compilato* [sic] *metrificata docens quid communis [?] et vtilius continetur in vnoquoque capitulo tocius biblie vnum quodlibet verbum vnius capituli summam [?] tenet. Incipit liber Genesis et habet versus 9 et capitula 50.* Sex .1. dierum opera/ Prohibet 2 fructum ligni scientie [?] boni et mali./ Peccant .3. Adam et Eua/ . . . [concludes with *Apocalipsis habet versus 4 et capitula 22*:] Sponsam 21 ornatam viro suo/ Venio iam 22 dicit sponsus.

Metrical summary of the Bible based on Alexander of Villa Dei, *Summarium Bibliae*, arranged by books and chapters (cf. Stegmüller, nos. 1175–82, where similar biblical summaries and commentaries are cited); here the text is written in three columns.

3. f. 62r .1. Genesis habet versus .9. capitula .50./ .2. Exodus habet versus .7. capitula .40./ . . . 56 Apocalypsis versus .4. capitula 22. f. 62v blank

Tabular chart for art. 2.

4. ff. 63r–73v *Prohemium testamentorum vndecim patriarcharum.* Hec abscondita et celata fuerunt per longa tempora ita quod tam doctores et antiqui . . . ad honorem dei in lucem prorumpunt. *Testamenta duodecim filiorum Iacob et Primo de Ruben.* Testamentum Ruben de hijs que habebat in mente de fornicatione/ . . . Testamentum Beniamin de mente inuidia [*sic*]. *Incipit tabula testamentorum vndecim Patriarcharum.* Aduentus christi in Iuda/ . . . Zabulon pietas et miseria in zabulon. *Explicit tabula testamentorum xii patriarcharum.* [text, f. 64r:] Transcriptum testamenti ruben quecumque mandauit filijs suis priusquam moreretur . . . in terra egypti vsque ad diem exitus eorum de terra egypti.

Testamenta XII Patriarcharum, Lat. tr. of Robert Grosseteste; see S. Harrison Thomson, *The Writings of Robert Grosseteste* (Cambridge, 1940) pp. 42–44; Stegmüller 87.7; PG 2.1038–1150. Text here is defective; two leaves with portions of Testaments II–III missing between ff. 64–65.

5. ff. 74r–80v In primo creauit deus celum et terram et statim cum deei [*sic*] primo articulo fecit deus lucem spiritualem et materialem et naturam angelicam . . . et hoc vsque ad Rothomagum in Normannia. f. 81r–v blank

World chronicle, beginning with the creation and ending with John of Lancaster, Duke of Bedford (1389–1435).

Parchment, ff. ii (paper) + 81 + ii (paper), 294 x 200 (220 x 145) mm. 2 columns, 50 lines (art. 2 = 3 columns; art. 3 = 11 columns). Single horizontal and vertical bounding lines; ruled in crayon. Remains of prickings.

Binding too tight for certain collation. Perhaps: $I–II^{12}$, III^{12}, (–1; –11, no loss of text), IV^{12} (–6, 11), V^{4}, VI^{12}, VII^{12} (–5, 6), VIII^{12} (–12).

Written in small neat secretary script with anglicana features; cf. Parkes, *Cursive Book Hands*, pls. 11 (ii) and 20 (i). Headings in large gothic bookhand.

One decorative initial, 8-line, gold with border of gold and colors extending across upper and down inner margins; details of illumination marred by extensive damage. Blue initials with intricate red penwork flourishes throughout. Headings underlined in red. Nicely painted heraldic shields, art. 1; paragraph marks alternate red and blue, arts. 2, 4–5.

Severe water staining throughout the text affects decoration, which has faded or bled, but rarely obscures the text.

Binding: England, s. xix. Red, hard-grained goatskin, blind- and gold-tooled, with arms of Elmhirst on both covers (later addition). Title arranged in panels down spine: "Tractatus varii. viz./ I. Upton De re militari./ II. Summaria metrificata./ III. Test. XI. [*sic*] Patriarcharum./ IV. Chronicon ab orig. mundi/ Ad Ann. 1332."

Written in England in the middle of the 15th century, sometime after 1435 (see. art. 5). Unidentified early painting (mark of ownership?) consisting of a single green leaf with red diagonal bar through the center and the number "4" written in red below, lower margin of f. 2r. Belonged to Henry Fitzalan, 12th earl of Arundel (1511?–80; inscription "Arundel" in upper margin, f. 1r); the manuscript presumably passed through his daughter to the Howard family when she married Thomas Howard, 4th duke of Norfolk. It was subsequently owned by their son Lord William Howard of Naworth (1563–1640; E. Bernard, *Catalogi librorum manuscriptorum Angliae et Hiberniae* [1697], no. 35). The codex remained in the family until the sale of the library of the Earl of Carlisle, Naworth Castle, Cumberland (Sotheby's, 28 Oct. 1947, no. 528). For more information and bibliography on this early provenance see A. S. G. Edwards and B. A. Shailor, "Marginalia," *Gazette* 65 (1991) pp. 190–91. Armorial bookplate of Edward Mars Elmhirst (b. 1915); bookplate added after 1939 when Dr. Elmhirst was granted the bastardized arms appearing therein: Elmhirst quarterly with those of Elmhirst-Baxter (*Burke's Landed Gentry*, 1952, p. 755). Purchased from L. C. Witten (who bought it from E. P. Goldschmidt, London?) in 1959 by Thomas E. Marston (bookplate).

secundo folio: ff [*sic*] de constitutis

Bibliography: Faye and Bond, p. 94, no. 255.

Marston MS 256 — Venice, s. XV/XVI
Life and Miracles of the Virgin Mary, in It., etc.

1. ff. 1r–23v [f. 1r:] *Qua dice Santo Epifanio del stado della vergene maria et como Ella vine diredo l'asension del so fiolo*, Dice Santo Epifanio che de diredo l'asension de yesu christo benedeto la vergene maria madre de dio demora in Ierusalem et stete in caxa de San zuane Evangelista perseverando sempre in oracione et contemplatione in le cose celestial . . . ;

   [f. 1v:] *Qua dice Santo epifanio como la vergene maria vegniua Spese fiade vixitada da l'ançolo de dio*, Dice Santo Epifanio che yhesu fiolo de dio Spese fiade mandaua el suo ançolo da ciello In terra a uiritar la vergene maria per consolarla . . . ;

   [f. 2r:] *Qua dice Santo Epifanio de le uestimente che portaua la ve[r]gene maria*, Dice Santo Epifanio che la uergene maria portaua en rava [?] le sue uestimente mondissime si de lino como de lana . . . ;

   [f 2r:] *de la charitade et della humilitade della vergene maria*, Dice Santo çuane damaseeno [*sic*] che la vergene maria fo Sempre piena de charitade e de humilitade E fo sempre conpiacente et piatora a li poveri . . . ;

   [f. 2v:] *Qua dice Santo Epifanio con chi demora la vergene maria driedo l'asension del suo fiolo yhesu christo*, Santo Epifanio dice de la vergene maria demorando In ierusalem ella stete pluxor anni cuon [*sic*] san çuane In una sua chaxa . . . ;

   [f. 3r] *Qua dice Santo germano che la vergene maria mando San çuane euançelista a pridicar per lo mondo*, Dice Santo germano che lla priecioxa vergene maria manda san çuane Euançeellista [*sic*] a predichar per lo mondo. mo [*sic*] San çuane abandonaua mal uolentira la madre de dio . . . ;

   [f. 4r:] *Qua dice Santo epifanio delle bone hoperacion de san simion çusto et como la vergene maria stete in chaxa sua*, Dice Santo Epifanio che simeon çusto si era uno homo molto deuoto et in boni costumi et in bone operation . . . ;

[f. 4v:] *Qua diee* [sic] *Santo germano delli Segni et delli miracoli che fece la vergene maria viuando al mondo,* In quel tempo viuando la vergene maria al mondo ella fece molti miracoli et segni li quali el segnor idio demostraua per ella che li infermi de diuerse infirmitade elle li curaua . . . ;

[f. 5r:] *Qua didice* [sic] *Santo germano che la vergene maria resusita el fiolo de pouera vedoua,* Una dona pouerissima la qualle era vedoua vene dalla vergene maria piançando molto forte et lamentandose de uno suo fiolo che era morto . . . ;

[f. 5v:] *Como la vergene maria resusita una çouene vergene,* Dice Santo germano che in [ie]rusalem si ear [*sic*] uno homo el quale si era fedellissimo che auea nome simion et questo si era batiçado da li apostoli . . . ;

[f. 6r:] *Como la vergene maria resusita una dona la qualle era morta, la qualle auea fato dui fioli in uno portado,* Una dona la qualle aueua nome matrona parturando ella dui fioli per caxone de quello dolor del porto l'anema si parti dal corpo . . . ;

[f. 6r:] *Qua dice Santo Ignatio che per li meriti de la vergene maria nasete uno fantolino de una dona morta,* Anchora una dona la qualle era forntissimamente [*sic*] grauida E del suo parto ella per quello doloro [*sic*] si pasa de questa uita auanti ch'ella parturise la criatura . . . ;

[f. 7r:] *Como la vergene maria libra le fiolo de una pouera dona che uno lion l'aueua portado via,* Una dona pouerissima la qualle era molto deuota della vergene maria la quialle [*sic*] aueua uno fiolo che era piçolo el qualle si ando in un canpo [*sic*] vene uno lione et portalo via . . . ;

[f. 7v] *Qua dice Santo Ignatio Como la vergen maria libera tre çoueni li qual era condanadi a la morte innocentemente,* In quel tempo tre çoueni innocentemente era condanadi a la morte et çudegadi per inuidia . . . ;

[f. 8r:] *Como la vergene maria libera una dona la quale era stada acuxada de adulterio,* Una dona la qual era stada acuxada de adulterio da farixei et condanada a morte per quello adulterio . . . ;

[f. 8v:] *Qua dice Santo theofillo como la vergene maria libera uno homo el quale era prexo per fruto* [sic], Uno homo lo quale era prexo per fruto et fo metudo in carcere In grosissimi feri . . . ;

[f. 9r:] *Qua dice Santo theofillo como molti neofici* [sic] *et incredulli de diuerse prouintie vene a ueder la pretioxa vergene maria,* In quel tempo molti nofici et molti increduli si ride [?] elli le vertude della vergene maria de lu[n]tana parte Elli uene per vederlla . . . ;

[f. 9v:] *Qua dice Santo Ignatio como san paulo retorna anchora in In* [sic] *ierusalem a uixitar la vergene maria,* Siando pasado un certo tempo ancora retorna san paolo In ierusalem a uixitar la vergene maria madre de dio, Et ancora san paolo mena cosi molti altri disipoli . . . ;

[f. 10r:] *Como san paulo se parti dalla vergene maria per andar a predichar la fede de yhesu christo benedeto,* Abiando san paolo demorado alguni di in In [*sic*] ierusalem, Siando ello ben instrutu [*sic*] della santa fe de christo ello domanda la benedicione dalla vergene . . . ;

[f. 10v:] *Como Santo Ignatio scrise una letera e mandala a la vergene maria pregandola la irescriua indriedo,* Santo Ignatio disipolo de san çuan euangelista si a e[?] conuertido a la fe con reuerentia ne saluta con eterna pace, Madone notificando, O regina dolcissima io ho gran desiderio de esser un poco con vuj . . . ;

[f. 11r:] *Como la vergene maria scrise a santo Ignatio co' la soa man propio questa letera dignado,* Al suo dileto et amado disipolo Ignatio elleto a la soprana gratia della fe chatolicha, Maria humelle deuota et ançellicha de christo te saluda con perfeto amaistramento de uertude, orandote . . . ;

[f. 12r:] *Como Santo epifanio li ani e 'l tempo che la vergene maria viue in questo mondo,* Dice e deschiara Santo epifanio che la vergene maria uiue in questo mondo lxxii anni . . . ;

[f. 12v:] *Qua dice san çuane damaseno della morte et della asuncione della vergene maria,* E Siando peruengnudo el tenpo ch'el nostro segnor misier yhesu christo receue la sua madre in la celestial gloria . . . ;

[f. 13v:] *Como la vergene maria anoncia a li sui amici et a le sue conp[a]gne la sua morte,* Allora siando l'ançolo montado in ciello la vergene maria fece convochar tuti li sui amici e parenti . . . ;

[f. 14r:] *Como li apostoli per spirito santo se congrega in ierusalem et como elle fo portadi auanti la porta della vergene maria,* Dice santo dionixio che statiando la vergene maria in oration et contenpiando ella in le scose [*sic*] dcelestial [*sic*] con quelli sui amici . . . ;

[f. 16r:] *Qua cice* [sic] *santo germano del pianto che fe li apostoli veçando aprosimar la morte della vergene maria,* Allora ueçando li apostoli ch'el se aprosimaua la morte della vergene maria elli comença tuti a pianςer amaramente dicedo . . . ;

[f. 16v:] *Como yhesu fiolo de dio aparse a la madre in hora della sua morte,* E Siando peruegnudo el tenpo et l'ora ch'el nostro segnor misier yhesu christo uolse receuer la sua dileta madre in la celiestal [*sic*] gloria, Et Ello con tuta la celestial corte desexe de cielo in tera . . . ;

[f. 17v:] *Como san michiel archançolo recomanda el corpo della vergene maria a li apostoli*, E Abiando christo benedeto portada quella anema glorifichada in la gloria de uita eterna, Alora san michiel archançolo recomanda el corpo santissimo . . . ;

[f. 18r:] *Como li apostoli porta quel glorioxo corpo de la uergene maria a sepelir in la vale iosafa*, Alora siando uia san michiel arcanço[lo] con el suo celestial spiendor, Et siando ben reuegnudi li apostoli et tornadi in perfeto seno . . . ;

[f. 18v:] *Como li çudei uolse andar per far uiolentia al corpo della vergene maria e deuenta tuti ciegi*, E Oldando li çudei li apostoli che andaua cantando et dicendo salmi et horation elli comença a domandar li altri çudei . . . ;

[f. 20r:] *Como una biancha nuuoleta couerse el corpo della vergene maria e li apostoli che lla portaua in aere con tuta la sepoltura*, Alora voitando [?] li apostoli et li altri disipoli el corpo della preciola [*sic*] vergene maria subitamente dio li manda una biancha nuuoleta . . . ;

[f. 20v:] *Como li apostoli sepeli el corpo della vergene maria in la vale de iosafa*, E Siando cusi couerti li apostoli con lo molumento [*sic*], Alora elli con deuota oracion et con salmi et suavissimi chanti . . . ;

[f. 20v:] *Qua dice san çuane damaseno chomo el fiolo de dio porta el corpo della vergene maria in cielo*, E Siando pasado el terço di adi xv anosto [*sic*] in eror del di. Subitamente el fiolo de dio desexe de cielo in tera . . . ;

[f. 21v:] *Como fo demostrado a san tomado el corpo della uergene precioxa maria vegnando ella portada in ciello*, E In quella hora quando la precioxa uergene maria uegniua exaltata in cielo. In quella propria hora uno delli apostoli de yhesu lo qual aueua nome san tomado . . . Et a lui piaqua per la sua misericordia et per lo benedeto transito della uergene maria a condurne anche nui a la gloria de uita eterna Amen. *Fenito lo libro del transito della gloriosa uergene maria madre de dio.*

Life and miracles of the Virgin Mary, in It.

2. ff. 24r–30r Litanies of the Virgin, of Christ on Ascension Day, of St. Jerome on his feast day.

3. ff. 30r–34v El grande esscelso confessor miser sancto magno secondo chome recita la sua istoria li fo de la citade de altino Et in el principio de la sua etade çoe ne li ani puerili si chomenço a cerchar idio . . . Si che per tanto chadauno che se retornera a lui ne le sue tribulatione

hover afani de uota mente [*sic*] serano exaudidi da miser yhesu christo per li meriti de questo glorioxo sancto miser santo magno El qual con idio padre uiue in secula senculorum [*sic*] Amen.

An account of the visions of St. Magnus that prompted him to found the Venetian churches of San Pietro, Raffaele Arcangelo, San Salvatore, Santa Maria Formosa, San Zaccaria, Santa Giustina and Santi Apostoli, and the story of St. Magnus's burial and subsequent translation to the church of San Geremia in Venice.

4. ff. 34v–40r El paradixo diliciano çi[o]e terresto si e in terra in questo mondo ne le parte de orient [*sic*] in su'n uno [*sic*] monte altissimo sopra tuto el mondo, Del quello [*sic*] paradixo excono quatro fiumni [*sic*] . . . Et poi passando de questa misera uita andarano [*sic*] alla Eterna beatitudine Alla quale ne conducha christo yhesu benedeto El qualle uiue Et regna in secula seculorum Amen.

   Legend of the three monks in Paradise, in It.; a version of this story is published by F. Zambrini, ed., "Leggenda del viaggio di tre santi monaci al Paradiso terrestre," in *Miscellanea di opuscoli inediti o rari dei secoli XIV e XV, Prose* (Turin, 1861) v. 1, pp. 161–79.

5. ff. 40r–43v *Como ogni male Et maximamente de infirmita sono da portare con patientia,* E douemo sapere che douemo auere patientia generalmente in ogni tribulatione E questo E contra alquanti stolti che certe cose patino assai bene Et alcune altra [*sic*] per nesuno modo sanno aconciare a patire . . . Et sagino al cielo si che li canti meno Et comentiarono a udire bene adunquale infermitade sono utile Et pero ci douiamo auere perfecta patientia.

   Exhortation to suffer illness patiently citing three *exempla* from St. Gregory's *Dialogues* (about Servulus always sick; Spes the blind father; Romula with angelic choirs at her death).

6. ff. 44r–45r Lists of the 7 works of spiritual mercy, the 7 works of corporal mercy, the 7 sacraments, the 7 virtues, the 7 mortal sins, the 5 senses, the 7 gifts of the Holy Spirit.

7. ff. 45r–48r Amantissima [cancellation?] como fiola mia carissima christo yhesu Il cui sancto feruente spirito sempre sia nel tuo cuore, l'apostolo çentilissimo san paulo cum summo ardore de caritade dice ne la Epistola ai galati, michi mundus crrcifixus [*sic*] est et ego mundo, oue aper[t]amente demostra che lo stado che colei che perfecta mente serve a christo yhesu . . . anima che per sola gratia a questo grado saliste non ti dementegare li infermi peccatori ma pregando per loro de me te

ricorda como de colui che posto nel profondo abisso dimanda per gratia de Esser a luce reuelato, Amen. Christus Yhesu sit in spiritu Omnium nostrorum.

Unidentified sermon or exhortation, in It., addressed to a woman.

8. f. 48r–v *Admonicio santi anselmi,* Interroga: frater, letaris quod in fide cristiana morieris? Respondet: etiam. Gaudes quod morieris in habitu religionis? Etiam. Fateris te non bene uixisse quam debuisses? etiam ... Dic ter: In manus tuas domine commendo spiritum meum. Conuentu id ipsum respondente: Securus moritur cui ante mortem hee dicitur, nec uidebit mortem in eternum. *Explicit recommendacio sancti Anselmi.*

Anselm of Canterbury, *Commendatio animae*; F.S. Schmitt, ed., *Ein neues unvollendetes Werk des hl. Anselm von Canterbury* (Munster, 1936) pp. 5–6 with text from "Conuentu id..." added in Marston MS 256.

9. f. 48v In dilectione dei necessario tenenda est fides et uita; in dileilectione [*sic*] autem proximi debet ... benigna uero ut sua bona proximis desiderabiliter impendat. Gregorius.

Short unidentified text attributed to Gregory I.

Parchment, ff. i (contemporary parchment; palimpsest; upper edge trimmed) + 48, 201 x 126 (129 x 77) mm. 30 long lines. Single vertical bounding lines ruled in hard point. Text lines ruled in ink. The placement of a single pricking along outer edge of leaf suggests text lines may have been drawn with a ruling device. Remains of prickings in lower margin. Folios 47–48 ruled in 4 columns perpendicular to present text.

I-IV^{10}, V^{6}, VI^{2} (+ 1 leaf, probably rear flyleaf, now removed).

Written in small round gothic bookhand, below top line.

Crudely executed initials, red with blue and/or red penwork designs and vice versa; initials on ff. 7v–8v have green added. Blue headings accompany red initials and red accompany blue. Initial letters stroked with red throughout. Line filler in red, blue and yellow on f. 6r.

Binding: Italy. s. xvi. Original sewing on three tawed skin, kermes pink, slit straps laced through tunnels in the edge to channels on the outside of beech boards and pegged twice. Yellow edges. Plain wound endbands are sewn on tawed skin cores laid in grooves on the outside of the boards. Spine is lined with leather between supports.

Covered in brown goatskin, blind-tooled with a triple cross in a central rectangle in concentric frames. Two fastenings; holes from pins on the lower board, the upper one cut in for straps which are fastened with star-headed nails. Spine: supports defined with double fillets; an *X* of triple fillets in the panels which are bordered with double fillets on the sides.

Written at the end of the 15th or beginning of the 16th century in Venice to judge from the dialect and the contents of art. 3; early provenance otherwise unknown. H. P. Kraus (*List 189*, no. 105; from the collection of Giuseppe [Joseph] Martini?). Purchased from L.C. Witten in 1959 by Thomas E. Marston (bookplate).

secundo folio: *Qua dice*

Bibliography: Faye and Bond. p. 94, no. 256.

Marston MS 257 Rome [?], s. $XV^{2/4\text{-med}}$
Leonardo Bruni, De militia

ff. 1r–20r Fateor clarissime uir. et mihi ipsi iam sepe indubium uenisse hanc nostri temporis militiam que dignitatis honorisque loco prestantibus . . . dicendum fore premisimus. Que cum ita sint finem dicendi aliquando faciamus. f. 20v blank

Baron, pp. 166–67; text edited by M. Maccioni, *Osservazioni e dissertazioni varie sopra il diritto feudale* (Livorno, 1764) pp. 81–106.

Parchment, ff. ii (modern paper) + i (early paper) + 20 (early foliation 1–20) + ii (modern paper), 258 x 189 (184 x 90) mm. 25 long lines. Double vertical and single horizontal bounding lines (Derolez 13.33), though on several leaves there are no horizontal bounding lines (13.31). Ruled in hard point on hair side. Remains of prickings in outer margins.

$I\text{–}II^8$, III^4. Horizontal catchwords in lower margin, right of center, verso (Derolez 12.2).

Written in a round humanistic bookhand by a single scribe, above top line.

One illuminated initial, 7-line, gold (partly flaked) on blue, green and pale mauve ground, with white vine-stem ornament and grey-green dots. Rubbed in upper right corner. Possibly by the same artist as the initials in Marston MS 85.

Folio 1r stained with loss of a few letters; outer margin repaired.

Binding: Austria, s. xix. Half bound by Ferd Bakala of Vienna, in cream color calf with green paper sides. A green, gold-tooled label on spine.

Written probably in Rome in the second quarter or middle of the 15th century; early modern provenance unknown. Note, s. xvii, written in ink on f. iii recto: "Orazioni latine manoscritte del Padre Giovanni Leonardo della Congregatione dell' Oratorio di S. Filippo Neri in tempo che era secolare." Two modern typewritten notes (blue ink). The first pasted inside front cover gives much the same information, in Italian, as the note above; the second, in German: "Codex aus der ersten Hälfte des 15. Jahrh., Derselbe besteht aus zwei Abhandlungen, die erste "De instituenda militia," die zweite "de principatu Graeciae," ausgezeichnet definiert, in klassischem Latein geschrieben, können sie als Mustertexte der besten Epoche der humanistischen Schule gelten - Die Arbeit ist dem Abte Leonardo Giovanni ir rtümlicherweise [*sic*] zugeschrieben denn derselbe wurde erst 1541 zu Lucca geboren und starb 1609 zu Rom - sehr wahrscheinlich ist der Verfasser. Leonardo Bruni - Genannt Aretino. Der Codex dürfte unediert sein." It is possible that Marston MS 85, with its label on spine reading "De principatu graeciae" and with foliation from 21–46, formerly comprised the second part of what was once a composite manuscript before modern rebinding. Although the two manuscripts were not written by the same scribe, they are of a similar size and contain decorative initials that may be by the same artist. (See also description of Marston MS 85.) In pencil on f. i recto: "gis/ KTS". Purchased in 1959 from Bernard M. Rosenthal by Thomas E. Marston (bookplate).

secundo folio: [quem]admodum nostra

Bibliography: Faye and Bond, p. 94, no. 257.

Marston MS 258 — Italy, s. $XV^{2/4}$
Cicero, De amicitia, Paradoxa Stoicorum

1. ff. 1r–25r [Heading, much faded:] *De amicitia lelij et scipionis amicissimorum omnique genere* [next word illegible] *prestantissimorum uirorum felicissime incipit. ad brutum Acticum.* Quintus Mutius sceuola augur multa narrare ... nichil prestabilius in amicitia esse putetis. [followed by erasure in following line: "laus deo patri. Amen"] Finis./ Liber de amicitia ad acticum marci tullij ciceronis feliciter explicit. laus deo patri Amen [added in red:] *Et uirgini marie. Amen.* f. 25v blank

   Cicero, *De amicitia*; K. Simbeck, ed., Teubner fasc. 47 (1917) pp. 46c–86c. The texts of both arts. 1 and 2 are accompanied by interlinear and marginal glosses and some variant readings, all in contemporary hands.

2. ff. 26r–39v *Incipit liber de paradoxis.* Animaduerti brute sepe Catonem

auunculum tuum cum in senatu ... sed etiam pauperes atque inopes extimandi [*sic*] sunt. Laus deo patri amen. Explicit liber de paradoxis. [added in red:] *Et uirgini Marie. Amen.* [added in lower margin:] Mei Karoli Reguardati Nursinj ex manu propria. [visible under ultra-violet light:] 1444. [the final catchword has been erased]

Cicero, *Paradoxa Stoicorum*; C. F. W. Müller, ed., Teubner (1878) pp. 197–213.

Paper (watermarks: similar in design to Piccard Schere III.918–19), ff. i (paper) + 39 + i (paper), 217 x 147 (128 x 87) mm. 19 long lines. Single horizontal and vertical bounding lines (Derolez 13.13); ruled in lead. Prickings in upper, lower, and outer margins.

I $(-1)^8$, II–V^8. Perpendicular catchwords along inner vertical bounding line by the scribe who wrote text (Derolez 12.6); horizontal catchwords within decorative scrolls, red and black, added in center of lower margin.

Written in poorly formed humanistic script with some gothic and cursive elements, perhaps by more than one scribe, above top line.

Decoration, all of poor quality, executed by several contemporary hands. On f. 1r, black penwork initial with floral design in center, on square pale red-orange ground, outlined in black; large rectangular frame, in black, connects initial to unidentified arms (or a castle [tower?] proper surrounded by vine, in chief azure [with label of cadency of 4 points argent?] with charge [stars or crosses?] argent) in lower margin. On f. 26r, angular scroll, green with pale red and orange trim, unfurls to form the letter *A*, 5-line, with an arrow shot through the two shafts to serve as crossbar; green foliage sprouting above. Initials, 5- to 2-line, of similar scroll design for each *paradoxon*. Rubric on f. 1r in a different hand from those in rest of manuscript. Many elegant pointing hands with fancy cuffs in margins.

Binding: Italy, s. xix. Quarter bound in vellum with blue, red, and yellow woodblock paste-paper sides. Traces of inscription on fore-edge [contemporary?] and on vellum strip.

Written in Italy in the second quarter of the 15th century sometime before 1444, as part of a longer codex (final catchword now erased). Arms on f. 1r were identified by T. E. Marston (note on front pastedown) as those of the Casati family of Milan (we have been unable to verify this). Belonged to Karolus Reguardatus whose ex-libris dated 1444 was added in the lower margin of f. 39v. Although Karolus Reguardatus has been listed as the scribe of this manuscript (*Colophons*, v. 1, no. 2496), his ex-libris is not in the same hand as the text. Other manuscripts owned by him include London, B. L. Burney 172 (dated 1460), and three manuscripts cited by L. Bertalot, "Zur Bibliographie der Übersetzungen des Leonardus Brunus Aretinus," *Studien zum italienischen und deutschen Humanismus*, P. O. Kristeller, ed. (Rome, 1975) v. 2, pp. 270–71, n. 1: Stuttgart Privatbesitz Baurat Kyriss (dated 1464); Florence, Biblioteca Laurenziana Ashb. 1233 (dated 1457); Vatican City, Biblioteca Apostolica Vaticana, Ottoboni 2867 (dated 1467). The Cicero manuscript also cited by Bertalot from the catalogue of Jacques Rosenthal in Munich (cat. 90, 1929, no. 130) is now Marston MS 258 (see also below). Partially erased inscription, s. xviii, in lower margin, f. 1r: "della Chiesa...". Inscription in purple ink on f. 1r: "Acquistato a li 15 Novembre 1888." No. 6 in the sale catalogue of A. Rosenthal (I, 1939: *Secular Thought in the Middle Ages*). From the collection of James P. R. Lyell (1871–1943; bookplate; for further information on his manuscripts see *Lyell Cat.*, pp. xv–xxix); no. 40 in the sale of his estate (Quaritch, cat. 699 [1952]). Traces of 2 [or 3?] labels on spine; "21596" in pencil on back pastedown. "T. M." and "14" within circle, in pencil, on f. 1r. Purchased from Bernard Quaritch Ltd. in 1954 by L. C. Witten (inv. no. 526), who sold it in 1956 to Thomas E. Marston (bookplate).

secundo folio: Lelij

Bibliography: Faye and Bond, p. 94, no. 258.

Marston MS 259 — Italy, s. XV[1]
Cecco d'Ascoli, L'Acerba

ff. 1r–120v [Rubric, only partially legible:] *Incipit acerba ... capitulum primum de ordinacione cellorum.* Oltra non segue piu la nostra luce/ ... Segnendo el bene qual morte sperona. [f.19r:] *Incipit liber secondus in quo tractat de multis rebus utillis [?] et primo de fortuna.* Torno nel canto delle prime note/ ... dicendo unde procede e che amore. [f. 50v:] *Incipit Liber tercius in quo tractat de amore et de Animalibus et de Lapidibus preciosis.* [Partially erased line, in red:] *V*[three letters?]*mano de Rinciis.* [text, f.51r:] Dal terzo cielo se moue tal uirtute/ ... da qui inanti qual el to uolere. [f. 89v:] *Incipit liber quartus in quo tractat//* [rubric unfinished]. [*I* in red ink drawn in left margin] No voglio qui chel quare trouel quia/ ... E piu ueloce la ove el temeire// catchwords: E io a te or qui del

Cecco d'Ascoli (Francesco Stabili), *L'Acerba*, Bks. 1–4 with the final 214 lines of Bk. 4 and all of the fragmentary Bk. 5 missing. A. Crespi, ed., *L'Acerba* (Ascoli Piceno, 1927); Marston MS 259 ends at line 4473 of this edition.

Paper (polished; watermarks: unidentified cherries [?] in upper margin, trimmed), ff. ii (paper) + 120 (early foliation, Arabic numerals) + ii (paper), 206 x 138 (110 x 76) mm. 21 lines of verse. Double vertical and single horizontal bounding lines (Derolez 13.33). Ruled in lead. Prickings in outer and inner margins.

I–XII^{10}. Vertical catchwords with elaborate penwork designs between inner vertical bounding lines (Derolez 12.5).

Written by a single scribe in *mercantesca* script, above top line.

Blue initial, 6-line, with nice penwork designs, f. 1r. Smaller initials, 2-line, red with purple designs or blue with red designs, alternate throughout. Headings in pale red. Paragraph marks alternate red and blue. Later addition of arms in lower margin, f. 1r, effaced and covered with mending strips.

Binding: Italy, s. xix. Vellum stays adhered inside and outside of quires. Backs of quires cut in for original sewing. Bookblock tacketed to a semi-limp paper case, reinforced at the spine. Handwritten paper label with title and a printed medallion with Flora [?] standing on an anchor and globe [?], both on spine.

Written in Italy in the first half of the 15th century; early provenance unknown. Purchased from B. M. Rosenthal in 1959 by Thomas E. Marston (bookplate).

secundo folio: Qual

Bibliography: Faye and Bond, p. 94, no. 259.

Marston MS 260 — France, s. XIV[1]
Sydrach, La fontaine de toutes sciences

ff. 1r–63r [Prologue:] *Cest le prologue de sydrac.* La porueance de dieu le pere tout puissant de toutes choses a este du comancement du monde de sauuer et gouerner si par eulx ne deuient [?]. Espandit sa grace et sa misericorde pour tout le monde par quoy les gentz sauant et seussent la manere de viure en cest monde par quoy ils puissent venir a la gloire que ia ne faudra . . . Et atollete l'an nostre seigneur. Mil. C. C. xliii. par les meillours mestres furent fetz les prologues et les chapitres de cest liure tout selonc que le roy boctus fist les demandes a sydrac le philosophe. Et mant est le liure chapitre selonc les demandes qui touchant a vne raison mes tout l'un aupres l'autre come le roy boctus les demanda et a ce acordirent les mestres. [table of chapters, f. 3v:] *Ici comancent les chapitres des demandes que le roy boctus demanda de sydrac le philosophe. i.* Fut dieu touz iours et sera. *ii.* Puet dieu estre veu. *iii* ... Que doit l'en dire quant l'enleue de dormir. *ccclii.* Qui n'a que vne coille puet il engendrer. *cccliij* [catchwords: Pour quoy (?)]//[remainder of table missing, text begins imperfectly, f. 9r:] auchune home l'enfant luy resanblera. *lxiij.* Quele chose est la meillure que home puet auoir en soy. R. Leaute en dieu quar qui est leaux en dieu il est leaux en soy maisines et a la gent pour [?] cele le aute ... sa mort et la mort sydrach par langue du diable guerpirent dieu et retournirent es ydoles des quex enfer est plein et sera touz iours sanz fin. [colophon:] Ici finit le liure de sydrach le sage philosophe le quel lessa la science ampres luy la quele est profitable aus gens. f. 63v blank, except for inscription cited in provenance

Le livre de Sidrach, ou la fontaine de toutes sciences is a popular adaptation of an Old French *Lucidaire*, a translation of Honorius Augustodunensis, *Elucidarium*; the text here consists of 519 questions, of which 1–lxii are wanting. For a brief discussion and classification of the manuscripts of the French version see R. Marichal, "Les traductions provençales du "Livre de Sidrach" précédées d'un classement des manuscrits français," *Positions de thèses, l'École nationale des Chartes* (1927) pp. 80–81. For a modern edition of the complete Old French Sidrach, based on Paris B. N. fr. 1160, see two dissertations from the University of North Carolina: H. S. Treanor, "Le Roman de Sydrac, fontaine de toutes sciences" (1939); W. M. Holler, "Le Livre de Sydrac, fontaine de toutes sciences, Folios 57–112" (1972). Extracts of the texts can be found in E. Renan and G. Paris, *Histoire littéraire de la France* 31, pp. 285–318.

Parchment, ff. ii (i = parchment pastedown; ii = parchment flyleaf) + 63 (modern pagination 1–125, in ink; modern foliation 1–63, in pencil, lower right corner), 251 x 159 (186 x 122) mm. 2 columns, 37 lines. Single vertical and upper horizontal bounding lines. Ruled in ink. Prominent prickings (slashes) in upper, lower and outer margins.

I^8, II missing, III-VIII^8, IX^8 (–8, no loss of text). Catchwords under inner column, verso.

Written in gothic bookhand, below top line.

Initial, 4-line, in red with purple penwork incorporating a human head in inner margin, f. 1r; plain 2-line initials alternate red and blue for each question; paragraph marks alternate red and blue for table. Headings, Roman numerals for questions, initial strokes and paragraph marks within text, all in red. Remains of instructions for rubricator and guide letters.

Binding: England [?], s. xx. Quarter bound in vellum over oak boards with title, in ink, on spine: "Boccus and Sydrach/ France Saec. XIV." Discoloration from turn-ins of earlier binding on f. i recto.

Written in France in the first half of the 14th century; belonged in the 16th century to an unidentified individual who wrote in English on f. 63v: "Ihesus marcy Ihesus marcy/ Ihesus haue marcy one/ The mayster of Thys boke/ And send hym longe leyf." Head of king added (s. xiv?) to f. ii verso. Traces of clipping (from sale catalogue?) formerly attached to f. i recto. Miscellaneous modern notes in pencil, including "[1159]," "21634" crossed out, "24315," and "rs/-/-." Purchased from the Seven Gables Bookshop in 1959 by Thomas E. Marston (bookplate).

secundo folio: dist. non

Bibliography: Faye and Bond, pp. 94–95, no. 260.

Marston MS 261 — Florence, 1464
Petrarch, Rerum vulgarium fragmenta, Triumphi — Pl. 22

1. ff. 1r–142r Voi ch' ascoltate in rime sparse il suono/ ... [f. 123v:] che piu bel corpo occider nun potea. *Finita la canzone. Seguita i sonetti.* Orai facto lextremo di tua possa/ ... [f. 142r:] Ch' aceolga il mio spirto ultimo in pace. Deo gratias. *Finito le canzone et sonetti di messer francesco petrarca. Incomincia i triumphi.* f. 142v ruled, but blank

   Petrarch, *Rerum vulgarium fragmenta*, nos. 1–325 (ff. 1r–123v), 326–36, 350, 355, 337–49, 356–65, 351–52, 354, 353, 366; G. Contini, ed., *Il canzoniere di Francesco Petrarca* (Torino, 1964; 6th ed., 1975).

2. ff. 143r–181v *Franc. Petrarcche poete cl. de amore triumphus primus incipit.* Nel tempo che rinoua i miei sospiri/ ... Vien cathenato Ioue innanzi al carro. [*Tr. cup.* 1]; f. 145v: *Secunda pars huius triumphi.* Era sì pieno il cor di marauiglie/ ... Et quale è il mele temperato collo assentio. [*Tr. cup.* 3]; f. 149r: *Tertia pars primi triumphi.* Poscia che mia fortuna in forza altrui/ ... Che 'l pie' ua inanzi et l' occhio torna adietro. [*Tr. cup.* 4]; f. 152r: *Quarta pars primi triumphi.* Stanco già di mirar non satio anchora/ ... Et d' un pomo beffata al fin cylippe. [*Tr. cup.* 2]; f. 155v: *Triumphus secundus de domina laura.* Quando ad un giogo et un tempo quiui/ ... Fra quali io uidi Ipolito et Ioseppe. [*Tr. pud.*]; f. 159r: *Triumphus tertius. de morte.* Questa leggiadra et gratiosa donna/ ... Morte bella parea nel suo bel uiso. [*Tr. mort.* 1]; f. 162r: *Secunda pars huius triumphi.* La nocte che seguì l' orribil caso/ ... Tu starai in terra senza me gran tempo. [*Tr. mort.* 2]; f. 165v: *Tertia pars tertius triumphi.* Nel cor pien d' amarissima dolcezza/ ... Poi alla fine uidi Arturo et Karlo. [fragment of *Tr. fam.* 1]; f. 168v: *Quartus triumphus. de fama.* Da poi che

morte triumphò nel uolto/ . . . Sì come auiene a chi uirtù relinque. [*Tr. fam.* 1]; f. 170v: *Secunda pars huius triumphi.* Pieno d' infinita et nobil marauiglia/ . . . Magnanimo gentil constante et largo. [*Tr. fam.* 2]; f. 173v: *Tertia pars.* Io non sapea di tal uista leuarme/ . . . Qui lascio et più dilor non dico auante. [*Tr. fam.* 3]; f. 176r: *Quintus triumphus de tempore.* Nel taureo albergo colla aurora inanzi/ . . . Cosi il tempo triumpha e' nomi e 'l mondo. [Tr. temp.]; f. 178v: *Sestus et ultimus triumphus de diuinitate.* Da poi che sotto il ciel cosa non uidi/ . . . Or che fia dunque a riuederla in cielo. [Tr. et.]. Deo gratias. *Franc. petrarcche poete clarissimi triumphi expliciunt.* [colophon:] Die vigesimo optauo [*sic*] iullij Me CCCC° LXIIII°. [f. 181v, remainder of colophon erased but visible under ultra-violet light:] Ego Carolus palle Guidi domini Francisci de forestis della foresta Hunc librum transcripsi. laus deo. [written above a rayed sun drawn in red].

Petrarch, *Triumphi*; F. Neri, ed., in *Rime, Trionfi e poesie latine* (Milan and Naples, 1951) pp. 481–578.

Parchment (speckled on hair side), ff. i (paper) + i (parchment) + 181 + i (parchment), 250 x 155 (160 x 75) mm. 28 verses per page. Double vertical bounding lines and rulings for text in pale brown ink (Derolez 13.31). Single pricking at bottom of inner margin, ca. 23 mm. from gutter.

I–XV^{10}, XVI^{8}, XVII–XVIII^{10}, XIX^{3} [?]. Unadorned horizontal catchwords in center of lower margin (Derolez 12.1). Remains of quire and leaf signatures (e.g., a 1, a 2, a 3, etc.) in red, lower right corner, recto.

Written by Carlo di Palla Guidi in a round humanistic script, above top line. For other manuscripts copied by this scribe see de la Mare, *New Research*, App. I, 12.

Illuminated by Antonio di Niccolò di Lorenzo. The decoration consists of an illuminated title page with full border, white vine-stem ornament on blue, red and green ground with white, blue and pale yellow dots, respectively, with a thin gold bar in all margins, forming a diamond (black) in inner and a roundel with a profile head of a young woman against blue sky with some clouds in the outer margin. In the lower border a medallion (erased) framed in gold and supported by four round-faced putti with multicolored wings in green and red. Superimposed on the border are a variety of multicolored birds, a lion and two putti. These animals are related to animals in contemporary Florentine manuscripts and perhaps reflect the use of a model book. Historiated initial, 10-line, gold, on blue green and red ground with white vine-stem ornament attached to the inner border, with a half-length portrait of Petrarch holding a book against a blue sky with white cloud formations. Six illuminated initials (ff.

143r, 155v, 159r, 168v, 176r, 178v), 6- and 5-line, gold on blue, red and green grounds with white vine-stem ornament extending into margin, and gold dots with hair-line extensions. On f. 143r, initial joined to partial border, same as above. Plain initials in blue, paragraph marks alternate red and blue. Headings in red.

Binding: Italy, s. xix. Brown calf, blind- and gold-tooled. Gilt edges. Title on spine: "Petrarca".

Written in Florence in 1464 by Carlo di Palla Guidi for Francesco della Foresta (see colophon in art. 2), for whom he copied other manuscripts between 1449 and 1484 (see de la Mare, *New Research*, p. 490, no. 12), and illuminated by Antonio di Niccolò di Lorenzo. From the Carmelite monastery of St. Paul's in Florence (library stamp on f. 1r within erased medallion). Unidentified small circular stamp containing the letters "CR" on second front flyleaf and back pastedown. Belonged to Mary (d. 1924) and Charles (1853–1933) Lacaita; bookplate inside front cover: "Caroli ac Mariae Lacaitae filiorumque. Selham, Sussex"; sold in London in 1936. Acquired from H. P. Kraus in 1960 by Thomas E. Marston (bookplate).

secundo folio: Quei che

Bibliography: Faye and Bond, p. 95, no. 261.
Dutschke, pp. 190–92, no. 75.

Marston MS 262 — Italy, s. XV²
Gaspare da Verona, Regulae de constructione — Pl. 60

ff. 1r–52v Actiuum uerbum est quod in /o/ desinit et format passiuum in or vt lego legor amo amor licet non [*est* deleted] sit in usu dor ut plurimum autem uerba actiua. . . . quod nomen in quacumque declinatione et genere feminino tam arborem quam fructum significat. Reperitur etiam ficus in declinatione secunda et genere masculino pro fructu./ Finis deo gratias. [colophon:] Laus tibi sit christe quoniam liber explicit iste/ Explicit hic totum pro pena da mihi potum/ . . . Pro tanto pretio numquam plus scribere uolo/ Explicit expliceat quis uult plus scribere scribat.
ff. 53r–60v blank

Printed in Milan by Philippus de Lavagna ca. 1476 and thereafter (GKW, v. 9, no. 10557). Names of Latin authors cited (Nonius Marcellus, Statius, et al.) added in margins. Marston MS 262 not listed in Bursill-Hall, *Census*.

Paper (watermarks, buried in gutter: similar in design to Briquet Fleur

6647–49, Briquet Croix grecque 5576 and Piccard Kreuz II.607, Piccard Einhorn III.1648), ff. 60 (stubs of parchment front and rear flyleaves?), 214 x 143 (138 x 84) mm. Double vertical bounding lines, full length (Derolez 13.31); lines impressed on a ruling board.

I–VI[10]. Catchwords perpendicular to text between vertical rulings (Derolez 12.5); those on f. 50v erased, then written horizontally below written space. Remains of quire and leaf signatures (e.g., f 1, f 2, etc.) in lower right corner, recto.

Written in humanistic cursive script with gothic features by a single scribe, above top line.

Plain red initials, 3- to 1-line, throughout. Guide letters for initials in margin.

Binding: Italy, s. xv. Parchment stays adhered inside each quire. Original wound sewing on three tawed skin, slit straps laced through tunnels in the edge to channels on the outside of beech boards and nailed. A natural color endband, caught up on the spine, is sewn on a tawed skin core which is laid in grooves on the outside of the boards and pegged. Tied down through brown leather.

Quarter bound in mottled brown tawed skin cut out around the head and tail supports. Two fastenings, the leaf-shaped catches (wanting) on the lower board, the upper one cut in for the red fabric straps. The letter *R* written in ink on head edge. Binding illustrated in *The Medieval Book*, p. 65 (no. 67).

Written in Italy in the second half of the 15th century; contemporary inscription, mostly illegible, beginning "ho . . . ," on lower board. Remains of oval book label, white with blue edge: "109 [?]" in red ink. Purchased from Bernard M. Rosenthal in 1959 by Thomas E. Marston (bookplate).

secundo folio: Compero as ui

Bibliography: Faye and Bond, p. 95, no. 262.

Marston MS 263 — Italy, 1493
Jerome, Epistolae, etc., **in It. tr.**

1. ff. 1r–2v ruled, but blank; f. 3r–v *Inchomincia la tauola delle pistole di Messere Santo Girolamo traslatate di latino In uolghare pel uenerabile huomo Ser niccholaio di berto martini da santo gimigniano Notaio fiorentino. .j.* Prima epistola a Daliodero del dispregio del mondo e commenda la uita solitaria . . . *Lxxvij.* A Lucino Ispagniuolo della uita Romiticha E de suoi libri molte chose//

Table of contents for art. 2, ending imperfectly.

2. ff. 4r–312v *Inchominciano le pistole del glorioso messere Sancto Girolamo dottore della sancta chiese ... la uita solitaria.* Con quanto amore io mi sforçai che tu e io insieme dimorassimo nell'ermo. Sallo il petto della tua carita ... [f. 312v:] Ma ggia l'anghoscia della epistola debbe auiere fine. Amen. [colophon:] Finite di scriuere l'epistole familiare del glorioso messer santo Ierolimo questo di xxij di maggio 1493. per me don benedetto de serragli indegnamente priore del monasterio di san saluij nell'eta d'anni. 58. preghando ciascuno che lle leggie prieghi per me/ e trouando qualche ischorrezione di penna lo inputi e ssì dalla chopia e ssì alla mia pocha sufficienzia. *Deo Graçias. Iesu christe fili dei uiui miserere mei o gloriosa mater dei memento mei.*

Jerome, *Epistolae*, etc., translated into Italian by Ser Nicolaus Berti Martini de Gentiluzis de Sanctogeminiano, a notary in Florence (ca. 1388–1468). Other manuscripts containing his translation are Florence, Biblioteca Riccardiana 1681; Paris, Bibliothèque Nationale ital. 83. For his scribal career see de la Mare, *New Research*, pp. 516–18 (this manuscript cited on p. 518).

In the following concordance of the contents of this article we list the works as they appear in the manuscript, citing in square brackets the appropriate references to CSEL or to PL (the former number also used by B. Lambert, *Bibliotheca Hieronymiana Manuscripta* [Steenbrugge, 1969–72] 7 vols., with Marston MS 263 cited in v. 3B, p. 765, no. 968; this work hereafter cited as BHM). For each text listed below we compared the Italian translation with the Latin original; unless otherwise noted, all texts are complete. f. 4r [14]; f. 6v [125]; f. 11r [PL 30.15–45 (16–46): BHM 301]; f. 24v [22]; f. 41v [148]; f. 48v [PL 30.61–75 (63–77): BHM 305]; f. 57v [127]; f. 61r [PL 30.239–42 (247–49): BHM 332]; f. 62v [PL 30.145–47 (150–52): BHM 311]; f. 64r [68]; f. 65r [129]; f. 68v [123, sections 1–11 only]; f. 72r [122]; f. 76r [25]; f. 76r [34]; f. 77v [38]; f. 78v [23]; f. 79r [24]; f. 80r [59]; f. 81v [40]; f. 82r [41]; f. 82v [42]; f. 83v [27]; f. 84r [44]; f. 84r [PL 30.278–82 (287–90): BHM 340]; f. 86r [61]; f. 87v [?]; f. 88v [PL 30.116–22 (121–24): BHM 308]; f. 91v [39]; f. 95v [77]; f. 99v [78]; f. 111r [107]; f. 115v [74]; f. 117r [72]; f. 118v [6]; f. 119r [8]; f. 119r [2]; f. 119v [10]; f. 120r [7]; f. 121r [140, section 16 and following only]; f. 122v [1]; f. 124r [81]; f. 124v [108]; f. 137r [PL 30.282–88 (291–97): BHM 341]; f. 140v [126]; f. 141v [3]; f. 142v [PL 20.1037–41*: BHM 358]; f. 144v [118]; f. 147v [41, 619–60; PL 40.591–610]; f. 156v [PL 30.122–42 (126–47): BHM 309]; f. 168r [17]; f. 169r [146]; f. 170r [PL 30.294–95 (304–6): BHM 347, section 1 only); f. 170r [PL 30.292–93 (301–2): BHM 343]; f. 170v [15];

f. 171v [16]; f. 172r [18B]; f. 173v [18A]; f. 178v [21]; f. 186r [9]; f. 186v [79]; f. 191r [117]; f. 194v [66]; f. 198v [PL 16.367ff., sections 1–38 only: BHM 320]; f. 200v [12]; f. 201r [11]; f. 201v [13]; f. 201v [48, for another version of this text see also f. 219v below]; f. 202v [97]; f. 203v [45]; f. 204v [62]; f. 205r [PL 30.288–92 (297–301): BHM 342]; f. 207r [73]; f. 209v [58]; f. 212v [53]; f. 217r [47]; f. 217v [71]; f. 219v [48, for another version of this text see also f. 201v above]; f. 220r [50]; f. 222r [26]; f. 222v [28]; f. 223r [32]; f. 223v [75]; f. 225r [PL 30.182–88 (188–94): BHM 318 and 155]; f. 228r [36]; f. 232r [PL 23.1173–85: BHM 206]; f. 237r [PL 23.1185–96: BHM 206]; f. 243r [84]; f. 247r [147]; f. 251r [119]; f. 257v [54]; f. 262v [60]; f. 268r [64]; f. 274v [65]; f. 282r [69]; f. 287v [52]; f. 293r [19]; f. 293v [PL 23.397–456 (415–78): BHM 255, text appears to be an abridgement of Parts I and II only]; f. 303r [102, sections 1–2 only]; f. 303v [103]; f. 304r [105]; f. 305r [134]; f. 305v [141]; f. 306r [142]; f. 306r [143]; f. 306v [PL 39.2181–83; PL 30.176: BHM 316]; f. 308r [55]; f. 310r [145]; f. 310v [70].

3. ff. 312v–316v *Epistola dello Egregio dottore santo Aughustino Mandata a Cirillo secondo Vescouo di gierusaleme.... della Vita e morte del prestante dottore beato Girolamo.* Stimi tu beatissimo padre Cyrillo che le laulde de girolamo gia presbitero ... ne fraudate le sue uoglie per infinita secula seculorum Amen. f. 317r–v ruled, but blank

Ps.-Augustine, *Epistola ad Cyrillum*, concerning the death of St. Jerome; PL 22.281–89 and BHM 903C.

Paper (watermarks: similar to Piccard Schere III.710, Briquet Chapeau 3387; unidentified eagle), ff. i (contemporary parchment) + 317 (contemporary foliation vi–cccxviii, one leaf from index missing), 332 x 230 (224 x 149) mm. 2 columns, 40 lines. Single vertical bounding lines (Derolez 13.11); ruled in pale brown ink or crayon. Single pricking in upper margin, 8 mm. left of inner bounding line, and single pricking in outer margin, 5 mm. below bottom line.

I^4 (-4), $II–XX^{10}$, XXI^6, $XXII–XXXII^{10}$, XXXIII^8. Horizontal catchwords in center of lower margin. Leaf signatures (e. g., a i, a ii, a iii, etc.) added later in lower margin, directly beneath text column, recto, for second and third gatherings only.

Written by a single scribe in a small upright gothic script with both notarial and humanistic influence, above top line.

One illuminated initial, f. 4r, 6-line, gold, filled with red and blue penwork in geometric patterns. The penwork extends the whole length of the text column to form a partial border, terminating in the upper and lower margins in a scroll of blue penwork with small flowers, heart-shaped leaves, and red dots. Numerous penwork initials of good quality, 5- to 2-line, alternate in red and blue with purple and red penwork respectively, often extending into the margins. Headings in red. Majuscules and display script touched with yellow.

Binding: Florence, s. xv/xvi. Sewn on three tawed skin, slit straps attached to oak boards, with brown and natural color endbands [later additions?] sewn on tawed skin cores laid in grooves on the outside of the boards.

Covered in orange/brown sheepskin neatly blind-tooled with rope interlace in concentric frames. Spine: double fillets at head and tail and outlining the supports on the spine; fine diapering with double fillets in the panels. Four flower-shaped catches on the lower board, two wanting. Remains of vellum label (wormeaten) on the spine and pieces of string used as place marks. Off-set impressions of medieval liturgical manuscript on front and back pastedowns. Orange edges. Sticky from excessive oiling.

Written in Italy in 1493 by the prior Benedetto de' Serragli (colophon, art. 2) of the Vallombrosan house of San Salvi (Cottineau, v. 2, cols. 2875–76); ownership inscription on front pastedown and on front flyleaf (partially effaced): "Iste liber monasterij *** [Sancti Salvi?] vallis umbrose." Unidentified oval white label with blue scalloped edge with "2" written in red ink, on spine. Purchased from B. M. Rosenthal in 1959 by Thomas E. Marston (bookplate).

secundo folio: [index:] leaf missing
[text, f. 5:] [ghan]natore la qual

Bibliography: Faye and Bond, p. 95, no. 263.

Marston MS 264 — Spain or Southern France, s. XV^{med}
Jean Gerson, De potestate ecclesiastica

ff. 1r–32v *Incipit tractatus de potestate ecclesiastica et de origine iuris et legum per M. Io. de Iarsanno* [sic]. [prologue:] Potestas ecclesiastica debet ab ecclesiastis quid et qualis et quanta sit cognosci ... [heading in outer margin:] Describitur potestas ecclesiastica. [text:] Potestas ecclesiastica est potestas que a christo supernaturaliter et spiritualiter collata est ... Ratus vero dupliciter vel de iure vel de facto. [colophon:] Explicit tractatulus de potestate ecclesiastica et dorigine [*sic*] iuris et legum ... pro tempore magistri Jo. de gersonno cancellarij ecclesie Parisiensis Anno a natiuitate domini M cccc. xvij die februarii.

P. Glorieux, ed., *Jean Gerson, oeuvres complètes* (Paris, 1965) v. 6, pp. 210–50; see v. 1 (1960) for list of manuscripts and previous editions.

Parchment (irregularly trimmed pieces), ff. ii (bifolium, original parchment flyleaves) + 32 + ii (bifolium, original parchment flyleaves), ca. 240 x 167 (175 x 85) mm. 34 long lines. Double vertical and double (often widely spaced) horizontal bounding lines, full across. Two additional vertical rulings in outer margin to delineate column for marginal notes and headings. Prickings spaced every three lines in outer margin suggest that text lines were drawn with a ruling device. All rulings in pale red ink.

I–IV^{8}. Quires signed with Roman numerals, center of lower margin, verso; catchwords to right of signatures. Quire and leaf signatures (e.g., .a. j, .a. ij., etc.) in lower right corner, recto.

Written by a single scribe in fere-humanistic script, below top line.

Crude initial, red with an asymmetrical configuration of red and black penwork designs. Floral line-filler at conclusion of prologue. Plain red initials, 3- to 2-line, mark text divisions. Heading, f. 1r, in red. Majuscules stroked with yellow. Contemporary sketches of intertwining snakes on ff. i recto and ii verso.

Binding: Spain [?], s. xv. Sewn on three tawed skin support, two pink, the central one green, laced into a thick parchment wrapper. Contemporary title written in ink on back cover: "Tractatus de potestate eclesiastica***." Rodent damage at tail.

Written in the middle of the 15th century, perhaps in Spain or Southern France; 16th-century inscription upside down on upper cover: "monsieur de uendre Canbourne [?]." Purchased from L. C. Witten in 1959 by Thomas E. Marston (bookplate).

secundo folio: denique quo

Bibliography: Faye and Bond, p. 95, no, 264.

Marston MS 265 — Northern Spain, s. $XIII^{4/4}$

Thomas Aquinas, Super Metaphysicam, Super De causis

I. 1. ff. 1r–120v Sicut docet philosophus in politicis suis quando aliqua plura ordinantur ad unum ... et primum bonum quid supra dixit deum. qui est benedictus in secula seculorum Amen.

Super Metaphysicam; H. V. Shooner, *Codices manuscripti operum Thomae de Aquino* (Montreal and Paris, 1985) v. 3, p. 35. Numerous corrections, erasures and annotations by at least three contemporary hands, one of which also annotated art. 2 (see provenance).

II. 2. ff. 121r–132v [S]icud [*sic*] dicit philosophus in .x. ethicorum ultima felicitas hominis consistit in optima hominis operitione ... Primo cunctorum. sint grates principiorum. A quo nostrorum riuus fuit eloquiorum. Explicit liber de causis. editus a ffratre Thoma de aquino. ordinis ffratrum predicatorum.

Super de causis; Shooner, *op. cit.*, p. 35.

Composed of two distinct parts, parchment (poor quality), 305 x 218 mm.

Part I: ff. 1–120 (medieval foliation 1–122 omits 37, 38; modern foliation 1–120), written space 227 x 146 mm. 2 columns, 51 lines. Single vertical bounding lines full length; an additional pair of vertical rulings in outer margin. Ruled in lead or crayon; remains of prickings in upper and lower margins and on f. 8 in inner margin. I–IX^{12}, X^{4}, XI^{8}. Catchwords, some enclosed in rectangles, either vertical and perpendicular to text along inner bounding line or horizontal between line and gutter. First leaves of gatherings usually marked in red with different styles of signatures (e.g., ff. 49–54 have a sequence of one to six small circles between columns just below written space). Written by a single scribe in small gothic book hand. One illuminated initial, rubbed, f. 1r: blue with white highlights on dark red ground with white highlights; terminals of ground extend up and down as modest border in blue, dark red and gold. Flourished initials of various sizes, styles and quality: blue with red penwork designs, red with blue, red with purple (ff. 75r–119r) and red and blue divided with penwork in purple (e.g., f. 88v); some flourished initials with border extensions (e.g., f. 110v). Running headlines in red and blue; paragraph marks alternate red and blue. Traces of guide letters for decorator.

Part II: ff. 121–132 (medieval foliation for 123–124 only, modern foliation 121–132), written space 235 x 150 mm. 2 columns, 62 lines. Frame-ruled in crayon. Remains of prickings in upper, lower and outer margins. A single gathering of twelve leaves. Written in a less accomplished gothic script than that in Part I. Spaces for decorative initials remain unfilled.

Binding: Spain, s. xiv–xv. Original sewing on five tawed skin, double supports laced into beech boards. Plain, wound natural color endbands. Single parchment leaf (front) and bifolium (rear), from what appear to be two different Hebrew Bible manuscripts, serve as pastedowns and spinelining; they have been cut out around the sewing supports. Yellow edges.

Covered in what was originally blue tawed skin (now faded) with two fastenings, the catches on the lower board and the straps attached with star-headed nails. Traces of title [?] scratched onto skin of upper board.

Parts I and II were written in Northern Spain in the fourth quarter of the 13th century. One of the correctors in Part I, who gives his name on f. 24v ("Istum quarternum correxit ffrater S. de saranyena..."), apparently came from Sariñena, a town 56 miles northeast of Saragossa. The two parts were together soon after they were written, since another contemporary hand has annotated the entire codex and the Spanish binding dates from the 14th or 15th century. The manuscript was formerly "24–39" in the Biblioteca del Cabildo in Saragossa where it was located until the 1950s when it was photographed by the Leonine Commission; at that time it contained the following information that is no longer in the codex: 1. note of the decorator on f. 120v: "Sicut hic litere maiores xxvj. minores vero c.l. et par. c.lxxxviij ***"; 2. contemporary title on first flyleaf: "Sanctus tomas super methaphysicam et super libro de causis N. 5"; 3. a modern booklabel: "Biblioteca del Cabildo Metropolitano de Zaragoza, Armario 24, No. del registro 1620, No. de orden 39." Sold by Dawsons of Pall Mall (cat. 102, n. 9, pl. 8) in 1959; acquired from C. A. Stonehill in the same year by Thomas E. Marston (bookplate).

secundo folio: memoriam

Bibliography: Faye and Bond, p. 95, no. 265.
H. V. Shooner, *Codices manuscripti operum Thomae de Aquino* (Montreal and Paris, 1985) v. 3, p. 35.

Marston MS 266 — Southern France or Spain, s. $XIII^{1/3}$

Durand of Huesca, Biblical Distinctiones

1. f. i recto Short quotations in a contemporary hand from Lev. 24.15–16 ("Homo qui maledixerit ... morte moriatur"); Dan. 3.96 ("A me ergo positum est ... et domus eius vastetur"); Isidore of Seville, *Etymologiae* 20.4.2, on the verb *fingere*: "Fingere enim est facere ... et vas fictile dicitur"; f. i verso unidentified 3-line text beginning "deus diligit eos qui diligunt eum.... "

2. f. 1r–v [A]lta supernorum/ de stirpe creata deorum/ Alloquor ista chorum/ sermonis arte decorum/ Lux. dux. sermonis/ distinctio fons rationis/ Artibus et donis/ locuples sceptrum salomonis/ ... Alfa sit in primis summis qui regnat et imis/ Cum sit sublimis/ donis me ditet opimis.

Rhymed life of Peter of Capua (d. 1214), in quatrains, composed by Durand of Huesca (ca. 1160–1224?). For a detailed discussion of the texts in this manuscript see M. A. Rouse and R. H. Rouse, "The Schools of the Waldensians: A New Work of Durand of Huesca," forthcoming, 1991. The first and third lines of each quatrain are placed on the left, the second and fourth in the center, and the common ending for all four verses on the right. The three columns are connected by a network of lines across the page.

3. ff. 1v–284r [Table of words for the letter A:] Incipiunt capitule prima littera. i Alpha. ii Altissimus. iii Altum. iiij Absconditum. v Arguere. vi Aduentus christi ... cxv Aliud. cxvi Amen. cxvij Apotheca. [text, f. 2r:] Alpha deus est. vnde apocalypsis [*i* added above]. Ego sum alpha et omega. et cetera. Alpha est prima littera alphabeti ... [f. 284r:] Zizania ... hereticum hominem post primam et secundam ammonitionem de uita. f. 284v blank, but with pen trials and quotations.

Durand of Huesca, Biblical *distinctiones*, which according to R. H. and M. A. Rouse (*op. cit.*) is an early 13th-century revision of Peter of Capua's *Alphabetum in artem sermocinandi*. Marston MS 266 is apparently the only known witness to Durand's revision. The text is arranged alphabetically with one chapter per word numbered in Roman numerals. Each letter of the alphabet is preceded by table, also numbered in Roman numerals. The text appears to be in progress since the scribe has left space at the end of most letters for additional material and since the tables that precede each letter and the actual contents of the chapters do not correspond to one another (e.g., the table for the letter C runs from i. creatio through cxx. cortex, whereas the text ends with entries for lxxxiij. casus, lxxxiiij. compedes, lxxxv. confessio, none of which are listed in the table; there are, however, forty additional entries in the table [lxxxi cataracta through cxx cortex] that are not in the text, although some space was allotted on ff. 41v–42v). Other pages were left blank after the letters D (ff. 53r–54v), F (f. 81v, followed by stub between ff. 81–82), G (stub between ff. 88–89), H (f. 96v), I (f. 108v), N (f. 136v), O (f. 145r–v), P (f. 162v), Q (stub between ff. 164–165), S (f. 195v, followed by 2 stubs), T (f. 228v), X (f. 278v), Y (ff. 281v–282r). All the stubs were presumably blank. At least one quire containing most of the text for the letter M lost between ff. 128 and 129.

Parchment, ff. ii (parchment: i = pastedown; ii = flyleaf) + 284, 250 x 177 (162 x 125) mm. 2 columns, 31 lines. Double vertical outer bounding lines, full length; 3 rulings between columns; ruled in lead or crayon. Prickings in upper, lower, and outer margins.

I-VIII^{10}, IX^{10} (-2, 10, both blanks), X-XIII^{10} (at least one quire lost here), XIV-XVI^{10}, XVII^{10} (-7, blank), XVIII-XIX^{10}, XX^{10} (-9 10, both blanks), XXI-XXVIII^{10}, XXIX^{8} (+ 1 leaf added at end). Catchwords center of lower edge.

Written in a fine early gothic bookhand by several scribes, above top line.

Nice penwork initials, 7- to 3-line, for each letter of the alphabet, blue with red or vice versa. Smaller initials, 2-line, in similar but less intricate designs for chapter divisions. Chapter numbers, some initials, plain line fillers, and text divisions in red. Ornamental border, in red, encloses common ending for verses on f. 1r-v. Spaces for rubrics left unfilled. Majuscules in text stroked with pale yellow.

Beginning and end of codex worm and rodent damaged.

Binding: Place and date uncertain. Fragmentary binding. Resewn with a chain stitch and the spine lined with coarse cloth. Plain, wound endbands and paste boards (composed of paper and parchment fragments of manuscripts), that once were covered with brick red tawed skin. Traces of two ties. Outline of rectangular label, now missing, on upper cover.

Written in the first third of the 13th century in Southern France or Spain to judge from certain Spanish features in the script and decoration (e.g., tironian *et* with long horizontal stroke; tall, vertically oriented ampersand with small, angular top loop; style of initials on ff. 61r, 63r, 109r, 199r, 240r); it is likely, given the nature and presentation of the text and the date of the manuscript, that Marston MS 266 is a fair copy made at Durand's request, and belonged to either him or one of his companions. Effaced inscription (Arabic or Hebrew?) on f. 284v. Purchased from Enzo Ferrajoli, Barcelona, in 1959 by L. C. Witten (inv. no. 2541), who sold it the same year to Thomas E. Marston (bookplate).

secundo folio: Alpha

Bibliography: Faye and Bond, p. 95, no. 266.

Marston MS 267 — Flanders or Northeastern France, s. XII/XIII
Vitae Sanctorum

For the following collection of Saints' lives we provide the appropriate reference in BHL; incipits or explicits in the manuscript are given only when they differ from those recorded in BHL.

1. ff. 1r-2r [St. Thomas Apostle:] *Incipit miraculum de sancto thoma apos-*

tolo. Temporibus Kalixti pape secundi et anno eius quarto res noua . . . hec de beato apostolo thoma enarrasset mirabilia que per eum deus facit sua clementia. kalixtus papa cum clero et populo. gracias reddit deo. BHL 8145?; this text also found in Paris, Bibliothèque Mazarine 624, f. 36r.

2. f. 2v *In hoc volumine continentur hec. I.* Vita sancti Augustini episcopo. et confessoris . . . *xxxii.* Lucie et Geminiani martyrum.

   Table of contents [explicit or ownership inscription, in red, erased].

3. ff. 3r–15v St. Augustine. BHL 791, here divided into 22 chapters. This very rare text attributed to Rupert of Deutz also appears in Brussels, Bibl. Roy. 9368, a manuscript from Liège.

4. ff. 16r–28r St. Jerome. BHL 3871, here divided into 15 chapters and preceded by a list of chapters.

5. ff. 28r–36v St. Pantaleon. BHL 6440.

6. ff. 36v–40v Sts. Fides, Spes, and Charitas. BHL 2971.

7. ff. 40v–46v St. Taurinus, Vita, BHL 7990 (lacking the prologue); ff. 46v–48r St. Taurinus, Inventio, BHL 7994, with explicit: " . . . a sancto tauryno mirabiliter est curata. unde benedicens est dominus laude sua. Iterum. die tercia mulier altera aduenit clauda. que statim meritis sancti est curata die tercia"; f. 48r–v St. Taurinus, Miracula, *Miracula de mutis animalibus.* Erat quidem homo. in monasterio sancte crucis Audoeny qui comparauit bouem cecum . . . ut participes illius summi ac ueri dei inueniamus, cui tu fideliter seruisti in uita tua . . . Amen. *Finiunt miracula post mortem sancti taurini facta.*

8. ff. 48v–52r Sts. Agape, Chionia and Irene. BHL 118.

9. ff. 52r–54r St. Anastasia. BHL 401e (Passio Pars IV).

10. ff. 54r–59r St. Erasmus. BHL 2582.

11. ff. 59r–64v Sts. Marianus and James. BHL 131.

12. ff. 64v–67r Sts. Parthenius and Calocerus. BHL 1534.

13. ff. 67r–73v Sts. Lucius, Flavianus, Montanus, et al. F. Dolbeau, ed., "La Passion des saints Lucius et Montanus," *Revue des études augustiniennes* 29 (1983) pp. 67–82 (Marston MS 267 = Y).

14. ff. 73v–75r St. Lambert, Vita, BHL 4688. (Prologue); ff. 75r–98r St. Lambert, Passio, divided into 17 chapters and preceded by list of chapters. Explicit: " . . . Circa cuius sepulchrum. tantam considerabant gloriam et magnificentiam. . ."

15. ff. 98v–99r Virgin Mary, Vita. BHL 5334; ff. 99r–107r Virgin Mary, Nativitas. BHL 5335, explicit: "... Non post tempus multum. dixit angelus ad ioseph ... mortui enim sunt omnes. qui querebant animam pueri."; ff. 107r–112r Virgin Mary, Transitus. BHL 5351, explicit: "... narrantes et praedicantes magnalia dei, qui in trinitate perfecta ... Amen."

16. ff. 112r–120v St. Mary Magdalen. BHL 5457 and 5457a, explicit: "... Transiit autem beatus maxyminus sexto idus iunij. a domino feliciter coronatus ... Amen."

17. ff. 120v–139r St. Basil. BHL 1023, here divided into 17 chapters and preceded by list of chapters.

18. ff. 139r–141r Sts. Donatianus and Rogatianus. BHL 2275.

19. ff. 141r–143r St. Sisinnius. BHL 7796.

20. ff. 143r–146r St. Photinus, etc. BHL 6839, with the following differences: preceding the prologue are five lines: "Anno septimo decimo imperii antonyni in multas Romane urbis prouincias ex acclamatione et seditione uulgi ... litteris mandata repperimus"; explicit: "Igitur hii omnes per martyrii coronam. ad celestem gloriam. ducente domino peruenerunt ... Amen."

21. ff. 146r–148r Sts. Cantius, Cantianus, Cantianilla. BHL 1544.

22. ff. 148r–152r [Sts. Quiricus and Julitta:] *Incipit passio beati cyrici et Iulyte matris eius.* In diebus alexandri presydis. surrexit fuit que terre motus magnus. in ecclesia christi. Iulyta quidem matrona timens deum [cf. BHL 1803 bis] ... Complevit igitur beatus cyricus puer martyrium suum media nocte. et coronatus est. cum matre sua beata iulyta ... Amen. [cf. BHL 1806].

23. ff. 152r–156r St. Alexius. BHL 286.

24. ff. 156r–177v St. Julianus. BHL 4529. The text begins as in BHL 4530 (the version without a prologue) but the prologue follows and the vita continues as in BHL 4529.

25. ff. 177v–178v Sts. Peter, Andrew, Paul, Dionysius. BHL 6716.

26. ff. 179r–183v St. William of Bourges, Vita. BHL 8904; ff. 183v–193v St. William of Bourges, Miracula. BHL 8901.

27. ff. 194r–204r St. Matthew, Apostle and Evangelist. BHL 5700, explicit: "... qui saluat omnes fideles, uidelicet illos. qui non confidunt in medicis, sed totam spem et uirtutem suam. non in uanis et caducis

rebus expendunt. sed tantummodo confidunt in illum per quem mundus saluatus est . . . Amen."

28. ff. 204r–210r St. Ignatius. BHL 4258, with slightly differing explicit: ". . . celebratur, et reliquie quidem corporis eius relate antyochie. iacent in cymiterio extra portam dafnyticam ad gloriam Domini . . . Amen."

29. ff. 210r–217v St. Achatius. BHL 20 (explicit: 21, 22).

30. ff. 217v–235v St. Paula. BHL 6548.

31. ff. 235v–238v St. Barbara. BHL 917.

32. ff. 238v–245v Sts. Lucy and Geminianus. BHL 4985.

Parchment (thick, furry; many leaves repaired), ff. i (paper) + 245 + i (paper), 247 x 175 (174 x 111) mm. 29 long lines. Double horizontal and single vertical bounding lines, with three horizontal rulings through center of written space. Prominent prickings in upper, lower and outer margins, with double prickings in outer margins for three medial horizontal rulings.

I^2, II^8, III^{10} (-2, 8, no loss of text), IV–XXX^8, XXXI^{12} (-2; no loss of text). Quires signed with bold Roman numerals between dots, along lower edge, verso. Remains of more modest signatures and catchwords along lower edge, verso (e.g., f. 34v).

Written by multiple scribes in early gothic book hand, above top line; an early hand has sporadically added running headlines and some notes in lead.

Red and medium blue split initials with penwork designs in red and/or blue on ff. 3r, 107r, 194r, 217v; red and/or blue initials, most lacking penwork designs, appear for major text divisions; initial on f. 139r in red and yellow. Numerous smaller initials in green, red, blue and sometimes yellow, a few with simple void designs or in ink of a contrasting color. Rubrics throughout, some written perpendicular to text when there was insufficient space. Numbers and initial letters for chapter lists in red, blue, yellow and/or green. Remains of guide letters and notes to rubricator.

Binding: Flanders or France, s. xv [?]. Wooden boards with a faint rectangular panel design on each board; fastenings may be later additions? Original sewing on double cords. Remains of tawed skin saddle stitched around the tail endband and brown leather added at the head. Paper pastedowns and flyleaves added later. Traces of corner fittings from an earlier binding on first and last parchment leaves.

Written in Flanders or Northeastern France at the of the 12th or beginning of the 13th century; according to F. Dolbeau (*op. cit.*, p. 43) the manuscript can probably be attributed to an Augustinian house of canons regular in the ancient region of Lotharingia (see also arts. 3 and 13). Early provenance otherwise unknown. Inscription, s. xvii–xviii, on f. 1r: "Vita Sanctorum Nr. 5219." Modern note, in pencil, on front pastedown [*bis*]: "Gf6/24." From the library of the ducs d'Arenberg; for a discussion of this collection see C. Lemaire, "La bibliothèque des ducs d'Arenberg, une première approche," *Liber amicorum Herman Liebaers 1984* (Brussels, 1984) pp. 81–106 (Marston MS 267 cited on p. 104). Purchased from H. P. Kraus (notes on rear pastedown; Cat. 85, no. 117) by Thomas E. Marston (bookplate).

secundo folio: sanatur

Bibliography: Faye and Bond, p. 95, no. 267.

Marston MS 268 — Northern France, s. $XII^{3/4}$

Arnald, abbot of Bonneval, De septem verbis Domini in cruce, De laudibus B. Mariae virginis — Pl. 57

1. ff. 1r–47r *de verbis domini in cruce*. Vltima christi uerba que cruci affixus noui testamenti heredibus tractanda proposuit ... et qui diu fuerant cineres. fiant doctores. et qui sepulti magistri.

   Tractatus de septem verbis domini in cruce; PL 189.1677–1726B.

2. ff. 47r–52v Si linguis hominum loquar et angelorum nichil digne. nichil proprie de sancte ... ut sua dispendia non attenderet dum erroneum lucraretur.

   Libellus de laudibus de B. Mariae virginis; PL 189.1725C–35. Text missing between ff. 48 and 49 (" ... in celestibus circumamicta uarietatibus inde aura // locaustum. penitentie tutum omnibus...") corresponding to PL 189.1727B–30A.

Parchment, ff. 52, 220 x 150 (156 x 98) mm. 21 long lines. Double horizontal and narrowly spaced double vertical bounding lines, full across. Additional pairs of rulings in upper, lower and outer margins. Ruled in lead. Remains of prominent prickings in upper, lower and outer margins.

I–VI^8, VII^6 (–1, 2, with loss of text). Quires signed in Roman numerals with a dot on either side (I and II also decorated with symmetrically arranged red circles and flourishes), center of lower margin, verso.

Written in a neat late caroline minuscule that is written above the text ruling, not on it.

Red initial, 4-line, with red and green arabesque designs on f. 1r; red monochrome initials with simple decorative designs, ff. 2v, 9r, 14r; less elaborate red initials, ff. 18v, 23r, 29v, 47r. Heading in red for art. 1 only. Initials stroked with red.

Binding: France, s. xiii–xiv [?]. Original sewing on four tawed skin, slit straps laced from out to inside the boards and wedged at an angle. Pastedowns sewn with book. The upper board is beech, the lower oak. The grooves on the inside of the boards have been burned as well as gouged out. A blue and natural color endband is sewn in a chevron pattern. The primary core is laced into grooves parallel to the edges of the boards but not fastened and the endband is sewn through the cover. Fragment of an unidentified text (France, s. XII$^{2/4\text{-med}}$) used for front pastedown; portion of a document dated 1225 [?] involving Theobaldus, abp. of Rouen (1221–29) and the Cistercian nunnery of Fontaine-Guérard (Fontes Guerardi) for rear pastedown.

Covered in very thick tawed skin, neatly patched and pieced out. The turn-ins are nailed near the corners. There are two strap-and-pin fastenings, the pins on the lower board and the kermes pink, tawed skin strap ending in a catch with a twisted, tawed skin cord and tassel attached, later additions [?]. Remains of later title, in ink, on spine. The rear cover of this binding is illustrated in *The Medieval Book*, p. 64, no. 63.

Written in Northern France in the third quarter of the 12th century. Belonged soon thereafter to the Cistercian nunnery of Fontaine-Guérard, founded in the diocese of Rouen ca. 1198 (Cottineau, v. 1, col. 1173); its early ex-libris on f. 52v: "iste liber est de fontibus geradi [*sic*]." Presumably the manuscript was bound while at Fontaine-Guérard given the contents of the document used for the back pastedown. According to the notes of T. E. Marston, the manuscript came from the Benedictine priory at Charsay, Angoulême; we find no evidence in the manuscript to support this provenance. Signature of B. Monnet, s. xviii, on ff. 1r and 52v. Purchased from L. C. Witten in 1960 by Thomas E. Marston (bookplate).

secundo folio: efficientia

Bibliography: Faye and Bond, p. 95, no. 268.

Marston MS 269 France, s, XIII^2

Didymus of Alexandria, De spiritu sancto, Lat. tr. Jerome, etc.

1. ff. 1r–22r //Dominus inquit dabit sapientiam et a facie eius sapiencia et inte[remainder of word effaced] cum ea sapiencia que ab hominibus

uenit non sit spiritualis ... nostri non ignorantie sermonis.

Didymus of Alexandria, *De spiritu sancto,* Lat. tr. Jerome; PG 39.1042(C)–86; Lambert BHM, v. 2, no. 258 (cited incorrectly on p. 425 as Marston MS 17). Text in Marston MS 269 is divided into three books, with the first beginning imperfectly.

2. ff. 22r–26r *Incipit prologus boetij in librum de trinitate ad symachum patricium socerum suum.* Inuestigatam diutissime questionem quantum nostre mentis igniculum lux diuina dignata est formatam rationibus ... Ac de proposita questione. hinc sumamus inicium. [text, f. 22v:] *Incipit liber.* Christiane religionis reuerentiam plures usurpant. Set ea fides pollet maxime ... quantum inbecillitas subtrahit. uota supplebunt.

   Boethius, *De trinitate* (*Trinitas unus Deus ac non tres dii*); E. K. Rand and S. J. Tester, eds., Loeb Classical Library (Cambridge, Mass., 1978) pp. 2–31.

3. f. 26r–v *Incipit eiusdem liber de eodem ad iohannem romane eclesie diaconum.* Quero an pater et filius et spiritus sanctus de diuinitate substantialiter predicentur ... et fidem si poteris rationemque coniunge.

   Boethius, *Utrum pater et filius ac spiritus sanctus de divinitate* ... ; Rand and Tester, *op. cit.*, pp. 32–37.

4. ff. 26v–28v *Incipit liber eiusdem ad eundem de ebdomadibus id est animi conceptionibus.* Postulas ut ex ebdomadibus nostris eius questionis obscuritatem que continet modum ... que sequuntur efficiam. *quasi argumentum.* Communis animi conceptio est enuntiatio quam quisque probat auditam ... Iccirco [*sic*] alia quidem iusta. alia ad aliud omnia bona.

   Boethius, *Quomodo substantiae in eo quod sint bonae sint* ... ; Rand and Tester, *op. cit.*, pp. 38–51.

5. ff. 28v–31v *Incipit liber eiusdem de christiana religione.* Christianam fidem noui ac ueteris testamenti pandit auctoritas. Et quamuis ipsum nomen christi uetus.... atque gaudium sempiternum delectatio. cibus. opus. laus perpetua creatoris.

   Boethius, *De fide catholica* (*De hebdomatibus*); Rand and Tester, *op. cit.*, pp. 52–71.

6. ff. 31v–40v *Incipit liber eiusdem ad eundem de duabus naturis et una persona in christo. contra diuersas heteres* [?] *nestorij et euthicetis.* Anxie te quidem diu quod sustinui. ut de ea que in conuentu mota est questione loqueremur ... bonitas atque omnium bonorum causa perscribit.

Boethius, *De duobus naturis et una persona in Christo* (*Liber contra Eutychen et Nestorium*). Rand and Tester, *op. cit.*, pp. 72–129; Marston MS 269 has the additional phrase "quod nullus hereticus adhuc attigit" (as noted on p. 120).

Parchment, ff. 40, 192 x 146, greatly trimmed (146 x 108) mm. 2 columns, 34 lines. Single vertical bounding lines, with additional vertical ruling between columns, triple upper and lower horizontal bounding lines and two or three medial horizontal rulings, all full across. A pair of horizontal rulings in upper margin (for running headlines) and a pair in lower margin, often trimmed. Ruled in lead.

I-V^{8} (a gathering missing at beginning?).

Written in a fine gothic bookhand by a single scribe, below top line.

Red and/or blue flourished initials, some divided, of good quality (e.g., ff. 15v, 26r). Running headlines, incipits, and initial strokes in red.

Binding: France, date uncertain. Random sewing and attachment to three vellum straps laced into paste boards. Impressed on each board a rectangular panel with seven heraldic shields; in the center of panel a crowned lion rampant with tongue extended and brandishing a sword. Remains of two green ribbon ties.

Written in France in the second half of the 13th century; early provenance unknown. The manuscript was already incomplete when it belonged to the Jesuit College of Clermont, Paris, since its inscriptions appear on f. 1r: "Colegij Paris. Soc. Jesu" and "Paraphe au desir de l'arrest du 5. juillet 1763. Mesnil." Signature, s. xviii, on front pastedown: "J. J. Vaissiere"; modern pencil note on front pastedown: "S 18/11/57." Purchased from L. C. Witten in 1960 by Thomas E. Marston (bookplate).

Bibliography: Faye and Bond, pp. 95–96, no. 269.

Marston MS 270 — Paris [?], s. XIII$^{3/3}$

Petrus de Tarentasia, In quartum librum Sententiarum Petri Lombardi, etc. — Pl. 45

1. ff. 1r–201r [Prologue:] *Haurietis aquas in gaudio de fontibus saluatoris et dicetis in illa die confitemini domino et inuocate nomen eius* ysa. xii. in istis uerbis duplex effectus sacramentorum. de quo in hoc quarto libro agitur sufficienter exprimitur . . . qui est benedictus in secula seculorum amen. [text, f. 1v:] *Samaritanus*. et cet. liber ista sentenciarum tamquam

fluuius paradisi in quatuor capita diuiditur ... Iohannes xiiij. ad quam uitam ipse qui est uia nos perducat cui est honor ... amen.

Petrus de Tarentasia (Pope Innocent V), *In quartum librum Sententiarum Petri Lombardi*; Kaeppeli SOPMA, v. 3, no. 3340, with Marston MS 270 listed as Yale University, Reinecke [*sic*] Library Marston 21 [270]); Stegmüller, *Sent.*, no. 690. A contemporary hand has written the number of the relevant *distinctio* in the upper right corner, recto.

2. ff. 201v–202v **** auaricia [?] non uidetur curiosa sed fructuosa uel inflaciam sed edificatiam ... uita scolastica// [ending abruptly in portion of text designated "14" in margin]

Distinctiones on the scholastic and monastic life, entered in a later highly abbreviated script; portions of text, including beginning, partially effaced.

3. ff. 203r–206v Distinctio .j. Quid sit sacramentum et de iiij^{or}. distinctionibus./ 2 In quibus consistit sacramentum./ 3 Quare sit institutum./ ... [trails off at end with additions in several hands]. f. 207r blank

Table of contents to art. 1.

4. ff. 207v–208v Psalmus David iste penitentialis atribuitur David prophete respicienti in finem id est in christum qui est finis legis aut prophetarum ... diuini sermonis assidue in cordibus eorum reuolucio [or *reuoluens*?].

Anonymous commentary on the Psalms; Stegmüller, no. 8476 (Miserere), citing Bamberg, Staatliche Bibliothek Bibl. 66.

Parchment, ff. ii (parchment) + 208 (foliation, s. xvi, 1–207 with 18 *bis*) + ii (parchment), 211 x 150 (154 x 109) mm. 2 columns, 46 lines. Single vertical and upper horizontal bounding lines, full across. Ruled in lead. Prickings in upper and lower margins.

I–XVI^{12}, XVII^{12} (–11, 12), XVIII^{6} (4 singletons followed by a bifolium). Remains of catchwords along lower edge near gutter, verso. Quires signed with Arabic numerals, in center of lower margin, verso; majuscules (e.g., A, B, C, etc.) in lower right corner, recto, added by a later hand. Quire XI has leaf signatures in red (e.g., a, b, c) starting on second folio, in lower right hand corner, recto.

Written in small gothic bookhand; arts. 2 and 4 in less formal scripts.

Two historiated initials, 7– and 4–line. Folio 1r: mauve initial with white filigree on blue ground with white filigree, edged in gold, showing a man drawing water from a well, against gold ground, illustrating the Biblical passage "Haurietis aquas. . . . " Serifs, ending in heart-shaped red leaves, on blue and red cusped grounds, with gold balls, extending along the inner margin to form a partial bar border. Perched on the top of the initial is a small bird, grey with red wings. Folio 1v: blue initial with white shading against dark red ground with white filigree. Ascender blue against dark red ground, extending along text column to form a partial bar border. The initial shows the good Samaritan riding on a donkey, against gold ground. For a similar initial style see Oxford, Bodl. Lib.. Canon. Bibl. Lat. 41 (Pächt and Alexander, v. 1, no. 547). Numerous flourished initials, 4- to 3-line, alternate red and blue with penwork designs in the opposite color. Running headlines in red and blue. Paragraph marks alternate red and blue. Guide letters for decorator visible beneath initials.

Binding: Germany or Italy [?], s. xvi. Resewn (early) on three tawed skin slit straps laced through tunnels in the edge of beech boards to channels on the outside and pegged; channels filled with glue. A pink, green and white, five core endband is sewn through a leather lining on a tawed skin core laced into the boards and pegged.

Covered in brick red sheepskin with corner tongues; blind-tooled with an *X* and sparse use of oak-leaf edging tool. Two truncated diamond catches on lower board, the upper board cut in for the red fabric clasp straps which were attached with star-headed nails. Corner fittings and six-petalled central medallion. Traces of title, in ink, on spine. Spine of the bookblock partially eaten by rodents.

Written in the last third of the 13th century, probably in Paris, since art. 1 was copied from a stationer's exemplar *secundum pecias*. Pecia numbers (most trimmed) appear only at the beginning of the codex: ij (f. 10v), iiij (f. 19r), vj (f. 23r), ix (f. 35v), ? (f. 43v), xij (f. 47r), xiiij (f. 55r), xvi (f. 63r). The style of the binding and notes in Italian on front and back flyleaves suggest an Italian provenance, s. xvi–xviii. Belonged to comte Chandon de Briailles (bookplate). Purchased from B. M. Rosenthal in 1960 by Thomas E. Marston (bookplate).

secundo folio: hic de

Bibliography: Faye and Bond, p. 96, no. 270.

Marston MS 271 — Northern Italy, s. $XI^{2/3}$

Passion of St. Secundus, in Lat.

ff. 1r–24v *Incipit prologus sancti secundi martyris*. Gloriosa beatorum martyrum gesta . . . que dominus noster ihesus christus eisdem seruis suis dignatus est prerogare; [f. 4v:] *Incipit passio sancti secundi martyris christi.* Sub Diocleciano igitur et maximiano imperatoribus fuit quidam uir spectabilis ... Passus est autem beatissimus christi martyr secundus .y. kalendas septembris sub diocleciano et maximiano imperatoribus. Regnante [erasure?] uero domino nostro cui est honor.

Life of St. Secundus, second version still unpublished; see *Acta Sanctorum, Aug.*, v. 5, pp. 792–95, where it is quoted, and BHL no. 7569 (note: the explicit given in BHL is on f. 24r, l. 13; there is therefore more text in Marston MS 271). The *Acta Sanctorum* states that a manuscript from the monastery of St. Maurice, Magdeburg is its source (p. 792, 3).

Parchment (yellow, speckled on hairside), ff. i (modern parchment) + 24 + i (modern parchment), 207 x 165 (136 x 104) mm. 18 long lines. Double vertical and horizontal bounding lines, full across. Ruled in hard point on hair side before folding. Prickings (slits) in upper, lower and outer margins.

Three gatherings of eight leaves.

Written in well-formed caroline minuscule.

Plain red initial, 2-line, at beginning of text, f. 1r; similar 2- to 1-line initials for text divisions. Headings in red majuscules. Initials stroked with red, ff. 1r–20r.

First leaf stained and wormeaten, with loss of an isolated letter or two.

Binding: Place uncertain, s. xix. Dark red plush case.

Written in Northern Italy in the second third of the 11th century; early provenance unknown. Inscription, s. xvi [?], on f. 1r: "Fr. Marcus An. Taffinus sacre Theologie Professor [?]." Belonged to Giuseppe (Joseph) Martini of Lugano from whom it was purchased by H. P. Kraus (Cat. 75, no. 95); sold by Kraus in 1960 to Thomas E. Marston (bookplate).

secundo folio: [rece]dens uenerat

Bibliography: Faye and Bond, p. 96, no. 271.

Marston MS 273 — Germany, s. XV^2

Reformatio Sigismundi, in Ger.

ff. 1r–24v [Text:] Allmechtiger Schopffer himels vnd des Ertriths Gib kraft vnd tu genad ... Sy tragen in dem kor Schetter daz in die mentel singent vnd lesent//

Reformatio Sigismundi, originally written in 1439 at the alleged instigation of the Holy Roman Emperor Sigismund (1368–1437) for the Council of Basel. The text of Marston MS 273 is the vulgate version (V), composed around 1440; for the text of all versions, see H. Koller, ed., *Reformation Kaiser Siegmunds*, MGH Staatsschriften des späteren Mittelalters, Band VI (Stuttgart, 1964). The text of Marston MS 273 breaks off at p. 213 of this edition. As with other versions, the author of this text is supposedly Friedrich von Lantnau or Lantzenau (see f. 6r), who claims to have undertaken the translation of it into German from the "original" Latin. The identity of this person is still uncertain (see Koller, *op. cit.*, p. 6), and the idea of a Latin "original" is rejected by the editor (Koller, *op. cit.*, p. 17).

Paper (watermarks: similar in general design but not in proportions to Briquet Char 3539), ff. i (paper) + 24, 270 x 194 (190 x 140) mm. 35 long lines. Frame-ruled in pale brownish yellow ink.

Accurate collation impossible due to brittle nature of binding and leaves.

Written by a single scribe in a neat hybrida script, without loops and with very few abbreviations.

Spaces for title on f. 1r and elsewhere remain unfilled, as do spaces for initials; some rubrics within text in red.

Binding: Germany, s. xix. Bluish green marbled paper wrapper.

Written in Germany in the second half of the 15th century; ownership inscription "Des buch gehort dem [*L*M*Z*?]" partially erased. Later titles on front flyleaf. Two labels, one with title in ink wrapped around spine: "Reformation der geistlichen Personen M.S." and white rectangular label with blue border and "No. 4." Purchased from B. M. Rosenthal in 1960 by Thomas E. Marston (bookplate).

secundo folio: peters

Bibliography: Faye and Bond, p. 96, no. 273.

Marston MS 274 — France, s. XV^2

Leonardo Bruni, De bello punico, Fr. tr. Jean Lebègue

f. 1r [Title for table of contents:] Cy dedens est contenuë la table du liure de la premiere partie bataille punique . . . Et premierement commencent les Rubriches ou chappictres [*sic*]. *Premierement Le prologue du transla-*

teur ou liure ... Et premierement la table du premier liure. [table:] De la premiere guerre punique, Cest adire ... et fut la cite de agrigentum prinse; ff. 1v–2r *Cy fine le premier liure ... et de la male fortune de cornelius consul Roumain.* [table:] Comment tantost apres la prinse de cornelius ... Les condictions de la paix entre les Roumains et les cartagiens; ff. 2r–v *Cy fine la premiere partie du premier liure ... qui furent diuerses.* [text:] Comment hanibal conquist le pont et la cite ... et son ost desconffit; f. 2v *Cy commence la seconde partie ... apres la paix faicte entre eulx et les cartagiens.* [table:] Comment les Roumains conquirent ... Et puis tout vint a leur abaissance; ff. 2v–4v *Cy fine la Table. Cy apres ensuyt le prologue ... premierement:* [prologue:] A Treshault et souuerain prince Charles septiesme de cest nom ... Et vieus a la desclairacion fe de son liure; ff. 4v–74r *Cy commence la* [*desclairacion* crossed out] *translacion ... la dicte translacion faicte en l'an mil.iiij^{c}. xlv.* [text:] Certes je doubte que aucuns ne cuident fort ... aucun pou de lieux wider et partir hors de toute la Region. Amen deo gratias. *Explicit. Cy fine le liure de la premiere guerre punicque.* ff. 74v–75v ruled, but blank

Leonardo Bruni, *De bello punico*, Fr. tr. by Jean Lebègue; made, and presented in 1445, for Charles VII of France (1422–1461).

Paper (watermarks: closest to Briquet Armoiries-Trois fleurs de lis 1686), ff. ii (paper) + 76 (f. iii, 1–75, modern foliation), 285 x 193 (199 x 125) mm. 33 long lines. Single vertical and horizontal bounding lines. All rulings in pale red ink. Prickings in upper and lower margins.

I^{12} (ff. iii, I–11), II–VI^{12}, VII^{4}. Catchwords to right of center in lower margin, verso. Quire and leaf signatures (e.g., a j., a ij., ... a vj., X for central bifolium) in lower left corner, recto.

Written by a single scribe in an elegant bâtarde script that sits above the line, rather than on it.

Red and blue divided initials, 5-line, on ff. 1r, 2v, 4v, and for major text divisions thereafter. 3- to 2-line plain red or blue initials throughout. Initials alternate red and blue for tables on ff. 1r–2v. Multi-line headings in red sharply indented toward right. Guide letters for illuminator.

Binding: France, s. xvi. Olive-green goatskin, roughly gold-tooled with the arms of Claude d'Urfé in the center and a monogram of his initial [C] with that of his wife, Jeanne de Balzac, [I] in the corners, together with cornucopiae, caducei, laurel and flaming altars. (See J. Guignard, *Nouvel armorial du bibliophile* [Paris, 1890] pp. 460–61.) Gilt edges. Corners repaired.

Written in France in the second half of the 15th century. It was perhaps commissioned by Louis Malet de Graville, amiral de France (1441/50–1516); the inscription, s. xvi, along upper edge of f. iii verso indicates that he bequeathed the volume to his daughter Anne Malet de Graville (before 1506–before 1540): "A anne de Grauille de la succession de feu monsieur L'admiral V^{c} xviij." See E. Quentin-Bauchert, *Les femmes bibliophiles de France* [Paris, 1886] pp. 386–87, for a similar inscription in Paris, B. N. fr. 254. She bequeathed her library to Claude d'Urfé (1501–58), who married her daughter Jeanne de Balzac and whose arms appear on the binding (see above). For a history of the d'Urfé library and a list of the surviving books (including Marston MS 274 on pp. 89, 94), see A. Vernet, "Les Manuscrits de Claude d'Urfé (1501–58) au Château de la Bastie," *Académie des Inscriptions et Belles-Lettres: Comptes-Rendus* (Paris, 1976) pp. 81–97. Note in purple ink on f. i recto: "R [?] Barbet/308 b[?]"; note with date "1754" on back pastedown. Belonged to Lucius Wilmerding; purchased at the sale of his estate (Parke-Bernet, 5 March 1951, no. 42) by H. P. Kraus (Cat. 80, no. 26) who sold it in 1960 to Thomas E. Marston (bookplate).

secundo folio: gastez

Bibliography: Faye and Bond, p. 96, no. 274.

Marston MS 275 — Northern Italy [?], s. XVI [?]
Solinus, Collectanea rerum memorabilium

ff. 1r–41r Cum et aurium clementia et optimarum artium studijs prestare te ceteris sentiam. idque opido [*sic*] expertus de beniuolentia tua nichil temere precipere me reputaui ... Deinde cum monstra illa putredine tabefacta sunt omnia illic inficit tetro odore ideoque non penitus ad nuncupationem congruam insularum qualitatem. C. iulij. solini finis. f. 41v blank

T. Mommsen, ed., (Berlin, 1864; 2nd ed. 1896). Text is missing the following passages: f. 39v "fragmenta scalptoribus ... nitellam pinguiorem ut," f. 39v "margaritis scatet ... regionibus offendit," f. 40v "hoc locorum ... non caret vitibus."

Paper (thin, sized, no watermarks visible; f. 41 only, thick, coarse paper with indistinguishable watermark), ff. ii (paper) + 41 + ii (paper), 275 x 209 (178 x 115) mm. 40 long lines. Single vertical bounding lines ruled in crayon; text rulings in lead.

I–IV^{10} (+ 1 leaf at end). Horizontal catchwords centered along lower edge, verso.

Written by a single scribe in a very stylized round humanistic bookhand with gothic features and fine hair-line appendages to many letters, above top line. Script perhaps influenced by printing.

Plain red initials, 8- to 3-line; guide letters for decorator. Space for heading, f. 1r, left unfilled.

Binding: England or France, s. xviii. Bluish green goatskin, gold-tooled, with two red gold-tooled labels: "Solini Memor. Mundi" and "MSS Chart. 1468." Yellow tail edge.

Written perhaps in Northern Italy in the 16th [?] century, though the very stylized script and lack of watermarks make it difficult to localize and date with certainty. The date on the binding, 1468, does not appear in the text of the manuscript. Unidentified notes include: "21" in red crayon on f. 41r at conclusion of text; "V24/ 69" in pencil on first front flyleaf, verso; "D" in a circle, written in pencil on f. 1r. Purchased in 1960 from Nicolas Rauch, Geneva, by L. C. Witten (inv. no. 3101), who sold it the same year to Thomas E. Marston (bookplate).

secundo folio: pastorali

Bibliography: Faye and Bond, p. 96, no. 275.

Marston MS 276 Italy, s. XIV^2

Jerome, Epistola ad Eustochium, It. tr. Domenico Cavalca, etc.

1. ff. 1r–43r *Incomincia la pistola la quale sancto ieronimo mando ad heustochio nobilissima uergine di roma inducendola a l'amore de la uerginita. prolago.* [translator's prologue and chapter list:] Volendo per utilitade d'alquante donne relegiose et altre uergini et oneste persone che gramatica non sanno recare in uolgare quella bella pistola. la quale san geronimo mandoe ad eustochio ... [text, f. 2r:] Audi filia et uide et inclina aurem tuam et obliuiscere populum tuum. et domum patris tui. et concupiscet rex decorem tuum. Per le predette parole le quali [added in a modern hand in the margin: *sono scritte*] nel quadragesimo quarto salmo. parla iddio all'anima et dicele dolcemente ... Et cosi incominciando qui uita gloriosa n'andrai poscia col tuo sposo a godere in uita eternale. Qui est benedictus in secula seculorum Amen. *Finisce la pistola di sancto ieronimo la quale e' mando ad heustochio nobilissima vergine di roma.*

Jerome, *Epistola ad Eustochium*, It. tr. Domenico Cavalca (b. ca. 1270); Kaeppeli, SOPMA, 834. This translation first printed in *Volgarizzamento del Dialogo di San Gregorio e dell'Epistola di S. Girolamo ad Eustochio, opera di fra Domenico Cavalca, con alcune poesie dello stesso* (Milan, 1840): on the letter to Eustochio, see introduction on pp. 13–22; text of letter on pp. 390–480, based on three manuscripts, signalled *G* (= Senator Filippo Guadagni, base manuscript), *S* (= in the library of the late Carlo Strozzi), *Ser.* (= Abate Serassi). Folios 39v–40r in Marston MS 276 are blank, but with no loss of text; text annotated in red crayon by a later hand. Marston MS 276 cited by B. Lambert, *Bibliotheca Hieronymiana Manuscripta* (Steenbrugge, 1970) v. IIIB, p. 765, no. 968.

2. ff. 43v–45v Priegoti che ricorri nel cospecto della diuina uolontade rimettendo [?] in essa tutta la tua prouedença et salute. Impercio che ttutte le cose che cci occorrono o buone o ree ci debbono sança dimorare in esse riducere a la [*sic*] semplice principio cioe del solo uolere di dio ... et poi la fortifica. a farglele operare et poi la trasforma in se in tale modo che cio che pensa vede et ode, fauella deus est qui per tempora et nell'altra sine tempore. Qui est sibi solus in se et per se et solummodo propter se. honor et gloria in secula seculorum Amen.

   Exhortation to free submission to the will of God, through practice of spiritual exercises.

3. ff. 45v–46v [R?]accomandomi alle orazioni uostre secondo la uolontade di dio in lui et per lui et co' llui. Et si com'io posso ti priego et conforto per dio che tu guardi la mente tua et la lingua tua dalle novitadi che soprauengono di subito come temposta di mare si nello stato spirituale come nel temporale. Et impero mi penso che sia molto necessario che noi ci raccolglamo in uno ... Adunque ad cio che noj non ci tocchino et da esso fuocho non siamo ritracti solamente a llui ricorriamo et in lui ci trasformiamo et in lui et per lui et da lui et solamente per lui Accio ch'esso medesimo solo sanza nulla altra cosa. sia ad noj dio et sia tucte le cose il quale e a se medesimo gloria in secula seculorum Amen. f. 47r–v ruled, but blank, except for pentrial alphabet on f. 47v

   Exhortation to adhere to divine unity, by rejecting multiple distractions of life.

Paper (thick, coarse; watermarks indistinguishable), ff. i (paper) + 47 (modern foliation, upper right corner; modern pagination, lower right corner) + i (paper), 208 x 138 (145 x 102) mm. 23 long lines. Single horizontal and vertical bounding lines ruled in lead; text rulings in hard point or lead. Remains of prickings for bounding lines.

I-II^{16}, III^{15} [?]. Horizontal catchwords in center of lower margin, verso.

Art. 1 written by a single scribe in mercantesca script; arts. 2–3 added by another hand.

Crude penwork initial, in red and black, with upper and inner marginal extensions on f. 43v for art. 2. Plain red initials, 2-line, in art. 1; headings, paragraph marks, initial strokes in red.

Binding: Place uncertain, s. xx. Brown and beige printed paper case.

Written in Italy in the second half of the 14th century; early provenance unknown. Unidentified notes on front pastedown, in pencil: "WW 2/3/30 [crossed out]"; written below "Vt 3/2/50." Acquired from Giuseppe (Joseph) Martini of Lugano by H. P. Kraus (collation notes on f. 47v), who sold it in 1960 to Thomas E. Marston (bookplate).

secundo folio: Audi

Bibliography: Faye and Bond, p. 96, no. 276.

Marston MS 277 — Italy, s. XV^{ex}; France, s. XVI^{1}
Franciscan Archive

Due to the errors and confusion in the early foliation, the following description uses the modern folio references, in pencil, in the lower right corner.

I. 1. f. i recto, formerly front pastedown: portion of a notarized Franciscan document dated 1491 (text rubbed and obscured by stains; portion of same document used for back pastedown). f. i verso blank; f. 1r ruled, but blank, except for notes relating to provenance; stub between ff. i and 1 reveals that the leaf removed contained written text(s).

2. ff. 1v–70r Unidentified text added on f. 1v by one "Marturinus robini clericus maleacensis dyocesis." [upper margin, f. 2r:] *Extracta de verbo ad verbum de primo originali sub plumbo in Conuentu de Araceli.* Nicolaus Episcopus seruus seruorum dei delictis filiis Generali et Prouincialibus.... [ff. 2–3, with contemporary foliation 52–53, are presumably out of order; the beginning of the text appears to occur on f. 4r:] *Maremagnum Alexandri pape....* Sixtus episcopus seruus seruorum dei ad perpetuam rei memoriam Regimini Vniuersalis ecclesie meritis licet ... hunc paginem. ff. 50v and 70v ruled, but blank

Collection of some 200 papal documents relating to the Franciscan Order.

3. ff. 71r–80v *Incipit prologus In uita et regula Sororum pauperum Sancte Clare virginis.* Clemens episcopus seruus seruorum dei Ad perpetuam dei memoriam. Cruorem quarundam harum felicis recordationis Clementis pape ... qui talis est. *Incipit vita et regula Sororum pauperum Sancte Clare. Capitulum primum.* Forma vite ordinis sororum pauperum quam beatus franciscus constituit hec est ... Clara indigna ancilla Christi....

   Rule for Poor Clares divided into 15 chapters (ff. 71r–74r), followed by papal bulls, mandates, etc., pertaining to the sisters. See I. Omaechevarria, O. F. M., *Escritos de Santa Clara* (Madrid, 1970), for arts 3 and 4, especially pp. 268–89 and 238–59.

4. ff. 81r–90v *Incipit prologus regule sancte Clare sororum sine earum que dicuntur minorisse.* Urbanus episcopus seruus seruorum dei dilectis in christo filiabus vniuersis abbatissis et sororibus inclusis ordinis sancte Clare Salutem et apostolicam benedictionem. Beata Clara virtute clarens et nomine, diuina inspiratione preuenta ... Que regula talis est. *In nomine domini Incipit regula sororum ordinis S. Clare.* Imnes [*sic*] que seculi vanitate relicta religionem vestram intrare voluerit ... Anno domini 1495 Pontificatus nostri Anno Tertio.

   Rule for Poor Clares (see also art. 3 above); includes order of the service for inducting sisters into the order (f. 87r–v). The rule is preceded by the Bull of Pope Urban IV that serves as introduction and is followed by various related documents, the last of which is dated 1495.

5. ff. 91r–104v *Incipit Regula seu modus vivendi fratrum et sororum tertij ordinis* [sic] *beatissimi francisci Per dominum papam Nicolaum 3^m^ confirmata.* Nicolaus episcopus seruus seruorum dei dilectis filijs fratribus et dilectis in christo filiabus sororibus ordinis.... Super montem catholice fidei quam populis gentium qui ambulabant in tenebris ... populum humilem bonorum operum//

   Rule of the Tertiaries of St. Francis, followed by papal bulls, etc.; ends imperfectly in sections on the canonization and stigmata of St. Francis.

II. 6. ff. 105r–130r Incipit recollectio priuilegiorum ordinis nostre in tabula alphabeti per vererendum [?] patrem fratrem Io. Iarnigon ... annotata. [prologue:] Omissis quam pluribus que potius vite relaxationem quam mentis pacem ... [signed:] Frater Iohannes Iarnigon Commissarius nominatus. Incipit littera A. *Abbatissa* monialium sancte Clare elegi debet a maiori parte sororum vocalium et . . . [concludes with sections on *visitare, vota*]. ff. 130v–132v ruled, but blank

An alphabetical list of definitions for ecclesiastical terms and positions pertaining to the Franciscan Order as compiled by Johannes Iarnigon.

III. 7. ff. 133r–175r Pope John XXII, extracts from his *Extravagantes*; papal documents relating to the Franciscan Order. f. 175v blank

IV. 8. ff. 176r–210v Incunable, *Minorica elucidatiua racionabilis separationis fratrum minorum de observantia ab aliis fratribus eiusdem ordinis.* The title page has a woodcut and the four Evangelists and *IHS.* Printed in Deventer by Jacobus de Breda, not before 1497; Hain-Copinger 11172. f. 211r blank; f. 211v blank except for a later addition: "Mors tua. mors christi. transitus mundi gaudia celi/ Et dolor inferni. sint meditenda tibi."

V. 9. ff. 212r–241r *Sequuntur articuli responsiui pro fratribus de obseruantia ordinis minorum compilati et propositi in consilio basiliensi per venerandum sacre theologie doctorem magistrum petrum Reginaldeti ac eiusdem obseruancie professorem contra allegationes friuolas in eodem consilio propositas per magistrum franciscum futz* [?] *fratrem conuentualium eiusdem ordinis generalem ministrum* . . . Et in terra pax hominibus . . . [Luc. 2]. Reuerendissimi reuerendique patres solito more in hac responsione coram vestri reuerendissimis . . . que exsuperat omnem sensum custodiat corda vestra et intelligencias vestras in eternum. Amen. Deo gracias.

Treatise by Petrus Reginaldetus, divided into 15 chapters; for the author see L. Wadding, *Scriptores ordinis minorum* . . . (Rome, 1906) p. 192, and *Supplementum* (Rome, 1921) pp. 362–63.

10. ff. 241v–245v Extracts from Bulls and indulgences (s. $XVI^{1/4}$), with continuations in a hand similar to (if not the same as) the hand of Rioche (see provenance). ff. 246r–247v ruled, but blank

VI. 11. ff. 248r–251v Si cupit agnoscere principium et originem observancie regularis ordinis minorum nunc vigentis in prouinciis francie. turonie et burgundie . . . sinodus basiliensis in spiritu sancto legittime congregata et cetera. ff. 252r–253v frame-ruled, but blank

Unidentified treatise on the Franciscan Order in France.

VII. 12. ff. 254r–259r [Heading:] *Casus.* [text:] Circa annum domini m.

400. Dum ordo fratrum minorum tantum pateretur ruinam ... *Explicit Consultacio dominj Antonij de Caffarellis vtriusque Iuris doctoris et aduocati....*

Antonius de Caffarellis, *Consultacio* including canon law decisions.

13. ff. 259r–265r *Incipit alia Consultacio nuper agitata.* Queritur an diuersus et strictior viuendi modus obseruancium fratrum quam conuentualium ... Ad huius questionis [?] tria erant videnda ... a conuentualibus separati. f. 265v blank

Unidentified *Consultacio.*

Composed of seven parts, measuring ca. 210 x 145 mm., iv (contemporary parchment, i = front pastedown, now free standing, ii = stub, a few letters of text remain, iii = f. 1, art. 1, iv = stub) + 265 (continuous modern foliation in lower right corner) + i (contemporary parchment pastedown, now freestanding).

Part I: ff. 2–104, parchment (fine, shiny flesh side), written space 155 x 100 mm. Ca. 42 long lines. Single vertical bounding lines ruled faintly in ink or lead, with an additional vertical ruling in outer margin. Text rulings in ink. I^{2} (conjugate, ff. 2–3 have contemporary foliation 52–53), $II–V^{10}$ (contemporary foliation 1–40), VI^{10} (–10, blank; contemporary foliation 41–49), VII^{8} (51–58), $VIII–X^{10}$ (59–88), XI^{10} (contemporary foliation, now incorrect, 89–98 replaces another series 59–68), XII^{8} (–5 through 8, blank?; 99–102, replacing 69, 80–82?). Written by several scribes in small gothic text hands. Two illuminated initials, 9- to 5-line, formed of stylized foliage, pink and green with white highlights on gold ground, filled with blue ground with white filigree. Terminals extending into the margins to form partial floral borders, stylized foliage, blue, green and pink, with gold balls with hair-line extensions. Pen-and-ink initials, alternating in blue and red with red and light green penwork. Plain initials in red or blue.

Part II: ff. 105–132, paper (watermarks, in gutter: very similar to Briquet Sirène 13882), written space 160 x 105 mm. Ca. 39 lines. Single vertical bounding lines ruled in lead; text rulings in ink. I^{20}, II^{8}. Written in small upright gothic script; words being defined written in larger, more formal style of script. Red and blue divided initial, 4-line, f. 105r, smaller initials in red or blue. Underlining and paragraph marks in red. Letters and words stroked with yellow.

Part III: ff. 133–175, paper (watermarks, in gutter: similar to Briquet Sirène 13882 [cf. Part II] and to Sirène 13883), written space 138 x 92 mm. Ca. 37 long lines. Single vertical bounding lines in red, text rulings in ink. Single prickings in outer margins (for a ruling device?); remains of prickings in lower margin for bounding lines. I^{14}, II^{16}, III^{12}. Vertical catchwords along lower edge near gutter, verso. Written in a style of script similar to that in Part II. Crude red initial with simple penwork designs, 8- to 2-line. Paragraph marks and underlining in red.

Part IV: ff. 176–211 (Incunabulum: see art. 8 above).

Part V: ff. 212–247, paper (watermarks, in gutter: similar in design to Briquet Main 11417–29), written space 139 x 92 mm. Ca. 40 long lines. Single vertical and upper horizontal bounding lines; ruled in lead. I–III^{12}. Remains of quire and leaf signatures (e.g., b j, b 2, etc.). Written in a small round gothic text hand with humanistic features. Red initial, 11-line, with simple designs, f. 212r; 2-line initials, headings, underlining, marginal notes, paragraph marks in red. Majuscules touched with yellow and stroked with red.

Part VI: ff. 248–253, paper (deckle edges; watermarks: unidentified unicorn, in gutter), 205 x 142 (140 x 89) mm. 38 long lines. Frame-ruled in lead. A single gathering of six leaves. Written in cramped and hastily written gothic script.

Part VII: ff. 254–265, paper (watermarks: unidentified mermaid, in gutter), written space 140 x 90 mm. 38 long lines. Frame-ruled in hard point; remains of prickings in upper, lower and outer margins. A single gathering of twelve leaves. Written in small gothic text hand. Paragraph marks and underlining in red.

Binding: France [?], s. xvi. Bound in tan goatskin over paste boards. Very faint blind tooling and four fastenings, two of them ribbon. Catches on the lower board. Front pastedown (and possibly back pastedown?): portion of a document dated 1491. Spine: tying-up marks at head, tail, and around the supports.

Written primarily in Italy at the end of the 15th century, to judge from the watermarks, script, and decoration of Parts I–III. The incunable constituting Part IV was printed in Deventer, not before 1497. Parts V–VII were probably written in France in the first half of the 16th century when all the parts appear to have been bound together into the present volume. Inscription, s. xvi, of Brother Iohannes Rioche inside back cover ("Simplici Vsui fratris Iohannis Rioche Iunioris post cuius obitum fiat de Conuentu Sancti brioci") indicates that the volume was to go, upon his death, to the Franciscan convent of S. Brieuc in Brittany; continuations added to art. 10 appear to have been written by Rioche. Provenance otherwise unknown. Purchased from L. C. Witten (date unknown) by Thomas E. Marston (bookplate).

secundo folio: [Part I, f. 5:] fratres
[Part II, f. 106:] quem
[Part III, f. 134:] Ihohannes
[Part V, f. 213:] assumptum
[Part VI, f. 249:] multipliciter
[Part VII, f. 255:] et inter illos

Marston MS 278 Florence, ca. 1425–30
Cicero, Partitiones oratoriae; Topica, etc. Pl. 15

I. 1. ff. 1r–37r *M. Tul. Ciceronis partitionum oratoriarum liber incipit.* Studeo mi pater latine ex te audire ea quae mihi tu de ratione dicendi graece tradidisti ... ex tuis praeclarissimis muneribus nullum maius expecto. *M. T. Ciceronis de partitionibus oratoriis ad c. filium liber explicit.*

Cicero, *Partitiones oratoriae*; W. Friedrich, ed., Teubner, v. 2 (1902) pp. 389–424. Abbreviations for names of interlocutors (*Cl, Tul, C, T*) in red. Text is divided by headings, in red, and decorative initials as follows: Cicero (f. 1v), *De praeceptis orationis* (ch. 8, sect. 27; f. 7v), *De quaestione* (ch. 18, sect. 61, f. 15v). Spaces for Greek left unfilled.

2. ff. 37v–63v *M. Tul. Ciceronis ad C. Trebatium iure consultum topica incipiunt.* Maiores nos res scribere ingressos. C. Trebati et his libris quos breui tempore satis multos ... quod quasi mancipio debuimus ornamenta quaedam uoluimus non debita accedere. *M. T. Ciceronis Topica ad .C. Trebatium expliciunt feliciter.* f. 64r–v ruled, but blank

Cicero, *Topica*; Friedrich, *op. cit.*, pp. 425–49. Spaces left blank for Greek words, some of which have been filled with words written in Roman letters; decorative initials to designate text divisions occur at beginnings of ch. 4, sect. 25; ch. 5, sect. 26; ch. 8, sect. 33; ch. 8, sect. 35; ch. 10, sect. 41; ch. 11, sect. 46; ch. 11, sect. 47; ch. 11, sect. 50; ch. 12, sect. 53; ch. 14, sect. 58; ch. 16, sect. 62; ch. 16, sect. 63; ch. 17, sect. 65; ch. 18, sect. 67; ch. 18, sect. 68; ch. 18, sect. 71; ch. 19, sect. 73; ch. 21, sect. 79 (2 initials); ch. 21, sect. 81; ch. 24, sect. 90.

II. 3. ff. 65r–87r *P. Rutilii Lupi schemata dianoeas ex graeco uorsa Gorgia.* Prosapodosis. Hoc schema duobus modis fieri et tractari potest. Nam sententiis duabus aut pluribus propositis ... hos necessitudine opitulandi astrinxit hosque ignotos iuxta beniuolentiae causa inlesit. *P. Rutilii. Lupi. schemata. dianoeas. ex. graeco. Gorgia. uorsa. explicit.*

P. Rutilius Lupus, *De figuris sententiarum et elocutionis*; edited with prolegomena and commentary by E. Brooks (Leiden, 1970), text on pp. 5–45. Greek terms are written by the scribe in Roman capitals; a second person, probably the same person who wrote arts. 5–6, neatly wrote the Greek words in the margins. The second scribe exhibits a better knowledge of Greek than the first, who often transliterated the Greek words into Roman letters incorrectly. This is one of the earliest manuscript witnesses to the text of Rutilius Lupus, which was rediscovered about the same time as Petronius and which was first noted in a letter of Ambrogio Traversari to Niccolò Niccoli datable to 1421. See A. C. de la Mare, "The Return of Petronius to Italy," *Medieval Learning and Literature: Essays Presented to Richard William Hunt*, ed. J. J. G. Alexander and M. T. Gibson (Oxford, 1976) pp. 220–54.

4. ff. 87r–108v *Incipit Romani Aquilae. Rhetoricos.* Petis longioris morae ac diligentiae quam pro angustis temporis quo me profecto urget. ideoque postea plenum hoc tibi munus reddemus ... M. Tullio. nec dum copiam imitamur in nimietatem incidamus cauendum est. *Explicit Aquilae.*

   Aquila Romanus, *De figuris sententiarum et elocutionis*; K. Halm, ed., *Rhetores Latini Minores*, Teubner (1863) pp. 22–37. The hand which has added Greek words in the margins is that of the second scribe who copied arts. 5–6.

5. f. 109r–v [I]n monosyllabis inspiciendum utrum finalis breuis sit an longa. Si longa est praeire debet trocheus. quae tamen apta est conclusio pendente adhuc sensu ... bona clausula fit; Sed In hac clausula cauendum // ne pro trocheo spondeus ponatur.

   Martianus Capella, *De figuris sententiarum et elocutionis*, extracts from V.520 and 522; A. Dick, ed., Teubner (1925) pp. 257–59. Followed by an unidentified text on f. 109v: Item non corrigas caput uersus heroici finemque. Quinque longas et totidem breues non improbes. Trocheum triplicem ascondes ... et istud est praedicare inter humanas dictiones.

6. ff. 109v–110v *Priscianus. de figuris numerorum.* [S]ciendum quod quom ab uno ad mille mille [*sic*] numeri notentur apud latinos

non plus tredecim eos figuris notari inuenimus. Nam principales reperiuntur quater singuli tam ante quinarios ... dicitur ut dardanus docet scrupulos esse idest sex siliquae dragma siue argenteus scripuli tres. Vncia// ff. 111r–114v ruled, but blank

Priscian, *De figuris numerorum (quos antiquissimi habent codices)*, sections 1–10 only and omitting portions of the long Greek quotations. H. Keil, ed., *Grammatici Latini*, v. 3, Teubner (1859) pp. 405–8. The same scribe who wrote arts. 5–6 added the Greek words in the margins of arts. 3–4.

Composed of two distinct parts; parchment, ff. iii (paper) + ii (parchment) + i (contemporary parchment) + 114 + ii (parchment) + iii (paper), 189 x 117 mm.

Part I: ff. 1–64, written space = 129 x 81 mm. 21 long lines. Double vertical and single horizontal bounding lines, full length and full width (Derolez 13.33). Ruled in hard point on hair side. Remains of prickings in upper, lower, and outer margins. I–VI^{10}, VII^{4}. Letters of the alphabet (A–F) with a single dot on each side of the letter serve as quire signatures in lower right corner of verso and lower left corner of recto (e. g., .A. on ff. 10v and 11r). Written in a well formed round humanistic script by a single scribe, above top line. Illumination in the early style of Bartolomeo di Antonio Varnucci (1410–79). Two large illuminated initials (ff. 1r and 37v), 5-line, gold on blue, green and peach ground with white vine-stem ornament, touched with green and white dots. On f. 1r a partial border incorporating a butterfly, grasshopper, moth, and a flying putto with bow and arrow who appears to be propelled by lozenge-shaped blue clouds. 25 small initials, 2-line, gold on blue, green and peach ground with white vine-stem ornament and white dots. Headings in pale red, the first on f. 1r partially obscured by the decoration.

Part II: ff. 65–114, written space = 131 x 72 mm. 20 long lines. Double vertical and single (or double) upper horizontal bounding lines (Derolez 13.33 and 35). Ruled in hard point on hair side. Remains of prickings in upper, lower and outer margins. I–V^{10}. Catchwords in lower margin, right of center (Derolez 12.2). Scribe 1 wrote arts. 3–4 in a neat round humanistic script, above top line. Scribe 2 added arts. 5–6 in an upright humanistic script bordering on cursive; he also added the Greek words in the margins for arts. 3–4. Display headings and key grammar words in majuscules; no decoration or rubrication.

Binding: France, s. xix. Bound in red goatskin, blind- and gold-tooled, by L. Guétant. Gilt edges.

Part I was written in Florence and decorated by Bartolomeo Varnucci early in his career, probably ca. 1425–30; the style of the illumination is very close to that of three of his manuscripts dated to 1426: Vatican City, Vat. Pal. lat. 1516 (Cicero, philosophical works); Florence, Bib. Laur. plut. 76, 35 (Seneca, philosophical works); Vatican City, Vat. lat. 2208 (Seneca, *Epistolae*); see de la Mare, *New Research*, p. 398, n. 17. Arts. 3–4 of Part II appear to be contemporary, but the portions by Scribe 2 (arts. 5–6 and Greek marginalia) may be a later addition. Although a modern note in pencil on f. i verso states: "Cicero (Nu. 33 Mss.). Aus Sammlung C. de Medici. LB 83557," we have not located the manuscript in the inventories published by F. Ames-Lewis ("The Inventories of Piero di Cosimo de' Medici's Library," *La Bibliofilia* 84 [1982] pp. 103–42) nor is there an ex-libris inscription of Piero de' Medici. With respect to the text, Marston MS 278 contains the same contents in arts. 1–6, in the same order and with the same series of extracts from Martianus Capella, Priscian and an unidentified text, as Vatican City, Biblioteca Apostolica Vaticana, Reg. lat. 2062, which is also an early 15th-century manuscript from Italy (see E. Pellegrin, et al., *Les manuscrits classiques latins de la Bibliothèque Vaticane* 2,1 [Paris, 1978] pp. 494–95); Marston MS 278 is, however, lacking the commentaries of Antonio Loschi on Cicero's orations added at the conclusion of the Vatican codex. Rectangular white tag with gold border on f. i recto: "aee" and "ade" written in ink, s. xix. "253" in pencil on f. i verso and "Impr. Temp. N o 21-del 3-3-933" and "3555" (erased) on final flyleaf, recto. Belonged to Thomas E. Marston (bookplate); his source and date of acquisition unknown.

secundo folio: [f. 2:] uocas locos
[f. 66:] grauis ad

Marston MS 279 — Verona [?], 1430s

Justinus, Epitoma historiarum Pompeii Trogi, etc.

I. 1. ff. 1r–2v The original text on f. 1r–v was Seneca, *Phaedra* 353–58, 360–404, 359: "// Nihil immune est. odiumque perit/ Cum iussit amor ueteres cedunt ... [f. 1v:] Regia. seuis modus quis est flammis." The recto, however, has been mostly erased and another hand has added: "Non ignara mali miseris sucurere disco" (Vergil, *Aeneid* 1.630) as well as some other verses no longer legible. Folio 2r contains another passage from Seneca, *Phaedra* 717–41: "// Non ipse toto magnus occeano pater/ Tantum expirarit sceleris. o silue: o furor ... Conferat tecum decus omne priscum//" f. 2v [in another hand]: "//postera cum primum sparge musa/ in modo mihi similis qui fui tempore belli/ Dic mihi musa uirum troie qui primus aboris [*sic*]/ [in another hand:] Dic mihi musa//".

II. 2. ff. 3r–130r *Liber primus iustini feliciter incipit.* Cum multi ex romanis etiam consularis dignitatis uiri res romanas . . . ac ferum legibus ad cultiorem uite usum traductum in formam prouincie redegit. Finis. f. 130v blank

Justinus, *Epitoma historiarum Pompeii Trogi*; F. Ruehl and O. Seel, eds., Teubner (1972) pp. 1–302. Minor discrepancies in the text include: f. 68v (beginning of Bk. 19), the introductory initial is omitted and the running headlines giving the book number still read 18; f. 102r (beginning of Bk. 33), decorative initial is omitted, but the numbering continues, still one off; f. 113r, a decorative initial marks Bk. 38.8.2 ("Tunc in egypto mortuo. . ."); f. 124r, Bk. 43.1.1–2 is omitted. The text has been corrected and annotated by several contemporary hands throughout.

Parchment, ff. i (paper) + ii (contemporary parchment, ff. 1–2) + 128 (modern foliation 3–130) + i (paper).

Part I: ff. 1–2 (palimpsest), 243 x 167 (165 x 98) mm. 26 lines of verse. Double horizontal and vertical bounding lines (Derolez 13.36); ruled in hard point on hair side. Written by several scribes (see art. 1) in humanistic bookhand; for the passages from Seneca, the initial letter for each verse is set between vertical bounding lines.

Part II: ff. 3–130, 245 x 169 (163 x 100) mm. 34 long lines. Double horizontal and vertical bounding lines (Derolez 13.36). Ruled in hard point on hair side. Prickings in upper, lower and outer margins (Derolez 18.1). I-XII^{10}, XIII^{8}. Horizontal catchwords written across inner vertical rulings (Derolez 12.3). Written by a single scribe, below top line, in humanistic bookhand that sits somewhat above the ruled line; the conclusion of the text on ff. 129v–130r was added by a different hand. One large illuminated initial, f. 3r, 9-line, pink with white highlights on irregular angular ground, blue with white filigree and a thin white line outlining the ground. Filled with a stylized interlacing pattern of white vine-stem, white with green and yellow shading against gold ground. This initial is in the same style as those in London, B. L. Add. 12012 (we thank A. C. de la Mare for this information), but in different colors. Numerous small initials, 3-line, yellow, on blue or blue and pink grounds with white filigree. Initial heading in gold; running headlines for book numbers in red.

Binding: Italy, s. xix. Rigid vellum binding, gold-tooled. Traces of turn-ins and bosses from earlier binding on f. 130 and possibly on f. 1.

Written in Italy, probably in Verona in the 1430s. Contemporary inscription, in gold, in upper margin of f. 2r in Part I: "Ceneura [*sic*] a nogarolis scripsi manu mea immaculata" was apparently added by Genevra Nogarola (1419–1465?; Cosenza, v. 3, p. 2484; R. Avesani, *Verona nel Quattrocento. La civiltà delle lettere* [Verona e il suo territorio IV, 2] 1984, pp. 60–76, with this manuscript cited on p. 63). The script of this inscription does not, however, seem to correspond to other hands in either Part I or II. Since the design of the initial on f. 3r (see above) is close to that of those in London, B.L. Add. 12012, a manuscript of Justinus copied in 1433 for Martino Rizzoni (tutor to the Nogarola sisters), Part II was probably written and decorated in Verona in the same period. It is not clear at what point Parts I and II were joined together. Note, s. xv, partially visible under ultra-violet light on f. 130v: "* * * qui in loco est brac[?]dini * * */ * * * Antonius de [?]zen[?]b[us?]* * *." Clipping from an unidentified sale catalogue, in German, in library files. Acquired from L. C. Witten in 1954 by Thomas E. Marston (bookplate).

secundo folio: [Part II:] ademit

Marston MS 280 France, s. XV²
Chroniques depuis le commencement du monde

1. f. 1r blank; f. 1v [Title:] Cest le liure des croniques depuis le commancement du monde et des Roys de france. ff. 2r–5r *Sensuiuent Les noms des Roys qui ont regne en france Premierement.* Pharamon eleue premier Roy des francois Regna paien xi. ans et trespassa l'an iiii°. et xxx ... Charles VI e filx de charles le quint tresaine et de bonnaire regna xlij^z^ ans et trespassa l'an mil iiij° xxij^z^.

   List of Kings of France from Pharamond to the death of Charles VI in 1422.

2. ff. 5r–81r [Space for rubric left unfilled]. *Au commencement.* Du monde puis que dieu eut fait ciel et terre tenebres et lumiere et les. iiii. elemens diuisez l'un de l'autre. Si fist diuerses creatures herbes et arbres poissons oiseaux et bestes ... Apres liij sint l'empire gracien .vi. ans Cils ama moult dieu et moult fut a saincte eglise propice. Si estoit plain de toutes bonnes meurs et de cheualerie alosez durement. *Cy finent les croniques Sainct Jherome/ ccc*[*c* crossed out] *iiij xx. /ccc iiii xx. I.*

History of the world from the creation to A.D. 380/81.

3. ff. 81r–207v *Au premier*. An Gracien l'empereure Commaince ses Croniques Sigibers qui fut moyne de gemblois . . . En cest an mesme [1307] le Iour de la conuersion Saint pol furent les noces faites en l'eiglise nostre dame en Bouloigne du roy d'angleterre et de madame ysabel fille du roy de france . . . li quens Robert de flandres. Et li quens de haynau. *Et sic est finis huius presentis operis*.

Chronicle of France from 381 A.D. to 1308 (the imprisonment of the Templars and the marriage of Edward II of England to Isabel, daughter of Philip the Fair).

Paper (watermarks obscured by text: similar in general design to Briquet Boeuf 2782–86 and Briquet Main 11493–505) with parchment outer bifolia, ff. i (paper) + ii (contemporary parchment, i with modern paper pasted to recto, ii = f. 1) + 207 + i (contemporary parchment with modern paper pasted to verso) + i (paper), 272 x 200 (203 x 133) mm. ca. 28 long lines. Frame-ruled in hard point or lead; generally four prickings at outer corners of written space.

I^{2} (ff. i and 1, bifolium), II^{16}, III^{18}, IV^{16}, V^{18}, VI^{20}, VII^{16}, $VIII–X^{20}$, XI^{18}, XII^{20}, XIII^{4} [structure uncertain]. Horizontal catchwords often enclosed by red rectangles in lower margin near inner bounding line, verso.

Written in bâtarde script; first words of each section written in large gothic bookhand.

Crude decorative initials, outlined in red and sometimes with red dots within the outline, at major text divisions. Headings, 1-line initials, Roman numerals to designate years, initial strokes, and some punctuation, all in red.

Ink has bled through paper leaves with minor loss of text.

Bindings: France, s. xviii. Tan calf with a gold-tooled spine and a red leather label "Regne des Rois de France." Red edges and gold-tooled turn-ins. Discoloration from turn-ins and fastenings of early binding visible on front and rear flyleaves.

Written in France in the second half of the 15th century; early provenance unknown. Belonged to Sir Thomas Phillipps (no. 14882; inscription in lower margin, f. 2r), who acquired it from Quaritch in 1859. Clipping from an unidentified French sale catalogue, no. 1770, on front pastedown. Bookplate of the Bibliotheca Richteriana on front pastedown. White oval tag with scalloped edge on spine, in ink "29[?]10," in pencil below "H3." Miscellaneous modern pencil notes on f. i verso, many erased, include: "MS. 201," "No. 12," "MHC"; in ink: "13 o cit 6 H 12." Purchased from

B. M. Rosenthal at an unknown date by Thomas E. Marston (bookplate).

secundo folio: Clouis

Marston MS 281 — Northern Italy, 1399

Augustine, De libero arbitrio, etc.

1. ff. 1r–42r *Incipit liber primus beati Augustini de libero arbitrio.* Dic michi queso te. Vtrum deus non sit auctor mali ... Iam fidem facere et ab hac disputacione requiescere aliquando compellit. et cet. et cet. *Explicit liber Augustini de libero arbitrio.*

   Augustine, *De libero arbitrio*; W. M. Green, ed., CC ser. lat. 29 (1970) pp. 211–321.

2. ff. 42r–56r *Incipit liber eiusdem de fide ad petrum.* Epistolam fili Petre tue caritatis accepi in qua te significasti uelle Ierosolimam pergere et poposcisti te litteris nostris ... illi deus reuelabit. Deo gracias. *Explicit liber beati Augustini de fide ad petrum.*

   Fulgentius of Ruspe, *De fide ad Petrum*; J. Fraipont, ed., CC ser. lat. 91A (1968) pp. 711–60; Bloomfield, *Virtues and Vices*, no. 1926 (Marston MS 281 not cited).

3. ff. 56r–90r *Incipit prefatio libri retractationum beati Augustini episcopi.* Iam diu istud facere cogito atque dispono quod nunc adiuuante domino aggredior ... ut possit hoc opere quantum potuoro [*sic*] curabo ut eundem ordinem nouerit et cet. [text:] *De achademicis libri iij.* Cum ergo reliquissem uel que adeptus fueram in cupiditatibus huius mundi ... ad populum alios dictatos alios a me dictos retractare cepissem. Deo Gracias Amen. *Explicit liber beati Augustini episcopi de retractacionibus.*

   Augustine, *Retractationes*; A. Mutzenbecher, ed., CC ser. lat. 57 (1984) pp. 3–143.

4. f. 90r–v *Retractacio Sancti Augustini in libris de doctrina christiana.* Libros de doctrina christiana cum inperfectos comperissem perficere malui quam eis ... quem de sacramentis siue de philosophia scripsit. Hoc opus sic Incipit Sunt precepta quedam. *Explicit retractacio sancti Augustini episcopi.*

   Augustine, *Retractationes* XXX; Mutzenbecher, *op. cit.*, pp. 92–93.

5. ff. 90v–143r *Incipit prohemium sancti Augustini episcopi in quattuor libris de doctrina christiana. et. cet.* Sunt precepta quedam tractandarum

scripturarum que studiosis earum uideo non incomode [*sic*] posse tradi ... orate pro anima huius scriptoris si placet amore dei et cet. [f. 92r:] *Explicit prohemium incipit liber primus sancti Augustini episcopi de doctrina christiana.* Due sunt res quibus nittitur [*sic*] omnis tractacio [*spiritus*? crossed out] scripturarum Modus intelligendi inueniendi que intelligenda sunt ... et alijs eciam laborare studet quantulacumque potui facultate disserui et cet. Deo gracias. [colophon:] Explicit liber beati Augustini episcopi de doctrina christiana Scriptus per me leonardum Rosenheyn de Basilea de allamania M ccc° lxxxx° viiij° die xviij decembris deo gracias. f. 143v blank; f. 144r–v ruled, but blank

Augustine, *De doctrina christiana*; J. Martin, ed., CC ser. lat. 32 (1962) pp. 1–167.

Parchment, ff. i (paper) + 144 (modern pagination, in ink; foliation, in pencil, lower right) + i (paper), 291 x 213 (192 x 136) mm. 2 columns, 34 lines. Single vertical bounding lines ruled in lead or crayon. Guide lines for text ruled in pale brown ink. Remains of prickings in upper margin.

I-XII^{10}, XIII^{12}, XIV (11 original leaves + 1 tipped in). Catchwords, touched with yellow, lower margin, left of inner bounding line, verso.

Written by a single scribe in semi-round gothic bookhand.

Ten illuminated initials of good quality, 11- to 4-line, pink and mauve with white filigree against blue ground with white filigree. Body of initials filled with stylized foliage or palmettes, orange, green and/or blue with black accents and/or white highlights against parchment ground. Foliage serifs, pink, mauve, green, blue and orange with white highlights extending into the margins to form partial borders. Folio 1r, an illuminated initial (later addition or overpainting of original) of poor quality, 5-line, dark grey and brown with black filigree against gold ground, filled with a stylized scroll in light green, with flowers, brown and blue, against parchment ground. Foliage serifs, brown, green and dark blue with black accents and gold balls extending into inner and upper margins to form partial border. In center of lower margin unidentified arms (later addition; barry of six or and azur, a lion rampant, bordure argent) within a quatrefoil, gold (mostly rubbed) edged in blue and black with gold balls. Numerous flourished initials, 2-line, alternate red and blue with purple and red penwork. Paragraph marks alternate red and blue. Headings in red in a clumsy humanistic script; initials touched with yellow. Notes to rubricator in margins.

Binding: Italy, s. xviii. Brown tree calf with a gold-tooled border and turn-ins. Gilt edges. Rebacked and a new gold-tooled spine with a red label ("Augustine Opera MS: In Membranis") added.

Written in Northern Italy by Leonardus Rosenheyn of Basel (*Colophons*, v. 4, no. 12504, and J. W. Bradley, *Dictionary of Miniaturists* ... [London, 1889] v. 3, p. 172, both citing this manuscript) who signed and dated the codex 1399 (see colophon, art. 5); early provenance unknown. Two unidentified inscriptions, s. xv–xvi?, partially visible under ultra-violet light, f. 143v. Belonged to Maffeo Pinelli of Venice (1736–85); see J. Morelli, *Bibliotheca Maphaei Pinellii Veneti* (Venice, 1787) pt. 3, p. 349, no. 7901. James Edwards sale of the Bibliotheca Pinelliana, London 1889–90, no. 12807. Bookplate of I. [or J?] T. Hand. From the collection of Charles A. Baldwin, Broadmoor, Colorado Springs, Colorado (booklabel; De Ricci, *Census*, v. 1, p. 150, no. 4). Purchased from L. C. Witten (date unknown) by Thomas E. Marston (bookplate).

secundo folio: fac michi

Marston MS 282 — Southern France, 1448
Ars dictandi

ff. 1r–19v *Incipiunt aliqua dicta cum aliquibus exemplis extracta de libro quj vocatur aurea gemma de arte dictandi. Ordo litterarum talis est. Quicumque.* litteras alieni persone dirigere voluerit ... ipsius presentia simul fuerimus. [colophon:] Explicit aurea gemma deo gracias scripta per me anthonium vincentj dyocesis Mimatiensis [precise form and spelling unclear] anno dominj m° cccc^{mo} xlviij In mense aprilis In domo domini abbatis deydiaco aux. [Latin abbreviation for Auch] In ciuitate commorantem.

Epistolary forms extracted from an unidentified *Aurea gemma de arte dictandi*. Leaves of the text have been misbound, with ff. 5, 6, 7 now at conclusion. The text appears to be complete.

Paper (watermarks, in gutter: unidentified bull's head), ff. ii (1 = front pastedown paper, with French accounts dated 1791) + 19 + ii (paper, with French records; ii = rear pastedown), 225 x 155 (152 x 103) mm. Ca. 32 long lines. Frame-ruled in ink. Prickings in upper, lower and outer margins.

Collation difficult due to fragile condition of leaves and incorrect rebinding: I^{3} (horizontal catchwords enclosed in red decorative rectangle, below written space near gutter), II^{20} (includes ff. 5–7 bound at end; quire and leaf signatures, cj, cij. etc. in lower right corner, recto; wanting 17–20, blanks).

Written in hasty bâtarde script by a single scribe.

Crude initials, 3- to 2- line, headings, underlining, paragraph marks, in red.

Binding: France, s. xix. Semi-limp vellum case made from French document, with only dorse visible.

Written in 1448 by the scribe Antonius Vincentius from the diocese of Mende in Southern France while residing in Auch (see *Colophons*, v. 1, no. 1279, another [?] manuscript cited as "Paris, Au Velin d'Or, cat. 26, n. 9379, cf. ibidem n. 9315)." Quire and leaf signatures indicate the text was formerly part of a longer manuscript. Purchased from Bernard M. Rosenthal at an unknown date by Thomas E. Marston (bookplate).

secundo folio: monasterij

Marston MS 283 — Northern Italy, s. XV^2
Vocabularius breviloquus

ff. 1r–88r //Aliquando. penu. cor./ Alabatrum [*sic*]. tri. est genus marmoris candidi et perlucidi uarijs coloris [*sic*] quod incorrupta seruat unguenta. ne. g./ Alonge. media. cor./ ... [f. 88r, under heading DE. ZO.:] Zona. ne. est cingulus. latus . et est etiam pars terre . . . / Zorobabel. est ex integris. tribus nominibus. [*z* crossed out] zo. dicitur iste. ro. magister.. babel. babilonia. iste. magister. de babilonia./ finis. Amen. f. 88v blank

Unidentified *Vocabularius breviloquus*, imperfect at beginning; arranged alphabetically according to the first two letters of a word. Most entries are very short, 1- to 2-lines; lengthy entries include those for Allegoria (ff. 1v–2r); Bubo (f. 8v); Eletrum (*sic*, f. 26r); Ferculum (f. 32v); Pellicanus (*sic*, f. 60v); Saphirus (f. 74r–v); Vnicornis (f. 86v).

Paper (watermarks, in gutter: similar in design to Briquet Balance 2502; Piccard Horn VII.226, 229–30; Briquet Tour 15911; Briquet Monts 11881–82; unidentified 6-pointed star in a circle), ff. i (later addition) + 88 + i (later addition), 211 x 143 (135 x 81) mm. 31 long lines. Double vertical bounding lines (Derolez 13.31); lines impressed on a ruling board.

I^{12} (–1 through 4, loss of text), $II–VII^{12}$, VIII^{8}. Vertical catchwords surrounded by squiggles, between inner bounding lines (Derolez 12.5).

Written in a highly abbreviated and cramped humanistic cursive script with some gothic features by a single scribe, above top line.

Headings in majuscules.

Binding: Italy, date uncertain (s. xv?). Original sewing on three tawed skin supports, with plain, natural color wound endbands sewn on tawed skin cores. The boards are wooden, the upper one cut in for the straps.

Covered in brown sheepskin with corner tongues, very faintly blind-tooled. Traces of two catches on lower board. Repaired at head and tail of spine.

Written in Italy in the second half of the 15th century; early provenance unknown. Purchased from Bernard M. Rosenthal (date unknown) by Thomas E. Marston (bookplate).

Marston MS 284 — Northern Italy, s. XV[1]

Differentiae verborum

ff. 1r–9v Arbor feret frutum. sine fructu dicitur arbos./ Aastam [*sic*] dic tereten. pomum dic esse retondum./ Artus id est strictus sed membrum dicitur artus./ ... Regulus est serpens paruus rex atque uolucris/ Rete sagena solet. sed solet uas esse lagena.

Unidentified list (incomplete) of homonyms, synonyms, and similar word types, arranged alphabetically *A–N, Q–R*. One entry per line. The list was intended to be expandable, since spaces were left after each letter where additions could be and were made. A few glosses in Italian.

Paper (coarse, brown; watermarks, buried in gutter and obscured by binding repairs: similar in design to Briquet Tête de boeuf 14507 but with normally spaced eyes), ff. i (paper) + 9 + i (paper), 200 x 143 (157 x 121) mm. Format irregular; rulings in lead.

Collation impossible; each leaf mounted on a modern stub.

Written in an upright *mercantesca* script.

First initial for each letter of alphabet, 2- to 1-line, in red. Paragraph marks, initial strokes, decorative flourishes after each entry, in red.

Worn, stained, repaired, with some loss of text.

Binding: Germany [?] s. xix. Greenish brown paste-paper case with a square blank paper label on spine. The paste paper is the same as that used on Marston MS 249.

Written in Northern Italy in the first half of the 15th century; an owner-produced manuscript given the format and nature of the text. Inscription on f. 6r: "hoc opus est scriptum de zanchis [or *manchis*?] per me Tadiolum." Early provenance otherwise unknown. Belonged to Thomas E. Marston (bookplate; date and place of his acquisition not recorded).

secundo folio: Biçi

Marston MS 285 Italy, s. XIV–XV
Vincent of Beauvais, De laudibus seu de gestis Beatae Virginis Mariae, etc.

I. 1. ff. 1r–38r *Prologus in opus singularissimum de speculabilibus Beatissime Virginis marie matris domini nostri yhesu Christi....* [prologue:] Quoniam de gestis beatissime virginis dei genitricis ad modum pauca in euangelica reperiuntur ystoria quedam uero antiqua scripta que uitam eius et originem et assumptionem cum quibusdam miraculis ystorico modo describere uidentur olim ... intentio dirigatur de facili totum opus per capitula subiecta distinxi. [list of chapters:] De laudibus uirginis matris *i.* Qualiter oraculis predicta est diuinis. *ii* ... Oratio specialis pro se ad eandem. *141.* Oratio ad filium pariter et matrem. *142.* [text:] *Capitulum primum de laudibus beatissime virginis Marie.* Si deum ore prophetico iubemur sanctis suis. laudare multo magis in memoria virginis matris eius ... ut in eternum psallat tota substantia mea. Amen.

Vincent of Beauvais, *De laudibus seu de gestis Beatae Virginis Mariae,* with text divided into 142 chapters. In arts. 1 and 3 the author and/or text quoted is cited in the margin. Copinger 6259; J. Quétif and J. Echard, *Scriptores ordinis praedicatoris* (Paris, 1719), v. 1, pp. 236–38, no. 2.

2. f. 38r [Title, in margin:] Petrus comestor. in laudem Beate uirginis. [text:] Si fieri possit que arene puluis et unde/ ... Que tua sit pietas nec littera nec dabit etas. Explicit feliciter.

Petrus Comestor, *Carmen in laudem Beatae Virginis* (10 lines); Walther, *Initia* 17728; PL 198.1045.

3. ff. 38r–44r [No rubric; prologue:] Completo diligenter ex dictis sanctorum patrum pro modulo uirium nostrarum auxiliante domino tractatu diffusiori de beatissima Virgine dei genitrice ... habet autem capitula uiginti quinque. [list of chapters:] De origine sancti iohannis euangeliste. 1./ De arte ipsius et priori conuersatione. 2. ... De ipso apostolo interpellando a nobis et imitando. 24. [text:] *De origine sancti iohannis euangeliste.* Beatus Iohannes euangelista uirgo est a domino electus ... per caritatem dei filius descendit in uirginem. nos exaltet ad paterne glorie caritatem. Amen. Explicit opus cum gracia yhesu christi.

Vincent of Beauvais, *De laudibus seu de gestis Iohannis evangeliste,* with text divided into 26 chapters. Copinger 6259; Quétif-Echard, *op.cit.,* v. 1, pp. 236–38, no. 3.

4. f. 44r–v Pictures of St. Barbara and Thomas Aquinas, and a medieval illuminated initial *S* (England [?], s. XV) pasted to blank pages.

II. 5. ff. 45r–56r [Heading:] Incipit opus domini Stephani Parisiensis Episcopi contra impugnantes scientiam sancti Thome de Aquino ordinis predicatorum et eam non intelligentes. [text:] [D]istinccione prima. questione quarta dicitur quod subiectum theologie est ens cognoscibile per inspiracionem. In prima parte summe questione prima articulo septimo dicitur quod deus sit subiectum theologie ... qui concordia facit in sublimibus cui est honor et gloria in secula seculorum. amen. ff. 56v–57r ruled, but blank

Stephanus Parisiensis [?], unidentified text supporting the theology of Thomas Aquinas.

6. ff. 57v–58v [Heading:] Incipit sermo sancti augustini de diuinatione demonum. [text:] [Q]uodam die in diebus sanctis octauarum cum apud me mane fuissent ... contradictiones peruenerint quantum deus adiuvabit respondebimus. Amen.

Augustine, *De divinatione daemonum*; J. Zycha, ed., CSEL 41 (1900) p. 597.

III. 7. ff. 59r–60r [No heading, text begins:] [Q]ueritur de ssensu [*sic*] communi Et primo queritur que sit necessitas ponendi sensum communem. Ad quod dicendum quod in omni natura ... sed communis quia per posterius sentit omnia.

Albertus Magnus, *De sensu communi*; I. Brady, ed., "Two Sources of the 'Summa de homine' of St. Albert the Great," *Recherches de théologie ancienne et médiévale* 20, 3–4 (1953) pp. 222–71; I. Brady, "Source or Extract? A Note on St. Albert," *Recherches de théologie ancienne et médiévale*, 25 (1958) pp. 142–43.

8. ff. 60r–62v [No heading, text begins:] [S]unt autem secundum philosophum partes anime sensibiles que sunt aprehensiue ... et est in subiecto cum eodem cum memoria. Explicit tractatus de sensu communi et quinque potentijs anime interioribus editus a fratre Alberto ordinis predicatorum. ff. 63r–64v ruled, but blank

Albertus Magnus, *De quinque potentiis anime interioribus*; for bibliography see art. 7.

IV. 9. f. 66r–v (col. a not legible; col. b:) //La turba questa meraveglia odendo/ S[?] credeva nel so detto/ C[?] piu de lui seguir ardita/

Questa cosa da i farisei odita/ ... Cantando osana filio davit/ Ch'en el intravit/ Sia benedetto nella sua vertute/ Alora ebbe yesu si grande honore/ Ch'en questa vita no l'ebbe magiore/ Di lune [ema?] che po questo [mute?]/ Cristo in ierusalem demora fece//; f. 65r–v //Un poco fo aperto mal dolore/ Volse che senpre stesse a lui sogietta/ Ch'era in lei demessa ogne valore/ ... *Ploratus matris christi cum aliquibus dominabus. Rubrica.* Era cum quella asai persone sante/ Piangendo cristo forte se dolendo/ Ch'eran venute in compagnia sua tante/ ... Io mo te faccio la devota laude/ Che prestamente teco me spilisca/ En la spultura [*sic*] tua costor me chiavi/ E questo mondo piu no me nutrisca//

Fragment of an account of the Passion of Christ; on f. 66r–v: concern of the Pharisees; death proposed by Caiaphas; dinner in the house of Simon, with Martha serving and Mary Magdalen pouring out ointment; decision of Judas to betray Jesus; entry into Jerusalem; on f. 65r–v: Christ on the cross; Mary entrusted to the care of John the Evangelist; Christ ignores Mary's sorrow; lament of the Virgin with the Holy Women; deposition from the cross by Joseph of Arimathea and Nicodemus; entombment; lament of the Virgin. The text is partially (on f. 65r–v) in terza rima.

V. 10. f. 67r–v ruled, but blank; ff. 68r–80v [A]bstinencia multipliciter inuenitur. *42.* c./ [A]bscondunt se quidam diuersitade. *151.* g./ [A]borsus peccatorum. *66.* d./ Accusatores peccatorum tres. *5.* g./ ... [Z]elus triplex. *19.* b./ [Z]izania habet tria mala. *28.* f. [Z]izania oritur tribus de causis. *29.* g.

Alphabetical index to an unidentified work.

Composed of five distinct parts, ff. ii (paper) + 80 (old foliation, Arabic numerals 1–79, in ink, skipping leaf between ff. 26 and 28) + ii (paper).

Part I: ff. 1–44, parchment, 250 x 180 (177 x 136) mm. 2 columns, 48 lines. Frame-ruled in lead. Remains of prickings in upper, lower and outer margins. I–III^{10}, IV^{14}. Horizontal catchwords in center of lower margin, verso. Written by a single scribe in small gothic bookhand, below top line. Blue initial, 6-line, with parchment designs and red penwork harping patterns on f. 1r. Plain initials, 4- to 3-line alternate red and blue. Headings, underlining, paragraph marks and chapter numbers, some initial strokes, in red. Guide letters for decorator in margins.

Part II: ff. 45–58, parchment, 248 x 182 (218 x 140) mm. 2 columns, 69 lines. Frame-ruled in lead. Prickings at four corners of written space. I^{10}, II^{8} (–5 through 8, blanks). Written by two scribes, one for art. 5, the other for art. 6, in small, tight gothic cursive scripts. Spaces left for decorative initials remain unfilled.

Part III: ff. 59–64, paper (watermarks: unidentified balance), 250 x 180 (190 x 142) mm. 2 columns, 51 lines. Single vertical bounding lines; ruled in hard point or lead. A single gathering of six leaves. Written by a single scribe in a small gothic text hand. Spaces left for decorative initials remain unfilled.

Part IV: ff. 65–66, parchment, 247 x 180 (195 x 155) mm. 2 columns, 37 lines. Remains of prickings in outer margin, f. 66. The two leaves, perhaps removed from a binding, are not conjugate: f. 66 is glued to the conjugate stub of f. 65. Written in round gothic bookhand. One initial, 2-line, on f. 65v and remains of another on conjugate stub: red with crudely drawn penwork designs in black and red. Headings, paragraph marks and initial strokes in orange-tinged red.

Part V: ff. 67–80, parchment, 248 x 182 (188 x 137) mm. 2 columns, 35 lines. Single or double vertical bounding lines in lead. Text rulings in ink. Remains of prickings in upper margin. A single gathering of 14 leaves. Written in a neat gothic bookhand. On ff. 68r–69r every other entry begins with a 1-line plain blue initial; second letter of each entry washed with yellow; citations of Arabic numerals in red. Guide letters for decorator.

Binding: England, s. xix–xx. Semi-limp vellum case with a gold-tooled title. Bound by Pierson [remainder of stamp on front pastedown difficult to read]. On spine: "Miscellanea Theologica. Stephanus Parisiensis. S. Augustinus. Albertus Magnus etc. Mss XIVe S."

Parts I–V all written in Italy in different periods. Part I: s. XIV^2; Parts II–III, s. XIV/XV; Part IV, s. XV; Part V: s. XIV. It is unclear when the parts were joined together. According to the modern note of Baron C. A. de Cosson (see below) on front flyleaf, the volume belonged to the Dominican convent of San Zanipolo in Venice ("From the Library of S. S. Giovanni e Paolo, Venice. See note in a 14th century M.S. of the Golden Legend bought at the same time, 1876"). Bookplate of de Cosson on front pastedown; his sale (Sotheby's, 27 March 1950, no. 32). No. 165 in an unidentified sale catalogue (copy in library files). Shelf-mark, in pencil, f. 1r: "N.1." Date and place of purchase by Thomas E. Marston (bookplate) unknown.

secundo folio: indignus

Marston MS 286 Venice [?], s. $XV^{2/4}$

Guarino da Verona, Regulae grammaticales, etc.

1. ff. 1r–22v Partes gramatice sunt quatuor videlicet littera. syllaba. Dictio et oratio. Littera ut u . . . Vt me uel prope me latet liber petrum uel petro.

   Guarino of Verona, *Regulae grammaticales*; numerous early printed editions of arts. 1–3. Beginning on f. 13v rubrics divide the text into the following sections: *Incipiunt Aduerbia, De comparatiuis, De superlatiuis, De participijs, De Inchoatiuis, De meditatiuis, De frequentatiuis, De desideratis, De figuris, De Patronomicis* [sic], *De etheroclitis.*

2. f. 22v–23r *Incipit orthographia.* A separans m uel n [?] abs q. c. t. cetera uult ab . . . extruit exanguis excindit et expuit expes.

   Guarino of Verona, *De orthographia.*

3. ff. 23r–28r *Incipiunt versus differentiales.* Dicitur esse nepos de nepa luxuriosus/ Ast natum grati post natum dic esse nepotem/ . . . Nauis. tris imbris pontis sic dicito partis/ Rarius is reliqua. plus pluris lis quoque litis. Expliciunt carmina differentialia Guarinj Veronensis. f. 28v blank except for pen trials

   Guarino of Verona, *Carmina differentialia.*

Parchment, ff. ii (paper) + 28 + ii (paper), 210 x 140 (136 x 86–89) mm. 31 long lines traced. Single vertical bounding lines ruled in hard point or lead (Derolez 13.11); rulings for text in brown ink. Prickings in upper and lower margin. A single pricking in outer margin, 80 mm. below top line (Derolez 18.3).

$I\text{-}II^{10}$, III^{8}.

Written in humanistic bookhand, below top line; marginal annotations in humanistic cursive.

One illuminated initial of poor quality, f. 1r, 11-line, purple with white filigree on gold and blue ground; filled with a stylized flower red and green with white filigree, upper terminal extending into pen-and-ink inkspray with gold balls and a mauve flower in upper border; pen-and-ink flourish with gold balls, ending in a bird's head, mauve, green and blue. Plain initials and paragraph marks alternate in blue and red; headings in red. Arms of the Valaresso family of Venice in lower border (azure, 3 bars gemelles or); partially effaced arms of Cardinal Bessarion in outer margin (azure, a cross botonny gules, a chief or; crest, cardinal's hat and crozier).

Binding: place uncertain, s. xix [?]. Rigid vellum case. Remains of a brick red label.

Written probably in Venice in the second quarter of the 15th century, perhaps as early as the 1430s. According to A. C. de la Mare the script resembles that of Nicolaus de Salveldia (Colophons, v. 5, nos. 14554–55) who signed Florence, Biblioteca Laurenziana Edili 215, at Venice in 1441, and St. Gall, Bibl. Vadiana MSS 306–8, at Padua in 1442–43; if Marston MS 286 was copied by him, it is probably earlier than his dated manuscripts. Belonged to a member of the Valaresso family of Venice (arms in lower margin, f. 1r). Subsequently owned by Cardinal Bessarion (d. 1472) whose arms were added in the outer margin of f. 1r. Since the arms include the cardinal's insignia, they were probably added by Bessarion after ca. 1441 (see C. Bianca, "La formazione della biblioteca latina del Bessarione," in *Scrittura biblioteche e stampa a Roma nel Quattrocento. Aspetti e problemi*. Atti del Seminario, 1979 [Vatican City, 1980: Littera Antiqua 1, 1] pp. 116–17). Inscription of "W. Oothont/ Verona 1873" on front pastedown. Bookplate of Thomas E. Marston; the date and source of acquisition unknown.

secundo folio: Accidentia verbi

Marston MS 287 Northern Belgium, 1470s
Collection of Texts on St. Barbara Pl. 64

We thank A. Derolez for his assistance with this manuscript.

1. f. 1r [Added in a later hand:] Vita Sanctae Virginis ac Martyris Barbarae per Nijchasium de Pomerio Capellanum Sancti Spiritus in Begginagio Herentalensi. f. 1v ruled, but blank

2. ff. 2r–4v [Short texts, primarily about St. Barbara, include but are not limited to the following:] Turrim sacre uirginis et martyris barbare. quidam deuotus. iamdicte virginis venerator. nobis contemporaneus. sacri palacij apostolici notarius ... Eximie virginis et martiris christi barbare genitor. in veteribus historiis. rex cuiusdam regni fuisse narratur. Quidque sic solet versibus dici: Pollet sublime regali barbara stirpe./ Namque dyoscorus. hanc genuit. dux nobilis et rex./ ... ; [f. 2v:] *Augustinus ad Jheronimum*. Cum enim hominem christiana caritate flagrantem ... in deo manet et deus in eo. [Unidentified extract concerning Jews:] *Item ex quatuor causis sustinemus iudeos. vtque in hijs uersibus*. Quatuor ex causis. iudeis parcitur ut sint ... quod christum crucifixerunt. sustinentur in terra christianorum. [Poem on the German cities of Trier, Cologne, Mainz:] Ante romam treueris. mille ducentis annis/ Treueris etate [gloss above: *id est antiquior est*]: sed rerum

prosperitate [gloss: id est diuicijs]/ Est agripina [gloss: id est colonia]: sed honore [gloss: *id est dignitate*] maguncia prima [Walther, *Initia*, 1307]. *Nota inferius scripta*. Virginis intacte dum veneris ante figuram/ Pretereundo caue. ne sileatur aue. [Walther, *Initia* 20471]; *Ysidorus*. Non enim sunt fideles in amicicia . . . procul absit auaricia; [quotes from Jerome and Augustine, f. 3r:] *Iheronimus. ad augustinum*. Superest ut diligas diligentem . . . Quod bos lassus. fortiter figat pedem . . . tibi messe video; [f. 4r:] Nichasius de pomerio. ordine sacerdos. Capellanus sancti spiritus in beghinagio herentaliensi. ob precipuam ac singularem deuocionem . . . et sic ad locum priscinum reportare debebit. Sunt etenim voces. bonarum mencium ortamenta [*sic*] . . . quod prefertur. [f. 4v:] Nota sacri corporis eximie virginis et martiris christi barbare quedam reliquie in summo altari ecclesie pontificalis ciuitatis reatine . . . ad consolationem fidelium. reseruata. [List of nine comets:] Nouem sunt nomina cometarum. Argentum. Dominus [?] . . . Tempore egemus ut aliquid maturius peragamus. [Note on St. Barbara's tower:] Nota Turris eximie virginis et martiris barbare . . . qui eam cum pluribus alijs ab intus et extra vidit.

Arts. 3–8 constitute the Life of St. Barbara compiled by John of Wakkerzeel, in five parts with interpolated texts (art. 7); see B. de Gaiffier, "La légende latine de Sainte Barbe par Jean de Wackerzeele," *Analecta Bollandiana* 77 (1959) pp. 5–41.

3. ff. 5r–8v *Prologus hystorie beatissime virginis et martiris barbare*. Viro cuidam deuoto . . . et omne donum perfectum descendens a patre luminum: Cui sit honor et gloria in secula seculorum. Amen.

Prologue; BHL 918.

4. ff. 8v–26v *Incipit historia beatissime virginis et martiris christi barbare. Et primo de vita eius et passione. Capittulum primum*. Veridicti ewangelij sanctione comperitur . . . non sinat iuri subiacere alieno: ad laudem et gloriam nominis sui. qui cum patre et spiritu sancto viuit et regnat in secula seculorum. Amen.

Vita Barbare; BHL 920.

5. ff. 26v–30r *Sequitur de translatione beatissime virginis et martiris christi barbare Capittulum primum*. Benedictus dominus deus israhel . . . Quod nobis ipse largiri dignetur. qui per infinita viuit et regnat deus secula seculorum. Amen.

History of the Translation of St. Barbara's relics to the West; BHL 926.

6. ff. 30r–44v *Sequuntur ex innumerabilibus quedam miracula de beatissima*

virgine et martire barbara. Promere cupiens laudes excellentissime virginis et martiris barbare ... tempore quo humatum fuerat mortuum iacuisset.

Description of the 23 miracles performed by St. Barbara; BHL 932–55.

7. f. 44v *Sequuntur rigmata de virgine barbara.* O Beata barbara o mea patrona/ ... Sed celesti gaudio tecum fruar amen [AH 52.335; F. J. Mone, ed., *Hymni Latini Medii Aevi*, v. 3, pp. 215–16); Ave terre lucifera ... [texts for a proper mass of St. Barbara.] *Beatus et sapiens pater augustinus.* Si vnus homo omnium hominum peccata perpetrasset ... ueniam non denegasset. hec ille: Ave barbara virgo egregia dominus tecum ... pulchritudinis ihesus christus. Amen.

8. ff. 45r–48r *Incipit breuiloquus epilogus de progenie. vita. passione. et prerogatiua excellentissime gloriosissime virginis et martiris christi barbare.* Origenes in multis libris narrat ... quod nobis praestare dignetur pater et filius et spiritus sanctus amen.

   A series of testimonies about St. Barbara incorrectly attributed to Origen ("*Dicta Origenis*"); BHL 919. Marston MS 287 is the earliest witness for this text, which was previously known only through two 16th-century manuscripts from the Benedictine abbey of St. Trond in Northeastern Belgium.

9. f. 48r–v [Added in margin: Nota genealogiam barbare.] In illo tempore quo regnabant titus et vespasianus ... Et hec de vita. progenie et passione sancte barbare virginis gloriose.

   Genealogia barbare, an expansion of BHL 919; de Gaiffier, *op. cit.*, pp. 25–27.

10. ff. 49r–55r *Presens legenda in honorem gloriose virginis et martiris christi barbare edita est: fideliterque per me verbotenus conscripta. et a viris fide dignis ex partibus napulie transmissa.* Imperante namque maximiano. qui maximus christianorum persecutor extitit ... Pater vero eius dyoscorus a demonibus in aere leuatus fuit: vox audita de eo, ve ve ve michi. quod unquam natus fui. Explicit hystoria virginis gloriosissime et martiris christi barbare.

    Otherwise unattested life of St. Barbara; text to be published by A. Derolez.

11. ff. 55r–57v *Sequuntur metra ad laudem virginis barbare descripta.* Barbara diuina regnans cum rege supremo/ ... Ad mea gaudia fine carencia suscipiantur. *Item miraculum* [three brief miracles follow.] *Sequuntur*

rigmata. Gaude sancta puellarum/ Barbara que es sacraum [*sic*] ... [AH 29.135]; *Sequuntur cuncta gaudia gloriose virginis barbare.* Gaude virgo gloriosa. barbaraque generosa ... ; O miranda pietas. et laudanda caritatis ... ; O quam gloriosa in sexu fragili barbare ... ; Gaude. felix barbara virginum preclara: que pro christo verbera ... ; Gaude barbara regina ... [RH 6714; Mone, *op. cit.*, p. 213].

Series of antiphons, verses and collects for Barbara followed by brief citations from Aristotle, Augustine, and Apuleius.

12. ff. 58r–62r *Sermo In annunciatione beate marie virginis.* Anno iubilei redeant ad possessiones suas: Leuitici uicesimo quinto. In quibus quidem verbis. prout presenti congruit festiuitati duo precipue tanguntur ... prestante eius vnigenito cum patre et spiritu sancto. Amen.

Unrecorded scholarly homily on Lev. 25.13.

13. f. 62r–v *Epistola beati thome de aquino missa cuidam suo discipulo.* Quia quesiuisti a me qualiter te incedere oporteat ... luxuriat raro non bene pasca caro.

Thomas Aquinas, *De modo studendi*; P. Mandonnet, ed., *Opera omnia* (Paris, 1927) v. 4, p. 535.

14. f. 63r–v *Humilitas.* Tu tibi displiceas, nec pompam dilige. nullum/ ... lubrica. te macules. nec gere mundiciem. *Castitas.*

Anacyclic or retrograde poem on the virtues and vices; cf. Walther, *Initia*, 19538, and Bloomfield, *Virtues and Vices*, no. 6112.

15. f. 63v *Sequuntur metra artificialiter composita.* Deice perpera probra puerpera virgula yesse ... ut tuo patrocinatu liberati. patriam consequamur.

Poem on the Virgin Mary followed by grammatical commentary and prose paraphrase.

16. ff. 63v–64r *Donum linguarum apostolorum.* Item apostoli non proferebant vna voce gallicum ... quia vnusquisque in ydromate suo intellexit linguagium apostolorum.

17. f. 64r–v *Sequitur doctrina magistri iohannis varenackere.* Qui sue ignorancie consulere velit ... Hec venerabilis vir magister iohannes varenackere. Sacre theologie professor.

Quotation dealing with moral subjects extracted from an unidentified work of Johannes Varenacker, Professor of Theology in Louvain (d. 1475).

18. f. 64v *Sequitur doctrina ambrosij.* Item secundam beatum ambrosium sacre theologie investigatorem validissimum ... plus exhortatio quam commocio. plus caritas quam potestas. Hec ille.

19. ff. 64v–65r *Item. xij. fuerunt sibille diuersarum etatum. que prophetauerunt deum de virgine matre futurum et cetera.* Sibilla. Ecce bestia conculcaberis. et gignetur dominus in orbe terrarum ... et nascetur ex matre ut deus. et conuersabitur ut peccator.

Twelve Sibylline prophecies.

20. f. 65r *Sancta maria.* Adorna templum tuum syon ... ; *Jheremias.* Hic est inque [?] deus noster ... *Ysaias.* Ecce uirgo concipiet.

Short texts complementing Sibylline prophecies in art. 19.

21. ff. 65v–66v Legimus in gestis secundiani. quod cum togatus ... et ad normam arcioris equitatis breuem vitam presentem dirigamus.

Passio sancti Secundiani; BHL 7550–52; the text here differs significantly from that printed in the *Acta Sanctorum, Junii* 1.35–37 (2nd ed.: 34–36).

22. f. 66v *Crisostomus super matheum.* Per bonam conuersationem ascenditur sine dubio ad scienciam ... sine scientia videmus nullum. *Augustinus in libro ad comitem quemdam sibi carissimum. Capitulo tercio.* Ne diu sine anima [?] nostri maneamus amplexu ... Quid superbus terra et cuius hec ille. *Origenes.* Hec est semper humane duricie incredulitas ... penitencia preparetur. *Augustinus ad quemdam comitem.* Elige tibi consiliarios bonos ... consiliarius autem vnus.

Short quotations from John Chrysostom, Augustine, Origen.

23. ff. 67r–68r *Dubitatur vtrum expediat beghinis omni dominica die communicare et ad hoc precepto astringi superioris siue curati.* Hec questio duplicem potest habere intellectum ... cum saluti opitulatur. alias nequaquam. Hec venerabilis vir magister iohannes varenackere plebanus louaniensis. et sacre theologie professor eximius.

Johannes Varenacker, *Questio* (see also arts. 17 and 24).

24. ff. 68r–70v Nota. quam plures confessores habent emulacionem dei ... Unius bernardus rara auis in terris distinctio ... sed moribus.

Short selections from Origen, Basil, Augustine, Jerome, Bernard, and Ambrose, followed by a *questio* of Johannes Varenacker beginning: "Quesitum fuit primo. An expediat Beghinis herentalensibus vouere suo curato obedientiam in omnibus. ... "

25. ff. 70v–71r Hec est salutaris et credenda professio. Et hoc solum credere non sufficit. nisi credas filium dei ... Tu autem hec intellige. intellectam crede et cetera.

26. f. 71v Fulget amica dei plus ipso sole diei/ ... Ense discoreo cesa superna colo.

Walther, *Initia*, 6960.

27. ff. 72r–73v Plura insignia dona. que diuisim sancti plures a domino meruerunt. hec coniunctim beate barbare in laudibus ecclesie. cantu vel lectione. vberius donata inueniuntur ... et trinitatem in personis et vnitatem diuine nature confitebatur.

List of gifts bequeathed to St. Barbara by God, listed in 21 short paragraphs.

Parchment (thick, but good quality), ff. 73, 214 x 148 (135 x 96) mm. 33 long lines or lines of verse. Single vertical and double horizontal bounding lines. Ruled in ink. Remains of prickings in upper, lower and outer margins.

I^4, $II–VIII^8$, IX^7 [?], X^6. Horizontal catchwords in lower margin near inner ruling. Remains of quire and leaf signatures (e.g., c i, c ii, c iii, etc.) in lower right corner, recto.

Written in a regular heavy *hybrida formata* script with features of *bastarda* by a single scribe who placed small circular flourishes above the letter *u*.

10-line illuminated initial on f. 5r, blue and mauve with white designs and highlights on gold cusped ground, a blue and gold bar border extending into the left-hand margin and terminating in acanthus leaves in the lower margin; interior of initial in orange, blue and gold checkered pattern. Fine red and blue divided initials, 8- to 7-line, with parchment designs and extensive pale purple flourishes, for major texts. Smaller plain initials in red or blue with parchment designs. Headings and initial strokes in red. Some instructions to rubricator in outer margins.

Binding: Belgium, s. xv/xvi. Covered in brown calf with corner tongues over wooden boards, a central panel diapered with blind-tooled triple fillets. Center and corner fittings and title written in a careful gothic bookhand under a brass-framed window on the upper board: "liber gloriose uirginis et martyris christi barbare." Lower board cut in for the straps which are attached with metal plates. Hasp of a chain on the lower board. Rebacked. Binding illustrated in *The Medieval Book*, p. 65, no. 65.

Written in Northern Belgium in the 1470s. According to the preface on f.

4r the texts of the manuscript were compiled, partially composed, and written into Marston MS 287 by Nicasius de Pomerio (Bogaerts), priest and chaplain of the Altar of the Holy Ghost in the Beguinage of Herentals, who specified that the manuscript was to be donated to the church of the Beguinage with the condition that it not be sold. It is unclear when the manuscript became separated from the Beguinage, where it would have been attached to a desk (see binding description above). Belonged to the library of the ducs d'Arenberg (shelf-number "54" on red square label on spine and hand-written on front pastedown); not noted by C. Lemaire, "La bibliothèque des ducs d'Arenberg, une première approche," in *Liber amicorum Herman Liebaers* (Brussels, 1984) pp. 81–106. Purchased from B. M. Rosenthal (date unknown) by Thomas E. Marston (bookplate).

secundo folio: [f. 3:] *Iheronimus*

Bibliography: A. Derolez, "A Devotee of Saint Barbara in a Belgian Beguinage (Marston MS 287)," ed. R. Babcock, *Gazette*, Supplement to v. 66 entitled *Beinecke Studies in Early Manuscripts* (forthcoming 1991).

Indices

Numbers in the index entries refer to the manuscript number rather than to the page number.

Index I
Manuscripts by Places and Periods

Index II

Dated Manuscripts

Index III
General Index

Index IV
Illuminators and Scribes

Index V
Provenance

Index VI
Other Manuscripts Cited

Index VII
Incipits

PLATES

Plates

PLATE 1

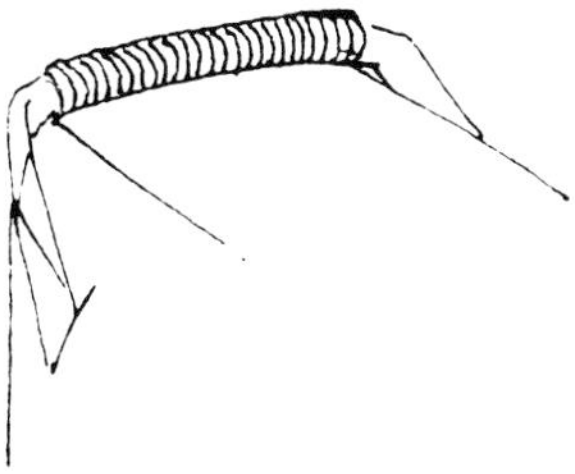

Plain wound; England and the Continent, Marston MSS 27, 29, 31, 37, 74, 82, 83 89, 95, 105, 123, 129, 140, 150, 176, 194, 196, 219, 231, 248, 256, 265, 277, 283; also used as a base for further embroidery

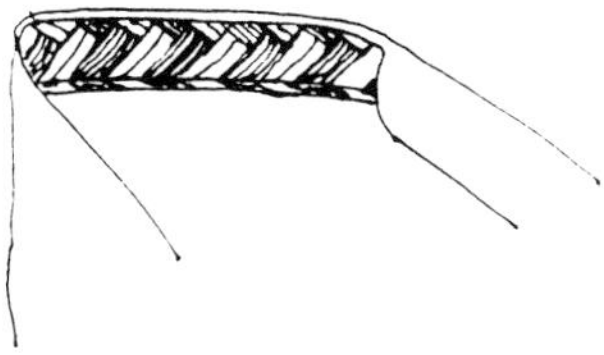

Beaded chevron; Italy, Marston MSS 39, 160, 251; Spain [?], Marston MS 51

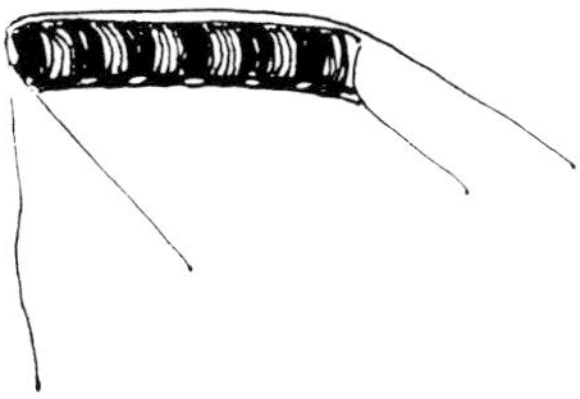

Beaded; England and the Continent, Marston MSS 40, 94, 154, 162, 175, 243, 247, 263

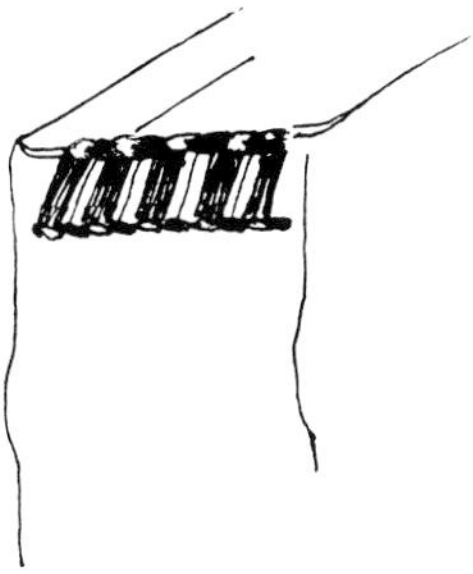

Monastic; France, Marston MS 268

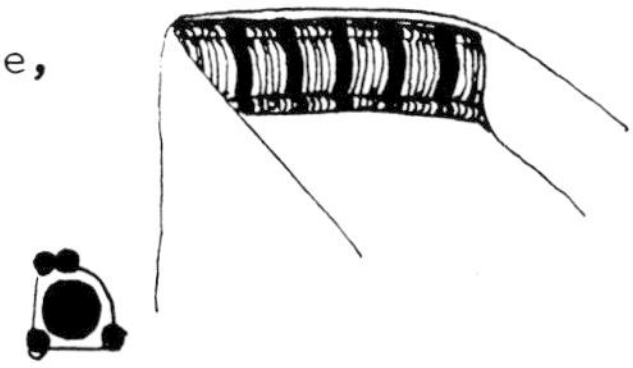

Cross section

Five core; Italy, Marston MSS 73, 247; Italy or Germany [?], Marston MS 270; Spain, Marston MSS 154, 164

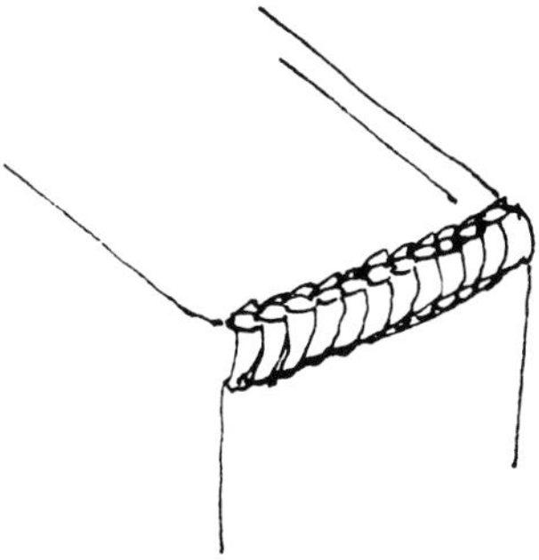

Braided; Germany, Marston MS 141

Endbands

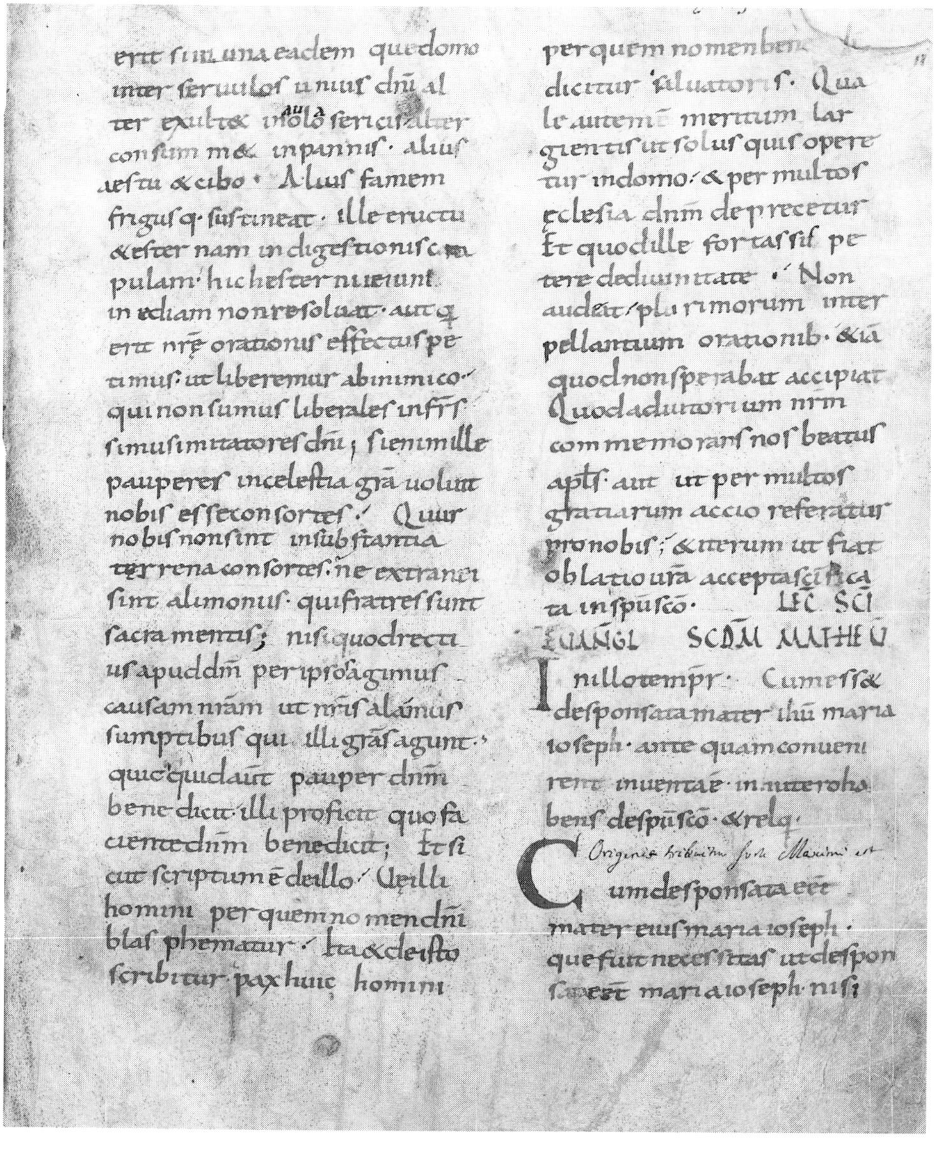

Marston MS 151, f. 11r (2/5 natural size)
Northern Italy, s. IX/X

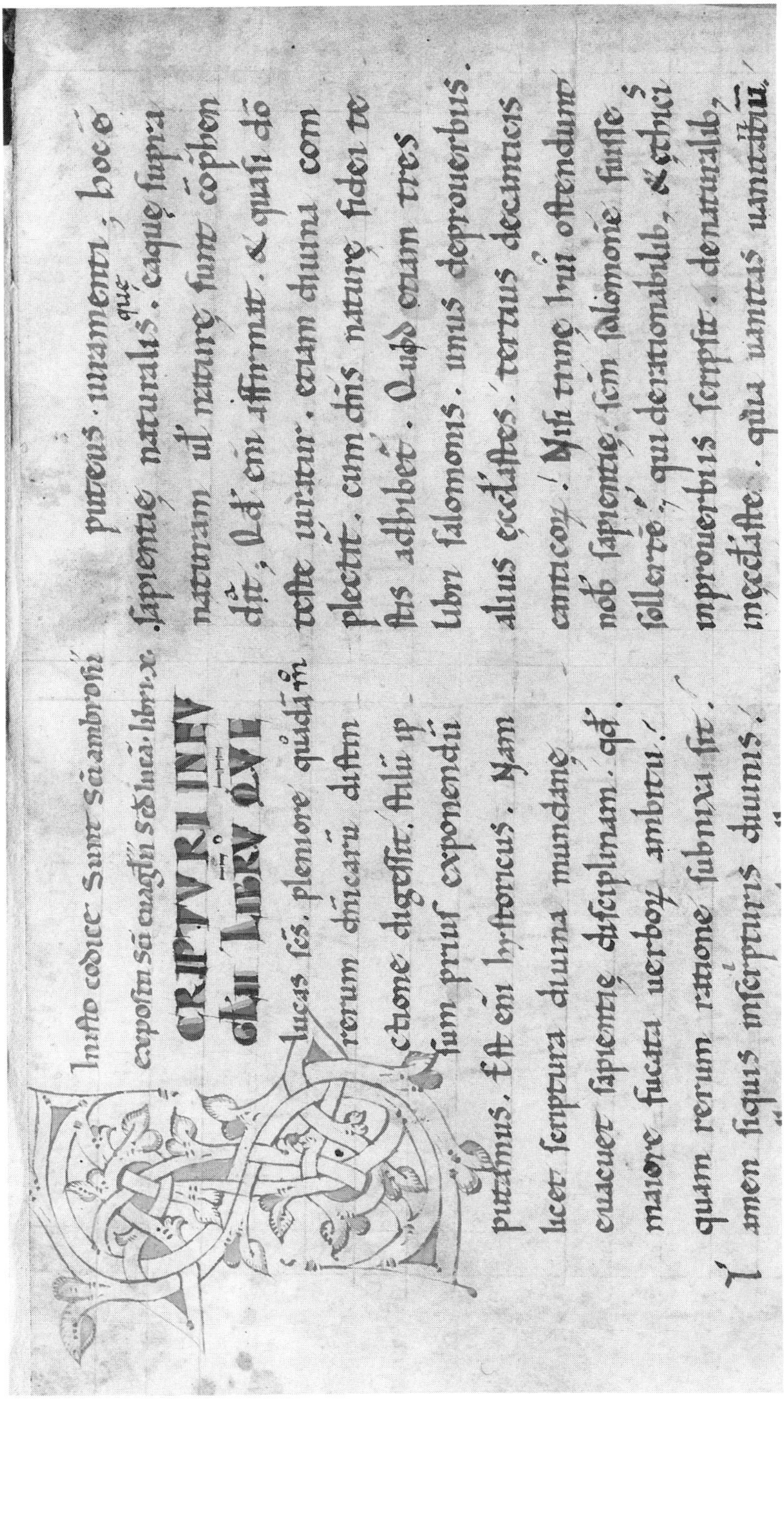

Marston MS 158, f. 1v (5/6 natural size)
Northern Italy, s. XI/XII

PLATE 4

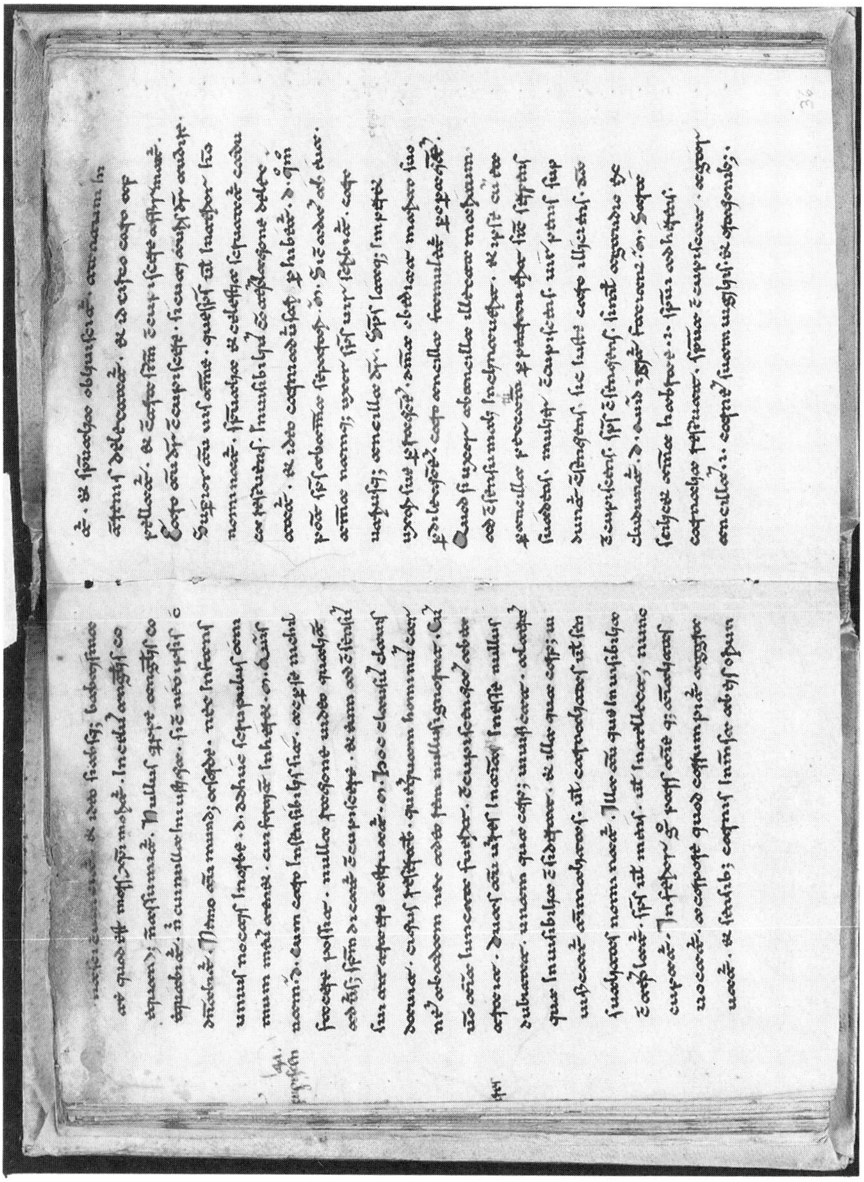

Marston MS 112, ff. 35v–36r (3/5 natural size)
Southern Italy, s. XII#1

PLATE 5

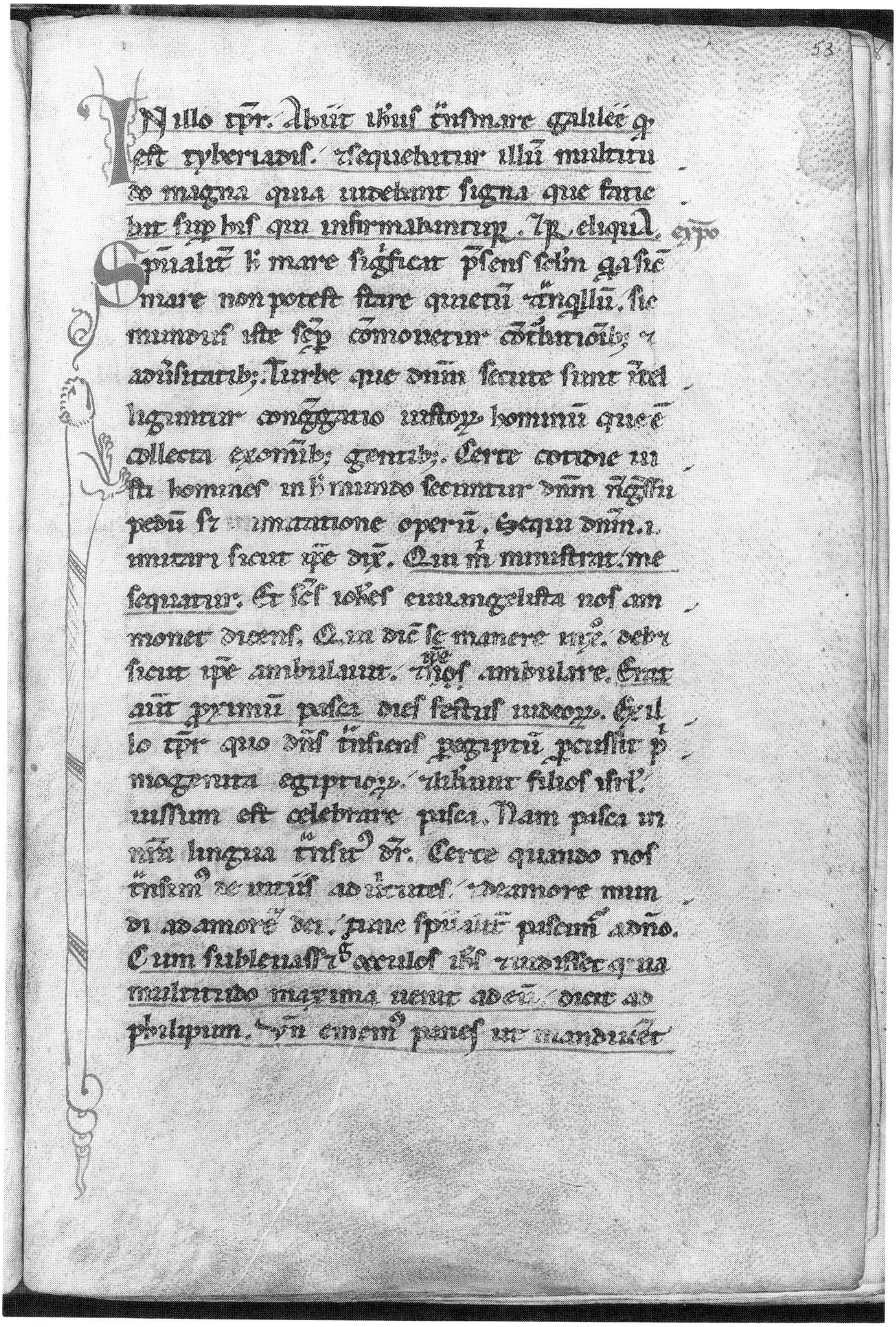

Marston MS 69, f. 53r (2/3 natural size)
Northern Italy, s. XIII#i#n

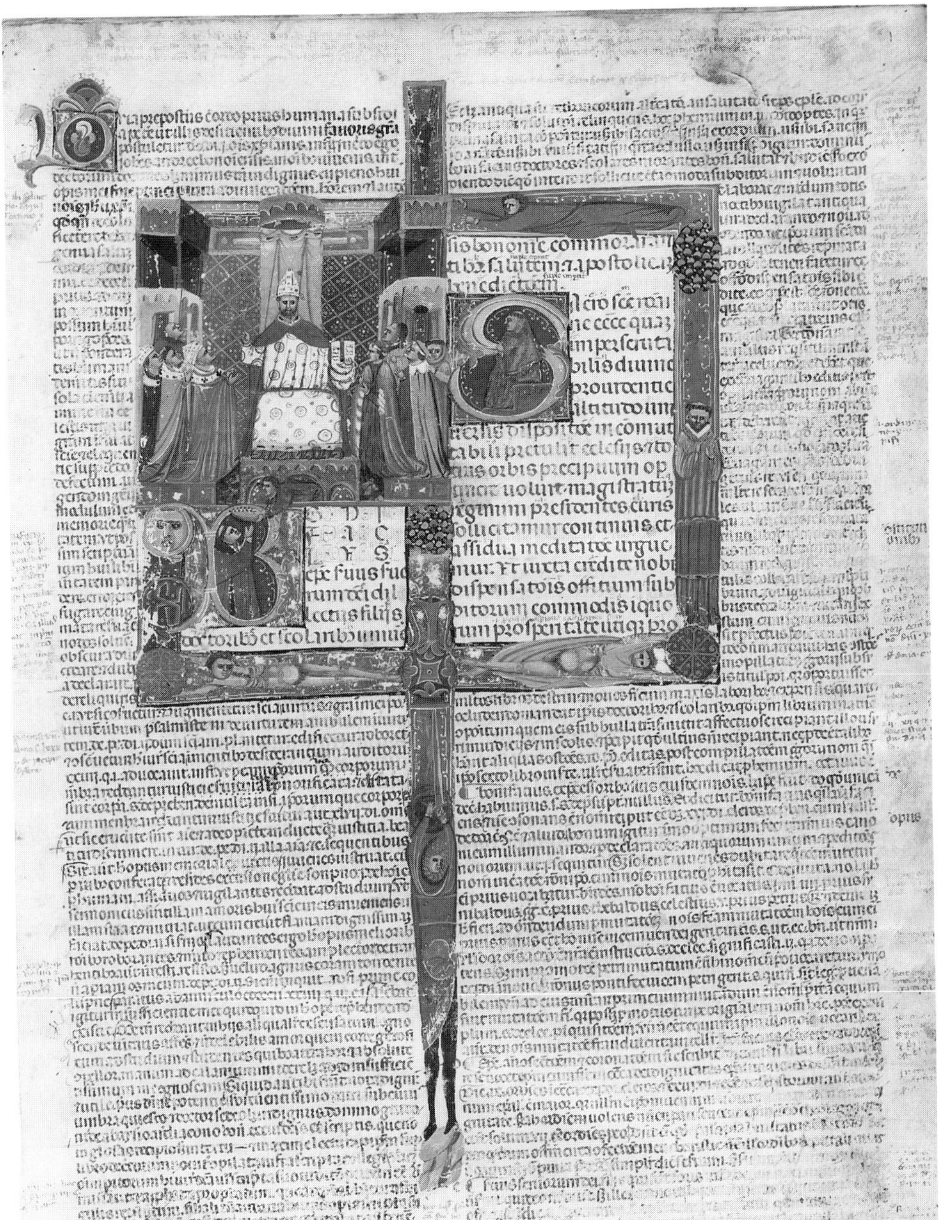

Marston MS 155, f. 1r (2/5 natural size)
Bologna, ca. 1325

PLATE 7

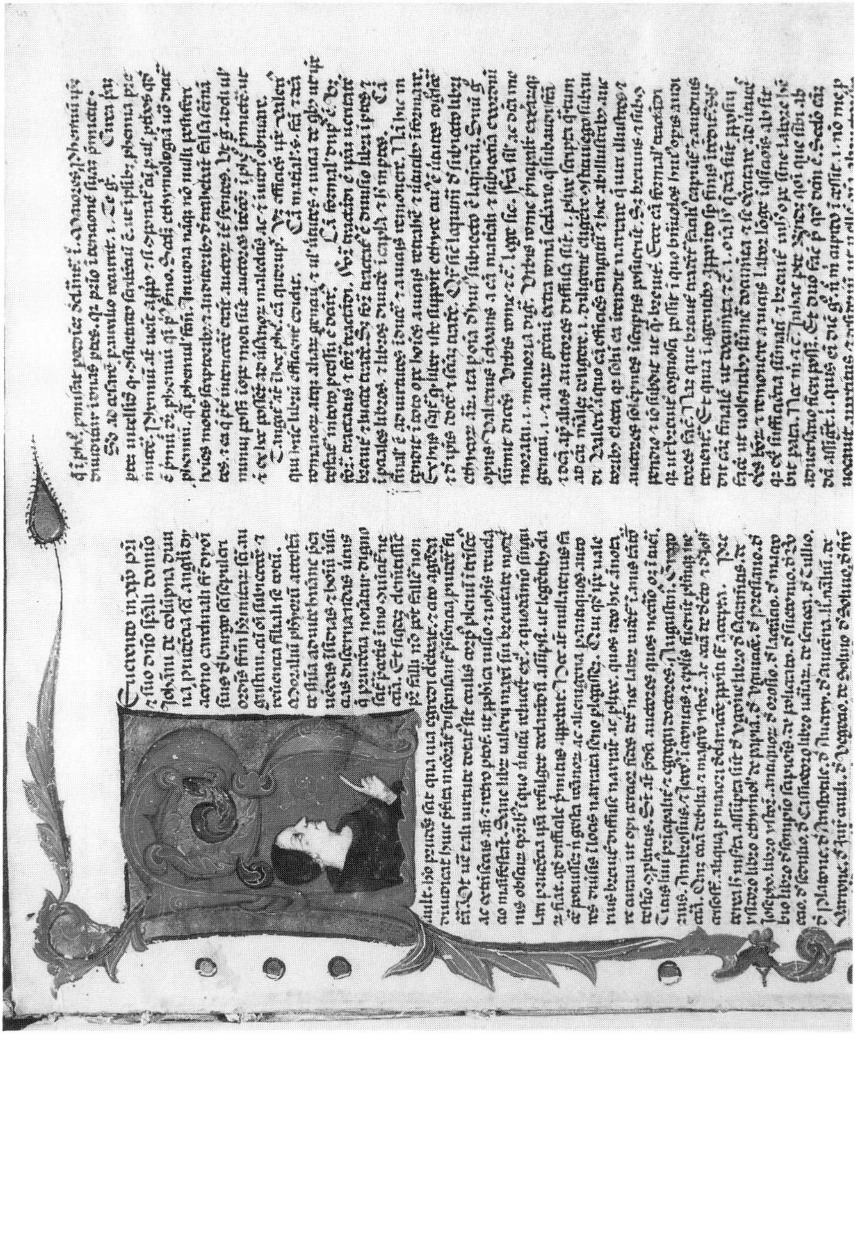

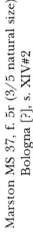

Marston MS 37, f. 5r (3/5 natural size)
Bologna [?], s. XIV#2

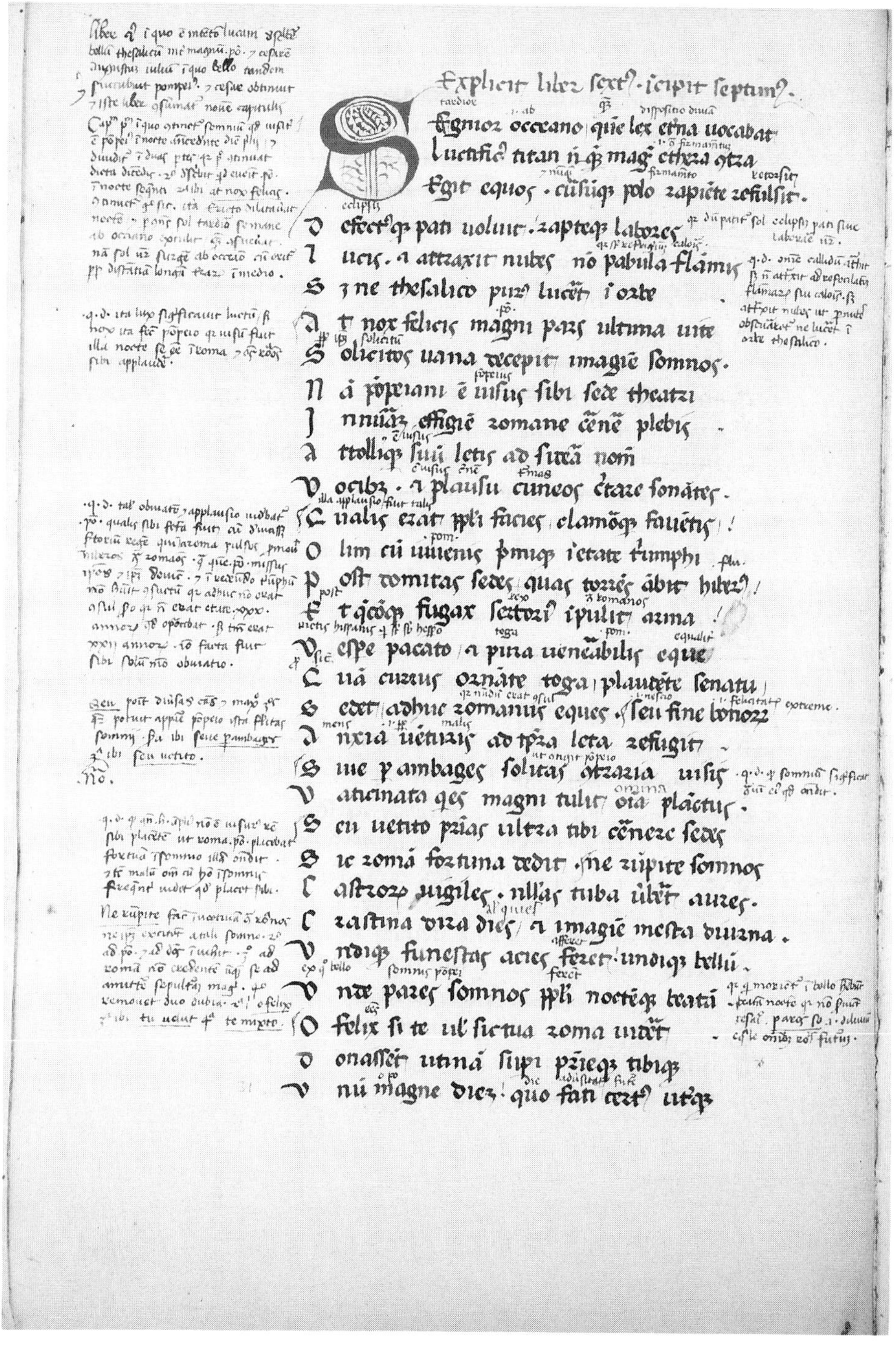

Marston MS 29, f. 75v (3/4 natural size)
Northern Italy, 1402

PLATE 9

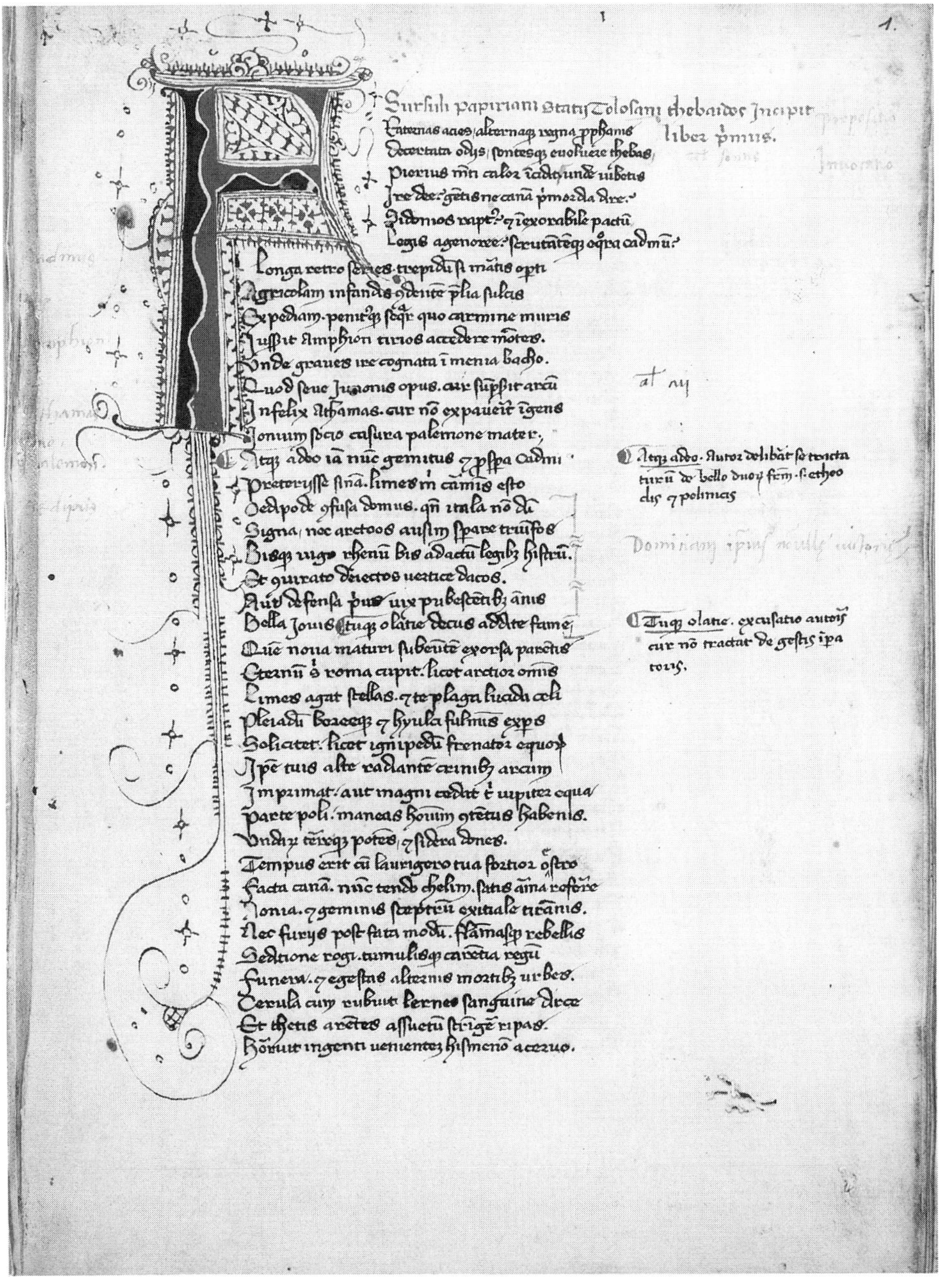

Marston MS 42, f. 1r (3/5 natural size)
Italy, 1406

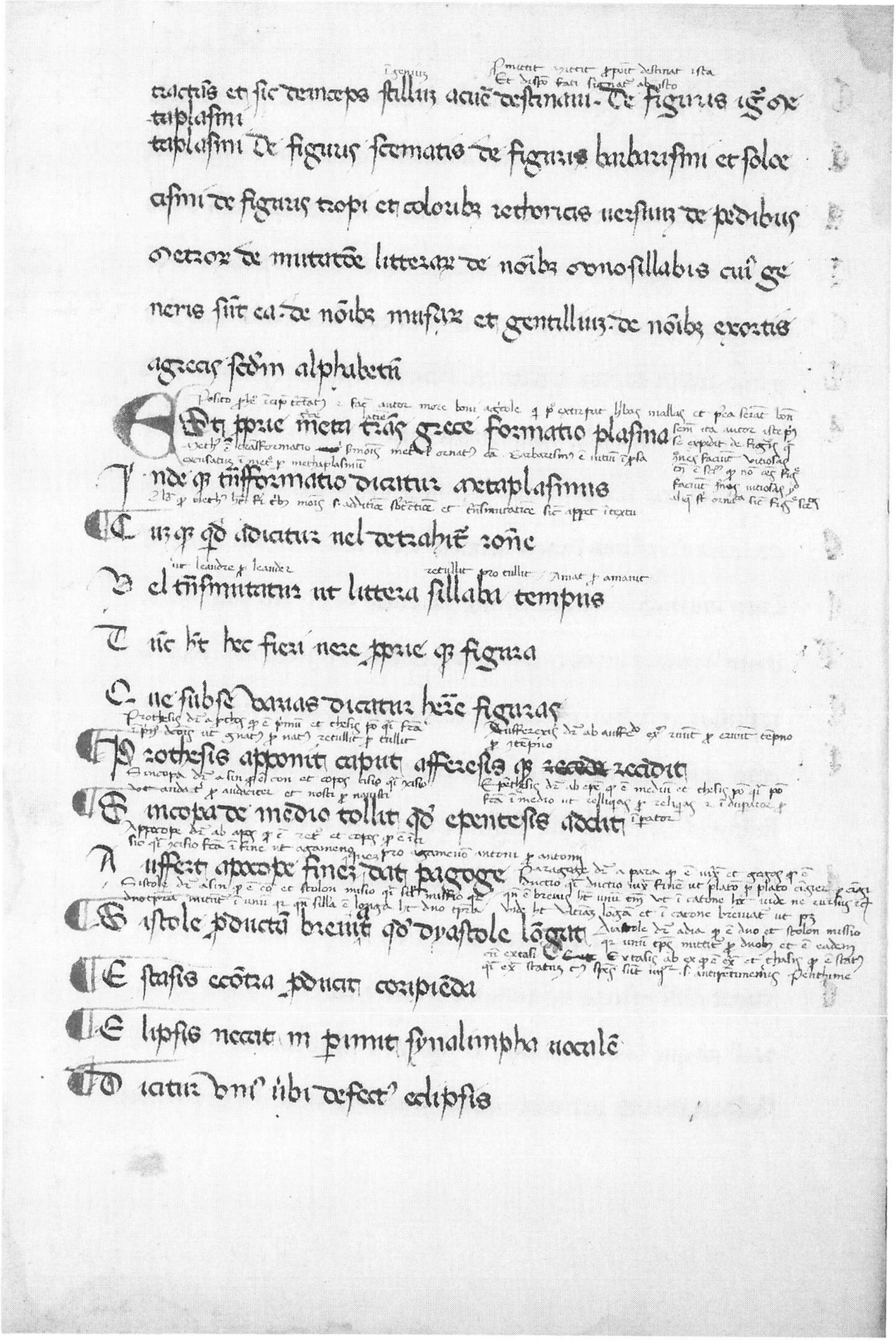

Marston MS 46, f. 1v (3/5 natural size)
Northern Italy, 1426

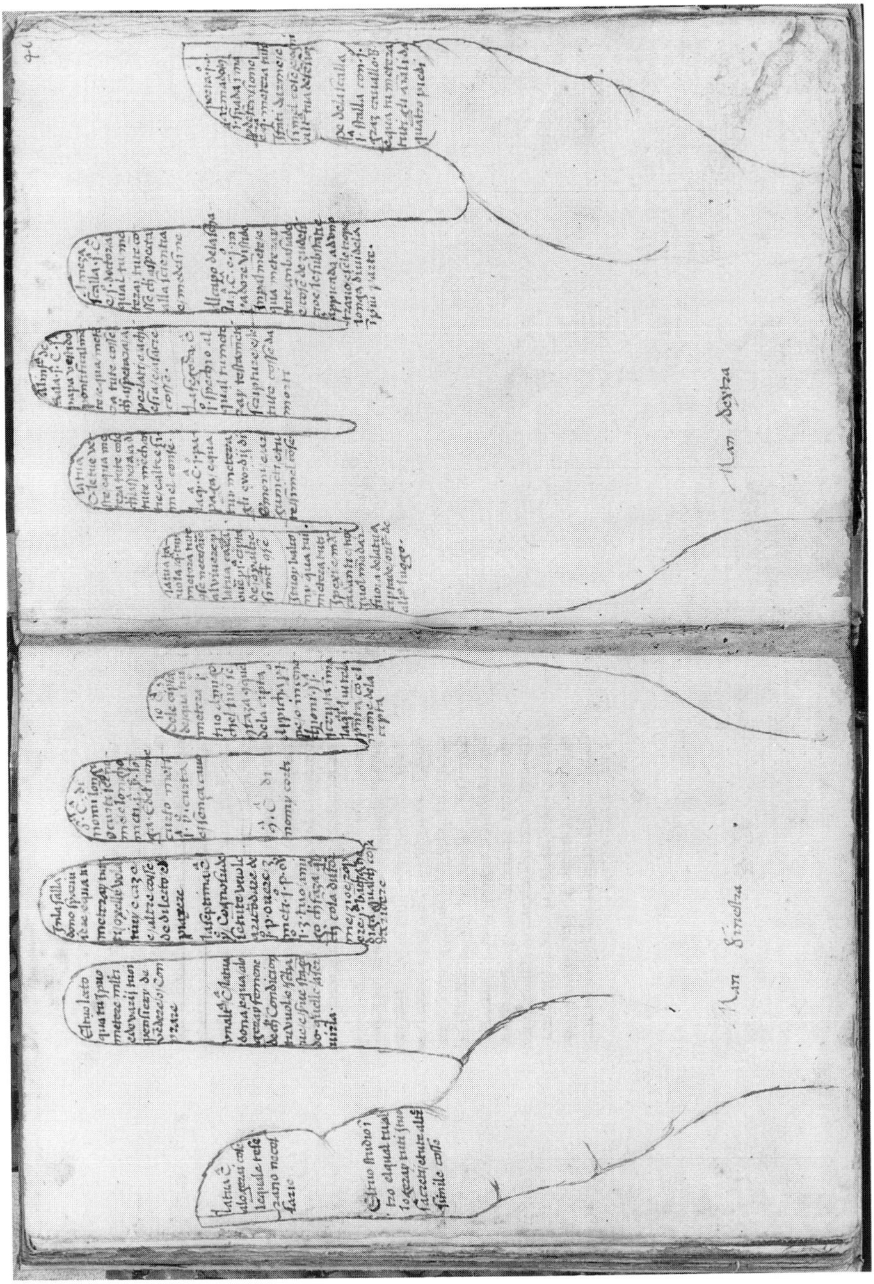

Marston MS 30, ff. 45v–46r (3/5 natural size)
Italy, s. XV#1

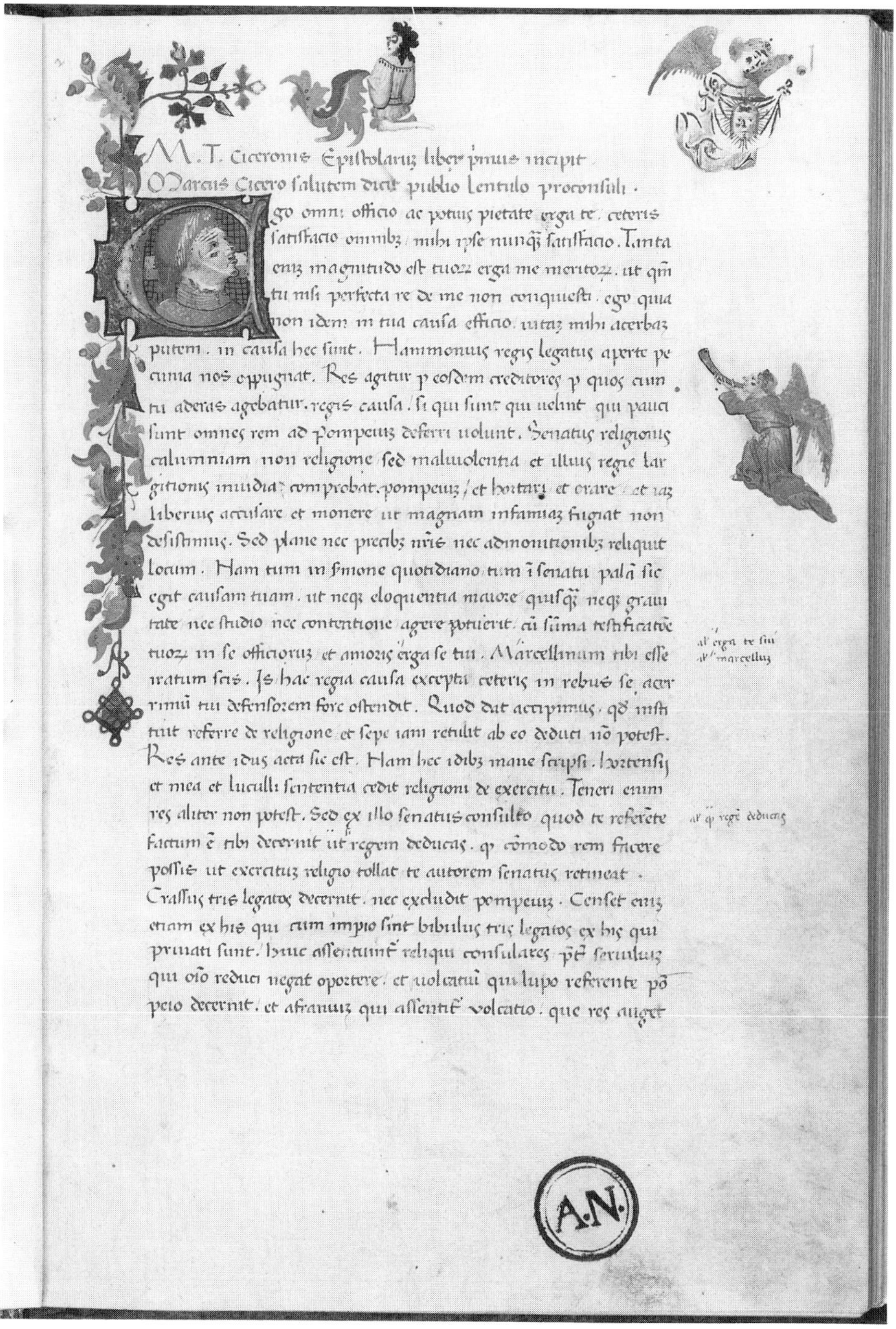

M. T. Ciceronis Epistolarum liber primus incipit.
Marcus Cicero salutem dicit publio Lentulo proconsuli.
Ego omni officio ac potius pietate erga te, ceteris
satisfacio omnibus mihi ipse numquam satisfacio. Tanta
enim magnitudo est tuorum erga me meritorum. ut quoniam
tu nisi perfecta re de me non conquiesti. ego quia
non idem in tua causa efficio. vitam mihi acerbam
putem. In causa hec sunt. Hammonius regis legatus aperte pe
cunia nos expugnat. Res agitur per eosdem creditores per quos cum
tu aderas agebatur. regis causa si qui sunt qui velint qui pauci
sunt omnes rem ad pompeium deferri volunt. Senatus religionis
calumniam non religione sed malivolentia et illius regie lar
gitionis invidia comprobat. pompeium et hortari et orare et iam
liberius accusare et monere ut magnam infamiam fugiat non
desistimus. Sed plane nec precibus nostris nec admonitionibus reliquit
locum. Nam cum in sermone quotidiano tum in senatu palam sic
egit causam tuam. ut neque eloquentia maiore quisquam neque gravi
tate nec studio nec contentione agere potuerit. cum summa testificatione
tuorum in se officiorum et amoris erga se tui. Marcellinum tibi esse
iratum scis. Is hac regia causa excepta ceteris in rebus se acer
rimum tui defensorem fore ostendit. Quod dat accipimus. quod insti
tuit referre de religione et sepe iam retulit ab eo deduci non potest.
Res ante idus acta sic est. Nam hec idibus mane scripsi. hortensij
et mea et luculli sententia cedit religioni de exercitu. Teneri enim
res aliter non potest. Sed ex illo senatusconsulto quod te referente
factum est tibi decernit ut regem deducas. quod commodo rem facere
possis. ut exercitum religio tollat te autorem senatus retineat.
Crassus tris legatos decernit. nec excludit pompeium. Censet enim
etiam ex his qui cum imperio sint. bibulus tris legatos ex his qui
privati sunt. huic assentiuntur reliqui consulares preter servilium
qui omnino reduci negat oportere. et volcatium qui lupo referente pom
peio decernit. et afranium qui assentitur volcatio. que res auget

al' erga te sui
al' marcellus
al' quod regem deducens

A.N.

Marston MS 59, f. 25r (3/5 natural size)
Northwestern Italy, ca. 1400; Netherlands, s. XV#1#/#2

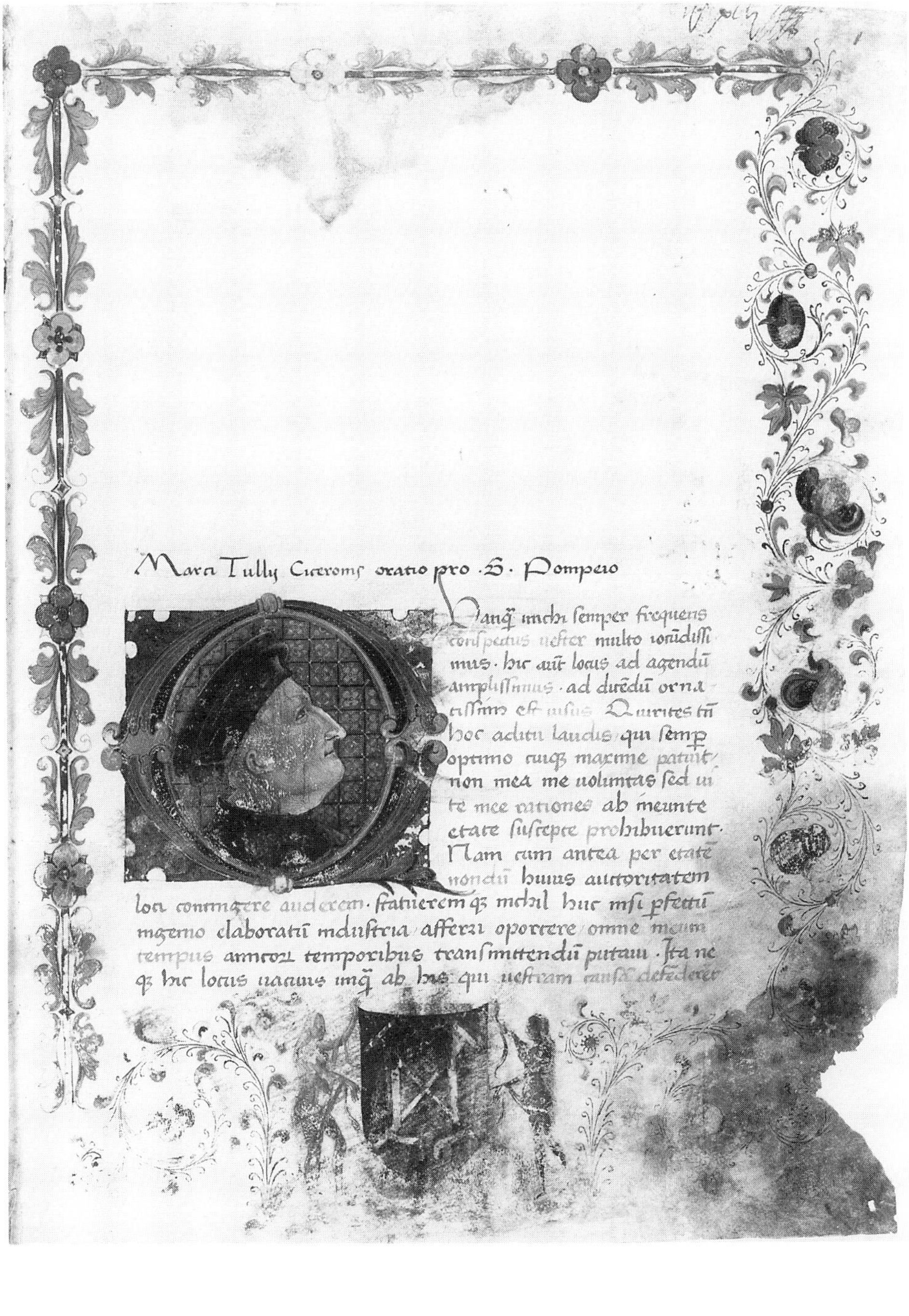

Marston MS 6, f. 1r (1/2 natural size)
Northern Italy, 1420s and s. XV#m#e#d

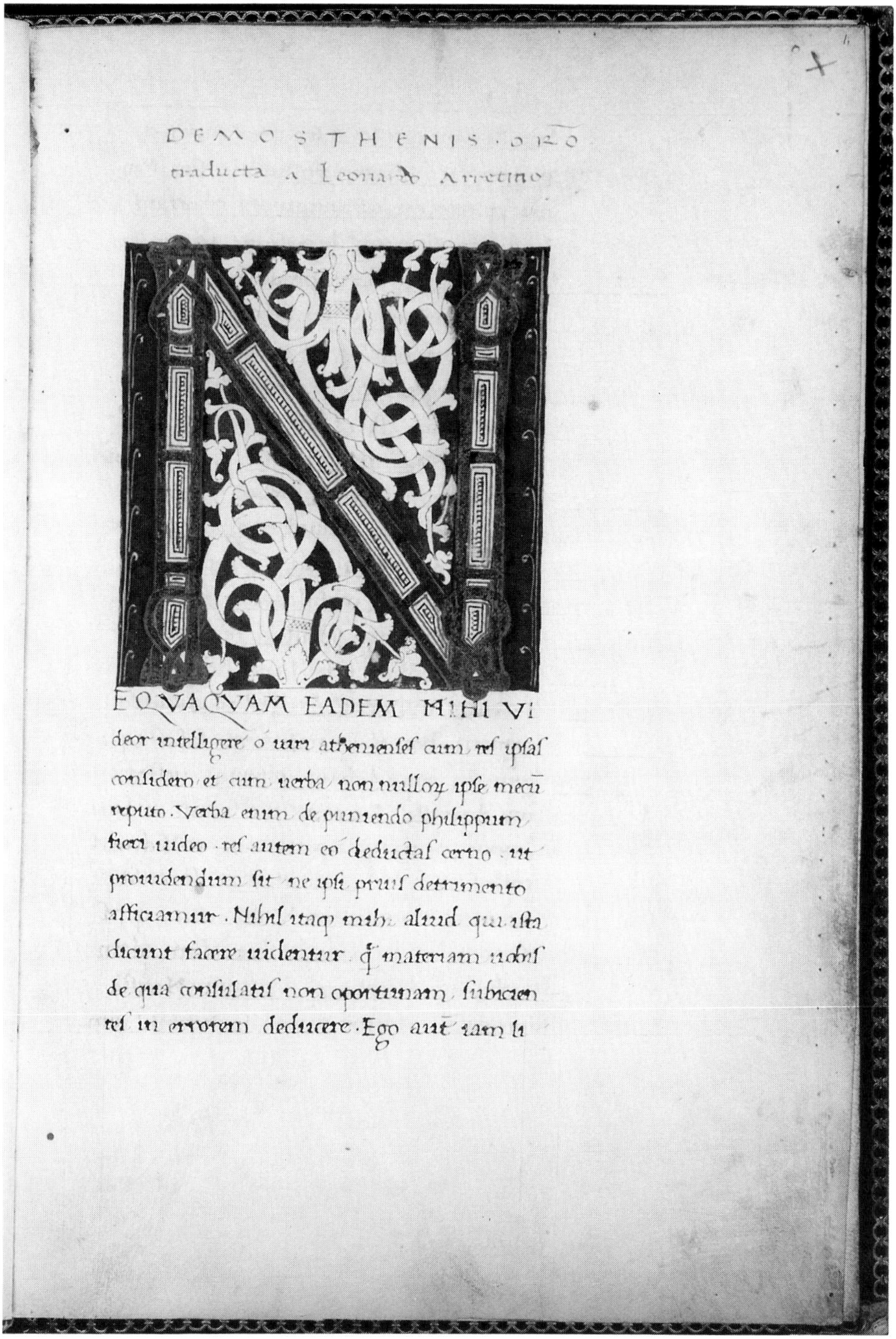

Marston MS 10, f. 1r (2/3 natural size)
Florence, ca. 1415–20

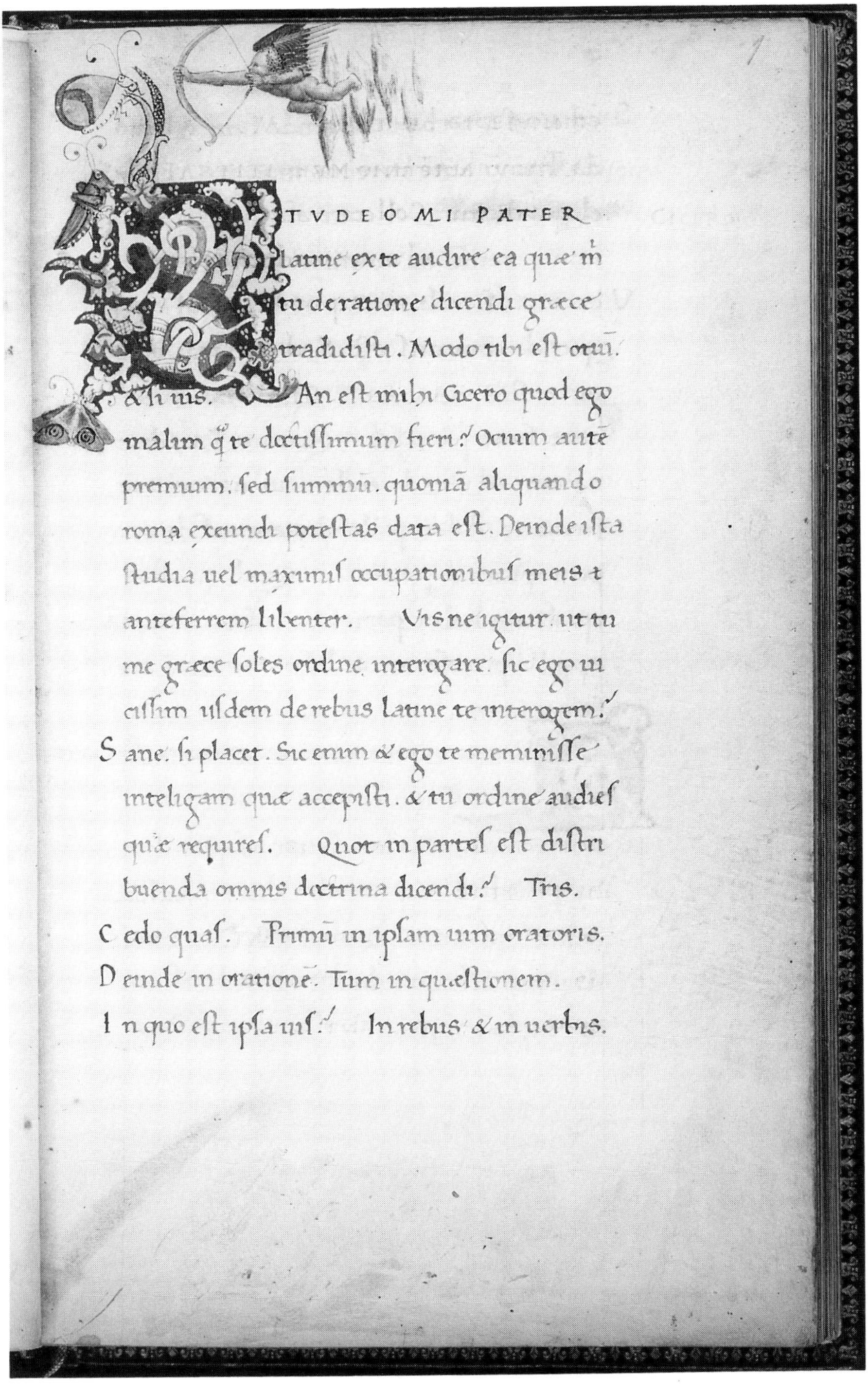
STUDEO MI PATER
latine ex te audire ea quae mi
tu de ratione dicendi graece
tradidisti. Modo tibi est otiū.
& si uis. An est mihi Cicero quod ego
malim q̄ te doctissimum fieri? Ocium autē
premium. sed summū. quoniā aliquando
roma exeundi potestas data est. Deinde ista
studia uel maximis occupationibus meis t
anteferrem libenter. Visne igitur ut tu
me graece soles ordine interogare. sic ego in
uicissim iisdem de rebus latine te interogem?
Sane. si placet. Sic enim & ego te meminisse
inteligam quae accepisti. & tu ordine audies
quae requires. Quot in partes est distri
buenda omnis doctrina dicendi? Tris.
Cedo quas. Primū in ipsam uim oratoris.
Deinde in orationē. Tum in questionem.
In quo est ipsa uis? In rebus & in uerbis.

Marston MS 278, f. 1r (5/6 natural size)
Florence, ca. 1425–30

PLATE 16

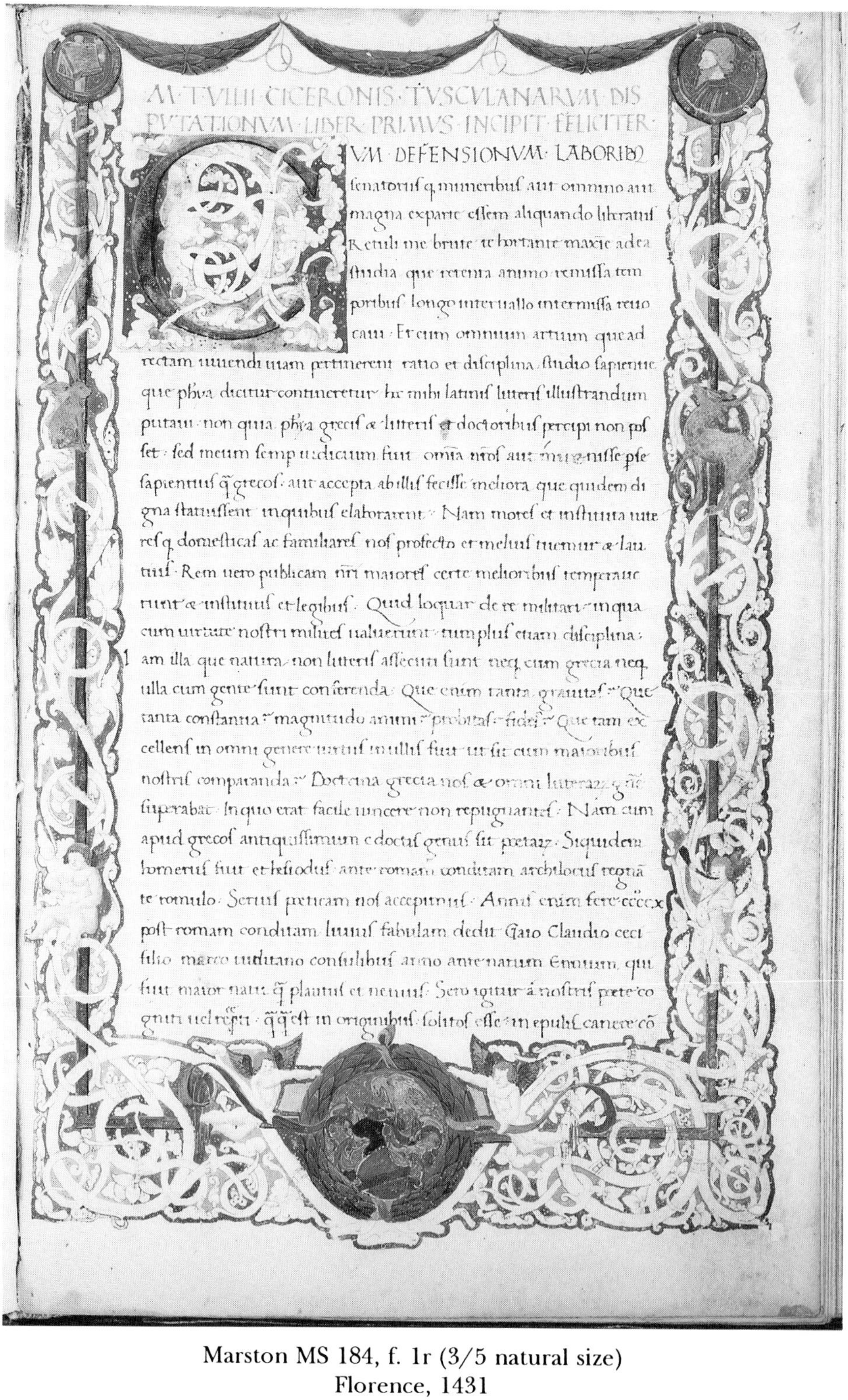
M·T·VLLII·CICERONIS·TVSCVLANARVM·DIS
PVTATIONVM·LIBER·PRIMVS·INCIPIT·FELICITER·
CVM·DEFENSIONVM·LABORIBꝫ
senatoriis q muneribus aut omnino aut
magna ex parte essem aliquando liberatus
Retuli me brute te hortante maxie ad ea
studia que retenta animo remissa tem
poribus longo interuallo intermissa reuo
caui. Et cum omnium artium que ad
rectam uiuendi uiam pertinerent ratio et disciplina studio sapientie
que phia dicitur contineretur hc mihi latinis litteris illustrandum
putaui non quia phia grecis & litteris et doctoribus percipi non pos
set. sed meum semp iudicium fuit omia nros aut inuenisse pse
sapientius q grecos aut accepta ab illis fecisse meliora que quidem di
gna statuissent in quibus elaborarent. Nam mores et instituta uite
resq domesticas ac familiares nos profecto et melius tuemur & lau
tius. Rem uero publicam nri maiores certe melioribus temperaue
runt & institutis et legibus. Quid loquar de re militari in qua
cum uirtute nostri milites ualuerunt tum plus etiam disciplina.
I am illa que natura non litteris assecuti sunt neq cum grecia neq
ulla cum gente sunt conferenda. Que enim tanta grauitas. Que
tanta constantia. magnitudo animi. probitas. fides. Que tam ex
cellens in omni genere uirtus in ullis fuit ut sit cum maioribus
nostris comparanda. Doctrina grecia nos & omni litterarum genere
superabat. In quo erat facile uincere non repugnantes. Nam cum
apud grecos antiquissimum e doctis genus sit poetarum. Siquidem
homerus fuit et hesiodus ante romam conditam archilocus regna
te romulo. Serius poeticam nos accepimus. Annis enim fere dx
post romam conditam liuius fabulam dedit Gaio Claudio ceci
filio marco tuditano consulibus anno ante natum Ennium qui
fuit maior natu q plautus et neuius. Sero igitur a nostris poete co
gniti uel recepti. quamquam est in originibus solitos esse in epulis canere co

Marston MS 184, f. 1r (3/5 natural size)
Florence, 1431

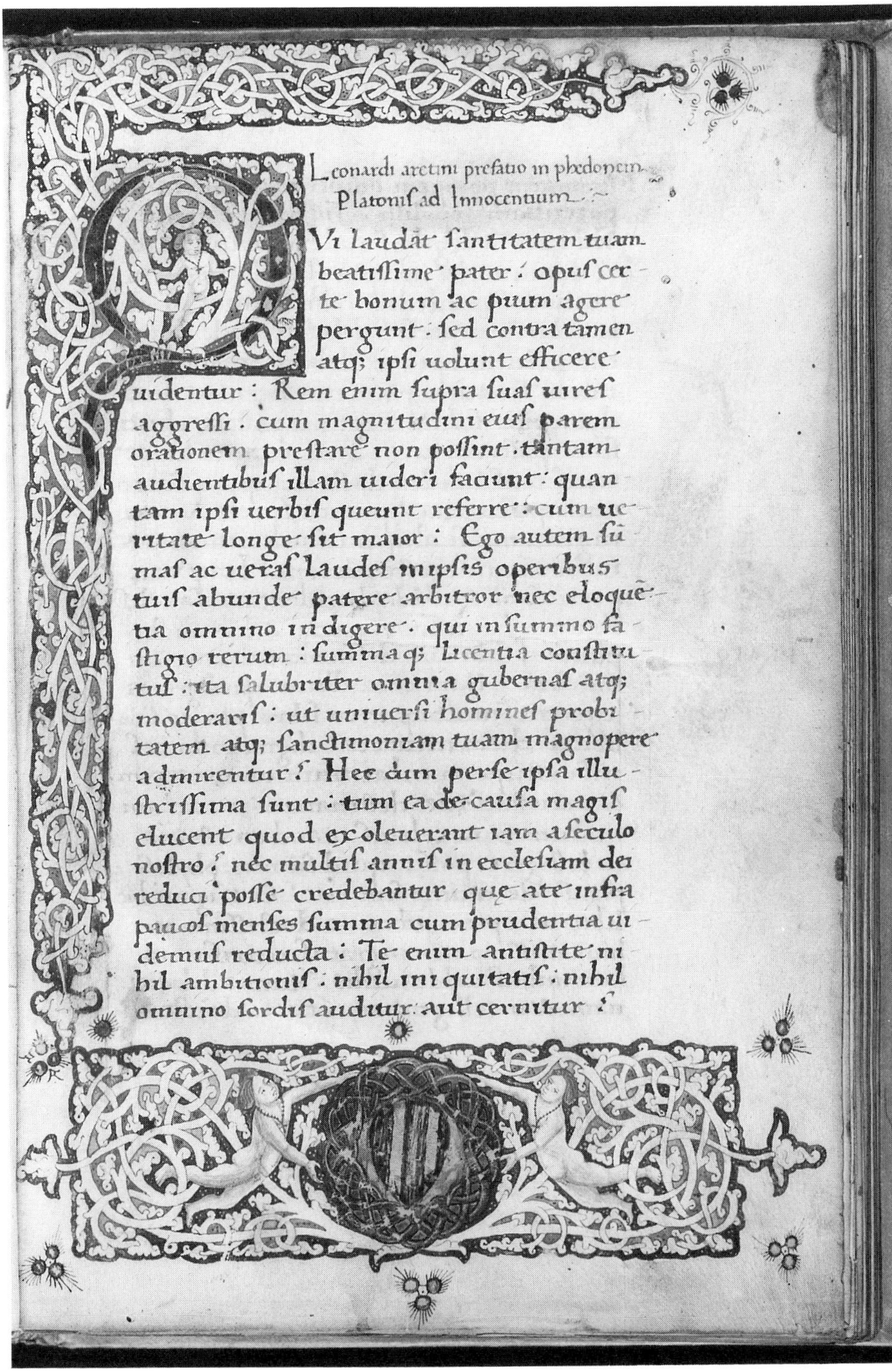
Leonardi aretini prefatio in phedonem
Platonis ad Innocentium.
Qui laudant santitatem tuam
beatissime pater: opus certe bonum ac pium agere
pergunt. sed contra tamen
atq; ipsi uolunt efficere
uidentur: Rem enim supra suas uires
aggressi. cum magnitudini eius parem
orationem prestare non possint. tantam
audientibus illam uideri faciunt: quantam ipsi uerbis queunt referre: cum ueritate longe sit maior: Ego autem sum-
mas ac ueras laudes in ipsis operibus
tuis abunde patere arbitror nec eloquentia omnino indigere. qui in summo fa-
stigio rerum: summaq; licentia constitutus: ita salubriter omnia gubernas atq;
moderaris: ut uniuersi homines probi-
tatem atq; sanctimoniam tuam magnopere
admirentur: Hec dum per se ipsa illu-
strissima sunt: tum ea de causa magis
elucent quod exoleuerant iam a seculo
nostro: nec multis annis in ecclesiam dei
reduci posse credebantur que a te infra
paucos menses summa cum prudentia uidemus reducta: Te enim antistite nihil ambitionis: nihil iniquitatis: nihil
omnino sordis auditur: aut cernitur:

Marston MS 78, f. 1r (7/10 natural size)
Florence, ca. 1440–50

PLATE 18

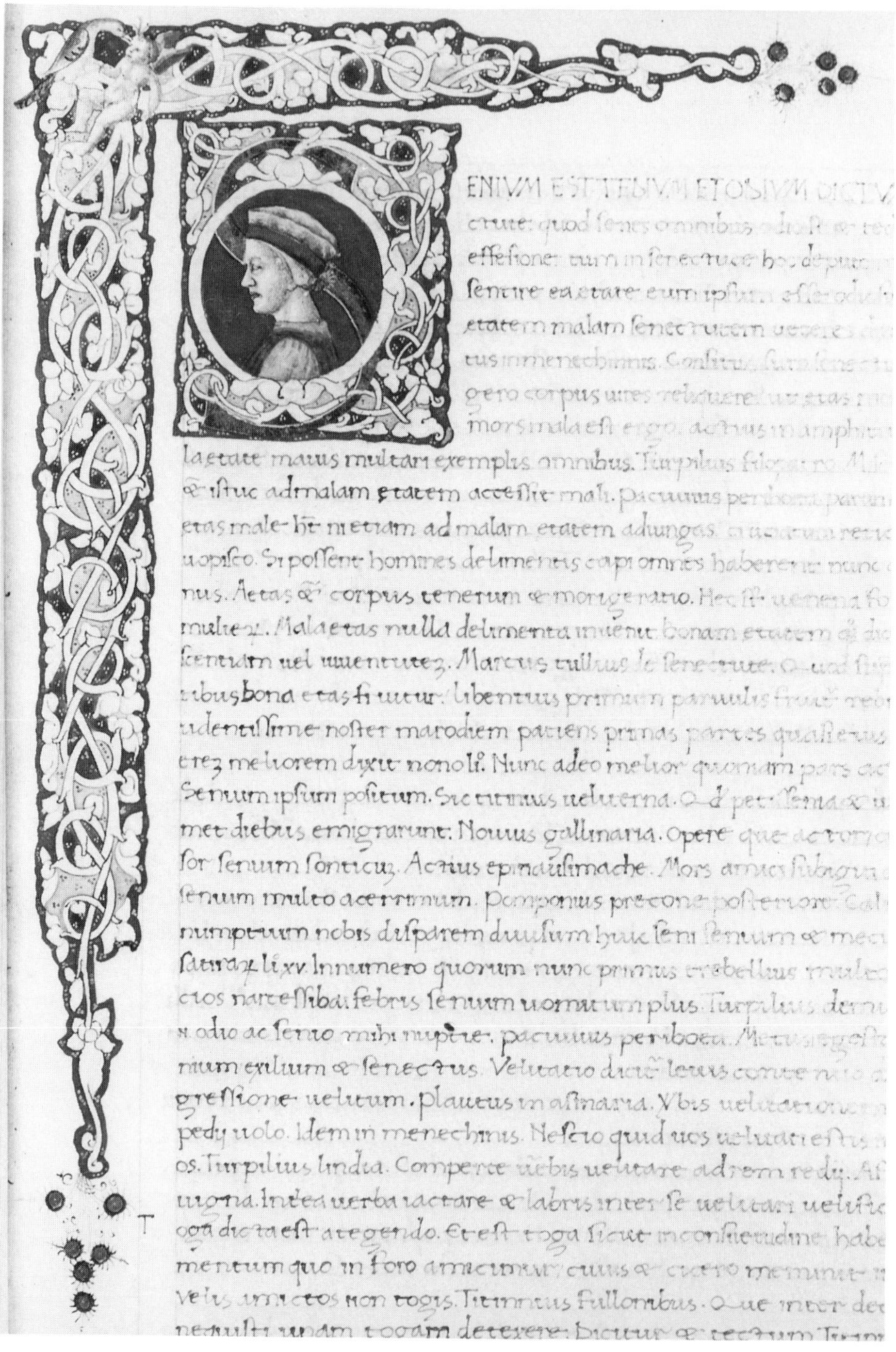

Marston MS 55, f. 1r (slightly reduced)
Florence, ca. 1445–50

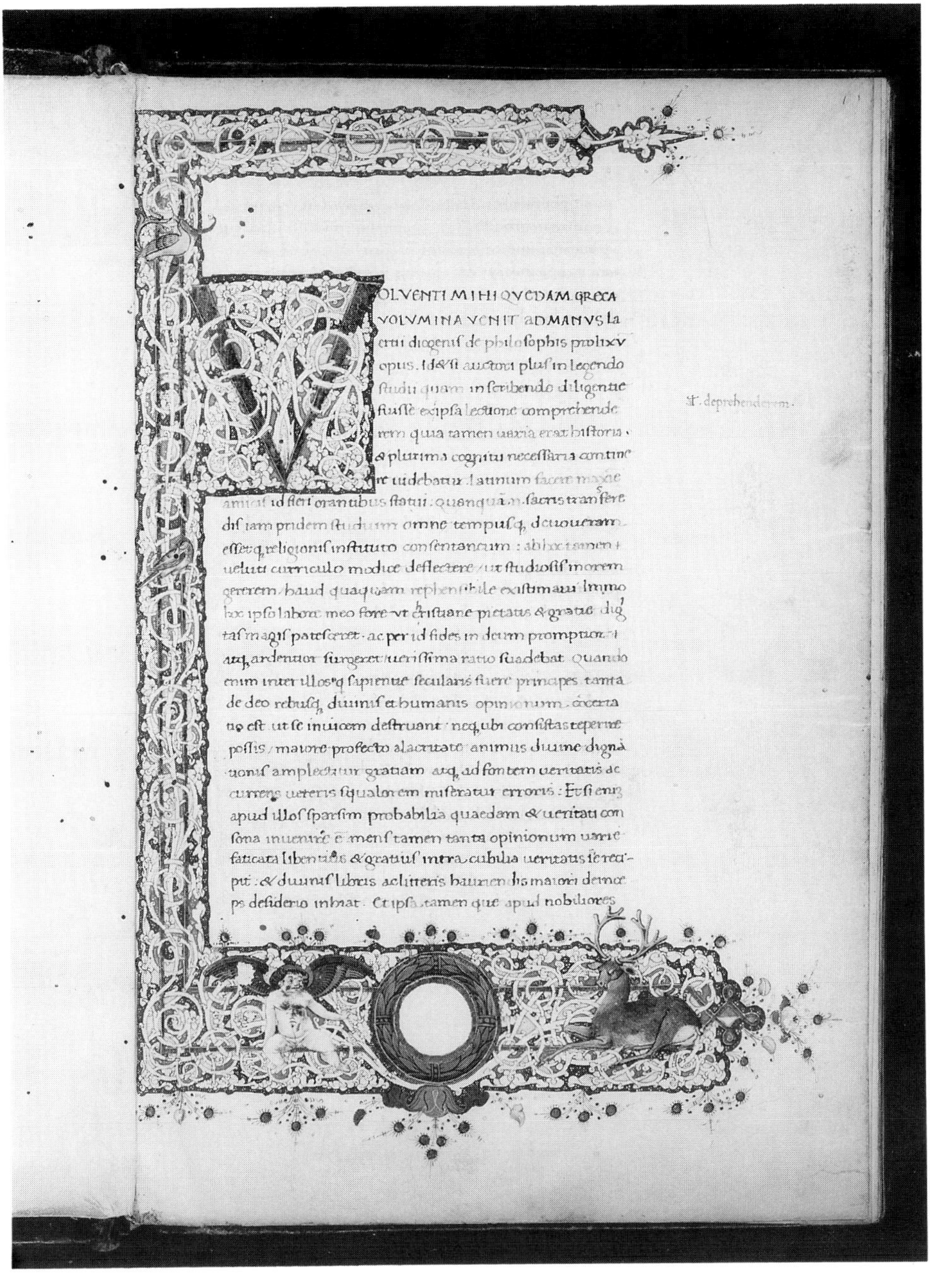
VOLVENTI MIHI QVEDAM GRECA
VOLVMINA VENIT AD MANVS La
ertii diogenis de philosophis prolixum
opus. Id & si auctori plus in legendo
studii quam in scribendo diligentie
fuisse ex ipsa lectione comprehende
rem quia tamen uaria erat historia
& plurima cognitu necessaria contine
re uidebatur. latinum facere maxime
amicis id fieri orantibus statui. quanquam a sacris transfere
dis iam pridem studium omne tempusque deuoueram
esseque religionis instituto consentaneum : ab hoc tamen
ueluti curriculo modice deflectere, ut studiosis morem
gererem, haud quaquam reprehensibile existimaui. Immo
hoc ipso labore meo fore ut christiane pietatis & gratie dig
tas magis patesceret. ac per id fides in deum promptior
atque ardentior surgeret, uerissima ratio suadebat. Quando
enim inter illos qui sapientie secularis fuere principes tanta
de deo rebusque diuinis et humanis opinionum concerta
tio est ut se inuicem destruant, neque ubi consistas reperire
possis, maiore profecto alacritate animus diuine digna
tionis amplectitur gratiam atque ad fontem ueritatis ac
currens ueteris squalorem miseratur erroris. Etsi enim
apud illos sparsim probabilia quaedam & ueritati con
sona inuenire est, mens tamen tanta opinionum uarie
faticata libentius & gratius intra cubilia ueritatis se reci
pit. & diuinis libris ac litteris hauriendis maiori deinde
ps desiderio inhiat. Et ipsa tamen que apud nobiliores
al. deprehenderem.

Marston MS 38, f. 1r (2/5 natural size)
Florence, ca. 1450–60

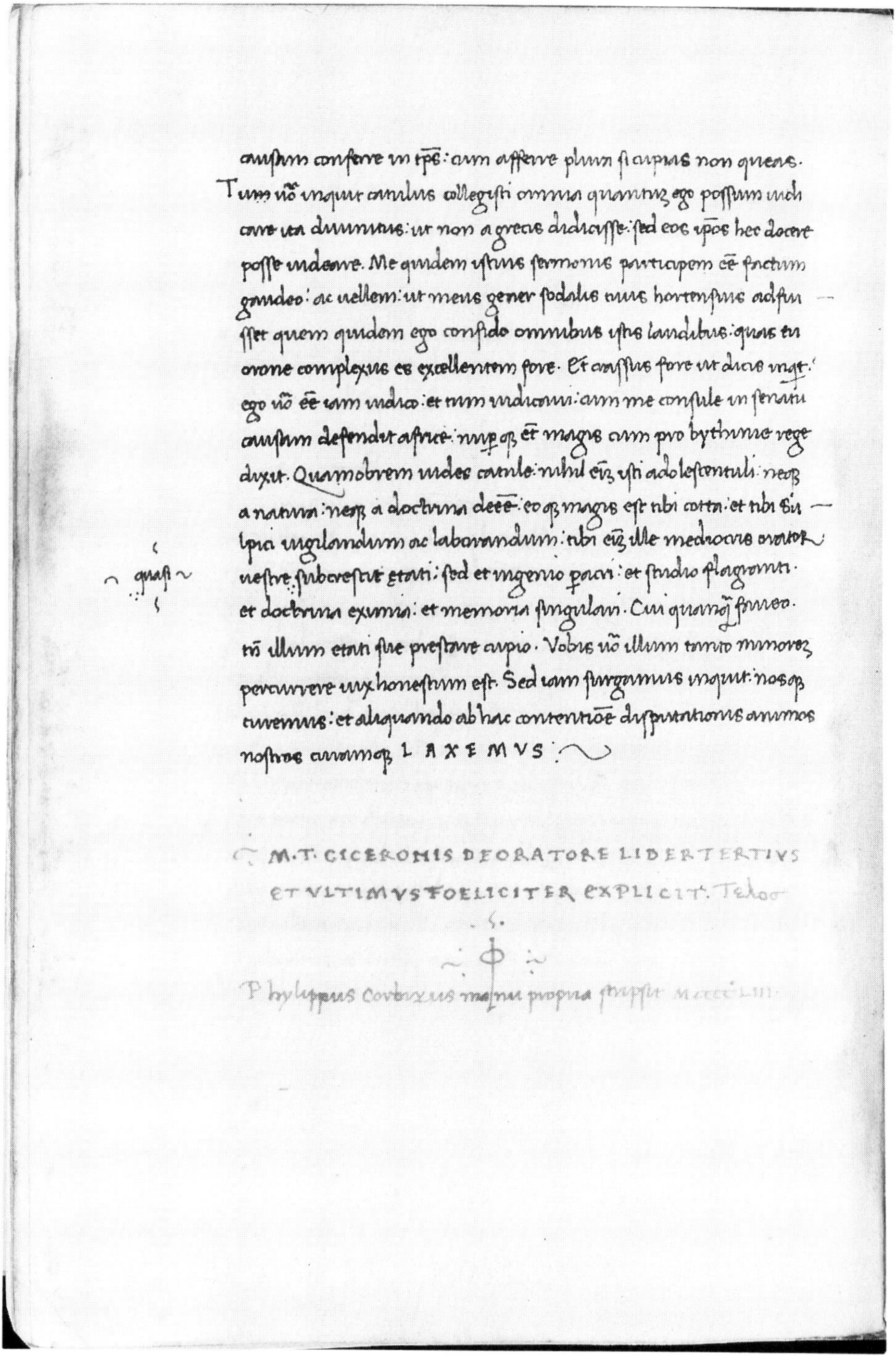
causam conferre in tempus: cum afferre plura si cupias non queas. Tum vero inquit catulus collegisti omnia quanta ego possum iudicare ita divinitus: ut non a grecis didicisse: sed eos ipsos hec docere posse videare. Me quidem istius sermonis participem esse factum gaudeo: ac vellem: ut meus gener sodalis tuus hortensius adfuisset quem quidem ego confido omnibus istis laudibus: quas tu oratione complexus es excellentem fore. Et crassus fore ut dicis inquit. ego vero esse iam iudico: et tum iudicavi: cum me consule in senatu causam defendit africe: nuperque etiam magis cum pro bythinie rege dixit. Quamobrem vides catule: nihil enim isti adolescentuli: neque a natura: neque a doctrina deesse: eoque magis est tibi cotta: et tibi sulpici vigilandum ac laborandum: non enim ille mediocris orator vestre quasi succrescit etati: sed et ingenio peracri: et studio flagranti: et doctrina eximia: et memoria singulari. Cui quamquam faveo: tamen illum etati sue prestare cupio. Vobis vero illum tanto minorem percurrere vix honestum est. Sed iam surgamus inquit: nosque curemus: et aliquando ab hac contentione disputationis animos nostros curamque LAXEMUS.

M. T. CICERONIS DE ORATORE LIBER TERTIUS ET ULTIMUS FOELICITER EXPLICIT. Τελος

Phylippus Corbizus manu propria scripsit MCCCCLIII

Marston MS 39, f. 121v (slightly reduced)
Florence, 1453

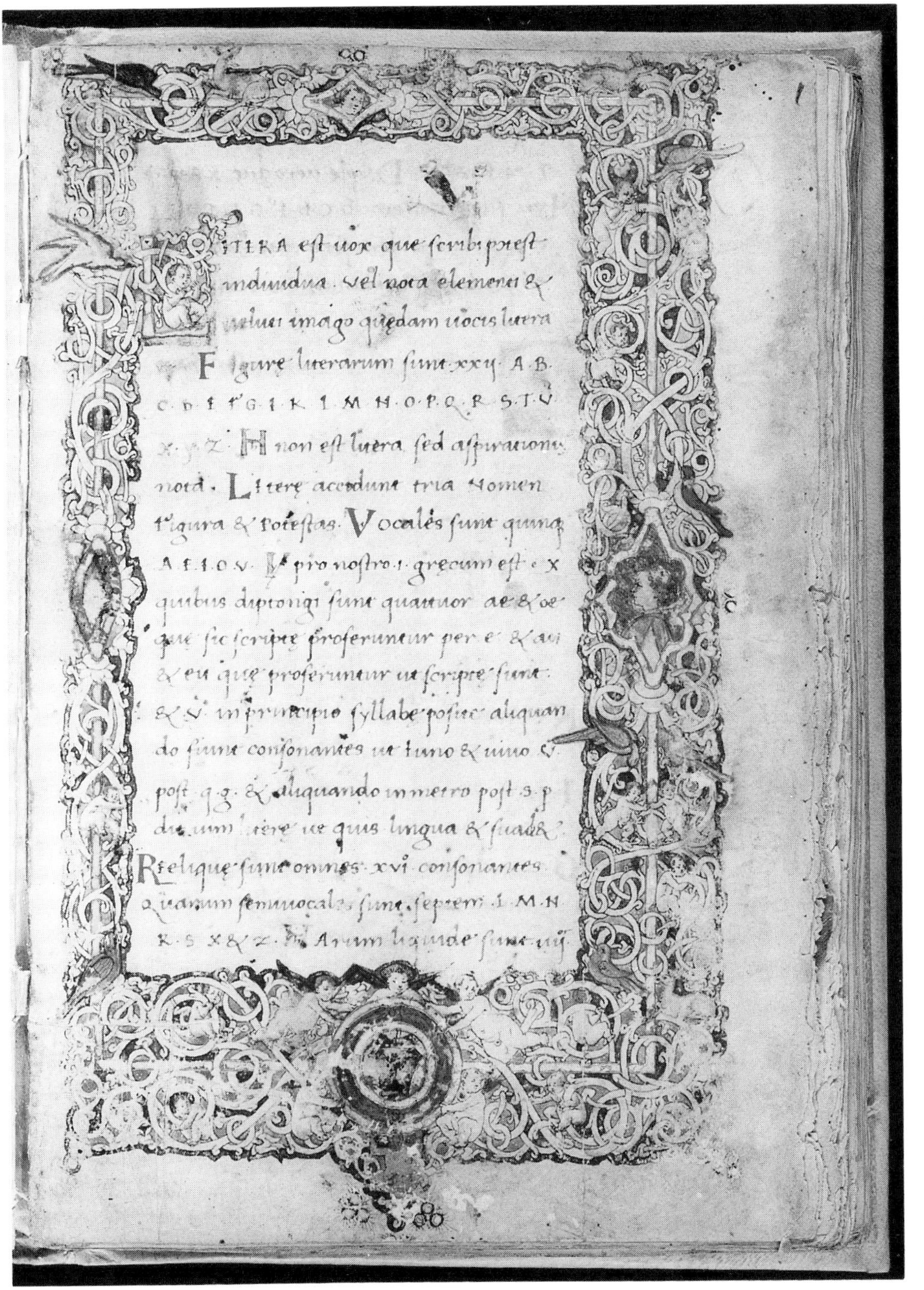

Marston MS 111, f. 1r (slightly reduced)
Florence, ca. 1460s [?]

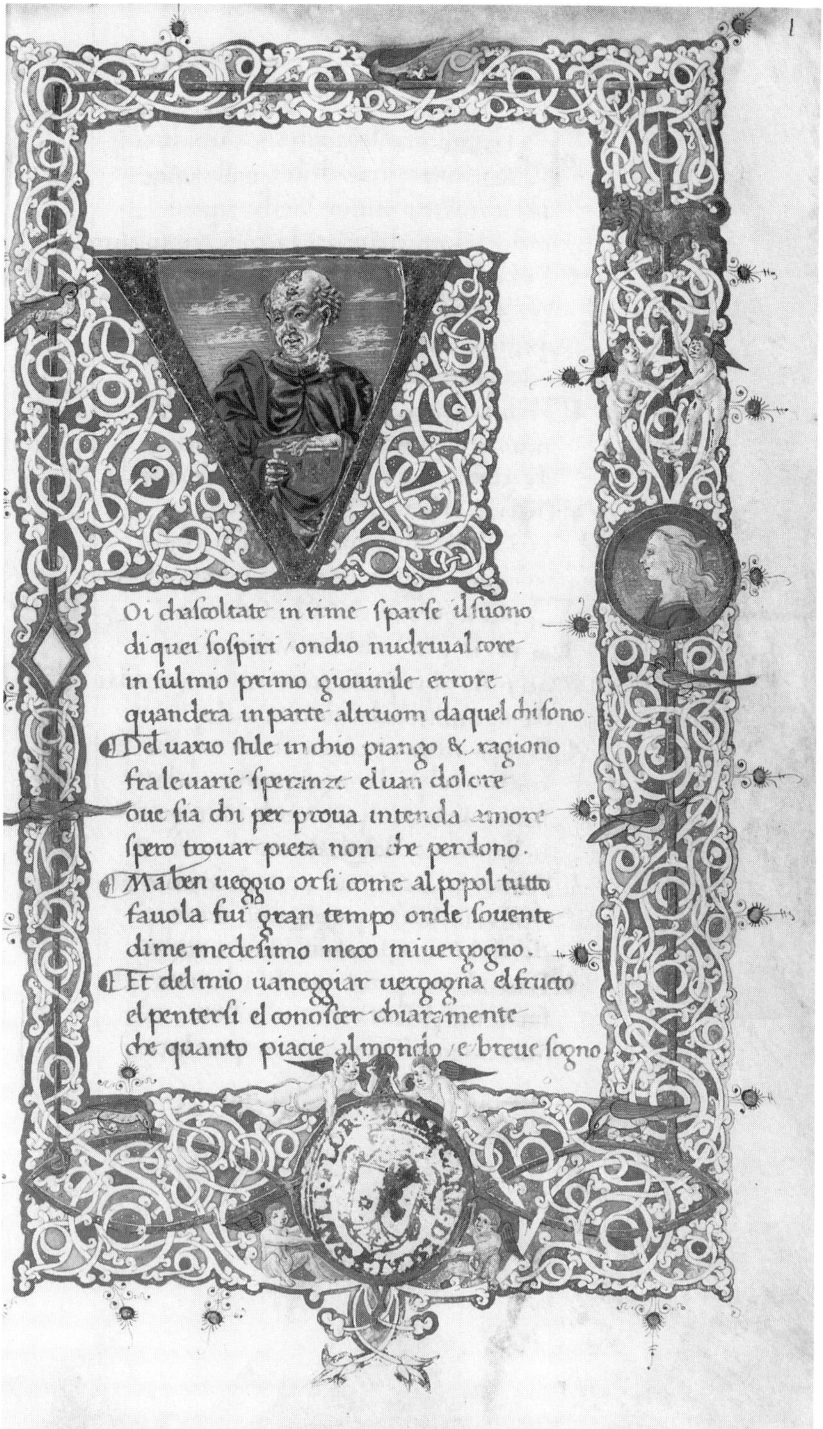
Oi chascoltate in rime sparse il suono
di quei sospiri ondio nudriua il core
in sul mio primo giouinile errore
quandera in parte altruom da quel chi sono.
Del uario stile inchio piango & ragiono
fra le uarie speranze e luan dolore
oue sia chi per proua intenda amore
spero trouar pieta non che perdono.
Ma ben ueggio orsi come al popol tutto
fauola fui gran tempo onde souente
di me medesimo meco miuergogno.
Et del mio uaneggiar uergogna el fructo
el pentersi el conoscer chiaramente
che quanto piacie al mondo e breue sogno.

Marston MS 261, f. 1r (7/10 natural size)
Florence, 1464

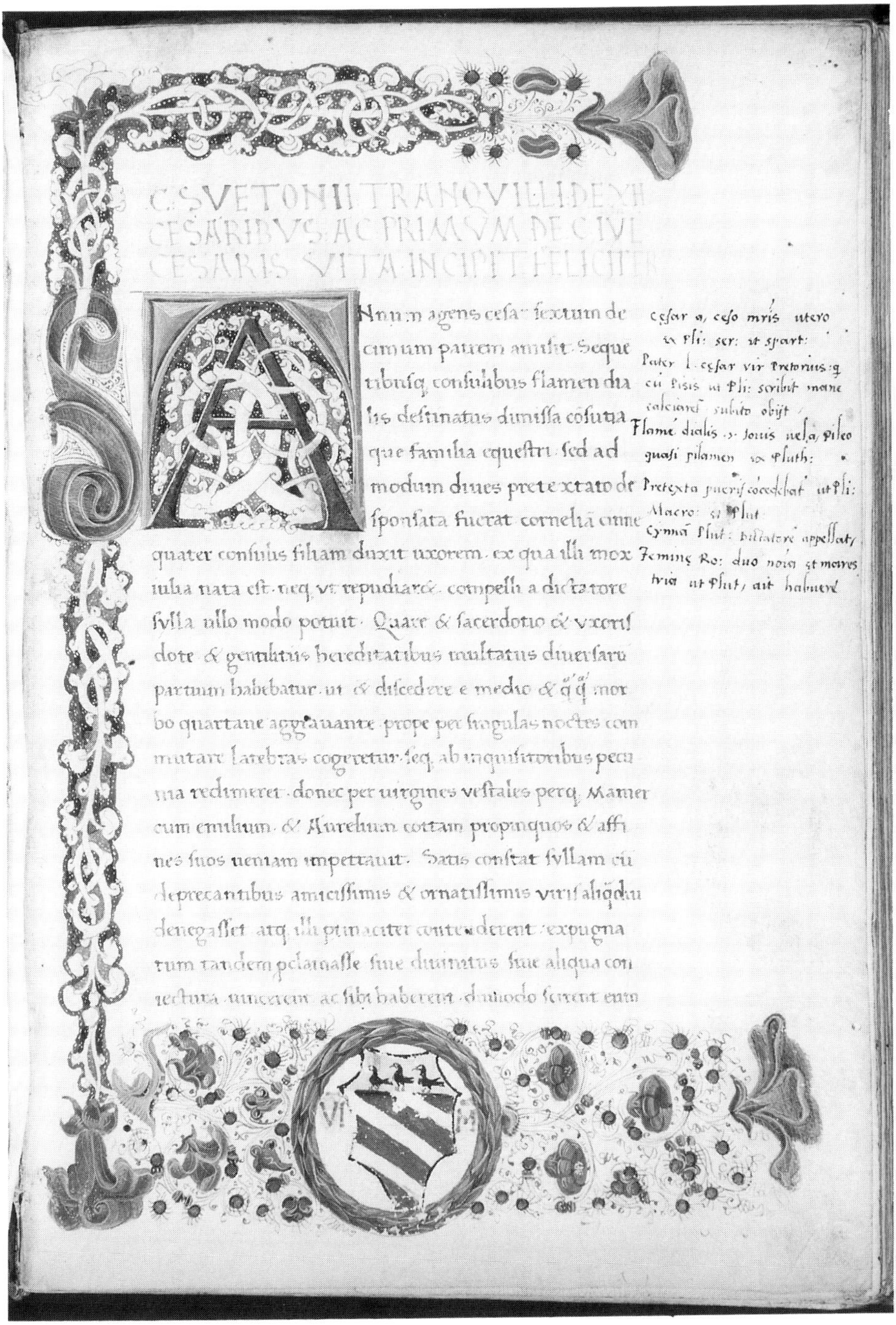

Marston MS 52, f. 1r (3/5 natural size)
Bologna, s. XV#m#e#d

PLATE 24

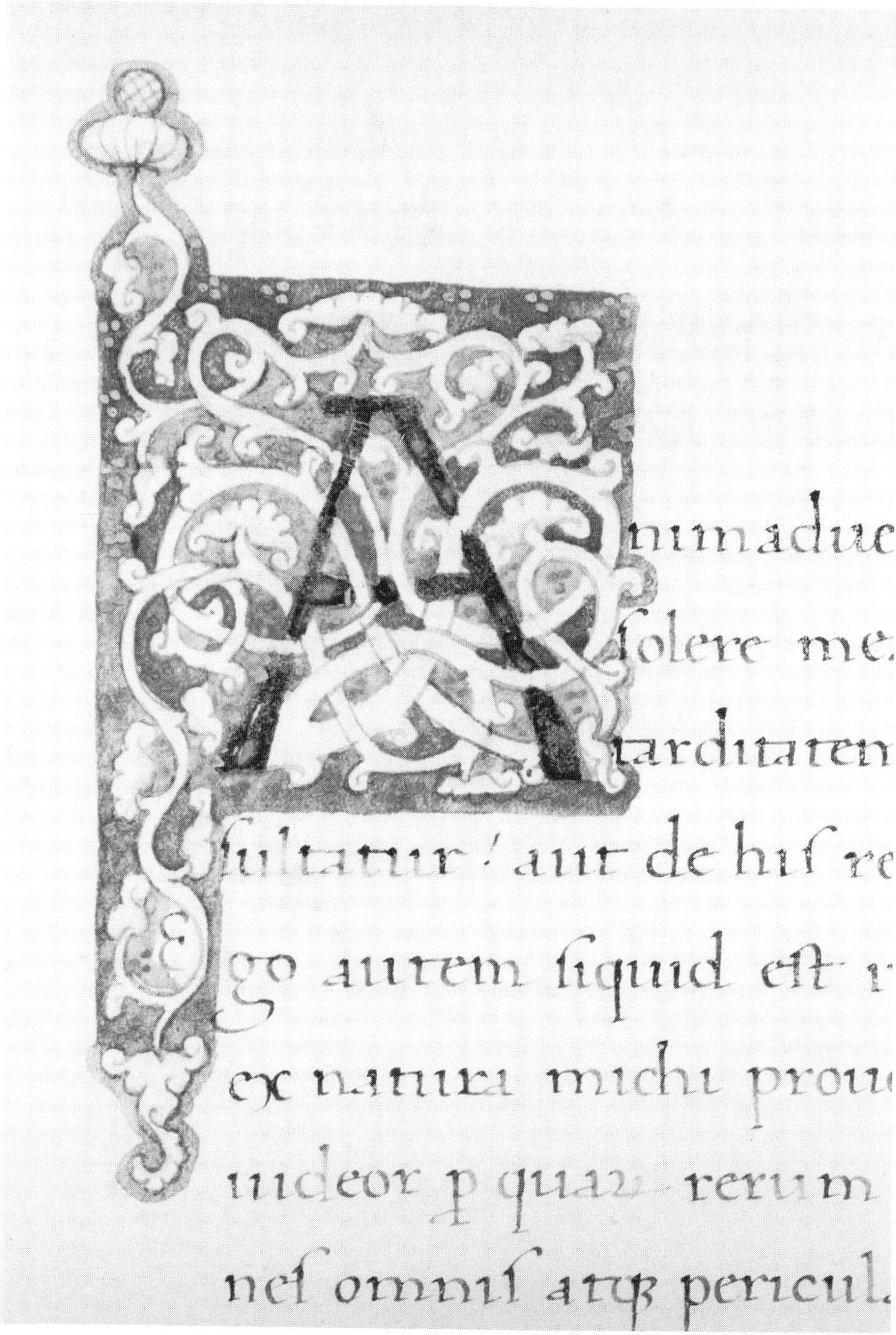

Marston MS 85, f. 1r (enlarged detail)
Rome [?]. s. XV#2#/#4#-#m#e#d

PLATE 25

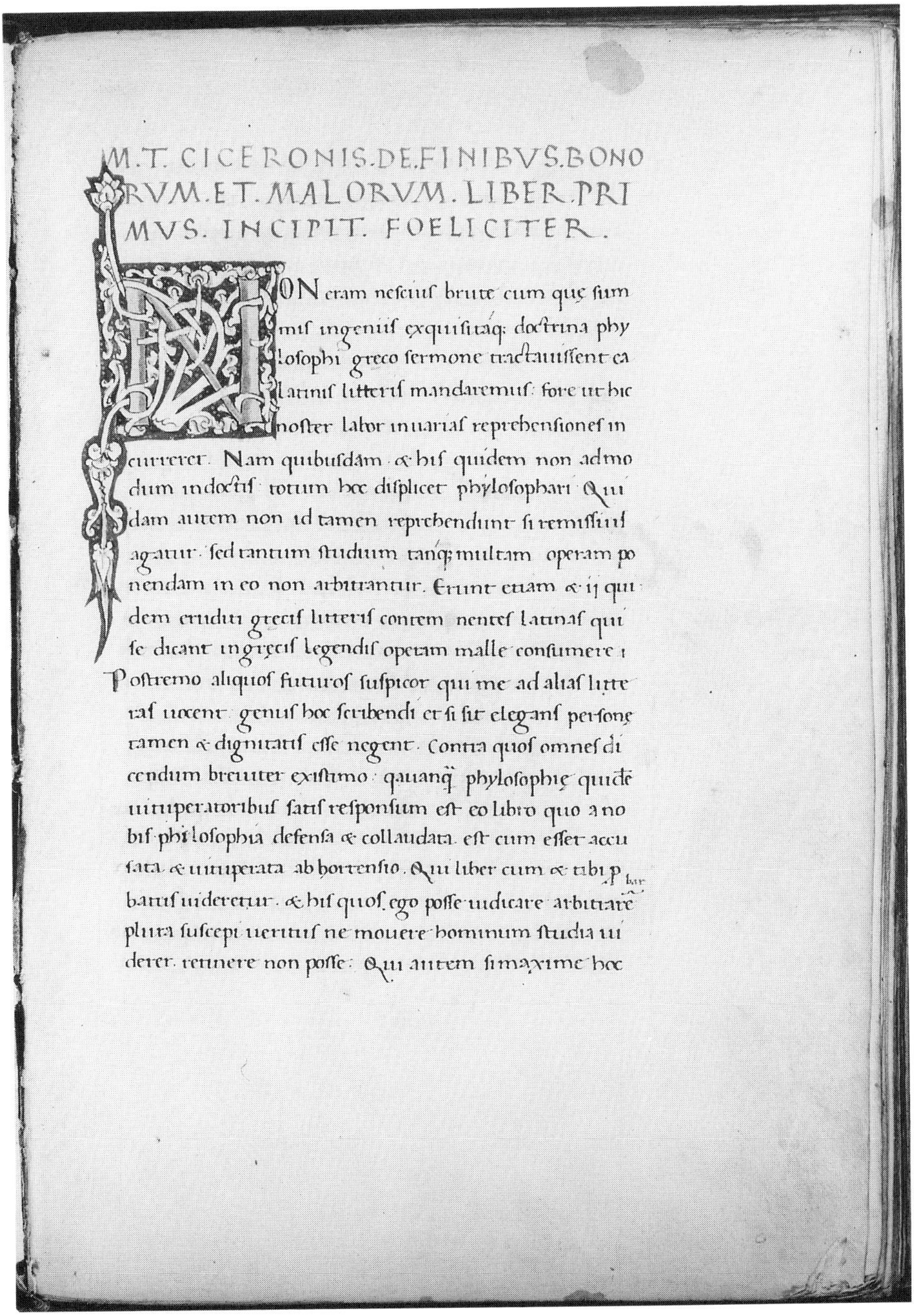
M.T. CICERONIS.DE.FINIBVS.BONO
RVM.ET.MALORVM.LIBER.PRI
MVS. INCIPIT. FOELICITER.

NON eram nescius brute cum que sum
mis ingeniis exquisitaque doctrina phy
losophi greco sermone tractauissent ea
latinis litteris mandaremus: fore ut hic
noster labor in uarias reprehensiones in
curreret. Nam quibusdam & his quidem non admo
dum indoctis totum hoc displicet phylosophari. Qui
dam autem non id tamen reprehendunt si remissius
agatur. sed tantum studium tanque multam operam po
nendam in eo non arbitrantur. Erunt etiam & ii qui
dem eruditi grecis litteris contem nentes latinas qui
se dicant in grecis legendis operam malle consumere.
Postremo aliquos futuros suspicor qui me ad alias litte
ras uocent genus hoc scribendi et si sit elegans persone
tamen & dignitatis esse negent. Contra quos omnes di
cendum breuiter existimo: quanquam phylosophie quidem
uituperatoribus satis responsum est eo libro quo a no
bis philosophia defensa & collaudata est cum esset accu
sata & uituperata ab hortensio. Qui liber cum & tibi p bar
batus uideretur. & his quos ego posse iudicare arbitrarem
plura suscepi ueritus ne mouere hominum studia ui
derer. retinere non posse: Qui autem si maxime hoc

Marston MS 72, f. 1r (2/3 natural size)
Rome, 1460

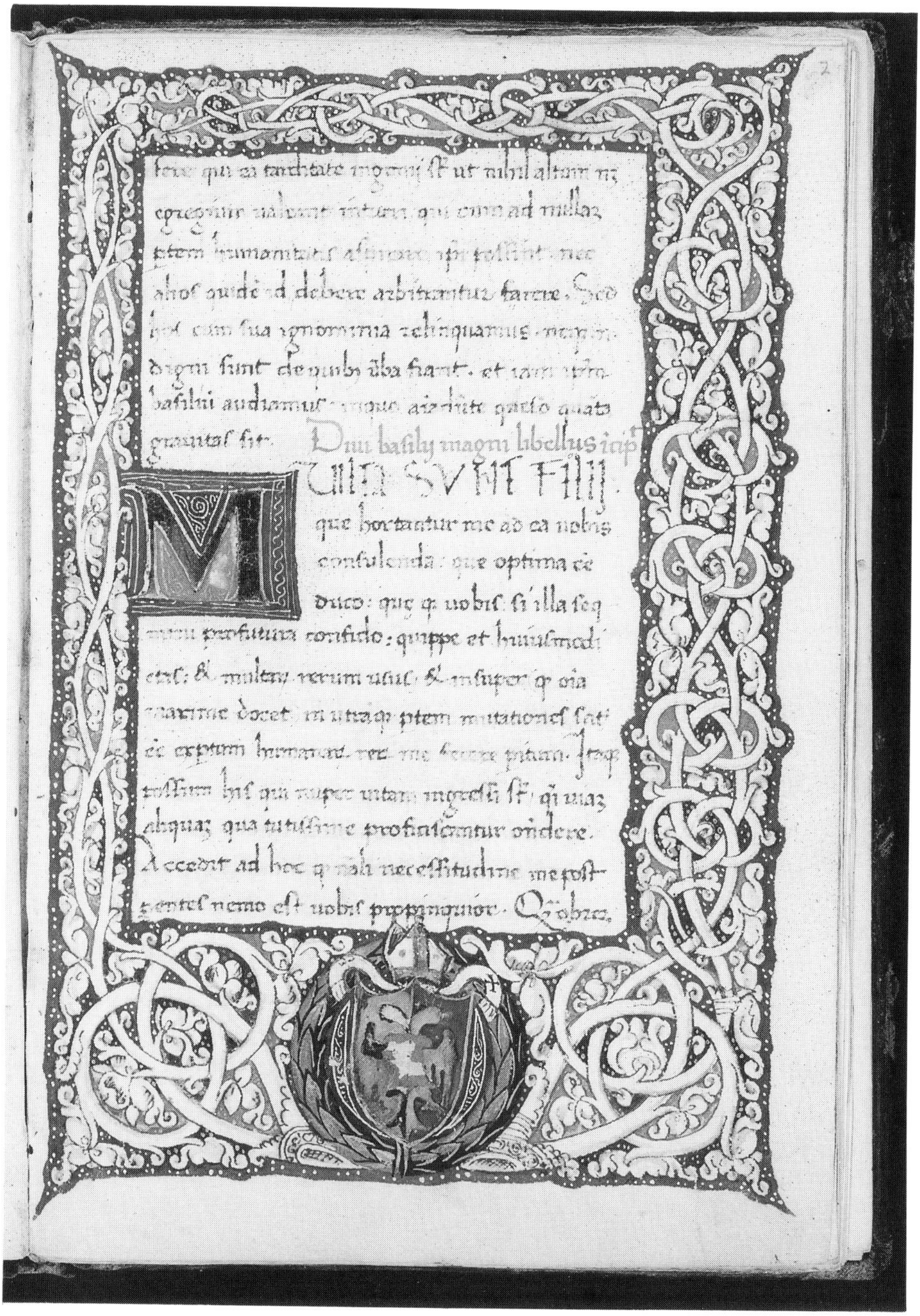

Marston MS 105, f. 2r (4/5 natural size)
Rome, s. XV#2

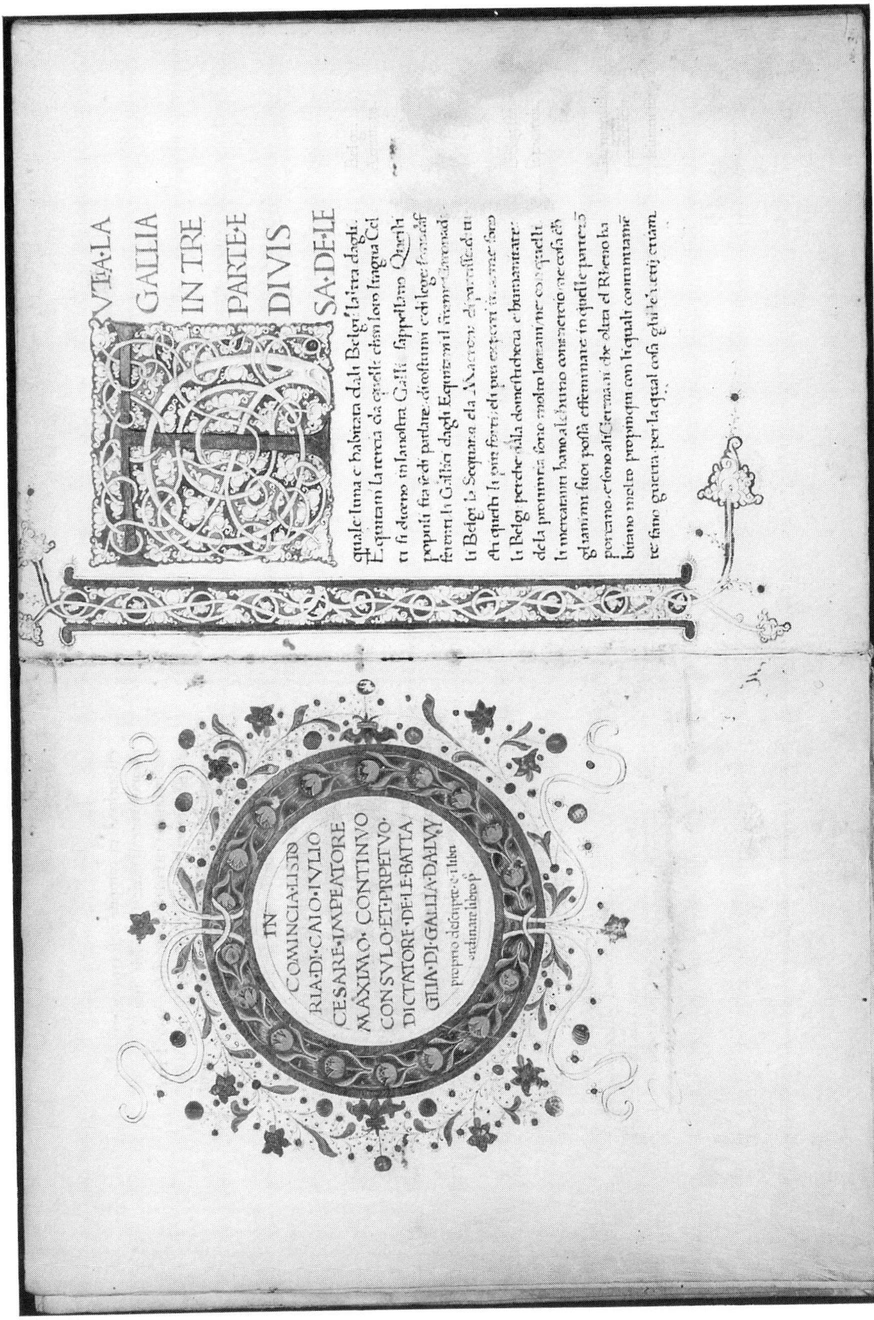

Marston MS 179, ff. 2v–3r (2/5 natural size)
Naples, s. XV#2

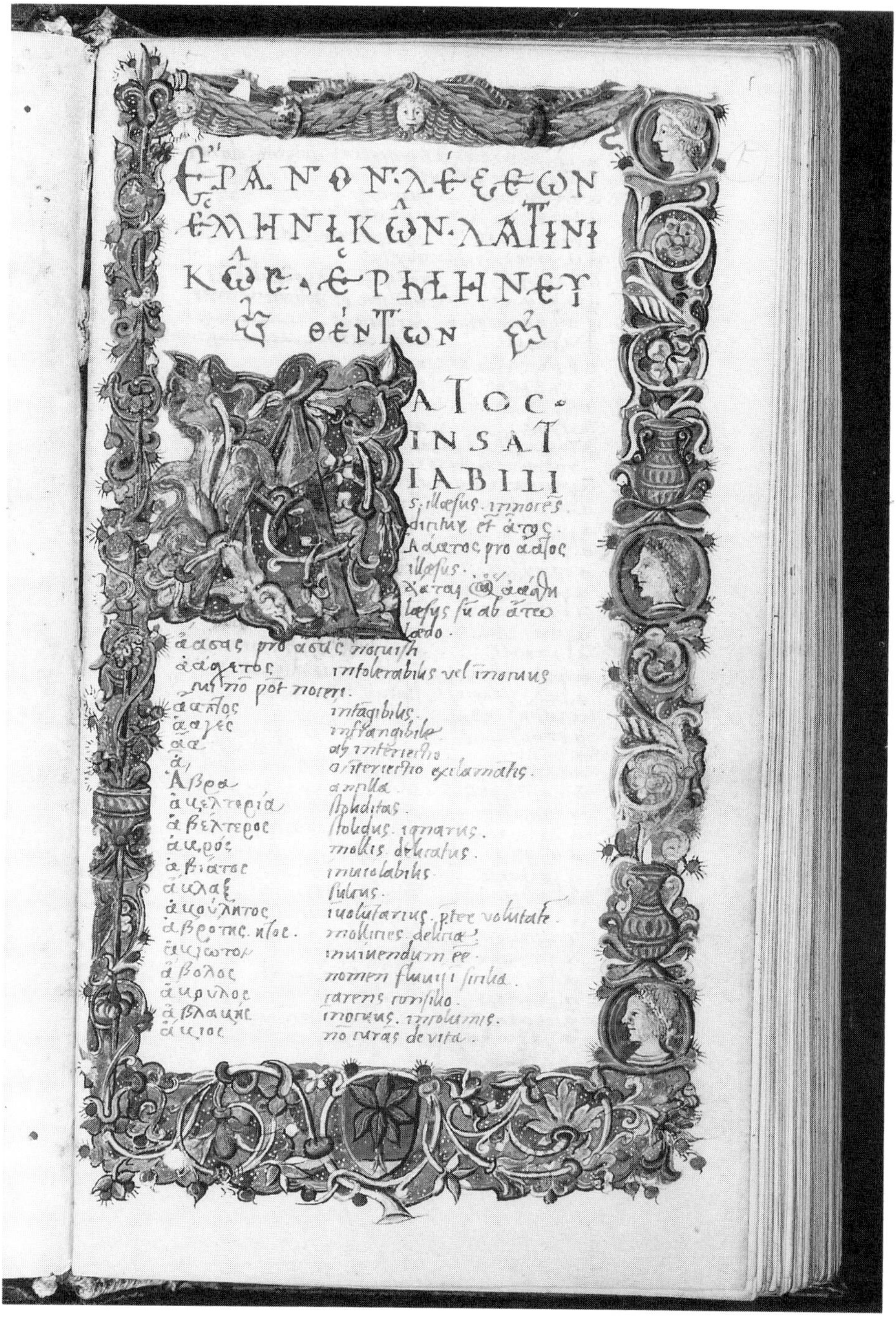

Marston MS 94, f. 1r (9/11 natural size)
Verona, ca. 1460

PLATE 29

Marston MS 201, f. 2r (6/7 natural size)
Verona, 1460s

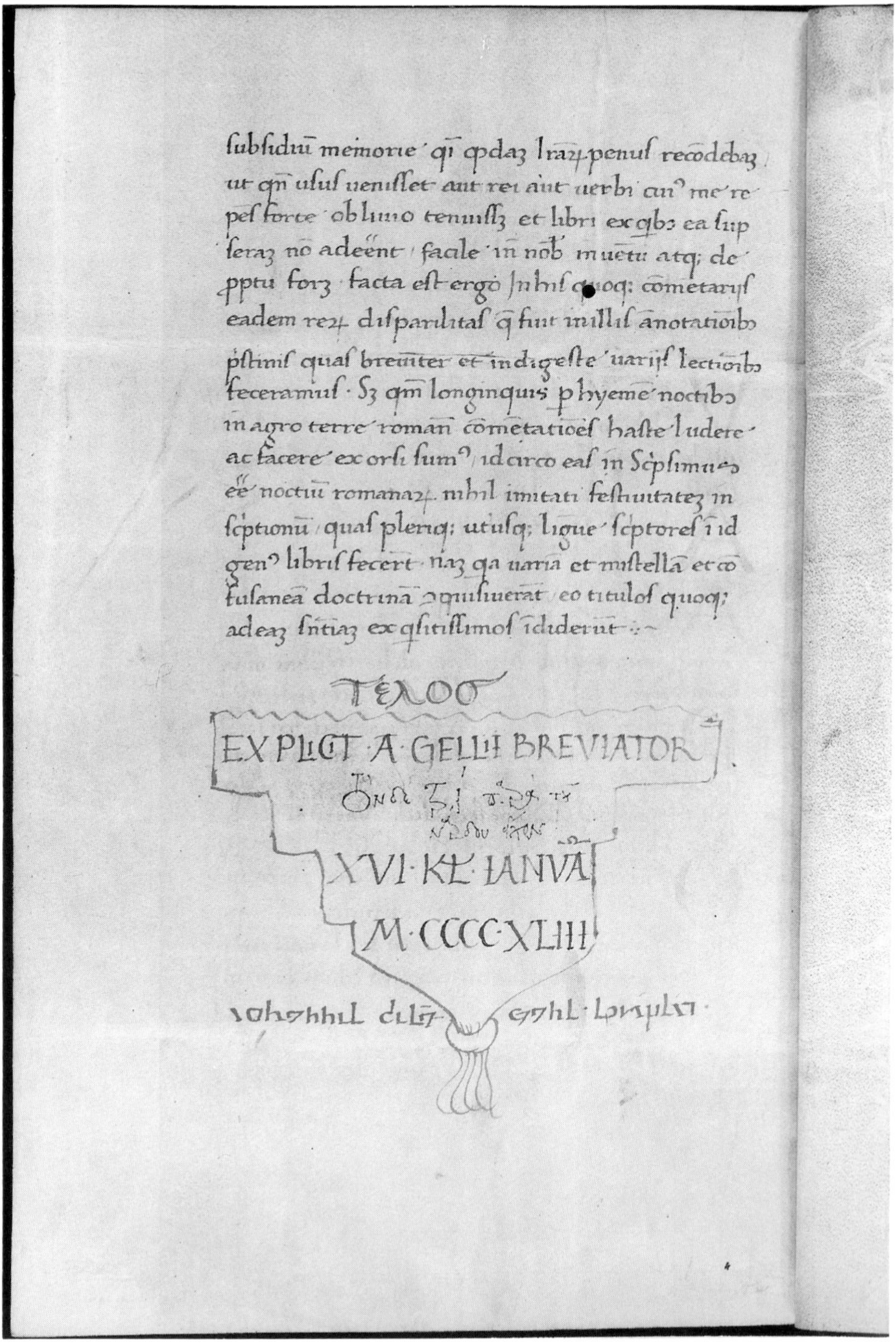

Marston MS 167, f. 61v (2/3 natural size)
Northwestern Italy, 1443

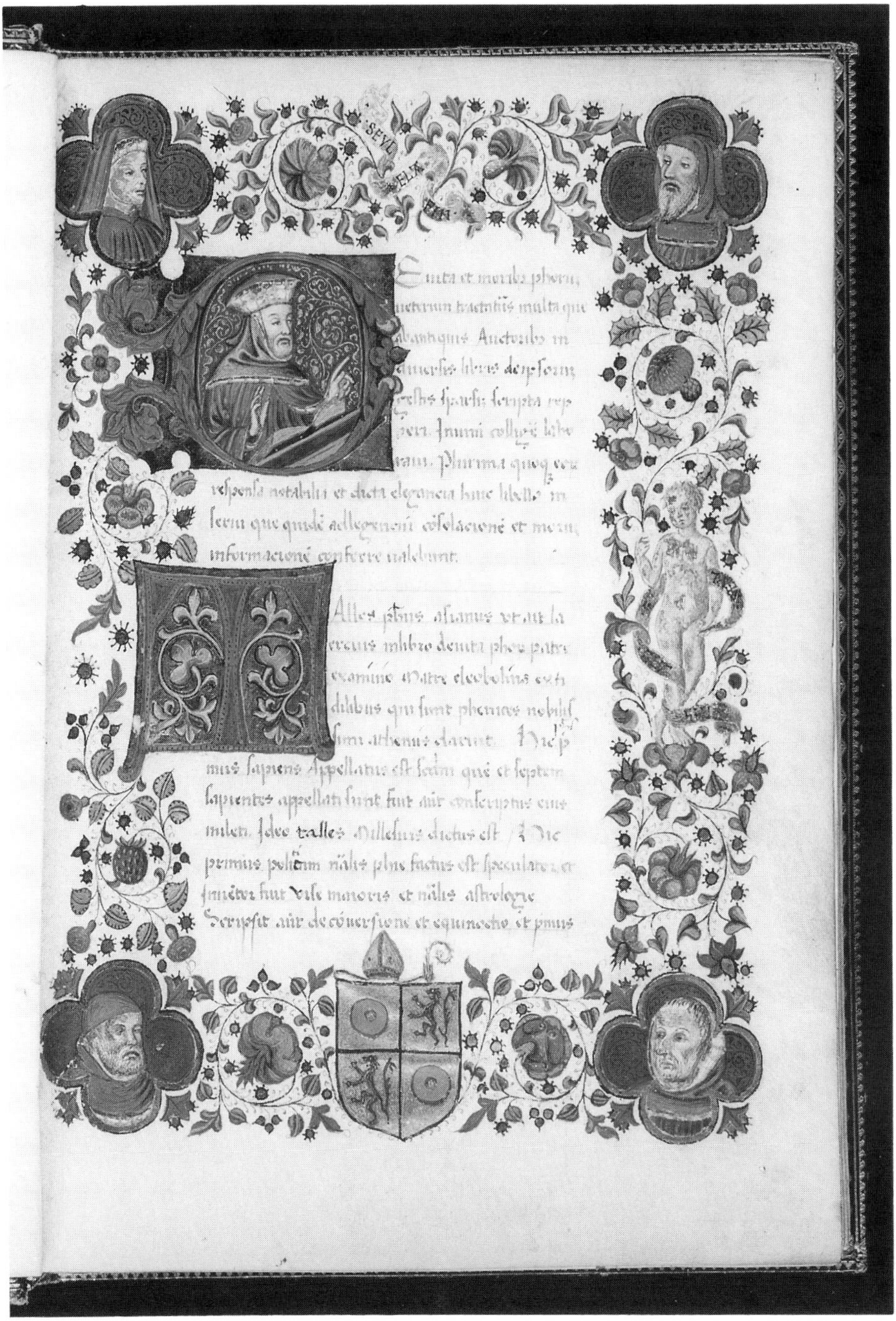

Marston MS 91, f. 1r (7/10 natural size)
Milan, s. XV#m#e#d#-#3#/#4

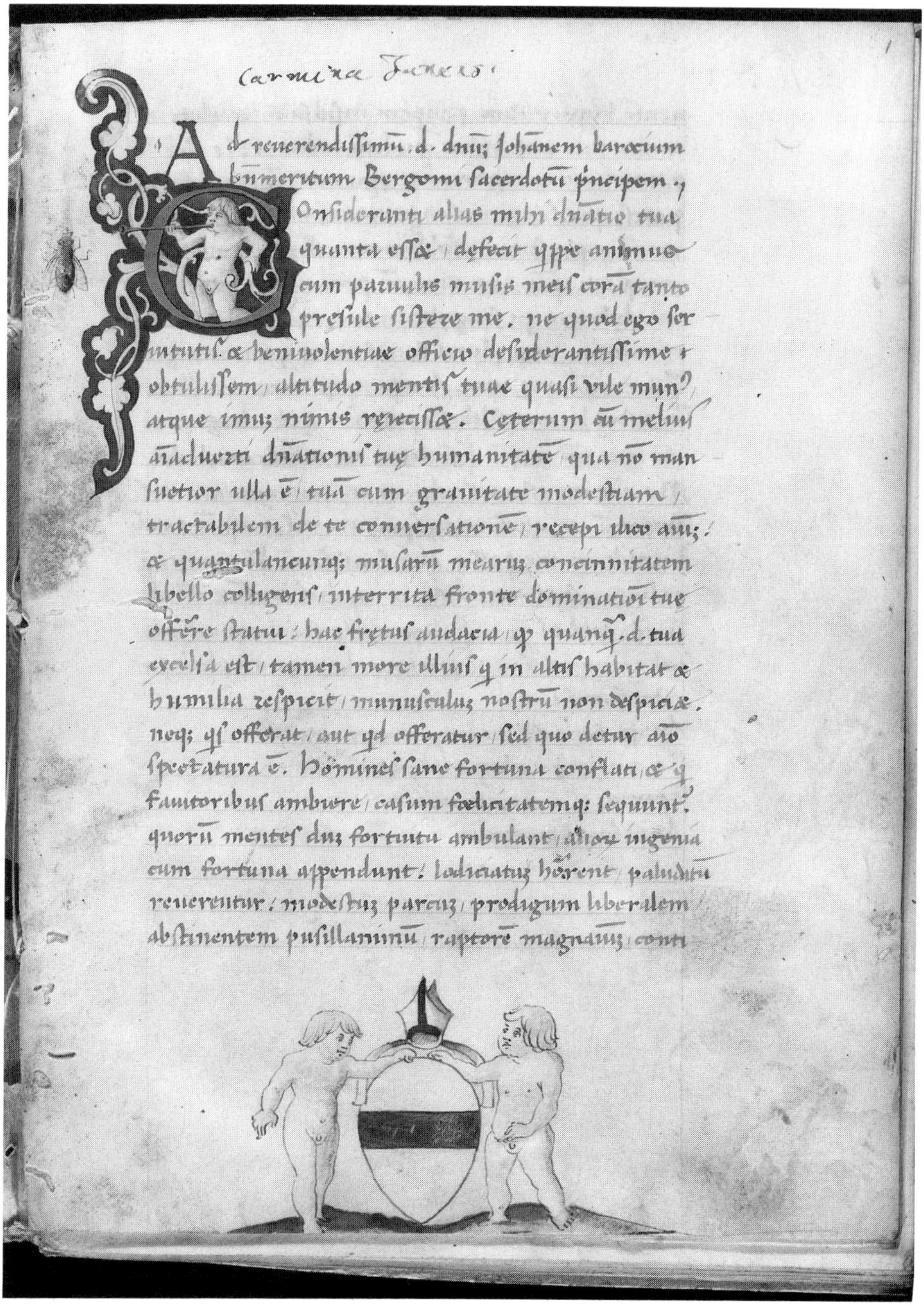

Ad reuerendissimu d. dnu Johanem barocium
bnmeritum Bergomi sacerdotu pncipem.
Considerati alias mihi dnatio tua
quanta esset, defecit ipse animus
cum paruulis musis meis cora tanto
presule sistere me. ne quod ego ser
uitutis et beniuolentiae officio desiderantissime
obtulissem, altitudo mentis tuae quasi vile mun
atque imu nimis reiecisset. Ceterum cu melius
aiaduerti dnationis tue humanitate qua no man
suetior ulla e tua cum grauitate modestiam
tractabilem de te conuersatione, recepi illico anim
et quantulancumq musaru mearu concinnitatem
libello colligens, interrita fronte dominatioi tue
offerre statui. hac fretus audacia q quanq d. tua
excelsa est, tamen more illius q in altis habitat et
humilia respicit, munusculu nostru non despiciet.
neq qs offerat aut qd offeratur sed quo detur aio
spectatura e. Homines sane fortuna conflati et q
fautoribus ambiere, casum faelicitatemq sequunt.
quoru mentes du fortuitu ambulant, alioru ingenia
cum fortuna appendunt. ladicatu horent, paludatu
reuerentur, modestu parcu, prodigum liberalem
abstinentem pusillanimu, raptore magnanimu, conti

Marston MS 188, f. 1r (4/5 natural size)
Northern Italy, ca. 1454–65

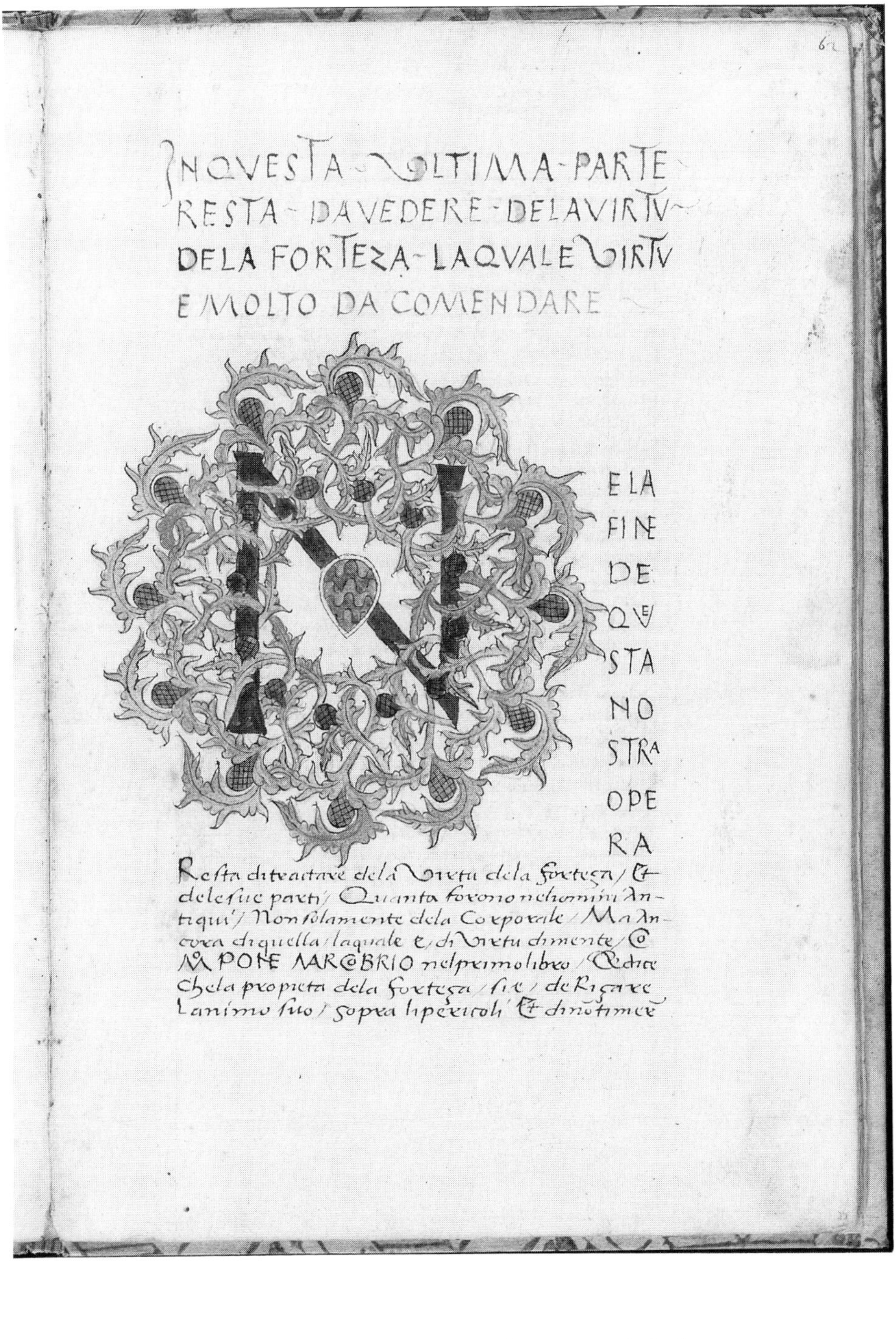
[I]NQVESTA VLTIMA PARTE
RESTA DAVEDERE DELA VIRTV
DELA FORTEZA LAQVALE VIRTV
E MOLTO DA COMENDARE

N
ELA
FINE
DE
QVE
STA
NO
STRA
OPE
RA

Resta ditractare dela vertu dela fortega / Et
dele sue parti / Quanta forono nehomini antiqui / Non solamente dela Corporale / Ma ancora diquella / laquale e / di vertu dimente / Co
mo pone MARCOBRIO nelpremolibro / Oe dice
Chela propreta dela fortega / sie / de Rigare
Lanimo suo / sopra lipericoli Et dinotimere

Marston MS 43, f. 25r (3/5 natural size)
Northeastern Italy, s. XV#2

~Vbus.~

SANCTISSIMO .D. N. DOMINO NICOLAO. Q. SVMM
O PONT. BLONDVS FLAVIVS FORLIVIENSIS.~

VM MVLTI HISTORIAM
beatissime pater variis extollant:
celebrentque sententiis: tum maxime
eam Alexander antonius Mamea
genitus christiana Imperator Romanus omnium iuditio optimus
unica ratione eam amplissime vide
tur laudasse: qui historicos & suos
appellavit: & habere voluit consilia
rios: quorum prudentia & exemplorum
copia gerendis imperii rebus permaxime uteretur. Clarissimi etiam
plerique Senatores consulares quoque viri: & nonnulli gloriosissimi prin
cipes qui bellicis artibus res gesserunt eterna digni memoria: dele
ctati sunt historia usque adeo ut non solum historias libenter legerint
sed eas quoque scribendo tam preclari muneris gloriam cum rerum
scriptoribus communem habere voluerint. Nam ut ceteros taceam
Fabius patricie gentis decus cognomento pictor. Lucius Lucullus. Au
lus Albinus. Asinius Pollio. Cornelius Nepos. et Gaius Cesar. eiusque ne
pos Octavius Augustus ac Adrianus scripsere historiam. Sed maxi
mam tantum manus preteritorum longe seculorum malitia & infelicitate
incurrit iniuriam: quod urbe Roma a variis gentibus sicut in historiis
accuratius a nobis est scriptum oppressa. & si bonarum artium studia
intermissa fuerunt: sola imperium omnino cessavit: extinctaque est
historia: factumque est: ut barbaris omnia evertentibus. et nullo
interim a que gererentur litterarum monumentis ad posteros trans
mittente: nedum mille qui effluxerunt annorum gesta sciamus. sed
Italie regiones urbes oppida lacus. flumina: montesque, quorum nomina

Alexander antonius.

Fabius pictor.
Lucius Lucullus.
Aulus Albinus.
Asinius pollio.
Cornelius nepos.
Gaius cesar.
Octavius Augustus.
Adrianus.

Marston MS 35, f. 1r (3/5 natural size)
Ferrara, ca. 1460–75

PLATE 35

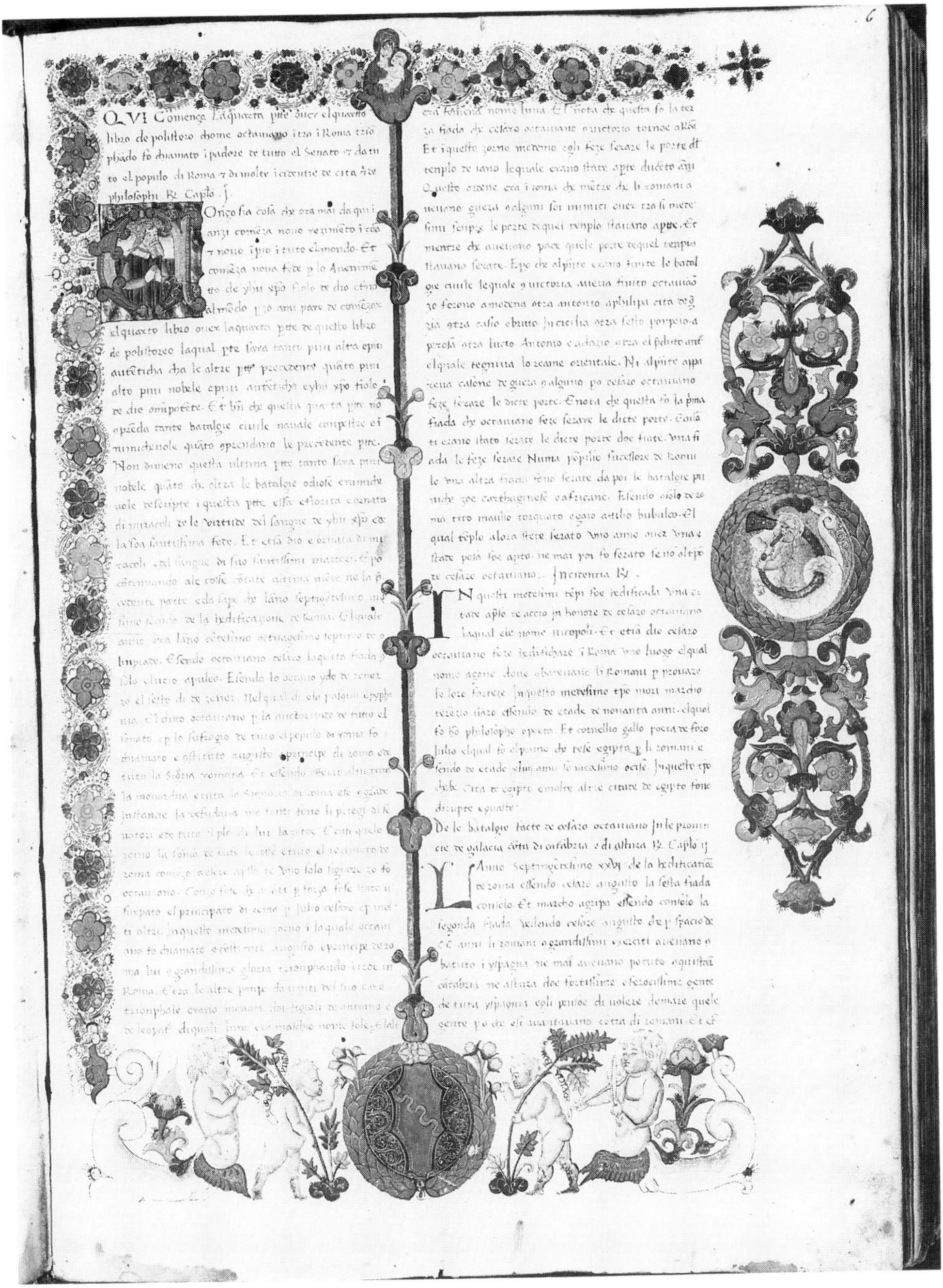

Marston MS 31, f. 6r (2/5 natural size)
Venice, 1470s

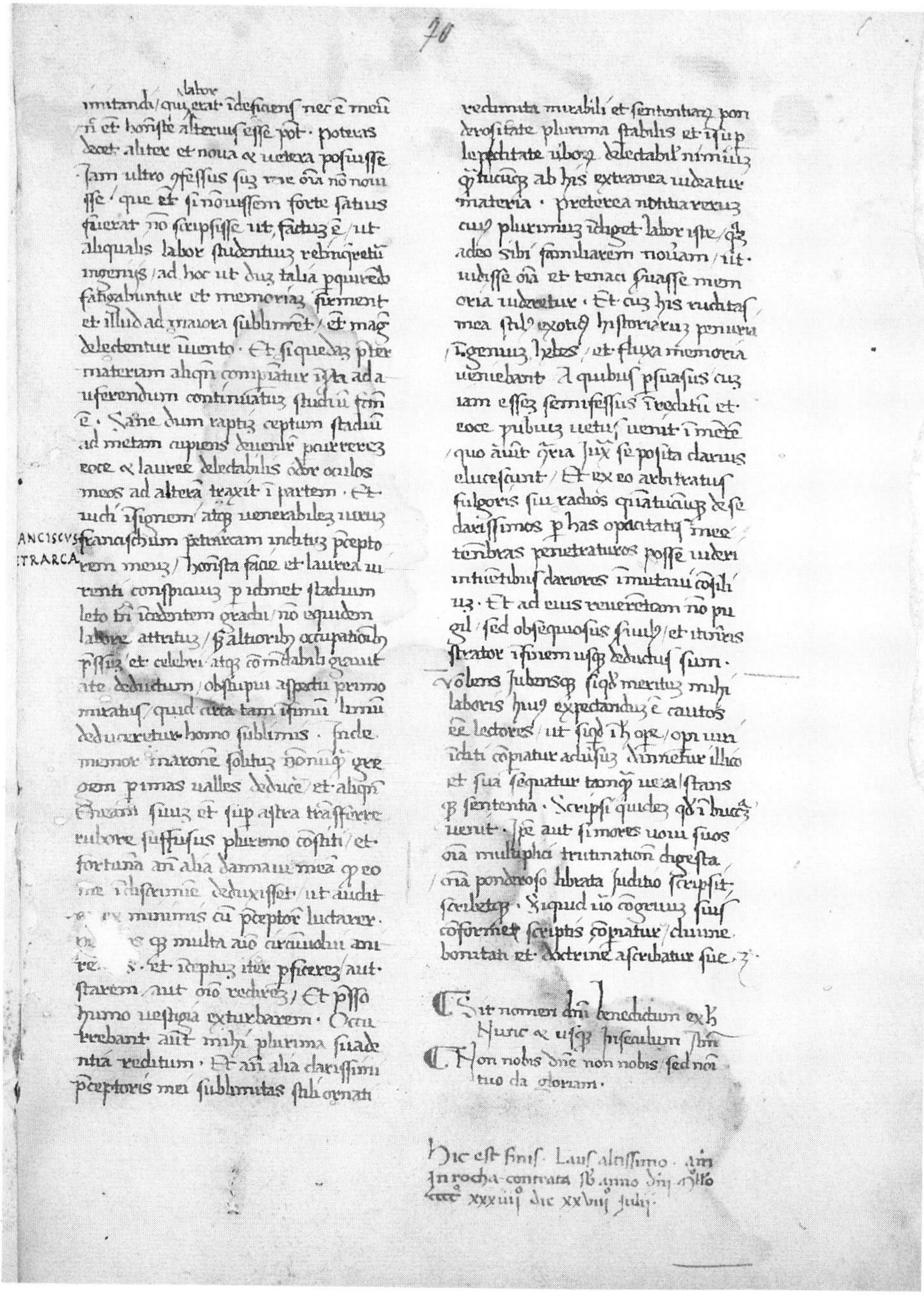

Marston MS 17, f. 70r (3/5 natural size)
Roccacontrada, 1434

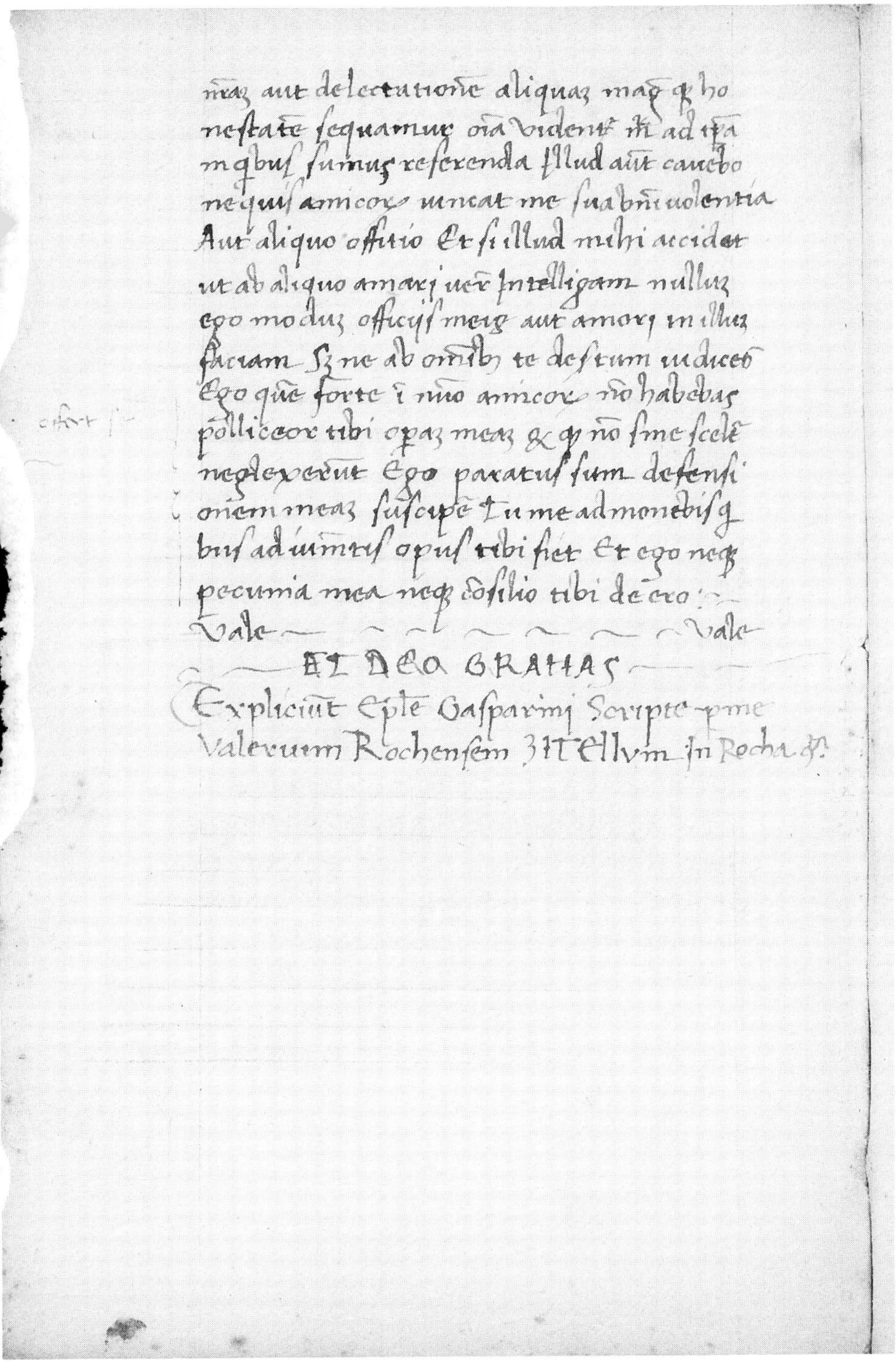

meā aut delectatione aliquā magis quam ho
nestate sequamur oīa videntur mihi ad ipsa
in quibus sumus referenda Illud autem cavebo
ne quis amicorum vincat me sua benivolentia
Aut aliquo offitio Et si illud mihi accidat
ut ab aliquo amari vere intelligam nullum
ego modum officiis meis aut amoris in illum
faciam Sed ne ab omnibus te destitutum iudices
Ego quem forte in numero amicorum non habebas
polliceor tibi operam meam et quam non sine scelere
neglexerunt Ego paratus sum defensi
onem meam suscipere Tu me admonebis qui
bus ad iuvenis opus tibi fiet Et ego neque
pecunia mea neque consilio tibi deero
Vale — Vale
ET DEO GRATIAS
Explicit Epistole Gasparini Scripte per me
Valerium Rochensem [illegible] in Rocha [illegible]

Marston MS 169, f. 83r (3/4 natural size)
Roccacontrada, s. XV#2

Marston MS 157, f. 19v (slightly reduced)
Northern France, s. XII#2#/#4

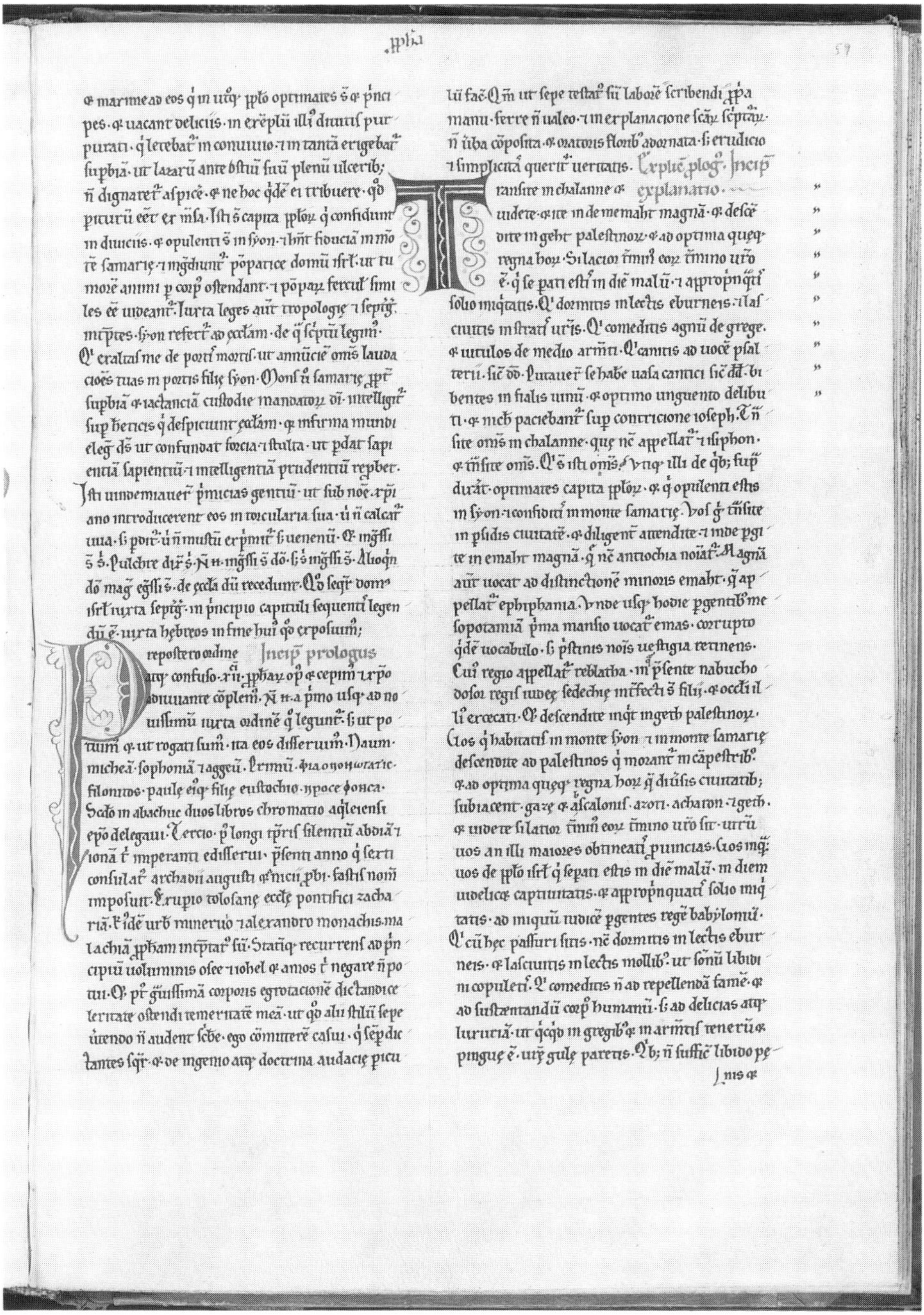

Marston MS 197, vol. 1, f. 59r (2/5 natural size)
Hautecombe [?], s. XII#m#e#d

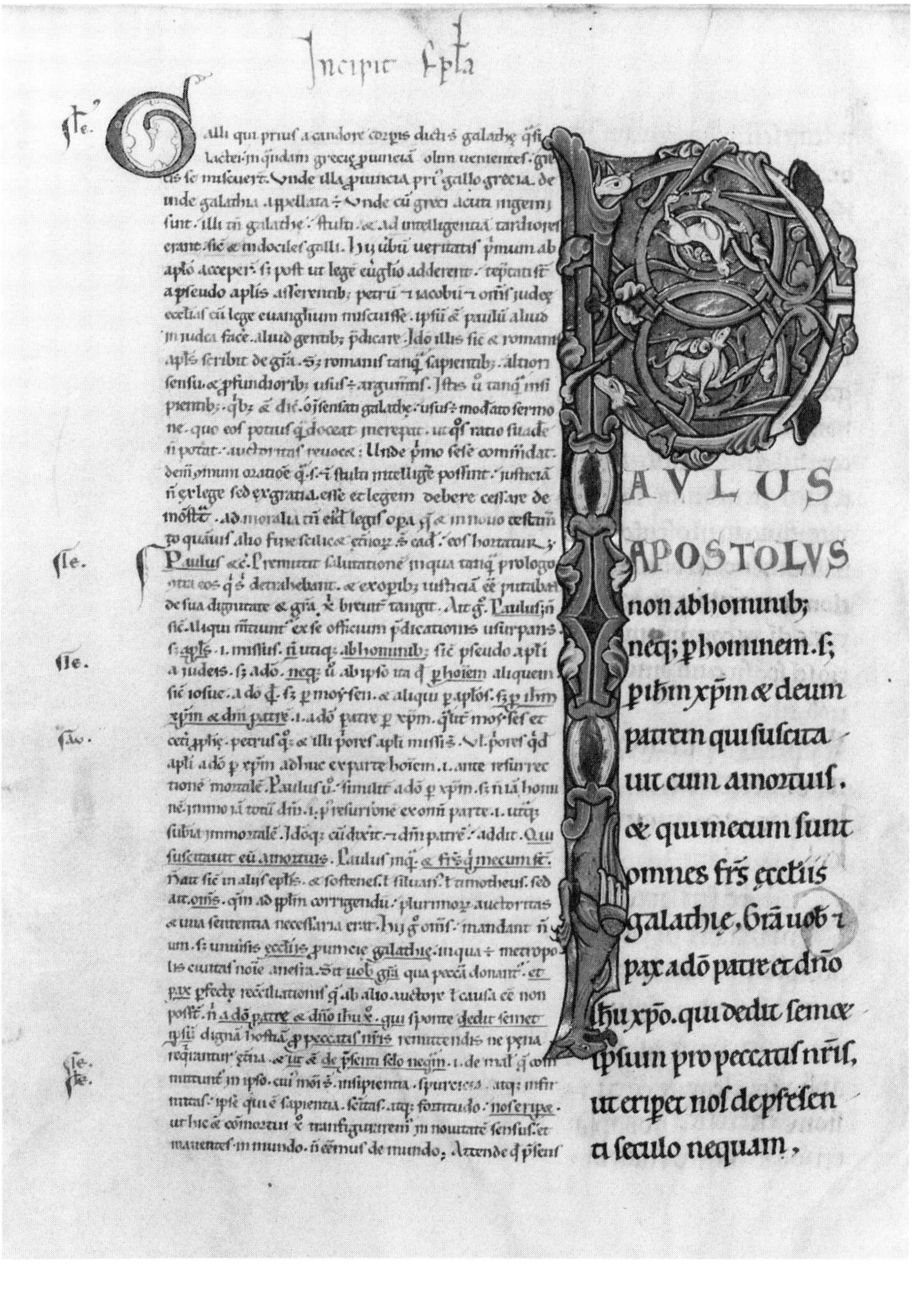
Incipit Epla

PAVLUS
APOSTOLVS
non ab hominib;
neq; p hominem. s;
p ihm xpm & deum
patrem qui suscita
uit eum a mortuis.
& qui mecum sunt
omnes frs ecctiis
galathie. Gra uob &
pax a do patre et dno
ihu xpo. qui dedit seme
ipsum pro peccatis nris,
ut eripet nos de psesen
ti seculo nequam.

Marston MS 152, f. 86v (3/5 natural size)
France, s. XII#m#e#d

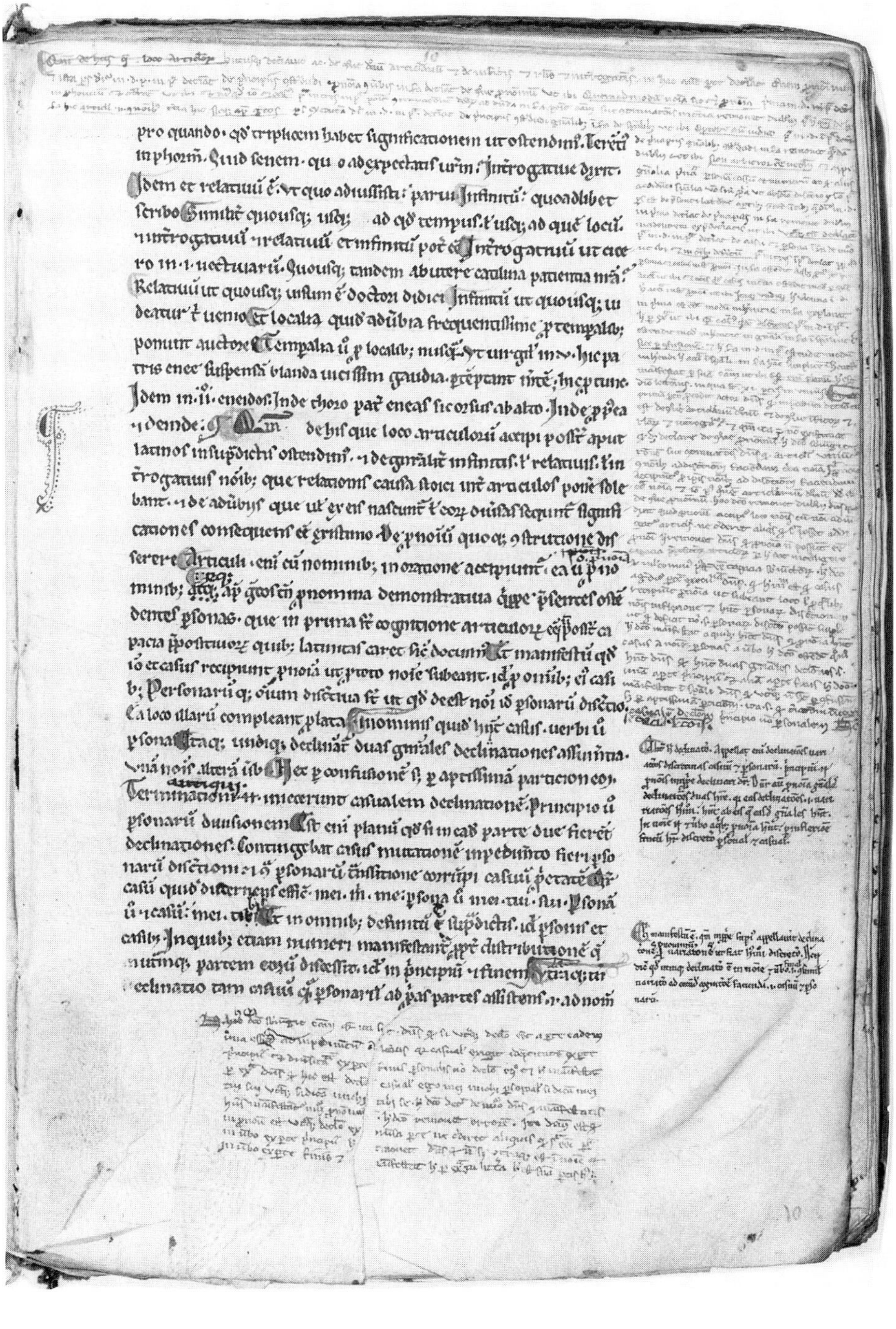

Marston MS 67, f. 10r (2/3 natural size)
Eastern France, s. XII#4#/#4

PLATE 42

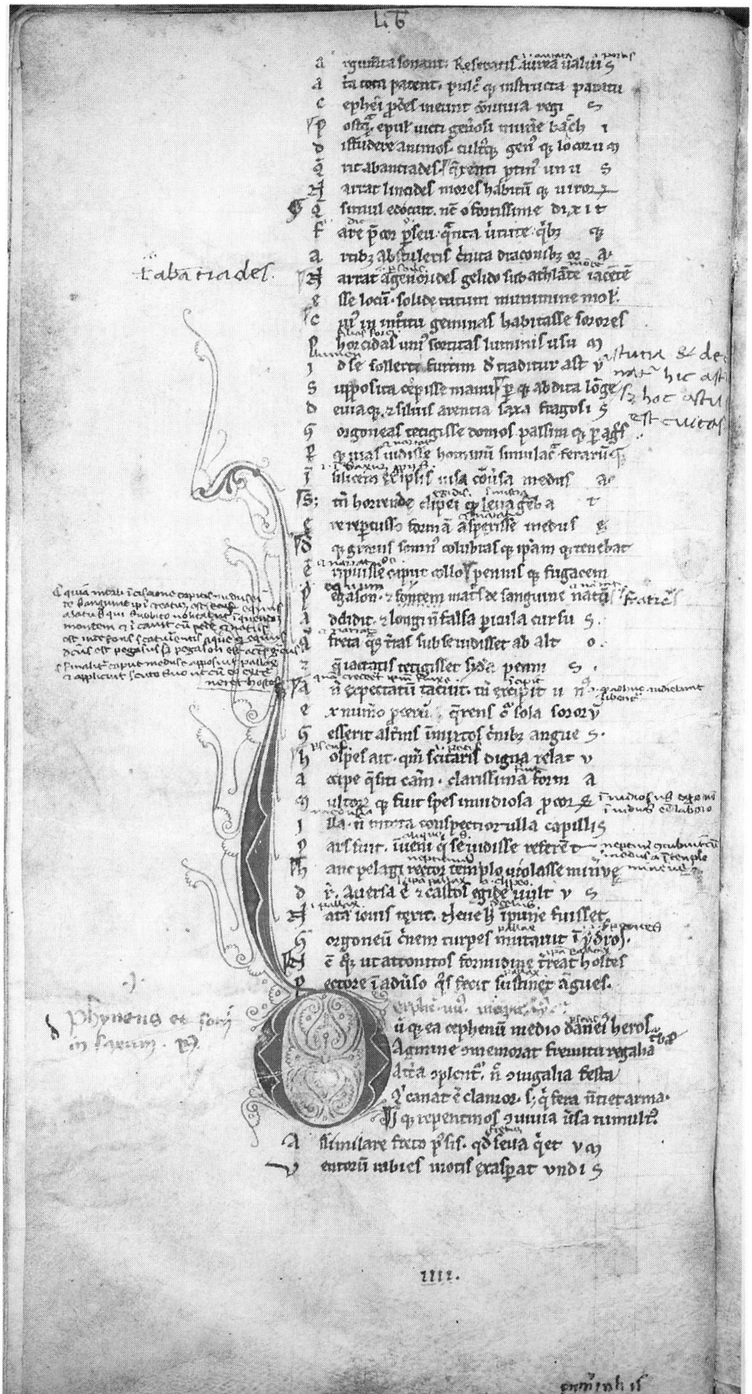

Marston MS 47, f. 32v (3/5 natural size)
France or Italy [?], s. XII/XIII

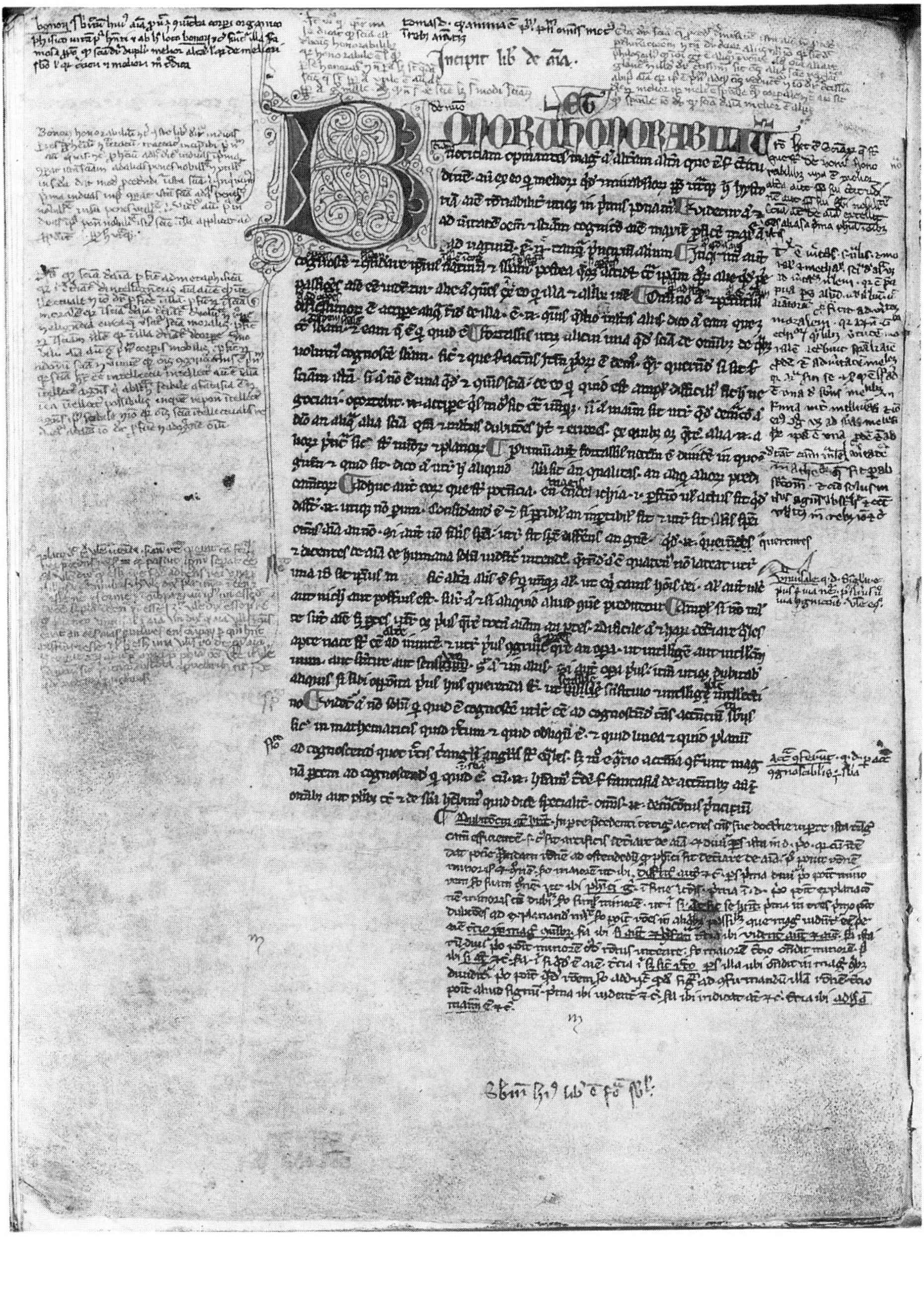

Marston MS 88, f. 66v (3/4 natural size)
Northern France, s. XIII#2#/#4

PLATE 44

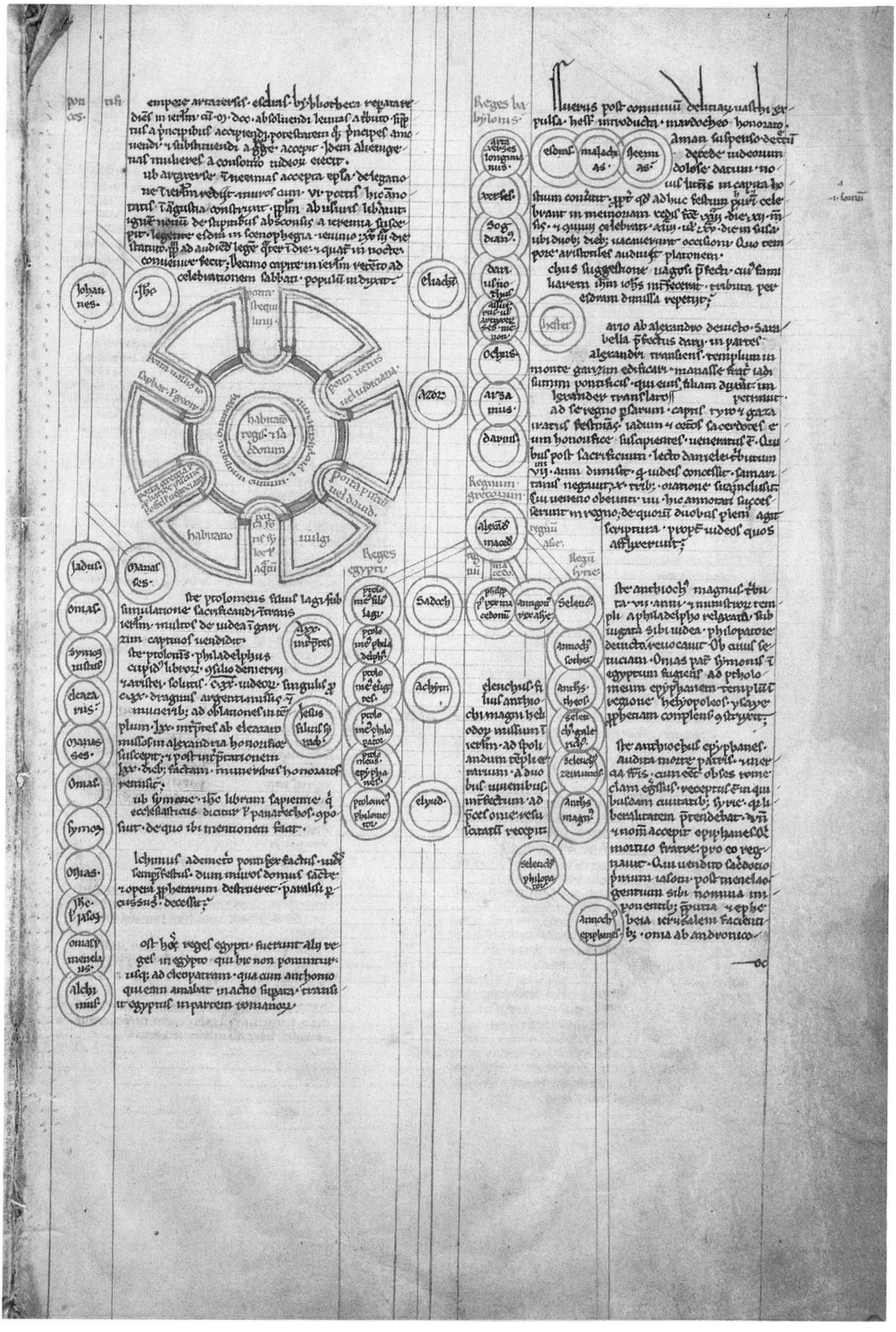

Marston MS 26, f. 4r (1/2 natural size)
France, s. XIII#2#/#4

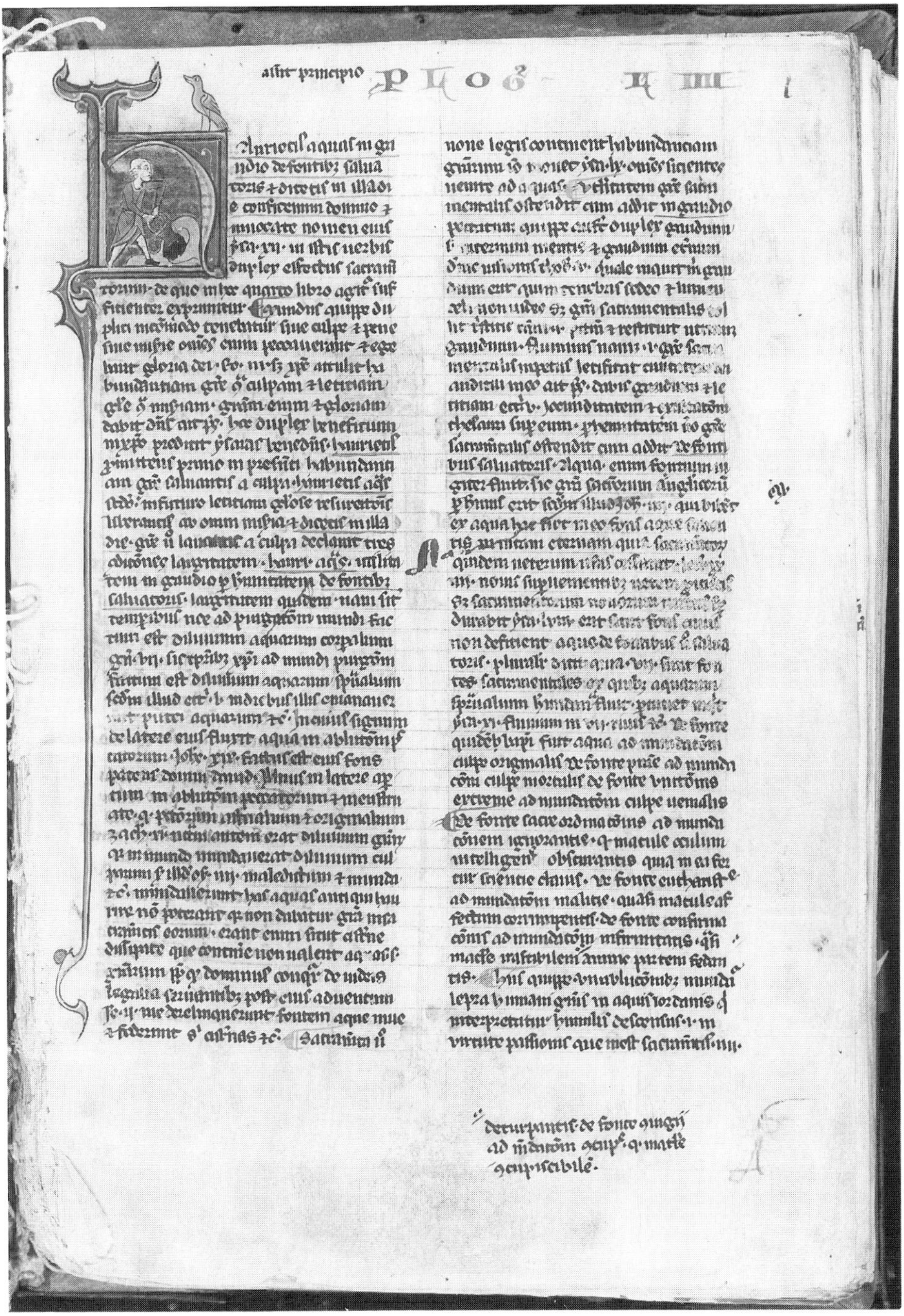

Marston MS 270, f. 1r (3/4 natural size)
Paris, s. XIII#3#/#3

PLATE 46

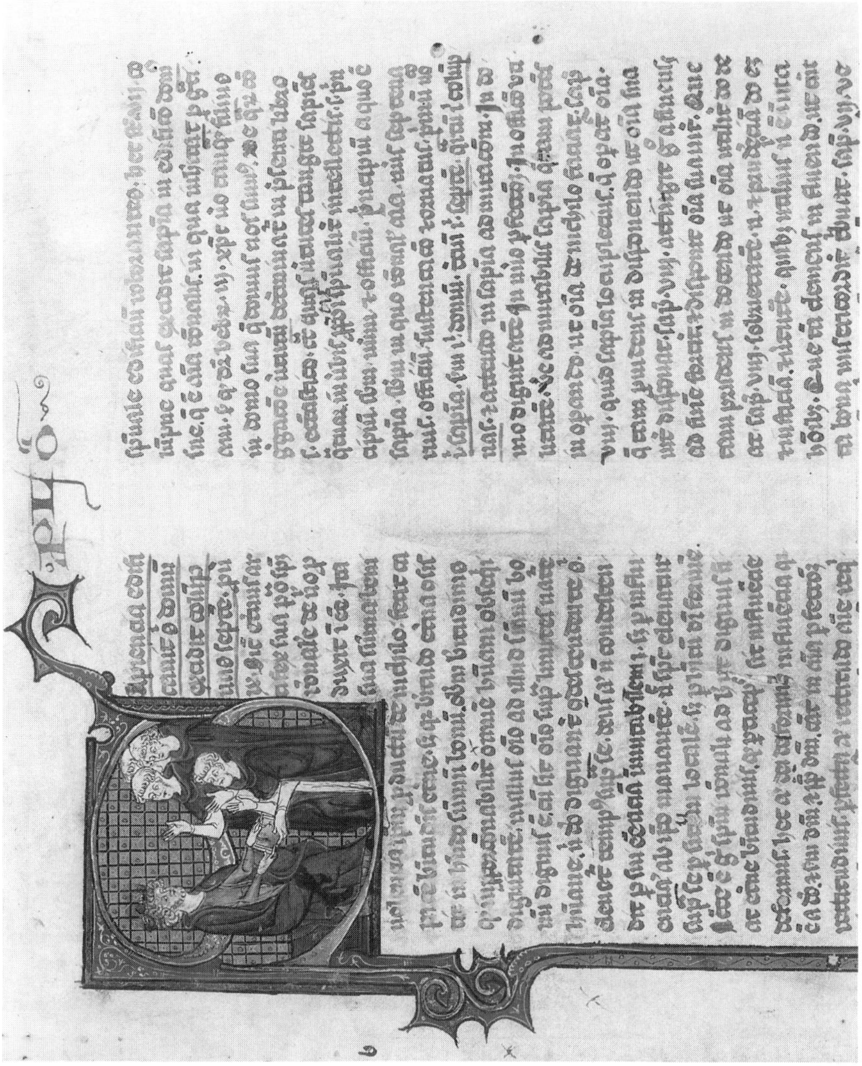

Marston MS 154, f. 1r (4/5 natural size)
Paris, s. XIV#1#/#4

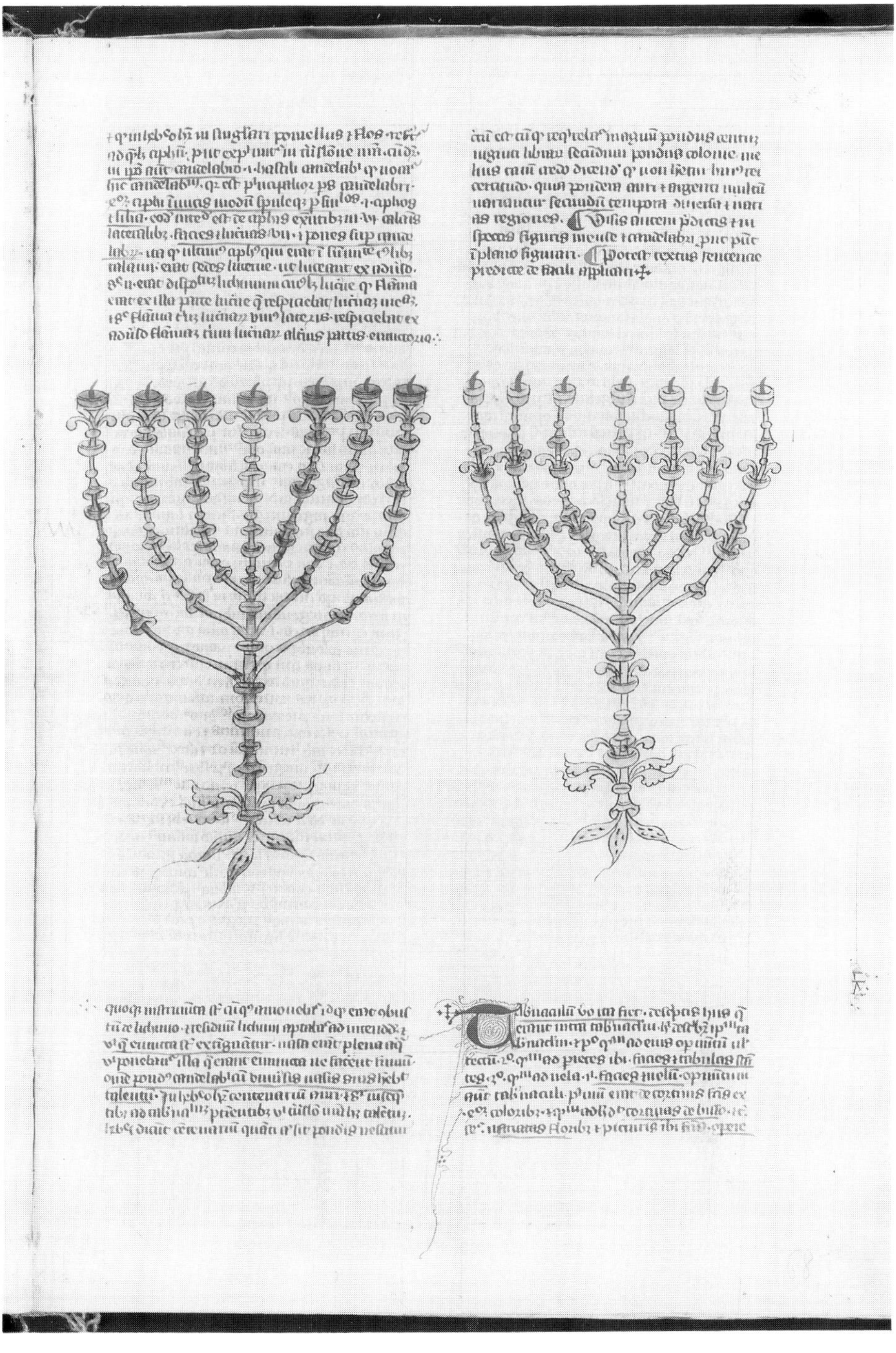

Marston MS 215, f. 68r (3/7 natural size)
Northern France, s. XIV#2#/#4

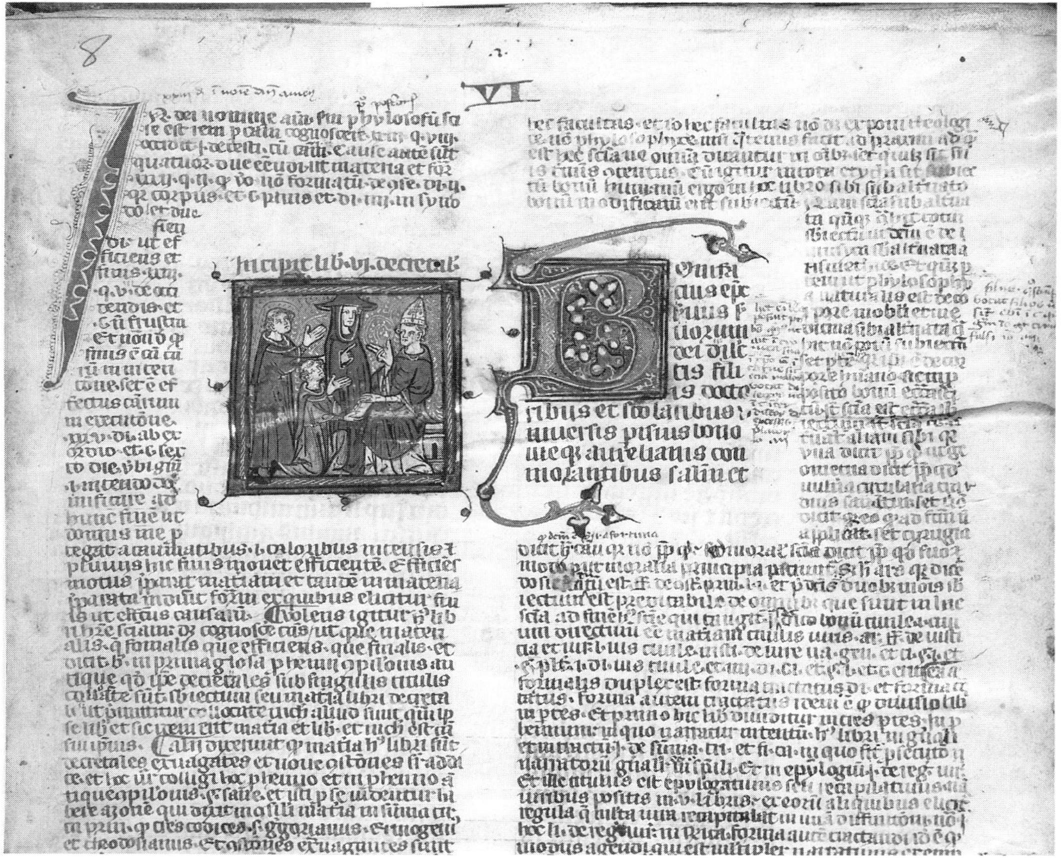

Marston MS 176, f. 1r (6/11 natural size)
France, s. XIV#2#/#4

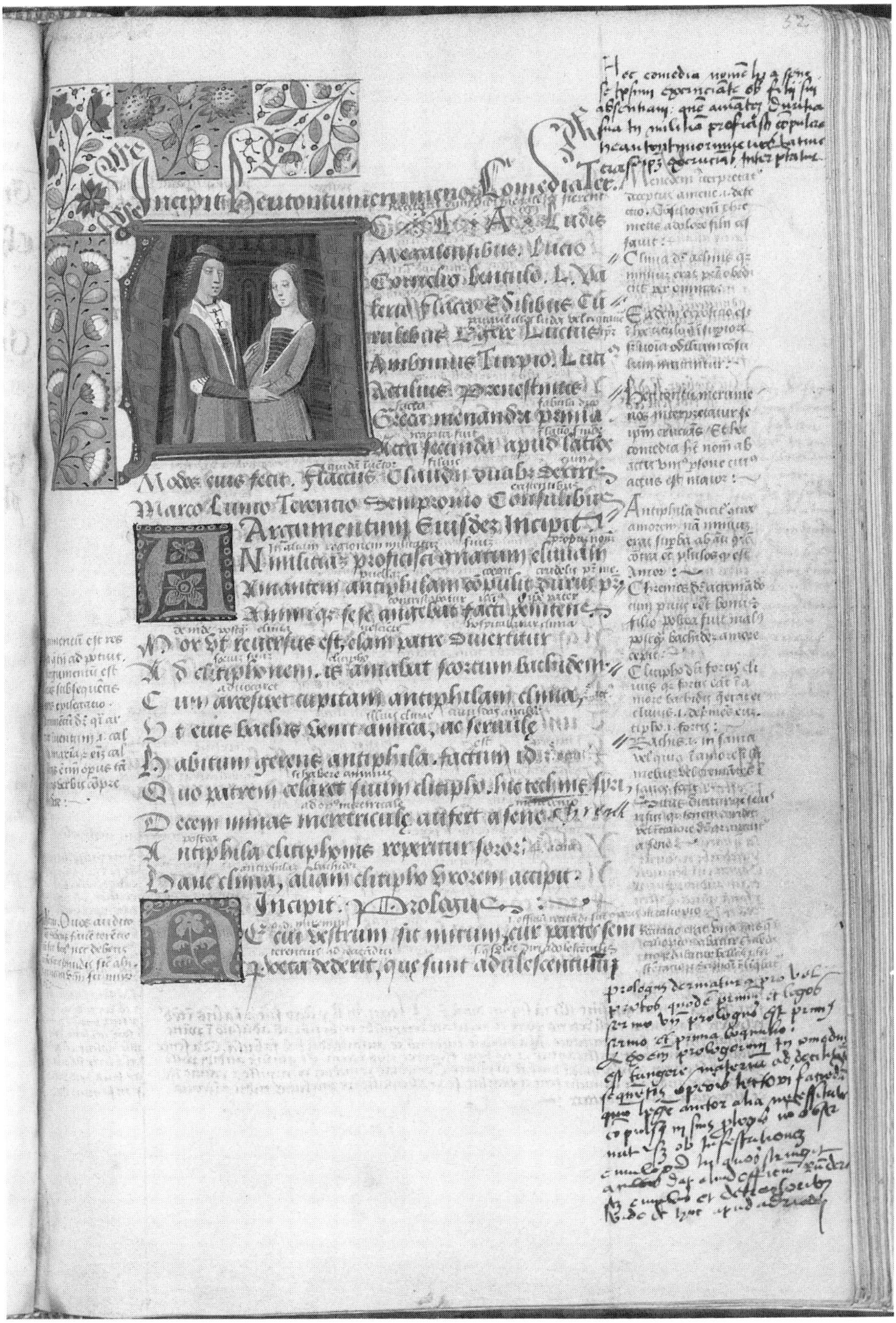

Marston MS 229, f. 52r (4/5 natural size)
Northern France, s. XV/XVI

PLATE 50

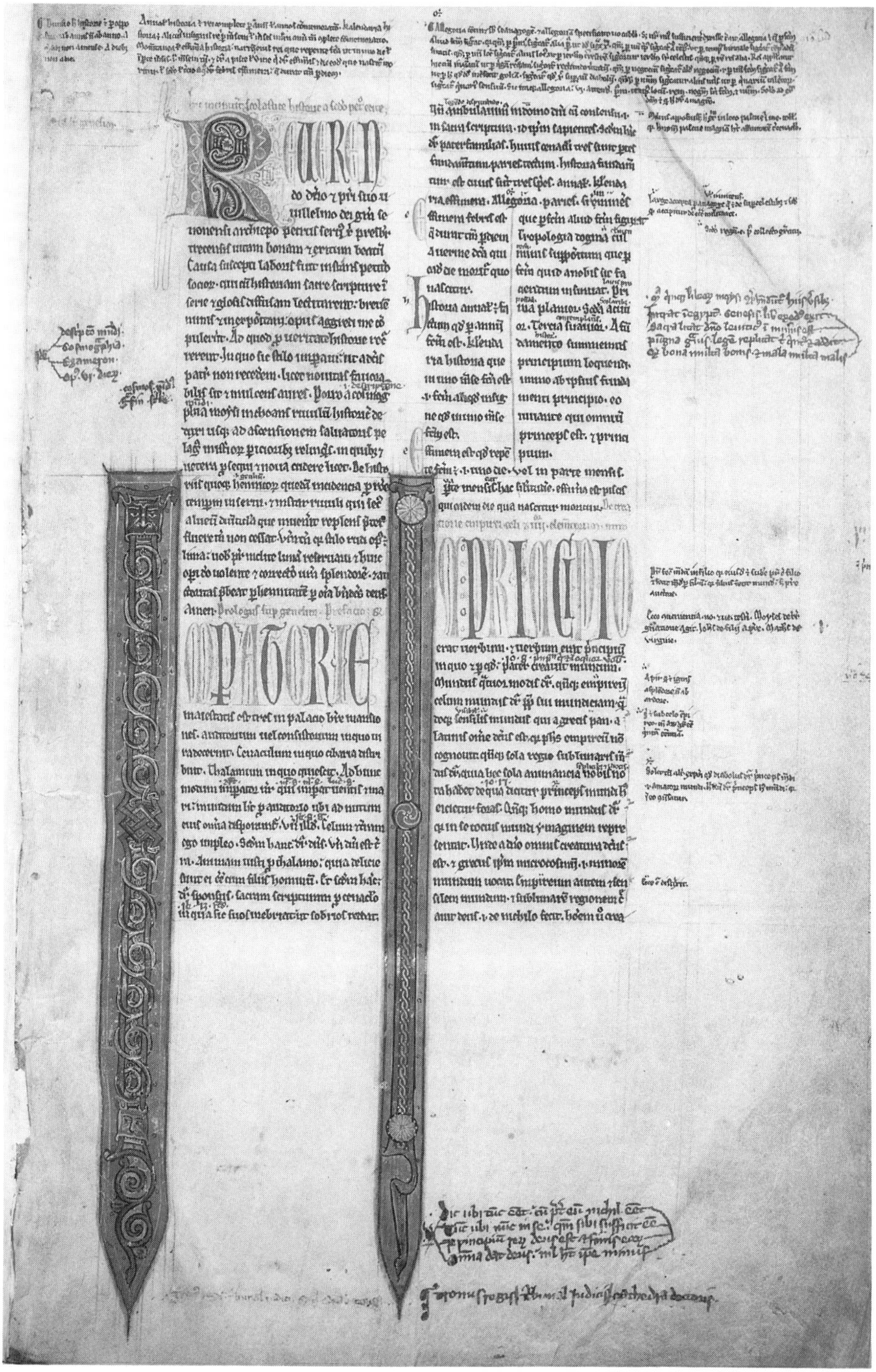

Marston MS 220, f. 1r (3/7 natural size)
England, s. XIII#i#/#n

PLATE 51

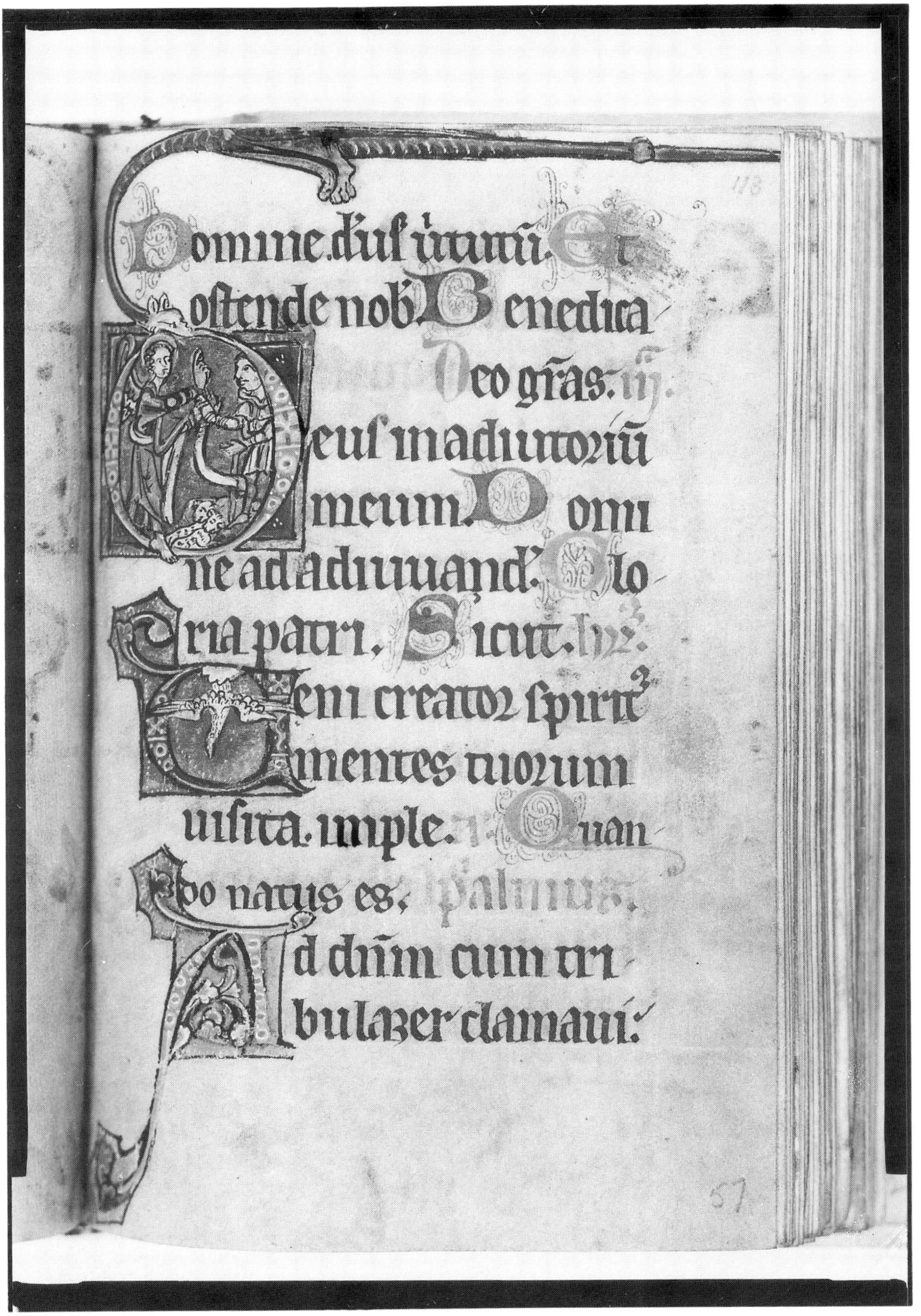
Domine. d'us uirtutu. Et
ostende nob'. Benedica
Deo gras. iij.
Deus in adiutoriu
meum. Domi
ne ad adiuuand'. Glo
ria patri. Sicut. hy.
Veni creator spirit'
mentes tuorum
uisita. imple. Quan
do natus es. psalmus.
Ad d'nm cum tri
bularer clamaui.

Marston MS 22, f. 57r
Oxford [?], s. XIII#m#e#d

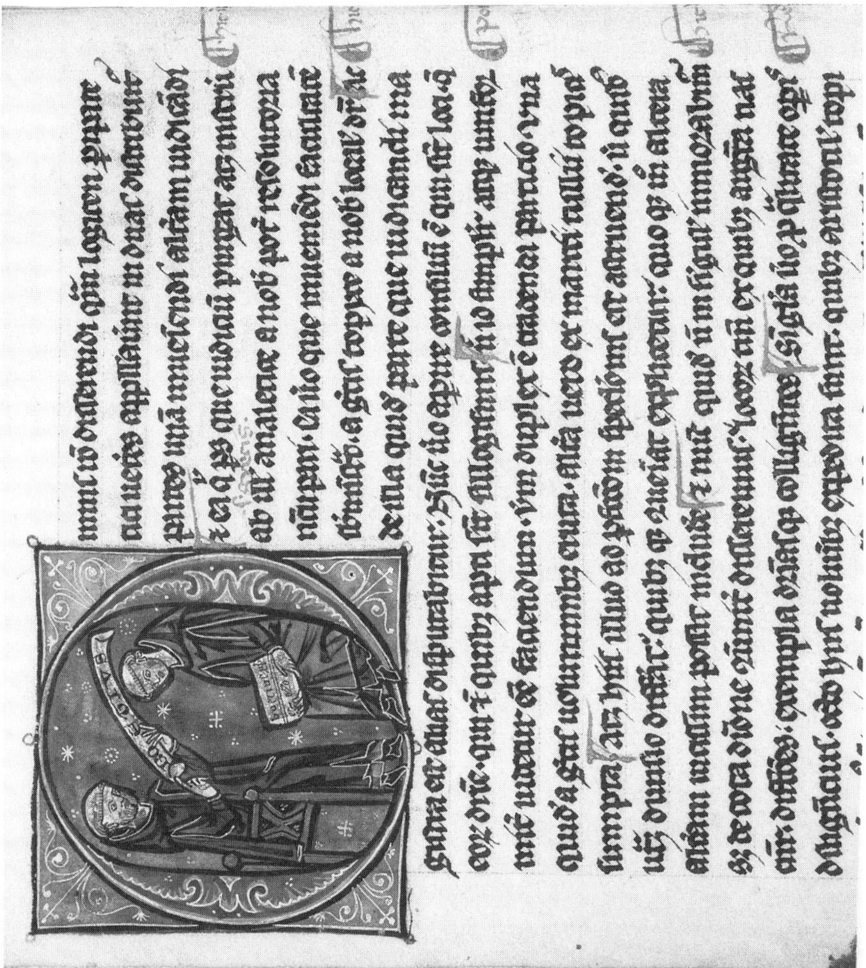

Marston MS 117, f. 1v (enlarged detail)
England, s. XIII#3#/#4

Marston MS 213, f. 60r (4/5 natural size)
Austria, s. XIII#3#/#4

PLATE 54

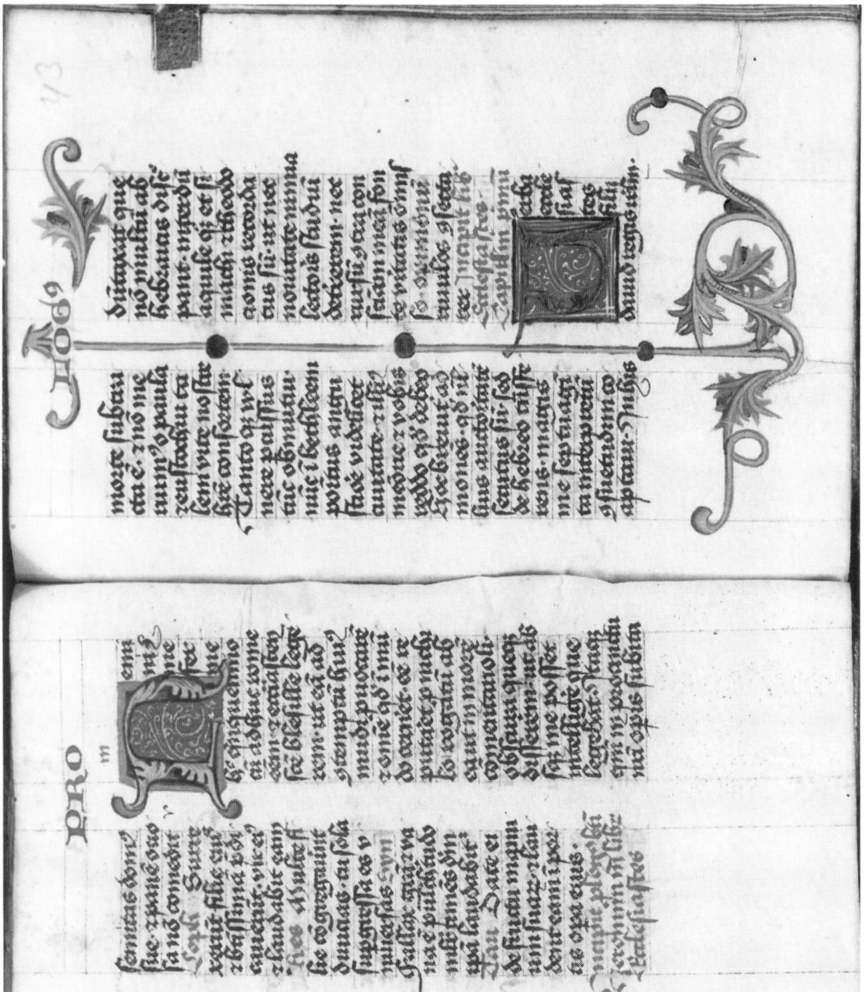

Marston MS 245, ff. 42v–43r (6/7 natural size)
Bohemia, s. XV#1

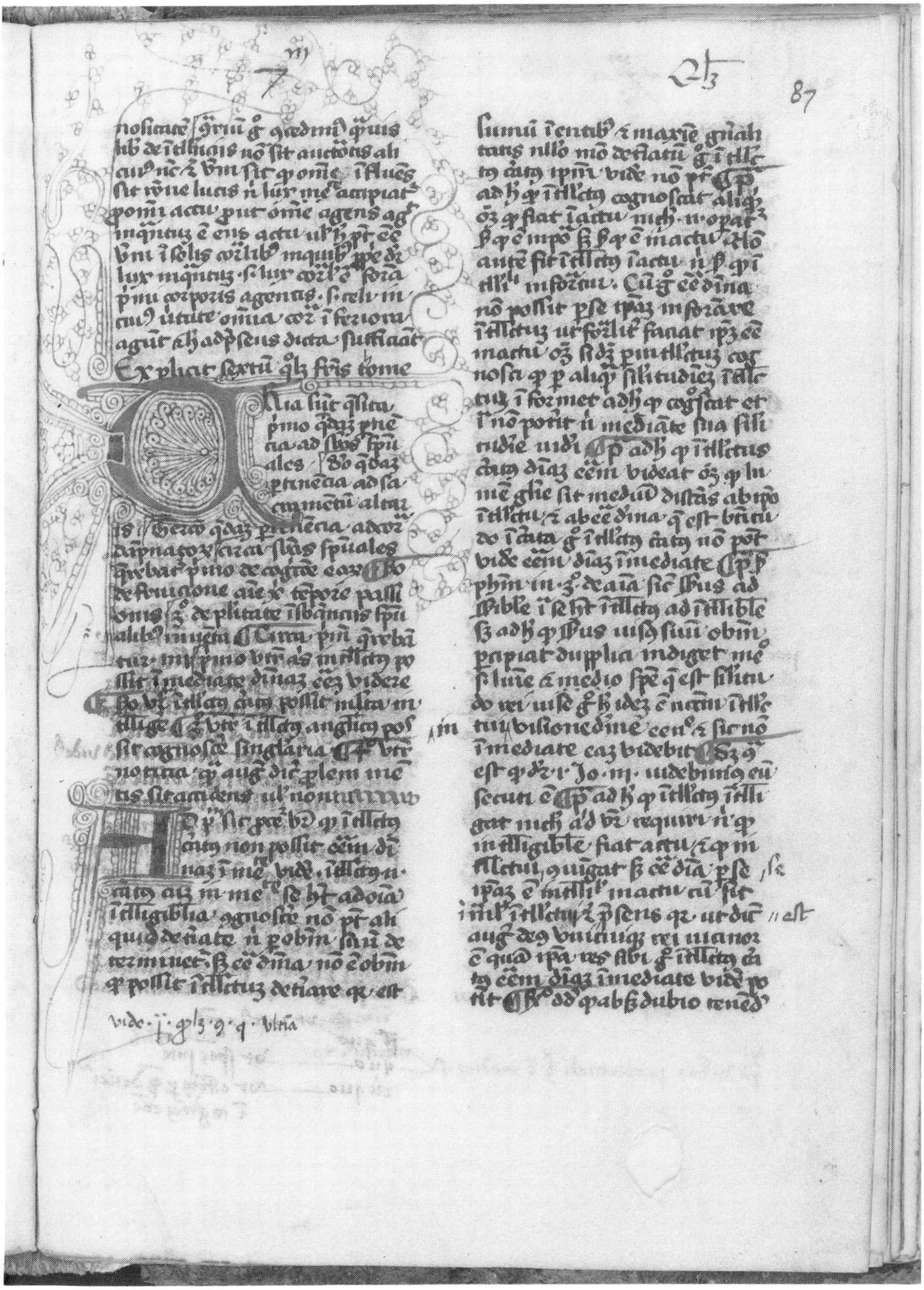

Marston MS 231, f. 87r (6/7 natural size)
Spain, s. XIII/XIV

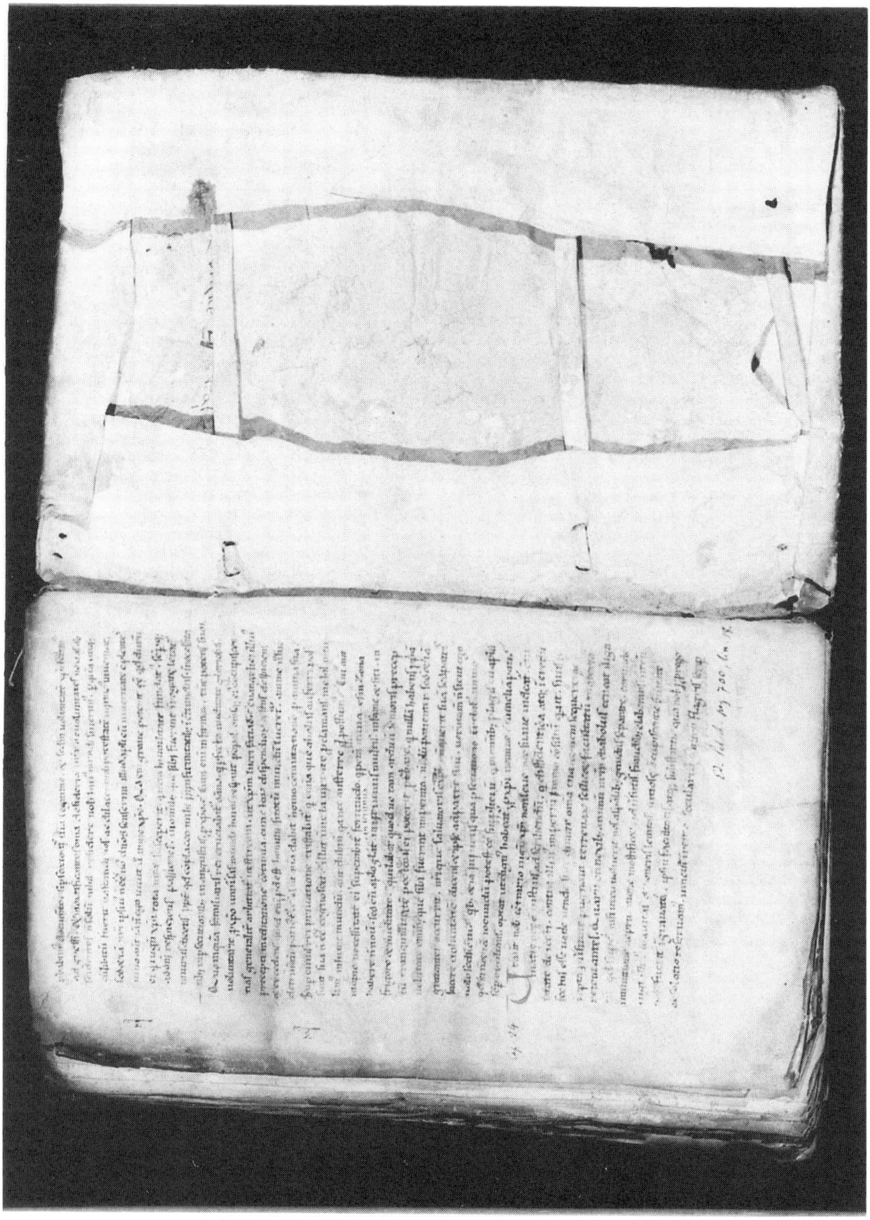

Marston MS 24, f. 90v and inside lower cover (1/3 natural size)
Italy, s. XII#i#n

PLATE 57

Marston MS 268, upper cover (2/3 natural size)
France, s. XIII–XIV [?]

Marston MS 73, lower cover (2/3 natural size)
Italy, s. XV#2

Marston MS 93, lower cover (3/4 natural size)
Florence or Tuscany, s. XV#2

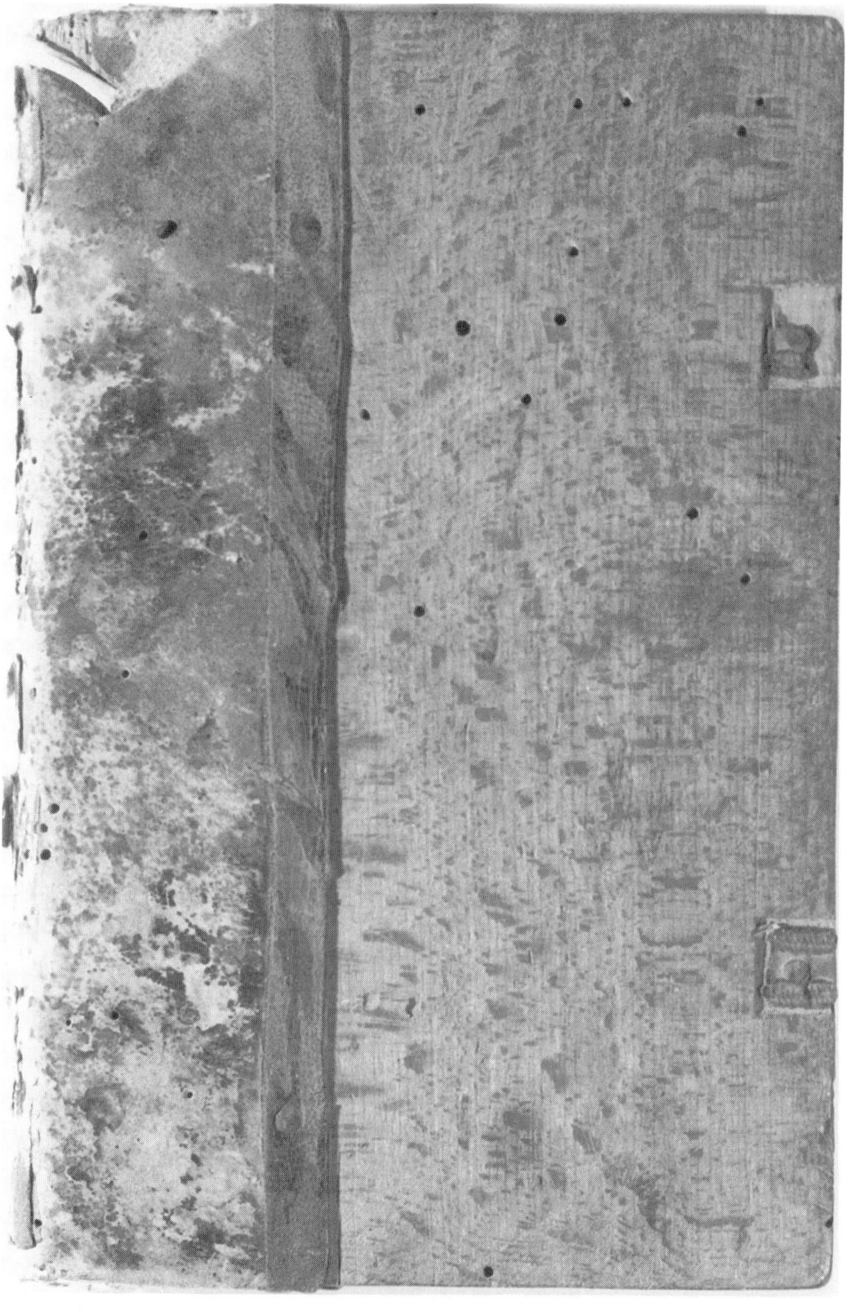

Marston MS 262, upper cover (8/11 natural size)
Italy, s. XV#2

Marston MS 51, lower cover (1/2 natural size)
Spain [?], s. XV#2

Marston MS 245, lower cover (7/8 natural size)
Bohemia, s. XV

Marston MS 141, binding (2/3 natural size)
Southern Germany [Amorbach?], s. XV#2

PLATE 64

Marston MS 287, upper cover (7/12 natural size)
Belgium, s. XV/XVI

Medieval and Renaissance Manuscripts in the Beinecke Rare Book and Manuscript Library, Yale University is a three-volume catalogue describing in detail 500 manuscripts in the general collection (vols. 1 and 2) and the 234 manuscripts in the Marston collection (vol. 3).

Volume III: Marston Manuscripts includes the Marston Collection, an impressive group of some 230 manuscripts acquired in the 1940s and '50s by the late Thomas E. Marston (1904–84), and purchased by Yale in 1962. The collection is very strong in twelfth-century monastic manuscripts; humanistic texts from fifteenth-century Italy; and representative texts illustrating thirteenth- and fourteenth-century intellectual interests. In addition to the works of Cicero, Sallust, Seneca, Servius, and Valerius Maximus, Marston actively sought out texts, translations, and commentaries by Leonardo Bruni, Ambrogio Traversari, Guarino of Verona, Lorenzo Valla, and other members of their circles. The volume includes sixty-four pages of plates of various manuscripts in the collection.

Barbara A. Shailor is Professor of Classics and Vice President for Student Services at Bucknell University, as well as Adviser, Medieval and Renaissance Manuscripts at the Beinecke. She was senior lecturer at the Dartmouth College Humanities Research Institute (1991), co-director of an NEH Summer Seminar for College Teachers at Yale University (summer 1989), and Councillor, the Medieval Academy of America (1988-91). She has published articles too numerous to list; her study, *The Medieval Book* (New Haven, 1988; repr. Toronto, 1991) was awarded first prize (1990) in the "American Book Prizes Current" competition of the American Library Association.

Iste coll[us]
q[ua]rtus
a divisa c[um]
ietus gla
dys et ho
mo mone[n]s
incisione[m]
rose tam[en]
siccab[itur] sic
rosa inci
dens rosa[m]
annis mo
tus tribu[s]
et cum t[er]tia littera t[er]cium elementum signi
ficat manus et falx una p[ri]ma litt[er]a in ad[ver]t
rosam lati · orat · miserum clericum vid[e]z
recipiens p[ri]ncipium ut inciderem florem
nō miserebi[tur] tui · quamvis in p[ri]ncipatu mane
as · vide cum iste incipiet colligere rosam an
te fereris in omnibus finem h[uius] in quo leta
re multum frustra ·